Renault Laguna
Service and Repair Manual

John S. Mead

Models covered

(3252 - 5AG4 - 440)

Renault Laguna Hatchback and Estate models with petrol and diesel engines, including special/limited editions

Petrol engines: 1.6 litre (1598 cc, 16-valve), 1.8 litre (1783 cc and 1794 cc, 8- and 16-valve), 2.0 litre (1948 cc and 1998 cc, 8- and 16-valve)

Diesel engines: 1.9 litre (1870 cc turbo), 2.2 litre (2188 cc turbo and non-turbo)

Does not cover 2963 cc V6 petrol engine, 2.0 litre 16-Valve VVT engine, or 1.9 litre common rail (dCi) diesel engine

© Haynes Publishing 2003

ABCDE
FG

A book in the **Haynes Service and Repair Manual Series**

ISBN **1 85960 599 0**

British Library Cataloguing in Publication Data
A catalogue record for this book is available from the British Library.

Printed in the USA

Haynes Publishing
Sparkford, Yeovil, Somerset BA22 7JJ, England

Haynes North America, Inc
861 Lawrence Drive, Newbury Park, California 91320, USA

Editions Haynes
4, Rue de l'Abreuvoir
92415 COURBEVOIE CEDEX, France

Haynes Publishing Nordiska AB
Box 1504, 751 45 UPPSALA, Sverige

Contents

LIVING WITH YOUR RENAULT LAGUNA

Roadside repairs

Weekly checks

MAINTENANCE

Routine maintenance and servicing

Contents

The Renault Laguna model range was introduced into the UK in 1994 to supersede the ageing Renault 21. All models are of five-door Hatchback or Estate design.

A range of four-cylinder petrol engines and diesel engines are available (a V6 petrol engine is available, but is not covered by this manual). All engines are of single or double overhead camshaft design, and are mounted transversely at the front of the vehicle.

Models may be fitted with five-speed manual, or four-speed automatic transmissions, mounted at the left-hand side of the engine.

All models have front-wheel-drive with fully-independent front and semi-independent rear suspension.

All models have a high trim level, which is very comprehensive in the upper model range. Central locking, electric windows, an electric sunroof, a trip computer, anti-lock brakes, air conditioning and cruise control are all available. A supplementary restraint system comprising air bag(s) and seat belt pre-tensioners is available on later models.

For the home mechanic, the Renault Laguna is a relatively straightforward vehicle to maintain and repair since design features have been incorporated to reduce the actual cost of ownership to a minimum, and most of the items requiring frequent attention are easily accessible.

Renault Laguna 2.2D RXE

Renault Laguna 1.8 RN

Your Renault Laguna Manual

The aim of this manual is to help you get the best value from your vehicle. It can do so in several ways. It can help you decide what work must be done (even should you choose to get it done by a garage), provide information on routine maintenance and servicing, and give a logical course of action and diagnosis when random faults occur. However, it is hoped that you will use the manual by tackling the work yourself. On simpler jobs, it may even be quicker than booking the car into a garage and going there twice, to leave and collect it. Perhaps most important, a lot of money can be saved by avoiding the costs a garage must charge to cover its labour and overheads.

The manual has drawings and descriptions to show the function of the various components, so that their layout can be understood. Then the tasks are described and photographed in a clear step-by-step sequence.

References to the 'left' or 'right' of the vehicle are in the sense of a person in the driver's seat, facing forwards.

The Renault Laguna Team

Haynes manuals are produced by dedicated and enthusiastic people working in close co-operation. The team responsible for the creation of this book included:

Author	John S. Mead
Page make-up	Steve Churchill
Workshop manager	Paul Buckland
Photo Scans	John Martin Steve Tanswell
Cover illustration & Line Art	Roger Healing
Wiring diagrams	Matthew Marke

We hope the book will help you to get the maximum enjoyment from your car. By carrying out routine maintenance as described you will ensure your car's reliability and preserve its resale value.

Acknowledgements

Certain illustrations are the copyright of the Renault (UK) Ltd, and are used with their permission. Thanks are also due to Kings of Taunton Ltd, who provided technical assistance, to Draper Tools Limited, who provided some of the workshop tools, and to all those people at Sparkford who helped in the production of this manual.

We take great pride in the accuracy of information given in this manual, but vehicle manufacturers make alterations and design changes during the production run of a particular vehicle of which they do not inform us. No liability can be accepted by the authors or publishers for loss, damage or injury caused by any errors in, or omissions from, the information given.

Project vehicles

The main vehicle used in the preparation of this manual, and which appears in many of the photographic sequences, was a Renault Laguna RT 2.2D 12V. Also used were Renault Laguna RTi 2.0 16V and RT 1.9 dTi models.

Working on your car can be dangerous. This page shows just some of the potential risks and hazards, with the aim of creating a safety-conscious attitude.

General hazards

Scalding

• Don't remove the radiator or expansion tank cap while the engine is hot.
• Engine oil, automatic transmission fluid or power steering fluid may also be dangerously hot if the engine has recently been running.

Burning

• Beware of burns from the exhaust system and from any part of the engine. Brake discs and drums can also be extremely hot immediately after use.

Crushing

• When working under or near a raised vehicle, always supplement the jack with axle stands, or use drive-on ramps. *Never venture under a car which is only supported by a jack.*
• Take care if loosening or tightening high-torque nuts when the vehicle is on stands. Initial loosening and final tightening should be done with the wheels on the ground.

Fire

• Fuel is highly flammable; fuel vapour is explosive.
• Don't let fuel spill onto a hot engine.
• Do not smoke or allow naked lights (including pilot lights) anywhere near a vehicle being worked on. Also beware of creating sparks (electrically or by use of tools).
• Fuel vapour is heavier than air, so don't work on the fuel system with the vehicle over an inspection pit.
• Another cause of fire is an electrical overload or short-circuit. Take care when repairing or modifying the vehicle wiring.
• Keep a fire extinguisher handy, of a type suitable for use on fuel and electrical fires.

Electric shock

• Ignition HT voltage can be dangerous, especially to people with heart problems or a pacemaker. Don't work on or near the ignition system with the engine running or the ignition switched on.

• Mains voltage is also dangerous. Make sure that any mains-operated equipment is correctly earthed. Mains power points should be protected by a residual current device (RCD) circuit breaker.

Fume or gas intoxication

• Exhaust fumes are poisonous; they often contain carbon monoxide, which is rapidly fatal if inhaled. Never run the engine in a confined space such as a garage with the doors shut.
• Fuel vapour is also poisonous, as are the vapours from some cleaning solvents and paint thinners.

Poisonous or irritant substances

• Avoid skin contact with battery acid and with any fuel, fluid or lubricant, especially antifreeze, brake hydraulic fluid and Diesel fuel. Don't syphon them by mouth. If such a substance is swallowed or gets into the eyes, seek medical advice.
• Prolonged contact with used engine oil can cause skin cancer. Wear gloves or use a barrier cream if necessary. Change out of oil-soaked clothes and do not keep oily rags in your pocket.
• Air conditioning refrigerant forms a poisonous gas if exposed to a naked flame (including a cigarette). It can also cause skin burns on contact.

Asbestos

• Asbestos dust can cause cancer if inhaled or swallowed. Asbestos may be found in gaskets and in brake and clutch linings. When dealing with such components it is safest to assume that they contain asbestos.

Special hazards

Hydrofluoric acid

• This extremely corrosive acid is formed when certain types of synthetic rubber, found in some O-rings, oil seals, fuel hoses etc, are exposed to temperatures above 400ºC. The rubber changes into a charred or sticky substance containing the acid. *Once formed, the acid remains dangerous for years. If it gets onto the skin, it may be necessary to amputate the limb concerned.*
• When dealing with a vehicle which has suffered a fire, or with components salvaged from such a vehicle, wear protective gloves and discard them after use.

The battery

• Batteries contain sulphuric acid, which attacks clothing, eyes and skin. Take care when topping-up or carrying the battery.
• The hydrogen gas given off by the battery is highly explosive. Never cause a spark or allow a naked light nearby. Be careful when connecting and disconnecting battery chargers or jump leads.

Air bags

• Air bags can cause injury if they go off accidentally. Take care when removing the steering wheel and/or facia. Special storage instructions may apply.

Diesel injection equipment

• Diesel injection pumps supply fuel at very high pressure. Take care when working on the fuel injectors and fuel pipes.

⚠ *Warning: Never expose the hands, face or any other part of the body to injector spray; the fuel can penetrate the skin with potentially fatal results.*

Remember...

DO

• Do use eye protection when using power tools, and when working under the vehicle.

• Do wear gloves or use barrier cream to protect your hands when necessary.

• Do get someone to check periodically that all is well when working alone on the vehicle.

• Do keep loose clothing and long hair well out of the way of moving mechanical parts.

• Do remove rings, wristwatch etc, before working on the vehicle – especially the electrical system.

• Do ensure that any lifting or jacking equipment has a safe working load rating adequate for the job.

DON'T

• Don't attempt to lift a heavy component which may be beyond your capability – get assistance.

• Don't rush to finish a job, or take unverified short cuts.

• Don't use ill-fitting tools which may slip and cause injury.

• Don't leave tools or parts lying around where someone can trip over them. Mop up oil and fuel spills at once.

• Don't allow children or pets to play in or near a vehicle being worked on.

The following pages are intended to help in dealing with common roadside emergencies and breakdowns. You will find more detailed fault finding information at the back of the manual, and repair information in the main chapters.

If your car won't start and the starter motor doesn't turn

- ☐ If it's a model with automatic transmission, make sure the selector is in P or N.
- ☐ Open the bonnet and make sure that the battery terminals are clean and tight.
- ☐ Switch on the headlights and try to start the engine. If the headlights go very dim when you're trying to start, the battery is probably flat. Get out of trouble by jump starting (see next page) using a friend's car.

If your car won't start even though the starter motor turns as normal

- ☐ Is there fuel in the tank?
- ☐ Is there moisture on electrical components under the bonnet? Switch off the ignition, then wipe off any obvious dampness with a dry cloth. Spray a water-repellent aerosol product (WD-40 or equivalent) on ignition and fuel system electrical connectors like those shown in the photos. Pay special attention to the ignition coil wiring connector and HT leads. (Note that Diesel engines don't normally suffer from damp.)

A Check the condition and security of the battery connections.

B Check that the spark plug HT leads are securely connected by pushing them onto the ignition coils.

C Check that the wiring connectors are securely connected to the ignition coils.

Check that electrical connections are secure (with the ignition switched off) and spray them with a water dispersant spray like WD-40 if you suspect a problem due to damp

D Check that the idle speed control valve wiring is secure.

E Check that the MAP sensor wiring plug is securely connected.

When jump-starting a car using a booster battery, observe the following precautions:

✔ Before connecting the booster battery, make sure that the ignition is switched off.

✔ Ensure that all electrical equipment (lights, heater, wipers, etc) is switched off.

✔ Take note of any special precautions printed on the battery case.

Jump starting

✔ Make sure that the booster battery is the same voltage as the discharged one in the vehicle.

✔ If the battery is being jump-started from the battery in another vehicle, the two vehicles MUST NOT TOUCH each other.

✔ Make sure that the transmission is in neutral (or PARK, in the case of automatic transmission).

1 Connect one end of the red jump lead to the positive (+) terminal of the flat battery

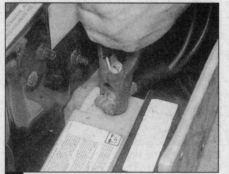

2 Connect the other end of the red lead to the positive (+) terminal of the booster battery.

3 Connect one end of the black jump lead to the negative (-) terminal of the booster battery

4 Connect the other end of the black jump lead to a bolt or bracket on the engine block, well away from the battery, on the vehicle to be started.

5 Make sure that the jump leads will not come into contact with the fan, drive-belts or other moving parts of the engine.

6 Start the engine using the booster battery and run it at idle speed. Switch on the lights, rear window demister and heater blower motor, then disconnect the jump leads in the reverse order of connection. Turn off the lights etc.

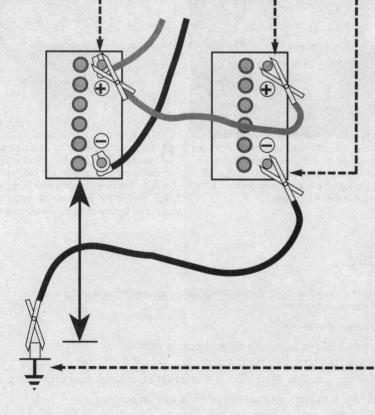

Wheel changing

Some of the details shown here will vary according to model. For instance, the location of the spare wheel and jack is not the same on all cars. However, the basic principles apply to all vehicles.

 Warning: Do not change a wheel in a situation where you risk being hit by another vehicle. On busy roads, try to stop in a lay-by or a gateway. Be wary of passing traffic while changing the wheel - it is easy to become distracted by the job in hand.

Preparation

☐ When a puncture occurs, stop as soon as it is safe to do so.

☐ Park on firm level ground, if possible, and well out of the way of other traffic.

☐ Use hazard warning lights if necessary.

☐ If you have one, use a warning triangle to alert other drivers of your presence.

☐ Apply the handbrake and engage first or reverse gear (or Park on models with automatic transmission).

☐ Chock the wheel diagonally opposite the one being removed – a couple of large stones will do for this.

☐ If the ground is soft, use a flat piece of wood to spread the load under the jack.

Changing the wheel

1 In the boot, lift the floor panel for access to the spare wheel. Engage the handle with the hook on the rear seat back to hold the floor panel open. Where applicable, lift out the storage box.

2 Unhook the elastic retaining cord, and engage it with the hook on the bottom of the floor panel to hold it clear of the spare wheel. Lift out the spare wheel.

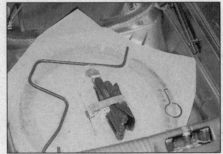

3 The jack, handle, wheel bolt spanner and wheel trim removal tool are all located underneath the spare wheel. The jack is secured by a rubber strap. Lift out the tools.

4 Where applicable, use the tool provided to pull off the wheel trim, then loosen each wheel bolt by half a turn, using the spanner provided.

5 Locate the jack head below the reinforced jacking point and on firm ground (don't jack the car at any other point on the sill). Ensure the lug on the jack head engages with the cut-out in the jacking point.

6 Engage the end of the jack handle with the jack, then turn the wheel brace clockwise until the wheel is raised clear of the ground. Remove the bolts and lift the wheel clear, then fit the spare wheel. Refit the wheel bolts and tighten moderately with the spanner.

7 Lower the car to the ground, then finally tighten the wheel bolts in a diagonal sequence, and where applicable, fit the wheel trim.

Finally...

☐ Note that the wheel bolts should be slackened and retightened to the specified torque at the earliest opportunity.

☐ Remove the wheel chocks.

☐ Stow the jack and tools in the correct locations in the car.

☐ Check the tyre pressure on the wheel just fitted. If it is low, or if you don't have a pressure gauge with you, drive slowly to the nearest garage and inflate the tyre to the right pressure.

☐ Have the damaged tyre or wheel repaired as soon as possible.

Identifying leaks

Puddles on the garage floor or drive, or obvious wetness under the bonnet or underneath the car, suggest a leak that needs investigating. It can sometimes be difficult to decide where the leak is coming from, especially if the engine bay is very dirty already. Leaking oil or fluid can also be blown rearwards by the passage of air under the car, giving a false impression of where the problem lies.

 Warning: Most automotive oils and fluids are poisonous. Wash them off skin, and change out of contaminated clothing, without delay.

> **HAYNES HiNT** *The smell of a fluid leaking from the car may provide a clue to what's leaking. Some fluids are distinctively coloured. It may help to clean the car carefully and to park it over some clean paper overnight as an aid to locating the source of the leak.*
> *Remember that some leaks may only occur while the engine is running.*

Sump oil

Engine oil may leak from the drain plug...

Oil from filter

...or from the base of the oil filter.

Gearbox oil

Gearbox oil can leak from the seals at the inboard ends of the driveshafts.

Antifreeze

Leaking antifreeze often leaves a crystalline deposit like this.

Brake fluid

A leak occurring at a wheel is almost certainly brake fluid.

Power steering fluid

Power steering fluid may leak from the pipe connectors on the steering rack.

Towing

When all else fails, you may find yourself having to get a tow home – or of course you may be helping somebody else. Long-distance recovery should only be done by a garage or breakdown service. For shorter distances, DIY towing using another car is easy enough, but observe the following points:

☐ Use a proper tow-rope – they are not expensive. The vehicle being towed must display an ON TOW sign in its rear window.
☐ Always turn the ignition key to the 'on' position when the vehicle is being towed, so that the steering lock is released, and that the direction indicator and brake lights will work.
☐ A towing eye is supplied as part of the vehicle tool kit. The towing eye is clipped into the bottom of the storage tray on the left-hand side of the luggage compartment.

☐ To fit the towing eye to the front of the vehicle, use the screwdriver blade on the end of the towing eye to unscrew the cover screw at the lower left-hand corner of the front spoiler. Unclip the cover, and screw in the towing eye as far as it will go.
☐ To fit the towing eye to the rear of the vehicle, unclip the cover from the rear bumper, and screw in the towing eye as far as it will go.
☐ Before being towed, release the handbrake and select neutral on the transmission.
☐ Note that greater-than-usual pedal pressure will be required to operate the brakes, since the vacuum servo unit is only operational with the engine running.
☐ On models with power steering, greater-than-usual steering effort will also be required.

☐ The driver of the car being towed must keep the tow-rope taut at all times to avoid snatching.
☐ Make sure that both drivers know the route before setting off.
☐ Only drive at moderate speeds and keep the distance towed to a minimum. Drive smoothly and allow plenty of time for slowing down at junctions.
☐ On models with automatic transmission, special precautions apply. If in doubt, do not tow, or transmission damage may result.

 Warning: To prevent damage to the catalytic converter, a vehicle must not be push-started, or started by towing, when the engine is at operating temperature. Use jump leads (see Jump starting).

Introduction

There are some very simple checks which need only take a few minutes to carry out, but which could save you a lot of inconvenience and expense.

These 'Weekly checks' require no great skill or special tools, and the small amount of time they take to perform could prove to be very well spent, for example;

☐ Keeping an eye on tyre condition and pressures, will not only help to stop them wearing out prematurely, but could also save your life.

☐ Many breakdowns are caused by electrical problems. Battery-related faults are particularly common, and a quick check on a regular basis will often prevent the majority of these.

☐ If your car develops a brake fluid leak, the first time you might know about it is when your brakes don't work properly. Checking the level regularly will give advance warning of this kind of problem.

☐ If the oil or coolant levels run low, the cost of repairing any engine damage will be far greater than fixing the leak, for example.

Underbonnet check points

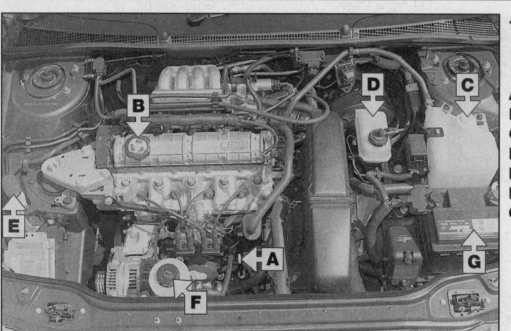

◀ **2.0 litre (8-valve) petrol (1.8 litre similar)**

A *Engine oil level dipstick*
B *Engine oil filler cap*
C *Coolant expansion tank*
D *Brake fluid reservoir*
E *Washer fluid reservoir*
F *Power steering fluid reservoir*
G *Battery*

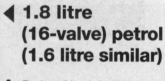

◀ **1.8 litre (16-valve) petrol (1.6 litre similar)**

A *Engine oil level dipstick*
B *Engine oil filler cap*
C *Coolant expansion tank*
D *Brake fluid reservoir*
E *Screen washer fluid reservoir*
F *Power steering fluid reservoir*
G *Battery*

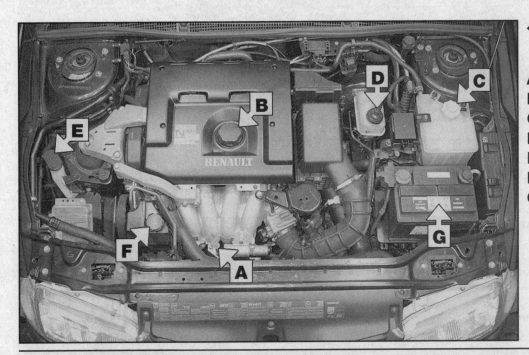

◀ 2.0 litre 16-valve petrol

A *Engine oil level dipstick*

B *Engine oil filler cap*

C *Coolant expansion tank*

D *Brake fluid reservoir*

E *Screen washer fluid reservoir*

F *Power steering fluid reservoir*

G *Battery*

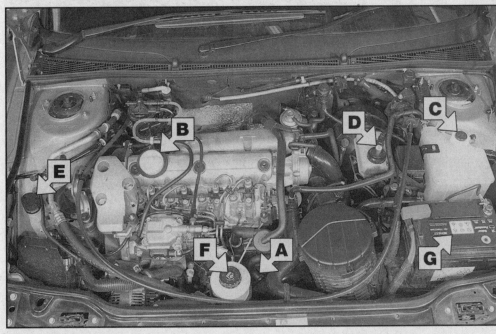

◀ 1.9 litre turbo diesel

A *Engine oil level dipstick*

B *Engine oil filler cap*

C *Coolant expansion tank*

D *Brake fluid reservoir*

E *Screen washer fluid reservoir*

F *Power steering fluid reservoir*

G *Battery*

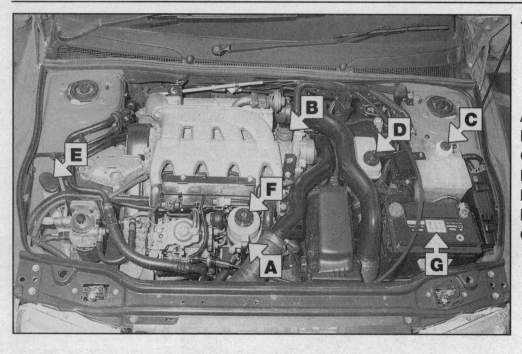

◀ **2.2 litre
turbo diesel
(non-turbo
similar)**

A *Engine oil level dipstick*
B *Engine oil filler cap*
C *Coolant expansion tank*
D *Brake fluid reservoir*
E *Screen washer fluid reservoir*
F *Power steering fluid reservoir*
G *Battery*

Engine oil level

Before you start

✔ Make sure that your car is on level ground.
✔ Check the oil level before the car is driven, or at least 5 minutes after the engine has been switched off.

 HAYNES HiNT *If the oil is checked immediately after driving the vehicle, some of the oil will remain in the upper engine components, resulting in an inaccurate reading on the dipstick!*

The correct oil

Modern engines place great demands on their oil. It is very important that the correct oil for your car is used (See Lubricants and fluids).

Car Care

● If you have to add oil frequently, you should check whether you have any oil leaks. Place some clean paper under the car overnight, and check for stains in the morning. If there are no leaks, the engine may be burning oil.

● Always maintain the level between the upper and lower dipstick marks (see photo 3). If the level is too low severe engine damage may occur. Oil seal failure may result if the engine is overfilled by adding too much oil.

1 The dipstick is located in a tube at the front of the engine (see *Underbonnet Check Points* for exact location). Withdraw the dipstick.

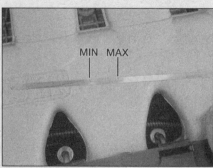

3 Note the oil level on the end of the dipstick, which should be between the upper (MAX) mark and the lower (MIN) mark.

2 Using a clean rag or paper towel, wipe all the oil from the dipstick. Insert the clean dipstick into the tube as far as it will go, then withdraw it again.

4 Oil is added through the filler cap. Unscrew the filler cap, then top-up the level. A funnel may help to reduce spillage. Add the oil slowly, checking the level on the dipstick often. Don't overfill (see *Car Care*).

Coolant level

⚠️ *Warning: DO NOT attempt to remove the expansion tank pressure cap when the engine is hot, as there is a very great risk of scalding. Do not leave open containers of coolant about, as it is poisonous.*

Car Care

● Adding coolant should not be necessary on a regular basis. If frequent topping-up is required, it is likely there is a leak. Check the radiator, all hoses and joint faces for signs of staining or wetness, and rectify as necessary.

● It is important that antifreeze is used in the cooling system all year round, not just during the winter months. Don't top-up with water alone, as the antifreeze will become too diluted.

1 The coolant level varies with engine temperature. The level is checked in the expansion tank, which is at the rear right-hand corner of the engine compartment. When the engine is cold, the level should be between the MAX and MIN markings.

2 If topping up is necessary, wait until the engine is cold, then turn the pressure cap on the expansion tank slowly anti-clockwise, and pause until any pressure remaining in the system is released. Unscrew the cap and lift off.

3 Add a mixture of water and antifreeze to the expansion tank, until the coolant is up to the MAX mark. Refit the cap, turning it clockwise as far as it will go until it is secure. Re-check that the cap is securely tightened once the engine is warm.

Power steering fluid level

Before you start:
✔ Park the vehicle on level ground.
✔ Set the steering wheel straight-ahead.
✔ The engine should be turned off.

HAYNES HiNT *For the check to be accurate, the steering must not be turned once the engine has been stopped.*

Safety First!
● The need for frequent topping-up indicates a leak, which should be investigated immediately.

1 The power steering fluid reservoir is located at the front of the engine. The fluid level should be checked with the engine stopped. A translucent reservoir is fitted, to most models with MAX and MIN markings on the side of the reservoir. On 2.0 litre (16-valve) models, the reservoir filler cap incorporates a dipstick for level checking.

2 The fluid level should be between the MAX and MIN marks on the reservoir, or between the upper and lower marks on the dipstick. Before removing the cap for level checking or topping-up, wipe the surrounding area so that dirt does not enter the reservoir.

3 Unscrew the cap, allowing the fluid to drain from the bottom of the cap as it is removed. Top up the fluid level to the MAX mark, or upper dipstick mark, using the specified type of fluid (do not overfill the reservoir), then refit and tighten the filler cap.

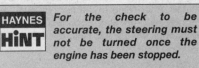

Brake fluid level

Warning:
● **Brake fluid can harm your eyes and damage painted surfaces, so use extreme caution when handling and pouring it.**

● **Do not use fluid that has been standing open for some time, as it absorbs moisture from the air, which can cause a dangerous loss of braking effectiveness.**

HAYNES HiNT
• *Make sure that your car is on level ground.*
• *The fluid level in the reservoir will drop slightly as the brake pads wear down, but the fluid level must never be allowed to drop below the "MIN" mark.*

Safety First!

● If the reservoir requires repeated topping-up this is an indication of a fluid leak somewhere in the system, which should be investigated immediately.

● If a leak is suspected, the car should not be driven until the braking system has been checked. Never take any risks where brakes are concerned.

1 The MAX and MIN marks are indicated on the side of the reservoir, which is located at the rear left-hand side of the engine compartment. The fluid level must be kept between these two marks.

2 If topping-up is necessary, first wipe the area around the filler cap with a clean rag, then disconnect the fluid level sensor wires before removing the cap. When adding fluid, it's a good idea to inspect the reservoir. The system should be drained and refilled if dirt is seen in the fluid (see Chapter 9).

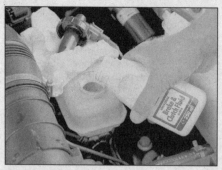

3 Carefully add fluid, avoiding spilling it on surrounding paintwork. Use only the specified hydraulic fluid; mixing different types of fluid can cause damage to the system and/or a loss of braking effectiveness. Bear in mind that the level in the reservoir will rise slightly when the cap/float assembly is refitted. After filling to the correct level, refit the cap securely and reconnect the sensor wires. Wipe off any spilt fluid.

4 When checking the fluid level it is a good idea to check the operation of the low fluid level warning light. Switch on the ignition and ask an assistant to press the test button on top of the brake fluid reservoir cap. When the button is pressed, the brake fluid level/handbrake 'on' warning light should come on - if not, the level switch, wiring or bulb may be faulty. If the warning light comes on and the fluid level is not low, check that the handbrake is not on (but note that certain models have a separate warning light for the handbrake). Switch off the ignition after testing.

Tyre condition and pressure

It is very important that tyres are in good condition, and at the correct pressure - having a tyre failure at any speed is highly dangerous. Tyre wear is influenced by driving style - harsh braking and acceleration, or fast cornering, will all produce more rapid tyre wear. As a general rule, the front tyres wear out faster than the rears. Interchanging the tyres from front to rear ("rotating" the tyres) may result in more even wear. However, if this is completely effective, you may have the expense of replacing all four tyres at once! Remove any nails or stones embedded in the tread before they penetrate the tyre to cause deflation. If removal of a nail does reveal that the tyre has been punctured, refit the nail so that its point of penetration is marked. Then immediately change the wheel, and have the tyre repaired by a tyre dealer.

Regularly check the tyres for damage in the form of cuts or bulges, especially in the sidewalls. Periodically remove the wheels, and clean any dirt or mud from the inside and outside surfaces. Examine the wheel rims for signs of rusting, corrosion or other damage. Light alloy wheels are easily damaged by "kerbing" whilst parking; steel wheels may also become dented or buckled. A new wheel is very often the only way to overcome severe damage.

New tyres should be balanced when they are fitted, but it may become necessary to re-balance them as they wear, or if the balance weights fitted to the wheel rim should fall off. Unbalanced tyres will wear more quickly, as will the steering and suspension components. Wheel imbalance is normally signified by vibration, particularly at a certain speed (typically around 50 mph). If this vibration is felt only through the steering, then it is likely that just the front wheels need balancing. If, however, the vibration is felt through the whole car, the rear wheels could be out of balance. Wheel balancing should be carried out by a tyre dealer or garage.

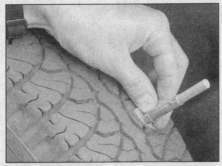

1 Tread Depth - visual check
The original tyres have tread wear safety bands (B), which will appear when the tread depth reaches approximately 1.6 mm. The band positions are indicated by a triangular mark on the tyre sidewall (A).

2 Tread Depth - manual check
Alternatively, tread wear can be monitored with a simple, inexpensive device known as a tread depth indicator gauge.

3 Tyre Pressure Check
Check the tyre pressures regularly with the tyres cold. Do not adjust the tyre pressures immediately after the vehicle has been used, or an inaccurate setting will result. Tyre pressures are shown on page 0•19.

Tyre tread wear patterns

Shoulder Wear

Underinflation (wear on both sides)
Under-inflation will cause overheating of the tyre, because the tyre will flex too much, and the tread will not sit correctly on the road surface. This will cause a loss of grip and excessive wear, not to mention the danger of sudden tyre failure due to heat build-up.
Check and adjust pressures
Incorrect wheel camber (wear on one side)
Repair or renew suspension parts
Hard cornering
Reduce speed!

Centre Wear

Overinflation
Over-inflation will cause rapid wear of the centre part of the tyre tread, coupled with reduced grip, harsher ride, and the danger of shock damage occurring in the tyre casing.
Check and adjust pressures

If you sometimes have to inflate your car's tyres to the higher pressures specified for maximum load or sustained high speed, don't forget to reduce the pressures to normal afterwards.

Uneven Wear

Front tyres may wear unevenly as a result of wheel misalignment. Most tyre dealers and garages can check and adjust the wheel alignment (or "tracking") for a modest charge.
Incorrect camber or castor
Repair or renew suspension parts
Malfunctioning suspension
Repair or renew suspension parts
Unbalanced wheel
Balance tyres
Incorrect toe setting
Adjust front wheel alignment
Note: *The feathered edge of the tread which typifies toe wear is best checked by feel.*

Washer fluid level

Screenwash additives not only keep the winscreen clean during foul weather, they also prevent the washer system freezing in cold weather - which is when you are likely to need it most. Don't top up using plain water as the screenwash will become too diluted, and will freeze during cold weather. *On no account use coolant antifreeze in the washer system - this could discolour or damage paintwork.*

1 The windscreen/tailgate/headlight washer fluid reservoir is located at the right-hand side of the engine compartment. If topping-up is necessary, open the cap.

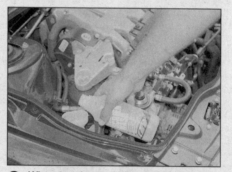

2 When topping-up the reservoir a screen-wash additive should be added in the quantities recommended on the bottle.

Wiper blades

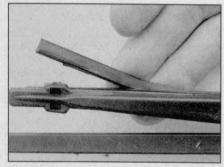

1 Check the condition of the wiper blades; if they are cracked or show any signs of deterioration, or if the glass swept area is smeared, renew them. For maximum clarity of vision, wiper blades should be renewed annually, as a matter of course.

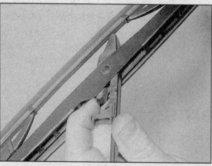

2 To remove a windscreen wiper blade, pull the arm fully away from the screen until it locks. Swivel the blade through 90°, then depress the locking clip at the base of the mounting block.

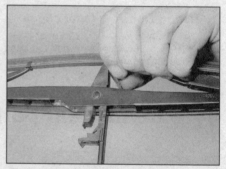

3 Swivel the mounting block through 90° then release the retaining clip at the top of the mounting block.

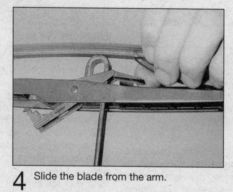

4 Slide the blade from the arm.

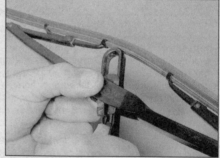

5 Don't forget to check the tailgate wiper blade as well. The blade can be removed by swivelling the blade through 90°, then depressing the retaining clips and sliding the blade from the arm.

Bulbs and fuses

✔ Check all external lights and the horn. Refer to the appropriate Sections of Chapter 12 for details if any of the circuits are found to be inoperative.

✔ Visually check all accessible wiring connectors, harnesses and retaining clips for security, and for signs of chafing or damage.

 HAYNES HiNT *If you need to check your brake lights and indicators unaided, back up to a wall or garage door and operate the lights. The reflected light should show if they are working properly.*

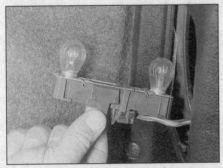

1 If a single indicator light, brake light or headlight has failed, it is likely that a bulb has blown and will need to be replaced. Refer to Chapter 12 for details. If both brake lights have failed, it is possible that the brake light switch operated by the brake pedal has failed. Refer to Chapter 9 for details.

2 If more than one indicator light or headlight has failed, it is likely that either a fuse has blown or that there is a fault in the circuit (see Chapter 12). The fuses are in a panel at the lower driver's side of the facia under a cover. Press the two catches to release the cover.

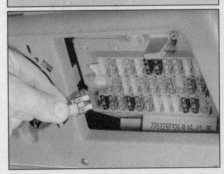

3 To replace a blown fuse, remove it, where applicable, using the plastic tool provided. Fit a new fuse of the same rating, available from car accessory shops. If the fuse blows again, it is important that you find out why - a complete checking procedure is given in Chapter 12.

Battery

Caution: Before carrying out any work on the vehicle battery, read the precautions given in Safety first at the start of this manual.

✔ Make sure that the battery tray is in good condition, and that the clamp is tight. Corrosion on the tray, retaining clamp and the battery itself can be removed with a solution of water and baking soda. Thoroughly rinse all cleaned areas with water. Any metal parts damaged by corrosion should be covered with a zinc-based primer, then painted.

✔ Periodically (approximately every three months), check the charge condition of the battery as described in Chapter 5A.

✔ If the battery is flat, and you need to jump start your vehicle, see *Roadside Repairs*.

1 The battery is located at the front left-hand corner of the engine compartment. The exterior of the battery should be inspected periodically for damage such as a cracked case or cover.

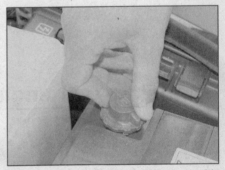

2 Check the tightness of the battery cable clamps to ensure good electrical connections. You should not be able to move them. Also check each cable for cracks and frayed conductors.

HAYNES HiNT

Battery corrosion can be kept to a minimum by applying a layer of petroleum jelly to the clamps and terminals after they are reconnected.

3 If corrosion (white fluffy deposits) is evident, remove the cables from the battery terminals, clean them with a small wire brush, then refit them. Automotive stores sell a useful tool for cleaning the battery post and terminals.

4 Note that the battery positive lead terminal can be disconnected by unscrewing the nut located under the plastic cover.

Lubricants and fluids

Petrol engine . . . . Multigrade engine oil, viscosity SAE 10W/30 to 15W/50, to API SH/SJ and/or ACEA-A2/A3

Diesel engine . . . . Multigrade engine oil, viscosity SAE 10W/30 to 15W/50, to API CF and/or ACEA-B2/B3

Cooling system . . . . Ethylene glycol-based antifreeze - RX Glaceol type D coolant

Manual transmission . . . . Elf Tranself TRX 75W/80W gear oil

Automatic transmission
AD4 transmission:
   Main transmission . . . . Elf Renaultmatic D2, Dexron II ATF
   Final drive (sealed for life) . . . . Elf Tranself Type B 80W
DPO transmission (sealed for life) . . . . Elf Renaultmatic D3 SYN, Dexron III ATF

Braking system . . . . Hydraulic fluid to SAE J1703F or DOT 4

Power steering . . . . Elf Renaultmatic D2, Dexron II ATF

Choosing your engine oil

Engines need oil, not only to lubricate moving parts and minimise wear, but also to maximise power output and to improve fuel economy.

HOW ENGINE OIL WORKS

• Beating friction

Without oil, the moving surfaces inside your engine will rub together, heat up and melt, quickly causing the engine to seize. Engine oil creates a film which separates these moving parts, preventing wear and heat build-up.

• Cooling hot-spots

Temperatures inside the engine can exceed 1000° C. The engine oil circulates and acts as a coolant, transferring heat from the hot-spots to the sump.

• Cleaning the engine internally

Good quality engine oils clean the inside of your engine, collecting and dispersing combustion deposits and controlling them until they are trapped by the oil filter or flushed out at oil change.

OIL CARE - FOLLOW THE CODE

To handle and dispose of used engine oil safely, always:

OIL CARE

FOLLOW THE CODE

OIL BANK LINE
0800 66 33 66
www.oilbankline.org.uk

• *Avoid skin contact with used engine oil. Repeated or prolonged contact can be harmful.*
• *Dispose of used oil and empty packs in a responsible manner in an authorised disposal site. Call 0800 663366 to find the one nearest to you. Never tip oil down drains or onto the ground.*

Tyre pressures (cold)

Note: *Recommended tyre pressures are marked on a label attached to the driver's door edge or frame. Pressures apply to original-equipment tyres, and may vary if any other make or type of tyre is fitted; check with the tyre manufacturer or supplier for correct pressures if necessary.*
Note: *If a space-saver emergency spare tyre is fitted, it should be inflated to a pressure of 4.2 bars (61 psi).*

	Front	Rear
Petrol engine Hatchback models:		
1.6 litre, 1.8 litre and 2.0 litre (8-valve) manual transmission models:		
Normal use	2.0 bars (29 psi)	2.0 bars (29 psi)
Fully laden or motorway driving	2.2 bars (32 psi)	2.2 bars (32 psi)
2.0 litre (8-valve) automatic transmission and 2.0 litre (16-valve) models:		
Normal use	2.3 bars (33 psi)	2.1 bars (30 psi)
Fully laden or motorway driving	2.4 bars (35 psi)	2.2 bars (32 psi)
Petrol engine Estate models:		
1.6 litre, 1.8 litre and 2.0 litre (8-valve) models:		
Normal use	2.0 bars (29 psi)	2.0 bars (29 psi)
Fully laden or motorway driving	2.2 bars (32 psi)	2.6 bars (38 psi)
2.0 litre (16-valve) models:		
Normal use	2.3 bars (33 psi)	2.1 bars (30 psi)
Fully laden or motorway driving	2.4 bars (35 psi)	2.6 bars (38 psi)
Diesel engine Hatchback models:		
1.9 litre models:		
Normal use	2.0 bars (29 psi)	2.0 bars (29 psi)
Fully laden or motorway driving	2.2 bars (32 psi)	2.2 bars (32 psi)
2.2 litre models:		
Normal use	2.3 bars (33 psi)	2.1 bars (30 psi)
Fully laden or motorway driving	2.4 bars (35 psi)	2.2 bars (32 psi)
Diesel engine Estate models:		
Normal use	2.3 bars (33 psi)	2.1 bars (30 psi)
Fully laden or motorway driving	2.4 bars (35 psi)	2.6 bars (38 psi)

Advanced driving

Many people see the words 'advanced driving' and believe that it won't interest them or that it is a style of driving beyond their own abilities. Nothing could be further from the truth. Advanced driving is straightforward safe, sensible driving - the sort of driving we should all do every time we get behind the wheel.

An average of 10 people are killed every day on UK roads and 870 more are injured, some seriously. Lives are ruined daily, usually because somebody did something stupid. Something like 95% of all accidents are due to human error, mostly driver failure. Sometimes we make genuine mistakes - everyone does. Sometimes we have lapses of concentration. Sometimes we deliberately take risks.

For many people, the process of 'learning to drive' doesn't go much further than learning how to pass the driving test because of a common belief that good drivers are made by 'experience'.

Learning to drive by 'experience' teaches three driving skills:

☐ Quick reactions. (Whoops, that was close!)
☐ Good handling skills. (Horn, swerve, brake, horn).
☐ Reliance on vehicle technology. (Great stuff this ABS, stop in no distance even in the wet...)

Drivers whose skills are 'experience based' generally have a lot of near misses and the odd accident. The results can be seen every day in our courts and our hospital casualty departments.

Advanced drivers have learnt to control the risks by controlling the position and speed of their vehicle. They avoid accidents and near misses, even if the drivers around them make mistakes.

The key skills of advanced driving are **concentration,** effective all-round **observation, anticipation** and **planning.** When **good vehicle handling** is added to

these skills, all driving situations can be approached and negotiated in a safe, methodical way, leaving nothing to chance.

Concentration means applying your mind to safe driving, completely excluding anything that's not relevant. Driving is usually the most dangerous activity that most of us undertake in our daily routines. It deserves our full attention.

Observation means not just looking, but seeing and seeking out the information found in the driving environment.

Anticipation means asking yourself what is happening, what you can reasonably expect to happen and what could happen unexpectedly. (One of the commonest words used in compiling accident reports is 'suddenly'.)

Planning is the link between seeing something and taking the appropriate action. For many drivers, planning is the missing link.

If you want to become a safer and more skilful driver and you want to enjoy your driving more, contact the Institute of Advanced Motorists at www.iam.org.uk, phone 0208 996 9600, or write to IAM House, 510 Chiswick High Road, London W4 5RG for an information pack.

Chapter 1 Part A:
Routine maintenance and servicing - petrol models

Contents

1A

Degrees of difficulty

Easy, suitable for novice with little experience	**Fairly easy,** suitable for beginner with some experience	**Fairly difficult,** suitable for competent DIY mechanic	**Difficult,** suitable for experienced DIY mechanic	**Very difficult,** suitable for expert DIY or professional

Lubricants and fluids

Refer to *Weekly checks* on page 0•18

Capacities

Engine oil

Excluding filter:

1.6 litre (16-valve) engines	4.2 litres
1.8 litre (8-valve) engines	5.7 litres
1.8 litre (16-valve) engines	5.0 litres
2.0 litre (8-valve) engines	5.5 litres
2.0 litre (16-valve) engines	5.7 litres

Including filter:

1.6 litre (16-valve) engines	4.7 litres
1.8 litre (8-valve) engines	6.2 litres
1.8 litre (16-valve) engines	5.5 litres
2.0 litre (8-valve) engines	6.0 litres
2.0 litre (16-valve) engines	6.2 litres

Cooling system (approximate)

1.6 litre (16-valve) engines	6.5 litres
1.8 litre (8-valve) engines	7.4 litres
1.8 litre (16-valve) engines	7.0 litres
2.0 litre (8-valve) engines	7.0 litres
2.0 litre (16-valve) engines	8.0 litres

Transmission

Manual transmission:

JB3-type gearbox	3.4 litres
JC5-type gearbox	3.1 litres

AD4 automatic transmission:

From dry:

Main transmission	4.6 litres
Final drive	1.0 litre

Drain and refill:

Main transmission	3.5 litres
Final drive	1.0 litre
DPO automatic transmission	6.0 litres

Fuel tank .... 66.0 litres

Engine

Auxiliary drivebelt tension (measured using Renault tool Mot. 1273):

1.8 and 2.0 litre (8-valve) engines:

Fitting/checking value:

Without air conditioning	112 ± 6 SEEM units
With air conditioning	114 ± 5 SEEM units
Minimum operating value	62 SEEM units

1.6 litre (16-valve) engines:

Fitting/checking value:

Without air conditioning	108 ± 6 SEEM units
With air conditioning	N/A (controlled by automatic tensioner)
Minimum operating value	60 SEEM units

1.8 litre (16-valve) engines:

Fitting/checking value:

Without air conditioning	102 ± 6 SEEM units
With air conditioning	N/A (controlled by automatic tensioner)
Minimum operating value	48 SEEM units

2.0 litre (16-valve) engines:

Fitting/checking value - with/without air conditioning	49 to 76 SEEM units

Cooling system

Antifreeze mixture:
35% antifreeze .... Protection down to -23°C
50% antifreeze .... Protection down to -40°C

Fuel system

Idle speed (not adjustable - controlled by ECU) .... 750 ± 50 rpm
Idle mixture CO content .... Less than 1.0 % (controlled by ECU)

Ignition system

Ignition timing .... Controlled by ECU - see Chapter 5B

Spark plugs:	Type	Electrode gap
1.6 litre	Bosch FR 7 D+	0.9 mm
1.8 litre:		
8-valve	Bosch WR 8 D+	0.8 mm
16-valve	Bosch FR 7 LD+	0.9 mm
2.0 litre:		
8-valve	Bosch WR 8 D+	0.8 mm
16-valve	Bosch FR 7 D+	0.9 mm

Brakes

Front disc brakes:
  Pad thickness (including backing):
    New .... 18.0 mm
    Minimum thickness .... 6.0 mm
Rear disc brakes:
  Pad thickness (including backing):
    New .... 15.0 mm
    Minimum thickness .... 6.0 mm
Rear drum brakes:
  Shoe thickness (including backing):
    New .... 7.0 mm
    Minimum thickness .... 2.5 mm

Torque wrench settings

	Nm	lbf ft
Roadwheel bolts	100	74
Spark plugs	25	18

1A

The maintenance intervals in this manual are provided with the assumption that you, not the dealer, will be carrying out the work. These are the minimum maintenance intervals recommended by us for vehicles driven daily. If you wish to keep your vehicle in peak condition at all times, you may wish to perform some of these procedures more often. We encourage frequent maintenance, because it enhances the efficiency, performance and resale value of your vehicle.

If the vehicle is driven in dusty areas, used to tow a trailer, or driven frequently at slow speeds (idling in traffic) or on short journeys, more frequent maintenance intervals are recommended.

When the vehicle is new, it should be serviced by a factory-authorised dealer service department, in order to preserve the factory warranty.

Every 250 miles (400 km) or weekly
☐ Refer to Weekly Checks

Every 6000 miles (10 000 km)
☐ Renew the engine oil and filter (Section 3)

Note: *Renault recommend that the oil filter is renewed every 12 000 miles (20 000 km), but it is advisable to renew the filter whenever the engine oil is renewed.*

☐ Check the front brake pad thickness (Section 4)
☐ Check the rear brake pad thickness - models with rear disc brakes (Section 5)
☐ Check the operation of the handbrake (Section 6)
☐ Check the operation of the clutch (Section 7)
☐ Check the condition of the auxiliary drivebelts (Section 8)
☐ Check the automatic transmission fluid level (Section 9)
☐ Check the idle speed and mixture setting (exhaust CO emissions) (Section 10)
☐ Check the condition of the seat belts (Section 11)
☐ Check the operation of all electrical systems (Section 12)
☐ Check the condition of the exhaust system and mountings (Section 13)
☐ Check the suspension and steering components (Section 14)
☐ Check the tightness of the roadwheel bolts (Section 15)

Every 12 000 miles (20 000 km)
Carry out all the operations listed under the 6000 mile (10 000 km) service, along with the following:
☐ Renew the air filter element (Section 16)
☐ Renew the spark plugs and check the ignition system (Section 17)
☐ Check the manual transmission oil level (Section 18)
☐ Check all underbonnet components and hoses for fluid leaks (Section 19)
☐ Renew the pollen filter (Section 20)
☐ Check the operation of the air conditioning system (Section 21)

Every 36 000 miles (60 000 km)
Carry out all the operations listed under the 6000 mile (10 000 km), and 12 000 mile (20 000 km) services, along with the following:
☐ Check the spare fuses are in place (Section 22)
☐ Check the front wheel alignment (Section 23)
☐ Check the rear brake shoe thickness - models with rear drum brakes (Section 24)
☐ Renew the automatic transmission fluid on AD4 type transmissions (Section 25)
☐ Renew the brake fluid (Section 26)
☐ Renew the fuel filter (Section 27)
☐ Carry out a road test (Section 28)
☐ Renew the timing belt (Section 29)

Note: *Although the normal interval for timing belt renewal is 72 000 miles (120 000 km), it is strongly recommended that the interval is halved to 36 000 miles (60 000 km) on vehicles which are subjected to intensive use, ie, mainly short journeys or a lot of stop-start driving. The actual belt renewal interval is therefore very much up to the individual owner, but bear in mind that severe engine damage may result if the belt breaks.*

Every 2 years
In addition to all the items listed previously, carry out the following:
☐ Renew the coolant (Section 30)

Underbonnet view of a 2.0 litre (8-valve) model - 1.8 litre models similar

1 Engine oil filler cap
2 Engine oil level dipstick
3 Battery
4 Brake fluid reservoir
5 Electrical connector box
6 Coolant expansion tank
7 Suspension strut upper mounting
8 Air filter housing
9 Engine oil filter
10 Power steering fluid reservoir
11 Alternator
12 Engine management electronic control unit
13 Washer fluid reservoir
14 Idle speed control valve
15 MAP sensor
16 Ignition coils

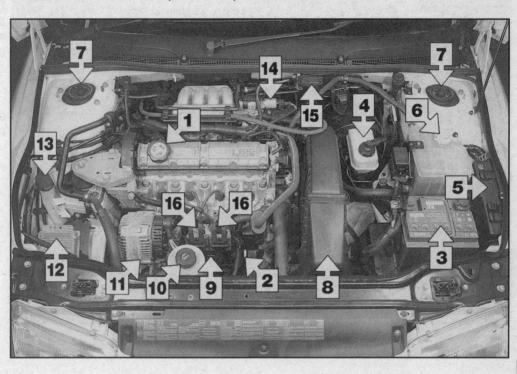

1A

Underbonnet view of a 1.8 litre (16-valve) model - 1.6 litre models similar

1 Engine oil filler cap
2 Engine oil level dipstick
3 Battery
4 Brake fluid reservoir
5 Electrical connector box
6 Coolant expansion tank
7 Suspension strut upper mounting
8 Air filter housing
9 Power steering fluid reservoir
10 Alternator
11 Washer fluid reservoir
12 Idle speed control valve

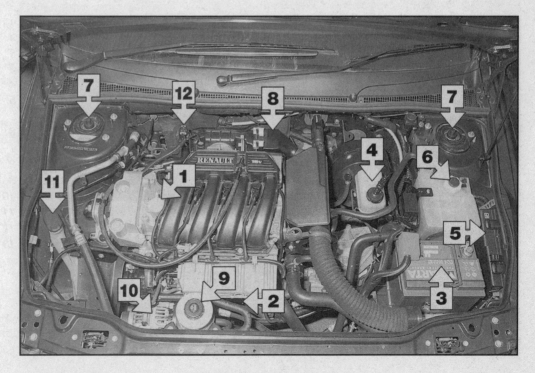

Underbonnet view of a 2.0 litre (16-valve) model

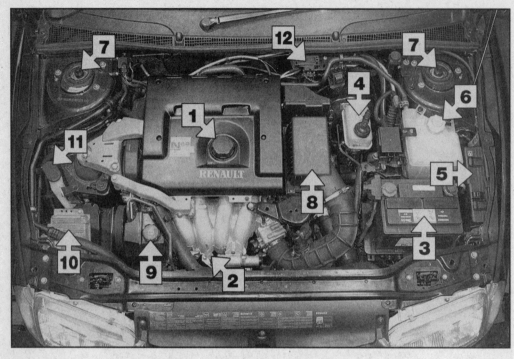

1 Engine oil filler cap
2 Engine oil level dipstick
3 Battery
4 Brake fluid reservoir
5 Electrical connector box
6 Coolant expansion tank
7 Suspension strut upper mounting
8 Air filter housing
9 Power steering fluid reservoir
10 Engine management electronic control unit
11 Washer fluid reservoir
12 MAP sensor

Front underbody view of a 2.0 litre (16-valve) model

1 Washer fluid reservoir
2 Air conditioning compressor
3 Engine oil cooler
4 Engine oil filter
5 Power steering fluid cooler pipes
6 Brake caliper
7 Suspension lower arm
8 Track-rod end
9 Anti-roll bar
10 Gearchange rod
11 Right-hand driveshaft
12 Engine mounting bracket
13 Engine oil drain plug

Rear underbody view of a 2.0 litre (16-valve) model

1 Handbrake cable equaliser
2 Exhaust expansion box
3 Rear suspension mounting
4 Rear brake pressure
regulating valve
5 Rear suspension
crossmember
6 Rear suspension torsion
bar
7 Rear shock absorber
8 Fuel tank
9 Fuel filter

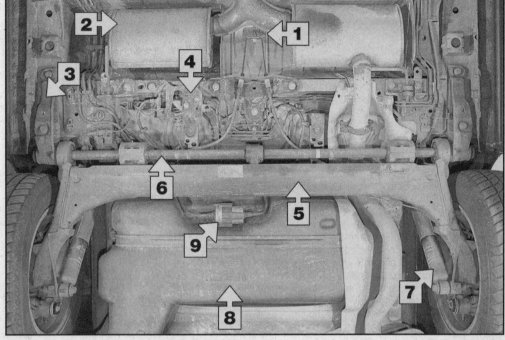

Maintenance procedures

1 Introduction

1 This Chapter is designed to help the home mechanic maintain his/her vehicle for safety, economy, long life and peak performance.
2 The Chapter contains a master maintenance schedule, followed by Sections dealing specifically with each task in the schedule. Visual checks, adjustments, component renewal and other helpful items are included. Refer to the accompanying illustrations of the engine compartment and the underside of the vehicle for the locations of the various components.
3 Servicing your vehicle in accordance with the mileage/time maintenance schedule and the following Sections will provide a planned maintenance programme, which should result in a long and reliable service life. This is a comprehensive plan, so maintaining some items but not others at the specified service intervals, will not produce the same results.
4 As you service your vehicle, you will discover that many of the procedures can - and should - be grouped together, because of the particular procedure being performed, or because of the close proximity of two otherwise-unrelated components to one another. For example, if the vehicle is raised for any reason, the exhaust can be inspected at the same time as the suspension and steering components.

5 The first step in this maintenance programme is to prepare yourself before the actual work begins. Read through all the Sections relevant to the work to be carried out, then make a list and gather together all the parts and tools required. If a problem is encountered, seek advice from a parts specialist, or a dealer service department.

2 Regular maintenance

1 If, from the time the vehicle is new, the routine maintenance schedule is followed closely, and frequent checks are made of fluid levels and high-wear items, as suggested throughout this manual, the engine will be kept in relatively good running condition, and the need for additional work will be minimised.
2 It is possible that there will be times when the engine is running poorly due to the lack of regular maintenance. This is even more likely if a used vehicle, which has not received regular and frequent maintenance checks, is purchased. In such cases, additional work may need to be carried out, outside of the regular maintenance intervals.
3 If engine wear is suspected, a compression test (refer to the relevant Part of Chapter 2) will provide valuable information regarding the overall performance of the main internal components. Such a test can be used as a basis to decide on the extent of the work to

be carried out. If, for example, a compression test indicates serious internal engine wear, conventional maintenance as described in this Chapter will not greatly improve the performance of the engine, and may prove a waste of time and money, unless extensive overhaul work is carried out first.
4 The following series of operations are those most often required to improve the performance of a generally poor-running engine:

Primary operations

a) Clean, inspect and test the battery (See Weekly checks).
b) Check all the engine-related fluids (See Weekly checks).
c) Check the condition and tension of the auxiliary drivebelt (Section 8).
d) Check the condition of the air filter element, and renew if necessary (Section 16).
e) Check the fuel filter (Section 27).
f) Check the condition of all hoses, and check for fluid leaks (Section 19).
g) Check the idle speed and mixture settings (Section 10).

5 If the above operations do not prove fully effective, carry out the following secondary operations:

Secondary operations

All items listed under Primary operations, plus the following:
a) Check the charging system (Chapter 5A).
b) Check the ignition system (Chapter 5B).
c) Check the fuel system (Chapter 4A).

Every 6000 miles (10 000 km)

3 Engine oil and filter renewal

1 Frequent oil and filter changes are the most important preventative maintenance procedures which can be undertaken by the DIY owner. As engine oil ages, it becomes diluted and contaminated, which leads to premature engine wear.

2 Before starting this procedure, gather together all the necessary tools and materials. Also make sure that you have plenty of clean rags and newspapers handy, to mop up any spills. Ideally, the engine oil should be warm, as it will drain more easily, and more built-up sludge will be removed with it. Take care not to touch the exhaust or any other hot parts of the engine when working under the vehicle. To avoid any possibility of scalding, and to protect yourself from possible skin irritants and other harmful contaminants in used engine oils, it is advisable to wear gloves when carrying out this work.

3 Firmly apply the handbrake then jack up the front of the vehicle and support it on axle stands (see *Jacking and vehicle support*). Undo the retaining screws and remove the plastic undercover from underneath the engine/transmission.

4 Remove the oil filler cap.

5 Using a spanner, or preferably a suitable socket and bar, slacken the drain plug about half a turn. Position the draining container under the drain plug, then remove the plug completely **(see Haynes Hint below)**. Note that on some engines an 8 mm square section drain plug key will be needed to unscrew the drain plug.

6 Allow some time for the oil to drain, noting that it may be necessary to reposition the container as the oil flow slows to a trickle.

7 After all the oil has drained, wipe the drain plug and the sealing washer with a clean rag.

Examine the condition of the sealing washer, and renew it if it shows signs of scoring or other damage which may prevent an oil-tight seal. Clean the area around the drain plug opening, and refit the plug complete with the washer and tighten it securely.

8 Move the container into position under the oil filter which is located on the front of the cylinder block.

9 Use an oil filter removal tool to slacken the filter initially, then unscrew it by hand the rest of the way **(see illustration)**. Empty the oil from the old filter into the container.

10 Use a clean rag to remove all oil, dirt and sludge from the filter sealing area on the engine. Check the old filter to make sure that the rubber sealing ring has not stuck to the engine. If it has, carefully remove it.

11 Apply a light coating of clean engine oil to the sealing ring on the new filter, then screw the filter into position on the engine. Tighten the filter firmly by hand only - **do not** use any tools.

12 Refit the undercover and securely tighten its retaining screws. Remove the old oil and all tools from under the vehicle then lower the vehicle to the ground.

13 Fill the engine through the filler hole, using the correct grade and type of oil (refer to *Weekly Checks* for details of topping-up). Pour in half the specified quantity of oil first, then wait a few minutes for the oil to drain into the sump. Continue to add oil, a small quantity at a time, until the level is up to the lower mark on the dipstick. Adding approximately a further 1.0 litre will bring the level up to the upper mark on the dipstick.

14 Start the engine and run it for a few minutes, while checking for leaks around the oil filter seal and the sump drain plug. Note that there may be a delay of a few seconds before the low oil pressure warning light goes out when the engine is first started, as the oil circulates through the new oil filter and the engine oil galleries before the pressure builds up.

15 Stop the engine, and wait a few minutes for the oil to settle in the sump once more. With the new oil circulated and the filter now completely full, recheck the level on the dipstick, and add more oil as necessary.

16 Dispose of the used engine oil safely with reference to *General repair procedures*.

4 Front brake pad check

1 Apply the handbrake, then jack up the front of the car and support it securely on axle stands (see *Jacking and vehicle support*). Remove the front roadwheels.

2 For a comprehensive check, the brake pads should be removed and cleaned. The operation of the caliper can then also be checked, and the condition of the brake disc itself can be fully examined on both sides. Refer to Chapter 9 for further information **(see Haynes Hint at foot of page)**.

3 On completion refit the roadwheels and lower the car to the ground.

5 Rear brake pad check - models with rear disc brakes

1 Jack up the rear of the car and support it securely on axle stands (see *Jacking and vehicle support*). Remove the rear roadwheels.

> **HAYNES HINT** *For a quick check, the thickness of friction material remaining on each brake pad can be measured through the aperture in the caliper body.*

2 For a comprehensive check, the brake pads should be removed and cleaned. The operation of the caliper can then also be checked, and the condition of the brake disc itself can be fully examined on both sides. Refer to Chapter 9 for further information.

3 On completion refit the roadwheels and lower the car to the ground.

As the drain plug threads release, move it sharply away so the stream of oil issuing from the sump runs into the container, not up your sleeve!

3.9 Using an oil filter removal tool to slacken the oil filter

For a quick check, the thickness of friction material remaining on each brake pad can be measured through the aperture in the caliper body.

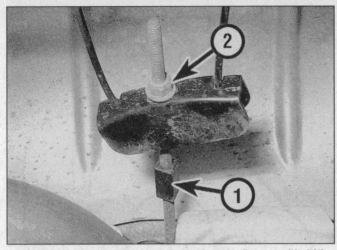

6.6 Hold the handbrake operating rod on the flats provided (1) and slacken the adjuster nut (2)

6.7 Check the operation of the handbrake lever (arrowed) - rear drum brake model

6 Handbrake check

General

1 The handbrake will normally be kept in adjustment by the action of the drum brakes automatic adjuster, or by the self-adjusting action of the rear disc calipers. Occasionally, the handbrake mechanism may require adjustment to compensate for cable stretch.
2 Chock the front wheels, then jack up the rear of the vehicle, and support securely on axle stands (see *Jacking and vehicle support*).
3 Fully release the handbrake and check that the wheels can be rotated easily by hand. The wheels may drag slightly, but there should be no binding.
4 If the wheels bind, it is likely that the handbrake mechanism is partially seized, or the mechanism is incorrectly adjusted. If the operation of the mechanism is not satisfactory, proceed as follows, according to type.

Models with rear drum brakes

5 Working under the vehicle, where applicable, remove the exhaust heat shields to expose the handbrake equaliser.
6 Counterhold the handbrake operating rod using the flats provided, then slacken the adjuster nut until there is no tension in the handbrake cables **(see illustration)**.
7 Remove the brake drums as described in Chapter 9, and check the operation of the handbrake lever on the trailing shoe **(see illustration)**. The lever should move freely.
8 If necessary, dismantle the components and clean them, then reassemble as described in Chapter 9.
9 Check that the adjuster star wheel rotates freely in both directions, then back off the star wheel by five or six teeth.

10 Check that the handbrake cables slide freely in their sheaths.
11 Check that the handbrake operating levers are resting correctly on the shoes.
12 Temporarily refit the brake drums (there is no need to fit the hub nuts), then operate the adjustment mechanism by depressing the brake pedal firmly several times. It should be possible to hear the adjustment mechanism clicking as the pedal is depressed.
13 Remove the brake drums again.
14 Working under the vehicle floor, turn the cable adjuster until handbrake operating levers on the brake shoes begin to move when the handbrake lever is pulled between the first and second notches. There should be no free-play in the handbrake cables once the lever is pulled beyond the second notch.
15 Tighten the adjuster locknuts.
16 Refit the brake drums as described in Chapter 9, then refit the roadwheels, and lower the vehicle to the ground.
17 With the vehicle resting on its wheels, again depress the brake pedal repeatedly to operate the self-adjusting mechanism. It should be possible to hear the adjusting mechanism click as the brake pedal is depressed.

Models with rear disc brakes

18 Proceed as described in paragraphs 5 and 6.
19 Remove the roadwheels.
20 Check that the handbrake cables slide freely in their sheaths, and that the operating levers on the calipers move freely.
21 Push the handbrake operating levers on the calipers as far as they will go against their bottom stops.
22 Working under the vehicle floor, turn the cable adjuster sleeve until the handbrake cable end fittings just contact the operating levers on the calipers, without moving the levers **(see illustration)**.

23 Continue to turn the adjuster sleeve until the handbrake operating levers on the calipers begin to move when the handbrake lever is pulled between the first and second notches. There should be no free-play in the handbrake cables once the lever is pulled beyond the second notch.
24 Tighten the adjuster locknuts.
25 Refit the roadwheels, and lower the vehicle to the ground.

7 Clutch check

1 Check and adjust the clutch cable as described in Chapter 6. Check that the cable moves freely and easily and lubricate its exposed section with multi-purpose grease.

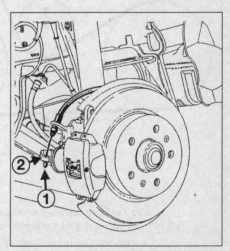

6.22 The handbrake cable end fittings (1) should just contact the operating levers (2) - rear disc brake model

1A

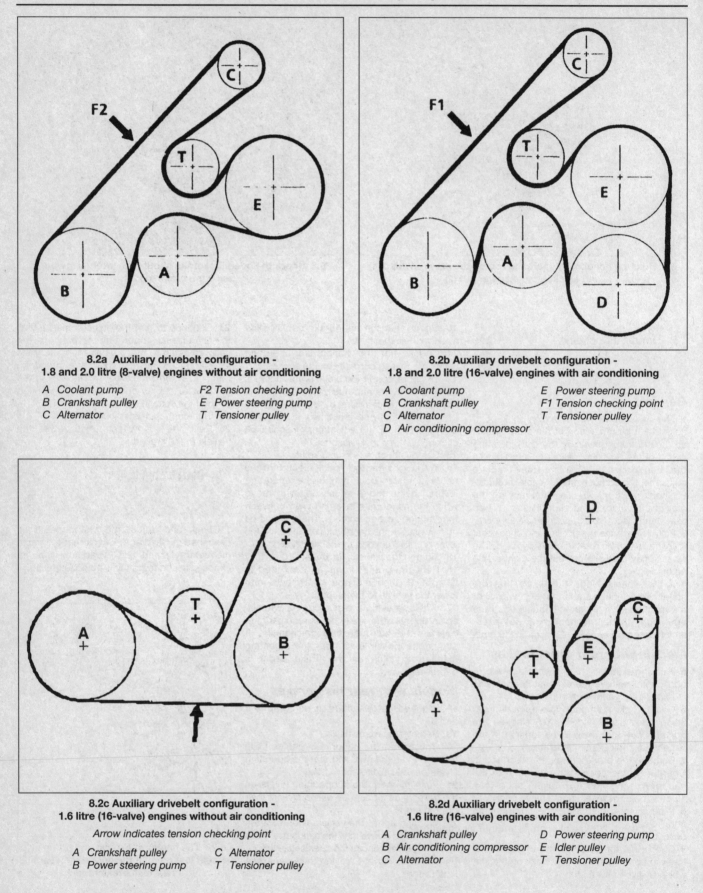

**8.2a Auxiliary drivebelt configuration -
1.8 and 2.0 litre (8-valve) engines without air conditioning**

A   Coolant pump
B   Crankshaft pulley
C   Alternator
F2 Tension checking point
E   Power steering pump
T   Tensioner pulley

**8.2b Auxiliary drivebelt configuration -
1.8 and 2.0 litre (16-valve) engines with air conditioning**

A   Coolant pump
B   Crankshaft pulley
C   Alternator
D   Air conditioning compressor
E   Power steering pump
F1 Tension checking point
T   Tensioner pulley

**8.2c Auxiliary drivebelt configuration -
1.6 litre (16-valve) engines without air conditioning**

Arrow indicates tension checking point

A   Crankshaft pulley
B   Power steering pump
C   Alternator
T   Tensioner pulley

**8.2d Auxiliary drivebelt configuration -
1.6 litre (16-valve) engines with air conditioning**

A   Crankshaft pulley
B   Air conditioning compressor
C   Alternator
D   Power steering pump
E   Idler pulley
T   Tensioner pulley

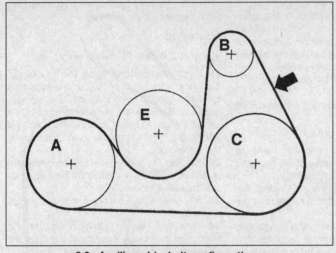

**8.2e Auxiliary drivebelt configuration -
1.8 litre (16-valve) engines without air conditioning**

Arrow indicates tension checking point

A   *Crankshaft pulley*   C   *Power steering pump*
B   *Alternator*   E   *Coolant pump*

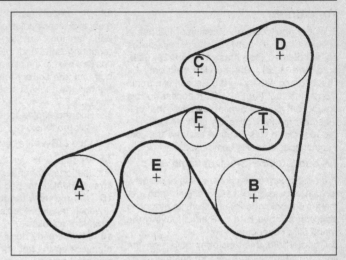

**8.2f Auxiliary drivebelt configuration -
1.8 litre (16-valve) engines with air conditioning**

A *Crankshaft pulley*   D *Power steering pump*
B *Air conditioning*   E *Coolant pump*
   compressor   F *Idler pulley*
C *Alternator*   T *Tensioner pulley*

8   Auxiliary drivebelt check and renewal

Note: *Renault recommend that a belt is renewed whenever it is slackened or removed.*

Checking

1 The auxiliary drivebelt is located at the right-hand side of the engine.
2 Numerous different drivebelt configurations may be encountered, depending on engine type and whether or not the vehicle is equipped with air conditioning **(see illustrations)**.
3 Due to their function and material makeup, drivebelts are prone to failure after a period of time and should therefore be inspected and, where applicable, periodically adjusted.
4 Since the drivebelt is located very close to the right-hand side of the engine compartment, it is possible to gain better access by raising the front of the vehicle (see *Jacking and vehicle support*) and removing the right-hand wheel, then removing the engine undercover (where applicable), and removing the splash shield from inside the wheelarch.
5 With the engine stopped, inspect the full length of the drivebelt for cracks and separation of the belt plies. It will be necessary to turn the engine (using a spanner or socket and bar on the crankshaft pulley bolt) in order to move the belt from the pulleys so that the belt can be inspected thoroughly. Twist the belt between the pulleys so that both sides can be viewed. Also check for fraying, and glazing which gives the belt a shiny appearance. Check the pulleys for nicks, cracks, distortion and corrosion.

1A

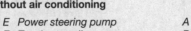

**8.2g Auxiliary drivebelt configuration -
2.0 litre (16-valve) engines without air conditioning**

A *Crankshaft pulley*   E *Power steering pump*
C *Idler pulley*   F *Tensioner pulley*
D *Alternator*

**8.2h Auxiliary drivebelt configuration -
2.0 litre (16-valve) engines with air conditioning**

A *Crankshaft pulley*   D *Alternator*
B *Air conditioning compressor*   E *Power steering pump*
C *Idler pulley*   F *Tensioner pulley*

Tensioning

6 Where applicable, the tension of the belt is checked midway between the pulleys at the point indicated (see illustrations 8.2a, 8.2b, 8.2c and 8.2e). The tension can only be checked and set, using the Renault electronic measuring tool (Mot. 1273). If access to this equipment is not available, have the belt tension checked by a Renault dealer. The procedures in this Section assume that the Renault special tool is being used.

1.8 and 2.0 litre (8-valve) engines

7 If adjustment is required, where necessary, to gain access, release the engine management electronic control unit from its mounting strap, and move it to one side, leaving the wiring plug connected.

8 Counterhold the tensioner pulley on the flats provided, using a 22 mm spanner, then slacken the pulley bolt using a 7 mm Allen key. Move the tensioner pulley as required to relieve or apply tension to the belt (see illustration).

9 Hold the pulley in position and tighten the pulley bolt to lock the tensioner pulley in position.

10 Run the engine for about 5 minutes, then recheck the tension.

1.6 litre (16-valve) engines

11 On models with air conditioning, an automatic tensioner is used to maintain the correct drivebelt tension, and an actual tension value is not given by Renault. If problems with belt squeal or slip are encountered, the belt should be renewed. If the problem continues, it will be necessary to renew the tensioner assembly.

12 On models without air conditioning, a manual drivebelt adjuster is fitted. To adjust the belt tension, slacken the two tensioner mounting bolts and the adjuster bolt locknut (located next to the alternator). Turn the adjuster bolt until the correct tension is obtained, then tighten the locknut and tensioner mounting bolts.

13 Run the engine for about 5 minutes, then recheck the tension.

1.8 litre (16-valve) engines

14 Models with air conditioning have an automatic tensioner assembly of the type and arrangement described in paragraph 11.

15 On models without air conditioning, the drivebelt tension is adjusted by means of the alternator as follows.

16 If not already done, apply the handbrake, then jack up the front of the car and support it on axle stands (see *Jacking and vehicle support*). Remove the right-hand wheel, then remove the engine undercover (where applicable), and the splash shield from inside the wheelarch.

17 From under the wheelarch, slacken the alternator lower mounting bolt.

18 From within the engine compartment, slacken the adjustment bolt, then move the alternator as required to obtain the correct belt tension. Tighten the mounting and adjustment bolts, refit the disturbed components and lower the car to the ground.

19 Run the engine for about 5 minutes, then recheck the tension.

2.0 litre (16-valve) engines

20 Models with and without air conditioning incorporate an automatic tensioner to maintain the correct drivebelt tension. If the drivebelt tension is not as specified, the tensioner should be renewed.

Renewal

1.8 and 2.0 litre (8-valve) engines

21 If not already done, apply the handbrake, then jack up the front of the car and support it on axle stands (see *Jacking and vehicle support*). Remove the right-hand wheel, then remove the engine undercover (where applicable), and the splash shield from inside the wheelarch.

22 Slacken the belt tension fully as described previously. Note the routing of the belt, then slip the belt off the pulleys.

23 Fit the new belt ensuring that it is routed correctly.

24 With the belt in position, adjust the tension as previously described, then refit the splash shield, undercover and roadwheel, and lower the car to the ground.

1.6 litre (16-valve) engines

25 If not already done, apply the handbrake, then jack up the front of the car and support it on axle stands (see *Jacking and vehicle support*). Remove the right-hand wheel, then remove the engine undercover (where applicable), and the splash shield from inside the wheelarch.

26 On models with air conditioning, using a 13 mm spanner or socket, turn the tensioner as shown to release the belt tension (see illustration). Align the holes in the tensioner and bracket and insert a 6 mm Allen key through the holes to lock the tensioner in the released position.

27 Note the routing of the belt, then slip the belt off the pulleys.

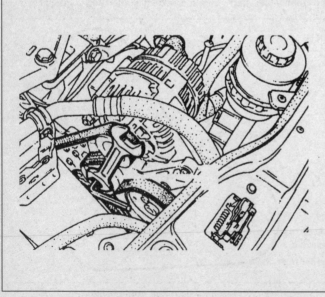

8.8 Use a spanner and an Allen key to slacken the auxiliary drivebelt tensioner on 1.8 and 2.0 litre (8-valve) engines

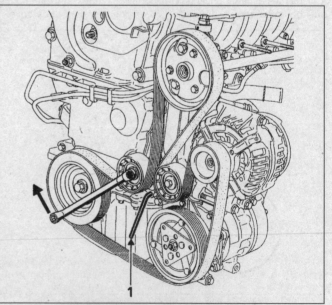

8.26 Releasing the drivebelt tensioner on 1.6 litre (16-valve) engines with air conditioning

Move the tensioner in the direction of the arrow then insert an Allen key (1) to lock the tensioner

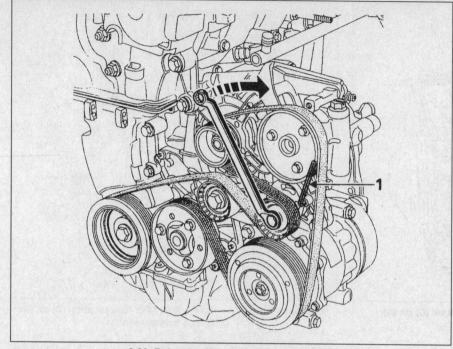

**8.33 Releasing the drivebelt tensioner on
1.8 litre (16-valve) engines with air conditioning**

*Move the tensioner in the direction of the arrow then insert an Allen key (1) to
lock the tensioner*

28 Fit the new belt ensuring that it is routed correctly, then release the tensioner to automatically tension the belt. Refit the splash shield, undercover and roadwheel, and lower the car to the ground.

29 On models without air conditioning, slacken the belt tension fully as described previously. Note the routing of the belt, then slip the belt off the pulleys.

30 Fit the new belt ensuring that it is routed correctly. Note that the drivebelt has five teeth and the alternator and power steering pump pulleys have six. When positioning the belt, ensure that the tooth at the end of the pulleys (furthest away from the engine) remains free.

31 With the belt in position, adjust the tension as previously described, then refit the splash shield, undercover and roadwheel, and lower the car to the ground.

1.8 litre (16-valve) engines

32 If not already done, apply the handbrake, then jack up the front of the car and support it on axle stands (see *Jacking and vehicle support*). Remove the right-hand wheel, then remove the engine undercover (where applicable), and the splash shield from inside the wheelarch.

33 On models with air conditioning, using a 13 mm spanner or socket, turn the tensioner as shown to release the belt tension **(see illustration)**. Align the holes in the tensioner and bracket and insert a 6 mm Allen key through the holes to lock the tensioner in the released position.

34 Note the routing of the belt, then slip the belt off the pulleys.

35 Fit the new belt ensuring that it is routed correctly. Note that the drivebelt has five teeth and the alternator, power steering pump and air conditioning pulleys have six. When positioning the belt, ensure that the tooth at the inside of the pulleys (nearest to the engine) remains free.

36 Release the tensioner to automatically tension the belt, then refit the splash shield, undercover and roadwheel, and lower the car to the ground.

37 On models without air conditioning, slacken the belt tension fully as described previously. Note the routing of the belt, then slip the belt off the pulleys.

38 Fit the new belt ensuring that it is routed correctly. Note that the drivebelt has five teeth and the alternator and power steering pump pulleys have six. When positioning the belt, ensure that the tooth at the inside of the pulleys (nearest to the engine) remains free.

39 With the belt in position, adjust the tension as previously described, then refit the splash shield, undercover and roadwheel, and lower the car to the ground.

2.0 litre (16-valve) engines

40 If not already done, apply the handbrake, then jack up the front of the car and support it on axle stands (see *Jacking and vehicle support*). Remove the right-hand wheel, then remove the engine undercover (where applicable), and the splash shield from inside the wheelarch.

41 To release the tensioner to allow removal of the belt, observe the tensioner bracket arm which will have either a three eighths inch, or three quarter inch square hole in its centre. This is to allow the Renault special tool (or the square end of a standard socket set extension bar) to be inserted into the hole to move the bracket and release the belt tension. However, clearance in this area is very restricted and a preferred alternative method is engage a spanner on the lug projecting from the base of the tensioner bracket arm.

42 Turn the tensioner bracket arm to release the belt tension. Align the holes in the arm and bracket and insert a suitable roll pin or drill bit through the holes to lock the tensioner in the released position.

43 Note the routing of the belt, then slip the belt off the pulleys.

44 Fit the new belt ensuring that it is routed correctly, then release the tensioner to automatically tension the belt. Refit the splash shield, undercover and roadwheel, and lower the car to the ground.

**9 Automatic transmission
fluid level check**

Transmission fluid

Note 1: *The transmission fluid level checking procedure is particularly complicated, and the home mechanic would be well-advised to take the vehicle to a Renault dealer to have the work carried out. To ensure accuracy, special test equipment is necessary to measure the fluid temperature when carrying out the check. However, the following procedure is given for those who may have access to this equipment.*

Note 2: *The following procedure is mainly applicable to the AD4 type transmission. The DPO type transmission is a 'sealed-for-life' unit and level checking will only be necessary if there has been a slight leak, or if it is suspected, for any reason, that the fluid level might be low.*

Note 3: *Refer to Chapter 7B for transmission type identification.*

1 On AD4 type transmissions, remove the plug from the top of the filler tube D on the front of the transmission. On DPO type transmissions, remove the air cleaner assembly as described in Chapter 4A, then unscrew the plug D from the top of the transmission **(see illustrations overleaf)**. Add 0.5 litre of the specified fluid to the transmission via the filler tube or opening, using a clean funnel with a fine-mesh filter, then refit the plug.

2 Position the vehicle over an inspection pit, on a ramp, or jack it up and support it on axle stands (see *Jacking and vehicle support*), ensuring that the vehicle remains level. If necessary, undo the retaining screws and remove the plastic undercover from beneath the engine/transmission.

1A

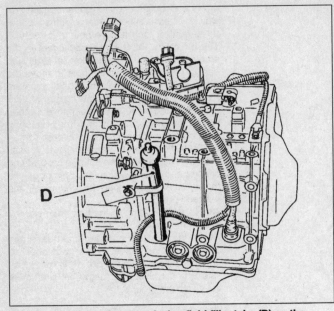

9.1a Automatic transmission fluid filler tube (D) on the AD4 type transmission

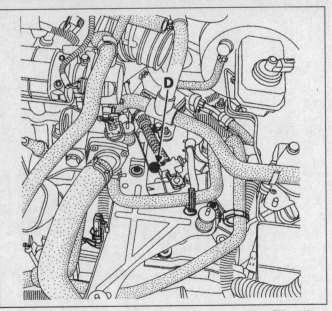

9.1b Automatic transmission fluid filler plug location (D) on the DPO type transmission

3 Connect the Renault XR25 test meter to the diagnostic socket, and enter DO4 (AD4 transmission) or D14 (DPO transmission) then number 04. With the selector lever in Park, run the engine at idle speed until the fluid temperature, as shown on the test meter, reaches 60ºC.

4 With the engine still running, unscrew the level plug from the transmission **(see illustrations)**. On the DPO type transmission, the drain plug and level plug are incorporated into one unit - the level plug is the smaller of the two hexagonal headed plugs forming the draining/level checking unit. Allow the excess fluid to run out into a calibrated container drop-by-drop, then refit the plug. The amount of fluid should be more than 0.1 litre; if it is not, the fluid level in the transmission is incorrect.

5 If the level is incorrect, add an extra 0.5 litre of the specified fluid to the transmission, as described in paragraph 1. Allow the transmission to cool down to 50ºC, then repeat the checking procedure again as described in the previous paragraphs. Repeat the procedure as required until more than the specified amount of fluid is drained as described in the previous paragraphs, indicating that the transmission fluid level is correct, then securely tighten the level plug. Where necessary, refit the engine undercover and the air cleaner assembly.

Final drive oil - AD4 type transmission only

6 This is not a routine operation, but it may be considered necessary if there is reason to suspect that the oil level is incorrect - for instance if there has been an oil leak.

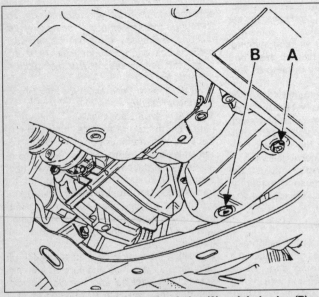

9.4a Automatic transmission level plug (A) and drain plug (B) on the AD4 type transmission

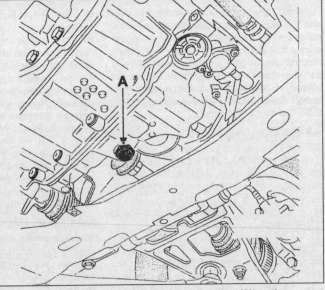

9.4b Combined drain plug and level plug (A) on the DPO type transmission

The level plug is the smaller of the two hexagonal headed plugs

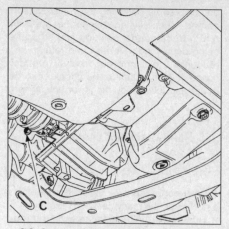

9.8 Automatic transmission final drive filler/level plug (C) on the AD4 type transmission

7 Either position the vehicle over an inspection pit, or jack up the front and rear of the vehicle and support it on axle stands (see *Jacking and vehicle support*). The vehicle must be level for the check to be accurate.

8 Unscrew the final drive filler/level plug located behind the right-hand driveshaft on the right-hand side of the transmission **(see illustration)**.

9 Check that the level of the oil is up to the bottom of the plug hole. If not, inject oil of the correct grade into the hole until if overflows.

10 Wipe clean the plug, then refit and tighten it.

11 Lower the vehicle to the ground.

10 Idle speed and mixture check

1 Both the idle speed and mixture (exhaust gas CO level) are automatically controlled by the engine management ECU and cannot be adjusted. If either the idle speed or mixture settings are thought to be incorrect then a fault is present in the engine management system and the vehicle should be taken to a Renault dealer for testing (see Chapter 4A).

11 Seat belt check

1 Carefully examine the seat belt webbing for cuts, or any signs of serious fraying or deterioration. If the belt is of the retractable type, pull the belt all the way out of the inertia reel, and examine the full extent of the webbing.

2 Fasten and unfasten the belt, ensuring that the locking mechanism holds securely, and releases properly when intended. If the belt is of the retractable type, check also that the retracting mechanism operates correctly when the belt is released.

3 Check the security of all seat belt mountings and attachments which are accessible without removing any trim or other components **(see illustration)**.

12 Electrical systems check

1 Check the operation of all electrical equipment, ie, lights, direction indicators, horn, etc. Refer to the appropriate Sections of Chapter 12 for details if any of the circuits are found to be inoperative.

2 Note that stop-light switch adjustment is described in Chapter 9.

3 Visually check all accessible wiring connectors, harnesses and retaining clips for security, and for signs of chafing or damage. Rectify any faults found.

13 Exhaust system check

1 With the engine cold (at least an hour after the vehicle has been driven), check the complete exhaust system from the engine to the end of the tailpipe. The exhaust system is most easily checked with the vehicle raised on a hoist, or suitably supported on axle stands, so that the exhaust components are readily visible and accessible.

2 Check the exhaust pipes and connections for evidence of leaks, severe corrosion and damage. Make sure that all brackets and mountings are in good condition, and that all relevant nuts and bolts are tight. Leakage at any of the joints or in other parts of the system will usually show up as a black sooty stain in the vicinity of the leak.

3 Rattles and other noises can often be traced to the exhaust system, especially the brackets and mountings. Try to move the pipes and silencers. If the components are able to come into contact with the body or suspension parts, secure the system with new mountings. Otherwise separate the joints (if possible) and twist the pipes as necessary to provide additional clearance.

14 Suspension and steering check

Front suspension and steering check

1 Raise the front of the vehicle, and securely support it on axle stands (see *Jacking and vehicle support*).

2 Visually inspect the balljoint dust covers and the steering rack-and-pinion gaiters for splits, chafing or deterioration. Any wear of these components will cause loss of lubricant,

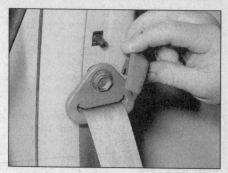

11.3 Check the security of the seat belt mountings

together with dirt and water entry, resulting in rapid deterioration of the balljoints or steering gear.

3 On vehicles with power steering, check the fluid hoses for chafing or deterioration, and the pipe and hose unions for fluid leaks. Also check for signs of fluid leakage under pressure from the steering gear rubber gaiters, which would indicate failed fluid seals within the steering gear.

4 Grasp the roadwheel at the 12 o'clock and 6 o'clock positions, and try to rock it **(see illustration)**. Very slight free play may be felt, but if the movement is appreciable, further investigation is necessary to determine the source. Continue rocking the wheel while an assistant depresses the footbrake. If the movement is now eliminated or significantly reduced, it is likely that the hub bearings are at fault. If the free play is still evident with the footbrake depressed, then there is wear in the suspension joints or mountings.

5 Now grasp the wheel at the 9 o'clock and 3 o'clock positions, and try to rock it as before. Any movement felt now may again be caused by wear in the hub bearings or the steering track-rod balljoints. If the outer balljoint is worn, the visual movement will be obvious. If the inner joint is suspect, it can be felt by placing a hand over the rack-and-pinion rubber gaiter and gripping the track-rod. If the wheel is now rocked, movement will be felt at the inner joint if wear has taken place.

6 Using a large screwdriver or flat bar, check for wear in the suspension mounting bushes

1A

14.4 Check for wear in the hub bearings by grasping the wheel and trying to rock it

by levering between the relevant suspension component and its attachment point. Some movement is to be expected, as the mountings are made of rubber, but excessive wear should be obvious. Also check the condition of any visible rubber bushes, looking for splits, cracks or contamination of the rubber.

7 With the car standing on its wheels, have an assistant turn the steering wheel back and forth, about an eighth of a turn each way. There should be very little, if any, lost movement between the steering wheel and roadwheels. If this is not the case, closely observe the joints and mountings previously described. In addition, check the steering column universal joints for wear, and also check the rack-and-pinion steering gear itself.

Rear suspension check

8 Chock the front wheels, then jack up the rear of the vehicle and support securely on axle stands (see *Jacking and vehicle support*).
9 Working as described previously for the front suspension, check the rear hub bearings, the suspension bushes and the shock absorber mountings for wear.

Shock absorber check

10 Check for any signs of fluid leakage around the shock absorber body, or from the rubber gaiter around the piston rod. Should any fluid be noticed, the shock absorber is defective internally, and should be renewed. **Note:** *Shock absorbers should always be renewed in pairs on the same axle.*
11 The efficiency of the shock absorber may

be checked by bouncing the vehicle at each corner. Generally speaking, the body will return to its normal position and stop after being depressed. If it rises and returns on a rebound, the shock absorber is probably suspect. Also examine the shock absorber upper and lower mountings for any signs of wear.

15 Roadwheel bolt check

1 Where applicable, remove the wheel trims, and slacken the roadwheel bolts slightly.
2 Tighten the bolts to the specified torque, using a torque wrench.

Every 12 000 miles (20 000 km)

16 Air filter element renewal

1.8 and 2.0 litre (8-valve) engines

1 Release the retaining clips, remove the lid from the top of the air cleaner housing and lift out the air filter element.
2 Wipe clean the filter housing and fit the new filter. Refit the filter cover and secure it in position with the retaining clips.

1.6 and 1.8 litre (16-valve) engines

3 Disconnect the air intake hose from the resonator, detach the resonator from the air filter housing and withdraw the resonator from its location.
4 Undo the two screws securing the air filter housing to the intake housing (see illustration).
5 Lift up the air filter housing, and lift out the air filter element.
6 Wipe clean the filter housing and fit the new filter. Locate the housing in position and secure with the two screws.

7 Refit the resonator and air intake hose.

2.0 litre (16-valve) engines

8 Undo the four screws, remove the lid from the top of the air cleaner housing and lift out the air filter element (see illustrations).
9 Wipe clean the filter housing and fit the new filter. Refit the filter cover and secure it in position with the four screws.

17 Spark plug renewal and ignition system check

Spark plug renewal

1 The correct functioning of the spark plugs is vital for the correct running and efficiency of the engine. It is essential that the plugs fitted are appropriate for the engine (a suitable type is specified at the beginning of this Chapter). If this type is used and the engine is in good condition, the spark plugs should not need attention between scheduled replacement intervals. Spark plug cleaning is rarely necessary, and should not be attempted unless specialised equipment is available, as damage can easily be caused to the firing ends.
2 Spark plug removal and refitting requires a spark plug socket, with an extension which can be turned by a ratchet handle or similar. This socket is lined with a rubber sleeve, to protect the porcelain insulator of the spark plug, and to hold the plug while it is removed or inserted into the spark plug hole. A torque wrench to tighten the plugs to the specified torque will also be required (see illustration). On 8-valve engines, a set of feeler blades or a spark plug electrode gap adjusting tool will be needed to check and adjust the electrode gap. On 16-valve engines, spark plugs with specially-shaped multiple electrodes are used and it is not necessary or possible to adjust the electrode gap on these types.

16.4 Air filter housing retaining screws (arrowed) on 1.6 and 1.8 litre (16-valve) engines

16.8a On 2.0 litre (16-valve) engines, undo the four screws (arrowed) . . .

16.8b . . . then lift up the lid and remove the filter element

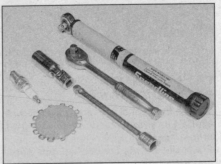

17.2 Tools required for spark plug removal, gap adjustment and refitting

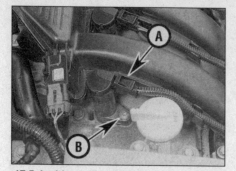

17.5 Ignition coil wiring connector (A) and retaining screw (B) on 1.6 and 1.8 litre (16-valve) engines

17.12a Measuring the spark plug gap with a wire gauge

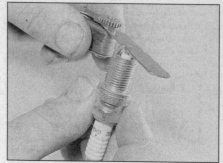

17.12b Measuring the spark plug gap with a feeler blade

3 To remove the spark plugs, open the bonnet and on 2.0 litre (16-valve) engines, remove the plastic engine cover from the top of the cylinder head. Note how the HT leads or ignition coil wiring harnesses are routed and secured by clips along the top of the cylinder head or inlet manifold. To prevent the possibility of mixing up the HT leads or wiring, it is a good idea to try to work on one spark plug at a time.

4 On 8-valve engines and 2.0 litre (16-valve) engines, disconnect the HT leads from the plugs by gripping the end fitting, not the lead, otherwise the lead connection may be fractured.

5 On 1.6 and 1.8 litre (16-valve) engines, each spark plug has a separate ignition coil located over the top of the plug and secured to the cylinder head with a retaining screw. Disconnect the wiring connector at the ignition coil, then undo the retaining screw and pull the coil upwards from the spark plug and cylinder head **(see illustration)**.

6 It is advisable to remove the dirt from the spark plug recesses using a clean brush, vacuum cleaner or compressed air before removing the plugs, to prevent dirt dropping into the cylinders.

7 Unscrew the plugs, ensuring that the socket is kept in alignment with each plug - if the socket is forcibly moved to either side, the porcelain top of the plug may be broken off.

8 As each plug is removed, examine it as follows - this will give a good indication of the condition of the engine. If the insulator nose of the spark plug is clean and white, with no deposits, this is indicative of a weak mixture or too hot a plug (a hot plug transfers heat away from the electrode slowly, a cold plug transfers heat away quickly).

9 If the tip and insulator nose are covered with hard black-looking deposits, then this is indicative that the mixture is too rich. Should the plug be black and oily, then it is likely that the engine is fairly worn, as well as the mixture being too rich.

10 If the insulator nose is covered with light tan to greyish-brown deposits, then the mixture is correct and it is likely that the engine is in good condition.

11 On 8-valve engines, the spark plug electrode gap is of considerable importance as, if it is too large or too small, the size of the spark and its efficiency will be seriously impaired. The gap should be set to the value given in the Specifications at the beginning of this Chapter.

12 To set the gap, where possible, measure it with a feeler blade or gap adjusting tool and then bend open, or closed, the outer plug electrode until the correct gap is achieved **(see illustrations)**. The centre electrode should never be bent, as this may crack the insulator and cause plug failure, if nothing worse.

13 Before fitting the spark plugs, check that the threaded connector sleeves are tight, and that the plug exterior surfaces and threads are clean.

14 Insert each spark plug into the cylinder head and screw them in by hand, taking extra care to enter the plug threads correctly **(see Haynes Hint)**.

It is very often difficult to insert spark plugs into their holes without cross-threading them. To avoid this possibility, fit a short length of 5/16 inch internal diameter rubber hose over the end of the spark plug. The flexible hose acts as a universal joint to help align the plug with the plug hole. Should the plug begin to cross-thread, the hose will slip on the spark plug, preventing thread damage to the aluminium cylinder head

15 When each spark plug is started correctly on its threads, screw it down until it just seats lightly, then tighten it to the specified torque wrench setting.

16 On 1.6 and 1.8 litre (16-valve) engines, check the condition of the O-ring seal on the end of each ignition coil and renew them if necessary. Locate the coils over the spark plugs and secure with the retaining screws. Connect the ignition coil wiring connectors in their correct order.

17 On all other engines, reconnect the HT leads in their correct order, pressing each one firmly into position. Where applicable, refit the plastic engine cover.

Ignition system check

> ⚠ *Warning: Voltages produced by an electronic ignition system are considerably higher than those produced by conventional ignition systems. Extreme care must be taken when working on the system with the ignition switched on. Persons with surgically-implanted cardiac pacemaker devices should keep well clear of the ignition circuits, components and test equipment.*

Models with a distributor

18 The spark plug (HT) leads should be checked whenever new spark plugs are fitted.

19 Ensure that the leads are numbered before removing them, to avoid confusion when refitting. Pull the leads from the plugs by gripping the end fitting, not the lead, otherwise the lead connection may be fractured.

20 Check inside the end fitting for signs of corrosion, which will look like a white crusty powder. Push the end fitting back onto the spark plug, ensuring that it is a tight fit on the plug. If not, remove the lead again and use pliers to carefully crimp the metal connector inside the end fitting until it fits securely on the end of the spark plug.

21 Using a clean rag, wipe the entire length of the lead to remove any built-up dirt and grease. Once the lead is clean, check for burns, cracks and other damage. Do not bend the lead excessively, nor pull the lead lengthwise - the conductor inside might break.

1A

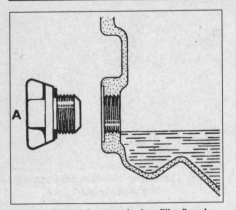

18.3 Manual transmission filler/level plug (A) - correct oil level shown

22 Disconnect the other end of the lead from the distributor cap. Again, pull only on the end fitting. Check for corrosion and a tight fit in the same manner as the spark plug end. If an ohmmeter is available, check the resistance of the lead by connecting the meter between the spark plug end of the lead and the segment inside the distributor cap. Refit the lead securely on completion.

23 Check the remaining leads one at a time, in the same way.

24 If new spark plug (HT) leads are required, purchase a set for your specific car and engine.

25 Unscrew its retaining screws and remove the distributor cap. Wipe it clean, and carefully inspect it inside and out for signs of cracks, black carbon tracks (tracking) and worn, burned or loose contacts; check that the cap's carbon brush is unworn, free to move against spring pressure, and making good contact with the rotor arm. Also inspect the cap seal for signs of wear or damage, and renew if necessary. Remove the rotor arm from the end of the camshaft and inspect it. It is common practice to renew the cap and rotor arm whenever new spark plug (HT) leads are fitted. When fitting a new cap, remove the leads from the old cap one at a time, and fit them to the new cap in the exact same location - do not simultaneously remove all the leads from the old cap, or firing order confusion may occur. When refitting, ensure

that the arm is securely pressed onto the camshaft, and tighten the cap retaining screws securely.

26 Even with the ignition system in first-class condition, some engines may still occasionally experience poor starting attributable to damp ignition components. To disperse moisture, a water-dispersant aerosol can be very effective.

Models with a static (distributorless) ignition system

27 Check the condition of the HT leads (where applicable) as described above in paragraphs 18 to 23.

18 Manual transmission oil level check

1 Either position the vehicle over an inspection pit, or jack up the front and rear of the vehicle and support it on axle stands (see *Jacking and vehicle support*). The vehicle must be level for the check to be accurate.

2 Undo the retaining screws and remove the undercover from beneath the engine/transmission.

3 Clean the area around the filler/level plug on the left-hand side of the transmission, then slacken and remove the plug from the transmission **(see illustration)**.

4 The transmission oil level should be up to the lower edge of the filler/level plug aperture.

5 If necessary, top-up using the specified type of lubricant until the transmission oil level is correct. Fill the transmission until oil starts to flow out and allow excess oil to drain out **(see illustration)**.

6 Once the transmission oil level is correct, refit the filler/level plug and tighten it securely.

7 Refit the engine undercover then lower the vehicle to the ground. Note that frequent need for topping-up indicates a leakage, possibly through an oil seal. The cause should be investigated and rectified.

19 Hose and fluid leak check

1 Visually inspect the engine joint faces, gaskets and seals for any signs of water or oil leaks. Pay particular attention to the areas around the cylinder head cover, cylinder head, oil filter and sump joint faces. Bear in mind that, over a period of time, some very slight seepage from these areas is to be expected - what you are really looking for is any indication of a serious leak **(see Haynes Hint)**. Should a leak be found, renew the offending gasket or oil seal by referring to the appropriate Chapters in this manual.

2 Also check the security and condition of all the engine-related pipes and hoses, and all braking system pipes and hoses. Ensure that

all cable-ties or securing clips are in place, and in good condition. Clips which are broken or missing can lead to chafing of the hoses, pipes or wiring, which could cause more serious problems in the future.

3 Carefully check the radiator hoses and heater hoses along their entire length. Renew any hose which is cracked, swollen or deteriorated. Cracks will show up better if the hose is squeezed. Pay close attention to the hose clips that secure the hoses to the cooling system components. Hose clips can pinch and puncture hoses, resulting in cooling system leaks. If the crimped-type hose clips are used, it may be a good idea to replace them with standard worm-drive clips.

4 Inspect all the cooling system components (hoses, joint faces, etc) for leaks.

5 Where any problems are found on system components, renew the component or gasket with reference to Chapter 3.

6 With the vehicle raised, inspect the fuel tank and filler neck for punctures, cracks and other damage. The connection between the filler neck and tank is especially critical. Sometimes a rubber filler neck or connecting hose will leak due to loose retaining clamps or deteriorated rubber.

7 Carefully check all rubber hoses and metal fuel lines leading away from the fuel tank. Check for loose connections, deteriorated hoses, crimped lines, and other damage. Pay particular attention to the vent pipes and hoses, which often loop up around the filler neck and can become blocked or crimped. Follow the lines to the front of the vehicle, carefully inspecting them all the way. Renew damaged sections as necessary. Similarly, whilst the vehicle is raised, take the opportunity to inspect all underbody brake fluid pipes and hoses.

8 From within the engine compartment, check the security of all fuel, vacuum and brake hose attachments and pipe unions, and inspect all hoses for kinks, chafing and deterioration.

9 Where applicable, check the condition of the power steering fluid pipes and hoses.

18.5 Topping-up the manual transmission oil level

A leak in the cooling system will usually show up as white- or rust-coloured deposits on the area adjoining the leak.

20 Pollen filter renewal

Models with one-piece scuttle cover panel

1 Remove the scuttle cover panels as described in Chapter 11, Section 23.
2 Unclip the water deflector from the heater air inlet for access to the pollen filter.
3 Withdraw the filter from its housing.
4 Refitting is a reversal of removal.

Models with two-piece scuttle cover panel

5 Open the bonnet.
6 Remove the three screws securing the smaller scuttle cover panel, which covers the pollen filter housing **(see illustration)**.
7 Carefully pull the weatherstrip from the front edge of the scuttle panel (as far as the windscreen washer jet), then lift the scuttle cover panel, and pull it forwards to release it from the scuttle. Unclip the windscreen washer fluid hose.

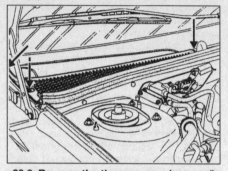

20.6 Remove the three screws (arrowed) securing the scuttle cover panel - left-hand-drive model shown

8 Remove the water deflector, by pulling it towards the centre of the vehicle, then pulling it forwards to release the securing clips at the inner end.
9 Use the tab provided to pull the pollen filter from its housing **(see illustration)**.
10 Fit the new filter, ensuring that it is correctly located in the housing. The top of the filter must be flat, and the tab should be visible at the top.
11 Refit the water deflector, then refit the

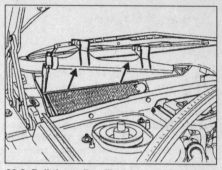

20.9 Pull the pollen filter from its housing - left-hand-drive model shown

scuttle cover panel using a reversal of the removal procedure. Make sure that the water deflector is securely refitted.

21 Air conditioning system check

The air conditioning system must be checked by a Renault dealer using dedicated test equipment.

1A

Every 36 000 miles (60 000 km)

22 Spare fuse check

Check that spare fuses are in place in the locations provided in the fusebox cover (see Chapter 12). It is advisable to carry at least one spare of each rating of fuse fitted. Spare fuses can be obtained from most car accessory shops, or from a Renault dealer.

23 Front wheel alignment check

Refer to the information given in Chapter 10.

24 Rear brake shoe thickness check - models with rear drum brakes

Remove the rear brake drums, and check the brake shoes for signs of wear or contamination. At the same time, also inspect the wheel cylinders for signs of leakage, and the brake drum for signs of wear. Refer to the

relevant Sections of Chapter 9 for further information.

25 Automatic transmission fluid renewal - AD4 type transmission

Note 1: *Refer to Section 9 to find out what is involved in checking the transmission fluid level before draining the transmission. Note that the final drive oil does not need to be renewed.*
Note 2: *The following procedure is only applicable to the AD4 type transmission. The DPO type transmission is a 'sealed-for-life' unit and fluid renewal is not a service operation.*
Note 3: *Refer to Chapter 7B for transmission type identification.*
1 Take the vehicle on a short run, to warm the transmission up to normal operating temperature.
2 Park the car on level ground, then switch off the ignition and apply the handbrake firmly. Jack up the front of the car and support it securely on axle stands (see *Jacking and vehicle support*). Note that, when refilling and checking the fluid level, the car must be level to ensure accuracy.

3 Undo the retaining screws and remove the plastic undercover from beneath the engine/transmission.
4 Position a suitable container under the transmission. Unscrew the transmission drain plug from the sump and allow the fluid to drain completely into the container.

⚠️ *Warning: If the fluid is hot, take precautions against scalding.*

5 Clean the drain plug, being especially careful to wipe any metallic particles off the magnetic insert. Discard the original sealing washer; this should be renewed whenever it is disturbed.
6 When the fluid has finished draining, clean the drain plug threads and those of the transmission casing. Fit a new sealing washer to the drain plug, and refit the plug to the transmission, tightening it securely.
7 Make sure the vehicle is level then refill the transmission with the specified type and amount of fluid via the filler tube (see Section 9). Refilling the transmission is an awkward operation, use a funnel with a fine mesh gauze, to avoid spillage, and to ensure that no foreign matter enters the transmission. Allow plenty of time for the fluid level to settle properly.
8 Check the transmission fluid level as described in Section 9.

26 Brake fluid renewal

⚠️ **Warning: Brake hydraulic fluid can harm your eyes and damage painted surfaces, so use extreme caution when handling and pouring it. Do not use fluid that has been standing open for some time, as it absorbs moisture from the air. Excess moisture can cause a dangerous loss of braking effectiveness.**

1 The procedure is similar to that for the bleeding of the hydraulic system as described in Chapter 9, except that the brake fluid reservoir should be emptied by siphoning, using a clean poultry baster or similar before starting, and allowance should be made for the old fluid to be expelled when bleeding a section of the circuit.

2 Working as described in Chapter 9, open the first bleed screw in the sequence, and pump the brake pedal gently until nearly all the old fluid has been emptied from the master cylinder reservoir. Top-up to the MAX level with new fluid, and continue pumping until only the new fluid remains in the reservoir, and new fluid can be seen emerging from the bleed screw. Tighten the screw, and top the reservoir level up to the MAX level line.

HAYNES HINT | Old hydraulic fluid is invariably much darker in colour than the new, making it easy to distinguish the two.

3 Work through all the remaining bleed screws in the sequence until new fluid can be seen at all of them. Be careful to keep the master cylinder reservoir topped-up to above the MIN level at all times, or air may enter the system and greatly increase the length of the task.

4 When the operation is complete, check that all bleed screws are securely tightened, and that their dust caps are refitted. Wash off all traces of spilt fluid, and recheck the master cylinder reservoir fluid level.

5 Check the operation of the brakes before taking the car on the road.

27 Fuel filter renewal

⚠️ **Warning: Before carrying out the following operation refer to the precautions given in Safety first! at the beginning of this manual and follow them implicitly. Petrol is a highly dangerous and volatile liquid and the precautions necessary when handling it cannot be overstressed.**

1 The fuel filter is located underneath the vehicle where it is mounted just in front of the fuel tank.

2 Bearing in mind the information given on depressurising the fuel system in Chapter 4A, disconnect the hoses from the fuel filter. The hoses are equipped with quick-release fittings to ease removal. To disconnect each hose, slide out the locking tab (where fitted) from the collar then depress the collar and detach each hose. Disconnect both hoses, noting the correct fitted position of the sealing rings and plug the hose ends to minimise fuel loss.

3 Slacken the clamp bolt then slide the filter out of position, noting its correct fitted orientation. The arrow on the filter should point in the direction of fuel flow (towards the throttle body/fuel rail).

4 Slide the new filter into position making sure its arrow is pointing in the direction of fuel flow. Make sure the rubber mounting is correctly positioned then securely tighten the clamp bolt.

5 Ensure that the sealing rings are in position and reconnect the hoses to the fuel filter. Check the end fittings are clipped securely in position and (where necessary) refit the locking tabs to the collars.

6 Lower the vehicle to the ground then start the engine and check the filter for signs of fuel leakage.

28 Road test

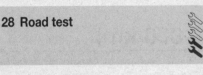

Instruments and electrical equipment

1 Check the operation of all instruments and electrical equipment.

2 Make sure that all instruments read correctly, and switch on all electrical equipment in turn, to check that it functions properly.

Steering and suspension

3 Check for any abnormalities in the steering, suspension, handling or road 'feel'.

4 Drive the vehicle, and check that there are no unusual vibrations or noises.

5 Check that the steering feels positive, with no excessive 'sloppiness', or roughness, and check for any suspension noises when cornering and driving over bumps.

Drivetrain

6 Check the performance of the engine, clutch, transmission and driveshafts.

7 Listen for any unusual noises from the engine, clutch and transmission.

8 Make sure that the engine runs smoothly when idling, and that there is no hesitation when accelerating.

9 Check that, where applicable, the clutch action is smooth and progressive, that the drive is taken up smoothly, and that the pedal travel is not excessive. Also listen for any noises when the clutch pedal is depressed.

10 Check that all gears can be engaged smoothly without noise, and that the gear lever action is not abnormally vague or 'notchy'.

11 On automatic transmission models, make sure that all gearchanges occur smoothly, without snatching, and without an increase in engine speed between changes. Check that all of the gear positions can be selected with the vehicle at rest. If any problems are found, they should be referred to a Renault dealer.

12 Listen for a metallic clicking sound from the front of the vehicle, as the vehicle is driven slowly in a circle with the steering on full-lock. Carry out this check in both directions. If a clicking noise is heard, this indicates wear in a driveshaft joint (see Chapter 8).

Check the operation and performance of the braking system

13 Make sure that the vehicle does not pull to one side when braking, and that the wheels do not lock prematurely when braking hard.

14 Check that there is no vibration through the steering when braking.

15 Check that the handbrake operates correctly, without excessive movement of the lever, and that it holds the vehicle stationary on a slope.

16 Test the operation of the brake servo unit as follows. Depress the footbrake four or five times to exhaust the vacuum, then start the engine. As the engine starts, there should be a noticeable 'give' in the brake pedal as vacuum builds up. Allow the engine to run for at least two minutes, and then switch it off. If the brake pedal is now depressed again, it should be possible to detect a hiss from the servo as the pedal is depressed. After about four or five applications, no further hissing should be heard, and the pedal should feel considerably harder.

29 Timing belt renewal

Refer to the relevant Part of Chapter 2.

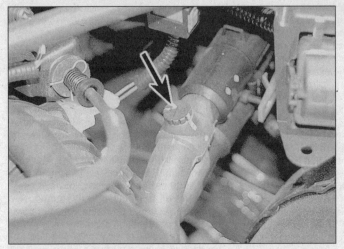

30.4a Coolant bleed screw (arrowed) in the heater matrix hose

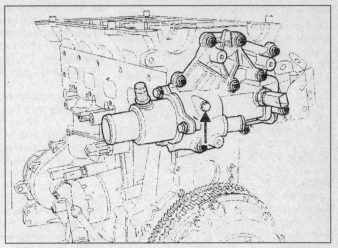

30.4b Coolant bleed screw (arrowed) in the thermostat housing

Every 2 years

30 Coolant renewal

Cooling system draining

⚠️ **Warning: Wait until the engine is cold before starting this procedure. Do not allow antifreeze to come in contact with your skin, or with the painted surfaces of the vehicle. Rinse off spills immediately with plenty of water. Never leave antifreeze lying around in an open container, or in a puddle in the driveway or on the garage floor. Children and pets are attracted by its sweet smell, but antifreeze can be fatal if ingested.**

Note: *Renault do not specify renewal intervals for the coolant, but it is advisable to drain and refill the system every two years to ensure that the corrosion inhibiting properties of the coolant are maintained.*

1 With the engine completely cold, remove the expansion tank filler cap. Turn the cap anti-clockwise, wait until any pressure remaining in the system is released, then unscrew it and lift it off.
2 Where applicable, remove the engine undershield, then position a suitable container beneath the radiator bottom hose connection.
3 Slacken the hose clip, pull off the hose and allow the coolant to drain into the container.
4 To assist draining, open the cooling system bleed screws. These are located in the following positions according to engine type:

1.8 and 2.0 litre (8-valve) engines

In the heater matrix outlet hose, and in the top left-hand side of the radiator (see illustration).

1.6 and 1.8 litre (16-valve) engines

In the heater matrix outlet hose, in the thermo- stat housing and in the top left-hand side of the radiator *(see illustration).*

2.0 litre (16-valve) engines

In the radiator top hose, in the heater matrix outlet hose, and in the top right-hand side of the radiator.

5 When the flow of coolant stops, reposition the container below the cylinder block drain plug. This is located at the front of the cylinder block on the left-hand side on 1.6 litre (16-valve) engines, and at the rear of the cylinder block on the right-hand side on all other engines **(see illustration).**
6 Remove the drain plug, and allow the coolant to drain into the container.
7 If the coolant has been drained for a reason other than renewal, then provided it is clean and less than two years old, it can be re-used, though this is not recommended.
8 Refit the radiator bottom hose and cylinder block drain plug on completion of draining.

Cooling system flushing

9 If coolant renewal has been neglected, or if the antifreeze mixture has become diluted, then in time, the cooling system may gradually lose efficiency, as the coolant passages become restricted due to rust, scale deposits, and other sediment. The cooling system efficiency can be restored by flushing the system clean.
10 The radiator should be flushed independently of the engine, to avoid unnecessary contamination.

Radiator flushing

11 Disconnect the top and bottom hoses and any other relevant hoses from the radiator, with reference to Chapter 3.
12 Insert a garden hose into the radiator top inlet. Direct a flow of clean water through the radiator, and continue flushing until clean water emerges from the radiator bottom outlet.
13 If after a reasonable period, the water still does not run clear, the radiator can be flushed with a good proprietary cleaning agent. It is important that their manufacturer's instructions are followed carefully. If the contamination is particularly bad, insert the hose in the radiator bottom outlet, and reverse-flush the radiator.

Engine flushing

14 To flush the engine, first refit the cylinder block drain plug, and tighten the cooling system bleed screw(s).
15 Remove the thermostat as described in Chapter 3, then temporarily refit the top hose at its engine connection.
16 With the top and bottom hoses disconnected from the radiator, insert a garden hose into the radiator top hose. Direct a clean flow of water through the engine, and continue flushing until clean water emerges from the radiator bottom hose.
17 On completion of flushing, refit the thermostat and reconnect the hoses with reference to Chapter 3.

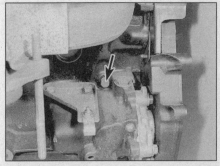

30.5 Coolant drain plug location (arrowed) on the rear of the cylinder block - viewed with engine removed from vehicle

1A

Cooling system filling

18 Before attempting to fill the cooling system, make sure that all hoses and clips are in good condition, and that the clips are tight. Note that an antifreeze mixture must be used all year round, to prevent corrosion of the engine components. Also check that the cylinder block drain plug is in place and tight.

19 Remove the expansion tank filler cap.

20 Open the cooling system bleed screws (see paragraph 4).

21 Place a container under the vehicle, below the expansion tank, to catch any coolant which may be spilt during the topping up procedure. Also place a wad of rags around the expansion tank.

22 Slowly fill the system until the coolant level reaches the top of the expansion tank filler neck.

23 Where applicable, close the bleed screws when coolant free from air bubbles emerges. Close the screws in sequence, starting with the lowest screw in the system.

24 Start the engine, and run it at a fast idle speed (do not exceed 1500 rpm) for approximately 4 minutes. Keep the level topped up to the top of the expansion tank filler neck.

25 Refit and tighten the expansion tank filler cap.

26 Allow the engine to run for approximately 20 minutes (until the cooling fan cuts in and out).

27 Stop the engine and check the coolant level, which should be up to the MAX mark on the side of the tank. Check that the expansion tank filler cap is tight.

28 Allow the engine to cool, then re-check the coolant level with reference to *Weekly checks*. Top-up the level if necessary and refit the expansion tank filler cap. Where applicable, refit the engine undershield.

Antifreeze mixture

29 The antifreeze should always be renewed at the specified intervals. This is necessary not only to maintain the antifreeze properties, but also to prevent corrosion which would otherwise occur as the corrosion inhibitors become progressively less effective.

30 Always use an ethylene-glycol based antifreeze which is suitable for use in mixed-metal cooling systems. The quantity of antifreeze and levels of protection are given in the Specifications.

31 Before adding antifreeze, the cooling system should be completely drained, preferably flushed, and all hoses checked for condition and security.

32 After filling with antifreeze, a label should be attached to the expansion tank, stating the type and concentration of antifreeze used, and the date installed. Any subsequent topping-up should be made with the same type and concentration of antifreeze.

33 Do not use engine antifreeze in the windscreen/tailgate washer system, as it will cause damage to the vehicle paintwork. A screenwash additive should be added to the washer system in the quantities stated on the bottle.

Chapter 1 Part B:
Routine maintenance and servicing - diesel models

Contents

1B

Degrees of difficulty

| Easy, suitable for novice with little experience | Fairly easy, suitable for beginner with some experience | Fairly difficult, suitable for competent DIY mechanic | Difficult, suitable for experienced DIY mechanic | Very difficult, suitable for expert DIY or professional |

Lubricants and fluids

Refer to *Weekly checks* on page 0•18

Capacities

Engine oil

	Excluding filter	Including filter
1.9 litre engines	4.1 litres	4.6 litres
2.2 litre non-turbo engines	5.8 litres	6.55 litres
2.2 litre turbo engines	7.2 litres	7.7 litres

Cooling system (approximate)
1.9 litre engines .... 7.5 litres
2.2 litre engines .... 9.0 litres

Transmission
JC5-type gearbox .... 3.1 litres
PK1-type gearbox:
    Minimum .... 2.3 litres
    Maximum .... 2.8 litres

Fuel tank .... 66.0 litres

Cooling system

Antifreeze mixture:
    35% antifreeze .... Protection down to -23ºC
    50% antifreeze .... Protection down to -40ºC

Fuel system

Idle speed:
    1.9 litre engines .... 850 ± 25 rpm (controlled by injection ECU)
    2.2 litre non-turbo engines .... 775 ± 25 rpm
    2.2 litre turbo engines .... 725 ± 25 rpm
Fast idle speed:
    1.9 litre engines .... Controlled by injection ECU
    2.2 litre non-turbo engines .... 875 ± 25 rpm
    2.2 litre turbo engines .... Controlled by injection ECU

Brakes

Front disc brakes:
    Pad thickness (including backing):
        New .... 18.0 mm
        Minimum thickness .... 6.0 mm
Rear disc brakes:
    Pad thickness (including backing):
        New .... 15.0 mm
        Minimum thickness .... 6.0 mm
Rear drum brakes:
    Shoe thickness (including backing):
        New .... 7.0 mm
        Minimum thickness .... 2.5 mm

Torque wrench setting

	Nm	lbf ft
Roadwheel bolts	100	74

The maintenance intervals in this manual are provided with the assumption that you, not the dealer, will be carrying out the work. These are the minimum maintenance intervals recommended by us for vehicles driven daily. If you wish to keep your vehicle in peak condition at all times, you may wish to perform some of these procedures more often. We encourage frequent maintenance, because it enhances the efficiency, performance and resale value of your vehicle.

If the vehicle is driven in dusty areas, used to tow a trailer, or driven frequently at slow speeds (idling in traffic) or on short journeys, more frequent maintenance intervals are recommended.

When the vehicle is new, it should be serviced by a factory-authorised dealer service department, in order to preserve the factory warranty.

Every 250 miles (400 km) or weekly

☐ Refer to Weekly Checks

Every 5000 miles (8000 km)

☐ Renew the engine oil and filter (Section 3)

Note: *Renault recommend that the oil filter is renewed every 10 000 miles (16 000 km), but it is advisable to renew the filter whenever the engine oil is renewed.*

☐ Drain any water from the fuel filter (Section 4)
☐ Check the front brake pad thickness (Section 5)
☐ Check the rear brake pad thickness - models with rear disc brakes (Section 6)
☐ Check the operation of the handbrake (Section 7)
☐ Check the operation of the clutch (Section 8)
☐ Check the condition of the auxiliary drivebelts (Sections 9 and 10)
☐ Check the condition of the seat belts (Section 11)
☐ Check the operation of all electrical systems (Section 12)
☐ Check the condition of the exhaust system and mountings (Section 13)
☐ Check the suspension and steering components (Section 14)
☐ Check the tightness of the roadwheel bolts (Section 15)
☐ Check the operation of the air conditioning system (Section 16)

Every 10 000 miles (16 000 km)

Carry out all the operations listed under the 5000 mile (8000 km) service, along with the following:
☐ Renew the air filter element (Section 17)
☐ Renew the fuel filter (Section 18)
☐ Check the manual transmission oil level (Section 19)
☐ Check all underbonnet components and hoses for fluid leaks (Section 20)
☐ Renew the pollen filter (Section 21)

Every 15 000 miles (24 000 km)

Carry out all the operations listed under the 5000 mile (8000 km) service, along with the following:
☐ Check the idle speed and anti-stall speed (Section 22)

Every 40 000 miles (64 000 km)

Carry out all the operations listed under the 5000 mile (8000 km), and 10 000 mile (16 000 km) services, along with the following:
☐ Check the spare fuses are in place (Section 23)
☐ Check the front wheel alignment (Section 24)
☐ Check the rear brake shoe thickness - models with rear drum brakes (Section 25)
☐ Renew the brake fluid (Section 26)
☐ Carry out a road test (Section 27)
☐ Renew the timing belt (Section 28)

Note: *Although the normal interval for timing belt renewal is 70 000 miles (112 000 km), it is strongly recommended that the interval is reduced to 40 000 miles (64 000 km) on vehicles which are subjected to intensive use, ie, mainly short journeys or a lot of stop-start driving. The actual belt renewal interval is therefore very much up to the individual owner, but bear in mind that severe engine damage may result if the belt breaks.*

Every 2 years

In addition to all the items listed previously, carry out the following:
☐ Renew the coolant (Section 29)

Underbonnet view of a 1.9 litre turbo diesel model

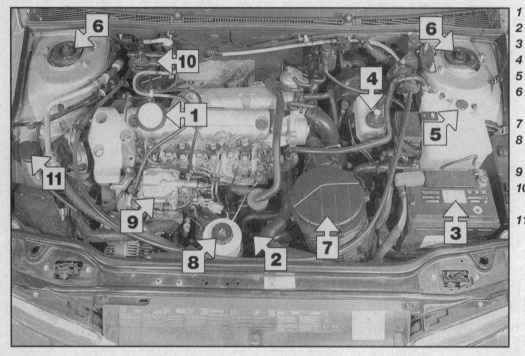

1 Engine oil filler cap
2 Engine oil level dipstick
3 Battery
4 Brake fluid reservoir
5 Coolant expansion tank
6 Suspension strut upper mounting
7 Air filter housing
8 Power steering fluid reservoir
9 Fuel injection pump
10 Fuel filter housing and priming button
11 Washer fluid reservoir

Underbonnet view of a 2.2 litre non-turbo diesel model

1 Engine oil filler cap
2 Engine oil level dipstick
3 Battery
4 Brake fluid reservoir
5 Coolant expansion tank
6 Suspension strut upper mounting
7 Air filter housing
8 Brake vacuum pump/power steering pump drivebelt cover
9 Power steering fluid reservoir
10 Fuel injection pump
11 Fuel filter housing and priming button
12 Washer fluid reservoir

Front underbody view of a 2.2 litre non-turbo diesel model

1   Washer fluid reservoir
2   Air conditioning compressor
3   Engine oil cooler
4   Engine oil filter
5   Power steering fluid cooler pipes
6   Brake caliper
7   Suspension lower arm
8   Track-rod end
9   Anti-roll bar
10 Gearchange rod
11 Right-hand driveshaft
12 Engine mounting bracket
13 Engine oil drain plug

Rear underbody view of a 2.2 litre non-turbo diesel model

1   Handbrake cable equaliser
2   Exhaust expansion box
3   Rear suspension mounting bolts
4   Rear brake pressure regulating valve
5   Rear suspension crossmember
6   Rear suspension torsion bar
7   Rear shock absorber
8   Fuel tank

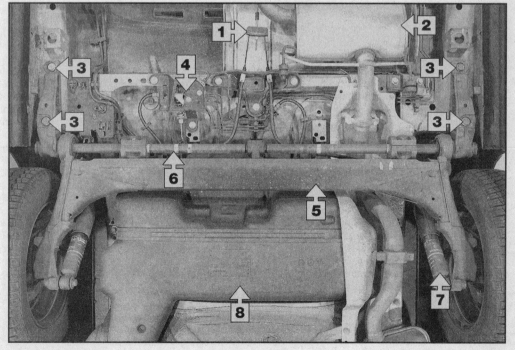

1 Introduction

1 This Chapter is designed to help the home mechanic maintain his/her vehicle for safety, economy, long life and peak performance.
2 The Chapter contains a master maintenance schedule, followed by Sections dealing specifically with each task in the schedule. Visual checks, adjustments, component renewal and other helpful items are included. Refer to the accompanying illustrations of the engine compartment and the underside of the vehicle for the locations of the various components.
3 Servicing your vehicle in accordance with the mileage/time maintenance schedule and the following Sections will provide a planned maintenance programme, which should result in a long and reliable service life. This is a comprehensive plan, so maintaining some items but not others at the specified service intervals, will not produce the same results.
4 As you service your vehicle, you will discover that many of the procedures can - and should - be grouped together, because of the particular procedure being performed, or because of the close proximity of two otherwise-unrelated components to one another. For example, if the vehicle is raised for any reason, the exhaust can be inspected at the same time as the suspension and steering components.

5 The first step in this maintenance programme is to prepare yourself before the actual work begins. Read through all the Sections relevant to the work to be carried out, then make a list and gather together all the parts and tools required. If a problem is encountered, seek advice from a parts specialist, or a dealer service department.

2 Regular maintenance

1 If, from the time the vehicle is new, the routine maintenance schedule is followed closely, and frequent checks are made of fluid levels and high-wear items, as suggested throughout this manual, the engine will be kept in relatively good running condition, and the need for additional work will be minimised.
2 It is possible that there will be times when the engine is running poorly due to the lack of regular maintenance. This is even more likely if a used vehicle, which has not received regular and frequent maintenance checks, is purchased. In such cases, additional work may need to be carried out, outside of the regular maintenance intervals.
3 If engine wear is suspected, a compression test or leakdown test (refer to Chapter 2D) will provide valuable information regarding the overall performance of the main internal components. Such a test can be used as a basis to decide on the extent of the work to

be carried out. If, for example, a compression test indicates serious internal engine wear, conventional maintenance as described in this Chapter will not greatly improve the performance of the engine, and may prove a waste of time and money, unless extensive overhaul work is carried out first.
4 The following series of operations are those most often required to improve the performance of a generally poor-running engine:

Primary operations

a) Clean, inspect and test the battery (See Weekly checks).
b) Check all the engine-related fluids (See Weekly checks).
c) Check the condition and tension of the auxiliary drivebelt (Sections 9 and 10).
d) Check the condition of the air filter element, and renew if necessary (Section 17).
e) Check the fuel filter (Section 18).
f) Check the condition of all hoses, and check for fluid leaks (Section 20).
g) Check the idle speed and anti-stall speed (Section 22).

5 If the above operations do not prove fully effective, carry out the following secondary operations:

Secondary operations

All items listed under Primary operations, plus the following:
a) Check the charging system (Chapter 5A).
b) Check the pre-heating system (Chapter 5C).
c) Check the fuel system (Chapter 4B).

Every 5000 miles (8000 km)

3 Engine oil and filter renewal

1 Frequent oil and filter changes are the most important preventative maintenance procedures which can be undertaken by the DIY owner. As engine oil ages, it becomes diluted and contaminated, which leads to premature engine wear.
2 Before starting this procedure, gather together all the necessary tools and materials. Also make sure that you have plenty of clean rags and newspapers handy, to mop up any spills. Ideally, the engine oil should be warm, as it will drain more easily, and more built-up sludge will be removed with it. Take care not to touch the exhaust or any other hot parts of the engine when working under the vehicle. To avoid any possibility of scalding, and to protect yourself from possible skin irritants and other harmful contaminants in used engine oils, it is advisable to wear gloves when carrying out this work.
3 Firmly apply the handbrake then jack up the front of the vehicle and support it on axle stands (see *Jacking and vehicle support*).

Undo the retaining screws and remove the plastic undercover from underneath the engine/transmission.
4 Remove the oil filler cap, and on 1.9 litre engines, the plastic engine cover.
5 Using a spanner, or preferably a suitable socket and bar, slacken the drain plug about half a turn. Position the draining container under the drain plug, then remove the plug completely **(see Haynes Hint)**. Note that on some engines

As the drain plug threads release, move it sharply away so the stream of oil issuing from the sump runs into the container, not up your sleeve!

an 8 mm square section drain plug key will be needed to unscrew the drain plug.
6 Allow some time for the oil to drain, noting that it may be necessary to reposition the container as the oil flow slows to a trickle.
7 After all the oil has drained, wipe the drain plug and the sealing washer with a clean rag. Examine the condition of the sealing washer, and renew it if it shows signs of scoring or other damage which may prevent an oil-tight seal. Clean the area around the drain plug opening, and refit the plug complete with the washer and tighten it securely.
8 Move the container into position under the oil filter which is located on the front of the cylinder block.
9 Use an oil filter removal tool to slacken the filter initially, then unscrew it by hand the rest of the way. Empty the oil from the old filter into the container.
10 Use a clean rag to remove all oil, dirt and sludge from the filter sealing area on the engine. Check the old filter to make sure that the rubber sealing ring has not stuck to the engine. If it has, carefully remove it.
11 Apply a light coating of clean engine oil to the sealing ring on the new filter, then screw the filter into position on the engine. Tighten the filter firmly by hand only - **do not** use any tools.

12 Refit the undercover and securely tighten its retaining screws. Remove the old oil and all tools from under the vehicle then lower the vehicle to the ground.

13 Fill the engine through the filler hole, using the correct grade and type of oil (refer to *Weekly Checks* for details of topping-up). Pour in half the specified quantity of oil first, then wait a few minutes for the oil to drain into the sump. Continue to add oil, a small quantity at a time, until the level is up to the lower mark on the dipstick. Adding approximately a further 1.0 litre will bring the level up to the upper mark on the dipstick. Refit the oil filler cap.

14 Note that when a non-turbo engine is first started, there may be a delay of a few seconds before the oil pressure warning light goes out as the oil circulates through the new oil filter and the engine oil galleries (for turbo engines, the procedure described in the following paragraph must be followed).

15 On turbo engines, the following procedures must be observed before starting the engine:

a) *Disconnect the wiring from the stop solenoid on the injection pump and insulate the connector.*

b) *Crank the engine on the starter motor until the oil pressure warning light goes out (this may take several seconds).*

c) *Reconnect the wiring to the stop solenoid, then start the engine using the normal procedure.*

d) *Run the engine at idle speed and check the turbocharger oil and coolant unions for leakage. Rectify any problems without delay.*

16 Run the engine for a few minutes, and check that there are no leaks around the oil filter seal and the sump drain plug.

17 Stop the engine, and wait a few minutes for the oil to settle in the sump once more. With the new oil circulated and the filter now completely full, recheck the level on the dipstick, and add more oil as necessary.

18 On 1.9 litre engines, refit the plastic engine cover.

19 Dispose of the used engine oil safely with reference to *General repair procedures*.

4 Fuel filter water draining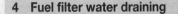

HAYNES HiNT *This is not a pleasant task, unless you like the smell of diesel fuel on your skin. Wear a pair of light plastic disposable gloves, like those available at the diesel pumps of most filling stations, to protect your hands and have plenty of newspaper or clean rag handy for mopping up spills. Ensure that diesel fuel does not spill on to the* *coolant hoses, electrical wiring, alternator, engine mountings or the auxiliary drivebelt - protect them, if necessary, with a plastic sheet. Drain the fuel into a clean container so that you can be sure of seeing any water or other foreign bodies which might be present in the system.*

1 A water drain screw s provided on the base of the fuel filter.

2 Place a suitable container beneath the drain screw. To make draining easier, a suitable length of tubing can be attached to the outlet on the screw to direct the fuel flow.

3 Loosen the fuel filter bleed screw, then open the drain screw by turning it anti-clockwise. On models where there is no bleed screw, loosen the fuel inlet union on the filter head.

4 Allow the entire contents of the filter to drain into the container, then securely tighten the drain screw and the bleed screw/fuel filter inlet union (as applicable).

5 Prime and bleed the fuel system as described in Chapter 4B.

6 Dispose of the used fuel safely with reference to *General repair procedures*.

5 Front brake pad check

1 Apply the handbrake, then jack up the front of the car and support it securely on axle stands (see *Jacking and vehicle support*). Remove the front roadwheels.

2 For a comprehensive check, the brake pads should be removed and cleaned. The operation of the caliper can then also be checked, and the condition of the brake disc itself can be fully examined on both sides. Refer to Chapter 9 for further information **(see Haynes Hint)**.

3 On completion refit the roadwheels and lower the car to the ground.

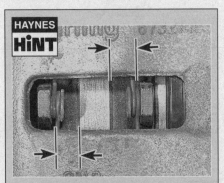

For a quick check, the thickness of friction material remaining on each brake pad can be measured through the aperture in the caliper body.

6 Rear brake pad check - models with rear disc brakes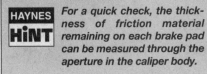

1 Jack up the rear of the car and support it securely on axle stands (see *Jacking and vehicle support*). Remove the rear road-wheels.

HAYNES HiNT *For a quick check, the thickness of friction material remaining on each brake pad can be measured through the aperture in the caliper body.*

2 For a comprehensive check, the brake pads should be removed and cleaned. The operation of the caliper can then also be checked, and the condition of the brake disc itself can be fully examined on both sides. Refer to Chapter 9 for further information.

3 On completion refit the roadwheels and lower the car to the ground.

7 Handbrake check

General

1 The handbrake will normally be kept in adjustment by the action of the drum brakes automatic adjuster, or by the self-adjusting action of the rear disc calipers. Occasionally, the handbrake mechanism may require adjustment to compensate for cable stretch.

2 Chock the front wheels, then jack up the rear of the vehicle, and support securely on axle stands (see *Jacking and vehicle support*).

3 Fully release the handbrake and check that the wheels can be rotated easily by hand. The wheels may drag slightly, but there should be no binding.

4 If the wheels bind, it is likely that the handbrake mechanism is partially seized, or the mechanism is incorrectly adjusted. If the operation of the mechanism is not satisfactory, proceed as follows, according to type.

Models with rear drum brakes

5 Working under the vehicle, where applicable, remove the exhaust heat shields to expose the handbrake equaliser.

6 Counterhold the handbrake operating rod using the flats provided, then slacken the adjuster nut until there is no tension in the handbrake cables **(see illustration)**.

7 Remove the brake drums as described in Chapter 9, and check the operation of the handbrake lever on the trailing shoe **(see illustration)**. The lever should move freely.

8 If necessary, dismantle the components and clean them, then reassemble as described in Chapter 9.

1B

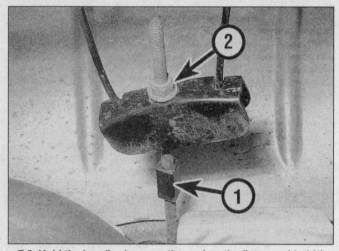

7.6 Hold the handbrake operating rod on the flats provided (1) and slacken the adjuster nut (2)

7.7 Check the operation of the handbrake lever (arrowed) - rear drum brake model

9 Check that the adjuster star wheel rotates freely in both directions, then back off the star wheel by five or six teeth.
10 Check that the handbrake cables slide freely in their sheaths.
11 Check that the handbrake operating levers are resting correctly on the shoes.
12 Temporarily refit the brake drums (there is no need to fit the hub nuts), then operate the adjustment mechanism by depressing the brake pedal firmly several times. It should be possible to hear the adjustment mechanism clicking as the pedal is depressed.
13 Remove the brake drums again.
14 Working under the vehicle floor, turn the cable adjuster until handbrake operating levers on the brake shoes begin to move when the handbrake lever is pulled between

the first and second notches. There should be no free-play in the handbrake cables once the lever is pulled beyond the second notch.
15 Tighten the adjuster locknuts.
16 Refit the brake drums as described in Chapter 9, then refit the roadwheels, and lower the vehicle to the ground.
17 With the vehicle resting on its wheels, again depress the brake pedal repeatedly to operate the self-adjusting mechanism. It should be possible to hear the adjusting mechanism click as the brake pedal is depressed.

Models with rear disc brakes

18 Proceed as described in paragraphs 5 and 6.
19 Remove the roadwheels.

20 Check that the handbrake cables slide freely in their sheaths, and that the operating levers on the calipers move freely.
21 Push the handbrake operating levers on the calipers as far as they will go against their bottom stops.
22 Working under the vehicle floor, turn the cable adjuster sleeve until the handbrake cable end fittings just contact the operating levers on the calipers, without moving the levers **(see illustration)**.
23 Continue to turn the adjuster sleeve until the handbrake operating levers on the calipers begin to move when the handbrake lever is pulled between the first and second notches. There should be no free-play in the handbrake cables once the lever is pulled beyond the second notch.
24 Tighten the adjuster locknuts.
25 Refit the roadwheels, and lower the vehicle to the ground.

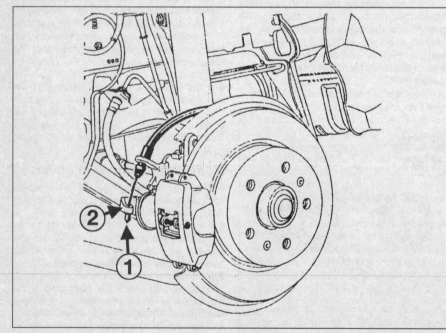

7.22 The handbrake cable end fittings (1) should just contact the operating levers (2) - rear disc brake model

| 8 | Clutch check | 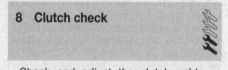 |

Check and adjust the clutch cable as described in Chapter 6. Check that the cable moves freely and easily and lubricate its exposed section with multi-purpose grease.

9 Auxiliary drivebelt check and renewal - 1.9 litre engines

Note: *Renault recommend that a belt is renewed whenever it is slackened or removed.*

Checking

1 The auxiliary drivebelt is located at the right-hand side of the engine.
2 Two different drivebelt configurations may be encountered, depending on whether or not the vehicle is equipped with air conditioning (see illustrations).

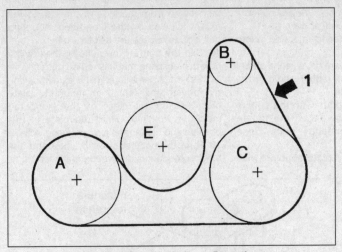

**9.2a Auxiliary drivebelt configuration -
1.9 litre models without air conditioning**

1 Tension checking point for the
  auxiliary drivebelt
A Crankshaft pulley

B Alternator
C Power-assisted steering pump
E Coolant pump

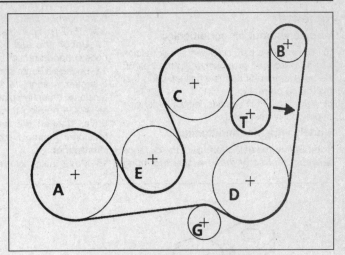

**9.2b Auxiliary drivebelt configuration -
1.9 litre models with air conditioning**

A Crankshaft pulley
B Alternator
C Power-assisted steering
  pump

D Air conditioning compressor
E Coolant pump
G Roller
T Tensioner

1B

3 Due to their function and material makeup, drivebelts are prone to failure after a period of time and should therefore be inspected, and if necessary adjusted periodically.

4 Since the drivebelt is located very close to the right-hand side of the engine compartment, it is possible to gain better access by raising the front of the vehicle (see *Jacking and vehicle support*) and removing the right-hand wheel, then removing the splash shield from inside the wheelarch. On certain models it will also be necessary to remove the lower timing belt cover.

5 With the engine switched off, inspect the full length of the drivebelt for cracks and separation of the belt plies. It will be necessary to turn the crankshaft (using a socket or spanner on the crankshaft pulley bolt) in order to move the belt from the pulleys so that the full length of the belt can be inspected thoroughly. Twist the belt between the pulleys so that both sides can be viewed. Also check for fraying, and glazing which gives the belt a shiny appearance. Check the pulleys for nicks, cracks, distortion and corrosion.

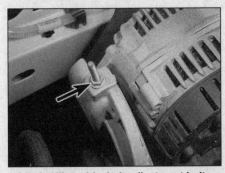

**9.7 Auxiliary drivebelt adjustment bolt -
1.9 litre models without air conditioning**

Tensioning

6 The tension of each drivebelt is checked midway between the pulleys at the point indicates in illustration 9.2a or 9.2b. For models without air conditioning, the belt tension can only be checked or set accurately by using the Renault electronic measuring tool (Mot. 1273).

7 If adjustment is necessary on models without air conditioning, loosen the alternator mounting and pivot bolts, then loosen the adjustment locknut and turn the adjustment bolt as required until the tension is correct. Tighten the adjustment, mounting and pivot bolts on completion (see illustration). Run the engine for about 5 minutes, then recheck the tension.

8 On models with air conditioning, a spring loaded tensioner is fitted to automatically maintain the correct tension on the belt. If there is any reason to suspect that the drivebelt tension is incorrect, it will be necessary to have this checked by a Renault dealer. A special gauge, tool Mot. 1387, is used to check the centreline distance between the tensioner mounting plate bolts, which then records on the gauge as correct or incorrect (see illustration). As an actual centreline distance measurement is not specified by Renault, having this checked by use of the gauge is the only alternative. In practice, however, as long as the tensioner is initially set as described below when refitting the belt, no problems should be encountered.

9 If the gauge is available, proceed as follows. Slacken the gauge's knurled locking wheel, fit the gauge to the tensioner as illustrated so that the ends of its arms engage on the heads of the tensioner mounting bolts, then tighten the knurled wheel to lock the

gauge. Withdraw the gauge and check that the distances between centres is within the indicated tolerance range (see illustrations overleaf). If the distance is below the minimum tolerance check first that the tensioner mounting plate is positioned correctly (rotated clockwise to the limit of the elongated mounting bolt slot), that the belt is of the correct type (not too short) and that it is correctly routed. If the distance is above the maximum tolerance check first that the tensioner mounting plate is positioned correctly, that the belt is of the correct type (not too long) and that it is correctly routed - if the distance is still incorrect, the belt must be renewed.

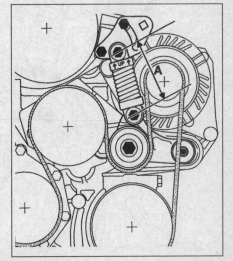

**9.8 The operation of the auxiliary drivebelt
automatic tensioner is checked by
measuring the distance (A) -
1.9 litre models with air conditioning**

Renewal

Models without air conditioning

10 To remove a belt, slacken the belt tension fully as described previously. Slip the belt off the pulleys, then fit the new belt ensuring that it is routed correctly.

11 With the belt in position, adjust its tension as previously described.

Models with air conditioning

Note: *Before the belt is removed, the distance between centres of the tensioner mounting* bolts must be checked using the Renault tool Mot. 1387 (see paragraph 9 above).

12 Unbolt the fuel filter-to-injection pump hose support bracket.

13 Engage a 9 mm square drive (ie the end of a socket wrench) in the square hole in the tensioner mounting plate.

14 While holding the plate with the square drive, slacken the lower, then the upper, tensioner plate mounting bolts **(see illustration)**.

15 Move the tensioner plate anticlockwise (as viewed from the side of the car) to the extent allowed by the elongated mounting bolt slot, to release the belt tension.

16 Slip the belt off the pulleys, then fit the new belt ensuring that it is routed correctly.

17 Set the automatic adjuster initial position by moving the tensioner mounting plate clockwise to the limit of the elongated mounting bolt slot. Hold the plate in this position and tighten the two mounting bolts.

18 Refit the hose support bracket and any other components disturbed for access.

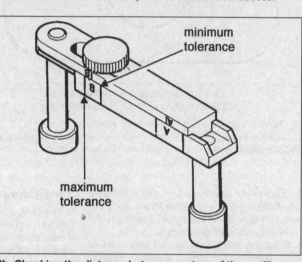

9.9b Checking the distance between centres of the auxiliary drivebelt automatic tensioner - 1.9 litre models with air conditioning

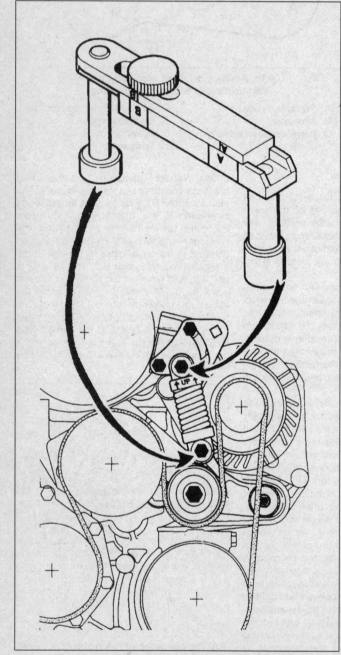

9.9a Fitting the special tool Mot. 1387 to check the operation of the auxiliary drivebelt automatic tensioner - 1.9 litre models with air conditioning

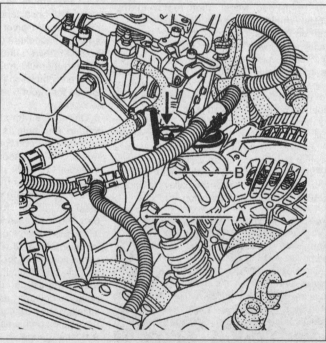

9.14 Auxiliary drivebelt automatic tensioner mounting plate - 1.9 litre models with air conditioning

A Lower mounting bolt   B Upper mounting bolt

Arrow indicates fuel hose support bracket bolt.

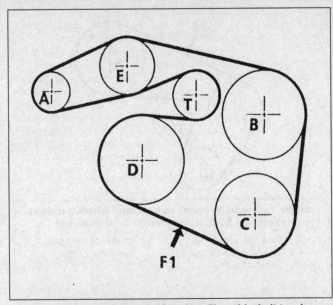

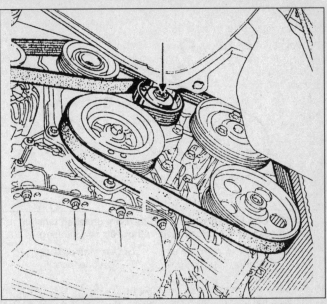

10.7 Right-hand (timing belt) end auxiliary drivebelt tension checking - 2.2 litre models

10.8 Right-hand (timing belt) end auxiliary drivebelt tensioner location (arrowed) - 2.2 litre models

A Alternator
B Coolant pump
C Air conditioning compressor or power steering pump
D Crankshaft pulley
E Idler pulley
F1 Tension checking point
T Tensioner pulley

10 Auxiliary drivebelt check and renewal - 2.2 litre engines

Note: *On models with a belt-driven brake vacuum pump, driven from the camshaft, Renault recommend that the vacuum pump drivebelt is renewed whenever the timing belt is renewed.*

General

1 On models with a belt-driven brake vacuum pump, two auxiliary drivebelts are fitted. The main auxiliary drivebelt is located at the right-hand (timing belt) end of the engine, and drives the alternator and coolant pump. On models without air conditioning, the main drivebelt also drives the power steering pump. On models with air conditioning, the main drivebelt also drives the air conditioning compressor. The second drivebelt is driven from the left-hand (flywheel) end of the camshaft, and drives the brake vacuum pump, and on models with air conditioning, the power steering pump.

2 On models with a brake vacuum pump driven directly from the camshaft, a single auxiliary drivebelt is fitted, which drives the alternator, power steering pump and, where applicable, the air conditioning compressor.

Right-hand (timing belt) end auxiliary drivebelt

Checking

3 Various different drivebelt configurations may be encountered, depending on model.

4 Due to their function and material makeup, drivebelts are prone to failure after a period of time and should therefore be inspected, and if necessary adjusted periodically.

5 Since the drivebelt is located very close to the right-hand side of the engine compartment, it is possible to gain better access by raising the front of the vehicle and removing the right-hand wheel, then removing the splash shield from inside the wheelarch, and the engine undercover(s), where applicable.

6 With the engine stopped, inspect the full length of the drivebelt for cracks and separation of the belt plies. It will be necessary to turn the engine (using a spanner or socket and bar on the crankshaft pulley bolt) in order to move the belt from the pulleys so that the belt can be inspected thoroughly. Twist the belt between the pulleys so that both sides can be viewed. Also check for fraying, and glazing which gives the belt a shiny appearance. Check the pulleys for nicks, cracks, distortion and corrosion.

Tensioning

Note: *Renault recommend that a belt is renewed whenever it is slackened.*

7 Where applicable, the tension of the belt is checked midway between the pulleys at the point indicated **(see illustration)**. The tension can only be checked and set, using the Renault electronic measuring tool (Mot. 1273). If access to this equipment is not available, have the belt tension checked by a Renault dealer. The procedures in this Section assume that the Renault special tool is being used.

8 If adjustment is necessary, counterhold the

tensioner pulley on the flats provided, using a 22 mm spanner, then slacken the pulley bolt using a 7 mm Allen key. Move the tensioner to relieve the tension in the belt **(see illustration)**.

9 To apply tension to the belt, move the tensioner pulley as required, then hold the pulley in position using the spanner on the flats. Tighten the pulley bolt to lock the tensioner pulley in position.

10 Run the engine for about 5 minutes, then recheck the tension.

Renewal

11 To remove a belt, slacken the belt tension fully as described previously. Note the routing of the belt, then slip the belt off the pulleys.

12 Fit the new belt ensuring that it is routed correctly.

13 With the belt in position, adjust the tension as previously described.

Left-hand (flywheel) end auxiliary drivebelt

Checking

14 The checking procedure is as described previously for the right-hand auxiliary drivebelt, noting the following points:
   a) *For access to the belt, it will be necessary to unscrew the oil filler cap, then unscrew the securing bolts and withdraw the belt cover.*
   b) *Note that the belt is of the toothed type.*

Tensioning

Note: *Renault recommend that a belt is renewed whenever it is slackened, and whenever the timing belt is renewed.*

1B

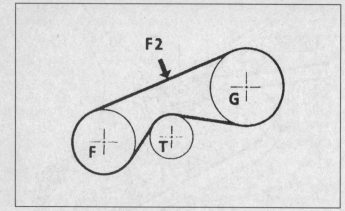

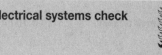

10.15a Left-hand (flywheel) end auxiliary drivebelt tension checking - 2.2 litre models without air conditioning

F Brake vacuum pump   G Camshaft pulley
F2 Tension checking point   T Tensioner pulley

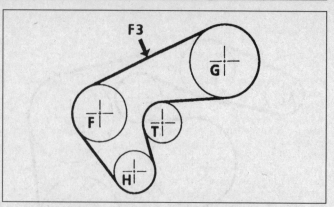

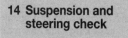

10.15b Left-hand (flywheel) end auxiliary drivebelt tension checking - 2.2 litre models with air conditioning

F Brake vacuum pump   H Power steering pump
F3 Tension checking point   T Tensioner pulley
G Camshaft pulley

15 Proceed as described in paragraphs 7 to 10, using the accompanying illustrations to identify the tension checking points **(see illustrations)**.

Renewal

16 Proceed as described in paragraphs 11 to 13.

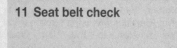

11 Seat belt check

1 Carefully examine the seat belt webbing for cuts, or any signs of serious fraying or deterioration. If the belt is of the retractable type, pull the belt all the way out of the inertia reel, and examine the full extent of the webbing.
2 Fasten and unfasten the belt, ensuring that the locking mechanism holds securely, and releases properly when intended. If the belt is of the retractable type, check also that the retracting mechanism operates correctly when the belt is released.
3 Check the security of all seat belt mountings and attachments which are accessible without removing any trim or other components **(see illustration)**.

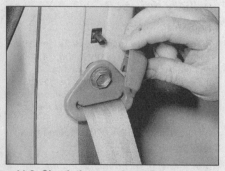

11.3 Check the security of the seat belt mountings

12 Electrical systems check

1 Check the operation of all electrical equipment, ie, lights, direction indicators, horn, etc. Refer to the appropriate Sections of Chapter 12 for details if any of the circuits are found to be inoperative.
2 Refer to Chapter 9 for stop-light adjustment.
3 Visually check all accessible wiring connectors, harnesses and retaining clips for security, and for signs of chafing or damage. Rectify any faults found.

13 Exhaust system check

1 With the engine cold (at least an hour after the vehicle has been driven), check the complete exhaust system from the engine to the end of the tailpipe. The exhaust system is most easily checked with the vehicle raised on a hoist, or suitably supported on axle stands (see *Jacking and vehicle support*), so that the exhaust components are readily visible and accessible.
2 Check the exhaust pipes and connections for evidence of leaks, severe corrosion and damage. Make sure that all brackets and mountings are in good condition, and that all relevant nuts and bolts are tight. Leakage at any of the joints or in other parts of the system will usually show up as a black sooty stain in the vicinity of the leak.
3 Rattles and other noises can often be traced to the exhaust system, especially the brackets and mountings. Try to move the pipes and silencers. If the components are able to come into contact with the body or suspension parts, secure the system with new mountings. Otherwise separate the joints (if possible) and twist the pipes as necessary to provide additional clearance.

14 Suspension and steering check

Front suspension and steering check

1 Raise the front of the vehicle, and securely support it on axle stands (see *Jacking and vehicle support*).
2 Visually inspect the balljoint dust covers and the steering rack-and-pinion gaiters for splits, chafing or deterioration. Any wear of these components will cause loss of lubricant, together with dirt and water entry, resulting in rapid deterioration of the balljoints or steering gear.
3 On vehicles with power steering, check the fluid hoses for chafing or deterioration, and the pipe and hose unions for fluid leaks. Also check for signs of fluid leakage under pressure from the steering gear rubber gaiters, which would indicate failed fluid seals within the steering gear.
4 Grasp the roadwheel at the 12 o'clock and 6 o'clock positions, and try to rock it **(see illustration)**. Very slight free play may be felt, but if the movement is appreciable, further investigation is necessary to determine the

14.4 Check for wear in the hub bearings by grasping the wheel and trying to rock it

source. Continue rocking the wheel while an assistant depresses the footbrake. If the movement is now eliminated or significantly reduced, it is likely that the hub bearings are at fault. If the free play is still evident with the footbrake depressed, then there is wear in the suspension joints or mountings.

5 Now grasp the wheel at the 9 o'clock and 3 o'clock positions, and try to rock it as before. Any movement felt now may again be caused by wear in the hub bearings or the steering track-rod balljoints. If the outer balljoint is worn, the visual movement will be obvious. If the inner joint is suspect, it can be felt by placing a hand over the rack-and-pinion rubber gaiter and gripping the track-rod. If the wheel is now rocked, movement will be felt at the inner joint if wear has taken place.

6 Using a large screwdriver or flat bar, check for wear in the suspension mounting bushes by levering between the relevant suspension component and its attachment point. Some movement is to be expected, as the mountings are made of rubber, but excessive wear should be obvious. Also check the condition of any visible rubber bushes, looking for splits, cracks or contamination of the rubber.

7 With the car standing on its wheels, have an assistant turn the steering wheel back and forth, about an eighth of a turn each way. There should be very little, if any, lost movement between the steering wheel and roadwheels. If this is not the case, closely observe the joints and mountings previously described. In addition, check the steering column universal joints for wear, and also check the rack-and-pinion steering gear itself.

Rear suspension check

8 Chock the front wheels, then jack up the rear of the vehicle and support securely on axle stands (see *Jacking and vehicle support*).
9 Working as described previously for the front suspension, check the rear hub bearings, the suspension bushes and the shock absorber mountings for wear.

Shock absorber check

10 Check for any signs of fluid leakage around the shock absorber body, or from the rubber gaiter around the piston rod. Should any fluid be noticed, the shock absorber is defective internally, and should be renewed.
Note: *Shock absorbers should always be renewed in pairs on the same axle.*

11 The efficiency of the shock absorber may be checked by bouncing the vehicle at each corner. Generally speaking, the body will return to its normal position and stop after being depressed. If it rises and returns on a rebound, the shock absorber is probably suspect. Also examine the shock absorber upper and lower mountings for any signs of wear.

15 Roadwheel bolt check

1 Where applicable, remove the wheel trims, and slacken the roadwheel bolts slightly.
2 Tighten the bolts to the specified torque, using a torque wrench.

16 Air conditioning system check

The air conditioning system must be checked by a Renault dealer using dedicated test equipment.

Every 10 000 miles (16 000 km)

1B

17 Air filter element renewal

1 On 1.9 litre engines, press the tab on the side of the lid, turn the lid anti-clockwise and lift the lid from the air cleaner housing **(see illustrations)**.
2 On 2.2 litre models, release the retaining clip then undo the retaining screws and remove the lid from the top of the air cleaner housing.
3 Lift out the air filter element and wipe clean the filter housing.

4 Fit the new filter, making sure it is correctly located, then refit the housing lid, securing it in position with the retaining screws and clip, on 2.2 litre engines.

18 Fuel filter renewal
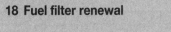

Caution: Do not allow dirt to enter the fuel system during this procedure.
1 Drain the contents of the fuel filter as described in Section 4.
2 Unscrew the filter and remove it from the base of the fuel filter housing. Recover the

filter sealing ring. To improve access, unscrew the retaining nuts and free the filter housing from its mounting bracket. If the filter is tight, use an oil filter removal tool to unscrew it.
3 Smear the sealing ring of the new filter with fuel and screw the new filter onto the housing. Tighten the filter firmly by hand only - **do not use any tools.**
4 Refit the filter housing to its mounting bracket and securely tighten the retaining nuts.
5 Prime and bleed the fuel system as described in Chapter 4B.

19 Manual transmission oil level check
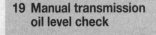

1 Either position the vehicle over an inspection pit, or jack up the front and rear of the vehicle and support it on axle stands (see *Jacking and vehicle support*). The vehicle must be level for the check to be accurate. Refer to Chapter 7A for information on transmission identification.

JC5 transmission

2 Undo the retaining screws and remove the undercover from beneath the engine/transmission.

17.1a On 1.9 litre engines, press the tab on the side of the air cleaner housing lid . . .

17.1b . . . then turn the lid anti-clockwise and lift it lid from the housing

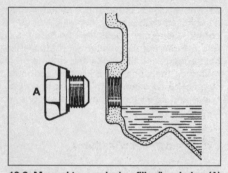

19.3 Manual transmission filler/level plug (A) - JC5 transmission (correct oil level shown)

3 Clean the area around the filler/level plug on the left-hand side of the transmission, then slacken and remove the plug from the transmission **(see illustration)**.
4 The transmission oil level should be up to the lower edge of the filler/level plug aperture.
5 If necessary, top-up using the specified type of lubricant until the transmission oil level is correct. Fill the transmission until oil starts to flow out and allow excess oil to drain out **(see illustration)**.
6 Once the transmission oil level is correct, refit the filler/level plug and tighten it securely.
7 Refit the engine undercover then lower the vehicle to the ground. Note that frequent need for topping-up indicates a leakage, possibly through an oil seal. The cause should be investigated and rectified.

PK1 transmission

8 Clean the area around the transmission oil dipstick which is situated at the rear of the unit, behind the left-hand driveshaft joint.
9 Withdraw the dipstick from the transmission and wipe all the oil from its end with a clean rag or paper towel. Insert the clean dipstick back in as far as it will go, then withdraw it once more. Note the oil level on the end of the dipstick; it should be between the upper and lower marks **(see illustration)**.
10 If topping up is necessary, clean the area around the filler plug on the transmission end cover, then slacken and remove the plug along with its sealing washer. If necessary, undo the retaining screws and remove the engine undercover to improve access to the plug.

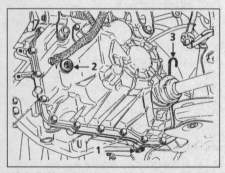

19.9 PK1 transmission drain plug (1), filler plug (2) and oil level dipstick (3)

19.5 Topping-up the manual transmission oil level - JC5 transmission

11 Top-up the transmission oil level with the specified type of lubricant via the filler plug hole. Once the level is up to the upper level mark, refit the filler plug and sealing washer and tighten it securely. Where necessary, refit the undercover and securely tighten its retaining screws. Note that frequent need for topping-up indicates a leakage, possibly through an oil seal. The cause should be investigated and rectified.

20 Hose and fluid leak check

1 Visually inspect the engine joint faces, gaskets and seals for any signs of water or oil leaks. Pay particular attention to the areas around the cylinder head cover, cylinder head, oil filter and sump joint faces. Bear in mind that, over a period of time, some very slight seepage from these areas is to be expected - what you are really looking for is any indication of a serious leak **(see Haynes Hint)**. Should a leak be found, renew the offending gasket or oil seal by referring to the appropriate Chapters in this manual.
2 Also check the security and condition of all the engine-related pipes and hoses, and all braking system pipes and hoses. Ensure that all cable-ties or securing clips are in place, and in good condition. Clips which are broken or missing can lead to chafing of the hoses, pipes or wiring, which could cause more serious problems in the future.
3 Carefully check the radiator hoses and heater hoses along their entire length. Renew any hose which is cracked, swollen or deteriorated. Cracks will show up better if the hose is squeezed. Pay close attention to the hose clips that secure the hoses to the cooling system components. Hose clips can pinch and puncture hoses, resulting in cooling system leaks. If the crimped-type hose clips are used, it may be a good idea to replace them with standard worm-drive clips.
4 Inspect all the cooling system components (hoses, joint faces, etc) for leaks.
5 Where any problems are found on system components, renew the component or gasket with reference to Chapter 3.

6 With the vehicle raised, inspect the fuel tank and filler neck for punctures, cracks and other damage. The connection between the filler neck and tank is especially critical. Sometimes a rubber filler neck or connecting hose will leak due to loose retaining clamps or deteriorated rubber.
7 Carefully check all rubber hoses and metal fuel lines leading away from the fuel tank. Check for loose connections, deteriorated hoses, crimped lines, and other damage. Pay particular attention to the vent pipes and hoses, which often loop up around the filler neck and can become blocked or crimped. Follow the lines to the front of the vehicle, carefully inspecting them all the way. Renew damaged sections as necessary. Similarly, whilst the vehicle is raised, take the opportunity to inspect all underbody brake fluid pipes and hoses.
8 From within the engine compartment, check the security of all fuel, vacuum and brake hose attachments and pipe unions, and inspect all hoses for kinks, chafing and deterioration.
9 Where applicable, check the condition of the power steering fluid pipes and hoses.

21 Pollen filter renewal

Models with one-piece scuttle cover panel

1 Remove the scuttle cover panels as described in Chapter 11, Section 23.
2 Unclip the water deflector from the heater air inlet for access to the pollen filter.
3 Withdraw the filter from its housing.
4 Refitting is a reversal of removal.

Models with two-piece scuttle cover panel

5 Open the bonnet.
6 Remove the three screws securing the smaller scuttle cover panel, which covers the pollen filter housing **(see illustration)**.

HAYNES HiNT

A leak in the cooling system will usually show up as white- or rust-coloured deposits on the area adjoining the leak.

7 Carefully pull the weatherstrip from the front edge of the scuttle panel (as far as the windscreen washer jet), then lift the scuttle cover panel, and pull it forwards to release it from the scuttle. Unclip the windscreen washer fluid hose.

8 Remove the water deflector, by pulling it towards the centre of the vehicle, then pulling it forwards to release the securing clips at the inner end.

9 Use the tab provided to pull the pollen filter from its housing **(see illustration)**.

10 Fit the new filter, ensuring that it is correctly located in the housing. The top of the filter must be flat, and the tab should be visible at the top.

11 Refit the water deflector, then refit the scuttle cover panel using a reversal of the removal procedure. Make sure that the water deflector is securely refitted.

22 Idle speed and anti-stall speed check and adjustment

Note: *On 1.9 litre engines, the idle speed and anti-stall speed are controlled by the injection electronic control unit and are not adjustable.*

1 The usual type of tachometer (rev counter), which works from ignition system pulses, cannot be used on diesel engines. A diagnostic socket is provided for the use of Renault test equipment, but this will not normally be available to the home mechanic. If it is not felt that adjusting the idle speed 'by ear' is satisfactory, one of the following alternatives may be used.

a) *Purchase or hire of an appropriate tachometer.*

b) *Delegation of the job to a Renault dealer or other specialist.*

2 Before making adjustments warm up the engine to normal operating temperature. Make sure that the accelerator cable is correctly adjusted (see Chapter 4B).

Idle speed check and adjustment

Note: *On 2.2 litre turbo engines, the injection pump load potentiometer must be re-calibrated using Renault diagnostic test equipment whenever the position of the anti-stall adjustment screw is altered.*

3 With the accelerator lever resting against the idle stop, check that the engine idles at the specified speed. If necessary adjust as follows.

4 Loosen the locknut and unscrew the anti-stall adjustment screw until it is clear of the pump accelerator lever **(see illustration)**.

5 Loosen the locknut and turn the idle speed adjustment screw as required, then retighten the locknut.

6 Make the anti-stall adjustment as described later in this Section.

7 Stop the engine and disconnect the tachometer, where applicable.

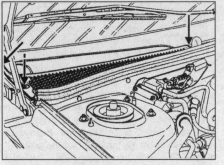

21.6 Remove the three screws (arrowed) securing the scuttle cover panel - left-hand-drive model shown

Anti-stall check and adjustment

8 Make sure that the engine is at normal operating temperature, and idling at the specified speed, as described previously.

9 Insert a 1 mm shim or feeler blade between the pump accelerator lever and the anti-stall adjustment screw. The idle speed should rise by approximately 10 to 20 rpm.

10 If adjustment is necessary, loosen the locknut and turn the anti-stall adjustment screw as required. Retighten the locknut.

11 Remove the shim and move the pump accelerator lever to increase the engine speed to approximately 3000 rpm, then quickly release the lever and check that the engine returns to the specified idle speed. Recheck the anti-stall speed setting and readjust, if necessary.

12 With the anti-stall speed correctly set, move the fast idle lever fully towards the

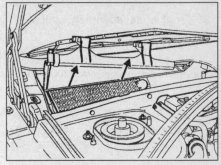

21.9 Pull the pollen filter from its housing - left-hand-drive model shown

flywheel end of the engine and check that the engine speed increases to the specified fast idle speed, where applicable. If necessary loosen the locknut and turn the fast idle adjusting screw as required, then retighten the locknut.

13 Disconnect the tachometer on completion.

23 Spare fuse check

Check that spare fuses are in place in the locations provided in the fusebox cover (see Chapter 12). It is advisable to carry at least one spare of each rating of fuse fitted. Spare fuses can be obtained from most car accessory shops, or from a Renault dealer.

1B

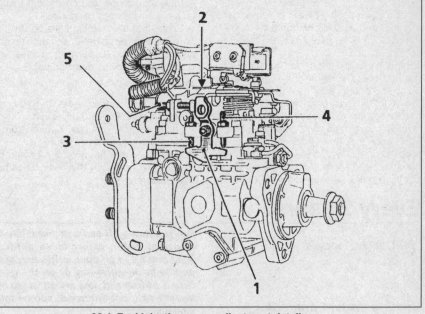

22.4 Fuel injection pump adjustment details - 2.2 litre non-turbo model shown

1 *Idle speed lever*	4 *Fast idle speed adjusting screw*
2 *Accelerator lever*	5 *Anti-stall speed adjusting screw*
3 *Idle speed adjusting screw*	

24 Front wheel alignment check

Refer to the information given in Chapter 10.

25 Rear brake shoe thickness check -
models with rear drum brakes

Remove the rear brake drums, and check the brake shoes for signs of wear or contamination. At the same time, also inspect the wheel cylinders for signs of leakage, and the brake drum for signs of wear. Refer to the relevant Sections of Chapter 9 for further information.

26 Brake fluid renewal

⚠ **Warning: Brake hydraulic fluid can harm your eyes and damage painted surfaces, so use extreme caution when handling and pouring it. Do not use fluid that has been standing open for some time, as it absorbs moisture from the air. Excess moisture can cause a dangerous loss of braking effectiveness.**

1 The procedure is similar to that for the bleeding of the hydraulic system as described in Chapter 9, except that the brake fluid reservoir should be emptied by siphoning, using a clean poultry baster or similar before starting, and allowance should be made for the old fluid to be expelled when bleeding a section of the circuit.
2 Working as described in Chapter 9, open the first bleed screw in the sequence, and pump the brake pedal gently until nearly all the old fluid has been emptied from the master cylinder reservoir. Top-up to the MAX level with new fluid, and continue pumping until only the new fluid remains in the reservoir, and new fluid can be seen emerging from the bleed screw. Tighten the screw, and top the reservoir level up to the MAX level line.

HAYNES HiNT *Old hydraulic fluid is invariably much darker in colour than the new, making it easy to distinguish the two.*

3 Work through all the remaining bleed screws in the sequence until new fluid can be seen at all of them. Be careful to keep the master cylinder reservoir topped-up to above the MIN level at all times, or air may enter the system and greatly increase the length of the task.
4 When the operation is complete, check that all bleed screws are securely tightened, and that their dust caps are refitted. Wash off all traces of spilt fluid, and recheck the master cylinder reservoir fluid level.
5 Check the operation of the brakes before taking the car on the road.

27 Road test

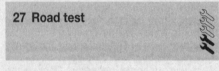

Instruments and electrical equipment

1 Check the operation of all instruments and electrical equipment.
2 Make sure that all instruments read correctly, and switch on all electrical equipment in turn, to check that it functions properly.

Steering and suspension

3 Check for any abnormalities in the steering, suspension, handling or road 'feel'.
4 Drive the vehicle, and check that there are no unusual vibrations or noises.
5 Check that the steering feels positive, with no excessive 'sloppiness', or roughness, and check for any suspension noises when cornering and driving over bumps.

Drivetrain

6 Check the performance of the engine, clutch, transmission and driveshafts.
7 Listen for any unusual noises from the engine, clutch and transmission.
8 Make sure that the engine runs smoothly when idling, and that there is no hesitation when accelerating.

9 Check that the clutch action is smooth and progressive, that the drive is taken up smoothly, and that the pedal travel is not excessive. Also listen for any noises when the clutch pedal is depressed.
10 Check that all gears can be engaged smoothly without noise, and that the gear lever action is not abnormally vague or 'notchy'.
11 Listen for a metallic clicking sound from the front of the vehicle, as the vehicle is driven slowly in a circle with the steering on full-lock. Carry out this check in both directions. If a clicking noise is heard, this indicates wear in a driveshaft joint (see Chapter 8).

Check the operation and performance of the braking system

12 Make sure that the vehicle does not pull to one side when braking, and that the wheels do not lock prematurely when braking hard.
13 Check that there is no vibration through the steering when braking.
14 Check that the handbrake operates correctly, without excessive movement of the lever, and that it holds the vehicle stationary on a slope.
15 Test the operation of the brake servo unit as follows. Depress the footbrake four or five times to exhaust the vacuum, then start the engine. As the engine starts, there should be a noticeable 'give' in the brake pedal as vacuum builds up. Allow the engine to run for at least two minutes, and then switch it off. If the brake pedal is now depressed again, it should be possible to detect a hiss from the servo as the pedal is depressed. After about four or five applications, no further hissing should be heard, and the pedal should feel considerably harder.

28 Timing belt renewal

Note: *On early models with a belt-driven brake vacuum pump, driven from the camshaft, Renault recommend that the vacuum pump drivebelt is renewed whenever the timing belt is renewed.*

Refer to the relevant Part of Chapter 2, and Section 10 of this Chapter if necessary.

Every 2 years

29 Coolant renewal

Cooling system draining

⚠ **Warning: Wait until the engine is cold before starting this procedure. Do not allow antifreeze to come in contact with your skin, or with the painted surfaces of the**

vehicle. **Rinse off spills immediately with plenty of water. Never leave antifreeze lying around in an open container, or in a puddle in the driveway or on the garage floor. Children and pets are attracted by its sweet smell, but antifreeze can be fatal if ingested.**
Note: *Renault do not specify renewal intervals for the coolant, but it is advisable to drain and refill the system every two years to ensure that the corrosion inhibiting properties of the coolant are maintained.*

1 With the engine completely cold, remove the expansion tank filler cap. Turn the cap anti-clockwise, wait until any pressure remaining in the system is released, then unscrew it and lift it off.
2 Remove the plastic engine cover (1.9 litre engines) and the engine undershield, then position a suitable container beneath the radiator bottom hose connection.
3 Slacken the hose clip, pull off the hose and allow the coolant to drain into the container.
4 To assist draining, open the cooling system

bleed screws. These are located in the heater matrix outlet hose, and/or in the radiator top and bottom hoses, and/or in the top of the radiator, depending on model **(see illustration)**.

5 If the coolant has been drained for a reason other than renewal, then provided it is clean and less than two years old, it can be re-used, though this is not recommended.

6 Refit the radiator bottom hose on completion of draining.

Cooling system flushing

7 If coolant renewal has been neglected, or if the antifreeze mixture has become diluted, then in time, the cooling system may gradually lose efficiency, as the coolant passages become restricted due to rust, scale deposits, and other sediment. The cooling system efficiency can be restored by flushing the system clean.

8 The radiator should be flushed independently of the engine, to avoid unnecessary contamination.

Radiator flushing

9 Disconnect the top and bottom hoses and any other relevant hoses from the radiator, with reference to Chapter 3.

10 Insert a garden hose into the radiator top inlet. Direct a flow of clean water through the radiator, and continue flushing until clean water emerges from the radiator bottom outlet.

11 If after a reasonable period, the water still does not run clear, the radiator can be flushed with a good proprietary cleaning agent. It is important that their manufacturer's instructions are followed carefully. If the contamination is particularly bad, insert the hose in the radiator bottom outlet, and reverse-flush the radiator.

Engine flushing

12 To flush the engine, first tighten the cooling system bleed screw(s).

13 Remove the thermostat as described in Chapter 3, then temporarily refit the top hose at its engine connection.

14 With the top and bottom hoses disconnected from the radiator, insert a garden hose into the radiator top hose. Direct a clean flow of water through the engine, and continue flushing until clean water emerges from the radiator bottom hose.

15 On completion of flushing, refit the thermostat and reconnect the hoses with reference to Chapter 3.

Cooling system filling

16 Before attempting to fill the cooling system, make sure that all hoses and clips are in good condition, and that the clips are tight. Note that an antifreeze mixture must be used all year round, to prevent corrosion of the engine components.

17 Remove the expansion tank filler cap.

18 Open the cooling system bleed screw(s) (see paragraph 4).

19 Place a container under the vehicle, below the expansion tank, to catch any coolant which may be spilt during the topping up procedure. Also place a wad of rags around the expansion tank.

20 Slowly fill the system until the coolant level reaches the top of the expansion tank filler neck.

21 Where applicable, close the bleed screws when coolant free from air bubbles emerges. Close the screws in sequence, starting with the lowest screw in the system.

22 Start the engine, and run it at a fast idle speed (do not exceed 1500 rpm) for approximately 4 minutes. Keep the level topped up to the top of the expansion tank filler neck.

23 Refit and tighten the expansion tank filler cap.

24 Allow the engine to run for approximately 20 minutes (until the cooling fan cuts in and out several times).

25 Stop the engine and check the coolant level, which should be up to the MAX mark on the side of the tank. Check that the expansion tank filler cap is tight.

26 Allow the engine to cool, then re-check the coolant level with reference to *Weekly*

29.4 Typical coolant bleed screw locations (arrowed)

checks. Top-up the level if necessary and refit the expansion tank filler cap. Where applicable, refit the engine undershield.

Antifreeze mixture

27 The antifreeze should always be renewed at the specified intervals. This is necessary not only to maintain the antifreeze properties, but also to prevent corrosion which would otherwise occur as the corrosion inhibitors become progressively less effective.

28 Always use an ethylene-glycol based antifreeze which is suitable for use in mixed-metal cooling systems. The quantity of antifreeze and levels of protection are given in the Specifications.

29 Before adding antifreeze, the cooling system should be completely drained, preferably flushed, and all hoses checked for condition and security.

30 After filling with antifreeze, a label should be attached to the expansion tank, stating the type and concentration of antifreeze used, and the date installed. Any subsequent topping-up should be made with the same type and concentration of antifreeze.

31 Do not use engine antifreeze in the windscreen/tailgate washer system, as it will cause damage to the vehicle paintwork. A screenwash additive should be added to the washer system in the quantities stated on the bottle.

1B

Chapter 2 Part A:
1.8 and 2.0 litre (8-valve) petrol engine in-car repair procedures

Contents

Degrees of difficulty

Easy, suitable for novice with little experience	**Fairly easy,** suitable for beginner with some experience	**Fairly difficult,** suitable for competent DIY mechanic	**Difficult,** suitable for experienced DIY mechanic	**Very difficult,** suitable for expert DIY or professional

2A

Specifications

General

Type	Four-cylinder, in-line, single overhead camshaft
Designation:	
1.8 litre engines	F3P
2.0 litre engines	F3R
Bore	82.7 mm
Stroke:	
1.8 litre engines:	
F3P 678 engine	83.0 mm
All other F3P engines	83.5 mm
2.0 litre engines	93.0 mm
Capacity:	
1.8 litre engines:	
F3P 678	1783 cc
All other F3P engines	1794 cc
2.0 litre engines	1998 cc
Firing order	1-3-4-2 (No 1 cylinder at transmission end of engine)
Direction of crankshaft rotation	Clockwise, viewed from timing belt end

Camshaft

Drive	Toothed belt
Number of bearings	5
Camshaft endfloat	0.048 to 0.133 mm

Valve clearances (engine cold)

Inlet	0.20 mm
Exhaust	0.40 mm

Lubrication system

Minimum oil pressure at 80°C:
  At 1000 rpm .... 1.2 bars (17 psi)
  At 3000 rpm .... 3.5 bars (50 psi)
Oil pump clearances:
  Gear-to-body:
    Minimum .... 0.10 mm
    Maximum .... 0.24 mm
  Gear endfloat:
    Minimum .... 0.02 mm
    Maximum .... 0.085 mm

Torque wrench settings

	Nm	lbf ft
Auxiliary shaft sprocket bolt	50	37
Camshaft sprocket	50	37
Camshaft bearing caps:		
8 mm diameter bolts	20	15
6 mm diameter bolts	10	7
Connecting rod (big-end) caps	50	37
Crankshaft pulley bolt	95	70
Cylinder head bolts:*		
1.8 litre engines:		
Stage 1	30	22
Stage 2	70	52
Wait for 3 minutes, fully slacken all bolts then tighten:		
Stage 3	20	15
Stage 4	Angle-tighten through 123° ± 2°	
2.0 litre engines:		
Stage 1	30	22
Stage 2	Angle-tighten through 50° ± 4°	
Wait for 3 minutes, slacken each bolt by 180° then tighten:		
Stage 3	25	18
Stage 4	Angle-tighten through 123° ± 7°	
Engine/transmission mountings:		
Right-hand mounting:		
Engine bracket-to-cylinder head bolts	25	18
Mounting bracket-to-engine bracket bolts	60	44
Mounting bracket-to-rubber mounting nut	40	30
Rubber mounting-to-body bolts	60	44
Left-hand mounting:		
Mounting bracket-to-transmission bolts	60	44
Mounting stud nut	80	59
Rubber mounting bolts	70	52
Rear mounting:		
Mounting bracket-to-transmission bolts	55	41
Mounting link rear bolt	110	81
Flywheel/driveplate bolts	55	41
Flywheel/driveplate cover plate bolts	24	18
Main bearing caps	65	48
Oil pump bolts:		
6 mm diameter bolts	10	7
8 mm diameter bolts	22	16
Roadwheel bolts	See Chapter 1A or 1B	
Sump bolts	13	10
Timing belt idler pulley bolts	20	15
Timing belt tensioner pulley nut	50	37
Valve cover nuts/bolts	5	4

* New bolts must be used

1 General information

This Part of Chapter 2 is devoted to in-car repair procedures for the 8-valve petrol engines. Similar information covering the 16-valve petrol engines, and the diesel engines will be found in Chapters 2B to 2E. All procedures concerning engine removal and refitting, and engine block/cylinder head overhaul for petrol and diesel engines can be found in Chapters 2F, 2G and 2H as applicable.

Refer to Vehicle identification in the Reference Section of this manual for details of engine code locations.

Most of the operations included in Chapter 2A are based on the assumption that the engine is still installed in the car. Therefore, if this information is being used during a complete engine overhaul, with the engine already removed, many of the steps included here will not apply.

Engine description

The engine is of four-cylinder, in-line, single overhead camshaft type, mounted transversely at the front of the vehicle.

The crankshaft is supported in five shell-type main bearings. Thrustwashers are fitted to control crankshaft endfloat.

The connecting rods are attached to the crankshaft by horizontally-split shell-type big-end bearings, and to the pistons by gudgeon pins. The gudgeon pins are a press fit in the connecting rods on 1.8 litre engines; on 2.0 litre engines the gudgeon pins are a sliding fit in the pistons and are secured in position with circlips. The aluminium alloy pistons are of the slipper type, and are fitted with three piston rings - two compression rings and a scraper-type oil control ring.

The single overhead camshaft is mounted directly in the cylinder head, and is driven by the crankshaft via a toothed timing belt.

The camshaft operates the valves via inverted bucket-type followers, which operate in bores machined directly in the cylinder head. Valve clearance adjustment is by shims located externally between the followers and the cam lobes. The inlet and exhaust valves are mounted vertically in the cylinder head, and are each closed by a single valve spring.

An auxiliary shaft located alongside the crankshaft is also driven by the timing belt, and actuates the oil pump via a skew gear.

A semi-closed crankcase ventilation system is employed; crankcase fumes are drawn from an oil separator on the cylinder block, and passed via a hose to the inlet manifold.

Engine lubrication is by pressure feed from a gear-type oil pump located beneath the crankshaft. Engine oil is fed through an externally-mounted oil filter to the main oil gallery feeding the crankshaft, auxiliary shaft and camshaft.

Repair operations possible with the engine in the vehicle

The following operations can be carried out without having to remove the engine from the vehicle:
a) Removal and refitting of the cylinder head.
b) Removal and refitting of the timing belt and sprockets.
c) Renewal of the camshaft oil seal.
d) Removal and refitting of the camshaft.
e) Removal and refitting of the sump.
f) Removal and refitting of the connecting rods and pistons*.
g) Removal and refitting of the oil pump.
h) Renewal of the crankshaft oil seals.
i) Renewal of the engine mountings.
j) Removal and refitting of the flywheel.
* Although the operation marked with an asterisk can be carried out with the engine in the car after removal of the sump, it is better for the engine to be removed, in the interests of cleanliness and improved access. For this reason, the procedure is described in Chapter 2F.

2 Compression test - description and interpretation

1 When engine performance is down, or if misfiring occurs which cannot be attributed to the ignition or fuel systems, a compression test can provide diagnostic clues as to the engine's condition. If the test is performed regularly, it can give warning of trouble before any other symptoms become apparent.
2 The engine must be fully warmed-up to normal operating temperature, the battery must be fully charged, and all the spark plugs must be removed (Chapter 1A). The aid of an assistant will also be required.
3 On models with a distributor, disable the ignition system by disconnecting the ignition HT coil lead from the distributor cap and earthing it on the cylinder block. Use a jumper lead or similar wire to make a good connection.
4 On models with a static (distributorless) ignition system, disable the ignition system by disconnecting the LT wiring connectors from the ignition HT coils, referring to Chapter 5B for further information.
5 Fit a compression tester to the No 1 cylinder spark plug hole - the type of tester which screws into the plug thread is to be preferred.
6 Have the assistant hold the throttle wide open, and crank the engine on the starter motor; after one or two revolutions, the compression pressure should build up to a maximum figure, and then stabilise. Record the highest reading obtained.
7 Repeat the test on the remaining cylinders, recording the pressure in each.
8 All cylinders should produce very similar pressures; a difference of more than 2 bars between any two cylinders indicates a fault. Note that the compression should build up quickly in a healthy engine; low compression on the first stroke, followed by gradually-increasing pressure on successive strokes, indicates worn piston rings. A low compression reading on the first stroke, which does not build up during successive strokes, indicates leaking valves or a blown head gasket (a cracked head could also be the cause). Deposits on the undersides of the valve heads can also cause low compression.
9 Although Renault do not specify exact compression pressures, as a guide, any cylinder pressure of below 10 bars can be considered as less than healthy. Refer to a Renault dealer or other specialist if in doubt as to whether a particular pressure reading is acceptable.
10 If the pressure in any cylinder is low, carry out the following test to isolate the cause. Introduce a teaspoonful of clean oil into that cylinder through its spark plug hole, and repeat the test.
11 If the addition of oil temporarily improves the compression pressure, this indicates that bore or piston wear is responsible for the pressure loss. No improvement suggests that leaking or burnt valves, or a blown head gasket, may be to blame.
12 A low reading from two adjacent cylinders is almost certainly due to the head gasket having blown between them; the presence of coolant in the engine oil will confirm this.
13 If one cylinder is about 20 percent lower than the others and the engine has a slightly rough idle, a worn camshaft lobe could be the cause.
14 If the compression reading is unusually high, the combustion chambers are probably coated with carbon deposits. If this is the case, the cylinder head should be removed and decarbonised.
15 On completion of the test, refit the spark plugs and reconnect the ignition system.

3 Top dead centre (TDC) for No 1 piston - locating

1 Top dead centre (TDC) is the highest point in the cylinder that each piston reaches as the crankshaft turns. Each piston reaches TDC at the end of the compression stroke and again at the end of the exhaust stroke. However, for the purpose of timing the engine, TDC refers to the position of No 1 piston at the end of its compression stroke. On all engines in this Part of Chapter 2, No 1 piston (and cylinder) is at the transmission end of the engine.
2 Disconnect the battery negative terminal (refer to *Disconnecting the battery* in the Reference Section of this manual).
3 Apply the handbrake, then jack up the front of the car and support it on axle stands (see *Jacking and vehicle support*). Remove the right-hand roadwheel, then remove the plastic cover from within the right-hand wheel arch, to gain access to the crankshaft pulley bolt.
4 Remove the air cleaner assembly as described in Chapter 4A to gain access to the flywheel/driveplate marking in the transmission housing aperture.
5 The crankshaft must now be turned until the timing mark on the front of the camshaft sprocket is positioned vertically at its highest point, and the flywheel/driveplate is aligned with the TDC (0º) mark on the transmission bellhousing. To view the camshaft sprocket timing mark on most models, it is necessary to unscrew the retaining bolts and release the clips (where applicable) and remove the timing belt upper cover. Note that on some models, it may be possible to align the sprocket mark with a pointer on the outer timing belt cover aperture.
6 The crankshaft can be turned by using a spanner or socket on the pulley bolt. Note that the crankshaft must always be turned in a clockwise direction (viewed from the right-hand side of vehicle).
7 Turn the crankshaft whilst keeping an eye on the camshaft sprocket. When the sprocket

2A

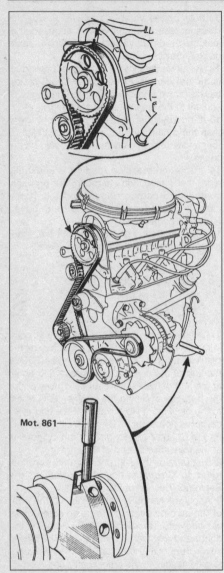

3.8 With number 1 cylinder positioned at TDC the crankshaft can be locked in positioned using a suitable dowel rod (Renault tool Mot 861 shown)

timing mark is correctly positioned, check the flywheel/driveplate mark is correctly aligned with the TDC (0°) mark on the transmission.

4.4 Unscrew the retaining nuts and remove the valve cover

The engine is now positioned with No1 piston at TDC on its compression stroke.

8 If necessary, the crankshaft can be locked in position to prevent unnecessary rotation. To do this, unscrew the access bolt from the left-hand end of the front of the cylinder block, located just to the left of the oil filter, and insert a dowel rod of suitable diameter to be a snug fit in the hole. Engage the rod in the timing slot provided for this purpose in the crankshaft, noting that it may be necessary to rotate the crankshaft slightly to do this **(see illustration)**. Once in place it should be impossible to turn the crankshaft. If the crankshaft will still move to and fro slightly, then the dowel rod has entered a balance hole in the crankshaft, instead of the timing slot. **Note:** *Do not attempt to rotate the engine whilst the crankshaft is locked in position. If the engine is to be left in this state for a long period of time, it is a good idea to place warning notices inside the vehicle, and in the engine compartment. This will reduce the possibility of the engine being accidentally cranked on the starter motor, which is likely to cause damage with the locking rod in place.*

4 Valve clearances - adjustment

Note: *This operation is not part of the maintenance schedule. It should be undertaken if noise from the valvegear becomes evident, or if loss of performance gives cause to suspect that the clearances*

may be incorrect. A new valve cover gasket may be required on refitting.

1 On multi-point injection models unclip and remove the wiring loom plastic cover which is situated between the inlet manifold and cylinder head.

2 On single-point injection models, disconnect the accelerator cable from the throttle housing as described in Chapter 4A.

3 Where applicable, disconnect the crankcase ventilation hose from the valve cover.

4 Unscrew the nuts from the valve cover, and withdraw the cover from the engine **(see illustration)**.

5 Remove the spark plugs with reference to Chapter 1A, in order to make turning the engine easier.

6 Draw the valve positions on a piece of paper, numbering them 1 to 8 from the transmission end of the engine. Identify them as inlet or exhaust (ie 1E, 2I, 3E, 4I, 5I, 6E, 7I, 8E) **(see illustration)**.

7 To improve access to the crankshaft pulley, apply the handbrake, then jack up the front of the car and support it on axle stands (see *Jacking and vehicle support*). Undo the retaining screws and remove the plastic undercover from beneath the engine/transmission.

8 Using a socket or spanner on the crankshaft pulley bolt, turn the engine until the valves of No 1 cylinder (transmission end) are 'rocking'. The exhaust valve will be closing, and the inlet valve will be opening. The piston of No 4 cylinder will be at the top of its compression stroke, with both valves fully closed. The clearances for both valves of No 4 cylinder may be checked at the same time.

9 Insert a feeler blade of the correct thickness (see *Specifications*) between the cam lobe and the shim on the top of the follower, and check that it is a firm sliding fit **(see illustration)**. If it is not, use the feeler blades to ascertain the exact clearance, and record this for use when calculating the new shim thickness required. Note that the inlet and exhaust valve clearances are different (see *Specifications*).

10 With No 4 cylinder valve clearances checked, turn the engine through half a turn so that No 3 valves are 'rocking', then check the valve clearances of No 2 cylinder in the

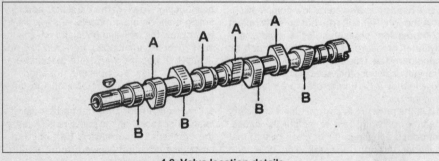

4.6 Valve location details

A Inlet   *B Exhaust*

4.9 Measuring a valve clearance

same way. Similarly check the remaining valve clearances in the following sequence:

Valves rocking on cylinder	Check clearances on cylinder
1	4
3	2
4	1
2	3

11 Where a valve clearance differs from the specified value, then the shim for that valve must be replaced with a thinner or thicker shim accordingly. The shim size is stamped on the bottom face of the shim **(see illustration)**; however, it is good practice to use a micrometer to measure the true thickness of any shim removed, as it may have been reduced by wear.

12 The size of shim required is calculated as follows. If the measured clearance is less than specified, subtract the measured clearance from the specified clearance, and deduct the result from the thickness of the existing shim. For example:

Sample calculation - clearance too small

Clearance measured (A) = 0.15 mm
Desired clearance (B) = 0.20 mm
Difference (B – A) = 0.05 mm
Shim thickness fitted = 3.70 mm
Shim thickness required =
3.70 – 0.05 = 3.65 mm

13 If the measured clearance is greater than specified, subtract the specified clearance from the measured clearance, and add the result to the thickness of the existing shim. For example:

Sample calculation - clearance too big

Clearance measured (A) = 0.50 mm
Desired clearance (B) = 0.40 mm
Difference (A – B) = 0.10 mm
Shim thickness fitted = 3.45 mm
Shim thickness required =
3.45 + 0.10 = 3.55 mm

14 The shims can be removed from their locations on top of the followers without removing the camshaft if the Renault tool shown can be borrowed, or a suitable alternative fabricated **(see illustration)**.

15 To remove the shim, the follower has to be pressed down against valve spring pressure, just far enough to allow the shim to be slid out. Theoretically, this could be done by levering against the camshaft between the cam lobes with a suitable pad to push the bucket down, but this is not recommended by the manufacturers.

16 An arrangement similar to the Renault tool can be made by bolting a bar to the camshaft bearing studs, and levering down against this with a stout screwdriver. The contact pad should be a triangular-shaped metal block, with a lip filed along each side to contact the edge of the buckets. Levering down against this will open the valve and allow the shim to be withdrawn.

17 Make sure that the cam lobe peaks are uppermost when depressing a follower, and rotate the follower so that the notches are at right-angles to the camshaft centre-line.

4.11 Shim thickness is stamped on the underside of each shim

When refitting the shims, ensure that the size markings face the followers (ie face downwards).

18 If the Renault tool cannot be borrowed or a suitable alternative made up, then it will be necessary to remove the camshaft to gain access to the shims, as described in Section 9.

19 Remove the socket or spanner from the crankshaft pulley bolt. Refit the undercover and lower the vehicle to the ground.

20 Refit the spark plugs with reference to Chapter 1A, then refit the valve cover, together with a new gasket where necessary.

21 Reconnect the crankcase ventilation hose to the cover and refit any components removed/disconnected to improve access.

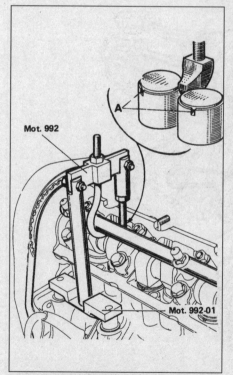

4.14 Renault tool for depressing followers and removing shims

Position follower notches (A) at right-angles to the camshaft before depressing them

5 Timing belt - removal and refitting

Note: *Renault specify the use of a special electronic tool (SEEM C.TRONIC type 105 belt tensioning measuring tool) to correctly set the timing belt tension. If access to this equipment cannot be obtained, an approximate setting can be achieved using the method described below. If the method described is used, the tension must be checked using the special electronic tool at the earliest possible opportunity. Do not drive the vehicle over large distances, or use high engine speeds, until the belt tension is known to be correct. Refer to a Renault dealer for advice.*

Note: *The timing belt should renewed whenever it is disturbed; never refit a belt which has already been used.*

Removal

1 Disconnect the battery negative terminal (refer to *Disconnecting the battery* in the Reference Section of this manual).

2 Apply the handbrake, then jack up the front of the car and support it on axle stands (see *Jacking and vehicle support*). Remove the right-hand front roadwheel.

3 Undo the retaining screws and remove the engine undercover and the front and rear protective covers from the right-hand wheelarch.

4 Remove the auxiliary drivebelt as described in Chapter 1A.

5 Position number 1 cylinder at TDC on its compression stroke and lock the crankshaft in position as described in Section 3.

6 Place a jack beneath the engine, with a block of wood on the jack head. Raise the jack until it is supporting the weight of the engine. Alternatively, attach a support bar to the engine and use the bar to support the weight of the engine/transmission.

7 Slacken and remove the retaining nut and bolts and remove the right-hand engine mounting bracket. Undo the three retaining bolts and remove the rubber mounting from the body.

8 Undo the retaining bolts and remove the timing belt upper cover.

9 Temporarily remove the crankshaft locking rod and slacken and remove the crankshaft pulley retaining bolt. To prevent crankshaft rotation whilst the retaining bolt is slackened, remove the lower cover plate and lock the flywheel/driveplate ring gear, using an arrangement similar to that shown **(see illustrations)**. On manual transmission models, if the engine is in the vehicle the crankshaft can be retained by selecting top gear and applying the brakes firmly. *Do not* be tempted to use the crankshaft locking pin to prevent the crankshaft from rotating (see Section 3). Remove the crankshaft pulley then refit the pulley bolt to the end of the crankshaft. Refit the locking rod making sure it is correctly located.

2A

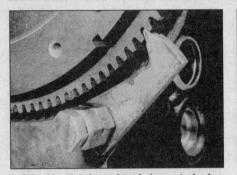

5.9a Use fabricated tool shown to lock flywheel/driveplate ring gear and prevent crankshaft rotation

5.9b Removing the crankshaft pulley

10 Undo the retaining bolts and remove the timing belt lower cover.

11 Undo the retaining bolts and remove the support strut from the front of the engine mounting bracket on the cylinder block. Undo the bolts and remove the mounting bracket.

12 Loosen the nut, rotate the timing belt tensioner clockwise to relieve the tension from the belt, and re-tighten the nut.

13 Release the belt from the camshaft sprocket, idler pulley, auxiliary shaft sprocket and crankshaft sprocket, and remove it from the engine.

14 Clean the sprockets and tensioners, and wipe them dry. Do not apply excessive amounts of solvent to the tensioner wheels, otherwise the bearing lubricant may be contaminated. Also clean the front of the cylinder head and block.

Refitting

15 In order to enable the tensioner to be adjusted easily, screw a 6 mm bolt into the threaded hole provided in the timing belt cover. The bolt will bear against the rear of the tensioner pulley and enable fine adjustments of the belt tension to be made.

16 Ensure that the crankshaft is at the TDC position for No 1 cylinder, and that the crankshaft is locked in this position using the metal rod through the hole in the crankcase, as described previously.

17 Check that the timing mark on the camshaft sprocket is in line with the corresponding mark on the timing belt rear cover or the valve cover, as applicable.

18 Align the timing mark bands on the belt with those on the sprockets, noting that the running direction arrows on the belt should be positioned between the auxiliary shaft sprocket and the tensioner pulley. The crankshaft sprocket mark is in the form of a notch in its rear guide perimeter. The auxiliary shaft sprocket has no timing mark. Fit the timing belt over the crankshaft sprocket first, then the auxiliary shaft sprocket, followed by the camshaft sprocket **(see illustration)**.

19 Check that all the timing marks are still aligned and remove all slack from the timing belt by screwing in the previously fitted 6mm bolt in the timing cover.

Tensioning without the special electronic measuring tool

Note: *If this method is used, ensure that the belt tension is checked by a Renault dealer at the earliest possible opportunity.*

20 In the absence of the special electronic tool, an approximate setting may be achieved by tensioning the belt until it is just possible to twist the timing belt through 90° by finger and thumb, midway between the auxiliary shaft sprocket and tensioner pulley. Under firm thumb pressure the deflection of the belt at the mid-point should be approximately 6.0 mm.

21 Adjust the position of the tensioner pulley as required then tighten its retaining nut to the specified torque setting.

22 Remove the crankshaft locking rod and, using a suitable socket and extension bar on the crankshaft sprocket bolt, rotate the crankshaft through two complete rotations in a clockwise direction (viewed from the right-hand end of the engine). Do not at any time rotate the crankshaft anti-clockwise.

23 Refit the crankshaft locking rod and check that the sprocket timing marks are correctly positioned. Recheck the belt tension as described in paragraph 20. If necessary slacken the tensioner pulley nut and repeat the procedures in paragraphs 21 and 22.

24 Once the belt is correctly tensioned, remove the crankshaft locking rod and refit its access plug, tightening it securely. Unscrew the bolt used to position the tensioner pulley.

25 Refit the engine mounting bracket and support rod to the cylinder block and tighten the retaining bolts to the specified torque.

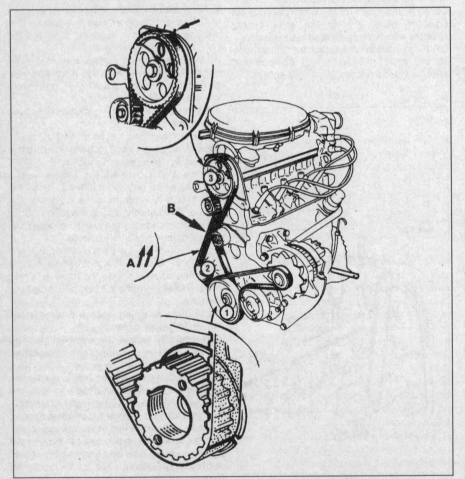

5.18 Timing belt and sprocket alignment markings

1 *Crankshaft pulley*   2 *Auxiliary shaft sprocket*   3 *Camshaft sprocket*
A *Arrows showing belt running direction*   B *Point to check timing belt tension*

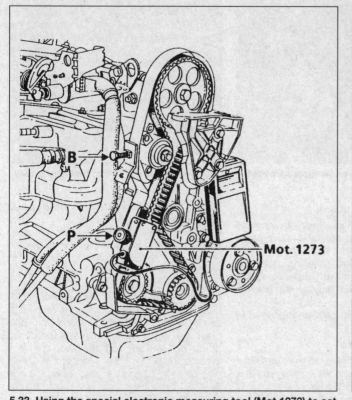

5.33 Using the special electronic measuring tool (Mot 1273) to set the timing belt tension

B Tensioner pulley adjustment bolt
P Measuring tool screw

6.2 Renault tool for holding the sprocket stationary using the old timing belt

26 Refit the timing belt lower cover and securely tighten its retaining bolts.

27 Refit the crankshaft pulley and tighten its retaining bolt to the specified torque, using the method employed on removal to prevent rotation. Where necessary, refit the flywheel/driveplate lower cover plate and tighten its retaining bolts to the specified torque.

28 Refit the timing belt upper cover and securely tighten its retaining bolts.

29 Refit the rubber mounting to the body and tighten its retaining bolts to the specified torque. Install the mounting bracket and loosely tighten its mounting nut and bolts. Ensure that the bracket is positioned centrally in relation to the rubber mounting lug then tighten its retaining nut and bolts to their specified torque settings. Remove the jack/engine support bar (as applicable).

30 Refit the auxiliary drivebelt as described in Chapter 1A.

31 Refit the undercover and wheelarch covers and fit the roadwheel.

32 Lower the vehicle to the ground and tighten the wheel bolts to the specified torque. Reconnect the battery.

Tensioning using the special electronic measuring tool

33 Fit the special belt tensioning measuring equipment to the timing belt, just above the auxiliary shaft sprocket **(see illustration)**. Position the tensioner pulley so that the belt is tensioned to a setting of 25 units on 1.8 litre models and 29 units on 2.0 litre models. Once the tensioner is correctly positioned, tighten its retaining nut to the specified torque.

34 Remove the locking rod from the crankshaft and remove the measuring tool from the belt.

35 Using a suitable socket and extension bar on the crankshaft sprocket bolt, rotate the crankshaft through four complete rotations in a clockwise direction (viewed from the right-hand end of the engine). *Do not* at any time rotate the crankshaft anti-clockwise.

36 Refit the belt measuring tool to the belt (see paragraph 33) and check the belt operating tension. The belt should now have a **minimum** tension of 22 units on 1.8 litre models and 27 units on 2.0 litre models. If not, slacken the tensioner pulley retaining nut and repeat paragraphs 33 to 36.

37 Once the belt tension is correctly set, refit the locking rod and check that the sprocket timing marks are correctly positioned. If all is well, remove the locking rod and refit its access plug, tightening it securely. Unscrew the bolt used to position the tensioner pulley.

38 Carry out the operations described in paragraphs 25 to 32.

6 Timing belt sprockets and tensioners - removal, inspection and refitting

Note: *A new timing belt must be used on refitting.*

Removal

1 Remove the timing belt as described in Section 5.

Camshaft sprocket

2 Slacken the sprocket retaining bolt and remove the bolt and washer. To prevent rotation as the bolt is slackened, a sprocket-holding tool will be required. In the absence of the special Renault tool, an acceptable substitute can be fabricated as follows. Use two lengths of steel strip (one long, the other short), and three nuts and bolts; one nut and bolt forms the pivot of a forked tool, with the remaining two nuts and bolts at the tips of the 'forks' to engage with the sprocket spokes as shown. Alternately, the sprocket can be retained using the old timing belt and a pair or grips **(see illustration)**.

3 With the retaining bolt removed, slide off the sprocket and recover the sprocket Woodruff key. Examine the oil seal for signs of oil leakage and, if necessary, renew it as described in Section 7.

2A

6.4 Removing the bolt from the auxiliary shaft

6.5 Removing the crankshaft sprocket

6.7 Removing the timing belt idler pulley

Auxiliary shaft sprocket

4 Remove the sprocket as described in paragraphs 2 and 3, retaining the sprocket using the timing belt and a pair of grips **(see illustration)**. Note that on some models the Woodruff key is an integral part of the sprocket.

Crankshaft sprocket

5 A puller may be necessary to remove the crankshaft sprocket. Make up a puller using two bolts, a metal bar and the existing crankshaft pulley bolt. By unscrewing the crankshaft pulley bolt, the sprocket is pulled from the end of the crankshaft. If necessary, remove the Woodruff key from the slot in the crankshaft **(see illustration)**. Examine the oil seal for signs of oil leakage and, if necessary renew as described in Section 13.

Tensioner pulley

6 Unscrew the large retaining nut and the retaining bolt and remove the timing belt tensioner pulley.

Idler pulley

7 Unscrew the retaining bolts securing the idler pulley backplate to the cylinder block and remove the pulley assembly **(see illustration)**.

Inspection

8 Inspect the teeth of the sprockets for signs of nicks and damage. The teeth are not prone to wear, and should normally last the life of the engine.

9 Spin the tensioner and idler pulley by hand, and check for any roughness or tightness. Do not attempt to clean them with solvent, as this may enter the bearings. If wear is evident, renew the tensioner and/or idler pulley as necessary.

Refitting

Camshaft sprocket

10 Refit the Woodruff key to the camshaft groove and refit the sprocket, making sure its slot engages correctly with the key.

11 Refit the sprocket retaining bolt and tighten it to the specified torque setting, using the holding tool to prevent rotation.

12 Fit the new timing belt as described in Section 5.

Auxiliary shaft sprocket

13 Refit the Woodruff key (where fitted) to the shaft and slide on the sprocket making sure its is correctly engaged with the shaft.

14 Refit the sprocket retaining bolt and tighten it to the specified torque using the method employed on removal to prevent rotation.

15 Fit the new timing belt as described in Section 5.

Crankshaft sprocket

16 Refit the Woodruff key to the crankshaft slot and slide of the sprocket, making sure it is correctly engaged with the key.

17 Fit the new timing belt as described in Section 5.

Tensioner pulley

18 Fit the tensioner pulley over its stud and refit the retaining nut and bolt.

19 Fit the new timing belt as described in Section 5.

Idler pulley

20 Fit the idler pulley to the cylinder block and securely tighten its retaining bolts.

21 Fit the new timing belt as described in Section 5.

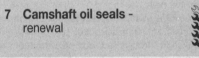

7 Camshaft oil seals - renewal

Front (timing belt end) oil seal

Note: *A new timing belt must be used on refitting.*

1 Remove the camshaft sprocket as described in Section 6.

2 Make a note of the correct fitted depth of the seal then punch or drill two small holes opposite each other in the oil seal. Screw a self-tapping screw into each and pull on the screws with pliers to extract the seal. **Note:** *On some models it may be necessary to unbolt and remove the timing belt rear upper cover to allow the seal to be withdrawn. If this is the case, remove the tensioner and idler pulleys (see Section 6) then unbolt and remove the cover.*

3 Clean the seal housing and polish off any

burrs or raised edges which may have caused the seal to fail in the first place.

4 Lubricate the lips of the new seal with clean engine oil and ease it into position on the end of the shaft. Press the seal into its housing until it is positioned at the same depth as the original was prior to removal. If necessary, a suitable tubular drift, such as a socket, which bears only on the hard outer edge of the seal can be used to tap the seal into position. Take great care not to damage the seal lips during fitting and ensure that the seal lips face inwards. Note that if the surface of the shaft was noted to be badly scored, press the new seal slightly further into its housing so that its lip is running on an unmarked area of the shaft.

5 Where necessary, refit the timing belt rear upper cover and install the idler and tensioner pulleys as described in Section 6

6 Refit the camshaft sprocket as described in Section 6 and fit the new timing belt as described in Section 5.

Rear (flywheel/driveplate end) oil seal

7 On models with a distributor, remove the distributor cap and rotor arm as described in Chapter 5B.

8 On models with a static (distributorless) ignition system, disconnect the wiring connector from the camshaft position sensor then undo the retaining screws and remove the sensor housing from the left-hand end of the cylinder head. Remove the toothed sensor ring from the end of the camshaft.

9 On all models, remove the insulating plate from the head to gain access to the oil seal.

10 Make a note of the correct fitted depth of the seal then punch or drill two small holes opposite each other in the oil seal. Screw a self-tapping screw into each and pull on the screws with pliers to extract the seal.

11 Clean the seal housing and polish off any burrs or raised edges which may have caused the seal to fail in the first place.

12 Lubricate the lips of the new seal with clean engine oil and ease it into position on the end of the shaft. Press the seal into its housing until it is positioned at the same depth as the original was prior to removal. If necessary, a suitable tubular drift, such as a socket, which bears only on the hard outer

edge of the seal can be used to tap the seal into position. Take great care not to damage the seal lips during fitting and ensure that the seal lips face inwards. Note that if the surface of the shaft was noted to be badly scored, press the new seal slightly further into its housing so that its lip is running on an unmarked area of the shaft.

13 Refit the insulating plate to the head and refit the rotor arm and distributor cap or the camshaft toothed sensor ring and sensor housing (as applicable).

8 Auxiliary shaft oil seal - renewal

1 Remove the auxiliary shaft sprocket as described in Section 6.

2 Make a note of the correct fitted depth of the seal then punch or drill two small holes opposite each other in the oil seal. Screw a self-tapping screw into each and pull on the screws with pliers to extract the seal. **Note:** *On some models it may be necessary to unbolt and remove the timing belt rear lower cover to allow the seal to be withdrawn. If this is the case, remove the crankshaft sprocket and idler pulleys (see Section 6) then unbolt and remove the cover.*

3 Clean the seal housing and polish off any burrs or raised edges which may have caused the seal to fail in the first place.

4 Lubricate the lips of the new seal with clean engine oil and ease it into position on the end of the shaft. Press the seal into its housing until it is positioned at the same depth as the original was prior to removal. If necessary, a suitable tubular drift, such as a socket, which bears only on the hard outer edge of the seal can be used to tap the seal into position. Take great care not to damage the seal lips during fitting and ensure that the seal lips face inwards. Note that if the surface of the shaft was noted to be badly scored, press the new seal slightly further into its housing so that its lip is running on an unmarked area of the shaft.

5 Where necessary, refit the timing belt rear cover and install the idler pulley and crankshaft sprocket as described in Section 6.

6 Refit the auxiliary shaft sprocket as described in Section 6 and fit the new timing belt as described in Section 5.

9 Camshaft and followers - removal, inspection and refitting

Note: *New camshaft oil seals, a new valve cover gasket and a new timing belt must be used on refitting. Suitable sealant will be required for the camshaft bearing caps and the bearing cap bolts.*

Removal

1 On multi-point injection models unclip and remove the wiring loom plastic cover which is situated between the inlet manifold and cylinder head.

2 On single-point injection models, to improve access disconnect the accelerator cable from the throttle housing as described in Chapter 4A.

3 Where applicable, disconnect the crankcase ventilation hose from the valve cover.

4 Unscrew the nuts from the valve cover, and withdraw the cover from the engine.

5 Remove the timing belt as described in Section 5.

6 On models with a distributor, disconnect the HT leads, and remove the distributor cap and rotor arm (Chapter 5B). Where applicable, also remove the insulating plate.

7 On models with a static (distributorless) ignition system, disconnect the wiring connector from the camshaft position sensor then undo the retaining screws and remove the sensor housing from the left-hand end of the cylinder head. Remove the toothed sensor ring from the end of the camshaft along with the insulating plate.

8 Remove the camshaft sprocket with reference to Section 6.

9 Using a dial gauge, measure the camshaft endfloat, and compare with the value given in the *Specifications*. This will give an indication of the amount of wear present on the thrust surfaces.

10 Make identifying marks on the camshaft bearing caps, so that they can be refitted in the same positions and the same way round.

11 Progressively slacken the bearing cap bolts until the valve spring pressure is relieved. Remove the bolts and the bearing caps noting the cap locating dowels **(see illustrations)**.

12 Note the position of the cam lobes. The lobes for No 1 cylinder (transmission end) will be pointing upwards. Lift out the camshaft, together with the oil seals.

13 Remove the followers, keeping each with its shim **(see illustration)**. Place them in a compartment box, or on a sheet of card marked into eight sections, so that they may be refitted to their original locations. Write down the shim thicknesses - they will be needed later if any of the valve clearances are incorrect. The shim size is stamped on the bottom face of the shim, but it is prudent to use a micrometer to measure the true thickness of any shim removed, as it may have been reduced by wear.

Inspection

14 Examine the camshaft bearing surfaces and lobes for wear ridges, pitting or scoring. Renew the camshaft if evident.

15 Renew the oil seals at the ends of the camshaft as a matter of course. Lubricate the lips of the new seals before fitting them, and store the camshaft so that its weight is not resting on the seals.

16 Examine the camshaft bearing surfaces in the cylinder head and bearing caps. Deep scoring or other damage means that the cylinder head must be renewed.

17 Inspect the followers and shims for scoring, pitting and wear ridges. Renew as necessary.

Refitting

18 Oil the followers, and fit them to the bores from which they were removed. Fit the correct shim, numbered side downwards, to each follower.

19 Oil the camshaft bearings. Place the camshaft with its oil seals onto the cylinder head. The oil seals must be positioned so that they are flush with the cylinder head faces. The cam lobes must be positioned as noted before removal (paragraph 12).

Caution: If the cam lobes are not positioned correctly, the valves may be forced into the pistons when the bearing caps are tightened.

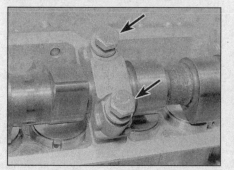

9.11a Slacken the retaining bolts ...

9.11b ... and lift off camshaft bearing caps

9.13 Removing a camshaft follower

2A

20 Ensure that the locating dowels are in position and refit the camshaft bearing caps to their original locations, applying a little sealant to the end caps where they meet the cylinder head.

21 Apply sealant to the threads of the bearing cap bolts. Fit the bolts and tighten them evenly and progressively to the specified torque.

22 If a new camshaft has been fitted, measure the endfloat using a dial gauge, and check that it is within the specified limits.

23 Refit the camshaft sprocket with reference to Section 6.

24 Fit the new timing belt with reference to Section 5.

25 Check and adjust the valve clearances as described in Section 4.

26 Refit the valve cover, together with a new gasket where necessary. Reconnect the crankcase ventilation hose to the cover and refit any components removed/disconnected to improve access.

27 On models with a distributor, refit the insulating plate, rotor arm and distributor cap, with reference to Chapter 5B.

28 On models with a static (distributorless) ignition system, refit the insulating plate and toothed sensor wheel then refit the camshaft sensor housing and securely tighten its retaining bolts. Connect the wiring connector to the camshaft position sensor.

29 Reconnect the battery.

10 Cylinder head -
removal and refitting

Note: *New cylinder head bolts and a new timing belt will be required on refitting.*

Removal

1 Disconnect the battery negative terminal (refer to *Disconnecting the battery* in the Reference Section of this manual).

2 Drain the cooling system with reference to Chapter 1A.

3 Remove the timing belt with reference to Section 5 noting that it will be necessary to support the engine weight with a jack rather than the support bar.

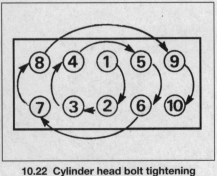

10.22 Cylinder head bolt tightening sequence

4 Remove the air cleaner assembly and inlet duct as described in Chapter 4A.

5 Remove the inlet and exhaust manifolds as described in Chapter 4A.

6 Remove the amplifier unit, distributor cap and HT leads (models with a distributor) or the ignition HT coils complete with leads (models with static ignition) as described in Chapter 5B.

7 Disconnect the wiring connectors from the cylinder head coolant temperature sensor, the MAP sensor and the knock sensor. Free the wiring loom from its retaining clips, noting its correct routing, and position it clear of the cylinder head.

8 Slacken and remove the two bolts securing the timing belt rear upper cover to the cylinder block. The upper cover is then free to be removed with the cylinder head.

9 Slacken the retaining clips and disconnect the coolant hoses from the thermostat housing on the left-hand end of the cylinder head.

10 Working in the **reverse** of the sequence shown in **illustration 10.22**, progressively slacken the cylinder head bolts by half a turn at a time until all nuts and bolts can be unscrewed by hand and removed.

11 Lift the cylinder head upwards and off the cylinder block. If it is stuck, tap it upwards using a hammer and block of wood. Do not try to turn it (it is located by two dowels), nor attempt to prise it free using a screwdriver inserted between the block and head faces. If the locating dowels are a loose fit, remove them and store them with the head for safe-keeping

Preparation for refitting

12 The mating faces of the cylinder head and cylinder block must be perfectly clean before refitting the head. Use a soft putty knife to remove all traces of gasket and carbon, and also clean the piston crowns. Take particular care during the cleaning operations as aluminium alloy is easily damaged. Also, make sure that debris is not allowed to enter the oil and water passages - this is particularly important for the lubrication system, as carbon could block the oil supply to the engine's components. Using adhesive tape and paper, seal the water, oil and bolt holes in the cylinder block. To prevent carbon entering the gap between the pistons and bores, smear a little grease in the gap. After cleaning each piston, use a small brush to remove all traces of grease and carbon from the gap, then wipe away the remainder with a clean rag. Clean all the pistons in the same way.

13 Check the mating surfaces of the cylinder block and cylinder head for nicks, deep scratches and other damage. If slight, they may be removed carefully with a file, but if excessive, machining may be the only alternative to renewal.

14 If warpage of the cylinder head gasket surface is suspected, use a straight-edge to check it for distortion. Refer to the overhaul information given in Part F of this Chapter if necessary.

15 Examine the cylinder head bolt threads in the cylinder block for damage. If necessary, use the correct-size tap to chase out the threads in the block. Ensure that the bolt holes are clean and free of oil. Syringe or soak up any oil left in the bolt holes. This is most important in order that the correct bolt tightening torque can be applied and to prevent the possibility of the block being cracked by hydraulic pressure when the bolts are tightened.

16 Note that the cylinder head bolts must be discarded and renewed, regardless of their apparent condition.

Refitting

17 Ensure that the mating faces of the cylinder block and head are spotlessly clean, that the retaining bolt threads are also clean and dry, and that they screw easily in and out of their locations.

18 Check that No 1 piston is still at TDC, and that the camshaft sprocket timing mark is correctly aligned with the cover (see Section 3)

Caution: If the camshaft/crankshaft is incorrectly positioned, there is a risk of the valves being forced into the pistons as the head is refitted.

19 Ensure that the locating dowels are correctly fitted to the block and fit a new cylinder head gasket, making sure it is the right way up.

20 Carefully lower the cylinder head onto the block, engaging it over the dowels. As the head is lowered into position make sure the timing belt rear cover is correctly engaged with the cylinder block.

21 Lightly oil the new cylinder head bolts, both on their threads and under their heads. Allow excess oil to drain off then insert the bolts, and tighten them finger-tight. Tighten the bolts as described under the relevant sub-heading.

1.8 litre models

22 Working progressively and in the sequence shown, tighten the cylinder head bolts to their Stage 1 torque setting, using a torque wrench and suitable socket **(see illustration)**.

23 Once all the bolts have been tightened to their Stage 1 setting, working again in the given sequence, tighten the bolts to the specified Stage 2 setting.

24 Wait for approximately 3 minutes then go around in the **reverse** of the specified sequence and fully slacken each bolt.

25 Once all the bolts are slack, go around in the specified sequence and tighten the bolts to the specified Stage 3 torque setting.

26 Finally go around again in the specified sequence and angle-tighten the bolts through the specified Stage 4 angle, using a socket and extension bar. It is recommended that an angle-measuring gauge is used during this stage of the tightening, to ensure accuracy **(see illustration)**.

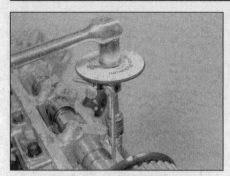

10.26 Using an angle-tightening measuring gauge to accurately tighten the cylinder head bolts

2.0 litre models

27 Working progressively and in the sequence shown in **illustration 10.22**, tighten the cylinder head bolts to their Stage 1 torque setting, using a torque wrench and suitable socket.

28 Once all the bolts have been tightened to their Stage 1 setting, working again in the given sequence, angle-tighten the bolts through the specified Stage 2 angle, using a socket and extension bar. It is recommended that an angle-measuring gauge is used during this stage of the tightening, to ensure accuracy.

29 Wait for approximately 3 minutes then go around in the **reverse** of the specified sequence and slacken each bolt by 180° (half-a-turn).

30 Working again in the specified sequence, tighten each bolt to the specified Stage 3 torque setting.

12.2 Removing the oil pump

12.3a Unbolt and remove the oil pump drivegear cover plate . . .

31 Finally go around again in the specified sequence and angle-tighten the bolts through the specified Stage 4 angle, using a socket and extension bar. It is recommended that an angle-measuring gauge is used during this stage of the tightening, to ensure accuracy.

All models

32 Reconnect the coolant hoses to the thermostat housing and securely tighten their retaining clips.

33 Refit the bolts securing the timing belt rear cover to the block and tighten them securely.

34 Ensure that the wiring is correctly routed and reconnect the connectors to the MAP sensor, coolant temperature sensor and knock sensor.

35 Refit the amplifier unit, distributor cap and leads or the ignition HT coils and leads (as applicable) as described in Chapter 5B.

36 Refit the inlet and exhaust manifolds as described in Chapter 4A.

37 Refit the air cleaner assembly and inlet duct as described in Chapter 4A.

38 Fit the new timing belt as described in Section 5.

39 Reconnect the battery and refill the cooling system as described in Chapter 1A.

40 On completion, check the oil level (see *Weekly checks*).

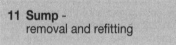

11 Sump -
removal and refitting

Removal

1 Apply the handbrake, then jack up the front of the car and support it on axle stands (see *Jacking and vehicle support*). Undo the retaining screws and remove the plastic under-cover from beneath the engine/transmission.

2 Drain the engine oil as described in Chapter 1A, then refit and tighten the drain plug.

3 Unscrew the bolts, including the bolts securing the support rods to the side of the cylinder block, and remove the flywheel/driveplate cover plate.

4 Unscrew and remove the bolts securing the sump to the crankcase. Tap the sump with a hide or plastic mallet to break the seal, then

12.3b . . . and withdraw the drivegear from the block

remove the sump along with its gasket. discard the gasket, a new one must be used on refitting.

Refitting

5 Remove all traces of dirt and oil from the mating surfaces of the sump and cylinder block.

6 Locate the new gasket on the top of the sump and lift the sump into position.

7 Insert the bolts and tighten them progressively to the specified torque.

8 Refit the undercover and lower the vehicle to the ground.

9 Fill the engine with fresh oil, with reference to Chapter 1A.

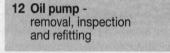

12 Oil pump -
removal, inspection and refitting

Removal

1 Remove the sump as described in Section 11.

2 Unscrew the four retaining bolts at the ends of the pump body, and withdraw the pump from the crankcase and drivegear **(see illustration)**. Note the locating dowel which is fitted over the pump driveshaft.

3 If necessary, unscrew the two retaining bolts and remove the oil pump drivegear cover and sealing ring from the rear of the cylinder block. Withdraw the drivegear and remove it from the block; the drivegear can be removed by screwing a 12 mm bolt into its threads and using the bolt to pull out the gear **(see illustrations)**. Discard the sealing ring; a new one should be used on refitting.

Inspection

4 Unscrew the retaining bolts, and lift off the pump cover.

5 Withdraw the idler gear and the drivegear/shaft. Mark the idler gear so that it can be refitted in its same position **(see illustration)**.

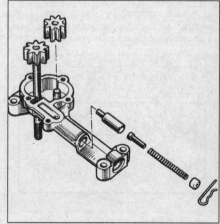

12.5 Exploded view of the oil pump

2A

12.8a Measuring the oil pump gear to body clearance

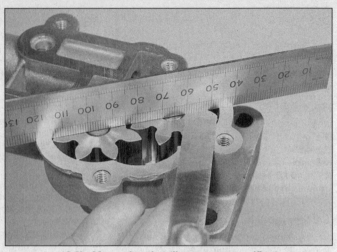

12.8b Measuring the oil pump gear endfloat

6 Extract the retaining clip, and remove the oil pressure relief valve spring retainer, spring, spring seat and plunger.

7 Clean the components, and carefully examine the gears, pump body and relief valve plunger for any signs of scoring or wear. Renew the complete pump assembly if excessive wear is evident.

8 If the components appear serviceable, measure the clearance between the pump body and the gears using feeler blades. Also measure the gear endfloat, and check the flatness of the end cover **(see illustrations)**. If the clearances exceed the specified tolerances, the pump must be renewed.

9 If the pump is satisfactory, reassemble the components in the reverse order of removal. Fill the pump with clean engine oil, then refit the cover and tighten the bolts securely. Thoroughly prime the oil pump by adding additional engine oil whilst rotating the driveshaft.

Refitting

10 Where necessary, refit the pump drivegear to the cylinder block making sure it is correctly engaged with the auxiliary shaft.

12.12 Refit the oil pump to the cylinder block and tighten its retaining bolts to the specified torque

Refit the drivegear cover using a new sealing ring and securely tighten its retaining bolts.

11 Wipe clean the mating faces of the oil pump and cylinder block.

12 Ensure that the locating dowel is correctly fitted to the pump then lift the oil pump into position. Engage the pump shaft with the drivegear splines and seat the pump fully in position. Refit the pump retaining bolts and tighten them to the specified torque **(see illustration)**.

13 Refit the sump as described in Section 11.

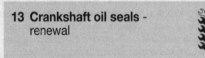

13 Crankshaft oil seals - renewal

Front (timing belt end) oil seal

1 Remove the crankshaft sprocket as described in Section 6.

2 Make a note of the correct fitted depth of the seal then punch or drill two small holes opposite each other in the oil seal. Screw a self-tapping screw into each and pull on the screws with pliers to extract the seal. **Note:** *On some models it may be necessary to unbolt and remove the timing belt rear lower cover to allow the seal to be withdrawn. If this is the case, remove the auxiliary shaft sprocket and idler pulleys (see Section 6) then unbolt and remove the cover.*

3 Clean the seal housing and polish off any burrs or raised edges which may have caused the seal to fail in the first place.

4 Lubricate the lips of the new seal with clean engine oil and ease it into position on the end of the shaft. Press the seal into its housing until it is positioned at the same depth as the original was prior to removal. If necessary, a suitable tubular drift, such as a socket, which

bears only on the hard outer edge of the seal can be used to tap the seal into position. Take great care not to damage the seal lips during fitting and ensure that the seal lips face inwards. Note that if the surface of the shaft was noted to be badly scored, press the new seal slightly further into its housing so that its lip is running on an unmarked area of the shaft.

5 Where necessary, refit the timing belt rear lower cover and install the idler pulley and auxiliary shaft sprocket as described in Section 6.

6 Refit the crankshaft sprocket as described in Section 6 and fit the new timing belt as described in Section 5.

Rear (flywheel/driveplate end) oil seal

7 Remove the flywheel/driveplate as described in Section 14.

8 Prise out the old oil seal using a small screwdriver, taking care not to damage the surface of the crankshaft. Alternatively, the oil seal can be removed as described in paragraph 2.

9 Inspect the seal rubbing surface on the crankshaft. If it is grooved or rough in the area where the old seal was fitted, the new seal should be fitted slightly less deeply, so that it rubs on an unworn part of the surface.

10 Wipe clean the oil seal seating, then dip the new seal in fresh engine oil. Locate it over the crankshaft, making sure its sealing lip is facing inwards. Make sure that the oil seal lip is not damaged as it is located on the crankshaft.

11 Using a metal tube, drive the oil seal squarely into the bore until flush. A block of wood cut to pass over the end of the crankshaft may be used instead.

12 Refit the flywheel/driveplate with reference to Section 14.

14 Flywheel/driveplate - removal, inspection and refitting

Note: *New flywheel/driveplate retaining bolts will be required on refitting.*

Removal

1 Remove the transmission as described in the relevant Part of Chapter 7. On manual transmission models remove the clutch assembly as described in Chapter 6.

2 Prevent the flywheel/driveplate from turning by locking the ring gear teeth with a similar arrangement to that shown in **illustration 5.9**. Alternatively, bolt a strap between the flywheel/ driveplate and the cylinder block/ crankcase. **Note:** *Do not attempt to lock the crankshaft in position using the locking rod described in Section 3.* Make alignment marks between the flywheel/driveplate and crankshaft using paint or a suitable marker pen.

3 Slacken and remove the flywheel/driveplate retaining bolts and remove the flywheel. Do not drop it, as it is very heavy. If the locating dowel (where fitted) is a loose fit in the crankshaft end, remove and store it with the flywheel for safe-keeping. Discard the bolts as they should be renewed whenever they are disturbed.

Inspection

4 On models with manual transmission, examine the flywheel for scoring of the clutch face, and for wear or chipping of the ring gear teeth. If the clutch face is scored, the flywheel may be surface-ground, but renewal is preferable. Seek the advice of a Renault dealer or engine reconditioning specialist to see if machining is possible. If the ring gear is worn or damaged, the flywheel must be renewed, as it is not possible to renew the ring gear separately.

5 On models with automatic transmission, check the torque converter driveplate carefully for signs of distortion. Look for any hairline cracks around the bolt holes or radiating outwards from the centre, and inspect the ring gear teeth for signs of wear or chipping. If any sign of wear or damage is found, the driveplate must be renewed.

Refitting

6 Clean the mating surfaces of the flywheel/driveplate and crankshaft.

7 Ensure that the locating dowel is in position (where fitted) and offer up the flywheel, locating it on the dowel, and fit the new retaining bolts. If the original is being refitted align the marks made prior to removal.

8 Lock the flywheel using the method employed on dismantling, and tighten the retaining bolts to the specified torque.

9 On manual transmission models, refit the clutch as described in Chapter 6.

10 Remove the locking tool, and refit the transmission as described in Chapter 7A or 7B as applicable.

15 Engine mountings - inspection and renewal

Inspection

1 If improved access is required, apply the handbrake, then jack up the front of the car and support it on axle stands (see *Jacking and vehicle support*).

2 Check the mounting rubber to see if it is cracked, hardened or separated from the metal at any point; renew the mounting if any such damage or deterioration is evident.

3 Check that all the mounting's fasteners are securely tightened; use a torque wrench to check if possible.

4 Using a large screwdriver or a crowbar, check for wear in the mounting by carefully levering against it to check for free play. Where this is not possible, enlist the aid of an assistant to move the engine/transmission back and forth, or from side to side, while you watch the mounting. While some free play is to be expected even from new components, excessive wear should be obvious. If excessive free play is found, check first that the fasteners are correctly secured, then renew any worn components as described below.

Renewal

Right-hand mounting

5 Disconnect the battery negative terminal (refer to *Disconnecting the battery* in the Reference Section of this manual).

6 Place a jack beneath the engine, with a block of wood on the jack head (remove the undercover to improve access to the sump). Raise the jack until it is supporting the weight of the engine. Alternately, attach an engine support bar to the lifting brackets and support the weight of the engine with the bar.

7 Slacken and remove the three bolts securing the right-hand engine mounting bracket to the bracket on the cylinder block. Remove the nut securing the bracket to the mounting rubber, and lift off the bracket.

8 Unscrew the three retaining bolts and remove the rubber mounting from the body. If necessary, unbolt the bracket and support rod and remove them from the end of the cylinder block.

9 Check carefully for signs of wear or damage on all components, and renew them where necessary.

10 On reassembly, refit the bracket and support rod to the cylinder block (where removed) and tighten their retaining bolts to the specified torque

11 Fit the rubber mounting to the body and tighten its retaining bolts to the specified torque.

12 Refit the mounting bracket and lightly tighten its retaining bolts and nut. Ensure that the bracket is positioned centrally in relation

to the rubber mounting lug then tighten its retaining nut and bolts to their specified torque settings.

13 Remove the jack from underneath the engine or the engine support bar (as applicable), and reconnect the battery negative terminal.

Left-hand mounting

14 Disconnect the battery negative terminal (refer to *Disconnecting the battery* in the Reference Section of this manual).

15 Place a jack beneath the transmission, with a block of wood on the jack head. Raise the jack until it is supporting the weight of the transmission.

16 Slacken and remove the mounting rubber's centre nut, and two retaining bolts and remove the mounting from the engine compartment.

17 If necessary, undo the retaining bolts and remove the mounting bracket from the top of the transmission housing. The mounting stud can be separated from the bracket once its lower retaining nut has been undone.

18 Check carefully for signs of wear or damage on all components, and renew them where necessary.

19 Refit the stud to the mounting bracket and tighten its to the specified torque.

20 Refit the bracket to the transmission, tightening its mounting bolts to the specified torque.

21 Fit the mounting rubber to the bracket and tighten its retaining bolts and centre nut to the specified torque.

22 Remove the jack from underneath the transmission and reconnect the battery negative terminal.

Rear mounting

23 Disconnect the battery negative terminal (refer to *Disconnecting the battery* in the Reference Section of this manual).

24 If not already done, apply the handbrake, then jack up the front of the car and support it on axle stands (see *Jacking and vehicle support*).

25 Position a jack with a block of wood on its head underneath the sump. Raise the jack until it is supporting the weight of the engine.

26 Slacken and remove the nut and bolt from each end of the mounting link and remove the link from underneath the vehicle. If necessary, undo the retaining nuts and bolts and remove the mounting bracket and support rod from the engine/transmission.

27 Check carefully for signs of wear or damage on all components, and renew them where necessary.

28 On reassembly, fit the mounting bracket (where removed) to the rear of the transmission and tighten its retaining bolts to the specified torque. Refit the support rod.

29 Fit the mounting link, and tighten both its bolts to their specified torque settings.

30 Lower the vehicle to the ground and reconnect the battery negative terminal.

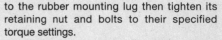

2A

Chapter 2 Part B:
1.6 and 1.8 litre (16-valve) petrol engine in-car repair procedures

Contents

Degrees of difficulty

Easy, suitable for novice with little experience	Fairly easy, suitable for beginner with some experience	Fairly difficult, suitable for competent DIY mechanic	Difficult, suitable for experienced DIY mechanic	Very difficult, suitable for expert DIY or professional

Specifications

General
Type . . . . Four-cylinder, in-line, double overhead camshaft
Designation:
 1.6 litre engines K4M
 1.8 litre engines F4P
Bore:
 1.6 litre engines . . . . 79.5 mm
 1.8 litre engines . . . . 82.7 mm
Stroke:
 1.6 litre engines . . . . 80.5 mm
 1.8 litre engines . . . . 83.0 mm
Capacity:
 1.6 litre engines . . . . 1598 cc
 1.8 litre engines . . . . 1783 cc
Compression ratio:
 1.6 litre engines 10.0:1
 1.8 litre engines 9.8:1
Firing order . . . . 1-3-4-2 (No 1 cylinder at flywheel end of engine)
Direction of crankshaft rotation . . . . Clockwise, viewed from timing belt end

Camshafts
Drive . . . . Toothed belt
Number of bearings 6
Camshaft bearing journal diameters:
 No 1 to No 5 bearings . . . . 24.979 to 25.000
 No 6 bearing . . . . 27.979 to 28.000
Camshaft endfloat . . . . 0.08 to 0.178 mm

Lubrication system

Minimum oil pressure at 80°C:	
At 1000 rpm	1.0 bars (14.5 psi)
At 3000 rpm	3.0 bars (43.5 psi)
Oil pump clearances:	
Gear-to-body:	
Minimum	0.110 mm
Maximum	0.249 mm
Gear endfloat:	
Minimum	0.020 mm
Maximum	0.086 mm

Torque wrench settings

	Nm	lbf ft
1.6 litre engines		
Auxiliary components mounting bracket bolts:		
Short side bolts	53	39
Main side bolt	110	81
Front bolts	21	15
Camshaft sprocket nuts:*		
Stage 1	30	22
Stage 2	Angle-tighten through 84°	
Connecting rod (big-end) caps*	43	32
Crankshaft pulley bolt:		
Stage 1	20	15
Stage 2	Angle-tighten through 135°	
Cylinder head lower section to block:		
Stage 1	20	15
Stage 2	Angle-tighten through 240°	
Cylinder head upper section to lower section **(see illustration 6.42 on page 2B•16)**:		
Stage 1 (bolts 22, 23, 20 and 13 in sequence)	8	6
Stage 2 (bolts 1 to 12, 14 to 19, 21 and 24 in sequence)	12	9
Stage 3 (bolts 22, 23, 20 and 13)	Slacken completely	
Stage 4 (bolts 22, 23, 20 and 13 in sequence)	12	9
Engine/transmission mountings:		
Right-hand mounting:		
Engine bracket-to-cylinder head bolts	62	46
Engine bracket-to-rubber mounting nut	105	77
Rubber mounting-to-body bolts	62	46
Left-hand mounting:		
Mounting bracket-to-transmission bolts	60	44
Mounting stud nut	67	49
Rubber mounting bolts	70	52
Rear mounting:		
Mounting bracket-to-transmission bolts	62	46
Mounting link bolts	105	77
Flywheel bolts*	55	41
Main bearing cap bolts:*		
Stage 1	25	18
Stage 2	Angle-tighten through 47°	
Oil pump-to-cylinder block bolts	22	16
Oil seal housing bolts (timing belt end)	11	8
Oil separator to cylinder head upper section	13	10
Sump bolts:		
Stage 1	8	6
Stage 2	14	10
Timing belt idler pulley bolt	45	33
Timing belt tensioner pulley nut	27	20
Timing belt upper cover	41	30
* New nuts/bolts must be used		
1.8 litre engines		
Auxiliary components mounting bracket bolts	44	32
Camshaft sprocket nuts:*		
Stage 1	30	22
Stage 2	Angle-tighten through 84°	

Torque wrench settings (continued)

	Nm	lbf ft
1.8 litre engines (continued)		
Connecting rod (big-end) caps:*		
Stage 1	20	15
Stage 2	Angle-tighten through 40º	
Crankshaft pulley bolt:		
Stage 1	20	15
Stage 2	Angle-tighten through 115º	
Cylinder head lower section to block:		
Stage 1	20	15
Stage 2	Angle-tighten through 165º	
Cylinder head upper section to lower section **(see illustration 6.42 on page 2B•16):**		
Stage 1 (bolts 22, 23, 20 and 13 in sequence)	8	6
Stage 2 (bolts 1 to 12, 14 to 19, 21 and 24 in sequence)	12	9
Stage 3 (bolts 22, 23, 20 and 13)	Slacken completely	
Stage 4 (bolts 22, 23, 20 and 13 in sequence)	12	9
Engine/transmission mountings:		
Right-hand mounting:		
Engine bracket-to-cylinder head bolts	62	46
Engine bracket-to-rubber mounting nut	40	30
Rubber mounting-to-body bolts	105	77
Left-hand mounting:		
Mounting bracket-to-transmission bolts	60	44
Mounting stud nut	67	49
Rubber mounting bolts	70	52
Rear mounting:		
Mounting bracket-to-transmission bolts	62	46
Mounting link bolts	105	77
Flywheel bolts*	55	41
Main bearing cap bolts*	65	48
Oil pump-to-cylinder block bolts	22	16
Oil seal housing bolts (timing belt end)	15	11
Oil separator to cylinder head upper section	13	10
Roadwheel bolts	See Chapter 1A or 1B	
Sump bolts:		
Stage 1	8	6
Stage 2	14	10
Timing belt idler pulley bolts	45	33
Timing belt tensioner pulley nut	27	20
Timing belt upper cover:		
M10 nuts/bolts	38	28
M8 bolts	18	13
Timing belt lower cover	20	15
Transmission-to-engine bolts	50	37

New bolts must be used

1 General information

This Part of Chapter 2 is devoted to in-car repair procedures for the 1.6 and 1.8 litre, 16-valve petrol engines. Similar information covering the 8-valve petrol engines, the 2.0 litre 16-valve petrol engine, and the diesel engines will be found in Chapters 2A, and 2C to 2E. All procedures concerning engine removal and refitting, and engine block/cylinder head overhaul for petrol and diesel engines can be found in Chapters 2F, 2G and 2H as applicable.

Refer to *Vehicle identification* in the *Reference Section* of this manual for details of engine code locations.

Most of the operations included in Chapter 2B are based on the assumption that the engine is still installed in the car. Therefore, if this information is being used during a complete engine overhaul, with the engine already removed, many of the steps included here will not apply.

Engine description

The two 16-valve engines covered in this Part of Chapter 2 are of four-cylinder, in-line, double overhead camshaft type, incorporating two inlet valves and two exhaust valves per cylinder. The engines are mounted transversely at the front of the vehicle with the transmission bolted to their left-hand side. Both engines are virtually identical in the cylinder head and timing gear arrangement, although there are some slight differences in the bottom end construction.

The crankshaft is supported in five shell-type main bearings. Crankshaft endfloat is controlled by thrustwashers fitted to the centre main bearing on 1.6 litre engines, and to No 2 main bearing on 1.8 litre engines.

The connecting rods are attached to the crankshaft by horizontally-split shell-type big-end bearings, and to the pistons by gudgeon pins. On 1.6 litre engines the gudgeon pins are a sliding fit in the pistons and are secured in position with circlips. On 1.8 litre engines, the gudgeon pins are a press fit in the connecting rods. The aluminium alloy pistons are of the slipper type, and are fitted with three piston rings - two compression rings and a scraper-type oil control ring.

The cylinder head comprises an upper and lower section, mated along the centre line of the camshafts. The upper section of the cylinder head functions as a combined valve cover and camshaft cover, the camshafts run in plain bearings integral to the two cylinder head sections. The camshafts operate the inlet and exhaust valves via roller rocker arms which are supported at their pivot ends by hydraulic self-adjusting tappets.

2B

Drive to the camshaft is by a toothed timing belt and sprockets and incorporating an automatic tensioning mechanism. On 1.6 litre engines, the timing belt also drives the coolant pump. All accessories are driven from the crankshaft pulley by a single multi-ribbed auxiliary drivebelt.

A semi-closed crankcase ventilation system is employed; crankcase fumes are drawn from an oil separator on the cylinder head, and passed via a hose to the inlet manifold.

The lubrication system is of the full-flow, pressure-feed type. Oil is drawn from the sump by a chain-driven gear-type oil pump located beneath the crankshaft. Oil under pressure passes through a filter before being fed to the various shaft bearings and to the valve gear.

Repair operations possible with the engine in the car

The following work can be carried out with the engine in the car:

a) Compression pressure - testing.
b) Timing belt and sprockets - removal and refitting.
c) Camshaft oil seals - renewal.
d) Camshafts, tappets and rocker arms - removal and refitting.
e) Cylinder head - removal and refitting.
f) Cylinder head and pistons - decarbonising.
g) Crankshaft oil seals - renewal.
h) Sump - removal and refitting.
i) Pistons and connecting rods - removal and refitting.*
j) Oil pump - removal and refitting.
k) Flywheel - removal and refitting.
l) Engine mountings - removal and refitting.

* Although the operation marked with an asterisk can be carried out with the engine in the car after removal of the sump, it is better for the engine to be removed, in the interests of cleanliness and improved access. For this reason, the procedure is described in Chapter 2G.

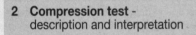

2 Compression test - description and interpretation

1 When engine performance is down, or if misfiring occurs which cannot be attributed to the ignition or fuel systems, a compression test can provide diagnostic clues as to the engine's condition. If the test is performed regularly, it can give warning of trouble before any other symptoms become apparent.
2 The engine must be fully warmed-up to normal operating temperature, the battery must be fully charged, and all the spark plugs must be removed (see Chapter 1A). The aid of an assistant will also be required.
3 Disable the ignition system by disconnecting the crankshaft sensor wiring at the connector located on the left-hand side of the engine. Also disconnect the wiring connectors to each fuel injector to prevent

unburned fuel from damaging the catalytic converter.
4 Fit a compression tester to the No 1 cylinder spark plug hole - the type of tester which screws into the plug thread is to be preferred.
5 Have the assistant hold the throttle wide open, and crank the engine on the starter motor; after one or two revolutions, the compression pressure should build up to a maximum figure, and then stabilise. Record the highest reading obtained.
6 Repeat the test on the remaining cylinders, recording the pressure in each.
7 All cylinders should produce very similar pressures; a difference of more than 2 bars between any two cylinders indicates a fault. Note that the compression should build up quickly in a healthy engine; low compression on the first stroke, followed by gradually-increasing pressure on successive strokes, indicates worn piston rings. A low compression reading on the first stroke, which does not build up during successive strokes, indicates leaking valves or a blown head gasket (a cracked cylinder head could also be the cause). Deposits on the undersides of the valve heads can also cause low compression.
8 If the pressure in any cylinder is low, carry out the following test to isolate the cause. Introduce a teaspoonful of clean oil into that cylinder through its spark plug hole, and repeat the test.
9 If the addition of oil temporarily improves the compression pressure, this indicates that bore or piston wear is responsible for the pressure loss. No improvement suggests that leaking or burnt valves, or a blown head gasket, may be to blame.
10 A low reading from two adjacent cylinders is almost certainly due to the head gasket having blown between them; the presence of coolant in the engine oil will confirm this.
11 If one cylinder is about 20 percent lower than the others and the engine has a slightly rough idle, a worn camshaft lobe could be the cause.
12 If the compression reading is unusually high, the combustion chambers are probably coated with carbon deposits. If this is the case, the cylinder head should be removed and decarbonised.
13 On completion of the test, refit the spark plugs and reconnect the ignition system and fuel injectors.

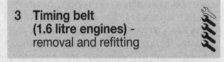

3 Timing belt (1.6 litre engines) - removal and refitting

Note: *This is a complicated operation requiring the use of certain special tools. Read through the entire procedure to familiarise yourself with the work involved then either obtain the manufacturers special tools or, where applicable, fabricate the home-made alternatives described, before proceeding.*

General information

1 The function of the timing belt is to drive the camshafts and the coolant pump. Should the belt slip or break in service, the valve timing will be disturbed and piston-to-valve contact will occur, resulting in serious engine damage.
2 The timing belt should be renewed at the specified intervals (see Chapter 1A), or earlier if it is contaminated with oil, or if it is at all noisy in operation (a 'scraping' noise due to uneven wear). Note that the manufacturer recommends that the timing belt should be renewed whenever it is removed, and that the timing belt tensioner and idler pulley should also be renewed at the same time. Additionally, new camshaft sealing caps will be required, and a new crankshaft pulley retaining bolt and camshaft sprocket retaining nuts may be needed, depending on the condition of the components and/or the tensioning method being used when refitting.
3 Before carrying out this procedure, it will be necessary to obtain a crankshaft TDC positioning pin, and to obtain or fabricate a camshaft holding tool, as described later in this Section. Do not attempt to remove the timing belt unless the special tools or their alternatives are available.
4 The design of the camshaft and crankshaft timing belt sprockets are slightly unusual in that no method of positive location of the sprockets (such as that afforded by a Woodruff key) is employed. Instead, the sprockets are retained purely by the clamping action of the sprocket retaining bolts/nuts. Due to this arrangement, there are two different procedures for tensioning the timing belt when refitting. The first method is used for routine timing belt renewal when the camshaft sprockets have not been disturbed. The second method is used if either of the camshaft sprockets have been removed, or their retaining nuts slackened prior to refitting the timing belt.

Removal

5 Disconnect the battery negative terminal (refer to *Disconnecting the battery* in the Reference Section of this manual).
6 Apply the handbrake, then jack up the front of the car and support it on axle stands (see *Jacking and vehicle support*). Remove the right-hand front roadwheel, the undo the retaining screws and remove the engine undercover and the front and rear protective covers from the right-hand wheelarch.
7 Remove the auxiliary drivebelt as described in Chapter 1A.
8 Remove the complete air cleaner assembly and inlet ducts as described in Chapter 4A.
9 Position an engine hoist, or an engine lifting beam across the engine compartment and attach the jib to the right hand engine lifting eyelet. Raise the lifting gear to take up the slack, so that it is just supporting the weight of the engine.
10 Undo the three bolts securing the right-

hand engine mounting bracket to the cylinder head **(see illustration)**. Similarly, undo the three bolts securing the rubber mounting to the body **(see illustration)**. Release the relevant cable clips and remove the complete mounting assembly.

11 Disconnect the wiring connectors at the idle speed stepper motor, throttle position sensor and MAP sensor, then unclip the wiring harness from the upper timing belt cover and move the harness to one side **(see illustration)**.

12 Release the fuel pipes from the clips on the lower timing belt cover.

13 Prise the sealing caps from the left hand end of the cylinder head, to expose the ends of both camshafts. The caps cannot be reused, so the easiest way to remove them is to punch a small hole in the centre of each cap and lever them out with a stout screwdriver **(see illustration)**.

14 With the help of an assistant to slowly turn the crankshaft using a socket or spanner on the

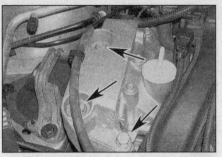

3.10a Undo the three bolts (arrowed) securing the right-hand engine mounting bracket to the cylinder head . . .

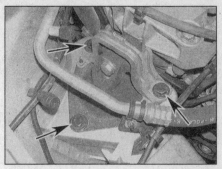

3.10b . . . and the three bolts (arrowed) securing the rubber mounting to the body

3.11 Disconnect the wiring connectors at the idle speed stepper motor, throttle position sensor and MAP sensor (arrowed)

3.13 Using a screwdriver, prise the camshaft sealing caps from the left hand end of the cylinder head

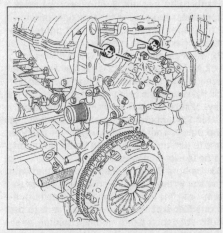

3.14 Turn the crankshaft until the slots in the camshafts are initially positioned at approximately a 30° angle from the horizontal, with the offsets below the centreline

crankshaft pulley bolt, observe the position of the slots in the ends of the camshafts. Turn the crankshaft in a clockwise direction (as viewed from the timing belt end), until the camshaft slots are positioned at approximately a 30° angle from the horizontal, with the offset below the centreline **(see illustration)**.

15 Unscrew the plug from the TDC pin hole on the left-hand end of the front of the cylinder block, located just below the engine identification plate. Screw the crankshaft TDC pin (Renault special tool Mot. 1489) into the hole as far as it will go.

16 With the TDC pin in place, continue to turn the crankshaft clockwise until it contacts the

TDC pin. The slots in the ends of the camshafts should now be horizontal (ie parallel to the join between the upper and lower cylinder head sections) with their offsets below the centreline **(see illustrations)**.

17 Using a socket and extension bar, slacken the crankshaft pulley bolt. Hold the crankshaft stationary while the bolt is unscrewed by engaging a screwdriver with the flywheel ring gear teeth through the opening at the lower rear of the cylinder block. Unscrew the bolt and remove the washer and crankshaft pulley.

18 Unscrew the nuts and bolts and remove the lower timing belt cover followed by the upper cover **(see illustration)**.

2B

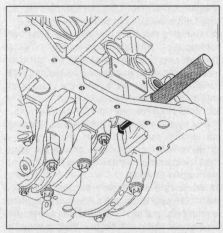

3.16a Fit the TDC pin and turn the crankshaft until it contacts the pin . . .

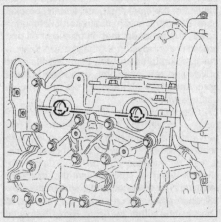

3.16b . . . and check that the camshaft slots are now horizontal with their offsets below the centreline

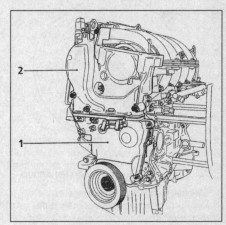

3.18 Unscrew the nuts and bolts and remove the lower timing belt cover (1) followed by the upper cover (2)

TOOL TiP

Tip 1: To make a camshaft holding tool, obtain a length of steel strip and cut it to length so that it will fit across the rear of the cylinder head. Obtain a second length of steel strip of suitable thickness to fit snugly in the slots in the camshafts. Cut the second strip into two lengths and drill accordingly so that they can be bolted to the first strip in the correct position to engage with the camshaft slots. Secure a suitably drilled small piece of steel angle to the first strip so that the tool can be bolted to the threaded hole in the cylinder head upper section.

19 Slacken the timing belt tensioner pulley centre retaining nut.

20 Unscrew the mounting bolt and remove the timing belt idler pulley.

21 Slip the timing belt off the sprockets and remove it. Clearance is very limited at the crankshaft sprocket and a certain amount of manipulation is necessary. Do not rotate the crankshaft or camshafts with the belt removed, as there is the risk of piston to valve contact.

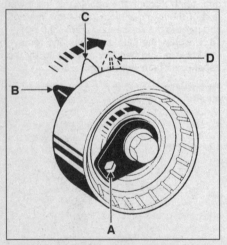

3.33 Timing belt tensioner pulley details

A *Slot for Allen key in tensioner arm*
B *Position of moving index pointer in the 'at rest' position*
C *Fixed index pointer*
D *Moving index pointer positioned 7.0 to 8.0 mm to the right of the fixed index pointer*

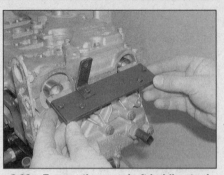

3.29a Engage the camshaft holding tool with the camshaft slots . . .

22 Obtain a new timing belt, new tensioner and idler pulleys and new camshaft sealing caps prior to refitting. If method two is being used for the refitting and tensioning procedure, new camshaft sprocket retaining nuts will also be required.

23 Measure the length of the crankshaft pulley retaining bolt, from the underside of the head to the end of the thread. The bolt must be renewed if the length exceeds 49.1 mm.

Refitting and tensioning

Method one

Note: *Method one should be used for refitting and tensioning the timing belt when the camshaft sprockets have not been disturbed. If either of the camshaft sprockets have been removed, or their retaining nuts slackened prior to refitting the timing belt, method two described later in this Section should be used instead.*

24 Fit the new tensioner pulley to the mounting stud then screw on the retaining nut, finger tight only at this stage.

25 Check that the crankshaft is still in contact with the TDC pin. Slip the crankshaft sprocket off the end of the crankshaft and check that the keyway in the crankshaft is uppermost. Note that although there is a keyway in both the crankshaft and crankshaft sprocket, a Woodruff key is not used.

26 Using a suitable solvent, thoroughly clean the end of the crankshaft, crankshaft sprocket bore, and the crankshaft and sprocket mating faces. It is essential that all traces of oil and grease are removed from these areas to allow the sprocket to be securely clamped when the pulley and retaining bolt are refitted. If the sprocket slips in service, serious engine damage will result.

27 Check that the camshafts are still correctly positioned with the slots parallel to the join between the upper and lower cylinder head sections, with their offsets below the centreline. It may be necessary to turn the camshafts slightly using a spanner on the sprocket retaining nuts, to correctly align the slots.

28 The camshafts must now be retained in this position either by using Renault special tool Mot. 1496, or by fabricating a home-made alternative **(see Tool Tip 1)**.

29 Engage the Renault special tool or the

3.29b . . . and secure the tool using a suitable bolt screwed into the cylinder head

home-made alternative with the slots in the camshafts and secure the tool to the cylinder head using a suitable bolt **(see illustrations)**. With the crankshaft against the TDC pin and the camshafts secured with the holding tool, refit the crankshaft sprocket to the end of the crankshaft.

30 Locate the new timing belt over the crankshaft, coolant pump and camshaft sprockets, and around the tensioner pulley.

31 Fit the new idler pulley and tighten the retaining bolt to the specified torque.

32 Refit the crankshaft pulley and the retaining bolt and washer. If the original bolt is being re-used, lightly lubricate the threads with engine oil. If a new bolt is being used it should be fitted dry. Tighten the bolt so there is approximately 2.0 to 3.0 mm clearance between the bolt and the pulley. The crankshaft sprocket must be free to turn on the crankshaft for the timing belt to be tensioned correctly.

33 Using a 6.0 mm Allen key engaged with the slot in the tensioner pulley arm, rotate the arm until the moving index pointer is positioned approximately 7.0 to 8.0 mm to the right of the fixed index pointer **(see illustration)**. Hold the tensioner in this position and initially tighten the retaining nut to 7.0 Nm (5.0 lbf ft).

34 Tighten the crankshaft pulley retaining bolt to the Stage 1 torque setting, then through the Stage 2 angle as given in the Specifications. The TDC pin can be used to retain the crankshaft as the bolt is tightened.

35 Remove the TDC pin and the camshaft holding tool. Turn the crankshaft clockwise through two complete revolutions, but just before completing the second revolution, refit the TDC pin. Continue turning the crankshaft until it contacts the TDC pin.

36 Hold the tensioner pulley arm with the Allen key and slacken the tensioner retaining nut a maximum of one turn. Align the tensioner moving index pointer with the fixed index pointer then tighten the retaining nut to the specified torque.

37 Remove the TDC pin and turn the crankshaft clockwise through a further two complete revolutions, but just before completing the second revolution, refit the TDC pin once again. Continue turning the crankshaft until it contacts the TDC pin.

38 Check that the tensioner moving index pointer is still aligned with the fixed index pointer. If not, realign it as described in paragraph 36.

39 With the belt correctly tensioned, recheck the timing by removing the TDC pin, turning the crankshaft through two complete revolutions, and refitting the TDC pin just before completing the second revolution. Continue turning the crankshaft until it contacts the TDC pin.

40 Check that with the crankshaft contacting the TDC pin, it is possible to fit the camshaft holding tool to the slots in the camshafts without force. If the slots are not correctly positioned and the tool will not fit, repeat the complete refitting and tensioning procedure.

41 If the timing is correct, remove the TDC pin and camshaft holding tool and continue with the refitting procedure from paragraph 62 onwards.

Method two

Note: *Method two should be used for refitting and tensioning the timing belt if either of the camshaft sprockets have been removed, or their retaining nuts slackened for any reason prior to refitting the belt. If the camshaft sprockets have not been disturbed, method one described earlier in this Section should be used instead.*

42 Check that the crankshaft is still in contact with the TDC pin. Slip the crankshaft sprocket off the end of the crankshaft and check that the keyway in the crankshaft is uppermost. Note that although there is a keyway in both the crankshaft and crankshaft sprocket, a Woodruff key is not used.

43 Using a suitable solvent, thoroughly clean the end of the crankshaft, crankshaft sprocket bore, and the crankshaft and sprocket mating faces. Similarly clean the camshaft ends, camshaft sprocket bores and mating faces. It is essential that all traces of oil and grease are removed from these areas to allow the sprockets to be securely clamped when the pulley and retaining bolt/nuts are refitted. If the sprockets slip in service, serious engine damage will result.

44 Check that the camshafts are still correctly positioned with the slots parallel to the join between the upper and lower cylinder head sections, with their offsets below the centreline. If necessary, temporarily refit the old camshaft sprocket retaining nuts and turn the camshafts slightly using a spanner on the nuts, to correctly align the slots.

45 The camshafts must now be retained in this position either by using Renault special tool Mot. 1496, or by fabricating a home-made alternative **(see Tool Tip 1)**.

46 Engage the Renault special tool or the home-made alternative with the slots in the camshafts and secure the tool to the cylinder head using a suitable bolt. With the crankshaft against the TDC pin and the camshafts secured with the holding tool, refit the crankshaft sprocket to the end of the crank-shaft **(see illustrations 3.29a and 3.29b)**.

47 Refit the camshaft sprockets and new retaining nuts. Tighten the nuts so there is approximately 0.5 to 1.0 mm clearance between the nuts and the sprockets, and the sprockets are free to turn. Position the sprockets so that the Renault logo stamped one of the spokes is vertically uppermost.

48 Fit the new tensioner pulley to the mounting stud then screw on the retaining nut, finger tight only at this stage.

49 Locate the new timing belt over the crankshaft, coolant pump and camshaft sprockets, and around the tensioner pulley. Ensure that the camshaft sprockets remain correctly positioned (Renault logo uppermost) as the belt is fitted.

50 Fit the new idler pulley and tighten the retaining bolt to the specified torque.

51 Refit the crankshaft pulley and the retaining bolt and washer. If the original bolt is being re-used, lightly lubricate the threads with engine oil. If a new bolt is being used it should be fitted dry. Tighten the bolt so there is approximately 2.0 to 3.0 mm clearance between the bolt and the pulley. The crankshaft and camshaft sprockets must all be free to turn for the timing belt to be tensioned correctly.

52 Using a 6.0 mm Allen key engaged with the slot in the tensioner pulley arm, rotate the arm until the moving index pointer is positioned approximately 7.0 to 8.0 mm to the right of the fixed index pointer **(see illustration 3.33)**. Hold the tensioner in this position and initially tighten the retaining nut to 7.0 Nm (5.0 lbf ft).

53 Turn the exhaust camshaft sprocket through six complete revolutions to initially settle and pre-tension the timing belt. The sprocket can be turned using a suitable forked tool engaged with the holes in the sprocket as described in paragraph 56. During this operation ensure that the sprocket retaining nuts remain slack to allow the sprockets to turn freely.

54 Hold the tensioner pulley arm with the Allen key and slacken the tensioner retaining nut a maximum of one turn. Align the tensioner moving index pointer with the fixed index pointer then tighten the retaining nut to the specified torque **(see illustration 3.33)**.

55 Check that the crankshaft is still contacting the TDC pin then tighten the crankshaft pulley retaining bolt to the Stage 1 torque setting, then through the Stage 2 angle as given in the Specifications. The TDC pin can be used to retain the crankshaft as the bolt is tightened.

56 Similarly tighten both camshaft sprocket retaining nuts to the Stage 1 torque setting, then through the Stage 2 angle as given in the Specifications. The sprocket can be held stationary as the nuts are tightened using a suitable forked tool engaged with the holes in the sprocket **(see Tool Tip 2)**.

57 Remove the TDC pin and the camshaft holding tool. Turn the crankshaft clockwise through two complete revolutions, but just

Tip 2: *To make a camshaft sprocket holding tool, obtain two lengths of steel strip about 6 mm thick by 30 mm wide or similar, one 600 mm long, the other 200 mm long (all dimensions approximate). Bolt the two strips together to form a forked end, leaving the bolt slack so that the shorter strip can pivot freely. At the end of each 'prong' of the fork, drill a suitable hole and fit a nut and bolt to engage with the holes in the sprocket.*

before completing the second revolution, refit the TDC pin. Continue turning the crankshaft until it contacts the TDC pin.

58 Remove the TDC pin and check that the tensioner moving index pointer is still aligned with the fixed index pointer. If not, hold the tensioner pulley arm with the Allen key and slacken the tensioner retaining nut a maximum of one turn. Align the tensioner moving index pointer with the fixed index pointer then tighten the retaining nut to the specified torque.

59 With the belt correctly tensioned, recheck the timing by removing the TDC pin, turning the crankshaft through two complete revolutions, and refitting the TDC pin just before completing the second revolution. Continue turning the crankshaft until it contacts the TDC pin.

60 Check that with the crankshaft contacting the TDC pin, it is possible to fit the camshaft holding tool to the slots in the camshafts without force. If the slots are not correctly positioned and the tool will not fit, repeat the complete refitting and tensioning procedure.

61 If the timing is correct, remove the TDC pin and camshaft holding tool and continue with the refitting procedure as follows.

62 Refit new camshaft sealing caps to the left-hand end of the cylinder head and carefully tap them into place using a large socket or similar tool **(see illustration)**.

63 Apply sealing compound to the TDC pin plug then refit the plug to the cylinder block, tightening it securely.

64 Refit the timing belt upper cover followed by the lower cover and tighten the retaining nuts and bolts to the specified torque, where applicable.

65 Secure the fuel pipes with the clips on the lower timing belt cover.

2B

3.62 Fit new sealing caps to the cylinder head and tap them into place using a large socket

66 Reconnect the wiring connectors at the idle speed stepper motor, throttle position sensor and MAP sensor, then clip the wiring harness to the upper timing belt cover.

67 Locate the right-hand engine mounting assembly into position and refit the bolts securing the mounting bracket to the cylinder head. Tighten the bolts to the specified torque. Refit the three bolts securing the rubber mounting to the body. Ensure that the movement limiter is positioned centrally over the mounting rubber then tighten the three bolts to the specified torque.

68 Remove the engine hoist or lifting beam from the engine compartment.

69 Refit the auxiliary drivebelt as described in Chapter 1A, and the air cleaner components as described in Chapter 4A.

70 Refit the engine undercover and wheel arch covers then refit the right-hand road-wheel. Tighten the wheel bolts to the specified torque.

71 Lower the car to the ground and reconnect the battery.

**4 Timing belt
(1.8 litre engines) -
removal and refitting**

Note: *This is a complicated operation requiring the use of certain special tools. Read through the entire procedure to familiarise yourself with the work involved then either obtain the manufacturers special tools or, where applicable, fabricate the home-made alternatives described, before proceeding.*

General information

1 The function of the timing belt is to drive the camshafts. Should the belt slip or break in service, the valve timing will be disturbed and piston-to-valve contact will occur, resulting in serious engine damage.

2 The timing belt should be renewed at the specified intervals (see Chapter 1A), or earlier if it is contaminated with oil, or if it is at all noisy in operation (a 'scraping' noise due to uneven wear). Note that the manufacturer recommends that the timing belt should be renewed whenever it is removed, and that the timing belt tensioner and idler pulley should also be renewed at the same time. Additionally, new camshaft sealing caps will be required, and a new crankshaft pulley retaining bolt and camshaft sprocket retaining nuts may be needed, depending on the condition of the components and/or the tensioning method being used when refitting.

3 Before carrying out this procedure, it will be necessary to obtain or fabricate a crankshaft TDC positioning pin and a camshaft holding tool, as described later in this Section. Do not attempt to remove the timing belt unless the special tools or their alternatives are available.

4 The design of the camshaft and crankshaft timing belt sprockets are slightly unusual in that no method of positive location of the sprockets (such as that afforded by a Woodruff key) is employed. Instead, the sprockets are retained purely by the clamping action of the sprocket retaining bolts/nuts. Due to this arrangement, there are two different procedures for tensioning the timing belt when refitting. The first method is used for routine timing belt renewal when the camshaft sprockets have not been disturbed. The second method is used if either of the camshaft sprockets have been removed, or their retaining nuts slackened prior to refitting the timing belt.

Removal

5 Carry out the operations described in paragraphs 5 to 13 in Section 3.

6 With the help of an assistant to slowly turn the crankshaft using a socket or spanner on the crankshaft pulley bolt, observe the position of the slots in the ends of the camshafts. Turn the crankshaft in a clockwise direction (as viewed from the timing belt end), until the camshaft slots are nearly horizontal, with the offset below the centreline **(see illustration)**.

7 Unscrew the plug from the TDC pin hole on the left-hand end of the front of the cylinder block, located just below the engine identification plate. Insert the crankshaft TDC pin (Renault special tool Mot. 1054) into the hole until it contacts the crankshaft. Alternatively, insert a dowel rod of suitable diameter to be a snug fit in the hole **(see illustrations)**.

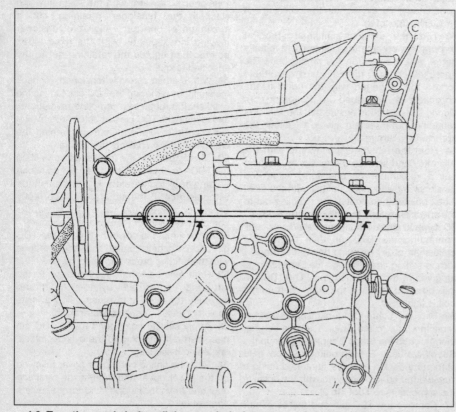

4.6 Turn the crankshaft until the camshaft slots are nearly horizontal, with the offset below the centreline

4.7a Unscrew the plug from TDC pin hole on the left-hand end of the front of the cylinder block . . .

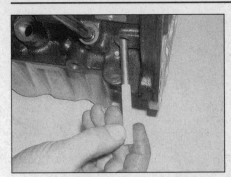

4.7b . . . and insert the special tool or a dowel rod of suitable diameter to be a snug fit in the hole

4.8a Turn the crankshaft until the special tool or dowel rod (A) enters the crankshaft setting slot (B) . . .

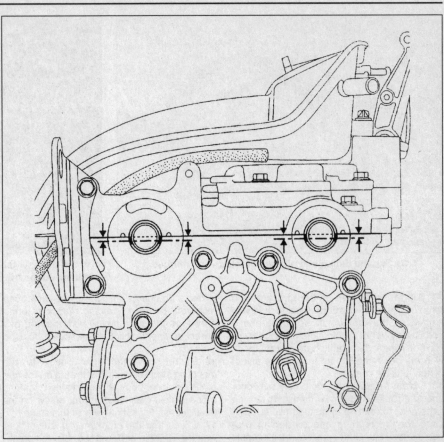

4.8b . . . and check that the slots in the ends of the camshafts are horizontal with their offsets below the centreline

2B

8 While maintaining slight pressure on the TDC pin or dowel rod, continue to turn the crankshaft clockwise very slightly until the pin or rod enters the slot provided for this purpose in the crankshaft web. Note that there is a balance hole in the crankshaft web adjacent to the TDC setting slot. If care is not taken, it is very easy for the TDC pin or dowel rod to engage with the balance hole and not the setting slot. If the tool has entered the setting slot, the slots in the ends of the camshafts should now be horizontal (ie parallel to the join between the upper and lower cylinder head sections) with their offsets below the centreline (**see illustrations**).
9 Using a socket and extension bar, slacken the crankshaft pulley bolt. Hold the crankshaft stationary while the bolt is unscrewed by engaging a screwdriver with the flywheel ring gear teeth through the opening at the lower rear of the cylinder block. Unscrew the bolt and remove the washer and crankshaft pulley.
10 Unscrew the nuts and bolts and remove the lower timing belt cover followed by the upper cover, then collect the spacers from the mounting studs (**see illustrations**).
11 Slacken the timing belt tensioner pulley centre retaining nut.
12 Unscrew the mounting bolt and remove the timing belt idler pulley and the spacer (**see illustration**).

4.10a Unscrew the nuts and bolts and remove the lower timing belt cover . . .

4.10b . . . followed by the upper cover . . .

4.10c . . . then collect the spacers from the studs

4.12 Unscrew the bolt and remove the timing belt idler pulley and the spacer

4.13 Slip the timing belt off the sprockets and remove it

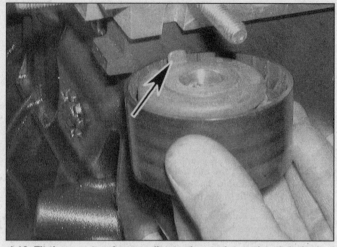

4.16 Fit the new tensioner pulley to the stud ensuring that the lug (arrowed) on the tensioner engages in the cylinder head slot

13 Slip the timing belt off the sprockets and remove it **(see illustration)**. Clearance is very limited at the crankshaft sprocket and a certain amount of manipulation is necessary. Do not rotate the crankshaft or camshafts with the belt removed, as there is the risk of piston to valve contact.

14 Obtain a new timing belt, new tensioner and idler pulleys and new camshaft sealing caps prior to refitting. If method two is being used for the refitting and tensioning procedure, new camshaft sprocket retaining nuts will also be required.

15 Measure the length of the crankshaft pulley retaining bolt, from the underside of the head to the end of the thread. The bolt must be renewed if the length exceeds 49.1 mm.

Refitting and tensioning

Method one

Note: *Method one should be used for refitting and tensioning the timing belt when the camshaft sprockets have not been disturbed. If either of the camshaft sprockets have been removed, or their retaining nuts slackened prior to refitting the timing belt, method two described later in this Section should be used instead.*

16 Fit the new tensioner pulley to the mounting stud ensuring that the lug on the rear of the tensioner body engages in the slot in the cylinder head **(see illustration)**. Screw on the retaining nut, finger tight only at this stage.

17 Check that the crankshaft is still locked with the TDC pin or dowel rod. Slip the crankshaft sprocket off the end of the crankshaft and check that the keyway in the crankshaft is uppermost. Note that although there is a keyway in both the crankshaft and crankshaft sprocket, a Woodruff key is not used.

18 Using a suitable solvent, thoroughly clean the end of the crankshaft, crankshaft sprocket bore, and the crankshaft and sprocket mating faces. It is essential that all traces of oil and grease are removed from these areas to allow the sprocket to be securely clamped when the pulley and retaining bolt are refitted. If the sprocket slips in service, serious engine damage will result.

19 Check that the camshafts are still correctly positioned with the slots parallel to the join between the upper and lower cylinder head sections, with their offsets below the centreline. It may be necessary to turn the camshafts slightly using a spanner on the sprocket retaining nuts, to correctly align the slots.

20 The camshafts must now be retained in this position either by using Renault special tool Mot. 1496, or by fabricating a home-made alternative **(see Tool Tip 1 in Section 3)**.

21 Engage the Renault special tool or the home-made alternative with the slots in the camshafts and secure the tool to the cylinder head using a suitable bolt **(see illustration)**. With the crankshaft against the TDC pin and the camshafts secured with the holding tool, refit the crankshaft sprocket to the end of the crankshaft.

22 Locate the new timing belt over the crankshaft and camshaft sprockets, and around the tensioner pulley **(see illustration)**.

4.21 Engage the camshaft holding tool with the camshaft slots and secure the tool using a suitable bolt screwed into the cylinder head

4.22 Locate the new timing belt over the sprockets and around the tensioner pulley

4.23 Fit the new idler pulley and spacer ensuring that the spacer is fitted the correct way round

23 Fit the new idler pulley and spacer and tighten the retaining bolt to the specified torque. Ensure that the spacer is fitted the correct way round **(see illustration)**.
24 Refit the crankshaft pulley and the retaining bolt and washer. If the original bolt is being re-used, lightly lubricate the threads with engine oil. If a new bolt is being used it should be fitted dry. Tighten the bolt so there is approximately 2.0 to 3.0 mm clearance between the bolt and the pulley. The crankshaft sprocket must be free to turn on the crankshaft for the timing belt to be tensioned correctly.
25 Using a 6.0 mm Allen key engaged with the slot in the tensioner pulley arm, rotate the arm clockwise until the indentation on the pulley arm is aligned with the notch on the pulley body **(see illustrations)**. Hold the tensioner in this position and initially tighten the retaining nut to 7.0 Nm (5.0 lbf ft).
26 Initially tighten the crankshaft pulley retaining bolt to the Stage 1 torque setting as given in the Specifications.
27 Using quick-drying paint, make alignment marks between the camshaft sprockets and cylinder head upper section to use as reference marks in the following procedure **(see illustration)**.
28 Remove the TDC pin or dowel rod and the camshaft holding tool, then finally tighten the

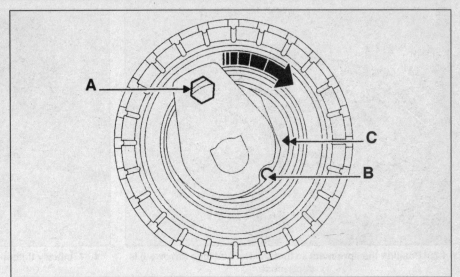

4.25a Using an Allen key in the tensioner arm slot (A) rotate the arm until the indentation (B) is aligned with the notch (C) in the pulley body

crankshaft pulley bolt through the Stage 2 angle as given in the Specifications. Lock the crankshaft using a screwdriver engaged with the flywheel ring gear to prevent crankshaft rotation as the bolt is tightened.
29 Turn the crankshaft clockwise through two complete revolutions, but just before completing the second revolution, ie half a tooth before the previously made reference marks on the sprockets and cylinder head upper section align, refit the TDC pin or dowel rod. Continue turning the crankshaft until the pin or rod fully engage with the crankshaft setting slot.
30 Remove the TDC pin or dowel rod and check that the indentation on the tensioner pulley arm is still aligned with the notch on the pulley body. If not, slacken the tensioner nut and repeat the procedure in paragraphs 25 and 29. If the tensioner pulley is correctly positioned, finally tighten the retaining nut to

the specified torque.
31 With the belt correctly tensioned, recheck the timing by once again turning the crankshaft clockwise through two complete revolutions, and stopping just before completing the second revolution, (just before the previously made sprocket reference marks align). Refit the TDC pin or dowel rod, then continue turning the crankshaft until the pin or rod fully engage with the crankshaft setting slot.
32 Check that with the crankshaft locked with the TDC pin or dowel rod, it is possible to fit the camshaft holding tool to the slots in the camshafts without force. If the slots are not correctly positioned and the tool will not fit, repeat the complete refitting and tensioning procedure.
33 If the timing is correct, remove the TDC pin and camshaft holding tool and continue with the refitting procedure as described in Section 3, paragraphs 62 to 71.

2B

4.25b Hold the tensioner and tighten the retaining nut

4.27 Make alignment marks between the camshaft sprockets and cylinder head upper section to use as reference marks

4.39 Position the sprockets so that the Renault logo (arrowed) is uppermost

4.47 Initially tighten the crankshaft pulley retaining bolt to the Stage 1 torque setting

Method two

Note: *Method two should be used for refitting and tensioning the timing belt if either of the camshaft sprockets have been removed, or their retaining nuts slackened for any reason prior to refitting the belt. If the camshaft sprockets have not been disturbed, method one described earlier in this Section should be used instead.*

34 Check that the crankshaft is still locked with the TDC pin or dowel rod. Slip the crankshaft sprocket off the end of the crankshaft and check that the keyway in the crankshaft is uppermost. Note that although there is a keyway in both the crankshaft and crankshaft sprocket, a Woodruff key is not used.

35 Using a suitable solvent, thoroughly clean the end of the crankshaft, crankshaft sprocket bore, and the crankshaft and sprocket mating faces. Similarly clean the camshaft ends, camshaft sprocket bores and mating faces. It is essential that all traces of oil and grease are removed from these areas to allow the sprockets to be securely clamped when the pulley and retaining bolt/nuts are refitted. If the sprockets slip in service, serious engine damage will result.

36 Check that the camshafts are still correctly positioned with the slots parallel to the join between the upper and lower cylinder

4.49 Finally tighten the pulley bolt through the Stage 2 angle

head sections, with their offsets below the centreline. If necessary, temporarily refit the old camshaft sprocket retaining nuts and turn the camshafts slightly using a spanner on the nuts, to correctly align the slots.

37 The camshafts must now be retained in this position either by using Renault special tool Mot. 1496, or by fabricating a home-made alternative **(see Tool Tip 1 in Section 3)**.

38 Engage the Renault special tool or the home-made alternative with the slots in the camshafts and secure the tool to the cylinder head using a suitable bolt **(see illustration 4.21)**. With the crankshaft against the TDC pin and the camshafts secured with the holding tool, refit the crankshaft sprocket to the end of the crankshaft.

39 Refit the camshaft sprockets and new retaining nuts. Tighten the nuts so there is approximately 0.5 to 1.0 mm clearance between the nuts and the sprockets, and the sprockets are free to turn. Position the sprockets so that the Renault logo stamped on one of the spokes is vertically uppermost **(see illustration)**.

40 Fit the new tensioner pulley to the mounting stud ensuring that the lug on the rear of the tensioner body engages in the slot in the cylinder head **(see illustration 4.16)**. Screw on the retaining nut, finger tight only at this stage.

41 Locate the new timing belt over the crankshaft and camshaft sprockets, and around the tensioner pulley. Ensure that the camshaft sprockets remain correctly positioned (Renault logo uppermost) as the belt is fitted.

42 Fit the new idler pulley and spacer and tighten the retaining bolt to the specified torque. Ensure that the spacer is fitted the correct way round **(see illustration 4.23)**.

43 Refit the crankshaft pulley and the retaining bolt and washer. If the original bolt is being re-used, lightly lubricate the threads with engine oil. If a new bolt is being used it should be fitted dry. Tighten the bolt so there is approximately 2.0 to 3.0 mm clearance

between the bolt and the pulley. The crankshaft and camshaft sprockets must all be free to turn for the timing belt to be tensioned correctly.

44 Using a 6.0 mm Allen key engaged with the slot in the tensioner pulley arm, rotate the arm clockwise until the indentation on the pulley arm is aligned with the notch on the pulley body **(see illustrations 4.25a and 4.25b)**. Hold the tensioner in this position and initially tighten the retaining nut to 7.0 Nm (5.0 lbf ft).

45 Turn the exhaust camshaft sprocket through six complete revolutions to initially settle and pre-tension the timing belt. The sprocket can be turned using a suitable forked tool engaged with the holes in the sprocket **(see Tool Tip 2 in Section 3)**. During this operation, ensure that the sprocket retaining nuts remain slack to allow the sprockets to turn freely.

46 Check that the indentation on the tensioner pulley arm is still aligned with the notch on the pulley body. If not, slacken the tensioner nut and repeat the procedure in paragraphs 44 and 45. If the tensioner pulley is correctly positioned, finally tighten the retaining nut to the specified torque.

47 Initially tighten the crankshaft pulley retaining bolt to the Stage 1 torque setting as given in the Specifications **(see illustration)**.

48 Using quick-drying paint, make alignment marks between the camshaft sprockets and cylinder head upper section to use as reference marks in the following procedure **(see illustration 4.27)**.

49 Remove the TDC pin or dowel rod and finally tighten the crankshaft pulley bolt through the Stage 2 angle as given in the Specifications **(see illustration)**. Lock the crankshaft using a screwdriver engaged with the flywheel ring gear to prevent crankshaft rotation as the bolt is tightened.

50 Turn the crankshaft clockwise through two complete revolutions, but just before completing the second revolution, ie half a tooth before the previously made reference

4.51a Tighten both camshaft sprocket retaining nuts to the Stage 1 torque setting . . .

4.51b . . . then through the stage 2 angle

4.53 Hold the tensioner arm and tighten the retaining nut to the specified torque

marks on the sprockets and cylinder head upper section align, refit the TDC pin or dowel rod. Continue turning the crankshaft until the pin or rod fully engage with the crankshaft setting slot.

51 Tighten both camshaft sprocket retaining nuts to the Stage 1 torque setting, then through the Stage 2 angle as given in the Specifications. The forked tool described in Section 3 can be used to hold the sprockets as the nuts are tightened **(see illustrations)**.

52 Remove the TDC pin or dowel rod and the camshaft holding tool. Turn the crankshaft clockwise through two complete revolutions, but just before completing the second revolution, ie half a tooth before the previously made reference marks on the sprockets and cylinder head upper section align, refit the TDC pin or dowel rod. Continue turning the crankshaft until the pin or rod fully engage with the crankshaft setting slot.

53 Remove the TDC pin or dowel rod and check that the indentation on the tensioner pulley arm is still aligned with the notch on the pulley body. If not, slacken the tensioner nut and realign the indentation and notch as described in paragraph 44. Tighten the tensioner nut to the specified torque, then turn the crankshaft through a further two revolutions and recheck the setting **(see illustration)**.

54 With the belt correctly tensioned, recheck the timing by once again turning the crankshaft clockwise through two complete revolutions, and stopping just before completing the second revolution, (just before the

previously made sprocket reference marks align). Refit the TDC pin or dowel rod, then continue turning the crankshaft until the pin or rod fully engage with the crankshaft setting slot.

55 Check that with the crankshaft locked with the TDC pin or dowel rod, it is possible to fit the camshaft holding tool to the slots in the camshafts without force. If the slots are not correctly positioned and the tool will not fit, repeat the complete refitting and tensioning procedure.

56 If the timing is correct, remove the TDC pin and camshaft holding tool and continue with the refitting procedure as described in Section 3, paragraphs 62 to 71.

5 Camshaft front oil seals - renewal

1 Remove the timing belt as described in Section 3 or 4 as applicable.

2 If both camshaft sprockets are to be removed, suitably mark them inlet and exhaust for identification when refitting. On all engines, the inlet sprocket is nearest the front of the car.

3 Undo the retaining nut and remove the appropriate camshaft sprocket for access to the failed seal. Restrain the sprocket with a suitable forked tool as described in Section 3, which will engage with the sprocket holes. Note that new sprocket retaining nut will be required for refitting.

4 Withdraw the appropriate sprocket from the camshaft **(see illustration)**.

5 Carefully extract the seal by prising it out with a small screwdriver or hooked tool. Take great care to avoid damaging the shaft sealing face.

6 Clean the seal seat. Examine the shaft sealing face for wear or damage which could cause premature failure of the new seal.

7 Lubricate the new oil seal. Fit the seal over the shaft, lips inwards, and tap it home using a large socket or piece of tube until its outer face is flush with the housing **(see illustrations)**.

8 Refit the camshaft sprocket and timing belt using the 'method two' refitting and tensioning procedure described in Section 3 or Section 4, as applicable.

6 Camshafts tappets and rocker arms - removal, inspection and refitting

Note: *For this procedure, Renault special tool Mot.1367 will be required to support the engine from below while the engine mounting and lifting brackets are removed. Details for fabricating a home-made alternative are given in the text. A tube of the specified type of liquid gasket, and a short-haired application roller (available from Renault dealers) will be required when refitting the cylinder head upper section and the oil separator housing. New gaskets, seals and O-rings will also be required for refitting certain other components.*

2B

5.4 Withdraw the appropriate sprocket from the camshaft for access to the oil seal

5.7a Fit the new oil seal over the camshaft . . .

5.7b . . . and tap it home using a large socket or piece of tube

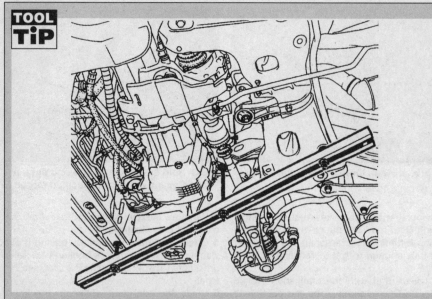

TOOL TIP

To make an engine support tool, obtain a suitable length of square section steel tube. Drill the tube at both ends so that it can be bolted to the crossmember below the radiator at the front, and to the suspension crossmember at the rear, using suitable nuts, bolts and spacers. Drill a third hole to allow a length of threaded rod to be attached using nuts and washers. The position of the hole should be directly below a suitable location on the engine to allow the upper end of the threaded bar to be attached, either directly with nuts and washers, or by means of a small bracket.

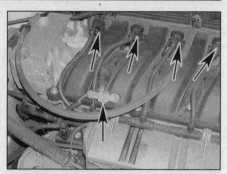

6.9 Disconnect the wiring connectors at the inlet air temperature sensor and at each of the four ignition coils (arrowed)

6.10 Undo the nuts and remove the fuel injector and fuel rail protective cover (arrowed) at the front of the inlet manifold

Removal

1 Disconnect the battery negative terminal (refer to *Disconnecting the battery* in the Reference Section of this manual).

2 Drain the cooling system as described in Chapter 1A.

3 Remove the timing belt as described in Section 3 or Section 4 as applicable.

4 Suitably mark the inlet and exhaust camshaft sprockets for identification when refitting. On all engines, the inlet sprocket is nearest the front of the car.

5 Undo the retaining nuts and remove both sprockets from the camshafts. Restrain the sprockets with a suitable forked tool as described in Section 3, which will engage with the sprocket holes. Note that new sprocket retaining nuts will be required for refitting.

6 The engine must now be supported from below so that the engine hoist or lifting beam used for timing belt removal can be removed for access to the top of the engine. If possible, obtain Renault special tool Mot.1367, or fabricate a home-made alternative out of square-section steel tube **(see Tool Tip)**.

7 Disconnect the accelerator cable from the throttle housing and inlet manifold as described in Chapter 4A.

8 Detach the power steering fluid reservoir from its mounting and move it to one side without disconnecting the fluid hoses.

9 Disconnect the wiring connector at the inlet air temperature sensor on the front of the inlet manifold, and the wiring connectors at each of the four ignition coils **(see illustration)**. Release the ignition coil wiring from the clips on the inlet manifold upper section and move the wiring clear.

10 Undo the nuts securing the fuel injector and fuel rail protective cover at the front of the inlet manifold. Release the wiring harness from the cable clips and remove the cover **(see illustration)**.

11 Undo the bolts and remove the engine lifting brackets from the right-hand and left-hand ends of the cylinder head.

12 Disconnect the brake servo vacuum hose from the inlet manifold upper section.

13 Undo the two bolts at the base of the throttle housing and remove the housing from the inlet manifold upper section **(see illustration)**. Recover the gasket or O-ring as applicable.

6.13 Inlet manifold upper section and throttle housing attachments

1 to 7 Inlet manifold upper section retaining bolts (numbers also indicate bolt tightening sequence when refitting)

A Throttle housing retaining bolts

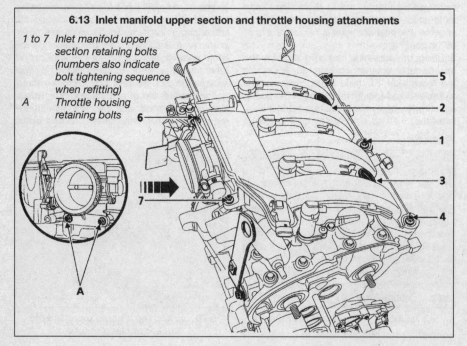

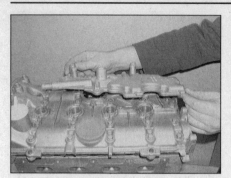

6.16 Undo the eight bolts and remove the oil separator housing

6.18 Gently tap and prise the cylinder head upper section upwards off the lower section

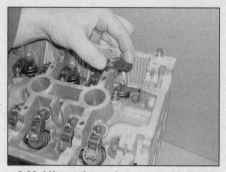

6.23 Lift out the rocker arms and place them in a marked box or containers

14 Undo the five bolts at the front and two bolts at the rear securing the inlet manifold upper section to the lower section and to the oil separator housing. Lift off the manifold and recover the seals.

15 Undo the mounting bolts and remove the four ignition coils from the spark plugs and cylinder head upper section.

16 Undo the eight bolts and remove the oil separator housing from the cylinder head upper section **(see illustration)**.

17 In a progressive sequence, slacken then remove all the bolts securing the cylinder head upper section.

18 Using a soft faced mallet and a protected screwdriver, gently tap and prise the cylinder head upper section upwards off the lower section **(see illustration)**. Note that parting lugs are provided to allow the upper section to be struck or prised against without damage. Do not insert the screwdriver or similar tool into the joint between the two sections as a means of separation. The upper section will be quite tight as it is located on several dowels.

19 Once the upper section is free, lift it squarely from the cylinder head. The camshafts will rise up slightly under the pressure of the valve springs - be careful they don't tilt and jam in either section.

20 Suitably mark the camshafts, inlet and exhaust and lift them out complete with the front oil seals. Be careful of the lobes, which may have sharp edges.

21 Remove the oil seals from the camshafts, noting their fitted positions. Obtain new seals for reassembly.

22 Have ready two suitable boxes divided into sixteen segments each, or some containers or other means of storing and identifying the rocker arms and hydraulic tappets after removal. The box or containers for the hydraulic tappets must be oil tight and deep enough to allow the tappets to be almost totally submerged in oil. Mark the segments in the boxes or the containers with the number for each rocker arm and tappet (ie 1 to 8 inlet and 1 to 8 exhaust).

23 Lift out the rocker arms and place them in their respective positions in the box or containers **(see illustration)**.

24 Similarly lift out the tappets and place them upright in their respective positions in the box or containers **(see illustration)**. Once all the tappets have been removed, add clean engine oil to the box or container so that the tappet is submerged.

Inspection

25 Inspect the cam lobes and the camshaft bearing journals for scoring or other visible evidence of wear. Once the surface hardening of the cam lobes has been eroded, wear will occur at an accelerated rate. **Note:** *If these symptoms are visible on the tips of the camshaft lobes, check the corresponding rocker arm, as it will probably be worn as well.*

26 If the camshafts appear satisfactory, measure the bearing journal diameters and compare the figures obtained with those given in the Specifications. If the diameters are not as specified, consult a Renault dealer or engine overhaul specialist. Wear of the camshaft bearings will almost certainly be accompanied by similar wear of the bearings in the cylinder head, which will entail renewal of the cylinder head upper and lower sections together with the camshafts.

27 Inspect the rocker arms and tappets for scuffing, cracking or other damage and renew any components as necessary. Also check the condition of the tappet bores in the cylinder head. As with the camshafts, any wear in this area will necessitate cylinder head renewal.

Refitting

28 Thoroughly clean the sealant from the mating surfaces of the upper and lower cylinder head sections. Use a suitable liquid gasket dissolving agent (available from Renault dealers) together with a soft putty knife; do not use a metal scraper or the faces will be damaged. As there is no conventional gasket used, the cleanliness of the mating faces is of the utmost importance.

29 Clean off any oil, dirt or grease from both components and dry with a clean lint free cloth. Ensure that all the oilways are completely clean.

30 To prevent any possibility of the valves contacting the pistons when the camshafts

are refitted, remove the TDC pin or dowel rod used to lock the crankshaft, and turn the crankshaft clockwise a quarter turn.

31 Liberally lubricate the tappet bores in the cylinder head lower section with clean engine oil.

32 Prior to refitting each tappet, remove it from its container, place it on the bench the correct way up and press down on the top of the tappet (the stop piston) with your thumb. If it is possible to depress the stop piston then the tappet must be primed by inserting it in a container of diesel fuel before refitting.

33 Insert the tappets into their original bores in the cylinder head lower section unless they have been renewed.

34 Lubricate the rocker arms and place them over their respective tappets and valve stems.

35 Lubricate the camshaft journals in the cylinder head lower section sparingly with oil, taking care not to allow the oil to spill over onto the upper and lower section contact areas.

36 Lay the camshafts in their correct locations in the lower section, remembering that the inlet camshaft must be at the front of the engine. If new camshafts are being fitted, or if the identification marks made during removal have been lost, the camshafts can be identified by referring to the markings located between two of the cam lobes. The markings consist of a series of manufacturers numbers and letters together with a code to identify the camshaft. On 1.6 litre engines, the two letters

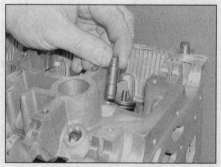

6.24 Similarly lift out the tappets and place them upright in a marked box or containers filled with oil

2B

6.36a Refit the camshafts in the cylinder head lower section, with the inlet camshaft at the front of the engine

6.36b Camshaft identification code marking A (arrowed). 1.8 litre engine inlet camshaft shown

at the end of the series denote the camshaft code - AM for inlet camshaft and EM for exhaust camshaft. On 1.8 litre engines, the camshaft code is the fourth digit in the series - A for inlet camshaft and E for exhaust camshaft **(see illustrations)**.

37 Turn the camshafts so that the slot in the end of each camshaft is horizontal (ie parallel to the join between the upper and lower cylinder head sections) with the offset below the centreline **(see illustration)**.

38 Ensure that the mating faces of both cylinder head sections are clean and free of any oil or grease.

39 Using the short-haired roller, apply an even coating of Loctite 518 liquid gasket solution to the mating face of the cylinder head upper section only **(see illustration)**.

Ensure that the whole surface is coated to a reddish colour, but take care to keep the solution out of the oilways.

40 With the camshafts correctly positioned, lay the upper section in place on the lower section.

41 Insert all the upper section retaining bolts and progressively tighten them just sufficiently to pull the upper section down into contact with the lower section.

42 The upper section retaining bolts must now be tightened in four stages in the order given in the Specifications **(see illustration)**. First tighten the four bolts indicated in the Specifications in the correct sequence to the setting given (Stage 1). Tighten the remaining bolts in the correct sequence to the setting given (Stage 2). Slacken the original four bolts

completely (Stage 3), then finally tighten the original four bolts in the correct sequence to the setting given (Stage 4).

43 Ensure that the mating faces of oil separator housing and cylinder head upper section are clean and free of any oil or grease.

44 Using the short-haired roller, apply an even coating of Loctite 518 liquid gasket solution to the mating face of the oil separator housing until it is reddish in colour **(see illustration)**.

45 Refit the oil separator housing to the cylinder head upper section. Insert the retaining bolts and tighten them to the specified torque in the sequence shown **(see illustration)**.

46 Lubricate the lips of the two new camshaft oil seals. Fit each seal the correct way round over the camshaft, and tap it home with a large socket or piece of tube until its outer face is flush with the housing; refer to the information in Section 5 for guidance.

47 Refit the four ignition coils to the spark plugs and cylinder head upper section and secure with the retaining bolts tightened securely.

48 Using new seals, refit the inlet manifold upper section to the lower section and secure with the seven retaining bolts. Tighten the bolts to the specified torque (see Chapter 4A) in the sequence shown **(see illustration 6.13)**.

49 Using a new gasket or O-ring as applicable, refit the throttle housing to the inlet manifold and secure with the two bolts tightened to the specified torque (see Chapter 4A).

6.37 Position the camshafts so that the slots are horizontal with the offset below the centreline

6.39 Apply an even coating of Loctite 518 gasket solution to the mating face of the cylinder head upper section

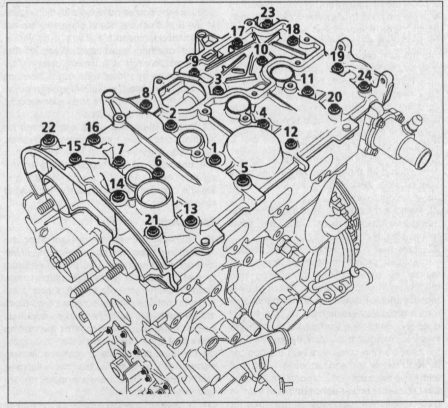

6.42 Cylinder head upper section retaining bolt identification

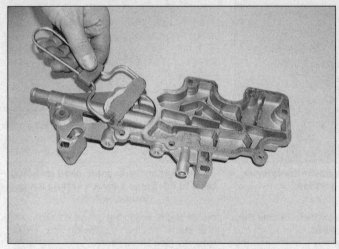

6.44 Apply an even coating of Loctite 518 gasket solution to the mating face of the oil separator housing

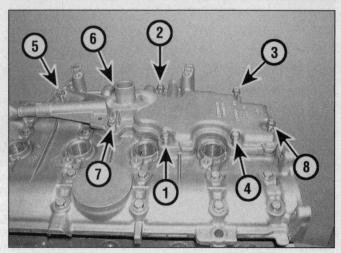

6.45 Oil separator housing retaining bolt tightening sequence

50 Reconnect the brake servo vacuum hose to the inlet manifold.

51 Refit the engine lifting brackets to the right-hand and left-hand ends of the cylinder head. The engine can now be re-attached to the engine hoist or lifting beam allowing the support tool to be removed from below. Alternatively, the tool can be left in position until after the timing belt is refitted.

52 Reconnect the wiring to the four ignition coils and the inlet air temperature sensor on the front of the inlet manifold. Secure the wiring harness with the clips provided on the manifold.

53 Refit the fuel injector and fuel rail protective cover to the front of the inlet manifold, and secure the wiring harness with the cable clips.

54 Refit the power steering fluid reservoir to its mounting.

55 Refer to Chapter 4A and reconnect the accelerator cable.

56 Turn the crankshaft back a quarter of a turn to the TDC position then, referring to the information given in Section 3 or Section 4 as applicable, lock the crankshaft with the TDC pin.

57 Refit the timing belt using the 'method two' refitting and tensioning procedure described in Section 3 or Section 4 as applicable.

58 On completion, refill the cooling system as described in Chapter 1A.

---

7 Cylinder head - removal and refitting

Removal

1 Remove the camshafts tappets and rocker arms as described in Section 6.

2 Remove the inlet and exhaust manifolds as described in Chapter 4A.

3 Disconnect the radiator top hose, the heater hoses and expansion tank hose from the thermostat housing on the left-hand end of the cylinder head.

4 Disconnect the wiring connector at the coolant temperature sensor on the side of the thermostat housing.

5 Undo the retaining bolts and release the wiring harness support bracket from the left-hand end of the cylinder head.

6 Working in the **reverse** of the sequence shown in **illustration 7.21b**, progressively slacken the cylinder head bolts by half a turn at a time until all the bolts can be unscrewed by hand and removed.

7 Lift the cylinder head upwards and off the cylinder block. If it is stuck, tap it upwards using a hammer and block of wood. Do not try to turn it (it is located by two dowels), nor attempt to prise it free using a screwdriver inserted between the block and head faces. If the locating dowels are a loose fit, remove them and store them with the head for safe-keeping

8 Remove the cylinder head gasket from the cylinder block.

9 If the cylinder head is to be dismantled for overhaul, refer to Part G of this Chapter.

Preparation for refitting

10 The mating faces of the cylinder head and cylinder block must be perfectly clean before refitting the head. Use a soft putty knife to remove all traces of gasket and carbon; also clean the piston crowns. Take particular care during the cleaning operations, as aluminium alloy is easily damaged. Also, make sure that the carbon is not allowed to enter the oil and water passages - this is particularly important for the lubrication system, as carbon could block the oil supply to the engine's components. Using adhesive tape and paper, seal the water, oil and bolt holes in the cylinder block. To prevent carbon entering the gap between the pistons and bores, smear a

little grease in the gap. After cleaning each piston, use a small brush to remove all traces of grease and carbon from the gap, then wipe away the remainder with a clean rag. Clean all the pistons in the same way.

11 Check the mating surfaces of the cylinder block and the cylinder head for nicks, deep scratches and other damage. If slight, they may be removed carefully with a file, but if excessive, machining may be the only alternative to renewal.

12 If warpage of the cylinder head gasket surface is suspected, use a straight-edge to check it for distortion. Refer to the overhaul information given in Part G of this Chapter if necessary.

13 Examine the cylinder head bolt threads in the cylinder block for damage. If necessary, use the correct-size tap to chase out the threads in the block. Ensure that the bolt holes are clean and free of oil. Syringe or soak up any oil left in the bolt holes. This is most important in order that the correct bolt tightening torque can be applied and to prevent the possibility of the block being cracked by hydraulic pressure when the bolts are tightened.

14 Check the condition of the cylinder head bolts, and particularly their threads, whenever they are removed. Wash the bolts in a suitable solvent, and wipe them dry. Check each bolt for any sign of visible wear or damage, renewing them if necessary.

15 If the bolt condition is satisfactory, measure the length of each bolt, from the underside of the head to the end of the thread. If the length of any bolt exceeds 117.7 mm, all the bolts must be renewed.

Refitting

16 Ensure that the mating faces of the cylinder block and head are spotlessly clean, that the retaining bolt threads are also clean and dry, and that they screw easily in and out of their locations.

2B

7.17 Locate a new cylinder head gasket on the cylinder block . . .

7.18 . . . and carefully lower the cylinder head into position

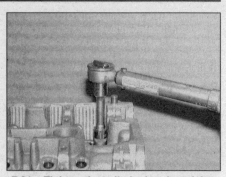

7.21a Tighten the cylinder head retaining bolts to the Stage 1 torque setting using a torque wrench

17 Ensure that the locating dowels are correctly fitted to the block and fit a new cylinder head gasket, making sure it is the right way up **(see illustration)**.

18 Carefully lower the cylinder head onto the block, engaging it over the dowels **(see illustration)**.

19 If new cylinder head bolts are being used, they should be fitted dry. If the original bolts are being re-used, lightly oil them, both on their threads and under their heads and allow any excess oil to drain off.

20 Fit the bolts and screw them in until they just contact the cylinder head.

21 Working progressively and in the sequence shown, tighten the cylinder head bolts to their Stage 1 torque setting, using a torque wrench and suitable socket **(see illustrations)**.

22 Once all the bolts have been tightened to their Stage 1 setting, working again in the given sequence, angle-tighten the bolts through the specified Stage 2 angle, using a socket and extension bar. It is recommended

that an angle-measuring gauge is used during this stage of the tightening, to ensure accuracy **(see illustration)**.

23 Reconnect the coolant hoses to the thermostat housing and securely tighten their retaining clips.

24 Refit the wiring harness support bracket to the left-hand end of the cylinder head and reconnect the coolant temperature sensor wiring connector.

25 Refit the inlet and exhaust manifolds as described in Chapter 4A.

26 Refit the camshafts tappets and rocker arms as described in Section 6.

8 Sump -
removal and refitting
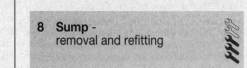

Removal

1 Apply the handbrake, then jack up the front of the car and support it on axle stands (see *Jacking and vehicle support*). Undo the retaining screws and remove the plastic undercover from beneath the engine/transmission.

2 Drain the engine oil as described in Chapter 1A, then refit and tighten the drain plug.

3 Unscrew the bolts securing the left-hand end of the sump to the transmission bellhousing flange.

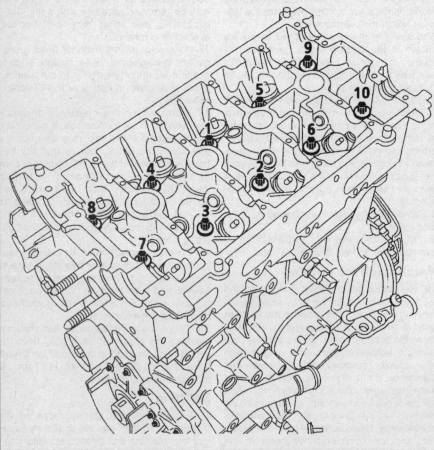

7.21b Cylinder head retaining bolt tightening sequence

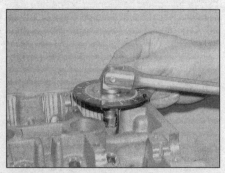

7.22 Using an angle tightening gauge to tighten the cylinder head retaining bolts through the Stage 2 angle

4 Unscrew the bolts securing the sump to the cylinder block. Tap the sump with a hide or plastic mallet to break the seal, then remove the sump along with its gasket. discard the gasket, a new one must be used on refitting.

Refitting

5 Remove all traces of dirt and oil from the mating surfaces of the sump and cylinder block.

6 Apply a bead of Rhodorseal 5661 sealant (available from Renault dealers) to the join between the crankshaft front oil seal housing and cylinder block, and to the join between the rear main bearing cap and cylinder block **(see illustrations)**.

7 Locate the new gasket on the top of the sump and lift the sump into position **(see illustration)**.

8 Insert the bolts and initially tighten them all to the Stage 1 torque setting given in the Specifications. If the engine is in the car, ensure that the left-hand end of the sump is in contact with the transmission bellhousing flange. If the engine is removed from the car, use a straight-edge to maintain the alignment between the left-hand end of the sump and cylinder block **(see illustration)**.

9 Progressively tighten the bolts to the Stage 2 torque setting in an anti-clockwise spiral pattern starting at the centre and working outwards.

10 Refit the undercover and lower the vehicle to the ground.

11 Fill the engine with fresh oil, with reference to Chapter 1A.

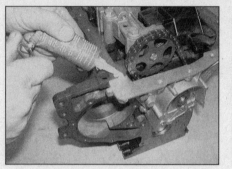

8.6a Apply a bead of sealant to the join between the crankshaft front oil seal housing and cylinder block . . .

8.6b . . . and to the join between the rear main bearing cap and cylinder block

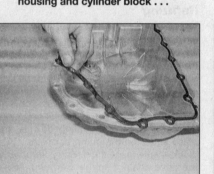

8.7 Locate the new gasket on the top of the sump and lift the sump into position

8.8 If the engine is removed, use a straight-edge to maintain the alignment between the left-hand end of the sump and cylinder block

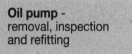

9 Oil pump - removal, inspection and refitting

Removal

1 To remove the oil pump alone, first remove the sump as described in Section 8.

2 Unscrew the oil pump mounting bolts and the additional bolt(s) securing the anti-emulsion plate to the crankcase **(see illustration)**.

3 Withdraw the oil pump slightly and remove the anti-emulsion plate. Tilt the pump to disengage its sprocket from the drive chain and lift away the pump **(see illustrations)**. If the locating dowels are displaced, refit them in their locations.

4 To remove the pump complete with its drive chain and sprockets, first remove the sump as described in Section 8, then remove the crankshaft timing belt end oil seal housing as described in Section 10.

5 Remove the oil pump as described in paragraphs 1 and 2 above.

6 Slide the drive sprocket together with the chain from the crankshaft **(see illustration)**. Note that the drive sprocket is not keyed to the crankshaft, but relies on the pulley bolt being tightened correctly to clamp the sprocket.

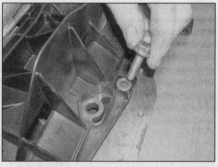
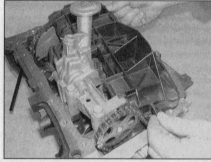

9.2 Unscrew the anti-emulsion plate retaining bolt(s)

9.3a Remove the anti-emulsion plate . . .

9.3b . . . then tilt the pump to disengage its sprocket from the drive chain

9.6 Slide the drive sprocket together with the chain from the crankshaft

2B

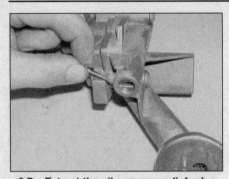

9.7a **Extract the oil pressure relief valve retaining clip . . .**

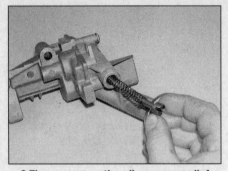

9.7b **. . . remove the oil pressure relief valve spring retainer and spring . . .**

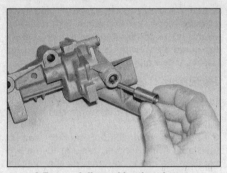

9.7c **. . . followed by the plunger**

Inspection

7 Extract the retaining clip, and remove the oil pressure relief valve spring retainer, spring and plunger **(see illustrations)**.

8 Unscrew the retaining bolts, and lift off the pump cover **(see illustration)**.

9 Carefully examine the gears, pump body and relief valve plunger for any signs of scoring or wear. Renew the pump complete if excessive wear is evident.

10 If the components appear serviceable, measure the clearance between the pump body and the gears using feeler blades. Also measure the gear endfloat, and check the flatness of the end cover **(see illustrations)**. If the clearances exceed the specified tolerances, the pump must be renewed.

11 If the pump is satisfactory, reassemble the components in the reverse order of removal. Fill the pump with oil, then refit the cover and tighten the bolts securely **(see illustration)**.

Refitting

12 Wipe clean the oil pump and cylinder block mating surfaces.

13 Locate the drive sprocket onto the end of the crankshaft, ensuring that it is fitted with the projecting boss facing away from the crankshaft **(see illustration)**. Engage the chain with the sprocket and push the sprocket fully home.

14 Check that the locating dowels are in place either on the pump or on the cylinder block, then engage the oil pump sprocket with the drive chain. Engage the pump with the dowels, fit the two retaining bolts and tighten them to the specified torque.

15 Refit the anti-emulsion plate and secure with the retaining bolt(s).

16 Refit the oil seal housing as described in Section 10.

17 Refit the sump as described in Section 8.

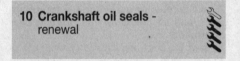

10 Crankshaft oil seals - renewal

Front (timing belt end) oil seal

1 Remove the timing belt as described in Section 3 or Section 4 as applicable, the withdraw the sprocket from the end of the crankshaft.

2 Make a note of the correct fitted depth of the seal then punch or drill two small holes opposite each other in the oil seal. Screw a self-tapping screw into each and pull on the screws with pliers to extract the seal.

3 Clean the seal housing and polish off any burrs or raised edges which may have caused the seal to fail in the first place.

4 Lubricate the lips of the new seal with clean engine oil and ease it into position on the end of the shaft. Press the seal into its housing until it is positioned at the same depth as the original was prior to removal.

5 If necessary, a suitable tubular drift, such as a socket, which bears only on the hard outer edge of the seal can be used to tap the seal into position. Take great care not to damage the seal lips during fitting and ensure that the seal lips face inwards. Note that if the surface of the shaft was noted to be badly scored, press the new seal slightly further into its housing so that its lip is running on an unmarked area of the shaft.

6 Refit and tension the new timing belt using the 'method one' procedure described in Section 3 or Section 4 as applicable.

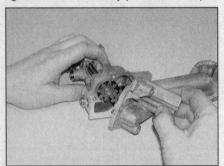

9.8 **Unscrew the retaining bolts, and lift off the oil pump cover**

9.10a **Using feeler blades, measure the clearance between the pump body and the gears . . .**

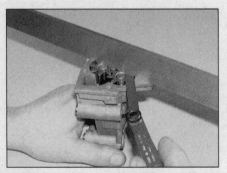

9.10b **. . . and measure the gear endfloat**

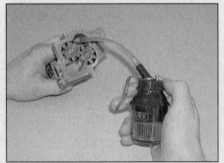

9.11 **Fill the pump with oil, then refit the cover**

9.13 **Ensure that the oil pump drive sprocket is fitted with the projecting boss facing away from the crankshaft**

Front (timing belt end) oil seal housing

7 Remove the timing belt as described in Section 3 or Section 4 as applicable, the withdraw the sprocket from the end of the crankshaft.

8 Remove the sump as described in Section 8.

9 Unscrew the retaining bolts and withdraw the oil seal housing, noting the locating dowels around its two lower bolt holes. If it is stuck in place, a leverage point is provided on the upper edge (near the timing belt idler pulley) to allow a screwdriver to be used to gently prise the housing free.

10 Note the presence of the oil pump drive chain guide block and of its two locating dowels, Check that the guide block is fit for further use and renew it if there is any doubt about its condition.

11 The oil seal should be renewed whenever the housing is removed. Note the fitted position of the old seal then prise it out with a screwdriver and wipe clean the seating.

12 Lubricate the outer surface of the new seal then locate it squarely on the housing with its closed side facing outwards. Place the housing on blocks of wood, then use a suitable socket or metal tube to drive in the oil seal **(see illustration)**.

13 Clean all traces of sealant from the housing and cylinder block mating faces. Check that the chain guide block is correctly fitted and that the housing locating dowels are in place. Refit the housing as described in the following sub-Sections according to engine type.

1.6 litre engines

14 Apply a 0.6 to 1.0 mm diameter bead of Loctite 518 sealant to the housing mating surface ensuring that the sealant is applied around the inner edges of the bolt holes.

15 Lubricate the lips of the oil seal then locate the housing on the cylinder block.

16 Refit the housing retaining bolts and progressively tighten them in a diagonal sequence to the specified torque.

17 Refit the sump as described in Section 8.

18 Refit and tension the new timing belt using the 'method one' procedure described in Section 3.

1.8 litre engines

19 Lightly coat the housing mating surface with Rhodorseal 5661 sealant (available from Renault dealers). Do not allow the sealant to block the small oil channel at the top of the housing **(see illustrations)**.

20 Lubricate the lips of the oil seal then locate the housing on the cylinder block. Refit the retaining bolts and tighten them progressively to the specified torque.

21 Refit the sump as described in Section 8.

22 Refit and tension the new timing belt using the 'method one' procedure described in Section 4.

Rear (flywheel end) oil seal

23 Remove the flywheel as described in Section 11.

24 Prise out the old oil seal using a small screwdriver, taking care not to damage the surface of the crankshaft. Alternatively, the oil seal can be removed as described in paragraph 2.

25 Inspect the seal rubbing surface on the crankshaft. If it is grooved or rough in the area where the old seal was fitted, the new seal should be fitted slightly less deeply, so that it rubs on an unworn part of the surface.

26 Wipe clean the oil seal seating, then dip the new seal in fresh engine oil. Locate it over the crankshaft, making sure its sealing lip is facing inwards. Make sure that the oil seal lip is not damaged as it is located on the crankshaft.

27 Using a metal tube, drive the oil seal squarely into the bore until flush. A block of wood cut to pass over the end of the crankshaft may be used instead.

28 Refit the flywheel with reference to Section 11.

---

11 Flywheel -
removal, inspection
and refitting

Note: *New flywheel retaining bolts will be required on refitting.*

Removal

1 Remove the transmission as described in Chapter 7A, then remove the clutch assembly as described in Chapter 6.

2 Prevent the flywheel from turning by locking the ring gear teeth with a screwdriver. Alternatively a home-made tool similar to that shown in Chapter 2A, Section 5 can be used. Make alignment marks between the flywheel and crankshaft using paint or a suitable marker pen.

3 Slacken and remove the flywheel retaining bolts and remove the flywheel. Do not drop it, as it is very heavy. If the locating dowel (where

10.12 Use a suitable socket or metal tube to drive the new crankshaft front oil seal into the housing

fitted) is a loose fit in the crankshaft end, remove and store it with the flywheel for safe-keeping. Discard the bolts as they should be renewed whenever they are disturbed.

Inspection

4 Examine the flywheel for scoring of the clutch face, and for wear or chipping of the ring gear teeth. If the clutch face is scored, the flywheel may be surface-ground, but renewal is preferable. Seek the advice of a Renault dealer or engine reconditioning specialist to see if machining is possible. If the ring gear is worn or damaged, the flywheel must be renewed, as it is not possible to renew the ring gear separately.

Refitting

5 Clean the mating surfaces of the flywheel and crankshaft.

6 Ensure that the locating dowel is in position (where fitted) and offer up the flywheel, locating it on the dowel, and fit the new retaining bolts. If the original is being refitted align the marks made prior to removal.

7 Lock the flywheel using the method employed on dismantling, and tighten the retaining bolts to the specified torque.

8 Refit the clutch as described in Chapter 6.

9 Remove the locking tool, and refit the transmission as described in Chapter 7A.

2B

10.19a On 1.8 litre engines, lightly coat the oil seal housing mating surface with sealant . . .

10.19b . . . taking care not to allow the sealant to block the small oil channel (arrowed) at the top of the housing

12 Engine mountings - inspection and renewal

Inspection

1 If improved access is required, apply the handbrake, then jack up the front of the car and support it on axle stands (see *Jacking and vehicle support*).

2 Check the mounting rubber to see if it is cracked, hardened or separated from the metal at any point; renew the mounting if any such damage or deterioration is evident.

3 Check that all the mounting's fasteners are securely tightened; use a torque wrench to check if possible **(see illustration)**.

4 Using a large screwdriver or a crowbar, check for wear in the mounting by carefully levering against it to check for free play. Where this is not possible, enlist the aid of an assistant to move the engine/transmission back and forth, or from side to side, while you watch the mounting. While some free play is to be expected even from new components, excessive wear should be obvious. If excessive free play is found, check first that the fasteners are correctly secured, then renew any worn components as described below.

Renewal

Right-hand mounting

5 Disconnect the battery negative terminal (refer to *Disconnecting the battery* in the Reference Section of this manual).

6 Place a jack beneath the engine, with a block of wood on the jack head (remove the undercover to improve access to the sump). Raise the jack until it is supporting the weight of the engine. Alternately, attach an engine support bar to the lifting brackets and support the weight of the engine with the bar.

7 Undo the bolt securing the rubber mounting to the engine mounting bracket. Slacken and remove the three bolts securing the engine mounting bracket to the cylinder head/timing cover. Release the accelerator cable from the cable clip and lift off the bracket.

8 Unscrew the three retaining bolts and remove the rubber mounting and movement limiter from the body.

9 Check carefully for signs of wear or damage on all components, and renew them where necessary.

10 On reassembly, refit the bracket to the cylinder head/timing cover and tighten the retaining bolts to the specified torque.

11 Fit the rubber mounting and movement limiter to the body, insert the retaining bolts but tighten them finger tight only at this stage.

12 Refit the bolt securing the rubber mounting to the engine mounting bracket and tighten it to the specified torque.

13 Centralise the movement limiter around the rubber mounting then tighten the three bolts to the specified torque.

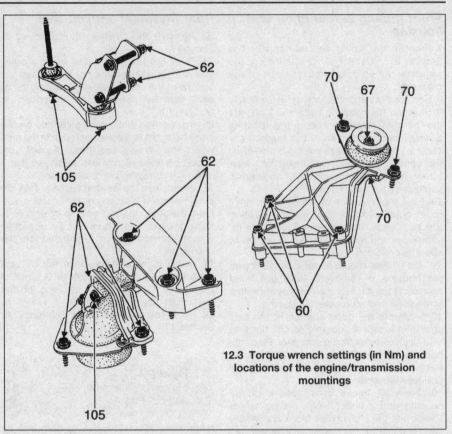

12.3 Torque wrench settings (in Nm) and locations of the engine/transmission mountings

14 Remove the jack from underneath the engine or the engine support bar (as applicable), and reconnect the battery negative terminal.

Left-hand mounting

15 Disconnect the battery negative terminal (refer to *Disconnecting the battery* in the Reference Section of this manual).

16 Refer to Chapter 4A and remove the air cleaner and inlet components as necessary for access to the mounting.

17 Place a jack beneath the transmission, with a block of wood on the jack head. Raise the jack until it is supporting the weight of the transmission.

18 Slacken and remove the mounting rubber's centre nut, and two retaining bolts and remove the mounting from the engine compartment.

19 If necessary, undo the retaining bolts and remove the mounting bracket from the top of the transmission housing. The mounting stud can be separated from the bracket once its lower retaining nut has been undone.

20 Check carefully for signs of wear or damage on all components, and renew them where necessary.

21 Refit the stud to the mounting bracket and tighten its to the specified torque.

22 Refit the bracket to the transmission, tightening its mounting bolts to the specified torque.

23 Fit the mounting rubber to the bracket and tighten its retaining bolts and centre nut to the specified torque.

24 Refit the air cleaner and inlet components removed for access.

25 Remove the jack from underneath the transmission and reconnect the battery negative terminal.

Rear mounting

26 Disconnect the battery negative terminal (refer to *Disconnecting the battery* in the Reference Section of this manual).

27 If not already done, apply the handbrake, then jack up the front of the car and support it on axle stands (see *Jacking and vehicle support*).

28 Position a jack with a block of wood on its head underneath the sump. Raise the jack until it is supporting the weight of the engine.

29 Slacken and remove the nut and bolt from each end of the mounting link and remove the link from underneath the vehicle. If necessary, undo the retaining nuts and bolts and remove the mounting bracket from the engine/transmission.

30 Check carefully for signs of wear or damage on all components, and renew them where necessary.

31 On reassembly, fit the mounting bracket (where removed) to the rear of the transmission and tighten its retaining bolts to the specified torque.

32 Fit the mounting link, and tighten both its bolts to their specified torque settings.

33 Lower the vehicle to the ground and reconnect the battery negative terminal.

Chapter 2 Part C:
2.0 litre (16-valve) petrol engine in-car repair procedures

Contents

Degrees of difficulty

Easy, suitable for novice with little experience	**Fairly easy,** suitable for beginner with some experience	**Fairly difficult,** suitable for competent DIY mechanic	**Difficult,** suitable for experienced DIY mechanic	**Very difficult,** suitable for expert DIY or professional

2C

Specifications

General

Type	Four-cylinder, in-line, double overhead camshaft
Designation	N7Q
Bore	83.0 mm
Stroke	90.0 mm
Capacity	1948 cc
Compression ratio	10.5:1
Firing order	1-3-4-2 (No 1 cylinder at timing belt end of engine)
Direction of crankshaft rotation	Clockwise, viewed from timing belt end

Camshafts

Drive	Toothed belt
Number of bearings	5
Camshaft endfloat	0.08 to 0.178 mm

Lubrication system

Minimum oil pressure at 80°C:	
At 750 rpm	0.8 bar (11.6 psi)
At 3000 rpm	3.2 bar (46.4 psi)
Oil pump type	Gear, driven from crankshaft
Pressure relief valve opening pressure	5 bar (73 psi)
Pressure relief valve spring, free height	82.13 mm
Outer rotor-to-housing clearance	0.35 mm

Torque wrench settings

	Nm	lbf ft
Auxiliary components mounting bracket bolts	25	18
Auxiliary drivebelt tensioner bracket assembly	25	18
Camshaft position sensor housing	20	15
Camshaft position sensor rotor plate	17	13
Camshaft sprocket bolts	20	15
Connecting rod (big-end) caps:*		
Stage 1	20	15
Stage 2	Tighten through a further 90°	
Crankshaft pulley-to-sprocket bolts:		
Stage 1	25	18
Stage 2	Tighten through a further 30°	
Crankshaft sprocket centre nut	180	133
Cylinder head lower section to block:*		
Stage 1	20	15
Stage 2	60	44
Stage 3	Tighten through a further 150°	
Cylinder head upper section to lower section	17	13
Engine/transmission mountings:		
Right-hand mounting:		
Attachment bracket-to-cylinder head bolts	60	44
Mounting bracket-to-attachment bracket and cylinder head bolts	56	41
Mounting bracket-to-rubber mounting nut	37	27
Rubber mounting-to-body bolts	56	41
Acoustic tie-rod bolts	20	15
Left-hand mounting:		
Mounting bracket-to-transmission bolts	60	44
Mounting stud nut	67	49
Rubber mounting bolts	70	52
Rear mounting:		
Mounting bracket-to-transmission bolts	62	46
Mounting link bolts	150	111
Flywheel*:		
Stage 1	45	33
Stage 2	Tighten through a further 65°	
Intermediate section to cylinder block:		
Stage 1 (M10 bolts only)*	20	15
Stage 2 (M10 bolts only)	45	33
Stage 3 (M8 bolts only)	25	18
Stage 4 (M7 bolts only)	17	13
Stage 5 (M10 bolts only)	Tighten through a further 90°	
Oil filter housing centre bolt	60	44
Oil pick-up pipe bolts	18	13
Oil pump cover bolts	17	13
Oil pump to cylinder block	12	9
Roadwheel bolts	See Chapter 1A or 1B	
Sump bolts	17	13
Timing belt idler pulley	25	18
Timing belt tensioner bolts	25	18
Timing belt tensioner pulley	25	18
Transmission-to-engine bolts	50	37

*New nuts/bolts must be used

1 General information

How to use this Chapter

This Part of Chapter 2 is devoted to in-car repair procedures for the 2.0 litre, 16-valve petrol engine. Similar information covering the 8-valve petrol engines, the 1.6 and 1.8 litre 16-valve petrol engines, and the diesel engines will be found in Chapters 2A, and 2B, 2D and 2E. All procedures concerning engine removal and refitting, and engine block/cylinder head overhaul for petrol and diesel engines can be found in Chapters 2F, 2G and 2H as applicable.

Most of the operations included in Chapter 2C are based on the assumption that the engine is still installed in the car. Therefore, if this information is being used during a complete engine overhaul, with the engine already removed, many of the steps included here will not apply.

Engine description

The 16-valve engine covered in this Part of Chapter 2 is a 4-cylinder, in-line unit, of the double overhead camshaft type incorporating two inlet valves and two exhaust valves per cylinder. The engine is mounted transversely at the front of the vehicle with the transmission bolted to the left-hand side.

The entire engine is constructed of aluminium and consists of five sections. The cylinder head comprises an upper and lower section, with the cylinder block, intermediate section and sump forming the other three. The upper and lower sections of the cylinder head are mated along the centre line of the camshafts, while the cylinder block and intermediate section are mated along the crankshaft centre line. A conventional cylinder head gasket is used between the cylinder head and block, with liquid gaskets being used in the joints between the other main sections.

The cylinder block incorporates four cast iron dry cylinder liners which are cast into the block and cannot be replaced. Cast iron reinforcements are also used in the intermediate section as strengthening agents in the main bearing areas.

Drive to the camshaft is by a toothed timing belt and sprockets and incorporating an automatic tensioning mechanism. The timing belt also drives the coolant pump. All accessories are driven from the crankshaft pulley by a single multi-ribbed auxiliary drivebelt.

The cylinder head is of the crossflow type, the inlet ports being at the front of the engine and the exhaust ports at the rear. The upper section of the cylinder head functions as a combined valve cover and camshaft cover, the camshafts run in plain bearings integral to the two cylinder head sections. Valve actuation is by maintenance free hydraulic tappets acted upon directly by the camshaft lobes.

The crankshaft runs in five shell type main bearings; the connecting rod big-end bearings are also of the shell type. Crankshaft endfloat is taken by thrustwashers which are an integral part of the No 4 main bearing shells.

The lubrication system is of the full-flow, pressure-feed type. Oil is drawn from the sump by a gear type pump, driven from the front of the crankshaft. Oil under pressure passes through a filter before being fed to the various shaft bearings and to the valve gear. An external oil cooler is also fitted between the oil filter and oil filter housing.

Repair operations possible with the engine in the car

The following work can be carried out with the engine in the car:

a) Compression pressure - testing.
b) Timing belt - removal and refitting.
c) Camshaft oil seals - renewal.
d) Camshafts and tappets - removal and refitting.
e) Cylinder head - removal and refitting.
f) Cylinder head and pistons - decarbonising.
g) Crankshaft oil seals - renewal.
h) Oil pump - removal and refitting.
i) Flywheel - removal and refitting.
j) Engine mountings - removal and refitting.

2 Compression test - description and interpretation

1 When engine performance is down, or if misfiring occurs which cannot be attributed to the ignition or fuel systems, a compression test can provide diagnostic clues as to the engine's condition. If the test is performed regularly, it can give warning of trouble before any other symptoms become apparent.
2 The engine must be fully warmed-up to normal operating temperature, the battery must be fully charged, and all the spark plugs must be removed (see Chapter 1A). The aid of an assistant will also be required.
3 Disable the ignition system by disconnecting the crankshaft sensor at the wiring connector. Also disconnect the wiring connectors to each fuel injector to prevent unburned fuel from damaging the catalytic converter.
4 Fit a compression tester to the No 1 cylinder spark plug hole - the type of tester which screws into the plug thread is to be preferred.
5 Have the assistant hold the throttle wide open, and crank the engine on the starter motor; after one or two revolutions, the compression pressure should build up to a maximum figure, and then stabilise. Record the highest reading obtained.
6 Repeat the test on the remaining cylinders, recording the pressure in each.
7 All cylinders should produce very similar pressures; a difference of more than 2 bars between any two cylinders indicates a fault. Note that the compression should build up quickly in a healthy engine; low compression on the first stroke, followed by gradually-increasing pressure on successive strokes, indicates worn piston rings. A low compression reading on the first stroke, which does not build up during successive strokes, indicates leaking valves or a blown head gasket (a cracked cylinder head could also be the cause). Deposits on the undersides of the valve heads can also cause low compression.
8 If the pressure in any cylinder is low, carry out the following test to isolate the cause. Introduce a teaspoonful of clean oil into that cylinder through its spark plug hole, and repeat the test.
9 If the addition of oil temporarily improves the compression pressure, this indicates that bore or piston wear is responsible for the pressure loss. No improvement suggests that leaking or burnt valves, or a blown head gasket, may be to blame.
10 A low reading from two adjacent cylinders is almost certainly due to the head gasket having blown between them; the presence of coolant in the engine oil will confirm this.
11 If one cylinder is about 20 percent lower than the others and the engine has a slightly rough idle, a worn camshaft lobe could be the cause.

12 If the compression reading is unusually high, the combustion chambers are probably coated with carbon deposits. If this is the case, the cylinder head should be removed and decarbonised.
13 On completion of the test, refit the spark plugs and reconnect the ignition system and fuel injectors.

3 Timing belt - removal and refitting

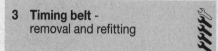

Note: *This is a complicated operation requiring the use of certain special tools. Read through the entire procedure to familiarise yourself with the work involved then either obtain the manufacturers special tools or, where applicable, fabricate the home-made alternatives described, before proceeding.*

General information

1 The function of the timing belt is to drive the camshafts and the coolant pump. Should the belt slip or break in service, the valve timing will be disturbed and piston-to-valve contact will occur, resulting in serious engine damage.
2 The timing belt should be renewed at the specified intervals (see Chapter 1A), or earlier if it is contaminated with oil, or if it is at all noisy in operation (a 'scraping' noise due to uneven wear).
3 Before carrying out this procedure, it will be necessary to obtain or fabricate an engine support tool, a crankshaft pulley holding tool and a camshaft locking tool. Details for fabricating home-made alternatives to the manufacturers special tools are given in the text. A crankshaft timing position setting tool will also be required, but due to the shape of this tool it is not practical to fabricate a home-made alternative and in this instance, the manufacturer's special tool (Mot. 1340) will be required. Do not attempt to remove the timing belt unless the special tools or their alternatives are available.

Removal

4 Disconnect the battery negative terminal (refer to *Disconnecting the battery* in the Reference Section of this manual).
5 Apply the handbrake, then jack up the front of the car and support it on axle stands (see *Jacking and vehicle support*). Remove the right-hand front roadwheel, the undo the retaining screws and remove the engine undercover and the front and rear protective covers from the right-hand wheel arch.
6 Remove the auxiliary drivebelt as described in Chapter 1A.
7 The engine must now be supported from below so that the right-hand engine mounting can be removed, and to allow unobstructed access to the top of the engine. If possible, obtain Renault special tool Mot.1290, or fabricate a home-made alternative out of square-section steel tube **(see Tool Tip 1)**.

2C

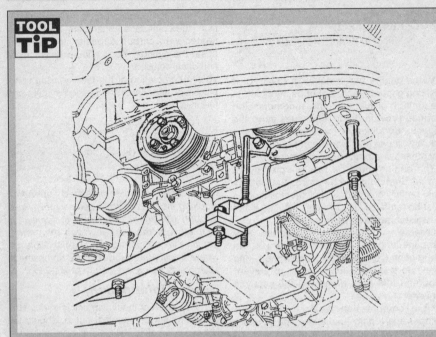

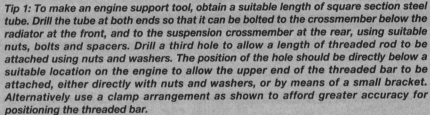

TOOL TiP

Tip 1: To make an engine support tool, obtain a suitable length of square section steel tube. Drill the tube at both ends so that it can be bolted to the crossmember below the radiator at the front, and to the suspension crossmember at the rear, using suitable nuts, bolts and spacers. Drill a third hole to allow a length of threaded rod to be attached using nuts and washers. The position of the hole should be directly below a suitable location on the engine to allow the upper end of the threaded bar to be attached, either directly with nuts and washers, or by means of a small bracket. Alternatively use a clamp arrangement as shown to afford greater accuracy for positioning the threaded bar.

3.8 Attach the engine support tool and adjust its position to support the weight of the engine

8 Fit the tool to the underside of the vehicle and engine and adjust its position to support the weight of the engine **(see illustration)**.

9 Undo the four screws and lift off the plastic cover from the top of the engine **(see illustration)**.

10 Undo the three bolts and remove the right-hand engine mounting acoustic tie-rod **(see illustration)**.

11 Undo the three bolts securing the right-hand engine mounting bracket to the cylinder head attachment bracket and cylinder head upper section. Similarly undo the three bolts securing the rubber mounting to the body and lift off the complete mounting assembly **(see illustration)**.

12 Release the two screws securing the fuel pipe mounting brackets and upper timing belt cover to the cylinder head upper section. Lift up the fuel pipes and remove the timing belt upper cover **(see illustrations)**.

3.9 Undo the four screws and remove the engine top cover

3.10 Remove the right-hand engine mounting acoustic tie-rod . . .

3.11 . . . and the engine mounting bracket and rubber mounting assembly

3.12a Undo the fuel pipe bracket and upper timing belt cover retaining screws . . .

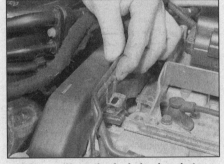

3.12b . . . lift up the fuel pipe bracket . . .

3.12c . . . and remove the upper timing belt cover

TOOL TiP

Tip 2: To make a crankshaft pulley holding tool, obtain two lengths of steel strip about 6 mm thick by 30 mm wide or similar, one 600 mm long, the other 200 mm long (all dimensions approximate). Bolt the two strips together to form a forked end, leaving the bolt slack so that the shorter strip can pivot freely. At the end of each 'prong' of the fork, drill a suitable hole to enable the tool to be bolted to the pulley.

13 The crankshaft pulley must now be held stationary while its retaining nut is slackened. To do this make up a forked tool that can be bolted to the pulley **(see Tool Tip 2)**.
14 Undo the four crankshaft pulley retaining bolts and use two of them to attach the home-made tool to the pulley. Hold the tool securely and undo the pulley centre retaining nut using a socket and bar **(see illustrations)**. Remove the tool and lift the pulley off the sprocket.
15 Undo the two bolts and remove the

3.14a Undo the four crankshaft pulley retaining bolts (arrowed) . . .

auxiliary drivebelt tensioner bracket assembly from the front of the engine **(see illustration)**.
16 Remove the air cleaner assembly and inlet ducts as described in Chapter 4A for access to the left-hand side of the cylinder head.
17 Disconnect the camshaft position sensor wiring at the connector located adjacent to the sensor **(see illustration)**.
18 Undo the two screws and remove the camshaft position sensor housing from the left-hand end of the cylinder head. Undo the bolt and remove the sensor rotor plate from the end of the exhaust camshaft **(see illustration)**.
19 Prise the sealing cap from the left-hand end of the cylinder head, to expose the end of the inlet camshaft. The cap cannot be reused, so the easiest way to remove it is to punch a small hole in the centre of the cap and lever it out with a stout screwdriver **(see illustration)**.

3.14b . . . attach the forked holding tool to the pulley and undo the pulley centre retaining nut

Take care to ensure that no debris falls into the camshaft oil return hole.
20 Undo the retaining bolt in the upper centre of the lower timing belt cover. Disengage the retaining tabs at the base and around the periphery of the cover and manipulate the cover out from under the wheel arch **(see illustration)**.
21 Undo the two anti-fall back bolts securing the timing belt lower guard plate to the oil pump housing and remove the guard plate **(see illustrations)**.
22 Temporarily refit the crankshaft pulley retaining nut to allow the crankshaft to be turned to the timing position.
23 With the help of an assistant to slowly turn the crankshaft using a socket or spanner on the crankshaft pulley nut, observe the position of the slots in the left-hand ends of the camshafts. Turn the crankshaft in a clockwise direction (as

2C

3.15 Undo the two bolts (arrowed) and remove the auxiliary drivebelt tensioner bracket

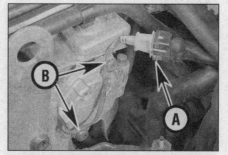

3.17 Camshaft position sensor wiring connector (A) and sensor housing retaining bolts (B)

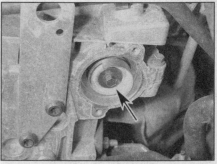

3.18 Undo the bolt (arrowed) and remove the camshaft position sensor rotor plate

3.19 Using a screwdriver, prise out the inlet camshaft sealing cap from the cylinder head

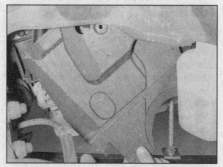

3.20 Remove the lower timing belt cover from under the wheel arch

3.21a Undo the two anti-fall back bolts (arrowed) . . .

3.21b . . . and remove the timing belt lower guard plate

viewed from the timing belt end), until the camshaft slots are positioned horizontally (ie parallel to the join between the upper and lower cylinder head sections). Note that the camshaft slots are very slightly offset from the centreline. In the correct timing position, the inlet camshaft slot offset must be slightly above the centreline,

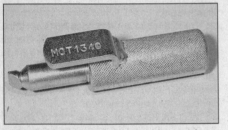

3.25b Using the timing position setting tool (Mot. 1340) . . .

3.25c . . . insert the tool into the setting hole as far as it will go

3.26 With the setting tool in place, the timing marks (arrowed) on the crankshaft sprocket and oil pump housing should be aligned

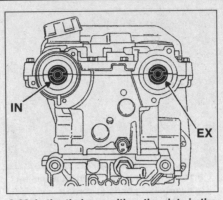

3.23 In the timing position, the slots in the camshafts should be horizontal with the inlet camshaft slot offset above the centreline and the exhaust camshaft slot offset below the centreline

and the exhaust camshaft slot slightly below **(see illustration)**.

24 Remove the starter motor as described in Chapter 5A.

25 Unscrew the plug from the crankshaft timing position setting hole on the front of the cylinder block (behind the starter motor location). Insert the timing position setting tool (Renault special tool Mot. 1340) fully into the hole **(see illustrations)**. If the tool will not fully enter the hole, continue to turn the crankshaft clockwise very slightly until the tool enters.

26 With the position setting tool in place, turn the crankshaft anti-clockwise until the

TOOL TiP

Tip 3: To make a camshaft locking tool, obtain a length of angle iron and cut it to length so that it will fit across the rear of the cylinder head. Mark and drill the angle iron so that it can be bolted to a threaded hole in the cylinder head upper section. Obtain a length of steel strip of suitable thickness to fit snugly in the slots in the camshafts. Cut the strip into two lengths and drill accordingly so that both strips can be bolted to the angle iron. Using spacer washers, nuts and bolts, position and secure the strips to the angle iron so that the camshafts can be locked with their slots horizontal. Pack out the strips with spacers to cater for the offset of the slots.

3.25a Unscrew the plug from the crankshaft timing position setting hole on the front of the cylinder block

crankshaft web is felt to contact the tool. Check that the camshaft slots are positioned as described in paragraph 23 and also check that the timing mark on the crankshaft sprocket is aligned with the projection cast into the outer surface of the oil pump housing **(see illustration)**.

27 The camshafts must now be locked to retain them in the timing position. To do this, obtain Renault special tool Mot. 1337 or fabricate a home-made alternative to engage with the slots in the camshafts **(see Tool Tip 3)**.

28 With the crankshaft correctly positioned against the setting tool, engage the Renault special tool or the home-made alternative with the slots in the camshafts and secure the tool to a threaded hole in the cylinder head upper section using a suitable bolt and washers **(see illustrations)**.

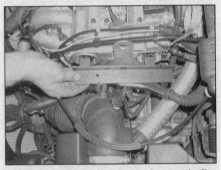

3.28a Attach the home-made camshaft locking tool to the rear of the cylinder head . . .

3.28b . . . ensuring that the tool fully engages with the slots (arrowed) in the camshafts

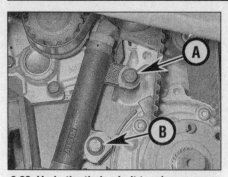

3.29 Undo the timing belt tensioner upper retaining bolt (A) and slacken the lower bolt (B)

3.31 Slip the timing belt off the sprockets, tensioner and idler pulleys and remove it

3.36 Lock the compressed tensioner using a 2.0 mm roll pin

29 Undo the timing belt tensioner upper retaining bolt and slacken the lower one. Move the tensioner assembly anti-clockwise to free it from the tensioner pulley **(see illustration)**.

30 Remove the previously slackened tensioner lower bolt and remove the tensioner. Collect the plastic horseshoe shaped spacer collar fitted to the top of the tensioner.

31 Mark the running direction of the belt if it is to be re-used, then slip it off the sprockets, tensioner and idler pulleys and remove it **(see illustration)**.

32 Spin the tensioner and idler pulleys and check for roughness or shake; renew if necessary. Check that the tensioner pulley arm is free to move up and down under the action of the tensioner. If the arm is at all stiff, remove the unit, clean it thoroughly, then lubricate sparingly and refit.

33 Check the timing belt carefully for any signs of uneven wear, splitting, or oil contamination. Pay particular attention to the roots of the teeth. Renew the belt if there is the slightest doubt about its condition. If the engine is undergoing an overhaul, and has covered more than 36 000 miles (60 000 km) with the existing belt fitted, renew the belt as a matter of course, regardless of its apparent condition. The cost of a new belt is negligible when compared to the cost of engine repairs, should the belt break in service. If signs of oil contamination are found, trace the source of

the oil leak, and rectify it. Wash down the engine timing belt area and all related components, to remove all traces of oil.

34 Renew the tensioner assembly if there are signs of oil leaks, if there is no resistance to compression of the plunger, or if the plunger cannot be compressed.

Refitting and tensioning

35 Prior to refitting the timing belt, it will be necessary to compress and lock the tensioner plunger, before the tensioner assembly is refitted to the engine.

36 To do this, mount the assembly in a vice with protected jaws; the jaws in contact with the tensioner body and the plunger. Tighten the vice until resistance is felt, then tighten it very slowly a little further. Pause for a few seconds and tighten slowly a little further again. Continue this procedure until the hole in the tensioner body and corresponding hole in the plunger are aligned. It will probably take about five minutes to do this; don't rush it or the internal seals will be damaged by trying to force oil between the internal chambers too quickly. When the two holes are finally aligned, insert a 2.0 mm roll pin or twist drill through all the holes to lock the assembly **(see illustration)**.

37 Refit the horseshoe shaped spacer collar to the tensioner, then refit the locked tensioner to the engine and secure with the two bolts tightened to the specified torque **(see illustration)**.

38 Before refitting the timing belt, ensure that the crankshaft is still contacting the setting

tool and the camshafts are secured with the locking tool.

39 Slacken the three bolts securing each camshaft sprocket to its respective camshaft so that the sprockets are free to move within the limits of the elongated bolt holes. Position the sprockets so that the bolts are at the centre of their elongated holes. If necessary, remove one of the bolts completely from each sprocket so that the bolt holes can be more easily observed. To hold the sprockets while the bolts are slackened, use the tool described earlier for removal of the crankshaft pulley, but fit a nut and bolt to the holes drilled in the ends of the 'prongs' of the fork. The bolts will then engage with the holes in the sprocket to hold the sprocket stationary **(see illustration)**.

40 Slip the belt over the crankshaft sprocket, keep it taught and feed it over the idler pulley, inlet camshaft sprocket, exhaust camshaft sprocket, coolant pump sprocket and finally over the tensioner pulley. Try and keep the sprocket bolts centred in their holes as the belt is fitted, and observe the correct running direction if the old belt is being re-used.

41 With the belt correctly positioned, release the tensioner by sharply pulling out the locking pin with pliers **(see illustration)**. Check that the tensioner plunger moves out to tension the belt.

42 Refit the remaining bolt to each camshaft sprocket (if removed) and tighten all three bolts to the specified torque.

43 Remove the crankshaft setting tool and the locking tool from the rear of the camshafts.

3.37 Refit the horseshoe shaped spacer collar to the tensioner, then refit the locked tensioner to the engine

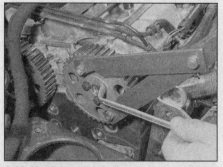

3.39 Hold the camshaft sprockets with the forked tool to allow the retaining bolts to be slackened

3.41 Release the timing belt tensioner by sharply pulling out the locking pin with pliers

2C

3.48a Ensure that the tabs on the timing belt cover right-hand side (arrowed) . . .

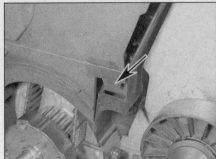

3.48b . . . and left-hand side (arrowed) engage with the slots on the inner cover

44 Turn the crankshaft clockwise through two complete revolutions and align the timing mark on the crankshaft sprocket with the projection on the oil pump housing. Refit the crankshaft setting tool and bring the crankshaft into contact with the tool. Check that it is possible to fit the camshaft locking tool to the slots in the camshafts without force. If the slots are not correctly positioned and the tool will not fit, repeat the complete refitting and tensioning procedure.

45 With the timing belt correctly fitted and tensioned, remove the crankshaft setting tool and the camshaft locking tool. Refit the plug to the crankshaft timing position setting hole.

46 Refit the starter motor as described in Chapter 5A.

47 Refit the timing belt lower guard to the oil pump housing and secure with the anti-fall back bolts.

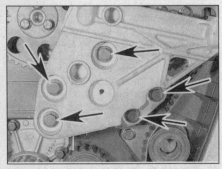

4.2a Undo the five engine mounting attachment bracket retaining bolts (arrowed) . . .

48 Refit the lower timing belt cover ensuring that the lower tabs engage with the slots on the inner timing cover, and the tabs around the periphery clip into place **(see illustrations)**. Secure the cover with the retaining bolt tightened securely.

49 Refit a new camshaft sealing cap to the inlet camshaft at the left-hand end of the cylinder head and carefully tap it into place using a large socket or similar tool.

50 Refit the camshaft position sensor rotor plate to the exhaust camshaft and secure with the retaining bolt tightened to the specified torque. Refit the sensor housing, secure with the two screws and reconnect the wiring connector.

51 Refit the air cleaner assembly and inlet ducts as described in Chapter 4A.

52 Refit the auxiliary drivebelt tensioner bracket and secure with the two screws tightened to the specified torque.

53 Refit the crankshaft pulley and tighten the four securing bolts and centre nut to the specified torque.

54 Place the upper timing belt cover in position and secure the cover and the two fuel pipe mounting brackets with the two bolts, securely tightened.

55 Locate the right-hand engine mounting assembly into position and refit the bolts securing the mounting bracket to the cylinder head attachment bracket and cylinder head upper section. Tighten the bolts to the specified torque. Refit the three bolts securing the rubber mounting to the body. Ensure that the movement limiter is positioned centrally then tighten the three bolts to the specified torque.

56 Refit the acoustic tie-rod and tighten the three bolts to the specified torque.

57 Remove the support tool from beneath the engine.

58 Refit the auxiliary drivebelt as described in Chapter 1A.

59 Refit the plastic cover to the top of the engine.

60 Refit the engine undercover and wheel arch covers then refit the right-hand roadwheel. Tighten the wheel bolts to the specified torque.

61 Lower the car to the ground and reconnect the battery.

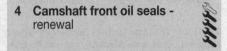

4 Camshaft front oil seals - renewal

1 Remove the timing belt as described in Section 3.

2 Undo the five bolts and remove the right-hand engine mounting attachment bracket from the cylinder head. Withdraw the bracket from under the wheel arch **(see illustrations)**. Note that the bracket is located on dowels and clearance is very limited, requiring a certain degree of manipulation. Note also that two of the bolts cannot be completely withdrawn with the bracket in place, but can be unscrewed sufficiently to allow the bracket to be removed.

3 If both camshaft sprockets are to be removed, suitably mark them inlet and exhaust for identification when refitting. On all engines, the inlet sprocket is nearest the front of the car.

4 Undo the three bolts and remove the appropriate camshaft sprocket for access to the failed seal. To hold the sprockets while the bolts are slackened, use the tool described in Section 3 for removal of the crankshaft pulley, but fit a nut and bolt to the holes drilled in the ends of the 'prongs' of the fork. The bolts will then engage with the holes in the sprocket to hold the sprocket stationary **(see illustration)**.

5 Withdraw the appropriate sprocket from the camshaft **(see illustration)**.

6 Punch or drill a small hole in the oil seal. Screw a self-tapping screw into the hole, and pull on the screw with pliers to extract the seal **(see illustration)**.

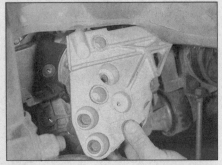

4.2b . . . and manipulate the bracket out from under the wheel arch

4.4 Hold the camshaft sprocket with the forked tool and undo the retaining bolts

4.5 Withdraw the sprocket from the camshaft

4.6 Screw a self-tapping screw into the oil seal, and pull on the screw with pliers to extract the seal

4.8a Fit the new oil seal over the camshaft, with the seal lips inwards . . .

4.8b . . . and tap it home with a large socket or piece of tube

7 Clean the seal seat. Examine the shaft sealing face for wear or damage which could cause premature failure of the new seal.
8 Lubricate the new oil seal. Fit the seal over the shaft, lips inwards, and tap it home with a large socket or piece of tube until its outer face is flush with the housing **(see illustrations)**.
9 Refit the camshaft sprocket(s) and secure with only two of the retaining bolts for each sprocket, tightened finger tight only at this stage.
10 Refit the right-hand engine mounting attachment bracket and secure with the five bolts tightened to the specified torque.
11 Refit and tension the timing belt as described in Section 3.

5 Camshaft rear oil seals - renewal

1 Disconnect the battery negative terminal (refer to *Disconnecting the battery* in the Reference Section of this manual).
2 Refer to Chapter 4A and remove the complete air cleaner assembly and inlet ducts as necessary for clear access to the rear end of both camshafts (left-hand side of the cylinder head).

Exhaust camshaft oil seal

3 Disconnect the camshaft position sensor wiring at the connector located adjacent to the sensor.
4 Undo the two screws and remove the camshaft position sensor housing from the left-hand end of the cylinder head. Undo the bolt and remove the sensor rotor plate from the end of the exhaust camshaft.
5 Punch or drill a small hole in the oil seal. Screw a self-tapping screw into the hole, and pull on the screw with pliers to extract the seal.
6 Clean the seal seat. Examine the shaft sealing face for wear or damage which could cause premature failure of the new seal.
7 Lubricate the new oil seal. Fit the seal over the shaft, lips inwards, and tap it home with a large socket or piece of tube.

8 Refit the camshaft position sensor rotor plate and secure with the retaining bolt tightened to the specified torque. Refit the sensor housing, secure with the two screws and reconnect the wiring connector.
9 Refit the air cleaner assembly and inlet ducts as described in Chapter 4A, then reconnect the battery.

Inlet camshaft oil seal

10 The inlet camshaft does not have a rear oil seal as such, but instead a composite rubber sealing cap is used to seal the opening at the end of the cylinder head.
11 To renew the cap, punch a small hole in the centre and lever it out with a stout screwdriver. Take care to ensure that no debris falls into the camshaft oil return hole.
12 Clean the opening in the cylinder head and locate a new sealing cap in position. Carefully tap the cap into place using a large socket or similar tool.
13 Refit the air cleaner assembly and inlet ducts as described in Chapter 4A, then reconnect the battery.

6 Camshafts and tappets - removal, inspection and refitting

Note: *For this procedure, various special tools will be required, however details for fabricating home-made alternatives are given*

6.6 Disconnect the fuel return hose from the fuel pressure regulator on the fuel rail

in the text. Do not attempt to carry out the work without these tools. A tube of the specified type of liquid gasket, and a short-haired application roller (available from Renault dealers) will be required when refitting the cylinder head upper section.

⚠ **Warning: Some of the procedures in this Section require the removal of fuel lines and connections, which may result in fuel spillage. Before carrying out any operation on the fuel system components, refer to the precautions given in Safety first! at the beginning of this manual, and follow them implicitly. Petrol is a highly dangerous and volatile liquid, and the precautions necessary when handling it cannot be overstressed.**

Removal

1 Disconnect the battery negative terminal (refer to *Disconnecting the battery* in the Reference Section of this manual).
2 Remove the timing belt as described in Section 3.
3 Undo the five bolts and remove the right-hand engine mounting attachment bracket from the cylinder head. Withdraw the bracket from under the wheel arch.
4 Suitably mark the camshaft sprockets, inlet and exhaust, for identification when refitting. The inlet sprocket is nearest the front of the car.
5 Undo the three bolts and remove the sprockets from the camshafts. Restrain the sprockets with a suitable tool through the holes in their faces. Refer to Section 3 for details of fabricating a suitable sprocket restraining tool.
6 Release the retaining clip and disconnect the fuel return hose from the fuel pressure regulator on the fuel rail **(see illustration)**. Suitably seal the ends of the hose and the regulator to prevent dirt ingress.
7 Place absorbent cloth around the fuel supply hose at the end of the fuel rail. Using a screwdriver, carefully prise the fuel hose coupling from the fuel rail and recover the O-ring **(see illustration)**. Note that a new O-ring will be required for refitting. Be prepared for an initial release of fuel which may be ejected under pressure. Suitably seal the coupling and the fuel rail to prevent dirt ingress.

2C

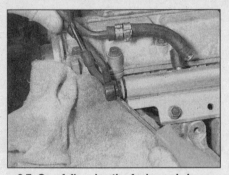

6.7 Carefully prise the fuel supply hose coupling from the fuel rail and recover the O-ring

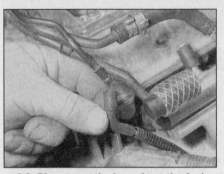

6.8 Disconnect the hose from the fuel vapour pipe coupling adjacent to the end of the fuel rail

6.11 Undo the screw (arrowed) securing the air injection pipe to the cylinder head upper section

8 Disconnect the hose from the fuel vapour pipe at the coupling adjacent to the end of the fuel rail **(see illustration)**.

9 Move the disconnected hoses and pipes away from the cylinder head upper section.

10 Remove all four spark plugs as described in Chapter 1A, then remove the two ignition coils as described in Chapter 5B.

11 On models fitted with secondary air injection, undo the screw securing the air injection pipe to the top of the cylinder head upper section **(see illustration)**.

12 Release the hoses and pipes from the guides on the left-hand end of the ignition coil support bracket and move them to one side. Similarly release the clip on the right-hand side of the support bracket and move the wiring harness clear **(see illustration)**.

13 Undo the retaining bolts and lift up the ignition coil support bracket **(see illustration)**.

14 On models with secondary air injection, detach the vacuum hose and air hose from the shut-off valve, and undo the bolt securing the air hose clamp at the rear of the ignition coil support bracket. As access is difficult with the support bracket in place, the easiest way to do this is as the bracket is lifted off the cylinder head. The secondary air injection components can then remain attached to the ignition coil support bracket **(see illustrations)**. Recover the small O-ring from the end of the air injection pipe as it is released from the cylinder head upper section. Note that a new O-ring will be required for refitting.

15 Disconnect the crankcase ventilation hose from the cylinder head upper section.

16 The camshafts must now be secured to the cylinder head upper section so that as the upper section is removed, the camshafts will be removed with it, as an assembly. The camshafts should still be secured at their left-hand (flywheel) end by the locking tool used during timing belt removal. If not, refit the locking tool as described in Section 3.

17 To retain the camshafts at their right-hand (timing belt) end, either obtain Renault special tool Mot. 1338, or make up a retaining strap out of welding rod **(see Tool Tip 1)**.

18 With the camshafts securely retained, undo the 34 bolts securing the cylinder head upper section to the lower section, working in a progressive diagonal sequence.

19 Using a soft faced mallet, gently tap, or alternatively prise, the cylinder head upper section upwards off the lower section. Note that parting lugs are provided at each corner and in the centre to allow the upper section to be struck or prised against without damage. Do not insert a screwdriver or similar tool into the joint between the two sections as a means of separation. The upper section will be quite tight as it is located on numerous dowels.

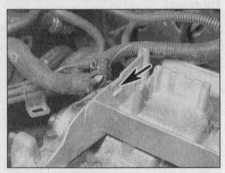

6.12 Release the clip (arrowed) on the ignition coil support bracket and move the wiring harness clear

6.13 Undo the retaining bolts and lift off the ignition coil support bracket

6.14a When sufficient clearance exists, disconnect the secondary air injection vacuum hose . . .

6.14b . . . then undo the hose clamp bolt and disconnect the air hose (arrowed) from the shut-off valve

TOOL TiP

Tip 1: To retain the camshafts in the cylinder head upper section at the front, make a retaining strap out of welding rod, bent to shape, which will locate under the camshaft projections at the front and can be secured to the upper section with two bolts.

6.20 Lift the upper section squarely from the cylinder head

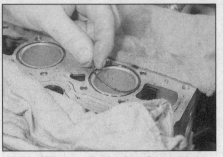

6.21 Withdraw the sealing O-rings from the top of the spark plug recesses in the lower section

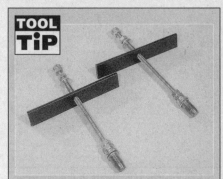

Tip 2: *To pull the cylinder head upper section down against valve spring pressure, obtain two old spark plugs and carefully break away all the porcelain so that only the lower threaded portion remains. Drill out the centre of the spark plugs as necessary, then fit a long bolt or threaded rod to each, and secure tightly with nuts. The bolts or rods must be long enough to project up from the spark plug wells to above the level of the assembled cylinder head. Drill a hole in the centre of two 6 mm thick strips of steel which are long enough to fit across the cylinder head upper section. Fit the strips then fit a nut and locknut to each bolt or rod.*

20 Once the upper section is free, lift it squarely from the cylinder head **(see illustration)**. The camshafts will rise up under the pressure of the valve springs - be careful they don't tilt and jam, particularly at the timing belt end.

21 Withdraw the sealing O-rings from the top of the spark plug recesses in the lower section. Obtain new O-rings for reassembly **(see illustration)**.

22 Remove the locking and holding tools, then suitably mark the camshafts, inlet and exhaust. Lift them out of the cylinder head upper section complete with front and rear oil seals. Be careful of the lobes, which may have sharp edges.

23 Remove the oil seals from the camshafts, noting their fitted positions. Obtain new seals for reassembly.

24 Have ready a suitable box divided into sixteen segments, or some containers or other means of storing and identifying the hydraulic tappets after removal. The box or containers must be oil tight and deep enough to allow the tappets to be almost totally submerged in oil. Mark the segments in the box or the containers with the cylinder number for each tappet, together with identification for its position in the cylinder head (ie 1 to 8 inlet and 1 to 8 exhaust).

25 Lift out the tappets, using a suction cup or magnet if necessary. Keep them identified for position and place them upright in their respective positions in the box or containers. Once all the tappets have been removed, add clean engine oil to the box or container so that the oil hole in the side of the tappet is submerged.

Inspection

26 Inspect the cam lobes and the camshaft bearing journals for scoring or other visible evidence of wear. Once the surface hardening of the cam lobes has been eroded, wear will occur at an accelerated rate. **Note:** *If these symptoms are visible on the tips of the camshaft lobes, check the corresponding tappet, as it will probably be worn as well*

27 No specific bearing journal diameters or running clearances are specified by Renault for the camshafts or journals. However, if there is a visual deterioration, then component renewal will be necessary.

28 Inspect the tappets for scuffing, cracking or other damage; measure their diameter in several places with a micrometer. Renew the tappets if they are damaged or worn.

Preparation for refitting

29 Thoroughly clean the sealant from the mating surfaces of the upper and lower cylinder head sections. Use a suitable liquid gasket dissolving agent (available from Renault dealers) together with a soft putty knife; do not use a metal scraper or the faces will be damaged. As there is no conventional gasket used, the cleanliness of the mating faces is of the utmost importance.

30 Clean off any oil, dirt or grease from both components and dry with a clean lint free cloth. Ensure that all the oilways are completely clean.

31 For reassembly, the camshafts are installed in the upper section and retained in place, in the correct position, using the special tools already obtained or fabricated for removal. This assembly is then fitted to the lower section, clamped in place against the pressure of the valve springs with an additional special tool, and finally bolted down.

32 To allow the upper section to be clamped down against the pressure of the valve springs, either obtain Renault special tool Mot. 1339 or make up an alternative **(see Tool Tip 2)**.

Refitting

33 To aid refitting, undo the two bolts and remove left-hand engine lifting bracket from the cylinder head lower section.

34 Commence refitting by liberally oiling the

tappet bores and the camshaft bearings in the cylinder head lower section with clean engine oil.

35 Insert the tappets into their original bores unless they have been renewed **(see illustration)**. Fill new tappets with oil through the oil hole in their side before fitting.

36 Ensure that the mating faces of both cylinder head sections are clean and free of any oil or grease.

37 Check that the crankshaft is still correctly positioned in contact with the setting tool as described in Section 3.

38 Using a short-haired roller, apply an even coating of Loctite 518 liquid gasket solution to the mating face of the cylinder head upper section only **(see illustration)**. Ensure that the whole surface is coated to a reddish colour, but take care to keep the solution out of the oilways.

6.35 Lubricate the tappets and insert them into their bores in the cylinder head

6.38 Using a short-haired roller, apply an even coating of Loctite 518 to the mating face of the cylinder head upper section only

2C

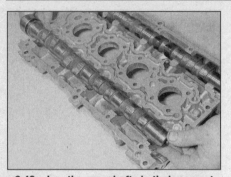

6.40a Lay the camshafts in their correct locations in the cylinder head upper section

39 Lubricate the camshaft journals in the upper section sparingly with oil, taking care not to allow the oil to spill over onto the liquid gasket.

40 Lay the camshafts in their correct locations in the upper section, remembering that the inlet camshaft must be at the front of the engine **(see illustration)**. If new camshafts are being fitted, or if the identification marks made during removal have been lost, the camshafts can be identified by referring to the markings located at the slotted (flywheel) end of each camshaft . The markings consist of a series of manufacturers numbers and letters together with a code to identify the camshaft. The letter at the end of the series denotes the camshaft code - I for the inlet camshaft and E for the exhaust camshaft **(see illustration)**.

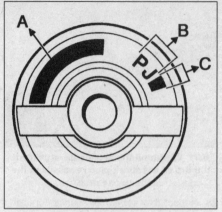

6.40b Camshaft identification markings

A Manufacturing reference code
B Factory reference code
C Camshaft identification code - inlet 'I', exhaust 'E'

41 Turn the camshafts so that their slots are parallel to the upper section join, noting that the slots in each camshaft are offset with regards to the centreline. When viewing the upper section the right way up, ie as it would be when fitted, the slot on the inlet camshaft is offset above the centreline and the exhaust camshaft slot is offset below the centreline **(see illustrations)**. Verify this by looking at the other end of the camshafts. Again, with the upper section the right way up, there should

be two sprocket bolt holes above the centre-line on the inlet camshaft, and two bolt holes below the centreline on the exhaust camshaft.

42 With the camshafts correctly positioned, secure them at the front using the retaining strap, and lock them at the rear by fitting the locking tool **(see illustrations)**. It should not be possible to rotate the camshafts at all with the tools in place.

43 Place new sealing O-rings into the recesses around each spark plug well in the lower section **(see illustration)**.

44 Lift up the assembled upper section, with camshafts, and lay it in place on the lower section.

45 Insert the pull-down tools into Nos 1 and 4 spark plug holes and tighten securely **(see illustration)**. If using the home-made tool, make sure that the bolt or threaded rod is a secure fit in the spark plug or you will not be able to remove the tool later.

46 Lay the pull-down tool top plates, or the home-made steel strips, over the bolts or threaded rods and secure with the nuts. Slowly and carefully tighten the nuts, a little at a time, so that the tools pull the upper section down onto the lower section **(see illustrations)**. Remember there will be considerable resistance from the valve springs. Make sure that the upper section stays level or the locating dowels will jam.

47 Refit the upper section retaining bolts and tighten them in a progressive diagonal sequence, working outwards, to the specified torque.

6.41a Position the inlet camshaft with the slot offset above the centreline . . .

6.41b . . . and position the exhaust camshaft with the slot offset below the centreline

6.42a Secure the camshafts to the cylinder head upper section at the front using the retaining strap . . .

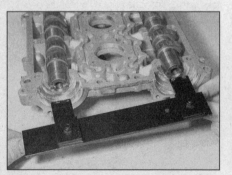

6.42b . . . and at the rear using the locking tool

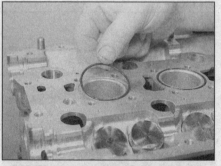

6.43 Place new sealing O-rings into the recesses around each spark plug well in the lower section

6.45 Insert the pull-down tools into Nos 1 and 4 spark plug holes and tighten securely

6.46a Lay the pull-down tool steel strips, over the threaded rods and secure with the nuts . . .

6.46b . . . then tighten the nuts, a little at a time, so that the tools pull the upper section down onto the lower section

6.51 Fit a new O-ring to the end of the secondary air injection pipe

48 With the upper section secure, remove the pull-down tool and the camshaft front end retaining strap. Leave the rear locking tool in place.

49 Lubricate the lips of the new right-hand (timing belt end) oil seals. Fit each seal the correct way round over the camshaft, and tap it home with a large socket or piece of tube until its outer face is flush with the housing; refer to the information in Sections 4 and 5 for guidance.

50 Reconnect the crankcase ventilation hose to the cylinder head upper section.

51 On models with secondary air injection fit a new O-ring to the end of the air injection pipe **(see illustration)**.

52 Place the ignition coil support bracket on the cylinder head upper section. On models with secondary air injection, attach the vacuum hose, air hose and hose clamp, as

the support bracket is fitted. Ensure that the air injection pipe engages with its location in the cylinder head upper section. Refit the retaining bolts and tighten securely.

53 Refit the hoses and pipes to the guides on the left-hand end of the ignition coil support bracket and secure the wiring harness on the right-hand side with the retaining clip.

54 Refit the ignition coils and spark plugs as described in Chapter 5B and 1A respectively.

55 Reconnect the hose to the fuel vapour pipe at the coupling adjacent to the end of the fuel rail.

56 Using a new O-ring, refit the fuel supply hose coupling to the end of the fuel rail by pushing it firmly home until it locks into place.

57 Reconnect the fuel return hose to the fuel pressure regulator on the fuel rail and secure with the retaining clip.

58 Refit the camshaft sprockets and two of the retaining bolts for each. Tighten the bolts so that they just touch the sprockets, but allow the sprockets to turn within the limits of their elongated bolt holes. Position the sprockets so that the bolts are centred in their holes.

59 Refit the right-hand engine mounting engine bracket and secure with the five bolts tightened to the specified torque.

60 Refit and tension the timing belt as described in Section 3. During the timing belt refitting procedure, remember to refit the left-hand engine lifting bracket to the cylinder head lower section once the camshaft locking tool has been removed, and to fit a new exhaust camshaft left-hand oil seal before refitting the camshaft position sensor components.

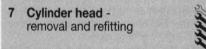

7 Cylinder head -
removal and refitting

Note: *New cylinder head retaining bolts will be required for refitting.*

Removal

1 Disconnect the battery negative terminal (refer to *Disconnecting the battery* in the Reference Section of this manual).

2 Drain the cooling system as described in Chapter 1A.

3 Slacken the clips and remove the radiator top hose from the thermostat housing and radiator. Remove the expansion tank hose from the thermostat housing.

4 Remove the timing belt as described in Section 3.

5 Remove the camshafts and tappets as described in Section 6.

6 Remove the inlet manifold and exhaust manifolds as described in Chapter 4A.

7 Undo the pivot bolt and remove the timing belt tensioner pulley **(see illustration)**.

8 Undo the two bolts and remove the timing belt idler pulley **(see illustration)**.

9 Undo the remaining two bolts securing the timing belt inner cover to the cylinder block and remove the cover **(see illustrations)**.

10 Undo the two bolts securing the coolant pipe flange to the right-hand rear of the cylinder head.

11 Disconnect the wiring at the coolant temperature sensor at the left-hand end of the cylinder head.

7.7 Undo the pivot bolt (arrowed) and remove the timing belt tensioner pulley

2C

7.8 Undo the two bolts and remove the timing belt idler pulley

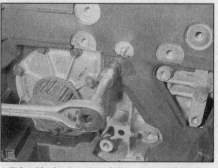

7.9a Undo the remaining upper bolt . . .

7.9b . . . and lower bolt and remove the inner timing belt cover

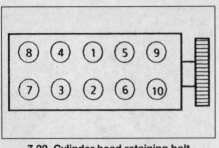

7.22 Cylinder head retaining bolt tightening sequence

12 Working in the **reverse** of the sequence shown in **illustration 7.22**, progressively slacken the cylinder head bolts by half a turn at a time until all the bolts can be unscrewed by hand and removed. Note that new bolts will be required for refitting.

13 Lift the cylinder head upwards and off the cylinder block. If it is stuck, tap it upwards using a hammer and block of wood. Do not try to turn it (it is located by two dowels), nor attempt to prise it free using a screwdriver inserted between the block and head faces. If the locating dowels are a loose fit, remove them and store them with the head for safe-keeping. Remove the cylinder head gasket.

14 If the cylinder head is to be dismantled for overhaul, refer to Part G of this Chapter.

Preparation for refitting

15 The mating faces of the cylinder head and cylinder block must be perfectly clean before refitting the head. Use a soft putty knife to remove all traces of gasket and carbon; also clean the piston crowns. Take particular care during the cleaning operations, as aluminium alloy is easily damaged. Also, make sure that the carbon is not allowed to enter the oil and water passages - this is particularly important for the lubrication system, as carbon could block the oil supply to the engine's components. Using adhesive tape and paper, seal the water, oil and bolt holes in the cylinder block. To prevent carbon entering the gap between the pistons and bores, smear a little grease in the gap. After cleaning each piston, use a small brush to remove all traces of grease and carbon from the gap, then wipe away the remainder with a clean rag. Clean all the pistons in the same way.

16 Check the mating surfaces of the cylinder block and the cylinder head for nicks, deep scratches and other damage. If slight, they may be removed carefully with a file, but if excessive, machining may be the only alternative to renewal.

17 If warpage of the cylinder head gasket surface is suspected, use a straight-edge to check it for distortion. Refer to the overhaul information given in Part G of this Chapter if necessary.

18 Examine the cylinder head bolt threads in the cylinder block for damage. If necessary, use the correct-size tap to chase out the threads in the block. Ensure that the bolt holes are clean and free of oil. Syringe or soak up any oil left in the bolt holes. This is most important in order that the correct bolt tightening torque can be applied and to prevent the possibility of the block being cracked by hydraulic pressure when the bolts are tightened.

Refitting

19 Commence refitting by placing a new head gasket on the cylinder block. Make sure it is the right way up; the surface marked with the word TOP should face upwards.

20 Check that the crankshaft is still correctly positioned in contact with the setting tool as described in Section 3.

21 Lower the cylinder head into position then oil the threads of the new cylinder head bolts. Insert the bolts and screw them in until they just contact the cylinder head.

22 Working progressively and in the sequence shown, tighten the cylinder head bolts to their Stage 1 torque setting, using a torque wrench and suitable socket **(see illustration)**.

23 In the same sequence, tighten the bolts to the Stage 2 torque setting, then wait three minutes to allow the gasket to settle. After this time, working again in the given sequence, angle-tighten the bolts through the specified Stage 3 angle, using a socket and extension bar. It is recommended that an angle-measuring gauge is used during this stage of the tightening, to ensure accuracy.

24 Using a new gasket, refit the coolant pipe flange to the rear of the cylinder head and secure with the two bolts.

25 Reconnect the coolant temperature sensor wiring connector.

26 Attach the radiator top hose and expansion tank hose to the thermostat housing and radiator securely tighten their retaining clips.

27 Place the timing belt inner cover in position and secure with the two bolts that locate in the cylinder block.

28 Refit the timing belt tensioner pulley and idler pulley and tighten the retaining bolts to the specified torque.

29 Refit the inlet manifold and exhaust manifolds as described in Chapter 4A.

30 Refit the camshafts and tappets as described in Section 6.

31 Refit the timing belt as described in Section 3.

32 On completion, refill cooling system as described in Chapter 1A.

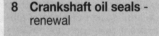

8 Crankshaft oil seals - renewal

Front oil seal

1 Remove the timing belt as described in Section 3.

2 Re-insert two of the crankshaft pulley retaining bolts and draw the sprocket off the crankshaft using a universal puller. Engage the puller legs with the protruding bolts at the rear **(see illustration)**. Avoid damaging the sprocket teeth.

3 With the sprocket removed, carefully prise out the old oil seal **(see illustration)**. Do not damage the oil pump housing or the surface of the crankshaft. Alternatively, punch or drill two small holes opposite each other in the oil seal. Screw a self-tapping screw into each, and pull on the screws with pliers to extract the seal.

4 Clean the oil seal location and the crankshaft. Inspect the crankshaft for a wear groove or ridge left by the old seal.

5 Lubricate the housing, the crankshaft and the new seal. Fit the seal, lips inwards, and use a piece of tube (or the old seal, inverted) to tap it into place until flush **(see illustrations)**.

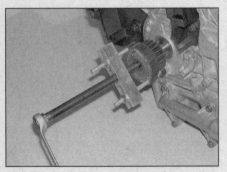

8.2 Draw the crankshaft sprocket off using a universal puller

8.3 Carefully prise out the old oil seal

8.5a Fit the new seal over the crankshaft . . .

6 Refit the crankshaft sprocket and tap it fully into position. Note that the crankshaft nose has a master spline to ensure that the sprocket is correctly refitted **(see illustration)**.
7 Refit the timing belt as described in Section 3.

Rear oil seal

8 Remove the flywheel or driveplate as described in Section 10.
9 Remove the old seal and fit the new one using the procedure described previously in paragraphs 3 to 5 **(see illustrations)**.
10 Refit the flywheel or driveplate (Section 10).

9 Oil pump -
removal, inspection and refitting

Removal

1 Carry out the operations described in Section 8, paragraphs 1 and 2.
2 Undo the four bolts securing the oil pump to the front of the cylinder block.
3 Carefully withdraw the pump assembly by levering behind the upper and lower parting lugs using a screwdriver. Remove the pump and recover the gasket.
4 Thoroughly clean the pump and cylinder block mating faces and remove all traces of old gasket.

Inspection

5 Remove the two screws which hold the two halves of the pump together **(see illustration)**.
6 Remove the gear cover from the pump body. Be prepared to catch the pressure relief valve spring **(see illustration)**.
7 Remove the relief valve spring and plunger and the pump gears **(see illustrations)**.
8 Remove the crankshaft front oil seal by carefully levering it out of the cover **(see illustration)**. Obtain a new seal for refitting.
9 Clean all components thoroughly, then inspect the gears, body and gear cover for signs of wear or damage.

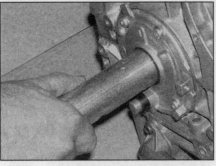

8.5b . . . and use a piece of tube to tap it into place until it is flush with its housing

8.6 Note that the crankshaft nose has a master spline (arrowed) to ensure that the sprocket is correctly refitted

8.9a Fit the new oil seal over the crankshaft . . .

8.9b . . . and use a length of wood to tap it into place until it is flush with its housing

9.5 Remove the two screws which hold the two halves of the pump together

9.6 Remove the gear cover from the pump body

9.7a Remove the relief valve spring and plunger . . .

9.7b . . . and inner . . .

9.7c . . . and outer pump gears

9.8 Remove the crankshaft front oil seal by carefully levering it out of the cover

2C

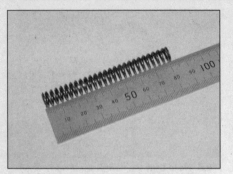

9.10 Measure the free height of the pressure relief valve spring

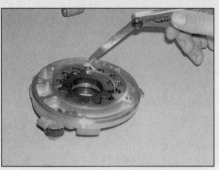

9.11 Check the clearance between the outer gear and its housing

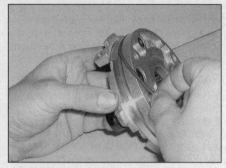

9.13 Fit a new O-ring seal to the pump body

10 Measure the free height of the pressure relief valve spring, and compare the dimension with that given in the Specifications. Renew it if it is weak or distorted. Also inspect the plunger for scoring or other damage **(see illustration)**.

11 Refit the gears to the pump body, with the markings on the large gear uppermost. Using feeler blades, check the clearance between the large gear and the pump body. If the clearance is outside the specified limit, renew the pump **(see illustration)**.

12 If the clearance is satisfactory, liberally lubricate the gears. Lubricate and fit the relief valve plunger and spring.

13 Fit a new O-ring seal to the pump body then fit the cover and secure with the two screws **(see illustration)**.

Refitting

14 Using a new gasket, fit the pump to the block. Apply suitable sealant to the pump retaining bolts, then use the bolts as guides and draw the pump into place with the crankshaft pulley nut and spacers. With the pump seated, tighten the retaining bolts diagonally to the specified torque **(see illustrations)**.

15 Lubricate the cover, crankshaft and the new oil seal. Fit the seal, lips inwards, and use a piece of tube (or the old seal, inverted) to tap it into place until flush.

16 Refit the crankshaft sprocket and tap it fully into position. Note that the crankshaft nose has a master spline to ensure that the sprocket is correctly refitted.

17 Refit the timing belt as described in Section 3.

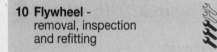

10 Flywheel -
removal, inspection
and refitting

Note: *New flywheel retaining bolts will be required for refitting.*

Removal

1 Remove the transmission as described in Chapter 7A.

2 Remove the clutch assembly as described in Chapter 6.

3 Make alignment marks so that the flywheel can be refitted in the same position relative to the crankshaft.

4 Unbolt the flywheel and remove it. Prevent crankshaft rotation by inserting a large screwdriver in the ring gear teeth and in contact with an adjacent dowel in the engine/transmission mating face.

Inspection

5 If the flywheel's clutch mating surface is deeply scored, cracked or otherwise damaged, the flywheel must be renewed. However, it may be possible to have it surface-ground; seek the advice of a Renault dealer or engine reconditioning specialist. If the ring gear is badly worn or has missing teeth, flywheel renewal will also be necessary.

Refitting

6 Clean the mating surfaces of the flywheel and crankshaft. Remove any remaining locking compound from the threads of the crankshaft holes, using the correct-size tap, if available.

9.14a Using a new gasket . . .

9.14b . . . fit the pump to the block

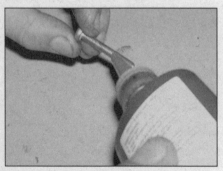

9.14c Apply suitable sealant to the pump retaining bolts

9.14d Insert the retaining bolts . . .

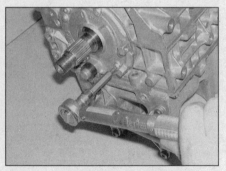

9.14e . . . and tighten them diagonally to the specified torque

If a suitable tap is not available, cut two slots into the threads of one of the old flywheel bolts and use the bolt to remove the locking compound from the threads.

7 Continue refitting by reversing the removal operations. Note that the flywheel is located by a roll pin pressed into the crankshaft mating surface. Apply liquid gasket to the threads of the new flywheel retaining bolts (to prevent oil seepage) and then tighten them to the specified torque and angle **(see illustrations)**.

8 Refit the clutch as described in Chapter 6, and the transmission as described in Chapter 7A.

10.7a The flywheel is located by a roll pin pressed into the crankshaft mating surface

10.7b Insert the new flywheel retaining bolts . . .

11 Engine mountings - inspection and renewal

Inspection

1 If improved access is required, apply the handbrake, then jack up the front of the car and support it on axle stands (see *Jacking and vehicle support*).

2 Check the mounting rubber to see if it is cracked, hardened or separated from the metal at any point; renew the mounting if any such damage or deterioration is evident.

3 Check that all the mounting's fasteners are securely tightened; use a torque wrench to check if possible **(see illustration)**.

4 Using a large screwdriver or a crowbar, check for wear in the mounting by carefully levering against it to check for free play. Where this is not possible, enlist the aid of an assistant to move the engine/transmission back and forth, or from side to side, while you watch the mounting. While some free play is to be expected even from new components, excessive wear should be obvious. If excessive free play is found, check first that the fasteners are correctly secured, then renew any worn components as described below.

Renewal

Right-hand mounting

5 Disconnect the battery negative terminal (refer to *Disconnecting the battery* in the Reference Section of this manual).

6 Place a jack beneath the engine, with a block of wood on the jack head (remove the undercover to improve access to the sump). Raise the jack until it is supporting the weight of the engine. Alternately, attach an engine support bar to the lifting brackets and support the weight of the engine with the bar.

7 Undo the four screws and lift off the plastic cover from the top of the engine.

8 Undo the three bolts and remove the

10.7c . . . and tighten them to the specified torque . . .

10.7d . . . and through the specified angle

acoustic tie-rod from the mounting bracket and cylinder head.

9 Undo the centre nut securing the mounting bracket to the rubber mounting

10 Undo the three bolts securing the mounting bracket to the cylinder head attachment bracket and cylinder head upper section and remove the bracket.

11 Undo the three bolts securing the rubber mounting and movement limiter to the body and remove the mounting.

12 Check carefully for signs of wear or damage on all components, and renew them where necessary.

13 Fit the rubber mounting and movement limiter to the body, insert the retaining bolts but tighten them finger tight only at this stage.

14 Locate the mounting bracket over the rubber mounting stud and position it on the cylinder head attachment bracket. Refit the retaining bolts and tighten them to the specified torque.

2C

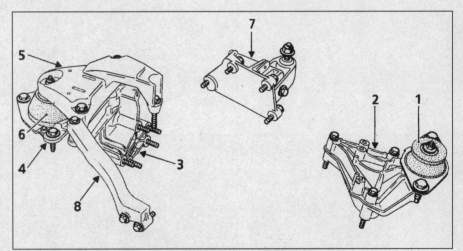

11.3 Engine/transmission mounting details

1 *Left-hand mounting rubber*
2 *Left-hand mounting transmission bracket*
3 *Right-hand mounting attachment bracket*
4 *Right-hand mounting movement limiter*
5 *Right-hand mounting bracket*
6 *Right-hand mounting rubber*
7 *Rear mounting assembly*
8 *Acoustic tie-rod*

15 Secure the mounting bracket to the rubber mounting by tightening the centre nut to the specified torque.

16 Centralise the movement limiter around the rubber mounting then tighten the three bolts to the specified torque.

17 Refit the acoustic tie-rod and tighten the three bolts to the specified torque.

18 Refit the engine cover, then remove the jack from underneath the engine or the engine support bar (as applicable), and reconnect the battery negative terminal.

Left-hand mounting

19 Disconnect the battery negative terminal (refer to *Disconnecting the battery* in the Reference Section of this manual).

20 Refer to Chapter 4A and remove the air cleaner and inlet components as necessary for access to the mounting.

21 Place a jack beneath the transmission, with a block of wood on the jack head. Raise the jack until it is supporting the weight of the transmission.

22 Slacken and remove the mounting rubber's centre nut, and two retaining bolts and remove the mounting from the engine compartment.

23 If necessary, undo the retaining bolts and remove the mounting bracket from the top of the transmission housing.

24 Check carefully for signs of wear or damage on all components, and renew them where necessary.

25 Refit the bracket to the transmission, tightening its mounting bolts to the specified torque.

26 Fit the mounting rubber to the bracket and tighten its retaining bolts and centre nut to the specified torque.

27 Refit the air cleaner and inlet components removed for access.

28 Remove the jack from underneath the transmission and reconnect the battery negative terminal.

Rear mounting

29 Disconnect the battery negative terminal (refer to *Disconnecting the battery* in the Reference Section of this manual).

30 If not already done, apply the handbrake, then jack up the front of the car and support it on axle stands (see *Jacking and vehicle support*).

31 Position a jack with a block of wood on its head underneath the sump (remove the undercover to improve access to the sump). Raise the jack until it is supporting the weight of the engine.

32 Slacken and remove the nut and bolt from each end of the mounting link and remove the link from underneath the vehicle. If necessary, undo the retaining bolts and remove the mounting bracket from the engine/transmission.

33 Check carefully for signs of wear or damage on all components, and renew them where necessary.

34 On reassembly, fit the mounting bracket (where removed) to the rear of the transmission and tighten its retaining bolts to the specified torque.

35 Fit the mounting link, and tighten both its bolts to their specified torque settings.

36 Lower the vehicle to the ground and reconnect the battery negative terminal.

Chapter 2 Part D:
1.9 litre diesel engine in-car repair procedures

Contents

Degrees of difficulty

Easy, suitable for novice with little experience	**Fairly easy,** suitable for beginner with some experience	**Fairly difficult,** suitable for competent DIY mechanic	**Difficult,** suitable for experienced DIY mechanic	**Very difficult,** suitable for expert DIY or professional

Specifications

General

Type	Four-cylinder, in-line, single overhead camshaft
Designation	F9Q 716
Bore	80.0 mm
Stroke	93.0 mm
Capacity	1870 cc
Compression ratio	18.3:1

Compression pressure (engine warm - approximately 80° C):

Normal	22.0 bars
Minimum	20.0 bars
Maximum difference between cylinders	4.0 bars
Firing order	1-3-4-2 (No 1 cylinder at flywheel end of engine)
Direction of crankshaft rotation	Clockwise, viewed from timing belt end

Valve clearances (engine cold)

Inlet	0.20 mm
Exhaust	0.40 mm

Timing belt tension value (see text)

Fitting/checking value	42 SEEM units
Minimum operating value	37 SEEM units

Camshaft

Drive	Toothed belt
Endfloat	0.05 to 0.13 mm

Lubrication system

Minimum oil pressure at 80°C:

At 1000 rpm	1.2 bars
At 3500 rpm	3.5 bars

Oil pump clearances:

Gear-to-body:

Minimum	0.10 mm
Maximum	0.24 mm

Gear endfloat:

Minimum	0.020 mm
Maximum	0.085 mm

Torque wrench settings

	Nm	lbf ft
Camshaft bearing caps:		
8 mm diameter fasteners	20	15
6 mm diameter fasteners	10	7
Camshaft sprocket bolt	60	44
Connecting rod (big-end) cap bolts	45 to 50	33 to 37
Crankshaft pulley bolt	90 to 100	66 to 74
Cylinder head bolts (see illustration 9.49 on page 2D•12)*:		
Stage 1 - all bolts, in the order shown	30	22
Stage 2	Tighten all bolts through a further 50° ± 4°	
Stage 3	Wait for at least 3 minutes for the gasket to settle	
Stage 4	Slacken fully bolts 1 and 2	
Stage 5	Tighten bolts 1 and 2 to a torque setting of 25 Nm/18 lbf ft	
Stage 6	Tighten bolts 1 and 2 through a further 213° ± 7°	
Stage 7	Slacken fully bolts 3 and 4	
Stage 8	Tighten bolts 3 and 4 to a torque setting of 25 Nm/18 lbf ft	
Stage 9	Tighten bolts 3 and 4 through a further 213° ± 7°	
Stage 10	Slacken fully bolts 5 and 6	
Stage 11	Tighten bolts 5 and 6 to a torque setting of 25 Nm/18 lbf ft	
Stage 12	Tighten bolts 5 and 6 through a further 213° ± 7°	
Stage 13	Slacken fully bolts 7 and 8	
Stage 14	Tighten bolts 7 and 8 to a torque setting of 25 Nm/18 lbf ft	
Stage 15	Tighten bolts 7 and 8 through a further 213° ± 7°	
Stage 16	Slacken fully bolts 9 and 10	
Stage 17	Tighten bolts 9 and 10 to a torque setting of 25 Nm/18 lbf ft	
Stage 18	Tighten bolts 9 and 10 through a further 213° ± 7°	
Cylinder head cover nuts/bolts	12	9
Engine/transmission mountings:		
Right-hand mounting:		
Engine bracket-to-cylinder head bolts	62	46
Engine bracket-to-rubber mounting nut	105	77
Rubber mounting-to-body bolts	62	46
Left-hand mounting:		
Mounting bracket-to-transmission bolts	60	44
Mounting stud nut	67	49
Rubber mounting bolts	70	52
Rear mounting:		
Mounting bracket-to-transmission bolts	62	46
Mounting link bolts	105	77
Flywheel bolts *	50 to 55	37 to 41
Injection pump sprocket nut	See Chapter 4B	
Main bearing caps	60 to 65	44 to 48
Oil pump bolts:		
6 mm diameter bolts	10	7
8 mm diameter bolts	22	16
Piston oil spray jet securing bolts	20 ± 2	15 ± 2
Roadwheel bolts	See Chapter 1A or 1B	
Sump bolts:		
Stage 1	8	6
Stage 2	14	10
Timing belt idler sprocket bolt	50	37
Timing belt tensioner nut	50	37

*New nuts/bolts must be used

1 General information

How to use this Chapter

This Part of Chapter 2 is devoted to in-car repair procedures for the 1.9 litre diesel engine. Similar information covering the 2.2 litre diesel engines and the petrol engines will be found in Chapters 2A, 2B, 2C and 2E. All procedures concerning engine removal and refitting, and engine block/cylinder head overhaul for petrol and diesel engines can be found in Chapters 2F, 2G and 2H as applicable.

Most of the operations included in Chapter 2D are based on the assumption that the engine is still installed in the car. Therefore, if this information is being used during a complete engine overhaul, with the engine already removed, many of the steps included here will not apply.

Engine description

The engine is of four-cylinder, in-line, single overhead camshaft type, mounted transversely at the front of the vehicle with the transmission bolted to the left-hand side.

The crankshaft is supported in five shell-type main bearings. Thrustwashers are fitted to No 2 main bearing to control crankshaft endfloat.

The connecting rods are attached to the crankshaft by horizontally-split shell-type big-end bearings and to the pistons by gudgeon pins. The gudgeon pins are fully floating and are retained by circlips. The aluminium alloy pistons are of the slipper type and are fitted with three piston rings; two compression rings and a scraper-type oil control ring.

The single overhead camshaft is mounted in five plain bearings machined directly in the aluminium alloy cylinder head and is driven by the crankshaft via a toothed timing belt.

The camshaft operates the valves via inverted bucket-type followers, which operate in bores machined directly in the cylinder head. Valve clearance adjustment is by shims located externally between the followers and the cam lobes. The inlet and exhaust valves are mounted vertically in the cylinder head and are each closed by a single valve spring.

The fuel injection pump is driven by the timing belt and is described in further detail in Chapter 4B.

A semi-closed crankcase ventilation system is employed and crankcase fumes are drawn from an oil separator on the cast iron cylinder block and passed via a hose (and in certain cases, a second oil separator) to the inlet tract (see Chapter 4C for further details).

The lubrication system is of the full-flow, pressure-feed type. Oil is drawn from the sump by a chain-driven gear-type oil pump located beneath the crankshaft. Engine oil is fed through an externally-mounted oil filter to the main oil gallery feeding the crankshaft and camshaft. Oil spray jets are fitted to the cylinder block to supply oil to the underside of the pistons. Certain models are fitted with an oil cooler mounted on the cylinder block.

Repair operations possible with the engine in the vehicle

The following operations can be carried out without having to remove the engine from the vehicle:

a) Removal and refitting of the cylinder head
b) Removal and refitting of the timing belt and sprockets
c) Renewal of the camshaft oil seals
d) Removal and refitting of the camshaft
e) Removal and refitting of the sump
f) Removal and refitting of the connecting rods and pistons *
g) Removal and refitting of the oil pump
h) Renewal of the crankshaft oil seals
i) Renewal of the engine mountings

* Note: Although the operation marked with an asterisk can be carried out with the engine in the car after removal of the sump, it is better for the engine to be removed in the interests of cleanliness and improved access. For this reason, the procedure is described in Chapter 2H.

2 Compression and leakdown tests - description and interpretation

Compression test

Note: *A compression tester specifically designed for diesel engines must be used for this test.*

1 When engine performance is down, or if misfiring occurs which cannot be attributed to a fault in the fuel system, a compression test can provide diagnostic clues as to the engine's condition. If the test is performed regularly it can give warning of trouble before any other symptoms become apparent.

2 A compression tester specifically intended for diesel engines must be used, because of the higher pressures involved. The tester is connected to an adapter which screws into the glow plug or injector hole **(see illustration)**. It is unlikely to be worthwhile buying such a tester for occasional use, but it may be possible to borrow or hire one - if not, have the test performed by a garage.

3 Unless specific instructions to the contrary are supplied with the tester, observe the following points:

a) *The battery must be in a good state of charge, the air filter must be clean and the engine should be at normal operating temperature*
b) *All the injectors or glow plugs should be removed before starting the test. If removing the injectors, also remove the fire seal washers (which must be renewed when the injectors are refitted - see Chapter 4B), otherwise they may be blown out*
c) *It is advisable to disconnect the stop solenoid on the pump to reduce the amount of fuel discharged as the engine is cranked*

4 The actual compression pressures measured are not as important as the balance between cylinders. Values are given in the Specifications.

5 The cause of poor compression is less easy to establish on a diesel engine than on a petrol one. The effect of introducing oil into the cylinders ('wet' testing) is not conclusive, because there is a risk that the oil will sit in the swirl chamber or in the recess on the piston crown instead of passing to the rings. However, the following can be used as a rough guide to diagnosis.

6 All cylinders should produce very similar pressures; any difference greater than that specified indicates the existence of a fault. Note that the compression should build up quickly in a healthy engine; low compression on the first stroke, followed by gradually increasing pressure on successive strokes, indicates worn piston rings. A low compression reading on the first stroke, which does not build up during successive strokes, indicates leaking valves or a blown head gasket (a cracked head could also be the cause).

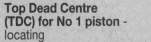
2.2 Carrying out a compression test

7 A low reading from two adjacent cylinders is almost certainly due to the head gasket having blown between them.

8 If the compression reading is unusually high, the cylinder head surfaces, valves and pistons are probably coated with carbon deposits. If this is the case, the cylinder head should be removed and decarbonised (see Chapter 2H).

Leakdown test

9 A leakdown test measures the rate at which compressed air fed into the cylinder is lost. It is an alternative to a compression test and in many ways it is better, since the escaping air provides easy identification of where pressure loss is occurring (piston rings, valves or head gasket).

10 The equipment needed for leakdown testing is unlikely to be available to the home mechanic. If poor compression is suspected, have the test performed by a suitably equipped garage.

3 Top Dead Centre (TDC) for No 1 piston - locating

TOOL TiP *If the special Renault timing pin tool (Mot. 1054) mentioned in this Section is not available, an 8 mm diameter rod or drill bit can be used instead. On some engines, however, an 8 mm diameter rod may be too slack a fit in the blanking plug aperture in the cylinder block for the crankshaft position to be determined accurately - it will therefore be necessary in such cases to have a stepped pin made up, with an 8 mm diameter at its tip to engage in the crankshaft slot and a larger diameter as necessary to fit precisely in the cylinder block aperture*

Caution: These timing pins are intended SOLELY for the purpose of checking the position of the crankshaft during various engine overhaul procedures. DO NOT use them as locking tools to prevent crankshaft rotation while the pulley or flywheel bolts are unscrewed or tightened

2D

3.4 Flywheel timing mark aligned with TDC (0°) mark on bellhousing

1 Top Dead Centre (TDC) is the highest point in the cylinder that each piston reaches as the crankshaft turns. Each piston reaches TDC at the end of the compression stroke and again at the end of the exhaust stroke; however, for the purpose of timing the engine, TDC refers to the position of No 1 piston at the end of its compression stroke. No 1 piston is at the flywheel end of the engine.

2 When No 1 piston is at TDC, the timing mark on the camshaft sprocket should be aligned with the pointer on the timing belt outer cover (the pulley mark can be viewed through the cut-out in the cover, below the pointer). Additionally, the timing mark on the flywheel should be aligned with the TDC mark on the gearbox bellhousing.

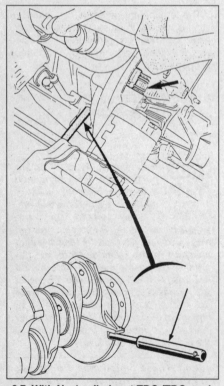

3.7 With No 1 cylinder at TDC (TDC mark on flywheel can be viewed through bellhousing aperture) the crankshaft position can be checked using a timing pin, Renault tool Mot. 1054

3.6 Camshaft sprocket timing mark aligned with pointer on timing belt outer cover

3 To align the timing marks, the crankshaft must be turned. This should be done by using a spanner on the crankshaft pulley bolt. Improved access to the pulley bolt can be obtained by jacking up the front right-hand corner of the vehicle and removing the roadwheel and the wheel arch lower liner (secured by plastic clips). If desired, to enable the engine to be turned more easily, remove the glow plugs (Chapter 5C) or the fuel injectors (Chapter 4B).

4 Look through the timing aperture in the gearbox bellhousing and turn the crankshaft until the timing mark on the flywheel is aligned with the TDC (0°) mark on the bellhousing **(see illustration)**.

5 Unscrew the retaining nuts and withdraw the engine sound-insulating cover.

6 Check that the timing mark on the camshaft sprocket is aligned with the pointer on the timing belt outer cover **(see illustration)**. The engine is now positioned with No 1 piston at TDC on its compression stroke.

7 For absolute accuracy, the crankshaft position should be checked by inserting a timing pin - Renault tool Mot. 1054. To do this, unscrew the blanking plug from the front left-hand end of the cylinder block, next to the base of the oil level dipstick tube, and insert the timing pin so that it engages in the timing slot provided for this purpose in the crankshaft. It may be necessary to rock the crankshaft very slightly backwards or forwards to do this **(see illustration)**. Note that there is a balance hole in the crankshaft web adjacent to the timing slot. If care is not taken, it is very easy for the pin to engage with the balance hole and not the timing slot.

8 Once in place it should be impossible to turn the crankshaft - if the crankshaft will still move to and fro slightly, then the timing pin has entered the balance hole instead of the timing slot. **Note:** *Do not attempt to rotate the engine whilst the timing pin is in place. If the engine is to be left in this state for a long period of time, it is a good idea to place warning notices inside the vehicle and in the engine compartment. This will reduce the possibility of the engine being accidentally cranked on the starter motor, which will cause severe damage if done with the timing pin in place.*

9 On completion, remove the timing pin and refit all removed components.

Note: *This operation is not part of the maintenance schedule. It should be undertaken if noise from the valvegear becomes evident, or if loss of performance gives cause to suspect that the clearances may be incorrect. A new cylinder head cover gasket may be required on refitting.*

Checking

1 Where necessary for improved access, unclip any hoses which are routed across the top of the cylinder head cover and move them to one side out of the way. If fuel lines are disconnected, cover open unions to prevent dirt ingress.

2 Unscrew the retaining nuts and withdraw the engine sound-insulating cover.

3 Unscrew the bolts from the cylinder head cover and withdraw the cover from the engine. Recover the gasket.

4 During the following procedure, the crankshaft must be turned, using a spanner on the crankshaft pulley bolt. Improved access to the pulley bolt can be obtained by jacking up the front right-hand corner of the vehicle (see *Jacking and vehicle support*) and removing the roadwheel and the wheel arch lower liner (secured by plastic clips).

5 If desired, to enable the crankshaft to be turned more easily, remove the glow plugs (Chapter 5C) or the fuel injectors (Chapter 4B).

6 Draw the valve positions on a piece of paper, numbering them 1 to 8 from the flywheel end of the engine. Identify them as inlet or exhaust (i.e. 1E, 2I, 3E, 4I, 5I, 6E, 7I, 8E) **(see illustration)**.

7 Turn the crankshaft until the valves of No 1 cylinder (flywheel end) are 'rocking' - the exhaust valve will be closing and the inlet valve will be opening. The piston of No 4 cylinder will be at the top of its compression stroke, with both valves fully closed - the clearances for both valves of No 4 cylinder may now be checked.

8 Insert a feeler gauge of the correct thickness (see Specifications) between the

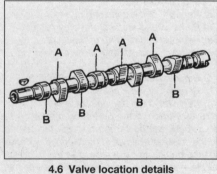

4.6 Valve location details

A Inlet   *B Exhaust*

cam lobe and the shim on the top of the follower and check that it is a firm sliding fit **(see illustration)**. If it is not, use the feeler gauges to ascertain the exact clearance and record this for use when calculating the new shim thickness required. Note that the inlet and exhaust valve clearances are different (see Specifications).

9 With No 4 cylinder valve clearances checked, turn the engine through half a turn so that No 3 valves are 'rocking', then check the valve clearances of No 2 cylinder in the same way. Similarly check the remaining valve clearances in the sequence shown **(see illustration)**.

Adjustment

Note: *A micrometer will be required for this operation.*

10 Where a valve clearance differs from the specified value, then the shim for that valve must be replaced with a thinner or thicker shim accordingly. Each shim's thickness is normally etched on the shim, but it is prudent to use a micrometer to measure the true thickness of any shim removed, as it may have been reduced by wear **(see illustration)**.

11 The thickness of shim required is calculated as follows. If the measured clearance is less than specified, subtract the measured clearance from the specified clearance and deduct the result from the thickness of the existing shim. For example:

Sample calculation - clearance too small
Clearance measured (A) = 0.15 mm
Desired clearance (B) = 0.20 mm
Difference (B – A) = 0.05 mm
Shim thickness fitted = 3.70 mm
Shim required = 3.70 – 0.05 = 3.65 mm

12 If the measured clearance is greater than specified, subtract the specified clearance from the measured clearance and add the result to the thickness of the existing shim. For example:

Sample calculation - clearance too big
Clearance measured (A) = 0.50 mm
Desired clearance (B) = 0.40 mm
Difference (A – B) = 0.10 mm
Shim thickness fitted = 3.45 mm
Shim required = 3.45 + 0.10 = 3.55 mm

4.8 Measuring a valve clearance

13 The shims have a round projection on their lower face which locates in a recess in the follower. This arrangement makes it very difficult to remove the shims with the camshaft installed. The procedure requires the use of the Renault special tool shown **(see illustration)**, or a suitable home-made alternative, but it is first necessary to remove the inlet and exhaust manifolds and the turbocharger (see Chapter 4B).

14 To remove the shim, turn the crankshaft in the normal direction of rotation until the valve to be adjusted is fully open. Insert the tool through the cylinder head port so that the shaped end of the tool locates on the valve seat **(see illustration)**.

15 If removing an inlet valve shim, turn the crankshaft a further 180°, in the normal direction of rotation, to allow the valve to close and contact the tool. The tool will trap the valve, preventing it from closing fully, which will allow sufficient clearance for the shim to be removed with a screwdriver. The same procedure is used for the exhaust valves except that the crankshaft must be turned 180° in the **opposite** direction to normal rotation.

16 Before refitting the shims, wipe the top of the follower and ensure that all the oil is removed from the shim locating recess in the follower's upper face. Fit the shim to the follower with the projection on the shim engaged with the follower's recess.

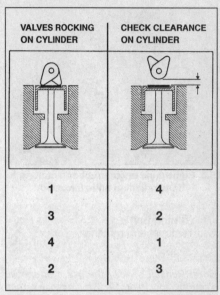

VALVES ROCKING ON CYLINDER	CHECK CLEARANCE ON CYLINDER
1	4
3	2
4	1
2	3

4.9 Valve clearance checking sequence

17 If the Renault tool cannot be borrowed or a suitable alternative improvised, then it will be necessary to remove the camshaft to gain access to the shims, as described in Section 8.

18 Remove the spanner from the crankshaft pulley bolt.

19 Refit the cylinder head cover, using a new gasket where necessary - tighten the cover retaining bolts evenly to the specified torque wrench setting.

20 Where applicable, refit the fuel injectors (as described in Chapter 4B), or the glow plugs (Chapter 5C).

21 Refit the inlet and exhaust manifolds and the turbocharger as described in Chapter 4B.

22 Refit/reconnect any hoses which were moved for access. If fuel lines were disconnected, reconnect them, then prime and bleed the fuel system as described in Chapter 4B.

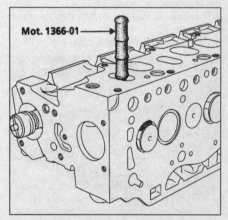

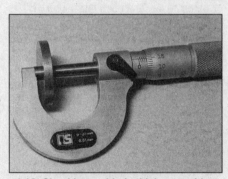

4.10 Checking a shim's thickness with a micrometer

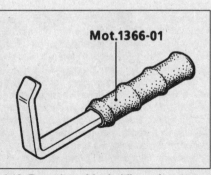

4.13 Renault tool for holding valves open

4.14 Method of inserting and using Renault tool to hold valves open

2D

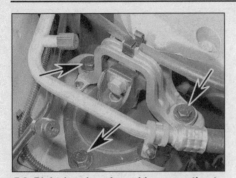

5.6 Right-hand engine rubber mounting to body retaining bolts (arrowed)

5 Timing belt -
removal and refitting

Note: *Renault specify the use of a special electronic tool (Mot. 1273) to correctly set the timing belt tension. If access to this equipment cannot be obtained, an approximate setting can be achieved using the method described below. If the method described is used, the tension must be checked using the special electronic tool at the earliest possible opportunity. Do not drive the vehicle over large distances, or use high engine speeds, until the belt tension is known to be correct. Refer to a Renault dealer for advice.*

Note: *The timing belt should renewed whenever it is disturbed; never refit a belt which has already been used.*

Removal

1 Disconnect the battery negative terminal (refer to *Disconnecting the battery* in the Reference Section of this manual).
2 Apply the handbrake, then jack up the front of the car and support it on axle stands (see *Jacking and vehicle support*). Remove the right-hand front roadwheel, the undo the retaining screws and remove the engine undercover and the front and rear protective covers from the right-hand wheelarch.
3 Unscrew the retaining nuts and withdraw the engine sound-insulating cover.
4 Remove the auxiliary drivebelt as described in Chapter 1B.
5 Position an engine hoist, or an engine lifting

5.13 Loosen the timing belt tensioner nut

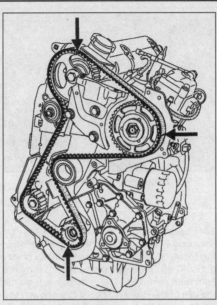

5.11 Sprocket timing mark positions with No 1 piston at TDC

beam across the engine compartment and attach the jib to the right-hand engine lifting eyelet. Raise the lifting gear to take up the slack, so that it is just supporting the weight of the engine.
6 Undo the three bolts securing the right-hand engine mounting bracket to the cylinder head. Similarly, undo the three bolts securing the rubber mounting to the body **(see illustration)**. Release the relevant cable clips and remove the complete mounting assembly.
7 Disconnect the wiring plug from the injection control unit located at the front right-hand side of the engine compartment. Undo the mounting bolts and remove the control unit. Similarly, unbolt the pre/post heating system control unit, adjacent to the injection control unit, and move it to one side.
8 Using a socket and extension bar, slacken the crankshaft pulley bolt. Hold the crankshaft stationary while the bolt is unscrewed by engaging a screwdriver with the flywheel ring gear teeth through the opening at the lower rear of the cylinder block. Unscrew the bolt and remove the washer and crankshaft pulley.
9 Temporarily refit the crankshaft pulley bolt. Turn the crankshaft to position No 1 piston at

5.17 M6 bolt fitted to timing belt inner cover to adjust timing belt tension

TDC on the compression stroke and insert a timing pin to check the crankshaft position as described in Section 3.
10 Unscrew the securing bolts and withdraw the timing belt outer covers.
11 With No 1 piston at TDC on the compression stroke (see paragraph 9), note the position of the timing marks on the camshaft, fuel injection pump and crankshaft sprockets **(see illustration)**.
12 If the original belt is to be re-used (contrary to Renault's recommendation), check that the belt is marked with arrows to indicate its running direction and if necessary mark it. Similarly, note that the belt should be marked with bands across its width to act as timing marks corresponding to the timing marks on the camshaft, fuel injection pump and crankshaft sprockets. If the original belt is to be refitted (contrary to Renault's recommendation) and the timing bands have deteriorated (in which case, it is likely that the belt is in need of renewal in any case), make accurate alignment marks on the belt.
13 Loosen its retaining nut and bolt, then push back the tensioner to relieve the tension on the timing belt **(see illustration)**. Re-tighten the nut.
14 Release the belt first from the camshaft sprocket, then from the fuel injection pump sprocket, upper idler pulley, crankshaft sprocket and lower idler sprocket, and remove it from the engine.
15 Do not turn the camshaft or the crankshaft whilst the timing belt is removed, as there is a risk of piston-to-valve contact. If it is necessary to turn the camshaft for any reason, before doing so, remove the timing pin and turn the crankshaft anti-clockwise (viewed from the timing belt end of the engine) by a quarter-turn to position all four pistons halfway down their bores.
16 Clean the sprockets, idler pulley and tensioner and wipe them dry - **do not** apply excessive amounts of solvent to the idler pulley and tensioner otherwise the bearing lubricant may be removed. Also clean the timing belt inner cover and the related surfaces of the cylinder head and block.

Refitting

17 Ensure that the crankshaft is at the TDC position for No 1 cylinder, with the timing pin in place to ensure complete accuracy, as described previously. If the pistons have been positioned halfway down their bores (see paragraph 15), temporarily refit the timing belt outer cover which covers the camshaft sprocket and check that the timing mark on the pulley is aligned with the pointer on the timing belt outer cover, then turn the crankshaft clockwise (viewed from the timing belt end of the engine) until the timing pin can be refitted. To enable the tensioner to be adjusted, screw a 6 mm bolt into the threaded hole provided in the timing belt inner cover. The bolt will bear against the rear of the tensioner pulley and enable adjustments of the belt tension to be made **(see illustration)**.

18 Align the timing bands on the belt with the marks on the crankshaft, camshaft and fuel injection pump sprockets, ensuring that the running direction arrows on the belt are pointing clockwise (viewed from the timing belt end of the engine). Fit the timing belt over the crankshaft sprocket first, followed by the lower idler pulley, fuel injection pump sprocket, camshaft sprocket, tensioner and upper idler sprocket.

19 Check that all the timing marks are still aligned and remove all slack from the timing belt by tightening the bolt fitted to the timing belt inner cover. **Note:** *As a further check, count the number of timing belt teeth between the camshaft pulley's timing mark and the injection pump pulley's timing mark - if the valve timing is correct, there will be 30 teeth.*

20 The belt tension must now be checked - this can be set or checked accurately **only** by using the Renault tool Mot. 1273 **(see illustration)**. If this equipment is not available, set the belt's tension as carefully as possible using the method outlined below, then take the vehicle to a Renault dealer as soon as possible for the tension to be checked by qualified personnel using the special equipment. Do not take the vehicle on any long journeys or rev the engine to high speeds until the timing belt's tension has been checked and is known to be correct.

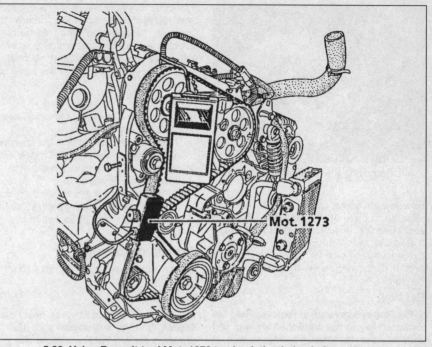

5.20 Using Renault tool Mot. 1273 to check the timing belt tension

With experience, timing belt tension may be judged to be approximately correct when the belt can be twisted 45 to 90° with moderate pressure between the finger and thumb, checking midway between the pulleys on the belt's longest run. If the special tool is not available and there is any doubt about the tension of the timing belt, the vehicle should be taken to a Renault dealer as soon as possible for the tension to be checked by qualified personnel using the special equipment.

21 If the adjustment is incorrect, the tensioner will have to be repositioned by loosening the tensioner nut and by screwing in or out the bolt fitted to the timing belt inner cover.

22 With the correct tension applied, re-tighten the tensioner nut to the specified torque. This torque is critical, since if the nut were to come loose, considerable engine damage would result. Loosen the bolt fitted to the timing belt inner cover so that it no longer bears on the tensioner roller bracket.

23 Remove the crankshaft timing pin, then refit the crankshaft pulley and securing bolt. Prevent the crankshaft turning using the method described previously and tighten the bolt to the specified torque.

24 Check that the crankshaft is still positioned with No 1 piston at TDC (by refitting temporarily the crankshaft timing pin), then remove the timing pin and turn the crankshaft three complete turns in the normal direction of rotation, returning it to the TDC position again. Re-insert the timing pin in the cylinder block.

25 Temporarily refit the timing belt outer cover which covers the camshaft sprocket and check that the pulley timing mark still aligns with the pointer on the cover, as noted before removal (see Section 3).

26 Re-check the belt tension as described previously. If the tension is incorrect, the setting and checking procedure must be repeated until the correct tension is achieved.

27 With the belt tensioned correctly, remove the M6 bolt from the timing belt inner cover and remove the timing pin from the cylinder block, if not already done. Refit the blanking plug to the cylinder block and tighten it securely, also tighten the tensioner retaining bolt.

28 Check the fuel injection pump timing as described in Chapter 4B.

29 Refit the timing belt upper outer covers, ensuring that any brackets secured by the bolts are in position as noted before removal.

30 Locate the right-hand engine mounting assembly into position and refit the bolts securing the mounting bracket to the cylinder head. Tighten the bolts to the specified torque. Refit the three bolts securing the rubber mounting to the body. Ensure that the movement limiter is positioned centrally over the mounting rubber then tighten the three bolts to the specified torque.

31 Remove the engine hoist or lifting beam used to support the engine.

32 Refit the auxiliary drivebelt as described in Chapter 1B.

33 Refit the injection control unit and the wiring plug, and the pre/post heating control unit. Refit the engine sound-insulating cover.

34 Refit the engine compartment undershield, then refit the wheel arch liner and the roadwheel and lower the vehicle to the ground.

35 Reconnect the battery negative terminal.

6 Timing belt sprockets and tensioner - removal and refitting

Note: *A new timing belt must be used on refitting.*

Crankshaft sprocket

Removal

1 Remove the timing belt as described in Section 5.

2 It should be possible simply to pull the sprocket off the crankshaft **(see illustration)**.

2D

6.2 Removing the crankshaft sprocket

However in some cases a puller may be required to draw off the sprocket - one can easily be made up as shown **(see Tool Tip)**.

3 Recover the Woodruff key if it is loose. Examine the oil seal for signs of oil leakage and, if necessary renew it as described in Section 7.

Refitting

4 Refitting is a reversal of removal. Refit the Woodruff key to the crankshaft keyway and slide on the sprocket, making sure it is correctly engaged with the key and with its flange against the cylinder block/timing belt inner cover.

5 Fit the new timing belt as described in Section 5.

Fuel injection pump sprocket

Note: *Renault special tool Mot. 1200-01 will be required to hold the injection pump sprocket during removal and refitting. Refer to Chapter 4B for additional information.*

Removal

6 Remove the timing belt as described in Section 5.

7 Fit the Renault sprocket holding tool (Mot. 1200-01) to prevent the injection pump sprocket from rotating.

8 Unscrew the sprocket nut to draw off the sprocket - the nut will slacken at first and then

It is easy to make up a puller for the crankshaft sprocket using two bolts, a strip of metal and the existing crank-shaft pulley bolt. By unscrewing the pulley bolt against the metal strip, the sprocket is drawn off the crankshaft

tighten as its extracting action is brought to bear against the sprocket centre bolt. Continue 'unscrewing' the nut until the sprocket is free of the pump shaft's taper.

9 Remove the sprocket and recover the Woodruff key from the end of the pump shaft if it is loose.

Refitting

10 Refitting is a reversal of removal, bearing in mind the following points:
a) *Tighten the sprocket nut to the specified torque wrench setting (see Chapter 4B).*
b) *Fit and tension the new timing belt as described in Section 5.*
c) *Before refitting the timing belt outer cover over the injection pump sprocket, check the injection timing as described in Chapter 4B.*

Camshaft sprocket

Note: *A suitable puller will be required for this operation.*

Removal

11 Remove the timing belt as described in Section 5. If it is necessary to turn the camshaft for any reason, before doing so, remove the timing pin and turn the crankshaft anti-clockwise (viewed from the timing belt end of the engine) by a quarter-turn to position all four pistons halfway down their bores.

12 On models with air conditioning, unbolt the auxiliary drivebelt tensioner mounting plate (see Chapter 1B), then unscrew the associated alternator/fuel injection pump mounting bolt.

13 Unscrew the bolts securing the engine right-hand mounting main bracket to the engine and withdraw the bracket.

14 Unscrew the camshaft sprocket bolt. The sprocket can be held using a suitable socket and extension bar engaged with one of the timing belt inner cover securing bolts, or by making up a sprocket holding tool as shown in Chapter 2B, Section 3. Alternatively, use the old timing belt wrapped around the pulley. Recover the washer.

15 Remove the bolt, washer and sprocket from the camshaft. A suitable puller may be required, in which case ensure that the legs of the puller act on the holes in the pulley, **not** on the pulley teeth.

16 Recover the Woodruff key from the end of the camshaft if it is loose - note that on later engines the key is an integral part of the pulley.

Refitting

17 Refit the Woodruff key (where separate) to the camshaft keyway. Refit the sprocket with its projecting hub towards the cylinder head and ensuring that the key engages correctly with the keyway.

18 Ensure that the washer is in place, then refit the sprocket bolt and tighten it to the specified torque, holding the pulley as during removal.

19 Refit the engine right-hand mounting main bracket to the engine and tighten the securing bolts. Where applicable, refit the upper two bolts to the holes in the bracket before the bracket is refitted.

20 Refit the bolts securing the auxiliary drivebelt tensioner mounting plate and the alternator/fuel injection pump mounting bolt disturbed on removal.

21 Fit the new timing belt as described in Section 5.

Idler sprocket/pulley

Removal

22 Remove the timing belt as described in Section 5.

23 To remove the idler sprocket, undo the retaining bolt and withdraw the sprocket. To remove the idler pulley, unscrew the two securing bolts and withdraw the idler pulley assembly, manipulating it out from the timing belt inner covers.

Refitting

24 Refitting is a reversal of removal, but check that the sprocket/pulley turns freely without binding or excessive play.

25 Fit the new timing belt as described in Section 5.

Tensioner

Removal

26 Remove the timing belt as described in Section 5.

27 Unscrew the securing nut and its washer, unscrew the retaining bolt, then withdraw the tensioner assembly.

Refitting

28 Refitting is a reversal of removal, but check that the roller turns freely without binding or excessive play. Ensure that the peg on the cylinder block engages with the hole in the tensioner bracket.

29 Fit the new timing belt as described in Section 5.

| 7 | Camshaft oil seals - renewal | |

Timing belt end oil seal

1 Remove the camshaft sprocket as described in Section 6.

2 Remove the Woodruff key (where separate) from the end of the camshaft, if not already done.

3 Make a note of the fitted depth of the old seal then, using a small screwdriver, prise it out of the cylinder head, taking care not to damage the surface of the camshaft. Alternatively, the oil seal can be removed by drilling a small hole and inserting a self-tapping screw. A pair of grips can then be used to pull out the oil seal, by pulling on the screw **(see illustrations)**. If difficulty is

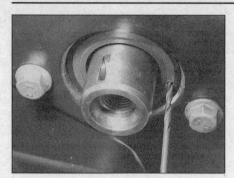

7.3a Drill a small hole . . .

7.3b . . . and use a screw and pliers to pull out the seal

experienced, insert two screws diagonally opposite each other.

4 Wipe clean the oil seal seating in the cylinder head, then dip the new seal in fresh engine oil and locate it over the camshaft with its closed side facing outwards. Make sure that the oil seal lip is not damaged as it is located on the camshaft.

5 Using a tube of suitable diameter, drive the oil seal squarely into the housing to the previously noted depth. A block of wood cut to pass over the end of the camshaft may be used instead.

6 Refit the camshaft sprocket as described in Section 6.

Flywheel end oil seal

7 No oil seal is fitted to the flywheel end of the camshaft. The sealing is provided by a gasket between the cylinder head and the brake vacuum pump housing and on certain models by an O-ring fitted between the pump and the housing. The gasket and the O-ring, where applicable, can be renewed after unbolting the pump from the cylinder head (see Chapter 9).

8 Camshaft and followers - removal, inspection and refitting

Note: *A new camshaft timing belt end oil seal should be fitted and a new cylinder head cover gasket may be required on refitting. Suitable sealant will be required for the camshaft bearing caps and thread-locking compound for the bearing cap bolts.*

Removal

1 Remove the camshaft sprocket as described in Section 6.

2 Remove the timing belt tensioner as described in Section 6 **(see illustration)**.

3 Unscrew the two bolts securing the timing belt upper inner cover to the cylinder head **(see illustration)**.

4 Unscrew the lower bolt(s) securing the timing belt upper inner cover to the cylinder block.

5 Remove the timing belt idler pulley securing bolt which also passes through the timing belt inner cover.

6 Manipulate the timing belt inner cover from the camshaft end and, where possible, withdraw the cover from the engine.

7 Remove the brake vacuum pump as described in Chapter 9.

8 Where necessary for improved access, unclip any hoses which are routed across the top of the cylinder head cover and move them to one side out of the way. If any fuel lines are disconnected, cover the open unions to prevent dirt ingress.

9 Unscrew the cylinder head cover bolts and withdraw the cover. Recover the gasket.

10 Using a dial gauge, measure the camshaft endfloat and compare with the value given in the Specifications **(see illustration)**. This will give an indication of the amount of wear present on the thrust surfaces.

11 If the original camshaft is to be refitted, it is advisable to measure the valve clearances at this stage, as described in Section 4, so that any shims required can be obtained before the camshaft is refitted.

12 Check the camshaft bearing caps for identification marks and if none are present, make identifying marks so that they can be refitted in their original positions and the same way round. Number the caps from the flywheel end of the engine.

13 Progressively slacken the bearing cap bolts and studs until the valve spring pressure is relieved. Remove the bolts and studs (noting their locations to ensure correct refitting) and the bearing caps themselves. Note that No 1 bearing cap is secured by two studs and two additional bolts.

14 Lift out the camshaft with the oil seal **(see illustration)**.

15 Remove the followers, keeping each with its shim **(see illustration)**. Place them in a compartment box, or on a sheet of card

2D

8.2 Withdraw the timing belt tensioner

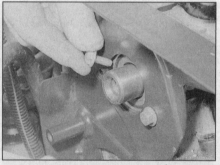

8.3 Remove the bolts securing the timing belt upper inner cover to the cylinder head

8.10 Measuring camshaft endfloat

8.14 Lifting out the camshaft

8.15 Lifting out a cam follower

marked into eight sections, so that they may be refitted to their original locations. Write down the shim thicknesses - they will be needed later if any of the valve clearances are incorrect. The shim thickness is usually etched on the bottom face of the shim, but it is prudent to use a micrometer to measure the true thickness of any shim removed, as it may have been reduced by wear.

Inspection

16 Examine the camshaft bearing surfaces and cam lobes for wear ridges, pitting or scoring. Renew the camshaft if evident.

17 Renew as a matter of course the oil seal at the timing belt end of the camshaft. Lubricate the lips of the new seal before fitting and store the camshaft so that its weight is not resting on the seal.

18 Examine the camshaft bearing surfaces in the cylinder head and bearing caps. Deep scoring or other damage means that the cylinder head must be renewed.

19 Inspect the followers and shims for scoring, pitting and wear ridges. Renew as necessary.

Refitting

20 Ensure that the pistons are positioned halfway down their bores, as described for sprocket removal in Section 6.

21 Oil the followers and fit them to the bores from which they were removed. Fit the correct shim, numbered side downwards, to each follower.

22 Oil the camshaft bearings. Place the camshaft with its oil seal onto the cylinder head. The oil seal must be positioned so that it is flush with the cylinder head face.

23 Apply sealant (Rhodorseal 5661, available from Renault dealers) to the cylinder head mating faces of the camshaft right- and left-hand bearing caps (Nos 1 and 5).

24 Refit the camshaft bearing caps to their original locations, ensuring that the right-hand oil seal is correctly located in the bearing cap.

25 Apply a few drops of thread-locking compound to the threads of the bearing cap bolts and studs. Fit the bolts and studs and tighten them progressively to the specified torque.

26 If a new camshaft has been fitted, measure the endfloat using a dial gauge and check that it is within the specified limits.

27 Refit the brake vacuum pump with reference to Chapter 9.

28 Refit the timing belt upper inner cover, then refit and tighten the bolts securing it to the cylinder block and to the head.

29 Refit and tighten the bolt securing the timing belt idler pulley assembly.

30 Refit the timing belt tensioner, ensuring that the peg on the cylinder block engages with the hole in the tensioner bracket.

31 Refit the camshaft sprocket as described in Section 6.

32 Check the valve clearances as described in Section 4 and take any corrective action necessary.

33 Refit the cylinder head cover, using a new gasket where necessary - tighten the cover retaining nuts or bolts evenly to the specified torque wrench setting.

34 Refit/reconnect any hoses which were moved for access. If fuel lines were disconnected, reconnect them, then prime and bleed the fuel system as described in Chapter 4B.

35 Reconnect the battery negative terminal.

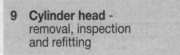

9 Cylinder head - removal, inspection and refitting

Note: *A new cylinder head gasket and cylinder head bolts must be fitted and a new cylinder head cover gasket may be required on refitting - see text.*

Removal

1 The following procedure describes removal and refitting of the cylinder head complete with manifolds and the fuel injection pump.

2 Disconnect the battery negative terminal (refer to *Disconnecting the battery* in the Reference Section of this manual). Unscrew the retaining nuts and withdraw the engine sound-insulating cover.

3 Drain the cooling system as described in Chapter 1B.

4 Remove the auxiliary drivebelt as described in Chapter 1B.

5 On models with air conditioning, unbolt the auxiliary drivebelt tensioner mounting plate (see Chapter 1B), then unscrew the associated alternator/fuel injection pump mounting bolt.

6 Unbolt the earth strap from the rear of the engine.

7 Disconnect the two fuel hoses from the top of the fuel filter assembly. The unions are equipped with quick-release fittings which are intended to be uncoupled using the Renault tool Mot. 1311-06 - this is a small forked implement which is passed between the two outer 'spokes' of the fitting and pressed to disengage the retaining claws. The hose can then be pulled off the union. If the tool is not available, the very careful use of two small electrical screwdrivers should serve to release

9.16 Unbolt the thermostat housing and move it to one side

the union. To stop diesel fuel from spilling, cover the open ends of the hoses.

8 Release the disconnected fuel hoses from any support clips and position them clear of the cylinder head.

9 Disconnect the air trunking running from the air cleaner to the inlet manifold, or turbocharger, as applicable and remove the trunking (note that, where applicable, the breather hoses which connect to the trunking will also have to be disconnected).

10 Disconnect the air trunking running from the intercooler to the turbocharger and remove the trunking.

11 Remove the timing belt as described in Section 5 and the timing belt tensioner as described in Section 6.

12 The engine must now be supported from below so that the engine hoist or lifting beam used for timing belt removal can be removed for access to the top of the engine. If possible, obtain Renault special tool Mot.1367, or fabricate a home-made alternative out of square-section steel tube as shown in Chapter 2B, Section 6.

13 Unbolt the hose bracket from the front of the fuel injection pump mounting bracket and move the hoses and bracket clear of the pump.

14 Disconnect the breather hose(s) from the crankcase oil separator(s) and where applicable, disconnect the hose from the boost pressure corrector on the injection pump. Similarly, disconnect the corresponding ends of the hoses from the manifold.

15 Unclip the hose bracket from the engine front lifting bracket, unbolt the remaining hose bracket from the brake vacuum pump and remove the hose assembly from the engine.

16 Unbolt the thermostat housing from the cylinder head and move it to one side, leaving the hoses and sensor wiring connected **(see illustration)**.

17 Disconnect the coolant hose from the left-hand rear corner of the cylinder head and move the hose clear.

18 Disconnect the vacuum hose from the brake vacuum pump.

19 Disconnect all relevant wiring from the fuel injection pump by disconnecting the wiring connectors at the brackets on the pump. Label all connections to aid correct refitting.

20 Disconnect the electrical feed wires from the relevant glow plugs.

21 Disconnect all relevant pipes and hoses from the manifolds and the turbocharger, with reference to the relevant Section(s) of Chapter 4B. Label all pipes and hoses to aid correct refitting.

22 Where applicable, unbolt any hose brackets from the manifolds and surrounding area and move the hoses to one side.

23 Remove the two bolts securing the turbocharger inlet elbow to the bracket on the gearbox. Remove the nut and bolt securing the bracing bracket to the turbocharger and the inlet elbow and remove the elbow.

24 Remove the bolts securing the timing belt upper inner cover to the cylinder block.

25 Remove the timing belt idler pulley securing bolt which also passes through the timing belt inner cover.

26 Remove the exhaust front section as described in Chapter 4B.

27 Unscrew the union nut securing the turbocharger oil feed pipe to the union on the cylinder block and remove the pipe/hose assembly.

28 Remove the bolts securing the turbocharger support bracket to the turbocharger and the engine and remove the support bracket.

29 If not already done, remove the timing pin from the cylinder block and turn the crankshaft anti-clockwise (viewed from the timing belt end of the engine) by a quarter-turn to position all four pistons halfway down their bores.

30 Working in the **reverse** of the sequence shown in illustration 9.49, progressively slacken the cylinder head bolts by half a turn at a time until all bolts can be unscrewed by hand and removed. Note that new bolts must be used for refitting.

31 The cylinder head assembly complete with ancillaries is heavy and it is advisable to attach a hoist and suitable lifting tackle to the lifting brackets on the cylinder head to lift it from the engine.

32 Lift the cylinder head (complete with manifolds, injection pump and timing belt upper inner cover) upwards and off the cylinder block. If it is stuck, tap it upwards using a hammer and block of wood (taking care not to damage the fuel injection pump). **Do not** try to turn the cylinder head (it is located by two dowels), nor attempt to prise it free using a screwdriver inserted between the block and head faces. If the locating dowels are a loose fit, remove them and store them with the head for safe-keeping.

33 If desired, the manifolds, turbocharger and fuel injection pump can be removed from the cylinder head with reference to the relevant Sections of Chapter 4B.

Inspection

34 The mating faces of the cylinder head and block must be perfectly clean before refitting the head. Use a scraper to remove all traces of gasket and carbon and also clean the tops of the pistons. Take particular care with the aluminium cylinder head, as the soft metal is damaged easily. Also, make sure that debris is not allowed to enter the oil and water channels - this is particularly important for the oil circuit, as carbon could block the oil supply to the camshaft or crankshaft bearings. Using adhesive tape and paper, seal the water, oil and bolt holes in the cylinder block. Clean the piston crowns in the same way.

 HAYNES HiNT *To prevent carbon entering the gap between the pistons and bores, smear a little grease in the gap. After*

cleaning the piston, rotate the crankshaft so that the piston moves down the bore, then wipe out the grease and carbon with a cloth rag

35 Check the block and head for nicks, deep scratches and other damage. If slight, they may be removed carefully with a file. More serious damage may be repaired by machining, but this is a specialist job.

36 If warpage of the cylinder head is suspected, use a straight-edge to check it for distortion. Refer to Chapter 2H if necessary.

37 Clean out the cylinder head bolt holes in the block using a pipe cleaner, or a rag and screwdriver. Make sure that all oil is removed, otherwise there is a possibility of the block being cracked by hydraulic pressure when the bolts are tightened.

38 Examine the cylinder head bolt threads in the cylinder block for damage - if necessary, use the correct-size tap to chase out the threads in the block. The cylinder head bolts must be discarded and renewed, regardless of their apparent condition.

Gasket selection

39 Turn the crankshaft to bring piston Nos 1 and 4 to just below the TDC position (just below the top face of the cylinder block). Position a dial test indicator (DTI) on the cylinder block and zero it on the block face. Transfer the probe to the centre of No 1 piston, then slowly turn the crankshaft back and forth past TDC, noting the highest reading produced on the indicator. Record this reading.

40 Repeat this measurement procedure on No 4 piston, then turn the crankshaft half a turn (180°) and repeat the procedure on Nos 2 and 3 pistons **(see illustration)**. Ensure that all measurements are taken along the longitudinal centreline of the crankshaft (this will eliminate errors due to piston slant).

41 If a dial test indicator is not available, piston protrusion may be measured using a straight-edge and feeler gauges or vernier calipers. However, these methods are inevitably less accurate and cannot therefore be recommended.

42 Ascertain the greatest piston protrusion measurement and use this to determine the

9.40 Measuring piston protrusion

appropriate thickness cylinder head gasket from the following table. The identification holes are located at the front corner of the gasket, at the flywheel end **(see illustrations)**. **Note:** *The gasket thickness identification holes are located in an area 25 mm from the flywheel end of the gasket. Do not take into account any other holes outside this area.*

Piston protrusion	Gasket identification
Up to 0.868 mm	*2 holes*
0.868 to 1.000 mm	*1 hole*
More than 1.000 mm	*3 holes*

Cylinder head bolts

43 The manufacturer recommends that the cylinder head bolts are renewed as a matter of course whenever they are disturbed, in view of the severe stresses to which they are subjected.

Refitting

44 Where applicable, refit the manifolds, turbocharger and fuel injection pump to the cylinder head, with reference to the relevant Sections of Chapter 4B.

45 Turn the crankshaft clockwise (viewed from the timing belt end) until Nos 1 and 4 pistons pass bottom dead centre (BDC) and begin to rise, then position them halfway up their bores (this is to prevent the possibility of piston-to-valve contact). Nos 2 and 3 pistons will also be at their midway positions, but descending their bores. Do not turn the crankshaft again until the timing belt is to be refitted.

2D

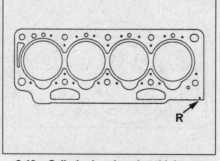

9.42a Cylinder head gasket thickness marking location (R)

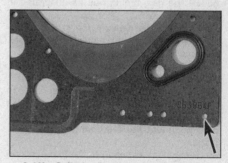

9.42b Cylinder head gasket thickness marking - '1 hole' type shown (ignore remaining holes - see text)

46 Ensure that the cylinder head locating dowels are fitted to the cylinder block, then fit the correct gasket the right way round on the cylinder block with the identification mark(s) at the front corner of the engine at the flywheel end **(see illustration)**.

47 Lower the cylinder head onto the block. Ensure that the timing belt upper inner cover engages correctly with the lower inner cover on the cylinder block. Where applicable, disconnect the lifting tackle and hoist.

48 Lightly oil the new cylinder head bolts, both on their threads and under their heads. Allow excess oil to drain off then insert the bolts, with their washers, and tighten them finger-tight.

49 Tighten the cylinder head bolts to the specified torques in the sequence shown and in the stages given in the Specifications at the beginning of this Chapter **(see illustration)**. The initial stages pre-compress the gasket and the remaining stages are the main tightening procedure. When angle-tightening the bolts, it is recommended that an angle-tightening gauge is used to ensure accuracy. Note that provided the bolts are tightened exactly as specified, there will be no need to retighten them once the engine has been started and run after reassembly.

⚠ *Warning: The final tightening stages involve very high forces. Ensure that the tools used are in good condition. If the engine has been removed from the vehicle, it is recommended that the final tightening stages are carried out with the engine refitted to the vehicle (it may be necessary to remove the engine right-hand mounting upper bracket for access to one of the bolts with the engine in the vehicle)*

50 Refit the turbocharger support bracket and tighten the securing bolts.

51 Refit the turbocharger oil feed pipe/hose assembly and tighten the union to the cylinder block.

52 Refit the exhaust front section with reference to Chapter 4B.

53 Refit the timing belt idler pulley securing bolt.

54 Refit the bolts securing the timing belt upper inner cover to the cylinder block, then refit the timing belt tensioner as described in Section 6.

55 Fit the new timing belt as described in Section 5.

56 Examine the sealing ring in the turbocharger inlet elbow and renew it if necessary. Refit the elbow and the bracing bracket.

57 Refit any hose brackets to the manifolds, as noted before removal.

58 Reconnect all relevant pipes and hoses to the manifolds and the turbocharger where applicable, as noted before removal.

59 Reconnect the feed wires to the glow plugs.

60 Reconnect all wiring to the fuel injection pump.

61 Reconnect the engine earth lead.

62 Reconnect the coolant hose to the

cylinder head and the brake vacuum hose to the vacuum pump.

63 Reconnect the air trunking between the air cleaner, inlet manifold, turbocharger and intercooler, as applicable. Ensure that any breather hoses are correctly reconnected.

64 Examine the sealing ring between the thermostat housing and the cylinder head and renew it if necessary. Refit the thermostat housing to the cylinder head.

65 Reconnect the crankcase breather hose(s) and the boost pressure corrector hose, ensuring that the connections are securely made. Refit the brackets to the engine lifting bracket and the brake vacuum pump.

66 Refit the hose bracket to the fuel injection pump mounting bracket.

67 Reconnect the fuel supply and return hoses to the fuel filter.

68 Refit the auxiliary drivebelt tensioner and bracket, followed by the drivebelt (refer to Chapter 1B if necessary).

69 Refill and bleed the cooling system as described in Chapter 1B.

70 Reconnect the battery negative terminal.

71 Prime and bleed the fuel system as described in Chapter 4B.

72 Follow the procedure described in Chapter 4B (priming the turbocharger oil circuit) before starting the engine.

73 Refit the engine sound-insulating cover.

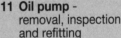

9.46 Cylinder head locating dowel positions (A)

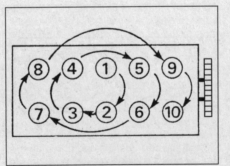

9.49 Cylinder head bolt tightening sequence

---

10 Sump - removal and refitting

Removal

1 Apply the handbrake, then jack up the front of the car and support it on axle stands (see *Jacking and vehicle support*). Undo the retaining screws and remove the plastic undercover from beneath the engine/transmission.

2 Drain the engine oil as described in Chapter 1B, then refit and tighten the drain plug.

3 Unscrew the bolts securing the left-hand end of the sump to the transmission bellhousing flange.

4 Unscrew the bolts securing the sump to the cylinder block. Tap the sump with a hide or plastic mallet to break the seal, then remove the sump along with its gasket. discard the gasket, a new one must be used on refitting.

Refitting

5 Remove all traces of dirt and oil from the mating surfaces of the sump and cylinder block.

6 Apply a bead of Rhodorseal 5661 sealant (available from Renault dealers) to the join between the crankshaft front oil seal housing and cylinder block, and to the join between the rear main bearing cap and cylinder block.

7 Locate the new gasket on the top of the sump and lift the sump into position.

8 Insert the bolts and initially tighten them all to the Stage 1 torque setting given in the Specifications. If the engine is in the car, ensure that the left-hand end of the sump is in contact with the transmission bellhousing flange. If the engine is removed from the car, use a straight-edge to maintain the alignment between the left-hand end of the sump and cylinder block.

9 Progressively tighten the bolts to the Stage 2 torque setting in an anti-clockwise spiral pattern starting at the centre and working outwards.

10 Refit the undercover and lower the vehicle to the ground.

11 Fill the engine with fresh oil, with reference to Chapter 1B.

11 Oil pump - removal, inspection and refitting

Removal

1 To remove the oil pump alone, first remove the sump, referring to Section 10.

2 Unscrew the oil pump mounting bolts and the additional bolt(s) securing the anti-emulsion plate to the crankcase.

3 Withdraw the oil pump slightly and remove the anti-emulsion plate. Tilt the pump to disengage its sprocket from the drive chain

11.11a Measuring the oil pump gear-to-body clearance

11.11b Measuring the oil pump gear endfloat

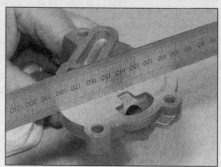

11.11c Checking the flatness of the oil pump cover

and lift away the pump. If the locating dowels are displaced, refit them in their locations.

4 To remove the oil pump complete with its drive chain and sprockets, first remove the sump (Section 10), then unbolt the crankshaft timing belt end oil seal housing, as described in Section 12. Note the presence of the chain guide block and of its two locating dowels.

5 Unscrew the bolts securing the sprocket to the oil pump hub. Use a screwdriver through one of the holes in the sprocket to hold it stationary.

6 Slide the drive sprocket from the crankshaft and the driven sprocket from the oil pump. Withdraw both sprockets and the chain. Note that the drive sprocket is not keyed to the crankshaft, but relies on the pulley bolt being tightened correctly to clamp the sprocket. It is most important that the pulley bolt is correctly tightened otherwise there is the possibility of the oil pump not functioning.

7 Unbolt the oil pump as described in paragraph 2 above.

Inspection

8 Unscrew the retaining bolts and lift off the pump cover. Withdraw the idler gear and the drivegear/shaft. Mark the idler gear before removal, so that it can be refitted in its original position.

9 Extract the retaining clip and remove the oil pressure relief valve spring retainer, spring, spring seat and plunger.

10 Clean the components and carefully examine the gears, pump body and relief valve plunger for any signs of scoring or wear. Renew the complete pump assembly if excessive wear is evident (no spare parts are available).

11 If the components appear serviceable, measure the clearance between the pump body and the gears using feeler gauges. Also measure the gear endfloat and check the flatness of the end cover **(see illustrations)**. If the clearances exceed the specified tolerances, the pump must be renewed. There should be no discernible wear or distortion of the end cover.

12 If the pump is satisfactory, reassemble the components in the reverse order of removal. Fill the pump with oil, then refit the cover and tighten the bolts securely. Prime the oil pump

by filling it with clean engine oil whilst rotating the driveshaft.

Refitting

13 Wipe clean the oil pump and cylinder block mating surfaces.

14 Check that the two locating dowels are fitted in the cylinder block, then position the oil pump on them and insert the two mounting bolts. Tighten the bolts securely.

15 Engage the sprockets on the chain (if removed), then refit both sprockets and the chain as an assembly. Slide the drive sprocket fully onto the crankshaft and locate the driven sprocket on the oil pump hub.

16 Align the holes, then insert the sprocket bolts and tighten them securely while holding the sprocket stationary with a screwdriver.

17 Refit the anti-emulsion plate and secure with the retaining bolt(s).

18 Refit the oil seal housing as described in Section 12 - do not forget the chain guide block and its two locating dowels - and the sump (refer to Section 10).

---

12 Crankshaft oil seals - renewal

Timing belt end oil seal

1 Remove the crankshaft sprocket, as described in Section 6.

2 Note the fitted position of the old seal, then prise it out of the oil seal housing using a screwdriver or suitable hooked instrument. An alternative method of removing the oil seal is to drill carefully two small holes opposite each other in the oil seal and insert self-tapping screws, then pull on the screws with grips. Take care not to damage the surface of the crankshaft or spacer or the seal housing. **Note:** *On some models it may be necessary to remove the timing belt lower inner cover to allow the seal to be withdrawn. If this is the case, remove the idler sprocket and idler pulley (see Section 6) then unbolt the cover.*

3 Clean the seal housing and polish off any burrs or raised edges which may have caused the seal to fail in the first place. Inspect the seal rubbing surface on the crankshaft. If it is

grooved or rough in the area where the old seal was fitted, the new seal should be fitted slightly less deeply, so that it rubs on an unworn part of the crankshaft surface.

4 Wipe clean the oil seal seating, then dip the new seal in fresh engine oil and locate it over the crankshaft with its closed side facing outwards. Make sure that the oil seal lip is not damaged as it is located on the crankshaft.

5 Using a tube of suitable diameter, drive the oil seal squarely into the housing to the previously noted position - take great care not to damage the seal lips during fitting. Note that if the surface of the shaft was noted to be badly scored, press the new seal slightly further into its housing so that its lip is running on an unmarked area of the shaft.

6 Where necessary, refit the timing belt lower inner cover and install the idler pulley and idler sprocket as described in Section 6. Refit the crankshaft sprocket as described in Section 6 and fit the new timing belt as described in Section 5.

Timing belt end oil seal housing

7 Remove the timing belt as described in Section 5 and the crankshaft and idler sprockets and the idler pulley with reference to Section 6. Remove the Woodruff key from the crankshaft keyway, then unbolt the timing belt lower inner cover from the cylinder block.

8 Unscrew the bolts securing the sump to the oil seal housing.

9 Unscrew the retaining bolts and carefully withdraw the oil seal housing, noting the locating dowels around its two lower bolt holes. If it is stuck in place a leverage point is provided on its upper edge (near the timing belt idler pulley) to allow a screwdriver or similar to be used gently to prise the housing away from the cylinder block without risking damage to the delicate mating surfaces of either. If the sump gasket is damaged, the sump will have to be removed to renew it. Note the presence of the oil pump drive chain guide block and of its two locating dowels - check that the guide block is fit for further use and renew it if there is any doubt about its condition.

10 The oil seal should be renewed whenever the housing is removed. Note the fitted position of the old seal, then prise it out with a screwdriver and wipe clean the seating.

2D

Smear the outer perimeter of the new seal with fresh engine oil and locate it squarely on the housing with its closed side facing outwards. Place the housing on a block of wood, then use a socket or metal tube to drive in the oil seal.

11 On refitting, clean all traces of sealant from the housing, sump and block mating faces. Check that the chain guide block is correctly fitted and that the housing's locating dowels are in place.

12 Apply a 0.6 to 1.0 mm diameter bead of Rhodorseal 5661 (available from Renault dealers) to the housing's gasket surfaces, around the inner edges of the bolt holes and apply a smear of sealant to the threads of the two bolts (nearest the oil seal) which project inside the cylinder block. Do **NOT** allow sealant to foul the oil gallery at the upper end of the housing. Refit the housing to the cylinder block and sump, tightening the bolts securely and evenly.

13 Refit the Woodruff key to the crankshaft keyway, then refit the timing belt lower inner cover to the cylinder block, tightening securely its retaining bolts.

14 Refit the crankshaft and idler sprockets and the idler pulley and fit the new timing belt with reference to Sections 6 and 5.

Flywheel end oil seal

15 Remove the flywheel as described in Section 13.

16 Prise out the old oil seal using a small screwdriver, taking care not to damage the surface of the crankshaft. Alternatively, the oil seal can be removed as described in paragraph 2.

17 Inspect the seal rubbing surface on the crankshaft. If it is grooved or rough in the area where the old seal was fitted, the new seal should be fitted slightly less deeply, so that it rubs on an unworn part of the surface.

18 Wipe clean the oil seal seating, then dip the new seal in fresh engine oil. Locate it over the crankshaft, making sure its sealing lip is facing inwards. Make sure that the oil seal lip is not damaged as it is located on the crankshaft.

19 Using a metal tube, drive the oil seal squarely into the bore until flush. A block of wood cut to pass over the end of the crankshaft may be used instead.

20 Refit the flywheel with reference to Section 13.

13 Flywheel - removal, inspection and refitting

Note: *New flywheel retaining bolts will be required on refitting.*

Removal

1 Remove the transmission as described in Chapter 7A, then remove the clutch assembly as described in Chapter 6.

2 Prevent the flywheel from turning by locking the ring gear teeth with a screwdriver. Alternatively a home-made tool similar to that shown in Chapter 2A, Section 5 can be used. Make alignment marks between the flywheel and crankshaft using paint or a suitable marker pen.

3 Slacken and remove the flywheel retaining bolts and remove the flywheel. Do not drop it, as it is very heavy. If the locating dowel (where fitted) is a loose fit in the crankshaft end, remove and store it with the flywheel for safe-keeping. Discard the bolts as they should be renewed whenever they are disturbed.

Inspection

4 Examine the flywheel for scoring of the clutch face, and for wear or chipping of the ring gear teeth. If the clutch face is scored, the flywheel may be surface-ground, but renewal is preferable. Seek the advice of a Renault dealer or engine reconditioning specialist to see if machining is possible. If the ring gear is worn or damaged, the flywheel must be renewed, as it is not possible to renew the ring gear separately.

Refitting

5 Clean the mating surfaces of the flywheel and crankshaft.

6 Ensure that the locating dowel is in position (where fitted) and offer up the flywheel, locating it on the dowel, and fit the new retaining bolts. If the original is being refitted align the marks made prior to removal.

7 Lock the flywheel using the method employed on dismantling, and tighten the retaining bolts to the specified torque.

8 Refit the clutch as described in Chapter 6.

9 Remove the locking tool, and refit the transmission as described in Chapter 7A.

14 Engine/transmission mountings - renewal

Refer to Chapter 2B, Section 12.

Chapter 2 Part E:
2.2 litre diesel engine in-car repair procedures

Contents

Degrees of difficulty

Easy, suitable for novice with little experience	**Fairly easy,** suitable for beginner with some experience	**Fairly difficult,** suitable for competent DIY mechanic	**Difficult,** suitable for experienced DIY mechanic	**Very difficult,** suitable for expert DIY or professional

2E

Specifications

General

Type	Four-cylinder, in-line, single overhead camshaft, 12-valve
Designation:	
Non-turbo engines (2.2 D models):	
Early models	G8T 706, G8T 790
Later models	G8T 752, G8T 794
Turbo engines (2.2 Dt models)	G8T 760 turbo
Bore	87.0 mm
Stroke	92.0 mm
Capacity	2188 cc
Compression ratio:	
G8T	23.0:1
G8T turbo	22.0:1
Firing order	1-3-4-2 (No 1 cylinder at flywheel end of engine)
Direction of crankshaft rotation	Clockwise, viewed from timing belt end

Camshaft

Drive	Toothed belt
Number of bearings	5
Camshaft endfloat	0.04 to 0.13 mm

Lubrication system

Minimum oil pressure at 80°C:	
At 1000 rpm	1.6 bars
At 3000 rpm	4.0 bars

Torque wrench settings

	Nm	lbf ft
Auxiliary drivebelt idler pulley nut	40	30
Auxiliary drivebelt tensioner pulley bolts	55	41
Camshaft bearing cap bolts	21	15
Camshaft cover nuts and bolts	9	7
Camshaft timing belt sprocket bolt:		
Stage 1	20	15
Stage 2	Angle-tighten through 105°	
Camshaft vacuum pump sprocket - G8T 706 and 790 engines	80	59
Connecting rod (big-end) cap bolts:		
Stage 1	20	15
Stage 2	Angle-tighten through 70°	
Crankshaft front oil seal housing bolts	9	7
Crankshaft pulley bolt:		
Stage 1	25	18
Stage 2	Angle-tighten through 64°	
Cylinder block main bearing casting bolts:		
Large (12 mm) inner bolts:		
Stage 1	20	15
Stage 2	Angle-tighten through 140°	
Smaller (8 mm) outer bolts	21	15
Cylinder head bolts (see illustration 10.23a on page 2E•13)*:		
Stage 1	20	15
Stage 2:		
Bolts number 1, 5, 9, 13 and 17 in tightening sequence	Angle-tighten a further 215°	
Bolts number 2, 6, 10, 14 and 18	Angle-tighten a further 240°	
Bolts number 3, 7, 11 and 15	Angle-tighten a further 160°	
Bolts number 4, 8, 12 and 16	Angle-tighten a further 246°	
Wait for 3 minutes then in the specified order:		
Stage 3	20	15
Stage 4:		
Bolts number 1, 5, 9, 13 and 17 in tightening sequence	Angle-tighten a further 296°	
Bolts number 2, 6, 10, 14 and 18	Angle-tighten a further 301°	
Bolts number 3, 7, 11 and 15	Angle-tighten a further 243°	
Bolts number 4, 8, 12 and 16	Angle-tighten a further 322°	
Engine/transmission mountings:		
Right-hand mounting:		
Engine bracket bolts	45	33
Mounting bracket-to-engine bracket bolts	55	41
Mounting bracket-to-rubber mounting nut	35	26
Rubber mounting-to-body bolts	55	41
Left-hand mounting:		
Mounting bracket-to-transmission bolts	60	44
Mounting stud lower nut	115	85
Mounting stud upper nut	65	48
Rubber mounting retaining bolts	70	52
Rear mounting:		
Connecting link bolts	150	111
Mounting-to-cylinder block bolts	65	48
Flywheel bolts	60	44
Flywheel cover plate bolts	24	18
Oil hose union bolt - G8T 706 and 790 engines	20	15
Oil pump:		
Pump mounting bolts	22	16
Pump driven sprocket bolts	9	7
Roadwheel bolts	See Chapter 1A or 1B	
Sump bolts	9	7
Timing belt tensioner pulley nut	32	24

*Refer to the specific instructions contained in Section 10 when tightening the cylinder head bolts. New bolts must be used.

1 General information

How to use this Chapter

This Part of Chapter 2 is devoted to in-car repair procedures for the 2.2 litre diesel engine. Similar information covering the 1.9 litre diesel engines and the petrol engines will be found in Chapters 2A, 2B, 2C and 2D. All procedures concerning engine removal and refitting, and engine block/cylinder head overhaul for petrol and diesel engines can be found in Chapters 2F, 2G and 2H as applicable.

Most of the operations included in Chapter 2E are based on the assumption that the engine is still installed in the car. Therefore, if this information is being used during a complete engine overhaul, with the engine already removed, many of the steps included here will not apply.

Engine description

The 2.2 litre diesel engine is a four-cylinder overhead camshaft 12-valve design, mounted transversely at the front of the vehicle with the transmission bolted to the left-hand side **(see illustration)**. On early versions of the non-turbo engine (G8T 706 and 790) the coolant pump is driven by the main auxiliary drivebelt, and the brake servo vacuum pump is driven by a second auxiliary drivebelt via a sprocket on the left-hand (flywheel) end of the camshaft. On later versions (G8T 752 and 794) the coolant pump is driven by the timing belt and the brake servo vacuum pump is driven directly by the camshaft. Turbo engines are virtually identical to the later non-turbo engines apart from minor differences in the pistons and connecting rods.

On all engines, the crankshaft is supported in five shell-type main bearings. Thrust-washers are fitted to No 2 main bearing to control crankshaft endfloat.

The connecting rods are attached to the crankshaft by horizontally-split shell-type big-end bearings, and to the pistons by gudgeon pins. The gudgeon pins are a sliding fit in the connecting rods and are retained by circlips. The aluminium alloy pistons are of the slipper type, and are fitted with three piston rings - two compression rings and a scraper-type oil control ring.

The single overhead camshaft is mounted directly in the cylinder head, and is driven by the crankshaft via a toothed timing belt. The timing belt also drives the fuel injection pump and, on turbo and later non-turbo models, the coolant pump.

The camshaft operates the 12 valves, which are mounted vertically in the head, through followers situated directly underneath the camshaft. The opposite end of the each follower is in contact with a hydraulic tappet which automatically adjusts the valve clearance.

Engine lubrication is by pressure feed from a gear-type oil pump, the pump is chain driven off the timing belt end of the crankshaft. Engine oil is fed through an externally-mounted oil filter and oil cooler to the main oil gallery feeding the crankshaft and camshaft. The oil cooler helps keep the oil temperature constant under arduous operating conditions.

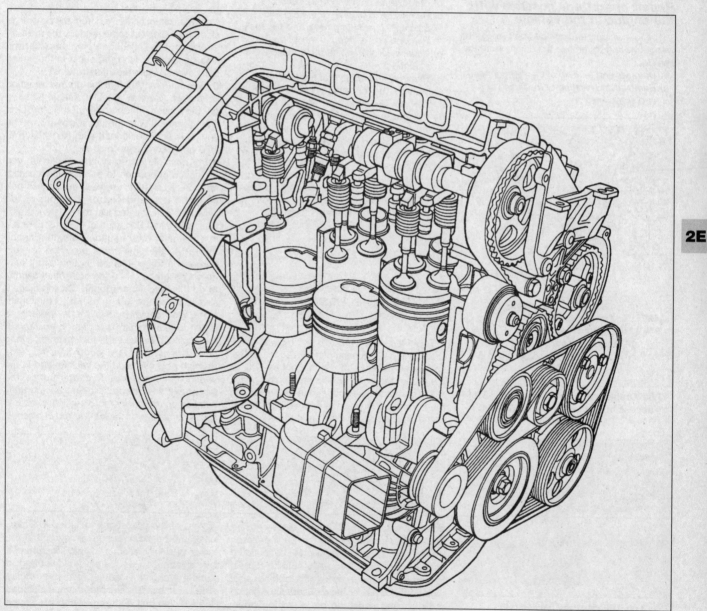

1.3 Cutaway view of G8T 706 non-turbo diesel engine

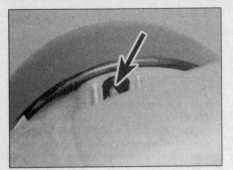

3.4a Number 1 cylinder is positioned at TDC on its compression stroke when the timing mark on the rear of the camshaft sprocket is aligned with the pointer on the camshaft cover (arrowed)

Repair operations possible with the engine in the vehicle

The following operations can be carried out without having to remove the engine from the vehicle:

a) *Removal and refitting of the cylinder head.*
b) *Removal and refitting of the timing belt and sprockets.*

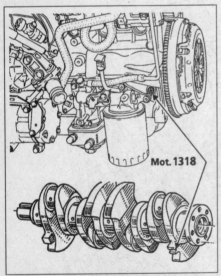

3.6a Crankshaft locking rod (Mot. 1318) access bolt location and crankshaft locating slot

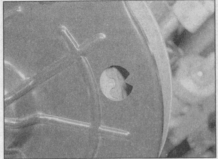

3.4b On some models there is also a TDC pointer on the injection pump sprocket cover

c) *Removal and refitting of the camshaft, followers and hydraulic tappets*
d) *Removal and refitting of the sump.*
e) *Removal and refitting of the big-end bearings, connecting rods, and pistons*.*
f) *Removal and refitting of the oil pump.*
g) *Renewal of the engine/transmission mountings.*
h) *Removal and refitting of the flywheel.*

* Although the operation marked with an asterisk can be carried out with the engine in the car after removal of the sump, it is better for the engine to be removed, in the interests of cleanliness and improved access. For this reason, the procedure is described in Chapter 2H.

2 Compression test - description and interpretation

Refer to Chapter 2D, Section 2.

3 Top Dead Centre (TDC) for No 1 piston - locating

1 Top dead centre (TDC) is the highest point in the cylinder that each piston reaches as the crankshaft turns. Each piston reaches TDC at the end of the compression stroke and again at the end of the exhaust stroke. However, for the purpose of timing the engine, TDC refers to the position of No 1 piston at the end of its compression stroke. On all engines in this Part of Chapter 2, No 1 piston (and cylinder) is at the flywheel end of the engine.

2 Disconnect the battery negative terminal (refer to *Disconnecting the battery* in the Reference Section of this manual). Apply the handbrake, then jack up the front of the car and support it on axle stands (see *Jacking and vehicle support*). Remove the right-hand roadwheel.

3 Remove the plastic cover from within the right-hand wheel arch, to gain access to the crankshaft pulley bolt.

4 The crankshaft must now be turned until the index mark on the rear of the camshaft sprocket is aligned with the timing mark cast into the aperture in the end of the camshaft cover. The crankshaft can be turned by using a spanner or socket on the pulley bolt. Note that the crankshaft must always be turned in a clockwise direction (viewed from the right-hand side of vehicle). On some models, the mark on the front of the injection pump sprocket will also be aligned with the pointer in the timing belt cover aperture **(see illustrations)**.

5 Turn the crankshaft in the normal direction of rotation (clockwise) whilst keeping an eye on the cover window. Align the sprocket timing mark(s) with the cover pointer(s). The engine is now positioned with No1 piston at TDC on its compression stroke.

6 For absolute accuracy, the crankshaft can be locked in position to prevent unnecessary rotation. To do this, unscrew the access bolt from the left-hand end of the front of the cylinder block, located just to the left of the oil filter, and insert Renault tool Mot. 1318, or a 7 mm diameter rod of suitable length. Engage the rod in the timing slot provided for this purpose in the crankshaft, noting that it may be necessary to rotate the crankshaft slightly to do this **(see illustrations)**. Once in place it should be impossible to turn the crankshaft. **Note:** *Do not attempt to rotate the engine whilst the crankshaft is locked in position. If the engine is to be left in this state for a long period of time, it is a good idea to place warning notices inside the vehicle, and in the engine compartment. This will reduce the possibility of the engine being accidentally cranked on the starter motor, which is likely to cause damage with the locking rod in place.*

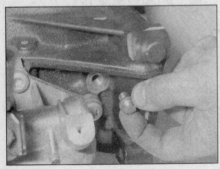

3.6b Unscrew the access bolt . . .

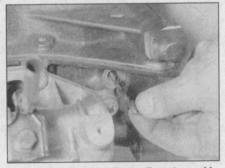

3.6c . . . and insert a 7 mm diameter rod in through the cylinder block . . .

3.6d . . . so that it engages with the timing slot in the crankshaft web (arrowed)

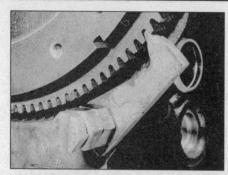

4.4 Use a fabricated tool to lock the flywheel ring gear and stop crankshaft rotation

4.8a Tighten the crankshaft pulley bolt to the specified Stage 1 torque setting . . .

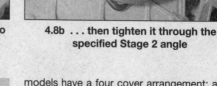

4.8b . . . then tighten it through the specified Stage 2 angle

4 Crankshaft pulley - removal and refitting

Note: *A new pulley retaining bolt will be required on refitting.*

Removal

1 Disconnect the battery negative terminal (refer to *Disconnecting the battery* in the Reference Section of this manual). Apply the handbrake, then jack up the front of the car and support it on axle stands (see *Jacking and vehicle support*). Remove the right-hand roadwheel.

2 Unbolt and remove the plastic undercover from the beneath the engine/transmission and the plastic cover from within the right-hand wheelarch.

3 Remove the auxiliary drivebelt as described in Chapter 1B.

4 Slacken the crankshaft pulley retaining bolt. To prevent crankshaft rotation whilst the retaining bolt is slackened, select top gear and have an assistant apply the brakes firmly. If this fails to prevent rotation, remove the lower cover plate and lock the flywheel ring gear, using an arrangement similar to that shown **(see illustration)**. *Do not* be tempted to use the crankshaft locking rod to prevent the crankshaft from rotating (see Section 3).

5 Remove the retaining bolt and pulley from the end of the crankshaft. Discard the bolt, a new one should be used on refitting.

Refitting

6 Remove all traces of locking compound from the crankshaft threads.

7 Clean the threads of the new crankshaft pulley retaining bolt and apply a few drops of locking compound (Renault recommend the use of Loctite Autoform).

8 Refit the pulley to the crankshaft and screw in the retaining bolt. Tighten the bolt first to the specified Stage 1 torque and then through the specified Stage 2 angle, using the method employed on removal to prevent rotation **(see illustrations)**.

9 Refit the auxiliary drivebelt as described in Chapter 1B.

5 Timing belt covers - removal and refitting

Note: *The timing belt cover retaining bolts must be renewed whenever they are disturbed.*

Removal

1 Depending on engine type, there are two possible timing belt cover arrangements. Non-turbo models fitted with G8T 706 and 790 engines have a three cover arrangement; a top cover, an injection pump sprocket cover and the main cover **(see illustration)**. All other models have a four cover arrangement; a top cover, and injection pump sprocket cover, the camshaft sprocket cover and the crankshaft sprocket cover.

2 Access to the timing belt covers is poor. To improve access it will be necessary to remove the mounting bracket from the engine mounting (see Section 15) and support the engine transmission with a jack/engine support bar. Also unbolt the fuel filter housing from its mounting bracket and position it clear of the cover.

Top cover

3 Undo the retaining nut then free the wiring loom from its retaining clips and position it clear of the timing belt covers.

2E

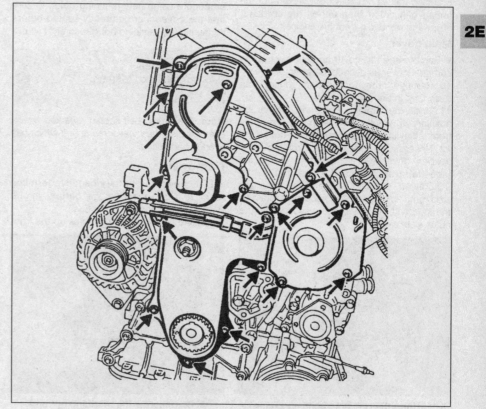

5.1 Timing belt cover bolt locations on G8T 706 and 790 engine models

5.4 Removing the timing belt top cover

5.6 Removing the timing belt injection pump sprocket cover

4 Undo the retaining screws and remove the cover from the engine **(see illustration)**.

Injection pump sprocket cover

5 Remove the top cover as described in paragraphs 3 and 4.
6 Unclip the wiring loom from the side of the timing belt cover then unbolt the sprocket cover and remove it from the engine **(see illustration)**.

Camshaft sprocket cover

7 Remove the top cover as described in paragraphs 3 and 4.
8 Unclip the wiring loom from the side of the timing belt cover then unbolt the sprocket cover and remove it from the engine.

Main cover

9 Remove the top cover and injection pump sprocket cover as described earlier.
10 Remove the crankshaft pulley as described in Section 4.
11 Undo the retaining bolts and remove the auxiliary drivebelt tensioner pulley assembly from the cylinder block **(see illustration)**.
12 Unscrew the retaining nut and remove the auxiliary drivebelt idler pulley from the engine **(see illustration)**. As the retaining nut is unscrewed, ensure that the pulley mounting stud remains in position; if necessary retaining the stud with an open-ended spanner as the nut is slackened.

13 Unscrew the retaining bolts, noting the correct fitted location of the wiring loom holder, and remove the main cover from the engine **(see illustration)**.

Crankshaft sprocket cover

14 Remove the top cover, injection pump sprocket cover and camshaft sprocket cover as described earlier.
15 Remove the cover as described in paragraphs 10 to 13.

Refitting

16 Refitting is a reverse of the removal procedure using new retaining bolts. Ensure that the cover(s) are correctly seated before tightening the retaining bolts securely.

---

6 Timing belt -
removal and refitting

Note: *The timing belt should renewed whenever it is disturbed; never refit a belt which has already been used.*

Removal

1 Disconnect the battery negative terminal (refer to *Disconnecting the battery* in the Reference Section of this manual).
2 Apply the handbrake, then jack up the front

of the car and support it on axle stands (see *Jacking and vehicle support*). Remove the right-hand front roadwheel.
3 Undo the retaining screws and remove the engine undercover and the front and rear protective covers from the right-hand wheelarch
4 Remove the auxiliary drivebelt as described in Chapter 1B. On models where the coolant pump is driven by the auxiliary drivebelt, unbolt the drivebelt pulley and remove it from the pump.
5 Position number 1 cylinder at TDC on its compression stroke and lock the crankshaft in position as described in Section 3.
6 Place a jack beneath the engine, with a block of wood on the jack head. Raise the jack until it is supporting the weight of the engine. Alternatively, attach and support bar to the engine and use the bar to support the weight of the engine/transmission.
7 Slacken and remove the retaining nut and bolts and remove the right-hand engine mounting bracket. Undo the three retaining bolts and remove the rubber mounting from the body.
8 Remove the crankshaft pulley as described in Section 4 then refit the pulley bolt to the crankshaft. As a precaution, when slackening the pulley retaining bolt, temporarily remove the locking rod from the crankshaft. Once the bolt is loose, slide the rod back into position.

5.11 Undo the retaining bolts and remove the auxiliary drivebelt tensioner

5.12 Unscrew the retaining nut and remove the auxiliary drivebelt idler pulley

5.13 Removing the timing belt main cover

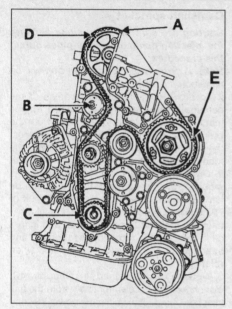

6.10 Timing belt sprocket timing mark locations with No 1 cylinder positioned at TDC on its compression stroke (G8T 706 engine shown)

A *Camshaft sprocket rear timing mark*
B *Timing belt tensioner pulley nut*
C *Crankshaft sprocket*
D *Camshaft sprocket front timing mark*
E *Injection pump sprocket timing mark*

9 Remove the timing belt covers as described in Section 5, noting that all the retaining bolts should be renewed on refitting.
10 Check the crankshaft, camshaft and injection pump sprocket timing marks are positioned as shown **(see illustration)**. The injection pump sprocket mark should be aligned with the mark on the pump mounting bracket and the crankshaft sprocket Woodruff key should be uppermost with the sprocket timing mark at the bottom. The mark on the **rear** of the camshaft sprocket should be aligned with the pointer in the camshaft cover aperture and the mark on the **front** of the sprocket should be aligned with the lug on the cylinder head.
11 Slacken the tensioner pulley retaining nut and, where necessary, slacken the locknut

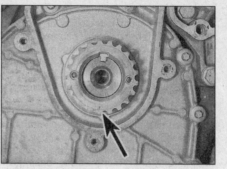

6.14a Ensure the crankshaft sprocket timing mark (arrowed) is at the bottom . . .

6.14c . . . and the injection pump sprocket mark aligned with the mark on the bracket

and unscrew the tensioner pulley adjuster bolt.
12 Slip the timing belt **off** the sprockets and remove it from the engine. If signs of oil contamination are found, trace the source of the oil leak and rectify it. Wash down the engine timing belt area and all related components, to remove all traces of oil. Check that the tensioner and idler pulley rotates freely, without any sign of roughness. If necessary, renew as described in Section 7.

Refitting

13 Clean the sprockets and tensioners, and wipe them dry. Do not apply excessive amounts of solvent to the tensioner wheels, otherwise the bearing lubricant may be contaminated. Also clean the front of the cylinder head and block.
14 Ensure that the crankshaft is at the TDC

6.14b . . . the camshaft sprocket marks (arrowed) are correctly positioned . . .

6.15a Ensure the timing belt arrows are pointing in the direction of normal rotation

position for No 1 cylinder and is locked in this position using the metal rod through the hole in the crankcase and that the sprocket timing marks are correctly positioned (see paragraph 10) **(see illustrations)**.
15 Offer up the new belt making sure the arrows marked on it are pointing in the direction of rotation. Starting with the crankshaft sprocket, align the mark on the **inside** of the new belt with the sprocket mark then route the belt around the idler pulley and over the injection pump and camshaft sprockets. Ensure that the marks on the outside of the timing belt are correctly aligned with both sprockets and slide the belt fully into position **(see illustrations)**.
16 With the timing marks correctly aligned, and the belt located around all the sprockets and pulleys, make sure the tensioner pulley is correctly engaged with the

2E

6.15b Align the belt inner mark with the crankshaft sprocket timing mark . . .

6.15c . . . and the second mark with the injection pump sprocket mark (arrowed) . . .

6.15d . . . and the third mark with the camshaft sprocket mark (arrowed)

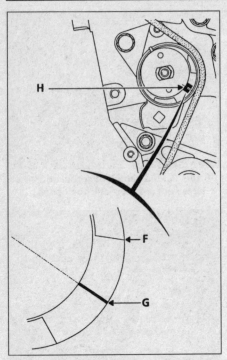

6.16a Timing belt tensioner pulley details

F *Backplate maximum tension mark*
  (used to preload the belt)
G *Backplate correct tension mark*
  (used to correctly set the belt tension)
H *Indicator arm*

upper peg then remove all slack from the timing belt by pivoting the tensioner into contact with the belt. Position the tensioner so that tensioner indicator arm contacts its backplate maximum tension stop lightly and tighten the pulley retaining nut to the specified torque. Do not force the tensioner pulley against the stop. On early models adjust the tensioner by levering between the tensioner and cylinder block lugs with a suitable bar, on later models screw in the adjuster bolt **(see illustrations)**.

17 Remove the crankshaft locking rod and, using a suitable socket and extension bar on the crankshaft sprocket bolt, rotate the crankshaft through three complete rotations in a clockwise direction (viewed from the right-

hand end of the engine). *Do not* at any time rotate the crankshaft anti-clockwise.

18 Hold the tensioner pulley in position and carefully slacken its retaining nut. Slowly release the tensioner pulley until its indicator arm is aligned with the reference mark on the backplate **(see illustration)**. Hold the tensioner pulley in position and tighten its retaining nut to the specified torque setting. On later models, tighten the adjuster bolt locknut securely.

19 Rotate the crankshaft through another complete rotation then refit the locking rod and check that all the sprocket timing marks are correctly position (see paragraph 10).

20 Remove the locking rod and refit the access plug to the front of the cylinder block.

21 Refit the timing belt covers as described in Section 5.

22 Refit the crankshaft pulley as described in Section 4.

23 Refit the rubber mounting to the body and tighten its retaining bolts to the specified torque. Install the mounting bracket and loosely tighten its mounting nut and bolts. Ensure that the bracket is positioned centrally in relation to the rubber mounting lug then tighten its retaining nut and bolts to their specified torque settings. Remove the jack/engine support bar (as applicable).

24 Refit the coolant pump pulley (where necessary) and refit auxiliary drivebelt as described in Chapter 1B.

25 Refit the undercover and wheelarch covers and fit the roadwheel.

26 Lower the vehicle to the ground and tighten the wheel bolts to the specified torque. Reconnect the battery.

---

7 Timing belt sprockets and tensioner - removal, inspection and refitting

Note: *A new timing belt must be used on refitting.*

Removal

1 Remove the timing belt as described in Section 6 noting that all the timing belt cover retaining bolts should be renewed on refitting.

Camshaft sprocket

Caution: Be careful not to allow dirt into the injection pump or injector pipes during this procedure.

Note: *A new camshaft sprocket bolt will be required on refitting.*

2 To provide clearance for removal of the camshaft sprocket, the right-hand engine mounting bracket must be released from the cylinder head. On G8T 706 and 790 engines, the fuel injection pump is also attached to the mounting bracket and must be removed with it. On all other engines the injection pump is mounted on a separate bracket and can be left in position. If working on the G8T 706 or 790 engines, proceed as follows. On all other engines, proceed to paragraph 6, and ignore all references to connections and attachments on the fuel injection pump when refitting.

3 Working as described in Chapter 4B, disconnect the accelerator cable from the fuel injection pump, then unclip the power steering fluid reservoir and position it clear of the pump. Unbolt the reservoir mounting bracket and remove it.

4 Wipe clean the pipe unions then slacken the union nut securing the injector pipes to the top of each injector and the four union nuts securing the pipes to the rear of the injection pump; as each pump union nut is slackened, retain the adapter with a suitable open-ended spanner to prevent it being unscrewed from the pump. With all the union nuts undone remove the injector pipe assembly from the engine and mop up and spilt fuel.

5 Undo the retaining bolts and remove the rear mounting bracket from the fuel injection pump.

6 Slacken and remove the retaining bolts securing the injection pump/engine mounting bracket to the cylinder head. Release the pump/bracket assembly and position it clear of the camshaft sprocket. Support the assembly to avoid placing strain on the fuel hoses and recover the locating dowels which are fitted between the bracket and head. If the bracket assembly is to be removed it will be necessary to disconnect the fast idle cable (models with a thermostatic fast idle valve) or the vacuum hose (models with a vacuum-operated fast idle system) from the pump.

7 Slacken the sprocket retaining bolt and remove. To prevent rotation as the bolt is slackened, a sprocket-holding tool will be required. In the absence of the special Renault tool, an acceptable substitute can be fabricated as follows. Use two lengths of steel strip (one long, the other short), and three nuts and bolts; one nut and bolt forms the pivot of a forked tool, with the remaining two nuts and bolts at the tips of the 'forks' to engage with the sprocket spokes as shown **(see illustration)**. Alternately, the sprocket can be retained using the old timing belt and a pair or grips.

6.16b On early models adjust the tensioner using a suitable lever in-between the tensioner and cylinder block lugs as shown

6.18 Back off the tensioner and align the indicator arm with the correct tensioner mark on the backplate (arrowed)

7.7 Retain the camshaft sprocket with a tool similar to that shown whilst slackening the retaining bolt

8 With the retaining bolt removed, slide off the sprocket. Examine the oil seal for signs of oil leakage and, if necessary, renew it as described in Section 8.

Injection pump sprocket

9 Loosen the sprocket retaining nut whilst prevent rotation by holding the sprocket hub with a large open-ended spanner. Alternately prevent rotation using the holding tool described in paragraph 7.

10 Attach a suitable puller to the injection pump sprocket hub and carefully free the hub from the pump shaft taper. The Renault puller is attached to the sprocket hub using three 8 mm bolts once the sprocket rim bolts have been removed; make alignment marks between the bolts and sprocket before unscrewing them **(see illustrations)**.

7.10a Using a three-legged puller to free the injection pump sprocket from its shaft

11 Once the sprocket is free remove the puller then unscrew the retaining nut and withdraw the sprocket. Remove the Woodruff key from the injection pump and store it with the sprocket for safe-keeping **(see illustrations)**.

Crankshaft sprocket

12 Slide the sprocket off from the end of the crankshaft **(see illustration)**. Examine the oil seal for signs of oil leakage and, if necessary, renew it as described in Section 14.

Tensioner pulley

13 Unscrew the retaining nut and remove the tensioner pulley assembly from the engine **(see illustration)**. If the tensioner stud requires renewal it will be necessary to unbolt the injection pump bracket from the cylinder block (see paragraphs 2 to 6).

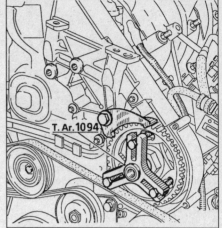

7.10b Renault puller (T. Ar. 1094) for removing injection pump sprocket

Idler pulley

14 Unscrew the retaining nut and remove the pulley **(see illustration)**. If necessary, unscrew the pulley stud and remove it from the engine.

Toothed idler pulley - G8T 706 and 790 engines

15 Unscrew the mounting stud and remove the pulley from the cylinder block **(see illustration)**.

Coolant pump pulley

16 Refer to Chapter 3.

2E

7.11a Remove the retaining nut . . .

7.11b . . . then slide off the sprocket taking care not to lose the Woodruff key (arrowed)

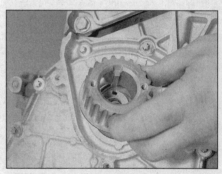

7.12 Removing the crankshaft sprocket

7.13 Removing the timing belt tensioner pulley

7.14 Unscrew the retaining nut and remove the idler pulley

7.15 On G8T 706 and 790 engines, unscrew the mounting stud and remove the toothed idler pulley

7.20a Tighten the camshaft sprocket retaining bolt first to the specified Stage 1 torque . . .

7.20b . . . and then through the specified Stage 2 angle

7.33 Refit the tensioner pulley making sure its backplate is correctly located on the peg (arrowed)

Inspection

17 Inspect the teeth of the sprockets for signs of nicks and damage. The teeth are not prone to wear, and should normally last the life of the engine.

18 Spin the tensioner and idler pulley by hand, and check for any roughness or tightness. Do not attempt to clean them with solvent, as this may enter the bearings. If wear is evident, renew the tensioner and/or idler wheel as necessary.

Refitting

Camshaft sprocket

19 Refit the camshaft sprocket making sure it is correctly engaged with the camshaft slot.

20 Fit the new sprocket retaining bolt and, using the holding tool to prevent rotation, tighten it first to the specified Stage 1 torque setting and then through the specified Stage 2 angle. It is recommended that an angle-measuring gauge is used during Stage 2 to ensure accuracy (see illustrations).

21 Ensure that the locating dowels are in position and refit the injection pump/engine mounting bracket to the head, tightening its retaining bolts to the specified torque setting.

22 Refit the injection pump rear mounting bracket and securely tighten its mounting nuts/bolts.

23 Although not strictly necessary, it is recommended that the injection pump timing is checked as described in Chapter 4B.

24 Ensure that the unions are clean and dry then refit the injector pipes and securely tighten

their unions nuts. Refit the power steering reservoir to its bracket and clip it in position.

25 Reconnect the accelerator cable and adjust as described in Chapter 4B.

26 Fit the new timing belt as described in Section 6.

Injection pump sprocket

27 Fit the Woodruff key to injection pump shaft and slide on the sprocket making sure it is correctly engaged with the key.

28 Fit the sprocket retaining nut and tighten it to the specified torque, preventing rotation with the method used on removal (Chapter 4B).

29 Fit the new timing belt as described in Section 6.

Crankshaft sprocket

30 Align the sprocket into position with the crankshaft groove and slide it into position.

31 Fit the new timing belt as described in Section 6.

Tensioner pulley

32 Where necessary, fit the new mounting stud and refit the injection pump bracket (see paragraphs 21 to 25).

33 Fit the pulley, making sure the backplate is correctly engaged with the locating peg and lightly tighten its retaining nut (see illustration). Fit the new timing belt as described in Section 6.

Idler pulley

34 Where necessary, fit the stud and tighten securely having applied a few drops of locking compound to its threads.

35 Fit the pulley, tightening its retaining nut securely, then fit the new timing belt as described in Section 6.

Toothed idler pulley - G8T 706 and 790 engines

36 Apply a few drops of locking compound to the mounting stud threads then fit the pulley to its bracket and securely tighten the stud.

37 Fit the new timing belt as described in Section 6.

Coolant pump pulley

38 Refer to Chapter 3.

8 Camshaft oil seals - renewal

Front (timing belt end) oil seal

Note: *A new timing belt must be used on refitting.*

1 Remove the camshaft sprocket as described in Section 7.

2 Make a note of the correct fitted depth of the seal then punch or drill two small holes opposite each other in the oil seal. Screw a self-tapping screw into each and pull on the screws with pliers to extract the seal.

3 Clean the seal housing and polish off any burrs or raised edges which may have caused the seal to fail in the first place.

4 Lubricate the lips of the new seal with clean engine oil and ease it into position on the end of the shaft. Press the seal into its housing until it is positioned at the same depth as the original was prior to removal. If necessary, a suitable tubular drift, such as a socket, which bears only on the hard outer edge of the seal can be used to tap the seal into position (see illustrations). Take great care not to damage the seal lips during fitting and ensure that the seal lips face inwards. Note that if the surface of the shaft was noted to be badly scored, press the new seal slightly further into its housing so that its lip is running on an unmarked area of the shaft.

5 Refit the camshaft sprocket as described in Section 7 and fit the new timing belt as described in Section 6.

8.4a Carefully ease the new seal over the end of the camshaft . . .

8.4b . . . and tap it into position with a suitable tubular drift such as a socket

9.13 Ensure that the oil pressure relief valve (arrowed) is in position in the left-hand end of the cylinder head

9.14a Refit the hydraulic tappets . . .

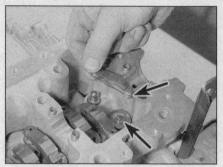

9.14b . . . then fit the followers making sure the follower groove is correctly engaged with the valve (arrowed)

Rear (flywheel end) oil seal

G8T 706 and 790 engines

Note: *A new pulley retaining bolt and drivebelt will be required on refitting.*

6 Remove the auxiliary drivebelt as described in Chapter 1B.

7 Slacken the sprocket retaining bolt whilst preventing rotation using the holding tool described in paragraph 7 of Section 7.

8 Remove the retaining bolt and slide off the drivebelt sprocket.

9 Renew the oil seal as described in paragraphs 2 to 4.

10 Refit the sprocket, making sure it is correctly engaged with the camshaft, and fit the new retaining bolt. Hold the sprocket and tighten the retaining bolt to the specified torque.

11 Fit the new drivebelt as described in Chapter 1B.

All other engines

12 On all engines except G8T 706 and 790, the braking system vacuum pump is mounted directly on the end of the camshaft. If oil is leaking remove the pump and investigate the cause as described in Chapter 9.

---

9 Camshaft, followers and hydraulic tappets - removal, inspection and refitting

Note: *New camshaft oil seals and a new timing belt must be used on refitting.*

Removal

1 Remove the inlet manifold as described in Chapter 4B.

2 Remove the camshaft sprocket as described in Section 7.

3 On G8T 706 and 790 engines, remove the drivebelt sprocket from the rear of the camshaft as described in paragraphs 6 to 8 of Section 8.

4 On all other engines, remove the braking system vacuum pump as described in Chapter 9.

5 Unscrew the retaining nuts and bolts and lift off the camshaft cover along with its seal. If the seal shows damage, renew it.

6 The camshaft bearing caps should be numbered 1 to 5 from the flywheel end of the engine. If the caps are not already numbered, identify them, numbering them from the flywheel end of the engine, and making the marks on the manifold side.

7 Evenly and progressively unscrew the camshaft bearing cap bolts by a turn at a time to gradually relieve the valve spring pressure. Once the bolts are loose, unscrew and remove them, noting their correct fitted locations, and remove the bearing caps. If the cap locating dowels are a loose-fit, remove them and store them with the caps for safe-keeping.

8 Lift the camshaft from the cylinder head. Remove the oil seal(s) from the end(s) of the camshaft and discard: it/they must be renewed.

9 Obtain twelve small, clean plastic containers, and number them 1 to 12; alternatively, divide a larger container into twelve compartments. Lift out each follower and hydraulic tappet in turn, and place them in their respective container. Do not interchange the cam followers, or the rate of wear will be much-increased.

Inspection

10 Examine the camshaft bearing surfaces and cam lobes for signs of wear ridges and scoring. Renew the camshaft if any of these conditions are apparent. Examine the condition of the bearing surfaces, both on the camshaft journals and in the cylinder head/bearing caps. If the head bearing surfaces are worn excessively, the cylinder head will need to be renewed.

11 Examine the cam follower bearing surfaces which contact the camshaft lobes for wear ridges and scoring. Renew any follower on which these conditions are apparent. If a follower bearing surface is badly scored, also examine the corresponding lobe on the camshaft for wear, as it is likely that both will be worn. Renew worn components as necessary.

12 If the hydraulic tappets are thought to be faulty they should be renewed; testing of the tappets is not possible.

Refitting

13 Prior to refitting check that the oil pressure relief valve is present in the left-hand end of the cylinder head; the valve is retained by the lug on number 1 camshaft bearing cap **(see illustration)**.

14 Lubricate the hydraulic tappets and their cylinder head bores with clean engine oil. Refit the tappets to the cylinder head, making sure they are fitted in their original locations. Refit each follower to the top of its respective tappet, ensuring that the follower groove is correctly engaged with the top of the valve **(see illustrations)**.

15 Lubricate the cam lobes and bearing journals with clean engine oil of the specified grade and fit the camshaft to the head **(see illustration)**.

16 Position the camshaft so that its sprocket locating key groove is uppermost and check the crankshaft is still locked in position (see Section 3) **(see illustration)**.

9.15 Lubricate the camshaft bearings with clean engine oil . . .

9.16 . . . then fit the camshaft to the head and position it so that its sprocket locating keyway (arrowed) is uppermost

9.18 Refit the camshaft bearing caps using the identification numbers to ensure each cap is refitted in its original position

9.21a Apply a smear of sealant to the areas where the end bearing caps meet the cylinder head surface . . .

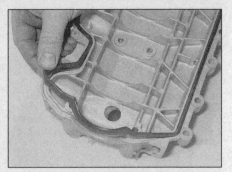

9.21b . . . then fit the seal to the camshaft cover groove and refit the cover to the head

17 Remove the crankshaft locking rod and rotate the crankshaft backwards through 90° (a quarter of a turn) so that all the pistons are positioned halfway up their bores. This will prevent the valves being forced against the pistons as the camshaft cap bolts are tightened.

18 Ensure that the locating dowels are in position then refit the bearing caps, making sure they are fitted in their original locations and the correct way around **(see illustration)**. Screw in the retaining bolts noting that the bolts with the studs should be fitted to bearing caps 2 to 4. Evenly and progressively tighten the bolts so the camshaft is pulled squarely down onto the head. Once all the bearing caps are in contact with the cylinder head go around in a diagonal sequence, starting at the centre and working outwards, and tighten the camshaft bearing cap retaining bolts to the specified torque.

19 If the original tappets have been refitted, all of the valves will now be forced open due to the hydraulic lock inside each tappet (this shouldn't be a problem if new tappets are being installed). Leave the engine for at least 15 minutes, to allow the hydraulic pressure in each tappet to be released and the valves to return to their correct positions.

20 Carefully rotate the crankshaft through 90° in the correct direction of rotation, to bring No. 1 and 4 cylinders back to TDC, and refit the crankshaft locking rod (see Section 3).

21 Apply a smear of sealant (Renault recommend the use of Rhodorseal 5661) to the areas where the camshaft end bearing caps meet the cylinder head. Refit the camshaft cover and seal and tighten its retaining nuts and bolts to the specified torque setting **(see illustrations)**.

22 Fit a new camshaft front oil seal then refit the camshaft sprocket and fit the new timing belt as described in Sections 6, 7 and 8.

23 On G8T 706 and 790 engines, fit a new camshaft rear oil seal and refit the drivebelt sprocket as described in Section 8.

24 On all other engines refit the vacuum pump as described in Chapter 9.

25 Refit the inlet manifold as described in Chapter 4B.

26 On completion check the engine oil level as described in *Weekly checks*. Start the engine and check for noise from the hydraulic tappets. If the tappets are noisy, bleed them by running the engine at approximately 2500 rpm until the noise stops (this should not take more than 5 to 10 minutes). **Note:** *Do not run the engine at high speeds until the tappets are operating correctly and the valvegear is operating quietly.*

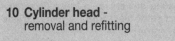

10 Cylinder head -
removal and refitting

Note: *New cylinder head bolts and a new timing belt will be required on refitting.*
Caution: Be careful not to allow dirt into the injection pump or injector pipes during this procedure.

Removal

1 Disconnect the battery negative terminal (refer to *Disconnecting the battery* in the Reference Section of this manual), then drain the cooling system with reference to Chapter 1B.

2 Remove the timing belt with reference to Section 6.

3 The engine must now be supported from below so that the engine hoist or lifting beam used for timing belt removal can be removed for access to the top of the engine. If possible, obtain Renault special tool Mot.1367, or fabricate a home-made alternative out of square-section steel tube as shown in Chapter 2B, Section 6.

4 Remove the air cleaner assembly and inlet duct as described in Chapter 4B. Undo the retaining nuts and bolts and remove the housing mounting bracket.

5 Remove the inlet and exhaust manifolds as described in Chapter 4B.

6 On G8T 706 and 790 engines, remove the auxiliary drivebelt from the left-hand end of the cylinder head as described in Chapter 1B. On all other engines, release the retaining clip and disconnect the hose from the vacuum pump on the left-hand end of the cylinder head.

7 Disconnect the wiring connectors from coolant temperature senders which are screwed into the coolant outlet housing on the left-hand end of the cylinder head. Slacken the retaining clips and disconnect the coolant hoses from the elbow.

8 Working as described in Chapter 4B, carry out the following.
a) *Disconnect the accelerator cable from the fuel injection pump.*
b) *Undo the union nuts and remove the metal pipes linking the pump to the injectors.*
c) *Undo the retaining bolts and remove the rear mounting bracket from the fuel injection pump.*
d) *Disconnect the injection pump wiring connector and the stop solenoid wiring connector from the rear of the pump.*
e) *Remove the injectors.*
f) *Disconnect the fast idle cable from the pump (models with a thermostatic valve) or the vacuum hose from the pump fast idle diaphragm (models with a vacuum-operated fast idle system.*

9 If the cylinder head is to be overhauled, remove the glow plugs as described in Chapter 5C. If not, disconnect the glow plug wiring connector from the preheating unit and free it from its retaining clips so it is free to removed with the cylinder head.

10 Unscrew the retaining nuts and bolts and lift off the camshaft cover along with its seal. If the seal shows damage, renew it.

11 Working in the **reverse** of the sequence shown in **illustration 10.23a**, progressively slacken the cylinder head bolts by half a turn at a time until all bolts can be unscrewed by hand and removed. Remove the baffle plate from the top of the cylinder head.

12 Lift the cylinder head upwards and off the cylinder block. If it is stuck, tap it upwards using a hammer and block of wood. *Do not* try to turn it (it is located by two dowels), nor attempt to prise it free using a screwdriver inserted between the block and head faces. If the locating dowels are a loose fit, remove them and store them with the head for safe-keeping. As the head is removed, take care to ensure that the swirl chambers do not fall out.

Inspection

13 The mating faces of the cylinder head and block must be perfectly clean before refitting the head. Use a scraper to remove all traces of gasket and carbon, and also clean the tops of the pistons. Take particular care with the aluminium cylinder head, as the soft metal is damaged easily. Also, make sure that debris is not allowed to enter the oil and water channels - this is particularly important for the oil circuit, as carbon could block the oil supply to the camshaft or crankshaft bearings. Using adhesive tape and paper, seal the water, oil and bolt holes in the cylinder block. To prevent carbon entering the gap between the pistons and bores, smear a little grease in the gap. After cleaning the piston, rotate the crankshaft so that the piston moves down the bore, then wipe out the grease and carbon with a cloth rag. Clean the piston crowns in the same way.

14 Check the block and head for nicks, deep scratches and other damage. If slight, they may be removed carefully with a file. More serious damage may be repaired by machining, but this is a specialist job.

15 If warpage of the cylinder head is suspected, use a straight-edge to check it for distortion. Refer to Chapter 2H if necessary.

16 Ensure that the cylinder head bolt holes in the crankcase are clean and free of oil. Syringe or soak up any oil left in the bolt holes. This is most important in order that the correct bolt tightening torque can be applied and to prevent the possibility of the block being cracked by hydraulic pressure when the bolts are tightened.

17 Examine the cylinder head bolt threads in the cylinder block for damage. If necessary, use the correct-size tap to chase out the threads in the block, and use a die to clean the threads on the bolts. The cylinder head bolts must be discarded and renewed, regardless of their apparent condition.

Refitting

18 Ensure that the mating faces of the cylinder block and head are spotlessly clean, that the retaining bolt threads are also clean and dry, and that they screw easily in and out of their locations.

19 Check that No 1 piston is still at TDC, and

10.20 Fitting a new cylinder head gasket

that the camshaft sprocket timing mark is correctly positioned (temporarily refit the camshaft cover to check this) (see Section 3). *Caution: If the camshaft and/or crankshaft are incorrectly positioned, there is a risk of valves being forced into pistons as the head is refitted.*

20 Ensure that the locating dowels are correctly fitted to the block and fit a new cylinder head gasket, making sure it is the right way up **(see illustration)**.

21 Carefully lower the cylinder head onto the block, engaging it over the dowels. If the swirl chambers are a loose fit, take care to ensure that they stay correctly positioned as the head is lowered into position.

22 Lightly oil the new cylinder head bolts, both on their threads and under their heads. Allow excess oil to drain off then refit the baffle plate to the top of the head and insert the bolts, tightening them finger-tight only **(see illustration)**.

23 Working progressively and in the sequence shown, tighten the cylinder head bolts to their Stage 1 torque setting, using a torque wrench and suitable socket **(see illustrations)**.

24 Once all bolts are tightened to the Stage 1 specified torque setting, working in the specified sequence, tighten each bolt through its specified Stage 2 angle, using a socket and extension bar. It is recommended that an angle-measuring gauge is used during this stage of the tightening, to ensure accuracy **(see illustration)**. **Note:** *The Stage 2 tightening angle differs depending on the bolt location.*

10.22 Refit the baffle plate and install the new head bolts

25 Wait approximately 3 minutes then fully slacken the bolts number 1 and 2 in the tightening sequence. Working in sequence, tighten both bolts first to the specified Stage 3 torque setting then angle-tighten them through the specified Stage 4 angle, using a socket and extension bar. It is recommended that an angle-measuring gauge is used during this stage of the tightening, to ensure accuracy. **Note:** *The Stage 4 tightening angles differ depending on the bolt/nut location.*

26 Fully slacken bolts number 3, 4, 5 and 6 in the tightening sequence. Working in the specified sequence tighten the slackened bolts first to the specified Stage 3 torque setting and then angle-tighten them through the specified Stage 4 angle (see paragraph 25).

27 Fully slacken bolts number 7, 8, 9 and 10 in the tightening sequence. Working in the specified sequence tighten the slackened bolts first to the specified Stage 3 torque setting and then angle-tighten them through the specified Stage 4 angle (see paragraph 25).

28 Fully slacken bolts number 11, 12, 13 and 14 in the tightening sequence. Working in the specified sequence tighten the slackened bolts first to the specified Stage 3 torque setting and then angle-tighten them through the specified Stage 4 angle (see paragraph 25).

29 Fully slacken bolts number 15, 16, 17 and 18 in the tightening sequence. Working in the specified sequence tighten the slackened bolts first to the specified Stage 3 torque setting and then angle-tighten them through the specified Stage 4 angle (see paragraph 25).

30 Apply a smear of sealant (Renault recommend the use of Rhodorseal 5661) to

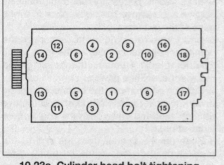

10.23a Cylinder head bolt tightening sequence

10.23b Working in the specified sequence, tighten the head bolts to the specified torque . . .

10.24 . . . then through the various angle-tightening stages as described in the text

2E

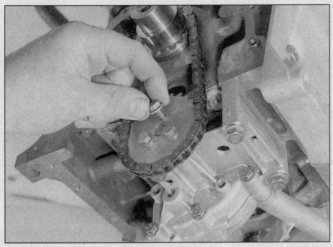

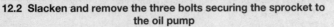

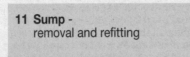

12.2 Slacken and remove the three bolts securing the sprocket to the oil pump

12.3 Remove the oil pump from the cylinder block and recover the locating dowels (1) and sealing ring (2)

the areas where the end camshaft bearing caps meet the cylinder head. Refit the camshaft cover and seal and tighten its retaining nuts and bolts to the specified torque setting.

31 Refit the glow plugs (where removed) as described in Chapter 5C and/or reconnect the wiring.

32 Working as described in Chapter 4B, carry out the following.

a) *Reconnect and adjust the fast idle cable or connect the diaphragm unit vacuum hose.*

b) *Refit the injectors.*

c) *Reconnect the injection pump wiring.*

d) *Refit the pump rear mounting bracket and securely tighten its retaining bolts.*

e) *Refit the metal pipes linking the injection pump to the injectors.*

f) *Reconnect and adjust the accelerator cable.*

33 Reconnect the coolant hoses to the outlet elbow and securely tighten their retaining clips. Reconnect the wiring connectors to the temperature sender units.

34 On G8T 706 and 790 engines, refit the vacuum pump auxiliary drivebelt as described in Chapter 1B. On all other engines, reconnect the vacuum hose to the vacuum pump.

35 Refit the exhaust and inlet manifolds as described in Chapter 4B.

36 Refit the air cleaner assembly components as described in Chapter 4B.

37 Fit the new timing belt as described in Section 6.

38 Refill the cooling system as described in Chapter 1B and reconnect the battery.

11 Sump -
removal and refitting

Removal

1 Apply the handbrake, then jack up the front of the car and support it on axle stands (see *Jacking and vehicle support*). Undo the retaining screws and remove the plastic undercover from beneath the engine/transmission.

2 Drain the engine oil as described in Chapter 1B, then refit and tighten the drain plug.

3 Unscrew the bolts, including the bolts securing the support rods to the side of the cylinder block, and remove the flywheel/driveplate cover plate.

4 Unscrew and remove the bolts securing the sump to the crankcase. Tap the sump with a hide or plastic mallet to break the seal, then remove the sump along with its gasket. discard the gasket, a new one must be used on refitting.

Refitting

5 Remove all traces of dirt and oil from the mating surfaces of the sump and cylinder block.

6 Locate the new gasket on the top of the sump and lift the sump into position.

7 Insert the bolts and tighten them progressively to the specified torque.

8 Refit the undercover and lower the vehicle to the ground.

9 Fill the engine with fresh oil, with reference to Chapter 1B.

12 Oil pump -
removal, inspection and refitting

Removal

Oil pump

1 Remove the sump as described in Section 11. Where necessary, undo the retaining screws and remove the baffle plate from the base of the cylinder block.

2 Undo the three bolts securing the pump sprocket to the pump and remove the sprocket **(see illustration)**.

3 Unscrew the oil pump retaining bolts and withdraw the pump from the crankcase. Recover the pump locating dowels and the sealing ring which are fitted between the pump and crankcase casting. Discard the sealing ring; a new one should be used on refitting **(see illustration)**.

Drive chain and sprockets

Note: *A new timing belt and crankshaft oil seal housing bolts will be required on refitting. It is also recommended that the crankshaft oil seal is renewed.*

4 Remove the crankshaft sprocket as described in Section 7

5 Remove the sump as described in Section 11. Where necessary, undo the retaining screws and remove the baffle plate from the base of the cylinder block.

6 Undo the retaining bolts securing the crankshaft oil seal housing to the front of the cylinder block. Remove the housing and recover the locating dowels.

7 Slacken and remove the bolts securing the driven sprocket to the oil pump and remove the sprocket and chain from the engine **(see illustration)**.

8 Slide off the spacer from the end of the crankshaft and remove the oil pump drive sprocket **(see illustrations)**. The oil pump can be unbolted and removed (see paragraph 3).

12.7 Remove the driven sprocket and chain . . .

12.8a . . . then slide off the spacer . . .

12.8b . . . and drive sprocket from the end of the crankshaft

12.14 Tighten the three pump body retaining bolts (1) to the specified torque then tighten the outlet union bolt (2)

Inspection

9 The oil pump must be treated as a sealed unit as no spare parts are available from Renault. If the pump assembly is thought to be faulty it must be renewed. If necessary the pump can be dismantled and checked as described in Part D of this Chapter.

10 Inspect the drive chain and sprockets for signs of wear or damage, such as hooked or missing teeth. If either sprocket is damaged or the chain is excessively stretched, renew both sprockets and the chain as a matched set. Note that it is false economy to fit a new chain to worn sprockets or new sprockets to a worn chain as the rate of wear will be dramatically increased.

Refitting

Oil pump

11 Ensure that the pump pick-up filter is clean and unblocked and prime the oil pump with clean engine oil. To do this fill the pump assembly through its upper hole and rotate the pump shaft until oil flows out through the pick-up filter.

12 Ensure that the locating dowels are in position and fit a new sealing ring to the pump outlet union.

13 Manoeuvre the pump into position and engage it with the drive chain. Ensure that the sealing ring remains correctly positioned and locate the pump on the base of the crankcase casting.

14 Refit the pump retaining bolts and tighten them by hand. Tighten the three bolts securing the main pump body to the crankcase casting to the specified torque first, then tighten the bolt securing the pump outlet union to the casting to the specified torque **(see illustration)**.

15 Align the sprocket with the oil pump flange then refit its retaining bolts and tighten them to the specified torque.

16 Refit the baffle plate (where fitted) and securely tighten its retaining bolts, then refit the sump as described in Section 11.

Drive chain and sprockets

17 Prior to refitting, clean the crankshaft oil seal housing bolt hole threads by running a tap of the correct diameter and pitch down them.

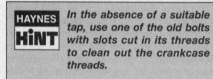

> **HAYNES HiNT**
>
> *In the absence of a suitable tap, use one of the old bolts with slots cut in its threads to clean out the crankcase threads.*

18 Where necessary, fit the oil pump as described in paragraphs 11 to 14.

19 Assemble the chain and sprockets making sure the sprockets are fitted the correct way around.

20 Slide the drive sprocket onto the crankshaft and locate the driven sprocket on the pump flange. Refit the sprocket retaining bolts and tighten them to the specified torque and slide the spacer back onto the crankshaft.

21 If the crankshaft oil seal is being renewed, note the correct fitted depth of the seal in the housing then carefully lever it out of position using a large, flat-bladed screwdriver. Fit the new seal to the housing, making sure its sealing lip is facing inwards and press it squarely into position until it is positioned at the same depth as the original **(see illustrations)**.

2E

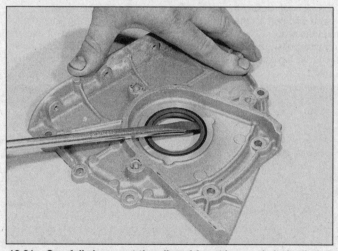

12.21a Carefully lever out the oil seal from the crankshaft oil seal housing . . .

12.21b . . . and tap in a new one using a tubular drift which bears only on the seals outside edge

12.22 Apply sealant to the mating surface of the oil seal housing . . .

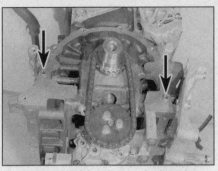

12.23a . . . then ensuring the locating dowels (arrowed) are in position . . .

12.23b . . . carefully refit the housing to the cylinder block

22 Ensure that the mating surfaces are clean and dry and apply a smear of sealant (Renault recommend the use of Loctite 518) to the housing mating surface (see illustration).

23 Ensure that the locating dowels are in position and lubricate the oil seal lip with clean engine oil. Carefully ease the housing over the end of the crankshaft and into position on the block (see illustrations).

24 Fit the new retaining bolts and tighten them to the specified torque setting.

25 Refit the baffle plate (where fitted) and securely tighten its retaining bolts then refit the sump as described in Section 11.

26 Refit the crankshaft sprocket as described in Section 7, and fit the new timing belt as described in Section 6.

13 Flywheel - removal, inspection and refitting

Removal

1 Remove the transmission as described in Chapter 7A, then remove the clutch assembly as described in Chapter 6.

2 Prevent the flywheel from turning by locking the ring gear teeth with a screwdriver. Alternatively a home-made tool similar to that shown in Chapter 2A, Section 5 can be used. Make alignment marks between the flywheel and crankshaft using paint or a suitable marker pen.

3 Slacken and remove the flywheel retaining bolts and remove the flywheel. Do not drop it, as it is very heavy. If the locating dowel (where fitted) is a loose fit in the crankshaft end, remove and store it with the flywheel for safe-keeping. Discard the bolts as they should be renewed whenever they are disturbed.

Inspection

4 Examine the flywheel for scoring of the clutch face, and for wear or chipping of the ring gear teeth. If the clutch face is scored, the flywheel may be surface-ground, but renewal is preferable. Seek the advice of a Renault dealer or engine reconditioning specialist to see if machining is possible. If the ring gear is worn or damaged, the flywheel must be

renewed, as it is not possible to renew the ring gear separately.

Refitting

5 Clean the mating surfaces of the flywheel and crankshaft.

6 Ensure that the locating dowel is in position (where fitted) and offer up the flywheel, locating it on the dowel, and fit the new retaining bolts. If the original is being refitted align the marks made prior to removal.

7 Lock the flywheel using the method employed on dismantling, and tighten the retaining bolts to the specified torque.

8 Refit the clutch as described in Chapter 6.

9 Remove the locking tool, and refit the transmission as described in Chapter 7A.

14 Crankshaft oil seals - renewal

Front (timing belt end) oil seal

Note: *A new timing belt will be required on refitting.*

1 Remove the crankshaft sprocket as described in Section 7.

2 Make a note of the correct fitted depth of the seal then punch or drill two small holes opposite each other in the oil seal. Screw a self-tapping screw into each and pull on the screws with pliers to extract the seal.

3 Clean the seal housing and polish off any burrs or raised edges which may have caused the seal to fail in the first place.

14.7a Screw in a self-tapping screw carefully into the oil seal . . .

4 Lubricate the lips of the new seal with clean engine oil and ease it into position on the end of the shaft. Press the seal into its housing until it is positioned at the same depth as the original was prior to removal. If necessary, a suitable tubular drift, such as a socket, which bears only on the hard outer edge of the seal can be used to tap the seal into position. Take great care not to damage the seal lips during fitting and ensure that the seal lips face inwards. Note that if the surface of the spacer was noted to be badly scored, press the new seal slightly further into its housing so that its lip is running on an unmarked area of the spacer.

5 Refit the crankshaft sprocket as described in Section 7 and fit the new timing belt as described in Section 6.

Rear (flywheel end) oil seal

6 Remove the flywheel as described in Section 13.

7 Prise out the old oil seal using a small screwdriver, taking care not to damage the surface of the crankshaft. Alternatively, the oil seal can be removed as described in paragraph 2 (see illustrations).

8 Inspect the seal rubbing surface on the crankshaft. If it is grooved or rough in the area where the old seal was fitted, the new seal should be fitted slightly less deeply, so that it rubs on an unworn part of the surface.

9 Wipe clean the oil seal seating, then dip the new seal in fresh engine oil. Locate it over the crankshaft, making sure its sealing lip is facing inwards. Make sure that the oil seal lip is not damaged as it is located on the crankshaft.

14.7b . . . then prise the seal out of position using a pair of pointed-nose pliers

10 Using a metal tube, drive the oil seal squarely into the bore until flush. A block of wood cut to pass over the end of the crankshaft may be used instead.

11 Refit the flywheel as described in Section 13.

15 Engine/transmission mountings - inspection and renewal

Inspection

1 If improved access is required, apply the handbrake, then jack up the front of the car and support it on axle stands (see *Jacking and vehicle support*).

2 Check the mounting rubber to see if it is cracked, hardened or separated from the metal at any point; renew the mounting if any such damage or deterioration is evident **(see illustration)**.

3 Check that all the mounting's fasteners are securely tightened; use a torque wrench to check if possible.

4 Using a large screwdriver or a crowbar, check for wear in the mounting by carefully levering against it to check for free play. Where this is not possible, enlist the aid of an assistant to move the engine/transmission back and forth, or from side to side, while you watch the mounting. While some free play is to be expected even from new components, excessive wear should be obvious. If excessive free play is found, check first that the fasteners are correctly secured, then renew any worn components as described below.

Renewal

Right-hand mounting

5 Disconnect the battery negative terminal (refer to *Disconnecting the battery* in the Reference Section of this manual).

6 Place a jack beneath the engine, with a block of wood on the jack head (remove the undercover to improve access to the sump). Raise the jack until it is supporting the weight of the engine. Alternately, attach an engine support bar to the lifting brackets and support the weight of the engine with the bar.

7 Slacken and remove the three bolts securing the right-hand engine mounting bracket to the bracket on the cylinder block. Remove the nut securing the bracket to the mounting rubber, and lift off the bracket.

8 Unscrew the three retaining bolts and remove the rubber mounting from the body.

9 To renew the cylinder head bracket, first remove the timing belt as described in Section 6. On G8T 706 and 790 engines, remove the fuel injection pump as described in Chapter 4B. Unbolt the engine mounting bracket and remove it from the cylinder head.

10 Check carefully for signs of wear or damage on all components, and renew them where necessary.

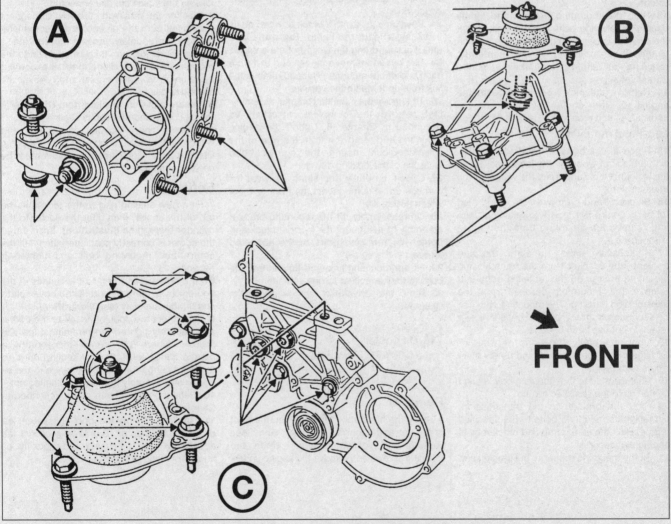

15.2 Engine mounting details (mounting nuts and bolts arrowed)

A Rear mounting assembly	*B Left-hand mounting assembly*	*C Right-hand mounting assembly*

2E

16.7 Fit a new seal to the oil cooler groove . . .

16.8 . . . and cover plate

11 On reassembly, refit the engine mounting bracket to the cylinder head and tighten its retaining bolts to the specified torque. Refit the injection pump (where applicable) as described in Chapter 4B, and fit a new timing belt as described in Section 6.

12 Fit the rubber mounting to the body and tighten its retaining bolts to the specified torque.

13 Refit the mounting bracket and lightly tighten its retaining bolts and nut. Ensure that the bracket is positioned centrally in relation to the rubber mounting lug then tighten its retaining nut and bolts to their specified torque settings.

14 Remove the jack from underneath the engine or the engine support bar (as applicable), and reconnect the battery.

Left-hand mounting

15 Place a jack beneath the transmission, with a block of wood on the jack head. Raise the jack until it is supporting the weight of the transmission.

16 Slacken and remove the mounting rubber's centre nut, and two retaining bolts and remove the mounting from the engine compartment.

17 If necessary, unbolt the earth strap and coolant pipe bracket from the transmission mounting then undo the retaining bolts and remove the mounting bracket from the transmission housing. The mounting stud can be separated from the bracket once its lower retaining nut has been undone.

18 Check carefully for signs of wear or damage on all components, and renew them where necessary.

19 Refit the stud to the mounting bracket and tighten its to the specified torque.

20 Refit the bracket to the transmission, tightening its mounting bolts to the specified torque. Refit the earth strap and bracket bolts and tighten securely.

21 Fit the mounting rubber to the bracket and tighten its retaining bolts and centre nut to the specified torque.

22 Remove the jack from underneath the transmission.

Rear mounting

23 If not already done, apply the handbrake, then jack up the front of the car and support it on axle stands (see *Jacking and vehicle support*).

24 Position a jack with a block of wood on its head underneath the sump. Raise the jack until it is supporting the weight of the engine.

25 Slacken and remove the nut and bolt from each end of the mounting link and remove the link from underneath the vehicle.

26 To remove the mounting bracket assembly, first remove the complete driveshaft as described in Chapter 8. Unbolt the engine mounting and remove it from the rear of the cylinder block, noting the correct fitted locations of the locating dowels.

27 Check carefully for signs of wear or damage on all components, and renew them where necessary.

28 On reassembly, fit the mounting bracket assembly to the rear of the cylinder block and tighten its retaining bolts to the specified torque.

29 Fit the mounting link, and tighten both its bolts to their specified torque settings.

30 Refit the driveshaft as described in Chapter 8.

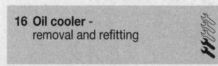

16 Oil cooler -
removal and refitting

Removal

1 Apply the handbrake, then jack up the front of the car and support it on axle stands (see *Jacking and vehicle support*). Undo the retaining screws and remove the engine under-cover to gain access to the oil cooler which is mounted on the front of the cylinder block.

2 Drain the engine oil as described in Chapter 1B, then refit and tighten the drain plug.

3 Drain the cooling system as described in Chapter 1B. Alternatively, clamp the oil cooler coolant hoses as close to the cooler as possible, and be prepared for some coolant loss as the hoses are disconnected.

4 Slacken the retaining clips and disconnect the hoses from the oil cooler. On some later models the coolant hoses incorporate a plastic flange joint; on these models undo the retaining nut then disconnect the coolant hose union from the cooler and recover the sealing rings.

5 Unscrew the cover plate from the base of the oil cooler and recover its sealing ring.

6 Unscrew the oil cooler centre bolt and withdraw the cooler along with its sealing ring. Discard all sealing rings; new ones must be used on refitting.

Refitting

7 Fit a new sealing ring to the recess in the top of the cooler, then offer the cooler to the cylinder block **(see illustration)**. Ensure that the cooler is correctly positioned then refit the centre bolt mounting bolt and tighten it securely.

8 Fit a new sealing ring to the recess in the cooler cover plate then refit the cover plate and tighten securely **(see illustration)**.

9 Reconnect the coolant hoses to the cooler and securely tighten the retaining clips. On models where the hoses incorporate a plastic flange joint, fit new sealing rings to the hose flange then refit the flange to the oil cooler and securely tighten its retaining nut.

10 Refill the engine with oil as described in Chapter 1B.

11 Refill or top-up the cooling system as described in Chapter 1B or *Weekly checks* (as applicable). Start the engine, and check the oil cooler for signs of leakage.

Chapter 2 Part F:
8-valve petrol engine removal and overhaul procedures

Contents

Degrees of difficulty

Easy, suitable for novice with little experience	Fairly easy, suitable for beginner with some experience	Fairly difficult, suitable for competent DIY mechanic	Difficult, suitable for experienced DIY mechanic	Very difficult, suitable for expert DIY or professional

Specifications

Cylinder head
Maximum gasket face distortion . . . . 0.05 mm
Cylinder head height . . . . 169.5 ± 0.2 mm

Valves
Valve head diameter:
    Inlet . . . . 40.0 mm
    Exhaust . . . . 32.5 mm
Valve stem diameter . . . . 8.0 mm
Valve guide bore diameter in cylinder head:
    Standard . . . . 13.00 mm
    Oversize . . . . 13.25 mm
Valve seat angle (included) . . . . 90°
Valve seat width . . . . 1.7 ± 0.2 mm

Auxiliary shaft
Endfloat . . . . 0.07 to 0.15 mm

Cylinder block
Cylinder bore diameter:
    Size group A . . . . 82.70 to 82.71 mm
    Size group B . . . . 82.71 to 82.72 mm
    Size group C . . . . 82.72 to 82.73 mm

Pistons
Piston diameter:
    Size group A . . . . 82.665 to 82.675 mm
    Size group B . . . . 82.675 to 82.685 mm
    Size group C . . . . 82.685 to 82.695 mm
Piston-to-bore clearance . . . . 0.035 to 0.065 mm

Crankshaft

Endfloat	0.07 to 0.23 mm
Main bearing journal diameter:	
Standard	54.795 mm
Undersize	54.545 mm
Big-end bearing journal diameter:	
Standard	48.000 mm
Undersize	47.750 mm
Maximum bearing journal out-of-round	0.01 mm
Main bearing running clearance*	0.025 to 0.050 mm
Big-end bearing running clearance*	0.025 to 0.050 mm

These are suggested figures, typical for this type of engine - no exact values are stated by Renault.

Piston rings

Thickness:	
Top compression ring	1.50 mm
Second compression ring	1.75 mm
Oil control ring	3.00 mm

Torque wrench settings

Refer to Chapter 2A Specifications

1 General information

Included in this Part of Chapter 2 are details of removing the engine/transmission from the car and general overhaul procedures for the cylinder head, cylinder block and all other engine internal components.

The information given ranges from advice concerning preparation for an overhaul and the purchase of replacement parts, to detailed step-by-step procedures covering removal, inspection, renovation and refitting of engine internal components.

After Section 6, all instructions are based on the assumption that the engine has been removed from the car. For information concerning in-car engine repair, as well as the removal and refitting of those external components necessary for full overhaul, refer to Part A of this Chapter and to Section 6. Ignore any preliminary dismantling operations described in Part A that are no longer relevant once the engine has been removed from the car.

Apart from torque wrench settings, which are given at the beginning of Part A, all specifications relating to engine overhaul are at the beginning of this Part of Chapter 2.

2 Engine overhaul - general information

It is not always easy to determine when, or if, an engine should be completely overhauled, as a number of factors must be considered.

High mileage is not necessarily an indication that an overhaul is needed, while low mileage does not preclude the need for an overhaul. Frequency of servicing is probably the most important consideration. An engine which has had regular and frequent oil and filter changes, as well as other required maintenance, should give many thousands of miles of reliable service. Conversely, a neglected engine may require an overhaul very early in its life.

Excessive oil consumption is an indication that piston rings, valve seals and/or valve guides are in need of attention. Make sure that oil leaks are not responsible before deciding that the rings and/or guides are worn. Perform a compression test, as described in Part A of this Chapter, to determine the likely cause of the problem.

Check the oil pressure with a gauge fitted in place of the oil pressure switch, and compare it with that specified. If it is extremely low, the main and big-end bearings, and/or the oil pump, are probably worn out.

Loss of power, rough running, knocking or metallic engine noises, excessive valve gear noise, and high fuel consumption may also point to the need for an overhaul, especially if they are all present at the same time. If a complete service does not remedy the situation, major mechanical work is the only solution.

An engine overhaul involves restoring all internal parts to the specification of a new engine. During an overhaul, the pistons and the piston rings are renewed. New main and big-end bearings are generally fitted; if necessary, the crankshaft may be renewed, to restore the journals. The valves are also serviced as well, since they are usually in less-than-perfect condition at this point. While the engine is being overhauled, other components, such as the starter and alternator, can be overhauled as well. The end result should be an as-new engine that will give many trouble-free miles. **Note:** *Critical cooling system components such as the hoses, thermostat and coolant pump should be renewed when an engine is overhauled.* *The radiator should be checked carefully, to ensure that it is not clogged or leaking. Also, it is a good idea to renew the oil pump whenever the engine is overhauled.*

Before beginning the engine overhaul, read through the entire procedure, to familiarise yourself with the scope and requirements of the job. Overhauling an engine is not difficult if you follow carefully all of the instructions, have the necessary tools and equipment, and pay close attention to all specifications. It can, however, be time-consuming. Plan on the car being off the road for a minimum of two weeks, especially if parts must be taken to an engineering works for repair or reconditioning. Check on the availability of parts and make sure that any necessary special tools and equipment are obtained in advance. Most work can be done with typical hand tools, although a number of precision measuring tools are required for inspecting parts to determine if they must be renewed. Often the engineering works will handle the inspection of parts and offer advice concerning reconditioning and renewal. **Note:** *Always wait until the engine has been completely dismantled, and until all components (especially the cylinder block and the crankshaft) have been inspected, before deciding what service and repair operations must be performed by an engineering works. The condition of these components will be the major factor to consider when determining whether to overhaul the original engine, or to buy a reconditioned unit. Do not, therefore, purchase parts or have overhaul work done on other components until they have been thoroughly inspected. As a general rule, time is the primary cost of an overhaul, so it does not pay to fit worn or sub-standard parts.*

As a final note, to ensure maximum life and minimum trouble from a reconditioned engine, everything must be assembled with care, in a spotlessly-clean environment.

3 Engine removal - methods and precautions

If you have decided that the engine must be removed for overhaul or major repair work, several preliminary steps should be taken.

Locating a suitable place to work is extremely important. Adequate work space, along with storage space for the car, will be needed. If a workshop or garage is not available, at the very least, a flat, level, clean work surface is required.

Cleaning the engine compartment and engine/transmission before beginning the removal procedure will help keep tools clean and organised.

An engine hoist or A-frame will also be necessary. Make sure the equipment is rated in excess of the combined weight of the engine and transmission. Safety is of primary importance, considering the potential hazards involved in lifting the engine/transmission out of the car.

If this is the first time you have removed an engine, an assistant should ideally be available. Advice and aid from someone more experienced would also be helpful. There are many instances when one person cannot simultaneously perform all of the operations required when lifting the engine out of the vehicle.

Plan the operation ahead of time. Before starting work, arrange for the hire of or obtain all of the tools and equipment you will need. Some of the equipment necessary to perform engine/transmission removal and installation safely and with relative ease (in addition to an engine hoist) is as follows: a heavy duty trolley jack, complete sets of spanners and sockets as described in the reference section of this manual, wooden blocks, and plenty of rags and cleaning solvent for mopping up spilled oil, coolant and fuel. If the hoist must be hired, make sure that you arrange for it in advance, and perform all of the operations possible without it beforehand. This will save you money and time.

Plan for the car to be out of use for quite a while. An engineering works will be required to perform some of the work which the do-it-yourselfer cannot accomplish without special equipment. These places often have a busy schedule, so it would be a good idea to consult them before removing the engine, in order to accurately estimate the amount of time required to rebuild or repair components that may need work.

During the engine removal procedure, it is advisable to make notes of the locations of all brackets, cable ties, earthing points etc, as well as how the wiring harnesses, hoses and electrical connections are attached and routed around the engine and engine compartment. An effective way of doing this is to take a series of photographs of the various components before they are disconnected or removed. A simple inexpensive disposable camera is ideal for this and the resulting photographs will prove invaluable when the engine is refitted.

Always be extremely careful when removing and refitting the engine/transmission. Serious injury can result from careless actions. Plan ahead and take your time, and a job of this nature, although major, can be accomplished successfully.

4 Engine/manual transmission - removal, separation, connection and refitting

Removal

Note: *The engine is removed upwards from the engine compartment as a complete unit with the transmission; the two are then separated for overhaul.*

1 Apply the handbrake, then jack up the front of the car and support it on axle stands (see *Jacking and vehicle support*). Remove both front roadwheels.

2 Set the bonnet in the upright position or, to improve access, remove it completely as described in Chapter 11.

3 Undo the retaining screws and remove the plastic undercover from beneath the engine/transmission. Also remove the plastic covers from the left- and right-hand wheelarches.

4 If the engine is to be dismantled, working as described in Chapter 1A, first drain the oil and remove the oil filter. Clean and refit the drain plug, tightening it securely.

5 Remove the battery as described in Chapter 5A. Trace the engine wiring harness back to the wiring connectors in the left-hand front corner of the engine compartment. Unclip the plastic cover and disconnect the wiring from the fusebox assembly then free the harness from all its retaining clips so that it is free to be removed with the engine.

6 Remove the air cleaner assembly and associated components as described in Chapter 4A.

7 Drain the transmission oil as described in Chapter 7A. Refit the drain and filler plugs, and tighten them securely.

8 On models equipped with air conditioning, remove the auxiliary drivebelt (see Chapter 1A) then unbolt the compressor, and position it clear of the engine. Support the weight of the compressor by tying it to the vehicle body, to prevent any excess strain being placed on the compressor lines whilst the engine is removed. *Do not* disconnect the refrigerant lines from the compressor (refer to the warnings given in Chapter 3).

9 Drain the cooling system as described in Chapter 1A. Slacken the retaining clips and disconnect the coolant hoses from the left-hand end of the cylinder head.

10 On models with power steering, referring to Chapter 10, slacken the retaining clip and disconnect the low pressure hose, linking the pump to the cooler, from the cooler. Slacken the union nut and disconnect the high pressure pipe from the pump, noting its sealing ring, then release the pipe from its retaining clips and position it clear of the engine/transmission. Plug the pipe ends to minimise fluid loss and prevent the entry of dirt into the system. Undo the retaining screws securing the fluid reservoir to its mounting bracket and tie the reservoir to the engine.

11 Referring to Chapter 4A, carry out the following operations.

a) *Disconnect the fuel hoses from the throttle body/fuel rail (as applicable).*

b) *Disconnect the accelerator cable from the throttle body/housing.*

c) *Remove the exhaust system front pipe.*

d) *Disconnect the vacuum hose and wiring connector from the MAP sensor and unclip the diagnostic wiring connector from its bracket. Release the electronic control unit (ECU) from its mounting bracket then release the wiring loom from its clips and tie the ECU to the engine. Disconnect the wiring connectors from the ignition HT coil so that the wiring loom and components are free to be removed with the engine.*

e) *Disconnect the relevant vacuum hoses from the inlet manifold.*

12 Working as described in Chapter 8, disconnect both driveshafts from the transmission. Note that it is not necessary to undo the driveshaft nut and remove the driveshaft completely, it can be left attached to the hub assembly and released from the transmission as the hub assembly is pulled outwards. **Note:** *Do not allow the shaft to hang down under its own weight as this could damage the constant velocity joints/gaiters.*

13 Disconnect the clutch cable from the transmission and position it clear (see Chapter 6).

14 Disconnect the gearchange linkage and the speedometer cable from the transmission as described in Chapter 7A. Undo the retaining bolt and disconnect the earth lead from the transmission housing.

15 Manoeuvre the engine hoist into position, and attach it to the lifting brackets bolted onto the cylinder head. Raise the hoist until it is supporting the weight of the engine.

16 From underneath the vehicle, undo the retaining bolts and remove the rear mounting link, connecting the engine/transmission mounting to the body. Also undo the retaining bolt and remove the mounting support rod from the engine bracket.

17 Unscrew the lower nut from the left-hand mounting stud then undo the bolts securing the mounting bracket to the top of the transmission housing and remove the bracket. Unbolt and remove the rubber mounting assembly and remove it from the vehicle body.

18 Unscrew the retaining nut and bolts and remove the mounting bracket from the right-hand engine/transmission mounting. Undo the retaining bolts and remove the rubber mounting from the vehicle body.

19 Make a final check that any components which would prevent the removal of the engine/transmission from the car have been removed or disconnected. Ensure that components such as the gearchange selector rod and driveshafts are secured so that they cannot be damaged on removal.

20 Lift the engine/transmission out of the car, ensuring that nothing is trapped or damaged. Enlist the help of an assistant during this procedure, as it will be necessary to tilt the assembly slightly to clear the body panels.

21 Once the engine is high enough, lift it out over the front of the body, and lower the unit to the ground.

Separation

22 With the engine/transmission assembly removed, support the assembly on suitable blocks of wood, on a workbench (or failing that, on a clean area of the workshop floor).

23 Undo the retaining bolts, and remove the flywheel lower cover plate from the transmission. On some models the plate has support struts attached to it, these will have to be unbolted from the side of the cylinder block.

24 Disconnect the wiring then undo the retaining bolts, and remove the starter motor from the transmission, noting the correct fitted position of the locating dowel (see Chapter 5A).

25 Ensure that both engine and transmission are adequately supported, then slacken and remove the remaining bolts securing the transmission housing to the engine. Note the correct fitted positions of each bolt (and the relevant brackets) as they are removed, to use as a reference on refitting.

26 Carefully withdraw the transmission from the engine, ensuring that the weight of the transmission is not allowed to hang on the input shaft while it is engaged with the clutch friction disc.

27 If they are loose, remove the locating dowels from the engine or transmission, and keep them in a safe place.

Connection

28 If the engine and transmission have not been separated, proceed as described from paragraph 35 onwards.

29 Ensure that the clutch plate and transmission input shaft splines are clean and dry. Do not apply grease to the splines as they have a special low-friction nickel coating.

30 Ensure that the locating dowels are correctly positioned prior to installation and make sure the clutch release mechanism components are correctly fitted (see Chapter 6).

31 Carefully offer the transmission to the engine, until the locating dowels are engaged. Ensure that the weight of the transmission is not allowed to hang on the input shaft as it is engaged with the clutch friction disc.

32 Refit the transmission housing-to-engine bolts, ensuring that all the necessary brackets are correctly positioned, and tighten them to the specified torque setting.

33 Refit the starter motor making sure its locating dowel is correctly positioned. Securely tighten its retaining bolts and reconnect the wiring (see Chapter 5A).

34 Refit the flywheel lower cover plate to the transmission, and tighten its retaining bolts to the specified torque.

Refitting

35 Reconnect the hoist and lifting tackle to the engine lifting brackets. With the aid of an assistant, lift the assembly over the engine compartment.

36 The assembly should be tilted as necessary to clear the surrounding components, as during removal; lower the assembly into position in the engine compartment, manipulating the hoist and lifting tackle as necessary.

37 With the engine/transmission in position, refit the left-hand mounting bracket to the top of the transmission and (where removed) the rubber mounting and tighten the retaining bolts to the specified torque. Fit the lower nut to the mounting stud tightening it by hand only at this stage.

38 Refit the right-hand mounting bracket, tightening its retaining nut and bolts by hand only.

39 Refit the rear mounting link and support rod and lightly tighten the retaining bolts.

40 Rock the engine to settle it on its mountings. Centralise the right-hand mounting bracket in relation to the rubber mounting lug then tighten its retaining nut and bolts to their specified torque settings. Go around and tighten all the remaining mounting nuts and bolts to their specified torque settings and detach the hoist from the engine.

41 The remainder of the refitting procedure is a direct reversal of the removal sequence, noting the following points:

a) *Ensure that the wiring loom is correctly routed and retained by all the relevant retaining clips; all connectors should be correctly and securely reconnected.*

b) *Prior to refitting the driveshafts to the transmission, renew the driveshaft oil seal(s) as described in Chapter 7A.*

c) *Ensure that all disturbed hoses are correctly reconnected, and securely retained by their retaining clips.*

d) *Adjust the clutch cable as described in Chapter 6.*

e) *Adjust the accelerator cable as described in the Chapter 4A.*

f) *Refill the engine and transmission with the correct quantity and type of oil, as described in Chapters 1A and 7A.*

g) *Refill the cooling system as described in Chapter 1A.*

---

5 Engine/automatic transmission - removal, separation, connection and refitting

Removal

Note: *The engine is removed upwards from the engine compartment as a complete unit with the transmission; the two are then separated for overhaul.*

Note: *Refer to Chapter 7B for transmission type identification.*

1 Carry out the operations described in paragraphs 1 to 11 of Section 4, noting that the transmission oil/fluid draining procedure for the AD4 type transmission is given in Chapter 1A. It is not necessary to drain the fluid on models equipped with the DPO type transmission.

2 Working as described in Chapter 8, disconnect left-hand driveshaft from the transmission. Note that it is not necessary to remove the driveshaft completely, it can be left attached to the hub assembly and released from the transmission flange as the hub assembly is pulled outwards. **Note:** *Do not allow the shaft to hang down under its own weight as this could damage the constant velocity joints/gaiters.*

3 Disconnect the right-hand driveshaft and remove the intermediate shaft and mounting bracket as described in Chapter 8.

4 Release the retaining clips and disconnect the coolant hoses from the transmission fluid cooler.

5 On the AD4 type transmission, release the retaining clip and disconnect the speedometer cable from its drive. On the DPO type transmission, disconnect the wiring connector at the vehicle speed sensor.

6 On the AD4 type transmission, release the retaining clips and disconnect the wiring connectors from the transmission electronic control unit (ECU) which is situated in the left-hand corner of the engine compartment. Free the first and fourth wiring connectors from the ECU loom; the remaining wiring connectors and loom are then free to be removed with the transmission. On the DPO type transmission, disconnect the wiring harness multiplug connector from the top of the transmission.

7 Disconnect the selector cable from the transmission and position it clear of the unit as described in Chapter 7B.

8 Remove the engine/transmission as described in paragraphs 15 to 21 of Section 4, noting there is no support rod on the rear mounting assembly.

Separation

9 With the engine/transmission assembly removed, support the assembly on suitable blocks of wood, on a workbench (or failing that, on a clean area of the workshop floor).

10 Disconnect the wiring then undo the retaining bolts, and remove the starter motor from the transmission, noting the correct fitted position of the locating dowel (see Chapter 5A).

11 Undo the retaining bolts and remove the driveplate lower cover plate from the base of the transmission housing. On some models the plate has support struts attached to it, these will have to be unbolted from the side of the cylinder block.

12 Slacken and remove the three nuts securing the torque converter to the engine driveplate. The nuts are accessible through the cover plate aperture. Unscrew the visible nut then, using a socket and extension bar to rotate the crankshaft pulley, undo the remaining nuts securing the torque converter to the driveplate as they become accessible. Note that new nuts will be required for refitting.

13 Ensure that both the engine and transmission are adequately supported, then slacken and remove the remaining bolts securing the transmission housing to the engine. Note the correct fitted positions of each bolt (and any relevant brackets) as they are removed, to use as a reference on refitting.

14 With the bolts removed, make sure the torque converter is pushed fully onto the transmission shaft, then carefully withdraw the transmission from the engine. If the locating dowels are a loose fit in the engine/transmission, remove them and keep them in a safe place. Secure the torque converter in position by bolting a length of metal bar to one of the housing holes.

Connection

15 If the engine and transmission have not been separated, proceed as described from paragraph 24 onwards.

16 Ensure that the torque converter centring ring is in good condition and apply a smear of high-melting point grease (Renault recommend the use of Molykote BR2) to its contact surface. Do not apply too much, otherwise there is a possibility of the grease contaminating the torque converter.

17 Ensure that the locating dowels are correctly positioned in the engine or transmission.

18 Remove the retaining strap (where fitted) and make sure the torque converter is pushed fully into position.

19 Carefully offer the transmission to the engine, aligning the torque converter studs with the driveplate holes, until the locating dowels are correctly engaged.

20 Refit the transmission housing-to-engine bolts, ensuring that all the necessary brackets are correctly positioned, and tighten them to the specified torque setting.

21 Apply thread locking compound (Renault recommend the use of Loctite Frenbloc) to the new torque converter retaining nuts and tighten them to the specified torque (see Chapter 7B).

22 Refit the driveplate lower cover plate and tighten its retaining bolts to the specified torque.

23 Refit the starter motor, making sure its locating dowel is correctly fitted. Securely tighten its retaining bolts and reconnect the wiring (see Chapter 5A).

Refitting

24 Refit the engine to the vehicle as described in paragraphs 35 to 40 of Section 4.

25 The remainder of the refitting procedure is a reversal of the removal sequence, noting the following points:

a) Ensure that the wiring loom is correctly

routed, and retained by all the relevant retaining clips; all connectors should be correctly and securely reconnected.

b) Ensure that all coolant hoses are correctly reconnected, and securely retained by their retaining clips.

c) Adjust the selector cable as described in Chapter 7B.

d) Adjust the accelerator cable as described in Chapter 4A.

e) Refill the engine and AD4 type transmission (including final drive) with correct quantity and type of lubricant, as described in Chapter 1A.

f) Refill the cooling system as described in Chapter 1A.

6 Engine overhaul - dismantling sequence

1 It is much easier to dismantle and work on the engine if it is mounted on a portable engine stand. These stands can often be hired from a tool hire shop. Before the engine is mounted on a stand, the flywheel/driveplate should be removed, so that the stand bolts can be tightened into the end of the cylinder block.

2 If a stand is not available, it is possible to dismantle the engine with it blocked up on a sturdy workbench, or on the floor. Be extra-careful not to tip or drop the engine when working without a stand.

3 If you intend to obtain a reconditioned engine, all ancillaries must be removed first, to be transferred to the replacement engine (just as they will if you are doing a complete engine overhaul yourself). These components include the following:

a) Alternator and mounting bracket(s).

b) Power steering pump and bracket(s) (Chapter 10).

c) Coolant pump, thermostat and housing, and coolant outlet chamber/elbow (Chapter 3).

d) Dipstick tube.

e) Fuel system components (Chapter 4A).

f) Wiring harness and all electrical switches and sensors.

g) Inlet and exhaust manifolds (Chapter 4A).

h) Oil filter (Chapter 1A).

i) Flywheel/driveplate (Part A of this Chapter).

Note: When removing the ancillary components from the engine, pay close attention to details that may be helpful or important during refitting. Note the fitted position of gaskets, seals, spacers, pins, washers, bolts, and other small items.

4 If you are obtaining a 'short' engine (ie. engine cylinder block, crankshaft, pistons and connecting rods all assembled), then the cylinder head, sump, oil pump, and timing belt will have to be removed also.

5 If you are planning a complete overhaul, the engine can be dismantled, in the order shown:

a) Inlet and exhaust manifolds.

b) Timing belt, sprockets and tensioner(s).

c) Cylinder head.

d) Flywheel/driveplate.

e) Auxiliary shaft.

f) Sump.

g) Oil pump.

h) Piston/connecting rod assemblies.

i) Crankshaft.

7 Cylinder head - dismantling

Note: New and reconditioned cylinder heads are available from the manufacturer, and from engine overhaul specialists. Be aware that some specialist tools are required for the dismantling and inspection procedures, and new components may not be readily available. It may therefore be more practical and economical for the home mechanic to purchase a reconditioned head, rather than dismantle, inspect and recondition the original head.

1 Remove the cylinder head as described in Part A of this Chapter.

2 Remove the camshaft, followers and shims as described in Part A of this Chapter.

3 Using a valve spring compressor, compress each valve spring in turn until the split collets can be removed. Release the compressor, and lift off the spring retainer, spring and spring seat. Using a pair of pliers, carefully extract the valve stem seal from the top of the guide.

4 If, when the valve spring compressor is screwed down, the spring retainer refuses to free and expose the split collets, gently tap the top of the tool, directly over the retainer, with a light hammer. This will free the retainer.

5 Withdraw the valve through the combustion chamber.

6 It is essential that each valve is stored together with its collets, retainer, spring, and spring seat **(see illustration)**. The valves should also be kept in their correct sequence, unless they are so badly worn that they are to be renewed. If they are going to be kept and used again, place each valve assembly in a labelled polythene bag or similar small container. Note that No 1 valve is nearest to the transmission (flywheel/driveplate) end of the engine.

7.6 Place each valve and its associated components in a labelled polythene bag

2F

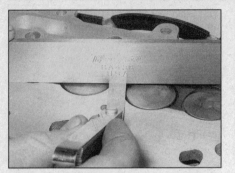

8.6 Checking the cylinder head gasket surface for distortion

8 Cylinder head and valves - cleaning and inspection

1 Thorough cleaning of the cylinder head and valve components, followed by a detailed inspection, will enable you to decide how much valve service work must be carried out during the engine overhaul. **Note:** *If the engine has been severely overheated, it is best to assume that the cylinder head is warped - check carefully for signs of this.*

Cleaning

2 Scrape away all traces of old gasket material from the cylinder head.
3 Scrape away the carbon from the combustion chambers and ports, then wash the cylinder head thoroughly with paraffin or a suitable solvent.
4 Scrape off any heavy carbon deposits that may have formed on the valves, then use a power-operated wire brush to remove deposits from the valve heads and stems.

Inspection

Note: *Be sure to perform all the following inspection procedures before concluding that the services of a machine shop or engine overhaul specialist are required. Make a list of all items that require attention.*

Cylinder head

5 Inspect the head very carefully for cracks, evidence of coolant leakage, and other damage. If cracks are found, a new cylinder head should be obtained.

8.11 Measuring a valve stem diameter

8.8 Checking the valve guides and valves for wear

6 Use a straight-edge and feeler blade to check that the cylinder head surface is not distorted **(see illustration)**. The manufacturers state that no resurfacing of the cylinder head surface is possible, therefore if distortion is evident, a new cylinder head will be required.
7 Examine the valve seats in each of the combustion chambers. If they are severely pitted, cracked, or burned, they will need to be re-cut by an engine overhaul specialist. If they are only slightly pitted, this can be removed by grinding-in the valve heads and seats with fine valve-grinding compound, as described below.
8 Check the valve guides for wear by inserting the relevant valve, and checking for side-to-side motion of the valve **(see illustration)**. A very small amount of movement is acceptable. If the movement seems excessive, remove the valve. Measure the valve stem diameter (see below), and renew the valve if it is worn. If the valve stem is not worn, the wear must be in the valve guide, and the guide must be renewed. The renewal of valve guides is best carried out by a Renault dealer or engine overhaul specialist, who will have the necessary tools available. Where no valve stem diameter is specified, seek the advice of a Renault dealer on the best course of action.
9 If renewing the valve guides, the valve seats should be re-ground only *after* the guides have been fitted.

Valves

10 Examine the head of each valve for pitting, burning, cracks, and general wear. Check the valve stem for scoring and wear ridges. Rotate the valve, and check for any obvious indication that it is bent. Look for pits or excessive wear on the tip of each valve stem. Renew any valve that shows any such signs of wear or damage.
11 If the valve appears satisfactory at this stage, measure the valve stem diameter at several points using a micrometer **(see illustration)**. Any significant difference in the readings obtained indicates wear of the valve stem. Should any of these conditions be apparent, the valve(s) must be renewed.
12 If the valves are in satisfactory condition, they should be ground (lapped) into their respective seats, to ensure a smooth, gas-

tight seal. If the seat is only lightly pitted, or if it has been re-cut, fine grinding compound *only* should be used to produce the required finish. Coarse valve-grinding compound should *not* be used, unless a seat is badly burned or deeply pitted. If this is the case, the cylinder head and valves should be inspected by an expert, to decide whether seat re-cutting, or even the renewal of the valve or seat insert (where possible) is required.
13 Valve grinding is carried out as follows. Place the cylinder head upside-down on a bench.
14 Smear a trace of (the appropriate grade of) valve-grinding compound on the seat face, and press a suction grinding tool onto the valve head. With a semi-rotary action, grind the valve head to its seat, lifting the valve occasionally to redistribute the grinding compound **(see illustration)**. A light spring placed under the valve head will greatly ease this operation.
15 If coarse grinding compound is being used, work only until a dull, matt even surface is produced on both the valve seat and the valve, then wipe off the used compound, and repeat the process with fine compound. When a smooth unbroken ring of light grey matt finish is produced on both the valve and seat, the grinding operation is complete. *Do not grind-in the valves any further than absolutely necessary, or the seat will be prematurely sunk into the cylinder head.*
16 When all the valves have been ground-in, carefully wash off *all* traces of grinding compound using paraffin or a suitable solvent, before reassembling the cylinder head.

Valve components

17 Examine the valve springs for signs of damage and discoloration. No minimum free length is specified by Renault, so the only way of judging valve spring wear is by comparison with a new component.
18 Stand each spring on a flat surface, and check it for squareness. If any of the springs are damaged, distorted or have lost their tension, obtain a complete new set of springs. It is normal to renew the valve springs as a matter of course if a major overhaul is being carried out.
19 Renew the valve stem oil seals regardless of their apparent condition.

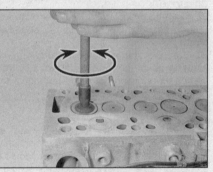

8.14 Grinding in a valve

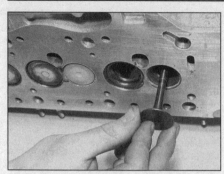

9.1 Lubricate the valve stem and insert the valve into the correct guide

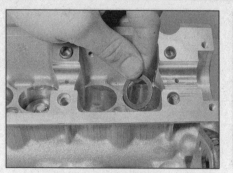

9.2a Fit the spring seat . . .

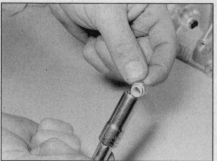

9.2b . . . then press on the new valve guide oil seal using a socket

9.3a Fit the valve spring . . .

9.3b . . . and the spring retainer . . .

9.4 . . . then compress the valve and fit the collets (diesel engine shown)

9 Cylinder head - reassembly

1 Lubricate the stems of the valves, and insert the valves into their original locations **(see illustration)**. If new valves are being fitted, insert them into the locations to which they have been ground.
2 Refit the spring seat then, working on the first valve, dip the new valve stem seal in fresh engine oil. Carefully locate it over the valve and onto the guide. Take care not to damage the seal as it is passed over the valve stem. Use a suitable socket or metal tube to press the seal firmly onto the guide **(see illustrations)**.
3 Locate the valve spring on top of its seat, then refit the spring retainer **(see illustrations)**.
4 Compress the valve spring, and locate the split collets in the recess in the valve stem **(see illustration)**. Release the compressor, then repeat the procedure on the remaining valves.

> **HAYNES HiNT**
> *Use a little dab of grease to hold the collets in position on the valve stem while the spring compressor is released.*

5 With all the valves installed, place the cylinder head on blocks on the bench and, using a hammer and interposed block of wood, tap the end of each valve stem to settle the components.

6 Refit the camshaft, followers and shims as described in Part A of this Chapter.
7 The cylinder head can then be refitted as described in Part A of this Chapter.

10 Auxiliary shaft - removal, inspection and refitting

Removal

1 Remove the timing belt, crankshaft and

auxiliary shaft timing sprockets and the idler pulley as described in Part A. Unbolt and remove the lower timing belt cover.
2 Unscrew the retaining bolts and withdraw the auxiliary shaft housing and gasket from the cylinder block. Note the housing locating dowels **(see illustration)**.
3 Unscrew the two bolts and withdraw the oil pump drivegear cover plate and sealing ring from the cylinder block. Screw a suitable bolt into the oil pump drivegear, or use a tapered wooden shaft, and withdraw the drivegear from its location.

2F

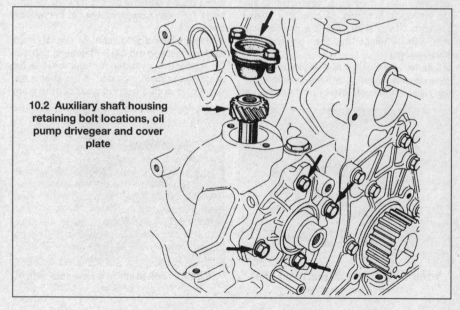

10.2 Auxiliary shaft housing retaining bolt locations, oil pump drivegear and cover plate

10.4a Remove the thrustplate . . .

10.4b . . . and slide the auxiliary shaft out from the block

4 Unscrew the two bolts and washers, and slide out the auxiliary shaft thrustplate. The auxiliary shaft can then be withdrawn from the block **(see illustrations)**.

Inspection

5 Examine the auxiliary shaft and oil pump driveshaft for pitting, scoring or wear ridges on the bearing journals, and for chipping or wear of the gear teeth. Renew as necessary. Check the auxiliary shaft bearings in the cylinder block for wear and, if worn, have these renewed by your Renault dealer or suitably-equipped engineering works. Wipe them clean if they are still serviceable.

6 Temporarily fit the thrustplate to its position on the auxiliary shaft, and use a feeler blade to check that the endfloat is as given in the *Specifications*. If it is greater than the upper tolerance, a new thrustplate should be obtained, but first check the thrust surfaces on the shaft to ascertain if wear has occurred here.

Refitting

7 Ensure that the mating surfaces of the housing and cylinder block are clean and dry.
8 Note the correct fitted location of the oil seal in the housing then carefully lever out the old seal. Install the new oil seal, making sure its sealing lip is facing inwards, and press it squarely into position until it is positioned at the same height as the original **(see illustrations)**.
9 Liberally lubricate the auxiliary shaft with clean engine oil and slide it into position.
10 Slide the thrustplate in position with its

curved edge away from the crankshaft, and refit the two retaining bolts, tightening them securely.
11 Place a new housing gasket in position over the dowels of the cylinder block. Liberally lubricate the oil seal lips and carefully ease the housing over the end of the shaft and into position. Refit the housing retaining bolts and tighten them securely.
12 Lubricate the oil pump drivegear, and lower the gear into its location. Ensure that the gear is correctly located then position a new sealing ring seal on the drivegear cover plate and fit the plate tightening its retaining bolts securely.
13 Refit the timing belt cover, sprockets and idler pulley and fit a new timing belt as described in Part A of this Chapter.

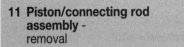

11 Piston/connecting rod assembly - removal

1 Remove the cylinder head, sump and oil pump as described in Part A of this Chapter.
2 If there is a pronounced wear ridge at the top of any bore, it may be necessary to remove it with a scraper or ridge reamer, to avoid piston damage during removal. Such a ridge indicates excessive wear of the cylinder bore.
3 Using quick drying paint or similar, mark each connecting rod big-end bearing cap with its respective cylinder number on the flat machined surface provided; if the engine has been dismantled before, note carefully any

identifying marks made previously **(see illustration)**. Note that No 1 cylinder is at the transmission (flywheel/driveplate) end of the engine.
4 Turn the crankshaft to bring pistons 1 and 4 to BDC (bottom dead centre).
5 Unscrew the bolts from No 1 piston big-end bearing cap. Take off the cap, noting the correct fitted positions of the locating pins, and recover the bottom half bearing shell. If the bearing shells are to be re-used, tape the cap and the shell together.
6 Using a hammer handle, push the piston up through the bore, and remove it from the top of the cylinder block. Recover the bearing shell, and tape it to the connecting rod for safe-keeping.
7 Loosely refit the big-end cap to the connecting rod, and secure with the bolts - this will help to keep the components in their correct order.
8 Remove No 4 piston assembly in the same way.
9 Turn the crankshaft through 180° to bring pistons 2 and 3 to BDC (bottom dead centre), and remove them in the same way.

12 Crankshaft - removal

1 Remove the timing belt, the crankshaft, auxiliary shaft and idler sprockets, the oil pump and the flywheel/driveplate as described in Part A of this Chapter. If the piston and connecting rod assemblies are also to be removed, remove the cylinder head.
2 Check the crankshaft endfloat as described in Section 15, then proceed as follows.
3 Remove the piston and connecting rod assemblies as described in Section 11. If no work is to be done on the pistons and connecting rods, unbolt the caps and push the pistons far enough up the bores that the connecting rods are positioned clear of the crankshaft journals.
4 Undo the retaining bolts and remove the timing belt lower cover from the cylinder block.
5 Slacken and remove the retaining bolts securing the crankshaft front oil seal housing

10.8a Prise out the oil seal using a flat-bladed screwdriver . . .

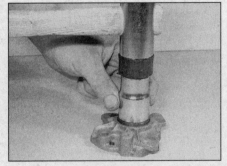

10.8b . . . and press in a new seal with a socket

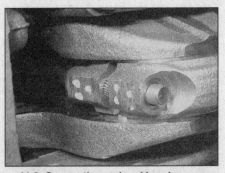

11.3 Connecting rod and bearing cap identification markings (No 3 shown)

to the cylinder block and remove the housing from the crankshaft end. If the cover locating dowels are a loose fit, remove and store them with the cover for safe-keeping.

6 The main bearing caps should be numbered 1 to 5 from the transmission (flywheel/driveplate) end of the engine. If not, mark them accordingly using paint in the same way as the connecting rods.

7 Unscrew and remove the main bearing cap retaining bolts, and withdraw the caps **(see illustration)**. Recover the lower main bearing shells, and tape them to their respective caps for safe-keeping.

8 Carefully lift out the crankshaft, taking care not to displace the upper main bearing shells, and discard the rear oil seal **(see illustration)**.

9 Recover the upper bearing shells from the cylinder block, and tape them to their respective caps for safe-keeping. Remove the thrustwasher halves from the side of crankcase main bearing, and store them with the bearing cap.

12.7 Removing a main bearing cap

12.8 Removing the crankshaft

---

13 Cylinder block -
cleaning and inspection

Cleaning

1 Remove all external components and electrical switches/sensors from the block. For complete cleaning, the core plugs should ideally be removed. Drill a small hole in the plugs, then insert a self-tapping screw into the hole. Pull out the plugs by pulling on the screw with a pair of grips, or by using a slide hammer.

2 Scrape all traces of gasket from the cylinder block, taking care not to damage the gasket/sealing surfaces.

3 Remove all oil gallery plugs (where fitted). The plugs are usually very tight - they may have to be drilled out, and the holes re-tapped. Use new plugs when the engine is reassembled.

4 If any of the castings are extremely dirty, all should be steam-cleaned.

5 After the castings are returned, clean all oil holes and oil galleries one more time. Flush all internal passages with warm water until the water runs clear. Dry thoroughly, and apply a light film of oil to all mating surfaces, to prevent rusting. Also oil the cylinder bores. If you have access to compressed air, use it to speed up the drying process, and to blow out all the oil holes and galleries.

 Warning: Wear eye protection when using compressed air!

6 If the castings are not very dirty, you can do an adequate cleaning job with hot (as hot as you can stand) soapy water and a stiff brush. Take plenty of time, and do a thorough job. Regardless of the cleaning method used, be sure to clean all oil holes and galleries very thoroughly, and to dry all components well.

Protect the cylinder bores as described above, to prevent rusting.

7 All threaded holes must be clean, to ensure accurate torque readings during reassembly. To clean the threads, run the correct-size tap into each of the holes to remove rust, corrosion, thread sealant or sludge, and to restore damaged threads. If possible, use compressed air to clear the holes of debris produced by this operation.

 Warning: Wear eye protection when cleaning out these holes in this way!

8 Apply suitable sealant to the new oil gallery plugs, and insert them into the holes in the block. Tighten them securely.

9 If the engine is not going to be reassembled right away, cover it with a large plastic bag to keep it clean; protect all mating surfaces and the cylinder bores as described above, to prevent rusting.

Inspection

10 Visually check the castings for cracks and corrosion. Look for stripped threads in the threaded holes. If there has been any history of internal water leakage, it may be worthwhile having an engine overhaul specialist check the cylinder block with special equipment. If

defects are found, have them repaired if possible, or renew the assembly.

11 Check the each cylinder bore for scuffing and scoring. Check for signs of a wear ridge at the top of the cylinder, indicating that the bore is excessively worn.

12 If the necessary measuring equipment is available, measure the bore diameter of each cylinder liner at the top (just under the wear ridge), centre, and bottom of the cylinder bore, parallel to the crankshaft axis.

13 Next, measure the bore diameter at the same three locations, at right-angles to the crankshaft axis. Compare the results with the figures given in the Specifications. If there is any doubt about the condition of the cylinder bores seek the advice of a Renault dealer or suitable engine reconditioning specialist.

14 At the time of writing, oversize pistons were not available for these engines. If the bores are worn, renewal of the block seems to be the only option. Seek the advice of a Renault dealer or engine overhaul specialist on the best course of action.

15 The size group of the cylinder bore can be determined from the 5 mm holes drilled into the side of the block **(see illustration)**. The distance from the block mating surface to the centre of the holes identifies the size group of

2F

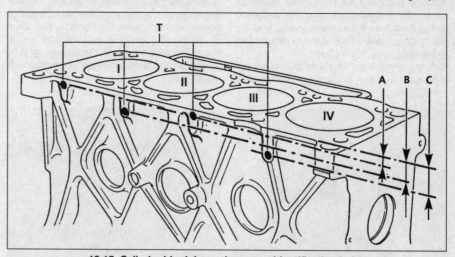
13.15 Cylinder block bore size group identification holes

A *Size group A axis*
B *Size group B axis*
C *Size group C axis*
T *Bore diameter identification holes*

the bore. On 1.8 litre models size group A holes are drilled 6 mm down from the mating surface, size group B holes 12 mm and size group C holes 18 mm. On 2.0 litre models size group A holes are drilled 18 mm down from the mating surface, size group B holes 24 mm and size group C holes 30 mm. Use the size group markings when purchasing new pistons.

14 Piston/connecting rod assembly - inspection

1 Before the inspection process can begin, the piston/connecting rod assemblies must be cleaned, and the original piston rings removed from the pistons.
2 Carefully expand the old rings over the top of the pistons. The use of two or three old feeler blades will be helpful in preventing the rings dropping into empty grooves. Be careful not to scratch the piston with the ends of the ring. The rings are brittle, and will snap if they are spread too far. They're also very sharp - protect your hands and fingers. Note that the third ring incorporates an expander. Always remove the rings from the top of the piston. Keep each set of rings with its piston if the old rings are to be re-used.
3 Scrape away all traces of carbon from the top of the piston. A hand-held wire brush (or a piece of fine emery cloth) can be used, once the majority of the deposits have been scraped away. The piston identification markings should now be visible **(see illustration)**.
4 Remove the carbon from the ring grooves in the piston, using an old ring. Break the ring in half to do this (be careful not to cut your fingers - piston rings are sharp). Be careful to remove only the carbon deposits - do not remove any metal, and do not nick or scratch the sides of the ring grooves.
5 Once the deposits have been removed, clean the piston/connecting rod assembly with paraffin or a suitable solvent, and dry thoroughly. Make sure that the oil return holes in the ring grooves are clear.
6 If the pistons and cylinder bores are not damaged or worn excessively, the original

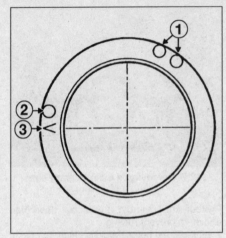

14.3 Piston identification markings

1 *Manufacturer's reference marking*
2 *Size group making*
3 *Correct fitting position marking*

pistons can be refitted. Normal piston wear shows up as even vertical wear on the piston thrust surfaces, and slight looseness of the top ring in its groove. New piston rings should always be used when the engine is reassembled.
7 Carefully inspect each piston for cracks around the skirt, around the gudgeon pin holes, and at the piston ring 'lands' (between the ring grooves).
8 Look for scoring and scuffing on the piston skirt, holes in the piston crown, and burned areas at the edge of the crown. If the skirt is scored or scuffed, the engine may have been suffering from overheating, and/or abnormal combustion which caused excessively high operating temperatures. The cooling and lubrication systems should be checked thoroughly. Scorch marks on the sides of the pistons show that blow-by has occurred. A hole in the piston crown, or burned areas at the edge of the piston crown, indicates that abnormal combustion (pre-ignition, knocking, or detonation) has been occurring. If any of the above problems exist, the causes must be investigated and corrected, or the damage will occur again.

9 Corrosion of the piston, in the form of pitting, indicates that coolant has been leaking into the combustion chamber and/or the crankcase. Again, the cause must be corrected, or the problem may persist in the rebuilt engine.
10 Examine each connecting rod carefully for signs of damage, such as cracks around the big-end and small-end bearings. Check that the rod is not bent or distorted. Damage is highly unlikely, unless the engine has been seized or badly overheated. Detailed checking of the connecting rod assembly can only be carried out by a Renault dealer or engine repair specialist with the necessary equipment.
11 On 1.8 litre engines the gudgeon pins are an interference fit in the connecting rod small-end bearing. Therefore, piston and/or connecting rod renewal should be entrusted to a Renault dealer or engine repair specialist, who will have the necessary tooling to remove and install the gudgeon pins. If new pistons are to be fitted, ensure that the correct size group piston is fitted to each bore (see Section 13).
12 On 2.0 litre engines the gudgeon pins are of the floating type, secured in position by two circlips. If necessary, the pistons and connecting rods can be separated as follows.
13 Using a small flat-bladed screwdriver, prise out the circlips, and push out the gudgeon pin **(see illustrations)**. Hand pressure should be sufficient to remove the pin. Identify the piston and rod to ensure correct reassembly. Discard the circlips - new ones *must* be used on refitting.
14 Examine the gudgeon pin and connecting rod small-end bearing for signs of wear or damage. Wear will mean both the pin and connecting rod will have to be renewed.
15 The connecting rods themselves should not be in need of renewal, unless seizure or some other major mechanical failure has occurred. Check the alignment of the connecting rods visually, and if the rods are not straight, take them to an engine overhaul specialist for a more detailed check.
16 Examine all components, and renew any worn parts. If new pistons are purchased, they will be supplied complete with gudgeon pins and circlips. Circlips can also be purchased individually. When purchasing new pistons, ensure that the correct size group piston is fitted to each bore (see Section 13).
17 Noting that the connecting rod bearing cap locating pins are positioned on the timing belt end of the connecting rod, fit the piston so that the V stamped on the piston crown **(see illustration 14.3)** is pointing towards the flywheel end. Apply a smear of clean engine oil to the gudgeon pin. Slide it into the piston and through the connecting rod small-end. Check that the piston pivots freely on the rod, then secure the gudgeon pin in position with two new circlips. Ensure that each circlip is correctly located in its groove in the piston.

14.13a On 2.0 litre engines, carefully prise out the circlip . . .

14.13b . . . then press out the gudgeon pin and separate the piston and connecting rod

15.2 Measuring the crankshaft endfloat using a dial gauge

15.3 Measuring the crankshaft endfloat using a feeler blade

15.10 Measuring a main bearing journal diameter using a micrometer

15 Crankshaft - inspection

Checking crankshaft endfloat

1 If the crankshaft endfloat is to be checked, this must be done when the crankshaft is still installed in the cylinder block, but is free to move.

2 Check the endfloat using a dial gauge in contact with the end of the crankshaft. Push the crankshaft fully one way, and then zero the gauge. Push the crankshaft fully the other way, and check the endfloat **(see illustration)**. The result can be compared with the specified amount, and will give an indication as to whether new thrustwashers are required.

3 If a dial gauge is not available, feeler blades can be used. First push the crankshaft fully towards the flywheel end of the engine, then use feeler blades to measure the gap between the web of the crankpin and the thrustwasher **(see illustration)**.

Inspection

4 Clean the crankshaft using paraffin or a suitable solvent, and dry it, preferably with compressed air if available. Be sure to clean the oil holes with a pipe cleaner or similar probe, to ensure that they are not obstructed.

 Warning: Wear eye protection when using compressed air.

5 Check the main and big-end bearing journals for uneven wear, scoring, pitting and cracking.

6 Big-end bearing wear is accompanied by distinct metallic knocking when the engine is running (particularly noticeable when the engine is pulling from low speed) and some loss of oil pressure.

7 Main bearing wear is accompanied by severe engine vibration and rumble - getting progressively worse as engine speed increases - and again by loss of oil pressure.

8 Check the bearing journal for roughness by running a finger lightly over the bearing surface. Any roughness (which will be accompanied by obvious bearing wear)

indicates that the crankshaft requires regrinding (where possible) or renewal.

9 If the crankshaft has been reground, check for burrs around the crankshaft oil holes (the holes are usually chamfered, so burrs should not be a problem unless regrinding has been carried out carelessly). Remove any burrs with a fine file or scraper, and thoroughly clean the oil holes as described previously.

10 Using a micrometer, measure the diameter of the main and big-end bearing journals, and compare the results with the Specifications **(see illustration)**. By measuring the diameter at a number of points around each journal's circumference, you will be able to determine whether or not the journal is out-of-round. Take the measurement at each end of the journal, near the webs, to determine if the journal is tapered. Compare the results obtained with those given in the Specifications.

11 Check the oil seal contact surfaces at each end of the crankshaft for wear and damage. If the seal has worn a deep groove in the surface of the crankshaft, consult an engine overhaul specialist; repair may be possible, but otherwise a new crankshaft will be required.

12 If the crankshaft journals have not already been reground, it may be possible to have the crankshaft reconditioned, and to fit oversize shells. Consult your Renault dealer or engine specialist for further information.

16 Main and big-end bearings - inspection

1 Even though the main and big-end bearings should be renewed during the engine overhaul, the old bearings should be retained for close examination, as they may reveal valuable information about the condition of the engine. The bearing shells are graded by thickness, the grade of each shell being indicated by the colour code marked on it.

2 Bearing failure can occur due to lack of lubrication, the presence of dirt or other foreign particles, overloading the engine, or corrosion **(see illustration)**. Regardless of the cause of bearing failure, the cause must be corrected (where applicable) before the engine is reassembled, to prevent it from happening again.

3 When examining the bearing shells, remove them from the cylinder block, the main bearing caps, the connecting rods and the connecting rod big-end bearing caps. Lay them out on a clean surface in the same general position as their location in the engine. This will enable you to match any bearing problems with the corresponding crankshaft journal.

4 Dirt and other foreign matter gets into the engine in a variety of ways. It may be left in

2F

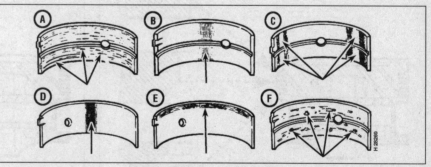

16.2 Typical bearing failures

A Scratched by dirt; dirt embedded in bearing material
B Lack of oil; overlay wiped out
C Improper seating; bright (polished) sections
D Tapered journal; overlay gone from entire surface
E Radius ride
F Fatigue failure; craters or pockets

the engine during assembly, or it may pass through filters or the crankcase ventilation system. It may get into the oil, and from there into the bearings. Metal chips from machining operations and normal engine wear are often present. Abrasives are sometimes left in engine components after reconditioning, especially when parts are not thoroughly cleaned using the proper cleaning methods. Whatever the source, these foreign objects often end up embedded in the soft bearing material, and are easily recognised. Large particles will not embed in the bearing, and will score or gouge the bearing and journal. The best prevention for this cause of bearing failure is to clean all parts thoroughly, and keep everything spotlessly-clean during engine assembly. Frequent and regular engine oil and filter changes are also recommended.

5 Lack of lubrication (or lubrication breakdown) has a number of interrelated causes. Excessive heat (which thins the oil), overloading (which squeezes the oil from the bearing face) and oil leakage (from excessive bearing clearances, worn oil pump or high engine speeds) all contribute to lubrication breakdown. Blocked oil passages, which usually are the result of misaligned oil holes in a bearing shell, will also oil-starve a bearing, and destroy it. When lack of lubrication is the cause of bearing failure, the bearing material is wiped or extruded from the steel backing of the bearing. Temperatures may increase to the point where the steel backing turns blue from overheating.

6 Driving habits can have a definite effect on bearing life. Full-throttle, low-speed operation (labouring the engine) puts very high loads on bearings, tending to squeeze out the oil film. These loads cause the bearings to flex, which produces fine cracks in the bearing face (fatigue failure). Eventually, the bearing

material will loosen in pieces, and tear away from the steel backing.

7 Short-distance driving leads to corrosion of bearings, because insufficient engine heat is produced to drive off the condensed water and corrosive gases. These products collect in the engine oil, forming acid and sludge. As the oil is carried to the engine bearings, the acid attacks and corrodes the bearing material.

8 Incorrect bearing installation during engine assembly will lead to bearing failure as well. Tight-fitting bearings leave insufficient bearing running clearance, and will result in oil starvation. Dirt or foreign particles trapped behind a bearing shell result in high spots on the bearing, which lead to failure.

9 As mentioned at the beginning of this Section, the bearing shells should be renewed as a matter of course during engine overhaul; to do otherwise is false economy.

17 Engine overhaul - reassembly sequence

1 Before reassembly begins, ensure that all new parts have been obtained, and that all necessary tools are available. Read through the entire procedure to familiarise yourself with the work involved, and to ensure that all items necessary for reassembly of the engine are at hand. In addition to all normal tools and materials, thread-locking compound will be needed. A suitable tube of liquid sealant will also be required for the joint faces that are fitted without gaskets. It is recommended that Renault's own product(s) are used, which are specially formulated for this purpose; the relevant product names are quoted in the text of each Section where they are required.

2 In order to save time and avoid problems, engine reassembly can be carried out in the following order:
  a) Crankshaft.
  b) Piston/connecting rod assemblies.
  c) Auxiliary shaft.
  d) Oil pump.
  e) Sump.
  f) Flywheel.
  g) Cylinder head.
  h) Timing belt tensioner and sprockets, and timing belt.
  i) Engine ancillary components.

3 At this stage, all engine components should be absolutely clean and dry, with all faults repaired. The components should be laid out (or in individual containers) on a completely clean work surface.

18 Piston rings - refitting

1 Fit the piston rings using the same technique as for removal. Fit the bottom (oil control) ring first, and work up. Ensure that both the top and second compression rings are fitted the correct way up **(see illustrations)**. **Note:** *Always follow any instructions supplied with the new piston ring sets - different manufacturers may specify different procedures. Do not mix up the top and second compression rings, as they have different cross-sections.*

2 With the piston rings correctly installed, check that each ring is free to rotate easily in its groove. Position the ring end gaps so that are spaced at 120° intervals.

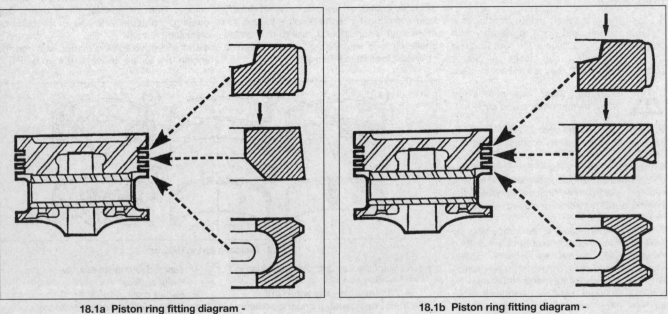

18.1a Piston ring fitting diagram - 1.8 litre engine

18.1b Piston ring fitting diagram - 2.0 litre engine

19 Crankshaft -
refitting and main bearing running clearance check

Note: *It is recommended that new main bearing shells are fitted regardless of the condition of the original ones.*

Selection of bearing shells

1 There are two different sizes of bearing shell available; the standard size shell for use with an original crankshaft and an oversize shell for use once the crankshaft has been reground.

2 The relevant set of bearing shells required can be obtained by measuring the diameter of the crankshaft main bearing journals (see Section 15). This will show if the crankshaft is original or whether its journals have been reground, identifying if either standard or oversize bearing shells are required.

3 If the access to the necessary measuring equipment cannot be gained, the size of the bearing shells can be identified by the markings stamped on the rear of each shell **(see illustration)**. Details of these markings should be supplied to your Renault dealer who will then be able to identify the size of shell fitted.

4 Whether the original shells or new shells are being fitted, it is recommended that the running clearance is checked as follows prior to installation.

Main bearing running clearance check

5 Clean the backs of the bearing shells and the bearing locations in both the cylinder block and the main bearing caps.

6 Press the bearing shells into their locations, noting that the shells with the holes should be fitted to the cylinder block, ensuring that the tab on each shell engages in the notch in the cylinder block or main bearing cap.

7 If the original bearing shells are being used for the check, ensure that they are refitted in their original locations. The clearance can be checked in either of two ways.

8 One method (which will be difficult to achieve without a range of internal micrometers or internal/external expanding calipers) is to refit the main bearing caps to the cylinder block, with bearing shells in place. With the cap retaining bolts correctly tightened, measure the internal diameter of each assembled pair of bearing shells. If the diameter of each corresponding crankshaft journal is measured and then subtracted from the bearing internal diameter, the result will be the main bearing running clearance.

9 The second (and more accurate) method is to use a product known as Plastigauge. This consists of a fine thread of perfectly round plastic which is compressed between the bearing shell and the journal. When the shell is removed, the plastic is deformed and can be measured with a special card gauge supplied

19.3 Typical marking on the back of a bearing shell

with the kit. The running clearance is determined from this gauge. Plastigauge is sometimes difficult to obtain but enquiries at one of the larger specialist quality motor factors should produce the name of a stockist in your area. The procedure for using Plastigauge is as follows.

10 With the main bearing upper shells in place, carefully lay the crankshaft in position. Do not use any lubricant; the crankshaft journals and bearing shells must be perfectly clean and dry.

11 Cut several lengths of the appropriate size Plastigauge (they should be slightly shorter than the width of the main bearings) and place one length on each crankshaft journal axis **(see illustration)**.

12 With the main bearing lower shells in position, refit the main bearing caps, tightening their retaining bolts to the specified torque. Take care not to disturb the Plastigauge and do not rotate the crankshaft at any time during this operation.

13 Remove the main bearing caps again taking great care not to disturb the Plastigauge or rotate the crankshaft.

14 Compare the width of the crushed Plastigauge on each journal to the scale printed on the Plastigauge envelope to obtain the main bearing running clearance **(see illustration)**. Compare the clearance measured with that given in the Specifications at the start of this Chapter.

15 If the clearance is significantly different from that expected, the bearing shells may be the wrong size (or excessively worn if the

19.14 Measuring the width of the deformed Plastigauge using the scale on the card provided

19.11 Plastigauge in place on a crankshaft main bearing journal

original shells are being re-used). Before deciding that the crankshaft is worn, make sure that no dirt or oil was trapped between the bearing shells and the caps or block when the clearance was measured. If the Plastigauge was wider at one end than at the other, the crankshaft journal may be tapered.

16 Note that Renault do not specify a running clearance for these engines. The figure given in the Specifications is a guide figure which is typical for this type of engine. Before condemning the components concerned, seek the advice of your Renault dealer or suitable engine repair specialist. They will also be able to inform as to the best course of action and whether it is possible to have the crankshaft journals reground (where possible) or whether renewal will be necessary.

17 Where necessary, obtain the correct size of bearing shell and repeat the running clearance checking procedure as described above.

18 On completion, carefully scrape away all traces of the Plastigauge material from the crankshaft and bearing shells using a fingernail or other object which is unlikely to score the bearing surfaces.

Final crankshaft refitting

19 Carefully lift the crankshaft out of the cylinder block once more.

20 Place the bearing shells in their locations as described above in paragraphs 6 and 7 **(see illustration)**. If new shells are being fitted, ensure that all traces of the protective grease are cleaned off using paraffin. Wipe dry the shells and caps with a lint-free cloth.

19.20 Fit the bearing shells to the block noting that the upper shells are the ones with oil holes in them

2F

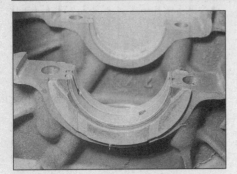

19.21 Stick the thrustwasher halves to the cylinder block using grease, making sure their oil grooves are facing outwards

21 Using a little grease, stick the thrust-washers to each side of the main bearing upper location; ensure that the oilway grooves on each thrustwasher face outwards (away from the cylinder block) **(see illustration).**

22 Liberally lubricate each bearing shell in the cylinder block with clean engine oil then lower the crankshaft into position ensuring that the bearing shells and thrustwashers remain correctly seated.

23 Check the crankshaft endfloat as described in Section 15.

24 Ensure that the cap locating dowels are in position and fit the main bearing caps numbers 2 to 5. Ensure that the caps are fitted in their correct locations and the correct way round. Insert the bearing cap bolts and tighten them to the specified torque setting **(see illustration).**

25 There are two possible ways of sealing the No 1 main bearing cap. The first is by fitting rubber sealing strips to the cap grooves, and the second is by filling the grooves with a special sealant kit available from your Renault dealer **(see illustration).** The second method using the sealant is extremely messy and if carried out carelessly can lead to the oilways being blocked. It is therefore recommended that the sealing strips are used as follows.

26 Two different thickness of sealing strip are available and it is first necessary to decide which size is needed. The thinner (5.1 mm thick) sealing strip is unmarked whereas the thicker (6.0 mm thick) sealing strip has a colour marking on it.

27 To select the correct size of sealing strip, ensure that the locating dowels are in position then fit the main bearing cap and lightly tighten the retaining bolts. Using a suitable twist drill, measure the gap between the inner edge of the main bearing cap seal groove and the cylinder block **(see illustration).** If this dimension is less than 5 mm then the thinner sealing strips will be required. If the dimension is greater than or equal to 5 mm then the thicker sealing strips will be required. Unbolt the bearing cap and remove.

28 Fit the correct rubber sealing strips to each groove in the bearing cap ensuring that the groove in each strip is facing outwards. Position each sealing strip so that is end protrudes approximately 0.2 mm above the upper (cylinder block) mating surface of the bearing cap **(see illustrations).**

29 To ease installation, obtain two thin metal strips of 0.25 mm thickness or less. These can then be used to prevent the strips moving as the cap is being fitted. Old feeler blades are ideal for this purpose, provided all burrs which may damage the sealing strips are first removed.

19.24 Fit bearing caps numbers 2 to 5 and tighten the retaining bolts to the specified torque

19.25 Renault sealing kit for main bearing cap grooves. Full instructions are supplied with the kit.

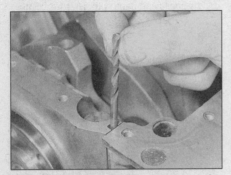

19.27 Using a twist drill to measure main bearing cap groove to cylinder block clearance

19.28a Fit the sealing strips to the bearing cap so that its groove is facing away from the cap . . .

19.28b . . . and position the strip so that it protrudes above the cap mating surface by approximately 0.2 mm

30 Apply a thin coating of sealant (Renault recommend the use of CAF 4/60 THIXO or Rhodorseal) to the mating surface of the cylinder block, taking great care not to block the oil return holes **(see illustration)**.

31 Oil both sides of the metal strips, and hold them on the sealing strips. Ease the main bearing cap into position and insert the bolts loosely **(see illustration)**. Just before the cap touches the cylinder block/mating surface, check that the sealing strips are still protruding from the cap. If not remove the cap and repeat the fitting procedure.

32 With the cap in position tighten the retaining bolts to the specified torque setting then carefully pull out the metal strips with a pair of pliers in a horizontal direction. Using a sharp knife, trim the lower end of each sealing strip so that the strips are flush with the sump mating surface **(see illustrations)**.

33 Note the correct fitted depth of the crankshaft front oil seal in the housing then carefully lever it out of position using a large, flat-bladed screwdriver. Fit the new seal to the housing, making sure its sealing lip is facing inwards and press it squarely into position until it is positioned at the same depth as the original.

34 Ensure that the mating surfaces are clean and dry and apply a smear of sealant (Renault recommend the use of CAF 4/60 THIXO or Rhodorseal) to the housing mating surface.

When applying the sealant, take care not to block the cover oilway **(see illustration)**.

35 Ensure that the locating dowels are in position and lubricate the oil seal lip with clean engine oil. Carefully ease the housing over the end of the crankshaft and into position on the block.

36 Coat the threads of the two oil seal housing lower bolts (those which screw into the locating dowel holes) with the sealant. Refit all the retaining bolts and tighten them securely.

37 Fit a new crankshaft rear oil seal as described in Part A of this Chapter.

38 Refit the timing belt lower cover and securely tighten its retaining bolts.

39 Refit the piston/connecting rod assemblies, auxiliary shaft, oil pump, flywheel/driveplate, cylinder head, timing belt sprockets and fit a new timing belt as described in Part A of this Chapter.

20 Piston/connecting rod assembly - refitting and big-end running clearance check

Note: *It is recommended that new piston rings and big-end bearing shells are fitted regardless of the condition of the original ones.*

Selection of bearing shells

1 See Section 19.

Big-end bearing running clearance check

2 Clean the backs of the bearing shells and the bearing locations in both the connecting rod and bearing cap.

3 Press the bearing shells into their locations, ensuring that the tab on each shell engages in the notch in the connecting rod and cap and taking care not to touch any shell's bearing surface with your fingers.

4 The upper shells, which are fitted to the connecting rods may or may not (depending on model) have an oil hole in them, the lower shells which are fitted to the bearing caps, are plain. If the original bearing shells are being used for the check ensure that they are refitted in their original locations. The clearance can be checked in either of two ways.

5 One method is to refit the big-end bearing cap to the connecting rod, with bearing shells in place. With the cap retaining bolts correctly tightened, use an internal micrometer or vernier caliper to measure the internal diameter of each assembled pair of bearing shells. If the diameter of each corresponding crankshaft journal is measured and then subtracted from the bearing internal diameter, the result will be the big-end bearing running clearance.

6 The second method is to use Plastigauge as described in Section 19, paragraphs 9 to 18.

19.30 Apply a smear of suitable sealant to the cylinder block/crankcase . . .

19.31 . . . then slide the bearing cap assembly into position using the metal strips to ensure the sealing strips are not displaced

19.32a Tighten the bearing cap retaining bolts to the specified torque . . .

19.32b . . . then carefully slide out the metal strips

19.32c Trim off the ends of the sealing strips so that each one is flush with the block face

19.34 Apply sealant to the crankshaft oil seal housing mating surface taking care not to apply any sealant to the area indicated by the arrow

2F

20.10 Tap the piston into the bore using a hammer handle

20.12a Refit the big-end bearing cap . . .

20.12b . . . and tighten its retaining bolts nuts to the specified torque

With the piston/connecting rod assemblies refitted as described below, place a strand of Plastigauge on each (cleaned) crankpin journal. Refit the (clean) bearing shells and big-end bearing caps, tightening the bolts to the specified torque wrench setting. Take care not to disturb the Plastigauge. Dismantle the assemblies without rotating the crankshaft and use the scale printed on the Plastigauge envelope to obtain the big-end bearing running clearance. On completion of the measurement, carefully scrape off all traces of Plastigauge from the journal and shells using a fingernail or other object which will not score the components.

Final piston/connecting rod assembly refitting

7 Ensure that the bearing shells are correctly refitted as described above in paragraphs 2 to 4. If new shells are being fitted, ensure that all traces of the protective grease are cleaned off using paraffin. Wipe dry the shells and connecting rods with a lint-free cloth.
8 Lubricate the bores, the pistons and piston rings then lay out each piston/connecting rod assembly in its respective position.
9 Starting with assembly number 1, make sure that the piston rings are still spaced as described in Section 18, then clamp them in position with a piston ring compressor.
10 Insert the piston/connecting rod assembly into the top of cylinder No 1 ensuring that the V stamped on the piston crown is pointing towards the flywheel end of the engine. Using a block of wood or hammer handle against

the piston crown, tap the assembly into the cylinder until the piston crown is flush with the top of the cylinder **(see illustration)**.
11 Taking care not to mark the cylinder bore, liberally lubricate the crankpin and both bearing shells, then pull the piston/connecting rod assembly down the bore and onto the crankpin. Ensure that the locating pins are in position then refit the big-end bearing cap.
12 Refit the bearing cap bolts and tighten them evenly and progressively to the specified torque setting **(see illustrations)**.
13 Refit the remaining three piston and connecting rod assemblies in the same way.
14 Rotate the crankshaft, and check that it turns freely, with no signs of binding or tight spots.
15 Refit the auxiliary shaft, oil pump, flywheel/driveplate, cylinder head, timing belt sprockets and fit a new timing belt as described in Part A of this Chapter.

21 Engine - initial start up after overhaul

1 With the engine refitted in the vehicle, double-check the engine oil and coolant levels. Make a final check that everything has been reconnected, and that there are no tools or rags left in the engine compartment.
2 Remove the spark plugs. On models with a distributor, disable the ignition system by disconnecting the ignition HT coil lead from the distributor cap, and earthing it on the

cylinder block. Use a jumper lead or similar wire to make a good connection. On models with a static (distributorless) ignition system, disable the ignition system by disconnecting the LT wiring connector from the ignition HT coil, referring to Chapter 5B for further information.
3 Turn the engine on the starter until the oil pressure warning light goes out. Refit the spark plugs, and reconnect the spark plug (HT) leads, referring to Chapter 1A for further information. Reconnect any HT leads or wiring which was disconnected in paragraph 2.
4 Start the engine, noting that this may take a little longer than usual, due to the fuel system components having been disturbed.
5 While the engine is idling, check for fuel, water and oil leaks. Don't be alarmed if there are some odd smells and smoke from parts getting hot and burning off oil deposits.
6 Assuming all is well, keep the engine idling until hot water is felt circulating through the top hose, then switch off the engine.
7 After a few minutes, recheck the oil and coolant levels as described in *Weekly checks*, and top-up as necessary.
8 If they were tightened as described, there is no need to re-tighten the cylinder head bolts once the engine has first run after reassembly.
9 If new pistons, rings or crankshaft bearings have been fitted, the engine must be treated as new, and run-in for the first 500 miles (800 km). *Do not* operate the engine at full-throttle, or allow it to labour at low engine speeds in any gear. It is recommended that the oil and filter be changed at the end of this period.

Chapter 2 Part G:
16-valve petrol engine removal and overhaul procedures

Contents

Degrees of difficulty

Easy, suitable for novice with little experience	Fairly easy, suitable for beginner with some experience	Fairly difficult, suitable for competent DIY mechanic	Difficult, suitable for experienced DIY mechanic	Very difficult, suitable for expert DIY or professional

2G

Specifications

1.6 litre engines

Cylinder head

Maximum gasket face distortion	0.05 mm
Cylinder head height	137.0 mm
Valve seat angle (included)	89°
Valve seat width:	
Inlet	1.3 to 2.7 mm
Exhaust	1.4 to 2.7 mm

Valves

	Inlet	Exhaust
Valve head diameter	32.58 to 32.82 mm	27.84 to 28.08 mm
Valve stem diameter	5.474 to 5.494 mm	5.463 to 5.483 mm
Valve length	109.32 mm	107.64 mm
Valve seat angle (included)	90° 15'	

Valve springs

External diameter	27.0 mm
Free length	41.30 mm

Cylinder block

Cylinder bore diameter:	
Class A	79.50 to 79.51 mm
Class B	79.51 to 79.52 mm
Class C	79.52 to 79.53 mm

Pistons

Piston diameter:	
Class A	79.47 to 79.48 mm
Class B	79.48 to 79.49 mm
Class C	79.49 to 79.50 mm
Piston-to-bore clearance	0.02 to 0.04 mm

Piston rings

	Thickness	End gap (measured in cylinder)
Top compression	1.2 mm	0.15 to 0.30 mm
Second compression	1.5 mm	0.40 to 0.60 mm
Oil control	2.5 mm	0.40 to 1.40 mm

Gudgeon pins

Length	61.7 to 62.0 mm
Diameter	19.986 to 19.991 mm

1.6 litre engines (continued)

Crankshaft

Endfloat	0.045 to 0.85 mm
Main bearing journal diameter:	
Class A	47.990 to 47.997 mm
Class B	47.997 to 48.003 mm
Class C	48.003 to 48.010 mm
Big-end bearing journal diameter	43.96 to 43.98 mm
Maximum bearing journal out-of-round*	0.01 mm
Main bearing running clearance*	0.025 to 0.050 mm
Big-end bearing running clearance*	0.025 to 0.050 mm

These are suggested figures, typical for this type of engine - no exact values are stated by Renault.

Torque wrench settings

Refer to Chapter 2B Specifications

1.8 litre engines

Cylinder head

Maximum gasket face distortion	0.05 mm
Cylinder head height	138.15 mm
Valve seat angle (included)	89°
Valve seat width:	
Inlet	1.3 to 2.7 mm
Exhaust	1.4 to 2.7 mm

Valves

	Inlet	Exhaust
Valve head diameter	33.38 to 33.62 mm	28.88 to 29.12 mm
Valve stem diameter	5.462 to 5.480 mm	5.438 to 5.456 mm
Valve length	109.93 to 110.23 mm	108.72 to 109.02 mm
Valve seat angle (included)	90°	

Valve springs

External diameter	27.0 mm
Free length	41.30 mm

Cylinder block

Cylinder bore diameter:	
Class 2	82.710 to 82.720 mm
Class 3	82.720 to 82.730 mm

Pistons

Piston diameter:	
Class 2	82.680 to 82.690 mm
Class 3	82.690 to 82.700 mm
Piston-to-bore clearance	0.02 to 0.04 mm

Piston rings

Thickness:	
Top compression	1.2 mm
Second compression	1.47 to 1.495 mm
Oil control	1.94 mm
End gap (measured in cylinder):	
Top compression	0.15 to 0.30 mm
Second compression	0.40 to 0.60 mm
Oil control	0.40 to 1.40 mm

Gudgeon pins

Length	60.7 to 61.0 mm
Diameter	20.995 to 21.000 mm

Crankshaft

Endfloat	0.07 to 0.23 mm
Main bearing journal diameter	54.785 to 54.805
Big-end bearing journal diameter	47.980 to 48.000 mm
Maximum bearing journal out-of-round*	0.01 mm
Main bearing running clearance*	0.025 to 0.050 mm
Big-end bearing running clearance*	0.025 to 0.050 mm

These are suggested figures, typical for this type of engine - no exact values are stated by Renault.

Torque wrench settings

Refer to Chapter 2B Specifications

2.0 litre engines

Cylinder head

Maximum gasket face distortion	0.05 mm
Cylinder head height	129.0 mm
Valve seat angle (included)	90º
Valve seat width:	
Inlet	1.4 to 1.8 mm
Exhaust	1.8 to 2.2 mm

Valves

Valve head diameter:	
Inlet	30.85 to 31.15 mm
Exhaust	26.85 to 27.15 mm
Valve stem diameter	6.90 to 6.94 mm
Valve seat angle (included)	90º

Valve springs

Free length	42.40 mm

Cylinder block

Cylinder bore diameter:	
Class C	83.000 to 83.010 mm
Class D	83.010 to 83.020 mm
Class E	83.020 to 83.030 mm
Class G	83.040 to 83.050 mm
Class 2 (oversize)	83.200 to 83.210 mm

Pistons

Piston diameter:	
Class C	82.980 to 82.990 mm
Class D	82.990 to 83.000 mm
Class E	83.000 to 83.010 mm
Class G	83.017 to 83.032 mm
Class 2 (oversize)	83.177 to 83.192 mm
Piston-to-bore clearance	0.01 to 0.03 mm

Piston rings

Thickness:	
Top compression	1.17 to 1.2 mm
Second compression	1.73 to 1.75 mm
Oil control	2.98 to 3.00 mm

Crankshaft

Endfloat	0.08 to 0.19 mm
Main bearing journal diameter	64.987 to 65.000
Big-end bearing journal diameter	49.984 to 50.000 mm
Maximum bearing journal out-of-round*	0.01 mm
Main bearing running clearance*	0.025 to 0.050 mm
Big-end bearing running clearance*	0.025 to 0.050 mm

*These are suggested figures, typical for this type of engine - no exact values are stated by Renault.

Torque wrench settings

Refer to Chapter 2C Specifications

1 General information

Included in this Part of Chapter 2 are details of removing the engine/transmission from the car and general overhaul procedures for the cylinder head, cylinder block and all other engine internal components.

The information given ranges from advice concerning preparation for an overhaul and the purchase of replacement parts, to detailed step-by-step procedures covering removal, inspection, renovation and refitting of engine internal components.

After Section 5, all instructions are based on the assumption that the engine has been removed from the car. For information concerning in-car engine repair, as well as the removal and refitting of those external components necessary for full overhaul, refer to Parts B and C of this Chapter and to Section 4. Ignore any preliminary dismantling operations described in Parts B or C that are no longer relevant once the engine has been removed from the car.

Apart from torque wrench settings, which are given at the beginning of Parts B or C, all specifications relating to engine overhaul are at the beginning of this Part of Chapter 2.

2 Engine/transmission removal - preparation and precautions

If you have decided that an engine must be removed for overhaul or major repair work, several preliminary steps should be taken.

Locating a suitable place to work is extremely important. Adequate work space, along with storage space for the car, will be needed. If a workshop or garage is not available, at the very least, a flat, level, clean work surface is required.

If possible, clear some shelving close to the work area and use it to store the engine

2G

components and ancillaries as they are removed and dismantled. In this manner the components stand a better chance of staying clean and undamaged during the overhaul. Laying out components in groups together with their fixing bolts, screws etc will save time and avoid confusion when the engine is refitted.

Clean the engine compartment and engine/transmission before beginning the removal procedure; this will help visibility and help to keep tools clean.

The help of an assistant should be available; there are certain instances when one person cannot safely perform all of the operations required to remove the engine from the vehicle. Safety is of primary importance, considering the potential hazards involved in this kind of operation. A second person should always be in attendance to offer help in an emergency. If this is the first time you have removed an engine, advice and aid from someone more experienced would also be beneficial.

Plan the operation ahead of time. Before starting work, obtain (or arrange for the hire of) all of the tools and equipment you will need. Access to the following items will allow the task of removing and refitting the engine/transmission to be completed safely and with relative ease: an engine hoist - rated in excess of the combined weight of the engine/ transmission, a heavy-duty trolley jack, complete sets of spanners and sockets as described in the reference section of this manual, wooden blocks, and plenty of rags and cleaning solvent for mopping up spilled oil, coolant and fuel. A selection of different sized plastic storage bins will also prove useful for keeping dismantled components grouped together. If any of the equipment must be hired, make sure that you arrange for it in advance, and perform all of the operations possible without it beforehand; this may save you time and money.

Plan on the vehicle being out of use for quite a while, especially if you intend to carry out an engine overhaul. Read through the whole of this Section and work out a strategy based on your own experience and the tools, time and workspace available to you. Some of the overhaul processes may have to be carried out by a Renault dealer or an engineering works - these establishments often have busy schedules, so it would be prudent to consult them before removing or dismantling the engine, to get an idea of the amount of time required to carry out the work.

During the engine removal procedure, it is advisable to make notes of the locations of all brackets, cable ties, earthing points etc, as well as how the wiring harnesses, hoses and electrical connections are attached and routed around the engine and engine compartment. An effective way of doing this is to take a series of photographs of the various components before they are disconnected or removed. A simple inexpensive disposable camera is ideal for this and the resulting photographs will prove invaluable when the engine is refitted.

Always be extremely careful when lifting the engine/transmission assembly from the engine bay. Serious injury can result from careless actions. If help is required, it is better to wait until it is available rather than risk personal injury and/or damage to components by continuing alone. By planning ahead and taking your time, a job of this nature, although major, can be accomplished successfully and without incident.

3 Engine and transmission - removal, separation, connection and refitting

Removal

Note: *The engine is removed upwards from the car as a complete unit with the transmission; the two are then separated for overhaul.*

1 Set the bonnet in the upright position (by tying it to the radio aerial) or, to improve access, remove it completely as described in Chapter 11.

2 Remove the battery as described in Chapter 5A, then remove the battery tray.

3 Where applicable, undo the screws and lift off the plastic cover from the top of the engine.

4 Apply the handbrake, then jack up the front of the car and support it on axle stands (see *Jacking and vehicle support*). Remove both front roadwheels.

5 Undo the retaining screws and remove the plastic undercover from beneath the engine/transmission. Also remove the plastic covers from the left- and right-hand wheel arches.

6 If the engine is to be dismantled, working as described in Chapter 1A, drain the engine oil. Clean and refit the drain plug, tightening it securely.

7 Drain the transmission oil as described in Chapter 7A. Refit the drain and filler plugs, and tighten them securely.

8 Drain the cooling system as described in Chapter 1A.

9 Working as described in Chapter 8, disconnect the left-hand driveshaft from the transmission. Note that it is not necessary to remove the driveshaft completely, it can be left attached to the hub assembly and released from the transmission as the hub assembly is pulled outwards. **Note:** *Do not allow the shaft to hang down under its own weight as this could damage the constant velocity joints/gaiters.*

10 Remove the complete right-hand driveshaft assembly as described in Chapter 8.

11 Remove the air cleaner assembly and air inlet ducts as described in Chapter 4A.

12 Remove the auxiliary drivebelt as described in Chapter 1A.

13 Disconnect the clutch cable from the transmission as described in Chapter 6 and position it clear.

14 Disconnect the gearchange linkage and the speedometer cable from the transmission as described in Chapter 7A.

15 Referring to Chapter 4A, carry out the following operations.

a) *Disconnect the fuel hoses from the fuel rail and release them from the clips/ support brackets. Move the hoses clear.*

b) *Disconnect the accelerator cable from the throttle housing.*

c) *Remove the exhaust system front pipe/catalytic converter.*

d) *On 2.0 litre engines, disconnect the camshaft position sensor wiring connector.*

e) *Disconnect the vacuum hose and wiring connector from the MAP sensor and unclip the diagnostic wiring connector from its bracket. Release the electronic control unit (ECU) from its mounting bracket then release the wiring loom from its clips and tie the ECU to the engine.*

f) *Disconnect the relevant vacuum hoses from the inlet manifold.*

16 On 2.0 litre engines with secondary air injection, refer to Chapter 4C and disconnect the vacuum hoses from the solenoid valve on the bulkhead and disconnect the air pump hose from the air pipe below the engine.

17 Remove the headlights as described in Chapter 12, Section 7.

18 Remove the front bumper as described in Chapter 11.

19 Disconnect the bonnet release cable from the bonnet lock on the front body panel.

20 Undo the bolts securing the wiring harness support brackets to the front body panel.

21 Where applicable, undo the retaining screws securing the power steering fluid reservoir to its mounting bracket and tie the reservoir to the engine.

22 Referring to the procedures described in Chapter 3, remove the electric cooling fans and the radiator. Note that once the front body panel has been released, it should be removed completely (do not lay it across the top of the engine).

23 Disconnect the coolant hoses from the expansion tank, then disconnect the heater hoses, and remaining coolant hoses from the engine. Release any support clips as necessary then move all the hoses clear of the engine.

24 Referring to Chapter 10, slacken the retaining clip and disconnect the power steering low pressure hose, linking the pump to the cooler, from the cooler. Slacken the union nut and disconnect the high pressure pipe from the pump, noting its sealing ring, then release the pipe from its retaining clips and position it clear of the engine/ transmission. Plug the pipe ends to minimise fluid loss and prevent the entry of dirt into the system.

25 Undo the retaining nuts/bolts and free the power steering pipes from the mounting brackets on the transmission. Check that the

3.26 Undo the bolt and release the wiring at the fusebox on the left-hand side of the engine compartment

3.27a Disconnect the wiring from the fusebox assembly by pulling out the relevant fuses . . .

3.27b . . . and releasing the fuse holders

pipes are released from all the relevant retaining clips and are positioned clear of the engine/transmission.

26 Trace the engine wiring harness back to the wiring connectors on the left-hand side of the engine compartment. Undo the supply wiring attachment bolt and release the wiring harness **(see illustration)**.

27 Unclip the plastic cover and disconnect the wiring from the fusebox assembly by pulling out the relevant fuses and releasing the fuse holders **(see illustrations)**.

28 Disconnect the wiring at the connector behind the expansion tank and at the main connector adjacent to the fuse holders **(see illustrations)**.

29 Unbolt the relay box from the side of the expansion tank, or disconnect the wiring at the two relays as applicable according to engine **(see illustration)**.

30 Undo the bolts on the battery support

platform and release the applicable earth cables **(see illustration)**. Similarly disconnect the earth cables on the front crossmember and transmission.

31 Where fitted, disconnect the wiring at the evaporative emission system purge valve solenoid on the bulkhead.

32 Check that all wiring connectors have been disconnected, then release the harness from all its retaining clips so that it is free to be removed with the engine.

33 Manoeuvre the engine hoist into position, and attach it to the lifting brackets bolted onto the cylinder head. Raise the hoist until it is supporting the weight of the engine.

34 Remove the plastic impact absorbers from each side of the front crossmember for access to the mounting nuts **(see illustration)**.

35 Check that all wiring, pipes and hoses are released from the crossmember, then undo

3.28a Disconnect the wiring at the connector behind the expansion tank . . .

the three mounting nuts each side. Where applicable remove the anti-theft alarm horn, then withdraw the crossmember off the mounting studs **(see illustrations)**.

2G

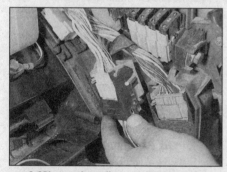

3.28b . . . then disconnect the main connector adjacent to the fuse holders . . .

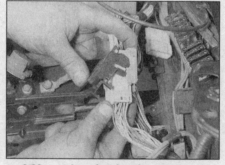

3.28c . . . by releasing the connector locking bar

3.29 Unbolt the relay box from the side of the expansion tank

3.30 Release the earth cables by undoing the bolts on the battery platform

3.34 Remove the plastic impact absorbers from each side of the front crossmember

3.35a Undo the three mounting nuts on each side of the front crossmember . . .

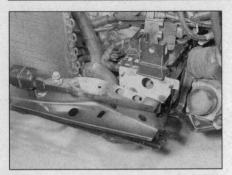

3.35b ... then withdraw the crossmember off the mounting studs

36 On models equipped with air conditioning, disconnect the compressor clutch wiring connector then unbolt the compressor from the auxiliary components mounting bracket on the engine. Carefully move the compressor, together with the condenser, away from the front of the engine and support them on blocks or by other suitable means at the front right-hand side of the car. It may be necessary to disconnect additional retaining clips or mountings to allow the assembly to be moved clear. Take care not to place excess strain on the various pipes and hoses and ensure that all the components are well supported or tied clear of the engine. *Do not* disconnect the refrigerant lines from the compressor (refer to the warnings given in Chapter 3).

37 From underneath the vehicle, undo the retaining bolts and remove the rear mounting link, connecting the engine/transmission mounting to the body.

38 Unscrew the nut from the transmission left-hand mounting stud then undo the bolts securing the rubber mounting assembly and remove it from the vehicle body.

39 On 2.0 litre engines, undo the three bolts and remove the right-hand engine mounting acoustic tie-rod

40 Undo the three bolts securing the right-hand engine mounting bracket to the cylinder head. Similarly, undo the three bolts securing the rubber mounting to the body. Release the relevant cable clips and remove the complete mounting assembly.

41 Make a final check that any components which would prevent the removal of the

3.42 Remove the engine/transmission unit upwards and forwards out of the engine compartment

engine/transmission from the car have been removed or disconnected. Ensure that components such as the gearchange selector rod and driveshafts are secured so that they cannot be damaged on removal.

42 With the help of an assistant, raise the hoist and lift the engine/transmission slightly, ensuring that nothing is trapped or damaged. Once the engine is high enough, turn it slightly as necessary and withdraw it forwards, out of the engine compartment and clear of the car **(see illustration)**.

Separation

43 With the engine/transmission assembly removed, support the assembly on suitable blocks of wood, on a workbench (or failing that, on a clean area of the workshop floor).

44 Disconnect the wiring then undo the retaining bolts, and remove the starter motor from the transmission, noting the correct fitted position of the locating dowel (see Chapter 5A).

45 Ensure that both engine and transmission are adequately supported, then slacken and remove the remaining bolts securing the transmission housing to the engine. Note the correct fitted positions of each bolt (and the relevant brackets) as they are removed, to use as a reference on refitting.

46 Carefully withdraw the transmission from the engine, ensuring that the weight of the transmission is not allowed to hang on the input shaft while it is engaged with the clutch friction plate.

47 If they are loose, remove the locating dowels from the engine or transmission, and keep them in a safe place.

Connection

48 If the engine and transmission have not been separated, proceed as described from paragraph 54 onwards.

49 Ensure that the clutch friction plate and transmission input shaft splines are clean and dry. Do not apply grease to the splines as they have a special low-friction nickel coating.

50 Ensure that the locating dowels are correctly positioned prior to installation and make sure the clutch release mechanism components are correctly fitted (see Chapter 6).

51 Carefully offer the transmission to the engine, until the locating dowels are engaged. Ensure that the weight of the transmission is not allowed to hang on the input shaft as it is engaged with the clutch friction plate.

52 Refit the transmission housing-to-engine bolts, ensuring that all the necessary brackets are correctly positioned, and tighten them to the specified torque setting.

53 Refit the starter motor making sure its locating dowel is correctly positioned. Securely tighten its retaining bolts and reconnect the wiring (see Chapter 5A).

Refitting

54 Reconnect the hoist and lifting tackle to the engine lifting brackets. With the aid of an

assistant, lift the assembly into the engine compartment, and manoeuvre it as necessary to clear the surrounding components, as during removal.

55 With the engine/transmission in position, refit the left-hand rubber mounting and tighten the retaining bolts to the specified torque. Fit the nut to the mounting stud tightening it by hand only at this stage.

56 Refit the right-hand rubber mounting and engine bracket assembly. Tighten the bracket to engine bolts to the specified torque, but only tighten the rubber mounting bolts by hand at this stage.

57 Refit the rear mounting link and support rod and lightly tighten the retaining bolts.

58 Rock the engine to settle it on its mountings. Centralise the right-hand mounting movement limiter, then tighten the three rubber mounting bolts to the specified torque. Go around and tighten all the remaining mounting nuts and bolts to their specified torque settings and detach the hoist from the engine.

59 The remainder of the refitting procedure is a direct reversal of the removal sequence, noting the following points:

a) *Ensure that the wiring loom is correctly routed and retained by all the relevant retaining clips; all connectors should be correctly and securely reconnected.*

b) *Prior to refitting the driveshafts to the transmission, renew the driveshaft oil seal(s) as described in Chapter 7A.*

c) *Ensure that all disturbed hoses are correctly reconnected, and securely retained by their retaining clips.*

d) *Adjust the clutch cable as described in Chapter 6.*

e) *Adjust the accelerator cable as described in the Chapter 4A.*

f) *Refill the engine and transmission with the correct quantity and type of oil, as described in Chapters 1A and 7A.*

g) *Refill the cooling system as described in Chapter 1A.*

---

4 Engine overhaul - preliminary information

It is much easier to dismantle and work on the engine if it is mounted on a portable engine stand. These stands can often be hired from a tool hire shop. Before the engine is mounted on a stand, the flywheel should be removed so that the stand bolts can be tightened into the end of the cylinder block.

If a stand is not available, it is possible to dismantle the engine with it suitably supported on a sturdy, workbench or on the floor. Be careful not to tip or drop the engine when working without a stand.

If you intend to obtain a reconditioned engine, all ancillaries must be removed first, to be transferred to the replacement engine (just as they will if you are doing a complete engine overhaul yourself). These components include the following.

 a) *Engine mountings and brackets (Chapter 2B or 2C).*
 b) *Alternator including auxiliary components mounting bracket (Chapter 5A).*
 c) *Starter motor (Chapter 5A).*
 d) *The ignition system and HT components including all sensors, coil modules and spark plugs (Chapters 1A and 5B).*
 e) *Exhaust manifold (Chapter 4A).*
 f) *Inlet manifold with fuel injection components (Chapter 4A).*
 g) *All electrical switches, actuators and sensors and the engine wiring harness (Chapters 4A, 4C and 5B).*
 h) *Coolant pump, thermostat, hoses, and distribution pipe (Chapter 3).*
 i) *Clutch components (Chapter 6).*
 j) *Flywheel (Chapter 2B or 2C).*
 k) *Oil filter (Chapter 1A).*
 l) *Dipstick, tube and bracket.*

Note: *When removing the external components from the engine, pay close attention to details that may be helpful or important during refitting. Note the fitting positions of gaskets, seals, washers, bolts and other small items.*

If you are obtaining a short engine (cylinder block, crankshaft, pistons and connecting rods all assembled), then the cylinder head, timing belt (together with tensioner, tensioner and idler pulleys and covers) and auxiliary drivebelt tensioner will have to be removed also.

If a complete overhaul is planned, the engine can be dismantled in the order given below.

 a) *Inlet and exhaust manifolds.*
 b) *Timing belt, sprockets, tensioner, pulleys and covers.*
 c) *Cylinder head.*
 d) *Flywheel.*
 e) *Sump.*
 f) *Oil pump.*
 g) *Oil pick-up pipe (2.0 litre engines).*
 h) *Intermediate section (2.0 litre engines).*
 i) *Pistons/connecting rods.*
 j) *Crankshaft.*

5 Cylinder head - dismantling, cleaning, inspection and reassembly

Note: *New and reconditioned cylinder heads are available from the manufacturer and from engine overhaul specialists. Specialist tools are required for the dismantling and inspection procedures, and new components may not be readily available. it may, therefore, be more practical and economical for the home mechanic to purchase a reconditioned head rather than dismantle, inspect and recondition the original head.*

Dismantling

1 Remove the cylinder head as described in Part B or C of this Chapter.

2 According to components still fitted, remove the thermostat housing (Chapter 3), the spark plugs (Chapter 1A) and any other unions, pipes, sensors or brackets as necessary.

3 Place the cylinder head on wooden blocks and tap each valve stem smartly, using a light hammer and drift, to free the spring and associated items.

4 Fit a deep reach type valve spring compressor to each valve in turn and compress each spring until the collets are exposed. Lift out the collets; a small screwdriver, a magnet or a pair of tweezers may be useful. Carefully release the spring compressor and remove it.

5 Remove the valve spring upper seat and the valve spring. Pull the valve out of its guide.

6 Pull off the valve stem oil seal with a pair of long-nosed pliers. Alternatively, a valve stem oil seal removal tool can be obtained from automotive accessory shops. The tool is basically a pair of pliers with specially shaped ends which grip the seal.

7 On 2.0 litre engines, recover the valve spring lower seat. If there is much carbon build-up round the outside of the valve guide, this will have to be scraped off before the seat can be removed. On 1.6 and 1.8 litre engines, the spring lower seat is integral with the valve stem oil seal.

8 It is essential that each valve is stored together with its collets, spring and seats. The valves should also be kept in their correct sequence, unless they are so badly worn or burnt that they are to be renewed. If they are going to be kept and used again, place each valve assembly in a labelled polythene bag or similar container.

9 Continue removing all the remaining valves in the same way.

Cleaning

10 Thoroughly clean all traces of old gasket material and sealing compound from the cylinder head upper and lower mating surfaces. Use a suitable liquid gasket dissolving agent (available from Renault dealers) together with a soft putty knife; do not use a metal scraper or the faces will be damaged.

5.15 Use a straight edge and feeler blade to check for distortion of the cylinder head gasket surface

11 Remove the carbon from the combustion chambers and ports, then clean all traces of oil and other deposits from the cylinder head, paying particular attention to the bearing journals, tappet bores, valve guides and oilways.

12 Wash the head thoroughly with paraffin or a suitable solvent. Take plenty of time and do a thorough job. Be sure to clean all oil holes and galleries very thoroughly and then dry the head completely.

13 Scrape off any heavy carbon deposits that may have formed on the valves, then use a power-operated wire brush to remove deposits from the valve heads and stems.

Inspection

Note: *Be sure to perform all the following inspection procedures before concluding that the services of an engineering works are required. Make a list of all items that require attention.*

Cylinder head

14 Inspect the head very carefully for cracks, evidence of coolant leakage, and other damage. If cracks are found, a new cylinder head should be obtained.

15 Use a straight edge and feeler blade to check that the cylinder head gasket surface is not distorted. If it is, it may be possible to re-surface it; consult your dealer or engine overhaul specialist **(see illustration)**.

16 Examine the valve seats in each of the combustion chambers. If they are severely pitted, cracked or burned, then they will need to be renewed or re-cut by an engine overhaul specialist. If they are only slightly pitted, this can be removed by grinding-in the valve heads and seats with fine valve-grinding compound, as described below.

17 If the valve guides appear worn, indicated by a side-to-side motion of the valve, new guides must be fitted. The renewal of valve guides should be carried out by an engine overhaul specialist.

18 If the valve seats are to be re-cut, this must be done *only after* the guides have been renewed.

19 The threaded holes in the cylinder head must be clean to ensure accurate torque readings when tightening fixings during reassembly. Carefully run the correct size tap (which can be determined from the size of the relevant bolt which fits in the hole) into each of the holes to remove rust, corrosion, thread sealant or other contamination, and to restore damaged threads. If possible, use compressed air to clear the holes of debris produced by this operation. Do not forget to clean the threads of all bolts and nuts as well.

20 Any threads which cannot be restored in this way can often be reclaimed by the use of thread inserts. If any threaded holes are damaged, consult your dealer or engine overhaul specialist and have them install any thread inserts where necessary.

2G

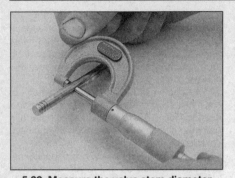

5.22 Measure the valve stem diameter using a micrometer

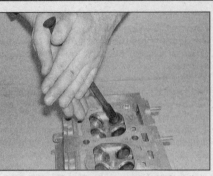

5.25 With a semi-rotary action, grind the valve head to its seat

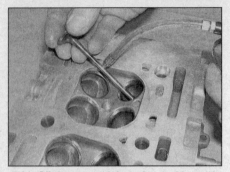

5.31 Oil the stem of the valve and insert it into the guide

Valves

21 Examine the head of each valve for pitting, burning, cracks and general wear, and check the valve stem for scoring and wear ridges. Rotate the valve, and check for any obvious indication that it is bent. Look for pits and excessive wear on the tip of each valve stem. Renew any valve that shows any such signs of wear or damage.

22 If the valve appears satisfactory at this stage, measure the valve stem diameter at several points, using a micrometer **(see illustration)**. Any significant difference in the readings obtained indicates wear of the valve stem. Should any of these conditions be apparent, the valve(s) must be renewed.

23 If the valves are in satisfactory condition, they should be ground (lapped) into their respective seats, to ensure a smooth gas-tight seal. If the seat is only lightly pitted, or if it has been re-cut, fine grinding compound *only* should be used to produce the required finish. Coarse valve-grinding compound should *not* be used unless a seat is badly burned or deeply pitted; if this is the case, the cylinder head and valves should be inspected by an expert, to decide whether seat re-cutting, or even the renewal of the valve or seat insert, is required.

24 Valve grinding is carried out as follows. Place the cylinder head upside-down on a bench, with a block of wood at each end to give clearance for the valve stems.

25 Smear a trace of (the appropriate grade) valve-grinding compound on the seat face,

and press a suction grinding tool onto the valve head. With a semi-rotary action, grind the valve head to its seat, lifting the valve occasionally to redistribute the grinding compound **(see illustration)**. A light spring placed under the valve head will greatly ease this operation.

26 If coarse grinding compound is being used, work only until a dull, matt even surface is produced on both the valve seat and the valve, then wipe off the used compound, and repeat the process with fine compound. When a smooth unbroken ring of light grey matt finish is produced on both the valve and seat, the grinding operation is complete. *Do not* grind in the valves any further than absolutely necessary, or the seat will be prematurely sunk into the cylinder head.

27 When all the valves have been ground-in, carefully wash off *all* traces of grinding compound, using paraffin or a suitable solvent, before reassembly of the cylinder head.

Valve components

28 Examine the valve springs for signs of damage and discoloration, and also measure their free length.

29 Stand each spring on a flat surface, and check it for squareness. If any of the springs are damaged, distorted, or have lost their tension, obtain a complete set of new springs. It is normal to fit new springs as a matter of course if a major overhaul is being carried out.

30 Renew the valve stem oil seals regardless of their apparent condition.

Reassembly

31 Oil the stem of the first valve to be fitted and insert it into the corresponding guide **(see illustration)**.

32 On 2.0 litre engines, fit the lower spring seat in position over the valve guide.

33 The new valve stem oil seals should be supplied with a plastic fitting sleeve to protect the seal when it is fitted over the valve **(see illustration)**. If not, wrap a thin piece of polythene around the valve stem allowing it to extend about 10 mm above the end of the valve stem.

34 With the fitting sleeve, or polythene in place around the valve, fit the valve stem oil seal and push it onto the valve guide by hand as far as it will go with a suitable socket or piece of tube **(see illustrations)**. On 1.6 and 1.8 litre engines the lower valve spring seat is integral with the stem oil seal and the internal diameter of the socket or tube used for fitting must be large enough to fit over the oil seal portion and contact the spring seat. Once the seal is seated, remove the protective sleeve or polythene.

35 Fit the valve spring and upper seat. Compress the spring and fit the two collets in the recesses in the valve stem. Carefully release the compressor **(see illustrations)**.

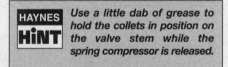

HAYNES HINT *Use a little dab of grease to hold the collets in position on the valve stem while the spring compressor is released.*

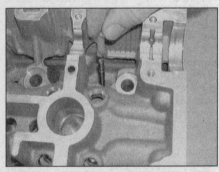

5.33 Fit a protective sleeve over the valve stem to aid fitting the valve stem oil seal

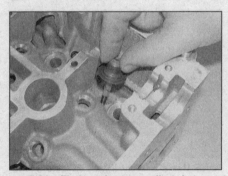

5.34a Fit the valve stem oil seal . . .

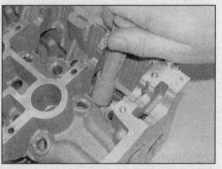

5.34b . . . and push it onto the valve guide with a suitable socket or tube

36 Cover the valve stem with a cloth and tap it smartly with a light hammer to verify that the collets are properly seated.

37 Repeat these procedures on all the other valves.

38 Refit the remainder of the disturbed components then refit the cylinder head as described in Part B or C of this Chapter.

6 Sump and intermediate section (2.0 litre engines) - removal

1 If not already done, drain the engine oil then remove the oil filter, referring to Chapter 1A if necessary.

2 Remove the oil pump as described in Part C of this Chapter.

3 If the pistons and connecting rods are to be removed later, rotate the crankshaft to position all the pistons approximately half way down their bores.

4 Undo the oil filter housing centre bolt and remove the housing and oil cooler assembly. Recover the O-ring seal from the housing.

5 Undo the bolts securing the sump to the intermediate section, noting the different bolt lengths and their locations.

6 Carefully tap the sump free using a rubber or hide mallet. Recover the O-ring seals.

7 Undo the mounting bracket bolt and remove the oil pick-up pipe. Recover the O-ring seal on the end of the pipe (see illustrations).

8 Undo all the M8 bolts securing the inter-mediate section to the cylinder block in the **reverse** order to that shown in **illustration 12.42c**. With all the M8 bolts removed, undo the four M7 bolts in a spiral pattern, starting at the centre and working outwards. Finally undo the M10 bolts in the same order as the M8 bolts (see illustrations).

9 Carefully tap the intermediate section free using a rubber or hide mallet. Lift off the intermediate section complete with crankshaft lower main bearing shells. If any of the shells have stayed on the crankshaft, transfer them to their correct locations in the intermediate section.

10 Remove the crankshaft rear oil seal.

5.35a Fit the valve spring . . .

5.35b . . . followed by the upper spring seat . . .

5.35c . . . then compress the spring using the spring compressors . . .

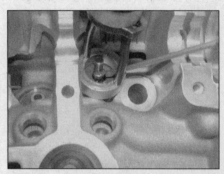

5.35d . . . and fit the two collets in the recesses in the valve stem, using a small screwdriver or similar

6.7a Undo the mounting bracket bolt . . .

6.7b . . . and remove the oil pick-up pipe

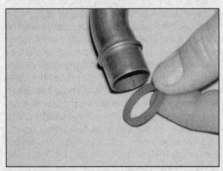

6.7c Recover the O-ring seal from the end of the pipe

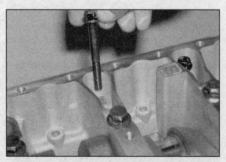

6.8a Undo all the M8 bolts securing the intermediate section to the cylinder block, followed by the four M7 bolts

6.8b With all the smaller bolts removed, undo the M10 bolts

2G

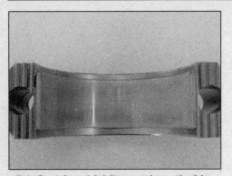

7.4 On 1.8 and 2.0 litre engines, the big-end bearing shells do not have locating tabs. Make a careful note of the position of the shell in the bearing cap - during refitting the shell must be refitted to the cap in exactly the same position

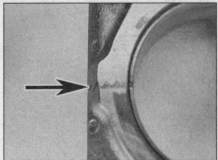

7.6 On 2.0 litre engines, the serrations on the bearing cap and connecting rod mating surfaces ensure that the cap can only be fitted the correct way round

7.7 The arrow on the piston crown points toward the flywheel on 1.6 and 1.8 litre engines, and toward the timing belt on 2.0 litre engines

7 Pistons and connecting rods - removal and inspection

Removal

1 On 1.6 and 1.8 litre engines, remove the cylinder head, sump, oil pump and flywheel as described in Part B of this Chapter. On 2.0 litre engines, remove the cylinder head, oil pump and flywheel as described in Part C of this Chapter, then remove the sump and intermediate section as described in Section 6.

2 Feel inside the tops of the bores for a pronounced wear ridge. It is recommended that you remove such a ridge (with a scraper or ridge reamer) before attempting to remove the pistons, as the pistons rings may jam beneath the ridge making removal difficult. Note that a ridge large enough to cause complications such as this will almost certainly mean that further attention to the cylinder block is necessary.

3 Check that there are identification numbers or marks on each connecting rod and cap; paint suitable marks if necessary, so that each rod can be refitted in the same position and the same way round.

4 Remove the two connecting rod nuts/bolts. Tap the cap with a soft-faced hammer to free it. Remove the bearing cap, and note that on 1.8 and 2.0 litre engines, the lower bearing

shell does not have locating tabs **(see illustration)**. Make a careful note of the position of the shell in the bearing cap - during refitting the shell must be refitted to the cap in exactly the same position; no alignment markings or locating tabs are provided. **Note**: *On all engines, new big-end bearing cap nuts or bolts (as applicable) will be needed for reassembly.*

5 Push the connecting rod and piston up and out of the bore, noting that on 1.8 and 2.0 litre engines, like the lower bearing shell, the upper bearing shell has no locating tabs or alignment markings. Make a careful note of the position of the shell in the connecting rod - during refitting the shell must be refitted to the rod in exactly the same position.

6 Refit the cap to the connecting rod, the correct way round, so that they do not get mixed up. On 2.0 litre engines, serrations are used on the bearing cap and connecting rod mating surfaces to ensure that the cap can only be fitted the correct way around **(see illustration)**.

7 Check to see if there is an arrow on the top of the piston which should be pointing toward the flywheel end of the cylinder block on 1.6 and 1.8 litre engines, and toward the timing belt end on 2.0 litre engines **(see illustration)**. If no arrow can be seen, make a suitable direction mark yourself.

8 Repeat the operations on the remaining connecting rods and pistons.

Inspection

9 Before the inspection process can be carried out, the piston/connecting rod assemblies must be cleaned, and the original piston rings removed from the pistons

10 Carefully expand the old rings and remove them from the top of the pistons. The use of two or three old feeler blades will be helpful in preventing the rings dropping into empty grooves **(see illustration)**. Be careful not to scratch the pistons with the ends of the ring. The rings are brittle and will snap if they are spread too far. They are also very sharp - protect your hands and fingers.

11 Scrape all traces of carbon from the top of the piston. A hand-held wire brush (or a piece

of fine emery cloth) can be used, once the majority of the deposits have been scraped away.

12 Remove the carbon from the ring grooves in the piston, using an old ring. Break the ring in half to do this (be careful not to cut your fingers - piston rings are sharp). Be careful to remove only the carbon deposits - do not remove any metal, and do not nick or scratch the sides of the ring grooves.

13 Once the deposits have been removed, clean the piston/rod assemblies with paraffin or a suitable solvent, and dry thoroughly. Make sure the oil return holes in the ring grooves, are clear.

14 If the pistons and cylinder bores are not damaged or worn excessively, and if the cylinder block does not need further attention, the original pistons can be refitted. Normal piston wear appears as even vertical wear on the piston thrust surfaces, and slight looseness of the top ring in its groove. New piston rings should always be used when the engine is reassembled.

15 Carefully inspect each piston for cracks around the skirt, around the gudgeon pin holes, and at the ring lands (between the ring grooves).

16 Look for scoring and scuffing on the piston skirt, holes in the piston crown, and burned areas at the edge of the crown. If the skirt is scored or scuffed, the engine may have been suffering from overheating and/or abnormal combustion, which caused excessively-high operating temperatures. The cooling and lubrication systems should be checked thoroughly. Scorch marks on the sides of the piston show that blow-by has occurred. A hole in the piston crown or burned areas at the edge of the piston crown, indicates that abnormal combustion (pre-ignition, knocking, or detonation) has been occurring. If any of the above problems exist, the causes must be investigated and corrected, or the damage will occur again. The causes may include inlet air leaks, incorrect fuel/air mixture or an emission control system fault.

17 Corrosion of the piston, in the form of pitting, indicates that coolant has been

7.10 Removing the piston rings using a feeler blade

leaking into the combustion chamber and/or the crankcase. Again, the cause must be corrected, or the problem may persist in the rebuilt engine.

18 Examine each connecting rod carefully for signs of damage, such as cracks around the big-end and small end bearings. Check that the rod is not bent or distorted. Damage is highly unlikely, unless the engine has been seized or badly overheated. Detailed checking of the connecting rod assembly can only be carried out by an engine overhaul specialist with the necessary equipment.

19 On 1.6 litre engines the gudgeon pins are an interference fit in the connecting rod small-end bearing. Therefore, piston and/or connecting rod renewal should be entrusted to a Renault dealer or engine repair specialist, who will have the necessary tooling to remove and install the gudgeon pins.

20 On 1.8 and 2.0 litre engines, the gudgeon pins are of the floating type, secured in position by two circlips. Where necessary, the pistons and connecting rods can be separated as follows.

21 Make a note of any identification marks on the connecting rod, in relation to the arrow on the piston crown, so that the connecting rod and piston can be refitted the correct way round on reassembly. Remove one of the circlips which secure the gudgeon pin and push the gudgeon pin out of the piston and connecting rod **(see illustration)**.

22 The diameter of the pistons should now be measured with a micrometer using the procedures described in the following sub-Sections, according to engine type **(see illustration)**.

1.6 litre engines

23 Using a micrometer, measure the diameter of all four pistons at a point 42 mm from the top of the crown, at right angles to the gudgeon pin axis. Compare the meas-

7.21 Push the gudgeon pin out of the piston and connecting rod

urements obtained, with those listed in the Specifications. Note that three standard size piston and cylinder bore classes are available, A, B and C - the class letter being stamped on the piston crown. The class of the corresponding cylinder bore can be determined from the group of four small identification holes drilled into the side of the block. The distance from the block mating surface to the centre of the holes identifies the class of the bore. Class A holes are drilled 17 mm down from the mating surface, class B holes 27 mm and class C holes 37 mm **(see illustration)**. If new pistons are to be obtained, they must be of the same class as the cylinder bore to which they will be fitted.

1.8 litre engines

24 Using a micrometer, measure the diameter of all four pistons at a point 43.8 mm from the top of the crown, at right angles to the gudgeon pin axis. Compare the measurements obtained, with those listed in the Specifications. Note that two standard size piston and cylinder bore classes are available, identified as 2 and 3 - the class number being stamped on the piston crown.

7.22 Measure the diameter of each piston using a micrometer (see text)

The class of the corresponding cylinder bore can be determined from the small identification holes drilled into the side of the block, one adjacent to each cylinder. The distance from the block mating surface to the centre of the holes identifies the class of the bore. Class 2 holes are drilled 13 mm down from the mating surface, and class 3 holes 19 mm **(see illustration)**. If new pistons are to be obtained, they must be of the same class as the cylinder bore to which they will be fitted.

2.0 litre engines

25 Using a micrometer, measure the diameter of all four pistons at a point 16 mm from the bottom of the skirt, at right angles to the gudgeon pin axis. Compare the measurements obtained, with those listed in the Specifications. Note that four standard size piston and cylinder bore classes are available, C, D, E and G, and one oversize class, O2. The class letter/number is stamped on the piston crown and into the rear of the cylinder block **(see illustration)**. If new pistons are to be obtained, they must be of the same class as the cylinder bore to which they will be fitted.

All engines

26 If the diameter of any of the pistons is out of the tolerance band listed for its particular class, then all four pistons must be renewed. Record the measurements and use them to check the piston-to-bore clearance when the cylinder bores are measured later in this Chapter.

2G

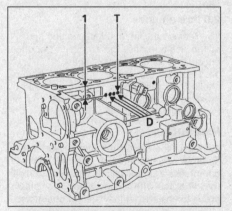

7.23 Piston/cylinder bore class group markings (1.6 litre engines)

1 *Distance from block mating surface to centre of class group identification holes*
D *Position of class group identification holes for each cylinder*
T *Class group identification holes*

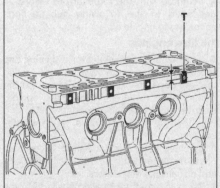

7.24 Piston/cylinder bore class group markings (1.8 litre engines)

T *Class group identification holes*
Arrows indicate distance from block mating surface to centre of holes

7.25 Piston/cylinder bore class group markings stamped on the edge of the cylinder block (2.0 litre engines)

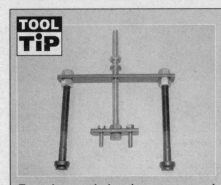

TOOL TIP

To make a main bearing cap removal tool for 1.8 litre engines, obtain a length of steel strip about 6 mm thick by 30 mm wide, and long enough to straddle the main bearing cap. Drill three holes in the strip as shown. Attach two suitable lengths of threaded rod, using two nuts each, to the outer two holes in the strip, or alternatively two old cylinder head bolts can be used instead. Make a lifting plate by cutting a second length of steel strip, long enough to fit over the bearing cap. Drill a hole in the centre, then mark and drill a hole each side so that the plate can be bolted to the holes in the cap. Attach a threaded rod to the lifting plate using two nuts and screw on another nut at the top.

27 On 1.8 and 2.0 litre engines, check the fit of the gudgeon pin in the connecting rod bush and in the piston. If there is perceptible play, a new bush or an oversize gudgeon pin must be fitted. Consult a Renault dealer or engine reconditioning specialist.

28 Examine all components and obtain any new parts required. If new pistons are purchased, they will be supplied complete with gudgeon pins and circlips. Circlips can also be purchased separately.

29 Oil the gudgeon pin. Reassemble the connecting rod and piston, making sure the rod is the right way round, and secure the gudgeon pin with the circlip. On 1.8 litre engines, position the circlip so that its opening is facing upward. On 2.0 litre engines, position the circlip so that its opening is facing downward, and with the lug located in the slot on the side of the piston.

8.10 Using the home-made tool to remove No 1 main bearing cap (1.8 litre engines)

30 Repeat these operations for the remaining pistons.

8 Crankshaft - removal and inspection

Removal

Note: *If no work is to be done on the pistons and connecting rods, then removal of the cylinder head and pistons will not be necessary. Instead, the pistons need only be pushed far enough up the bores so that they are positioned clear of the crankpins.*

1 With reference to Part B and C of this Chapter, and earlier Sections of this part as applicable, carry out the following:
 a) *Remove the sump (1.6 and 1.8 litre engines).*
 b) *Remove the oil pump drive chain and sprockets (1.6 and 1.8 litre engines).*
 c) *Remove the oil pump (2.0 litre engines).*
 d) *Remove the sump and intermediate section (2.0 litre engines).*
 e) *Remove the clutch components and flywheel (all engines).*
 f) *Remove the pistons and connecting rods (all engines - refer to the Note above).*

2 Before the crankshaft is removed, it is advisable to check the endfloat. To do this, temporarily refit the intermediate section (2.0 litre engines) then mount a dial gauge with the stem in line with the crankshaft and just touching the crankshaft nose.

3 Push the crankshaft fully away from the gauge, and zero it. Next, lever the crankshaft towards the gauge as far as possible, and check the reading obtained. The distance that the crankshaft moved is its endfloat; if it is greater than specified, check the crankshaft thrust surfaces for wear. If no wear is evident, new thrustwashers (which are integral with the main bearing shells on 2.0 litre engines) should correct the endfloat.

4 Continue with the removal procedure as described in the following sub-Sections according to engine type.

1.6 litre engines

5 Unscrew and remove the main bearing cap retaining bolts and withdraw the caps, noting that the caps are numbered 1 to 5 from the transmission (flywheel) end of the engine. Recover the lower main bearing shells, and tape them to their respective caps for safe-keeping.

6 Carefully lift out the crankshaft, taking care not to displace the upper main bearing shells, and discard the rear oil seal.

7 Recover the upper bearing shells from the cylinder block, and tape them to their respective caps for safe-keeping. Remove the thrustwasher halves from the side of crankcase main bearing, and store them with the bearing cap.

1.8 litre engines

8 On 1.8 litre engines, No 1 main bearing cap

(nearest the flywheel end of the engine) is sealed to the sides of the cylinder block with a semi-permanent silicone based sealant. As there is very little clearance between the crankshaft and cylinder block in this area, in which to tap or prise the cap free, it will be necessary to use Renault special tool Mot. 1423 for removal. Alternatively, fabricate a home-made alternative **(see Tool Tip)**.

9 Unscrew and remove the main bearing cap retaining bolts and carefully withdraw all the caps except No 1. The caps are numbered 1 to 5 from the transmission (flywheel) end of the engine. Note that the main bearing shells do not have locating tabs. If possible (assuming that the shell remains in the cap as the cap is removed) make a careful note of the position of the shell in the bearing cap and its fitted direction - during refitting the shell must be refitted to the cap in exactly the same position; no alignment markings or locating tabs are provided. Recover the lower main bearing shells if they remained on the crankshaft, and tape all the shells to their respective caps for safe-keeping.

10 Position the removal tool on the cylinder block and attach the lifting plate to the two threaded holes in No 1 main bearing cap using suitable bolts. Turn the nut on the threaded centre rod of the tool to withdraw the bearing cap from the cylinder block **(see illustration)**. Remove the tool, recover the lower main bearing shell (if still on the crankshaft) and tape it to the cap.

11 Carefully lift out the crankshaft, taking care not to displace the upper main bearing shells, and discard the rear oil seal.

12 Again, make a careful note of the fitted positions of the bearing shells and recover the upper shells from the cylinder block. Tape them the correct way round to their respective caps for safe-keeping. Remove the thrust washer halves from the side of crankcase main bearing, and store them with the bearing cap.

2.0 litre engines

13 Remove the intermediate section again, if still in position after the crankshaft endfloat check, then lift out the crankshaft.

14 Remove the upper half main bearing shells from their seats in the crankcase by pressing the end of the shell furthest from the locating tab. Keep all the shells in order.

Inspection

15 Clean the crankshaft using paraffin or a suitable solvent, and dry it, preferably with compressed air if available. Be sure to clean the oil holes with a pipe cleaner or similar probe to ensure that they are not obstructed.

⚠ *Warning: Wear eye protection when using compressed air!*

16 Check the main and big-end bearing journals for uneven wear, scoring, pitting and cracking.

17 Big-end bearing wear is accompanied by distinct metallic knocking when the engine is running (particularly noticeable when the engine is pulling from low speed) and some loss of oil pressure.

18 Main bearing wear is accompanied by severe engine vibration and rumble - getting progressively worse as engine speed increases - and again by loss of oil pressure.

19 Check the bearing journal for roughness by running a finger lightly over the bearing surface. Any roughness (which will be accompanied by obvious bearing wear) indicates that the crankshaft requires regrinding (where possible) or renewal.

20 Using a micrometer, measure the diameter of the main and big-end journals, and compare the results with the Specifications **(see illustration)**. By measuring the diameter at a number of points around each journal's circumference, you will be able to determine whether or not the journal is out-of-round. Take the measurement at each end of the journal, near the webs, to determine if the journal is tapered. Compare the results obtained with those given in the Specifications. If the crankshaft journals are outside the tolerance range specified, a new crankshaft will be needed as only, standard size bearing shells are available from the manufacturer. However, seek the advice of an engine overhaul specialist first, as to whether regrinding may be possible and whether suitable bearing shells can be supplied to match.

21 Check the oil seal contact surfaces at each end of the crankshaft for wear and damage. If either seal has worn a deep groove in the surface of the crankshaft, consult an engine overhaul specialist; repair may be possible, otherwise a new crankshaft will be required.

---

9 Cylinder block/crankcase - cleaning and inspection

Cleaning

1 Prior to cleaning, remove all external components and senders, and any gallery plugs or caps that may be fitted. On 1.8 litre engines, piston oil spray jets are fitted to the base of each cylinder **(see illustration)**. Numerous special tools are required to remove and refit these jets and if there is any doubt about their condition, have the jets renewed by an engine overhaul specialist.

2 If any of the castings are extremely dirty, all should be steam-cleaned.

3 After the castings are returned from steam-cleaning, clean all oil holes and oil galleries one more time. Flush all internal passages with warm water until the water runs clear. If you have access to compressed air, use it to speed the drying process, and to blow out all the oil holes and galleries.

 ⚠ *Warning: Wear eye protection when using compressed air!*

8.20 Use a micrometer to measure the crankshaft journal diameters

4 If the castings are not very dirty, you can do an adequate cleaning job with hot soapy water (as hot as you can stand!) and a stiff brush. Take plenty of time, and do a thorough job. Regardless of the cleaning method used, be sure to clean all oil holes and galleries very thoroughly, and to dry all components completely. Apply clean engine oil to the cylinder bores to prevent rusting.

5 The threaded holes in the cylinder block must be clean to ensure accurate torque readings when tightening fixings during reassembly. Carefully run the correct size tap (which can be determined from the size of the relevant bolt which fits in the hole) into each of the holes to remove rust, corrosion, thread sealant or other contamination, and to restore damaged threads. If possible, use compressed air to clear the holes of debris produced by this operation. Do not forget to clean the threads of all bolts and nuts as well.

6 Any threads which cannot be restored in this way can often be reclaimed by the use of thread inserts. If any threaded holes are damaged, consult your dealer or engine overhaul specialist and have them install any thread inserts where necessary.

7 If the engine is not going to be reassembled right away, cover it with a large plastic bag to keep it clean; protect the machined surfaces as described above, to prevent rusting.

Inspection

8 Visually check the castings for cracks and corrosion. Look for stripped threads in the threaded holes. If there has been any history of internal coolant leakage, it may be

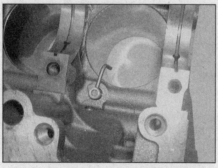

9.1 Piston oil spray jets are fitted to the base of each cylinder on 1.8 litre engines

worthwhile having an engine overhaul specialist check the cylinder block/crankcase for cracks with special equipment. If defects are found, have them repaired, if possible, or renew the assembly.

9 Check the condition of the cylinder head and sump or intermediate section mating surfaces. Check the surfaces for any possible distortion using the straight-edge and feeler blade method described earlier for cylinder head inspection. If distortion is slight, consult an engine overhaul specialist as to the best course of action.

10 Check each cylinder bore for scuffing and scoring. Check for signs of a wear ridge at the top of the cylinder, indicating that the bore is excessively worn.

11 If the necessary measuring equipment is available, measure the diameter of each cylinder at the top (just under the ridge area), centre and bottom of the cylinder bore, parallel to the crankshaft axis using a cylinder bore gauge. Next, measure the bore diameter at the same three locations across the crankshaft axis. Note the measurements obtained. Have this work carried out by an engine overhaul specialist if you do not have access to the measuring equipment needed.

12 To obtain the piston-to-bore clearance, measure the piston diameter as described earlier in this Chapter, and subtract the piston diameter from the largest bore measurement.

13 Repeat these procedures for the remaining pistons and cylinder bores.

14 Compare the results with the Specifications at the beginning of this Chapter; if any measurement is beyond the dimensions specified for that class, or if any bore measurement is significantly different from the others (indicating that the bore is tapered or oval), the piston or bore is excessively-worn. Note that each cylinder bore is identified by a class marking stamped into side or rear of the cylinder block. Refer to the information contained in Section 7 for details of interpretation of the class markings.

15 If any of the cylinder bores are badly scuffed or scored, or if they are excessively-worn, out-of-round or tapered, the usual course of action would be to have the cylinder block/crankcase rebored, and to fit new, oversized, pistons on reassembly. At the time of writing, however, oversize pistons were only available for the 2.0 litre engines. If the bores are worn on 1.6 and 1.8 litre engines, renewal of the block seems to be the only option. Seek the advice of a Renault dealer or engine overhaul specialist on the best course of action.

16 If the bores are in reasonably good condition and not excessively-worn, then it may only be necessary to renew the piston rings.

17 If this is the case, the bores should be honed, to allow the new rings to bed in correctly and provide the best possible seal. Honing is an operation that will be carried out for you by an engine reconditioning specialist.

2G

18 After all machining operations are completed, the entire block/crankcase must be washed very thoroughly with warm soapy water to remove all traces of abrasive grit produced during the machining operations. When the cylinder block/crankcase is completely clean, rinse it thoroughly and dry it, then lightly oil all exposed machined surfaces, to prevent rusting.

19 The final step is to renew the main bearing cap retaining bolts on 1.6 and 1.8 litre engines and the M10 bolts used to secure the intermediate section to the cylinder block on 2.0 litre engines. As with all bolts that are tightened to a very high torque setting or through a torque angle, they are prone to stretch, often up to the extent of their elastic limit. It is virtually impossible to judge the strain that this imposes on a particular bolt, and if any are in any way flawed, breakage when retightening, or failure in service could be the result.

10 Main and big-end bearings - inspection and selection

Inspection

1 Even though the main and big-end bearing shells should be renewed during the engine overhaul, the old shells should be retained for close examination, as they may reveal valuable information about the condition of the engine.

2 Bearing failure occurs because of lack of lubrication, the presence of dirt or other foreign particles, overloading the engine, and corrosion **(see illustration)**. Regardless of the cause of bearing failure, the cause must be corrected (where applicable) before the engine is reassembled, to prevent it from happening again.

3 When examining the bearing shells, remove them from the cylinder block/crankcase and main bearing caps, and from the connecting rods and the big-end bearing caps, then lay them out on a clean surface in the same general position as their location in the engine. This will enable you to match any bearing problems with the corresponding crankshaft journal. *Do not* touch any of the shell's bearing surface with your fingers while checking it, or the delicate surface may be scratched.

4 Dirt or other foreign matter gets into the engine in a variety of ways. It may be left in the engine during assembly, or it may pass through filters or the crankcase ventilation system. It may get into the oil, and from there into the bearings. Metal chips from machining operations and normal engine wear are often present. Abrasives are sometimes left in engine components after reconditioning, especially when parts are not thoroughly cleaned using the proper cleaning methods. Whatever the source, these foreign objects often end up embedded in the soft bearing material, and are easily recognised. Large particles will not embed in the material, and will score or gouge the shell and journal. The best prevention for this cause of bearing failure is to clean all parts thoroughly, and to keep everything spotlessly-clean during engine assembly. Frequent and regular engine oil and filter changes are also recommended.

5 Lack of lubrication (or lubrication breakdown) has a number of inter-related causes. Excessive heat (which thins the oil), overloading (which squeezes the oil from the bearing face) and oil leakage (from excessive bearing clearances, worn oil pump or high engine speeds) all contribute to lubrication breakdown. Blocked oil passages, which usually are the result of misaligned oil holes in a bearing shell, will also starve a bearing of oil, and destroy it. When lack of lubrication is the cause of bearing failure, the bearing material is wiped or extruded from the shell's steel backing. Temperatures may increase to the point where the steel backing turns blue from overheating.

6 Driving habits can have a definite effect on bearing life. Full-throttle, low-speed operation (labouring the engine) puts very high loads on bearings, which tends to squeeze out the oil film. These loads cause the shells to flex, which produces fine cracks in the bearing face (fatigue failure). Eventually, the bearing material will loosen in pieces, and tear away from the steel backing.

7 Short-distance driving leads to corrosion of bearings, because insufficient engine heat is produced to drive off condensed water and corrosive gases. These products collect in the engine oil, forming acid and sludge. As the oil is carried to the engine bearings, the acid attacks and corrodes the bearing material.

8 Incorrect shell refitting during engine assembly will lead to bearing failure as well. Tight-fitting shells leave insufficient bearing running clearance, and will result in oil starvation. Dirt or foreign particles trapped behind a bearing shell result in high spots on the bearing, which lead to failure.

9 *Do not* touch any shell's bearing surface with your fingers during reassembly; there is a risk of scratching the delicate surface, or of depositing particles of dirt on it.

Selection - main and big-end bearings

10 Although there are different crankshaft main bearing journal diameter classes, the main bearing shells supplied by the manufacturer are available in one standard size only. The big-end bearing shells are also only supplied in one standard size. As an actual running clearance dimension for the bearings is not specified, the only safe course of action is to fit new main and big-end bearing shells whenever an overhaul is being undertaken. Assuming that the relevant crankshaft journals are all within tolerance, the running clearances will then be correct. Before obtaining new bearing shells, consult a Renault dealer or engine reconditioning specialist as to the latest recommendations concerning bearing shell selection.

11 Engine overhaul - reassembly sequence

1 Before reassembly begins ensure that all new parts have been obtained and that all necessary tools are available. Read through the entire procedure to familiarise yourself with the work involved, and to ensure that all items necessary for reassembly of the engine are at hand. In addition to all normal tools and materials, thread locking compound will be needed in certain areas during engine reassembly. On 1.6 and 1.8 litre engines, a silicone sealant will be required to seal No 1 main bearing cap to the cylinder block, and on 2.0 litre engines, a liquid gasket solution together with a short-haired application roller will also be needed to assemble the main engine sections. Specific details of these sealants and compounds is given in the text of the applicable Section.

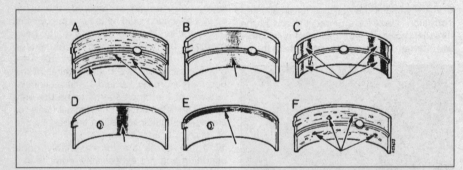

10.2 Typical bearing failures

A *Scratched by dirt; dirt embedded in bearing material*
B *Lack of oil; overlay wiped out*
C *Improper seating; bright (polished) sections*
D *Tapered journal; overlay gone from entire surface*
E *Radius ride*
F *Fatigue failure; craters or pockets*

2 In order to save time and avoid problems, engine reassembly can be carried out in the following order:

a) *Crankshaft.*
b) *Pistons/connecting rods.*
c) *Oil pump drive chain and sprockets (1.6 and 1.8 litre engines).*
d) *Sump (1.6 and 1.8 litre engines).*
e) *Intermediate section and sump (2.0 litre engines).*
f) *Oil pump (2.0 litre engines).*
g) *Flywheel.*
h) *Cylinder head.*
i) *Camshaft and tappets.*
j) *Timing belt, tensioner, sprockets and idler pulleys.*
k) *Engine external components.*

3 At this stage, all engine components should be absolutely clean and dry, with all faults repaired. The components should be laid out (or in individual containers) on a completely clean work surface.

12 Crankshaft - refitting

Note: *To obtain the correct main bearing running clearance, new main bearing shells should always be fitted regardless of the condition of the original ones.*

1 Crankshaft refitting is the first stage of engine reassembly following overhaul. It is assumed at this point that the cylinder block/crankcase and crankshaft have been cleaned, inspected and repaired or reconditioned as necessary. Position the cylinder block on a clean level work surface, with the crankcase facing upwards. The crankshaft can now be refitted as described in the following sub-Sections according to engine type.

1.6 litre engines

2 Clean the backs of the bearing shells and the bearing locations in both the cylinder block and the main bearing caps. If new shells are being fitted, ensure that all traces of the protective grease are cleaned off using paraffin. Wipe dry the shells and caps with a lint-free cloth.

3 Press the bearing shells into their locations, noting that the shells with the oil groves are fitted to the cylinder block and to main bearing caps 2 and 4. The shells without oil grooves are fitted to main bearing caps 1, 3 and 5 **(see illustration)**. Ensure that the tab on each shell engages in the notch in the cylinder block or main bearing cap. If the original bearing shells are being used they must be refitted in their original locations.

4 Using a little grease, stick the thrust-washers to each side of the centre main bearing upper location; ensure that the oilway grooves on each thrustwasher face outwards (away from the cylinder block).

5 Liberally lubricate each bearing shell in the cylinder block with clean engine oil then lower

12.3 Fitting a shell to No 1 main bearing cap (1.6 litre engines)

the crankshaft into position ensuring that the bearing shells and thrustwashers remain correctly seated.

6 Ensure that the cap locating dowels are in position and fit main bearing caps 2 to 5 to their correct locations and the correct way round.

7 Apply a thin coating of Rhodorseal 5661 sealant (available from Renault dealers) to the mating surface of No 1 main bearing cap, taking great care not to block the oil return grooves, then fit the cap **(see illustrations)**.

8 Insert the new main bearing cap bolts and tighten them to the specified Stage 1 torque setting using a torque wrench. Once all the bolts have been tightened to their Stage 1 setting, angle-tighten the bolts through the specified Stage 2 angle, using a socket and extension bar. It is recommended that an angle-measuring gauge is used during this stage of the tightening, to ensure accuracy.

9 Check that the crankshaft is free to turn without stiffness or tight spots.

10 Check the crankshaft endfloat with reference to Section 8.

11 Lubricate the rear oil seal location, the crankshaft, and a new oil seal. Fit the seal, lips inwards, and use a piece of tube (or the old seal, inverted) to tap it into place until flush.

12 Continue with the engine reassembly procedures as described in the relevant Sections of this Chapter and Chapter 2B.

1.8 litre engines

13 Before refitting the crankshaft a decision must be made as to the method to be used when fitting the main bearing shells to the

12.7b . . . then fit the cap to the block (1.6 litre engines)

12.7a Apply a thin coating of sealant to the mating surface of No 1 main bearing cap . . .

cylinder block and bearing caps. Renault specify the use of special tool Mot.1493 to accurately position the bearing shells in their locations. However, with care, it is possible to position the shells in their locations equally accurately without the tool. In the following procedure, both methods are described.

14 To seal the contact surfaces of No 1 main bearing cap to the cylinder block, a tube of Rhodorseal 5661 sealant, together with a hardening agent and application syringe will be required. This is available as a kit from Renault dealers **(see illustration)**.

15 Clean the backs of the bearing shells and the bearing locations in both the cylinder block and the main bearing caps. If new shells are being fitted, ensure that all traces of the protective grease are cleaned off using paraffin. Wipe dry the shells, block and caps with a lint-free cloth.

16 Lay out the bearing shells ready for fitting, noting that the shells with the oil groves are fitted to the cylinder block, and the shells without oil grooves are fitted to the main bearing caps. If the original bearing shells are being used they must be refitted in their original locations and in their original fitted direction as noted during removal.

17 If the Renault special tool is being used, place the tool over the bearing location in the cylinder block and insert the bearing shell into the tool. Hold the tool and press one end of the bearing shell until the shell seats fully in its location and its other end contacts the stop on the tool **(see illustrations)**. Refit all the remaining shells to the cylinder block in the same way.

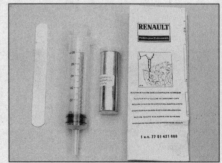

12.14 Renault sealing kit for No 1 main bearing cap (1.8 litre engines)

12.17a If the Renault special tool is being used to fit the main bearing shells to the block, place the tool over the bearing location . . .

12.17b . . . insert the bearing shell into the tool . . .

12.17c . . . and press one end of the shell until the other end contacts the tool (1.8 litre engines)

18 If the bearing shells are being fitted without the tool, press them into position in the cylinder block so that they are exactly centred in their locations and their edges are flush with the surface of the block.

19 Using a little grease, stick the thrustwashers to each side of No 2 main bearing upper location; ensure that the oilway grooves on each thrustwasher face outwards (away from the cylinder block) **(see illustrations)**.

20 Liberally lubricate each bearing shell in the cylinder block with clean engine oil then lower the crankshaft into position ensuring that the bearing shells and thrustwashers remain correctly seated **(see illustrations)**.

21 Fit the bearing shells to the main bearing caps using the same method as for the shells in the block **(see illustrations)**.

22 Lubricate the bearing shells in the caps with clean engine oil, then fit main bearing caps 2 to 5 to their correct locations and the correct way round **(see illustrations)**.

23 Insert the new main bearing cap bolts for

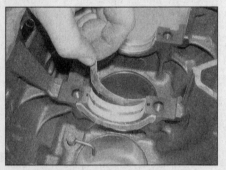

12.19a Smear a little grease on the crankshaft thrustwashers . . .

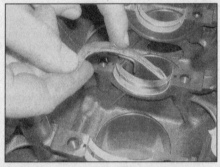

12.19b . . . and stick them to No 2 main bearing upper location (1.8 litre engines)

12.20a Liberally lubricate the upper main bearing shells . . .

12.20b . . . then lower the crankshaft into position (1.8 litre engines)

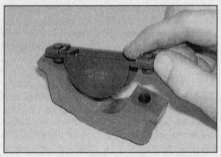

12.21a If the special tool is being used to fit the main bearing shells to the caps, fit the tool in the cap . . .

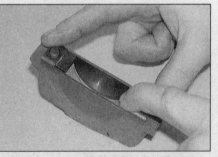

12.21b . . . insert the bearing shell into the tool . . .

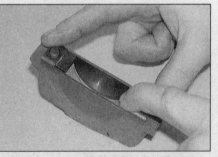

12.21c . . . then hold the tool and press one end of the shell until the other end contacts the tool (1.8 litre engines)

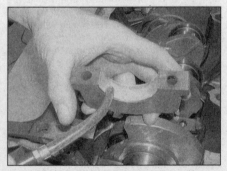

12.22a Liberally lubricate the bearing shells . . .

12.22b . . . then fit main bearing caps 2 to 5 (1.8 litre engines)

12.23 Insert the new bolts for bearing caps 2 to 5 and tighten them to the specified torque (1.8 litre engines)

12.26a Apply a thin coating of sealant to No 1 main bearing cap lower mating surface in the cylinder block . . .

12.26b . . . then fit No 1 main bearing cap (1.8 litre engines)

12.27 Using the syringe, inject the sealing mixture into the grooves on each side of No1 main bearing cap, until it flows out on both sides (1.8 litre engines)

12.28 When dry, cut away any surplus sealant from the sump mating face (1.8 litre engines)

caps 2 to 5 and tighten them to the specified torque **(see illustration)**.

24 Check that the crankshaft is free to turn without stiffness or tight spots, then check the crankshaft endfloat with reference to Section 8.

25 Thoroughly clean the contact surfaces of No 1 main bearing cap and its location in the cylinder block with methylated spirit and allow to dry thoroughly.

26 Apply a thin coating of Rhodorseal 5661 sealant to the bearing cap lower mating surface in the cylinder block, then fit the cap **(see illustrations)**. Insert the new main bearing cap bolts and tighten them to the specified torque.

27 Mix approximately half of the 100 g tube of Rhodorseal 5661 sealant together with half the hardener as described in the instructions

supplied with the kit. Using the syringe supplied, inject the mixture into the grooves on each side of the bearing cap, until it can be seen to flow out slightly on both sides of the grooves **(see illustration)**. Using a clean cloth, wipe away any surplus mixture from the inside and outside of the cylinder block.

28 Allow the sealant to dry for a few minutes, then cut away any surplus sealant from the sump mating face **(see illustration)**.

29 Check that the crankshaft is free to turn without stiffness or tight spots.

30 Lubricate the rear oil seal location, the crankshaft, and a new oil seal. Fit the seal, lips inwards, and use a piece of tube (or the old seal, inverted) to tap it into place until flush.

31 Continue with the engine reassembly procedures as described in the relevant Sections of this Chapter and Chapter 2B.

2.0 litre engines

32 If they're still in place, remove the old bearing shells from the block and the intermediate section.

33 Clean the backs of the bearing shells and the bearing locations in both the cylinder block and intermediate section. If new shells are being fitted, ensure that all traces of the protective grease are cleaned off using paraffin. Wipe dry the shells, block and intermediate section with a lint-free cloth.

34 Insert the previously selected upper shells into their correct position in the cylinder block. Press the shells home so that the tangs engage in the recesses provided **(see illustrations)**.

35 Liberally lubricate the bearing shells in the cylinder block with clean engine oil **(see illustration)**.

2G

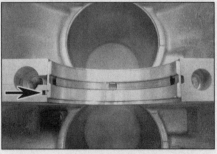

12.34a Insert the previously selected upper shells into their correct position in the cylinder block . . .

12.34b . . . then press the shells home so that the tangs (arrowed) engage in the recesses provided (2.0 litre engines)

12.35 Liberally lubricate the bearing shells in the cylinder block with clean engine oil (2.0 litre engines)

12.36 Lower the crankshaft into position, making sure that the bearing shells are not displaced (2.0 litre engines)

12.38 Using a short-haired roller, apply a coating of liquid gasket solution to the intermediate section (2.0 litre engines)

12.39a Insert the previously selected lower shells into their correct position in the intermediate section . . .

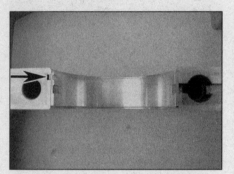

12.39b . . . then press the shells home so that the tangs (arrowed) engage in the recesses provided (2.0 litre engines)

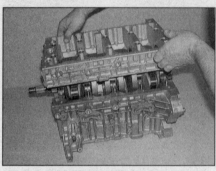

12.41 Lay the intermediate section on the crankshaft and cylinder block (2.0 litre engines)

36 Wipe clean the crankshaft journals, then lower the crankshaft into position (see illustration). Make sure that the shells are not displaced.

37 Inject oil into the crankshaft oilways then wipe any traces of excess oil from the crankshaft and intermediate section mating faces.

38 Using a short haired application roller, apply an even coating of Loctite 518 liquid gasket solution to the cylinder block mating face of the intermediate section (see illustration). Ensure that the whole surface is covered, but note that a thin coating is sufficient for a good seal.

39 Insert the previously selected lower shells into their correct position in the intermediate section. Press the shells home so that the

tangs engage in the recesses provided (see illustrations).

40 Lightly lubricate the bearing shells in the intermediate section, but take care to keep the oil away from the liquid gasket solution.

41 Lay the intermediate section on the crankshaft and cylinder block (see illustration).

42 Oil the threads of the intermediate section retaining bolts, then insert and tighten them in the stages listed in the Specifications, to the specified torque and torque angle, in the sequence shown (see illustrations). Note that new 10 mm diameter bolts must be used.

43 Rotate the crankshaft and check that it is free to turn without stiffness or tight spots.

44 It is a good idea at this stage, to once again check the crankshaft endfloat as described in Section 8. If the thrust surfaces

of the crankshaft have been checked and new bearing shells have been fitted, then the endfloat should be within specification.

45 Lubricate the rear oil seal location, the crankshaft, and a new oil seal. Fit the seal, lips inwards, and use a piece of tube (or the old seal, inverted) to tap it into place until flush.

46 Continue with the engine reassembly procedures as described in the relevant Sections of this Chapter and Chapter 2C.

13 Pistons and piston rings - assembly

1 At this stage it is assumed that the pistons have all been correctly assembled to their respective connecting rods. If not, refer to the end of Section 7.

2 Before the rings can be fitted to the pistons, the end gaps must be checked with the rings inserted into the cylinder bores. Note that no piston ring end gap dimensions are provided by the manufacturer for 2.0 litre engines, but the following checks should be carried out anyway, to ensure that the rings are not binding.

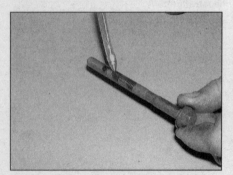

12.42a Oil the threads of the intermediate section retaining bolts . . .

12.42b . . . and tighten the intermediate section bolts to the specified torque in the correct sequence (2.0 litre engines)

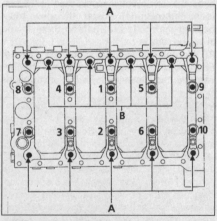

12.42c Intermediate section retaining bolt tightening sequence (2.0 litre engines)

A M8 bolts   1 to 10   Tightening
B M7 bolts   sequence for M8
                            and M10 bolts

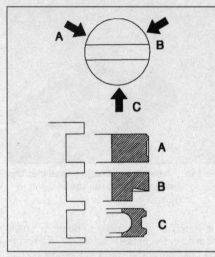

13.12 Piston ring identification and end gap positioning (2.0 litre engines)

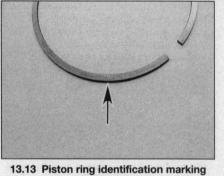

13.13 Piston ring identification marking (arrowed)

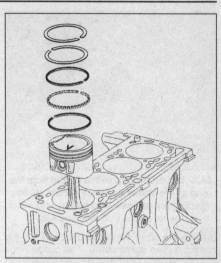

13.14 Piston ring end gap positioning (1.6 and 1.8 litre engines)

3 Lay out the piston assemblies and the new ring sets so the components are kept together in their groups, during and after end gap checking. Position the cylinder block on the work surface, on its side, allowing access to the top and bottom of the bores.

4 Take the No 1 piston top ring and insert it into the top of the first cylinder. Push it down the bore using the top of the piston; this will ensure that the ring remains square with the cylinder walls. Position the ring near the bottom of the cylinder bore, at the lower limit of ring travel.

5 Measure the ring gap using feeler blades.

6 Repeat the procedure with the ring at the top of the cylinder bore, at the upper limit of its travel and compare the measurements with the figures given in the Specifications.

7 If new rings are being fitted it is unlikely that the end gaps will be too small. If a measurement is found to be undersize, there is the risk that the ring ends may contact each other during engine operation, possibly resulting in engine damage. If the gaps are too small, check that you have the correct rings for your engine and for the cylinder bore size.

8 It is equally unlikely that the end gap will be too large. If the gaps are too large, again, check that you have the correct rings for your engine and for the cylinder bore size.

9 Repeat the checking procedure for each ring in the first cylinder, and then for the rings in the remaining cylinders. Remember to keep rings, pistons and cylinders matched up.

10 Once the ring end gaps have been checked, the rings can be fitted to the pistons. **Note:** *Always follow any instructions supplied with the new piston ring sets - different manufacturers may specify different procedures. Do not mix up the top and second compression rings, as they have different cross-sections.*

11 The oil control ring (lowest on the piston) is installed first. On 1.6 and 1.8 litre engines it is composed of three separate components. Slip

the expander into the groove, then install the lower side rail into the groove between the expander and the ring land, then install the upper side rail in the same manner. On 2.0 litre engines, a one-piece oil control ring is used. Carefully expand it and slip it into the bottom groove in the piston.

12 Install the second ring next. **Note:** *The second ring and top ring are different, and can be identified by their cross-sections.* Making sure the ring is the correct way up (on 2.0 litre engines, the second ring is bevelled and the bevel must face downwards when installed), fit the ring into the middle groove on the piston, taking care not to expand the ring any more than is necessary **(see illustration)**.

13 Install the top ring in the same way, making sure the ring is the correct way up. Where the ring is symmetrical, fit it with its identification marking facing upwards **(see illustration)**.

14 When all the rings are in position arrange the ring gaps 180° apart on 1.6 and 1.8 litre engines, and 120° apart on 2.0 litre engines **(see illustration)**.

15 Repeat the above procedure for the remaining pistons and rings.

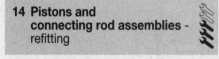

14 Pistons and connecting rod assemblies - refitting

1.6 litre engines

1 Before refitting the piston/connecting rod assemblies, the cylinder bores must be perfectly clean, the top edge of each cylinder must be chamfered, and the crankshaft must be in place.

2 Remove the big-end bearing cap from No 1 cylinder connecting rod, and remove the original bearing shells.

3 Clean the backs of the big-end bearing shells and the recesses in the connecting rods and big-end caps. If new shells are being fitted, ensure that all traces of the protective grease are cleaned off using paraffin. Wipe the shells and connecting rods dry with a lint-free cloth.

4 Press the bearing shells into the connecting rods and caps in their correct positions. Make sure that the location tabs are engaged with the cut-outs in the connecting rods.

5 Position the piston ring gaps in their correct positions around the piston, lubricate the piston and rings with clean engine oil, and attach a piston ring compressor to the piston. Leave the piston crown protruding slightly, to guide the piston into the cylinder bore. The rings must be compressed until they're flush with the piston.

6 Rotate the crankshaft until No 1 big-end journal is at BDC (Bottom Dead Centre), and apply a coat of engine oil to the cylinder walls.

7 Arrange the No 1 piston/connecting rod assembly so that the arrow on the piston crown points toward the flywheel end of the engine. Gently insert the assembly into the No 1 cylinder bore, and rest the bottom edge of the ring compressor on the cylinder block **(see illustration)**.

8 Tap the top edge of the ring compressor to make sure it's contacting the block around its entire circumference.

9 Gently tap on the top of the piston with the end of a wooden hammer handle, whilst

14.7 Insert the piston/connecting rod assembly into the cylinder bore, and rest the bottom edge of the ring compressor on the block (1.6 litre engines)

2G

14.9 Tap on the top of the piston with the end of a wooden hammer handle, whilst guiding the connecting rod big-end onto the crankpin (1.6 litre engines)

14.14a On 1.8 litre engines, if the special tool is being used to fit the big-end bearing shells to the connecting rods, place the rod on the tool . . .

14.14b . . . insert the bearing shell into the sliding part of the tool . . .

guiding the connecting rod big-end onto the crankpin **(see illustration)**. The piston rings may try to pop out of the ring compressor just before entering the cylinder bore, so keep some pressure on the ring compressor. Work slowly, and if any resistance is felt as the piston enters the cylinder, stop immediately. Find out what is binding (usually a ring), and fix it before proceeding. *Do not*, for any reason, force the piston into the cylinder - you might break a ring and/or the piston.

10 Make sure the bearing surfaces are perfectly clean, then apply a uniform layer of clean engine oil, to both of them. You may have to push the piston back up the cylinder bore slightly to expose the bearing surface of the shell in the connecting rod.

11 Slide the connecting rod back into place on the big-end journal and refit the big-end bearing cap. Lubricate the threads of the studs, fit the new nuts and tighten them to the specified torque

12 Repeat the entire procedure for the remaining piston/connecting rod assemblies. The important points to remember are:

a) *Keep the backs of the bearing shells and their locations in the connecting rods and caps perfectly clean when assembling them.*

b) *Make sure you have the correct piston/rod assembly for each cylinder.*

c) *The arrow on the piston crown must face the flywheel end of the engine.*

d) *Lubricate the cylinder bores with clean engine oil.*

e) *Lubricate the bearing surfaces before fitting the big-end bearing caps.*

13 After all the piston/connecting rod assemblies have been properly installed, rotate the crankshaft a number of times by hand, to check for any obvious binding.

1.8 and 2.0 litre engines

14 A decision must first be made as to the method to be used when fitting the big-end bearing shells to the connecting rods and caps. Renault specify the use of special tool Mot. 1492 (1.8 litre engines) or Mot. 1341 (2.0 litre engines) to accurately position the bearing shells in the rod and cap. However, with care, it is possible to position the shells in their locations equally accurately without the tool. If the special tools are being used, follow the instructions supplied with the tool to fit the shells to the connecting rod and cap as shown **(see illustrations)**. The following procedure describes fitting the shells without the use of the special tool.

15 Before refitting the piston/connecting rod assemblies, the cylinder bores must be perfectly clean, the top edge of each cylinder must be chamfered, and the crankshaft (and intermediate section on 2.0 litre engines) must be in place.

16 Remove the original bearing shells (observing the notes in Section 7, relating to the position of the shells in the bearing cap and connecting rod) and wipe the bearing recesses of the connecting rod and cap with a clean, lint-free cloth. They must be kept spotlessly-clean. Ensure that new big-end bearing cap retaining bolts are available.

17 Clean the back of the new upper bearing shell, fit it to No 1 connecting rod, then fit the other shell of the bearing to the big-end bearing cap. Position the shells in the rod and cap so that they are exactly centred in their locations and their edges are flush with the rod and cap mating surfaces. If the original bearing shells are being used they must be refitted in exactly the same position as noted during removal.

18 Position the piston ring gaps in their correct positions around the piston, lubricate the piston and rings with clean engine oil, and attach a piston ring compressor to the piston **(see illustration)**. Leave the piston crown protruding slightly, to guide the piston into the cylinder bore. The rings must be compressed until they're flush with the piston.

19 Rotate the crankshaft until No 1 big-end journal is at BDC (Bottom Dead Centre), and apply a coat of engine oil to the cylinder walls. Note that on 1.8 litre engines, No 1 cylinder is at the flywheel end of the cylinder block, and on 2.0 litre engines No 1 cylinder is at the timing belt end.

20 Arrange the No 1 piston/connecting rod

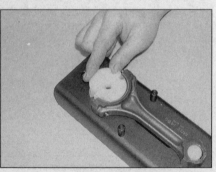

14.14c . . . then push the tool sliding part and bearing shell into the connecting rod. Fit the shells to the caps in the same way

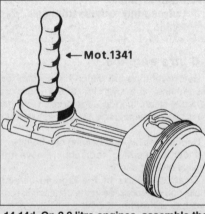

← Mot.1341

14.14d On 2.0 litre engines, assemble the bearing shells into the connecting rod and cap, the special tool is then used to centre the shells

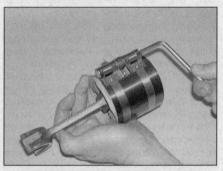

14.18 Attach a ring compressor to the piston

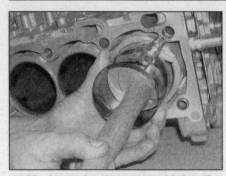

14.22a Insert the piston assembly into the No 1 cylinder bore, and gently tap on the top of the piston with the end of a wooden hammer handle

14.22b Guide the connecting rod big-end onto the crankpin with the aid of a long screwdriver

14.23 Apply clean engine oil to the bearing cap surfaces

assembly so that the arrow on the piston crown points toward the flywheel end (1.8 litre engines) or timing belt end (2.0 litre engines). Gently insert the assembly into the No 1 cylinder bore, and rest the bottom edge of the ring compressor on the cylinder block.

21 Tap the top edge of the ring compressor to make sure it's contacting the block around its entire circumference.

22 Gently tap on the top of the piston with the end of a wooden hammer handle, whilst guiding the connecting rod big-end onto the crankpin with the aid of a long screwdriver **(see illustrations)**. The piston rings may try to pop out of the ring compressor just before entering the cylinder bore, so keep some pressure on the ring compressor. Work slowly, and if any resistance is felt as the

piston enters the cylinder, stop immediately. Find out what is binding (usually a ring), and fix it before proceeding. *Do not*, for any reason, force the piston into the cylinder - you might break a ring and/or the piston. Take care also not to let the connecting rod foul the piston oil spray jets on 1.8 litre engines, as it approaches the crankshaft.

23 Make sure the bearing surfaces are perfectly clean, then apply a uniform layer of clean engine oil, to both of them **(see illustration)**. You may have to push the piston back up the cylinder bore slightly to expose the bearing surface of the shell in the connecting rod.

24 Slide the connecting rod back into place on the big-end journal and refit the big-end bearing cap. Lubricate the bolt threads, fit the new bolts and tighten them to the specified Stage 1 torque setting, then through the specified Stage 2 angle. It is recommended that an angle-measuring gauge is used during this stage of the tightening, to ensure accuracy **(see illustrations)**.

25 Repeat the entire procedure for the remaining piston/connecting rod assemblies. *Caution: Do not rotate the crankshaft until the first pair of big-end bearing caps have been tightened to their final torque settings, or the bearing shells may be dislodged.*

26 The important points to remember are:
a) *Keep the backs of the bearing shells and their locations in the connecting rods and caps perfectly clean when assembling them.*
b) *Ensure that the bearing shells are correctly positioned on the rods and caps.*
c) *Make sure you have the correct piston/rod assembly for each cylinder.*
d) *The arrow on the piston crown must face the flywheel end of the engine (1.8 litre engines) or timing belt end (2.0 litre engines).*
e) *Lubricate the cylinder bores with clean engine oil.*
f) *Lubricate the bearing surfaces before fitting the big-end bearing caps.*

27 After all the piston/connecting rod assemblies have been properly installed, rotate the crankshaft a number of times by hand, to check for any obvious binding.

2G

15 Sump (2.0 litre engines) - refitting

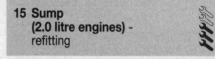

1 Place a new O-ring on the oil pick-up pipe and insert the pipe into its location. Secure

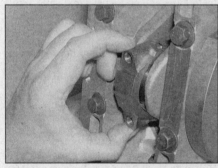

14.24a Refit the big-end bearing cap . . .

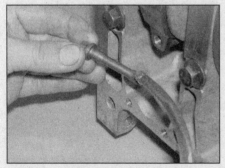

14.24b . . . lubricate the threads of the new bearing cap bolts . . .

14.24c . . . tighten them to the first stage torque . . .

14.24d . . . then angle-tighten them through the second stage angle

15.2 Locate new O-rings in the recesses in the intermediate section

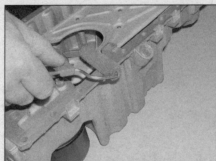

15.3 Using a short-haired roller, apply an even coating liquid gasket solution to the sump mating face

15.4 Place the sump in position on the intermediate section

15.5 Using a straight edge, ensure that the rear edges of the sump and cylinder block are flush

15.6 Refit the remaining bolts and tighten all progressively, working towards the centre, to the specified torque

with the bracket retaining bolt tightened to the specified torque.

2 Wipe off any oil smears from the sump and intermediate section joint faces, then locate new O-rings in the recesses in the intermediate section **(see illustration)**.

3 Using the short haired application roller, apply an even coating of Loctite 518 liquid gasket solution to the sump mating face **(see illustration)**. Ensure that the whole surface is covered, but note that a thin coating is sufficient for a good seal.

4 Place the sump in position and insert four of the retaining bolts tightened finger tight only **(see illustration)**.

5 Using a straight edge, ensure that the rear edges of the sump, cylinder block and intermediate section are flush, then tighten the four bolts to just hold the sump in position **(see illustration)**.

6 Refit the remaining bolts and tighten all progressively, working towards the centre, to the specified torque **(see illustration)**.

7 Fit new O-rings to the oil filter housing and centre retaining bolt. Refit the housing and tighten the centre bolt to the specified torque.

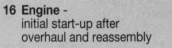

16 Engine -
initial start-up after
overhaul and reassembly

1 Refit the remainder of the engine components in the order listed in Section 11, with reference to the relevant Sections of this part of Chapter 2, and Part B or C. Refit the engine and transmission to the vehicle as described in Section 3 of this Part. Double-

check the engine oil and coolant levels and make a final check that everything has been reconnected. Make sure that there are no tools or rags left in the engine compartment.

2 Remove the spark plugs and disable the ignition system by disconnecting the crankshaft sensor wiring at the connector. Disconnect the fuel injector wiring connectors to prevent fuel being injected into the cylinders.

3 Turn the engine over on the starter motor until the oil pressure warning light goes out. If the light fails to extinguish after several seconds of cranking, check the engine oil level and oil filter security. Assuming these are correct, check the security of the oil pressure sensor wiring - do not progress any further until you are sure that oil is being pumped around the engine at sufficient pressure.

4 Refit the spark plugs and HT leads, and reconnect the crankshaft sensor and fuel injector wiring connectors.

5 Start the engine, noting that this also may

take a little longer than usual, due to the fuel system components being empty.

6 While the engine is idling, check for fuel, coolant and oil leaks. Don't be alarmed if there are some odd smells and smoke from parts getting hot and burning off oil deposits. Note also that it may initially be a little noisy until the hydraulic tappets fill with oil.

7 Keep the engine idling until hot water is felt circulating through the top hose, check that it idles reasonably smoothly and at the usual speed, then switch it off.

8 After a few minutes, recheck the oil and coolant levels, and top-up as necessary (see Chapter 1B).

9 If new components such as pistons, rings or crankshaft bearings have been fitted, the engine must be run-in for the first 500 miles (800 km). Do not operate the engine at full-throttle, or allow it to labour in any gear during this period. It is recommended that the oil and filter be changed at the end of this period.

Chapter 2 Part H:
Diesel engine removal and overhaul procedures

Contents

Degrees of difficulty

Easy, suitable for novice with little experience	**Fairly easy,** suitable for beginner with some experience	**Fairly difficult,** suitable for competent DIY mechanic	**Difficult,** suitable for experienced DIY mechanic	**Very difficult,** suitable for expert DIY or professional

Specifications

1.9 litre engines

Cylinder head

Maximum gasket face distortion .... 0.05 mm
Cylinder head height .... 162.00 ± 0.10 mm
Valve depth below cylinder head gasket face:
    Inlet .... 0.65 ± 0.09 mm
    Exhaust .... 0.57 ± 0.09 mm
Valve seat angle (included) .... 90°
Valve seat width .... 1.8 mm

Valves

Valve head diameter:
    Inlet .... 35.20 mm
    Exhaust .... 32.50 mm
Valve stem diameter .... 7.000 −0.010 mm to −0.020 mm

Valve springs

Free length .... 45.80 mm

Cylinder block

Cylinder bore diameter (nominal) .... 80.00 mm

Pistons

Piston-to-bore clearance .... 0.015 to 0.030 mm (suggested values)

Piston rings

Thickness:
    Top compression .... 2.50 mm
    Second compression .... 2.00 mm
    Oil control .... 3.00 mm
End gap (measured in cylinder) .... Rings supplied pre-set

1.9 litre engines (continued)

Crankshaft

Main bearing journal diameter:	
Standard	54.790 ± 0.01 mm
Undersize	Not available
Main bearing running clearance	0.020 to 0.058 mm
Big-end bearing journal diameter:	
Standard	48.00 mm +0.02 mm
Undersize	Not available
Big-end bearing running clearance	0.014 to 0.053 mm
Crankshaft endfloat	0.070 to 0.230 mm
Thrustwasher thicknesses	2.30, 2.35, 2.40 and 2.45 mm

Torque wrench settings

Refer to Chapter 2D Specifications

2.2 litre engines

Cylinder head

Maximum gasket face distortion	0.05 mm
Cylinder head height	147.0 ± 0.08 mm
Swirl chamber protrusion	0 to 0.04 mm
Valve seat angle (included)	90°
Valve seat width	1.55 to 1.90 mm

Valves

Valve head diameter:	
Inlet	32.10 mm
Exhaust	31.10 mm
Valve stem diameter	7.00 mm

Valve springs

Free length	48.13 mm

Cylinder block

Cylinder bore diameter (nominal):	
Size group 1	87.000 to 87.015 mm
Size group 2	87.015 to 87.030 mm

Pistons

Piston diameter (nominal):	
Size group 1	87.000 to 87.015 mm
Size group 2	87.015 to 87.030 mm
Piston-to-bore clearance	Not available

Piston rings

Thickness:	
Top compression	2.50 mm
Second compression	1.75 mm
Oil control	2.50 mm
End gap (measured in cylinder)	Rings supplied pre-set

Crankshaft

Main bearing journal diameter:	
Standard	57.980 to 58.000 mm
Undersize	Not available
Main bearing running clearance*	0.025 to 0.050 mm
Big-end bearing journal diameter:	
Standard	47.910 to 47.750 mm
Undersize	Not available
Big-end bearing running clearance*	0.025 to 0.050 mm
Maximum bearing journal out-of-round	0.01 mm
Crankshaft endfloat	0.042 to 0.215 mm

*These are suggested figures, typical for this type of engine - no exact values are stated by Renault.

Torque wrench settings

Refer to Chapter 2E Specifications

1 General information

Included in this Part of Chapter 2 are details of removing the engine/transmission from the car and general overhaul procedures for the cylinder head, cylinder block and all other engine internal components.

The information given ranges from advice concerning preparation for an overhaul and the purchase of replacement parts, to detailed step-by-step procedures covering removal, inspection, renovation and refitting of engine internal components.

After Section 5, all instructions are based on the assumption that the engine has been removed from the car. For information concerning in-car engine repair, as well as the removal and refitting of those external components necessary for full overhaul, refer to Parts D and E of this Chapter and to Section 5. Ignore any preliminary dismantling operations described in Parts D or E that are no longer relevant once the engine has been removed from the car.

Apart from torque wrench settings, which are given at the beginning of Parts D or E (as applicable), all specifications relating to engine overhaul are at the beginning of this Part of Chapter 2.

2 Engine overhaul - general information

It is not always easy to determine when, or if, an engine should be completely over-hauled, as a number of factors must be considered.

High mileage is not necessarily an indication that an overhaul is needed, while low mileage does not preclude the need for an overhaul. Frequency of servicing is probably the most important consideration. An engine which has had regular and frequent oil and filter changes, as well as other required maintenance, should give many thousands of miles of reliable service. Conversely, a neglected engine may require an overhaul very early in its life.

Excessive oil consumption is an indication that piston rings, valve seals and/or valve guides are in need of attention. Make sure that oil leaks are not responsible before deciding that the rings and/or guides are worn. Perform a compression test, as described in Part D of this Chapter, to determine the likely cause of the problem.

Check the oil pressure with a gauge fitted in place of the oil pressure switch, and compare it with that specified. If it is extremely low, the main and big-end bearings, and/or the oil pump, are probably worn out.

Loss of power, rough running, knocking or metallic engine noises, excessive valve gear noise, and high fuel consumption may also point to the need for an overhaul, especially if they are all present at the same time. If a complete service does not remedy the situation, major mechanical work is the only solution.

An engine overhaul involves restoring all internal parts to the specification of a new engine. During an overhaul, the pistons and the piston rings are renewed. New main and big-end bearings are generally fitted; if necessary, the crankshaft may need to be renewed also. The valves are serviced as well, since they are usually in less-than-perfect condition at this point. While the engine is being overhauled, other components, such as the starter and alternator, can be overhauled as well. The end result should be an as-new engine that will give many trouble-free miles. **Note:** *Critical cooling system components such as the hoses, thermostat and coolant pump should be renewed when an engine is overhauled. The radiator should be checked carefully, to ensure that it is not clogged or leaking. Also, it is a good idea to renew the oil pump whenever the engine is overhauled.*

Before beginning the engine overhaul, read through the entire procedure, to familiarise yourself with the scope and requirements of the job. Overhauling an engine is not difficult if you follow carefully all of the instructions, have the necessary tools and equipment, and pay close attention to all specifications. It can, however, be time-consuming. Plan on the car being off the road for a minimum of two weeks, especially if parts must be taken to an engineering works for repair or reconditioning. Check on the availability of parts and make sure that any necessary special tools and equipment are obtained in advance. Most work can be done with typical hand tools, although a number of precision measuring tools are required for inspecting parts to determine if they must be renewed. Often the engineering works will handle the inspection of parts and offer advice concerning reconditioning and renewal. **Note:** *Always wait until the engine has been completely dismantled, and until all components (especially the cylinder block and the crankshaft) have been inspected, before deciding what service and repair operations must be performed by an engineering works. The condition of these components will be the major factor to consider when determining whether to overhaul the original engine, or to buy a reconditioned unit. Do not, therefore, purchase parts or have overhaul work done on other components until they have been thoroughly inspected. As a general rule, time is the primary cost of an overhaul, so it does not pay to fit worn or sub-standard parts.*

As a final note, to ensure maximum life and minimum trouble from a reconditioned engine, everything must be assembled with care, in a spotlessly-clean environment.

3 Engine removal - methods and precautions

If you have decided that the engine must be removed for overhaul or major repair work, several preliminary steps should be taken.

Locating a suitable place to work is extremely important. Adequate work space, along with storage space for the car, will be needed. If a workshop or garage is not available, at the very least, a flat, level, clean work surface is required.

Cleaning the engine compartment and engine/transmission before beginning the removal procedure will help keep tools clean and organised.

An engine hoist or A-frame will also be necessary. Make sure the equipment is rated in excess of the combined weight of the engine and transmission. Safety is of primary importance, considering the potential hazards involved in lifting the engine/transmission out of the car.

If this is the first time you have removed an engine, an assistant should ideally be available. Advice and aid from someone more experienced would also be helpful. There are many instances when one person cannot simultaneously perform all of the operations required when lifting the engine out of the vehicle.

Plan the operation ahead of time. Before starting work, arrange for the hire of or obtain all of the tools and equipment you will need. Some of the equipment necessary to perform engine/transmission removal and installation safely and with relative ease (in addition to an engine hoist) is as follows: a heavy duty trolley jack, complete sets of spanners and sockets as described in the reference section of this manual, wooden blocks, and plenty of rags and cleaning solvent for mopping up spilled oil, coolant and fuel. If the hoist must be hired, make sure that you arrange for it in advance, and perform all of the operations possible without it beforehand. This will save you money and time.

Plan for the car to be out of use for quite a while. An engineering works will be required to perform some of the work which the do-it-yourselfer cannot accomplish without special equipment. These places often have a busy schedule, so it would be a good idea to consult them before removing the engine, in order to accurately estimate the amount of time required to rebuild or repair components that may need work.

During the engine removal procedure, it is advisable to make notes of the locations of all brackets, cable ties, earthing points etc, as well as how the wiring harnesses, hoses and electrical connections are attached and routed around the engine and engine compartment. An effective way of doing this is to take a series of photographs of the various components before they are disconnected or

2H

4.5a Unclip the plastic cover . . .

4.5b . . . to gain access to the engine wiring loom connectors

removed. A simple inexpensive disposable camera is ideal for this and the resulting photographs will prove invaluable when the engine is refitted.

Always be extremely careful when lifting the engine/transmission assembly from the engine bay. Serious injury can result from careless actions. If help is required, it is better to wait until it is available rather than risk personal injury and/or damage to components by continuing alone. By planning ahead and taking your time, a job of this nature, although major, can be accomplished successfully and without incident.

4 Engine and transmission - removal, separation, connection and refitting

Caution: Be careful not to allow dirt into the injection pump or injector pipes during this procedure.

Removal

Note: *The engine is removed upwards from the engine compartment as a complete unit with the transmission; the two are then separated for overhaul.*

1 Apply the handbrake, then jack up the front of the car and support it on axle stands (see *Jacking and vehicle support*). Remove both front roadwheels.

2 Set the bonnet in the upright position or, to improve access, remove it completely as described in Chapter 11.

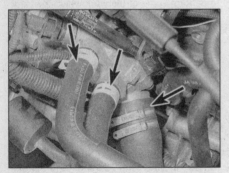

4.12 On models where the coolant pump is driven by the auxiliary drivebelt disconnect the hoses (arrowed) from the pump

3 Undo the retaining screws and remove the plastic undercover from beneath the engine/transmission. Also remove the plastic covers from the left- and right-hand wheelarches. On 1.9 litre engines, unscrew the retaining nuts and withdraw the engine sound-insulating cover.

4 If the engine is to be dismantled, working as described in Chapter 1B, first drain the oil and remove the oil filter. Clean and refit the drain plug, tightening it securely.

5 Remove the battery as described in Chapter 5A. Trace the engine wiring harness back to the wiring connectors in the left-hand front corner of the engine compartment. Unclip the plastic cover and disconnect the wiring from the fusebox assembly then free the harness from all its retaining clips so that it is free to be removed with the engine **(see illustrations)**.

6 Remove the air cleaner assembly and associated components as described in Chapter 4B.

7 Drain the transmission oil as described in Chapter 7A. Refit the drain and filler plugs, and tighten them securely.

8 On models equipped with air conditioning, remove the auxiliary drivebelt (see Chapter 1B).

9 Drain the cooling system as described in Chapter 1B. Slacken the retaining clips and disconnect the coolant hoses from the left-hand end of the cylinder head.

10 Remove the front bumper as described in Chapter 11.

11 Referring to the procedures described in Chapter 3, remove the electric cooling fans

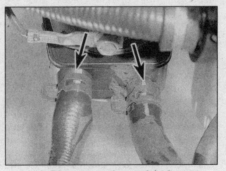

4.13 Disconnect the coolant hoses (arrowed) from the oil cooler

and the radiator. Note that once the front body panel has been released, it should be removed completely (do not lay it across the top of the engine).

12 On models where the coolant pump is driven by the auxiliary drivebelt, slacken the clip(s) and disconnect the hoses from the rear of the coolant pump **(see illustration)**.

13 Release the retaining clips and disconnect the hoses from the oil cooler **(see illustration)**. On some later models the coolant hoses incorporate a plastic flange joint; on these models undo the retaining nut then disconnect the coolant hose union from the cooler and recover the sealing rings.

14 Referring to Chapter 3, disconnect the coolant hoses from the expansion tank and heater matrix union then unbolt the hose mounting brackets from the top of the transmission and remove the hose assemblies from the engine compartment, where necessary, disconnecting the wiring connector from the coolant temperature sender as the hoses are removed.

15 Referring to Chapter 4B, carry out the following operations.

a) *Disconnect the accelerator cable from the injection pump (2.2 litre engines) or pedal position sensor (1.9 litre engines).*

b) *On 2.2 litre engines, disconnect the fuel feed and return hoses from the injection pump. Free the hose from its clip on the manifold.*

c) *On 1.9 litre engines, disconnect the two fuel hoses at the quick release fittings on the top of the fuel filter assembly.*

d) *Remove the exhaust system front pipe.*

16 On 2.2 litre engines, disconnect the wiring connectors from the pre/post heating unit, fuel filter heating element and switch, and the atmospheric pressure sensor and relay. Release the wiring harness from its retaining clips so it is free to be removed with the engine.

17 On 1.9 litre engines, disconnect the wiring plug from the injection control unit located at the front right-hand side of the engine compartment. Undo the mounting bolts and remove the control unit. Similarly, unbolt the pre/post heating system control unit, adjacent to the injection control unit, and move it to one side.

18 Release the retaining clip and disconnect the vacuum hose from the brake servo unit and (where necessary) the vacuum solenoid valve.

19 Referring to Chapter 10, unscrew the union nut and disconnect the fluid pipe from the power steering pump then release the clip and disconnect the hose from the front of the fluid reservoir **(see illustrations)**. Plug the pipe ends and steering gear unions to minimise fluid loss and prevent dirt entry.

20 On 1.9 litre engines, unbolt the power steering fluid reservoir from its mountings and move it to one side.

21 Undo the retaining nuts/bolts and free the power steering pipes from the mounting

4.19a Disconnect the fluid pipe from the power steering pump . . .

4.19b . . . and the hose from the front of the power steering reservoir

brackets on the transmission. Check that the pipes are released from all the relevant retaining clips and are positioned clear of the engine/transmission.

22 Free the diagnostic wiring connector from its mounting bracket on the engine compartment bulkhead so that it is free to be removed with the engine/transmission. On models with EGR it will also be necessary to disconnect the wiring and vacuum hose from the solenoid valve and relay mounted onto the bracket **(see illustration)**.

23 Working as described in Chapter 8, disconnect the left-hand driveshaft (2.2 litre engines) or right-hand driveshaft (1.9 litre engines) from the transmission. Note that it is not necessary to remove the driveshaft completely, it can be left attached to the hub assembly and released from the transmission as the hub assembly is pulled outwards. **Note:** *Do not allow the shaft to hang down under its own weight as this could damage the constant velocity joints/gaiters.*

24 Remove the complete right-hand driveshaft assembly (2.2 litre engines) or left-hand driveshaft assembly (1.9 litre engines) as described in Chapter 8.

25 Disconnect the clutch cable from the transmission and position it clear (see Chap-

ter 6). Where a hydraulic clutch is fitted, unbolt the slave cylinder from the side of the transmission and move it to one side after releasing the fluid hose from any support brackets or clips.

26 Disconnect the gearchange linkage and the speedometer cable from the transmission as described in Chapter 7A. Undo the retaining bolt and detach the earth strap from the top of the transmission.

27 Check that all wiring connectors have been disconnected, then release the harness from all its retaining clips so that it is free to be removed with the engine.

28 Manoeuvre the engine hoist into position, and attach it to the lifting brackets bolted onto the cylinder head. Raise the hoist until it is supporting the weight of the engine.

29 Remove the plastic impact absorbers from each side of the front crossmember for access to the mounting nuts.

30 Check that all wiring, pipes and hoses are released from the crossmember, then undo the three mounting nuts each side. Where applicable remove the anti-theft alarm horn, then withdraw the crossmember off the mounting studs.

31 On models equipped with air conditioning, disconnect the compressor clutch

wiring connector then unbolt the compressor from the auxiliary components mounting bracket on the engine. Carefully move the compressor, together with the condenser, away from the front of the engine and support them on blocks or by other suitable means at the front right-hand side of the car. It may be necessary to disconnect additional retaining clips or mountings to allow the assembly to be moved clear. Take care not to place excess strain on the various pipes and hoses and ensure that all the components are well supported or tied clear of the engine. *Do not disconnect the refrigerant lines from the compressor (refer to the warnings given in Chapter 3).*

32 From underneath the vehicle, undo the retaining bolts and remove the rear mounting link, connecting the engine/transmission mounting to the body.

33 Unscrew the nut from the transmission left-hand mounting stud then undo the bolts securing the rubber mounting assembly and remove it from the vehicle body.

34 Undo the three bolts securing the right-hand engine mounting bracket to the cylinder head. Similarly, undo the three bolts securing the rubber mounting to the body. Release the relevant cable clips and remove the complete mounting assembly.

35 Make a final check that any components which would prevent the removal of the engine/transmission from the car have been removed or disconnected. Ensure that components such as the gearchange selector rod and driveshafts are secured so that they cannot be damaged on removal.

36 With the help of an assistant, raise the hoist and lift the engine/transmission slightly, ensuring that nothing is trapped or damaged. Once the engine is high enough, turn it slightly as necessary and withdraw it forwards, out of the engine compartment and clear of the car **(see illustration)**.

2H

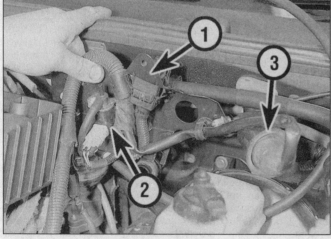

4.22 Free the diagnostic wiring connector (1) from the bracket. On models with EGR disconnect the solenoid valve (2) and relay (3)

4.36 Lifting the engine/transmission unit out from the vehicle

Separation

37 With the engine/transmission assembly removed, support the assembly on suitable blocks of wood, on a workbench (or failing that, on a clean area of the workshop floor).

38 Undo the retaining bolts, and remove the flywheel lower cover plate (where applicable) from the transmission. On some models the plate has support struts attached to it, these will have to be unbolted from the side of the cylinder block.

39 Disconnect the wiring then undo the retaining bolts, and remove the starter motor from the transmission, noting the correct fitted position of the locating dowel (see Chapter 5A).

40 Ensure that both engine and transmission are adequately supported, then slacken and remove the remaining bolts securing the transmission housing to the engine. Note the correct fitted positions of each bolt (and the relevant brackets) as they are removed, to use as a reference on refitting.

41 Carefully withdraw the transmission from the engine, ensuring that the weight of the transmission is not allowed to hang on the input shaft while it is engaged with the clutch friction plate. Note that on models with the PK1 transmission it will be necessary to unclip the clutch release fork from the clutch release bearing as the transmission is removed from the engine.

42 If they are loose, remove the locating dowels from the engine or transmission, and keep them in a safe place.

Connection

43 If the engine and transmission have not been separated, proceed as described from paragraph 49 onwards.

44 Ensure that the clutch friction plate and transmission input shaft splines are clean and dry. Do not apply grease to the splines as they have a special low-friction nickel coating.

45 Ensure that the locating dowels are correctly positioned prior to installation and make sure the clutch release mechanism components are correctly fitted (see Chapter 6).

46 Carefully offer the transmission to the engine, until the locating dowels are engaged. Ensure that the weight of the transmission is not allowed to hang on the input shaft as it is engaged with the clutch friction plate. **Note:** *On models with a PK1 transmission, ensure that the release fork lever and bearing are correctly positioned and engage correctly with each other as the transmission is fitted (see Chapter 7A, Section 8 for further information). Do not proceed any further until you are sure the release fork and bearing are correctly engaged.*

47 Refit the transmission housing-to-engine bolts, ensuring that all the necessary brackets are correctly positioned, and tighten them to the specified torque setting.

48 Refit the starter motor making sure its locating dowel is correctly positioned. Securely tighten its retaining bolts and reconnect the wiring (see Chapter 5A).

Refitting

49 Reconnect the hoist and lifting tackle to the engine lifting brackets. With the aid of an assistant, lift the assembly into the engine compartment, and manoeuvre it as necessary to clear the surrounding components, as during removal.

50 With the engine/transmission in position, refit the left-hand rubber mounting and tighten the retaining bolts to the specified torque. Fit the nut to the mounting stud tightening it by hand only at this stage.

51 Refit the right-hand rubber mounting and engine bracket assembly. Tighten the bracket to engine bolts to the specified torque, but only tighten the rubber mounting bolts by hand at this stage.

52 Refit the rear mounting link and support rod and lightly tighten the retaining bolts.

53 Rock the engine to settle it on its mountings. Centralise the right-hand mounting movement limiter, then tighten the three rubber mounting bolts to the specified torque. Go around and tighten all the remaining mounting nuts and bolts to their specified torque settings and detach the hoist from the engine.

54 The remainder of the refitting procedure is a direct reversal of the removal sequence, noting the following points:
a) Ensure that the wiring loom is correctly routed and retained by all the relevant retaining clips; all connectors should be correctly and securely reconnected.
b) Prior to refitting the driveshafts to the transmission, renew the driveshaft oil seal(s) as described in Chapter 7A.
c) Ensure that all disturbed hoses are correctly reconnected, and securely retained by their retaining clips.
d) Adjust the clutch cable as described in Chapter 6.
e) Adjust the accelerator cable as described in the Chapter 4A.
f) Refill the engine and transmission with the correct quantity and type of oil, as described in Chapters 1B and 7A.
g) Refill the cooling system as described in Chapter 1B.

5 Engine overhaul - dismantling sequence

It is much easier to dismantle and work on the engine if it is mounted on a portable engine stand. These stands can often be hired from a tool hire shop. Before the engine is mounted on a stand, the flywheel should be removed so that the stand bolts can be tightened into the end of the cylinder block.

If a stand is not available, it is possible to dismantle the engine with it suitably supported on a sturdy, workbench or on the floor. Be careful not to tip or drop the engine when working without a stand.

If you intend to obtain a reconditioned engine, all ancillaries must be removed first, to be transferred to the replacement engine (just as they will if you are doing a complete engine overhaul yourself). These components include the following.
a) Engine mountings and brackets (Chapter 2D or 2E).
b) Alternator including auxiliary components mounting bracket (Chapter 5A).
c) Power steering pump and bracket(s) (Chapter 10).
d) Coolant pump, thermostat and housing, and coolant outlet chamber/elbow (Chapter 3).
e) Oil filter (Chapter 1B).
f) Oil cooler housing (Chapter 2E).
g) Braking system vacuum pump (Chapter 9).
h) Dipstick tube.
i) Fuel system components (Chapter 4B).
j) Wiring harness and all electrical switches and sensors.
k) Inlet and exhaust manifolds (Chapter 4B).
l) Clutch components (Chapter 6).
m) Flywheel (Part D or E of this Chapter).

Note: *When removing the external components from the engine, pay close attention to details that may be helpful or important during refitting. Note the fitting positions of gaskets, seals, washers, bolts and other small items.*

If you are obtaining a short engine (cylinder block, crankshaft, pistons and connecting rods all assembled), then the cylinder head, timing belt (together with tensioner, tensioner and idler pulleys and covers) and auxiliary drivebelt tensioner will have to be removed also.

If a complete overhaul is planned, the engine can be dismantled in the order given below.
a) Inlet and exhaust manifolds.
b) Timing belt, sprockets, tensioner, pulleys and covers.
c) Cylinder head.
d) Flywheel.
e) Sump.
f) Oil pump.
g) Pistons/connecting rods.
h) Crankshaft.

6 Cylinder head - dismantling

Note: *New and reconditioned cylinder heads are available from the manufacturer, and from engine overhaul specialists. Be aware that some specialist tools are required for the dismantling and inspection procedures, and new components may not be readily available. It may therefore be more practical and economical for the home mechanic to purchase a reconditioned head, rather than dismantle, inspect and recondition the original head.*

1 Remove the cylinder head as described in Part D or E of this Chapter (as applicable).

2 Remove the camshaft, followers and shims/hydraulic tappets (as applicable) as described in Part D or E of this Chapter.

3 Using a valve spring compressor, compress each valve spring in turn until the split collets can be removed. Release the compressor, and lift off the spring retainer, spring and spring seat. Using a pair of pliers, carefully extract the valve stem seal from the top of the guide.

4 If, when the valve spring compressor is screwed down, the spring retainer refuses to free and expose the split collets, gently tap the top of the tool, directly over the retainer, with a light hammer. This will free the retainer.

5 Withdraw the valve through the combustion chamber.

6 It is essential that each valve is stored together with its collets, retainer, spring, and spring seat **(see illustration)**. The valves should also be kept in their correct sequence, unless they are so badly worn that they are to be renewed. If they are going to be kept and used again, place each valve assembly in a labelled polythene bag or similar small container. Note that No 1 valve is nearest to the transmission (flywheel) end of the engine.

6.6 Place each valve and its associated components in a labelled polythene bag

Inspection

Note: *Be sure to perform all the following inspection procedures before concluding that the services of a machine shop or engine overhaul specialist are required. Make a list of all items that require attention.*

Cylinder head

5 Inspect the head very carefully for cracks, evidence of coolant leakage, and other damage. If cracks are found, a new cylinder head should be obtained.

6 Use a straight-edge and feeler blade to check that the cylinder head surface is not distorted **(see illustration)**. Renault state that no resurfacing of the cylinder head surface is possible.

7 Examine the valve seats in each of the combustion chambers. If they are severely pitted, cracked, or burned, they will need to be re-cut by an engine overhaul specialist. If they are only slightly pitted, this can be removed by grinding-in the valve heads and seats with fine valve-grinding compound, as described below.

8 Check the valve guides for wear by inserting the relevant valve, and checking for side-to-side motion of the valve. A very small amount of movement is acceptable. If the movement seems excessive, remove the valve. Measure the valve stem diameter (see below), and renew the valve if it is worn. If the valve stem is not worn, the wear must be in the valve guide, and the guide must be renewed. The renewal of valve guides is best carried out by a Renault dealer or engine overhaul specialist, who will have the

necessary tools available. Where no valve stem diameter is specified, seek the advice of a Renault dealer on the best course of action.

9 If renewing the valve guides, the valve seats should be re-ground only *after* the guides have been fitted.

10 On 2.2 litre engines, inspect the swirl chambers for burning or damage such as cracking. Small cracks in the chambers are acceptable; renewal of the chambers will only be required if chamber tracts are badly burned and disfigured, or if they are no longer a tight fit in the cylinder head. If there is any doubt as to the swirl chamber condition, seek the advice of a Renault dealer or a suitable repairer who specialises in diesel engines. Using a dial test indicator, check that the swirl chamber protrusion is within the limits in the *Specifications*. Zero the dial test indicator on the gasket surface of the cylinder head, then measure the protrusion of the swirl chamber **(see illustration)**. If the protrusion is not within the specified limits first ensure that the chamber is fully seated in the head; if it is, the advice of a Renault dealer or suitable repairer who specialises in diesel engines should be sought. Each swirl chamber can be tapped out of position using a soft-metal drift inserted through the injector hole (some chambers may be loose already). Fit the swirl chamber, aligning its locating pin with the head cutout and tap it firmly into position. Also check that the oil pressure relief valve (located beneath number 1 camshaft bearing cap) is clear and unblocked; if necessary renew the valve.

Valves

11 Examine the head of each valve for pitting, burning, cracks, and general wear. Check the valve stem for scoring and wear ridges. Rotate the valve, and check for any obvious indication that it is bent. Look for pits or excessive wear on the tip of each valve stem. Renew any valve that shows any such signs of wear or damage.

12 If the valve appears satisfactory at this stage, measure the valve stem diameter at several points using a micrometer **(see illustration)**. Any significant difference in the readings obtained indicates wear of the valve stem. Should any of these conditions be apparent, the valve(s) must be renewed.

7 Cylinder head and valves - cleaning and inspection

1 Thorough cleaning of the cylinder head and valve components, followed by a detailed inspection, will enable you to decide how much valve service work must be carried out during the engine overhaul. **Note:** *If the engine has been severely overheated, it is best to assume that the cylinder head is warped - check carefully for signs of this.*

Cleaning

2 Scrape away all traces of old gasket material from the cylinder head.

3 Scrape away the carbon from the combustion chambers and ports, then wash the cylinder head thoroughly with paraffin or a suitable solvent.

4 Scrape off any heavy carbon deposits that may have formed on the valves, then use a power-operated wire brush to remove deposits from the valve heads and stems.

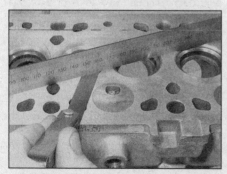

7.6 Checking the cylinder head gasket surface for distortion

7.10 Checking a swirl chamber protrusion - 2.2 litre engines

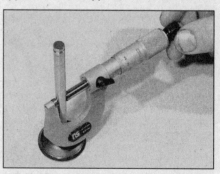

7.12 Measuring a valve stem diameter

2H

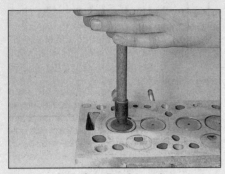

7.15 Grinding-in a valve

13 If the valves are in satisfactory condition, they should be ground (lapped) into their respective seats, to ensure a smooth, gas-tight seal. If the seat is only lightly pitted, or if it has been re-cut, fine grinding compound *only* should be used to produce the required finish. Coarse valve-grinding compound should *not* be used, unless a seat is badly burned or deeply pitted. If this is the case, the cylinder head and valves should be inspected by an expert, to decide whether seat re-cutting, or even the renewal of the valve or seat insert (where possible) is required.

14 Valve grinding is carried out as follows. Place the cylinder head upside-down on a bench.

15 Smear a trace of (the appropriate grade of) valve-grinding compound on the seat face, and press a suction grinding tool onto the valve head. With a semi-rotary action, grind

the valve head to its seat, lifting the valve occasionally to redistribute the grinding compound **(see illustration)**. A light spring placed under the valve head will greatly ease this operation.

16 If coarse grinding compound is being used, work only until a dull, matt even surface is produced on both the valve seat and the valve, then wipe off the used compound, and repeat the process with fine compound. When a smooth unbroken ring of light grey matt finish is produced on both the valve and seat, the grinding operation is complete. *Do not* grind-in the valves any further than absolutely necessary, or the seat will be prematurely sunk into the cylinder head.

17 When all the valves have been ground-in, carefully wash off *all* traces of grinding compound using paraffin or a suitable solvent, before reassembling the cylinder head.

Valve components

18 Examine the valve springs for signs of damage and discoloration and also measure their free length using vernier calipers or a steel rule or by comparing the existing spring with a new component.

19 Stand each spring on a flat surface, and check it for squareness. If any of the springs are damaged, distorted or have lost their tension, obtain a complete new set of springs. It is normal to renew the valve springs as a matter of course if a major overhaul is being carried out.

20 Renew the valve stem oil seals regardless of their apparent condition.

8 Cylinder head - reassembly

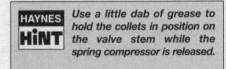

1 Lubricate the stems of the valves, and insert the valves into their original locations. If new valves are being fitted, insert them into the locations to which they have been ground.

2 Refit the spring seat then, working on the first valve, dip the new valve stem seal in fresh engine oil. Carefully locate it over the valve and onto the guide. Take care not to damage the seal as it is passed over the valve stem. Use a suitable socket or metal tube to press the seal firmly onto the guide **(see illustration)**.

3 Locate the valve spring on top of its seat, then refit the spring retainer **(see illustrations)**.

4 Compress the valve spring, and locate the split collets in the recess in the valve stem **(see illustration)**. Release the compressor, then repeat the procedure on the remaining valves.

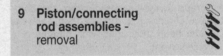

Use a little dab of grease to hold the collets in position on the valve stem while the spring compressor is released.

5 With all the valves installed, place the cylinder head on blocks on the bench and, using a hammer and interposed block of wood, tap the end of each valve stem to settle the components.

6 Refit the camshaft, followers and shims/hydraulic tappets (as applicable) as described in Part D or E of this Chapter.

7 The cylinder head can then be refitted as described in Part D or E of this Chapter.

9 Piston/connecting rod assemblies - removal

Note: *New connecting rod big-end cap bolts will be required on refitting.*

1 Remove the cylinder head, sump and oil pump as described in Part D or E of this Chapter as applicable.

2 If there is a pronounced wear ridge at the top of any bore, it may be necessary to remove it with a scraper or ridge reamer, to avoid piston damage during removal. Such a ridge indicates excessive wear of the cylinder bore.

3 Using quick-drying paint, mark each connecting rod and big-end bearing cap with its respective cylinder number on the flat machined surface provided; if the engine has been dismantled before, note carefully any identifying marks made previously **(see illustration)**. Note that No 1 cylinder is at the transmission (flywheel) end of the engine.

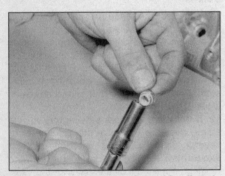

8.2 Press on the new valve guide oil seal using a socket

8.3a Fit the valve spring . . .

8.3b . . . and the spring retainer . . .

8.4 . . . then compress the valve and fit the collets

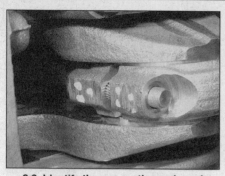

9.3 Identify the connecting rods and bearing caps using quick-drying paint

10.6 The main bearing caps should be numbered 1 to 5 from the transmission (flywheel) end of the engine - 1.9 litre engines

10.7 Unscrew and remove the main bearing cap retaining bolts, and withdraw the caps - 1.9 litre engines

4 Turn the crankshaft to bring pistons 1 and 4 to BDC (bottom dead centre).

5 Unscrew the bolts from No 1 piston big-end bearing cap. Take off the cap, noting its correct fitted position, and recover the bottom half bearing shell. If the bearing shells are to be re-used, tape the cap and the shell together.

6 Using a hammer handle, push the piston up through the bore, and remove it from the top of the cylinder block. Recover the bearing shell, and tape it to the connecting rod for safe-keeping.

7 Loosely refit the big-end cap to the connecting rod, and secure with the bolts - this will help to keep the components in their correct order.

8 Remove No 4 piston assembly in the same way.

9 Turn the crankshaft through 180° to bring pistons 2 and 3 to BDC (bottom dead centre), and remove them in the same way.

10 Crankshaft - removal

1.9 litre engines

1 Remove the timing belt, the crankshaft sprocket, the oil pump and the flywheel as described in Part D of this Chapter. If the piston and connecting rod assemblies are also to be removed, remove the cylinder head.

2 Check the crankshaft endfloat as described in Section 13, then proceed as follows.

3 Remove the piston and connecting rod assemblies as described in Section 9. If no work is to be done on the pistons and connecting rods, unbolt the caps and push the pistons far enough up the bores that the connecting rods are positioned clear of the crankshaft journals.

4 Undo the retaining bolts and remove the timing belt lower cover from the cylinder block.

5 Slacken and remove the retaining bolts securing the crankshaft front oil seal housing to the cylinder block and remove the housing

from the crankshaft end. If the cover locating dowels are a loose fit, remove and store them with the cover for safe-keeping.

6 The main bearing caps should be numbered 1 to 5 from the transmission (flywheel) end of the engine **(see illustration)**. If not, mark them accordingly using quick-drying paint in the same way as the connecting rods.

7 Unscrew and remove the main bearing cap retaining bolts, and withdraw the caps **(see illustration)**. Recover the lower main bearing shells, and tape them to their respective caps for safe-keeping. Note that No 1 main bearing cap is sealed to the sides of the cylinder block with a semi-permanent silicone based sealant. As there is very little clearance between the crankshaft and cylinder block in this area, in which to tap or prise the cap free, it may be necessary to use Renault special tool Mot. 1423 for removal. Alternatively, fabricate a home-made alternative as shown in Chapter 2G, Section 8.

8 Carefully lift out the crankshaft, taking care not to displace the upper main bearing shells, and discard the rear oil seal **(see illustration)**.

9 Recover the upper bearing shells from the cylinder block, and tape them to their respective caps for safe-keeping. Remove the thrustwasher halves from the side of crankcase main bearing, and store them with the bearing cap.

10.8 Lifting the crankshaft from the crankcase - 1.9 litre engines

2.2 litre engines

Note: *New cylinder block casting main bearing bolts and will be required on refitting.*

10 Remove the oil pump and drive chain and sprockets, the flywheel and the rear mounting bracket as described in Part E of this Chapter. If the piston and connecting rod assemblies are also to be removed, remove the cylinder head.

11 Check the crankshaft endfloat as described in Section 13, then proceed as follows.

12 On G8T 706 and 790 engines, unscrew the union bolt and disconnect the braking system vacuum pump oil supply hose from the oil cooler housing **(see illustration)**. Recover the sealing washer fitted on each side of the hose union and discard them; new ones should be used on refitting. Release the retaining clip and detach the return hose from the casting.

13 Undo the retaining bolt and remove the oil return pipe lower section from the base of the main bearing casting. Undo the bolt securing the upper section of the pipe to the cylinder block then remove the pipe and along with its sealing ring. Discard the sealing ring a new one should be used on refitting **(see illustrations)**.

14 Slacken and remove the smaller (8 mm) outer bolts securing the main bearing casting to the cylinder block **(see illustration)**.

10.12 Undo the union bolt and disconnect the vacuum pump oil hose from the oil cooler housing - G8T 706 and 790, 2.2 litre engines

2H

10.13a Unscrew the retaining bolts and remove the lower section . . .

10.13b . . . and upper section of the oil return pipe noting the sealing ring (arrowed) - 2.2 litre engines

10.14 Slacken and remove the smaller (8 mm) main bearing casting bolts . . .

15 Working in a diagonal sequence, evenly and progressively slacken the ten large (12 mm) main bearing casting retaining bolts by a turn at a time. Once all the bolts are loose, remove them from the casting. Discard the bolts; new ones must be used on refitting **(see illustration)**.

16 With all the retaining bolts removed, carefully lift the main bearing casting away from the base of the cylinder block and recover the sealing ring from the oilway. Recover the lower main bearing shells, and tape them to their respective locations in the casting. If the locating dowels are a loose fit, remove them and store them with the casting for safe-keeping.

17 Remove the piston and connecting rod assemblies as described in Section 9. If no work is to be done on the pistons and connecting rods, unbolt the caps and push the pistons far enough up the bores so that the connecting rods are positioned clear of the crankshaft journals.

18 Lift out the crankshaft, and discard the rear oil seal.

19 Recover the upper main bearing shells, and store them along with the relevant lower bearing shell. Also recover the two thrustwashers (one fitted either side of No 2 main bearing) from the cylinder block.

11 Cylinder block - cleaning and inspection

Cleaning

1 Remove all external components and electrical switches/sensors from the block. For complete cleaning, the core plugs should ideally be removed. Drill a small hole in the plugs, then insert a self-tapping screw into the hole. Pull out the plugs by pulling on the screw with a pair of grips, or by using a slide hammer.

2 Undo the retaining bolts and remove the piston oil jet spray tubes from inside the cylinder block.

3 Scrape all traces of gasket from the cylinder block, and from the main bearing casting (where fitted), taking care not to damage the gasket/sealing surfaces.

4 Remove all oil gallery plugs (where fitted). The plugs are usually very tight - they may have to be drilled out, and the holes re-tapped. Use new plugs when the engine is reassembled.

5 If any of the castings are extremely dirty, all should be steam-cleaned.

6 After the castings are returned, clean all oil holes and oil galleries one more time. Flush all internal passages with warm water until the water runs clear. Dry thoroughly, and apply a light film of oil to all mating surfaces, to prevent rusting. Also oil the cylinder bores. If you have access to compressed air, use it to speed up the drying process, and to blow out all the oil holes and galleries.

⚠ **Warning: Wear eye protection when using compressed air!**

7 If the castings are not very dirty, you can do an adequate cleaning job with hot (as hot as you can stand), soapy water and a stiff brush. Take plenty of time, and do a thorough job. Regardless of the cleaning method used, be sure to clean all oil holes and galleries very thoroughly, and to dry all components well. Protect the cylinder bores as described above, to prevent rusting.

8 All threaded holes must be clean, to ensure accurate torque readings during reassembly. To clean the threads, run the correct-size tap into each of the holes to remove rust, corrosion, thread sealant or sludge, and to restore damaged threads. If possible, use compressed air to clear the holes of debris produced by this operation.

10.15 . . . then unscrew and remove the ten larger (12 mm) bolts

⚠ **Warning: Wear eye protection when cleaning out these holes in this way!**

9 Apply suitable sealant to the new oil gallery plugs, and insert them into the holes in the block. Tighten them securely.

10 Refit the piston oil jet spray tubes to the cylinder block, making sure their locating pegs are correctly engaged, and securely tighten the retaining bolts **(see illustrations)**.

11 If the engine is not going to be reassembled right away, cover it with a large plastic bag to keep it clean; protect all mating surfaces and the cylinder bores as described above, to prevent rusting.

Inspection

12 Visually check the castings for cracks and corrosion. Look for stripped threads in the threaded holes. If there has been any history of internal water leakage, it may be worthwhile

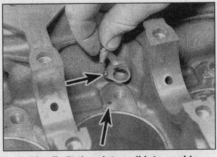

11.10a Refit the piston oil jets, making sure the locating pegs are correctly located in the block holes (arrowed) . . .

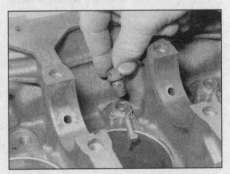

11.10b . . . and refit the retaining bolts

having an engine overhaul specialist check the cylinder block with special equipment. If defects are found, have them repaired if possible, or renew the assembly.

13 Check the each cylinder bore for scuffing and scoring. Check for signs of a wear ridge at the top of the cylinder, indicating that the bore is excessively worn.

14 If the necessary measuring equipment is available, measure the bore diameter of each cylinder at the top (just under the wear ridge), centre, and bottom of the cylinder bore, parallel to the crankshaft axis.

15 Next, measure the bore diameter at the same three locations, at right-angles to the crankshaft axis. Compare the results with the figures given in the Specifications. Where no tolerance figures are stated by Renault, if there is any doubt about the condition of the cylinder bores seek the advice of a Renault dealer or suitable engine reconditioning specialist.

16 Oversize pistons are not available for any of the diesel engines. If the bores are worn, it will be necessary to obtain a new cylinder block, together with new standard size pistons.

17 On 1.9 litre engines, seek the advice of a Renault dealer or engine overhaul specialist regarding standard size cylinder bore size groups and the availability of matching pistons.

18 On 2.2 litre engines, the size group of the cylinder bore can be determined from the 5 mm holes drilled into the rear of the block **(see illustration)**. If the holes are drilled into the upper flat (N) the cylinders bore is in size group 1 and if they are drilled into the lower flat (R) the cylinder bore is in size group 2. Use the size group markings when purchasing new pistons (see Section 12).

12 Piston/connecting rod assemblies - inspection

1 Before the inspection process can begin, the piston/connecting rod assemblies must be cleaned, and the original piston rings removed from the pistons.

2 Carefully expand the old rings over the top of the pistons. The use of two or three old feeler blades will be helpful in preventing the rings dropping into empty grooves. Be careful not to scratch the piston with the ends of the ring. The rings are brittle, and will snap if they are spread too far. They're also very sharp - protect your hands and fingers. Note that the third ring may incorporate an expander. Always remove the rings from the top of the piston. Keep each set of rings with its piston if the old rings are to be re-used.

3 Scrape away all traces of carbon from the top of the piston. A hand-held wire brush (or a piece of fine emery cloth) can be used, once the majority of the deposits have been scraped away. The piston identification markings should now be visible **(see illustration)**.

4 Remove the carbon from the ring grooves in the piston, using an old ring. Break the ring in half to do this (be careful not to cut your fingers - piston rings are sharp). Be careful to remove only the carbon deposits - do not remove any metal, and do not nick or scratch the sides of the ring grooves.

5 Once the deposits have been removed, clean the piston/connecting rod assembly with paraffin or a suitable solvent, and dry thoroughly. Make sure that the oil return holes in the ring grooves are clear.

6 If the pistons and cylinder bores are not damaged or worn excessively, the original pistons can be refitted. Normal piston wear shows up as even vertical wear on the piston thrust surfaces, and slight looseness of the top ring in its groove. New piston rings should always be used when the engine is reassembled.

7 Carefully inspect each piston for cracks around the skirt, around the gudgeon pin holes, and at the piston ring 'lands' (between the ring grooves).

8 Look for scoring and scuffing on the piston skirt, holes in the piston crown, and burned areas at the edge of the crown. If the skirt is scored or scuffed, the engine may have been suffering from overheating, and/or abnormal combustion which caused excessively high operating temperatures. The cooling and lubrication systems should be checked thoroughly. Scorch marks on the sides of the pistons show that blow-by has occurred. A hole in the piston crown, or burned areas at the edge of the piston crown, indicates that abnormal combustion has been occurring. If any of the above problems exist, the causes must be investigated and corrected, or the damage will occur again. The causes may include incorrect injection pump timing, or a faulty injector.

2H

11.18 Cylinder block bore size group identification holes - 2.2 litre engines

N Size group 1 flat   *R Size group 2 flat*

12.3 Piston identification markings

1 Height size group marking
2 Manufacturer's modification marking
3 Diameter size group marking
4 Manufacturer's date marking
5 Engine type marking

12.12a Carefully prise out the circlip . . .

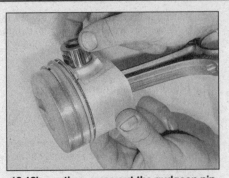

12.12b . . . then press out the gudgeon pin and separate the piston and connecting rod

9 Corrosion of the piston, in the form of pitting, indicates that coolant has been leaking into the combustion chamber and/or the crankcase. Again, the cause must be corrected, or the problem may persist in the rebuilt engine.

10 Examine each connecting rod carefully for signs of damage, such as cracks around the big-end and small-end bearings. Check that the rod is not bent or distorted. Damage is highly unlikely, unless the engine has been seized or badly overheated. Detailed checking of the connecting rod assembly can only be carried out by a Renault dealer or engine repair specialist with the necessary equipment.

11 The gudgeon pins are of the floating type, secured in position by two circlips. If necessary, the pistons and connecting rods can be separated as follows.

12 Using a small flat-bladed screwdriver, prise out the circlips, and push out the gudgeon pin **(see illustrations)**. Hand pressure should be sufficient to remove the pin. Identify the piston and rod to ensure correct reassembly. Discard the circlips - new ones *must* be used on refitting.

13 Examine the gudgeon pin and connecting rod small-end bearing for signs of wear or damage. Wear will mean both the pin and connecting rod will have to be renewed.

14 The connecting rods themselves should not be in need of renewal, unless seizure or some other major mechanical failure has occurred. Check the alignment of the connecting rods visually, and if the rods are not straight, take them to an engine overhaul specialist for a more detailed check.

15 Examine all components, and renew any worn parts. If new pistons are purchased, they will be supplied complete with gudgeon pins and circlips. Circlips can also be purchased individually.

16 On 1.9 litre engines, if the pistons and/or connecting rods are to be renewed, seek the advice of a Renault dealer or engine overhaul specialist regarding cylinder bore/piston size groups. The new pistons can then be refitted to the connecting rods as described in paragraph 25.

17 On 2.2 litre engines, if the pistons and/or connecting rods are to be renewed, permissible combinations of piston/connecting rod must be selected for each cylinder using the procedure described in paragraphs 18 to 24.

18 To enable the piston protrusion to be accurately set, the connecting rods and pistons are available in size groups. Depending on which size group it is in; the distance between the big-end and small-end bores (connecting rod) and gudgeon pin bore

and piston crown (piston) vary slightly. The piston size group marking can be found on the piston crown and the connecting rod size group marking is on the side of the rod **(see illustrations)**.

2.2 litre non-turbo engines

Connecting rod size groups	Distance between big-end and small-end bores (mm)
A	149.88 to 149.89
B	149.89 to 149.90
C	149.90 to 149.91
D	149.91 to 149.92
Piston size groups	**Distance from gudgeon pin bore to piston crown (mm)**
A	44.88 to 44.92
B	44.92 to 44.96
C	44.96 to 45.00
D	45.00 to 45.04
E	45.04 to 45.08
F	45.08 to 45.12

2.2 litre turbo engines

Connecting rod size groups	Distance between big-end and small-end bores (mm)
A	149.88 to 149.89
B	149.89 to 149.90
C	149.90 to 149.91
D	149.91 to 149.92
Piston size groups	**Distance from gudgeon pin bore to piston crown (mm)**
E	44.74 to 44.78
F	44.78 to 44.82
J	44.82 to 44.86
K	44.86 to 44.90
L	44.90 to 44.94
M	44.94 to 44.98

19 To select the correct size group of piston/connecting rod, it is necessary to measure the distance from the top of the crankshaft big-end journal to the cylinder head mating surface when the crankshaft is

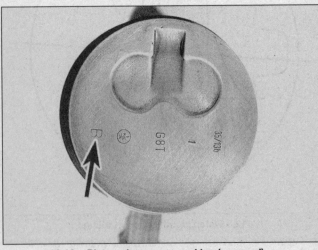

12.18a Piston size group marking (arrowed) . . .

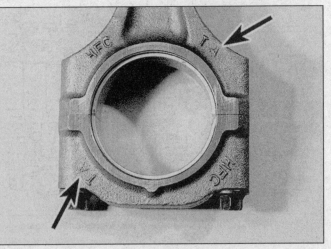

12.18b . . . and connecting rod size group marking (arrowed) - 2.2 litre engines

positioned at TDC for each cylinder. To do this accurately access to the special Renault service tool (Mot. 1319), which entails the use of a dial gauge and measuring rod to measure the height, will be needed (see illustration). Without access to this tool, it will be difficulty to obtain the measurements with the necessary degree of accuracy and it is therefore recommended that this task is entrusted to a Renault dealer.

20 Rotate the crankshaft until journals 1 and 4 are positioned at TDC then lock the crankshaft in position by inserting a suitable rod through the access hole in the front of the cylinder block (see Part D or E, Section 3).

21 Ensure that the cylinder block mating surface is clean and fit the measuring tool to the top of No 1 bore. Zero the dial gauge by measuring the distance between the top edge of the measuring tool and the cylinder block mating surface (points C and E in **illustration 12.19**); if the measurements differ take the average reading. With the gauge zeroed, insert the measuring rod through the centre of the tool until it contacts the crankshaft journal. Slide the dial gauge into position so it contacts the end of the rod and note the reading obtained. The relevant height can then be calculated by subtracting the reading obtained from the length of the rod. For example if a reading of 0.115 mm is obtained, subtract this from the length of the measuring rod which is 170.14 mm which gives a crankshaft journal to cylinder block mating surface height of 169.999 mm.

22 Repeat the operation described in paragraph 21 on No 4 cylinder.

23 Remove the locking rod then rotate the crankshaft through 180° to bring crankshaft journals 2 and 3 to TDC and measure the journal to cylinder block mating surface heights as described in paragraph 21.

24 Using the measurements obtained for each cylinder, use the table below to select the correct connecting rod and piston size group combinations allowed. **Note:** *On non-turbo engines, all new connecting rods supplied by Renault are size group B and new pistons are only available in size groups A, C or E. On turbo engines the connecting rods are all size group C and the pistons are only available in size groups E, J or L.*

2.2 litre non-turbo engines

Crankshaft journal height (mm)	Piston size group	Connecting rod size group
169.924 to 169.954	A	A
169.924 to 169.964	A	B
169.924 to 169.974	A	C
169.932 to 169.984	A	D
169.954 to 170.034	C	A
169.964 to 170.044	C	B
169.974 to 170.054	C	C
169.984 to 170.064	C	D
170.034 to 170.141	E	A
170.044 to 170.150	E	B
170.054 to 170.150	E	C
170.064 to 170.150	E	D

2.2 litre turbo engines

Crankshaft journal height (mm)	Piston size group	Connecting rod size group
169.924 to 169.984	E	A
169.924 to 169.984	E	B
169.924 to 169.994	E	C
169.924 to 170.004	E	D
169.984 to 170.054	J	A
169.984 to 170.064	J	B
169.994 to 170.074	J	C
170.004 to 170.084	J	D
170.054 to 170.150	L	A
170.064 to 170.150	L	B
170.074 to 170.150	L	C
170.084 to 170.150	L	D

25 On 1.9 litre engines, locate the piston on the connecting rod so that the oil hole in the rod faces away from the combustion chamber in the piston crown (see illustration). Apply a smear of clean engine oil to the gudgeon pin. Slide it into the piston and through the connecting rod small-end. Check that the piston pivots freely on the rod, then secure the gudgeon pin in position with two new circlips. Ensure that each circlip is correctly located in its groove in the piston.

26 On 2.2 litre non-turbo engines, noting that the connecting rod bearing cap locating pins are positioned on the timing belt end of the connecting rod, fit the piston so that the cutout on the piston skirt is offset towards the flywheel end; this will align the cutout with the piston oil jet fitted inside the cylinder block (see illustration). Apply a smear of clean engine oil to the gudgeon pin. Slide it into the piston and through the connecting rod small-end. Check that the piston pivots freely on the rod, then secure the gudgeon pin in position with two new circlips. Ensure that each circlip is correctly located in its groove in the piston.

27 On 2.2 litre turbo engines, locate the

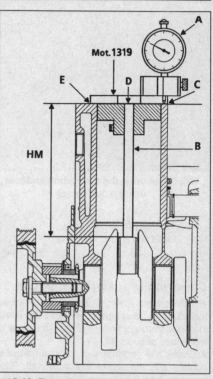

12.19 Renault equipment for measuring crankshaft journal to cylinder block distance (HM)

A Dial gauge
B Measuring rod
C Cylinder block mating surface
D Measuring point
E Cylinder block mating surface

piston on the connecting rod so that the combustion chamber in the piston crown is on the same side as the big-end bearing shell locating notches in the rod and cap. Apply a smear of clean engine oil to the gudgeon pin. Slide it into the piston and through the connecting rod small-end. Check that the piston pivots freely on the rod, then secure the gudgeon pin in position with two new circlips. Ensure that each circlip is correctly located in its groove in the piston.

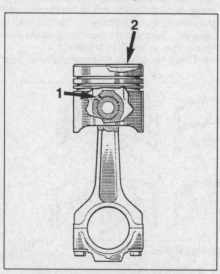

12.25 On 1.9 litre engines, oil hole (1) in connecting rod small-end should face away from combustion chamber (2) in piston crown

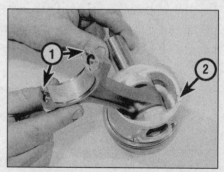

12.26 On 2.2 litre non-turbo engines, position the connecting rod bearing cap locating pins (1) on the timing belt side and the piston skirt cut-out (2) on the flywheel side

13.2 Measuring the crankshaft endfloat using a dial gauge

13.3 Measuring the crankshaft endfloat using a feeler blade

13 Crankshaft - inspection

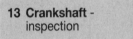

Checking crankshaft endfloat

1 If the crankshaft endfloat is to be checked, this must be done when the crankshaft is still installed in the cylinder block, but is free to move (see Section 10).

2 Check the endfloat using a dial gauge in contact with the end of the crankshaft. Push the crankshaft fully one way, and then zero the gauge. Push the crankshaft fully the other way, and check the endfloat **(see illustration)**. The result can be compared with the specified amount, and will give an indication as to whether new thrustwashers are required.

3 If a dial gauge is not available, feeler blades can be used. First push the crankshaft fully towards the flywheel end of the engine, then use feeler blades to measure the gap between the web of the crankpin and the thrustwasher **(see illustration)**.

Inspection

4 Clean the crankshaft using paraffin or a suitable solvent, and dry it, preferably with compressed air if available. Be sure to clean the oil holes with a pipe cleaner or similar probe, to ensure that they are not obstructed.

⚠️ **Warning: Wear eye protection when using compressed air.**

5 Check the main and big-end bearing journals for uneven wear, scoring, pitting and cracking.

6 Big-end bearing wear is accompanied by distinct metallic knocking when the engine is running (particularly noticeable when the engine is pulling from low speed) and some loss of oil pressure.

7 Main bearing wear is accompanied by severe engine vibration and rumble - getting progressively worse as engine speed increases - and again by loss of oil pressure.

8 Check the bearing journal for roughness by running a finger lightly over the bearing surface. Any roughness (which will be accompanied by obvious bearing wear) indicates that the crankshaft requires renewal.

9 Using a micrometer, measure the diameter of the main and big-end bearing journals, and compare the results with the Specifications. By measuring the diameter at a number of points around each journal's circumference, you will be able to determine whether or not the journal is out-of-round. Take the measurement at each end of the journal, near the webs, to determine if the journal is tapered. Compare the results obtained with those given in the Specifications.

10 Check the oil seal contact surfaces at each end of the crankshaft for wear and damage. If the seal has worn a deep groove in the surface of the crankshaft, consult an engine overhaul specialist; repair may be possible, but otherwise a new crankshaft will be required.

11 As no oversize bearing shells are produced by Renault, if the crankshaft has worn beyond the specified limits, it will have to be renewed, it cannot be reground. Consult your Renault dealer or engine specialist for further information on parts availability.

14 Main and big-end bearings - inspection and selection

Inspection

1 Even though the main and big-end bearings should be renewed during the engine overhaul, the old bearings should be retained for close examination, as they may reveal valuable information about the condition of the engine.

2 Bearing failure can occur due to lack of lubrication, the presence of dirt or other foreign particles, overloading the engine, or corrosion **(see illustration)**. Regardless of the cause of bearing failure, the cause must be corrected (where applicable) before the engine is reassembled, to prevent it from happening again.

3 When examining the bearing shells, remove them from the cylinder block, the main bearing casting/caps (as appropriate), the connecting rods and the connecting rod big-end bearing caps. Lay them out on a clean surface in the same general position as their location in the engine. This will enable you to match any bearing problems with the corresponding crankshaft journal.

4 Dirt and other foreign matter gets into the engine in a variety of ways. It may be left in the engine during assembly, or it may pass through filters or the crankcase ventilation system. It may get into the oil, and from there into the bearings. Metal chips from machining operations and normal engine wear are often present. Abrasives are sometimes left in engine components after reconditioning, especially when parts are not thoroughly cleaned using the proper cleaning methods. Whatever the source, these foreign objects often end up embedded in the soft bearing material, and are easily recognised. Large particles will not embed in the bearing, and will score or gouge the bearing and journal. The best prevention for this cause of bearing failure is to clean all parts thoroughly, and keep everything spotlessly-clean during engine assembly. Frequent and regular engine oil and filter changes are also recommended.

5 Lack of lubrication (or lubrication breakdown) has a number of interrelated causes. Excessive heat (which thins the oil), overloading (which squeezes the oil from the bearing face) and oil leakage (from excessive bearing clearances,

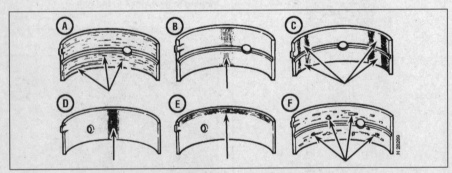

14.2 Typical bearing failures

A   Scratched by dirt; dirt embedded in
    bearing material
B   Lack of oil; overlay wiped out
C   Improper seating; bright (polished)
    sections

D   Tapered journal; overlay gone from
    entire surface
E   Radius ride
F   Fatigue failure; craters or pockets

worn oil pump or high engine speeds) all contribute to lubrication breakdown. Blocked oil passages, which usually are the result of misaligned oil holes in a bearing shell, will also oil-starve a bearing, and destroy it. When lack of lubrication is the cause of bearing failure, the bearing material is wiped or extruded from the steel backing of the bearing. Temperatures may increase to the point where the steel backing turns blue from overheating.

6 Driving habits can have a definite effect on bearing life. Full-throttle, low-speed operation (labouring the engine) puts very high loads on bearings, tending to squeeze out the oil film. These loads cause the bearings to flex, which produces fine cracks in the bearing face (fatigue failure). Eventually, the bearing material will loosen in pieces, and tear away from the steel backing.

7 Short-distance driving leads to corrosion of bearings, because insufficient engine heat is produced to drive off the condensed water and corrosive gases. These products collect in the engine oil, forming acid and sludge. As the oil is carried to the engine bearings, the acid attacks and corrodes the bearing material.

8 Incorrect bearing installation during engine assembly will lead to bearing failure as well. Tight-fitting bearings leave insufficient bearing running clearance, and will result in oil starvation. Dirt or foreign particles trapped behind a bearing shell result in high spots on the bearing, which lead to failure.

Selection - main and big-end bearings

9 The main and big-end bearing shells supplied by the manufacturer are only available in one standard size. Therefore, if the relevant crankshaft journals are all within tolerance, and new bearing shells are fitted, the bearing running clearances should then be correct. Before obtaining new bearing shells, consult a Renault dealer or engine reconditioning specialist as to the latest recommendations concerning bearing shell selection.

15 Engine overhaul - reassembly sequence

1 Before reassembly begins, ensure that all new parts have been obtained, and that all necessary tools are available. Read through the entire procedure to familiarise yourself with the work involved, and to ensure that all items necessary for reassembly of the engine are at hand. In addition to all normal tools and materials, thread-locking compound will be needed. A suitable tube of liquid sealant will also be required for the joint faces that are fitted without gaskets. It is recommended that Renault's own product(s) are used, which are specially formulated for this purpose; the relevant product names are quoted in the text of each Section where they are required.

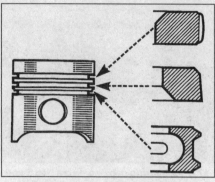

16.1 Piston ring fitting diagram

2 In order to save time and avoid problems, engine reassembly can be carried out in the following order:
  a) Crankshaft.
  b) Piston/connecting rod assemblies.
  c) Oil pump.
  d) Sump.
  e) Flywheel.
  f) Cylinder head.
  g) Timing belt tensioner and sprockets, and timing belt.
  h) Engine external components.

3 At this stage, all engine components should be absolutely clean and dry, with all faults repaired. The components should be laid out (or in individual containers) on a completely clean work surface.

16 Piston rings - refitting

1 Fit the piston rings using the same technique as for removal. Fit the bottom (oil control) ring first, and work up. Ensure that both the top and second compression rings are fitted the correct way up (see illustration). **Note:** Always follow any instructions supplied with the new piston

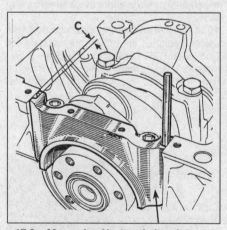

17.2a Measuring No 1 main bearing cap side seal groove using a dowel rod - 1.9 litre engines

Bearing cap (arrowed)
C Seal groove measurement

ring sets - different manufacturers may specify different procedures. Do not mix up the top and second compression rings, as they have different cross-sections.

2 With the piston rings correctly installed, check that each ring is free to rotate easily in its groove. Position the ring end gaps so that are spaced at 120° intervals.

17 Crankshaft - refitting

Note: To obtain the correct main bearing running clearance, new main bearing shells should always be fitted regardless of the condition of the original ones.

1 Crankshaft refitting is the first stage of engine reassembly following overhaul. It is assumed at this point that the cylinder block/crankcase and crankshaft have been cleaned, inspected and repaired or reconditioned as necessary. Position the cylinder block on a clean level work surface, with the crankcase facing upwards. The crankshaft can now be refitted as described in the following sub-Sections according to engine type.

1.9 litre engines

2 Before fitting the crankshaft and main bearings, decide whether the No 1 main bearing cap is to be sealed using butyl seals or silicone sealant. If butyl seals are to be used, it is necessary to determine the correct thickness of the seals to obtain from Renault. To do this, place the bearing cap in position without any seals and secure it with the two retaining bolts. Locate a twist drill, dowel rod or any other suitable implement which will just fit in the side seal groove (see illustration). Now measure the implement - this dimension is the side seal groove size. If the dimension is less than or equal to 5 mm, a 5.10 mm thick side seal is needed. If the dimension is more than 5 mm, a 5.4 mm thick side seal is required. If No 1 main bearing cap is to be fitted using sealant, a tube of Rhodorseal 5661 sealant, together with a hardening agent and application syringe will be required. This is available as a kit from Renault dealers (see illustration).

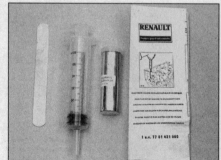

17.2b Renault sealing kit for No 1 main bearing cap grooves. Full instructions are supplied with the kit - 1.9 litre engines

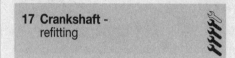
2H

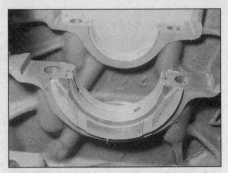

17.6 Stick the thrustwasher halves to the cylinder block using grease, making sure their oil grooves are facing outwards - 1.9 litre engines

17.8 Fit bearing caps numbers 2 to 5 and tighten the retaining bolts to the specified torque - 1.9 litre engines

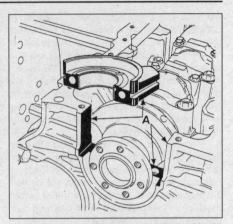

17.10 Thoroughly clean the cylinder block and No 1 main bearing cap mating faces (A) - 1.9 litre engines

3 Clean the backs of the bearing shells and the bearing locations in both the cylinder block and the main bearing caps. If new shells are being fitted, ensure that all traces of the protective grease are cleaned off using paraffin. Wipe dry the shells, block and caps with a lint-free cloth.

4 Lay out the bearing shells ready for fitting, noting that the shells with the oil holes are fitted to the cylinder block. If the original bearing shells are being used they must be refitted in their original locations and in their original fitted direction as noted during removal.

5 Press the bearing shells into their locations, ensuring that the tab on each shell engages in the notch in the cylinder block or main bearing cap.

6 Using a little grease, stick the thrustwashers to each side of the main bearing upper location; ensure that the oilway grooves on each thrustwasher face outwards (away from the cylinder block) **(see illustration).**

7 Liberally lubricate each bearing shell in the cylinder block with clean engine oil then lower the crankshaft into position ensuring that the bearing shells and thrustwashers remain correctly seated.

8 Ensure that the cap locating dowels are in position and fit the main bearing caps numbers 2 to 5. Ensure that the caps are fitted in their correct locations and the correct way round. Insert the bearing cap bolts and tighten

them to the specified torque setting **(see illustration).**

9 Check that the crankshaft is free to turn without stiffness or tight spots, then check the crankshaft endfloat with reference to Section 13.

10 Thoroughly clean the contact surfaces of No 1 main bearing cap and its location in the cylinder block with methylated spirit and allow to dry thoroughly **(see illustration).**

11 If fitting butyl seals to No 1 bearing cap, fit the seals with their grooves facing outwards. Position the seals so that approximately 0.2 mm of seal protrudes at the bottom-facing side (the side towards the crankcase). Apply a thin coating of Rhodorseal 5661 sealant to the bearing cap lower mating surface in the cylinder block, and lubricate the seals with a little oil **(see illustrations).** When the cap is being fitted, use the bolts as a guide by just starting them in their threads, then pressing the cap firmly into position. When the cap is almost fully home, check that the seals still protrude slightly at the cylinder block mating face.

12 Screw in the main bearing cap bolts and tighten them to the specified torque. Trim the protruding ends of the butyl seals flush with the surface of the cylinder block sump mating face.

13 If No 1 main bearing cap is to be fitted using sealant, apply a thin coating of Rhodorseal 5661 sealant to the bearing cap lower mating surface in the cylinder block, then fit the cap. Insert the main bearing cap

bolts and tighten them to the specified torque.

14 Mix approximately half of the 100 g tube of Rhodorseal 5661 sealant together with half the hardener as described in the instructions supplied with the kit. Using the syringe supplied, inject the mixture into the grooves on each side of the bearing cap, until it can be seen to flow out slightly on both sides of the grooves. Using a clean cloth, wipe away any surplus mixture from the inside and outside of the cylinder block.

15 Allow the sealant to dry for a few minutes, then cut away any surplus sealant from the sump mating face.

16 Fit a new seal to the crankshaft timing belt end oil seal housing and refit the housing with reference to Chapter 2D.

17 Fit a new crankshaft flywheel end oil seal, with reference to Chapter 2D.

18 Where applicable, refit the timing belt lower inner cover.

19 Refit the piston/connecting rod assemblies, oil pump, flywheel, cylinder head, timing belt sprockets and fit a new timing belt as described in Part D of this Chapter.

2.2 litre engines

20 Clean the backs of the bearing shells and the bearing locations in both the cylinder

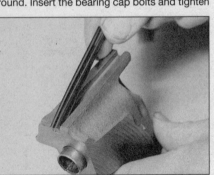

17.11a Fit the sealing strips to No 1 bearing cap so that its groove is facing away from the cap . . .

17.11b . . . and position the strip so that it protrudes above the cap mating surface by approximately 0.2 mm - 1.9 litre engines

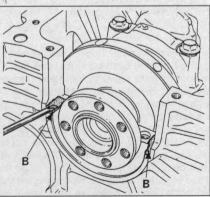

17.11c Apply sealant to No 1 bearing cap lower mating surface (B) in the cylinder block - 1.9 litre engines

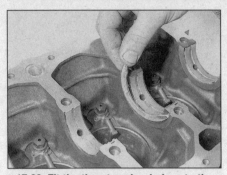

17.23 Fit the thrustwasher halves to the side of No 2 main bearing - 2.2 litre engines

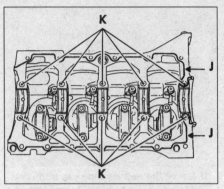

17.25 Apply a bead of sealant (J) to the cylinder block mating surface (K shows the locations of the ten main bearing bolts) - 2.2 litre engines

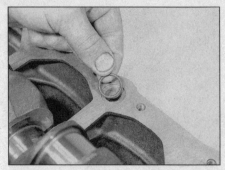

17.26 Fit a new sealing ring to the cylinder block oilway recess - 2.2 litre engines

block and the main bearing casting. If new shells are being fitted, ensure that all traces of the protective grease are cleaned off using paraffin. Wipe dry the shells, block and casting with a lint-free cloth.

21 Lay out the bearing shells ready for fitting, noting that the shells with the oil holes are fitted to the cylinder block. If the original bearing shells are being used they must be refitted in their original locations and in their original fitted direction as noted during removal.

22 Press the bearing shells into their locations, ensuring that the tab on each shell engages in the notch in the cylinder block or main bearing casting.

23 Using a little grease, stick the thrustwashers to each side of the main bearing upper location; ensure that the oilway grooves on each thrustwasher face outwards (away from the cylinder block) **(see illustration)**.

24 Liberally lubricate each bearing shell in the cylinder block with clean engine oil then lower the crankshaft into position ensuring that the bearing shells and thrustwashers remain correctly seated.

25 Ensure that the mating surfaces of the cylinder block and main bearing casting are clean and dry. Apply a bead of Loctite 518 sealant approximately 0.6 to 1.0 mm wide to the mating surface of the block as shown **(see illustration)**.

26 Fit a new sealing ring to the cylinder block oilway **(see illustration)**.

27 Ensure that the locating dowels are in position then carefully lower the main bearing casting onto the block.

28 Fit the ten new large (12 mm) casting bolts and screw in the smaller (8 mm) bolts, tightening all bolts lightly only.

29 Working in a diagonal sequence, starting at the centre and working outwards, tighten the ten large (inner) main bearing casting bolts to their specified Stage 1 torque setting. Once all bolts have been tightened, go around in the same sequence and tighten the bolts through the specified Stage 2 angle, using a socket and extension bar. It is recommended that an angle-measuring gauge is used during this stage of the tightening, to ensure accuracy **(see illustrations)**.

30 Once the casting large (12 mm) bolts are correctly tightened, go around and tighten the smaller (8 mm) bolts to the specified torque setting **(see illustration)**.

31 Check that the crankshaft is free to turn without stiffness or tight spots, then check the crankshaft endfloat with reference to Section 13.

32 Refit/reconnect the piston/connecting rod assemblies to the crankshaft as described in Section 18.

33 Fit a new crankshaft rear oil seal as described in Chapter 2E.

34 Fit a new sealing ring to the oil return pipe upper section then refit the pipe and securely

tighten its retaining bolt. Refit the lower section to the base of the main bearing casting and securely tighten its retaining bolt.

35 On G8T 706 and 790 engines, position a new sealing washer on each side of the braking system vacuum pump oil supply hose union then reconnect the hose to oil cooler and tighten the union bolt to the specified torque. Reconnect the return hose and secure in position with its retaining clip.

36 Refit the oil pump and drive chain (renew the crankshaft oil seal), flywheel, cylinder head, timing belt sprockets and fit a new timing belt as described in Chapter 2E.

18 Piston/connecting rod assemblies - refitting

Note: *To obtain the correct main bearing running clearance, new main bearing shells should always be fitted regardless of the condition of the original ones.*

1 Clean the backs of the big-end bearing shells and the recesses in the connecting rods and big-end caps. If new shells are being fitted, ensure that all traces of the protective grease are cleaned off using paraffin. Wipe the shells and connecting rods dry with a lint-free cloth.

2 Press the big-end bearing shells into the connecting rods and caps in their correct positions. Make sure that the location tabs are engaged with the cut-outs in the connecting rods.

17.29a Tighten the ten (12 mm) main bearing bolts first to the specified Stage 1 torque setting . . .

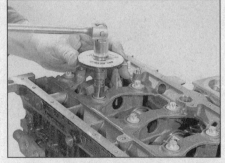

17.29b . . . and then through the specified Stage 2 angle - 2.2 litre engines

17.30 With the large (12 mm) bolts tightened correctly, tighten the smaller (8 mm) bolts to the specified torque - 2.2 litre engines

2H

18.5 Tap the piston into the bore using a hammer handle

18.8a Fit the new bearing cap bolts and tighten them first to the Stage 1 torque setting . . .

18.8b . . . and then through the Stage 2 angle setting

3 Lubricate the bores, the pistons and piston rings then lay out each piston/connecting rod assembly in its respective position.

4 Starting with assembly number 1, make sure that the piston rings are still spaced as described in Section 16, then clamp them in position with a piston ring compressor.

5 Insert the piston/connecting rod assembly into the top of cylinder No 1. Ensure that the combustion chamber recess on the piston crown is towards the front (oil filter side) of the cylinder block. Using a block of wood or hammer handle against the piston crown, tap the assembly into the cylinder until the piston crown is flush with the top of the cylinder/liner (see illustration).

6 Taking care not to mark the cylinder bore, liberally lubricate the crankpin and both bearing shells, then pull the piston/connecting rod assembly down the bore and onto the crankpin. Refit the big-end bearing cap to the connecting rod.

7 On 1.9 litre engines, fit the new bearing cap bolts and tighten them evenly and progressively to the specified torque.

8 On 2.2 litre engines, fit the new bearing cap bolts and tighten them evenly and progressively to the Stage 1 torque setting. Once both bolts have been tightened to the Stage 1 setting, angle-tighten them through the specified Stage 2 angle, using a socket

and extension bar. It is recommended that an angle-measuring gauge is used during this stage of the tightening, to ensure accuracy (see illustrations).

9 Refit the remaining three piston and connecting rod assemblies in the same way.

10 Rotate the crankshaft, and check that it turns freely, with no signs of binding or tight spots.

11 Refit the oil pump, sump and the cylinder head as described in Part D or E of this Chapter.

19 Engine - initial start up after overhaul

1 With the engine refitted in the vehicle, double-check the engine oil and coolant levels. Make a final check that everything has been reconnected, and that there are no tools or rags left in the engine compartment.

2 Disconnect the wiring from the stop solenoid on the injection pump (see Chapter 4B), then turn the engine on the starter motor until the oil pressure warning light goes out. Reconnect the wire to the stop solenoid.

3 Prime the fuel system as described in Chapter 4B.

4 Fully depress the accelerator pedal, turn

the ignition key and wait for the preheating warning light to go out.

5 Start the engine, noting that this may take a little longer than usual, due to the fuel system components having been disturbed.

6 While the engine is idling, check for fuel, water and oil leaks. Don't be alarmed if there are some odd smells and smoke from parts getting hot and burning off oil deposits.

7 Assuming all is well, keep the engine idling until hot water is felt circulating through the top hose, then switch off the engine.

8 Check the injection pump timing, and the idle speed settings (as appropriate), then switch the engine off.

9 After a few minutes, recheck the oil and coolant levels as described in Weekly checks, and top-up as necessary.

10 If they were tightened as described, there is no need to re-tighten the cylinder head bolts once the engine has first run after reassembly.

11 If new pistons, rings or crankshaft bearings have been fitted, the engine must be treated as new, and run-in for the first 500 miles (800 km). Do not operate the engine at full-throttle, or allow it to labour at low engine speeds in any gear. It is recommended that the oil and filter be changed at the end of this period.

Chapter 3
Cooling, heating and air conditioning systems

Contents

Degrees of difficulty

Easy, suitable for novice with little experience

Fairly easy, suitable for beginner with some experience

Fairly difficult, suitable for competent DIY mechanic

Difficult, suitable for experienced DIY mechanic

Very difficult, suitable for expert DIY or professional

Specifications

General
Maximum system pressure:
Brown expansion tank cap	1.2 bar
Blue expansion tank cap	1.6 bar

Thermostat
Opening temperatures:
Starts to open:
Petrol engines	89°C
Diesel engines	83°C

Fully open:
Petrol engines	99°C
Diesel engines	95°C

Torque wrench settings
	Nm	lbf ft
Coolant pump bolts (petrol engines):		
1.8 and 2.0 litre (8-valve) engines	17	13
1.6 litre (16-valve) engines:		
Stage 1	8	6
Stage 2 (M6 bolts)	11	8
Stage 3 (M8 bolts)	22	16
1.8 litre (16-valve) engines	17	13
2.0 litre (16-valve) engines	20	15

1 General information and precautions

General information

The cooling system is of pressurised type, comprising a coolant pump driven by the timing belt or the auxiliary drivebelt (depending on engine type), an aluminium crossflow radiator, expansion tank, electric cooling fan(s), a thermostat, heater matrix, and all associated hoses and switches.

The system functions as follows. Cold coolant in the bottom of the radiator passes through the bottom hose to the coolant pump, where it is pumped around the cylinder block and head passages, and through the oil cooler(s) (where fitted). After cooling the cylinder bores, combustion surfaces and valve seats, the coolant reaches the underside of the thermostat, which is initially closed. The coolant passes through the heater, and is returned via the cylinder block to the coolant pump.

When the engine is cold, the coolant circulates only through the cylinder block, cylinder head, and heater. When the coolant reaches a predetermined temperature, the thermostat opens, and the coolant passes through the top hose to the radiator. As the coolant circulates through the radiator, it is cooled by the inrush of air when the car is in forward motion. The airflow is supplemented by the action of the electric cooling fan(s) when necessary. Upon reaching the bottom of the radiator, the coolant has now cooled, and the cycle is repeated.

When the engine is at normal operating temperature, the coolant expands, and some of it is displaced into the expansion tank. Coolant collects in the tank, and is returned to the radiator when the system cools.

On models fitted with an engine oil cooler, the coolant is also passed through the oil cooler. Similarly, coolant also passes through the automatic transmission fluid cooler, where applicable.

The electric cooling fan(s) mounted in front of the radiator are controlled by a thermostatic switch. At a predetermined coolant temperature, the switch/sensor actuates the fan.

Precautions

 Warning: Do not attempt to remove the expansion tank filler cap, or to disturb any part of the cooling system, while the engine is hot, as there is a high risk of scalding. If the expansion tank filler cap must be removed before the engine and radiator have fully cooled (even though this is not recommended), the pressure in the cooling system must first be relieved. Cover the cap with a thick layer of cloth, to avoid scalding, and slowly unscrew the filler cap until a hissing sound is heard. When the hissing has stopped, indicating that the pressure has reduced, slowly unscrew the filler cap until it can be removed; if more hissing sounds are heard, wait until they have stopped before unscrewing the cap completely. At all times, keep well away from the filler cap opening, and protect your hands.

Warning: Do not allow antifreeze to come into contact with your skin, or with the painted surfaces of the vehicle. Rinse off spills immediately, with plenty of water. Never leave antifreeze lying around in an open container, or in a puddle in the driveway or on the garage floor. Children and pets are attracted by its sweet smell, but antifreeze can be fatal if ingested.

Warning: If the engine is hot, the electric cooling fan may start rotating even if the engine is not running. Be careful to keep your hands, hair, and any loose clothing well clear when working in the engine compartment.

Warning: Refer to Section 10 for precautions to be observed when working on models equipped with air conditioning.

2 Cooling system hoses - disconnection and renewal

Note: Refer to the warnings given in Section 1 of this Chapter before proceeding. Hoses should only be disconnected once the engine has cooled sufficiently to avoid scalding.

Conventional hose connections

1 If the checks described in the relevant part of Chapter 1 reveal a faulty hose, it must be renewed as follows.
2 First drain the cooling system (see the relevant part of Chapter 1). If the coolant is not due for renewal, it may be re-used, providing it is collected in a clean container.
3 To disconnect a hose, proceed as follows.
4 The clips used to secure the hoses in position may be either standard worm-drive clips or disposable crimped types. The crimped type of clip is not designed to be re-used and should be replaced with a worm drive type on reassembly.
5 To disconnect a hose, use a screwdriver to slacken or release the clips, then move them along the hose, clear of the relevant inlet/outlet **(see illustration)**. Carefully work the hose free. The hoses can be removed with relative ease when new - on an older car, they may have stuck.
6 If a hose proves to be difficult to remove, try to release it by rotating its ends before attempting to free it. Gently prise the end of the hose with a blunt instrument (such as a flat-bladed screwdriver), but do not apply too much force, and take care not to damage the pipe stubs or hoses. Note in particular that the radiator inlet stub is fragile; do not use excessive force when attempting to remove the hose. If all else fails, cut the hose with a sharp knife, then slit it so that it can be peeled off in two pieces. Although this may prove

expensive if the hose is otherwise undamaged, it is preferable to buying a new radiator. Check first, however, that a new hose is readily available.
7 When fitting a hose, first slide the clips onto the hose, then work the hose into position. If crimped-type clips were originally fitted, use standard worm-drive clips when refitting the hose. If the hose is stiff, use a little soapy water as a lubricant, or soften the hose by soaking it in hot water. Do not use oil or grease, which may attack the rubber.
8 Work the hose into position, checking that it is correctly routed, then slide each clip back along the hose until it passes over the flared end of the relevant inlet/outlet, before tightening the clip securely.
9 Refill the cooling system with reference to the relevant part of Chapter 1.
10 Check thoroughly for leaks as soon as possible after disturbing any part of the cooling system.

Heater matrix hose connector

11 Depress the (black plastic) locking tab, then pull the hose connector back sharply to release if from the matrix pipes. Take care not to damage the seals **(see illustrations)**.
12 Check the condition of the seals and renew if necessary.
13 When reconnecting, press the connector into position until the locking tab engages.

3 Radiator - removal, inspection and refitting

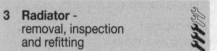

Removal

1 Apply the handbrake, then jack up the front of the vehicle and support securely on axle stands (see *Jacking and vehicle support*).
2 Disconnect the battery negative terminal (refer to *Disconnecting the battery* in the Reference Section of this manual).
3 Drain the cooling system as described in the relevant part of Chapter 1.
4 Remove the radiator grille panel as described in Chapter 11.

2.5 Disconnecting the radiator top hose

2.11a Depress the locking tab (arrowed) . . .

2.11b . . . and pull the hose connector from the heater matrix pipes

3.6 Unclip the battery tray

3.8 Withdraw the cover from the electrical connector box . . .

3.9 . . . then disconnect the wiring harness plug (arrowed)

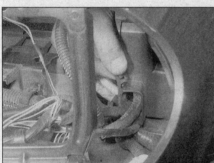

3.10 Release the wiring harness rubber clip

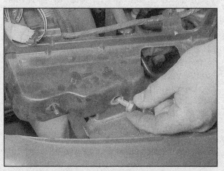

3.11 Unclip the weatherstrip from the front body panel

3.12 Remove the screws securing the front body panel to the radiator

5 Remove the direction indicator lights and the headlights as described in Chapter 12, Section 7.

6 Remove the battery, with reference to Chapter 5A if necessary, then unclip the battery tray from the body panel **(see illustration)**.

7 Unclip the throttle cable from the front body panel.

8 Depress the retaining clips, and withdraw the cover from the electrical connector box at the front left-hand corner of the engine compartment **(see illustration)**.

9 Release the locking clip, and disconnect the body front panel wiring harness plug from the connector in the box **(see illustration)**.

10 Release the rubber clip securing the wiring harness to the connector box **(see illustration)**.

11 Unclip the weatherstrip from the top edge of the front body panel **(see illustration)**.

12 Remove the two screws securing the front body panel to the top of the radiator **(see illustration)**.

13 Working under the right-hand front wheel arch, remove the screws securing the wheel arch liner to the bumper and the body, then pull the liner back for access to the washer fluid reservoir.

14 Disconnect the wiring plug from the washer fluid pump.

15 Unscrew the three bolts on each side, and the central bolt securing the front body panel assembly, then lift off the body panel, and lay it carefully across the engine (support the panel on rags to prevent the possibility of

damage to other components in the engine compartment) **(see illustrations)**.

16 Where applicable, lift off the deflector

panel from the top of the radiator.

17 Release the clip, and disconnect the top coolant hose from the radiator.

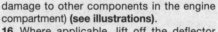

3.15a Unscrew the lower bolt . . .

3.15b . . . and the two upper bolts on each side . . .

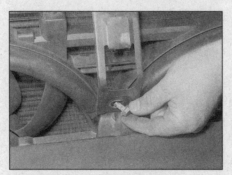

3.15c . . . and the central bolt . . .

3.15d . . . and lift off the front body panel assembly

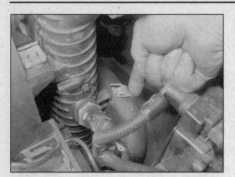

3.18 Release the clip securing the bottom hose to the lug on the radiator

3.19 Prise off the clips securing the radiator lugs to the lower body panel

3.21 Prise off the clips securing the cooling fan shroud to the radiator

3.22 Lifting the radiator from the vehicle

18 Release the clip securing the bottom hose to the lug on the radiator, and move the hose to one side **(see illustration)**.
19 Working under the vehicle, prise off the clips securing the radiator lower locating lugs to the lower body panel, and recover the washers **(see illustration)**.
20 Disconnect the wiring plug from the cooling fan switch mounted in the side of the radiator.
21 Undo the upper retaining bolts (where fitted), then prise off the clips and recover the washers securing the cooling fan shroud to the radiator. Carefully lift the cooling fan shroud and, where applicable, the air conditioning condenser from the lugs on the radiator **(see illustration)**.
22 Lift the radiator to release the lower locating lugs from the body panel, then withdraw the radiator upwards from the front of the vehicle **(see illustration)**.

Inspection

23 If the radiator has been removed due to suspected blockage, reverse-flush it as described in the relevant part of Chapter 1. Clean dirt and debris from the radiator fins, using an air line (in which case, wear eye protection) or a soft brush. Be careful, as the fins are sharp, and easily damaged.
24 If necessary, a radiator specialist can perform a 'flow test' on the radiator, to establish whether an internal blockage exists.
25 A leaking radiator must be referred to a specialist for permanent repair. Do not attempt to weld or solder a leaking radiator, as damage to the plastic components may result.
26 In an emergency, minor leaks from the radiator can be cured by using a suitable radiator sealant, in accordance with its manufacturer's instructions, with the radiator *in situ*.

4.5 Removing the thermostat and cover - 8-valve petrol engine models

4.6 Removing the thermostat sealing ring

27 If the radiator is to be sent for repair or renewed, remove all hoses, and the cooling fan switch (where fitted).
28 Inspect the condition of the radiator mounting rubbers, and renew them if necessary.

Refitting

29 Refitting is a reversal of removal, but on completion, refill and bleed the cooling system as described in the relevant part of Chapter 1.

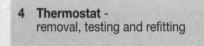

4 Thermostat -
removal, testing and refitting

Petrol engine models

Removal

1 The thermostat is located in a housing bolted to the front of the cylinder head on 2.0 litre (16-valve) engines, and to the left-hand side of the cylinder head on all other engines.
2 Where applicable to improve access, remove the air cleaner assembly as described in Chapter 4A.
3 Partially drain the cooling system to below the level of the thermostat housing, as described in Chapter 1A.
4 Where necessary, release any relevant wiring and hoses from the retaining clips, and position clear of the thermostat housing to improve access.
5 Unscrew the securing bolts, and carefully withdraw the thermostat housing cover, along with the thermostat **(see illustrations)**. Take care not to strain the coolant hose connected to the cover.
6 Lift the thermostat from the cover, and recover the sealing ring **(see illustration)**.

Testing

7 A rough test of the thermostat may be made by suspending it with a piece of string in a container full of water. Heat the water to bring it to the boil - the thermostat must open by the time the water boils. If not, renew it.
8 If a thermometer is available, the precise opening temperature of the thermostat may be determined; compare with the figures given in the *Specifications*. The opening temperature is also marked on the thermostat.
9 A thermostat which fails to close as the water cools must also be renewed.

Refitting

10 Refitting is a reversal of removal, bearing in mind the following points:
a) Examine the sealing ring for signs of damage or deterioration, and if necessary, renew.
b) On completion, refill the cooling system as described in Chapter 1A.

Diesel engine models

Removal

11 On 1.9 litre engines, the thermostat is located in a housing bolted to the left-hand side of the cylinder head. On early 2.2 litre engines, the thermostat is located in a housing bolted to the end of the coolant pump, and on later engines, located in a housing bolted to the power steering fluid reservoir bracket at the front left-hand side of the engine.

12 Proceed as described in paragraphs 3 to 6 (see illustrations).

Testing

13 Proceed as described in paragraphs 7 to 9.

Refitting

14 Refer to paragraph 10.

5	Electric cooling fan -
	testing, removal and refitting

Testing

1 Current supply to the cooling fan(s) is via the ignition switch (see Chapter 10) and a fuse (see Chapter 12). The circuit is completed by the cooling fan thermostatic switch, which is mounted in the radiator.

2 If a fan does not appear to work, run the engine until normal operating temperature is reached, then allow it to idle. The fan should cut in within a few minutes (before the temperature gauge needle enters the red section, or before the coolant temperature warning light comes on). If not, switch off the ignition and disconnect the wiring plug from the cooling fan switch. Bridge the two contacts in the wiring plug using a length of spare wire, and switch on the ignition. If the fan now operates, the switch is probably faulty, and should be renewed.

3 If the fan still fails to operate, check that battery voltage is available at the feed wire to the switch; if not, then there is a fault in the feed wire (possibly due to a fault in the fan motor, or a blown fuse). If there is no problem with the feed, check that there is continuity between the switch earth terminal and a good earth point on the body; if not, then the earth connection is faulty, and must be re-made.

4 If the switch and the wiring are in good condition, the fault must lie in the motor itself. The motor can be checked by disconnecting it from the wiring loom, and connecting a 12-volt supply directly to it.

Removal

5 Disconnect the battery negative terminal (refer to *Disconnecting the battery* in the Reference Section of this manual).

6 Proceed as described in Section 3, paragraphs 4 to 15, and remove the front body panel assembly.

4.12a Unscrew the securing bolts . . .

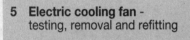

Slide a large piece of card in front of the radiator/air conditioning condenser (as applicable) to reduce the possibility of damaging the radiator/compressor fins during the remainder of the procedure.

7 On models fitted with air conditioning, working at the right-hand end of the shroud, unscrew the bolts securing the fan shroud to the air conditioning drier bottle (see illustration).

8 Prise off the clips and recover the washers securing the fan shroud to the radiator.

9 Disconnect the wiring plug from the cooling fan switch mounted in the side of the radiator (see illustration).

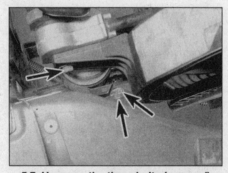

5.7 Unscrew the three bolts (arrowed) securing the air conditioning drier bottle to the fan shroud

5.10 Unscrew the bolt securing the wiring harness earth lead to the body

4.12b . . . and withdraw the thermostat and cover - early 2.2 litre diesel engine models

10 Working at the left-hand side of the fan shroud, unscrew the bolt securing the wiring harness earth lead to the body (see illustration).

11 On models fitted with air conditioning, prise off the clips securing the air conditioning condenser to the fan shroud, then lift up the air conditioning condenser from the lugs on the fan shroud - take care not to damage the condenser fins (see illustration). Note that on turbo diesel engines, the intercooler is also bolted to the condenser and care must also be taken not to damage the intercooler.

12 Again, on models with air conditioning, disconnect the wiring plug from the drier bottle (see illustration).

13 Carefully lift out the fan shroud assembly, taking care not to strain the wiring (see illustration).

5.9 Disconnecting the wiring plug from the cooling fan switch

5.11 Prise off the clips securing the air conditioning condenser to the fan shroud

3

5.12 Disconnect the wiring plug from the air conditioning drier bottle

5.13 Lifting out the cooling fan shroud

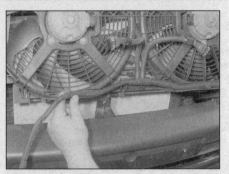

5.14 Release the wiring from the clips on the fan shroud

14 Disconnect the wiring plugs from the cooling fan motor(s), then release the wiring harness from the clips on the fan shroud **(see illustration)**.
15 Release the securing clips, and lift the relay cover from the housing at the bottom of the fan shroud, then unclip the relays from the housing **(see illustrations)**.
16 Withdraw the cooling fan/shroud assembly.
17 If desired, the motor can be separated from the shroud assembly by prising off the metal clip and removing the fan blades, then unscrewing the three nuts and bolts securing the motor to the shroud.

Refitting

18 Refitting is a reversal of removal, but ensure that all wiring is routed as noted during removal, and take care not to damage the radiator and, where applicable, the air conditioning condenser fins.

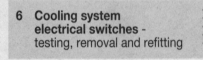

6 Cooling system electrical switches - testing, removal and refitting

Electric cooling fan thermostatic switch

Testing

1 Testing of the switch is described in Section 5, as part of the electric cooling fan test procedure.

Removal

Note: *A new sealing ring or sealing compound may be required on refitting.*
2 The switch is located in the left-hand side of the radiator.
3 Disconnect the battery negative terminal (refer to *Disconnecting the battery* in the Reference Section of this manual).
4 Partially drain the cooling system to just below the level of the switch (see the relevant part of Chapter 1). Alternatively, have ready a suitable bung to plug the switch aperture in the radiator when the switch is removed. If this method is used, take great care not to damage the radiator, and do not use anything which will allow foreign matter to enter the radiator.

5.15a Remove the cover . . .

5 Disconnect the wiring plug from the switch.
6 Carefully unscrew the switch from the housing, and recover the sealing ring, where applicable. If the system has not been drained, plug the switch aperture to prevent further coolant loss.

Refitting

7 If the switch was originally fitted using sealing compound, clean the switch threads thoroughly, and coat them with fresh sealing compound.
8 If the switch was originally fitted using a sealing ring, use a new sealing ring on refitting.
9 Refitting is a reversal of removal. Tighten the switch, and refill (or top-up) the cooling system as described in the relevant part of Chapter 1 or *Weekly Checks*.
10 On completion, start the engine and run it until it reaches normal operating temperature.

6.11 Typical temperature gauge/warning light sender (arrowed) in thermostat housing - diesel engine models

5.15b . . . then unclip the relays from the housing in the fan shroud

Continue to run the engine, and check that the cooling fan cuts in and out correctly.

Coolant temperature gauge/warning light sender

Testing

11 A combined temperature gauge/warning light sender is fitted and located as follows according to engine type **(see illustration):**
8-valve petrol engines - in the front of the cylinder head at the left-hand end.
1.6 and 1.8 litre (16-valve) petrol engines - in the thermostat housing on the left-hand side of the cylinder head.
2.0 litre (16-valve) petrol engines - in the thermostat housing on the front of the cylinder head.
1.9 litre diesel engines - in the thermostat housing on the left-hand side of the cylinder head.
2.2 litre diesel engines - in the thermostat housing on the end of the coolant pump on early models, and in the coolant housing at the left-hand end of the cylinder head on later models.
12 The temperature gauge is fed with a stabilised voltage from the instrument panel feed (via the ignition switch and a fuse). The gauge earth is controlled by the sender. The sender contains a thermistor - an electronic component whose electrical resistance decreases at a predetermined rate as its temperature rises. When the coolant is cold, the sender resistance is high, current flow through the gauge is reduced, and the gauge needle points towards the blue (cold) end of

the scale. As the coolant temperature rises and the sender resistance falls, current flow increases, and the gauge needle moves towards the upper end of the scale. If the sender is faulty, it must be renewed.

13 On models with a temperature warning light, the light is fed with a voltage from the instrument panel. The light earth is controlled by the sender. The sender is effectively a switch, which operates at a predetermined temperature to earth the light and complete the circuit. If the light is fitted in addition to a gauge, the senders for the gauge and light are incorporated in a single unit, with two wires, one each for the light and gauge earths.

14 If the gauge develops a fault, first check the other instruments; if they do not work at all, check the instrument panel electrical feed. If the readings are erratic, there may be a fault in the voltage stabiliser, which will necessitate renewal of the stabiliser (the stabiliser is integral with the instrument panel printed circuit board - see Chapter 12). If the fault lies in the temperature gauge alone, check it as follows.

15 If the gauge needle remains at the cold end of the scale when the engine is hot, disconnect the sender wiring plug, and earth the relevant wire to the engine. If the needle then deflects when the ignition is switched on, the sender unit is proved faulty, and should be renewed. If the needle still does not move, remove the instrument panel (Chapter 12) and check the continuity of the wire between the sender unit and the gauge, and the feed to the gauge unit. If continuity is shown, and the fault still exists, then the gauge is faulty, and the gauge unit should be renewed.

16 If the gauge needle remains at the hot end of the scale when the engine is cold, disconnect the sender wire. If the needle then returns to the cold end of the scale when the ignition is switched on, the sender unit is proved faulty, and should be renewed. If the needle still does not move, check the remainder of the circuit as described previously.

17 The same basic principles apply to testing the warning light. The light should illuminate when the relevant sender wire is earthed.

Removal and refitting

18 The procedure is similar to that described previously in this Section for the electric cooling fan thermostatic switch **(see illustration)**. On

6.18 Disconnecting the wiring plug from the temperature gauge/warning light switch - petrol engine models

some models, access to the switch(es) is poor, and surrounding components may need to be moved to one side before the sender unit can be reached.

Coolant temperature sensors - fuel system

19 Various sensors may be fitted to both petrol and diesel engines, depending on engine type. Refer to the relevant part of Chapter 4 for details of the sensor locations and function. Removal and refitting is as described previously in this Section for the electric cooling fan thermostatic switch.

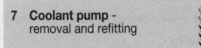

7 Coolant pump -
removal and refitting

1.8 and 2.0 litre (8-valve) and 1.8 litre (16-valve) petrol engine models

Note: *A new gasket will be required on refitting.*

Removal

1 The pump is mounted on the front of the cylinder block, at the timing belt end of the engine.

2 Remove the auxiliary drivebelt as described in Chapter 1A, noting that the coolant pump pulley retaining bolts should be slackened before the belt is removed **(see illustration)**.

3 Drain the cooling system as described in Chapter 1A.

7.2 Coolant pump pulley retaining bolts (arrowed) - 8-valve petrol engine models

4 Unscrew the securing bolts, and remove the pump pulley.

5 Unscrew the bolts securing the pump to the cylinder block, and withdraw the pump from the block **(see illustration)**. If the pump is stuck, tap it using a soft-faced mallet. Recover the gasket and discard it; a new one must be used on refitting.

Refitting

6 Commence refitting by thoroughly cleaning the mating faces of the pump and the cylinder block.

7 Refitting is a reversal of removal, bearing in mind the following points.
  a) Use a new pump gasket.
  b) Tighten the pump mounting bolts to the specified torque.
  c) Refit and tension the auxiliary drivebelt as described in Chapter 1A.
  d) On completion, refill the cooling system as described in Chapter 1A.

1.6 litre (16-valve) petrol engine models

Note: *A tube of Loctite 518 sealant will be required on refitting.*

Removal

8 The pump is mounted on the front of the cylinder block, at the timing belt end of the engine.

9 Drain the cooling system as described in Chapter 1A.

10 Remove the timing belt and timing belt tensioner as described in Chapter 2B.

11 Working in the reverse of the tightening sequence shown in illustration 7.16, undo the eight coolant pump retaining bolts, noting the locations of the different size bolts.

12 Withdraw the pump from the block, tapping it with a soft-faced mallet if it is stuck.

Refitting

13 Commence refitting by thoroughly cleaning the mating faces of the pump and the cylinder block, ensuring that all traces of sealant are removed.

14 Apply a 0.6 to 1.0 mm wide band of Loctite 518 sealant to the pump mating face as shown **(see illustration)**.

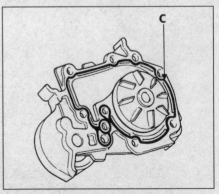

7.14 Apply a bead of sealant (C) to the coolant pump mating face as shown - 1.6 litre (16-valve) petrol engine models

7.5 Withdrawing the coolant pump - 8-valve petrol engine models

3

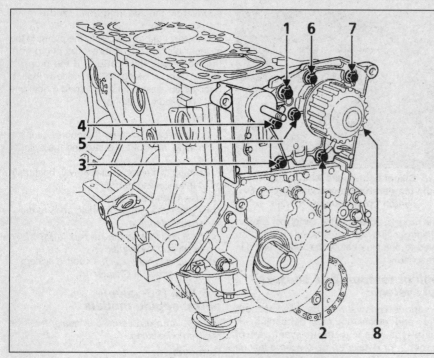

7.16 Coolant pump retaining bolt tightening sequence - 1.6 litre (16-valve) petrol engine models

15 Locate the pump in position and refit the retaining bolts to their correct locations. Note that a suitable thread sealant should be applied to the threads of bolts 1 and 4.

16 Working in the sequence shown tighten all the bolts to the specified Stage 1 torque setting **(see illustration)**. Again working in sequence tighten the M6 bolts to the torque setting given for Stage 2, then tighten the M8 bolts to the setting given for Stage 3.

17 Refit the timing belt tensioner and timing belt as described in Chapter 2B.

18 On completion, refill the cooling system as described in Chapter 1A.

2.0 litre (16-valve) petrol engine models

Note: *A new gasket will be required on refitting.*

Removal

19 The pump is mounted on the front of the cylinder block, at the timing belt end of the engine.

20 Drain the cooling system as described in Chapter 1A.

21 Remove the timing belt and timing belt tensioner as described in Chapter 2C.

22 Unscrew the bolts securing the pump to the cylinder block, and withdraw the pump from the block **(see illustration)**. If the pump is stuck, tap it using a soft-faced mallet. Recover the gasket and discard it; a new one must be used on refitting.

Refitting

23 Commence refitting by thoroughly cleaning the mating faces of the pump and the cylinder block, ensuring that all traces of gasket are removed.

24 Place a new gasket on the pump then locate the pump in position on the cylinder block. Refit the retaining bolts and tighten them to the specified torque.

25 Refit the timing belt as described in Chapter 2C.

26 On completion, refill the cooling system as described in Chapter 1A.

1.9 litre diesel engine models

Note: *A new gasket will be required on refitting.*

27 The pump is mounted on the front of the cylinder block, at the timing belt end of the engine.

28 Remove the auxiliary drivebelt as described in Chapter 1B, noting that the coolant pump pulley retaining bolts should be slackened before the belt is removed.

29 Drain the cooling system as described in Chapter 1B.

30 Unscrew the retaining bolts, and remove the pulley from the coolant pump **(see illustration)**.

31 Unscrew the retaining bolts, then manoeuvre the coolant pump out of position **(see illustrations)**. Note the correct fitted location of the pump locating dowels, and remove them for safe-keeping if they are loose. Recover the pump gasket and discard it; a new one must be used on refitting.

Refitting

32 Ensure that pump and cylinder block/housing mating faces are clean and dry,

7.22 Coolant pump retaining bolts (arrowed) - 2.0 litre (16-valve) petrol engine models

7.30 Unscrew the retaining bolts, and remove the pulley from the coolant pump - 1.9 litre diesel engine models

and that the locating dowels are correctly positioned.

33 Offer up the new gasket and fit the pump assembly, tightening its retaining bolts securely.

34 Refit the coolant pump pulley, refit the drivebelt and tension as described in Chapter 1B, then securely tighten the pulley retaining bolts.

35 Refill the cooling system as described in Chapter 1B.

2.2 litre diesel engine models - auxiliary belt-driven pump

Note: *A new pump housing O-ring will be required on refitting, and a new pump gasket, or suitable sealant may be required (depending on model).*

Removal

36 The pump is mounted on the front of the cylinder block, at the timing belt end of the engine.

37 Remove the auxiliary drivebelt as described in Chapter 1B, noting that the coolant pump pulley retaining bolts should be slackened before the belt is removed.

38 Drain the cooling system as described in Chapter 1B.

39 Disconnect the three coolant hoses from the thermostat housing (bolted to the rear of the coolant pump).

40 Disconnect the wiring plug from the coolant temperature sensor in the thermostat housing.

41 Unscrew the two nuts and two bolts securing the coolant pump, then withdraw the pump/housing assembly from the side of the cylinder block. Recover the O-ring **(see illustrations)**.

42 Unscrew the securing bolts, and separate the pump from the housing. Where applicable, recover the gasket **(see illustrations)**.

Refitting

43 Refitting is a reversal of removal, bearing in mind the following points.

  a) *Thoroughly clean the mating faces of the pump and housing.*
  b) *If the pump was originally fitted using a gasket, use a new gasket on refitting.*
  c) *If the pump was originally fitted using sealant, use suitable sealant on refitting.*
  d) *Use a new O-ring when refitting the pump housing.*
  e) *Refit and tension the auxiliary drivebelt as described in Chapter 1B.*
  f) *On completion, refill the cooling system as described in Chapter 1B.*

2.2 litre diesel engine models - timing belt-driven pump

Note: *A new gasket, or suitable sealant, as applicable, will be required on refitting.*

Removal

44 The pump is mounted on the front of the cylinder block, at the timing belt end of the engine.

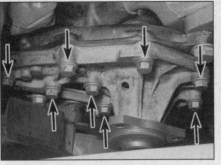

7.31a Unscrew the retaining bolts (arrowed - not all bolts visible) . . .

7.41a Withdraw the coolant pump/housing assembly . . .

45 Drain the cooling system as described in Chapter 1B.

46 Remove the timing belt as described in Chapter 2E.

47 Unscrew the securing bolts, and withdraw the coolant pump from its housing in the end of the cylinder block. If the pump is stuck, tap it lightly with a soft-faced mallet.

Refitting

48 Commence refitting by thoroughly cleaning the mating faces of the pump and block.

49 Lay a new gasket in position, or apply suitable sealant, as applicable, then refit the pump and securely tighten the bolts.

50 Refit the timing belt as described in Chapter 2E.

51 On completion, refill the cooling system as described in Chapter 1B.

7.42a Unscrew the securing bolts . . .

7.31b . . . then manoeuvre the coolant pump out of position - 1.9 litre diesel engine models

7.41b . . . and recover the O-ring - 2.2 litre diesel engine models with auxiliary belt-driven pump

8 Heating and ventilation system - general information

The heating/ventilation system consists of a four-speed blower motor (housed behind the facia), a control unit mounted in the facia, face level vents in the centre and at each end of the facia, and air ducts to the front and rear footwells.

The facia-mounted controls operate flap valves to deflect and mix the air flowing through the various parts of the heating/ventilation system. The flap valves are contained in the air distribution housing, which acts as a central distribution unit, passing air to the various ducts and vents.

3

7.42b . . . and withdraw the pump from the housing - 2.2 litre diesel engine models with auxiliary belt-driven pump

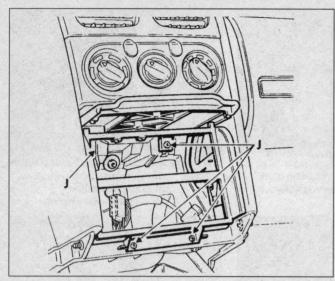

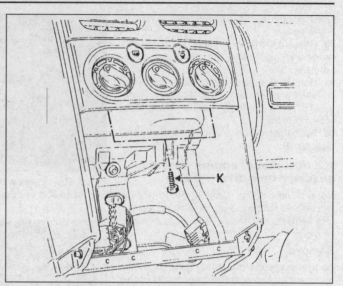

9.3 Remove the four securing screws (J) and withdraw the radio/cassette player housing

9.4 Unscrew the two heater/ventilation control panel securing screws (K)

Cold air enters the system through the grille at the top of the engine compartment scuttle. If required, the airflow is boosted by the blower motor, and then flows through the various ducts, according to the settings of the controls. Stale air is expelled via the vents in the rear of the vehicle. If warm air is required, the cold air is passed over the heater matrix, which is heated by the engine coolant. A recirculation position on blower motor switch enables the outside air supply to be closed off, while the air inside the vehicle is recirculated. This can be useful to prevent unpleasant odours entering from outside the vehicle, but should only be used briefly, as the recirculated air inside the vehicle will soon become stale.

Models with air conditioning may have a conventional heater/ventilation control unit, with a button which is used to switch on the air conditioning, or on higher specification models, a fully-electronic automatic air conditioning is fitted, with an electronic control panel. On models fitted with air conditioning, a Stop switch isolates the passenger compartment from the outside atmosphere. Further details of the air conditioning system can be found in Section 10.

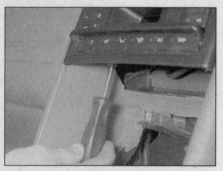

9.7 Unscrewing a securing screw from an electronic heater/ventilation control unit

9 Heating and ventilation system components - removal and refitting

Conventional heater/ ventilation control unit

Removal

1 Remove the centre console, as described in Chapter 11.
2 Where applicable, remove the radio/cassette player as described in Chapter 12.
3 Remove the four securing screws, and withdraw the radio/cassette player housing **(see illustration)**.
4 Working under the heater/ventilation control panel, unscrew the two securing screws, then withdraw the control unit from the facia **(see illustration)**.
5 Working at the rear of the control panel, disconnect the control cables, and the wiring plug(s), noting their locations, then withdraw the control unit.

Refitting

6 Refitting is a reversal of removal, but before reconnecting the cables, position the air distribution unit flaps against their stops, and position the heater/ventilation control knobs at their anti-clockwise stops. Check the operation of the heater controls before refitting the control unit securing screws.

Electronic heater/ventilation control unit (models with automatic air conditioning)

7 The procedure is as described previously for models with a conventional heater/ventilation control unit, but there are no control cables to disconnect **(see illustration)**. Once the wiring plugs have been disconnected, the unit can be removed.

Heater/ventilation control cables

Removal

8 Remove the heater/ventilation control unit as described previously in this Section.
9 On right-hand drive models, remove the facia as described in Chapter 11. On left-hand drive models, remove the glovebox as described in Chapter 11, Section 28, or the passenger's side air bag as described in Chapter 12, as applicable.
10 Disconnect the end of the relevant cable from the lever on the air distribution unit, then withdraw the cable, noting its routing to aid refitting **(see illustration)**.

Refitting

11 Refitting is a reversal of removal, bearing in mind the following points.
a) Before refitting the cables, position the air distribution unit flaps against their stops, and position the heater/ventilation control knobs at their anti-clockwise stops.

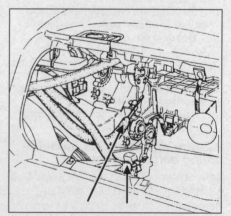

9.10 Two of the heater control cables (arrowed) accessible through the glovebox aperture on left-hand drive models

b) Route the cable(s) as noted before removal.
c) Where applicable, refit the passenger's side air bag as described in Chapter 12.
d) Check the operation of the heater controls before refitting the control unit securing screws.

Heater matrix - models without air conditioning

Removal

12 Drain the cooling system as described in the relevant part of Chapter 1.
13 Working in the engine compartment, release the securing lug, and disconnect the heater hose connector from the heater matrix pipes (refer to Section 2).
14 Remove the securing screws, and withdraw the pipe cover from the bulkhead **(see illustration)**.

HAYNES HINT *Drain as much coolant as possible from the heater matrix by applying compressed air to one of the heater matrix pipes (connect a clean hose to one of the pipes, and blow through the hose) - place a container under the pipes to catch escaping coolant.*

15 Working in the passenger compartment, remove the passenger's side lower facia panel.
16 Working under the facia, remove the clamp bolt and the screw securing the heater matrix pipes to the air distribution unit **(see illustration)**.

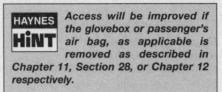

HAYNES HINT *Access will be improved if the glovebox or passenger's air bag, as applicable is removed as described in Chapter 11, Section 28, or Chapter 12 respectively.*

17 Remove the two screws securing the heater matrix cover to the air distribution unit.
18 Where applicable, carefully lever the four matrix cover securing clips, until they are disengaged from the air distribution unit.
19 Carefully manipulate the heater matrix pipes from the bulkhead (recover the grommets), then withdraw the matrix from the air distribution unit. Take care not to spill any remaining coolant inside the vehicle.

Refitting

20 If a new matrix is to be fitted to a Valeo-type heater unit, the cover/pipe assembly must be removed from the old matrix, and transferred to the new matrix.
21 Refitting is a reversal of removal, bearing in mind the following points.
 a) Ensure that the foam insulation strips are in place when fitting the matrix to the air distribution unit.
 b) Note that there is no need to refit the screw securing the pipes to the air distribution unit.
 c) On completion, refill the cooling system as described in the relevant part of Chapter 1.

Heater matrix - models with air conditioning

22 On models with air conditioning, to enable

9.14 Withdrawing the heater matrix pipe cover from the bulkhead

removal of the heater matrix, the complete facia and heater air distribution/air conditioning unit must be removed - this is a complex procedure, and the air conditioning system must be discharged before starting. The job should therefore be entrusted to a Renault dealer.

Heater blower motor - models without air conditioning

Removal

23 Disconnect the battery negative terminal (refer to *Disconnecting the battery* in the Reference Section of this manual).
24 Working inside the passenger compartment, remove the passenger's side lower facia panel.
25 Disconnect the blower motor wiring plug.
26 If a Behr-type blower motor is being removed, twist the motor cover anti-clockwise, then lower the motor/cover assembly from the air distribution unit **(see illustration)**.

3

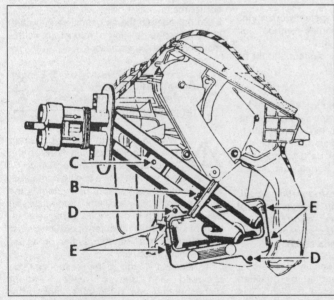

9.16 Heater matrix mounting details

B Pipe clamp bolt
C Pipe securing screw
D Matrix securing screws
E Matrix securing clips (not applicable to all models)

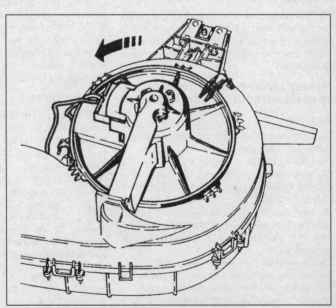

9.26 Twist the Behr-type blower motor anti-clockwise to remove - viewed with heater unit removed and inverted (left-hand-drive shown)

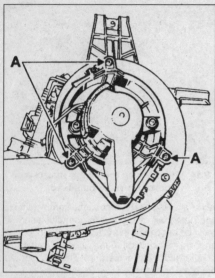

9.27 Valeo-type blower motor securing screws (A) - viewed with heater unit removed and inverted (left-hand-drive shown)

27 If a Valeo-type blower motor is being removed, unscrew the three screws securing the motor cover to the air distribution housing, then lower the motor/cover assembly from the air distribution unit **(see illustration)**. Note that an Allen key may be required to reach the rear securing screw.

Refitting

28 Refitting is a reversal of removal.

Heater blower motor - models with air conditioning

Removal

29 The procedure is as described previously for the Valeo-type blower motor on models without air conditioning, but note that the motor cover is secured by four screws **(see illustration)**.

Heater blower motor resistor - models without air conditioning

Removal

30 Disconnect the battery negative terminal (refer to *Disconnecting the battery* in the Reference Section of this manual).
31 The resistor is located on top of the blower motor housing, on the passenger's side of the facia.
32 Remove the glovebox as described in Chapter 11, Section 28, or the passenger's air bag unit as described in Chapter 12, as applicable.
33 Disconnect the resistor wiring plug.
34 Remove the screw securing the resistor to the blower motor housing, then twist the resistor clockwise, and withdraw it **(see illustration)**.

Refitting

35 Refitting is a reversal of removal.

Heater blower motor resistor/control unit - models with air conditioning

36 On models with air conditioning, the blower motor resistor/control unit is integral with the motor casing, and cannot be renewed separately.

---

10 Air conditioning system - general information and precautions

General information

1 An air conditioning system is available on certain models. It enables the temperature of incoming air to be lowered, and also dehumidifies the air, which makes for rapid demisting and increased comfort.
2 The cooling side of the system works in the same way as a domestic refrigerator. Refrigerant gas is drawn into a belt-driven compressor, and passes into a condenser mounted on the front of the radiator, where it loses heat and becomes liquid. The liquid passes through an expansion valve to an evaporator, where it changes from liquid under high pressure to gas under low pressure. This change is accompanied by a drop in temperature, which cools the evaporator. The refrigerant returns to the compressor, and the cycle begins again.
3 Air blown through the evaporator passes to the air distribution unit, where it is mixed with hot air blown through the heater matrix to achieve the desired temperature in the passenger compartment.
4 The heating side of the system works in the same way as on models without air conditioning (see Section 8).
5 Any problems with the system should be referred to a Renault dealer.

Precautions

6 When an air conditioning system is fitted, it is necessary to observe special precautions whenever dealing with any part of the system, or its associated components. If for any reason the system must be disconnected, entrust this task to your Renault dealer or a refrigeration engineer.

⚠ *Warning: The refrigeration circuit contains a liquid refrigerant, and it is therefore dangerous to disconnect any part of the system without specialised knowledge and equipment.*

7 The refrigerant is potentially dangerous, and should only be handled by qualified persons. If it is splashed onto the skin, it can cause frostbite. It is not itself poisonous, but

9.29 Removing the heater blower motor - models with air conditioning

9.34 Heater blower motor resistor (A) and securing screw (B)

in the presence of a naked flame (including a cigarette) it forms a poisonous gas. Uncontrolled discharging of the refrigerant is dangerous, and potentially damaging to the environment.
8 Do not operate the air conditioning system if it is known to be short of refrigerant, as this may damage the compressor.

---

11 Air conditioning system components - removal and refitting

⚠ *Warning: Do not attempt to open the refrigerant circuit. Refer to the precautions given in Section 10.*

The only operation which can be carried out easily without discharging the system is the renewal of the auxiliary (compressor) drivebelt, which is described in the relevant part of Chapter 1. All other operations must be referred to a Renault dealer or an air conditioning specialist.

If necessary, the compressor can be unbolted and moved aside, without disconnecting the refrigerant lines, after removing the drivebelt.

Chapter 4 Part A:
Fuel/exhaust systems - petrol engine models

Contents

Degrees of difficulty

Easy, suitable for novice with little experience	Fairly easy, suitable for beginner with some experience	Fairly difficult, suitable for competent DIY mechanic	Difficult, suitable for experienced DIY mechanic	Very difficult, suitable for expert DIY or professional

4A

Specifications

System type

Single-point injection models:	
1.8 litre (8-valve) engines	Bosch Monopoint
Multi-point injection models:	
1.8 and 2.0 litre (8-valve) engines	Siemens-Fenix 5 sequential multi-point injection
1.6 and 1.8 litre (16-valve) engines	Siemens SIRIUS sequential multi-point injection
2.0 litre (16-valve) engines	Siemens-Fenix 5 sequential multi-point injection

Fuel system data

Fuel pump type	Electric, immersed in tank
Fuel pump regulated constant pressure:	
Single-point injection models	1.06 ± 0.05 bar
Multi-point injection models:	
With fuel pressure regulator vacuum hose attached	2.5 ± 0.2 bar
With fuel pressure vacuum hose disconnected	3.0 ± 0.2 bar
Specified idle speed (not adjustable - controlled by ECU)	750 ± 50 rpm
Idle mixture CO content	Less than 1.0 % (controlled by ECU)

Recommended fuel

Minimum octane rating	95 RON unleaded (UK unleaded premium). Leaded fuel must **not** be used

Torque wrench settings

	Nm	lbf ft
1.8 and 2.0 litre (8-valve) engines		
Fuel pump/gauge sender locking ring	35	26
Fuel rail mounting nuts - multi-point injection models	10	7
Manifold retaining nuts	20	15
Throttle body/housing bolts:		
Single-point injection models	15	11
Multi-point injection models	20	15
1.6 and 1.8 litre (16-valve) engines		
Air cleaner intake housing to inlet manifold	10	7
Exhaust manifold bolts	18	13
Exhaust manifold heat shield bolts	10	7
Fuel pump/gauge sender locking ring	35	26
Fuel rail mounting bolts	10	7
Inlet manifold lower section bolts	21	15
Inlet manifold upper section bolts	10	7
Lambda sensor	45	33
Throttle housing bolts	13	10
2.0 litre (16-valve) engines		
Exhaust manifold nuts	24	18
Fuel pump/gauge sender locking ring	35	26
Inlet manifold to cylinder head	17	13
Throttle housing bolts	10	7

1 General information and precautions

The fuel system consists of a fuel tank (which is mounted under the rear of the car, with an electric fuel pump immersed in it), a fuel filter and the fuel feed and return lines. On single-point injection models the fuel is supplied by a throttle body assembly which incorporates the single fuel injector and the fuel pressure regulator. On multi-point injection models the fuel pump supplies fuel to the fuel rail, which acts as a reservoir for the four fuel injectors which inject fuel into the inlet tracts. In addition, there is an Electronic Control Unit (ECU) and various sensors, electrical components and related wiring.

Refer to Section 7 for further information on the operation of each fuel injection system, and to Section 19 for information on the exhaust system.

⚠️ **Warning: Many of the procedures in this Chapter require the removal of fuel lines and connections, which may result in some fuel spillage. Before carrying out any operation on the fuel system, refer to the precautions given in Safety first! at the beginning of this manual, and follow them implicitly. Petrol is a highly-dangerous and volatile liquid, and the precautions necessary when handling it cannot be overstressed.**

Note: *Residual pressure will remain in the fuel lines long after the vehicle was last used. When disconnecting any fuel line, first depressurise the fuel system as described in Section 8.*

2 Air cleaner assembly and inlet ducts - removal and refitting

Removal

1.8 and 2.0 litre (8-valve) engines

1 Detach the throttle body/housing duct from the top of the air cleaner housing. Where necessary, also disconnect the idle control valve air hose from the housing.

2 Free the inlet duct(s) from the base of the air cleaner housing then undo the retaining nut and remove the housing from the engine compartment. On single-point injection models note that it will be necessary to disconnect the vacuum hose from the air temperature control valve as the housing is removed.

3 If necessary, the various ducts and hoses can then be unclipped and removed from the engine compartment, the main inlet duct is secured to the left-hand side of the body by a bolt. The air cleaner mounting bracket is secured to the top of the transmission by a nut and two bolts.

1.6 and 1.8 litre (16-valve) engines

4 To remove the resonator and filter housing, disconnect the air intake hose from the resonator, detach the resonator from the air filter housing and withdraw the resonator from its location **(see illustration)**.

5 Undo the two screws and detach the filter housing from the intake housing.

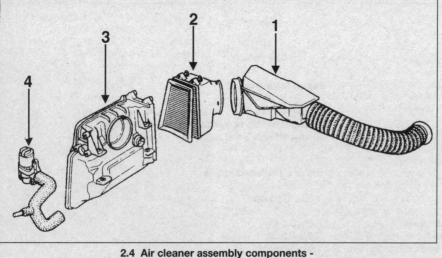

**2.4 Air cleaner assembly components -
1.6 and 1.8 litre (16-valve) engines**

1 Resonator	*3 Intake housing*
2 Air filter housing	*4 Auxiliary air valve*

2.11 Detach the throttle housing duct from the top of the air cleaner housing . . .

2.12 . . . Unscrew the air cleaner housing to mounting bracket nuts (left-hand nut arrowed) . . .

2.13 . . . free the inlet duct and remove the housing - 2.0 litre (16-valve) engines

6 To remove the intake housing, remove the resonator and filter housing as previously described.

7 Disconnect the brake servo vacuum hose from the inlet manifold.

8 Disconnect the hose and the wiring connector at the auxiliary air valve on the side of the intake housing.

9 At the left-hand end of the engine, unbolt the Lambda sensor connector mounting bracket to facilitate removal of the intake housing.

10 Undo the two bolts securing the intake housing to the inlet manifold. Withdraw the housing from the manifold and manipulate it out towards the left-hand side of the engine compartment.

2.0 litre (16-valve) engines

11 Detach the throttle housing duct from the top of the air cleaner housing **(see illustration)**.

12 Unscrew the nuts securing the air cleaner housing to the mounting brackets, and extract the small circlip securing the upper rubber support to the engine lifting bracket **(see illustration)**.

13 Free the inlet duct from the base of the air cleaner housing then remove the housing from the engine **(see illustration)**.

14 To remove the air cleaner to throttle housing duct, disconnect the inlet air temperature sensor wiring connector at the sensor in the duct. Release the crankcase ventilation hose connector from the duct by slackening the locking collar then turning the connector one eighth of a turn anti-clockwise to release it. Detach the idle speed control valve air hose, release the duct from the throttle housing and remove it from the engine.

15 If necessary, the remaining ducts and hoses can then be unclipped and removed from the engine compartment, the main air inlet duct is secured to the left-hand side of the body by a bolt. The air cleaner mounting bracket is secured to the top of the transmission by a nut and two bolts.

Refitting

16 Refitting is the reverse of removal making sure all the ducts and wiring connectors are securely reconnected.

---

3 Air cleaner air temperature control system (single-point injection models) - general

1 The system is controlled by a heat-sensitive vacuum switch, mounted in the air cleaner housing-to-throttle body duct. When the temperature of the air passing through the duct is cold (below approximately 20ºC), the vacuum switch is open, allowing inlet manifold depression to act on the air temperature control valve diaphragm in the base of the air cleaner housing. This vacuum causes the diaphragm to rise, drawing a flap valve across the cold-air inlet, allowing only (warmed) air to enter the air cleaner.

2 As the temperature of the exhaust-warmed air in the duct rises, the wax capsule in the vacuum switch deforms and closes the switch, cutting off the vacuum supply to the air temperature control valve assembly. As the vacuum supply is cut, the flap is gradually lowered across the hot-air inlet until, when the temperature of the air in the duct is fully warmed-up (approximately 40ºC) the control valve closes, allowing only cold air from the front of the car to enter the air cleaner.

3 To check the system, allow the engine to cool down completely, then slacken the retaining clip and disconnect the inlet ducts from the front of the control valve assembly; the flap valve in the duct should be securely seated across the hot-air inlet. Start the engine; the flap should immediately rise to close off the cold-air inlet, and should then lower steadily as the engine warms up, until it is eventually seated across the hot-air inlet again.

4 To check the vacuum switch, disconnect the vacuum pipe from the control valve when the engine is running, and place a finger over the pipe end. When the engine is cold, full inlet manifold vacuum should be present in the pipe, and when the engine is at normal operating temperature, there should be no vacuum in the pipe.

5 To check the air temperature control valve assembly, slacken the retaining clip and disconnect the inlet duct from the front of the valve assembly; the flap valve should be securely seated across the hot-air inlet. Disconnect the vacuum pipe and, using a

suitable length of hose, suck hard at the control valve stub; the flap should rise to shut off the cold-air inlet.

6 If either component is faulty, it must be renewed. The vacuum switch is an integral part of the inlet duct and the temperature control valve is an integral part of the air cleaner housing; neither component is available separately.

---

4 Accelerator cable - removal and refitting

Removal

1 Working in the engine compartment, free the accelerator inner cable from the throttle cam or throttle lever, then pull the outer cable out from its mounting bracket rubber grommet **(see illustration)**. Remove the spring clip from the end of the cable.

2 Working back along the length of the cable, free it from any retaining clips or ties, noting its correct routing.

3 From inside the vehicle, to improve access unclip the facia fusebox lid. Undo the retaining screws situated along the lower edge of the fusebox lid cover panel and unclip the panel assembly from the facia.

4 Reach up behind the facia and unclip the accelerator inner cable from the top of the accelerator pedal. Prise out the rubber sealing grommet from bulkhead and free it from the cable.

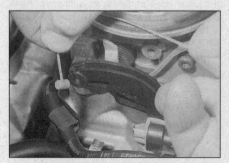

4.1 Disconnecting the accelerator cable from the throttle cam - single-point injection model shown

4A

5 Return to the engine compartment, release the outer cable from the bulkhead and withdraw the cable.

Refitting

6 Feed the cable into position from the engine compartment and seat the outer cable against the bulkhead.

7 From inside the vehicle, clip the inner cable into position in the pedal end then refit the rubber sealing making sure it is correctly located in the bulkhead. Check that the cable is securely retained, then refit the fusebox lid panel to the facia.

8 From within the engine compartment, ensure that the outer cable is correctly seated in the bulkhead, then work along the cable, securing it in position with the retaining clips and ties, and ensuring that the cable is correctly routed.

9 Pass the outer cable through its mounting bracket grommet, and reconnect the inner cable to the throttle cam. Adjust the cable as follows.

Adjustment

10 With the spring clip removed from the accelerator outer cable, ensure that the throttle cam or throttle lever is fully against its stop. Gently pull the cable out of its grommet until all free play is removed from the inner cable.

11 With the cable held in this position, refit the spring clip to the last exposed outer cable groove in front of the rubber grommet and washer. When the clip is refitted and the outer cable is released, there should be only a small amount of free play in the inner cable **(see illustration)**.

12 Have an assistant depress the accelerator pedal, and check that the throttle opens fully and returns smoothly to its stop.

5 Accelerator pedal - removal and refitting

Removal

1 To improve access unclip the facia fusebox lid. Undo the retaining screws situated along the lower edge of the fusebox lid cover panel and unclip the panel assembly from the facia.

2 Reach up behind the facia and unclip the accelerator cable from the top of the pedal.

3 Slacken and remove the pedal pivot retaining nuts and remove the pedal from underneath the facia.

4 Examine the pedal assembly for signs of wear and renew as necessary.

Refitting

5 Refitting is a reversal of the removal procedure, applying a little multi-purpose grease to the pedal pivot point. On completion, adjust the accelerator cable as described in Section 4.

4.11 Accelerator cable outer end fitting (arrowed)

6 Unleaded petrol - general information and usage

Note: *The information given in this Chapter is correct at the time of writing. If updated information is thought to be required, check with a Renault dealer. If travelling abroad, consult one of the motoring organisations (or a similar authority) for advice on the fuel available.*

1 The fuel recommended by Renault is given in the *Specifications* section of this Chapter, followed by the equivalent petrol currently on sale in the UK.

2 All petrol models are designed to run on fuel with a minimum octane rating of 95 (RON). All models have a catalytic converter, and so must be run on unleaded fuel only. Under no circumstances should leaded fuel (UK 4-star) be used, as this may damage the converter.

3 Super unleaded petrol (98 octane) can also be used in all models if wished, though there is no advantage in doing so.

7 Fuel injection systems - general information

Bosch Monopoint single-point injection system

1 Single-point injection models are equipped with a Bosch Monopoint engine management (fuel injection/ignition) system. The system incorporates a closed-loop catalytic converter and an evaporative emission control system, and complies with the latest emission control standards. The fuel injection side of the system operates as follows; refer to Chapter 5B for information on the ignition system.

2 The fuel pump, immersed in the fuel tank, pumps fuel from the fuel tank to the fuel injector, via a filter mounted underneath the rear of the vehicle. Fuel supply pressure is controlled by the pressure regulator in the throttle body assembly. The regulator operates by allowing excess fuel to return to the tank.

3 The electrical control system consists of the ECU, along with the following sensors.
- a) *Throttle potentiometer - informs the ECU of the throttle position, and the rate of throttle opening or closing.*
- b) *Coolant temperature sensor - informs the ECU of engine temperature.*
- c) *Inlet air temperature sensor - informs the ECU of the temperature of the air passing through the throttle body.*
- d) *Lambda sensor - informs the ECU of the oxygen content of the exhaust gases (explained in greater detail in Part C of this Chapter).*
- e) *Microswitch (built into idle speed stepper motor) - informs the ECU when the throttle valve is closed (ie when the accelerator pedal is released).*
- f) *Crankshaft sensor - informs the ECU of engine speed and crankshaft position.*
- g) *Power steering pressure switch - informs the ECU when the power steering pump is working so the engine idle speed can be increased to prevent stalling.*
- h) *Knock sensor - informs the ECU when pre-ignition (pinking) is occurring.*

4 All the above information is analysed by the ECU and, based on this, the ECU determines the appropriate ignition and fuelling requirements for the engine. The ECU controls the fuel injector by varying its pulse width - the length of time the injector is held open - to provide a richer or weaker mixture, as appropriate. The mixture is constantly varied by the ECU, to provide the best setting for cranking, starting (with either a hot or cold engine), warm-up, idle, cruising, and acceleration.

5 The ECU also has full control over the engine idle speed, via a stepper motor which is fitted to the throttle body. The motor pushrod rests against a cam on the throttle valve spindle. When the throttle valve is closed (accelerator pedal released), the ECU uses the motor to vary the opening of the throttle valve and so control the idle speed.

6 The ECU also controls the exhaust and evaporative emission control systems, which are described in detail in Part C of this Chapter.

7 If there is an abnormality in any of the readings obtained from either the coolant temperature sensor, the inlet air temperature sensor or the lambda sensor, the ECU enters its back-up mode. In this event, the ECU ignores the abnormal sensor signal, and assumes a pre-programmed value which will allow the engine to continue running (albeit at reduced efficiency). If the ECU enters this back-up mode, the warning light on the instrument panel will come on, and the relevant fault code will be stored in the ECU memory.

8 If the warning light comes on, the vehicle should be taken to a Renault dealer at the earliest opportunity. A complete test of the engine management system can then be carried out, using a special electronic diagnostic test unit which is simply plugged into the system's diagnostic connector (located on the engine compartment bulkhead).

9 A fuel cut-off inertia switch is incorporated into the fuel injection system. In the event of an impact the switch cuts off the electrical supply to the fuel pump and so prevents fuel being expelled should the fuel pipes/hoses be damaged in an accident.

Siemens-Fenix 5 multi-point injection system

10 The Siemens-Fenix 5 multi-point system is similar to the single-point system described in earlier paragraphs, however, there are four injectors (one per cylinder) located directly in the inlet manifold. All the injectors are fed from a common fuel rail, which also carries the fuel pressure regulator.

11 The system is of sequential design with each injector operating individually. A camshaft sensor is used in conjunction with the crankshaft position sensor to inform the ECU of engine speed, crankshaft position and cylinder phase. Information on engine speed and piston position relative to TDC are supplied to the ECU by the crankshaft position sensor. Information on which of the two pistons at TDC is on the inlet phase is supplied by the camshaft position sensor. From this data the ECU is able to determine the start of injection point for each cylinder in turn. Further information from additional sensors allows the ECU to calculate injector opening duration according to temperature, engine speed and load.

12 Engine idle speed is controlled via an auxiliary air valve which bypasses the throttle valve. When the throttle valve is closed, the ECU controls the opening of the valve, which in turn regulates the amount of air entering the manifold, and so controls the idle speed.

13 On 2.0 litre (16-valve) engines, secondary air injection is also incorporated into the system. Information on this is given in Part C of this Chapter.

Siemens SIRIUS multi-point injection system

14 The Siemens SIRIUS multi-point system is a development of the Siemens-Fenix 5 system described previously with a number of refinements, mainly in the area of exhaust emissions and in the control software within the ECU.

15 On the SIRIUS system, a camshaft sensor is not used for calculation of cylinder inlet phase. This function is carried out by the ECU based on information received from the crankshaft position sensor and by memorising which injector was last controlled each time the engine is stopped. On restart, the ECU remembers the reference cylinder and proceeds to the next cylinder in the firing sequence.

16 For enhanced control of the engine exhaust emissions, two lambda sensors are fitted, one upstream of the catalytic converter, and one downstream. From the information received, the ECU can carry out extremely precise calculations of fuel metering.

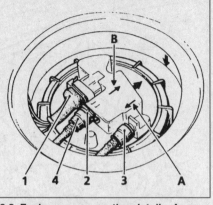

9.3 Fuel pump connection details. Arrows A and B show the direction of fuel flow

1 Wiring connector   3 Fuel supply hose
2 Locking tab   4 Fuel return hose

8 Fuel injection system - depressurisation

⚠️ *Warning: Refer to the warning in Section 1 before proceeding. The following procedure will merely relieve the pressure in the fuel system - remember that fuel will still be present in the system components, and take precautions accordingly before disconnecting any of them.*

1 The fuel system referred to in this Section is defined as the tank-mounted fuel pump, the fuel filter, the fuel injector(s) and the pressure regulator in the injector housing/fuel rail, and

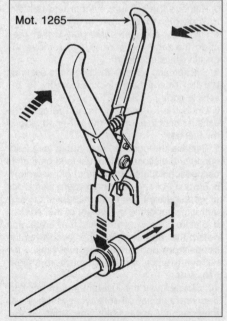

9.5 Renault special pliers (Mot. 1265) for releasing the fuel hose quick-release fittings

the metal pipes and flexible hoses of the fuel lines between these components. All these contain fuel which will be under pressure while the engine is running, and/or while the ignition is switched on. The pressure will remain for some time after the ignition has been switched off, and it must be relieved in a controlled fashion when any of these components are disturbed for servicing work.

2 Disconnect the battery negative terminal (refer to *Disconnecting the battery* in the Reference Section of this manual).

3 Place a suitable container beneath the connection or union to be disconnected, and have a large rag ready to soak up any escaping fuel not being caught by the container.

4 Slowly loosen the connection or union nut to avoid a sudden release of pressure, and position the rag around the connection, to catch any fuel spray which may be expelled. Once the pressure is released, disconnect the fuel line. Plug the pipe ends, to minimise fuel loss and prevent the entry of dirt into the fuel system.

9 Fuel pump - removal and refitting

⚠️ *Warning: Refer to the warning in Section 1 before proceeding.*

Removal

1 Disconnect the battery negative terminal (refer to *Disconnecting the battery* in the Reference Section of this manual).

2 Open up the tailgate and lift up the luggage compartment carpet to reveal the fuel pump access cover.

3 Using a screwdriver, carefully prise the plastic access cover from the floor to expose the fuel pump **(see illustration)**.

4 Disconnect the wiring connector from the fuel pump, and tape the connector to the vehicle body, to prevent it disappearing behind the tank.

5 Mark the fuel hoses for identification purposes. The hoses have quick-release fittings to ease removal **(see illustration)**. To disconnect each hose, slide out the locking tab (where fitted from the collar then, bearing in mind the information in Section 8, depress the collar and detach the hose from the pump. Disconnect both hoses from the top of the pump, noting the correct fitted position of the sealing rings and plug the hose ends to minimise fuel loss.

6 Noting the alignment marks on the pump cover and fuel tank, unscrew the locking ring and remove it from the tank. This is best accomplished by using a screwdriver on the raised ribs of the locking ring. Carefully tap the screwdriver to turn the ring anti-clockwise until it can be unscrewed by hand.

7 Carefully lift the fuel pump assembly out of

4A

the fuel tank, taking great care not to damage the fuel level gauge sender arm, or to spill fuel onto the interior of the vehicle. Recover the rubber sealing ring and discard it - a new one must be used on refitting.

8 Note that the fuel pump/fuel gauge sender unit is only available as a complete assembly - no components are available separately.

Refitting

9 Ensure that the fuel pump pick-up filter is clean and free of debris. Fit the new sealing ring to the top of the fuel tank.

10 Carefully manoeuvre the pump assembly into the fuel tank.

11 Align the mark on the fuel pump cover with the alignment marks on the fuel tank, then refit the locking ring. Securely tighten the locking ring, then recheck that the pump cover and tank marks are all correctly aligned. **Note:** *If the special Renault service tool (Mot. 1264) is available tighten the locking ring to the specified torque.*

12 Ensure that the sealing rings are in position and reconnect the feed and return hoses to the top of the fuel pump, using the marks made on removal to ensure that they are correctly reconnected. Check the end fittings are clipped securely in position and (where necessary) refit the locking tabs to the collars.

13 Reconnect the wiring connector.

14 Reconnect the battery negative terminal, and start the engine. Check the fuel pump feed and return hoses unions for signs of leakage.

15 If all is well, refit the plastic access cover and fold the carpet down into position.

10 Fuel gauge sender unit - removal and refitting

The fuel gauge sender unit is an integral part of the fuel pump assembly (see Section 9).

11 Fuel tank - removal and refitting

⚠️ *Warning: Refer to the warning in Section 1 before proceeding.*

Removal

1 Before removing the fuel tank, all fuel must be drained from the tank. Since a fuel tank drain plug is not provided, it is therefore preferable to carry out the removal operation when the tank is nearly empty. Before proceeding, disconnect the battery negative terminal (refer to *Disconnecting the battery* in the Reference Section of this manual), and syphon or hand-pump the remaining fuel from the tank.

2 Disconnect the fuel pipes and wiring from the fuel pump as described in paragraphs 1 to 5 of Section 9.

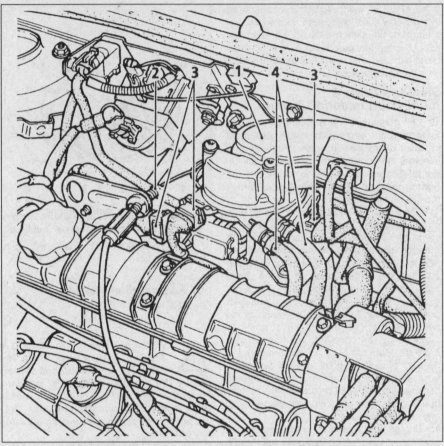

12.2 Throttle body assembly - single-point fuel injection engines

1 Inlet duct
2 Accelerator cable
3 Wiring connectors
4 Fuel feed and return hoses

3 Remove the exhaust system and relevant heat shield(s) as described in Section 19.

4 Remove the right-hand rear wheel then undo the retaining screws and remove the plastic wheelarch liner.

5 Slacken and remove the two bolts securing the top of the filler neck assembly to the vehicle body

6 Undo the retaining bolts and remove the exhaust heatshield from the left-hand side of the fuel tank.

7 Release the quick release fitting (see Section 9) and disconnect the fuel feed pipe at its connection situated just in front of the tank.

8 Place a trolley jack with an interposed block of wood beneath the tank, then raise the jack until it is supporting the weight of the tank.

9 Slacken and remove the retaining nuts/bolts and remove the two retaining straps from underneath the fuel tank. Also remove the tank mounting bolt from its left-hand side.

10 Slowly lower the fuel tank out of position, disconnecting any other relevant vent pipes as they become accessible (where necessary), and remove the tank from underneath the vehicle.

11 If the tank is contaminated with sediment

or water, remove the fuel pump/sender unit (Section 9), and swill the tank out with clean fuel. The tank is injection-moulded from a synthetic material - if seriously damaged, it should be renewed. However, in certain cases, it may be possible to have small leaks or minor damage repaired. Seek the advice of a specialist before attempting to repair the fuel tank.

Refitting

12 Refitting is the reverse of the removal procedure, noting the following points:

a) When lifting the tank back into position, take care to ensure that none of the hoses become trapped between the tank and vehicle body. Also ensure that the filler neck is correctly located as the tank is raised into position.

b) Ensure that all pipes and hoses are correctly routed. Make sure the sealing rings are in position in the quick-release fittings prior to fitting and make sure they are securely clipped in position.

c) On completion, refill the tank with a small amount of fuel, and check for signs of leakage prior to taking the vehicle out on the road.

12 Throttle body/housing - removal and refitting

⚠️ **Warning: Refer to the warning in Section 1 before proceeding.**

Removal

1 Disconnect the battery negative terminal (refer to *Disconnecting the battery* in the Reference Section of this manual).

1.8 litre (8-valve) engines with single-point fuel injection

2 Undo the retaining screws and detach the inlet duct from the top of the throttle body **(see illustration on opposite page)**. Recover the duct sealing ring.

3 Depress the retaining clips and disconnect the wiring connectors from the throttle potentiometer, the idle control stepper motor, and the injector wiring loom connector which is situated on the side of the throttle body.

4 Bearing in mind the information given in Section 8 about depressurising the fuel system, release the retaining clips and disconnect the fuel feed and return hoses from the throttle body assembly **(see illustration)**. If the original crimped-type Renault clips are still fitted, cut the clips and discard them; use standard worm-drive hose clips on refitting.

5 Disconnect the accelerator inner cable from the throttle cam, then withdraw the outer cable from the mounting bracket, along with its flat washer and spring clip.

6 Disconnect the breather/purge valve hoses from the throttle body (as applicable).

7 Slacken and remove the bolts securing the throttle body assembly to the inlet manifold, then remove the assembly along with its gasket spacer. Discard the gasket spacer, a new one should be used on refitting.

8 If necessary, undo the retaining bolts securing the throttle body mounting flange to the inlet manifold and remove the flange and gasket.

1.8 and 2.0 litre (8-valve) engines with multi-point fuel injection

9 Disconnect the idle control valve hose and breather hose from the top of the air cleaner housing. Disconnect the wiring connector from the inlet air temperature sensor then release the air cleaner housing lid retaining clips and remove the lid and duct assembly from the engine compartment.

10 Unclip and remove the wiring loom plastic cover from the top of the inlet manifold.

11 Disconnect the wiring connectors from the idle speed control valve and the throttle potentiometer.

12 Disconnect the wiring connectors from the injectors and position the wiring loom clear of the throttle housing.

13 Disconnect the accelerator inner cable from the throttle cam, then withdraw the outer

12.4 Fuel feed (1) and return (2) hose connections on the throttle body. Note fuel flow direction arrows on body- single-point fuel injection engines

cable from the mounting bracket, along with its flat washer and spring clip.

14 Slacken and remove the retaining bolts and remove the throttle housing from the inlet manifold. Recover the housing gasket spacer/gaskets and insulating plate (as applicable).

1.6 and 1.8 litre (16-valve) engines

15 Remove the air cleaner air intake housing as described in Section 2.

16 Disconnect the accelerator cable from the throttle lever as described in Section 4.

17 Disconnect the throttle potentiometer wiring connector.

18 Undo the two retaining bolts and remove the throttle housing from the inlet manifold **(see illustration)**. Recover the housing seal, noting that a new seal will be required for refitting.

2.0 litre (16-valve) engines

19 Remove the air cleaner to throttle housing duct as described in Section 2.

20 Disconnect the accelerator cable from the throttle cam as described in Section 4.

21 Disconnect the throttle potentiometer wiring connector.

22 Undo the four retaining bolts and remove the throttle housing from the inlet manifold **(see illustration)**. Recover the housing gasket.

Refitting

1.8 litre (8-valve) engines with single-point fuel injection

23 Refitting is the reverse of removal, noting the following points.

a) *Where applicable, ensure that the mating surfaces of the manifold and throttle body flange are clean and dry. Fit the flange to the manifold using a new gasket and tightening the retaining screws securely.*

b) *Ensure that the mating surfaces of the throttle body and flange are clean and dry, then fit a new gasket spacer. Refit the throttle body and tighten the retaining bolts to the specified torque.*

c) *Ensure that all hoses are correctly reconnected and, where necessary, that their retaining clips are securely tightened.*

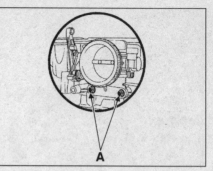

12.18 Throttle housing retaining bolts (A) - 1.6 and 1.8 litre (16-valve) engines

d) *On completion, adjust the accelerator cable using the information given in Section 4.*

1.8 and 2.0 litre (8-valve) engines with multi-point fuel injection

24 Refitting is a reversal of the removal procedure, noting the following points:

a) *Ensure that all mating surfaces are clean and dry.*

b) *On models with a gasket spacer, fit the housing using a new gasket spacer and tighten the retaining bolts to the specified torque.*

c) *On models with an insulating plate, position a new gasket on each side of the insulating plate then refit the throttle housing and tighten the retaining bolts to the specified torque.*

d) *Ensure that all hoses are correctly reconnected and, where necessary, are securely held in position by the retaining clips.*

e) *Ensure that all wiring is correctly routed, and that the connectors are securely reconnected.*

f) *On completion, adjust the accelerator cable as described in Section 4.*

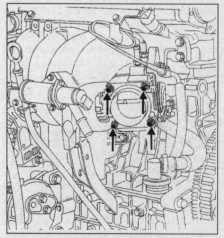

12.22 Throttle housing retaining bolts (arrowed) - 2.0 litre (16-valve) engines

4A

14.2 On single-point injection models remove the injector and recover the sealing rings

1.6, 1.8 and 2.0 litre (16-valve) engines

25 Refitting is a reversal of the removal procedure, noting the following points:
a) Ensure that all mating surfaces are clean and dry.
b) Use a new gasket or O-ring seal and tighten the housing retaining bolts to the specified torque.
c) Refit the air cleaner intake housing or air inlet duct with reference to Section 2.
d) Ensure that all hoses are correctly reconnected and, where necessary, are securely held in position by the retaining clips.
e) Ensure that all wiring is correctly routed, and that the connectors are securely reconnected.
f) On completion, adjust the accelerator cable as described in Section 4.

13 Fuel injection system - testing and adjustment

Testing

1 If a fault appears in the fuel injection system, first ensure that all the system wiring connectors are securely connected and free of corrosion. Ensure that the fault is not due to poor maintenance; ie, check that the air cleaner filter element is clean, the spark plugs are in good condition and correctly gapped, the cylinder compression pressures are

14.11 . . . then undo the screws (arrowed) and remove the idle control stepper motor (throttle body removed for clarity)

14.10 Disconnect the wiring connector . . .

correct, the ignition timing is correct, and that the engine breather hoses are clear and undamaged, referring to the relevant parts of Chapters 1, 2 and 5 for further information.

2 If these checks fail to reveal the cause of the problem, the vehicle should be taken to a suitably-equipped Renault dealer for testing. A diagnostic connector is incorporated in the engine management circuit, into which a special electronic diagnostic tester can be plugged; the connector is clipped onto the engine compartment bulkhead. The tester will locate the fault quickly and simply, alleviating the need to test all the system components individually, which is a time-consuming operation that carries a risk of damaging the ECU.

Adjustment

3 Whilst experienced home mechanics with a considerable amount of skill and equipment (including a tachometer and an accurately calibrated exhaust gas analyser) may be able to check the exhaust CO level and the idle speed. However, if these are found to be in need of adjustment, the car *must* be taken to a suitably-equipped Renault dealer for further testing. Neither the mixture adjustment (exhaust gas CO level) nor the idle speed are adjustable, and should either be incorrect, a fault must be present in the fuel injection system.

14 Single-point injection system components - removal and refitting

Note: *Check the availability of individual components with your Renault dealer before dismantling. At the time of writing it seems that the throttle body must be treated as a sealed unit with no individual components being available separately.*

Fuel injector

⚠ **Warning: Refer to the warning in Section 1 before proceeding.**

Note: *If a faulty injector is suspected, before condemning the injector, it is worth trying the effect of one of the proprietary injector-cleaning treatments.*

1 Remove the inlet air temperature sensor as described later in this Section.
2 Lift out the injector and recover its sealing rings **(see illustration)**.
3 Refitting is a reversal of the removal procedure ensuring that the injector sealing rings and injector cap O-ring are in good condition. When refitting the injector cap ensure that the injector pins are correctly aligned with the cap terminals, the terminals are marked '+' and '-' for identification.

Fuel pressure regulator

⚠ **Warning: Refer to the warning in Section 1 before proceeding.**

Note: *Although the unit can be dismantled for cleaning, if required, it should not be disturbed unless absolutely necessary (see Note at the start of this Section).*

4 Disconnect the battery negative terminal (refer to *Disconnecting the battery* in the Reference Section of this manual).
5 Undo the retaining screws then detach the inlet duct from the top of the throttle body and recover its sealing ring.
6 Using a marker pen, make alignment marks between the regulator cover and throttle body, then slacken and remove the cover retaining screws. As the screws are slackened, place a clean rag over the cover, to catch any fuel spray which may be released.
7 Lift off the cover, then remove the spring and withdraw the diaphragm, noting its correct fitted orientation. Remove all traces of dirt, and examine the diaphragm for signs of splitting. If damage is found, it will probably be necessary to renew the throttle body assembly.
8 Refitting is a reverse of the removal procedure, ensuring that the diaphragm and cover are fitted the correct way round, and that the retaining screws are securely tightened.

Idle control stepper motor

9 Disconnect the battery negative terminal (refer to *Disconnecting the battery* in the Reference Section of this manual).
10 Depress the retaining clip, and disconnect the wiring connectors from the idle control stepper motor and the injector wiring connector **(see illustration)**.
11 Unclip the plastic wiring loom connector then undo the retaining screws, and remove the motor from the front of the throttle body **(see illustration)**.
12 Refitting is a reverse of the removal procedure, ensuring that the motor retaining screws are securely tightened.

Throttle potentiometer

13 The throttle potentiometer is a sealed unit, and *under no circumstances* should it be disturbed. For this reason, on some models, it is secured to the throttle body assembly by tamperproof screws. If the throttle potentiometer is faulty, the complete throttle body assembly must be renewed - refer to your Renault dealer for the latest information.

Inlet air temperature sensor

 Warning: Refer to the warning in Section 1 before proceeding.

14 The inlet air temperature sensor is an integral part of the throttle body injector cap. To remove the cap, first disconnect the battery negative terminal.

15 Undo the retaining screws then free the inlet duct from the top of the throttle body. Position the duct clear of the throttle body and recover its sealing ring.

16 Depress the retaining clip and disconnect the wiring connector from the injector wiring connector (see illustration).

17 Undo the injector cap retaining screw then lift off the cap and recover the gasket and/or sealing ring (as applicable). Note that as the cap screw is slackened, place a rag over the injector to catch any fuel spray which may be released (see illustrations).

18 Refitting is a reversal of the removal procedure ensuring that the injector cap gasket and/or O-ring is in good condition. Take care to ensure that the cap terminals are correctly aligned with the injector pins and securely tighten the cap retaining screw.

Coolant temperature sensor

19 The coolant temperature sensor is screwed into the front, left-hand end of the cylinder head. Refer to Chapter 3, Section 6 for removal and refitting details.

Electronic control unit (ECU)

20 The ECU is located in the front right-hand corner of the engine compartment.

21 Disconnect the battery negative terminal (refer to *Disconnecting the battery* in the Reference Section of this manual).

22 Unhook the retaining strap and remove the plastic cover from the ECU.

23 Slacken and remove the ECU mounting bolts and free the unit from its mounting plate.

24 Release the retaining clip then disconnect the wiring connector and remove the ECU from the engine compartment.

25 Refitting is a reverse of the removal procedure ensuring that the wiring connector is securely reconnected.

Fuel injection system relay and fuel pump relay

26 The injection relay and fuel pump relay are clipped onto the ECU protective cover in the front right-hand corner of the engine compartment.

27 Release the retaining strap and free the protective cover from the ECU.

28 Free the relevant relay from the cover and disconnect it from the wiring connector.

29 Refitting is the reverse of removal, ensuring that the relay unit is securely clipped in position.

Crankshaft sensor

30 The crankshaft sensor is mounted onto the top of the transmission (clutch) housing at the left-hand end of the cylinder block.

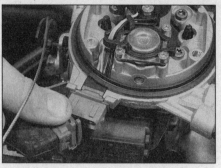

14.16 Disconnect the wiring connector . . .

31 To remove the sensor, disconnect the battery negative terminal (refer to *Disconnecting the battery* in the Reference Section of this manual), then remove the air cleaner housing as described in Section 2.

32 Trace the wiring back from the sensor to the wiring connector, and disconnect it from the main harness.

33 Slacken and remove the retaining bolts and remove the sensor from the top of the transmission.

34 Refitting is a reverse of the removal procedure. Ensure that the sensor retaining bolts are securely tightened.

Power steering pressure switch

35 The pressure switch is screwed into the power steering feed pipe from the pump to the steering gear (see illustration).

36 To remove the switch, disconnect the wiring connector.

37 Wipe clean the area around the switch then unscrew the switch and remove it from the pipe. Plug the pipe aperture to prevent excess fluid leakage and prevent dirt entry into the hydraulic system.

38 Refitting is the reverse of removal. On completion check the power steering fluid level as described in *Weekly checks*.

Knock sensor

39 The knock sensor is screwed into the front of the cylinder block.

40 Disconnect the wiring connector from the sensor then unscrew the sensor and remove it from the cylinder block.

14.17b . . . and remove the injector cap/ inlet air temperature sensor from the throttle body

14.17a . . . then undo the retaining screw . . .

41 Refitting is the reverse of removal making sure the sensor is securely tightened.

Fuel cut-off inertia switch

42 The fuel cut-off inertia switch is located in the engine compartment. To remove the switch first disconnect the battery negative terminal (refer to *Disconnecting the battery* in the Reference Section of this manual).

43 Slacken and remove the switch retaining screws then disconnect its wiring connector and remove the switch from the engine compartment.

44 Refitting is the reverse of removal. On completion, reset the switch by depressing its button.

15 Siemens-Fenix 5 multi-point injection system components - removal and refitting

Fuel rail and injectors

1.8 and 2.0 litre (8-valve) engines

 Warning: Refer to the warning in Section 1 before proceeding.

Note: *If a faulty injector is suspected, before condemning the injector, it is worth trying the effect of one of the proprietary injector-cleaning treatments.*

14.35 Power steering pressure switch location

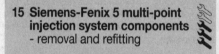

4A

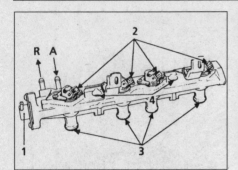

15.3 Fuel rail and injector assembly - 1.8 and 2.0 litre (8-valve) engines

1	Fuel pressure regulator	4	Retaining nuts
2	Fuel injectors	A	Fuel feed union
3	Sealing rings	R	Fuel return union

1 Disconnect the battery negative terminal (refer to *Disconnecting the battery* in the Reference Section of this manual).
2 Unclip and remove the plastic wiring loom cover from the top of the inlet manifold. To further improve access to the fuel rail, disconnect the breather hose(s) from the cylinder head.
3 Bearing in mind the information given in Section 8, slacken the retaining clips and disconnect the fuel feed and return hoses from the fuel rail. Where the original crimped-type Renault hose clips are still fitted, cut them and discard; replace them with standard jubilee-type hose clips on refitting **(see illustration)**.

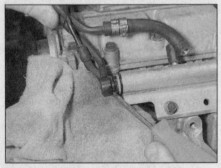

15.13 Prise the fuel supply hose union from the end of the fuel rail - 2.0 litre (16-valve) engines

15.11 Depress the retaining tangs and disconnect the wiring connectors from the fuel injectors - 2.0 litre (16-valve) engines

4 Depress the retaining tangs and disconnect the wiring connectors from the idle speed control valve, the inlet air temperature sensor and the injectors and position the wiring harness clear of the fuel rail.
5 Disconnect the vacuum hose from the fuel pressure regulator.
6 Slacken and remove the fuel rail retaining nuts then carefully ease the fuel rail and injector assembly **off** its studs and remove it from the manifold. Remove the sealing rings which are between the fuel rail and manifold and discard them; they must be renewed whenever they are disturbed.
7 Slacken the retaining plate bolts and withdraw the injector from the fuel rail. Remove the sealing rings and discard; all disturbed sealing rings must be renewed.
8 Refitting is a reversal of the removal procedure, noting the following points.
  a) Renew all sealing rings. When fitting the upper sealing rings to the injectors, use the seal protector supplied in the seal kit.
  b) Apply a smear of engine oil to the sealing rings to aid installation then ease the injectors and fuel rail into position ensuring that none of the sealing rings are displaced. Refit the retaining plates and securely tighten the retaining bolts.
  c) Refit the fuel rail assembly to the manifold, making sure the sealing rings remain correctly positioned, and tighten the retaining nuts to the specified torque.
  d) On completion start the engine and check for fuel leaks.

15.12 Disconnect the fuel return hose from the fuel pressure regulator - 2.0 litre (16-valve) engines

2.0 litre (16-valve) engines

⚠ *Warning: Refer to the warning in Section 1 before proceeding.*

Note: *If a faulty injector is suspected, before condemning the injector, it is worth trying the effect of one of the proprietary injector-cleaning treatments.*
9 Disconnect the battery negative terminal (refer to *Disconnecting the battery* in the Reference Section of this manual).
10 Remove the plastic cover from the top of the engine.
11 Depress the retaining tangs and disconnect the wiring connectors from the fuel injectors **(see illustration)**.
12 Bearing in mind the information given in Section 8, disconnect the fuel return hose from the fuel pressure regulator and suitably cover or plug the regulator and hose to prevent dirt ingress **(see illustration)**.
13 Carefully prise the fuel supply hose union from the end of the fuel rail and suitably cover or plug the hose and fuel rail to prevent dirt ingress **(see illustration)**.
14 Slacken and remove the two fuel rail retaining bolts then carefully ease the fuel rail and injector assembly from the manifold. Remove the sealing rings which are between the fuel rail and manifold and discard them; they must be renewed whenever they are disturbed. As the fuel rail is withdrawn, disconnect the vacuum hose from the base of the pressure regulator **(see illustrations)**.

15.14a Slacken and remove the two fuel rail retaining bolts . . .

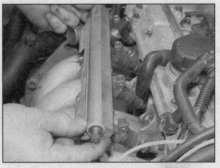

15.14b . . . carefully ease the fuel rail and injector assembly from the manifold . . .

15.14c . . . and disconnect the vacuum hose from the base of the pressure regulator - 2.0 litre (16-valve) engines

15 Undo the three retaining plate screws and remove the retaining plate from the fuel rail **(see illustrations)**.

16 Withdraw the injectors from the fuel rail and recover the sealing rings **(see illustrations)**. Discard the rings; all disturbed sealing rings must be renewed.

17 Refitting is a reversal of the removal procedure, noting the following points.

a) *Apply a smear of engine oil to the sealing rings to aid installation then ease the injectors into the fuel rail, ensuring that none of the sealing rings are displaced. Refit the retaining plate and tighten the retaining bolts.*

b) *Refit the fuel rail assembly to the manifold, making sure the sealing rings remain correctly positioned, and tighten the retaining bolts securely.*

c) *On completion start the engine and check for fuel leaks.*

Fuel pressure regulator

Warning: Refer to the warning in Section 1 before proceeding.

1.8 and 2.0 litre (8-valve) engines

18 Disconnect the battery negative terminal (refer to *Disconnecting the battery* in the Reference Section of this manual).

19 Disconnect the vacuum pipe from the regulator. Note that access to the regulator is poor with the fuel rail in position, if necessary, remove the fuel rail as described earlier then remove the regulator.

20 Place a wad of rag over the regulator, to catch any fuel spray which may be released, then carefully unscrew the retaining bolts and plate and ease the regulator out from the fuel rail. Recover the regulator sealing rings and discard them, they should be renewed whenever they are disturbed.

21 On refitting, fit the new sealing rings to the regulator grooves and apply a smear of engine oil to them to ease installation. Ease the regulator back into the end of the fuel rail and refit the retaining plate, tighten the retaining bolts securely.

2.0 litre (16-valve) engines

22 Remove the fuel rail and injectors as described previously.

23 If nor already done, undo the three retaining plate screws and remove the retaining plate from the fuel rail.

24 Withdraw the regulator from the fuel rail **(see illustration)**.

25 Remove the regulator sealing ring and discard it, a new sealing ring must be used on refitting.

26 On refitting, fit the new sealing ring to the regulator and apply a smear of engine oil to ease installation. Ease the regulator back into the fuel rail and refit the retaining plate. Tighten the retaining plate bolts securely.

Throttle potentiometer

27 Remove the throttle housing as described in Section 12.

15.15a Undo the three retaining plate screws (arrowed) . . .

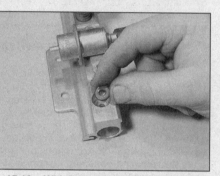

15.16a Withdraw the injectors from the fuel rail . . .

28 Undo the retaining screws and remove the potentiometer from the throttle housing.

29 Refitting is a reverse of the removal procedure ensuring that the potentiometer is correctly engaged with the throttle valve spindle. Note that Renault recommend that potentiometer operation should be checked using the special electronic (XR25) tester whenever it is disturbed.

Idle speed control valve

30 The idle speed control valve is mounted on the top or side of the inlet manifold.

31 Disconnect the battery negative terminal (refer to *Disconnecting the battery* in the Reference Section of this manual).

32 On 16-valve engines, remove the air cleaner-to-throttle housing duct as described in Section 2.

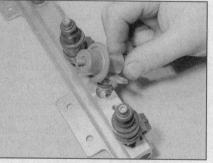

15.24 Withdraw the fuel pressure regulator from the fuel rail - 2.0 litre (16-valve) engines

15.15b . . . and remove the retaining plate from the fuel rail - 2.0 litre (16-valve) engines

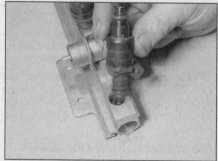

15.16b . . . and recover the sealing rings - 2.0 litre (16-valve) engines

33 Depress the retaining clip and disconnect the wiring connector from the valve **(see illustration)**.

34 Slacken and remove the control valve retaining bolts and remove the valve from the manifold. Recover the valve gasket and discard it; a new one should be used on refitting.

35 Refitting is a reversal of the removal procedure using a new gasket.

Manifold absolute pressure (MAP) sensor

36 The MAP sensor is mounted onto the engine compartment bulkhead.

37 Disconnect the battery negative terminal (refer to *Disconnecting the battery* in the Reference Section of this manual).

38 Undo the retaining nuts and free the MAP sensor from its bracket.

4A

15.33 Disconnect the wiring connector from the idle speed control valve - 2.0 litre (16-valve) engines

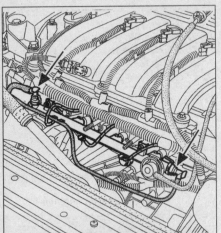

16.6 Fuel supply and return hose connections (arrowed) on the fuel rail - 1.6 and 1.8 litre (16-valve) engines

39 Disconnect the wiring connector and vacuum hose and remove the MAP sensor from the engine compartment.

40 Refitting is the reverse of the removal procedure.

Electronic Control Unit (ECU)

41 Refer to Section 14.

Coolant temperature sensor

42 The coolant temperature sensor is screwed into the front, left-hand end of the cylinder head on 8-valve engines, or into the thermostat housing on the front of the cylinder head on 16-valve engines. Refer to Chapter 3, Section 6 for removal and refitting details.

Inlet air temperature sensor

43 The inlet air temperature sensor is screwed into the air cleaner to throttle housing inlet duct.

44 Disconnect the battery negative terminal (refer to *Disconnecting the battery* in the Reference Section of this manual).

45 Disconnect the wiring connector then unscrew the sensor and remove it from the duct.

46 Refitting is the reverse of removal.

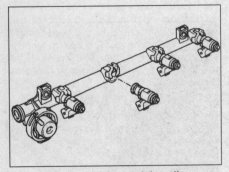

16.9 Extract the retaining clips, withdraw the injectors from the fuel rail and recover the sealing rings - 1.6 and 1.8 litre (16-valve) engines

Crankshaft sensor

47 Refer to Section 14.

Fuel injection system relay and fuel pump relay

48 The injection relay and fuel pump relay are clipped onto the ECU protective cover, or located next to the ECU, in the front right-hand corner of the engine compartment.

49 Where applicable, release the retaining strap and free the protective cover from the ECU.

50 Free the relevant relay from the cover or mounting bracket and disconnect it from the wiring connector.

51 Refitting is the reverse of removal, ensuring that the relay unit is securely clipped in position.

Power steering pressure switch

52 Refer to Section 14.

Camshaft position sensor

53 The camshaft position sensor is mounted onto the left-hand end of the cylinder head.

54 To gain access to the sensor, remove the air cleaner housing as described in Section 2.

55 Disconnect the wiring connector then undo the retaining bolt(s) and withdraw the sensor from the cylinder head.

56 Refitting is the reverse of removal.

Fuel cut-off inertia switch

57 Refer to Section 14.

---

16 Siemens SIRIUS multi-point injection system components - removal and refitting

Fuel rail and injectors

⚠ *Warning: Refer to the warning in Section 1 before proceeding.*

Note: *If a faulty injector is suspected, before condemning the injector, it is worth trying the effect of one of the proprietary injector-cleaning treatments.*

1 Disconnect the battery negative terminal (refer to *Disconnecting the battery* in the Reference Section of this manual).

2 Detach the power steering fluid reservoir from its mountings and move it to one side.

3 Undo the nuts securing the fuel injector and fuel rail protective cover at the front of the inlet manifold. Release the wiring harness from the cable clips and remove the cover.

4 Disconnect the vacuum hose from the fuel pressure regulator.

5 Depress the retaining tangs and disconnect the wiring connectors from the fuel injectors.

6 Bearing in mind the information given in Section 8, disconnect the fuel supply hose union from the right-hand end of the fuel rail and suitably cover or plug the hose and fuel rail to prevent dirt ingress **(see illustration)**.

7 Disconnect the fuel return hose from the

end of the fuel rail and suitably cover or plug the regulator and hose to prevent dirt ingress.

8 Slacken and remove the two fuel rail retaining bolts then carefully ease the fuel rail and injector assembly from the manifold. Remove the sealing rings which are between the fuel rail and manifold and discard them; they must be renewed whenever they are disturbed.

9 Extract the retaining clips, withdraw the injectors from the fuel rail and recover the sealing rings **(see illustration)**. Discard the rings; all disturbed sealing rings must be renewed.

10 Refitting is a reversal of the removal procedure, noting the following points.

a) *Apply a smear of engine oil to the sealing rings to aid installation then ease the injectors into the fuel rail, ensuring that none of the sealing rings are displaced. Refit the retaining clips.*

b) *Refit the fuel rail assembly to the manifold, making sure the sealing rings remain correctly positioned, and tighten the retaining bolts to the specified torque.*

c) *On completion start the engine and check for fuel leaks.*

Fuel pressure regulator

⚠ *Warning: Refer to the warning in Section 1 before proceeding.*

11 The fuel pressure regulator is an integral part of the fuel rail and cannot be renewed separately.

Throttle potentiometer

12 Remove the throttle housing as described in Section 12.

13 Undo the retaining screws and remove the potentiometer from the throttle housing.

14 Refitting is a reverse of the removal procedure ensuring that the potentiometer is correctly engaged with the throttle valve spindle. Note that Renault recommend that potentiometer operation should be checked using the special electronic (XR25) tester whenever it is disturbed.

Idle speed control valve

15 The idle speed control valve is mounted on the top of the inlet manifold.

16 Disconnect the battery negative terminal (refer to *Disconnecting the battery* in the Reference Section of this manual).

17 Disconnect the air hose and wiring connector from the valve.

18 Slacken and remove the three control valve retaining bolts and remove the valve from the manifold. Recover the O-ring and discard it; a new one should be used on refitting.

19 Refitting is a reversal of the removal procedure using a new O-ring.

Manifold absolute pressure (MAP) sensor

20 The MAP sensor is mounted in right-hand side of the inlet manifold.

21 Disconnect the battery negative terminal (refer to *Disconnecting the battery* in the Reference Section of this manual).
22 Disconnect the wiring connector, then carefully release the sensor from its location in the manifold.
23 Refitting is the reverse of the removal procedure.

Electronic Control Unit (ECU)

24 Refer to Section 14.

Coolant temperature sensor

25 The coolant temperature sensor is screwed into the thermostat housing on the left-hand side of the cylinder head. Refer to Chapter 3, Section 6 for removal and refitting details.

Inlet air temperature sensor

26 The inlet air temperature sensor is located in the front of the inlet manifold .
27 Disconnect the battery negative terminal (refer to *Disconnecting the battery* in the Reference Section of this manual).
28 Disconnect the wiring connector then carefully release the sensor from the manifold.
29 Refitting is the reverse of removal.

Crankshaft sensor

30 Refer to Section 14.

Fuel injection system relay

31 The injection relay is located on a bracket attached to the cooling system expansion tank.
32 Free the relay from the mounting bracket and disconnect it from the wiring connector.
33 Refitting is the reverse of removal, ensuring that the relay is securely clipped in position.

Power steering pressure switch

34 Refer to Section 14.

Fuel cut-off inertia switch

35 Refer to Section 14.

17 Manifolds (8-valve engines) - removal and refitting

1 Although the inlet and exhaust manifolds are separate, they are retained by the same nuts and share the same gasket. Therefore, in order to renew the gasket both manifolds must be removed at the same time.

Removal

Single-point injection models

2 Remove the throttle body as described in Section 12.
3 Unclip and remove the plastic cover from the throttle body fuel hoses then release the retaining clips and detach the lower end of the hoses from the metal pipes and remove the hoses from the engine.

4 Undo the retaining screws and free the pipe/wiring harness mounting bracket from the rear of the manifold.
5 Firmly apply the handbrake then jack up the front of the vehicle and support it on axle stands (see *Jacking and vehicle support*).
6 Disconnect the exhaust system from the manifold as described in Section 19.
7 Unscrew the retaining nut and bolt and remove the support bracket securing the left-hand end of the exhaust manifold to the cylinder block.
8 Undo the retaining bolt(s) and remove the heatshield from above the starter motor.
9 Slacken and remove all the manifold lower retaining nuts.
10 From above, noting each hoses correct fitted location disconnect the brake servo vacuum hose, the MAP sensor hose, and the breather/vacuum hoses from the inlet manifold.
11 Clamp the manifold coolant hoses to minimise coolant loss then slacken the retaining clips and disconnect the hoses from the manifold. Mop up any spilt coolant.
12 Slacken and remove the upper manifold retaining nuts then withdraw the inlet manifold from the engine.
13 Remove the exhaust manifold and recover the manifold gasket, noting which way around it is fitted.

Multi-point injection models

14 Remove the fuel rail and injector assembly as described in Section 15.
15 Firmly apply the handbrake then jack up the front of the vehicle and support it on axle stands (see *Jacking and vehicle support*).
16 Disconnect the exhaust system from the manifold as described in Section 19.
17 Undo the retaining bolt(s) and remove the heatshield from above the starter motor.
18 Slacken and remove all the manifold lower retaining nuts.
19 From above, noting each hoses correct fitted location disconnect the brake servo vacuum hose, the MAP sensor hose, and the breather/vacuum hoses from the manifold.
20 Slacken and remove the upper manifold retaining nuts then withdraw the inlet manifold from the engine.
21 Remove the exhaust manifold and recover the manifold gasket, noting which way around it is fitted.

Refitting

22 Refitting is a reverse of the removal procedure noting the following points.
  a) *Ensure that the manifold and cylinder mating surfaces are clean and dry and fit the new gasket so that its metallic side is facing towards the manifolds (crimped side against the cylinder head).*
  b) *Refit the manifolds and tighten the retaining nuts evenly and progressively to the specified torque.*
  c) *Ensure that all relevant hoses are reconnected to their original positions,*

and are securely held (where necessary) by their retaining clips.
  d) *On single-point injection models, refit the throttle body as described in Section 12 and on completion, top-up the cooling system as described in Weekly checks.*
  e) *On multi-point injection models refit the fuel rail and injector assembly as described in Section 15.*

18 Manifolds (16-valve engines) - removal and refitting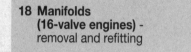

Inlet manifold - removal

1.6 and 1.8 litre engines

1 Disconnect the battery negative terminal (refer to *Disconnecting the battery* in the Reference Section of this manual).
2 To remove the manifold plastic upper section first remove the throttle housing as described in Section 12.
3 Release the accelerator cable from the inlet manifold mounting bracket and move it to one side.
4 Disconnect the wiring connectors at the idle speed control valve, throttle position sensor and MAP sensor.
5 Disconnect the wiring connector at the inlet air temperature sensor on the front of the inlet manifold, and the wiring connectors at each of the four ignition coils. Release the ignition coil wiring from the clips on the inlet manifold upper section and move the wiring clear.
6 Undo the five bolts at the front and two bolts at the rear securing the inlet manifold upper section to the lower section and to the oil separator housing **(see illustration overleaf)**. Lift off the manifold upper section and recover the seals.
7 To remove the manifold lower section, remove the upper section as previously described.
8 Remove the fuel rail and injectors as described in Section 16.
9 On 1.6 litre engines with air conditioning, remove the power steering pump as described in Chapter 10.
10 Undo the bolts securing the manifold to the cylinder head and the additional bolt securing the manifold to the upper timing cover. Withdraw the manifold from its location and manoeuvre it out from behind the auxiliary components mounting bracket. Recover the gasket.

2.0 litre engines

11 Disconnect the battery negative terminal (refer to *Disconnecting the battery* in the Reference Section of this manual).
12 Undo the four screws and lift off the plastic cover from the top of the engine.
13 Remove the air cleaner assembly and inlet ducts as described in Section 2.
14 Remove the throttle housing as described in Section 12.

4A

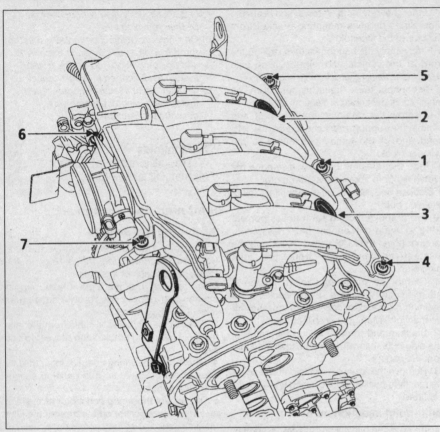

18.16 Undo the bolt to release power steering pipe support bracket (arrowed) from the strengthening bracket - 2.0 litre (16-valve) engines

18.17 Undo the bolt securing the dipstick tube to the manifold and withdraw the tube from the sump - 2.0 litre (16-valve) engines

18.6 Inlet manifold upper section attachment details - 1.6 and 1.8 litre (16-valve) engines

1 to 7   Inlet manifold upper section retaining bolts (numbers also indicate bolt tightening sequence when refitting)

15 Remove the fuel rail and injectors as described in Section 15.

16 Undo the bolt securing the power steering pipe support bracket to the strengthening bracket at the front of the manifold **(see illustration)**.

17 Undo the bolt securing the dipstick tube to the manifold and withdraw the tube from the sump **(see illustration)**. Recover the sealing O-ring from the end of the tube.

18 Unbolt and remove the strengthening bracket from the manifold and alternator mounting bracket **(see illustration)**.

19 Undo the three bolts and remove the right-hand engine mounting acoustic tie-rod.

20 Disconnect the wiring connector from the idle speed control valve.

21 From the top of the manifold behind the throttle housing location, disconnect the brake servo vacuum hose, the secondary air

injection vacuum hose and the MAP sensor vacuum hose **(see illustrations)**.

22 From the side of the manifold, disconnect the crankcase ventilation hose **(see illustration)**.

23 Apply the handbrake, then jack up the front of the car and support it on axle stands (see *Jacking and vehicle support*). Remove the engine undertray.

24 From under the car, undo the bolt

18.18 Unbolt and remove the strengthening bracket from the manifold and alternator mounting bracket - 2.0 litre (16-valve) engines

18.21a From the top of the manifold, disconnect the brake servo vacuum hose . . .

18.21b . . . and the secondary air injection vacuum hose and the MAP sensor vacuum hose - 2.0 litre (16-valve) engines

18.22 From the side of the manifold, disconnect the crankcase ventilation hose - 2.0 litre (16-valve) engines

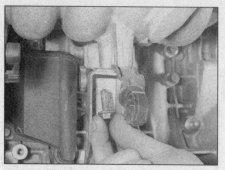

18.24 Undo the bolt securing the lower strengthening bracket to the manifold - 2.0 litre (16-valve) engines

18.25 Undo the three upper bolts securing the manifold to the cylinder head, and slacken the three lower bolts - 2.0 litre (16-valve) engines

18.26a Lift the manifold up and off the lower bolts and withdraw it from the cylinder head . . .

18.26b . . . when sufficient clearance exists, slacken the clip and disconnect the crankcase ventilation hose from the oil separator . . .

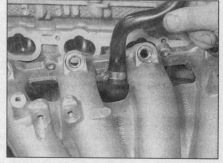

18.26c . . . and feed the hose through the manifold - 2.0 litre (16-valve) engines

securing the lower strengthening bracket to the manifold **(see illustration)**.

25 From within the engine compartment, undo the three upper bolts securing the manifold to the cylinder head, and slacken the three lower bolts **(see illustration)**. Note that the manifold lower bolt holes are slotted so it is not necessary to completely remove the lower bolts. Access to the lower bolt nearest to the power steering pump is very restricted and it will be necessary to use a socket and universal joint to unscrew it.

26 Lift the manifold up and off the lower bolts and withdraw it from the cylinder head. As soon as sufficient clearance exists, slacken the clip and disconnect the crankcase ventilation hose from the oil separator. Feed the hose through the manifold and remove the manifold from the engine compartment **(see illustrations)**.

27 With the manifold removed, undo the three lower retaining bolts and recover the gasket **(see illustrations)**.

Inlet manifold - refitting

28 Refitting is a reverse of the removal procedure noting the following points.

a) *Ensure that the manifold and cylinder mating surfaces are clean and dry and fit a new gasket or seals as applicable.*

b) *On 1.6 and 1.8 litre engines, ensure that the lower manifold is positioned so that the projections on the manifold inner side*

are in contact with the cylinder head upper section. Additionally, on 1.8 litre engines, ensure that the timing belt end face of the lower manifold is flush with the edge of the cylinder head.

c) *Refit the manifold and tighten the retaining bolts evenly and progressively to the specified torque. On 1.6 and 1.8 litre engines, tighten the manifold upper section retaining bolts in the sequence shown in illustration 18.6.*

d) *Ensure that all relevant hoses are reconnected to their original positions, and are securely held (where necessary) by their retaining clips.*

e) *Refit the fuel rail and injector assembly as described in Section 15 or 16 as applicable.*

f) *Refit the throttle housing as described in Section 12.*

g) *Refit the air cleaner assembly and inlet ducts as described in Section 2.*

h) *On 1.6 litre engines with air conditioning, refit the power steering pump as described in Chapter 10.*

Exhaust manifold - removal

1.6 and 1.8 litre engines

29 Disconnect the battery negative terminal (refer to *Disconnecting the battery* in the Reference Section of this manual).

30 Remove the air cleaner assembly and inlet ducts as described in Section 2.

31 Disconnect the lambda sensor wiring at the connector located at the left-hand end of

4A

18.27a With the manifold removed, undo the three lower retaining bolts . . .

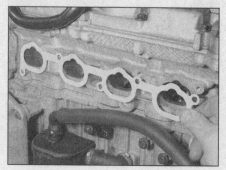

18.27b . . . and recover the gasket

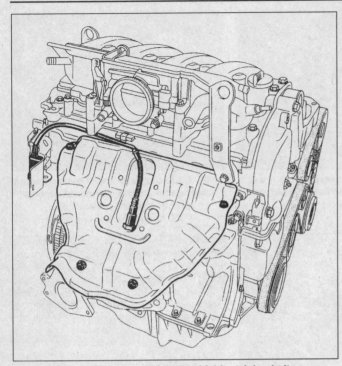

18.32 Exhaust manifold heat shield retaining bolts - 1.6 and 1.8 litre (16-valve) engines

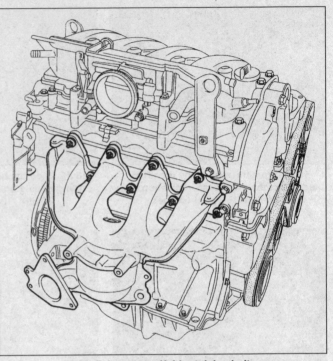

18.36 Exhaust manifold retaining bolts - 1.6 and 1.8 litre (16-valve) engines

the cylinder head. Unscrew the lambda sensor and remove it from the top of the manifold.

32 Undo the four bolts and remove the exhaust manifold heat shield **(see illustration)**.

33 Apply the handbrake, then jack up the front of the car and support it on axle stands (see *Jacking and vehicle support*). Remove the engine undertray.

34 Undo the retaining nuts and bolts and separate the exhaust system front pipe from the manifold. Move the front pipe away from the manifold slightly and suitably support it. Recover the flange gasket.

35 Unbolt the support strut from the base of the manifold.

36 Undo the bolts securing the manifold to the cylinder head **(see illustration)**. Pivot the manifold through approximately 45° and manipulate it from its location and out towards the right-hand side.

2.0 litre engines

37 Disconnect the battery negative terminal (refer to *Disconnecting the battery* in the Reference Section of this manual).

38 Undo the four screws and lift off the plastic cover from the top of the engine.

39 On engines with secondary air injection, undo the bolt securing the air injection pipe to the top of the cylinder head upper section and the bolt securing the pipe support bracket to the cylinder head upper section **(see illustrations)**.

40 Undo the bolts securing the clamp brackets for the two air hoses leading to the shut-off valve **(see illustration)**.

41 Undo the two bolts securing the non-return valve mounting bracket to the cylinder head upper section **(see illustration)**. Withdraw the air injection pipe from the cylinder head and carefully move the complete secondary air injection assembly to one side. Recover the small O-ring from the end of the air injection pipe as it is released from the cylinder head upper section. Note that a new O-ring will be required for refitting.

42 On all engines, undo the two lower plain bolts and two upper spring-loaded bolts and remove the heat shield from the manifold **(see illustration)**.

18.39a Undo the bolt securing the secondary air injection pipe to the top of the cylinder head upper section . . .

18.39b . . . and the bolt (arrowed) securing the pipe support bracket to the cylinder head upper section - 2.0 litre (16-valve) engines

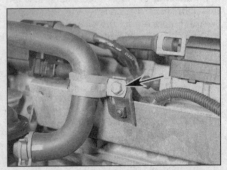

18.40 Undo the bolts securing the clamp brackets (one clamp arrowed) for the two air hoses leading to the secondary air injection shut-off valve - 2.0 litre (16-valve) engines

18.41 Undo the two bolts (arrowed) securing the secondary air injection non-return valve mounting bracket to the cylinder head upper section - 2.0 litre (16-valve) engines

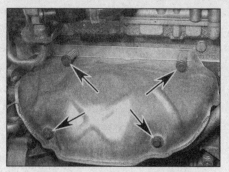

18.42 Heat shield mounting bolts (arrowed) - 2.0 litre (16-valve) engines

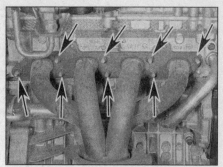

18.46 Exhaust manifold mounting nuts (arrowed) - 2.0 litre (16-valve) engines

43 Apply the handbrake, then jack up the front of the car and support it on axle stands (see *Jacking and vehicle support*). Remove the engine undertray.

44 Undo the retaining nuts and separate the exhaust system front pipe from the manifold. Move the front pipe away from the manifold slightly and suitably support it. Recover the flange gasket.

45 Undo the three bolts and remove the strengthening bracket from the base of the manifold.

46 Undo the nuts securing the manifold to the cylinder head **(see illustration)**. Withdraw the manifold off the studs and remove it from under the car. Recover the gasket.

Exhaust manifold - refitting

47 Refitting is a reverse of the removal procedure noting the following points.
 a) *Ensure that the manifold and cylinder mating surfaces are clean and dry and fit a new gasket or seals as applicable.*
 b) *Refit the manifold and tighten the retaining nuts/bolts evenly and progressively to the specified torque.*
 c) *On 1.6 and 1.8 litre engines, ensure that the heat shield is correctly located between the manifold and lambda sensor.*
 d) *On 2.0 litre engines, to assist in refitting the heat shield upper bolts, compress the springs in a vice until the coils touch. This will effectively shorten the spring length, making it easier to insert the bolts.*
 e) *Use a new gasket on the manifold to front pipe flange joint.*

19 Exhaust system - general information, removal and refitting

General information

1 On new vehicles the exhaust system consists of three sections; the front pipe, the catalytic converter and intermediate pipe and the tailpipe. All exhaust sections are joined by a flanged joint. The front pipe joints are secured by nuts and bolts, the manifold joint being of the spring-loaded ball type, to allow for movement in the exhaust system. The intermediate pipe joint-to-silencer joint is secured by a clamping ring. The system is suspended throughout its entire length by rubber mountings.

2 Although on new vehicles the catalytic converter and intermediate pipe are in the same exhaust section, when replacement is needed they are renewed individually which requires the original exhaust section to be cut into two halves (see paragraph 11).

Removal

3 Each exhaust section can be removed individually, or alternatively, the complete system can be removed as a unit. Even if only one part of the system needs attention, it is often easier to remove the whole system and separate the sections on the bench.

4 To remove the system or part of the system, first jack up the front or rear of the car, and support it on axle stands (see *Jacking and vehicle support*). Alternatively, position the car over an inspection pit, or on car ramps.

Front pipe

5 Trace the wiring back from the lambda sensor and disconnect it at the wiring connector. Free the wiring from any relevant retaining clips so the sensor is free to be removed with the front pipe.

6 Slacken and remove the nuts securing the front pipe flange joint to the manifold, and recover the conical springs, noting which way around they are fitted.

7 Slacken and remove the two nuts securing the front pipe flange joint to the catalytic converter. Remove the bolts, then withdraw the front pipe from underneath the vehicle, and recover the gasket from each end of the pipe.

Catalytic converter and intermediate pipe section (as fitted to new vehicles)

8 Slacken and remove the two nuts securing the front pipe flange joint to the catalytic converter. Remove the bolts, then separate the flange joint and recover the gasket.

9 Have an assistant support the front end of the pipe then slacken the mounting clamp nuts and detach the intermediate pipe from the tailpipe.

10 Unhook the section from its mounting rubber(s) and remove it from the underneath the vehicle.

11 If the section has been removed to enable it to be cut in half, locate the cutting area which is situated on the straight section of pipe approximately midway between the catalytic converter and silencer. The cutting point is marked with two circular punch marks on the side of the pipe. The punch marks are 90 mm apart and the exhaust section should be cut at the mid-point between the two punch marks. **Note:** *Ensure that the exhaust pipe is cut squarely else it will be difficult to obtain a gas-tight seal when the exhaust is refitted.*

Catalytic converter (replacement section)

12 Slacken and remove the two nuts securing the front pipe flange joint to the catalytic converter. Remove the bolts, then separate the flange joint and recover the gasket.

13 Slacken the clamping sleeve nut and bolt and slide the sleeve along the intermediate pipe.

14 Remove the catalytic converter and clamping sleeve. Discard the clamping sleeve; it must be renewed whenever it is disturbed.

Intermediate pipe (replacement section)

15 Slacken the clamping ring nuts and detach the intermediate pipe from the tailpipe.

16 Slacken the clamping sleeve nut and bolt and slide the sleeve along the catalytic converter.

17 Remove the intermediate pipe and clamping sleeve. Discard the clamping sleeve; it must be renewed whenever it is disturbed.

Tailpipe

18 Slacken the clamping ring nuts and detach the intermediate pipe from the tailpipe.

19 Free the tailpipe from its mounting rubbers and remove it from underneath the vehicle.

Complete system

20 Trace the wiring back from the lambda sensor and disconnect it at the wiring

4A

connector. Free the wiring from any relevant retaining clips so the sensor is free to be removed with the front pipe.

21 Slacken and remove the nuts securing the front pipe flange joint to the manifold, and recover the conical springs, noting which way around they are fitted. Separate the flange joint, and collect the gasket. Free the system from all its mounting rubbers, and lower it from under the vehicle.

Heat shield(s)

22 The heat shields are secured to the underside of the body by various nuts and bolts. Each shield can be removed once the relevant exhaust section has been removed. If a shield is being removed to gain access to a component located behind it, it may prove sufficient in some cases to remove the retaining nuts and/or bolts, and simply lower the shield, without disturbing the exhaust system.

Acoustic weight

23 2.0 litre (16-valve) models are fitted with an acoustic weight bolted to the intermediate exhaust section. The positioning of this weight is critical and must be positioned as shown whenever the intermediate section is renewed.

Refitting

24 Each section is refitted by reversing the removal sequence, noting the following points:

a) Ensure that all traces of corrosion have been removed from the flanges, and renew all necessary gaskets.

b) Inspect the rubber mountings for signs of damage or deterioration, and renew as necessary.

c) When refitting the front pipe to the manifold, ensure that the gasket and springs are fitted the correct way around and securely tighten the nuts so that they bear against the manifold shoulders.

d) When reconnecting the intermediate pipe to tailpipe joint, apply a smear of exhaust system jointing paste to the flange joint, to ensure a gas-tight seal. Tighten the clamping ring nuts evenly and progressively so that the clearance between the clamp halves remains equal on either side.

e) On models with a replacement catalytic converter/intermediate pipe section, apply a smear of exhaust system jointing paste (Renault recommend the use of Sodicam) to the inside of the new clamping ring. With the catalytic converter and intermediate pipe correct located at their outer ends, make sure both inner ends of the cut pipe are positioned squarely against the stop of the clamping sleeve. Position the sleeve bolt vertically on the left-hand side of the pipe and securely tighten the nut until it is heard to click; the clamp bolt has a groove in it to ensure that the nut is correctly tightened (equivalent to a tightening torque of around 25 Nm).

f) Prior to tightening the exhaust system fasteners, ensure that all rubber mountings are correctly located, and that there is adequate clearance between the exhaust system and vehicle underbody.

Chapter 4 Part B:
Fuel/exhaust systems - diesel engine models

Contents

Degrees of difficulty

Easy, suitable for novice with little experience	**Fairly easy,** suitable for beginner with some experience	**Fairly difficult,** suitable for competent DIY mechanic	**Difficult,** suitable for experienced DIY mechanic	**Very difficult,** suitable for expert DIY or professional

Specifications

General

Firing order .... 1-3-4-2 (No 1 cylinder at flywheel end of engine)

Maximum speed

With no load on engine:
1.9 litre engines .... not adjustable - controlled by ECU
2.2 litre non-turbo engines .... 5400 ± 100 rpm
2.2 litre turbo engines .... 5000 ± 100 rpm
With load on engine:
1.9 litre engines .... not adjustable - controlled by ECU
2.2 litre non-turbo engines .... 4800 ± 100 rpm
2.2 litre turbo engines .... 4500 ± 100 rpm

Injection pump

Direction of rotation .... Clockwise, viewed from sprocket end
Static timing:
Engine position .... No 1 piston at TDC
Pump timing measurement (stamped on pump accelerator lever):
1.9 litre engines .... 0.45 ± 0.02 mm
2.2 litre non-turbo engines .... 0.80 ± 0.04 mm
2.2 litre turbo engines .... 0.74 ± 0.04 mm

Injectors

Type .... Pintle
Opening pressure:
1.9 litre engines ....
2.2 litre non-turbo engines .... 130 ± 5 bar
2.2 litre turbo engines .... 150 ± 5 bar
Maximum difference between any two injectors .... 8 bar

Torque wrench settings

	Nm	lbf ft
1.9 litre engines		
Fuel pipe union nuts	25	18
Injection pump right-hand mounting bolts	22	16
Injection pump sprocket nut	45	33
Injector clamp bolts	27	20
Inlet/exhaust manifold nuts	28	21
Oil feed pipe-to-turbocharger union	20	15
Oil return pipe-to-turbocharger union	9	7
Turbocharger mounting nuts	26	19
2.2 litre non-turbo engines		
Exhaust manifold nuts	32	24
Fuel pipe union nuts	25	18
Injection pump right-hand mounting bolts	22	16
Injection pump sprocket nut	90	66
Injectors to cylinder head	70	52
Inlet manifold nuts	22	16
2.2 litre turbo engines		
Exhaust manifold nuts	22	16
Fuel pipe union nuts	25	18
Injection pump right-hand mounting bolts	22	16
Injection pump sprocket nut	90	66
Injectors to cylinder head	70	52
Inlet manifold nuts	22	16
Oil feed/return pipe-to-turbocharger union	20	15
Turbocharger mounting nuts	20	15

1 General information and precautions

General information

1.9 litre engines

The fuel system consists of a rear-mounted fuel tank, a fuel filter with integral water separator, a fuel injection pump, injectors and associated components. Before passing through the filter, the fuel is heated by an electric heating element which is fitted to the filter housing.

Fuel is drawn from the fuel tank to the fuel injection pump by a vane-type transfer pump incorporated in the fuel injection pump. Before reaching the pump, the fuel passes through a fuel filter, where foreign matter and water are removed. Excess fuel lubricates the moving components of the pump, and is then returned to the tank.

The fuel injection pump is driven at half-crankshaft speed by the timing belt. The high pressure required to inject the fuel into the compressed air in the swirl chambers is achieved by a cam plate acting on a single piston. The fuel passes through a central rotor with a single outlet drilling which aligns with ports leading to the injector pipes.

The four fuel injectors produce a homogeneous spray of fuel into the swirl chambers located in the cylinder head. The injectors are calibrated to open and close at critical pressures to provide efficient and even combustion. Each injector needle is lubricated by fuel, which accumulates in the spring chamber and is channelled to the injection pump return hose by leak-off pipes.

To enable the engine to meet stringent exhaust emission regulations, fuel metering and injection timing is controlled electronically by an injection electronic control unit (ECU). This highly sophisticated system is similar in operation to a full engine management system as used on petrol engine vehicles and uses similar sensors to provide data to the ECU on engine operating conditions. The sensors typically monitor coolant temperature, air temperature, fuel flow, engine speed, vehicle speed, atmospheric pressure, fuel temperature and accelerator pedal position. From the data received, the ECU controls injection pump fuel metering and injection advance, pre/post heating system, exhaust gas recirculation, the anti-theft system engine immobiliser, and the electric stop control. This allows precise control of all engine fuelling requirements providing optimum engine operation and minimal exhaust emissions under all engine operating conditions.

Provided that the specified maintenance is carried out, the fuel injection equipment will give long and trouble-free service. The injection pump itself may well outlast the engine. The main potential cause of damage to the injection pump and injectors is dirt or water in the fuel.

Servicing of the injection pump, injectors, and electronic equipment and sensors is very limited for the home mechanic, and any dismantling or adjustment other than that described in this Chapter must be entrusted to a Renault dealer or fuel injection specialist.

If a fault appears in the injection system, first ensure that all the system wiring connectors are securely connected and free of corrosion. Ensure that the fault is not due to poor maintenance; ie, check that the air cleaner filter element is clean, the cylinder compression pressures are correct, and that the engine breather hoses are clear and undamaged, referring to the relevant parts of Chapters 1, 2 and 5 for further information.

Should the fault persist, the vehicle should be taken to a suitably-equipped Renault dealer who can test the system on the Renault XR25 diagnostic tester. The tester will locate the fault quickly and simply, alleviating the need to test all the system components individually, which is a time-consuming operation that carries a risk of damaging the ECU. The tester uses a barchart configuration on a LCD screen; a fiche for the particular model is placed on the screen and each circuit can be checked instantly. It is also advisable to have any faulty components renewed by the dealer as in most instances the XR25 tester is required to re-program the ECU in the event of component or sensor renewal.

2.2 litre non-turbo engines

On 2.2 litre non-turbo engines, the mechanical configuration and operation of the diesel injection equipment is basically the same as described for the 1.9 litre engines. The main difference between the two installations is in the area of injection control, which is entirely mechanical on 2.2 litre non-turbo engines.

Fuel metering is controlled by a centrifugal governor, which reacts to accelerator pedal position and engine speed. The governor is linked to a metering valve, which increases or decreases the amount of fuel delivered at each pumping stroke.

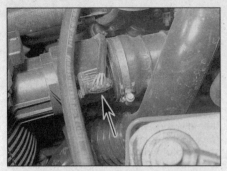

2.2 Disconnect the inlet air temperature sensor wiring connector - 1.9 litre engines

2.3 Release the retaining clip at the base of the air cleaner housing and lift the housing upward - 1.9 litre engines

2.5 Removing the manifold duct - 2.2 litre non-turbo engines

Basic injection timing is determined when the pump is fitted. When the engine is running, it is varied automatically to suit the prevailing engine speed by a mechanism which turns the cam plate or ring.

Cold starting is assisted by pre-heater or 'glow' plugs fitted to each swirl chamber. A thermostatic sensor in the cooling system operates a fast idle lever on the injection pump to increase the idling speed when the engine is cold.

A stop solenoid cuts the fuel supply to the injection pump rotor when the ignition is switched off.

Servicing of the injection pump and injectors is very limited for the home mechanic, and any dismantling or adjustment other than that described in this Chapter must be entrusted to a Renault dealer or fuel injection specialist.

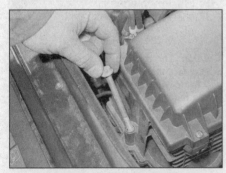

2.6a Undo the retaining bolt . . .

2.2 litre turbo engines

On 2.2 litre turbo engines the mechanical configuration and operation of the diesel injection equipment is basically the same as for non-turbo models, but with electronic control of certain functions. This is achieved by sensors which monitor crankshaft position, coolant temperature, air temperature and engine load. From the data received, the ECU controls pre/post heating system, injection pump cold start fuel metering, and exhaust gas recirculation.

Precautions

> ⚠️ **Warning: It is necessary to take certain precautions when working on the fuel system components, particularly the fuel injectors. Before carrying out any operations on the fuel system, refer to the precautions given in Safety first! at the beginning of this manual, and to any additional warning notes at the start of the relevant Sections.**

---

2 Air cleaner assembly and inlet ducts -
removal and refitting

Removal

1.9 litre engines

1 Slacken the hose clips and disconnect the air inlet hoses from the air cleaner housing.
2 Disconnect the inlet air temperature sensor wiring connector **(see illustration)**.

3 Release the retaining clip at the base of the air cleaner housing and lift the housing upward **(see illustration)**. Disconnect the air intake and remove the housing.
4 With the air cleaner housing removed, the air inlet hoses and plastic ducts can be individually removed after slackening the retaining clips and undoing the relevant retaining bolts.

2.2 litre non-turbo engines

5 Detach the inlet manifold duct from the rear of the air cleaner housing **(see illustration)**. Where necessary, also disconnect the breather hose(s) from the housing.
6 Slacken and remove the mounting bolt from the front of the air cleaner housing then unclip the housing and remove it from the mounting bracket **(see illustrations)**.
7 Free the inlet duct(s) from the air cleaner mounting bracket then undo the retaining nuts and remove the bracket from the top of the transmission. If necessary unbolt the inlet duct from the side of the engine compartment and remove it from the vehicle **(see illustrations)**.

2.2 litre turbo engines

8 Slacken the hose clips and disconnect the air inlet hoses from the plastic ducts on each side of the air cleaner housing.
9 Undo the mounting bolts and remove the plastic ducts from the engine compartment.
10 Slacken and remove the mounting bolt from the front of the air cleaner housing then unclip the housing and remove it from the mounting bracket.

4B

2.6b . . . and unclip the air cleaner housing from its mounting bracket - 2.2 litre non-turbo engines

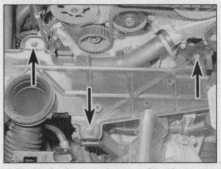

2.7a Undo the nuts (arrowed) and remove the air cleaner mounting bracket - 2.2 litre non-turbo engines

2.7b Removing the intake duct - 2.2 litre non-turbo engines

11 Free the inlet duct(s) from the air cleaner mounting bracket then undo the retaining nuts and remove the bracket from the top of the transmission. If necessary unbolt the inlet duct from the side of the engine compartment and remove it from the vehicle.

Refitting

12 Refitting is the reverse of removal making sure all the hoses and ducts are securely reconnected.

3 Accelerator cable - removal and refitting

Refer to Chapter 4A, Section 4 noting that on 1.9 litre engines the accelerator cable end is attached to the pedal position sensor on the rear left-hand side of the engine compartment, and on 2.2 litre engines the cable is clipped onto the injection pump accelerator lever balljoint with a plastic end fitting.

4 Accelerator pedal - removal and refitting

Refer to Chapter 4A, Section 5.

5 Fuel system - priming and bleeding

1 After disconnecting part of the fuel supply system or running out of fuel, it is necessary to prime the system and bleed off any air which may have entered the system components.

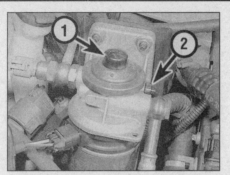

5.2 Fuel system priming pump (1) and bleed screw (2)

2 All models are fitted with a hand-operated priming pump to enable the system to be bled. On 1.9 litre engines this consists of a hand-operated priming bulb located next to the filter assembly on the right-hand side of the engine compartment bulkhead. On 2.2 litre engines, the pump consists of a plunger on the top of the fuel filter housing, which is located in the right-hand front corner of the engine compartment **(see illustration)**.

3 To prime the system, loosen the bleed screw located in the top of the fuel filter housing.

4 Pump the priming pump until fuel free from air bubbles emerges from the bleed screw. Retighten the bleed screw.

5 Switch on the ignition (to activate the stop solenoid) and continue pumping the priming plunger until firm resistance is felt, then pump a few more times.

6 If a large amount of air has entered the pump, place a wad of rag around the fuel return union on the pump (to absorb spilt fuel), then slacken the union. Operate the priming plunger (with the ignition switched on to activate the stop solenoid), or crank the

engine on the starter motor in 10 second bursts, until fuel free from air bubbles emerges from the fuel union. Tighten the union and mop up split fuel.

⚠️ **Warning: Be prepared to stop the engine if it should fire, to avoid excessive fuel spray and spillage.**

7 If air has entered the injector pipes, place wads of rag around the injector pipe unions at the injectors (to absorb spilt fuel), then slacken the unions. Crank the engine on the starter motor until fuel emerges from the unions, then stop cranking the engine and retighten the unions. Mop up spilt fuel.

Refer to the warning given in the previous paragraph.

8 Start the engine with the accelerator pedal fully depressed. Additional cranking may be necessary to finally bleed the system before the engine starts.

6 Fuel gauge sender unit - removal and refitting

Refer to Chapter 4A, Section 10.

7 Fuel tank - removal and refitting

Refer to Chapter 4A, Section 11.

8 Maximum speed - checking and adjustment

Caution: The maximum speed adjustment screw is sealed by the manufacturers at the factory, using paint or a locking wire and a lead seal. There is no reason why it should require adjustment. Do not disturb the screw if the vehicle is still within the warranty period, otherwise the warranty will be invalidated. This adjustment requires the use of a tachometer - refer to Chapter 1B, Section 22.

Note: *The following procedure is only applicable to 2.2 litre engines. On 1.9 litre engines, the maximum speed setting is controlled by the ECU.*

1 Run the engine to operating temperature.

2 Have an assistant fully depress the accelerator pedal, and check that the maximum engine speed is as given in the *Specifications*. Do not keep the engine at maximum speed for more than two or three seconds.

3 If adjustment is necessary, stop the engine, then loosen the locknut, turn the maximum speed adjustment screw as necessary, and retighten the locknut **(see illustration)**.

4 Repeat the procedure in paragraph 2 to check the adjustment.

5 Stop the engine and disconnect the tachometer.

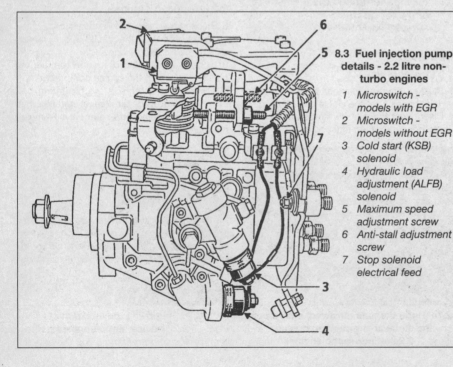

8.3 Fuel injection pump details - 2.2 litre non-turbo engines

1 *Microswitch - models with EGR*
2 *Microswitch - models without EGR*
3 *Cold start (KSB) solenoid*
4 *Hydraulic load adjustment (ALFB) solenoid*
5 *Maximum speed adjustment screw*
6 *Anti-stall adjustment screw*
7 *Stop solenoid electrical feed*

9 Fast idle system - removal, refitting and adjustment

Note: *The following procedure is only applicable to 2.2 litre engines. On 1.9 litre engines, the fast idle speed setting is controlled by the ECU.*

1 On models equipped with air conditioning and some later models not fitted with air conditioning, the fast idle system is vacuum-operated via a diaphragm unit and electrically-operated solenoid valve which is controlled by the pre-heating unit; the fast idle diaphragm is also used as a load corrector (LDA) to fine tune the injection pump fuel metering under certain conditions. On all other models the fast idle system is controlled by a thermostatic valve which is screwed into the front of the cylinder head.

Models with a thermostatic valve

Removal

2 To improve access to the valve, unclip the power steering reservoir and position it clear of its mounting bracket.
3 Drain the cooling system as described in Chapter 1B.
4 Loosen the clamp screw or nut (as applicable), and disconnect the fast idle cable end fitting from the inner cable at the fuel injection pump fast idle lever.
5 Slide the cable from the adjustment screw located in the bracket on the fuel injection pump.
6 Using a suitable open-ended spanner, unscrew the thermostatic valve from the cylinder head and withdraw the valve complete with the cable. Recover the sealing washer, where applicable.

Refitting

7 If sealing compound was originally used to fit the sensor in place of a washer, thoroughly clean all traces of old sealing compound from the sensor and cylinder head. Ensure that no traces of sealant are left in the internal coolant passages.
8 Fit the sensor, using suitable sealing compound or a new washer as applicable, and tighten it securely.
9 Insert the adjustment screw into the bracket on the fuel injection pump, and screw on the locknut finger-tight.
10 Insert the inner cable through the fast idle lever, and position the end fitting on the cable, but do not tighten the clamp screw or nut (as applicable).
11 Clip the power steering fluid reservoir back into position.
12 Refill the cooling system as described in Chapter 1B and adjust the cable as described under the following heading.

Adjustment

13 With the engine cold, push the fast idle lever fully towards the rear of the pump until it is in contact with the fast idle adjusting screw. Hold it in this position and slide the cable end fitting along the cable until its abuts the fast idle lever and securely tighten its clamp nut or screw (as applicable).
14 Start the engine, warm it up to its normal operating temperature. As the engine warms up the fast idle cable should extend so that the fast idle lever returns to is stop.
15 Once the cooling fan has cut in, measure the clearance between the fast idle lever and the cable end fitting. There should be a gap of 6 ± 1 mm. If not, slacken the clamp screw or nut (as applicable), move the end fitting to the correct position and securely retighten the screw or nut.
16 Switch off the engine and allow it to cool. As the engine cools the fast idle valve cable should retract and eventually pull the lever back against the fast idle adjustment screw.

Models with a vacuum-operated system

Removal

17 To remove the solenoid valve, disconnect the vacuum hoses and wiring connector then undo the retaining nuts and remove the valve from the front of the engine compartment.
18 To remove the vacuum diaphragm unit first disconnect the vacuum hose. Loosen the clamp screw or nut (as applicable), and disconnect the fast idle cable end fitting from the inner cable at the fuel injection pump fast idle lever Unscrew the retaining nut and remove the diaphragm and cable assembly from the pump bracket.

Refitting

19 Refit diaphragm and securely tighten its retaining nut. Reconnect the cable to the pump, making sure the cable end fitting is correctly located, but do not tighten the clamp screw/nut. Reconnect the vacuum hose to the diaphragm.
20 Refit the solenoid valve tightening its retaining nuts securely, and reconnect the vacuum hoses. Adjust the cable as follows.

Adjustment

21 Disconnect the vacuum hose from the diaphragm unit on the injection pump. Hold the diaphragm cable taut and position the end fitting so that is a clearance of 2 ± 1 mm between the end fitting and fast idle lever. Move the end fitting to the correct position and securely tighten its clamp screw/nut.
22 Reconnect the vacuum hose to the diaphragm and start the engine. When the engine is cold the diaphragm should pull the fast lever towards the rear of the pump until it is in contact with the fast idle adjustment screw. Once the engine warm, the solenoid valve should cut-off the vacuum supply to the diaphragm and the cable will extend, returning the fast idle lever to its stop against the idle speed screw. Check the clearance between the fast idle cable end fitting and lever is 2 ± 1 mm then switch off the engine.

10 Stop solenoid - description, removal and refitting

Caution: Be careful not to allow dirt into the injection pump during this procedure.

Description

1 The stop solenoid is located on the top of the fuel injection pump, at the rear. Its purpose is to cut the fuel supply when the ignition is switched off. If an open-circuit occurs in the solenoid or supply wiring, it will be impossible to start the engine, as the fuel will not reach the injectors. The same applies if the solenoid plunger jams in the stop position. If the solenoid jams in the run position, the engine will not stop when the ignition is switched off.
2 If the solenoid has failed and the engine will not run, a temporary repair may be made by removing the solenoid as described in the following paragraphs. Refit the solenoid body without the plunger and spring. Tape up the wire so that it cannot touch earth. The engine can now be started as usual, but it will be necessary to stall the engine to stop it.

Removal

3 Disconnect the battery negative terminal (refer to *Disconnecting the battery* in the Reference Section of this manual).
4 To improve access to the solenoid, release the retaining clip and position the power steering fluid reservoir clear of the injection pump.
5 Withdraw the rubber boot (where applicable), then unscrew the terminal nut and disconnect the wire from the top of the solenoid.
6 Carefully clean around the solenoid, then unscrew and withdraw the solenoid, and recover the sealing washer or O-ring (as applicable). Recover the solenoid plunger and spring if they remain in the pump. Operate the hand-priming pump as the solenoid is removed, to flush away any dirt.

Refitting

7 Refitting is a reversal of removal, using a new sealing washer/O-ring and tightening the solenoid securely.

11 Fuel injection pump - removal and refitting

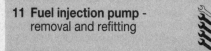

Caution: Be careful not to allow dirt into the injection pump or injector pipes during this procedure. New sealing rings should be used on the fuel pipe banjo unions when refitting.

Removal

1.9 litre engines

Note: *The following procedure describes pump removal and refitting using the special*

Renault injection pump sprocket holding tool (Mot 1200-01). This tool holds the sprocket securely in position whilst the pump is removed, keeping the timing belt correctly tensioned, and so removes the need to disturb the timing belt. If the procedure is to be attempted without the special tool, great care must be taken to ensure that the pump sprocket is held firmly in position so that it does not move in relation to the timing belt. If the sprocket moves or the timing belt tension is released it will be necessary to remove the timing belt cover and check the position of the sprocket timing marks prior to starting the engine (see Chapter 2D).

1 Disconnect the battery negative terminal (refer to *Disconnecting the battery* in the Reference Section of this manual).

2 Unscrew the retaining nuts and withdraw the engine sound-insulating cover.

3 Position an engine hoist, or an engine lifting beam across the engine compartment and attach the jib to the right-hand engine lifting eyelet. Raise the lifting gear to take up the slack, so that it is just supporting the weight of the engine.

4 Undo the three bolts securing the right-hand engine mounting bracket to the cylinder head. Similarly, undo the three bolts securing the rubber mounting to the body. Release the relevant cable clips and remove the complete mounting assembly.

5 Unscrew the securing bolts and withdraw the timing belt outer covers.

6 Turn the crankshaft to bring No 1 piston to TDC on the compression stroke, and fit a timing pin to check the crankshaft's position, as described in Chapter 2D, Section 3.

7 Disconnect the wiring plug from the ECU located at the front right-hand side of the engine compartment. Undo the mounting bolts and remove the unit. Similarly, unbolt the pre/post heating system control unit, adjacent to the ECU, and move it to one side. Remove the ECU mounting bracket.

8 Fit the injection pump sprocket holding tool (Renault tool Mot. 1200-01) to secure the pump sprocket.

9 Disconnect the two fuel hoses from the top of the fuel filter assembly. The unions are equipped with quick-release fittings which are intended to be uncoupled using the Renault tool Mot. 1311-06 - this is a small forked implement which is passed between the two outer 'spokes' of the fitting and pressed to disengage the retaining claws. The hose can then be pulled off the union. If the tool is not available, the very careful use of two small electrical screwdrivers should serve to release the union. To stop Diesel fuel from spilling cover the open ends of the hoses.

10 Disconnect the main fuel leak-off return hose from the relevant fuel injector.

11 Disconnect the pump wiring harness at the main socket connector and at the two connectors at the front of the pump. Release the wiring from the retaining clips and move it clear.

12 Unscrew the union nuts securing the

11.28a Unscrew the unions nut connecting the injector pipes to the pump . . .

injector pipes to the injection pump and injectors. Counterhold the unions on the pump, when unscrewing the pipe-to-pump union nuts. Remove the pipes as a set. Cover open unions to keep dirt out, using small plastic bags or fingers cut from discarded (but clean!) rubber gloves.

13 Unscrew the bolts securing the injection pump left-hand mounting bracket to the cylinder block.

14 Make alignment marks between the pump and the right-hand mounting. This will aid pump timing on refitting.

15 Using a suitable socket inserted through the slots in the pump sprocket, slacken the three pump right-hand mounting bolts.

16 Mark the sprocket in relation to the end of the pump shaft to ensure correct refitting, then slacken the centre nut securing the sprocket to the pump shaft.

17 Alternately, continue slackening the three pump mounting bolts then the sprocket retaining nut until they are completely released. Withdraw the pump from the sprocket and right-hand mounting and remove it from the engine, leaving the sprocket still in place and engaged with the timing belt. Recover the Woodruff key from the end of the pump shaft if it is loose.

2.2 litre engines

Note: *The following procedure describes pump removal and refitting using the special Renault injection pump sprocket holding tool (Mot 1317). This tool holds the sprocket securely in position whilst the pump is removed, keeping the timing belt correctly*

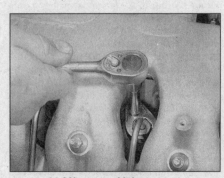

11.28b . . . and injectors . . .

tensioned, and so removes the need to disturb the timing belt. If the procedure is to be attempted without the special tool, great care must be taken to ensure that the pump sprocket is held firmly in position so that it does not move in relation to the timing belt. If the sprocket moves or the timing belt tension is released it will be necessary to remove the timing belt cover and check the position of the sprocket timing marks prior to starting the engine (see Chapter 2E).

Note: *New timing belt top and sprocket cover bolts will be required on refitting.*

18 Disconnect the battery negative terminal (refer to *Disconnecting the battery* in the Reference Section of this manual).

19 Position number 1 cylinder at TDC on its compression stroke and lock the crankshaft in position as described in Chapter 2E, Section 3. **Do not** attempt to rotate the engine once the crankshaft is locked in position.

20 Undo the retaining nut and disconnect the wiring connector from the injection pump stop solenoid terminal on the pump rear bracket.

21 On models with a thermostatic fast idle valve, disconnect the cable from the injection pump as described in Section 9.

22 On models with a vacuum-operated fast idle system, disconnect the vacuum hose from the pump diaphragm unit.

23 Unclip the accelerator inner cable end fitting from the injection pump lever then free the outer cable from mounting bracket and position it clear of the pump.

24 Disconnect the pump microswitch wiring connector and free the connector from its retaining clip.

25 Wipe clean the fuel feed and return unions on the injection pump. To improve access to the rear of the pump, unclip the power steering fluid reservoir and position it clear of the pump. Unbolt the reservoir bracket and remove it from the engine.

26 Slacken and remove the fuel feed hose union bolt from the pump. Recover the sealing washer from each side of the hose union and position the hose clear of the pump. Screw the union bolt back into position on the pump for safe-keeping and cover both the hose end and union bolt to prevent the ingress of dirt into the fuel system.

27 Detach the fuel return hose from the pump as described in the previous paragraph.

Note: *The injection pump feed and return hose union bolts are not interchangeable. Great care must be taken to ensure that the bolts are not swapped.*

28 Wipe clean the pipe unions then slacken the union nuts securing the injector pipes to the top of each injector and the four union nuts securing the pipes to the rear of the injection pump; as each pump union nut is slackened, retain the adapter with a suitable open-ended spanner to prevent it being unscrewed from the pump. With all the union nuts undone, remove the injector pipe assembly from the engine and mop up any spilt fuel (see illustrations).

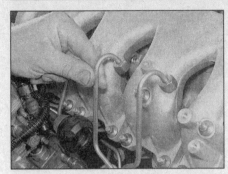

11.28c . . . and remove the pipes from the engine - 2.2 litre non-turbo engines

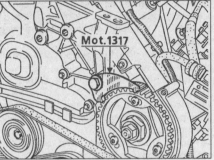

11.30a Renault special tool (Mot. 1317) for holding the injection pump sprocket stationary whilst the pump is removed - 2.2 litre non-turbo engines

11.30b If care is taken the sprocket can be held in position using wooden wedges (arrowed) whilst the pump is removed - 2.2 litre non-turbo engines

29 Undo the retaining nuts securing the fuel filter housing to its mounting bracket and position the filter clear of the timing belt cover. Undo the retaining bolts and remove the timing belt top cover and injection pump sprocket cover; discard the bolts as they must be renewed whenever they are disturbed.

30 With the cover removed, bolt the sprocket retaining tool *(see* **Note** *at the start of this Section)* in position on the engine mounting. In the absence of the special Renault tool, a suitable alternative can be fabricated out of a piece of angled-metal or alternately the sprocket can be held in position by firmly inserting two wooden wedges between the sprocket and bracket **(see illustrations)**.

31 With the injection sprocket locked in position, check the sprocket alignment mark is correctly aligned with the mark on the injection pump bracket then slacken and remove the sprocket retaining nut. If the Renault service tool is being used the sprocket will be held in position, if the tool is not being used, prevent rotation by holding the sprocket using a large open-ended spanner on the hub flats **(see illustration)**. Alternately prevent rotation using the tool described in Chapter 2E, Section 7.

32 Slacken and remove the retaining nuts/bolts and remove the pump rear mounting bracket **(see illustration)**.

33 Loosen the front retaining nuts/bolts (as applicable). **Note:** *On early (G8T 706 and 790 engine) models access to the lower pump nut/bolt can be improved by removing the coolant pump (see Chapter 3).*

34 Attach a suitable puller to the injection pump sprocket hub and carefully free the hub from the pump shaft taper. The Renault puller is attached to the sprocket hub using three 8 mm bolts once the sprocket rim bolts have been removed; make alignment marks between the bolts and sprocket before unscrewing them **(see illustrations)**.

35 Once the sprocket is free from the pump, remove the front mounting nuts/bolts and remove the pump assembly **(see illustrations)**. As the pump is removed take care to ensure that the sprocket Woodruff key is not lost; remove the key for safekeeping if it is a loose fit in the pump shaft.

11.31 Retain the pump sprocket with a large open-ended spanner as the retaining nut is slackened - 2.2 litre non-turbo engines

11.32 Unbolt the injection pump rear mounting bracket - 2.2 litre non-turbo engines

11.34a Using a puller to free the sprocket from the injection pump shaft - 2.2 litre non-turbo engines

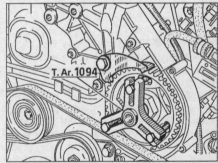

11.34b Renault special puller (T. Ar. 1094) for releasing the pump sprocket - 2.2 litre non-turbo engines

4B

11.35a With the sprocket freed, undo the front mounting bolts . . .

11.35b . . . and remove the injection pump from the engine - 2.2 litre non-turbo engines

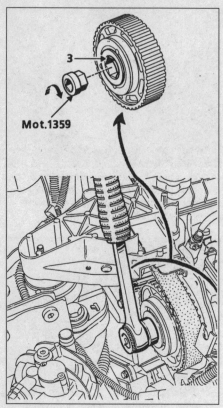

11.39 Renault tool for tightening the injection pump sprocket (3) centre bolt - 1.9 litre engines

Refitting

1.9 litre engines

36 Refit the Woodruff key to the end of the pump shaft. Make sure that the pump shaft is perfectly dry - otherwise degrease it.

37 Offer the pump to the right-hand mounting and engage the pump shaft with the sprocket. Be careful not to move the key while engaging the pump shaft. Align the marks made on the sprocket and the pump shaft before removal.

38 Where applicable, align the marks made on the pump and the right-hand mounting before removal. If a new pump is being fitted, transfer the mark from the old pump to give an approximate setting.

39 Tighten the pump right-hand mounting bolts lightly then refit the sprocket centre bolt using the Renault special tool Mot. 1359 **(see illustration)**. Tighten it to a torque of 90 Nm. Using the special Renault tool used on removal, lock the sprocket in place and refit the securing nut tightening it to the specified torque setting.

40 Refit and tighten the bolts securing the pump's left-hand mounting bracket to the cylinder head.

41 Refit and reconnect the injector fuel pipes, and tighten the unions. Counterhold the unions on the pump when tightening the pipe-to-pump union nuts.

42 Refit the timing belt covers and the engine upper right-hand mounting. Refer to Chapter 2D for details of the right-hand mounting refitting procedures.

43 Reconnect the fuel supply and return pipes and hoses.

44 Refit the ECU and reconnect all relevant wiring to the pump.

45 Reconnect the battery negative terminal then prime and bleed the fuel system as described in Section 5.

46 On completion check and adjust the injection timing (see Sections 12 and 13).

2.2 litre engines

47 Ensure that the Woodruff key is securely fitted to the pump shaft and position the shaft so the key will engage with the sprocket hub slot as the pump is refitted. If the key is a loose fit, hold it in position using a smear of grease.

48 Manoeuvre the pump into position, making sure the Woodruff key engages with the sprocket groove, and loosely refit its front mounting nuts/bolts.

49 Refit the injection pump sprocket nut and draw the sprocket fully onto the pump. Ensure that the Woodruff key does not fall out of the shaft as the sprocket is pulled onto the shaft.

50 Once the sprocket is correctly seated, securely tighten the pump front mounting nuts/bolts.

51 Refit the pump rear mounting bracket and securely tighten its mounting nuts/bolts.

52 With the pump in position, tighten the sprocket retaining nut to the specified torque setting. Where necessary, prevent rotation using the tool used on removal.

53 Set up the injection timing as described in Sections 12 and 13.

54 Ensure that the unions are clean and dry then refit the injector pipes and securely tighten their unions nuts.

55 Remove the injection pump sprocket locking tool(s) (as applicable) and refit the timing belt covers tightening its new retaining bolts securely. Refit the wiring loom clip to the

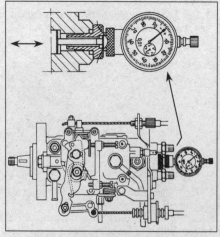

12.3 Dial test indicator and timing probe for timing the injection pump

cover and refit the fuel filter to its mounting bracket.

56 Reconnect all relevant wiring to the pump.

57 Reconnect the fuel feed and return hose unions to the pump, positioning a new sealing washer on each side of both unions, and securely tighten the union bolts. Refit the mounting bracket and clip the power steering fluid reservoir into position.

58 Reconnect the accelerator cable and, if necessary, adjust as described in Section 3.

59 On models with a thermostatic fast idle valve, reconnect the fast idle cable, and adjust it as described in Section 9.

60 On models with a vacuum-operated fast idle system, reconnect the vacuum hose to the diaphragm.

61 Reconnect the battery negative terminal and bleed the fuel system as described in Section 5.

62 Start the engine, and check the fuel injection pump adjustments as described in Chapter 1B, Section 22.

12 Injection timing - checking methods

1 Checking the injection timing is not a routine operation. It is only necessary after the injection pump has been disturbed.

2 Dynamic timing equipment does exist, but it is unlikely to be available to the home mechanic. The equipment works by converting pressure pulses in an injector pipe into electrical signals. If such equipment is available, use it in accordance with its maker's instructions.

3 Static timing as described in this Chapter gives good results if carried out carefully. A dial test indicator will be needed, with probes and adapters appropriate to the type of injection pump **(see illustration)**. Read through the procedures before starting work, to find out what is involved.

13 Injection timing - checking and adjustment

Caution: Some of the injection pump settings and access plugs may be sealed by the manufacturers at the factory, using paint or locking wire and lead seals. Do not disturb the seals if the vehicle is still within the warranty period, otherwise the warranty will be invalidated. Also do not attempt the timing procedure unless accurate instrumentation is available.

1.9 litre engines

Note: *Numerous Renault special tools are required for timing adjustment on these engines. Therefore, if no tools are available, it will be necessary to take the vehicle to a Renault dealer for adjustment of the injection* timing. A dial test indicator will be required, along with a special probe and adaptor to screw into the hole in the end of the pump on the left-hand side (Renault tool Mot. 856 or an alternative available from motor factors).

1 Disconnect the battery negative terminal (refer to *Disconnecting the battery* in the Reference Section of this manual).

2 Unscrew the retaining nuts and withdraw the engine sound-insulating cover.

3 Position an engine hoist, or an engine lifting beam across the engine compartment and attach the jib to the right-hand engine lifting eyelet. Raise the lifting gear to take up the slack, so that it is just supporting the weight of the engine.

4 Undo the three bolts securing the right-hand engine mounting bracket to the cylinder head. Similarly, undo the three bolts securing the rubber mounting to the body. Release the relevant cable clips and remove the complete mounting assembly.

5 Unscrew the securing bolts and withdraw the timing belt outer covers.

6 Turn the crankshaft to bring No 1 piston to TDC on the compression stroke, and fit a timing pin to check the crankshaft's position, as described in Chapter 2D, Section 3.

7 Cover the alternator with a plastic bag or rags as a precaution against spillage of fuel.

8 Remove the crankcase ventilation oil separator.

9 Unscrew the union nuts securing the injector pipes to the fuel injection pump. Counterhold the unions on the pump, when unscrewing the nuts. Cover the open unions to keep dirt out, using small plastic bags or fingers cut from discarded (but clean!) rubber gloves.

10 Unscrew the blanking plug from the left-hand side of the injection pump between the injector pipe connections. Be prepared for the loss of some fuel.

11 Insert the probe and connect it to the dial test indicator positioned directly over the inspection hole.

12 Remove the timing pin and turn the engine approximately a quarter-turn anti-clockwise (viewed from the timing belt end of the engine), then zero the dial test indicator.

13 Turn the crankshaft clockwise slowly (bringing the engine back to TDC) until the timing pin can be re-inserted.

14 Read the dial test indicator; the reading should correspond to the value given in the Specifications. Note that the timing value is also marked on the pump accelerator lever.

15 If the reading is not as specified, proceed as follows.

16 Disconnect the wiring plug from the ECU located at the front right-hand side of the engine compartment. Undo the mounting bolts and remove the unit. Similarly, unbolt the pre/post heating system control unit, adjacent to the ECU, and move it to one side. Remove the ECU mounting bracket.

17 Disconnect the two fuel hoses from the top of the fuel filter assembly. The unions are equipped with quick-release fittings which are intended to be uncoupled using the Renault tool Mot. 1311-06 - this is a small forked implement which is passed between the two outer 'spokes' of the fitting and pressed to disengage the retaining claws. The hose can then be pulled off the union. If the tool is not available, the very careful use of two small electrical screwdrivers should serve to release the union. To stop Diesel fuel from spilling cover the open ends of the hoses.

18 Disconnect the pump wiring harness at the main socket connector and at the two connectors at the front of the pump. Release the wiring from the retaining clips and move it clear.

19 Fit the injection pump sprocket holding tool (Renault tool Mot. 1200-01) to secure the pump sprocket (see Section 11).

20 The injection pump MAA-type sprocket (Micrometric Angular Adjustment) consists of a hub/plate and toothed rim which are locked together by a centre bolt (left-hand thread) **(see illustration)**. The plate incorporates

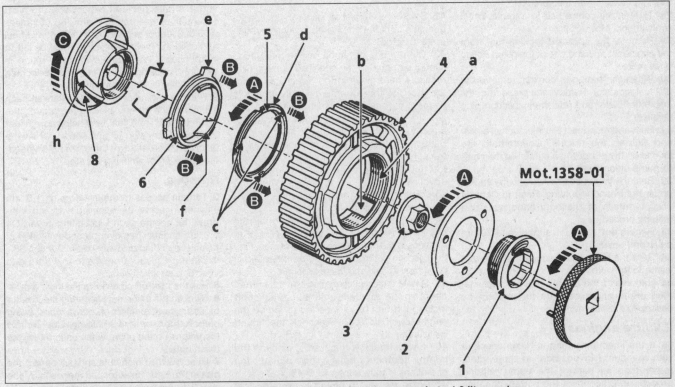

13.20 Exploded view of MAA-type injection pump sprocket - 1.9 litre engines

1 Centre bolt - left-hand thread	*7 Centre bolt locking spring*	*B Transverse movement of the rings*
2 Plate	*8 Sprocket hub*	*b Straight guide ramps for guide lugs e*
3 Sprocket nut		
4 Sprocket toothed rim	*A Anti-clockwise movement caused by tool operator*	*C Clockwise rotation exerted on the pump shaft*
5 Micrometric advance ring		
6 Angular adjustment ring	*a Thread for item d*	

c Slots for tool pins
d Thread for item a
e Guide lugs
f Helicoidal guide ramps for items h
h Helicoidal ramps for items f

4B

three holes into which a special tool (Renault Mot. 1358-01) is inserted to turn the pump shaft. First, the centre bolt must be loosened using Renault tool Mot. 1359 **(see illustration 11.39)** or a suitable equivalent.

21 Fit the special tool in the three holes and turn the tool/plate assembly so that the three claws of the tool engage in the three slots in the advance ring.

22 Now rotate the tool/plate assembly clockwise until the tool locks. This allows the sprocket to be set to the position for starting adjustment.

23 Remove the sprocket locking tool and turn the engine 2 turns (bringing No 1 piston back to TDC) until the timing probe can be reinserted.

24 Now turn the tool Mot. 1358-01 anti-clockwise until the correct timing value is obtained on the dial gauge. If the timing value is exceeded when the timing is carried out, turn it back 0.7 mm below the value before making the adjustment again.

25 Remove the special tool, then tighten the centre bolt (left-hand thread) to a torque of 20 Nm with another tool Mot. 1359.

26 Remove the timing pin.

27 Fit the tool Mot. 1200-01 to immobilise the sprocket. Turn the engine by hand in an anti-clockwise direction to bring the locking tool into contact with the sprocket.

28 Tighten the centre bolt to a torque of 90 Nm with tool Mot. 1359.

29 Remove the sprocket locking tool, turn the engine 2 turns and check the pump timing once more.

30 When the timing is correct, remove the dial test indicator. Remove the probe from the inspection hole, and refit the inspection plug securely.

31 Refit and reconnect the injector fuel pipes, and tighten the unions. Counterhold the unions on the pump when tightening the pipe-to-pump union nuts.

32 Refit the timing belt covers and the engine upper right-hand mounting. Refer to Chapter 2D for details of the right-hand mounting refitting procedures.

33 Reconnect the fuel supply and return pipes and hoses.

34 Refit the ECU and reconnect all relevant wiring to the pump.

35 Reconnect the battery negative terminal then prime and bleed the fuel system as described in Section 5.

2.2 litre engines

36 If the injection timing is being checked with the pump in position on the engine, rather than as part of the pump refitting procedure, Disconnect the battery negative terminal (refer to *Disconnecting the battery* in the Reference Section of this manual).

37 If not already having done so, slacken the clamp screw/nut (as applicable) and slide the fast idle cable end fitting arrangement along the cable so that its no longer in contact with the pump fast idle lever (ie. so the fast idle lever

returns to its stop against the idle speed screw) (see Section 9).

38 Referring to Chapter 2E, Section 3, position number 1 cylinder at TDC on its compression stroke and lock the crankshaft in position. Remove the locking pin and turn the crankshaft **backwards** (anti-clockwise) approximately a quarter of a turn.

39 Unscrew the access screw, situated in the centre of the four injector pipe unions, from the rear of the injection pump (access to the screw is greatly improved if the power steering reservoir is detached and secured to one side). As the screw is removed, position a container beneath the pump to catch any escaping fuel. Mop up any split fuel with a clean cloth.

40 Screw the adapter into the rear of the pump and mount the dial gauge in the adapter. If access to the special adapter and dial gauge cannot be gained (Renault tool No. Mot. 856), they can be purchased from most good motor factors. Position the dial gauge so that its plunger is at the mid-point of its travel and securely tighten the adapter locknut.

41 Slowly rotate the crankshaft back and forth whilst observing the dial gauge, to determine when the injection pump piston is at the bottom of its travel (BDC). When the piston is correctly positioned, zero the dial gauge.

42 Rotate the crankshaft slowly in the correct direction until the crankshaft locking tool can be re-inserted.

43 The reading obtained on the dial gauge should be equal to the specified pump timing measurement given in the *Specifications* at the start of this Chapter. If adjustment is necessary, remove the timing belt top cover and the injection pump sprocket cover (if not already having done so) as described in Section 11. Slacken the three bolts securing the sprocket rim to the hub and slowly rotate the hub until the point is found where the specified reading is obtained. When the sprocket hub is correctly positioned, tighten the three rim retaining bolts securely.

44 Remove the locking pin and rotate the crankshaft through one and three quarter rotations in the normal direction of rotation. Find the injection pump piston BDC as described in paragraph 41 and zero the dial gauge.

45 Rotate the crankshaft slowly in the correct direction of rotation until the crankshaft locking pin can be re-inserted (bringing the engine back to TDC). Recheck the timing measurement.

46 If adjustment is necessary, slacken the pump sprocket bolts and repeat the operations in paragraphs 43 to 45.

47 When the pump timing is correctly set unscrew the adapter and remove the dial gauge.

48 Refit the screw and sealing washer to the pump and tighten it securely.

49 If the procedure is being carried out as part of the pump refitting sequence, proceed as described in Section 11.

50 If the procedure is being carried out with the pump fitted to the engine, refit the timing belt covers tightening its new retaining bolts securely. Refit the wiring loom clip to the cover and refit the fuel filter to its mounting bracket. Reconnect the battery then bleed the fuel system as described in Section 5. Start the engine and adjust the idle speed and anti-stall speeds as described in Chapter 1B. Also adjust the fast idle cable as described in Section 9.

14 Fuel injectors - removal and refitting

⚠️ *Warning: Exercise extreme caution when working on the fuel injectors. Never expose the hands or any part of the body to injector spray, as the high working pressure can cause the fuel to penetrate the skin, with possibly fatal results. You are strongly advised to have any work which involves testing the injectors under pressure carried out by a dealer or fuel injection specialist.*

Testing

1 Injectors do deteriorate with prolonged use, and it is reasonable to expect them to need reconditioning or renewal after 60 000 miles (100 000 km) or so. Accurate testing, overhaul and calibration of the injectors must be left to a specialist. A defective injector which is causing knocking or smoking can be located without dismantling as follows.

2 Run the engine at a fast idle. Slacken each injector union in turn, placing rag around the union to catch spilt fuel, and being careful not to expose the skin to any spray. When the union on the defective injector is slackened, the knocking or smoking will stop.

Removal

3 To gain access to the injectors on 1.9 litre engines, unscrew the retaining nuts and withdraw the engine sound-insulating cover. On 2.2 litre engines, remove the upper section of the inlet manifold as described in Section 18.

4 Carefully clean around the injectors and injector pipe union nuts.

5 Pull the leak-off pipes from the injectors.

6 Slacken the union nuts securing the injector pipes to the fuel injection pump whilst being prepared for some fuel spillage. Counterhold the unions on the pump when unscrewing the union nuts.

7 Unscrew the union nuts and disconnect the pipes from the injectors. If necessary, the injector pipes may be completely removed. Note carefully the locations of the pipe clamps, for use when refitting. Cover the ends of the injectors, to prevent dirt ingress.

8 On 1.9 litre engines, unscrew the bolt securing each injector clamp plate to the cylinder head **(see illustration)**. Lift off the clamp plates and remove the injectors then

14.8 Unscrew the bolt (arrowed) securing each injector clamp plate to the cylinder head - 1.9 litre engines

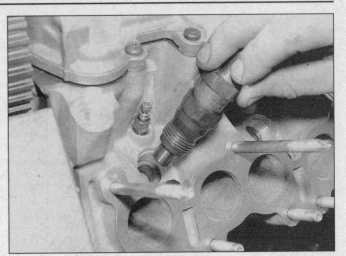

14.9a Unscrew the injector and remove it from the cylinder head . . .

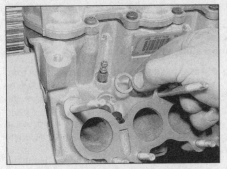

14.9b . . . then withdraw the copper washer . . .

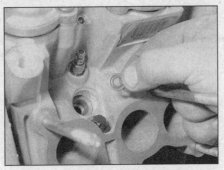

14.9c . . . and flame shield washer - 2.2 litre non-turbo engines

14.13 Ensure the flame shield washers are fitted with their convex surface downwards - 2.2 litre non-turbo engines

recover the sealing shims between the injectors and the cylinder head. If removing injector No 1, disconnect the needle lift sensor wiring connector.

9 On 2.2 litre engines, unscrew the injectors and remove them from the cylinder head. Recover the copper washers and flame seal washers from the cylinder head **(see illustrations)**, and the sleeves, if they are loose.

Refitting

10 On 1.9 litre engines, obtain new sealing shims. On 2.2 litre engines, obtain new copper washers and flame seal washers. Also renew the sleeves, if they are damaged.

11 Take care not to drop the injectors, or allow the needles at their tips to become damaged. The injectors are precision-made to fine limits, and must not be handled roughly. In particular, never mount them in a bench vice.

12 On 1.9 litre engines, fit new sealing shims between the injectors and the cylinder head. Insert the injectors then fit the clamp plates. Tighten the clamp plate bolts to the specified torque. Reconnect the wiring for No.1 injector.

13 On 2.2 litre engines, commence refitting by

inserting the sleeves (if removed) into the cylinder head, followed by the flame seal washers (convex face downwards), and copper washers **(see illustration)**. Insert the injectors, and tighten them to the specified torque.

14 Refit the injector pipes, and securely tighten the union nuts. Make sure the pipe clamps are in their previously-noted positions. Bearing in mind the high vibration levels with a diesel engine, if the clamps are wrongly positioned or missing, problems may be experienced with pipes breaking or splitting.

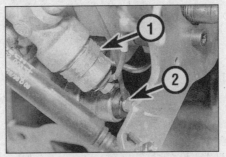

15.1a Injection pump cold start advance (KSB) solenoid (1) and hydraulic load adjustment (AFLB) solenoid (2)

15 Reconnect the leak-off pipes.

16 Refit the sound insulation cover or inlet manifold as applicable.

17 Start the engine. If difficulty is experienced, bleed the fuel system as described in Section 5.

15 Cold start advance (KSB) system - general information

On 2.2 litre engines, the fuel injection pump is equipped with a cold start advance (KSB) solenoid to advance the injection pump timing when the engine is cold; the cold start solenoid is the upper of the two solenoids fitted to the front of the injection pump. The solenoid is controlled by the pre-heating unit, which has an integral air temperature sensor, and a coolant temperature sender which is screwed into the coolant outlet housing on the left-hand end of the cylinder head **(see illustrations)**. The solenoid is operated when the ambient air temperature is less than 15°C and the engine coolant temperature less than 60°C.

4B

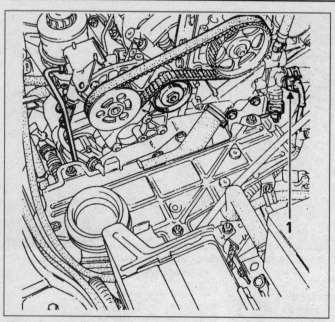

15.1b Coolant temperature sender (1) is screwed into the cylinder head coolant outlet

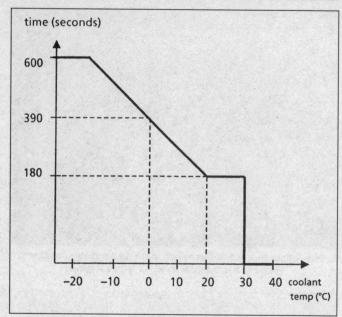

15.2 Cold start advance (KSB) solenoid operating time when air temperature sensor is faulty

If the system develops a fault, check the electrical feed to the solenoid valve and the condition of the wiring connecting the pre-heating unit, the coolant temperature sender and the solenoid. Note that if the air temperature sensor is faulty, the solenoid is operated for a set time depending on the engine coolant temperature **(see illustration).** If the coolant temperature sender is faulty the solenoid is operated for 3 minutes, regardless of the air temperature. More detailed testing of the system should be entrusted to a Renault dealer.

16 Hydraulic load adjustment (ALFB) system - general information

On 2.2 litre engines, the hydraulic load adjustment (ALFB) solenoid, the solenoid reduces the injection pump transfer pressure during at low engine speeds in order to reduce the pump timing advance. The solenoid is controlled by the pre-heating unit and coolant temperature sender (see Section 15) and also by the atmospheric pressure sensor and relay which are mounted on the right-hand side of the engine compartment, behind the headlight **(see illustration).** The hydraulic load adjustment solenoid is the lower of the two solenoids fitted to the front of the injection pump and operates under the following conditions.

a) When the air temperature is less than 15° and the engine coolant temperature is less than 70°C.

b) When the atmospheric pressure is less than 890 ± mb.

If the system develops a fault, check the electrical feed to the solenoid valve and the condition of the wiring connecting the pre-

heating unit, the coolant temperature sender and the solenoid. Note that if the air temperature sensor is faulty, the solenoid is operated when the engine coolant temperature is less than 70°C and if the coolant temperature sender is faulty the solenoid is operated for 10 minutes, regardless of the air temperature. More detailed testing of the system should be entrusted to a Renault dealer.

17 Inlet and exhaust manifolds (1.9 litre engines) - removal and refitting

Removal

1 Although the manifolds are separate, they are retained by the same nuts, since the stud holes are split between the manifold flanges.
2 Unscrew the retaining nuts and withdraw the engine sound-insulating cover.

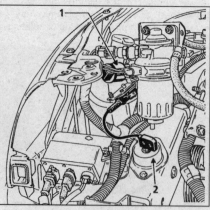

16.1 Hydraulic load adjustment relay (1) and atmospheric pressure sensor (2)

3 Apply the handbrake, then jack up the front of the car and support it on axle stands (see *Jacking and vehicle support*). Remove the engine undertray.
4 Note the location of any wiring or hose brackets/clips attached to the manifolds, and remove them.
5 Disconnect the breather hoses from the inlet manifold, noting their locations to aid refitting.
6 Remove the turbocharger as described in Section 21.
7 On models fitted with an EGR system, remove the recirculation valve and pipe as described in Chapter 4C.
8 Unbolt the engine earth strap from the engine lifting bracket at the right-hand end of the inlet manifold, then unbolt the bracket from the manifold.
9 Progressively unscrew the nuts securing the inlet and exhaust manifolds and withdraw them from the cylinder head. Recover the manifold gasket.

Refitting

10 Refitting is a reversal of removal, bearing in mind the following points.

a) Ensure that the cylinder head and manifold mating surfaces are clean and use a new gasket. Tighten all fixings to the specified torque.

b) Where applicable, refit the EGR recirculation valve and pipe with reference to Chapter 4C.

c) Refit the turbocharger as described in Section 21.

d) Ensure that the breather hoses are correctly reconnected as noted before removal.

e) Ensure that any wiring or hose brackets/clips are positioned as noted before removal.

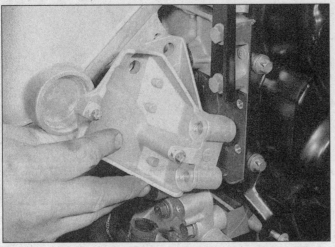

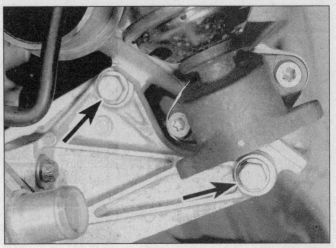

18.8 Unbolt and remove the right-hand mounting bracket . . .

18.9 . . . then undo the left-hand mounting bracket bolts (arrowed) and remove the intake chamber

18 Inlet manifold (2.2 litre engines) - removal and refitting

Removal

1 Disconnect the battery negative terminal (refer to *Disconnecting the battery* in the Reference Section of this manual), then undo the retaining nut and free the fuel return hose clip from the manifold.

2 On turbo engines, undo the bolts and remove the wiring harness support panel from the top of the manifold.

3 Evenly and progressively slacken and remove the nuts securing the manifold upper section to the cylinder head and inlet chamber.

4 Lift the manifold upwards and away from the engine, noting that on models with a vacuum-operated fast idle system it may be necessary to unbolt the solenoid valve and free it from the bracket to enable the manifold to be removed. Recover the gaskets which are fitted between the manifold and cylinder head/inlet chamber and discard them; new ones must be used on refitting.

5 To remove the inlet chamber, slacken and remove the oil separator mounting clamp screws and remove the mounting clamp securing the separator to the right-hand end of the inlet chamber.

6 Disconnect the breather hoses connecting the oil separator to the inlet chamber and camshaft cover.

7 On models equipped with an exhaust gas recirculation (EGR) system undo the retaining bolts and free the recirculation valve from the left-hand end of the chamber. Recover the gasket and discard it; a new one must be used on refitting.

8 Slacken and remove the retaining bolts and remove the inlet chamber right-hand mounting bracket **(see illustration)**.

9 Slacken and remove the bolts securing the left-hand mounting bracket to the inlet chamber and remove the chamber from the engine compartment **(see illustration)**. If necessary unbolt the left-hand mounting bracket and remove it from the cylinder head.

Refitting

10 Refitting is the reverse of removal noting the following.

a) If the inlet chamber has been removed, tighten the bolts securing the mounting brackets to the chamber by hand only when refitting the chamber. Securely tighten the bolts only after the inlet manifold nuts have been tightened to the specified torque.

b) Ensure that the manifold and cylinder head/inlet chamber mating surfaces are clean and dry and fit the new gaskets. Install the manifold and tighten its retaining nuts evenly and progressively to the specified torque.

c) On models with EGR, ensure that the mating surfaces are clean and dry then refit the recirculation valve, using a new gasket, and securely tighten its retaining bolts.

19 Exhaust manifold (2.2 litre engines) - removal and refitting

Removal

1 Remove the inlet manifold and inlet chamber as described in Section 18.

2 On turbo engines, remove the turbocharger as described in Section 21.

3 Remove the exhaust system front pipe as described in Section 23.

4 Undo the retaining bolts and remove the heatshield from the right-hand end of the manifold **(see illustration)**.

5 Slacken and remove the retaining nut and bolt and remove the support bracket from underneath the exhaust manifold **(see illustration)**.

6 On models equipped with an exhaust gas recirculation (EGR) system undo the retaining nuts/bolts and free the recirculation pipe from the left-hand side of the manifold. Remove the pipe assembly and recover the gasket; discard the gasket, a new one should be used on refitting **(see illustration)**.

4B

19.4 Removing the exhaust manifold heatshield

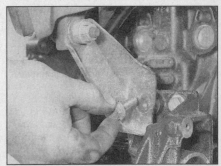

19.5 Undo the bolt and nut and remove the exhaust manifold support bracket

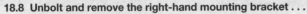

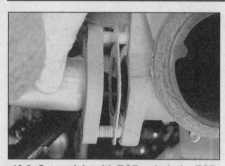

19.6 On models with EGR unbolt the EGR pipe from the manifold and remove it along with the gasket

19.7a Remove the exhaust manifold . . .

19.7b . . . and recover the gasket from the cylinder head studs

7 Slacken and remove the manifold retaining nuts and remove the exhaust manifold from the engine compartment. Recover the manifold gasket and discard it; a new one must be used on refitting **(see illustrations)**.

Refitting

8 Refitting is the reverse of removal, using a new gasket(s) and tightening the manifold retaining nuts to the specified torque.

20 Turbocharger -
description and precautions

Description

A turbocharger increases engine efficiency by raising the pressure in the inlet manifold above atmospheric pressure. Instead of the air simply being sucked into the cylinders, it is forced in. Additional fuel is supplied by the injection pump in proportion to the increased air intake.

Energy for the operation of the turbocharger comes from the exhaust gas. The gas flows through a specially-shaped housing (the turbine housing) and in so doing, spins the turbine wheel. The turbine wheel is attached to a shaft, at the end of which is another vaned wheel known as the compressor wheel. The compressor wheel spins in its own housing and compresses the inducted air on the way to the inlet manifold.

Between the turbocharger and the inlet manifold, the compressed air passes through an intercooler. This is an air-to-air heat exchanger, mounted in front of the radiator, and supplied with cooling air ducted through the front of the car. The purpose of the intercooler is to remove, from the inducted air, some of the heat gained in being compressed. Because cooler air is denser, removal of this heat further increases engine efficiency.

Boost pressure (the pressure in the inlet manifold) is limited by a wastegate, which diverts the exhaust gas away from the turbine wheel in response to a pressure-sensitive actuator.

The turbo shaft is pressure-lubricated by an oil feed pipe from the main oil gallery. The

shaft 'floats' on a cushion of oil. A drain pipe returns the oil to the sump.

The turbocharger bearings are cooled by circulating engine coolant. After switching off the ignition, an electric pump continues to circulate coolant for several minutes to prevent overheating of the bearings and to prolong their life.

Precautions

The turbocharger operates at extremely high speeds and temperatures. Certain precautions must be observed to avoid premature failure of the turbo or injury to the operator.

Do not race the engine immediately after start-up, especially if it is cold. Give the oil a few seconds to circulate.

Always allow the engine to return to idle speed before switching it off - do not blip the throttle and switch off, as this will leave the turbo spinning without lubrication.

Allow the engine to idle for several minutes before switching off after a high-speed run.

Observe the recommended intervals for oil and filter changing, and use a reputable oil of the specified quality. Neglect of oil changing, or use of inferior oil, can cause carbon formation on the turbo shaft and subsequent failure.

⚠️ **Warning: Do not operate the turbo with any parts exposed. Foreign objects falling onto the rotating vanes could cause excessive damage and (if ejected) personal injury.**

21 Turbocharger -
removal and refitting

Note: *New turbocharger-to-exhaust manifold nuts must be used on refitting. If a new turbocharger is to be fitted, new exhaust elbow-to-turbocharger nuts and new coolant pipe seals will be required.*

Removal

1 Whilst the engine is still warm, spray the turbocharger mounting bolts with a penetrating oil to ease removal.

2 Apply the handbrake, then jack up the front of the vehicle, and support securely on axle stands (see *Jacking and vehicle support*).
3 Ensure that the engine has cooled sufficiently to avoid scalding, then drain the cooling system as described in Chapter 1B.
4 Where applicable, remove the engine undershield.
5 Remove the exhaust front section and downpipe with reference to Section 23.
6 Working under the vehicle, unscrew the retaining bolts, and remove the turbocharger support brackets and the two lower heat shield retaining bolts.
7 Unscrew the turbocharger oil return pipe union from the outlet on the underside of the turbocharger. Be prepared for oil spillage.
8 Slacken the hose clamp, and disconnect the lower coolant hose from the turbocharger pipe. Be prepared for coolant spillage.
9 Remove the air cleaner assembly as described in Section 2.
10 Loosen the clamps, undo the bolts and remove the air ducts connecting the inlet manifold to the intercooler tube.
11 Loosen the clamps, and remove the air ducts connecting the air cleaner to the turbocharger. Also disconnect the breather hose connecting the air duct to the inlet manifold. Note the locations of any clips attached to the air trunking.
12 Loosen the clamp and disconnect the air outlet trunking (running to the intercooler) from the turbocharger.
13 On 2.2 litre engines, remove the inlet manifold as described in Section 18.
14 Undo the upper bolt and remove the heat shield from the turbocharger.
15 Unscrew the union nut, and disconnect the oil feed pipe from the top of the turbocharger. It may be necessary to remove the wastegate bracket bolts to enable access to the union nut.
16 Disconnect the upper turbocharger coolant hose.
17 Unscrew the four turbocharger-to-manifold nuts, slide the turbocharger from the manifold studs and manipulate it from its location. Access to the lower right-hand nut is easiest from underneath the vehicle. For improved access to the nuts, unbolt the exhaust elbow from the turbocharger.

18 If a new turbocharger is to be fitted, remove the coolant pipes and the exhaust elbow from the old unit, and transfer them to the new unit. Use new nuts when fitting the exhaust elbow, and new seals when fitting the coolant pipes.

Refitting

19 Refitting is a reversal of removal, but renew any damaged hose clamps, and use new turbocharger-to-exhaust manifold nuts which should be tightened to the specified torque. Tighten the oil feed and return pipe-to-turbocharger union nuts to the specified torque. Where applicable, the exhaust elbow should be refitted to the turbocharger using new nuts. Note that if the wastegate bracket bolts were removed, they must be refitted using a suitable thread-locking compound before tightening to the specified torque. Refill the cooling system as described in Chapter 1B.
20 On completion, the following procedure must be observed before starting the engine.
  a) *Disconnect the wiring from the stop solenoid on the injection pump, and insulate the connector.*
  b) *Crank the engine on the starter motor until the instrument panel oil pressure warning light goes out (this may take several seconds).*
  c) *Reconnect the wiring to the stop solenoid, then start the engine using the normal procedure.*
  d) *Run the engine at idle speed, and check the turbocharger oil and coolant unions for leakage. Rectify any problems without delay.*
21 After the engine has been run, check the engine oil level, and top up if necessary.

22 Intercooler (turbo engines) - removal and refitting

Removal

1 The intercooler is located at the front of the car between the electric cooling fan assembly and the radiator. To remove the intercooler, disconnect the air inlet ducts then refer to the procedures contained in Chapter 3, Section 5, paragraphs 5 to 11. Once access is gained, the intercooler can be unbolted and carefully removed from its location.

Refitting

2 Refitting is a reversal of removal.

23 Exhaust system - general information, removal and refitting

Refer to Chapter 4A, Section 19, ignoring all references to the lambda sensor. Note that not all models are fitted with a catalytic converter. On early models the catalytic converter is replaced by an ordinary silencer box.

4B

Chapter 4 Part C:
Emission control systems

Contents

Degrees of difficulty

Easy, suitable for novice with little experience	Fairly easy, suitable for beginner with some experience	Fairly difficult, suitable for competent DIY mechanic	Difficult, suitable for experienced DIY mechanic	Very difficult, suitable for expert DIY or professional

Specifications

Torque wrench setting	Nm	lbf ft
Lambda sensor - petrol models:		
Sensor mounted in exhaust front pipe	40	30
Sensor mounted in exhaust manifold	45	33

1 General information

All petrol engine models have the ability to use unleaded petrol and also have various other features built into the fuel system to help minimise harmful emissions. On top of this, all models are equipped with the crankcase emission-control system described below. All models are also equipped with a catalytic converter and an evaporative emission control system. 2.0 litre (16-valve) engine models also utilise a secondary air injection system to quickly bring the catalytic converter up to normal working temperature.

All diesel engine models are also designed to meet the strict emission requirements and are also equipped with a crankcase emission control system. In addition to this certain models may also be fitted with a catalytic converter to reduce exhaust emissions. To further reduce emissions, later models are also equipped with an exhaust gas recirculation (EGR) system.

The emission control systems function as follows.

Petrol models

Crankcase emission control

To reduce the emission of unburned hydrocarbons from the crankcase into the atmosphere, the engine is sealed and the blow-by gases and oil vapour are drawn from inside the crankcase, through a wire mesh oil separator, into the inlet tract to be burned by the engine during normal combustion.

Under conditions of high manifold depression (idling, deceleration) the gases will be sucked positively out of the crankcase. Under conditions of low manifold depression (acceleration, full-throttle running) the gases are forced out of the crankcase by the (relatively) higher crankcase pressure; if the engine is worn, the raised crankcase pressure (due to increased blow-by) will cause some of the flow to return under all manifold conditions.

Exhaust emission control

To minimise the amount of pollutants which escape into the atmosphere, all models are fitted with a catalytic converter in the exhaust system. The system is of the closed-loop type, in which one or two lambda sensors in the exhaust system provides the fuel-injection/ignition system ECU with constant feedback, enabling the ECU to adjust the mixture to provide the best possible conditions for the converter to operate.

The lambda sensors have a heating element built-in that is controlled by the ECU through the lambda sensor relay to quickly bring the sensor's tip to an efficient operating temperature. The sensor's tip is sensitive to oxygen and sends the ECU a varying voltage depending on the amount of oxygen in the exhaust gases; if the inlet air/fuel mixture is too rich, the exhaust gases are low in oxygen so the sensors sends a low-voltage signal, the voltage rising as the mixture weakens and the amount of oxygen rises in the exhaust gases. Peak conversion efficiency of all major pollutants occurs if the inlet air/fuel mixture is maintained at the chemically-correct ratio for the complete combustion of petrol of 14.7 parts (by weight) of air to 1 part of fuel (the 'stoichiometric' ratio). The sensor output voltage alters in a large step at this point, the ECU using the signal change as a reference point and correcting the inlet air/fuel mixture accordingly by altering the fuel injector pulse width.

Evaporative emission control

To minimise the escape into the atmosphere of unburned hydrocarbons, an evaporative emissions control system is also fitted to all models. The fuel tank filler cap is sealed and a charcoal canister is mounted behind the right-hand front wing. The canister collects the petrol vapours generated in the tank when the car is parked and stores them until they can be cleared from the canister (under the control of the fuel injection/ignition system ECU) via the purge valve into the inlet tract to be burned by the engine during normal combustion.

To ensure the engine runs correctly when it is cold and/or idling and to protect the catalytic converter from the effects of an over-rich mixture, the purge control valve is not opened by the ECU until the engine has warmed up, and the engine is under load; the valve solenoid is then modulated on and off to allow the stored vapour to pass into the inlet tract.

4C

Secondary air injection

Certain 2.0 litre (16-valve) engine models are also equipped with a secondary air injection system. This system is designed to reduce exhaust emissions in the period between first starting the engine, and until the catalytic converter reaches operating (functioning) temperature. Introduction of air into the exhaust system during the initial start-up period, creates an 'afterburner' effect which quickly increases the temperature in the exhaust system front pipe, thus bringing the catalytic converter up to normal operating temperatures very quickly.

The system is controlled by the fuel injection/ignition ECU and consists of an air pump, mounted under the left-hand front wing, a vacuum operated shut-off valve, a non-return valve, a solenoid valve and interconnecting air and vacuum hoses.

Diesel models

Crankcase emission control

Refer to paragraphs 4 and 5.

Exhaust emission control

To minimise the level of exhaust pollutants released into the atmosphere, a catalytic converter is fitted in the exhaust system of some models.

The catalytic converter consists of a canister containing a fine mesh impregnated with a catalyst material, over which the hot exhaust gases pass. The catalyst speeds up the oxidation of harmful carbon monoxide, unburnt hydrocarbons and soot, effectively reducing the quantity of harmful products released into the atmosphere via the exhaust gases.

Exhaust gas recirculation system

This system is designed to recirculate small quantities of exhaust gas into the inlet tract, and therefore into the combustion process. This process reduces the level of oxides of nitrogen present in the final exhaust gas which is released into the atmosphere.

The volume of exhaust gas recirculated is controlled by vacuum supplied from the brake servo vacuum pump, via a solenoid valve controlled by the pre-heating system control unit. A vacuum-operated valve is fitted to the exhaust manifold, to regulate the quantity of exhaust gas recirculated. The valve is operated by the vacuum supplied by the solenoid valve.

The system is controlled by the pre-heating system control unit or injection ECU which receives information from a coolant temperature sender unit, the post-heating microswitch and the clutch pedal switch and time delay relay. The EGR system operates only when all the following conditions are met.

a) When the engine coolant temperature is above 40ºC.
b) When the accelerator pedal is depressed beyond a travel of 12 mm (measured by the post-heating microswitch on the injection pump).

c) When the clutch pedal has been released for at least 2 seconds (measured by the clutch pedal switch via the time delay relay).

2 Petrol engine emission control systems - testing and component renewal

Crankcase emission control

1 The components of this system require no attention other than to check that the hose(s) are clear and undamaged at regular intervals.

Evaporative emission control system

Testing

2 If the system is thought to be faulty, disconnect the hoses from the charcoal canister and purge control valve and check that they are clear by blowing through them. If the purge control valve(s) or charcoal canister are thought to be faulty, they must be renewed.

Charcoal canister - renewal

3 The charcoal canister is located behind the right-hand front wing. To gain access to the canister, firmly apply the handbrake then jack up the front of the car and support it on axle stands (see Jacking and vehicle support).
4 Undo the retaining screws and remove the plastic cover from the front corner of the base of the wing.
5 Slacken and remove the retaining bolts and lower the canister out from underneath the wing. Mark the hoses for identification purposes then disconnect both hoses and remove the canister from the vehicle. Where the crimped-type hose clips are fitted, cut the clips and discard them, replace them with standard worm-drive hose clips on refitting. Where the hoses are equipped with quick-release fittings depress the centre collar of the fitting with a small flat-bladed screwdriver then detach the hose from the canister.

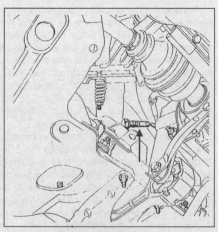

2.16 Lambda sensor location (arrowed) viewed from underneath the vehicle - petrol engine

6 Refitting is a reverse of the removal procedure ensuring that the hoses are correctly reconnected.

Purge valve - renewal

7 The purge valve is mounted onto the right-hand end of the engine compartment bulkhead, next to the suspension mounting turret.
8 To renew the purge valve, disconnect the battery negative terminal then depress the retaining clip and disconnect the wiring connector from the valve.
9 Disconnect the hoses from the valve, noting their correct fitted locations then release the valve from its retaining clip and remove it from the engine compartment.
10 Refitting is a reversal of the removal procedure ensuring that the valve is fitted the correct way around and the hoses are securely connected.

Exhaust emission control

Testing

11 The performance of the catalytic converter can be checked only by measuring the exhaust gases using a good-quality, carefully-calibrated exhaust gas analyser.
12 If the CO level at the tailpipe is too high, the vehicle should be taken to a Renault dealer so that the complete fuel-injection and ignition systems, including the lambda sensor, can be thoroughly checked using the special diagnostic equipment. Once these have been checked and are known to be free from faults, the fault must be in the catalytic converter, which must be renewed.

Catalytic converter - renewal

13 Refer to Chapter 4A, Section 19.

Lambda sensor - renewal

Note 1: The lambda sensor is delicate and will not work if it is dropped or knocked, if its power supply is disrupted, or if any cleaning materials are used on it.
Note 2: 1.6 and 1.8 litre (16-valve) engines are fitted with an 'upstream' lambda sensor screwed into the exhaust manifold. Refer to Chapter 4A for details of removal and refitting.
14 Firmly apply the handbrake then jack up the front of the vehicle and support it on axle stands (see Jacking and vehicle support).
15 Trace the wiring back from the lambda sensor, which is screwed into the exhaust front pipe and disconnect its wiring connector, freeing the wiring from any relevant retaining clips or ties.
16 Unscrew the sensor and remove it from the exhaust system front pipe (see illustration).
17 Refitting is a reverse of the removal procedure. Prior to installing the sensor apply a smear of high temperature grease to the sensor threads. Tighten the sensor to the specified torque and ensure that the wiring is correctly routed and in no danger of contacting either the exhaust system or engine.

Secondary air injection

Testing

18 The components of this system require no attention other than to check that the hose(s) are clear and undamaged at regular intervals.

19 Accurate testing of the system operation entails the use of diagnostic test equipment and should be entrusted to a Renault dealer.

Air pump - renewal

20 The air pump is located behind the left-hand front wing **(see illustration)**. To gain access to the pump, firmly apply the handbrake then jack up the front of the car and support it on axle stands (see *Jacking and vehicle support*).

21 Undo the retaining screws and remove the engine undertray and the plastic cover from the front corner of the base of the wing.

22 Slacken and remove the retaining bolts and withdraw the pump mounting bracket from its location. Undo the bolts securing the pump to the mounting bracket and remove the bracket.

23 Disconnect the air hoses and wiring connector and remove the pump.

24 Refitting is a reverse of the removal procedure ensuring that the hoses are correctly reconnected.

Valve and hose - renewal

25 Undo the four screws and lift off the plastic cover from the top of the engine.

26 Undo the bolt securing the air injection pipe to the top of the cylinder head upper section and the bolt securing the pipe support bracket to the cylinder head upper section.

27 Undo the bolts securing the clamp brackets for the two air hoses leading to the shut-off valve.

28 Release the clip and disconnect the air inlet hose from the shut-off valve. Disconnect the vacuum hose from the top of the valve.

29 Undo the two bolts securing the non-return valve mounting bracket to the cylinder head upper section. Withdraw the air injection pipe from the cylinder head and lift off secondary air injection components as an assembly from the cylinder head. Recover the small O-ring from the end of the air injection pipe as it is released from the cylinder head upper section. Note that a new O-ring will be required for refitting.

30 Separate the individual components as necessary after disconnecting the hoses and, where necessary, the air injection pipe.

31 Refitting is a reverse of the removal procedure using a new O-ring on the air injection pipe. Ensure that the hoses are correctly reconnected.

Inlet pipe - renewal

32 Firmly apply the handbrake then jack up the front of the car and support it on axle stands (see *Jacking and vehicle support*).

33 Undo the retaining screws and remove the engine undertray and the plastic cover from the front corner of the base of the wing.

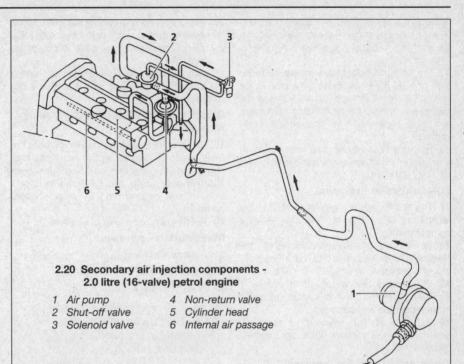

2.20 Secondary air injection components - 2.0 litre (16-valve) petrol engine

1 Air pump
2 Shut-off valve
3 Solenoid valve
4 Non-return valve
5 Cylinder head
6 Internal air passage

34 Disconnect the inlet pipe lower air hose at its connection on the air pump.

35 Undo the bolts securing the air pipe to the transmission mounting brackets and disconnect the upper air hose from the shut off valve. Remove the inlet pipe from the engine compartment.

36 Refitting is a reverse of the removal procedure.

Solenoid valve - renewal

37 The solenoid valve is located on the engine compartment bulkhead to the rear of the air cleaner housing.

38 To remove the valve, disconnect the vacuum and inlet hoses and the wiring connector.

39 Undo the retaining screws and remove the valve from the mounting bracket,

40 Refitting is a reverse of the removal procedure.

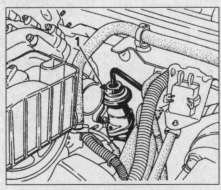

3.7 EGR recirculation valve (1) - diesel engine

3 Diesel engine emission control systems - testing and component renewal

Crankcase emission control

1 The components of this system require no attention other than to check that the hose(s) are clear and undamaged at regular intervals.

Exhaust emission control

Testing

2 The performance of the catalytic converter can be checked only by measuring the exhaust gases using a good-quality, carefully-calibrated exhaust gas analyser.

3 If the catalytic converter is thought to be faulty, before assuming the catalytic converter is faulty, it is worth checking the problem is not due to a faulty injector(s). Refer to your Renault dealer for further information.

Catalytic converter - renewal

4 Refer to Chapter 4B, Section 23.

Exhaust gas recirculation (EGR) system

Testing

5 Testing of the system should be entrusted to a Renault dealer.

Recirculation valve - renewal

6 Slacken the retaining clips and remove the duct connecting the air cleaner housing to the manifold inlet chamber.

7 Disconnect the vacuum hose from the EGR recirculation valve which is mounted on the left-hand end of the inlet chamber **(see illustration)**.

8 Slacken and remove the retaining bolts and free the valve from the inlet chamber. Recover the gasket and discard it; a new one must be used on refitting.

9 Either undo the bolts securing the valve to the pipe or undo the bolts securing the pipe to the exhaust manifold (as applicable). Recover the gasket and remove the recirculation valve/valve and pipe assembly from the engine compartment.

10 Refitting is the reverse of removal using new gaskets and ensuring that the bolts are securely tightened.

Solenoid valve - renewal

11 The EGR solenoid valve is located in the left-hand rear corner of the engine compartment.

12 To remove the solenoid, unscrew the retaining nuts and free the valve from its mounting bracket.

13 Disconnect the wiring connector and vacuum hoses from the valve and remove it from the engine compartment.

14 Refitting is the reverse of removal, ensuring that the vacuum hoses are securely reconnected.

Temperature sender - renewal

15 The EGR system temperature sender is situated directly beneath the fuel injection pump **(see illustration)**. Refer to Chapter 3, Section 6 for removal and refitting details.

Clutch pedal switch - renewal

16 Access to switch can be gained from underneath the facia. To improve access unclip the facia fusebox lid. Undo the retaining screws situated along the lower edge of the fusebox lid cover panel and unclip the panel assembly from the facia.

17 Reach up behind the facia and disconnect the wiring connector from the switch which is mounted onto the clutch pedal bracket. Twist the switch and carefully ease it out of its retaining clip.

18 Refitting is the reverse of removal pushing the switch into position until it contacts the clutch pedal stop.

Clutch pedal switch time delay relay - renewal

19 Disconnect the wiring connector from the relay which is located in the left-hand rear corner of the engine compartment **(see illustration)**. Undo the retaining bolt and remove the relay from the engine compartment.

20 Refitting is the reverse of removal.

Microswitch - renewal

21 Refer to Chapter 5C.

Pre-heating unit - renewal

22 Refer to Chapter 5C.

---

4   Catalytic converter -
general information
and precautions

The catalytic converter is a reliable and simple device which needs no maintenance in itself, but there are some facts of which an owner should be aware if the converter is to function properly for its full service life.

Petrol models

a) *DO NOT use leaded petrol in a car equipped with a catalytic converter - the lead will coat the precious metals, reducing their converting efficiency and will eventually destroy the converter.*
b) *Always keep the ignition and fuel systems well-maintained in accordance with the manufacturer's schedule.*
c) *If the engine develops a misfire, do not drive the car at all (or at least as little as possible) until the fault is cured.*
d) *DO NOT push- or tow-start the car - this will soak the catalytic converter in unburned fuel, causing it to overheat when the engine does start.*
e) *DO NOT switch off the ignition at high engine speeds.*
f) *DO NOT use fuel or engine oil additives - these may contain substances harmful to the catalytic converter.*
g) *DO NOT continue to use the car if the engine burns oil to the extent of leaving a visible trail of blue smoke.*
h) *Remember that the catalytic converter operates at very high temperatures. DO NOT, therefore, park the car in dry undergrowth, over long grass or piles of dead leaves after a long run.*
i) *Remember that the catalytic converter is FRAGILE - do not strike it with tools during servicing work.*
j) *In some cases a sulphurous smell (like that of rotten eggs) may be noticed from the exhaust. This is common to many catalytic converter-equipped cars and once the car has covered a few thousand miles the problem should disappear.*
k) *The catalytic converter, used on a well-maintained and well-driven car, should last for between 50 000 and 100 000 miles - if the converter is no longer effective it must be renewed.*

Diesel models

Refer to the information given in parts f, g, h and i of the petrol models information given above.

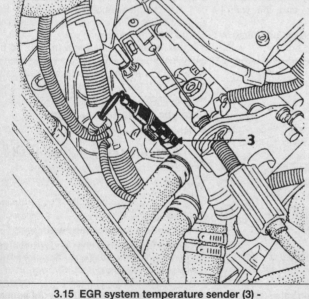

3.15 EGR system temperature sender (3) - diesel engine

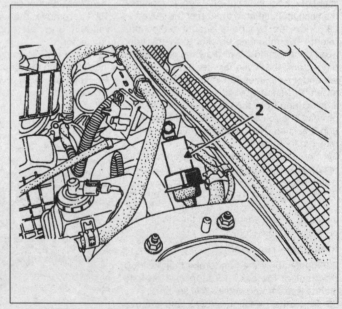

3.19 EGR system clutch pedal switch time delay relay (2) - diesel engine

Chapter 5 Part A:
Starting and charging systems

Contents

Degrees of difficulty

Easy, suitable for novice with little experience 	Fairly easy, suitable for beginner with some experience	Fairly difficult, suitable for competent DIY mechanic	Difficult, suitable for experienced DIY mechanic	Very difficult, suitable for expert DIY or professional 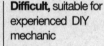

Specifications

System type . . . . 12-volt, negative earth

Battery

Type . . . . Lead-acid, low-maintenance or 'maintenance free'
Charge condition:
  Poor . . . . 12.5 volts
  Normal . . . . 12.6 volts
  Good . . . . 12.7 volts

Alternator

Type . . . . Valeo or Bosch (depending on model)
Output . . . . 60, 80 or 110 amps (depending on model)
Regulated voltage . . . . 13.5 to 14.8 volts

Starter motor

Type . . . . Valeo or Bosch (depending on model)

5A

1 General information and precautions

General information

The engine electrical system consists mainly of the charging and starting systems. Because of their engine-related functions, these components are covered separately from the body electrical devices such as the lights, instruments, etc (which are covered in Chapter 12). On petrol engine models refer to Part B for information on the ignition system, and on diesel models refer to Part C for information on the preheating system.

The electrical system is of the 12-volt negative earth type.

The battery is of the low maintenance or 'maintenance-free' (sealed for life) type and is charged by the alternator, which is belt-driven from the crankshaft pulley.

The starter motor is of the pre-engaged type incorporating an integral solenoid. On starting, the solenoid moves the drive pinion into engagement with the flywheel ring gear before the starter motor is energised. Once the engine has started, a one-way clutch prevents the motor armature being driven by the engine until the pinion disengages from the flywheel.

Precautions

Further details of the various systems are given in the relevant Sections of this Chapter. While some repair procedures are given, the usual course of action is to renew the component concerned. The owner whose

interest extends beyond mere component renewal should obtain a copy of the *Automobile Electrical & Electronic Systems Manual*, available from the publishers of this manual.

It is necessary to take extra care when working on the electrical system to avoid damage to semi-conductor devices (diodes and transistors), and to avoid the risk of personal injury. In addition to the precautions given in *Safety first!* at the beginning of this manual, observe the following when working on the system:

Always remove rings, watches, etc before working on the electrical system. Even with the battery disconnected, capacitive discharge could occur if a component's live terminal is earthed through a metal object. This could cause a shock or nasty burn.

Do not reverse the battery connections. Components such as the alternator, electronic control units, or any other components having semi-conductor circuitry could be irreparably damaged.

If the engine is being started using jump leads and a slave battery, connect the batteries positive-to-positive and negative-to-negative (see Jump starting). This also applies when connecting a battery charger.

Never disconnect the battery terminals, the alternator, any electrical wiring or any test instruments when the engine is running.

Do not allow the engine to turn the alternator when the alternator is not connected.

Never test for alternator output by 'flashing' the output lead to earth.

Never use an ohmmeter of the type incorporating a hand-cranked generator for circuit or continuity testing.

Always ensure that the battery negative lead is disconnected when working on the electrical system.

Before using electric-arc welding equipment on the car, disconnect the battery, alternator and components such as the fuel injection/ignition electronic control unit to protect them from the risk of damage.

Several systems fitted to the vehicle require battery power to be available at all times, either to ensure their continued operation (such as the clock) or to maintain security codes which would be wiped if the battery were to be disconnected. To ensure that there are no unforeseen consequences of this action, Refer to Disconnecting the battery in the Reference Section of this manual for further information.

2 Electrical fault finding - general information

Refer to Chapter 12.

3 Battery - testing and charging

Standard and low maintenance battery - testing

1 If the vehicle covers a small annual mileage, it is worthwhile checking the specific gravity of the electrolyte every three months, to determine the state of charge of the battery. Use a hydrometer to make the check, and compare the results with the following table. The temperatures quoted in the table are ambient (air) temperatures. Note that the specific gravity readings assume an electrolyte temperature of 15°C (60°F); for every 10°C (18°F) below 15°C (60°F), subtract 0.007. For every 10°C (18°F) above 15°C (60°F), add 0.007.

	Above 25°C (77°F)	Below 25°C (77°F)
Fully-charged	1.210 to 1.230	1.270 to 1.290
70% charged	1.170 to 1.190	1.230 to 1.250
Discharged	1.050 to 1.070	1.110 to 1.130

2 If the battery condition is suspect, first check the specific gravity of electrolyte in each cell. A variation of 0.040 or more between any cells indicates loss of electrolyte or deterioration of the internal plates.

3 If the specific gravity variation is 0.040 or more, the battery should be renewed. If the cell variation is satisfactory but the battery is discharged, it should be charged as described later in this Section.

Maintenance-free battery - testing

4 In cases where a 'sealed for life' maintenance-free battery is fitted, topping-up and testing of the electrolyte in each cell is not possible. The condition of the battery can therefore only be tested using a battery condition indicator or a voltmeter.

5 Certain models my be fitted with a Delco type maintenance-free battery, with a built-in charge condition indicator. The indicator is located in the top of the battery casing, and indicates the condition of the battery from its colour. If the indicator shows green, then the battery is in a good state of charge. If the indicator turns darker, eventually to black, then the battery requires charging, as described later in this Section. If the indicator shows clear/yellow, then the electrolyte level in the battery is too low to allow further use, and the battery should be renewed. **Do not** attempt to charge, load or jump start a battery when the indicator shows clear/yellow.

6 If testing the battery using a voltmeter, connect the voltmeter across the battery and compare the result with those given in the *Specifications* under 'charge condition'. The test is only accurate if the battery has not been subjected to any kind of charge for the previous six hours. If this is not the case, switch on the headlights for 30 seconds, then wait four to five minutes before testing the battery after switching off the headlights. All other electrical circuits must be switched off, so check that the doors and tailgate are fully shut when making the test.

7 If the voltage reading is less than 12.2 volts, then the battery is discharged, whilst a reading of 12.2 to 12.4 volts indicates a partially discharged condition.

8 If the battery is to be charged, remove it from the vehicle (Section 4) and charge it as described later in this Section.

Standard and low maintenance battery - charging

Note: *The following is intended as a guide only. Always refer to the manufacturer's recommendations (often printed on a label attached to the battery) before charging a battery.*

9 Charge the battery at a rate of 3.5 to 4 amps and continue to charge the battery at this rate until no further rise in specific gravity is noted over a four hour period.

10 Alternatively, a trickle charger charging at the rate of 1.5 amps can safely be used overnight.

11 Specially rapid 'boost' charges which are claimed to restore the power of the battery in 1 to 2 hours are not recommended, as they can cause serious damage to the battery plates through overheating.

12 While charging the battery, note that the temperature of the electrolyte should never exceed 37.8°C (100°F).

Maintenance-free battery - charging

Note: *The following is intended as a guide only. Always refer to the manufacturer's recommendations (often printed on a label attached to the battery) before charging a battery.*

13 This battery type takes considerably longer to fully recharge than the standard type, the time taken being dependent on the extent of discharge, but it can take anything up to three days.

14 A constant voltage type charger is required, to be set to 13.9 to 14.9 volts with a charger current below 25 amps. Using this method, the battery should be usable within three hours, giving a voltage reading of 12.5 volts, but this is for a partially discharged battery and, as mentioned, full charging can take considerably longer.

15 If the battery is to be charged from a fully discharged state (condition reading less than 12.2 volts), have it recharged by your Renault dealer or local automotive electrician, as the charge rate is higher and constant supervision during charging is necessary.

4 Battery - removal and refitting

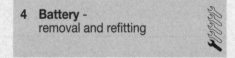

Note: *Refer to Disconnecting the battery in the Reference Section of this manual before proceeding.*

Removal

1 The battery is located on the left-hand side of the engine compartment.

2 Unscrew the large terminal nut and disconnect the clamp from the battery negative (earth) terminal.

3 Slacken the terminal nut and disconnect the positive terminal lead(s) in the same way.

4 Unscrew the nut/bolts (as applicable) and remove battery retaining clamp. On certain automatic transmission models it will be necessary to unclip the transmission ECU from the front of the battery to gain access to the clamp.

4.6 Removing the battery insulator plate (diesel model shown)

5 Lift the battery out of the engine compartment.

6 If necessary, unclip and remove the battery tray and unbolt and remove the insulator plate **(see illustration).**

Refitting

7 Refitting is a reversal of removal, but smear petroleum jelly on the terminals when reconnecting the leads, and always reconnect the positive lead first, and the negative lead last.

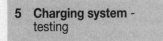

5 Charging system - testing

Note: *Refer to the warnings given in Safety first! and in Section 1 of this Chapter before starting work.*

1 If the ignition warning light fails to illuminate when the ignition is switched on, first check the alternator wiring connections for security. If satisfactory, check that the warning light bulb has not blown, and that the bulbholder is secure in its location in the instrument panel. If the light still fails to illuminate, check the continuity of the warning light feed wire from the alternator to the bulbholder. If all is satisfactory, the alternator is at fault and should be renewed or taken to an auto-electrician for testing and repair.

2 If the ignition warning light illuminates when the engine is running, stop the engine and check that the auxiliary drivebelt is correctly tensioned (see the relevant part of Chapter 1) and that the alternator connections are secure. If all is so far satisfactory, have the alternator checked by an auto-electrician for testing and repair.

3 If the alternator output is suspect even though the warning light functions correctly, the regulated voltage may be checked as follows.

4 Connect a voltmeter across the battery terminals and start the engine.

5 Increase the engine speed until the voltmeter reading remains steady; the reading should be approximately 12 to 13 volts, and no more than 14 volts.

6 Switch on as many electrical accessories (eg, the headlights, heated rear window and heater blower) as possible, and check that the alternator maintains the regulated voltage at around 13 to 14 volts.

7 If the regulated voltage is not as stated, the fault may be due to worn brushes, weak brush springs, a faulty voltage regulator, a faulty diode, a severed phase winding or worn or damaged slip rings. The alternator should be renewed or taken to an auto-electrician for testing and repair.

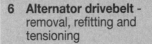

6 Alternator drivebelt - removal, refitting and tensioning

Refer to the procedure given for the auxiliary drivebelt in the relevant part of Chapter 1.

7 Alternator - removal and refitting

Removal

1 Disconnect the battery negative terminal (refer to *Disconnecting the battery* in the Reference Section of this manual).

2 Remove the auxiliary drivebelt as described in the relevant part of Chapter 1.

1.8 and 2.0 litre (8-valve) petrol engine models

3 Remove the rubber covers (where fitted) from the alternator terminals, then unscrew the retaining nuts and disconnect the wiring from the rear of the alternator.

4 On models with a manually-adjusted drivebelt, slacken and remove the bolt/nut and bolt securing the alternator to the threaded adjuster.

5 On models with a automatically-adjusted drivebelt, slacken and remove the alternator front mounting bolt.

6 On all models, unscrew the nut and through-bolt securing the alternator to the mounting bracket and remove the alternator from the engine compartment.

1.6 litre (16-valve) petrol engine models

7 On models equipped with air conditioning, release the power steering fluid reservoir from its location and move it to one side.

8 Remove the rubber covers (where fitted) from the alternator terminals, then unscrew the retaining nuts and disconnect the wiring from the rear of the alternator.

9 Undo the three bolts securing the alternator to the auxiliary components mounting bracket and withdraw the alternator from the engine.

1.8 litre (16-valve) petrol engine models

10 On models equipped with air conditioning, release the power steering fluid reservoir from its location and move it to one side. Referring to the procedures contained in Chapter 10, Section 21, remove the power steering pump pulley then, release the pump from its mountings and move it to one side without disconnecting the fluid pipe connections. It may be necessary to release the fluid pipes from their mounting brackets to enable the pump to be moved clear. With the pumped removed, unbolt the pump mounting bracket for access to the alternator.

11 Remove the rubber covers (where fitted) from the alternator terminals, then unscrew the retaining nuts and disconnect the wiring from the rear of the alternator.

12 Undo the alternator mounting bolts and withdraw the alternator from the engine.

2.0 litre (16-valve) petrol engine models

13 On models equipped with air conditioning, remove the power steering pump as described in Chapter 10.

14 Undo the bolts and remove the support bracket at the rear of the alternator and power steering pump location.

15 Apply the handbrake, then jack up the front of the car and support it on axle stands (see *Jacking and vehicle support*).

16 On models without air conditioning, remove the oil filter with reference to Chapter 1A.

17 Remove the rubber covers (where fitted) from the alternator terminals, then unscrew the retaining nuts and disconnect the wiring from the rear of the alternator.

18 Undo the alternator upper mounting through bolt and nut, and the lower rear bolt, then withdraw the alternator from its location.

1.9 litre diesel engine models

19 With the auxiliary drivebelt removed, undo the two drivebelt tensioner mounting plate bolts.

20 Remove the rubber covers (where fitted) from the alternator terminals, then unscrew the retaining nuts and disconnect the wiring from the rear of the alternator.

21 Undo the alternator mounting bolts and withdraw the alternator from the engine.

Diesel engine models

22 Although not strictly necessary, to improve access to the alternator remove the right-hand driveshaft as described in Chapter 8.

23 Undo the retaining nut and bolt and remove the exhaust manifold support bracket.

24 Remove the rubber covers (where fitted) from the alternator terminals, then unscrew the retaining nuts and disconnect the wiring from the rear of the alternator.

25 Slacken and remove the lower mounting bolt then unscrew the retaining nut and withdraw the upper mounting through-bolt.

26 Manoeuvre the alternator away from its mounting bracket and out from the engine compartment.

Refitting

27 Refitting is a reversal of removal, fitting a new drivebelt and tensioning it as described in the relevant part of Chapter 1.

5A

8 Alternator - testing and overhaul

If the alternator is thought to be suspect, it should be removed from the vehicle and taken to an auto-electrician for testing. Most auto-electricians will be able to supply and fit brushes at a reasonable cost. However, check on the cost of repairs before proceeding as it may prove more economical to obtain a new or exchange alternator.

9 Starting system - testing

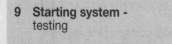

Note: *Refer to the precautions given in Safety first! and in Section 1 of this Chapter before starting work.*

1 If the starter motor fails to operate when the ignition key is turned to the appropriate position, the following possible causes may be to blame.
  a) *The battery is faulty.*
  b) *The electrical connections between the switch, solenoid, battery and starter motor are somewhere failing to pass the necessary current from the battery through the starter to earth.*
  c) *The solenoid is faulty.*
  d) *The starter motor is mechanically or electrically defective.*

2 To check the battery, switch on the headlights. If they dim after a few seconds, this indicates that the battery is discharged - recharge (see Section 3) or renew the battery.

If the headlights glow brightly, operate the ignition switch and observe the lights. If they dim, then this indicates that current is reaching the starter motor, therefore the fault must lie in the starter motor. If the lights continue to glow brightly (and no clicking sound can be heard from the starter motor solenoid), this indicates that there is a fault in the circuit or solenoid - see following paragraphs. If the starter motor turns slowly when operated, but the battery is in good condition, then this indicates that either the starter motor is faulty, or there is considerable resistance somewhere in the circuit.

3 If a fault in the circuit is suspected, disconnect the battery leads (including the earth connection to the body), the starter/solenoid wiring and the engine/transmission earth strap. Thoroughly clean the connections, and reconnect the leads and wiring, then use a voltmeter or test lamp to check that full battery voltage is available at the battery positive lead connection to the solenoid, and that the earth is sound. Smear petroleum jelly around the battery terminals to prevent corrosion - corroded connections are amongst the most frequent causes of electrical system faults.

4 If the battery and all connections are in good condition, check the circuit by disconnecting the wire from the solenoid blade terminal. Connect a voltmeter or test lamp between the wire end and a good earth (such as the battery negative terminal), and check that the wire is live when the ignition switch is turned to the 'start' position. If it is, then the circuit is sound - if not the circuit wiring can be checked as described in Chapter 12.

5 The solenoid contacts can be checked by connecting a voltmeter or test lamp between the battery positive feed connection on the starter side of the solenoid, and earth. When the ignition switch is turned to the 'start' position, there should be a reading or lighted bulb, as applicable. If there is no reading or lighted bulb, the solenoid is faulty and should be renewed.

6 If the circuit and solenoid are proved sound, the fault must lie in the starter motor. In this event, it may be possible to have the starter motor overhauled by a specialist, but check on the cost of spares before proceeding, as it may prove more economical to obtain a new or exchange motor.

10 Starter motor - removal and refitting

Removal

1 Disconnect the battery negative terminal (refer to *Disconnecting the battery* in the Reference Section of this manual).

1.8 and 2.0 litre (8-valve) petrol engine models

2 Remove the air cleaner assembly and inlet ducts as described in Chapter 4A.

3 Slacken and remove the three bolts securing the starter motor to the transmission housing.

4 Firmly apply the handbrake then jack up the front of the vehicle and support it on axle stands (see *Jacking and vehicle support*). To improve access, undo the retaining screws and remove the plastic undercover.

5 Unbolt and remove the support bracket which is situated at the rear of the starter motor.

6 Slacken and remove the two retaining nuts and disconnect the wiring from the starter motor solenoid. Recover the washers under the nuts.

7 Undo the bolt(s) securing the starter motor rear mounting bracket to the cylinder block then remove the motor downwards and out of position, noting the locating dowel which is fitted to the rear mounting bolt hole **(see illustration)**.

1.6 and 1.8 litre (16-valve) petrol engine models

8 Remove the air cleaner assembly and inlet ducts as described in Chapter 4A.

9 Remove the right-hand driveshaft as described in Chapter 8.

10 Slacken and remove the two retaining nuts and disconnect the wiring from the starter motor solenoid. Recover the washers under the nuts. Disconnect any adjacent wiring connectors to allow the wiring loom to be moved clear of the starter motor as necessary.

11 Undo the starter motor mounting bolts then remove the motor downwards and out of position, noting the position of the locating dowel.

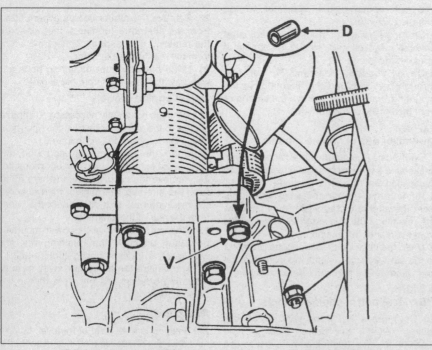

10.7 Locating dowel (D) location on the starter motor bolt hole (V)

2.0 litre
(16-valve) petrol engine models

12 Remove the air cleaner assembly and inlet ducts as described in Chapter 4A.

13 Slacken and remove the two retaining nuts and disconnect the wiring from the starter motor solenoid. Recover the washers under the nuts.

14 Slacken and remove the three bolts securing the starter motor to the transmission housing.

15 Remove the motor upwards and out of position, noting the locating dowel which is fitted to the rear mounting bolt hole.

1.9 litre diesel engine models

16 Remove the air cleaner assembly and inlet ducts as described in Chapter 4B.

17 Remove the exhaust front pipe as described in Chapter 4B.

18 Remove the right-hand driveshaft as described in Chapter 8.

19 Undo the two nuts and disconnect the turbocharger oil return pipe from the cylinder block. Recover the gasket. Plug the hole in the cylinder block to prevent dirt ingress.

20 Slacken and remove the two retaining nuts and disconnect the wiring from the starter motor solenoid. Recover the washers under the nuts.

21 Undo the starter motor mounting bolts then remove the motor downwards and out of position, noting the position of the locating dowel.

2.2 litre diesel engine models

22 Remove the air cleaner assembly and inlet ducts as described in Chapter 4B.

23 Undo the retaining screws and nut and remove the protective cover from the starter motor **(see illustration)**. Where necessary, withdraw the engine oil dipstick to improve access to the cover and release the coolant hoses and wiring loom from their retaining clips.

10.23 Unbolt and remove the protective cover from over the starter motor - 2.2 litre diesel engine models

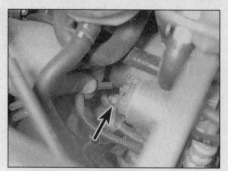

10.24 Disconnect the wiring connector from the solenoid then undo the nut (arrowed) and disconnect the main cable - 2.2 litre diesel engine models

24 Disconnect the wiring connector from the starter solenoid then undo the retaining nut and disconnect the main feed cable the solenoid. Recover the washer under the nut **(see illustration)**.

25 Undo the retaining nuts and bolts and remove the rear mounting bracket from the starter motor **(see illustration)**.

26 Slacken and remove the three bolts securing the starter motor to the transmission housing and remove the motor from the engine compartment **(see illustration)**. Recover the locating dowel which is fitted to the rear mounting bolt hole.

Refitting

27 Refitting is a reversal of removal, ensuring that the locating dowel is correctly positioned.

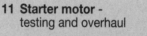

11 Starter motor -
testing and overhaul

If the starter motor is thought to be suspect, it should be removed from the vehicle and taken to an auto-electrician for testing. Most auto-electricians will be able to supply and fit brushes at a reasonable cost. However, check on the cost of repairs before proceeding as it may prove more economical to obtain a new or exchange motor.

12 Ignition switch -
removal and refitting

The ignition switch is integral with the steering column lock, and can be removed as described in Chapter 10.

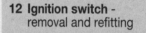

13 Oil pressure
warning light switch -
removal and refitting

Removal

1 The switch is located at the front of the cylinder block. On petrol engine models the switch is on the right-hand end of the cylinder block. On diesel engine models the switch is

10.25 Remove the rear mounting bracket . . .

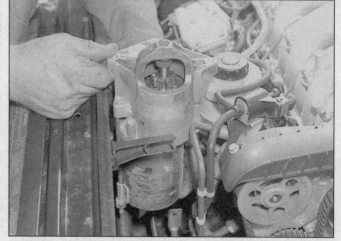

10.26 . . . then undo the front mounting bolts and remove the starter motor from the engine compartment - 2.2 litre diesel engine models

13.1 Oil pressure switch (arrowed) is situated at the rear of the injection pump - 2.2 litre diesel engine models

14.5 Removing the oil level sensor - 2.2 litre diesel engine models

located in the centre of the cylinder block and access is poor; to improve access remove the starter motor **(see illustration)**.

2 Disconnect the battery negative terminal (refer to *Disconnecting the battery* in the Reference Section of this manual).

3 Depress the retaining tabs and disconnect the wiring from the switch.

4 Unscrew the switch from the cylinder block, and recover the sealing washer. Be prepared for oil spillage, and if the switch is to be left removed from the engine for any length of time, plug the hole in the cylinder block.

Refitting

5 Examine the sealing washer for damage or deterioration and if necessary renew.

6 Refit the switch, complete with washer, and tighten it securely. Reconnect the wiring connector.

7 If necessary, top-up the engine oil as described in *Weekly checks*.

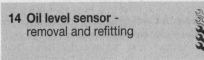

14 Oil level sensor - removal and refitting

Removal

1 The sensor is located on the front side of the cylinder block.

2 To gain access to the sensor, firmly apply the handbrake then jack up the front of the vehicle and support it on axle stands (see *Jacking and vehicle support*). Undo the retaining screws and remove the plastic under cover from beneath the engine/transmission.

3 Disconnect the wiring connector from the oil level sensor.

4 On petrol engine models, unscrew the sensor and withdraw it from the block.

5 On diesel engine models, undo the retaining bolts and carefully withdraw the sensor from the block **(see illustration)**. Recover the sensor sealing ring and discard it, a new one should be used on refitting.

Refitting

6 Refitting is the reverse of removal. On petrol engine models apply a smear of sealant to the threads of the sensor prior to refitting and on diesel engine models using a new sensor sealing ring.

Chapter 5 Part B:
Ignition system - petrol engine models

Contents

Degrees of difficulty

Easy, suitable for novice with little experience	Fairly easy, suitable for beginner with some experience	Fairly difficult, suitable for competent DIY mechanic	Difficult, suitable for experienced DIY mechanic	Very difficult, suitable for expert DIY or professional

Specifications

System type

1.8 and 2.0 litre (8-valve) engines:

Single-point injection, and early multi-point injection models ...... Electronic ignition system controlled by engine management ECU
Later multi-point injection models .... Static (distributorless) ignition system controlled by engine management ECU

1.6 and 1.8 litre (16-valve) engines .... Modular ignition system controlled by engine management ECU
2.0 litre (16-valve) engines .... Static (distributorless) ignition system controlled by engine management ECU

Firing order:

All engines except 2.0 litre (16-valve) .... 1-3-4-2 (No 1 cylinder at flywheel end of engine)
2.0 litre (16-valve) engines .... 1-3-4-2 (No 1 cylinder at timing belt end of engine)

Ignition system data

Ignition timing .... Controlled by the ECU - see text
Ignition HT coil resistances:
  1.8 and 2.0 litre (8-valve) engines:*
    Primary windings .... 1.5 ohms
    Secondary windings .... 6.5 k ohms
  1.6 and 1.8 litre (16-valve engines):
    Primary windings .... 0.5 ohms
    Secondary windings .... 7.5 k ohms
  2.0 litre (16-valve) engines:*
    Primary windings .... 1.5 ohms
    Secondary windings .... 6.5 k ohms

*These are suggested figures, typical for the coils used on these engines - no exact values are quoted by Renault

1 Ignition system - general information and precautions

The ignition system is integrated with the fuel injection system to form a combined engine management system under the control of one ECU (See Chapter 4A for further information). Depending on model, there are three possible types of ignition system.

Models with a distributor - early 1.8 and 2.0 litre (8-valve) engines

On models with a distributor, the ignition system comprises the amplifier unit, the HT coil, and the distributor (see illustration).

Depending on the information received from its various sensors, the ECU calculates the relevant ignition advance/coil charge time required for the engine speed and load. The ECU switches the amplifier unit to operate the ignition coil primary (LT) circuit. This causes a high voltage to be induced in the coil secondary (HT) windings which then travels down the HT lead to the distributor and onto the relevant spark plug. The distributor is driven off the left-hand end of the camshaft.

Static (distributorless) ignition system - later 1.8 and 2.0 litre (8-valve), and all 2.0 litre (16-valve) engines

On models with a static (distributorless) ignition system, the ignition system consists simply of a pair of two output ignition coils. Each coil supplies two cylinders (one coil

1.2 Ignition system HT coil and amplifier unit - models with a distributor

supplies cylinders 1 and 4, and the other cylinders 2 and 3). Under the control of the ECU, the ignition coil operates on the 'wasted spark' principle, ie. each spark plug sparks twice for every cycle of the engine, once on the compression stroke and once on the exhaust stroke. The ECU uses its inputs from various sensors to calculate the required ignition advance setting, and coil charging time.

Modular ignition system - 1.6 and 1.8 litre (16-valve) engines

On models with a modular ignition system, the ignition system consists of four individual 'pencil' type ignition coil modules, one for each cylinder, and fitted to the top of each spark plug. The engine management ECU uses its inputs from various sensors to calculate the ignition firing point for each ignition coil (and associated spark plug), the required ignition advance setting, and the coil charging time.

2 Ignition system - testing

⚠ **Warning: Voltages produced by an electronic ignition system are considerably higher than those produced by conventional ignition systems. Extreme care must be taken when working on the system with the ignition switched on. Persons with surgically-implanted cardiac pacemaker devices should keep well clear of the ignition circuits, components and test equipment.**

Models with a distributor

⚠ **Warning: Refer to the warning given in Section 1 of Part A of this Chapter before starting work. Always switch off the ignition before disconnecting or connecting any component and when using a multi-meter to check resistances.**

1 The components of electronic ignition systems are normally very reliable; most faults are far more likely to be due to loose or dirty connections or to 'tracking' of HT voltage due to dirt, dampness or damaged insulation than

to the failure of any components. **Always** check all wiring thoroughly before condemning an electrical component. Work methodically to eliminate all other possibilities before deciding that a particular component is faulty.

2 The old practice of checking for a spark by holding the live end of an HT lead a short distance away from the engine is not recommended; not only is there a high risk of a powerful electric shock, but the HT coil or ECU will be damaged. Similarly, **never** try to 'diagnose' misfires by pulling off one HT lead at a time.

Engine will not start

3 If the engine either will not turn over at all, or only turns very slowly, check the battery and starter motor as described in Chapter 5A.

4 If the engine turns over at normal speed but will not start, check the HT circuit by connecting a timing light (following the manufacturer's instructions) and turning the engine over on the starter motor; if the light flashes, voltage is reaching the spark plugs, so these should be checked first. If the light does not flash, check the HT leads themselves followed by the distributor cap, carbon brush and rotor arm using the information given in Chapter 1A, Section 17.

5 If there is still no spark, check the coil's primary and secondary winding resistance as described later in this Section; renew the coil if faulty, but be careful to check carefully the condition of the LT connections themselves before doing so, to ensure that the fault is not due to dirty or poorly-fastened connectors.

6 If these checks fail to reveal the cause of the problem the vehicle should be taken to a suitably equipped Renault dealer for testing. A wiring block connector is incorporated in the engine management circuit into which a special electronic diagnostic tester can be plugged. The tester will locate the fault quickly and simply alleviating the need to test all the system components individually which is a time consuming operation that carries a high risk of damaging the ECU. If necessary, the system wiring and wiring connectors can be checked as described in Chapter 12 ensuring that the ECU wiring connector(s) have first been disconnected.

Engine misfires

7 An irregular misfire suggests a loose connection or intermittent fault on the primary circuit, or an HT fault on the coil side of the rotor arm.

8 With the ignition switched off, check carefully through the system ensuring that all connections are clean and securely fastened. If the equipment is available, check the LT circuit as described above.

9 Check that the HT coil, the distributor cap and the HT leads are clean and dry. Check the leads themselves and the spark plugs (by substitution, if necessary), then check the distributor cap, carbon brush and rotor arm as described in Chapter 1A, Section 17.

10 Regular misfiring is likely due to a fault in the distributor cap, HT leads or spark plugs. Use a timing light (as described above) to check whether HT voltage is present at all leads.

11 If HT voltage is not present on any particular lead, the fault will be in that lead or in the distributor cap. If HT is present on all leads, the fault will be in the spark plugs; check and renew them if there is any doubt about their condition.

12 If no HT is present, check the HT coil; its secondary windings may be breaking down under load.

Static (distributorless) ignition system and modular ignition system

13 Check the ignition system as described in paragraphs 3 to 6, ignoring the references to the distributor cap and rotor arm.

3 Ignition HT coil - removal, testing and refitting

Removal

Models with a distributor

1 The ignition HT coil is bolted onto the front of the amplifier unit which is mounted onto the right hand side of the engine compartment bulkhead.

2 Disconnect the battery negative terminal (refer to *Disconnecting the battery* in the Reference Section of this manual), then disconnect the HT leads from the coil.

3 Slacken and remove the coil retaining bolts and carefully remove the coil from the amplifier unit.

Static (distributorless) ignition system

4 Disconnect the battery negative terminal (refer to *Disconnecting the battery* in the Reference Section of this manual).

5 On 2.0 litre (16-valve) engines, remove the plastic cover from the top of the engine.

6 Undo the retaining bolts and withdraw the coil from its mounting **(see illustration)**.

7 Disconnect the LT wiring connector and the HT leads and remove the coil **(see illustration)**.

3.6 Undo the retaining bolts and withdraw the coil from its mounting - static (distributorless) system

3.7 Disconnect the LT wiring connector and the HT leads and remove the coil - static (distributorless) system

Modular ignition system

8 Disconnect the battery negative terminal (refer to *Disconnecting the battery* in the Reference Section of this manual).
9 Disconnect the wiring connector at the relevant ignition coil.
10 Undo the mounting bolt and remove the relevant ignition coil from the spark plug and cylinder head upper section **(see illustration)**.

Testing

11 Testing of the coil consists of using a multimeter set to its resistance function, to check the primary (LT '+' to '-' terminals) and secondary (LT '+' to HT lead terminal) windings for continuity. Compare the results obtained to those given in the *Specifications* at the start of this Chapter. Note the resistance of the coil windings will vary slightly according to the coil temperature, the results in the *Specifications* for certain engines are approximate values only since no exact figures are quoted by Renault.
12 Check that there is no continuity between the HT lead terminal and the coil body/ mounting bracket.
13 If the coil is thought to be faulty, have your findings confirmed by a Renault dealer before renewing the coil.

Refitting

14 Refitting is a reversal of the relevant removal procedure ensuring that the wiring connectors and/or HT leads are correctly and securely connected.

4 Distributor - removal and refitting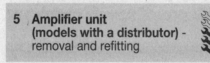

Removal

1 Slacken the distributor cap retaining screws and free the cap and cover assembly from the end of the cylinder head.
2 Remove the rotor arm from the end of the camshaft and remove the plastic shield.
3 If the cap is to be removed, ensure that the HT leads are marked with the relevant cylinder number then carefully disconnect the HT leads from the spark plugs and remove the cap and leads as an assembly.

Refitting

4 Refitting is the reverse of removal. If the distributor cap is to be renewed, transfer the HT leads one by one to the new cap to ensure that they are correctly positioned.

5 Amplifier unit (models with a distributor) - removal and refitting

Removal

1 Disconnect the battery negative terminal (refer to *Disconnecting the battery* in the Reference Section of this manual).
2 Disconnect the HT lead from the ignition coil then disconnect the wiring connectors from the amplifier unit.
3 Slacken and remove the nuts and remove the amplifier unit from its mounting studs on the

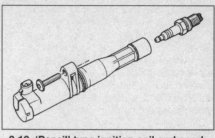

3.10 'Pencil' type ignition coil and spark plug arrangement - modular ignition system

engine compartment bulkhead. If necessary undo the retaining bolts and separate the ignition coil and amplifier unit (see Section 3).

Refitting

4 Refitting is the reverse of removal.

6 Ignition timing - checking and adjustment

The ignition timing is constantly being monitored and adjusted by the engine management ECU, and it is not possible for the home mechanic to check the ignition timing.

The only way in which the ignition timing can be checked is using special electronic test equipment, connected to the engine management system diagnostic connector (refer to Chapter 4A, Section 13 for further information). No adjustment of the ignition timing is possible. Should the ignition timing be incorrect, then a fault must be present in the engine management system.

5B

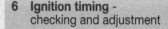

Chapter 5 Part C:
Pre-heating system - diesel engine models

Contents

Degrees of difficulty

Easy, suitable for novice with little experience	**Fairly easy,** suitable for beginner with some experience	**Fairly difficult,** suitable for competent DIY mechanic	**Difficult,** suitable for experienced DIY mechanic	**Very difficult,** suitable for expert DIY or professional

Specifications

Glow plugs	Bosch 0 250 202 025	
Torque wrench setting	**Nm**	**lbf ft**
Glow plugs	15	11

1 Pre/post heating system - description and testing

Description

1 Each swirl chamber has a heater plug (commonly called a glow plug) screwed into it. The plugs are electrically-operated before and during start-up when the engine is cold. According to engine, the glow plugs also operate after the engine has been started as described in the following sub-Sections.

1.9 litre engines

2 The pre-heating/post-heating system is controlled by the injection ECU located at the right-hand front of the engine compartment.
3 Pre-heating takes place in two phases. The first phase, during which time the warning light on the instrument panel is lit and there is a supply of current to the glow plugs, depends on coolant temperature. (If the coolant temperature sensor is faulty, the plugs are supplied with current automatically for 14 seconds). The second phase, after the warning light goes out, continues the current supply to the glow plugs for 8 seconds or until the engine is started. The glow plugs are supplied with current continuously whilst the starter motor is in action, but for no more than 20 seconds and only if the coolant temperature is below 60° C.
4 During the post-heating phase, after start-up, the supply of current to the glow plugs depends on coolant temperature and engine speed. Post-heating stops temporarily if engine speed exceeds 2500 rpm, and permanently when the coolant temperature exceeds a certain value.

2.2 litre non-turbo engines

5 The glow plugs provide a post-heating function, whereby the glow plugs remain switched on for a period after the engine has started. Once the starter has been switched the glow plugs begin a timed 210 second 'post-heating' cycle. The operation of the plugs cannot be cancelled for the first 10 seconds, but after the first 10 seconds, the supply to the plugs will be interrupted by:
a) Operation of the accelerator pedal beyond a travel of 14 mm (measured by the post-heating microswitch on the injection pump) for a duration of more than 3 seconds.
b) A coolant temperature of more than 70°C. If the coolant temperature sender is faulty, the post-heating will take place for the full 210 second period.
6 A warning light in the instrument panel tells the driver that pre-heating is taking place. When the light goes out, the engine is ready to start. The voltage supply to the glow plugs continues for a few seconds after the light goes out. If no attempt is made to start, the timer cuts off the supply, to avoid draining the battery and overheating the glow plugs.

2.2 litre turbo engines

7 The pre-heating/post-heating system is controlled by the same ECU which controls injection cold start fuel metering, fast idle and EGR.
8 Pre-heating takes place in two phases. The first phase, during which time the warning light on the instrument panel is lit and there is a supply of current to the glow plugs, depends on coolant temperature and altitude. (The control unit contains an altitude sensor). The second phase, after the warning light

goes out, continues the current supply to the glow plugs for 8 seconds or until the engine is started. The glow plugs are supplied with current continuously whilst the starter motor is in action.
9 Post-heating also takes place in two phases. In the first phase, after starting, all the glow plugs receive current for 10 seconds. In the second phase, the supply of current is determined by coolant temperature and by engine speed and load. Post-heating is temporarily interrupted if the control unit receives a '60% load' signal from the accelerator lever potentiometer on the injection pump; it will resume if the load reduces again. An excessive voltage supply (over 16V) will also cause post-heating to be interrupted. Post-heating stops altogether when the coolant temperature reaches 60° C or after 190 seconds, whichever comes first.

Testing

10 If the system malfunctions, testing is ultimately by substitution of known good units, but some preliminary checks may be made as follows.
11 Connect a voltmeter or 12-volt test lamp between the glow plug supply cable and earth (engine or vehicle metal). Make sure that the live connection is kept clear of the engine and bodywork.
12 Have an assistant switch on the ignition, and check that voltage is applied to the glow plugs. Note the time for which the warning light is lit, and the total time for which voltage is applied before the system cuts out. Switch off the ignition.
13 In general, at an under-bonnet temperature of 20°C, the warning light should operate for approximately 2 seconds,

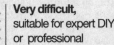
5C

2.3 Removing a glow plug

**3.1 Pre-heating control unit
(shown with headlight removed)**

followed by a further 8 seconds supply after the light goes out. Warning light time will increase with lower temperatures and decrease with higher temperatures.

14 If there is no supply at all, the relay, ECU or associated wiring is at fault.

15 To locate a defective glow plug, disconnect the main supply cable and the interconnecting wire or strap from the top of the glow plugs. Be careful not to drop the nuts and washers. On some engines, access to the glow plugs is poor, to improve access remove the inlet manifold as described in Chapter 4B.

16 Use a continuity tester, or a 12-volt test lamp connected to the battery positive terminal, to check for continuity between each glow plug terminal and earth. The resistance of a glow plug in good condition is very low (less than 1 ohm), so if the test lamp does not light or the continuity tester shows a high resistance, the glow plug is certainly defective.

17 If an ammeter is available, the current draw of each glow plug can be checked. After an initial surge of 15 to 20 amps, each plug should draw 12 amps. Any plug which draws much more or less than this is probably defective.

18 As a final check, the glow plugs can be removed and inspected as described in the following Section.

2 Glow plugs - removal, inspection and refitting

Removal

Caution: If the pre-heating system has just been energised, or if the engine has been running, the glow plugs will be very hot.

1 Disconnect the battery negative terminal (refer to *Disconnecting the battery* in the Reference Section of this manual). On 1.9 litre engines, unscrew the retaining nuts and withdraw the engine sound-insulating cover. On 2.2 litre engines, remove the inlet manifold as described in Chapter 4B.

2 Unscrew the nut from the relevant glow plug terminal(s), and recover the washer(s).

3 Unscrew the glow plug(s) and remove from the cylinder head **(see illustration)**.

Inspection

4 Inspect each glow plug for physical damage. Burnt or eroded glow plug tips can be caused by a bad injector spray pattern. Have the injectors checked if this sort of damage is found.

5 If the glow plugs are in good physical condition, check them electrically using a 12 volt test lamp or continuity tester as described in the previous Section.

6 The glow plugs can be energised by applying 12 volts to them to verify that they heat up evenly and in the required time. Observe the following precautions.

a) *Support the glow plug by clamping it carefully in a vice or self-locking pliers. Remember it will become red-hot.*

b) *Make sure that the power supply or test lead incorporates a fuse or overload trip to protect against damage from a short-circuit.*

c) *After testing, allow the glow plug to cool for several minutes before attempting to handle it.*

7 A glow plug in good condition will start to glow red at the tip after drawing current for 5

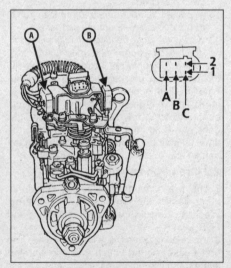

4.3 Injection pump microswitch and wiring connector details

A *Rear switch used on models without EGR*
B *Front switch used on models with EGR*

seconds or so. Any plug which takes much longer to start glowing, or which starts glowing in the middle instead of at the tip, is defective.

Refitting

8 Refit by reversing the removal operations. Apply a smear of copper-based anti-seize compound to the plug threads and tighten the glow plugs to the specified torque. Do not overtighten, as this can damage the glow plug element.

3 Pre-heating system control unit - removal and refitting

Removal

1 The unit is located on the right-hand side of the engine compartment where it is mounted behind the headlight **(see illustration)**.

2 Disconnect the battery negative terminal (refer to *Disconnecting the battery* in the Reference Section of this manual). To improve access to the unit on 2.2 litre engines, unscrew the retaining nuts and free the fuel filter housing from its mounting bracket.

3 Slacken and remove the retaining screws securing the unit to the body.

4 Disconnect the wiring connector from the base of the unit then unscrew the retaining nut and free the main feed wire from the unit. Remove the unit from the engine compartment.

Refitting

5 Refitting is a reversal of removal, ensuring that the wiring connectors are correctly connected.

4 Post-heating cut-out microswitch - testing, adjustment, removal and refitting

Note: *The post-heating cut-out microswitch is only fitted to 2.2 litre non-turbo engines.*

Testing and adjustment

1 Ensure that the idle speed and anti-stall settings are correctly adjusted as described in Chapter 1B.

2 To test and adjust the switch, first disconnect the switch wiring connector.

3 Connect a continuity tester or an ohmmeter across the switch wiring connector terminals of the injection pump connector **(see illustration)**. On models without an exhaust gas recirculation (EGR) system the rear switch is used and the tester should be connected across terminals B1 and C1, and on models with EGR the front switch is used and the tester should be connected across terminals B2 and C2.

4 Insert feeler blades of different thicknesses between the injection pump accelerator lever

and the anti-stall adjustment screw, and note the readings on the continuity tester or ohmmeter, as applicable **(see illustration)**. The readings obtained should be as follows.

Models without EGR

Spacer thickness	Test reading
Up to 13.1 mm	*Continuity/zero resistance*
Above 14.1 mm	*No continuity/infinite resistance*

Models with EGR

Spacer thickness	Test reading
Up to 11.7 mm	*Continuity/zero resistance*
Above 12.3 mm	*No continuity/infinite resistance*

5 To adjust the switch, bearing in mind the information in paragraph 3, slacken the switch retaining screws and repositioning the switch.
6 If the switch is permanently open or closed, renew it.

Removal

7 Disconnect the switch wiring connector, then remove the securing screws, and withdraw the switches from their brackets on the injection pump.

Refitting

8 Refitting is a reversal of removal. Adjust the switch as described above before tightening the retaining screws.

5 Fuel filter heating system - general information and component renewal

General information

1 An electrically-operated heating element is fitted between the fuel filter and filter housing, the heater is fitted to prevent the fuel 'waxing' at low temperatures. The heater is controlled by the temperature switch which is incorporated in the fuel filter feed hose union bolt **(see illustration)**. When the fuel temperature is below 0°C, the temperature switch supplies current to the heater which warms the fuel in the filter housing and filter. When the fuel temperature reaches 8°C, the temperature switch cuts off the supply to the heater.

Component renewal

Caution: Be careful not to allow dirt into the fuel system during the following procedures.

Fuel filter heating element

2 Disconnect the battery negative terminal (refer to *Disconnecting the battery* in the Reference Section of this manual) and remove the fuel filter as described in Chapter 1B. If the filter is damaged during removal, it must be renewed.
3 Disconnect the wiring connector then unscrew the centre bolt and remove the heating element from the base of the fuel filter

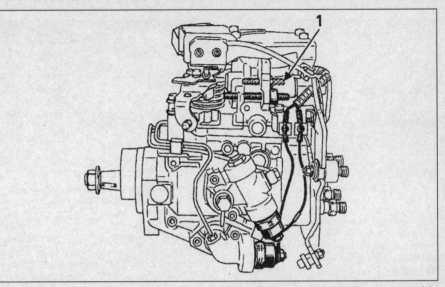

4.4 Insert a shim of the specified thickness between the anti-stall adjustment screw (1) and accelerator lever and adjust the microswitch as described in text

housing. Recover the sealing ring which is fitted between the element and filter housing and discard; a new one should be used on refitting.
4 On refitting, fit the new sealing ring to the groove in the heating element and refit the element to the filter housing, tightening the centre bolt securely.
5 Reconnect the wiring connector and fit the fuel filter as described in Chapter 1B.

Temperature switch

6 Disconnect the battery negative terminal (refer to *Disconnecting the battery* in the

Reference Section of this manual) then disconnect the wiring connector from the temperature switch.
7 Wipe clean the area around the temperature switch and fuel filter housing. Position a container to catch any spilt fuel then slacken and remove the switch from the fuel filter housing. Recover the sealing washers which are fitted on each side of the fuel hose union and discard them; new ones must be used on refitting.
8 Refitting is the reverse of removal, positioning a new sealing washer on each side of the fuel hose union.

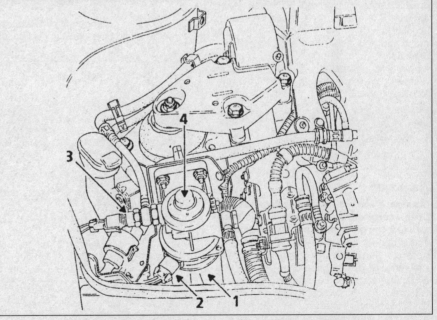

5.1 Fuel filter heating system components - 2.2 litre engine shown

1	*Fuel filter*	*3*	*Temperature switch*
2	*Heating element*	*4*	*Priming pump*

5C

Chapter 6
Clutch

Contents

Degrees of difficulty

Easy, suitable for novice with little experience	**Fairly easy,** suitable for beginner with some experience	**Fairly difficult,** suitable for competent DIY mechanic	**Difficult,** suitable for experienced DIY mechanic	**Very difficult,** suitable for expert DIY or professional

Specifications

General

Type	Single dry plate, with diaphragm spring and sealed ball release bearing in constant contact with diaphragm spring fingers.

Actuation:
All models except later 2.2 litre turbo diesel engines	Cable operated with semi-automatic wear compensator
Later 2.2 litre turbo diesel engines	Hydraulic with 'sealed-for-life' master and slave cylinder

Friction plate

Diameter:
1.8 and 2.0 litre (8-valve) petrol engines	200.0 mm
1.6 and 1.8 litre (16-valve) petrol engines	215.0 mm
2.0 litre (16-valve) petrol engines	220.0 mm
1.9 litre diesel engines	220.0 mm
2.2 litre non-turbo diesel engines	220.0 mm
2.2 litre turbo diesel engines	228.0 mm

Friction material thickness (new):
1.8 and 2.0 litre (8-valve) petrol engines	8.0 mm
1.6 and 1.8 litre (16-valve) petrol engines	6.8 mm
2.0 litre (16-valve) petrol engines	7.7 mm
1.9 litre diesel engines	7.7 mm
2.2 litre non-turbo diesel engines	7.7 mm
2.2 litre turbo diesel engines	8.0 mm

Torque wrench settings

	Nm	lbf ft
Pedal pivot bolt	38	28
Pressure plate cover to flywheel:		
1.8 and 2.0 litre (8-valve) petrol engines	22	16
1.6 litre (16-valve) petrol engines	18	13
1.8 litre (16-valve) petrol engines	20	15
2.0 litre (16-valve) petrol engines	25	18
1.9 litre diesel engines	18	13
2.2 litre non-turbo diesel engines	18	13
2.2 litre turbo diesel engines	10	7

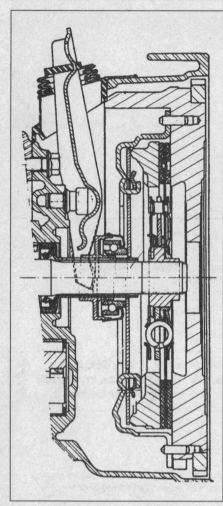

1.1a Cross-section of the JB3 and JC5 transmission clutch

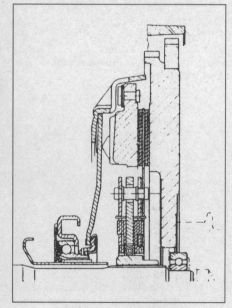

1.1b Cross-section of the PK1 transmission clutch

1 General information

The clutch consists of a friction plate, a pressure plate assembly, a release bearing and the release mechanism; all of these components are contained in the large cast-aluminium alloy bellhousing, sandwiched between the engine and the transmission **(see illustrations)**. The release mechanism is mechanical, operated by a cable, or hydraulic, operated by a master and slave cylinder.

The friction plate is fitted between the engine flywheel and the clutch pressure plate, and is allowed to slide on the transmission input shaft splines.

The pressure plate assembly is bolted to the engine flywheel. When the engine is running, drive is transmitted from the crankshaft, via the flywheel, to the friction plate (these components being clamped securely together by the pressure plate assembly) and from the friction plate to the transmission input shaft.

To interrupt the drive, the spring pressure must be relaxed. On models with a cable-operated clutch, at the transmission end of the clutch cable, the outer cable is retained by a fixed mounting bracket, and the inner cable is attached to the release fork lever. Depressing the clutch pedal pulls the control cable inner wire, and this pivots the release fork on its ball stud by acting on the lever at the fork's upper end. The release fork then presses the release bearing against the pressure plate spring fingers. This causes the springs to deform and releases the clamping force on the pressure plate.

The clutch cable is fitted with a semi-automatic wear compensation mechanism. Although the mechanism automatically adjusts the clutch cable clearance it still needs regular checking and resetting (see Section 2).

On models with a hydraulically operated clutch, the hydraulic components consist of a master cylinder mounted on the clutch pedal bracket and a slave cylinder mounted on the side of the transmission. A hydraulic fluid hose links the two cylinders, and a reserve of hydraulic fluid is provided by a small reservoir mounted adjacent to the master cylinder. The assembly is completely sealed and maintenance-free - topping-up of the fluid reservoir is not required. Depressing the clutch pedal forces the piston down the master cylinder bore which, by hydraulic action, in turn forces the slave cylinder piston down the slave cylinder bore. The slave cylinder piston acts on the clutch release fork, by means of a short pushrod, and actuates the release fork in the same way as the cable-operated version.

In some Sections of this Chapter, the operations differ depending on the type of transmission fitted. Refer to Chapter 7A, Section 1 for details of transmission identification.

2 Clutch cable - adjustment

1 The wear compensator mechanism fitted to the clutch cable is only semi-automatic and needs regular checking and, resetting as follows. The mechanism should also be reset every time the clutch is disturbed.

2 Depress the clutch pedal several times to ensure that the wear compensator is fully extended. If a new cable has been installed, depress the pedal approximately 30 times to remove the initial stretch from the cable and seat it in position.

3 Working in the engine compartment, locate the wear compensator which is situated near the engine compartment bulkhead. Inspect the scale on the side of the compensator which aligns with the edge of the com-pensator cover. The scale is marked 0 to 3 with maximum compensation being available at position 3 **(see illustration)**. The closer to position 0, the less compensation is available; when the scale reaches position 0, the wear compensator is no longer effective. The compensator can be reset as follows.

4 Ensure that the clutch pedal is in the at rest position. Rotate the compensator cover in the direction of the arrow marked on its side through 90° until the cover index mark is aligned with the ADJUSTING (REGLAGE) mark on the body. The cable should now slide freely, if not detach the cable from the clutch release fork, and free it before reconnecting it (see Section 3) **(see illustrations)**.

Caution: Never move the cable or depress the clutch pedal when the cover index mark is in the compensator zone marked with a warning triangle as this will damage the compensator mechanism.

5 With the cable sliding freely, rotate the compensator cover through a further 90° in the direction of the arrow until the cover index mark is realigned with the LOCKING (VERROUILLAGE) mark. The edge of the cover should now be aligned with the number 3 of the compensator scale, indicating that the compensator mechanism has been fully reset.

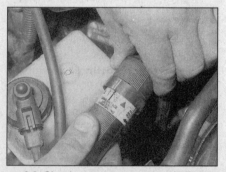

2.3 Clutch wear compensator in the LOCKING position

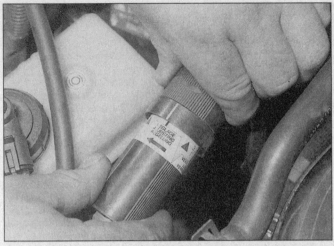

2.4a Rotate the compensator cover in the direction of the arrow until the index mark is aligned with the ADJUSTING mark . . .

2.4b . . . never depress the clutch pedal when the index mark is in the zone marked with the warning triangle

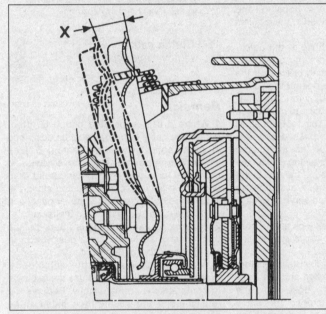

2.6a Checking the clutch release fork movement (X) - JB3 and JC5 transmission

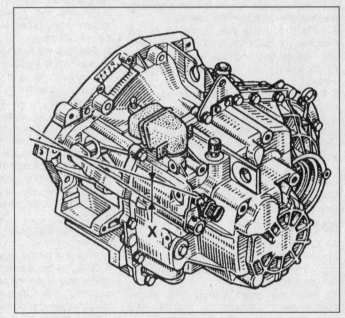

2.6b Checking the clutch release fork movement (X) - PK1 transmission

6 On completion, have an assistant fully depress and release the clutch pedal while you measure the travel of the clutch release fork **(see illustrations)**. If the compensator is functioning correctly, the fork travel should be 26 to 28 mm. If this is not the case, reset the compensator and repeat the check. If the release fork travel is still incorrect then it is likely that the compensator mechanism is faulty and the cable should be renewed.

3 Clutch cable - removal and refitting

Removal

1 Remove the switches from the side of the instrument panel and the instrument panel itself as described in Chapter 12. Undo the retaining screws and remove the heater vent from the driver's end of the facia.
2 Unclip the heater duct which runs along behind the instrument panel aperture and manoeuvre it out through the facia aperture.
3 Release the clutch cable wear compensator mechanism as described in paragraph 4 of Section 2 so the cable is free to slide easily.
4 To improve access to the transmission end of the cable, remove the air cleaner housing and mounting bracket as described in the relevant part of Chapter 4.
5 Detach the transmission end of the inner cable from the clutch release fork and free the outer cable from its mounting bracket **(see illustration)**.

3.5 Detaching the transmission end of the clutch cable from the release lever - JC5 transmission shown

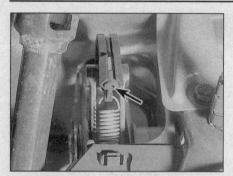

3.6 Pivot the notched segment of the pedal quadrant forwards and detach the cable end fitting (arrowed)

6 Working through the facia aperture, move the notched segment of the pedal quadrant forwards then detach the inner cable from the top of the clutch pedal **(see illustration)**.

7 Remove the rubber sealing grommet from the bulkhead then release the retaining tangs and free the cable from the bulkhead.

8 Return to the engine compartment and withdraw the cable forwards, releasing it from any relevant retaining clips and guides. Note its correct routing, and remove it from the vehicle.

9 Examine the cable, looking for worn end fittings or a damaged outer casing, and for signs of fraying of the inner wire. Check the cable's operation; the inner wire should move smoothly and easily through the outer casing. Remember that a cable that appears serviceable when tested off the car may well be much heavier in operation when in its working position. If the wear compensator is thought to faulty the cable must be renewed.

Refitting

10 Check that the cable wear compensator is released (see paragraph 4 of Section 2) and apply a thin smear of multi-purpose grease to the cable end fittings.

11 Pass the cable through the engine compartment bulkhead and clip the outer cable into position.

12 From inside the vehicle, make sure the outer cable is securely clipped in position then refit the rubber sealing grommet. Hook the inner cable onto the clutch pedal making sure it is correctly engaged with the pedal quadrant.

13 Ensuring that the cable is correctly routed and retained by all the relevant retaining clips and guides, pass the lower end through the mounting bracket and engage the inner cable with the clutch release fork.

14 Reset the cable compensator (see paragraph 5 of Section 2) and depress the cable several times to extend the compensator and adjust the cable freeplay. Refit the air cleaner housing as described in the relevant part of Chapter 4.

15 Manoeuvre the heater duct into position and refit the vent to the end of the facia. Make sure the duct is correctly connected at both ends then securely tighten the vent retaining screws.

16 Refit the instrument panel and switches as described in Chapter 12.

17 On completion, check the wear compensator as described in Section 2 and, if necessary, reset.

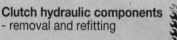

4 Clutch hydraulic components - removal and refitting

Removal

Note: *The clutch master cylinder and slave cylinder form one assembly connected by a hydraulic fluid hose. Although the hose incorporates a quick-release fitting to allow separation, none of the components are available separately.*

1 Disconnect the battery negative terminal (refer to *Disconnecting the battery* in the Reference Section of this manual).

2 Remove the air cleaner housing and mounting bracket as described in the relevant part of Chapter 4.

3 Separate the hydraulic hose at the quick-release fitting located under the previously removed air cleaner mounting bracket. If the hydraulic components are being renewed, a special tool is supplied with the new components to enable the quick-release fitting to be disconnected. This tool is a small forked implement which is passed between the two outer 'spokes' of the fitting and pressed to disengage the retaining claws. The fitting can then be separated. If the tool is not available, the very careful use of two small electrical screwdrivers should serve to release the fitting.

4 Apply the handbrake, then jack up the front of the car and support it on axle stands (see *Jacking and vehicle support*).

5 Undo the bolts securing the slave cylinder to the side of the transmission and the bolts securing the hydraulic hose to the transmission brackets. Remove the slave cylinder and lower section of hydraulic hose from under the car.

6 From within the engine compartment, remove the rubber sealing grommet from the bulkhead then release the retaining tangs and free the hydraulic hose from the bulkhead.

7 Remove the switches from the side of the instrument panel and the instrument panel itself as described in Chapter 12. Undo the retaining screws and remove the heater vent from the driver's end of the facia.

8 Unclip the heater duct which runs along behind the instrument panel aperture and manoeuvre it out through the facia aperture.

9 From inside the car, detach the master cylinder from its mounting bracket by turning it a quarter turn clockwise to release the bayonet fitting. Release the master cylinder pushrod from the balljoint on the clutch pedal.

10 Working through the facia aperture, unclip the master cylinder fluid reservoir from its mounting then withdraw the master cylinder, reservoir and upper section of hydraulic hose from inside the car.

Refitting

11 Refitting is the reverse of removal noting the following points.

a) Connect the master cylinder pushrod to the pedal balljoint before securing the master cylinder bayonet fitting.

b) Ensure that the hose grommet is correctly fitted to the bulkhead.

c) Check that the hose quick-release fitting is clean then push the two halves of the fitting together to secure.

d) Refit the instrument panel and switches as described in Chapter 12.

e) Refit the air cleaner components as described in the relevant part of Chapter 4.

f) Check the operation of the system by depressing the clutch pedal fully and slowly releasing it two or three times. While doing this, check that the clutch release fork is moving correctly.

5 Clutch pedal - removal and refitting

Removal

1 Where a cable-operated clutch is fitted, detach the cable from the pedal as described in paragraphs 1 to 6 of Section 3 **(see illustration opposite)**. To improve access to the pedal, unclip the facia fusebox lid then undo the retaining screws situated along the lower edge of the fusebox lid cover panel and unclip the panel assembly from the facia.

2 Where a hydraulic clutch is fitted, detach the master cylinder as described in paragraphs 7 to 9 of Section 4.

3 Wrap a cable-tie around the clutch pedal assist spring end fittings and use the cable-tie to compress the spring slightly. Remove the retaining clip and washer then slide out the pivot pin secure the spring end fitting to the pedal and remove the spring assembly.

4 Slacken and remove the pedal pivot bolt retaining nut.

5 Carefully withdraw the pivot bolt and slide the clutch pedal assembly out of position, On left-hand drive models, recover the spacer which is fitted between the brake and clutch pedals then slide the pivot bolt back into position to retain the brake pedal.

6 Slide out the spacer from the clutch pedal pivot and inspect the pedal assembly for signs of wear or damage, paying particular attention to the pivot bushes. Renew any components which show signs of wear.

Caution: If the assist spring assembly is to be dismantled, compress it in a vice before releasing the cable-tie.

Refitting

7 Ensure that the pivot bushes are pressed securely into the pedal then apply a smear of multi-purpose grease to the spacer and slide it into position.

8 Manoeuvre the pedal assembly into position and slide in the pivot bolt; on left-hand drive models make sure the spacer is correctly positioned between the brake and clutch pedals as the bolt is fitted. Refit the nut to the pivot bolt and tighten it to the specified torque setting.

9 Apply a smear of multi-purpose grease to the assist spring assembly end fittings and manoeuvre it into position. Make sure the front end fitting is correctly engaged with the mounting bracket then align the other end fitting with the pedal and slide in the retaining pin. Refit the washer to the pin and secure it in position with the retaining clip. Ensure that the assist spring assembly is correctly located then carefully release and remove the cable-tie.

10 Where applicable, reconnect the cable to the clutch pedal as described in paragraphs 12

to 17 of Section 3 and refit the fusebox lid panel to the facia. Alternatively refit the master cylinder as described in paragraph 11 of Section 4.

---

6   Clutch assembly -
   removal, inspection
   and refitting

⚠️ *Warning: Dust created by clutch wear and deposited on the clutch components may contain asbestos, which is a health hazard. DO NOT blow it out with compressed air, or inhale any of it. DO NOT use petrol or petroleum-based solvents to clean off the dust. Brake system cleaner or methylated spirit should be used to flush the dust into a suitable receptacle. After the clutch components are wiped clean with rags, dispose of the contaminated rags and cleaner in a sealed, marked container.*

Note: *Although some friction materials may no longer contain asbestos, it is safest to assume that they do, and to take precautions accordingly.*

Removal

1 Unless the complete engine/transmission is to be removed from the car and separated for major overhaul (see the relevant part of Chapter 2), the clutch can be reached by removing the transmission as described in Chapter 7A.

2 Before disturbing the clutch, use paint or a marker pen to mark the relationship of the pressure plate assembly to the flywheel.

3 On models with the PK1 transmission, using circlip pliers, open up the circlip and remove the release bearing from the centre of the pressure plate (see Section 6).

4 On all models, working in a diagonal sequence, slacken the pressure plate bolts by half a turn at a time, until spring pressure is

6

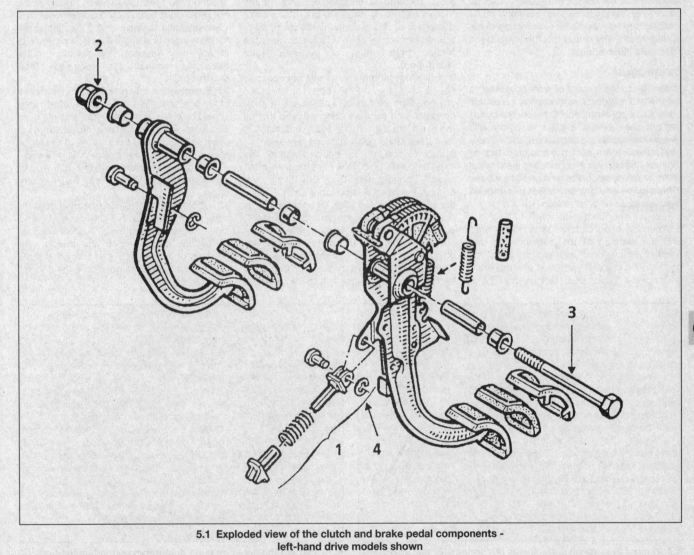

**5.1 Exploded view of the clutch and brake pedal components -
left-hand drive models shown**

| 1 | *Assist spring assembly* | 2 | *Pivot bolt nut* | 3 | *Pivot bolt* | 4 | *Assist spring pin retaining clip* |

6.4a Flywheel rotation can be prevented using a screwdriver (arrowed) as shown whilst the clutch bolts are slackened

6.4b Remove the pressure plate and withdraw the friction plate noting which way around it is fitted

released and the bolts can be unscrewed by hand. Prise the pressure plate assembly off its locating dowels, and collect the friction plate, noting which way round the friction plate is fitted **(see illustrations)**.

Inspection

Note: *Due to the amount of work necessary to remove and refit clutch components, it is usually considered good practice to renew the clutch friction plate, pressure plate assembly and release bearing as a matched set, even if only one of these is actually worn enough to require renewal. It is also worth considering the renewal of the clutch components on a preventive basis if the engine and/or transmission have been removed for some other reason.*

5 Remove the clutch assembly.

6 When cleaning clutch components, read first the warning at the beginning of this Section; remove dust using a clean, dry cloth, and working in a well-ventilated atmosphere.

7 Check the friction plate facings for signs of wear, damage or oil contamination. If the friction material is cracked, burnt, scored or damaged, or if it is contaminated with oil or grease (shown by shiny black patches), the friction plate must be renewed **(see illustration)**.

8 If the friction material is still serviceable, check that the centre boss splines are unworn, that the torsion springs are in good condition and securely fastened, and that all the rivets are tight. If any wear or damage is found, the friction plate must be renewed.

9 If the friction material is fouled with oil, this must be due to an oil leak from the crankshaft oil seal, from the sump-to-cylinder block joint, or from the transmission input shaft. Renew the seal or repair the joint, as appropriate, as described in the relevant parts of Chapters 2 or 7, before installing the new friction plate.

10 Check the pressure plate assembly for obvious signs of wear or damage; shake it to check for loose rivets or worn or damaged fulcrum rings, and check that the drive straps securing the pressure plate to the cover do not show signs (such as a deep yellow or blue discoloration) of overheating. If the diaphragm spring is worn or damaged, or if its pressure is in any way suspect, the pressure plate assembly should be renewed **(see illustration)**.

11 Examine the machined bearing surfaces of the pressure plate and of the flywheel; they should be clean, completely flat, and free from scratches or scoring **(see illustration)**. If either is discoloured from excessive heat, or shows signs of cracks, it should be renewed - although minor damage of this nature can sometimes be polished away using emery paper.

12 Check that the release bearing contact surface rotates smoothly and easily, with no sign of noise or roughness. Also check that the surface itself is smooth and unworn, with no signs of cracks, pitting or scoring. If there is any doubt about its condition, the bearing must be renewed.

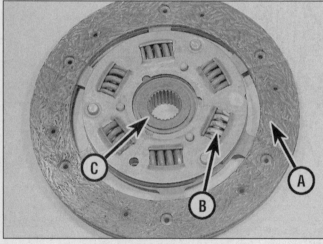

6.7 Inspect the friction plate linings (A), springs (B) and splines (C) for signs of wear or damage

6.10 Inspect the pressure plate diaphragm spring tips for signs of wear or damage

Refitting

13 On reassembly, ensure that the bearing surfaces of the flywheel and pressure plate are completely clean, smooth, and free from oil or grease. Use solvent to remove any protective grease from new components.

14 On all models except 2.2 litre turbo diesel engines, fit the friction plate so that its spring hub assembly faces away from the flywheel. On 2.2 litre turbo diesel engines fit the friction plate so that the longer offset on the hub faces toward the flywheel.

15 Refit the pressure plate assembly, aligning the marks made on dismantling (if the original pressure plate is re-used), and locating the pressure plate on its locating dowels. Fit the pressure plate bolts, but tighten them only finger-tight, so that the friction plate can still be moved.

16 The friction plate must now be centralised, so that when the transmission is refitted, its input shaft will pass through the splines at the centre of the friction plate.

17 Centralisation can be achieved by passing a screwdriver or other long bar through the friction plate and into the hole in the crankshaft; the friction plate can then be moved around until it is centred on the crankshaft hole. Alternatively, a clutch-aligning tool can be used to eliminate the guesswork; these can be obtained from most accessory shops. A home-made aligning tool can be fabricated from a length of metal rod or wooden dowel which fits closely inside the crankshaft hole, and has insulating tape wound around it to match the diameter of the friction plate splined hole. Renault clutch kits are supplied complete with a special centring tube **(see illustrations)**.

18 When the friction plate is centralised, tighten the pressure plate bolts evenly and in a diagonal sequence to the specified torque setting **(see illustration)**.

19 On PK1 transmissions, refit the release bearing as described in Section 6.

20 Refit the transmission as described in Chapter 7A.

6.11 Ensure the machined surface of the pressure plate is unmarked and free from discoloration

6.17b Using the centring tube supplied with the Renault clutch kit to centralise the friction plate

6.17a Using a clutch alignment tool to centralise the friction plate

6.18 Once the friction plate is centralised tighten the pressure plate bolts to the specified torque

bearing from the centre of the pressure plate **(see illustration)**.

Inspection

4 Check the release mechanism, renewing any component which is worn or damaged. Carefully check all bearing surfaces and points of contact.

5 When checking the release bearing itself, note that it is often considered worthwhile to renew it as a matter of course. Check that the contact surface rotates smoothly and easily, with no sign of noise or roughness, and that the surface itself is smooth and unworn, with no signs of cracks, pitting or scoring. If there is any doubt about its condition, the bearing must be renewed.

6 Where fitted, check the condition of the bearing in the centre of the crankshaft rear mounting flange for the flywheel. If it is worn or rattles, renew it. Draw the bearing out of position with a puller and tap the new one into position with a socket which bears only on the bearing outer race. If the bearing is a loose fit in the crankshaft/flywheel, apply thread locking compound to its outer circumference before fitting.

Refitting
JB3 and JC5 transmissions

7 Apply a little high-melting-point grease (Renault recommend the use of Molykote BR2

grease) to the contact surfaces of the release bearing, release fork, guide sleeve and pivot stud. Also pack the release fork stud gaiter with grease.

8 Slide the fork into position and clip it onto the pivot stud. Ensure that the fork is securely retained by its spring clip and the gaiter is correctly located in the stud groove **(see illustration)**.

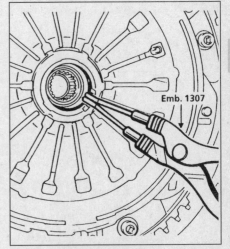

7.3 On PK1 transmission units, expand the circlip with a pair of circlip pliers and remove the release bearing from the pressure plate

7 Clutch release mechanism - removal, inspection and refitting

Removal

1 With the transmission removed in order to provide access to the clutch, attention can be given to the release bearing located in the clutch housing.

2 On JB3 and JC5 transmissions, tilt the release fork, then unclip the bearing and slide it from its guide tube. The release fork can then be simply slid from its pivot stud and removed along with its rubber gaiters.

3 On PK1 transmissions, using circlip pliers, open up the circlip and remove the release

9 Slide the release bearing into position making sure its retaining hook is correctly located behind the release fork **(see illustration)**.

10 Refit the release fork gaiter and seat it in the transmission housing.

11 Check the action of the release fork and bearing then refit the transmission as described in Chapter 7A.

PK1 transmission

12 Apply a little high-melting-point grease (Renault recommend the use of Molykote BR2 grease) to the contact surfaces of the release bearing, release fork and guide sleeve.

13 Slide the bearing onto the guide tube and clip it back into position in the pressure plate.

14 Refit the transmission as described in Chapter 7A making sure the release fork is correctly engaged with the bearing.

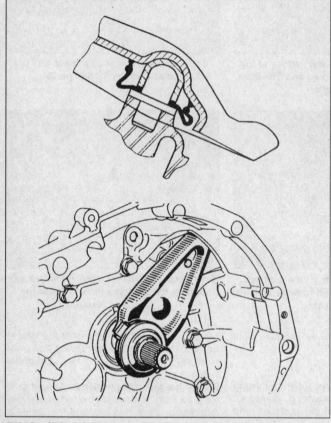

7.8 On JB3 and JC5 transmission units ensure the release fork is clipped securely in position so that its gaiter is correctly located in the pivot stud groove . . .

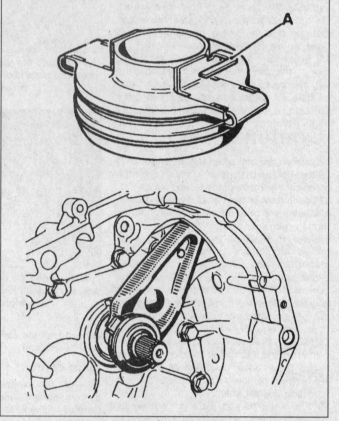

7.9 . . . then fit the release bearing making sure its retaining hook (A) is located behind the fork

Chapter 7 Part A:
Manual transmission

Contents

Degrees of difficulty

| **Easy,** suitable for novice with little experience | ⚒ | **Fairly easy,** suitable for beginner with some experience | ⚒ | **Fairly difficult,** suitable for competent DIY mechanic | ⚒ | **Difficult,** suitable for experienced DIY mechanic | ⚒ | **Very difficult,** suitable for expert DIY or professional | ⚒ |

Specifications

General

Type	Manual, five forward speeds and reverse. Synchromesh on all forward speeds

Designation:
  Petrol engine models:

1.6 litre (16-valve) and 1.8 litre (8-valve) engines	JB3
1.8 litre (16-valve) and 2.0 litre (8- and 16-valve) engines	JC5

  Diesel engine models:

1.9 litre engines	JC5
2.2 litre non-turbo engines	JC5
2.2 litre turbo engines	PK1

Note: *Transmission code is stamped on a plate attached to the transmission (see Section 1).*

Lubrication

Capacity (approximate):

JB3 transmission	3.4 litres
JC5 transmission	3.1 litres
PK1 transmission	2.6 litres

Torque wrench settings

	Nm	lbf ft
Clutch release bearing guide tube bolts - JC5 transmission	24	18
Engine-to-transmission bolts/nuts	50	37
Engine/transmission mountings	See the relevant part of Chapter 2	
Flywheel cover plate bolts	24	18
Gearchange lever:		
Housing nuts	13	10
Mounting plate nuts	13	10
Gearchange link rod:		
Link rod clamp bolt	30	22
Link rod-to-transmission bolt	30	22
Roadwheels bolts	See Chapter 1A or 1B	

7A

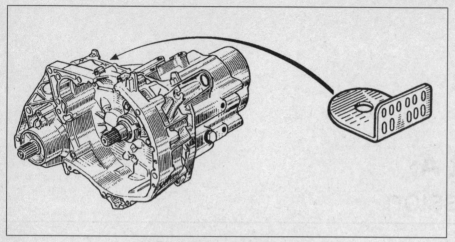

**1.1a Transmission identification plate -
JB3 and JC5 transmission**

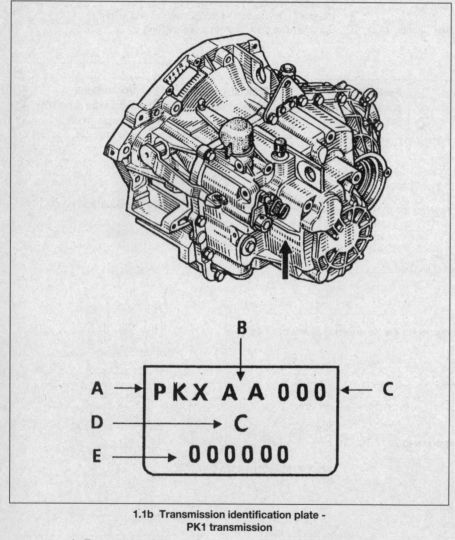

**1.1b Transmission identification plate -
PK1 transmission**

A Transmission type   D Manufacturer's code
B Homologation number   E Manufacturer's number
C Transmission suffix

1 General information

The transmission is contained in a cast-aluminium alloy casing bolted to the engine's left-hand end, and consists of the gearbox and final drive differential - often called a transaxle. Throughout this Chapter, the operations often differ depending on which type of transmission is fitted. The transmission type is stamped on an identification plate attached to the transmission **(see illustrations)**.

Drive is transmitted from the crankshaft via the clutch to the input shaft, which has a splined extension to accept the clutch friction plate, and rotates in sealed ball-bearings. From the input shaft, drive is transmitted to the output shaft, which rotates in a roller bearing at its right-hand end, and a sealed ball-bearing at its left-hand end. From the output shaft, the drive is transmitted to the differential crownwheel, which rotates with the differential case and planetary gears, thus driving the sun gears and driveshafts. The rotation of the planetary gears on their shaft allows the inner roadwheel to rotate at a slower speed than the outer roadwheel when the car is cornering.

The input and output shafts are arranged side by side, parallel to the crankshaft and driveshafts, so that their gear pinion teeth are in constant mesh. In the neutral position, the output shaft gear pinions rotate freely, so that drive cannot be transmitted to the crownwheel.

On JB3 and JC5 transmissions, gear selection is via a floor-mounted lever and selector rod mechanism. On the PK1 transmission, gear selection is via a lever and dual cable arrangement.

The transmission selector rod(s) causes the appropriate selector fork to move its respective synchro-sleeve along the shaft, to lock the gear pinion to the synchro-hub. Since the synchro-hubs are splined to the output shaft, this locks the pinion to the shaft, so that drive can be transmitted. To ensure that gear-changing can be made quickly and quietly, a synchro-mesh system is fitted to all forward gears, consisting of baulk rings and spring-loaded fingers, as well as the gear pinions and synchro-hubs. The synchro-mesh cones are formed on the mating faces of the baulk rings and gear pinions.

2 Manual transmission - draining and refilling

Note: *On JB3 and JC5 transmissions the filler plug is also used as the level plug. On PK1 transmissions the filler plug is used only for refilling the transmission, the oil level is checked using a dipstick (see the relevant part of Chapter 1).*

2.3a Transmission filler/level plug (arrowed) - JB3 and JC5 transmission

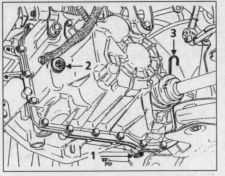

2.3b Transmission draining and refilling points - PK1 transmission

1 *Drain plug*   3 *Oil level*
2 *Filler plug*   *dipstick*

2.5 Slackening the transmission drain plug - JB3 and JC5 transmission

1 This operation is much quicker and more efficient if the car is first taken on a journey of sufficient length to warm the engine/ transmission up to operating temperature.

2 Park the car on level ground, switch off the ignition and apply the handbrake firmly. For improved access, jack up the front of the car and support it on axle stands (see *Jacking and vehicle support*). The car must be lowered to the ground and level, to ensure accuracy, when refilling and checking the oil level.

3 Undo the retaining screws and remove the undercover from beneath the engine/transmission. Remove all dirt then unscrew the filler/level plug from the front face of the transmission (JB3 and JC5 transmissions) or the filler plug from the left-hand end of the transmission (PK1 transmission) (as applicable). Recover the sealing washer **(see illustrations)**.

4 Position a suitable container under the drain plug situated on the base of the transmission housing.

5 Unscrew the drain plug and allow the oil to drain completely into the container **(see illustration)**. If the oil is hot, take precautions against scalding. Clean both the filler/level and the drain plugs, being especially careful to wipe any metallic particles off the magnetic inserts. Discard the original sealing washers; they should be renewed whenever they are disturbed.

6 When the oil has finished draining, clean the drain plug threads and those of the transmission casing, fit a new sealing washer and refit the drain plug, tightening it securely. It the car was raised for the draining operation, now lower it to the ground. Where necessary, refit the protective cover to the transmission.

7 Refilling the transmission is an extremely awkward operation. Above all, allow plenty of time for the oil level to settle properly before checking it. Note that the car must be parked on flat level ground when checking the oil level.

8 Refill the transmission with the exact amount of the specified type of oil (see *Weekly checks*) then check the oil level as described in the relevant part of Chapter 1. When the level is correct, refit the filler or filler level plug with a new sealing washer and

tighten securely. **Note:** *If the correct amount was poured into the transmission and a large amount flows out on checking the level, refit the filler or filler/level plug and take the car on a short journey so that the new oil is distributed fully around the transmission components, then check the level again on your return.*

| 3 | Gearchange mechanism - adjustment |

JB3 and JC5 transmissions

Note: *A special Renault service tool (B.Vi. 1133) will be required to accurately adjust the gearchange linkage.*

1 Firmly apply the handbrake, then jack up the front of the car and support it on axle stands (see *Jacking and vehicle support*).

2 Undo the retaining screws and remove the protective cover from the base of the transmission.

3 Select 1st gear on the transmission by moving the lever to the appropriate position.

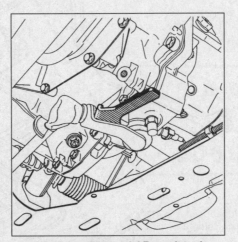

3.3 Using the special Renault tool (B.Vi. 1133) to hold the gearchange lever in position - JB3 and JC5 transmission

To hold the lever securely in position fit the Renault service tool (B.Vi. 1133) as shown **(see illustration)**. In the absence of the special tool, a suitable alternative tool can be made from flat metal bar or a piece of wood.

4 Using a feeler blade, check that the clearance between the reverse stop-ring on the gear lever and the inclined plane on the right-hand side of the gear lever housing is as shown **(see illustration)**.

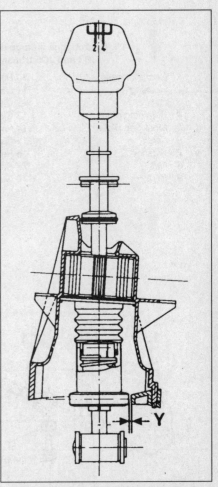

3.4 The clearance (Y) between the gearchange lever and housing should be 3 mm

5 If adjustment is necessary, unhook the return spring from the gear lever end of the link rod, then loosen the clamp bolt at the transmission end of the link rod so that the rod can be moved on the clevis.

6 Move the gear lever so that the reverse stop-ring is against the inclined plane on the housing, then insert a 3 mm feeler blade between the ring and plane. Hold the lever in this position, then tighten the clamp bolt to the specified torque setting.

7 Remove the holding tool then refit the return spring and recheck the clearance as described in paragraph 4.

8 Check that all gears can be selected, then refit the protective cover and/or undercover before lowering the vehicle to the ground.

PK1 transmission

9 On PK1 transmissions, if a stiff, sloppy or imprecise gearchange leads you to suspect that a fault exists within the mechanism, first remove the selector cables and lever, and check them as described in Section 4.

10 If this does not cure the fault, the car should be examined by an expert, as the fault must lie within the transmission itself. There is no adjustment as such in the mechanism.

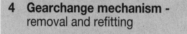

4 Gearchange mechanism - removal and refitting

Removal

JB3 and JC5 transmissions

1 Working inside the vehicle, carefully prise the gearchange lever gaiter out from the centre console. Pull the knob off from the top of the gearchange lever and remove it along with the gaiter **(see illustration)**.

2 Detach the reverse gear interlock cable from the lever slide then tap out the pins and remove the slide from the lever. If the roll pins are damaged on removal they must be renewed.

3 Firmly apply the handbrake, then jack up the front of the vehicle and support it securely on axle stands (see *Jacking and vehicle support*). Undo the retaining screws and remove the protective cover from underneath the transmission.

4 Remove the catalytic converter and intermediate pipe or the intermediate pipe front and rear sections (as applicable) as described in the relevant part of Chapter 4. Unbolt and remove the heatshield(s) to gain access to the underside of the gearchange lever.

5 Unhook the return spring and detach it from the link rod **(see illustration)**.

6 Release the retaining clip and fold back the

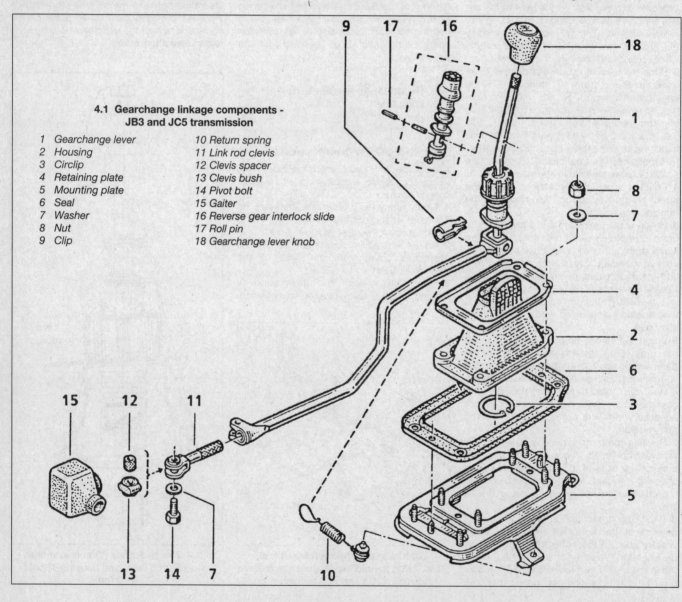

**4.1 Gearchange linkage components -
JB3 and JC5 transmission**

1 Gearchange lever
2 Housing
3 Circlip
4 Retaining plate
5 Mounting plate
6 Seal
7 Washer
8 Nut
9 Clip
10 Return spring
11 Link rod clevis
12 Clevis spacer
13 Clevis bush
14 Pivot bolt
15 Gaiter
16 Reverse gear interlock slide
17 Roll pin
18 Gearchange lever knob

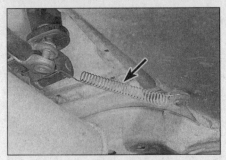

4.5 On JB3 and JC5 transmissions unhook the link rod return spring (arrowed) and remove it

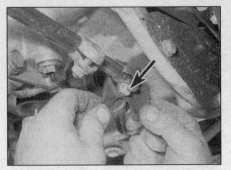

4.6a Peel back the rubber gaiter then undo the pivot bolt (arrowed) . . .

4.6b . . . and recover the spacer and bush from the lever

rubber gaiter from the transmission end of the link rod. Slacken and remove the pivot bolt then disconnect the link rod from the transmission lever and recover the bush and spacer **(see illustrations)**. Do not disturb the link rod clevis clamp bolt, if the clevis is to be removed make alignment marks with the link rod before removal.

7 From inside the vehicle, slacken and remove the nuts securing the gearchange lever mounting plate to the vehicle body then lower the link and gearchange lever assembly

out of position and remove it from underneath the vehicle. Recover the seal which is fitted between the housing and body. Renew the mounting plate.

8 To separate the lever from its housing, extract the circlip from the bottom of the gear lever, and withdraw the lever from the housing. If necessary, undo the retaining nuts and separate the housing from the mounting plate.

9 Examine all components for signs of wear or damage and renew as necessary.

PK1 transmission

10 Remove the centre console as described in Chapter 11.

11 Mark the cables for identification, then slide out the outer cable retaining clips **(see illustration)**. Unclip the inner cable balljoints and free both cables from the gearchange lever.

12 Slacken and remove the retaining nuts and spacers and remove the gearchange lever from the vehicle.

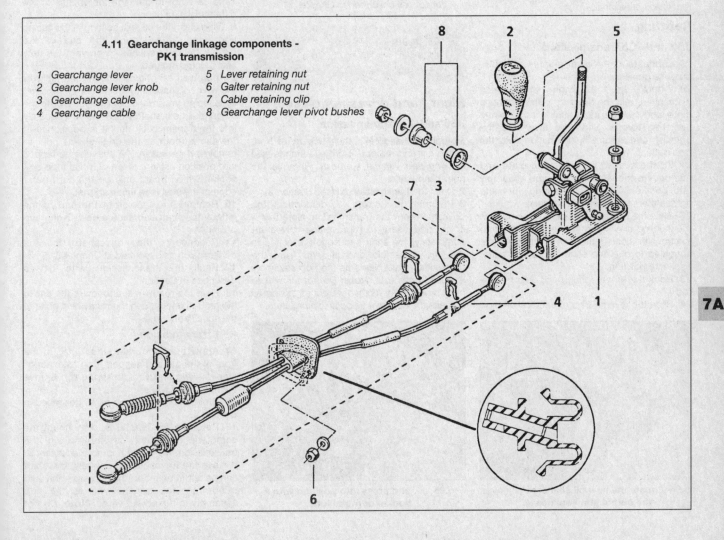

4.11 Gearchange linkage components - PK1 transmission

1 Gearchange lever	5 Lever retaining nut
2 Gearchange lever knob	6 Gaiter retaining nut
3 Gearchange cable	7 Cable retaining clip
4 Gearchange cable	8 Gearchange lever pivot bushes

7A

13 To remove the cables, remove the air filter housing as described in the relevant part of Chapter 4.

14 Firmly apply the handbrake then jack up the front of the vehicle and support it on axle stands (see *Jacking and vehicle support*).

15 Remove the left-hand front roadwheel then remove the retaining screws and fasteners and remove the wheelarch liner.

16 Slide out the outer cable retaining clips and detach each cable from its transmission selector lever balljoint.

17 Slacken and remove the nuts and washers securing the gearchange cable gaiter to the bulkhead and, noting each cable correct routing, withdraw the cable assembly from the engine compartment.

18 Examine the cables, looking for worn end fittings or a damaged outer casing, and for signs of fraying of the inner wire. Check each cable's operation; the inner wire should move smoothly and easily through the outer casing. Remember that a cable that appears serviceable when tested off the car may well be much heavier in operation when in its working position. The cables are renewed as an assembly. Check the gearchange lever assembly for signs of wear or damage and renew as necessary.

Refitting

JB3 and JC5 transmissions

19 Lubricate all the pivot points with multi-purpose grease.

20 Where the assembly has been dismantled, refit the housing to the mounting plate and tighten its retaining nuts to the specified torque. Slide the lever into the housing and secure it in position with the circlip.

21 Fit the seal to the mounting plate and manoeuvre the lever and link rod assembly into position. Refit the retaining nuts and tighten them to the specified torque.

22 Slide the bush and spacer into position in the link rod clevis and connect the clevis to the transmission. Tighten the pivot bolt to the specified torque and slide the rubber gaiter back into position.

23 Hook the return spring back onto the link rod.

24 Slide the reverse gear interlock slide onto

the lever and secure it in position with the roll pins. Reconnect the cable to the slide and check the operation of the gearchange lever.

25 Press the knob back onto the gearchange lever and clip the gaiter into the centre console.

26 Refit the disturbed heatshield(s) and exhaust section(s) as described in the relevant part of Chapter 4.

PK1 transmission

27 Refitting is the reverse of removal noting the following points.

a) *Prior to refitting lubricate the gearchange lever sliding surfaces with multi-purpose grease (Renault recommend the use of 33 Medium grease).* **Do not** *apply grease to the selector cable balljoints.*

b) *Manoeuvre the cables into position making sure they are correctly routed.*

c) *Tighten the gearchange lever nut to the specified torque.*

d) *Ensure that the selector cable balljoints are clipped securely onto the lever and transmission and secure the outer cables in position with the retaining clips.*

e) *Check the operation of the gearchange mechanism prior to refitting the centre console as described in Chapter 11.*

---

5 Oil seals - renewal

Right-hand driveshaft oil seal

JB3 and JC5 transmission

1 Apply the handbrake, then jack up the front of the car and support it on axle stands (see *Jacking and vehicle support*). Remove the right-hand wheel.

2 Drain the transmission oil (see Section 2).

3 Referring to Chapter 8, disconnect the driveshaft from the transmission. Note that it is not necessary to remove the driveshaft completely, the shaft can be left attached to the hub assembly and slid off from the differential gear splines as the hub assembly is pulled outwards. **Note:** *Do not allow it to hang down under its own weight as this could damage the constant velocity joints/gaiters.*

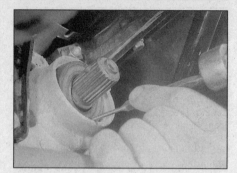

5.7 On JB3 and JC5 transmissions, tap the right-hand driveshaft oil seal with a small drift to remove it

4 Remove the O-ring from the side gear shaft.

5 Wipe clean the old oil seal.

6 Measure its fitted depth below the casing edge. This is necessary to determine the correct fitted position of the new oil seal, if the special Renault fitting tool is not being used.

7 Free the old oil seal, using a small drift to tap the outer edge of the seal inwards so that the opposite edge of the seal tilts out of the casing **(see illustration)**. A pair of pliers or grips can then be used to pull out the oil seal. Take care not to damage the splines of the differential side gear.

8 Wipe clean the oil seal seating in the casing and wrap tape around the end of the differential gear splines to prevent the new seal being damaged.

9 Apply a smear of grease to the sealing lip of the new oil seal and, making sure its sealing lip is facing inwards, carefully slide it onto the differential gear shaft. Press the seal squarely into the transmission until it is positioned at the same depth as the original was prior to removal. If necessary the seal can be tapped into position using a piece of metal tube or a socket which bears only on the hard outer edge of the seal **(see illustrations)**.

10 Remove the tape from the end of the differential shaft and slide a new O-ring into position.

11 Reconnect the driveshaft to the transmission as described in Chapter 8.

12 Refill the transmission with oil as described in Section 2.

13 Refit the roadwheel and lower the car to the ground and tighten the roadwheel bolts to the specified torque.

PK1 transmission

14 Apply the handbrake, then jack up the front of the car and support it on axle stands (see *Jacking and vehicle support*). Remove the right-hand wheel.

15 Drain the transmission oil as described in Section 2.

16 Referring to Chapter 8, disconnect the complete driveshaft assembly from the transmission. Note that it is not necessary to remove the driveshaft completely, the shaft can be left attached to the hub assembly and freed from the transmission as the hub assembly is pulled outwards. **Note:** *Do not*

5.9a Locate the new oil seal carefully over the output shaft splines . . .

5.9b . . . and press into position with a socket or metal tube

allow it to hang down under its own weight as this could damage the constant velocity joints/gaiters.

17 Note the correct fitted depth of the oil seal in the transmission then carefully lever it out of position using a flat-bladed screwdriver.

18 Wipe clean the oil seal seating in the casing. Press the new seal squarely into the transmission, making sure its sealing lip is facing inwards, until it is positioned at the same depth as the original was prior to removal. If necessary the seal can be tapped into position using a piece of metal tube or a socket which bears only on the hard outer edge of the seal.

19 Apply a smear of grease to the sealing lip of the seal and carefully refit the driveshaft assembly as described in Chapter 8.

20 Refill the transmission with oil as described in Section 2.

21 Refit the roadwheel and lower the car to the ground and tighten the roadwheel bolts to the specified torque.

Left-hand driveshaft oil seal

22 On the left-hand side of the transmission there is no oil seal. The seal is formed by the driveshaft gaiter. If oil is leaking from the left-hand driveshaft to the transmission joint, renew the gaiter as described in Chapter 8.

Input shaft oil seal

JB3 transmission

23 On the JB3 type transmission, it is not possible to renew the input shaft oil seal without first dismantling the transmission. The guide tube assembly is a press fit in the housing and is removed inwards. Oil seal renewal should therefore be entrusted to a Renault dealer or transmission overhaul specialist.

JC5 transmission

Note: *The release bearing guide tube is a press fit in the transmission housing and it is likely that the special Renault service tools (Emb.880 and Emb.1163) will be required to remove and refit it safely. Removal and refitting without the special tools is likely to lead to the guide tube/transmission casing being damaged.*

24 Remove the transmission as described in Section 8 and remove the clutch release mechanism as described in Chapter 6.

25 Slacken and remove the two bolts securing the release bearing guide tube to the transmission. Withdraw the guide tube from the transmission housing (see Note) and slide it off the input shaft; the Renault service tool is in the form of a slide hammer which clamps to the outside of the guide tube.

26 Where necessary, carefully lever out the oil seal, taking care not to mark the shaft or casing, and slide it off the end of the shaft. Discard the seal and guide tube, they must be renewed as an assembly.

27 Wrap tape around the end of the input shaft and slide the new seal and guide tube assembly into position.

28 Remove the tape from the input shaft and press the guide tube squarely into the transmission casing.

29 Refit the guide tube retaining bolts and tighten them to the specified torque.

30 Refit the clutch release mechanism as described in Chapter 6 then refit the transmission as described in Section 8.

PK1 transmission

31 Remove the transmission as described in Section 8.

32 Slacken and remove the retaining bolts and remove the clutch release bearing guide tube from the transmission.

33 Note the correct fitted position of the seal then carefully punch or drill two small holes opposite each other in the oil seal. Screw a self-tapping screw into each, and pull on the screws with pliers to extract the seal.

34 Clean the seal housing, and polish off any burrs or raised edges, which may have caused the seal to fail in the first place.

35 Wrap tape around the end of the input shaft and slide the new seal into position, making sure its sealing lip is facing inwards. Press the seal squarely into the transmission housing, if necessary, using a suitable tubular drift which bears only on the hard outer edge of the seal.

36 Remove the tape from the input shaft then refit the guide tube and securely tighten its retaining bolts.

37 Refit the transmission (see Section 8).

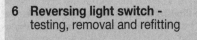

6 Reversing light switch -
testing, removal and refitting

Testing

1 The reversing light circuit is controlled by a plunger-type switch that is screwed into the left-hand side of the transmission casing, next to the driveshaft inner joint. If a fault develops in the circuit, first ensure that the circuit fuse has not blown.

2 To test the switch, disconnect the wiring connector, and use a multimeter (set to the resistance function) or a battery-and-bulb test circuit to check that there is continuity between the switch terminals only when reverse gear is selected. If this is not the case, and there are no obvious breaks or other damage to the wires, the switch is faulty, and must be renewed.

Removal

3 Firmly apply the handbrake then jack up the front of the vehicle and support it on axle stands (see *Jacking and vehicle support*).

4 To improve access, undo the retaining screws and remove the plastic undercover and/or protective cover from underneath the transmission (as applicable).

5 Disconnect the wiring connector, then unscrew it from the transmission casing along with its sealing washer **(see illustration)**.

Refitting

6 Fit a new sealing washer to the switch, then screw it back into position in the top of the transmission housing and tighten it securely. Reconnect the wiring connector, and test the operation of the circuit. Refit the protective cover and/or undercover (as applicable) and lower the vehicle to the ground. If any oil was lost when the switch was removed, check the oil level as described in the relevant part of Chapter 1.

7 Speedometer drive -
removal and refitting

JB3 and JC5 transmissions

1 On these transmissions it is not possible to renew the speedometer drive gears without first removing the transmission and dismantling the differential assembly. Therefore speedometer gear renewal should be entrusted to a Renault dealer or transmission overhaul specialist.

PK1 transmission

Removal

2 Remove the air cleaner housing as described in the relevant part of Chapter 4.

3 Unclip the speedometer cable from the drive which is located on the top of the transmission housing, towards the rear.

4 Slacken and remove the retaining bolt and withdraw the speedometer drive housing and driven gear assembly from the transmission housing, along with its O-ring. Take great care not to drop the gear.

5 If necessary, the gear can be slid out of the housing. Examine the gear for signs of damage, and renew if necessary. Renew the housing O-ring as a matter of course.

6 If the driven pinion is worn or damaged, also examine the drive pinion in the transmission housing for similar signs.

7 To renew the drive gear, the transmission must be dismantled and the differential gear removed. This task should therefore be entrusted to a Renault dealer or a transmission specialist.

7A

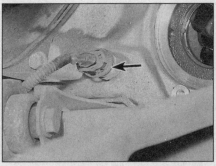

6.5 Reversing light switch (arrowed) -
JB3 and JC5 transmission

Refitting

8 Apply a smear of grease to the lips of the seal and to the driven gear shaft, and slide the gear into position in the speedometer drive.

9 Fit a new O-ring to the speedometer drive and refit it to the transmission, ensuring that the drive and driven pinions are correctly engaged.

10 Refit the retaining bolt and tighten it securely.

11 Reconnect the speedometer cable making sure it is clipped securely in position.

12 Refit the air cleaner housing as described in the relevant part of Chapter 4.

8 Manual transmission - removal and refitting

Removal

1 Remove the battery as described in Chapter 5A then remove the air cleaner housing and mounting bracket as described in the relevant part of Chapter 4.

2 Referring to Chapter 6, release the wear compensator and detach the lower end of the clutch cable from the transmission.

3 Firmly apply the handbrake then jack up the front of the vehicle and support it on axle stands (see *Jacking and vehicle support*). Remove both front roadwheels then undo the retaining screws and remove the plastic undercover and left-hand wheelarch liner.

4 Drain the transmission oil as described in Section 2.

5 Remove the starter motor as described in Chapter 5A.

6 Remove the left-hand driveshaft as described in Chapter 8.

7 Referring to Chapter 8, disconnect the right-hand driveshaft from the transmission. Note that it is not necessary to remove the driveshaft completely, the shaft can be left attached to the hub assembly and released from the transmission as the hub assembly is pulled outwards. **Note:** *Do not allow it to hang down under its own weight as this could damage the constant velocity joints/gaiters.*

8.8 On models with power steering, undo the nuts (arrowed) and free the steering pipes from the transmission brackets

8.10a Disconnect the wiring connector from the reversing light switch . . .

8 On models equipped with power steering, undo the retaining bolts securing the power steering pipes to the end of the transmission **(see illustration)**. Position the pipes clear of the transmission so they will not hinder removal.

9 Where applicable, release the retaining clip and disconnect the speedometer cable from its drive **(see illustration)**.

10 Disconnect the wiring connector from the reversing light switch. Undo the retaining nut/bolt and detach the earth strap from the transmission **(see illustrations)**.

11 Disconnect the gearchange linkage link rod (JB3 and JC5 transmission) or selector cables (PK1 transmission) from the transmission as described in Section 4. On PK1 transmissions unbolt the clutch slave cylinder and move it to one side. Release the

8.9 Depress the retaining clips and detach the speedometer cable

8.10b . . . and unbolt the earth strap from the top of the transmission

hydraulic fluid pipe from the bracket on top of the transmission.

12 On petrol engine models remove the crankshaft sensor as described in Chapter 4A, Section 14.

13 On diesel engine models, undo the retaining bolts and nuts and free the coolant pipe/wiring support brackets from the top of the transmission housing **(see illustrations)**.

14 Where a flywheel lower cover plate is fitted, undo the retaining bolts and remove the cover plate from the base of the transmission housing **(see illustration)**. On some models the plate has support struts attached to it, these will have to be unbolted from the side of the cylinder block.

15 Place a jack with a block of wood beneath the engine, to take the weight of the engine. Alternatively, attach a hoist or support bar to

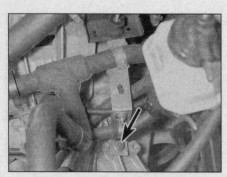

8.13a On diesel models, unscrew the retaining bolts (arrowed) . . .

8.13b . . . to release the coolant pipe/ wiring brackets from top of transmission

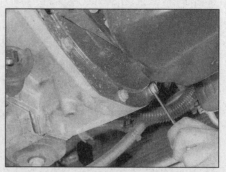

8.14 Unbolt the flywheel cover plate from the base of the transmission

8.15 Engine support bar fitted to support the engine's weight (diesel engine shown)

8.17a On diesel models, slacken and remove the nuts and bolts . . .

8.17b . . . and remove the rear mounting connecting link

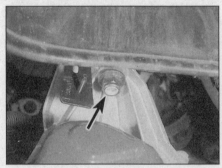

8.18a Unscrew the lower nut from the left-hand mounting . . .

8.18b . . . then undo the three mounting bolts . . .

8.18c . . . and remove the bracket from the top of the transmission housing

the engine lifting eyes to take the engine weight (see illustration). Also place a trolley jack and block of wood beneath the transmission, and raise the jack to take the weight of the transmission.

16 On petrol engine models, slacken and remove the bolts securing the engine/transmission rear mounting support rod in position and remove the rod. Loosen the nut securing either end of the mounting link in position then slacken and remove the mounting bracket retaining bolts and pivot the bracket away from the rear of the transmission.

17 On diesel engine models, slacken and remove the engine/transmission rear mounting connecting link nuts and bolts and remove the link from the vehicle (see illustrations).

18 On all models, slacken and remove the

8.20 Removing the transmission (JC5 transmission shown)

lower nut from the base of the left-hand engine/transmission engine mounting stud. Lower the transmission slightly then undo the bolts securing the mounting bracket to the transmission housing and manoeuvre it out of position (see illustrations).

19 With the jack positioned beneath the transmission taking the weight, slacken and remove the remaining nuts and bolts securing the transmission housing to the engine. Note the correct fitted positions of each nut/bolt, and the necessary brackets, as they are removed, to use as a reference on refitting. Make a final check that all components have been disconnected, and are positioned clear of the transmission so that they will not hinder the removal procedure.

20 With the nuts/bolts removed, move the trolley jack and transmission to the left, to free it from its locating dowels (see illustration). Note that on models with the PK1 transmission, it will be necessary to unclip the release fork from the clutch release bearing as the transmission is removed from the engine.

21 Once the transmission is free, lower the jack and manoeuvre the unit out from under the car. Remove the locating dowels from the transmission or engine if they are loose, and keep them in a safe place.

Refitting

22 The transmission is refitted by a reversal of the removal procedure, bearing in mind the following points:

a) Ensure that the clutch plate and

transmission input shaft splines are clean and dry. Do not apply grease to the splines as they have a special low-friction nickel coating.

b) Ensure that the locating dowels are correctly positioned prior to installation and make sure the clutch release mechanism components are correctly fitted (see Chapter 6).

c) On models with a PK1 transmission, prior to refitting, position the release fork lever as shown and make sure the release bearing clips are positioned correctly so they will align with the fork ends once the transmission is fitted (see illustration).

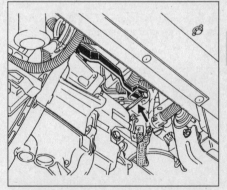

8.22 On PK1 transmission support the clutch release lever as shown when engaging the transmission with the engine to ensure that the lever correctly engages with the release bearing

7A

Manoeuvre the transmission into position and engage it carefully with the engine. Refit the lower transmission to engine nuts/bolts then move the clutch release lever sharply downwards to engage it with the release bearing clips; the fork should be heard to 'click' into position. Check the operation of the clutch. **Do not proceed any further until you are sure the release fork and bearing are correctly engaged.**

d) *Tighten all nuts and bolts to the specified torque (where given).*

e) *Refit the driveshafts as described in Chapter 8.*

f) *Connect and adjust the clutch cable as described in Chapter 6.*

g) *On completion, refill the transmission with the specified type and quantity of lubricant, as described in Section 2.*

9 Manual transmission overhaul - general information

1 Overhauling a manual transmission is a difficult and involved job for the DIY home mechanic. In addition to dismantling and reassembling many small parts, clearances must be precisely measured and, if necessary, changed by selecting shims and spacers. Internal transmission components are also often difficult to obtain, and in many instances, extremely expensive. Because of this, if the transmission develops a fault or becomes noisy, the best course of action is to have the unit overhauled by a specialist repairer, or to obtain an exchange reconditioned unit.

2 Nevertheless, it is not impossible for the more experienced mechanic to overhaul the transmission, provided the special tools are available, and the job is done in a deliberate step-by-step manner, so that nothing is overlooked.

3 The tools necessary for an overhaul include internal and external circlip pliers, bearing pullers, a slide hammer, a set of pin punches, a dial test indicator, and possibly a hydraulic press. In addition, a large, sturdy workbench and a vice will be required.

4 During dismantling of the transmission, make careful notes of how each component is fitted, to make reassembly easier and more accurate.

5 Before dismantling the transmission, it will help if you have some idea what area is malfunctioning. Certain problems can be closely related to specific areas in the transmission, which can make component examination and replacement easier. Refer to the Fault finding Section at the end of this manual for more information.

Chapter 7 Part B:
Automatic transmission

Contents

Degrees of difficulty

Easy, suitable for novice with little experience	Fairly easy, suitable for beginner with some experience	Fairly difficult, suitable for competent DIY mechanic	Difficult, suitable for experienced DIY mechanic	Very difficult, suitable for expert DIY or professional

Specifications

General

Type	Electronically-controlled with four forward speeds and reverse.
Designation:	
Up to 1998	AD4
From 1998 onward	DPO

Torque wrench settings

	Nm	lbf ft
AD4 type transmission		
Driveplate cover plate bolts	24	18
Driveplate-to-torque converter nuts	25	18
Engine-to-transmission bolts/nuts	50	37
Engine/transmission mounting bolts	60	44
Fluid cooler bolts	25	18
Roadwheel bolts	See Chapter 1A or 1B	
DPO type transmission		
Driveplate cover plate bolts	24	18
Driveplate-to-torque converter nuts	30	22
Engine-to-transmission bolts/nuts	44	32
Engine/transmission mounting bolts	60	44
Filter retaining bolts	5	4
Fluid cooler bolt	50	37
Modular connector mounting plate bolts	20	15
Multi-function switch mounting bolts	10	7
Roadwheel bolts	See Chapter 1A or 1B	
Sump retaining bolts	10	7

7B

1 General information

Two different types of automatic transmission are available on 2.0 litre (8-valve) engine models. Pre-1998 models are fitted with the AD4 type transmission, whereas later models have the DPO type transmission **(see illustrations)**. Both units are four-speed, electronically controlled, fully-automatic transmissions operating on similar principles, but with a number of additional features incorporated into the DPO unit.

The transmission consists of a torque converter, an epicyclic geartrain, hydraulically-operated clutches and brakes, and an electronic control unit (ECU).

The torque converter provides a fluid coupling between engine and transmission, which acts as an automatic clutch, and also provides a degree of torque multiplication when accelerating. On the DPO type transmission the torque converter incorporates a lock-up function whereby the engine and transmission can be directly coupled by means of a small clutch unit inside the torque converter. The lock-up function is controlled by the ECU according to vehicle operating conditions.

The epicyclic geartrain provides the forward gears or reverse gear, depending on which of its component parts are held stationary or allowed to turn. The components of the geartrain are held or released by brakes and clutches which are activated by a hydraulic control unit. A fluid pump within the transmission provides the necessary hydraulic pressure to operate the brakes and clutches.

Impulses from switches and sensors connected to the transmission throttle and selector linkages are directed to the ECU computer module, which determines the ratio to be selected from the information received. The computer activates solenoid valves, which in turn open or close ducts within the hydraulic control unit. This causes the clutches and brakes to hold or release the various components of the geartrain, and provide the correct ratio for the particular engine speed or load. The information from the computer module can be overridden by use of the selector lever, and a particular gear can be held if required, regardless of engine speed. On the DPO transmission, the selector lever also incorporates a shift-lock feature, which prevents the selector lever being moved from the P position unless the brake pedal is depressed.

The automatic transmission fluid is cooled by passing it through a cooler located on the top of the transmission. Coolant from the cooling system passes through the cooler.

Due to the complexity of the automatic transmission, any repair or overhaul work must be left to a Renault dealer with the necessary special equipment for fault diagnosis and repair. The contents of the following Sections are therefore confined to supplying general information, and any service information and instructions that can be used by the owner.

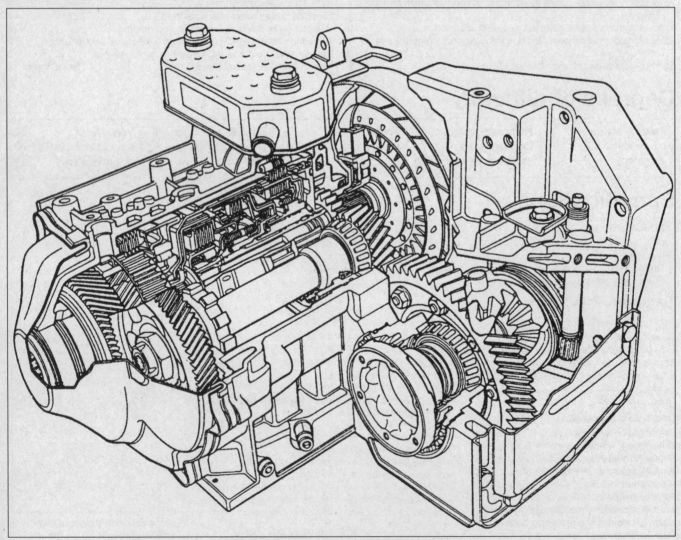

1.1a Cutaway view of the AD4 transmission unit

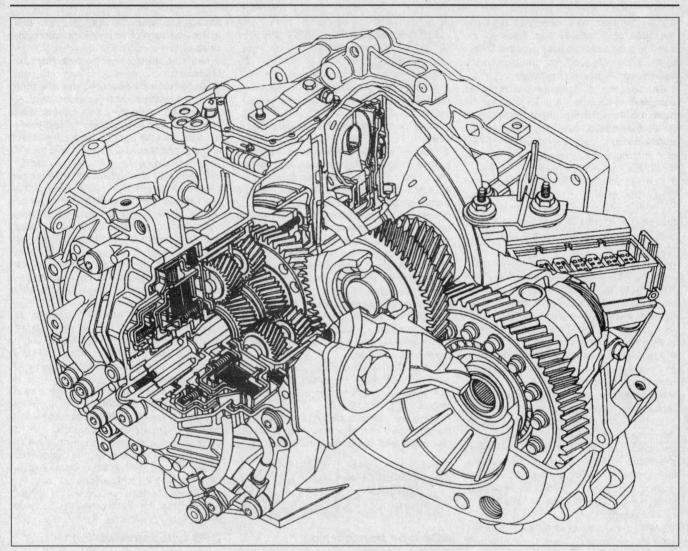

1.1b Cutaway view of the DPO transmission unit

2 Automatic transmission fluid (DPO transmission) - draining and refilling

Note 1: *The DPO type transmission is a 'sealed-for-life' unit and fluid renewal is not required. The following procedure should only be necessary if there is any reason to believe that the fluid may be contaminated, or if repair work requiring the fluid to be drained is to be carried out.*

Note 2: *The transmission fluid filling and level checking procedure is particularly complicated, and the home mechanic would be well-advised to take the vehicle to a Renault dealer to the draining and refilling work carried out. To ensure accuracy, special test equipment is necessary to measure the fluid temperature when carrying out the level check. However, the following procedure is given for those who may have access to this equipment.*

1 Take the vehicle on a short run, to warm the transmission up to normal operating temperature.

2 Park the car on level ground, then switch off the ignition and apply the handbrake firmly. Jack up the front of the car and support it securely on axle stands (see *Jacking and Vehicle Support*). Note that, when refilling and checking the fluid level, the car must be level to ensure accuracy.

3 Undo the retaining screws and remove the plastic undercover from beneath the engine/transmission.

4 Position a suitable container under the transmission. Unscrew the transmission drain plug and allow the fluid to drain completely into the container. Note that the drain plug and level checking plug are incorporated into one unit - the drain plug is the larger of the two hexagonal headed plugs forming the draining/level checking unit **(see illustration)**.

 Warning: If the fluid is hot, take precautions against scalding.

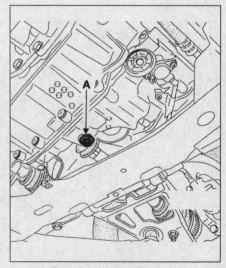

2.4 Combined drain plug and level checking plug unit (A) on the DPO transmission

7B

5 When the fluid has finished draining, clean the drain plug threads and those of the transmission casing. Fit a new sealing washer to the drain plug, and refit the plug to the transmission, tightening it securely.

6 Remove the air cleaner assembly as described in Chapter 4A, then unscrew the filler plug from the top of the transmission **(see illustration)**. Add 3.5 litres of the specified fluid to the transmission via the filler plug opening, using a clean funnel with a fine-mesh filter, then refit the plug.

7 Connect the Renault XR25 test meter to the diagnostic socket, and enter D14 then number 04. With the selector lever in Park, run the engine at idle speed until the fluid temperature, as shown on the test meter, reaches 60°C.

8 With the engine still running, unscrew the level plug from the centre of the draining/level checking unit. Allow the excess fluid to run out into a calibrated container drop-by-drop, then refit the plug. The amount of fluid should be more than 0.1 litre; if it is not, the fluid level in the transmission is incorrect.

9 If the level is incorrect, add an extra 0.5 litre of the specified fluid to the transmission, as described in paragraph 6. Allow the transmission to cool down to 50°C, then repeat the checking procedure again as described in the previous paragraphs. Repeat the procedure as required until more than the specified amount of fluid is drained as described in the previous paragraphs, indicating that the transmission fluid level is correct, then securely tighten the level plug. Refit the engine undercover and the air cleaner assembly.

10 With the XR25 test meter still connected, enter the command G74 then the date to reset the oil ageing counter in the electronic control unit. Disconnect the test meter on completion.

3 Transmission fluid filter (AD4 transmission) - renewal

1 The fluid filter should be changed whenever the transmission fluid has become contaminated.

2 Drain the transmission fluid as described in Chapter 1A.

3 Slacken and remove the sump retaining bolts and lower the sump away from the transmission. Recover the sump seal.

4 Unbolt the filter from the base of the transmission and recover the filter gasket.

5 Remove the magnet(s) from inside the sump, noting their correct fitted positions, and clean all traces of metal filings. The filings (if any) should be very fine; any sizeable chips of metal indicate a worn component in the transmission. Refit the magnet(s) in the correct position(s).

6 Fit a new gasket on top of the filter element, and offer the filter to the transmission. Refit the retaining bolts, ensuring that the gasket is still correctly positioned, and tighten them to the specified torque.

7 Ensure the seal is correctly located on the sump and refit the sump to the transmission, tightening its retaining bolts to the specified torque.

8 Lower the vehicle to the ground, then fill the transmission with the specified type and amount of fluid as described in Chapter 1A.

4 Selector cable - adjustment

AD4 type transmission

1 Apply the handbrake, then jack up the front of the car and support it on axle stands (see *Jacking and Vehicle Support*).

2 Remove the centre console as described in Chapter 11.

3 Move the selector lever inside the car to the D position.

4 Disconnect the selector cable end fitting from the transmission selector lever. To improve access to the cable, remove the air cleaner housing as described in Chapter 4A.

5 Check that the lever on the transmission is in the D position, and if necessary move the lever accordingly.

6 Check that the dimension between the cable end fitting and the outer cable location bracket is as shown **(see illustration)**. If this is not the case, loosen the bracket mounting nut(s) and move the bracket as necessary until the dimension is correct. Tighten the nut(s).

7 From inside the vehicle, release the selector adjuster by rotating its cover through a quarter of a turn and check that the cable slides freely.

8 Reconnect the selector cable to the transmission then lock the cable in position by rotating the adjuster cover back through a quarter of a turn. Where necessary, refit the air cleaner housing as described in Chapter 4A, then lower the car to the ground.

9 Check that the selector lever moves freely, and that the starter motor will only operate with P or N selected. Also check that the Park function operates correctly. Small adjustments may be made by turning the cable adjuster cover through a quarter-turn, then pulling or pushing the cable as required before locking the adjuster again.

10 Once the selector mechanism is correctly adjusted, refit the centre console as described in Chapter 11.

DPO type transmission

11 Move the selector lever inside the car to the N position.

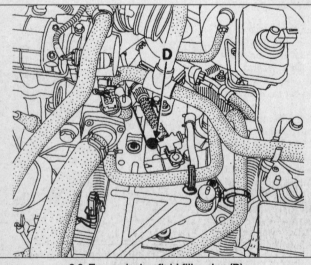

2.6 Transmission fluid filler plug (D) - DPO transmission

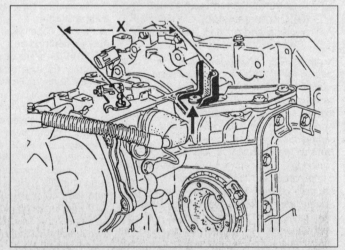

4.6 Adjust the position of the selector cable bracket (arrowed) so that the distance between the bracket and selector lever balljoint (X) is 118 mm - AD4 transmission

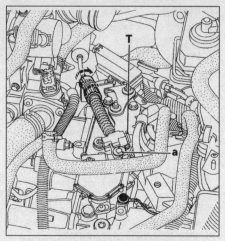

**4.14 Selector cable fitting details -
DPO transmission**

a End fitting on multi-function switch
T Adjuster tab
*Arrows indicate method of releasing locking
rings from cable support bracket*

12 Disconnect the selector cable end fitting
from the multi-function switch on top of the
transmission. To improve access to the cable,
remove the air cleaner housing as described
in Chapter 4A.
13 Check that the multi-function switch is in
the N position, and if necessary set it
accordingly.
14 Depress the tab on the side of the cable
end fitting and suitably retain it in the released
position **(see illustration)**.
15 Reconnect the selector cable to the multi-
function switch then release the tab on the
end fitting to lock the cable. Refit the air
cleaner housing as described in Chapter 4A.
16 Check that the selector lever moves
freely, and that the starter motor will only
operate with P or N selected. Also check that
the Park function operates correctly.

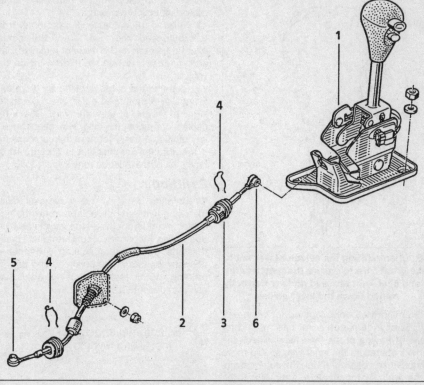

**5.2a Selector cable and lever components -
AD4 transmission**

1	*Lever assembly*	4	*Retaining clip*
2	*Cable*	5	*Cable transmission end*
3	*Cable adjuster*		*balljoint*
		6	*Cable selector lever end*
			balljoint

transmission mounting bracket **(see
illustration)**. To ease refitting, tie a length of
string to the end of the inner cable.
5 To achieve the necessary clearance
required to remove the cable, first undo the
retaining screws and remove the exhaust
system heatshield from underneath the
selector lever.

6 Release the cable sealing grommet from
the bulkhead then withdraw the cable,
releasing it from all the relevant retaining clips
and guides, and remove it from inside the
vehicle. When the end of the inner cable
appears, untie the string and leave it in
position in the vehicle; the string can then be
used to draw the new cable in position.

---

5 Selector cable -
removal and refitting

Removal

AD4 type transmission

1 Remove the centre console as described in
Chapter 11.
2 Release the outer cable adjuster retaining
clip then detach the inner cable balljoint and
free the cable from the selector lever. Undo
the retaining nut(s) and free the cable guide
from the floor **(see illustrations)**.
3 To gain access to the transmission end of
the cable, remove the air cleaner housing and
bracket as described in Chapter 4A.
4 Unclip the inner cable balljoint from the
transmission selector lever then remove the
retaining clip and free the cable from its

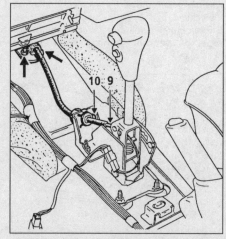

**5.2b Selector cable (9) and retaining clip
(10) at the lever end. Cable guide retaining
nuts are arrowed - AD4 transmission**

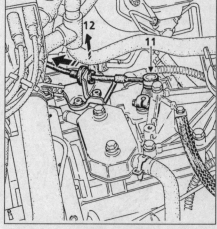

**5.4 Selector cable balljoint (11) and outer
cable fitting (12) at the transmission end -
AD4 transmission**

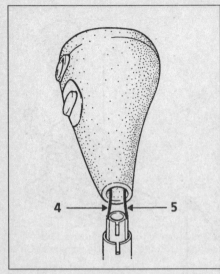

6.6 When refitting the selector lever knob, take great care to ensure the switch wires (4 and 5) are not crossed and are correctly routed down the lever guides

7 Examine the cable, looking for worn end fittings or a damaged outer casing, and for signs of fraying of the inner wire. Check the cable's operation; the inner wire should move smoothly and easily through the outer casing. If the adjuster mechanism is thought to be faulty the cable must be renewed.

DPO type transmission

8 Remove the selector lever assembly as described in Section 6.
9 Release the outer cable retaining clip then detach the inner cable balljoint and free the cable from the selector lever. Undo the retaining nuts and free the cable guide from the floor.
10 To gain access to the transmission end of the cable, remove the air cleaner housing and bracket as described in Chapter 4A.
11 Disconnect the selector cable end fitting from the multi-function switch on top of the transmission. Release the outer cable from the support bracket by turning the two locking rings in opposite directions **(see illustration 4.14)**. Do not move the orange ring as the locking rings are released. Note that if the orange ring

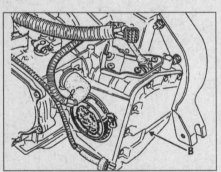

7.5 Remove the final drive housing cover plate (B) to gain access to the speedometer drive - AD4 transmission

breaks during removal, this will not adversely affect the operation of the cable and is not grounds for cable renewal.
12 Release the cable sealing grommet from the bulkhead then withdraw the cable, releasing it from all the relevant retaining clips and guides, and remove it from inside the vehicle.
13 Examine the cable, looking for worn end fittings or a damaged outer casing, and for signs of fraying of the inner wire. Check the cable's operation; the inner wire should move smoothly and easily through the outer casing. If the adjuster mechanism is thought to be faulty the cable must be renewed.

Refitting

14 Refitting is the reverse of removal, using the string (where applicable) to draw the new cable through from inside the vehicle and into position in the engine compartment. Ensure that the outer cable sealing grommet is correctly located in the bulkhead and prior to refitting the air cleaner housing, adjust the cable as described in Section 4.

---

6 Selector lever assembly - removal and refitting

Removal

1 Remove the centre console as described in Chapter 11.
2 If the control knob assembly is to be removed, disconnect the wiring connector then cut the sport mode switch wires. Undo the retaining screw and slide the knob off from the top of the selector lever, noting how the switch wires are routed down the channel on either side of the lever.
3 Release the outer cable retaining clip then detach the inner cable balljoint and free the cable adjuster from the selector lever.
4 Slacken and remove the retaining nuts and washers and remove the lever assembly from the vehicle.
5 Examine the selector lever assembly for signs of wear or damage and renew if necessary.

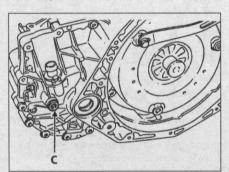

7.10 Final drive filler/level plug (C) - AD4 transmission

Refitting

6 Refitting is the reverse of removal, noting the following points.
a) *Prior to refitting, apply a smear of multi-purpose grease to the sliding surfaces of the selector lever mechanism.*
b) *If knob was removed, carefully feed the sport mode switch wires down the guides in the selector lever making sure the wires are not crossed* **(see illustration)**. *Seat the control knob in position and tighten its retaining screw. Crimp new wiring connectors onto the ends of the switch wires and locate the connectors in the wiring block.*
c) *On completion check the operation of the selector lever and, if necessary, adjust the cable as described in Section 4.*

---

7 Speedometer drive (AD4 transmission) - removal and refitting

Removal

1 The speedometer drive gear can be removed once the final drive cover plate has been unbolted from the rear of the transmission.
2 Firmly apply the handbrake then jack up the front of the vehicle and support it on axle stands (see *Jacking and vehicle support*). Undo the retaining screws and remove the plastic undercover from beneath the engine/transmission.
3 Disconnect the speedometer cable from the drive.
4 Place a suitable container under the final drive housing, to catch the fluid which will be released as the cover plate is removed.
5 Unscrew the securing bolts, and remove the final drive housing cover plate **(see illustration)**. Recover the gasket.
6 Unscrew the speedometer gear housing from the top of the transmission, then unclip the drive gear and withdraw the gear from inside the final drive housing. Recover the sealing ring.

Refitting

7 Fit a new sealing ring to the speedometer gear housing and insert the housing into the transmission. Clip the drive gear into the housing and seat the housing in position, making sure the gear is correctly engaged, and tighten securely.
8 Ensure the cover plate and transmission surfaces are clean and dry and refit the cover using a new gasket. Fit the cover bolts and tighten them securely.
9 Securely reconnect the speedometer cable to the drive.
10 It is now necessary to refill the final drive unit, the unit is refilled via the filler/level plug on the right-hand end of the transmission **(see illustration)**. Slacken and remove the filler/level plug and refill the final drive with the

exact amount of the specified type of oil (see *Lubricants and fluids*) until the fluid level is up to the lower edge of the filler/level plug hole. **Note:** *If the correct amount was poured into the final drive and a large amount flows out, refit the filler/level plug and take the car on a short journey so that the new oil is distributed fully around the transmission components, then check the level again on your return.* Refit the filler/level plug, tighten it securely and lower the vehicle to the ground.

11 Take the vehicle on a short drive. On your return, park the vehicle the vehicle on level ground and check the final drive unit oil level as described in Chapter 1A, Section 9.

8 Oil seals - renewal

AD4 type transmission

Right-hand differential oil seal

1 Apply the handbrake, then jack up the front of the car and support it on axle stands (see *Jacking and vehicle support*). Remove the right-hand wheel.

2 Referring to Chapter 8, disconnect the complete driveshaft assembly from the transmission. Note that it is not necessary to remove the driveshaft completely, the shaft can be left attached to the hub assembly and freed from the transmission as the hub assembly is pulled outwards. **Note:** *Do not allow it to hang down under its own weight as this could damage the constant velocity joints/gaiters.*

3 Carefully lever off the oil seal protector from the outside of the transmission housing **(see illustration)**. Note the fitted depth of the old seal, then carefully lever the seal out of position using a flat-bladed screwdriver.

4 Wipe clean the oil seal seating in the casing and apply a smear of oil to the seal lip. Making sure the seal lip is facing inwards, carefully ease the new seal into position over the differential shaft. Press the seal squarely into the transmission until it is positioned at the same depth as the original was prior to removal. If necessary the seal can be tapped into position using a piece of metal tube or a socket which bears only on the hard outer edge of the seal.

5 Fit the new seal protector making sure it is pressed securely into position.

6 Carefully refit the driveshaft assembly as described in Chapter 8.

7 Check and, if necessary, top-up the final drive oil level as described in Chapter 1A, Section 9.

8 Refit the roadwheel and lower the car to the ground and tighten the wheelbolts to the specified torque.

Left-hand differential oil seal

Note: *In order to renew the oil seal it will be necessary to obtain a suitable alternative to*

the *Renault service tool (B.Vi.1255)* **(see illustration).** *This is needed to compress the driveshaft flange spring to allow the retaining circlip to be removed and refitted.*

9 Apply the handbrake, then jack up the front of the car and support it on axle stands (see *Jacking and vehicle support*). Remove the left-hand front roadwheel.

10 Referring to Chapter 8, disconnect the driveshaft from the transmission. Note that it is not necessary to remove the driveshaft completely, the shaft can be left attached to the hub assembly and freed from the flange as the hub assembly is pulled outwards. **Note:** *Do not allow it to hang down under its own weight as this could damage the constant velocity joints/gaiters.*

11 Prise out the cap from the centre of the driveshaft flange to reveal the circlip. Discard the cap, a new one should be used on refitting.

12 Press the driveshaft flange into the transmission (see Note at the start of this Section) and remove the circlip.

13 Carefully release the driveshaft flange until all the spring tension is relieved then remove the driveshaft flange and spring from the transmission.

14 Note the correct fitted position of the original oil seal then carefully lever the seal out of position using a flat-bladed screwdriver.

15 Wipe clean the oil seal seating in the casing. Press the new seal squarely into the transmission, making sure its sealing lip is facing inwards, until it is positioned at the same depth as the original was prior to removal. If necessary the seal can be tapped into position using a piece of metal tube or a socket which bears only on the hard outer edge of the seal.

16 Apply a smear of grease to the sealing lip of the seal and the shoulder of the driveshaft flange. Carefully refit the driveshaft flange and spring to the transmission taking care not to damage the oil seal. Compress the spring and secure the flange in position with the circlip.

17 Make sure the circlip is correctly located in the shaft groove then tap a new cap into position in the centre of the flange.

18 Reconnect the driveshaft to the transmission as described in Chapter 8.

19 Check and, if necessary, top-up the final drive oil level as described in Chapter 1A, Section 9.

20 Refit the roadwheel and lower the car to the ground and tighten the wheelbolts to the specified torque.

Torque converter seal

21 Remove the transmission from the engine as described in Section 12.

22 Remove the retaining strap and carefully slide the torque converter off from the transmission shaft. Be prepared for fluid loss as the converter is removed.

23 Using a flat-bladed screwdriver carefully lever the seal out from the centre of the torque converter, taking great care not to mark the metal bush.

8.3 Removing the right-hand differential oil seal protector (A) - AD4 transmission

24 Press the new seal squarely into position making sure its sealing lip is facing inwards.

25 Lubricate the lip of the seal with clean transmission fluid and carefully slide the converter onto the transmission shaft.

26 Make sure the torque converter is correctly engaged with the transmission shaft splines then refit the transmission as described in Section 12.

DPO type transmission

Differential oil seals

27 Disconnect the battery negative terminal (refer to *Disconnecting the battery* in the Reference Section of this manual).

28 Apply the handbrake, then jack up the front of the car and support it on axle stands (see *Jacking and vehicle support*). Remove the relevant road wheel.

29 Drain the transmission fluid as described in Section 2.

30 Referring to Chapter 8, disconnect the complete driveshaft assembly from the transmission on the side being worked on.

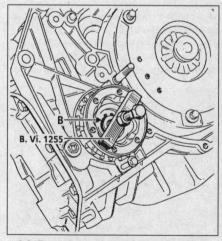

8.9 Renault special tool (B. Vi. 1255) to enable the left-hand drive shaft flange circlip (B) to be removed - AD4 transmission

7B

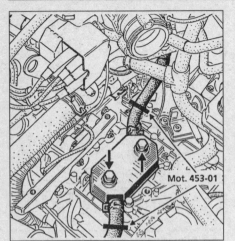

9.1 Fluid cooler is mounted onto the top of the transmission unit. The cooler hoses and mounting bolts are arrowed - AD4 transmission

Note that it is not necessary to remove the driveshaft completely, the shaft can be left attached to the hub assembly and freed from the transmission as the hub assembly is pulled outwards. **Note:** *Do not allow it to hang down under its own weight as this could damage the constant velocity joints/gaiters.*

31 Note the fitted depth of the old seal, then carefully lever the seal out of position using a flat-bladed screwdriver.

32 Wipe clean the oil seal seating in the casing and apply a smear of oil to the seal lip. Making sure the seal lip is facing inwards, carefully ease the new seal into position over the differential shaft. Press the seal squarely into the transmission until it is positioned at the same depth as the original was prior to removal. If necessary the seal can be tapped into position using a piece of metal tube or a socket which bears only on the hard outer edge of the seal.

33 Carefully refit the driveshaft assembly as described in Chapter 8.

34 Refill the transmission with new fluid as described in Section 2.

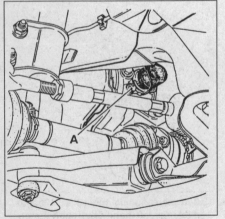

10.2 Multi-function switch and earth bolt (A) - AD4 transmission

35 Refit the roadwheel, lower the car to the ground and tighten the wheelbolts to the specified torque.

Torque converter seal

36 Proceed as described in paragraphs 21 to 26.

9 Fluid cooler - removal and refitting

Removal

1 The fluid cooler is located on top of the transmission on the AD4 unit, or on the rear left-hand side on the DPO unit **(see illustration)**. To gain access to the cooler, remove the air cleaner and mounting bracket as described in Chapter 4A.

2 To minimise coolant loss, clamp the coolant hoses on either side of the fluid cooler. Alternately, drain the cooling system as described in Chapter 1A.

3 Loosen the clips and disconnect the hoses from the fluid cooler - be prepared for some coolant spillage. Wash off any spilt coolant immediately with cold water, and dry the surrounding area before proceeding further.

4 Slacken and remove the mounting bolt(s), and remove the fluid cooler from the transmission. There will be some loss of fluid, so some clean rags should be placed around the cooler to absorb spillage. Make sure that dirt is prevented from entering the hydraulic system.

5 Remove the sealing ring from each mounting bolt and the sealing rings fitted between the cooler and transmission. Discard all sealing rings; new ones must be used on refitting.

Refitting

6 Lubricate the new seals with clean automatic transmission fluid, then fit the two new seals to the base of the fluid cooler, and a new seal to each mounting bolt.

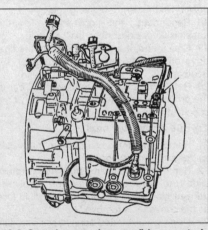

10.6 Speed sensor (arrowed) is mounted onto the top of the transmission unit - AD4 transmission

7 Locate the fluid cooler on the top of transmission housing, ensuring its lower seals remain in position. Refit the mounting bolt(s) and tighten them to the specified torque.

8 Reconnect the coolant hoses to the fluid cooler, and securely tighten their retaining clips. Remove the hose clamps.

9 Refit the air cleaner housing as described in Chapter 4A.

10 On completion, top-up the cooling system and check the automatic transmission fluid level as described in *Weekly checks* and Chapter 1A.

10 Electronic control components (AD4 transmission) - removal and refitting

Note: *Whenever any of the transmission electronic control components are renewed, on completion it is necessary to validate the no-load/full-load position of the transmission. To do this, the Renault (XR25) diagnostic equipment is needed. Therefore, it will be necessary to entrust the following work to a Renault dealer if access to the necessary equipment cannot be gained. Failure to validate the no-load/full-load position could lead to incorrect gearchange thresholds and the instrument panel warning light illuminating randomly.*

Removal

1 Disconnect the battery negative terminal (refer to *Disconnecting the battery* in the Reference Section of this manual).

Multi-function switch

2 The multi-function switch informs the electronic control unit of the selector lever position, prevents the starter motor operating when the transmission is in gear and also controls the reversing lights. The switch is located on the rear of the transmission, above the left-hand driveshaft **(see illustration)**.

3 To remove the switch, trace the wiring back from the switch and disconnect it at the connector.

4 Unscrew the mounting bolt and remove the clamp plate. Unscrew the earth wire bolt, then pull the switch out of the transmission along with its sealing ring.

Throttle potentiometer

5 Refer to Chapter 4A, Section 14, 15 or 16.

Vehicle speed sensor

6 The speed sensor is mounted onto the top of the transmission, on its front left-hand end **(see illustration)**.

7 If necessary, to improve access, remove the air cleaner assembly and mounting bracket, as described in Chapter 4A.

8 Trace the wiring back from the sensor and disconnect at the wiring connector.

9 Unscrew the mounting bolt and remove the clamp plate, then pull the switch out of the transmission along with its sealing ring.

Line pressure sensor

10 The line pressure sensor is fitted to the base of the transmission, on the front end **(see illustration)**.

11 To gain access to the sensor, firmly apply the handbrake then jack up the front of the vehicle and support it on axle stands. Undo the retaining screws and remove the plastic undercover.

12 Trace the wiring back from the sensor and disconnect it at the wiring connector.

13 Be prepared for some fluid loss as the sensor is removed then slacken the retaining bolts and remove the sensor retaining plate. Remove the sensor and recover the sealing ring.

Electronic control unit

14 The electronic control unit (ECU) is located in the front, left-hand corner of the engine compartment where it is clipped to the front of the battery **(see illustration)**.

15 Release the rubber retaining strap then disconnect the wiring connectors and remove the ECU from the engine compartment.

Refitting

16 Refitting is a reversal of the removal procedure. On completion reconnect the battery and validate the no-load/full-load position of the transmission.

---

11 Multi-function switch (DPO transmission) - removal and refitting

Removal

1 Disconnect the battery negative terminal (refer to *Disconnecting the battery* in the Reference Section of this manual).

2 The multi-function switch informs the electronic control unit of the selector lever

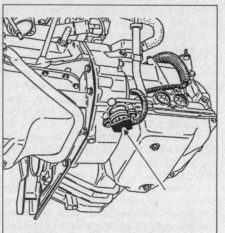

10.10 Line pressure sensor (arrowed) is located on the base of the transmission - AD4 transmission

position, prevents the starter motor operating when the transmission is in gear and also controls the reversing lights. The switch is located on the top of the transmission, below the air cleaner.

3 To gain access to the switch, remove the air cleaner and mounting bracket as described in Chapter 4A.

4 Disconnect the selector cable end fitting from the multi-function switch lever.

5 Pull out the locking tab and disconnect the transmission wiring harness modular connector **(see illustration)**.

6 Undo the three mounting bolts and release the modular connector mounting plate from the top of the transmission.

7 Undo the two multi-function switch mounting bolts and lift off the switch. Trace the switch wiring back to the modular connector plate and disconnect the 12-pin socket from the connector plate **(see illustration)**. Remove the multi-function switch from the transmission.

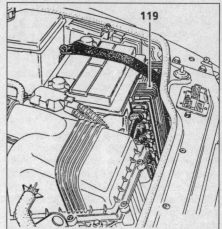

10.14 Transmission electronic control unit (ECU) (119) is strapped onto the front of the battery - AD4 transmission

Refitting

8 Reconnect the multi-function switch wiring to the modular connector plate, then refit the plate and attach the connector.

9 Position the multi-function switch on the transmission and refit the two mounting bolts, finger tight only at this stage.

10 Reconnect the selector cable end fitting to the multi-function switch lever.

11 With the gear selector lever and multi-function switch in position N, connect an ohmmeter across the two test terminals on the side of the multi-function switch **(see illustration)**.

12 Turn the switch body until the internal switch contacts close and 0 ohms is indicated on the ohmmeter. Hold the switch body in this position and tighten the two retaining bolts.

13 Refit the air cleaner and mounting bracket as described in Chapter 4A, then reconnect the battery.

14 Check that the starter motor will only operate with P or N selected.

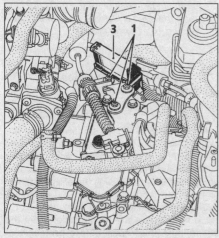

11.5 Transmission wiring harness modular connector (3) and mounting plate bolts (1) - DPO transmission

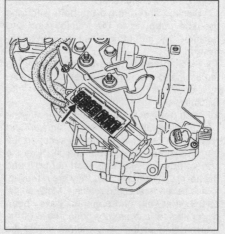

11.7 Multi-function switch wiring socket (arrowed) in the modular connector plate - DPO transmission

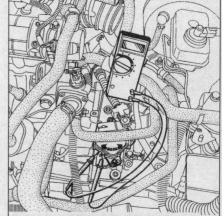

11.11 Using an ohmmeter to set the multi-function switch position - DPO transmission

7B

12 Automatic transmission - removal and refitting

Note: *On refitting it will be necessary to validate the no-load/full-load position of the transmission (see Note at the start of Section 10).*

Removal

1 Disconnect the battery negative terminal (refer to *Disconnecting the battery* in the Reference Section of this manual), then remove the air cleaner housing and mounting bracket as described in Chapter 4A.

2 Firmly apply the handbrake then jack up the front of the vehicle and support it on axle stands (see *Jacking and vehicle support*). Remove both front roadwheels then undo the retaining screws and remove the plastic undercover and left-hand wheelarch liner.

3 Remove the starter motor as described in Chapter 5A.

4 Remove the left-hand drive shaft as described in Chapter 8.

5 Referring to Chapter 8, disconnect the complete right-hand driveshaft from the transmission. Note that it is not necessary to remove the driveshaft completely, the shaft can be left attached to the hub assembly and released from the transmission as the hub assembly is pulled outwards. **Note:** *Do not allow it to hang down under its own weight as this could damage the constant velocity joints/gaiters.*

6 On models equipped with power steering, undo the retaining bolts securing the power steering pipes to the end of the transmission. Position the pipes clear of the transmission so they will not hinder removal. Disconnect the engine earth strap adjacent to the power steering fluid pipes

7 On the AD4 transmission, release the retaining clip and disconnect the speed-ometer cable from its drive. On the DPO transmission, disconnect the vehicle speed sensor connector.

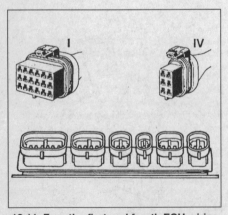

12.11 Free the first and fourth ECU wiring connectors from the wiring loom to enable the loom to be removed with the transmission unit - AD4 transmission

8 Remove the crankshaft sensor as described in Chapter 4A, Section 14, and disconnect the lambda sensor wiring connector.

9 Undo the retaining bolts and remove the driveplate lower cover plate from the base of the transmission housing. On some models the plate has support struts attached to it, these will have to be unbolted from the side of the cylinder block.

10 Clamp the hoses to minimise coolant loss then release the retaining clips and detach the coolant hoses from the transmission fluid cooler. Mop up any spilt coolant.

11 On the AD4 transmission, release the retaining clips and disconnect the wiring connectors from the transmission electronic control unit (ECU) which is situated in the left-hand corner of the engine compartment. Free the first and fourth wiring connectors from the ECU loom; the remaining wiring connectors and loom are then free to be removed with the transmission **(see illustration)**.

12 On the DPO transmission, pull out the locking tab and disconnect the transmission wiring harness modular connector. Protect the connector by placing it in a plastic bag.

13 Disconnect the selector cable from the transmission and position it clear of the unit (see Section 5).

14 Slacken and remove the three nuts securing the torque converter to the engine driveplate. The nuts are accessible through the cover plate aperture. Unscrew the visible nut then, using a socket and extension bar to rotate the crankshaft pulley, undo the remaining nuts securing the torque converter to the driveplate as they become accessible. Note that new nuts will be required for refitting.

15 Place a jack with a block of wood beneath the engine, to take the weight of the engine. Alternatively, attach a hoist or support bar to the engine lifting eyes take the engine weight.

16 Place a jack and block of wood beneath the transmission, and raise the jack to take the weight of the transmission.

17 Slacken and remove the bolts securing the rear mounting to the transmission and position the mounting clear of the transmission.

18 Slacken and remove the bolts securing the left-hand mounting bracket to the transmission housing then slightly lower the transmission.

19 With the jack positioned beneath the transmission taking the weight, slacken and remove the remaining nut/bolts securing the transmission housing to the engine. Note the correct fitted positions of each nut/bolt, and the necessary brackets, as they are removed, to use as a reference on refitting. Make a final check that all components have been disconnected, and are positioned clear of the transmission so that they will not hinder the removal procedure.

20 With the bolts removed, make sure the torque converter is pushed fully onto the

transmission shaft then move the trolley jack and transmission to the left, to free it from its locating dowels.

21 Once the transmission is free, lower the jack and manoeuvre the unit out from under the car. Remove the locating dowels from the transmission or engine if they are loose, and keep them in a safe place. Secure the torque converter in position by bolting a length of metal bar to one of the housing holes.

Refitting

22 The transmission is refitted by a reversal of the removal procedure, bearing in mind the following points

a) *Remove the retaining bar and ensure that the torque converter is pushed fully onto the transmission. Apply a smear of high-melting point grease (Renault recommend the use of Molykote BR2) to the converter centring ring.*

b) *Ensure the locating dowels are correctly positioned prior to installation and clean the torque converter to driveplate stud threads.*

c) *Aligning the torque converter studs with the driveplate holes as the transmission is refitted. Apply thread locking compound (Renault recommend the use of Loctite Frenbloc) to the new retaining nuts and tighten them to the specified torque.*

d) *Tighten all nuts and bolts to the specified torque (where given).*

e) *Refit the driveshafts as described in Chapter 8.*

f) *Connect the selector cable and adjust as described in Sections 5 and 4.*

g) *On completion, top-up/refill the transmission and final drive (as applicable) with the specified type and quantity of lubricant, as described in Section 2 and/or Chapter 1A.*

h) *On AD4 transmissions, validate the no-load/full-load position of the transmission using the special Renault equipment (see Section 10), on completion.*

13 Automatic transmission overhaul - general information

In the event of a fault occurring with the transmission, it is first necessary to determine whether it is of an electrical, mechanical or hydraulic nature, and to do this, special test equipment is required. It is therefore essential to have the work carried out by a Renault dealer if a transmission fault is suspected.

Do not remove the transmission from the car for possible repair before professional fault diagnosis has been carried out, since most tests require the transmission to be in the vehicle.

Chapter 8
Driveshafts

Contents

Degrees of difficulty

Easy, suitable for novice with little experience	**Fairly easy,** suitable for beginner with some experience	**Fairly difficult,** suitable for competent DIY mechanic	**Difficult,** suitable for experienced DIY mechanic	**Very difficult,** suitable for expert DIY or professional

Specifications

General

Type .... Tubular steel with constant velocity (CV) joint at each end
Lubrication .... Special grease supplied in sachets with gaiter kits - joints are otherwise pre-packed with grease, and sealed

Torque wrench settings

	Nm	lbf ft
Driveshaft nut	250	185
Left-hand driveshaft inner gaiter retaining plate bolts	25	18
Roadwheel bolts	See Chapter 1A or 1B	

1 General information

Drive is transmitted from the differential to the front wheels by means of two tubular steel driveshafts of unequal length.

Constant velocity (CV) joints are fitted to each end of the driveshafts, to ensure the smooth and efficient transmission of power at all suspension and steering angles.

Both driveshafts are fitted with ball-and-cage-type constant velocity (CV) joints at their outer ends. Each joint has an outer member, which is splined at its outer end to accept the wheel hub, and is threaded so that the hub can be fastened by a large nut.

On petrol engine models with a manual gearbox, except for 2.0 litre (16-valve) engines, different types of inner joint are fitted to each driveshaft. On the right-hand drive-shaft, a tripod-type CV joint is fitted to the inner end of the driveshaft - the joint outer member is splined, and is secured to the differential sun gear using roll-pins. On the left-hand side, the inner end of the driveshaft

also engages with a tripod-type joint, but the yoke in which the tripod is free to slide is an integral part of the differential sunwheel. The inner gaiter is secured to the transmission casing via a retaining plate and bolts, and to a ball-bearing on the driveshaft via a retaining clip. The bearing allows the driveshaft to turn within the gaiter, which does not revolve.

On diesel engine, and 2.0 litre (16-valve) petrol engine models, the left-hand driveshaft is of the same type as that described previously, but a two-piece right-hand driveshaft is fitted. The inner section of the right-hand driveshaft is splined, via a connecting sleeve, to the differential sunwheel, and is supported by an intermediate bearing, located in a bracket at its outer end. The inner and outer sections of the right-hand driveshaft are joined by a tripod-type CV joint.

On models with automatic transmission, a one-piece left-hand driveshaft is fitted - the outer member of the inner CV joint is bolted to the transmission drive flange, and the complete joint is protected by a gaiter, secured to the driveshaft and outer member. A two-piece right-hand driveshaft is fitted - the driveshaft outer section is bolted to the inner section via a

flange, and the driveshaft inner section splined to the differential sunwheel, and is supported by an intermediate bearing.

2 Right-hand driveshaft - removal and refitting

Manual gearbox models with one-piece driveshaft

Removal

Note: *A new driveshaft nut, new suspension strut-to-hub carrier nuts, and a new track-rod end balljoint nut will be required on refitting, and new roll-pins will be required to secure the inner end of the driveshaft on refitting. Sealant will be required to coat the outer end of the driveshaft. A balljoint separator tool will be required for this operation, and a hub puller may be required to free the end of the driveshaft from the hub.*

1 Apply the handbrake, then jack up the front of the vehicle and support securely on axle stands (see *Jacking and vehicle support*). Remove the relevant front roadwheel.

8

On models where access to the driveshaft nut can be obtained by removing the wheel trims, before jacking up the vehicle, loosen the driveshaft nut as follows:
a) *Chock the front wheels, and remove the wheel trim.*
b) *Have an assistant firmly apply the footbrake.*
c) *Loosen the driveshaft nut using a socket and extension.*

2 On models with ABS, it is advisable to remove the ABS wheel sensor as described in Chapter 9, to avoid any possibility of damage during the removal procedure.
3 If the driveshaft nut has been loosened, proceed to paragraph 5, otherwise proceed as follows.
4 Refit at least two roadwheel bolts to the front hub, and tighten them securely. Have an assistant firmly depress the brake pedal to prevent the front hub from rotating, then using a socket and a long extension bar, slacken and remove the driveshaft retaining nut. Alternatively, a tool can be fabricated from two lengths of steel strip (one long, one short) and a nut and bolt; the nut and bolt forming the

2.9 Drive out the double roll-pins securing the driveshaft to the sun gear shaft

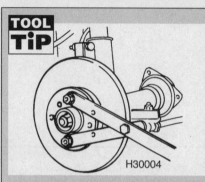

Using a fabricated tool to hold the front hub stationary whilst the driveshaft nut is slackened

pivot of a forked tool. Bolt the tool to the hub using two wheel bolts, and hold the tool to prevent the hub from rotating as the driveshaft retaining nut is undone **(see Tool Tip)**. This nut is very tight; make sure that there is no risk of pulling the car off the axle stands. (If the roadwheel trim allows access to the driveshaft nut, the initial slackening can be done with the wheels chocked and on the ground.)
5 Unbolt the brake caliper from the hub carrier as described in Chapter 9. Note that there is no need to disconnect the fluid hose - suspend the caliper from the suspension strut using wire or string, ensuring that the hose is not strained.
6 Slacken and partially unscrew the track-rod end balljoint nut (unscrew the nut as far as the end of the threads on the balljoint to prevent damage to the threads as the joint is released), then release the balljoint using a balljoint separator tool. Remove the nut, and discard it - a new nut must be used on refitting.
7 Unscrew the nut from the end of the upper suspension strut-to-hub carrier bolt. Note that the bolt is splined into the hub carrier. Temporarily screw the nut onto the end of the bolt to protect the bolt threads, then tap the bolt from the hub carrier, using a soft-faced

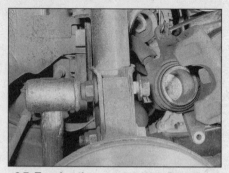

2.7 Tapping the upper suspension strut-to-hub carrier bolt from the hub carrier

hammer. Withdraw the bolt, and discard the nut - a new nut must be used on refitting **(see illustration)**.
8 Similarly, unscrew the lower suspension strut-to-hub carrier nut, and tap the bolt to free the splines from the hub carrier. Do not remove the bolt at this stage.
9 Working at the transmission end of the driveshaft, where applicable remove the sealant from the ends of the roll-pins securing the inner end of the driveshaft to the sun gear shaft, then drive out the double roll-pins, using a pin-punch **(see illustration)**.
10 Unscrew the driveshaft nut from the hub carrier end of the driveshaft. Recover the washer **(see illustration)**. Discard the nut, a new one must be used on refitting.
11 The driveshaft must now be released from the hub carrier **(see illustration)**. It should be possible to release the driveshaft by tapping the end of the driveshaft using a soft-faced hammer, or a hammer and a soft metal drift - **do not** strike the end of the driveshaft hard, as this may cause damage to the joints.
Note: *The driveshaft ends are fitted to the hub carriers using locking compound. Renault use a special extractor tool to release the driveshaft ends, but if the driveshaft cannot be released by hand, it should be possible to use a conventional hub puller as follows.*

2.10 Removing a driveshaft nut and washer

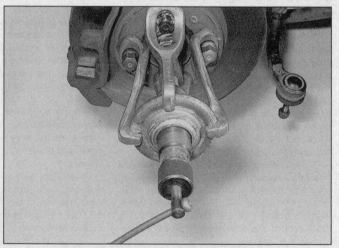

2.11 Using a hub puller to separate the driveshaft from the front hub

2.12 Withdrawing the end of the driveshaft from the hub

2.18 Fit a new O-ring to the sun gear shaft

2.19 Ensure that the roll-pin holes (arrowed) are correctly aligned

a) *Remove the brake disc with reference to Chapter 9.*

b) *Temporarily refit the driveshaft nut to protect the threads on the end of the driveshaft.*

c) *Fit the puller, with the arms bearing on the hub, and the centre screw bearing on the end of the driveshaft.*

d) *Use the puller to release the hub from the end of the driveshaft. Note that it is possible that the hub will be pulled from the hub bearing assembly (the bearing front half inner race will remain in position on the hub) - if this happens, a new bearing must be fitted as described in Chapter 10.*

12 Pivot the hub carrier downwards as necessary until the end of the driveshaft can be withdrawn from the hub **(see illustration)**. If necessary, unscrew the nut from the lower suspension strut-to-hub carrier bolt, and withdraw the bolt to enable the hub carrier to be pivoted further (discard the nut - a new nut must be used on refitting).

13 Place a container beneath the transmission end of the driveshaft to catch escaping oil/fluid which may be released as the end of the driveshaft is withdrawn.

14 Pull the driveshaft from the transmission, then withdraw the assembly from under the

vehicle. Where applicable, recover the O-ring from the end of the sun gear shaft.

Refitting

Note: *If a new driveshaft is being fitted, it may be supplied with a protective cardboard cover fitted over the outer driveshaft gaiter. In this case, do not remove the cover until the completion of the refitting procedure.*

15 Thoroughly clean all traces of old locking compound from the hub carrier end of the driveshaft.

16 Before installing the driveshaft, examine the driveshaft oil seal in the transmission for signs of damage or deterioration and, if necessary, renew it, referring to the appropriate part of Chapter 7 for further information. (Having got this far it is worth renewing the seal as a matter of course.)

17 Thoroughly clean the driveshaft splines, and the apertures in the transmission and hub assembly. Apply a thin film of grease to the oil seal lips, and to the driveshaft splines and shoulders. Check that all gaiter clips are securely fastened.

18 Where applicable, fit a new O-ring to the sun gear shaft **(see illustration)**.

19 Engage the inboard end of the driveshaft with the sun gear, ensuring that the roll-pin holes in the driveshaft and gear shaft are aligned **(see illustration)**.

20 Coat the hub end of the driveshaft with locking compound (Renault recommend the use of Loctite Scelbloc), then engage the end of the driveshaft with the hub. **Note:** *If the hub has been pulled from the bearing during the removal procedure, fit a new bearing as described in Chapter 10.*

21 Where applicable, refit the lower suspension strut-to-hub carrier bolt (noting that the bolts fits from the front of the vehicle), and screw a new nut onto the bolt. Do not screw the nut fully onto the bolt at this stage.

22 Secure the inner end of the driveshaft to the sun gear using new roll-pins. Coat the ends of the roll-pins with sealant **(see illustrations)**.

23 Screw the **new** driveshaft nut onto the end of the driveshaft as far as possible by hand, ensuring that the washer is in place, then tighten the nut until the end of the driveshaft is fully engaged with the hub. Do not fully tighten the nut at this stage.

24 Refit the upper suspension strut-to-hub carrier bolt (noting that the bolts fits from the front of the vehicle), and screw a new nut onto the bolt. Tap the bolts into position in the hub carrier (until the splines are engaged and the underside of the bolt head touches the suspension strut, then tighten the upper and lower suspension strut-to-hub carrier nuts to the specified torque (Chapter 10).

2.22b Seal the ends of the roll-pins with sealant

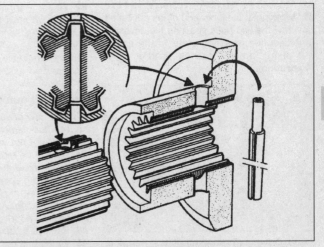

2.22a Right-hand driveshaft inner joint roll-pin arrangement

8

25 Reconnect the track-rod end to the hub carrier, and tighten a new balljoint nut to the specified torque (Chapter 10).

26 Where applicable, refit the brake disc, then refit the brake caliper, with reference to Chapter 9.

27 Use the method employed on removal to prevent the hub from rotating, and tighten the driveshaft retaining nut to the specified torque. Check that the hub rotates freely.

> **HAYNES HINT** *Where access to the drive-shaft nut can be gained by removing the wheel trim, the nut can be tightened with the footbrake firmly applied, and the vehicle resting on its wheels.*

28 Where applicable, refit the ABS wheel sensor, with reference to Chapter 9.

29 Where applicable, tear off the protective cover from the outer driveshaft joint gaiter. Do not use a sharp tool which may damage the gaiter.

30 Refit the roadwheel, then lower the vehicle to the ground and tighten the road-wheel bolts to the specified torque.

31 On completion, check the transmission oil/fluid level using the information in the relevant part of Chapter 1.

Manual gearbox models with two-piece driveshaft

Complete driveshaft - removal

Note: *On models with a two-piece driveshaft, the driveshaft can be removed as a complete assembly, as described in the following paragraphs, or the driveshaft outer section can be removed independently, as described later in this Section.*

Note: *A new driveshaft nut, new suspension strut-to-hub carrier nuts, and a new track-rod end balljoint nut will be required on refitting. Sealant will be required to coat the outer end of the driveshaft. A balljoint separator tool will be required for this operation.*

32 Proceed as described in paragraphs 1 to 8.

33 Working at the inner end of the driveshaft, unscrew the two bolts securing the driveshaft inner section retaining plate to the engine mounting bracket/bearing carrier **(see illustration)**.

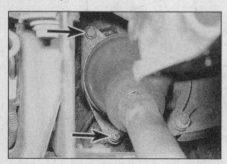

2.33 Driveshaft retaining plate-to-engine mounting bracket/bearing carrier bolts (arrowed)

34 Proceed as in paragraphs 10 to 13.

35 Pull the driveshaft from the transmission and the engine mounting bracket/bearing carrier, and recover the dust shield from the transmission end of the driveshaft.

Complete driveshaft - refitting

Note: *If a new driveshaft is being fitted, it may be supplied with a protective cardboard cover fitted over the outer driveshaft gaiter. In this case, do not remove the cover until the completion of the refitting procedure.*

36 Before refitting, thoroughly clean the mating faces of the driveshaft bearing and bearing carrier. Check the condition of the oil seal contact face on the driveshaft - if the driveshaft surface is excessively worn or deeply grooved, the driveshaft inner section should be renewed (as described later in this Section).

37 It is recommended that the differential output oil seal is renewed before refitting the driveshaft (see Chapter 7A).

38 Thoroughly clean all traces of old locking compound from the hub carrier end of the driveshaft.

39 Thoroughly clean the driveshaft splines, and the apertures in the transmission and hub assembly. Apply a thin film of grease to the oil seal lips, and to the driveshaft inner splines and shoulders. Check that all gaiter clips are securely fastened, and check that the dust seal is in position on the transmission end of the driveshaft.

40 Slide the inner end of the driveshaft into position in the transmission, and engage the intermediate bearing with the engine mounting bracket/bearing carrier, then secure with the retaining plate, and securely tighten the bolts. Slide the dust shield along the inner end of the shaft until it is flush with the transmission.

41 Coat the hub end of the driveshaft with locking compound (Renault recommend the use of Loctite Scelbloc), then engage the end of the driveshaft with the hub. **Note:** *If the hub has been pulled from the bearing during the removal procedure, fit a new bearing as described in Chapter 10.*

42 Where applicable, refit the lower suspension strut-to-hub carrier bolt (noting that the bolts fits from the front of the vehicle), and screw a new nut onto the bolt. Do not screw the nut fully onto the bolt at this stage.

43 Proceed as described in paragraphs 23 to 31.

Driveshaft outer section - removal

Note: *A new driveshaft nut, new suspension strut-to-hub carrier nuts, and a new track-rod end balljoint nut will be required on refitting. Sealant will be required to coat the outer end of the driveshaft, and a sachet of the appropriate grease (available from a Renault dealer) will be required to pack the driveshaft joint on refitting. A balljoint separator tool will be required for this operation.*

44 Proceed as described in paragraphs 1 to 8.

45 Working at the inner end of the driveshaft, cut the inner driveshaft gaiter securing clip, and slide the gaiter back from the joint.

46 Proceed as described in paragraphs 10 to 12.

47 Carefully withdraw the driveshaft outer section tripod joint from the driveshaft inner section. Be prepared to hold the rollers in place, otherwise they may fall off the tripod ends as the driveshaft outer section is withdrawn. If necessary, secure the rollers in place using tape. The rollers are matched to the tripod stems, and it is important that they are not interchanged.

Driveshaft outer section - refitting

Note: *If a new driveshaft is being fitted, it may be supplied with a protective cardboard cover fitted over the outer driveshaft gaiter. In this case, do not remove the cover until the completion of the refitting procedure.*

48 Thoroughly clean all traces of old locking compound from the hub carrier end of the driveshaft.

49 Wipe clean the driveshaft inner section and the joint spider, then pack about half of the sachet of new grease into the inner yoke, and around the joint spider. Insert the driveshaft outer section joint spider into the driveshaft inner section yoke, keeping the driveshaft horizontal as far as possible.

50 Pack the remainder of the grease evenly into the joint gaiter. Slide the gaiter over the end of the driveshaft inner section, then secure the gaiter with a new clip.

51 Coat the hub end of the driveshaft with locking compound (Renault recommend the use of Loctite Scelbloc), then engage the end of the driveshaft with the hub. **Note:** *If the hub has been pulled from the bearing during the removal procedure, fit a new bearing as described in Chapter 10.*

52 Where applicable, refit the lower suspension strut-to-hub carrier bolt (noting that the bolts fits from the front of the vehicle), and screw a new nut onto the bolt. Do not screw the nut fully onto the bolt at this stage.

53 Proceed as described in paragraphs 23 to 31.

Driveshaft inner section - removal

54 Remove the driveshaft outer section as described previously in this Section.

55 Unscrew the two bolts securing the driveshaft inner section retaining plate to engine mounting bracket/bearing carrier.

56 Slide the driveshaft inner section from the gearbox, and recover the dust shield from the inner end of the driveshaft.

Driveshaft inner section - refitting

57 Before refitting, thoroughly clean the mating faces of the driveshaft bearing and bearing housing. Check the condition of the oil seal contact face on the driveshaft - if the driveshaft surface is excessively worn or deeply grooved, the driveshaft inner section should be renewed.

58 It is recommended that the differential output oil seal is renewed before refitting the driveshaft inner section (see Chapter 7A).

59 Refitting is a reversal of removal, but securely tighten the driveshaft inner section retaining plate bolts, ensure that the dust shield is flush with the transmission, and refit the driveshaft outer section as previously in this Section.

Automatic transmission models

Complete driveshaft - removal

Note: *A new driveshaft nut, new suspension strut-to-hub carrier nuts, and a new track-rod end balljoint nut will be required on refitting. Sealant will be required to coat the outer end of the driveshaft. A balljoint separator tool will be required for this operation.*

60 Proceed as described in paragraphs 1 to 8.
61 Working at the inner end of the driveshaft, slacken the two intermediate bearing retaining bolt nuts, then rotate the bolts through 90°, so that their offset heads are clear of the bearing outer race.
62 Proceed as described in paragraphs 10 to 14.

Complete driveshaft - refitting

Note: *If a new driveshaft is being fitted, it may be supplied with a protective cardboard cover fitted over the outer driveshaft gaiter. In this case, do not remove the cover until the completion of the refitting procedure.*

63 Proceed as described in paragraphs 15 to 18.
64 Check that the intermediate bearing rotates smoothly, without any signs of roughness or undue free-play between its inner and outer races. If necessary, renew the bearing as described in Section 6.
65 Apply a smear of grease to the outer race of the intermediate bearing.
66 Pass the inner end of the shaft through the bearing mounting bracket, then carefully engage the inner driveshaft splines with the transmission, taking care not to damage the oil seal.
67 Align the intermediate bearing with its mounting bracket, and push the driveshaft fully into position. If necessary, use a soft-faced mallet to tap the outer race of the bearing into position in the mounting bracket.
68 Coat the hub end of the driveshaft with locking compound (Renault recommend the use of Loctite Scelbloc), then engage the end of the driveshaft with the hub. **Note:** *If the hub has been pulled from the bearing during the removal procedure, fit a new bearing as described in Chapter 10.*
69 Where applicable, refit the lower suspension strut-to-hub carrier bolt (noting that the bolts fits from the front of the vehicle), and screw a new nut onto the bolt. Do not screw the nut fully onto the bolt at this stage.
70 Ensure that that intermediate bearing is correctly seated, then rotate its retaining bolts back through 90° so that their offset heads are resting against the bearing outer race. Tighten the retaining bolts.
71 Proceed as described in paragraphs 23 to 31.

Driveshaft outer section - removal

Note: *A new driveshaft nut, new suspension strut-to-hub carrier nuts, and a new track-rod end balljoint nut will be required on refitting. Sealant will be required to coat the outer end of the driveshaft. A balljoint separator tool will be required for this operation.*

72 Proceed as described in paragraphs 1 to 8.
73 Working at the driveshaft flange, slacken and remove the six bolts and washers securing the driveshaft inner section to the outer section, rotating the shaft as necessary to gain access to the bolts.
74 Proceed as described in paragraphs 10 to 13.
75 Withdraw the driveshaft outer section.

Driveshaft outer section - refitting

Note: *If a new driveshaft is being fitted, it may be supplied with a protective cardboard cover fitted over the outer driveshaft gaiter. In this case, do not remove the cover until the completion of the refitting procedure.*

76 Ensure that the flange mating faces of the driveshaft inner and outer sections are clean and dry.
77 Engage the driveshaft outer section flange with the inner section flange, then refit the securing bolts (with washers). Securely tighten the bolts.
78 Thoroughly clean all traces of old locking compound from the hub carrier end of the driveshaft.
79 Thoroughly clean the driveshaft splines, and the aperture in the hub assembly.
80 Coat the hub end of the driveshaft with locking compound (Renault recommend the use of Loctite Scelbloc), then engage the end of the driveshaft with the hub. **Note:** *If the hub has been pulled from the bearing during the removal procedure, fit a new bearing as described in Chapter 10.*
81 Where applicable, refit the lower suspension strut-to-hub carrier bolt (noting that the bolts fits from the front of the vehicle), and screw a new nut onto the bolt. Do not screw the nut fully onto the bolt at this stage.
82 Proceed as described in paragraphs 23 to 31.

Driveshaft inner section - removal

83 Remove the driveshaft outer section as described previously in this Section.
84 Working at the inner end of the driveshaft, slacken the two intermediate bearing retaining bolt nuts, then rotate the bolts through 90°, so that their offset heads are clear of the bearing outer race.
85 Place a container beneath the transmission end of the driveshaft to catch escaping oil/fluid which may be released as the end of the driveshaft is withdrawn.
86 Pull the driveshaft from the transmission, then withdraw the assembly from under the vehicle. Where applicable, recover the O-ring from the end of the sun gear shaft.

Driveshaft inner section - refitting

Note: *If a new driveshaft is being fitted, it may*

be supplied with a protective cardboard cover fitted over the outer driveshaft gaiter. In this case, do not remove the cover until the completion of the refitting procedure.

87 Before installing the driveshaft, examine the driveshaft oil seal in the transmission for signs of damage or deterioration and, if necessary, renew it, referring to the appropriate part of Chapter 7 for further information. (Having got this far it is worth renewing the seal as a matter of course.)
88 Where applicable, fit a new O-ring to the sun gear shaft.
89 Check that the intermediate bearing rotates smoothly, without any signs of roughness or undue free-play between its inner and outer races. If necessary, renew the bearing as described in Section 6.
90 Apply a smear of grease to the outer race of the intermediate bearing.
91 Pass the inner end of the shaft through the bearing mounting bracket, then carefully engage the inner driveshaft splines with the transmission, taking care not to damage the oil seal.
92 Align the intermediate bearing with its mounting bracket, and push the driveshaft fully into position. If necessary, use a soft-faced mallet to tap the outer race of the bearing into position in the mounting bracket.
93 Ensure that that intermediate bearing is correctly seated, then rotate its retaining bolts back through 90°, so that their offset heads are resting against the bearing outer race. Tighten the retaining bolts.
94 Refit the driveshaft outer section as described previously in this Section.

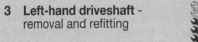

3 Left-hand driveshaft - removal and refitting

Manual gearbox models

Removal

Note: *A new driveshaft nut, new suspension strut-to-hub carrier nuts, and a new track-rod end balljoint nut will be required on refitting. Sealant will be required to coat the outer end of the driveshaft. A balljoint separator tool will be required for this operation.*

1 Drain the transmission oil/fluid, as described in the relevant part of Chapter 1.
2 Proceed as described in Section 2, paragraphs 1 to 8.
3 Working at the transmission end of the driveshaft, unscrew the three bolts securing the gaiter retaining plate to the transmission casing **(see illustration overleaf)**.
4 Proceed as described in Section 2, paragraphs 10 to 13.
5 Pull the driveshaft from the transmission, then withdraw the assembly from under the vehicle.

Refitting

Note: *If a new driveshaft is being fitted, it may*

8

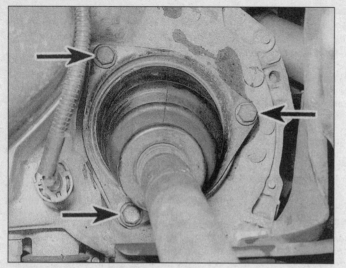

3.3 Unscrew the left-hand driveshaft inner joint gaiter retaining plate bolts (arrowed)

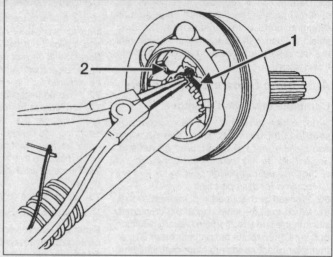

4.4 Extract the circlip (1) and tap exposed face of ball hub (2) to free the joint

be supplied with a protective cardboard cover fitted over the outer driveshaft gaiter. In this case, do not remove the cover until the completion of the refitting procedure.

6 Clean all traces of old locking compound from the hub carrier end of the driveshaft.

7 Wipe clean the side of the transmission. Insert the joint driveshaft joint spider into the sunwheel yoke, keeping the driveshaft horizontal as far as possible.

8 Align the gaiter retaining plate with its bolt holes in the transmission casing, then refit the retaining plate bolts, and tighten them to the specified torque. Ensure the gaiter is not twisted.

9 Coat the hub end of the driveshaft with locking compound (Renault recommend the use of Loctite Scelbloc), then engage the end of the driveshaft with the hub. **Note:** *If the hub has been pulled from the bearing during the removal procedure, fit a new bearing as described in Chapter 10.*

10 Where applicable, refit the lower suspension strut-to-hub carrier bolt (noting that the bolts fits from the front of the vehicle), and screw a new nut onto the bolt. Do not screw the nut fully onto the bolt at this stage.

11 Proceed as described in Section 2, paragraphs 23 to 31.

Automatic transmission models

Removal

Note: *A new driveshaft nut, new suspension strut-to-hub carrier nuts, and a new track-rod end balljoint nut will be required on refitting. Sealant will be required to coat the outer end of the driveshaft. A balljoint separator tool will be required for this operation.*

12 Proceed as described in Section 2, paragraphs 1 to 8.

13 On the AD4 type transmission, working at the transmission end of the driveshaft,

slacken and remove the six bolts and washers securing the driveshaft flange to the transmission flange, rotating the shaft as necessary to gain access to the bolts.

14 Proceed as described in Section 2, paragraphs 10 to 13.

15 Disengage the inner end of the driveshaft from the transmission flange, then withdraw the driveshaft from under the vehicle.

Refitting

Note: *If a new driveshaft is being fitted, it may be supplied with a protective cardboard cover fitted over the outer driveshaft gaiter. In this case, do not remove the cover until the completion of the refitting procedure.*

16 Thoroughly clean all traces of old locking compound from the hub carrier end of the driveshaft.

17 On the AD4 type transmission, ensure that the inner driveshaft joint flange and the transmission flange mating faces are clean and dry. Pack the joint recess with grease (Renault recommend the use of Molykote BR2).

18 Engage the driveshaft flange with the transmission flange then, where applicable, refit the securing bolts (with washers). Securely tighten the securing bolts, and wipe off any surplus grease.

19 Coat the hub end of the driveshaft with locking compound (Renault recommend the use of Loctite Scelbloc), then engage the end of the driveshaft with the hub. **Note:** *If the hub has been pulled from the bearing during the removal procedure, fit a new bearing as described in Chapter 10.*

20 Where applicable, refit the lower suspension strut-to-hub carrier bolt (noting that the bolts fits from the front of the vehicle), and screw a new nut onto the bolt. Do not screw the nut fully onto the bolt at this stage.

21 Proceed as described in Section 2, paragraphs 23 to 30.

4 Driveshaft rubber gaiters - renewal

Outer joint

Note: *Ensure that the appropriate gaiter repair kit is obtained before starting work.*

1 Remove the driveshaft as described in Section 2 or 3, as applicable.

2 Cut through the gaiter retaining clips, then slide the gaiter down the shaft to expose the outer constant velocity joint.

3 Scoop out as much grease as possible from the joint.

4 Using circlip pliers, expand the joint internal circlip **(see illustration)**. At the same time, tap the exposed face of the ball hub with a mallet to separate the joint from the driveshaft. Slide off the gaiter.

5 With the constant velocity joint removed from the driveshaft, clean the joint using paraffin, or a suitable solvent, and dry it thoroughly. Carry out a visual inspection of the joint.

6 Move the inner splined driving member from side to side, to expose each ball in turn at the top of its track. Examine the balls for cracks, flat spots or signs of surface pitting.

7 Inspect the ball tracks on the inner and outer members. If the tracks have widened, the balls will no longer be a tight fit. At the same time, check the ball cage windows for wear or cracking between the windows.

8 If on inspection any of the constant velocity joint components are found to be worn or damaged, it will be necessary to renew the joint (check on the availability of components with a Renault dealer). If the joint is in satisfactory condition, obtain a repair kit from your Renault dealer consisting of a new gaiter, rubber collar, clips, and the correct type and quantity of grease **(see illustration)**.

4.8 Renault driveshaft gaiter repair kit

9 Tape over the splines on the end of the driveshaft, then slide the smaller retaining clip and the gaiter onto the shaft. Locate the inner end of the gaiter in the groove on the driveshaft, and secure it in position with the retaining clip. A special tool is available to compress the retaining clip, but a satisfactory result can be achieved by carefully using a pair of side-cutters - take care not to cut the clip **(see illustration)**.

10 Remove the tape, then slide the constant velocity joint coupling onto the driveshaft until the internal circlip locates in the driveshaft groove.

11 Check that the circlip holds the joint securely on the driveshaft, then pack the joint with the grease supplied. Work the grease well into the ball tracks, and fill the gaiter with any excess.

12 Locate the outer lip of the gaiter in the groove on the joint outer member. With the coupling aligned with the driveshaft, lift the lip of the gaiter to equalise the air pressure. Secure the gaiter in position with the large retaining clip.

13 Check that the constant velocity joint moves freely in all directions, then refit the driveshaft to the vehicle as described in Section 2 or 3, as applicable.

Inner joint - manual gearbox models

Right-hand driveshaft - models with one-piece driveshaft

Note: *Ensure that the appropriate gaiter repair kit is obtained before starting work.*

14 Remove the driveshaft (see Section 2).

15 Using a pair of grips, bend up the metal joint cover at the points where it has been staked into the outer member recesses **(see illustration)**.

16 Using a pair of snips, cut the gaiter inner retaining clip.

17 Using a soft metal drift, tap the metal joint cover off the outer member **(see illustration)**. Slide the outer member off the end of the tripod joint. Be prepared to hold the rollers in place, otherwise they may fall off the tripod ends as the outer member is withdrawn. If necessary, secure the rollers in place using tape after removal of the outer member. The rollers are matched to the tripod stems, and it is important that they are not interchanged.

18 The tripod joint can now be removed. Where applicable, remove the circlip securing the tripod to the end of the driveshaft **(see illustration)**. Make alignment marks between the tripod and the shaft for use when refitting.

19 If the tripod is tight, draw the tripod off the driveshaft end using a puller. Ensure that the legs of the puller are located behind the tripod inner member and do not contact the joint rollers. Alternatively, support the tripod inner member, and press the shaft out using a hydraulic press, again ensuring that no load is applied to the joint rollers.

20 With the joint spider removed, slide the gaiter and inner retaining collar off the end of the driveshaft.

21 Wipe clean the joint components, taking care not to remove the alignment marks made on dismantling. **Do not** use paraffin or other solvents to clean this type of joint.

22 Examine the tripod joint, rollers and outer member for any signs of scoring or wear. Check that the rollers move smoothly on the tripod stems. If wear is evident, the tripod joint and roller assembly can be renewed, but it is not possible to obtain a replacement outer member (check with a Renault dealer on the availability of spares). Obtain a repair kit consisting of a gaiter, retaining clip, metal insert and joint cover, and the correct type and amount of special grease.

23 Fit the metal insert into the inside of the gaiter, then locate the gaiter assembly inside the metal joint cover.

24 Tape over the driveshaft splines, and slide

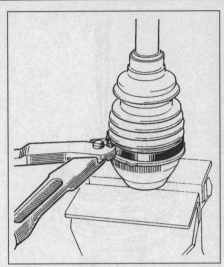

4.9 Securing a gaiter clip using side-cutters

the gaiter and joint cover assembly onto the driveshaft.

25 Remove the tape, then, aligning the marks made on dismantling, engage the tripod joint with the driveshaft splines. Use a hammer and soft metal drift to tap the joint onto the shaft, taking great care not to damage the driveshaft splines or joint rollers. Alternatively, support the driveshaft, and press the joint into position using a hydraulic press and suitable tubular spacer which bears only on the joint inner member.

26 Where applicable, secure the tripod joint in position with the circlip, ensuring that it is correctly located in the driveshaft groove.

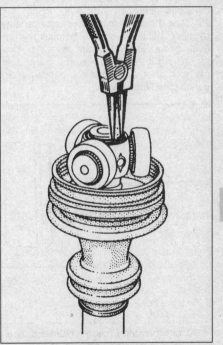

8

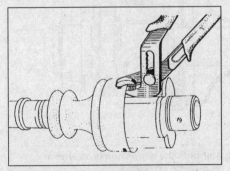

4.15 Bend up the metal joint cover using a pair of grips

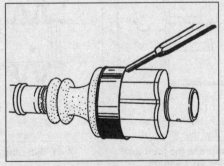

4.17 Tap the metal joint cover off the outer member

4.18 Where applicable, remove the circlip securing the tripod to end of driveshaft

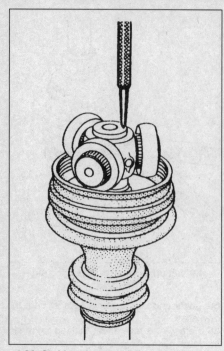

4.26 Staking the end of the driveshaft to secure the tripod joint

Where no circlip is fitted, secure the joint in position by staking the end of the driveshaft in three places, at intervals of 120°, using a hammer and punch **(see illustration)**.

27 Evenly distribute the special grease contained in the repair kit around the tripod joint and inside the outer member. Pack the gaiter with the remainder of the grease.

28 Slide the outer member into position over the tripod joint.

29 Slide the metal joint cover onto the outer member until it is flush with the outer member guide panel. Secure the joint cover in position by staking it into the recesses in the outer member, using a hammer and a round-ended punch **(see illustration)**.

30 Using a blunt rod, carefully lift the inner lip of the gaiter to equalise the air pressure. With the rod in position, compress the joint until the dimension from the inner end of the gaiter to the flat end face of the outer member is as shown **(see illustration)**. Hold the outer member in this position and withdraw the rod.

31 Fit the small retaining clip to the inner end of the gaiter. Remove any slack in the gaiter retaining clip by carefully compressing the raised section of the clip. In the absence of the special tool, a pair of side-cutters may be used - take care not to cut the clip.

32 Check that the constant velocity joint moves freely in all directions, then refit the driveshaft as described in Section 2.

Right-hand driveshaft - models with two-piece driveshaft

Note: *Ensure that the appropriate gaiter repair kit is obtained before starting work.*

33 Remove the driveshaft (see Section 2).

34 Using a pair of snips, cut through the gaiter securing clips (note that it may be necessary to saw through the larger clip).

35 Slide back the gaiter, and wipe out as much grease as possible from the joint.

36 Slide the outer member off the end of the tripod joint. Be prepared to hold the rollers in place, otherwise they may fall off the tripod ends as the outer member is withdrawn. If necessary, secure the rollers in place using tape after removal of the outer member. The rollers are matched to the tripod stems, and it is important that they are not interchanged.

37 Proceed as in paragraphs 18 to 22.

38 Tape over the driveshaft splines, and slide the gaiter (complete with the retaining clips) onto the driveshaft.

39 Proceed as in paragraphs 25 to 28.

40 Engage the inside of the gaiter with the groove in the outer member. Using a blunt rod, carefully lift the inner lip of the gaiter to equalise the air pressure.

41 With the rod in position, slide the outer end of the gaiter on the driveshaft until the

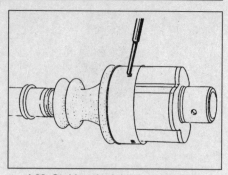

4.29 Staking the joint cover into the recesses in the outer member

dimension from the inner machined face of the outer member to the outer end of the driveshaft gaiter is as shown **(see illustration)**. Hold the gaiter in this position and withdraw the rod.

42 Fit the small retaining clip to the outer end of the gaiter. Remove any slack in the gaiter retaining clip by carefully compressing the raised section of the clip. In the absence of the special tool, a pair of side-cutters may be used - take care not to cut the clip.

43 Similarly fit the larger retaining clip to the gaiter and secure the gaiter in position in the outer member groove, as described previously.

44 Check that the constant velocity joint moves freely in all directions, then refit the driveshaft as described in Section 2.

Left-hand driveshaft

Note: *Ensure that the appropriate gaiter repair kit is obtained before starting work.*

45 Remove the driveshaft (see Section 3).

46 Using circlip pliers, extract the circlip securing the tripod joint to the driveshaft. Note that on some models, the joint may be staked in position; if so, relieve the stakings using a file.

47 Using a dab of paint or a hammer and punch, mark the tripod joint in relation to the driveshaft, to use as a guide to refitting.

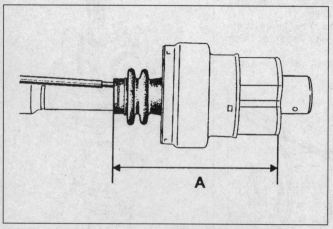

4.30 Lift the gaiter using a blunt rod, and compress the joint until the gaiter position is as shown - one-piece driveshaft

A = 156.0 ± 1.0 mm

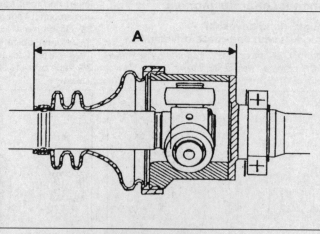

4.41 Slide the gaiter until the dimension is as shown - two-piece driveshaft

A = 156.0 ± 1.0 mm

48 The tripod joint can now be removed. If it is tight, draw the joint off the driveshaft end using a puller. Ensure that the legs of the puller are located behind the joint inner member and do not contact the joint rollers. Alternatively, support the inner member of the tripod joint and press the shaft out of the joint, again ensuring that no load is applied to the joint rollers.

49 The gaiter and bearing assembly is removed in the same way, either by drawing the bearing off the driveshaft, or by pressing the driveshaft out of the bearing. Remove the retaining plate, noting which way round it is fitted.

50 Obtain a new gaiter, which is supplied complete with the small bearing.

51 Owing to the lip-type seal used in the bearing, the bearing and gaiter must be pressed into position. If a hammer and tubular drift are used to drive the assembly onto the driveshaft, there is a risk of distorting the seal.

52 Refit the retaining plate to the driveshaft, ensuring that it is fitted the correct way round.

53 Support the driveshaft, and press the gaiter bearing onto the shaft, using a tubular spacer which bears only on the bearing inner race. Position the bearing so that the distance from the end of the driveshaft to the inner face of the bearing is as shown. The driveshaft can be supported using a clamp in the groove provided **(see illustrations)**.

54 Align the marks made on dismantling, and engage the tripod joint with the driveshaft splines. Use a hammer and soft metal drift to tap the joint onto the shaft, taking care not to damage the driveshaft splines or joint rollers. Alternatively, support the driveshaft, and press the joint into position using a tubular spacer which bears only on the joint inner member.

55 Secure the tripod joint in position with the circlip, ensuring that it is correctly located in the driveshaft groove. Where no circlip is fitted, secure the joint in position by staking the end of the driveshaft in three places, at intervals of 120°, using a hammer and punch.

56 Refit the driveshaft to the vehicle as described in Section 3.

Inner joint - automatic transmission models

57 At the time of writing, no information was available for the renewal of the driveshaft inner joint gaiter on these models. If gaiter renewal is necessary, the driveshaft should be removed from the vehicle and taken to a Renault dealer.

5 Driveshaft overhaul - general information

1 If any of the checks described in the relevant part of Chapter 1 reveal wear in a driveshaft joint, first remove the roadwheel trim or centre cap (as appropriate) and check

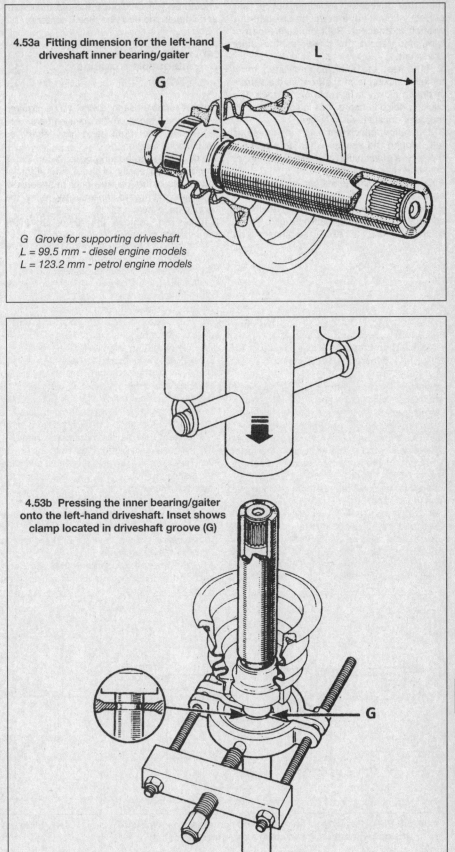

4.53a Fitting dimension for the left-hand driveshaft inner bearing/gaiter

G Grove for supporting driveshaft
L = 99.5 mm - diesel engine models
L = 123.2 mm - petrol engine models

4.53b Pressing the inner bearing/gaiter onto the left-hand driveshaft. Inset shows clamp located in driveshaft groove (G)

8

that the driveshaft retaining nut is still correctly tightened; if in doubt, use a torque wrench to check it. Refit the centre cap or trim, and repeat the check on the other driveshaft.

2 Road test the vehicle, and listen for a metallic clicking from the front as the vehicle is driven slowly in a circle on full-lock. If a clicking noise is heard, this indicates wear in the outer constant velocity joint.

3 If vibration, consistent with road speed, is felt through the vehicle when accelerating, there is a possibility of wear in the inner constant velocity joints.

4 Constant velocity joints can be dismantled and inspected for wear as described in Section 4. Check on the availability of components before dismantling a joint.

5 On models with ABS, the sensor ring should be removed from the old driveshaft and fitted to the new one. See Chapter 9.

6 Right-hand driveshaft intermediate bearing - renewal

Note: *A suitable bearing puller will be required to draw the bearing off the driveshaft end.*

1 Remove the right-hand driveshaft as described in Section 2.

2 Check that the bearing outer race rotates smoothly and easily, without any signs of roughness or undue free-play between the inner and outer races. If necessary, renew the bearing as follows.

3 If desired, remove the driveshaft inner section, with reference to Section 2.

4 Where applicable, remove the bearing retaining circlip.

5 Using a long-reach universal bearing puller, carefully draw the bearing off the inner end of the driveshaft.

6 Thoroughly clean the contact faces of the driveshaft and the new bearing.

7 Apply a smear of grease to the inner race of the new bearing, then fit the bearing over the end of the driveshaft.

8 Using hammer and a suitable piece of tubing, which bears only on the bearing inner race, tap the new bearing into position on the driveshaft until it contacts the locating shoulder on the shaft.

9 Where applicable, fit the bearing retaining circlip.

10 Check that the bearing rotates freely, then refit the driveshaft as described in Section 2.

Chapter 9
Braking system

Contents

Degrees of difficulty

Easy, suitable for novice with little experience | **Fairly easy,** suitable for beginner with some experience | **Fairly difficult,** suitable for competent DIY mechanic | **Difficult,** suitable for experienced DIY mechanic | **Very difficult,** suitable for expert DIY or professional

Specifications

General
System type . . . . Dual hydraulic circuit, split diagonally with servo assistance. Anti-lock braking system (ABS) available as an option. Front disc brakes on all models. Rear disc or drum brakes according to model. On diesel models, vacuum provided by engine-driven pump. Cable-operated handbrake acting on rear brakes

Front brakes
Disc thickness:
  All except 2.0 litre (16-valve) petrol engine models:
    New . . . . 22.0 mm
    Minimum thickness . . . . 19.8 mm
  2.0 litre (16-valve) petrol engine models:
    New . . . . 24.0 mm
    Minimum thickness . . . . 21.8 mm
Maximum disc run-out . . . . 0.07 mm
Pad thickness (including backing):
  New . . . . 18.0 mm
  Minimum thickness . . . . 6.0 mm

Rear disc brakes
Disc thickness:
  New . . . . 10.5 mm
  Minimum thickness . . . . 9.5 mm
Maximum disc run-out . . . . 0.07 mm
Pad thickness (including backing):
  New . . . . 15.0 mm
  Minimum thickness . . . . 6.0 mm

Rear drum brakes

Drum internal diameter:
New . . . . 203.4 mm
Maximum diameter . . . . 204.4 mm
Shoe thickness (including backing):
New . . . . 7.0 mm
Minimum thickness . . . . 2.5 mm

Torque wrench settings

	Nm	lbf ft
ABS electronic control unit bolts	5	4
ABS wheel sensor bolts	10	7
Brake disc securing screws	15	11
Brake fluid hose and pipe unions	13	10
Fluid bleed screws	7	5
Front brake caliper guide pin bolts	35	26
Front brake caliper mounting bracket-to-hub carrier bolts	100	74
Master cylinder-to-vacuum servo nuts	13	10
Rear caliper lower guide pin bolt	35	26
Rear caliper upper guide pin bolt	70	52
Rear hub nut:		
Non-ABS models with rear drum brakes	190	140
ABS models with rear drum brakes	175	129
Models with rear disc brakes	175	129
Rear stub axle securing bolts (models with rear drum brakes)	75	55
Vacuum servo bolts	23	17

1 General information

The braking system is of the servo-assisted, dual-circuit hydraulic type. The arrangement of the hydraulic system is such that each circuit operates one front and one rear brake from a tandem master cylinder. Under normal circumstances, both circuits operate in unison. However, in the event of hydraulic failure in one circuit, full braking force will still be available at two wheels.

Some models have disc brakes all round as standard; other models are fitted with front disc brakes and rear drum brakes. ABS is fitted as standard to certain models, and is offered as an option on most other models (refer to Section 23 for further information on ABS operation). ABS is available on models with both rear drum and rear disc brakes.

The front disc brakes are actuated by single-piston sliding type calipers, which ensure that equal pressure is applied to each disc pad.

On models with rear drum brakes, the rear brakes incorporate leading and trailing shoes, which are actuated by twin-piston wheel cylinders. A self-adjust mechanism is incorporated, to automatically compensate for brake shoe wear. As the brake shoe linings wear, the footbrake operation automatically operates the adjuster mechanism, which effectively lengthens the shoe strut and repositions the brake shoes, to remove the lining-to-drum clearance.

On models with rear disc brakes, the brakes are actuated by single-piston sliding calipers which incorporate mechanical handbrake mechanisms.

A load-sensitive pressure-regulating valve is fitted to regulate the hydraulic pressure applied to the rear brakes. The regulating valve helps to prevent rear wheel lock-up during emergency braking.

On all models, the handbrake provides an independent mechanical means of rear brake application.

On diesel engines, there is insufficient vacuum in the inlet manifold to operate the braking system servo effectively at all times. To overcome this problem, a vacuum pump is fitted to the engine, to provide sufficient vacuum to operate the servo unit. The vacuum pump is driven from the camshaft, either directly, or via a drivebelt, depending on model.

Note: *When servicing any part of the system, work carefully and methodically; also observe scrupulous cleanliness when overhauling any part of the hydraulic system. Always renew components (in axle sets, where applicable) if in doubt about their condition, and use only genuine Renault replacement parts, or at least those of known good quality. Note the warnings given in Safety first and at relevant points in this Chapter concerning the dangers of asbestos dust and hydraulic fluid.*

2 Hydraulic system - bleeding

Warning: Hydraulic fluid is poisonous; wash off immediately and thoroughly in the case of skin contact, and seek immediate medical advice if any fluid is swallowed or gets into the eyes. Certain types of hydraulic fluid are inflammable, and may ignite when allowed into contact with hot components; when servicing any hydraulic system, it is safest to assume that the fluid IS inflammable, and to take precautions against the risk of fire as though it is petrol that is being handled. Hydraulic fluid is also an effective paint stripper, and will attack plastics; if any is spilt, it should be washed off immediately, using copious quantities of clean water. Finally, it is hygroscopic (it absorbs moisture from the air). The more moisture is absorbed by the fluid, the lower its boiling point becomes, leading to a dangerous loss of braking under hard use. Old fluid may be contaminated and unfit for further use. When topping-up or renewing the fluid, always use the recommended type, and ensure that it comes from a freshly-opened sealed container.

Conventional braking system

General

1 The correct functioning of the brake hydraulic system is only possible after removing all air from the components and circuit; this is achieved by bleeding the system.
2 During the bleeding procedure, add only clean, fresh hydraulic fluid of the specified type; never re-use fluid that has already been bled from the system. Ensure that sufficient fluid is available before starting work.
3 If there is any possibility of incorrect fluid being used in the system, the brake lines and components must be completely flushed with uncontaminated fluid and new seals fitted to the components.
4 If brake fluid has been lost from the master cylinder due to a leak in the system, ensure that the cause is traced and rectified before proceeding further.
5 Park the vehicle on level ground, switch off the ignition and select first gear. Chock the wheels and release the handbrake.

6 Check that all pipes and hoses are secure, unions tight, and bleed screws closed. Remove the dust caps and clean any dirt from around the bleed screws.

7 Unscrew the brake fluid reservoir cap, and top-up the reservoir to the MAX level line. Refit the cap loosely, and remember to maintain the fluid level at least above the MIN level line throughout the procedure, otherwise there is a risk of further air entering the system.

8 There are a number of one-man, do-it-yourself, brake bleeding kits currently available from motor accessory shops. It is recommended that one of these kits is used wherever possible, as they greatly simplify the bleeding operation, and also reduce the risk of expelled air and fluid being drawn back into the system. If such a kit is not available, the basic (two-man) method must be used, which is described in detail below.

9 If a kit is to be used, prepare the vehicle as described previously, and follow the kit manufacturer's instructions, as the procedure may vary slightly according to the type being used; generally, they are as outlined below in the relevant sub-section.

10 Whichever method is used, the correct sequence must be followed to ensure that the removal of all air from the system.

Bleeding sequence

11 If the hydraulic system has only been partially disconnected and suitable precautions were taken to minimise fluid loss, it should only be necessary to bleed that part of the system (ie, the relevant caliper or wheel cylinder, or the primary or secondary circuit).

12 If the complete system is to be bled, then it should be done in the following sequence:
 a) *Rear right-hand brake.*
 b) *Front left-hand brake.*
 c) *Rear left-hand brake.*
 d) *Front right-hand brake.*

Bleeding - basic (two-man) method

13 Collect a clean glass jar and a suitable length of plastic or rubber tubing, which is a tight fit over the bleed screw, and a ring spanner to fit the screws. The help of an assistant will also be required.

14 If not already done, remove the dust cap from the bleed screw of the first wheel to be bled and fit the bleed tube to the screw. **(see illustration)**

15 Immerse the other end of the bleed tube in the jar, which should contain enough fluid to cover the end of the tube.

16 Ensure that the reservoir fluid level is maintained at least above the MIN level line throughout the procedure.

17 Open the bleed screw approximately half a turn, and have your assistant depress the brake pedal with a smooth steady stroke down to the floor, and then hold it there. When the flow of fluid through the tube stops, tighten the bleed screw and have your assistant release the pedal slowly.

18 Repeat this operation (paragraph 17) until clean brake fluid, free from air bubbles, can be seen flowing from the end of the tube.

19 When no more air bubbles appear, tighten the bleed screw, remove the bleed tube and refit the dust cap. Repeat these procedures on the remaining calipers in sequence until all air is removed from the system and the brake pedal feels firm again.

Bleeding - using a one-way valve kit

20 As their name implies, these kits consist of a length of tubing with a one-way valve fitted, to prevent expelled air and fluid being drawn back into the system; some kits incorporate a translucent container, which can be positioned so that the air bubbles can be more easily seen flowing from the end of the tube.

21 The kit is connected to the bleed screw, which is then opened. The user returns to the driver's seat, depresses the brake pedal with a smooth steady stroke, and slowly releases it; this is repeated until the expelled fluid is clear of air bubbles.

22 Note that these kits simplify work so much that it is easy to forget the reservoir fluid level; ensure that this is maintained at least above the MIN level line at all times.

Bleeding - using a pressure-bleeding kit

23 These kits are usually operated by the reserve of pressurised air contained in the spare tyre. However, note that it will probably be necessary to reduce the pressure to a lower level than normal; refer to the instructions supplied with the kit.

24 By connecting a pressurised, fluid-filled container to the fluid reservoir, bleeding is then carried out by simply opening each bleed screw in turn (in the specified sequence) and allowing the fluid to run out, rather like turning on a tap, until no air bubbles can be seen in the expelled fluid.

25 This method has the advantage that the large reservoir of fluid provides an additional safeguard against air being drawn into the system during bleeding.

26 Pressure bleeding is particularly effective when bleeding 'difficult' systems, or when bleeding the complete system at the time of routine fluid renewal. It is also the method recommended by Renault if the hydraulic system has been drained either wholly or partially.

All methods

27 When bleeding is completed, check and top-up the fluid level in the reservoir.

28 Check the feel of the brake pedal. If it feels at all spongy, air must still be present in the system, and further bleeding is indicated. Failure to bleed satisfactorily after a reasonable repetition of the bleeding operations may be due to worn master cylinder seals.

29 Discard brake fluid which has been bled from the system; it will not be fit for re-use.

ABS braking system

⚠ ***Warning: To bleed the ABS system it is necessary to use Renault diagnostic equipment. If only a brake caliper or wheel cylinder has been removed (and suitable precautions have been taken to minimise fluid loss), it is possible to bleed the hydraulic system conventionally as described in the following paragraphs. If the system is being bled for any other reason (fluid renewal, long pedal travel, master cylinder removal, hydraulic unit removal), bleeding should be entrusted to a Renault dealer equipped with the necessary diagnostic equipment.***

General

30 Refer to paragraphs 1 to 9.

Bleeding a brake caliper or wheel cylinder

31 Provided that the system has only been partially disconnected and suitable precautions were taken to minimise fluid loss, it should only be necessary to bleed that part of the system (ie, the relevant caliper or wheel cylinder), as follows.

32 Bleed the caliper or wheel cylinder in the conventional way, as described previously for the conventional braking system (two-man method, or using a one-way valve kit).

33 Fill the reservoir with brake fluid.

34 If a rear brake is being bled, clamp the rear pressure regulating valve operating arm (using a small clamp or a cable-tie) so that maximum brake pressure is applied to the rear wheels.

35 With the end of the bleed tube immersed in the jar, proceed as follows.
 a) *Open the bleed screw.*
 b) *Depress the brake pedal and hold it down.*
 c) *Close the bleed screw.*
 d) *Release the brake pedal.*
 e) *Wait for three seconds.*
 f) *Repeat the steps a) to e) at least ten times, until fluid emerges free from air bubbles.*

36 With the bleed screw closed, pump the brake pedal three times in succession.

37 Repeat the steps a) to d) in paragraph 35.

38 Where applicable, remove the clamp from the rear pressure regulating valve.

2.14 Rear wheel cylinder bleed screw (arrowed)

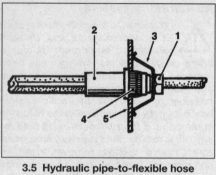

3.5 Hydraulic pipe-to-flexible hose connection

1 *Union nut*
2 *Flexible hose*
3 *Spring clip support*
4 *Splined end fitting*
5 *Mounting bracket*

39 Check the brake fluid level, and top-up if necessary (see *Weekly Checks*).

40 If the braking system performance is not satisfactory after bleeding, the vehicle should be taken to a Renault dealer to have the system bled using the appropriate diagnostic equipment.

3 Hydraulic pipes and hoses - inspection and renewal

Note: *Before starting work, refer to the warning at the beginning of Section 2 concerning the dangers of hydraulic fluid.*

Inspection

1 The hydraulic pipes, hoses, hose connections and pipe unions should be regularly examined.

2 First check for signs of leakage at the pipe unions, then examine the flexible hoses for signs of cracking, chafing and fraying.

3 The brake pipes should be examined carefully for signs of dents, corrosion or other damage. Corrosion should be scraped off, and if the depth of pitting is significant, the pipes renewed. This is particularly likely in those areas underneath the vehicle body where the pipes are exposed and unprotected.

Removal

4 If any pipe or hose is to be renewed, minimise fluid loss by removing the fluid reservoir cap and then tightening it down onto a piece of polythene (taking care not to damage the level sender unit) to obtain an airtight seal. Alternatively, flexible hoses can be sealed, if required, using a proprietary brake hose clamp; metal brake pipe unions can be plugged (if care is taken not to allow dirt into the system) or capped immediately they are disconnected. Place a wad of rag under any union that is to be disconnected, to catch any spilt fluid. If a section of pipe is to be removed from the master cylinder, the reservoir should be emptied by siphoning out the fluid or drawing out the fluid with a pipette.

5 If a flexible hose is to be disconnected, unscrew the brake pipe union nut before removing the spring clip which secures the hose to its mounting bracket **(see illustration)**.

6 To unscrew the union nuts, it is preferable to obtain a brake pipe spanner of the correct size (11 mm/13 mm split ring); these are available from motor accessory shops. Failing this, a close-fitting open-ended spanner will be required, though if the nuts are tight or corroded, their flats may be rounded off if the spanner slips. In such a case, a self-locking wrench is often the only way to unscrew a stubborn union, but it follows that the pipe and the damaged nuts must be renewed on reassembly. Always clean a union and surrounding area before disconnecting it. If disconnecting a component with more than one union, make a careful note of the connections before disturbing any of them.

7 If a brake pipe is to be renewed, it can be obtained, cut to length and with the union nuts and end flares in place, from Renault dealers. All that is then necessary is to bend it to shape, following the line of the original, before fitting it to the vehicle. Alternatively, most motor accessory shops can make up brake pipes from kits, but this requires very careful measurement of the original to ensure that the replacement is of the correct length. The safest answer is usually to take the original to the shop as a pattern.

Refitting

8 On refitting, do not overtighten the union nuts. The specified torque wrench settings (where given) are not high, and it is not necessary to exercise brute force to obtain a sound joint.

9 Ensure that the pipes and hoses are correctly routed with no kinks, and that they are secured in the clips or brackets provided. In the case of flexible hoses, make sure that they cannot contact other components during movement of the steering and/or suspension assemblies.

10 After fitting, remove the polythene from the reservoir (or remove the plugs or clamps, as applicable), and bleed the hydraulic system as described in Section 2. Wash off any spilt fluid, and check carefully for fluid leaks.

4 Front brake pads - renewal

⚠️ *Warning: Disc brake pads must be renewed on both front wheels at the same time - never renew the pads on only one wheel, as uneven braking may result. Also, the dust created by wear of the pads may contain asbestos, which is a health hazard. Never blow it out with compressed air and don't inhale any of it. An approved filtering mask should be worn when working on the brakes. DO NOT use petroleum based solvents to clean brake parts. Use brake cleaner or methylated spirit only.*

Note: *A new caliper guide pin bolt must be used on refitting.*

1 Apply the handbrake then jack up the front of the vehicle and support it securely on axle stands (see *Jacking and vehicle support*). Remove the front roadwheels.

2 Pull the caliper body outwards, away from the centre of the car. This will push the piston back into its bore to facilitate removal and refitting of the pads.

3 Disconnect the brake pad wear warning sensor wiring at the connector **(see illustration)**.

4 Unscrew the upper caliper guide pin bolt using a suitable spanner, while holding the guide pin with a second spanner. Discard the bolt - a new one must be used on refitting **(see illustrations)**.

4.3 Disconnecting the brake pad wear sensor wiring

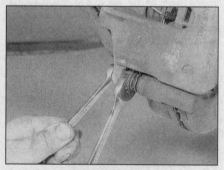

4.4a Counterhold the caliper guide pin . . .

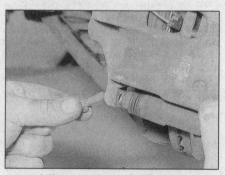

4.4b . . . and unscrew the bolt

4.5 Lift the caliper away from the pads

4.6a Lift out the inner . . .

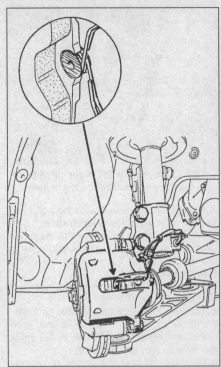

4.8 The anti-rattle springs on the pads must be located as shown

4.6b . . . and outer pads

4.6c Measuring brake pad friction material thickness

5 With the guide pin removed, pivot the caliper away from the brake pads **(see illustration)**.

6 Withdraw the two brake pads from the carrier bracket. If required, the thickness of the pads can be checked at this stage using a steel rule **(see illustrations)**.

7 Before refitting the pads, check that the guide pins are free to slide in the carrier bracket and check that the rubber dust excluders around the guide pins are undamaged. Brush the dust and dirt from the caliper and piston but do not inhale it as it is injurious to health. Inspect the dust excluder around the piston for damage and inspect the piston for evidence of fluid leaks, corrosion or damage. If attention to any of these components is necessary, refer to Section 10.

8 To refit the pads, place them in position on the carrier bracket, noting that the pad with the warning sensor wire must be nearest to

the centre of the car. The anti-rattle springs must be located as shown **(see illustration)**.

9 Make sure that the caliper piston is fully retracted in its bore. If not, carefully push it in, preferably using a G-clamp or, alternatively, using a flat bar or screwdriver as a lever **(see illustration)**. As the piston is retracted, the fluid level in the reservoir will rise - if necessary, syphon out some fluid to allow for this.

10 Position the caliper over the pads, then fit the new upper guide pin bolt. Tighten the bolt to the specified torque, counterholding the guide pin as during removal.

11 Reconnect the brake pad wear warning sensor wiring, then refit the roadwheel and repeat the renewal procedure on the remaining front brake.

12 On completion, check the fluid level in the reservoir, then depress the brake pedal two or three times to bring the pads into contact with the disc. Lower the car to the ground.

5 Rear brake pads - renewal

Warning: Disc brake pads must be renewed on both rear wheels at the same time - never renew the pads on only one wheel, as uneven braking may result. Also, the dust created by wear of the pads may contain asbestos, which is a health hazard. Never blow it out with compressed air and don't inhale any of it. An approved filtering mask should be worn when working on the brakes. DO NOT use petroleum based solvents to clean brake parts. Use brake cleaner or methylated spirit only.

Note: *Suitable thread-locking compound will be required to coat the threads of the caliper guide pin bolt.*

1 Chock the front wheels, engage reverse gear (or P on models with automatic transmission) and release the handbrake. Jack up the rear of the vehicle and support it securely on axle stands (see *Jacking and vehicle support*). Remove the relevant roadwheel.

2 Using a pair of pliers, disconnect the handbrake inner cable from the lever on the caliper, then slide the outer cable from the support bracket on the caliper **(see illustrations)**. If any difficulty is experienced in releasing the inner cable from the lever, slacken the adjuster nut on the handbrake operating rod with reference to Section 20.

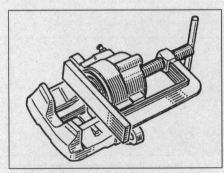

4.9 Using a G-clamp to retract a front caliper piston into its bore

5.2a Using a pair of pliers, disconnect the handbrake inner cable from the lever on the caliper . . .

9

5.2b ... then slide the outer cable from the support bracket on the caliper

5.3 Remove the locking clip from the pad retaining pin

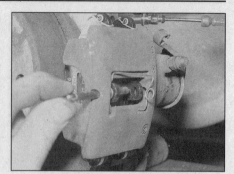

5.4 Tap out the pad retaining pin then withdraw the pin from the caliper

3 Using pliers, remove the locking clip from the pad retaining pin **(see illustration)**.

4 Working from the inside edge of the caliper, using a pin-punch, tap out the pad retaining pin then withdraw the pin from the caliper **(see illustration)**.

5 Recover the anti-rattle spring, noting its orientation to aid refitting.

6 Unscrew the upper caliper guide pin bolt.

7 Pull out the guide pin until it is clear of the caliper mounting bracket, then tilt the caliper downwards **(see illustrations)**.

8 Lift the pads from the caliper and remove the upper anti-rattle springs. If required, the thickness of the pads can be checked at this stage using a steel rule.

9 Before refitting the pads, brush the dust and dirt from the caliper and piston but do not inhale it as it is injurious to health. Inspect the dust excluder around the piston for damage and inspect the piston for evidence of fluid

leaks, corrosion or damage. Also check that the guide-pins are free to slide in the caliper bracket, and check that the rubber dust excluders around the guide pins are undamaged. If attention to any of these components is necessary, refer to Section 11. Thoroughly clean the threads of the upper caliper guide pin bolt.

10 The caliper piston must now be fully retracted into the cylinder. Do this by turning the piston clockwise, whilst simultaneously pressing the piston into the cylinder, until the piston continues to turn but will not go in any further. A special tool is available to retract the piston, but it should be possible to carry out the job using a pair of circlip pliers **(see illustration)**. As the piston is retracted, the fluid level in the reservoir will rise - if necessary, syphon out some fluid to allow for this.

11 Place the upper anti-rattle springs on the pads, then locate the pads in the caliper, beginning with the inner pad. Ensure that the ends of the upper anti-rattle springs are correctly positioned on the pads and caliper **(see illustration)**.

12 Coat the threads of the upper caliper guide pin bolt with thread-locking compound, then pivot the caliper into position over the disc, refit the guide pin bolt and tighten to the specified torque.

13 Place the anti-rattle spring in position on the caliper, ensuring that it is located as noted before removal. Working from the outside edge of the caliper, slide the pad retaining pin into position, threading it through the holes in the anti-rattle spring.

14 Tap the pad retaining pin fully into position, then refit the locking clip.

15 Reconnect the handbrake cable to the caliper bracket and handbrake lever.

16 Refit the roadwheel, then repeat the renewal procedure on the remaining rear brake.

17 On completion, check the hydraulic fluid level in the reservoir, then depress the brake pedal two or three times to bring the pads into contact with the disc. If the handbrake adjustment was disturbed to allow disconnection of the handbrake cable, adjust the handbrake as described in the relevant part of Chapter 1.

18 Lower the vehicle to the ground.

6 Rear brake shoes - inspection and renewal

⚠️ *Warning: Brake shoes must be renewed on both rear wheels at the same time - never renew the shoes on only one wheel, as uneven braking may result. Also, the dust created by wear of the shoes may contain asbestos, which is a health hazard. Never blow it out with compressed air and don't inhale any of it. An approved filtering mask should be worn when working on the brakes. DO NOT use petroleum based solvents to clean brake parts. Use brake cleaner or methylated spirit only.*

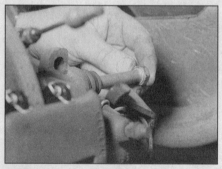

5.7a Unscrew the upper guide pin bolt until it is clear of the mounting bracket ...

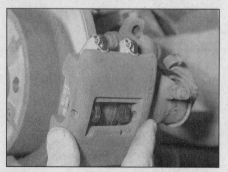

5.7b ... then tilt the caliper downwards

5.10 Using circlip pliers to retract the caliper piston

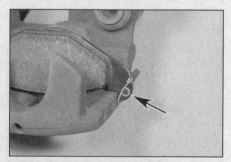

5.11 Ensure that the ends of the upper anti-rattle springs (arrowed) are positioned on the pads and caliper as shown

6.5 Rear drum brake component locations - left-hand side shown

6.6a Remove the shoe retainer spring cup and springs . . .

6.6b . . . then withdraw the retainer pins . . .

Inspection

1 Remove the brake drum (see Section 9).

2 Carefully remove all traces of brake dust from the brake drum, backplate and shoes.

3 Measure the thickness of each brake shoe (friction material and shoe) at several points. If either shoe is worn at any point to the specified minimum thickness or less, all four shoes must be renewed as a set. The shoes should also be renewed if they are fouled with oil or grease - there is no satisfactory way of degreasing friction material once contaminated.

4 If any of the brake shoes are worn unevenly, or fouled with oil or grease, trace and rectify the cause before reassembly.

Renewal

5 Make a note of the correct fitted positions of the springs and adjuster strut, to use as a guide on reassembly **(see illustration)**.

6 Using a pair of pliers, remove the leading and trailing shoe retainer spring cup by depressing and turning through 90°. With the cups removed, lift off the springs, then withdraw the retainer pins and remove the shoes, complete with the springs and adjuster components from the backplate **(see illustrations)**.

Wrap a strong elastic band or a cable-tie around the wheel cylinder pistons to retain them.

7 Disconnect the handbrake cable from the handbrake operating lever on the trailing shoe **(see illustration)**.

6.6c . . . and withdraw the shoe assembly

8 Carefully unhook both the upper and lower return springs, and remove them from the brake shoes.

9 Withdraw the trailing shoe.

10 Lift out the adjuster strut assembly.

11 Unhook the adjuster lever spring, noting that the shorter hooked end engages with the adjuster lever, and lift off the adjuster lever and rod.

12 If genuine Renault brake shoes are being installed, it may be necessary to remove the adjusting lever from the original leading shoe, and install it on the new shoe. All return springs should be renewed, regardless of their apparent condition; spring kits are also available from Renault dealers.

13 Withdraw the forked end from the adjuster strut, and carefully examine the assembly for signs of wear or damage. Pay particular attention to the threads and the knurled adjuster wheel, and renew if necessary. Note that left-hand and right-hand struts are not

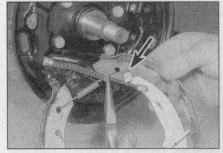

6.7 Disconnect the handbrake cable from the lever (arrowed) on the trailing shoe

interchangeable. The struts are marked L and R **(see illustration)**.

14 Peel back the rubber protective caps, and check the wheel cylinder for fluid leaks or other damage; check that both cylinder pistons are free to move easily. Refer to Section 12, if necessary, for information on wheel cylinder renewal.

15 Prior to installation, clean the backplate, and apply a thin smear of high-temperature brake grease or anti-seize compound to all those surfaces of the backplate which bear on the shoes, particularly the wheel cylinder pistons and lower pivot point **(see illustration)**. Do not allow the lubricant to foul the friction material.

16 Ensure that the handbrake lever stop-peg is correctly located against the edge of the trailing shoe, and remove the elastic band or cable-tie (as applicable) fitted to the wheel cylinder **(see illustration)**.

17 Engage the adjuster lever spring with the

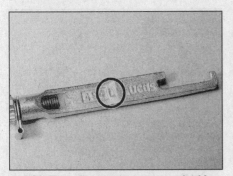

6.13 The adjuster struts are marked L and R

6.15 Apply brake grease to the shoe contact surfaces (arrowed) on the backplate

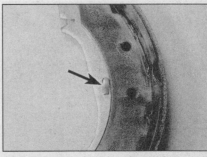

6.16 Ensure that the handbrake lever stop peg (arrowed) is located against the edge of the shoe as shown

9

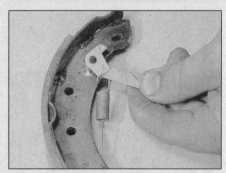

6.17 Engaging the adjuster lever with the peg on the brake shoe

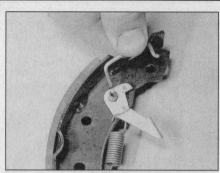

6.18 Refitting the adjuster lever rod

leading shoe and the adjuster lever, noting that the shorter hooked end engages with the adjuster lever, then engage the adjuster lever with the peg on the leading brake shoe **(see illustration)**.

18 Refit the adjuster lever rod **(see illustration)**.

19 Locate the adjuster strut in position on the shoes, ensuring that the cut-out in the end of the adjuster strut fork engages with the adjuster lever **(see illustrations)**.

20 Fit the upper and lower return springs to the shoes **(see illustrations)**.

21 Screw in the adjuster wheel until the minimum strut length is obtained.

22 Connect the handbrake cable to the operating lever on the trailing shoe, then offer the assembly into position on the backplate.

23 Slide the shoe assembly into position, ensuring that the upper ends of the shoes engage with the wheel cylinder piston.

24 Refit the shoe retainer pins, and secure the shoes in position with the springs and retainer cups.

25 Tap the components if necessary to seat them on the backplate.

26 Using a screwdriver, turn the strut adjuster wheel to expand the shoes until the brake drum just slides over the shoes.

27 Refit the brake drum as described in Section 9.

28 Repeat the above procedure on the remaining rear brake.

29 Once both sets of rear shoes have been renewed, adjust the lining-to-drum clearance by repeatedly depressing the brake pedal. Whilst depressing the pedal, have an assistant listen to the rear drums, to check that the adjuster strut is functioning correctly; if so, a clicking sound will be emitted by the strut as the pedal is depressed.

30 Check and, if necessary, adjust the

handbrake as described in the relevant part of Chapter 1.

31 On completion, check the hydraulic fluid level as described in the relevant part of Chapter 1.

32 New shoes will not give full braking efficiency until they have bedded in. Be prepared for this, and avoid hard braking as far as possible for the first hundred miles or so after shoe renewal.

---

7 Front brake disc - inspection, removal and refitting

Note: *Before starting work, refer to the warning at the beginning of Section 4 concerning the dangers of asbestos dust. If either disc requires renewal, both should be renewed at the same time, to ensure even and consistent braking. In principle, new pads should be fitted also.*

Inspection

1 Apply the handbrake, then jack up the front of the vehicle and support it securely on axle stands (see *Jacking and vehicle support*). Remove the appropriate front roadwheel.

2 Slowly rotate the brake disc so that the full area of both sides can be checked; remove the brake pads, as described in Section 4, if better access is required to the inboard surface. Light scoring is normal in the area swept by the brake pads, and can be removed using emery tape. If heavy scoring is found, the disc must be renewed.

3 It is normal to find a lip of rust and brake dust around the disc's perimeter; this can be scraped off if required. If, however, a lip has formed due to wear of the brake pad swept area, the disc thickness must be measured using a micrometer. Take measurements at several places around the disc at the inside and outside of the pad swept area; if the disc has worn at any point to the specified minimum thickness or less, it must be renewed.

4 If the disc is thought to be warped, it can be checked for run-out, ideally by using a dial gauge mounted on any convenient fixed

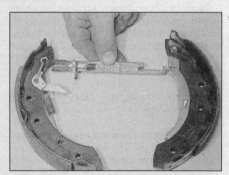

6.19a Locate the adjuster strut in position on the shoes . . .

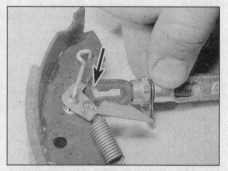

6.19b . . . ensuring that the cut-out (arrowed) engages with the adjuster lever

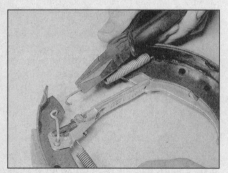

6.20a Refit the upper . . .

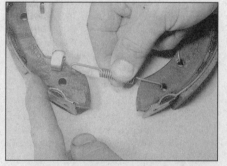

6.20b . . . and lower return springs

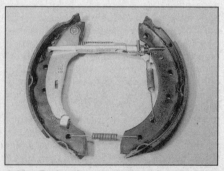

6.20c Brake shoe components assembled ready for fitting - viewed from rear

7.4 Checking disc run-out using a dial gauge

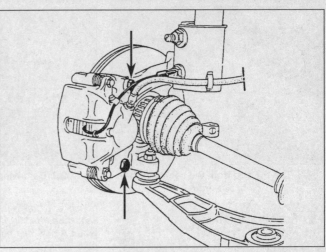

7.7 Brake caliper mounting bracket-to-hub carrier bolts (arrowed)

point, while the disc is slowly rotated **(see illustration)**. In the absence of a dial gauge, use feeler blades to measure (at several points all around the disc) the clearance between the disc and a fixed point such as the caliper mounting bracket. If the measurements obtained are at the specified maximum or beyond, the disc is excessively warped, and must be renewed; however, it is worth checking first that the hub bearing is in good condition (Section 14 in the relevant part of Chapter 1, and Chapter 10). Also try the effect of removing the disc and turning it through 180° to reposition it on the hub; if run-out is still excessive, the disc must be renewed.

5 Check the disc for cracks (especially around the wheel bolt holes), and for any other wear or damage. Renew the disc if necessary.

Removal

Note: *Suitable thread-locking compound will be required to coat the threads of the brake caliper mounting bracket bolts on refitting.*

6 If not already done, proceed as described in paragraph 1.

7 Unscrew the two bolts securing the brake caliper mounting bracket to the hub carrier, and slide the caliper assembly, complete with pads, off the disc (if necessary, pull the caliper body outwards, away from the centre of the car - this will push the piston back into its bore to allow the pads to pass over the disc) **(see illustration)**. Using a piece of wire or string, tie the caliper to the front suspension coil spring, to avoid placing any strain on the hydraulic brake hose or pad wear sensor wiring.

8 If the same disc is to be refitted, use chalk or paint to mark the relationship of the disc to the hub.

9 Remove the screw(s) securing the brake disc to the hub, and remove the disc. If it is tight, lightly tap its rear face with a hide or plastic mallet.

Refitting

10 Ensure that the mating surfaces of the disc and hub are clean and flat.

11 Offer the disc into position (where applicable, align the marks made on the disc and hub before removal), then refit and securely tighten the disc securing screw(s).

12 If a new disc has been fitted, use a suitable solvent to wipe any preservative coating from the disc before refitting the caliper.

13 Thoroughly clean the caliper mounting bracket bolt threads, then apply locking fluid to the bolt threads.

14 Slide the caliper and pad assembly into position over the disc, ensuring that the pads are correctly located, then refit the caliper mounting bracket bolts, and tighten to the specified torque.

15 Refit the roadwheel, then lower the vehicle to the ground and tighten the roadwheel bolts to the specified torque.

16 On completion, depress the brake pedal several times to bring the brake pads into contact with the disc.

8 Rear brake disc - inspection, removal and refitting

Note: *Before starting work, refer to the warning at the beginning of Section 4 concerning the dangers of asbestos dust. If either disc requires renewal, both should be renewed at the same time, to ensure even and consistent braking. In principle, new pads should be fitted also.*

Inspection

1 Chock the front wheels, engage reverse gear (or P on models with automatic transmission) and release the handbrake. Jack up the rear of the vehicle and support it securely on axle stands (see *Jacking and vehicle support*). Remove the relevant roadwheel.

2 Proceed as described for the inspection of the front brake discs in Section 7.

Removal

3 Disconnect the handbrake cable from the caliper and handbrake lever, with reference to Section 5.

4 Unscrew the upper caliper guide pin bolt.

5 Pull on the guide pin slightly until it is clear of the caliper mounting bracket, then tilt the caliper downwards, clear of the disc.

6 If the same disc is to be refitted, use chalk or paint to mark the relationship of the disc to the hub.

7 Remove the screw(s) securing the brake disc to the hub, and remove the disc. If it is tight, lightly tap its rear face with a hide or plastic mallet.

Refitting

8 Ensure that the mating surfaces of the disc and hub are clean and flat.

9 Offer the disc into position (where applicable, align the marks made on the disc and hub before removal), then refit and securely tighten the disc securing screw(s).

10 If a new disc has been fitted, use a suitable solvent to wipe any preservative coating from the disc before refitting the caliper.

11 Thoroughly clean the upper caliper guide pin bolt threads.

12 Coat the threads of the upper caliper guide pin bolt with thread-locking compound, then pivot the caliper into position over the disc, ensuring that the pads are correctly located. Refit the guide pin bolt and tighten to the specified torque.

13 Reconnect the handbrake cable to the caliper and handbrake lever.

14 Refit the roadwheel, then lower the vehicle to the ground and tighten the roadwheel bolts to the specified torque.

15 On completion, depress the brake pedal several times to bring the brake pads into contact with the disc.

9.2 Tap the cap from the centre of the brake drum

9.3 Removing the rear hub nut

9 Rear brake drum - removal, inspection and refitting

Note: *Before starting work, refer to the warning at the beginning of Section 6 concerning the dangers of asbestos dust. If either drum requires renewal, both should be renewed at the same time, to ensure even and* consistent braking. In principle, new shoes should be fitted also.

Note: *A new rear hub nut will be required on refitting.*

Removal

1 Chock the front wheels, engage reverse gear (or P on models with automatic transmission) and release the handbrake. Jack up the rear of the vehicle and support it securely on axle stands (see *Jacking and vehicle support*). Remove the appropriate rear wheel.
2 Using a hammer and suitable large flat-bladed screwdriver, carefully tap and prise the cap out of the centre of the brake drum **(see illustration)**.
3 Using a socket and long bar, slacken and remove the rear hub nut **(see illustration)**. Discard the hub nut; a new nut must used on refitting.
4 It should now be possible to withdraw the brake drum and hub bearing assembly from the stub axle by hand. It may be difficult to remove the drum due to the tightness of the hub bearing on the stub axle, or due to the brake shoes binding on the inner circumference of the drum. If the bearing is tight, tap the periphery of the drum using a hide or plastic mallet, or use a universal puller, secured to the drum with the wheel bolts, to pull it off. If the brake shoes are binding, proceed as follows.
5 First ensure that the handbrake is fully off. Working underneath the vehicle, counterhold the handbrake operating rod using the flats provided, and back off the adjuster nut at the cable equaliser (see the relevant part of

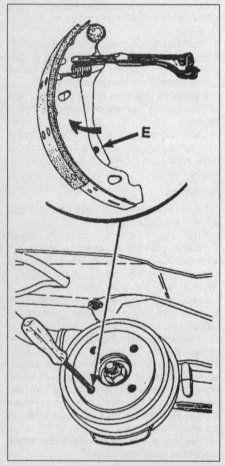

9.6a Using a screwdriver inserted through the brake drum to release the handbrake operating lever

E Handbrake operating lever stop peg location

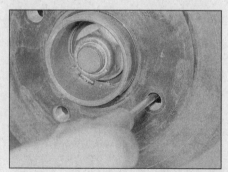

9.6b Releasing the handbrake operating lever

Chapter 1). Note that on some models, it will first be necessary to remove the mounting nut(s) and lower the exhaust heat shield to gain access to the adjuster nut.
6 Insert a screwdriver through one of the wheel bolt holes in the brake drum, so that it contacts the handbrake operating lever on the trailing brake shoe **(see illustrations)**. Push the lever until the stop-peg slips behind the brake shoe web, allowing the brake shoes to retract fully. Withdraw the brake drum.

Inspection

Note: *The drums on both sides must always be of the same internal diameter - therefore if one drum is machined to compensate for wear, the other drum must be machined to give the same finished internal diameter.*
7 Working carefully, remove all traces of brake dust from the drum, but *avoid inhaling the dust, as it is injurious to health.*
8 Scrub clean the outside of the drum, and check it for obvious signs of wear or damage such as cracks around the roadwheel bolt holes; renew the drum if necessary.
9 Carefully examine the inside of the drum. Light scoring of the friction surface is normal, but if heavy scoring is found, the drum must be renewed. It is usual to find a lip on the drum's inboard edge which consists of a mixture of rust and brake dust; this should be scraped away to leave a smooth surface which can be polished with fine (120 to 150 grade) emery paper. If the lip is due to the friction surface being recessed by wear, then the drum must be refinished (within the specified limits) or renewed.
10 If the drum is thought to be excessively worn or oval, its internal diameter must be measured at several points using an internal micrometer. Take measurements in pairs, the second at right-angles to the first, and compare the two to check for signs of ovality. Minor ovality can be corrected by machining; otherwise, renew the drum.

Refitting

11 If a new brake drum is to be installed, use a suitable solvent to remove any preservative coating that may have been applied to its interior.
12 Ensure that the handbrake lever stop-peg is correctly repositioned against the edge of the brake shoe web **(see illustration 6.16)**.
13 If necessary, using a screwdriver, rotate the adjuster wheel on the rear brake adjuster strut, to retract the brake shoes until the brake drum just slides over the shoes.
14 Apply a smear of gear oil to the stub axle, and slide on the brake drum, being careful not to get oil onto the brake shoes or the friction surface of the drum.
15 Fit a new hub nut, then tighten the nut to the specified torque.
16 Tap the hub cap into place in the centre of the brake drum.
17 Depress the footbrake several times to operate the self-adjusting mechanism.

18 Repeat the above procedure on the remaining rear brake assembly (where necessary), then adjust the handbrake as described in the relevant part of Chapter 1.

19 On completion, refit the roadwheel(s), lower the vehicle to the ground and tighten the roadwheel bolts to the specified torque.

10 Front brake caliper - removal, overhaul and refitting

⚠️ *Warning: Before starting work, refer to the warnings at the beginning of Sections 2 and 4 concerning the dangers of hydraulic fluid and asbestos dust.*

Note: *New caliper guide pin bolts must be used on refitting.*

Removal

1 Apply the handbrake, then jack up the front of the vehicle and support it securely on axle stands (see *Jacking and vehicle support*). Remove the appropriate roadwheel.

2 Minimise fluid loss by using a brake hose clamp, a G-clamp, or a similar tool with protected jaws, to clamp the flexible hose leading to the caliper.

3 Clean the area around the hose union on the caliper, then loosen the brake hose union nut.

4 Slacken and remove the upper and lower caliper guide pin bolts, using a slim open-ended spanner to prevent the guide pin itself from rotating. Discard the bolts - new ones must be used on refitting.

5 With the guide pin bolts removed, lift the caliper away from the brake disc, then unscrew the caliper from the end of the brake hose. Note that the brake pads need not be disturbed, and can be left in position in the caliper mounting bracket.

Overhaul

Note: *Make sure an appropriate overhaul kit can be obtained before dismantling the caliper.*

6 With the caliper on the bench, wipe away all traces of dust and dirt, but *avoid inhaling the dust, as it is injurious to health.*

7 Using a small flat-bladed screwdriver, carefully prise the dust seal retaining clip out of the caliper bore.

8 Withdraw the partially-ejected piston from the caliper body and remove the dust seal. The piston can be withdrawn by hand, or if necessary forced out by applying compressed air to the union bolt hole.

Caution: The piston may be ejected with some force. Only low pressure should be required, such as is generated by a foot pump. If the piston is forced out using compressed air, place a wooden block between the caliper body and the piston to prevent the possibility of damage to the piston as it is ejected.

9 Extract the piston hydraulic seal using a blunt instrument such as a knitting needle or a feeler blade, taking care not to damage the caliper bore **(see illustration)**.

10 Withdraw the guide pins from the caliper mounting bracket and remove the rubber gaiters.

11 Thoroughly clean all components using only methylated spirit, isopropyl alcohol or clean hydraulic fluid as a cleaning medium. Never use mineral-based solvents, such as petrol or paraffin, which will attack the hydraulic system rubber components. Dry the components immediately, using compressed air or a clean, lint-free cloth. Use compressed air to blow clear the fluid passages.

12 Check all components and renew any that are worn or damaged. Check particularly the cylinder bore and piston; if they are scratched, worn or corroded in any way, they must be renewed (note that this means the renewal of the complete body assembly). Similarly, check the condition of the guide pins and their bores; they should be undamaged and (when cleaned) a reasonably tight sliding fit in the caliper mounting bracket bores. If there is any doubt about the condition of a component, renew it.

13 If the assembly is fit for further use, obtain the appropriate repair kit; the components are available from Renault dealers, in various combinations.

14 Renew all rubber seals, dust covers and caps disturbed on dismantling as a matter of course; these should never be re-used.

15 Before starting reassembly, ensure that all components are absolutely clean and dry.

16 Dip the piston and the new piston (fluid) seal in clean hydraulic fluid. Smear clean fluid on the cylinder bore surface.

17 Fit the new piston (fluid) seal, using only the fingers to manipulate it into the cylinder bore groove. Fit the new dust seal to the piston. Refit the piston to the cylinder bore using a twisting motion, ensuring that the piston enters squarely into the bore. Press the piston fully into the bore, then press the dust seal into the caliper body.

18 Install the dust seal retaining clip, ensuring that it is correctly seated in the caliper groove.

19 Apply the grease supplied in the repair kit (or a good quality high-temperature brake grease or anti-seize compound) to the guide pins. Fit the pins to the caliper mounting bracket. Fit the new rubber gaiters, ensuring that they are correctly located in the grooves on both the pin, and mounting bracket.

Refitting

20 Screw the caliper body fully onto the flexible hose union nut. Check that the brake pads are still correctly fitted in the caliper mounting bracket.

21 Position the caliper over the pads. Fit the new lower caliper guide pin bolt, then press the caliper into position, and fit the upper guide pin bolt. Tighten the guide pin bolts to the specified torque, starting with the lower bolt.

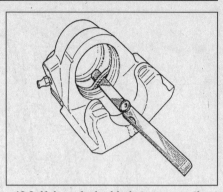

10.9 Using a feeler blade to remove the caliper hydraulic seal

22 Tighten the brake hose union nut to the specified torque.

23 Remove the clamp from the caliper fluid hose.

24 Apply the footbrake several times to position the pads against the discs.

25 Bleed the hydraulic system as described in Section 2. Providing the precautions described were taken to minimise brake fluid loss, it should only be necessary to bleed the relevant front brake.

26 Refit the roadwheel, then lower the vehicle to the ground and tighten the roadwheel bolts to the specified torque.

11 Rear brake caliper - removal, overhaul and refitting

⚠️ *Warning: Before starting work, refer to the warnings at the beginning of Sections 2 and 4 concerning the dangers of hydraulic fluid and asbestos dust.*

Note: *Suitable thread-locking compound will be required to coat the threads of the caliper guide pin bolts.*

Removal

1 Remove the brake pads as described in Section 5.

2 Minimise fluid loss by using a brake hose clamp, a G-clamp, or a similar tool with protected jaws, to clamp the flexible hose leading to the caliper.

3 Clean the area around the fluid hose union on the caliper, then loosen the fluid hose union nut.

4 Unscrew the lower caliper guide pin bolt **(see illustration overleaf)**.

5 Unscrew the bolt securing the caliper mounting bracket to the hub carrier, then withdraw the caliper, and unscrew the caliper from the end of the fluid hose.

Overhaul

6 At the time of writing, no information was available for the overhaul of the rear brake calipers. Consult a Renault dealer regarding the availability of spare parts.

9

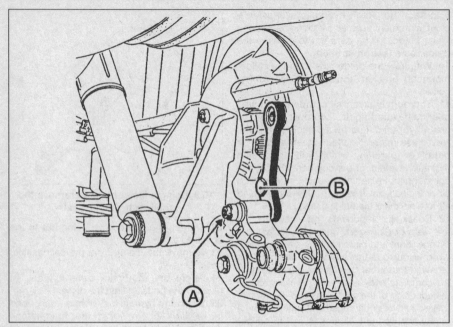

11.4 Rear brake caliper mounting details

A Lower guide pin bolt

B Mounting bracket-to-hub carrier bolt

Refitting

7 Thoroughly clean the threads of the caliper guide pin bolts and the bolt securing the caliper mounting bracket to the hub carrier.
8 Screw the caliper body fully onto the flexible hose union nut.
9 Coat the threads of the caliper mounting bracket bolt with locking compound, then offer the caliper mounting bracket into position, refit the bolt, and tighten securely.
10 Similarly, coat the threads of the lower caliper guide pin bolt with locking compound, then refit the bolt and tighten to the specified torque.
11 Refit the brake pads as described in Section 5.

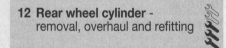

12 Rear wheel cylinder - removal, overhaul and refitting

Note: *Before starting work, refer to the warnings at the beginning of Section 2 concerning the dangers of hydraulic fluid, and at the beginning of Section 6 concerning the dangers of asbestos dust.*

Removal

1 Remove the brake drum as described in Section 9.
2 Using pliers, carefully unhook the brake shoe upper return spring and remove it from the brake shoes. Pull the upper ends of the shoes away from the wheel cylinder to disengage them from the pistons.
3 Minimise fluid loss, by using a brake hose clamp, a G-clamp or a similar tool with protected jaws to clamp the flexible hose at

the nearest convenient point to the wheel cylinder.
4 Wipe away all traces of dirt around the brake pipe union at the rear of the wheel cylinder, and unscrew the union nut. If the nut proves stubborn, soak it with penetrating oil for a while, then try again. Beware of using excessive force, as the brake pipe could become damaged. Consider buying a proper brake union spanner (also known as a flare nut spanner) which is designed specifically for this purpose. Carefully ease the pipe out of the wheel cylinder, and plug or tape over its end to prevent dirt entry. Wipe off any spilt fluid immediately.
5 Unscrew the two wheel cylinder retaining bolts from the rear of the backplate **(see illustration)**. Remove the cylinder, taking care not to allow hydraulic fluid to contaminate the brake shoe linings.

Overhaul

6 No spare parts are available for the wheel cylinder, and if faulty, a complete new unit must be fitted.

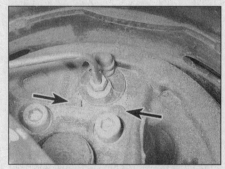

12.5 Rear wheel cylinder securing bolts (arrowed)

Refitting

7 Ensure that the backplate and wheel cylinder mating surfaces are clean, then spread the brake shoes and manoeuvre the wheel cylinder into position.
8 Engage the brake pipe, and screw in the union nut two or three turns to ensure that the thread has started.
9 Insert the two wheel cylinder retaining bolts, and tighten them securely. Now fully tighten the brake pipe union nut.
10 Remove the clamp from the brake hose.
11 Ensure that the brake shoes are correctly located in the cylinder pistons. Carefully refit the brake shoe upper return spring, using a screwdriver or long-nosed pliers to stretch the spring into position.
12 Refit the brake drum as described in Section 9.
13 Bleed the brake hydraulic system as described in Section 2. Providing suitable precautions were taken to minimise loss of fluid, it should only be necessary to bleed the relevant rear brake.

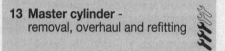

13 Master cylinder - removal, overhaul and refitting

Note: *Before starting work, refer to the warnings at the beginning of Section 2 concerning the dangers of hydraulic fluid.*
Note: *A new master cylinder-to-servo seal will be required on refitting.*

Removal

1 Syphon the fluid from the master cylinder reservoir. Use a syringe, a clean battery hydrometer or a poultry baster to do this, **never** use the mouth to suck the fluid out through a tube.
2 Disconnect the leads from the low fluid level warning light switch and pull the reservoir upwards out of the sealing grommets.
3 Note the locations of the hydraulic pipes and then disconnect them from the master cylinder by unscrewing the unions. Place a wad of rag under the master cylinder to catch any fluid which may drain out.
4 Unscrew the nuts securing the master cylinder to the front face of the vacuum servo, and withdraw the master cylinder.
5 Recover the seal.

Overhaul

6 A faulty master cylinder cannot be overhauled, as no spare parts are available. If the master cylinder is faulty or worn, the complete assembly must be renewed.

Refitting

7 Before fitting the master cylinder, check that the servo operating rod protrusion is as specified **(see illustration 14.14)**. If necessary adjust by turning the operating rod adjusting nut.

8 Place a new seal in position on the rear of the master cylinder.

9 Place the master cylinder in position on the servo, then refit and tighten the securing nuts.

10 Reconnect the brake fluid pipes and tighten the union nuts.

11 Push the reservoir firmly into its grommets, and reconnect the low fluid level warning light switch wires.

12 Fill the reservoir with clean fluid and bleed the complete hydraulic system as described in Section 2.

13 On completion, check that the length of the servo pushrod is as specified - see Section 14.

14 Vacuum servo unit - testing, removal and refitting

Left-hand-drive models

Testing

1 Operation of the servo can be checked in the following way.

2 With the engine stopped, depress the brake pedal several times. The pedal travel should remain the same each time the pedal is depressed.

3 Depress the brake pedal fully and hold it down, then start the engine. It should be possible to feel the pedal move down slightly.

4 Hold the pedal depressed with the engine running, then switch off the engine, whilst still holding the pedal depressed. The pedal should not rise nor fall.

5 Start the engine and run it for at least a minute. Stop the engine, then depress the brake pedal several times. The pedal travel should decrease with each application, and it should be possible to detect a 'hissing' sound from the servo as the pedal is depressed. After about four or five depressions of the pedal, no further hissing should be heard, and the pedal should feel considerably firmer.

6 If the foregoing tests do not prove satisfactory, check the servo vacuum hose and non-return valve for security and leakage at the valve grommet.

7 If the brake servo operates properly in the test, but still gives less effective service on the road, the air filter through which air flows into the servo should be inspected. A dirty filter will reduce the effectiveness of the servo.

8 The servo unit itself cannot be repaired and therefore renewal is necessary if the unit proves to be faulty.

Removal

9 Remove the master cylinder, as described in Section 13. Note that on some models, it may be possible to move the master cylinder to one side, without disconnecting the brake fluid pipes.

10 Disconnect the vacuum hose from the servo unit.

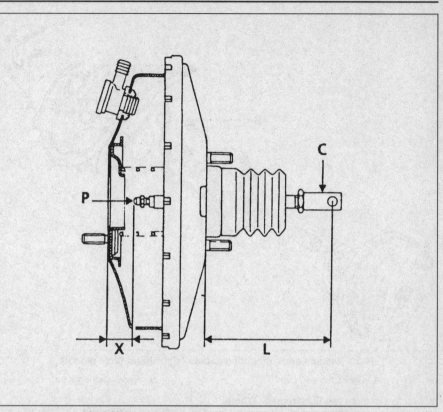

14.14 Vacuum servo operating rod and pushrod setting

C Servo pushrod   *P Servo operating rod*   *X = 22.3 mm*

L = 130.0 mm - right-hand-drive models   *L = 158.5 mm - left-hand-drive models*

11 Working in the driver's footwell, disconnect the servo pushrod from the brake pedal by extracting the split pin or spring clip (as applicable) and the clevis pin. Where a spring clip is fitted, prise out the locking lug, then pull off the clip.

12 Again working in the footwell, unscrew the brake servo mounting nuts.

13 Withdraw the servo from the engine compartment.

Refitting

14 Before refitting the servo, check that the protrusion of the servo operating rod is as specified **(see illustration)**. The protrusion is measured from the front face of the servo to the end of the operating rod. If necessary, adjust the operating rod protrusion by turning the adjuster nut on the end of the rod.

15 Similarly, check the length of the servo pushrod. The length is measured from the rear face of the servo to the centre of the hole in the pushrod clevis. If necessary, adjust the length of the pushrod by loosening the locknut and turning the clevis. Tighten the locknut on completion.

16 Refitting is a reversal of removal, but refit the master cylinder with reference to Section 13.

Right-hand-drive models

Testing

17 Proceed as described in paragraphs 1 to 8.

Removal

18 Proceed as described in paragraphs 9 and 10.

19 Working in the passenger's footwell, remove the lower facia trim panel, then pull off the securing clip (prise out the locking lug, then pull off the clip), and withdraw the clevis pin securing the servo pushrod to the pedal shaft **(see illustration)**.

20 Working in the engine compartment, reach behind the brake servo, and unscrew the four nuts securing the servo to the

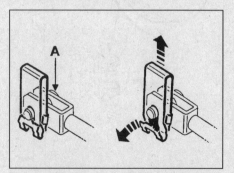

14.19 Prise out the locking lug, then pull off the clevis pin securing clip

A Clevis pin

9

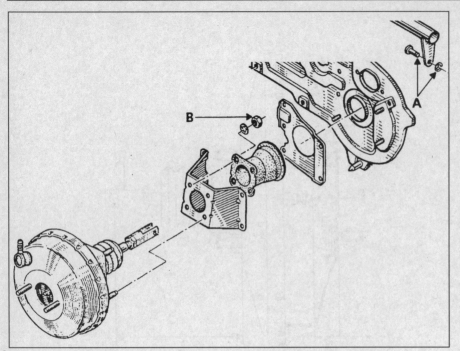

14.20 Vacuum servo mounting details - right-hand-drive models

A *Clevis pin and clip*   B *Servo securing nut*

mounting bracket **(see illustration)**. Where applicable, recover the washers.
21 Withdraw the servo from the mounting bracket. On some models it may be necessary to remove the air filter to provide sufficient clearance to remove the assembly.

Refitting

22 Proceed as in paragraphs 14 to 16.

15 Vacuum servo unit non-return valve - removal, testing and refitting

Removal

1 Slacken the clip and disconnect the vacuum hose from the non-return valve on the front face of the servo unit.
2 Withdraw the valve from its rubber sealing grommet by pulling and twisting. Pull the sealing grommet from the servo.

Testing

3 Examine the non-return valve and sealing grommet for damage and signs of deterioration, and renew if necessary. The valve can be tested by blowing through it in both directions - it should only be possible to blow from the servo end to the manifold end.

Refitting

4 Fit a new grommet to the servo, then push the valve into position in the grommet. A smear of rubber grease will aid fitting. Do not push too hard, as it is possible to push the sealing grommet into the servo.
5 Reconnect the vacuum hose.

16 Vacuum servo unit air filter - renewal

Left-hand-drive models

1 In the driver's footwell, remove the lower facia panel, pull the dust excluder from the rear of the servo, and slide it up the pushrod.
2 Using a scriber or similar pointed tool, prise

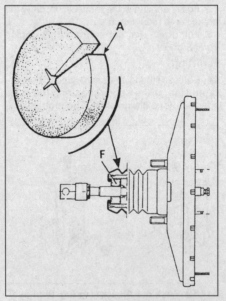

16.2 Vacuum servo air filter location (F)

Cut the new filter at A to enable fitting

the filter from its housing, and cut it to allow it to pass over the pushrod **(see illustration)**.
3 Cut the new filter, and push it into position, ensuring that it is correctly seated.
4 Push the dust excluder into position.

Right-hand-drive models

5 Remove the brake servo as described in Section 14.
6 Pull the dust excluder from the rear of the servo, and slide it up the pushrod.
7 Proceed as described in paragraphs 2 to 4.
8 Refit the servo as described in Section 14.

17 Brake pedal - removal and refitting

Left-hand-drive models

Removal

1 Working in the driver's footwell, disconnect the servo pushrod from the brake pedal arm by extracting the spring clip or split pin, as applicable, and pushing out the clevis pin.
2 Unscrew the nut from the end of the pedal pivot shaft, then slide the pivot shaft towards the side of the footwell until the pedal and mounting bushes can be withdrawn. Note that the pivot shaft also secures the clutch pedal (see Chapter 6).

Refitting

3 Examine the pedal pivot bushes, and renew if necessary.
4 Refitting is a reversal of removal. Ensure that the pivot bushes are refitted in their correct locations.

Right-hand-drive models

Removal

5 Remove the complete facia assembly as described in Chapter 11.
6 Remove the complete heater/air distribution assembly, as described in Chapter 3.
7 Working in the passenger's side footwell, prise off the securing clip, and withdraw the clevis pin securing the servo pushrod to the pedal shaft.
8 Working at the driver's side end of the pedal shaft, remove the circlip from the end of the shaft **(see illustration opposite)**.
9 Working in the engine compartment, unscrew the two bolts securing the pedal shaft mounting clamp.
10 Again working in the passenger compartment, disconnect the throttle cable from the pedal, with reference to the relevant part of Chapter 4 if necessary.
11 Where applicable, disconnect the clutch cable from the clutch pedal, with reference to Chapter 6.
12 Disconnect the speedometer cable from the transmission, with reference to Chapter 12 if necessary.

13 Ensure that the front wheels are in the straight-ahead position, then unscrew the steering column shaft-to-steering gear pinion clamp nut and bolt.

14 Working in the passenger compartment, unscrew the five nuts securing the pedal mounting bracket.

15 Working in the engine compartment, unscrew the remaining three nuts securing the pedal mounting bracket.

16 Pull the mounting bracket away from the bulkhead sufficiently to enable the pedal assembly to be withdrawn. If necessary, move the steering column shaft to one side to enable the pedal assembly to be withdrawn.

Refitting

17 Refitting is a reversal of removal, bearing in mind the following points.

a) *Ensure that the front wheels are in the straight-ahead position, and that the steering wheel is centralised when refitting the steering column shaft-to-steering gear pinion clamp nut and bolt.*

b) *Reconnect the throttle cable, and the clutch cable, where applicable, with reference to the relevant part of Chapters 4 and 6.*

c) *Refit the heater/air distribution assembly with reference to Chapter 3.*

d) *Refit the facia assembly with reference to Chapter 11.*

---

18 Rear brake pressure regulating valve -
adjustment, removal and refitting

Testing and adjustment

1 Testing and adjustment of the pressure regulating valve requires the use of special pressure gauges and adapters, and should be entrusted to a Renault dealer.

Removal

2 Chock the front wheels, engage reverse gear (or P on models with automatic transmission) and release the handbrake. Jack up the rear of the vehicle and support it securely on axle stands (see *Jacking and vehicle support*).

3 Minimise fluid loss by first removing the brake fluid reservoir cap, and then tightening it down onto a piece of polythene to obtain an airtight seal.

4 Working under the rear of the vehicle, wipe clean the area around the brake pipe unions on the valve.

5 Unscrew the two bolts securing the valve mounting bracket to the body **(see illustration)**.

6 Lower the assembly, taking care not to strain the brake fluid hose, then unclip the valve operating rod from the lever on the rear suspension.

7 Place absorbent rags beneath the pipe unions to catch any spilt fluid, then unscrew

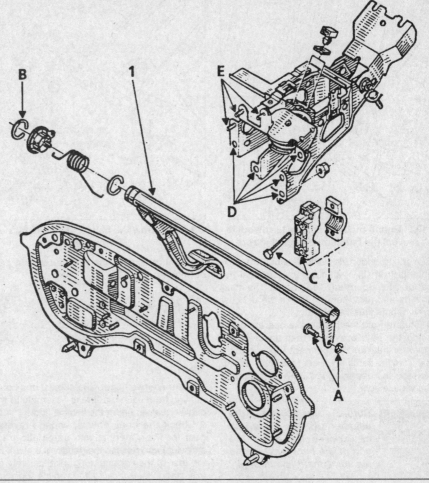

**17.8 Brake pedal mounting details -
right-hand-drive models**

1 Pedal shaft	*C Pedal shaft mounting clamp and bolt*
A Clevis pin and clip	*D Pedal mounting bracket nuts*
B Circlip	*E Pedal mounting bracket nuts*

the union nuts, and disconnect the brake fluid pipes from the valve.

8 Unscrew the two screws securing the valve to the mounting bracket, then withdraw the valve from under the vehicle. Ensure that the brake fluid hose (which should still be clipped to the valve mounting bracket) is not strained.

Refitting

9 Refitting is a reversal of removal, but on completion, have the adjustment of the valve checked by a Renault dealer at the earliest opportunity.

---

19 Handbrake lever -
removal and refitting

Removal

1 Jack up the car and support securely on axle stands (see *Jacking and vehicle support*).

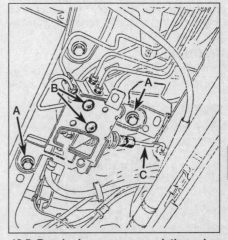

18.5 Rear brake pressure regulating valve

A Valve bracket securing bolts
B Valve-to-bracket securing screws
C Valve operating rod

9

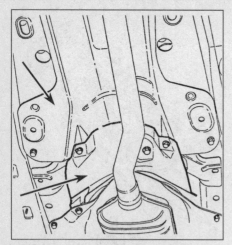

19.2 Unbolt the heat shields (arrowed) to reveal the handbrake operating rod

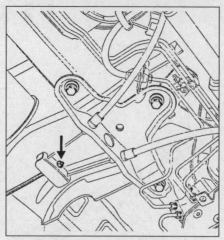
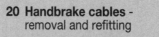

19.3 Unscrew the handbrake adjuster nut (arrowed)

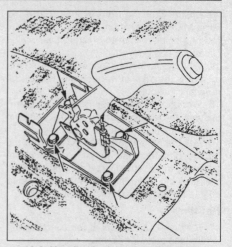

19.6 Handbrake lever securing bolts (arrowed)

2 Working under the vehicle, unbolt the heat shields from the vehicle floor to reveal the handbrake operating rod. Lower the heat shields and rest them on top of the exhaust system **(see illustration)**.

3 Counterhold the handbrake operating rod using the flats provided, then unscrew the adjuster nut, and disconnect the operating rod from the cable equaliser **(see illustration)**. Release the operating rod from the clip(s) on the vehicle floor.

> **HAYNES HINT**
> *Before unscrewing the adjuster nut, note the length of exposed thread on the end of the handbrake rod to aid adjustment on refitting.*

4 Working inside the vehicle, remove the centre console as described in Chapter 11.

5 Where necessary, carefully cut a slit in the carpet/sound insulation panels to expose the four handbrake lever securing bolts.

6 Unscrew the four bolts securing the handbrake lever assembly to the floor, then withdraw the handbrake lever/rod assembly **(see illustration)**.

Refitting

7 Refitting is a reversal of removal, but on completion, check the handbrake cable

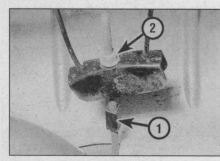

20.4 Counterhold the handbrake operating rod using the flats (1) and unscrew the adjuster nut (2)

adjustment as described in the relevant part of Chapter 1.

20 Handbrake cables - removal and refitting

Removal

1 There are two handbrake cables, one cable running from each rear brake assembly to the cable equaliser under the vehicle floor.

2 Chock the front wheels, engage reverse gear (or P on models with automatic transmission) and release the handbrake. Jack up the rear of the car and support it securely on axle stands (see *Jacking and vehicle support*).

3 Working under the rear of the vehicle, where applicable unbolt the heat shield from the vehicle floor to reveal the handbrake cable equaliser.

4 Counterhold the handbrake operating rod, using the flats provided, then unscrew the adjuster nut from the end of the operating rod **(see illustration)**.

5 Slide the end of the handbrake cable from the equaliser.

6 On models with rear drum brakes, remove the relevant brake drum(s) as described in Section 9, then disconnect the handbrake cable from the lever on the trailing shoe.

7 On models with rear disc brakes, disconnect the handbrake cable from the caliper as described in Section 5. Again, if necessary back-off the handbrake cable adjustment with reference to the relevant part of Chapter 1.

8 Release the cable from the clips on the body and suspension components, and withdraw the cable.

Refitting

9 Refitting is a reversal of removal, but lightly grease the end of the cable at the equaliser, and on completion, check the cable adjustment as described in the relevant part of Chapter 1.

21 Stop-light switch - adjustment, removal and refitting

Adjustment

1 The switch is self-adjusting.

2 If adjustment is required, reach up behind the facia and push the switch into the mounting bracket. Operate the brake pedal several times, which will automatically set the switch position.

Removal

3 Disconnect the battery negative terminal (refer to *Disconnecting the battery* in the Reference Section of this manual).

4 Reach up under the facia, and disconnect the wiring plug from the switch (where two switches are fitted to the brake pedal bracket, note that the upper switch controls the stop lights) **(see illustration)**.

5 Pull the switch from the mounting bracket.

Refitting

6 Push the switch into the mounting bracket, and reconnect the wiring plug.

7 Operate the brake pedal several times to set the position of the switch.

21.4 Stop light switch location (arrowed)

22 Handbrake 'on' warning light switch - removal and refitting

Removal

1 Disconnect the battery negative terminal (refer to *Disconnecting the battery* in the Reference Section of this manual).

2 Remove the centre console as described in Chapter 11.

3 Unscrew the four securing bolts, and lift up the handbrake lever until the switch securing nut can be unscrewed from the end of the stud (if necessary, back off the handbrake adjustment - see Section 19).

4 Unscrew the nut, then remove the switch and disconnect the wiring plug **(see illustration)**.

Refitting

5 Refitting is a reversal of removal but, where applicable, on completion check the handbrake adjustment as described in the relevant part of Chapter 1.

23 Anti-lock braking system (ABS) - general information

1 ABS is available as an option on certain models covered by this manual, and is fitted as standard equipment on others. The purpose of the system is to prevent the wheel(s) locking during heavy braking. This is achieved by automatic release of the brake on the relevant wheel, followed by re-application of the brake. The system comprises an electronic control module, a hydraulic modulator block, hydraulic solenoid valves and accumulators, an electrically-driven return pump, and four roadwheel sensors. A brake pedal travel sensor is also fitted, located in the brake vacuum servo.

22.4 Handbrake 'on' warning light switch securing nut (arrowed)

2 Models with ABS may be fitted with rear drum or rear disc brakes.

3 The solenoids (which control the fluid pressure to the calipers/wheel cylinders) are controlled by the electronic control unit, which itself receives signals from the wheel sensors. The wheel sensors monitor the speed of rotation of each wheel. By comparing these speed signals from the four wheels, the control unit can determine when a wheel is decelerating at an abnormal rate, compared to the speed of the vehicle. Using this information, the control unit can predict when a wheel is about to lock, and is able to reduce the fluid pressure to the brake on the relevant wheel to prevent it from locking.

4 During normal operation, the system functions in the same way as a conventional non-ABS braking system.

24 Anti-lock braking system (ABS) components - removal and refitting
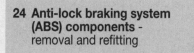

Front wheel sensor
Removal

1 Disconnect the battery negative terminal (refer to *Disconnecting the battery* in the Reference Section of this manual).

2 Apply the handbrake, then jack up the front of the vehicle and support securely on axle stands (see *Jacking and vehicle support*). To improve access, remove the relevant roadwheel.

3 Locate the sensor wiring connector, clipped to the front subframe, then separate the two halves of the connector. Release the wiring from any clips and support brackets.

4 Unscrew the securing bolt, then withdraw the sensor from the hub carrier **(see illustration)**.

Refitting

5 Refitting is a reversal of removal, bearing in mind the following points.
  a) *Smear the hub carrier contact faces of the sensor with a little grease before fitting.*
  b) *Tighten the securing bolt to the specified torque - do not overtighten the bolt.*
  c) *Ensure that the wiring connector is securely reconnected.*

Rear wheel sensor - models with rear drum brakes

Note: *New stub axle securing bolts will be required on refitting.*

Removal

6 Disconnect the battery negative terminal (refer to *Disconnecting the battery* in the Reference Section of this manual).

7 Chock the front wheels, engage reverse gear (or P on models with automatic transmission) and release the handbrake. Jack up the rear of the vehicle and support it securely on axle stands (see *Jacking and vehicle support*). Remove the appropriate rear wheel.

8 Locate the sensor wiring connector, clipped to a bracket under the rear floor of the vehicle, near the rear axle mounting, then separate the two halves of the connector **(see illustration)**. Release the wiring from any clips and support brackets.

9 Unscrew the sensor securing bolt **(see illustration)**.

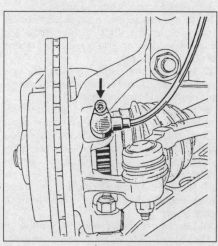

24.4 ABS front wheel sensor securing bolt (arrowed)

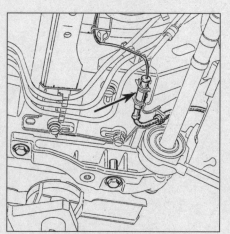

24.8 ABS rear wheel sensor wiring connector location (arrowed) - rear drum brake models

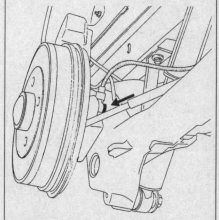

24.9 ABS rear wheel sensor securing bolt (arrowed) - rear drum brake model

9

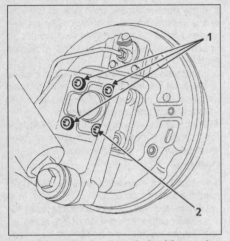

24.11 Unscrew the three bolts (1) securing the stub axle, then slacken bolt (2)

10 Release the sensor wiring, the brake pipe and the handbrake cable from the bracket on the trailing arm.

11 Working at the rear of the stub axle, unscrew and remove the three bolts shown securing the stub axle assembly to the trailing arm **(see illustration)**.

12 Slacken, but do not remove the remaining stub axle assembly securing bolt. Leave the bolt in place by two or three threads to retain the stub axle/brake assembly in position.

13 Carefully withdraw the wheel sensor by pushing it back towards the outside of the stub axle/brake assembly.

Refitting

14 Smear the trailing arm contact faces of the sensor with a little grease before fitting.

15 Push the sensor into position, using hand pressure only. **Do not** tap the sensor into position using tools.

16 Screw in three new bolts, by hand, to secure the stub axle, then unscrew the fourth bolt (left in position to retain the stub axle/brake assembly), and fit the fourth new securing bolt.

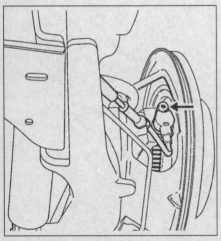

24.20 ABS rear wheel sensor securing bolt (arrowed) - rear disc brake model

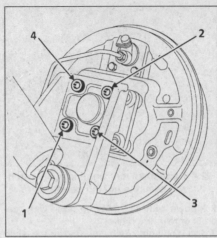

24.17 Tighten the stub axle securing bolts in the order shown

17 Tighten the four stub axle securing bolts, in the order shown, to the specified torque **(see illustration)**.

18 Further refitting is a reversal of removal, bearing in mind the following points.

a) *Tighten the securing bolt to the specified torque - do not overtighten the bolt.*

b) *Ensure that the wiring connector is securely reconnected.*

Rear wheel sensor - models with rear disc brakes

Removal

19 Proceed as described in paragraphs 6 to 8.

20 Unscrew the securing bolt, then withdraw the sensor from its housing **(see illustration)**.

Refitting

21 Refer to paragraph 5.

Front wheel sensor ring

Removal

22 Remove the driveshaft as described in Chapter 8.

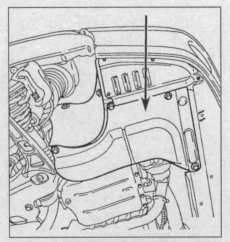

24.35 Remove the splash shield (arrowed) to access the ABS electronic control unit

23 Support the sensor ring, then press the driveshaft joint from the sensor ring. It is not advisable to drive the driveshaft from the ring, as this may result in damage to the driveshaft joint.

Refitting

24 If the original sensor ring is to be refitted, thoroughly clean the contact faces of the ring.

25 Coat the driveshaft contact faces of the sensor ring with locking compound, then press the ring onto the driveshaft joint, using a tube of suitable diameter, and the old driveshaft nut.

26 Refit the driveshaft (see Chapter 8).

Rear wheel sensor ring - models with rear drum brakes

Note: *A suitable puller will be required for this operation.*

Removal

27 Remove the brake drum as described in Section 9.

28 Using a suitable puller, pull the sensor ring from the rear of the drum.

Refitting

29 Thoroughly clean the contact faces of the sensor ring and the drum.

30 Press the sensor ring into position using a tube of suitable diameter.

Rear wheel sensor ring - models with rear disc brakes

31 The sensor ring is integral with the rear hub, and cannot be removed separately. Refer to Chapter 10 for details of rear hub removal and refitting.

Electronic control unit

Removal

32 The control unit is located under the right-hand or left-hand side of the vehicle, according to model, behind the bumper.

33 Disconnect the battery negative terminal (refer to *Disconnecting the battery* in the Reference Section of this manual).

34 To improve access, apply the handbrake, then jack up the front of the vehicle and support securely on axle stands (see *Jacking and vehicle support*).

35 Unscrew the securing screws, and withdraw the plastic splash shield to expose the control unit **(see illustration)**.

36 Unscrew the two bolts and the nut securing the ABS control assembly to the body, then carefully lower the assembly, taking care not to strain the fluid pipes or the wiring, for access to the control unit **(see illustration)**.

37 Release the securing clip, and disconnect the wiring plug from the top of the electronic control unit.

38 Unscrew the two securing bolts (four on later models), and withdraw the control unit from the ABS control assembly **(see illustration)**.

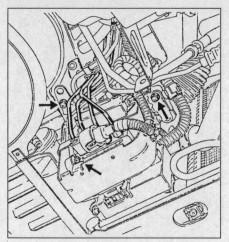

24.36 ABS control assembly securing bolts and nut (arrowed)

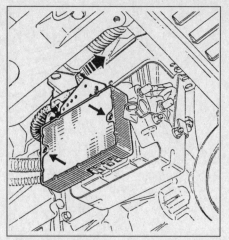

24.38 ABS electronic control unit securing bolts (arrowed)

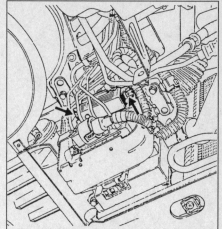

24.41 ABS relay block securing bolts (arrowed)

Refitting

39 Refitting is a reversal of removal, bearing in mind the following points.

a) *Ensure that the wiring plug is correctly reconnected.*

b) *Tighten the electronic control unit securing bolts to the specified torque. Do not overtighten the bolts.*

c) *On completion, have the system checked at the earliest opportunity by a suitably-equipped Renault dealer.*

Relay block

Removal

Note: *The relay block is only fitted to pre-May 1998 ABS systems.*

40 Proceed as described in paragraphs 32 to 36.

41 Unscrew the two relay block securing bolts **(see illustration).**

42 Disconnect the two wiring plugs, and withdraw the relay block.

Refitting

43 Refitting is a reversal of removal, but ensure that the wiring plugs are correctly reconnected and, on completion, have the system checked at the earliest opportunity by a suitably-equipped Renault dealer.

Hydraulic unit

Removal

⚠️ *Warning: Do not remove the hydraulic unit unless suitable arrangements can be made to have the system bled using Renault diagnostic equipment after refitting.*

44 Proceed as described in paragraphs 32 to 36.

45 Unscrew the two securing bolts (four on later models), and withdraw the electronic control unit from the ABS control assembly. There is no need to disconnect the wiring plug.

46 Where fitted, unscrew the secondary relay block mounting nut **(see illustration).**

47 Disconnect the two wiring plugs, and move the relay block to one side.

48 Place a suitable container beneath the hydraulic assembly to catch escaping fluid as the pipes are disconnected.

49 Note the locations of the fluid pipes (mark them if necessary), then unscrew the union nuts, and disconnect the fluid pipes from the hydraulic unit.

50 Withdraw the hydraulic unit, and plug or cover the open ends of the pipes and the apertures in the hydraulic unit to prevent dirt entry and further fluid loss.

Refitting

51 Refitting is a reversal of removal, bearing in mind the following points.

a) *Take great care not to allow dirt to enter the hydraulic circuit as the pipes are reconnected.*

b) *Ensure that the pipes are reconnected to their correct locations as noted before removal.*

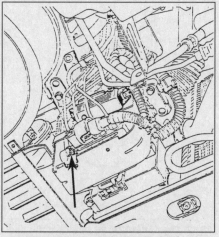

24.46 Secondary ABS relay block mounting nut (arrowed)

c) *Ensure that the wiring plug is correctly reconnected.*

d) *Tighten the electronic control unit securing bolts to the specified torque. Do not overtighten the bolts.*

e) *On completion, have the system checked at the earliest opportunity by a suitably-equipped Renault dealer.*

Brake pedal travel sensor

Removal

52 Disconnect the battery negative terminal (refer to *Disconnecting the battery* in the Reference Section of this manual), then disconnect the wiring plug from the sensor **(see illustration).**

53 Using a small flat-bladed screwdriver, release the sensor retaining clips, then withdraw the sensor from the vacuum servo.

Refitting

54 Refitting is a reversal of removal, but have the system checked at the earliest opportunity by a Renault dealer.

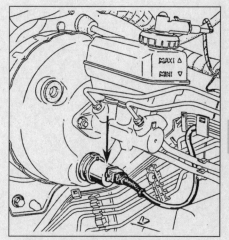

24.52 ABS brake pedal travel sensor location (arrowed)

9

25.3 Power steering fluid reservoir mounting details

2 Clip
3 Mounting bracket bolts

25 Brake vacuum pump (diesel engine models) - removal and refitting

Belt-driven pump

Removal

Note: *A three-legged puller will be required to remove the pump sprocket.*

1 Disconnect the battery negative terminal (refer to *Disconnecting the battery* in the Reference Section of this manual).

2 Remove the auxiliary (brake vacuum pump) drivebelt as described in Chapter 1B.

3 Release the securing clip, and move the power steering fluid reservoir to one side, taking care not to strain the fluid hoses **(see illustration)**.

4 Unscrew the two power steering fluid reservoir bracket mounting bolts, and remove the bracket. Where applicable, unscrew the

25.10 Brake vacuum pump securing bolts (arrowed)

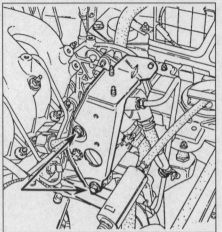

25.5 Unscrew the two bolts (arrowed) and remove the bracket from the vacuum pump

two nuts securing the fast idle solenoid to the top of the power steering reservoir mounting bracket, then move the valve to one side. If the hoses are disconnected, note their locations to ensure correct reconnection.

5 Unscrew the two securing bolts, and remove the bracket from the rear of the vacuum pump **(see illustration)**.

6 Place a suitable container beneath the pump oil feed pipe connection, then unscrew the union nut and disconnect the pipe. Recover the oil jet from the aperture in the pump if it is loose. Plug the open ends of the pipe and the pump to prevent dirt ingress and further oil spillage.

7 Similarly, remove the hose clip, and disconnect the oil return hose from the pump. Note the routing of the hose to aid refitting.

8 Remove the hose clip and disconnect the vacuum hose from the pump. Again, not the routing of the hose.

9 Fit a three-legged puller to the pump sprocket, then tighten the puller to release the sprocket from the taper on the pump shaft

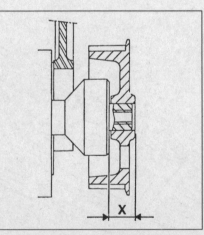

25.12 The dimension (x) between the end of the pump shaft and the outer face of the sprocket should be 16.5 mm

25.9 Using a puller to remove the brake vacuum pump sprocket

(see illustration). Withdraw the puller and sprocket.

10 Working at the front of the pump, unscrew the three bolts securing the pump to the mounting bracket, then withdraw the pump **(see illustration)**.

Refitting

11 Commence refitting by positioning the pump in the mounting bracket, refitting the three securing bolts.

12 The pump sprocket must now be refitted, and this can be achieved as follows.

a) *Place the sprocket on the end of the pump shaft.*

b) *Obtain a piece of flat metal bar, with a hole in the centre (of suitable size for an M8 bolt to pass through), and an M8 bolt (approx 125 mm long), large washer and nut.*

c) *Fit the washer to the bolt, then screw on the nut and pass the bolt through the steel bar. Screw the bolt into the threaded end of the pump shaft.*

d) *Screw the bolt into the pump shaft as far as possible, then tighten the nut until the washer touches the metal bar (prevent the sprocket from turning using an old drivebelt wrapped around the sprocket).*

e) *Tighten the nut to draw the sprocket onto the pump shaft. Take care not to draw the sprocket on too far - the dimension between the end of the pump shaft and the outer face of the sprocket should be as shown (see illustration).*

13 Further refitting is a reversal of removal, bearing in mind the following points.

a) *Ensure that the oil jet is in place in the pump aperture before reconnecting the oil supply pipe (see illustration).*

b) *Ensure that the oil return and vacuum hoses are routed as noted before removal.*

c) *Refit and tighten the pump drivebelt as described in Chapter 1B.*

25.13 Ensure that the oil jet (arrowed) is in position

Direct-drive pump

Removal

14 Release the retaining clip, and disconnect the vacuum hose from the pump.
15 Slacken and remove the three bolts and washers securing the pump to the left-hand end of the cylinder head, then remove the pump. Recover the O-rings, where applicable.

Refitting

16 Where applicable, fit new O-rings to the pump, then align the drive dog with the slot in the end of the camshaft, and refit the pump to the cylinder head, ensuring that the O-rings remain correctly seated, where applicable.

17 Refit the pump mounting bolts and washers, and tighten them securely.
18 Reconnect the vacuum hose to the pump, and tighten its securing clip.

26 Brake vacuum pump (diesel engine models) - testing and overhaul

Testing

Note: *A vacuum gauge will be required.*
1 The operation of the braking system vacuum pump can be checked using a vacuum gauge.
2 Disconnect the vacuum pipe from the pump, and connect the gauge to the pump union using a suitable length of tubing.
3 Start the engine and allow it to idle, then measure the vacuum created by the pump. As a guide, after one minute, a minimum of around 500 mm Hg should be registered. If the vacuum registered is significantly less than this, it is likely that the pump is faulty. However, seek the advice of a Renault dealer before condemning the pump.

Overhaul

4 Overhaul of the vacuum pump is not possible, since no components are available for it separately. If faulty, the complete pump assembly must be renewed.

9

Chapter 10
Suspension and steering

Contents

Degrees of difficulty

Easy, suitable for novice with little experience | **Fairly easy,** suitable for beginner with some experience | **Fairly difficult,** suitable for competent DIY mechanic | **Difficult,** suitable for experienced DIY mechanic | **Very difficult,** suitable for expert DIY or professional

Specifications

Front suspension

Type . . . . Independent, by MacPherson struts, with inclined coil springs and integral shock absorbers, located by lower arms. Anti-roll bar fitted to all models

Hub bearing free-play . . . . 0 to 0.05 mm

Rear suspension

Type . . . . Trailing arms, with transverse torsion bars (open-bar type) and telescopic shock absorbers. Rear anti-roll bars on all models

Hub bearing free-play . . . . 0 to 0.03 mm

Steering

Type . . . . Rack-and-pinion with collapsible safety column. Power steering fitted to all models

Wheel alignment and steering angles

Front wheel toe-setting . . . . 0°10' ± 10' (1.0 ± 1.0 mm) toe-in

10

Torque wrench settings

	Nm	lbf ft
Front suspension		
Anti-roll bar clamp bolts	20	15
Anti-roll bar drop link nuts	40	30
Driveshaft nut	250	185
Front subframe bracing plate bolts	65	48
Front subframe mounting bolts:		
Front bolts (M10)	37	27
Rear bolts (M12)	90	66
Lower arm balljoint nut	65	48
Lower arm front mounting bolt	210	155
Lower arm rear mounting nut and bolt	110	81
Rear engine mounting through-bolt and nut	50	37
Suspension strut piston rod nut	60	44
Suspension strut-to-hub carrier nuts and bolts:		
All except petrol engine models with manual gearbox		
from early 1995	200	148
Petrol engine models with manual gearbox from early 1995		
(M14 x 150 mm bolts)	170	125
Suspension strut upper mounting bolts	25	18
Rear suspension		
Hub nut:		
Non-ABS models with rear drum brakes	190	140
ABS models with rear drum brakes	175	129
Models with rear disc brakes	175	129
Shock absorber securing bolts and nut	100	74
Stub axle securing bolts (models with rear drum brakes)	75	55
Suspension assembly mounting bolts	85	63
Steering		
Steering column intermediate shaft-to-steering gear pinion clamp		
bolt and nut	25	18
Steering column securing nuts	15	11
Steering gear securing nuts	65	48
Steering wheel securing bolt	45	33
Track-rod end balljoint-to-hub carrier nut	40	30
Track-rod end clamp bolt	20	15
Track-rod inner balljoint	50	37
Roadwheels		
Roadwheel bolts	See Chapter 1A or 1B	

1 General information

The independent front suspension is of the MacPherson strut type, incorporating coil springs and integral telescopic shock absorbers. The MacPherson struts are located by transverse lower suspension arms, which utilise rubber inner mounting bushes and incorporate a balljoint at the outer ends. The front hub carriers, which carry the wheel bearings, brake calipers and the hub/disc assemblies, are bolted to the MacPherson struts and connected to the lower arms via the balljoints. A front anti-roll bar is fitted to all models. The anti-roll bar is rubber-mounted onto the subframe, and connects both the suspension struts.

The rear suspension consists of an open-bar rear axle comprising two torsion bars, two anti-roll bars and an L-section metal crossmember which is connected to both the trailing arms. The two torsion bars and two anti-roll bars are connected at the centre with a link, and at their outer ends to the trailing arms.

The steering column is connected by a universal joint to an integral intermediate shaft, which has a second universal joint at its lower end. The lower universal joint is attached to the steering gear pinion by means of a clamp bolt and nut.

The steering gear is mounted onto the front subframe. It is connected by two track-rods and balljoints to steering arms projecting rearwards from the hub carriers. The track-rod ends are threaded to enable wheel alignment adjustment.

Power-assisted steering is fitted as standard on all models. The power steering pump is belt-driven from the crankshaft pulley, or from the camshaft pulley on certain diesel models.

2 Front hub carrier - removal and refitting

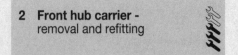

Removal

Note: *A new driveshaft nut will be required on refitting, and all Nyloc-type self-locking nuts should be renewed. A balljoint separator tool will be required for this operation. Sealant will be required to coat the outer end of the driveshaft.*

1 Apply the handbrake, then jack up the front of the vehicle and support securely on axle stands (see *Jacking and vehicle support*).

HAYNES HiNT *On models where access to the driveshaft nut can be obtained by removing the wheel trims, before jacking up the vehicle, loosen the driveshaft nut as follows.*
a) *Chock the front wheels, and remove the wheel trim.*
b) *Have an assistant firmly apply the footbrake.*
c) *Loosen the driveshaft nut using a socket and extension.*

2 On models with ABS, it is advisable to remove the ABS wheel sensor as described in Chapter 9, to avoid any possibility of damage during the removal procedure.

3 If the driveshaft nut has been loosened, proceed to paragraph 5, otherwise proceed as follows.

4 Refit at least two roadwheel bolts to the front hub, and tighten them securely. Have an assistant firmly depress the brake pedal to prevent the front hub from rotating, then using a socket and a long extension bar, slacken and remove the driveshaft retaining nut. Alternatively, a tool can be fabricated from two lengths of steel tubing (one long, one short) and a nut and bolt; the nut and bolt forming the pivot of a forked tool. Bolt the tool to the hub using two wheel bolts, and hold the tool to prevent the hub from rotating as the driveshaft retaining nut is undone **(see Tool Tip)**. This nut is very tight; make sure that there is no risk of pulling the car off the axle stands. (If the roadwheel trim allows access to the driveshaft nut, the initial slackening can be done with the wheels chocked and on the ground.)

5 If the hub bearings are to be disturbed, remove the brake disc as described in Chapter 9. If not, unbolt the brake caliper and move it to one side, as described in Chapter 9. Note that there is no need to disconnect the fluid hose - tie the caliper to the front suspension coil spring, using a piece of wire or string, to avoid straining the brake hose.

6 Slacken and partially unscrew the lower arm balljoint nut (unscrew the nut as far as the end of the threads on the balljoint to prevent damage to the threads as the joint is

released), then release the balljoint using a balljoint separator tool. Remove the nut, and discard it - a new nut must be used on refitting.

7 Similarly, release the balljoint and disconnect the track-rod from the steering arm on the hub carrier.

8 Unscrew the nut from the upper suspension strut-to-hub carrier bolt as far as the end of the bolt threads, then tap the end of the bolt (using the nut to protect the threads) to release the splines from the hub carrier. Withdraw the bolt, and discard the nut - a new nut must be used on refitting **(see illustration)**.

9 Similarly, unscrew the lower suspension strut-to-hub carrier nut, and tap the bolt to free the splines from the hub carrier. Do not remove the bolt at this stage.

10 Unscrew the driveshaft nut from the end of the driveshaft. Recover the washer. Discard the nut - a new one must be used on refitting.

11 The driveshaft must now be released from the hub carrier. It should be possible to release the driveshaft by tapping the end of the driveshaft using a soft-faced hammer, or a hammer and a soft metal drift - **do not** strike the end of the driveshaft hard, as this may cause damage to the joints.

Note: *The driveshaft ends are fitted to the hub carriers using locking compound. Renault use a special extractor tool to release the driveshaft ends, but if the driveshaft cannot be released by hand, it should be possible to use a conventional hub puller as follows* **(see illustration)**.
a) *If not already done, remove the brake disc with reference to Chapter 9.*
b) *Temporarily refit the driveshaft nut to protect the threads on the end of the driveshaft.*
c) *Fit the puller, with the arms bearing on the hub, and the centre screw bearing on the end of the driveshaft.*
d) *Use the puller to release the hub from the end of the driveshaft. Note that it is possible that the hub will be pulled from the hub bearing assembly (the bearing front half inner race will remain in position on the hub) - if this happens, a new bearing must be fitted as described in this Chapter.*

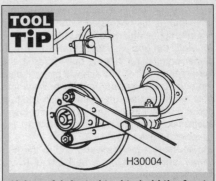
TOOL TiP

H30004

Using a fabricated tool to hold the front hub stationary whilst the driveshaft retaining nut is slackened

12 Pull the hub carrier from the lower arm balljoint, and tilt the hub carrier until the splined end of the driveshaft can be released from it **(see illustration)**.

13 Support the end of the driveshaft by suspending it using wire or string - do not allow the end of the driveshaft to hang down under its own weight, as this may damage the CV joints.

14 Remove the lower suspension strut-to-hub carrier bolt, and withdraw the hub carrier.

Refitting

15 Thoroughly clean all traces of old locking compound from the hub carrier end of the driveshaft, and from the splines in the hub.

16 Coat the hub end of the driveshaft with locking compound (Renault recommend the use of Loctite Scelbloc), then engage the end of the driveshaft with the hub. **Note:** *If the hub has been pulled from the bearing during the removal procedure, fit a new bearing as described in this Chapter.*

17 Refit the lower suspension strut-to-hub carrier bolt (noting that the bolts fits from the front of the vehicle), and screw a new nut onto the bolt. Do not tap the bolt into position or screw the nut fully onto the bolt at this stage.

18 Reconnect the lower arm balljoint to the hub carrier, then fit a new balljoint nut and tighten to the specified torque.

19 Screw the **new** driveshaft nut onto the end of the driveshaft as far as possible by hand, ensuring that the washer is in place,

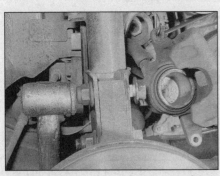
2.8 Tapping out the upper suspension strut-to-hub carrier bolt

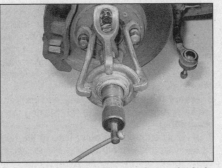
2.11 Using a hub puller to release the hub from the end of the driveshaft

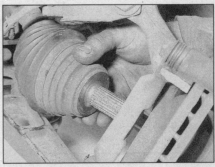
2.12 Releasing the end of the driveshaft from the hub carrier

10

then tighten the nut until the end of the driveshaft is fully engaged with the hub. Do not fully tighten the nut at this stage.

20 Refit the upper suspension strut-to-hub carrier bolt (noting that the bolts fits from the front of the vehicle), and screw a new nut onto the bolt. Tap the upper and lower bolts into position to engage the splines with the hub carrier, then tighten the upper and lower suspension strut-to-hub carrier nuts to the specified torque.

21 Reconnect the track-rod end to the hub carrier, and tighten a new balljoint nut to the specified torque.

22 Where applicable, refit the brake disc, then refit the brake caliper, with reference to Chapter 9.

23 Use the method employed on removal to prevent the hub from rotating, and tighten the driveshaft retaining nut to the specified torque. Check that the hub rotates freely.

 HAYNES HINT *On models where access to the driveshaft nut can be obtained by removing the wheel trim, the driveshaft nut can be tightened with the footbrake firmly applied, and the vehicle resting on its wheels.*

24 Where applicable, refit the ABS wheel sensor, with reference to Chapter 9.

25 Refit the roadwheel, then lower the vehicle to the ground and tighten the roadwheel bolts to the specified torque.

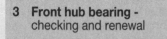

3 Front hub bearing - checking and renewal

Note: *The bearing is a sealed, pre-adjusted and pre-lubricated, double-row roller type, and is intended to last the car's entire service life*

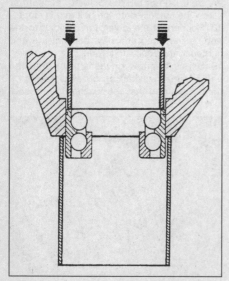

3.6 Pressing the front hub bearing from the hub - bearing retained by two circlips

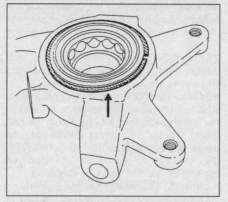

3.5 Front hub bearing retaining circlip (arrowed) - bearing retained by two circlips

without maintenance or attention. Do not attempt to remove the bearing unless absolutely necessary, as it will be damaged during the removal operation. Never overtighten the drive-shaft nut in an attempt to 'adjust' the bearing. A press will be required to dismantle and rebuild the assembly; if such a tool is not available, a large bench vice and suitable spacers (such as large sockets) will serve as an adequate substitute. The bearing's inner races are an interference fit on the hub; if the inner race remains on the hub when it is pressed out of the hub carrier, a suitable knife-edged bearing puller will be required to remove it.

Checking

1 Remove the brake disc as described in Chapter 9.

2 Wear in the front hub bearings can be checked by measuring the amount of side play present. To do this, a dial gauge should be fixed so that its probe is in contact with the disc contact face of the hub. The play should be between 0 and 0.05 mm. If the play is greater than specified, the bearings are worn excessively and must be renewed.

Renewal

All except petrol engine models from early 1995 (bearing retained by two circlips)

3 Remove the hub carrier as described in Section 2. Where applicable, undo the brake disc shield retaining screws and remove the shield from the hub carrier.

4 Support the hub carrier securely on blocks or in a vice. Using a suitable tubular spacer which bears only on the inner end of the hub flange, press the hub flange out of the bearing. If the bearing outboard inner race remains on the hub, remove it using a suitable bearing puller (see note above).

5 Extract the bearing retaining circlips from the inner and outer ends of the bearing **(see illustration)**.

6 Securely support the outer face of the hub carrier. Using a suitable tubular spacer which bears only on the outer race, press the complete bearing assembly out of the housing in the hub carrier **(see illustration)**.

7 Thoroughly clean the hub and hub carrier, removing all traces of dirt and grease. Polish away any burrs or raised edges which might hinder reassembly. Check for cracks or any other signs of wear or damage, and renew the components if necessary. As noted above, the bearing and its circlips must be renewed whenever they are disturbed. A replacement bearing kit, which consists of the bearing and circlips is available from Renault dealers.

8 On reassembly, check (if possible) that the new bearing is packed with grease. Apply a light film of oil to the bearing outer race and to the hub flange shaft.

9 Fit the inner bearing retaining circlip to the groove in the bearing.

10 Securely support the outer face of the hub carrier, and locate the bearing in its housing. Press the bearing into position, ensuring that it enters the housing squarely, using a suitable tubular spacer which bears only on the outer race. Press the bearing into position until the retaining circlip contacts the inner face of the hub carrier.

11 Once the bearing is correctly seated, secure it with the remaining outer retaining circlip.

12 Securely support the outer face of the hub flange.

13 Locate the stub axle carrier and the bearing inner race over the end of the hub flange. Press the bearing onto the hub flange, using a tubular spacer which bears only on the inner race, until it seats against the rear face of the flange. Check that the hub flange rotates freely. Wipe off any excess oil or grease.

14 Where applicable, refit the brake disc shield to the hub carrier, and tighten its retaining screws.

15 Refit the hub carrier (see Section 2).

Petrol engine models from early 1995 (bearing retained by single circlip at inner end)

16 Proceed as described in paragraphs 3 and 4.

17 Extract the bearing retaining circlip from the inner end of the hub carrier.

18 Securely support the inner face of the hub carrier. Using a suitable tubular spacer, which bears on the inner race, press the complete bearing assembly out of the housing in the hub carrier **(see illustration)**.

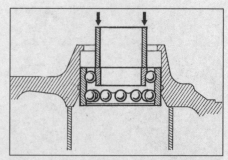

3.18 Pressing the front wheel bearing from the hub carrier - bearing retained by single circlip

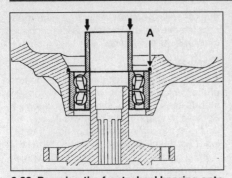

3.22 Pressing the front wheel bearing onto the hub flange - bearing retained by single circlip

A Bearing retaining circlip

19 Proceed as described in paragraphs 7 and 8.

20 Securely support the outer face of the hub carrier, and locate the bearing in its housing. Press the bearing into position, ensuring that it enters the housing squarely, using a suitable tubular spacer which bears only on the outer race. Press the bearing into position until it contacts the shoulder in the hub carrier.

21 Fit a new bearing retaining circlip to the groove in the inner end of the hub carrier.

22 Proceed as described in paragraphs 12 to 15 **(see illustration)**.

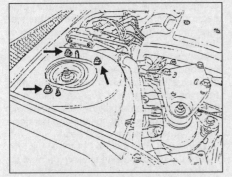

4.5 Unscrew the three nuts (arrowed) securing the suspension strut upper mounting

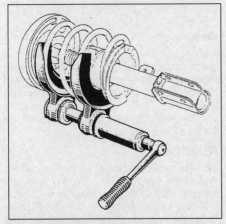

4.9 Spring compressor tool in position on suspension strut coil spring

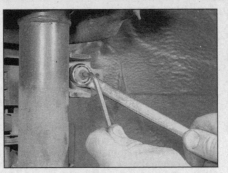

4.3 Unscrewing the anti-roll bar drop link-to-suspension strut nut

---

4 Front suspension strut - removal, overhaul and refitting

Note: *All Nyloc-type self-locking nuts should be renewed on refitting.*

Removal

1 Apply the handbrake, then jack up the front of the vehicle and support it securely on axle stands (see *Jacking and vehicle support*). Remove the appropriate roadwheel.

2 Unclip the brake fluid pipe and the brake pad wear indicator wiring from the brackets at the lower end of the suspension strut. Similarly, where applicable release the ABS sensor wiring from its clips on the suspension strut.

3 Unscrew the nut securing the anti-roll bar drop link to the suspension strut - if necessary, the drop link pin can be counterheld using an Allen key. Discard the nut - a new one must be used on refitting **(see illustration)**.

4 Unscrew the nut from the upper suspension strut-to-hub carrier bolt as far as the end of the bolt threads, then tap the end of the bolt (using the nut to protect the threads) to release the splines from the hub carrier. Withdraw the bolt, and discard the nut - a new nut must be used on refitting. Repeat the procedure on the lower suspension strut-to-hub carrier bolt, then support the hub carrier **(see illustration)**.

5 From within the engine compartment, unscrew the three nuts securing the strut upper mounting to the turret **(see illustration)**.

6 Release the strut from the stub axle carrier, and withdraw it from under the wheel arch, while pressing on the lower suspension arm to prevent damage to the driveshaft gaiter.

7 Once the strut has been removed, support the hub carrier to prevent damage to the driveshaft gaiter.

Overhaul

Note: *Spring compressor tools will be required for this operation.*

8 With the strut removed from the car as previously, clean away all external dirt then mount the strut upright in a vice.

4.4 Unscrewing the upper suspension strut-to-hub carrier nut

9 Fit the spring compressor tool and compress the coil spring until all tension is relieved from the upper mounting **(see illustration)**.

10 Where applicable, withdraw the plastic cap from the piston rod nut, then counterhold the piston rod with an Allen key or a hexagon bit, and unscrew the nut with a ring spanner.

11 Note the orientation and location of all components to aid refitting.

12 Lift off the washer, upper mounting, and spring seat assembly **(see illustration)**.

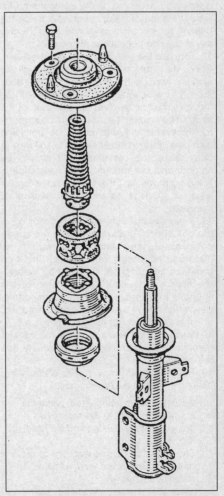

4.12 Front suspension strut components

10

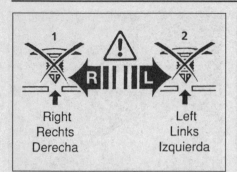

4.20 The appropriate plug must be removed from Renault 'exchange' struts

When fitting the strut to the right:
Remove plug 1
When fitting the strut to the left:
Remove plug 2

13 Lift off the spring and compressor tool. Do not remove the tool from the spring unless the spring is to be renewed.

14 Remove the convoluted dust cover, bump stop, and the lower spring seat and bearing components.

15 With the strut assembly now completely dismantled, examine all the components for wear, damage or deformation and check the bearing for smoothness of operation. Renew any of the components as necessary.

16 Examine the strut for signs of fluid leakage. Check the strut piston rod for signs of pitting along its entire length and check the strut body for signs of damage or elongation of the mounting bolt holes. Test the operation of the strut, while holding it in an upright position, by moving the piston rod through a full stroke and then through short strokes of 50 to 100 mm. In both cases the resistance felt should be smooth and continuous. If the resistance is jerky, or uneven, or if there is any visible sign of wear or damage to the strut, renewal is necessary.

17 If any doubt exists about the condition of the coil spring, gradually release the spring compressor, and check the spring for distortion and signs of cracking. Since no minimum free length is specified by Renault, the only way to check the tension of the spring is to compare it to a new component. Renew the spring if it is damaged or distorted, or if there is any doubt as to its condition.

18 Inspect all other components for signs of damage or deterioration, and renew any that are suspect.

19 Reassembly is a reversal of dismantling, bearing in mind the following points.

a) If a new strut is being fitted, prime the strut before refitting the spring, by compressing and extending the piston rod several times.

b) Ensure that all components are correctly orientated and positioned, as noted before dismantling.

c) Make sure that the spring ends are correctly located in the upper and lower seats.

d) Tighten the piston rod nut to the specified torque.

Refitting

20 If a Renault 'exchange' strut is being fitted (exchange struts can be fitted to either side of the vehicle), remove the appropriate plug from the assembly before refitting **(see illustration)**.

21 Manoeuvre the strut assembly into position, taking care not damage the drive-shaft gaiter. Ensure that the locating pins on the top mounting engage with the corresponding holes in the turret.

22 Refit the bolts securing the upper mounting to the turret, but do not fully tighten them at this stage.

23 Engage the hub carrier with the lower end of the strut, taking care not to damage the driveshaft gaiter, then insert the two hub carrier-to-suspension strut mounting bolts from the front side of the strut. Tap the bolts into position to engage the splines with the hub carrier, then fit the new nuts to the rear of the bolts, and tighten them to the specified torque.

24 Tighten the strut upper mounting bolts to the specified torque.

25 Reconnect the anti-roll bar drop link to the suspension strut, then fit a new nut and tighten to the specified torque (again, counterhold the drop link pin if necessary).

26 Clip the wiring and the brake pipe into the appropriate brackets on the strut.

27 Refit the roadwheel, then lower the vehicle to the ground and tighten the roadwheel bolts to the specified torque.

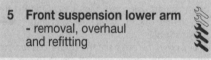

5   Front suspension lower arm
- removal, overhaul
and refitting

Note: *New lower arm mounting nuts and bolts must be used on refitting, and all Nyloc-type self-locking nuts should be renewed. Suitable*

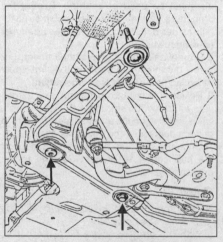

5.8 Loosen the two bolts (arrowed) securing the lower arm to the subframe

thread-locking compound will be required to coat the threads of the brake caliper mounting bracket bolts on refitting.

Removal

1 Apply the handbrake, then jack up the front of the vehicle and support it securely on axle stands (see *Jacking and vehicle support*). Remove the appropriate roadwheel.

2 Unbolt the brake caliper and move it to one side, as described in Chapter 9. Note that there is no need to disconnect the fluid hose - tie the caliper to the front suspension coil spring, using a piece of wire or string, to avoid straining the brake hose. Release the pad wear sensor wiring and the brake pipe from any clips or brackets as necessary to allow the caliper assembly to be moved.

3 Slacken and partially unscrew the lower arm balljoint nut (unscrew the nut as far as the end of the threads on the balljoint to prevent damage to the threads as the joint is released), then release the balljoint using a balljoint separator tool. Remove the nut, and discard it - a new nut must be used on refitting.

4 Similarly, release the balljoint and disconnect the track-rod from the steering arm on the hub carrier.

5 Where applicable, release the ABS sensor wiring from the clips on the suspension strut.

6 Unscrew the two nuts from the bolts securing the hub carrier to the suspension strut, noting that the nuts are positioned on the rear side of the strut. Withdraw the bolts, and support the hub carrier. Discard the nuts - new ones must be used on refitting.

7 Release the hub carrier/driveshaft assembly from the lower arm and the suspension strut, and support the assembly by suspending with wire or string from the coil spring. Take care not to damage the driveshaft gaiter.

8 Working at the inner end of the lower arm, loosen the bolts securing the lower arm to the subframe. If necessary, counterhold the nuts **(see illustration)**.

9 Withdraw the securing bolts, and nuts (recover the locking plates if they are loose), and manipulate the lower arm out from the subframe.

Overhaul

10 Special tools are required to renew the lower arm bushes. If the bushes are incorrectly fitted (if the bushes are no located centrally), the wheel alignment may be altered.

11 Renewal of the bushes should be entrusted to a Renault dealer.

Refitting

12 Manipulate the lower arm into position, then fit the new mounting nuts and bolts (the bolts fit from below the lower arm). Ensure that the reinforcement plate is in position under the front lower arm mounting nut **(see illustration)**. Tighten the bolts to the specified torque.

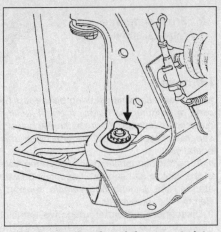

5.12 Ensure that the reinforcement plate (arrowed) is in position under the front lower arm mounting nut

13 Locate the lower end of the hub carrier/driveshaft assembly on the lower arm balljoint, and engage the upper end with the suspension strut, taking care not to damage the driveshaft gaiter.

14 Insert the two hub carrier-to-suspension strut mounting bolts from the front side of the strut, then tap them into position to engage the splines with the hub carrier. Fit the new nuts to the rear of the bolts, and tighten them to the specified torque.

15 Fit a new lower arm balljoint nut, and tighten to the specified torque.

16 Reconnect the track-rod to the steering arm on the hub carrier, then fit a new securing nut and tighten to the specified torque.

17 Refit the brake caliper, using new guide pin bolts, as described in Chapter 9.

18 Where applicable, reposition the brake pipe, pad wear sensor wiring and/or ABS sensor wiring in the appropriate clips or brackets.

19 Refit the roadwheel, then lower the vehicle to the ground and tighten the roadwheel bolts to the specified torque.

20 On completion, depress the brake pedal several times to bring the brake pads into contact with the disc, and check the front wheel alignment at the earliest opportunity (see Section 24).

6 Front suspension lower arm balljoint - renewal

Note: *The balljoint is a press-fit in the lower arm, and can only be renewed once - see paragraph 1.*

1 Original balljoints have no identifying marks. Replacement balljoints have a small cut-out in the edge of the lower bearing face (visible from under the balljoint) **(see illustration)**. If a marked balljoint is worn or damaged, it cannot be renewed independently, and the complete lower arm assembly must be renewed. A suitable puller will be required for this operation.

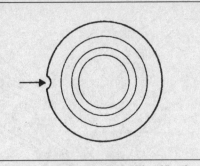

6.1 Replacement balljoint identification cut-out (arrowed)

2 To ease access, remove the lower arm as described in Section 5. Note that if the appropriate Renault puller tool is available (see following paragraph), it may be possible to renew the balljoint *in situ*, once the hub carrier/driveshaft assembly has been moved clear (see Section 5).

3 To remove and refit the balljoint, a puller will be required. A Renault special tool (T. Av. 1261) is available for this purpose, but it should be possible to improvise an alternative using suitable tubes, spacers, metal bar (with a thread cut in the centre to enable the bar to be screwed onto the balljoint pin), and two long bolts and nuts.

4 Screw the metal bar onto the balljoint pin, then assemble the puller components as shown (the hole in the bottom of the puller must be of sufficient diameter to allow the balljoint to pass through) **(see illustration)**.

5 Progressively tighten the puller nuts to force the balljoint from the lower end of the lower arm.

6 Thoroughly clean the mating faces of the balljoint and the housing in the lower arm.

7 Reassemble the puller components, noting the following.

 a) *Fit a spacer plate below the balljoint, so that the lower end of the puller contacts the lower edge of the balljoint.*

 b) *Fit a spacer tube between the upper end of the lower arm, and the puller metal bar, to prevent the metal bar from touching the balljoint pin.*

8 Progressively tighten the puller nuts to draw the balljoint into position in the lower arm.

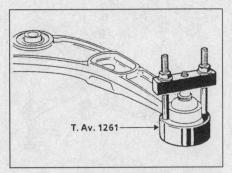

6.4 Renault lower arm balljoint puller tool assembled for use

Alternatively, the balljoint can be fitted by supporting the upper face of the lower arm, and pressing the balljoint in from below the arm, but in this care must be taken to ensure that the balljoint enters the housing in the lower arm squarely.

9 Where applicable, remove the puller assembly.

10 Refit the lower arm, or reconnect the hub carrier/driveshaft assembly, as applicable, as described in Section 5.

7 Front anti-roll bar components - removal and refitting

Anti-roll bar

Note: *All Nyloc-type self-locking nuts should be renewed on refitting.*

Removal

1 Apply the handbrake, then jack up the front of the vehicle and support it securely on axle stands (see *Jacking and vehicle support*). Remove the appropriate roadwheel.

2 Working under the vehicle, unscrew the bolt on each side, securing the subframe bracing plates to the vehicle floor **(see illustration)**.

3 Loosen the bolts securing the subframe bracing plates to the subframe, then pivot the bracing plates clear of the anti-roll bar.

4 Unscrew the bolts securing the anti-roll bar clamps to the subframe.

5 Unscrew the nuts securing the anti-roll bar to the drop links. If necessary, counterhold the drop link pins using an Allen key.

6 On models with manual transmission, disconnect the gear linkage as described in Chapter 7A to enable sufficient clearance to withdraw the anti-roll bar from under the car.

7 Remove the anti-roll bar from under the car.

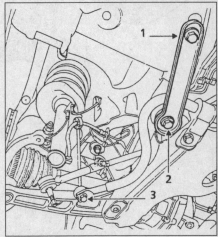

7.2 Subframe bracing plate and anti-roll bar mounting details

 1 *Bracing plate-to-floor bolt*
 2 *Bracing plate-to-subframe bolt*
 3 *Anti-roll bar-to-drop link nut*

10

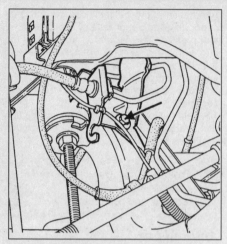

8.9 Brake pipe/wiring bracket-to-subframe bolt (arrowed)

Refitting

8 Refitting is a reversal of removal, but renew any Nyloc-type self-locking nuts, and tighten all fixings to the specified torque.

Drop link

Note: *New drop link securing nuts should be used on refitting.*

Removal

9 Apply the handbrake, then jack up the front of the car and support it on axle stands (see *Jacking and vehicle support*). If desired, remove the roadwheel to improve access.

8.10 Unscrew the through-bolt and nut (arrowed) securing the rear engine mounting to the subframe

10 Slacken and remove the upper and lower drop link securing nuts, and withdraw the drop link. If necessary, counterhold the drop link pins using an Allen key.

11 Examine the link for signs of damage or wear, paying particular attention to the balljoints. It is not possible to renew the bushes independently, and if the balljoints are worn, the complete link must be renewed.

Refitting

12 Refitting is a reversal of removal, but use new securing nuts, and tighten the nuts to the specified torque.

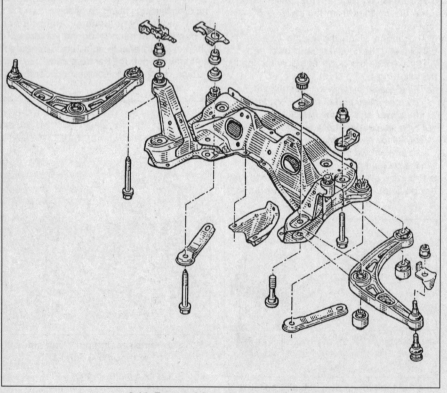

8.14 Front subframe mounting details

8 Front subframe - removal and refitting

Removal

Note: *New subframe securing bolts must be used on refitting. All Nyloc-type self-locking nuts should be renewed on refitting. A balljoint separator tool will be required for this operation.*

1 Apply the handbrake, then jack up the front of the vehicle and support it securely on axle stands (see *Jacking and vehicle support*). Remove the roadwheels.

2 Disconnect the battery negative terminal (refer to *Disconnecting the battery* in the Reference Section of this manual).

3 Fit clamps to the power steering fluid hoses as close as possible to the fluid reservoir. This will help to minimise fluid loss during subsequent operations.

4 Working in the passenger compartment, reach up under the facia, and unscrew the steering column-to-steering gear pinion pinch-bolt and nut.

5 Remove the track-rod ends as described in Section 22.

6 Working on each side of the vehicle in turn, unscrew the nuts securing the anti-roll bar drop links to the anti-roll bar. If necessary, counterhold the drop link pins using an Allen key.

7 Again working on each side of the vehicle, slacken and partially unscrew the lower arm balljoint nut (unscrew the nut as far as the end of the threads on the balljoint to prevent damage to the threads as the joint is released), then release the balljoint using a balljoint separator tool. Remove the nut, and discard it - a new nut must be used on refitting.

8 Where applicable, release the ABS sensor wiring from any clips on the lower arm and subframe. Note the routing of the wiring to aid refitting.

9 Unscrew the bolt(s) securing the brake pipe/wiring bracket to the subframe on each side of the vehicle, then release the brake pipes and the wiring from the clips on the subframe **(see illustration)**.

10 Working under the vehicle, unscrew the through-bolt and nut securing the rear engine mounting to the subframe **(see illustration)**.

11 Disconnect the gear linkage (Chapter 7A).

12 Position a jack under the centre of the subframe, and raise the jack to support the subframe.

13 Unscrew the securing bolts, and remove the bracing plates from the rear of the subframe.

14 Loosen the subframe bolts, and lower the subframe slightly (supporting with the jack) until the fuel pipe clip can be released from the top of the subframe **(see illustration)**.

15 Where applicable, reach up above the steering gear, and disconnect the oxygen sensor wiring connector and/or the variable power steering solenoid wiring connector.

16 Place a container beneath the steering gear, then unscrew the union nuts and disconnect the fluid pipes from the steering gear. Be prepared for some fluid spillage as the pipes are disconnected, and plug the pipe and steering gear openings to minimise fluid loss and to prevent the entry of dirt into the system.

17 Ensure that the subframe is adequately supported, then unscrew the securing bolts, lower the subframe on the jack, and withdraw the assembly, complete with the steering gear, from under the vehicle. **Note:** *When lowering the subframe, take care not to damage the brake pipes.*

Refitting

18 Refitting is a reversal of removal, bearing in mind the following points.

a) *If the steering gear has been removed from the subframe, refit it with reference to Section 18.*
b) *Alignment of the subframe is achieved using the two centring washers fitted to the rear subframe mountings. Ensure that these washers are in position, and when refitting the subframe mounting bolts, tighten the rear left-hand bolt first, then the rear right-hand bolt, then the remaining bolts.*
c) *Use new subframe securing bolts, and tighten all fixings to the specified torque.*
d) *Ensure that all wiring is correctly routed as noted before removal.*
e) *Reconnect the gear linkage with reference to Chapter 7A.*
f) *Use new lower arm balljoint nuts, and renew any Nyloc-type self-locking nuts disturbed during the removal procedure.*
g) *Refit the track-rod ends (see Section 22).*
h) *To aid refitting of the steering gear pinion gaiter to the body, ensure that it is securely attached to the pinion housing on the steering gear before refitting.*
i) *On completion, bleed the power steering hydraulic system as described in Section 20, and check the front wheel alignment as described in Section 24.*

9 Rear hub assembly - removal and refitting

Models with rear drum brakes

1 The hub assembly is integral with the brake drum. Removal and refitting of the brake drum is described in Chapter 9.

Models with rear disc brakes

Note: *A new rear hub nut will be required on refitting.*

Removal

2 The rear wheel bearings are integral with the rear hubs, and if the bearings are worn or damaged, or the hub is damaged, the complete hub/bearing assembly must be renewed as a unit.

3 Remove the brake disc (see Chapter 9).

4 Using a hammer and suitable large flat-bladed screwdriver, carefully tap and prise the cap out of the centre of the hub.

5 Using a socket and long bar, slacken and remove the rear hub nut. Discard the hub nut; a new nut must used on refitting.

6 It should now be possible to withdraw the hub/bearing assembly from the stub axle by hand. It may be difficult to remove the hub due to the tightness of the hub bearing on the stub axle. If the bearing is tight, tap the periphery of the hub using a hide or plastic mallet, or use a universal puller.

Refitting

7 Ensure that the contact faces of the stub axle and the wheel bearing are clean, then smear the stub axle with a little gear oil.

8 Slide the hub onto the stub axle and, if necessary, tap it into position using a soft-faced mallet.

9 Fit a new rear hub nut, and tighten it to the specified torque.

10 Tap the cap into position in the centre of the hub.

11 Refit the brake disc as described in Chapter 9.

10 Rear hub bearings - checking and renewal

Note: *The bearings are of sealed pre-adjusted and pre-lubricated type, and are intended to last the car's entire service life without maintenance. Never overtighten the hub nut in an attempt to 'adjust' the bearings.*

Models with rear drum brakes

Checking

1 Chock the front wheels and engage reverse gear (or P on automatic transmission models). Jack up the rear of the vehicle and support it securely on axle stands (see *Jacking and vehicle support*). Remove the appropriate rear roadwheel, and fully release the handbrake.

2 Wear in the rear hub bearings can be checked by measuring the amount of side play present. To do this, a dial test indicator should be fixed so that its probe is in contact with the drum outer face. The play should be between 0 and 0.03 mm. If the play is greater than specified, the bearings are worn excessively, and should be renewed.

Renewal

Note: *A new bearing retaining circlip, and a new rear hub nut must be used on refitting - these are normally supplied with the new bearing.*

3 The hub bearings are fitted to the brake drums.

4 Remove the appropriate brake drum as described in Chapter 9.

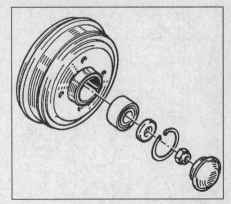

10.5 Rear brake drum and wheel bearing components

5 Using circlip pliers, extract the bearing retaining circlip from the centre of the brake drum **(see illustration)**.

6 Securely support the outer face of the brake drum. Press or drive the bearing out of the hub, using a tubular drift of suitable diameter (52.0 mm approximately) inserted through the rear of the brake drum, and in contact with the bearing outer race.

7 Thoroughly clean the hub, removing all traces of dirt and grease. Polish away any burrs or raised edges which might hinder reassembly. Check the drum assembly for cracks or any other signs of damage (with reference to Chapter 9), and renew if necessary.

8 The bearing and its circlip must be renewed whenever they are disturbed. A replacement bearing kit is available from Renault dealers, consisting of the bearing, circlip, hub nut and cap.

9 Commence reassembly by checking (if possible) that the new bearing is packed with grease. Apply a light film of gear oil to the bearing outer race, and to the stub axle.

10 Securely support the rear face of the brake drum, then press the bearing into position, using a suitable tube (approximately 54.0 mm outside diameter) in contact with the bearing outer race. Ensure that the bearing enters the drum squarely.

11 Ensure that the bearing is correctly seated against the shoulder in the drum, then secure the bearing in position with a new circlip. Ensure that the circlip is correctly seated in its groove.

12 Refit the brake drum (see Chapter 9).

Models with rear disc brakes

Checking

13 Remove the brake disc (see Chapter 9).

14 Wear in the rear hub bearings can be checked by measuring the amount of side play present. To do this, a dial test indicator should be fixed so that its probe is in contact with the hub outer face. The play should be between 0 and 0.03 mm. If the play is greater than specified, the bearings are worn excessively, and the complete hub/bearing assembly must be renewed.

10

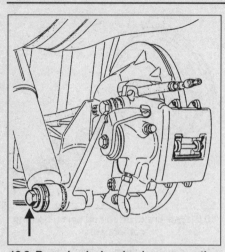

12.2 Rear shock absorber lower mounting bolt (arrowed)

Renewal

15 The bearings are integral with the rear hubs. If a bearing is worn or damaged, the complete hub/bearing assembly must be renewed as described in Section 9.

11 Rear suspension components - general

Although it is possible to remove the rear suspension torsion bars, trailing arms and anti-roll bars independently of the complete rear axle assembly, it is essential to have certain special tools available to complete the work successfully.

Due to the complexity of the tasks, and the requirement for special tools to accurately set the suspension geometry on refitting, the removal and refitting of individual rear suspension components is considered to be beyond the scope of DIY work, and should be entrusted to a Renault dealer.

Procedures for removal and refitting of the rear shock absorbers and the complete rear suspension assembly are given in Sections 12 and 13 respectively.

12 Rear shock absorber - removal, testing and refitting

Removal

1 Chock the front wheels and engage reverse gear (or P on automatic transmission models). Jack up the rear of the vehicle and support it securely on axle stands (see *Jacking and vehicle support*). Remove the appropriate rear roadwheel.
2 Using a jack, raise the trailing arm slightly until the shock absorber is slightly compressed. Remove the lower mounting bolt and recover the washer **(see illustration)**.

3 Working at the top end of the shock absorber, unscrew the upper securing bolt **(see illustration)**.
4 Withdraw the shock absorber from under the vehicle.

Testing

5 Examine the shock absorber for signs of fluid leakage. Check the piston for signs of pitting along its visible length, and check the shock absorber body for signs of damage. Test the operation of the shock absorber (mounting it in a vice if necessary), while holding it in an upright position, by moving the piston through a full stroke and then through short strokes of 50 to 100 mm. In both cases the resistance felt should be smooth and continuous. If the resistance is jerky, or uneven, or if there is any visible sign of wear or damage to the shock absorber, renewal is necessary. Note that the mounting bushes are not available separately.

Refitting

6 Prior to refitting the shock absorber, mount it upright in a vice, and operate it fully through several strokes in order to prime it. (This is necessary even if a new unit is being fitted, as it may have been stored horizontally, and so need priming). Apply a smear of multi-purpose grease to the shock absorber mounting bolts and nut.
7 Refitting is a reversal of removal, but delay tightening the mounting bolts until the unladen weight of the vehicle is on the suspension (ie, the vehicle is resting on its wheels), then tighten the bolts to the specified torque.

13 Rear suspension assembly - removal and refitting

Removal

1 Chock the front wheels and engage reverse gear (or P on automatic transmission models). Jack up the rear of the vehicle and support it securely on axle stands (see *Jacking and vehicle support*). Remove the roadwheels.
2 Working under the vehicle, where applicable, unbolt the heat shields from the vehicle floor to reveal the handbrake equaliser.
3 Counterhold the handbrake adjuster rod, using a spanner on the flats provided, then unscrew the adjuster nut, and disconnect the handbrake rod from the cable equaliser.

 HAYNES HiNT *Before unscrewing the locknut and adjuster nut, note the length of exposed thread on the end of the handbrake rod to aid adjustment on refitting.*

12.3 Unscrewing the rear shock absorber upper mounting bolt

4 Release the handbrake cables from the brackets on the vehicle floor.
5 Where applicable, disconnect the battery negative terminal (refer to *Disconnecting the battery* in the Reference Section of this manual), then disconnect the rear ABS wheel sensor wiring connectors (clipped to brackets under the floor).
6 To minimise fluid loss when the brake lines are disconnected, remove the brake fluid reservoir cap, and then tighten it down onto a piece of polythene (taking care not to damage the level sender unit) to obtain an airtight seal.
7 Unscrew the union nuts, and disconnect the flexible brake hoses from the pipes leading to the rear brake pressure regulating valve.
8 Disconnect the rear brake pressure regulating valve operating rod from the bracket on the rear suspension (see Chapter 9 - note that it may be necessary to unbolt the valve, but it should be possible to leave the pipes connected provided they are not strained).
9 Unscrew the two lower shock absorber mounting bolts, and recover the washers.
10 Make a final check to ensure that all relevant pipes, hoses and wires have been disconnected or moved clear to allow removal of the suspension assembly.
11 Position a trolley jack under the centre of the rear suspension crossmember to support the assembly, then unscrew the four mounting bolts, and lower the assembly from the vehicle **(see illustration)**.

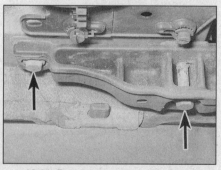

13.11 Rear suspension right-hand mounting bolts (arrowed)

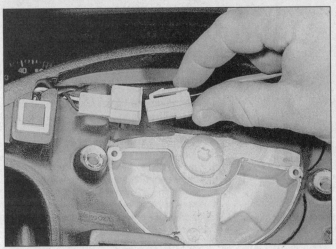

15.11a Disconnecting the horn push wiring connector

15.11b Using a Torx bit . . .

Refitting

12 Refitting is a reversal of removal, bearing in mind the following points.

a) *Do not fully tighten the lower shock absorber mounting bolts until the vehicle is resting on its wheels.*

b) *Tighten all fixings to the specified torque.*

c) *Take care not to twist the brake hoses when reconnecting them.*

d) *Adjust the handbrake mechanism as described in the relevant part of Chapter 1.*

e) *On completion, bleed the brake hydraulic system as described in Chapter 9.*

14 Vehicle ride height - checking and adjustment

Checking of the ride height requires the use of Renault special tools to accurately compress the suspension in a suspension checking bay.

Adjustment is made by altering the position of the trailing arms and the anti-roll bars. As it is not possible to carry out these procedures without the use of special tools (see Section 11), checking and adjustment of the vehicle ride height should be entrusted to a Renault dealer.

15 Steering wheel - removal and refitting

Models without air bag

Note: *A new steering wheel securing bolt must be used on refitting.*

Removal

1 Disconnect the battery negative terminal (refer to *Disconnecting the battery* in the Reference Section of this manual).

2 Ensure that the front wheels are in the straight-ahead position, with the steering column lock engaged.

3 Carefully prise the horn-push pad from the centre of the steering wheel.

4 Disconnect the wires from the rear of the horn-push pad and/or the cruise control switches, if applicable, and remove the pad.

5 On models with horn push buttons mounted in the steering wheel, disconnect the horn push wiring connector.

6 Slacken and remove the steering wheel securing bolt.

7 Mark the steering wheel and the steering column shaft in relation to each other, then lift the steering wheel off the column splines.

> **HAYNES HINT** *If the wheel is tight, tap it up near the centre, using the palms of your hands, or twist it from side-to-side, whilst pulling to release it from the splines.*

Refitting

8 Refitting is a reversal of removal, noting the following points.

a) *Ensure that the front wheels are still in the straight-ahead position, with the steering column lock engaged.*

b) *Align the marks made on the steering wheel and column shaft before removal.*

c) *Tighten a new steering wheel securing bolt to the specified torque.*

Models with air bag

> ⚠️ **Warning: Refer to the precautions given in Chapter 12, Section 25 before proceeding.**

Note: *A new steering wheel securing bolt must be used on refitting.*

Removal

9 Remove the air bag (see Chapter 12).

10 Ensure that the front wheels are in the straight-ahead position, with the steering column lock engaged.

11 Proceed as described in paragraphs 5 to 7 (see illustrations).

Refitting

12 Proceed as described in paragraph 8. Refit the air bag as described in Chapter 12.

16 Steering column and intermediate shaft - removal, inspection and refitting

Removal

1 The intermediate shaft is integral with the steering column assembly, and cannot be separated. Note that no spare parts are available for the column/intermediate shaft assembly, and if any components are worn or damaged, the complete assembly must be renewed.

2 Remove the steering wheel (see Section 15).

3 Working under the steering column, remove the three securing screws, and withdraw the lower steering column shroud.

4 Where applicable, unclip the cover from the radio/cassette player remote control switch, then remove the securing screw and withdraw the switch from the upper steering column shroud.

5 Remove the two securing screws, and withdraw the upper steering column shroud.

6 Release the securing clips, and lower the fusebox cover from the facia.

15.11c . . . unscrew the steering wheel securing bolt

10

16.9 Steering column shaft-to-steering gear pinion clamp nut (arrowed)

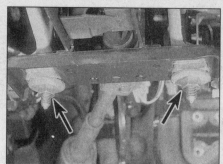

16.10 Steering column lower mounting nuts (arrowed)

7 To improve access, remove the three securing screws and withdraw the fusebox cover panel from the facia. Where applicable, disconnect the wiring from the voice synthesizer loudspeaker as the panel is withdrawn.

8 Working around the steering column, or through the fusebox aperture, as applicable, disconnect the following wiring connectors. Note the locations of the connectors and the routing of the wiring to aid refitting.

a) Ignition switch (for access to the ignition switch wiring connector(s), it may be necessary to disconnect the instrument panel lighting rheostat wiring connector).
b) Wash/wipe stalk switch.
c) Lighting stalk switch.
d) Air bag/cruise control rotary switch wiring connector (where applicable).

9 Working in the driver's footwell, unscrew the steering column shaft-to-steering gear pinion clamp nut and remove the bolt, and the safety clip, where applicable **(see illustration)**.

10 Working under the facia, unscrew the four securing nuts, and withdraw the steering column assembly, complete with the stalk switches **(see illustration)**.

Inspection

11 The steering column/intermediate shaft assembly incorporates a telescopic safety feature. In the event of a front-end crash, the shaft collapses and prevents the steering wheel injuring the driver. Before refitting the assembly, examine the column/intermediate

shaft assembly and its mountings for signs of damage and deformation and renew as necessary.

12 Check the steering shaft for signs of free-play in the column bushes, and check the universal joints for signs of damage or roughness in the joint bearings. If any damage or wear is found in the steering shaft/intermediate shaft universal joints or shaft bushes, the column must be renewed as an assembly.

Refitting

⚠️ **Warning: On models fitted with an air bag, do not reconnect the battery negative terminal until the air bag has been refitted as described in Chapter 12.**

13 Refitting is a reversal of removal, bearing in mind the following points.

a) Before refitting, ensure that the steering lock is applied to lock the steering shaft in the straight-ahead position, and ensure that the steering gear is centralised, with the front wheels in the straight-ahead position.
b) Tighten all fixings to the specified torque.
c) Ensure that all wiring is routed as noted before removal, and ensure that the connectors are correctly positioned.
d) When refitting the upper steering column shroud, ensure that the rubber seal at the rear of the shroud is correctly seated on the facia.
e) Refit the steering wheel as described in Section 15.

Removal

1 Disconnect the battery negative terminal (refer to *Disconnecting the battery* in the Reference Section of this manual).

2 Remove the steering wheel as described in Section 15.

3 Working under the steering column, remove the three securing screws, and withdraw the lower steering column shroud.

4 Where applicable, unclip the cover from the radio/cassette player remote control switch, then remove the securing screw and withdraw the switch from the upper steering column shroud.

5 Remove the two securing screws, and withdraw the upper steering column shroud.

6 Remove the plastic trim plate from the ignition switch assembly.

7 Release the securing clips, and lower the fusebox cover from the facia.

8 To improve access, remove the three securing screws and withdraw the fusebox cover panel. Where applicable, disconnect the wiring from the voice synthesizer loudspeaker as the panel is withdrawn.

9 Reach behind the facia, and disconnect the ignition switch wiring connectors - note that the two halves of the connector may be secured together by a plastic clip **(see illustration)**. For access to the ignition switch wiring connector(s), it may be necessary to disconnect the instrument panel lighting rheostat wiring connector. Note the locations of the connectors and the routing of the wiring to aid refitting.

10 Insert the ignition key, and turn the key to the arrow position (between A and M).

11 Unscrew the ignition switch securing screw from the top of the lock barrel **(see illustration)**.

12 Push the switch securing lug back towards the facia, then simultaneously depress the lug, and withdraw the lock assembly using the key. Feed the wiring through the switch housing as the switch is withdrawn **(see illustrations)**.

17.9 Ignition switch wiring connectors (arrowed) viewed through voice synthesizer loudspeaker aperture

17.11 Unscrewing the ignition switch/steering column lock securing screw

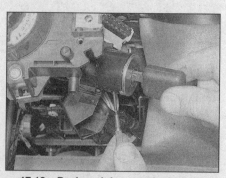

17.12a Push and depress the ignition switch/steering column lock securing lug . . .

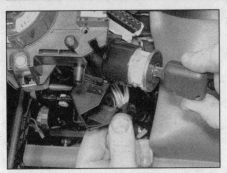

17.12b . . . and withdraw the assembly

13 If desired, the switch can be separated from the lock by unscrewing the two securing screws.

Refitting

⚠️ *Warning: On models fitted with an air bag, do not reconnect the battery negative terminal until the air bag has been refitted as described in Chapter 12.*

14 Refitting is a reversal of removal, bearing in mind the following points.

a) *If the switch has been separated from the lock, ensure that the switch wiper engages correctly with the lock on refitting.*
b) *Ensure that the wiring is correctly routed, and that the wiring connectors are correctly located as noted before removal.*
c) *Refit the steering wheel as described in Section 15.*

18 Steering gear assembly - removal, overhaul and refitting

Removal

Note: *New steering gear securing nuts must be used on refitting.*

1 Remove the front subframe as described in Section 8.
2 Unbolt the exhaust heat shield from the subframe.
3 Mark the position of the steering gear mounting lugs on the subframe, so that the steering gear can be refitted in exactly the same position.
4 Unscrew the four securing nuts, and remove the steering gear from the subframe **(see illustration)**.

Overhaul

5 Renewal procedures for the gaiters, the track-rod ends and the track-rods (complete with inner balljoints) are given in Sections 19, 22 and 23 respectively.
6 Examine the steering gear assembly for signs of wear or damage. Check that the rack moves freely over the full length of its travel, with no signs of roughness or excessive free

play between the steering gear pinion and rack. Internal wear or damage can only be cured by renewing the steering gear assembly.
7 Note that the steering gear is supplied as an assembly complete with track-rods, but the track-rod ends will have to be removed from the old assembly and transferred to the new steering gear, as described in Section 22.

Refitting

8 Refit the steering gear to the subframe, ensuring that the lugs are aligned with the marks made on the subframe before removal. Fit new securing nuts, and tighten to the specified torque.
9 Refit the heat shield.
10 Refit the subframe as described in Section 8.

19 Steering gear rubber gaiters - renewal

1 Remove the track-rod end as described in Section 22.
2 Mark the fitted position of the gaiter on the track-rod. Release the retaining clips, and slide the gaiter off the steering gear housing and track-rod end.
3 Thoroughly clean the track-rod and the steering gear housing, using fine abrasive paper to polish off any corrosion, burrs or sharp edges which might damage the sealing lips of the new gaiter on installation.
4 Where applicable, recover the grease from inside the old gaiter. If it is uncontaminated with dirt or grit, apply it to the track-rod inner balljoint. If the old grease is contaminated, or it is suspected that some has been lost, apply some new molybdenum disulphide grease.
5 Grease the inside of the new gaiter. Carefully slide the gaiter onto the track-rod, and locate it on the steering gear housing. Align the outer edge of the gaiter with the mark made on the track-rod prior to removal, then secure it in position with new retaining clips.
6 Refit the track-rod end as described in Section 22.

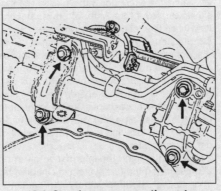

18.4 Steering gear mounting nuts (arrowed)

20 Power steering hydraulic system - bleeding

1 This procedure will only be necessary when any part of the hydraulic system has been disconnected, or if air has entered because of leakage.
2 Remove the fluid reservoir filler cap, and top-up the fluid level to the maximum mark, using only the specified fluid. Refer to *Lubricants and fluids* for fluid specifications, and to *Weekly checks* for details of the fluid reservoir markings.
3 With the engine stopped, slowly move the steering from lock-to-lock several times to expel trapped air, then top-up the level in the fluid reservoir. Repeat this procedure until the fluid level in the reservoir does not drop any further.
4 Start the engine. Slowly move the steering from lock-to-lock several times to expel any air remaining in the system. Repeat this procedure until bubbles cease to appear in the fluid reservoir.
5 If, when turning the steering, an abnormal noise is heard from the fluid pipes, it indicates that there is still air in the system. Check this by turning the wheels to the straight-ahead position and switching off the engine. If the fluid level in the reservoir rises, air is still present in the system, and further bleeding is necessary.
6 Once all traces of air have been removed, stop the engine and allow the system to cool. Once cool, check that the fluid level is up to the maximum mark on the power steering fluid reservoir; top-up if necessary.

21 Power steering pump - removal and refitting

8-valve petrol engine models

Removal

1 Disconnect the battery negative terminal (refer to *Disconnecting the battery* in the Reference Section of this manual).
2 Apply the handbrake, then jack up the front of the vehicle (see *Jacking and vehicle support*), and remove the right-hand roadwheel.
3 Where applicable, remove the securing screws, and withdraw the engine undershield. Remove the splash shield from under the wheel arch.
4 Slacken the three power steering pump pulley securing bolts.
5 Remove the auxiliary drivebelt as described in Chapter 1A.
6 Where applicable, release the fluid hoses/pipes from any clips or brackets to enable the hoses/pipes to be moved to one side, clear of the pump.

10

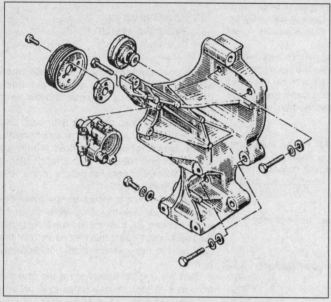

**21.10 Power steering pump mounting details -
8-valve petrol engine models**

**21.23 Disconnect the fuel supply hose from the fuel rail for
access to the pump rear mounting bolt -
1.6 litre (16-valve) petrol engine models with air conditioning**

7 Fit clamps to the power steering fluid hoses, as close as possible to the fluid reservoir to minimise fluid loss during the following operations.

8 Slacken the retaining clips, and disconnect the fluid supply and feed hoses from the pump. If necessary, to disconnect the feed pipe, unscrew the union nut and recover the O-ring. Be prepared for some fluid spillage as the hoses/pipes are disconnected; plug the hose/ pipe and pump openings to minimise fluid loss and to prevent the entry of dirt into the system.

9 Unscrew the three securing bolts, and remove the power steering pump pulley.

10 Unscrew the three securing bolts, and withdraw the power steering pump from its mounting bracket **(see illustration)**.

Refitting

11 Refitting is a reversal of removal, bearing in mind the following points.
a) *Where applicable, use a new O-ring when reconnecting the feed pipe union.*
b) *Refit the auxiliary drivebelt as described in Chapter 1A.*
c) *On completion, reconnect the battery then remove the hose clamps, and bleed the power steering hydraulic system as described in Section 20.*

1.6 litre (16-valve) petrol engine models without air conditioning

12 Proceed as described in paragraphs 1 to 11.

1.6 litre (16-valve) petrol engine models with air conditioning

Removal

13 Disconnect the battery negative terminal (refer to *Disconnecting the battery* in the Reference Section of this manual).

14 Apply the handbrake, then jack up the front of the vehicle (see *Jacking and vehicle support*), and remove the right-hand roadwheel.

15 Where applicable, remove the securing screws, and withdraw the engine undershield. Remove the splash shield from under the wheel arch.

16 Remove the auxiliary drivebelt as described in Chapter 1A.

17 Detach the power steering fluid reservoir from its mounting and move it to one side without disconnecting the fluid hoses.

18 Undo the nuts securing the fuel injector and fuel rail protective cover at the front of the inlet manifold. Release the wiring harness from the cable clips and remove the cover.

19 Where applicable, release the fluid hoses/pipes from any clips or brackets to enable the hoses/pipes to be moved to one side, clear of the pump.

20 Fit clamps to the power steering fluid hoses, as close as possible to the fluid reservoir to minimise fluid loss during the following operations.

21 Cover the alternator with a plastic sheet or similar to prevent the entry of power steering fluid when the hoses are disconnected.

22 Slacken the retaining clips, and disconnect the fluid supply and feed hoses from the pump. If necessary, to disconnect the feed pipe, unscrew the union nut and recover the O-ring. Be prepared for some fluid spillage as the hoses/pipes are disconnected; plug the hose/ pipe and pump openings to minimise fluid loss and to prevent the entry of dirt into the system.

23 Bearing in mind the information given on depressurising the fuel system in Chapter 4A, and taking suitable safety precautions, disconnect the fuel supply hose from the fuel rail **(see illustration)**.

24 Working through the openings in the pump pulley, unscrew the two bolts securing the front of the pump to the mounting bracket. Undo the rear mounting bolt and withdraw the power steering pump from its mounting bracket.

Refitting

25 Refitting is a reversal of removal, bearing in mind the following points.
a) *Where applicable, use a new O-ring when reconnecting the feed pipe union.*
b) *Refit the auxiliary drivebelt as described in Chapter 1A.*
c) *On completion, reconnect the battery then remove the hose clamps, and bleed the power steering hydraulic system as described in Section 20.*

1.8 litre (16-valve) petrol engine models

26 Proceed as described in paragraphs 1 to 11, noting that the pump is secured with four bolts.

2.0 litre (16-valve) petrol engine models

Removal

27 Disconnect the battery negative terminal (refer to *Disconnecting the battery* in the Reference Section of this manual).

28 Apply the handbrake, then jack up the front of the vehicle (see *Jacking and vehicle support*), and remove the right-hand roadwheel.

29 Where applicable, remove the securing screws, and withdraw the engine undershield. Remove the splash shield from under the wheel arch.

30 Remove the auxiliary drivebelt as described in Chapter 1A.

31 Where applicable, release the fluid hoses/pipes from any clips or brackets to enable the hoses/pipes to be moved to one side, clear of the pump.

32 Fit clamps to the power steering fluid hoses, as close as possible to the fluid reservoir to minimise fluid loss during the following operations.

33 Slacken the retaining clips, and disconnect the fluid supply and feed hoses from the pump. If necessary, to disconnect the feed pipe, unscrew the union nut and recover the O-ring. Be prepared for some fluid spillage as the hoses/pipes are disconnected; plug the hose/ pipe and pump openings to minimise fluid loss and to prevent the entry of dirt into the system.

34 Working through the openings in the pump pulley, unscrew the three bolts securing the front of the pump to the mounting bracket **(see illustration)**. Undo the additional front mounting bolt and the rear mounting bolt and withdraw the power steering pump from its mounting bracket.

Refitting

35 Refitting is a reversal of removal, bearing in mind the following points.
  a) *Where applicable, use a new O-ring when reconnecting the feed pipe union.*
  b) *Refit the auxiliary drivebelt as described in Chapter 1A.*
  c) *On completion, reconnect the battery then remove the hose clamps, and bleed the power steering hydraulic system as described in Section 20.*

1.9 litre diesel engine models without air conditioning

36 Proceed as described in paragraphs 1 to 11.

1.9 litre diesel engine models with air conditioning

Removal

Note: *To enable the pump to be removed from the mounting bracket, the pump pulley hub must be removed. To do this, a suitable puller will be required for removal, and Renault special tool Dir. 1083-01 will be required to refit the pulley hub to the pump.*

37 Disconnect the battery negative terminal (refer to *Disconnecting the battery* in the Reference Section of this manual).

38 Apply the handbrake, then jack up the front of the vehicle (see *Jacking and vehicle support*), and remove the right-hand roadwheel.

39 Where applicable, remove the securing screws, and withdraw the engine undershield. Remove the splash shield from under the wheel arch.

40 Unscrew the retaining nuts and withdraw the engine sound-insulating cover.

41 Slacken the three power steering pump pulley securing bolts.

42 Remove the auxiliary drivebelt as described in Chapter 1B.

43 Disconnect the wiring plug from the injection control unit located at the front right-hand side of the engine compartment. Undo the mounting bolts and remove the control unit. Similarly, unbolt the pre/post heating system control unit, adjacent to the injection control unit, and move it to one side.

44 From underneath the vehicle, undo the retaining bolts and remove the rear mounting link, connecting the engine/transmission mounting to the body.

45 Disconnect the exhaust system front pipe from the manifold as described in Chapter 4B.

46 Disconnect the gearchange linkage from the transmission as described in Chapter 7A.

47 Position an engine hoist, or an engine lifting beam across the engine compartment and attach the jib to the right-hand engine lifting eyelet. Raise the lifting gear to take up the slack, so that it is just supporting the weight of the engine.

48 Undo the three bolts securing the right-hand engine mounting bracket to the cylinder head. Similarly, undo the three bolts securing the rubber mounting to the body. Release the relevant cable clips and remove the complete mounting assembly.

49 Detach the power steering fluid reservoir from its mounting and move it to one side without disconnecting the fluid hoses.

50 Remove the alternator as described in Chapter 5A.

51 Raise the lifting gear to provide as much clearance as possible to the front of the power steering pump.

52 Undo the previously slackened pump pulley securing bolts and remove the pulley.

53 Where applicable, release the fluid hoses/pipes from any clips or brackets to enable the hoses/pipes to be moved to one side, clear of the pump.

54 Fit clamps to the power steering fluid hoses, as close as possible to the fluid reservoir to minimise fluid loss during the following operations.

55 Slacken the retaining clips, and disconnect the fluid supply and feed hoses from the pump. If necessary, to disconnect the feed pipe, unscrew the union nut and recover the O-ring. Be prepared for some fluid spillage as the hoses/pipes are disconnected; plug the hose/ pipe and pump openings to minimise fluid loss and to prevent the entry of dirt into the system.

56 Suitably hold the pump pulley hub and unscrew the pulley hub retaining nut.

57 Using a three-legged puller, draw the pulley hub off the pump shaft. Use a suitable packing piece to protect the end of the pump shaft when engaging the puller.

58 With the hub removed, undo the three mounting bolts and remove the pump from the mounting bracket.

Refitting

59 Fit the pump to the mounting bracket and secure with the three bolts.

60 Locate the pulley hub on the pump shaft and pull it fully into position using Renault tool Dir. 1083-01. To facilitate fitting the hub, insert a 25 mm shim between the tool body and the hub. To provide the correct fitting dimension, insert a 6.35 mm shim between the pulley hub and the pump.

61 Refit the pulley hub retaining nut and tighten it securely while holding the hub.

62 The remainder of refitting is a reversal of removal, bearing in mind the following points.
  a) *Where applicable, use a new O-ring when reconnecting the feed pipe union.*
  b) *Refit the alternator as described in Chapter 5A.*

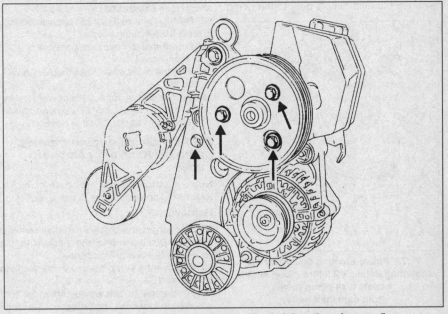

21.34 Power steering pump front mounting bolt locations (arrowed) - 2.0 litre (16-valve) petrol engine models

10

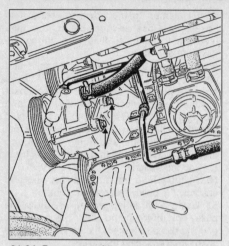

21.64 Power steering pump rear mounting bolts - 2.2 litre diesel engine models with pump driven from crankshaft pulley

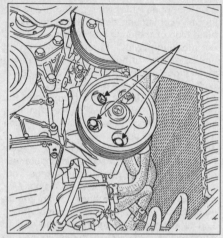

21.65 Power steering pump front mounting bolts - 2.2 litre diesel engine models with pump driven from crankshaft pulley

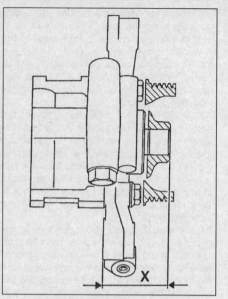

21.67 The dimension (x) between the end face of the pump and the end face of the pump hub must be 49.85 mm - 2.2 litre diesel engine models with pump driven from crankshaft pulley

c) Refit the right-hand engine mounting using the procedures described in Chapter 2D, Section 5.

d) Reconnect the gearchange linkage as described in Chapter 7A.

e) Refit the auxiliary drivebelt as described in Chapter 1B.

f) On completion, reconnect the battery then remove the hose clamps, and bleed the power steering hydraulic system as described in Section 20.

2.2 litre diesel engine models - pump driven from crankshaft pulley

Removal

63 Proceed as described in paragraphs 1 to 7, but note that there is no need to slacken the power steering pump pulley bolts, and the bolt securing the fluid supply pipe to the pump

mounting bracket must be unscrewed to allow the pipe to be disconnected.

64 Unscrew the two rear pump securing bolts **(see illustration)**.

65 Working through the holes in the power steering pump pulley, unscrew the three front pump securing bolts, then withdraw the pump from the mounting bracket **(see illustration)**.

Refitting

66 If a new pump is being fitted, the pump will be supplied without a pulley, therefore the pulley must be transferred from the old pump.

67 Use a suitable puller to remove the pulley from the old pump, then use a metal tube, or a suitable bolt, spacer and nut (screw the bolt into the end of the pump shaft) to press the sprocket onto the new pump shaft. The dimension between the end face of the pump and the end face of the pump hub **must** be as shown **(see illustration)**.

68 Refitting is a reversal of removal, bearing in mind the following points.

a) Ensure that all hoses are correctly reconnected.

b) Refit the drivebelt as described in Chapter 1B.

c) On completion, top-up the power steering fluid level (see Weekly Checks), and bleed the system as described in Section 20.

2.2 litre diesel engine models - pump driven from camshaft pulley

Note: A suitable puller will be required to remove the power steering pump sprocket.

Removal

69 Disconnect the battery negative terminal (refer to Disconnecting the battery in the Reference Section of this manual).

70 Remove the pump drivebelt as described in Chapter 1B.

71 Fit clamps to the power steering fluid hoses, as close as possible to the fluid reservoir to minimise fluid loss during the following operations.

72 Release the securing clip, and release the power steering fluid reservoir from its mounting clamp **(see illustration)**.

73 Unscrew the two bolts securing the clamp to the mounting bracket, and withdraw the clamp.

74 Where applicable, unscrew the two nuts securing the fast idle solenoid to the top of the power steering reservoir mounting bracket, then move the valve to one side. If the hoses are disconnected, note their locations to ensure correct reconnection.

75 Unscrew the two bolts securing the fluid reservoir mounting bracket to the pump mounting bracket, and withdraw the reservoir mounting bracket **(see illustration)**.

21.72 Power steering fluid reservoir mounting details - 2.2 litre diesel engine models with pump driven from camshaft pulley

2 Reservoir clamp clip
3 Reservoir clamp mounting bolts

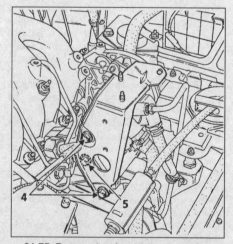

21.75 Power steering pump mounting bracket bolts (4) and rear pump mounting bolts (5) - 2.2 litre diesel engine models with pump driven from camshaft pulley

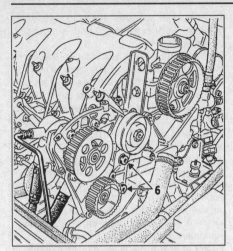

21.81 Front power steering pump/brake vacuum pump mounting bracket bolts (6) - 2.2 litre diesel engine models with pump driven from camshaft pulley

76 Place a suitable container beneath the pump oil feed pipe connection, then unscrew the union nut and disconnect the pipe. Recover the oil jet from the aperture in the pump if it is loose. Plug the open ends of the pipe and the pump to prevent dirt ingress and further oil spillage.
77 Similarly, remove the hose clip, and disconnect the oil return hose from the pump. Note the routing of the hose to aid refitting.
78 Remove the hose clip and disconnect the vacuum hose from the pump. Again, note the routing of the hose.
79 Similarly, disconnect the fluid pipes from the power steering pump - be prepared for fluid spillage.
80 Unscrew the rear power steering pump securing bolt.
81 Working at the front of the power steering pump/brake vacuum pump mounting bracket, unscrew the two securing bolts, and withdraw the complete mounting bracket/pump/tensioner assembly from the engine **(see illustration)**.
82 Using a suitable puller, pull the sprocket from the power steering pump shaft.
83 Unscrew the three securing bolts, and withdraw the pump from the mounting bracket **(see illustration)**.

Refitting

84 Commence refitting by positioning the pump on the mounting bracket, and securing with the three bolts.
85 Use a metal tube, or a suitable bolt, spacer and nut (screw the bolt into the end of the pump shaft) to press the sprocket onto the pump shaft. The dimension between the end face of the pump shaft hub and the end face of the pulley hub **must** be as shown **(see illustration)**.
86 Further refitting is a reversal of removal, bearing in mind the following points.
a) Ensure that all hoses are correctly reconnected.

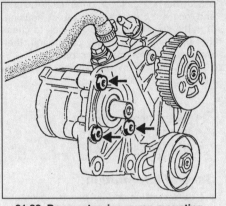

21.83 Power steering pump mounting bolts (arrowed) - 2.2 litre diesel engine models with pump driven from camshaft pulley

b) Refit the drivebelt as described in Chapter 1B.
c) On completion, top-up the power steering fluid level (see Weekly Checks), and bleed the system as described in Section 20.

22 Track-rod end - removal and refitting

Note: A balljoint separator tool will be required for this operation. A new balljoint nut will be required on refitting.

Removal

1 Apply the handbrake, then jack up the front of the vehicle and support it securely on axle stands (see Jacking and vehicle support). Remove the appropriate front roadwheel.
2 Count the number of exposed threads on the end of the track-rod to use as a guide when refitting.
3 Unscrew the track-rod end clamp bolt **(see illustration)**.
4 Remove the nut securing the track-rod end to the hub carrier. Release the balljoint tapered shank using a universal balljoint separator. If the track-rod end is to be re-used, protect the threaded end of the shank by screwing the nut back on a few turns before using the separator **(see illustration)**.

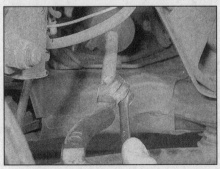

22.3 Unscrewing the track-rod end balljoint

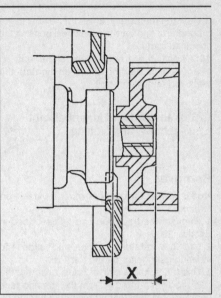

21.85 The dimension (x) between the end face of the pump shaft hub and the end face of the pulley hub must be 22.0 mm - 2.2 litre diesel engine models with pump driven from camshaft pulley

5 Counting the **exact** number of turns necessary to do so, unscrew the track-rod end from the track-rod. Counterhold the track-rod using a spanner on the flats provided.
6 Carefully clean the balljoint and the threads. Renew the track-rod end if the balljoint movement is sloppy or if it is too stiff, if it is excessively worn, or if it is damaged in any way. Carefully check the shank taper and threads. If the gaiter is damaged, the complete track-rod end must be renewed; it is not possible to obtain the gaiter separately.

Refitting

7 Screw the track-rod end into the track-rod by the number of turns noted on removal. This should leave the same number of threads exposed on the end of the track-rod as noted before removal.
8 Refit the balljoint shank to the hub carrier, and tighten the new retaining nut to the specified torque. If difficulty is experienced due to the balljoint shank rotating, jam it by exerting pressure on the top of the balljoint.

10

22.4 Using a balljoint separator tool to release the track-rod end balljoint

9 Refit the roadwheel, lower the vehicle to the ground and tighten the roadwheel bolts to the specified torque.

10 Check the front wheel alignment as described in Section 24, then tighten the track-rod end clamp-bolt.

23 Track-rod and inner balljoint - removal and refitting

Removal

Note: *A new lockwasher must be used on refitting.*

1 Remove the track-rod end as described in Section 22.

2 Cut the retaining clips, and slide the steering gear gaiter off the track-rod.

3 Using a suitable pair of grips, unscrew the track-rod inner balljoint from the steering rack end. Prevent the steering rack from turning by holding the balljoint lockwasher with a second pair of grips. Take care not to mark the surfaces of the rack and balljoint.

4 Remove the track-rod/inner balljoint assembly and discard the lockwasher; a new one must be used on refitting.

5 Examine the inner balljoint for signs of slackness or tight spots. Check that the track-rod itself is straight and free from damage. If necessary, renew the track-rod/inner balljoint; the new one will be supplied complete with a new lockwasher and a new end balljoint. It is also recommended that the steering gear gaiter is renewed.

Refitting

6 If a new track-rod is being installed, remove the outer balljoint from the track-rod end.

7 Locate the new lockwasher assembly on the end of the steering rack, ensuring that its locating tabs are correctly located with the flats on the rack end **(see illustration)**.

8 Apply a few drops of locking fluid to the inner balljoint threads. Screw the balljoint into the steering rack and tighten it securely. Again, take care not to damage or mark the balljoint or steering rack.

9 Slide the new gaiter onto the track-rod end, and locate it on the steering gear housing. Turn the steering from lock-to-lock to check that the gaiter is correctly positioned, then secure it with new retaining clips.

10 Refit the track-rod end balljoint as described in Section 22.

24 Wheel alignment and steering angles - general information

General information

1 A car's steering and suspension geometry is defined in four basic settings - all angles are expressed in degrees (toe settings are also expressed as a measurement); the relevant settings are camber, castor, steering axis inclination, and toe-setting. With the exception of toe-setting, none of these settings are adjustable.

Front wheel toe setting

Checking

2 Due to the special measuring equipment necessary to check the wheel alignment, and the skill required to use it properly, the checking and adjustment of these settings is best left to a Renault dealer or similar expert. Most tyre-fitting shops now possess sophisticated checking equipment.

3 For accurate checking, the vehicle must be at the kerb weight specified in *General dimensions and weights*.

4 Before starting work, check first that the tyre sizes and types are as specified, then check tyre pressures and tread wear. Also check roadwheel run-out, the condition of the hub bearings, the steering wheel free play and the condition of the front suspension components (see the relevant part of Chapter 1). Correct any faults found.

5 Park the vehicle on level ground, with the front roadwheels in the straight-ahead position. Rock the rear and front ends to settle the suspension. Release the handbrake and roll the vehicle backwards approximately

1 metre, then forwards again, to relieve any stresses in the steering and suspension components.

6 Two methods are available to the home mechanic for checking the front wheel toe setting. One method is to use a gauge to measure the distance between the front and rear inside edges of the roadwheels. The other method is to use a scuff plate, in which each front wheel is rolled across a movable plate which records any deviation, or scuff, of the tyre from the straight-ahead position as it moves across the plate. Such gauges are available in relatively-inexpensive form from accessory outlets. It is up to the owner to decide whether the expense is justified, in view of the small amount of use such equipment would normally receive.

7 Prepare the vehicle as described in paragraphs 3 to 5 above.

8 If the measurement procedure is being used, carefully measure the distance between the front edges of the roadwheel rims and the rear edges of the rims. Subtract the rear measurement from the front measurement, and check that the result is within the specified range. If not, adjust the toe setting as described in paragraph 10.

9 If scuff plates are to be used, roll the vehicle backwards, check that the roadwheels are in the straight-ahead position, then roll it across the scuff plates so that each front roadwheel passes squarely over the centre of its respective plate. Note the angle recorded by the scuff plates. To ensure accuracy, repeat the check three times, and take the average of the three readings. If the roadwheels are running parallel, there will of course be no angle recorded; if a deviation value is shown on the scuff plates, compare the reading obtained for each wheel with that specified. If the value recorded is outside the specified tolerance, the toe setting is incorrect, and must be adjusted as follows.

Adjustment

10 Apply the handbrake, then jack up the front of the vehicle and support it securely on axle stands (see *Jacking and vehicle support*). Turn the steering wheel onto full-left lock, and record the number of exposed threads on the end of the right-hand track-rod. Now turn the steering onto full-right lock, and record the number of threads on the left-hand side. If there are the same number of threads visible on both sides, then subsequent adjustment should be made equally on both sides. If there are more threads visible on one side than the other, it will be necessary to compensate for this during adjustment. **Note:** *It is important to ensure that, after adjustment, the same number of threads are visible on the end of each track-rod*.

11 First clean the track-rod threads; if they are corroded, apply penetrating fluid before starting adjustment. Release the steering gear rubber gaiter outboard clips, then peel back the gaiters and apply a smear of grease, so

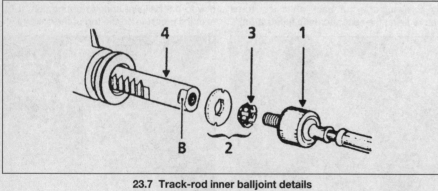

23.7 Track-rod inner balljoint details

1 Balljoint	*3 Lockwasher*	*B Flats on rack end*
2 Stop washer	*4 Steering rack*	

that both gaiters are free and will not be twisted or strained as their respective track-rods are rotated.

12 Use a straight-edge and a scriber or similar to mark the relationship of each track-rod to the track-rod end. Working on each track-rod end in turn, unscrew its clamp bolt.

13 Alter the length of the track-rods, bearing in mind the note in paragraph 10, by screwing them into or out of the track-rod ends. Rotate the track-rod using an open-ended spanner fitted to the flats provided. If necessary, counterhold the track-rod end using a second spanner **(see illustration)**. Shortening the track-rods (screwing them into their track-rod ends) will reduce toe-in and increase toe-out. Note that one full turn of the track-rods will alter the toe-setting by 30' (3.0 mm).

14 When the setting is correct, hold the track-rods and securely tighten the track-rod end clamp bolts. Check that the balljoints are seated correctly in their sockets, and count the exposed threads on the ends of the track-rods. If the number of threads exposed is not the same on both sides, then the adjustment has not been made equally, and problems will be encountered with tyre scrubbing in turns; also, the steering wheel spokes will no longer be horizontal when the wheels are in the straight-ahead position.

15 When the track-rod lengths are the same, lower the vehicle to the ground and re-check the toe setting; readjust if necessary. When the setting is correct, tighten the track-rod end clamp bolts. Ensure that the steering gear rubber gaiters are seated correctly and are not twisted or strained, then secure them in position with new retaining clips.

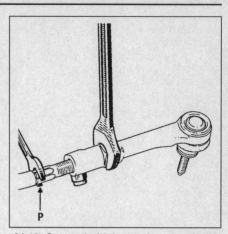

24.13 Counterhold the track-rod end and rotate the track rod using the flats (P) provided

10

Chapter 11
Bodywork and fittings

Contents

Degrees of difficulty

Easy, suitable for novice with little experience	Fairly easy, suitable for beginner with some experience	Fairly difficult, suitable for competent DIY mechanic	Difficult, suitable for experienced DIY mechanic	Very difficult, suitable for expert DIY or professional

Specifications

Torque wrench setting	Nm	lbf ft
Seat belt anchor bolts	25	18

1 General information

The bodyshell is of five-door Hatchback or Estate configuration, and is made of pressed steel sections. Most components are welded together, but some use is made of structural adhesives. The front wings are bolted on.

The bonnet, doors and some other vulnerable panels are made of zinc-coated metal, and are further protected by being coated with an anti-chip primer prior to being sprayed.

Extensive use is made of plastic materials, mainly in the interior, but also in exterior components. The front and rear bumpers and the front grille are injection-moulded from a synthetic material which is very strong, and yet light. Plastic components such as wheel arch liners are fitted to the underside of the vehicle, to improve the body's resistance to corrosion.

2 Maintenance - bodywork and underframe

The general condition of a vehicle's bodywork is the one thing that significantly affects its value. Maintenance is easy, but needs to be regular. Neglect, particularly after minor damage, can lead quickly to further deterioration and costly repair bills. It is important also to keep watch on those parts of the vehicle not immediately visible, for instance the underside, inside all the wheel arches, and the lower part of the engine compartment.

The basic maintenance routine for the bodywork is washing - preferably with a lot of water, from a hose. This will remove all the loose solids which may have stuck to the vehicle. It is important to flush these off in such a way as to prevent grit from scratching the finish. The wheel arches and underframe need washing in the same way, to remove any accumulated mud which will retain moisture and tend to encourage rust. Oddly enough, the best time to clean the underframe and wheel arches is in wet weather, when the mud is thoroughly wet and soft. In very wet weather, the underframe is usually cleaned of large accumulations automatically, and this is a good time for inspection.

Periodically, except on vehicles with a wax-based underbody protective coating, it is a good idea to have the whole of the underframe of the vehicle steam-cleaned, engine compartment included, so that a thorough inspection can be carried out to see what minor repairs and renovations are necessary. Steam-cleaning is available at many garages, and is necessary for the removal of the accumulation of oily grime, which sometimes is allowed to become thick in certain areas. If steam-cleaning facilities are not available, there are one or two excellent grease solvents available, which

11

can be brush-applied; the dirt can then be simply hosed off. Note that these methods should not be used on vehicles with wax-based underbody protective coating, or the coating will be removed. Such vehicles should be inspected annually, preferably just prior to Winter, when the underbody should be washed down, and any damage to the wax coating repaired. Ideally, a completely fresh coat should be applied. It would also be worth considering the use of such wax-based protection for injection into door panels, sills, box sections, etc, as an additional safeguard against rust damage, where such protection is not provided by the vehicle manufacturer.

After washing paintwork, wipe off with a chamois leather to give an unspotted clear finish. A coat of clear protective wax polish will give added protection against chemical pollutants in the air. If the paintwork sheen has dulled or oxidised, use a cleaner/polisher combination to restore the brilliance of the shine. This requires a little effort, but such dulling is usually caused because regular washing has been neglected. Care needs to be taken with metallic paintwork, as special non-abrasive cleaner/polisher is required to avoid damage to the finish. Always check that the door and ventilator opening drain holes and pipes are completely clear, so that water can be drained out. Brightwork should be treated in the same way as paintwork. Windscreens and windows can be kept clear of the smeary film which often appears, by the use of proprietary glass cleaner. Never use any form of wax or other body or chromium polish on glass.

3 Maintenance -
upholstery and carpets

Mats and carpets should be brushed or vacuum-cleaned regularly, to keep them free of grit. If they are badly stained, remove them from the vehicle for scrubbing or sponging, and make quite sure they are dry before refitting. Seats and interior trim panels can be kept clean by wiping with a damp cloth. If they do become stained (which can be more apparent on light-coloured upholstery), use a little liquid detergent and a soft nail brush to scour the grime out of the grain of the material. Do not forget to keep the headlining clean in the same way as the upholstery. When using liquid cleaners inside the vehicle, do not over-wet the surfaces being cleaned. Excessive damp could get into the seams and padded interior, causing stains, offensive odours or even rot. If the inside of the vehicle gets wet accidentally, it is worthwhile taking some trouble to dry it out properly, particularly where carpets are involved. Do not leave oil or electric heaters inside the vehicle for this purpose.

4 Minor body damage -
repair

Repairs of minor scratches in bodywork

If the scratch is very superficial, and does not penetrate to the metal of the bodywork, repair is very simple. Lightly rub the area of the scratch with a paintwork renovator, or a very fine cutting paste, to remove loose paint from the scratch, and to clear the surrounding bodywork of wax polish. Rinse the area with clean water.

Apply touch-up paint to the scratch using a fine paint brush; continue to apply fine layers of paint until the surface of the paint in the scratch is level with the surrounding paintwork. Allow the new paint at least two weeks to harden, then blend it into the surrounding paintwork by rubbing the scratch area with a paintwork renovator or a very fine cutting paste. Finally, apply wax polish.

Where the scratch has penetrated right through to the metal of the bodywork, causing the metal to rust, a different repair technique is required. Remove any loose rust from the bottom of the scratch with a penknife, then apply rust-inhibiting paint, to prevent the formation of rust in the future. Using a rubber or nylon applicator, fill the scratch with bodystopper paste. If required, this paste can be mixed with cellulose thinners, to provide a very thin paste which is ideal for filling narrow scratches. Before the stopper-paste in the scratch hardens, wrap a piece of smooth cotton rag around the top of a finger. Dip the finger in cellulose thinners, and quickly sweep it across the surface of the stopper-paste in the scratch; this will ensure that the surface of the stopper-paste is slightly hollowed. The scratch can now be painted over as described earlier in this Section.

Repairs of dents in bodywork

When deep denting of the vehicle's bodywork has taken place, the first task is to pull the dent out, until the affected bodywork almost attains its original shape. There is little point in trying to restore the original shape completely, as the metal in the damaged area will have stretched on impact, and cannot be reshaped fully to its original contour. It is better to bring the level of the dent up to a point which is about 3 mm below the level of the surrounding bodywork. In cases where the dent is very shallow anyway, it is not worth trying to pull it out at all. If the underside of the dent is accessible, it can be hammered out gently from behind, using a mallet with a wooden or plastic head. Whilst doing this, hold a suitable block of wood firmly against the outside of the panel, to absorb the impact from the hammer blows and thus prevent a large area of the bodywork from being 'belled-out'.

Should the dent be in a section of the bodywork which has a double skin, or some other factor making it inaccessible from behind, a different technique is called for. Drill several small holes through the metal inside the area - particularly in the deeper section. Then screw long self-tapping screws into the holes, just sufficiently for them to gain a good purchase in the metal. Now the dent can be pulled out by pulling on the protruding heads of the screws with a pair of pliers.

The next stage of the repair is the removal of the paint from the damaged area, and from an inch or so of the surrounding 'sound' bodywork. This is accomplished most easily by using a wire brush or abrasive pad on a power drill, although it can be done just as effectively by hand, using sheets of abrasive paper. To complete the preparation for filling, score the surface of the bare metal with a screwdriver or the tang of a file, or alternatively, drill small holes in the affected area. This will provide a really good 'key' for the filler paste.

To complete the repair, see the Section on filling and respraying.

Repairs of rust holes or gashes in bodywork

Remove all paint from the affected area, and from an inch or so of the surrounding 'sound' bodywork, using an abrasive pad or a wire brush on a power drill. If these are not available, a few sheets of abrasive paper will do the job most effectively. With the paint removed, you will be able to judge the severity of the corrosion, and therefore decide whether to renew the whole panel (if this is possible) or to repair the affected area. New body panels are not as expensive as most people think, and it is often quicker and more satisfactory to fit a new panel than to attempt to repair large areas of corrosion.

Remove all fittings from the affected area, except those which will act as a guide to the original shape of the damaged bodywork (eg headlamp shells etc). Then, using tin snips or a hacksaw blade, remove all loose metal and any other metal badly affected by corrosion. Hammer the edges of the hole inwards, in order to create a slight depression for the filler paste.

Wire-brush the affected area to remove the powdery rust from the surface of the remaining metal. Paint the affected area with rust-inhibiting paint; if the back of the rusted area is accessible, treat this also.

Before filling can take place, it will be necessary to block the hole in some way. This can be achieved by the use of aluminium or plastic mesh, or aluminium tape.

Aluminium or plastic mesh, or glass-fibre matting is probably the best material to use for a large hole. Cut a piece to the approximate size and shape of the hole to be filled, then position it in the hole so that its edges are below the level of the surrounding bodywork. It can be retained in position by several blobs of filler paste around its periphery.

Aluminium tape should be used for small or very narrow holes. Pull a piece off the roll, trim it to the approximate size and shape required, then pull off the backing paper (if used) and stick the tape over the hole; it can be overlapped if the thickness of one piece is insufficient. Burnish down the edges of the tape with the handle of a screwdriver or similar, to ensure that the tape is securely attached to the metal underneath.

Bodywork repairs - filling and respraying

Before using this Section, see the Sections on dent, deep scratch, rust holes and gash repairs.

Many types of bodyfiller are available, but generally speaking, those proprietary kits which contain a tin of filler paste and a tube of resin hardener are best for this type of repair. A wide, flexible plastic or nylon applicator will be found invaluable for imparting a smooth and well-contoured finish to the surface of the filler.

Mix up a little filler on a clean piece of card or board - measure the hardener carefully (follow the maker's instructions on the pack), otherwise the filler will set too rapidly or too slowly. Using the applicator, apply the filler paste to the prepared area; draw the applicator across the surface of the filler to achieve the correct contour and to level the surface. As soon as a contour that approximates to the correct one is achieved, stop working the paste - if you carry on too long, the paste will become sticky and begin to 'pick-up' on the applicator. Continue to add thin layers of filler paste at 20-minute intervals, until the level of the filler is just proud of the surrounding bodywork.

Once the filler has hardened, the excess can be removed using a metal plane or file. From then on, progressively-finer grades of abrasive paper should be used, starting with a 40-grade production paper, and finishing with a 400-grade wet-and-dry paper. Always wrap the abrasive paper around a flat rubber, cork, or wooden block - otherwise the surface of the filler will not be completely flat. During the smoothing of the filler surface, the wet-and-dry paper should be periodically rinsed in water. This will ensure that a very smooth finish is imparted to the filler at the final stage.

At this stage, the 'dent' should be surrounded by a ring of bare metal, which in turn should be encircled by the finely 'feathered' edge of the good paintwork. Rinse the repair area with clean water, until all of the dust produced by the rubbing-down operation has gone.

Spray the whole area with a light coat of primer - this will show up any imperfections in the surface of the filler. Repair these imperfections with fresh filler paste or

bodystopper, and once more smooth the surface with abrasive paper. If bodystopper is used, it can be mixed with cellulose thinners, to form a really thin paste which is ideal for filling small holes. Repeat this spray-and-repair procedure until you are satisfied that the surface of the filler, and the feathered edge of the paintwork, are perfect. Clean the repair area with clean water, and allow to dry fully.

The repair area is now ready for final spraying. Paint spraying must be carried out in a warm, dry, windless and dust-free atmosphere. This condition can be created artificially if you have access to a large indoor working area, but if you are forced to work in the open, you will have to pick your day very carefully. If you are working indoors, dousing the floor in the work area with water will help to settle the dust which would otherwise be in the atmosphere. If the repair area is confined to one body panel, mask off the surrounding panels; this will help to minimise the effects of a slight mis-match in paint colours. Bodywork fittings (eg chrome strips, door handles etc) will also need to be masked off. Use genuine masking tape, and several thicknesses of newspaper, for the masking operations.

Before commencing to spray, agitate the aerosol can thoroughly, then spray a test area (an old tin, or similar) until the technique is mastered. Cover the repair area with a thick coat of primer; the thickness should be built up using several thin layers of paint, rather than one thick one. Using 400 grade wet-and-dry paper, rub down the surface of the primer until it is really smooth. While doing this, the work area should be thoroughly doused with water, and the wet-and-dry paper periodically rinsed in water. Allow to dry before spraying on more paint.

Spray on the top coat, again building up the thickness by using several thin layers of paint. Start spraying at the top of the repair area, and then, using a side-to-side motion, work downwards until the whole repair area and about 2 inches of the surrounding original paintwork is covered. Remove all masking material 10 to 15 minutes after spraying on the final coat of paint.

Allow the new paint at least two weeks to harden, then, using a paintwork renovator or a very fine cutting paste, blend the edges of the paint into the existing paintwork. Finally, apply wax polish.

Plastic components

With the use of more and more plastic body components by the vehicle manufacturers (eg bumpers. spoilers, and in some cases major body panels), rectification of more serious damage to such items has become a matter of either entrusting repair work to a specialist in this field, or renewing complete components. Repair of such damage by the DIY owner is not really feasible, owing to the cost of the equipment and materials required

for effecting such repairs. The basic technique involves making a groove along the line of the crack in the plastic, using a rotary burr in a power drill. The damaged part is then welded back together, using a hot air gun to heat up and fuse a plastic filler rod into the groove. Any excess plastic is then removed, and the area rubbed down to a smooth finish. It is important that a filler rod of the correct plastic is used, as body components can be made of a variety of different types (eg polycarbonate, ABS, polypropylene).

Damage of a less serious nature (abrasions, minor cracks etc) can be repaired by the DIY owner using a two-part epoxy filler repair. Once mixed in equal, this is used in similar fashion to the bodywork filler used on metal panels. The filler is usually cured in twenty to thirty minutes, ready for sanding and painting.

If the owner is renewing a complete component himself, or if he has repaired it with epoxy filler, he will be left with the problem of finding a suitable paint for finishing which is compatible with the type of plastic used. At one time, the use of a universal paint was not possible, owing to the complex range of plastics encountered in body component applications. Standard paints, generally speaking, will not bond to plastic or rubber satisfactorily, but suitable paints to match any plastic or rubber finish, can be obtained from dealers. However, it is now possible to obtain a plastic body parts finishing kit which consists of a pre-primer treatment, a primer and coloured top coat. Full instructions are normally supplied with a kit, but basically, the method of use is to first apply the pre-primer to the component concerned, and allow it to dry for up to 30 minutes. Then the primer is applied, and left to dry for about an hour before finally applying the special-coloured top coat. The result is a correctly-coloured component, where the paint will flex with the plastic or rubber, a property that standard paint does not normally posses.

5 Major body damage - repair

Where serious damage has occurred, or large areas need renewal due to neglect, it means that complete new panels will need welding-in, and this is best left to professionals. If the damage is due to impact, it will also be necessary to check completely the alignment of the bodyshell, and this can only be carried out accurately by a Renault dealer using special jigs. If the body is left misaligned, it is primarily dangerous, as the car will not handle properly, and secondly, uneven stresses will be imposed on the steering, suspension and possibly transmission, causing abnormal wear, or complete failure, particularly to such items as the tyres.

11

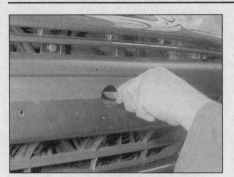

6.4 Unscrew the front bumper centre securing bolt

6.5 Remove the splash shield from the bottom of the bumper

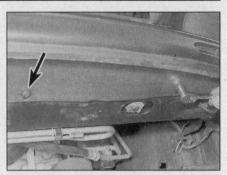

6.6 Unscrew the lower bumper securing screws

6.7a Unscrew the screws, and unclip the wheel arch liners . . .

6.7b . . . for access to the bumper side securing bolts (arrowed)

6 Bumpers - removal and refitting

Front bumper

Removal

1 To improve access, apply the handbrake, then jack up the front of the vehicle and support securely on axle stands (see *Jacking and vehicle support*). Remove the roadwheels.
2 On models with front foglights mounted in the bumper, disconnect the battery negative terminal (refer to *Disconnecting the battery* in the Reference Section of this manual).

3 Remove the number plate.
4 Unscrew the now-exposed centre bumper securing bolt **(see illustration)**.
5 Working at the bottom of the bumper, remove the securing screws, and withdraw the under-wing splash shields from the bottom of the bumper **(see illustration)**.
6 Unscrew the lower bumper securing screws **(see illustration)**.
7 Working under the wheel arches, unscrew the screws securing the wheel arch liners, then unclip the wheel arch liners from the wheel arches for access to the bumper side securing bolts **(see illustrations)**.
8 Unscrew the two bumper side securing bolts on each side of the vehicle.
9 Where applicable, working behind the lower edge of the bumper, unscrew the bumper rear securing bolts **(see illustration)**. For access to the right-hand bolt, it may be necessary to unbolt the washer fluid reservoir and move it

to one side. *Note that not all models have rear bumper securing bolts.*
10 Pull the bumper forwards from the body front panel to disengage the side locating lugs.
11 On models with front foglights mounted in the bumper, working at the rear of the light units, disconnect the wiring plugs and, where applicable, release the wiring from the clips at the rear of the bumper. Withdraw the bumper.

Refitting

12 Refitting is a reversal of removal, but where applicable ensure that the foglight wiring plugs are reconnected before refitting the bumper, and make sure that the bumper side locating lugs engage correctly with the clips on the body.

Rear bumper

Removal - Hatchback models

13 To improve access, chock the front wheels and engage reverse gear (or P on automatic transmission models). Jack up the rear of the vehicle and support it securely on axle stands (see *Jacking and vehicle support*).
14 Working in the luggage compartment, remove the securing screws, and withdraw the trim panel from the rear edge of the luggage compartment **(see illustration)**.
15 Where applicable, pull off the self-adhesive soundproofing blocks to expose the bumper rear securing nuts, then unscrew the nuts **(see illustration)**.
16 Working on the left-hand side of the luggage compartment, remove the securing

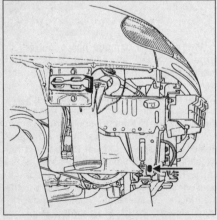

6.9 Front bumper rear securing bolt (arrowed) - not fitted to all models

6.14 Withdraw the trim panel from the rear edge of the luggage compartment . . .

6.15 . . . then unscrew the bumper rear securing nuts - Hatchback models

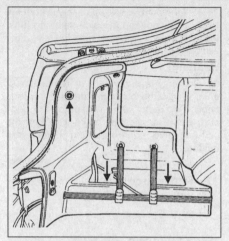

6.16 Unscrew the three screws (arrowed) and withdraw the side trim panel . . .

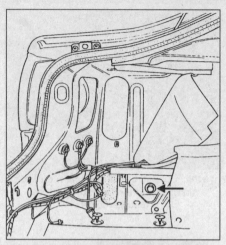

6.17 . . . for access to the bumper left-hand securing bolt (arrowed) - Hatchback models

6.18 Remove the splash shields/wheel arch liners . . .

screws, and withdraw the luggage compartment side trim panel **(see illustration)**.

17 Unscrew the now-exposed bumper left-hand securing bolt **(see illustration)**.

18 Working at each side of the bumper, remove the screws securing the splash shields/wheel arch liners to the rear and bottom edges of the bumper, and remove the splash shields/wheel arch liners **(see illustration)**.

19 Working underneath the vehicle, behind the right-hand wing panel, unscrew the bumper right-hand securing bolt **(see illustration)**.

20 Working under the rear of the bumper, unscrew the four lower bumper securing bolts **(see illustration)**.

21 Pull the bumper rearwards, away from the body, to disengage the side securing lugs, then withdraw the bumper from the rear of the vehicle.

Removal - Estate models

22 Where fitted, remove the rear mod flaps on each side.

23 Working at each side of the bumper, remove the screws under the wheel arch, and at the bumper bottom edges, securing the

splash shields/wheel arch liners to the bumper and underbody. Remove the splash shields/wheel arch liners **(see illustration)**.

24 Working under the rear of the bumper, unscrew the four lower bumper securing bolts **(see illustration)**.

25 Working underneath the vehicle, behind the right-hand wing panel, unscrew the bumper right-hand securing bolt **(see illustration)**.

26 Working on the left-hand side of the luggage compartment, remove the securing screws, and withdraw the luggage compartment side trim panel.

27 Unscrew the now-exposed bumper left-hand securing bolt **(see illustration)**.

28 Undo the two screws on the lower edge and single screw on each side, around the tailgate aperture **(see illustrations)**.

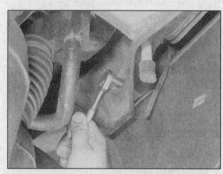

6.19 . . . for access to the bumper right-hand securing bolt - Hatchback models

6.20 Unscrewing a rear bumper lower securing bolt - Hatchback models

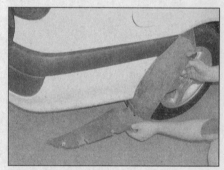

6.23 Removing the splash shield/ wheel arch liner - Estate models

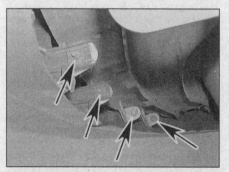

6.24 Unscrew the four lower bumper securing bolts (arrowed) - Estate models

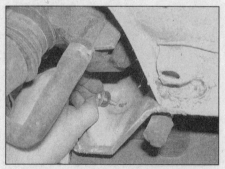

6.25 Unscrew the bumper right-hand securing bolt - Estate models

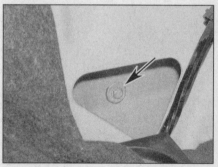

6.27 Unscrew the bumper left-hand securing bolt (arrowed) - Estate models

11

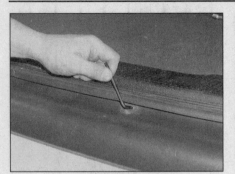

6.28a Undo the two screws on the bumper lower edge . . .

6.28b . . . and the single screw on each side, around the tailgate aperture - Estate models

6.29a Pull the bumper rearwards, away from the body, to disengage the side securing lugs . . .

6.29b . . . then withdraw the bumper from the rear of the vehicle - Estate models

7.2a Unscrew the radiator grille panel upper . . .

7.2b . . . and lower securing screws - pre-May 1998 models

7.3 Squeeze the grille panel securing clips . . .

7.4 . . . then pull the panel forwards - pre-May 1998 models

29 Pull the bumper rearwards, away from the body, to disengage the side securing lugs, then withdraw the bumper from the rear of the vehicle (see illustrations).

Refitting

30 Refitting is a reversal of removal, but ensure that the bumper side locating lugs engage correctly with the clips on the body and, where applicable, make sure that the self-adhesive sound-proofing blocks are refitted.

7 Radiator grille panel - removal and refitting

Pre-May 1998 models

Removal

1 Remove the direction indicator lights as described in Chapter 12, Section 7.
2 Unscrew the upper and lower grille panel securing screws. The lower screws can be reached through the slots in the bottom of the grille (note that the screws are captive in the grille panel) - a long screwdriver or Torx bit and extension will be required for access to the lower securing screws (see illustrations).
3 Working in the direction indicator light apertures, squeeze the securing clips to release the lower corners of the grille panel from the front wing panels (see illustration).
4 Carefully pull the grille panel forwards to release the securing lugs (take care, as the lugs are easily broken), and withdraw the panel (see illustration).
5 If desired, the two sections of the grille panel can be separated by removing the securing screws.

Refitting

6 Refitting is a reversal of removal, but make sure that the anti-rattle foam pads are intact on the rear of the panel.

May 1998 models onward

Removal

7 Undo the three bolts in the upper centre of the grill panel and the single bolt each side below the headlight.
8 Using a size 20 Torx bit and working through the small hole at the outer edge of the grille panel below the headlight, unscrew the bolt each side.
9 Carefully pull the outer edges of the grille panel forward to release the plastic securing lugs and remove the grille panel from the car.

Refitting

10 Prior to refitting, the grille panel end fittings (which will still be in place in the front wings) must be removed and re-attached to the grille. To do this, depress the plastic tabs on the top and bottom of the end fitting using a flat screwdriver and withdraw the fitting using pliers.

9.2 Bonnet release handle securing bolt (arrowed) viewed with facia removed

11 Refit the end fittings to the lugs on the radiator grille and secure with the retaining screws.
12 Refit the radiator grille panel to the car, engaging the end fittings first, then fit and tighten the grille panel retaining screws.

8 Bonnet and hinges - removal, refitting and adjustment

Bonnet

Removal

1 Open the bonnet, and support it in the open position using the bonnet stay.
2 Using a pencil, or felt-tipped pen, mark the outline of each bonnet hinge relative to the bonnet, to use as a guide on refitting.
3 Have an assistant support the bonnet, then working at each side of the bonnet in turn, unscrew the three bolts securing the hinge to the bonnet.
4 Unclip the bonnet stay then, with the aid of the assistant, lift the bonnet from the vehicle.

Refitting and adjustment

5 With the aid of an assistant, offer up the bonnet and loosely fit the securing bolts. Align the hinges with the marks made on removal, then tighten the securing bolts securely.
6 Close the bonnet and check for alignment with the surrounding body panels. If necessary, slacken the hinge bolts, and re-align the bonnet within the elongated holes in to suit. Once the bonnet is correctly aligned, tighten the hinge bolts securely.
7 Once the bonnet is correctly aligned, check that the bonnet fastens and releases in a satisfactory manner. If adjustment is necessary, slacken the bonnet lock striker securing bolts, and adjust the position of the strikers to suit (see Section 10). Once the lock operation is satisfactory, securely tighten the striker securing bolts.

Bonnet hinges

Removal

8 Remove the bonnet as described previously in this Section.
9 Unscrew the two bolts securing the hinge to the body.

Refitting

10 Refitting is a reversal of removal, but refit and adjust the bonnet as described previously in this Section.

9 Bonnet release cable - removal and refitting

Main cable

Removal

1 Remove the bonnet lock as described in Section 10.
2 Working in the passenger compartment, reach up behind the facia and locate the bonnet release handle securing bolt. Unscrew the release handle securing bolt (see illustration).
3 Working in the engine compartment, release the cable from any clips and brackets, noting its routing.

> **HAYNES HiNT** To aid refitting, tie a length of string to the end of the cable in the engine compartment. Pull the end of the string through into the passenger compartment as the cable is removed, then untie the string from the end of the release cable and leave it in position. The string can then be used to pull the cable through into the engine compartment on refitting.

4 Pull the cable through the bulkhead into the passenger compartment, and where applicable, untie the string from the end of the cable (see Haynes Hint).

Refitting

5 Refitting is a reversal of removal but, where applicable, use the string to pull the cable through the bulkhead into the engine compartment, and ensure that the cable is routed as noted before removal.

Lock connecting cable

Removal

6 Remove the passenger's side bonnet lock, with reference to Section 10.

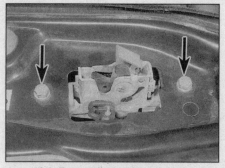

10.1 Bonnet lock securing bolts (arrowed)

7 Unclip the cable from any guides on the body front panel, then unhook the end of the cable from the driver's side lock, and withdraw the cable.

Refitting

8 Refitting is a reversal of removal, but refit the lock with reference to Section 10.

10 Bonnet lock components - removal and refitting

Bonnet lock

Removal

1 With the bonnet open, unscrew the two bolts securing the lock to the body front panel (see illustration).
2 Lift the lock out from under the body front panel, and disconnect the bonnet release cable(s). Withdraw the lock.

Refitting

3 Refitting is a reversal of removal.
4 On completion, check the operation of the lock. If necessary, adjust the position of the lock striker within the elongated holes in the bonnet to achieve satisfactory lock operation. Note also that the operation of the lock can be adjusted by altering the thickness of the shims fitted under the lock strikers.

Bonnet lock striker

Removal

5 With the bonnet open, mark the position of the striker using paint or a felt-tipped pen, to aid alignment on refitting.
6 Unbolt the striker from the bonnet, and recover the spacer shim.

Refitting

7 Refitting is a reversal of removal, but align the striker with the marks made before removal.
8 On completion, check the operation of the lock. If necessary, adjust the position of the lock striker within the elongated holes in the bonnet to achieve satisfactory lock operation. Note also that the operation of the lock can be adjusted by altering the thickness of the shims fitted under the lock strikers.

11 Door - removal, refitting and adjustment

Removal

1 Disconnect the battery negative terminal (refer to *Disconnecting the battery* in the Reference Section of this manual).
2 Open the door, then pull back the securing clip, and disconnect the door wiring connector.

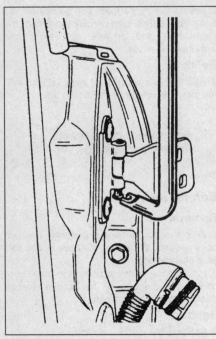

11.6 Using a cranked metal rod to remove a door hinge-pin - viewed with door removed

3 Unscrew the bolt securing the door check strap to the door pillar.

4 Support the door on blocks of wood, with rags positioned under the door to protect the paintwork.

5 Have an assistant steady the door, then remove the securing clips from the door hinge-pins.

6 Using a suitable pin-punch (note that Renault recommend the use of a cranked metal rod, with a cut-out to engage with the head of the hinge-pin), drive the hinge-pins from the hinges, then carefully lift the door from the vehicle **(see illustration)**.

Refitting and adjustment

7 Refitting is a reversal of removal, but check that the door is correctly aligned with the surrounding bodywork. Adjustment is made by altering the position of the hinges within the elongated bolt holes.

8 Check that the striker enters the lock centrally when the door is closed, and if necessary loosen the striker and reposition it until satisfactory lock operation is obtained.

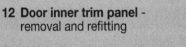

12 Door inner trim panel - removal and refitting

Front door

Removal

1 Disconnect the battery negative terminal (refer to *Disconnecting the battery* in the Reference Section of this manual).

2 Carefully prise the mirror trim plate from the front corner of the door **(see illustration)**.

3 On models with manual windows, note the position of the window regulator handle with the window shut, then remove the regulator handle. If necessary, use a forked tool, together with a piece of cloth to protect the door trim, to release the handle from the spindle.

4 Where applicable, remove the securing screw, then unclip the hand-grip plate/switch panel from the top of the armrest **(see illustration)**. If necessary, carefully lever the plate away using a flat-bladed screwdriver. Where applicable, disconnect the wiring from the switches in the panel, and withdraw the panel.

5 Starting at the bottom, carefully unclip the loudspeaker cover panel. Take care, as the clips are easily broken **(see illustration)**.

6 Unscrew the securing screws, then withdraw the loudspeaker from the housing in the door, and disconnect the wiring.

7 Unscrew the three door trim panel screws from the loudspeaker housing **(see illustration)**.

8 Lift up the inner door lock button then, using a small screwdriver, depress the retaining tab, and slide off the button **(see illustration)**.

9 Carefully unclip the door interior handle surround **(see illustration)**.

10 Working at the lower edge of the door trim panel, unscrew the four trim panel securing screws, then unscrew the remaining screw from the rear of the panel **(see illustrations)**.

11 Using a suitable forked tool, work around the edge of the door trim panel, and release the panel securing clips.

12.2 Prise the mirror trim plate from the door

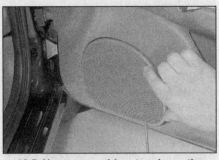

12.4 Unscrewing the hand grip plate-switch panel securing screw

12.5 Use a screwdriver to release the lower securing clip, then withdraw the loudspeaker cover panel

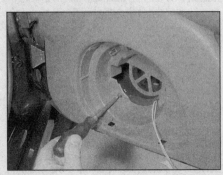

12.7 Unscrew the door trim panel securing screws from the loudspeaker housing

12.8 Lift the door lock operating button, and depress the retaining tab

12.9 Unclip the door interior handle surround

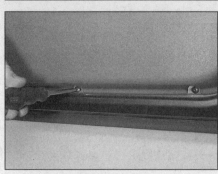

12.10a Unscrew the lower . . .

12.10b . . . and rear trim panel securing screws

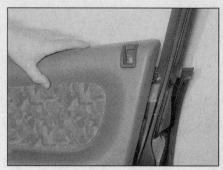

12.12 Lifting the trim panel from the door

12 Pull the panel upwards from the door **(see illustration)**.

13 If desired, the plastic sealing sheet can be removed from the door as follows.

   a) *Where applicable, disconnect the electric mirror wiring connector.*

   b) *Where applicable, unbolt the electric windows electronic control unit from the door, and disconnect the wiring plugs.*

   c) *Remove any wiring clips which protrude through the sealing sheet.*

   d) *Carefully peel the sealing sheet from the surface of the door. If this is done carefully, the sheet can be re-used.*

Refitting

14 Refitting is a reversal of removal, bearing in mind the following points.

   a) *Ensure that the plastic sealing sheet is securely refitted, and if necessary renew the sheet. Note that Renault recommend that both the plastic sheet and the sealing mastic are renewed.*

   b) *Before refitting, check whether any of the trim panel securing clips were broken on removal, and renew them as necessary.*

   c) *Where applicable, ensure that any wiring (electric mirrors and door-mounted switches) is fed through the holes in the trim panel as it is refitted.*

   d) *To refit the door lock operating button, first lock the door to ensure that the link rod is in its lowest position. Position the button locating tab in the lower of its two holes, then firmly push the button onto the rod, until is clips into position and the retaining tab appears in the upper hole.*

Rear door

Removal

15 Disconnect the battery negative terminal (refer to *Disconnecting the battery* in the Reference Section of this manual).

16 Carefully prise the trim plate from the rear corner of the door **(see illustration)**.

17 On models with manual windows, note the position of the window regulator handle with the window shut, then remove the regulator handle **(see illustration)**. If necessary, use a forked tool, together with a piece of cloth to protect the door trim, to release the handle from the spindle.

12.16 Prise the trim plate from the rear of the door

12.17 Pull off the window regulator handle

18 Where applicable, remove the securing screw, then unclip the hand-grip plate/switch panel from the top of the armrest. If necessary, carefully lever the plate away using a flat-bladed screwdriver. Where applicable, disconnect the wiring from the switches in the panel, and withdraw the panel.

19 Lift up the inner door lock operating button then, using a small screwdriver, depress the retaining tab, and slide off the button.

20 Carefully unclip the door interior handle surround.

21 Proceed as described in paragraphs 11 to 13.

Refitting

22 Refer to paragraph 14.

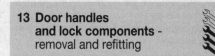

13 Door handles and lock components - removal and refitting

Door interior handle

Removal

1 Remove the door inner trim panel, and the plastic sealing sheet as described in Section 12.

2 Unscrew the interior handle securing screw **(see illustration)**.

3 Slide the handle forwards, then manipulate the handle out from its aperture in the door.

4 Release the securing clip, and disconnect the lock operating rod from the lever on the handle **(see illustration)**.

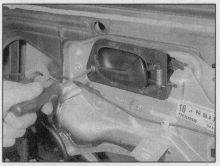

13.2 Unscrew the interior handle securing screw

13.4 Disconnecting the lock operating rod from the door interior handle

11

13.7a Prise out the grommet . . .

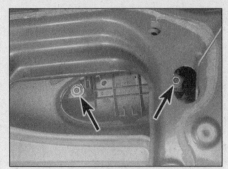

13.7b . . . then unscrew the exterior handle securing nuts (arrowed)

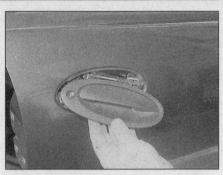

13.8 Withdrawing the exterior handle

Refitting

5 Refitting is a reversal of removal, but refit the plastic sealing sheet and the door inner trim panel with reference to Section 12.

Front door exterior handle

Removal

6 With the window glass fully raised, remove the door inner trim panel, and peel back the sealing sheet, as described in Section 12.

7 Prise out the door lock button operating rod grommet then, working through the door apertures, unscrew the two exterior handle securing nuts **(see illustrations)**.

8 Working through the aperture in the inside of the door, use a screwdriver to release the securing clips at the bottom of the handle, then manipulate the handle out from the door, and disconnect the lock operating rods **(see illustration)**.

13.12a Prise the securing clip from the rear of the lock cylinder . . .

Refitting

9 Refitting is a reversal of removal, bearing in mind the following points.

a) Reconnect the lock operating rod to the lock cylinder in the handle assembly before refitting the assembly to the door.

b) Ensure that the handle locating tabs engage with the lug on the door.

c) Refit the plastic sealing sheet and the door trim panel with reference to Section 12.

Rear door exterior handle

10 The removal and refitting procedures are as described previously for the front door exterior handle, except that to enable removal of the rear exterior handle, the door lock assembly must first be removed as described later in this Section.

Front door lock cylinder

Removal

11 Remove the door exterior handle as described previously in this Section.

12 Prise the securing clip from the rear of the lock cylinder, then withdraw the assembly from the handle **(see illustrations)**.

Refitting

13 Refitting is a reversal of removal but refit the door exterior handle as described previously in this Section.

Door lock

Note: *If the door lock is separated from the mounting plate, new securing rivets will be required on refitting.*

Removal

14 Remove the door inner trim panel and the plastic sealing sheet, referring to Section 12.

15 To improve access, remove the door interior and exterior handles as described previously in this Section.

16 Remove the door window glass as described in Section 14.

17 Unclip the window glass rear guide rail from the inside of the door **(see illustration)**.

18 Temporarily refit the window regulator handle, or reconnect the battery negative lead and the electronic control unit and switch, as applicable, and move the window regulator mechanism so that the window glass support rail is at approximately the half-open position.

19 Working at the rear edge of the door, unscrew the three lock securing screws **(see illustration)**.

20 Reach inside the door, and disconnect any lock operating rods as necessary, noting their locations and routing to aid refitting.

21 Where applicable, release the wiring clips from the door mechanism mounting plate **(see illustration)**.

22 Unscrew the five screws securing the door mechanism mounting plate to the inner door skin, then manipulate the mounting plate, complete with the lock, out through the door aperture **(see illustrations)**. Disconnect the wiring plugs from the lock motor and the window regulator motor, as applicable, as the assembly is withdrawn.

23 To separate the lock from the mounting plate, drill out the two securing rivets **(see illustration)**.

13.12b . . . then withdraw the assembly from the handle

13.17 Unclip the window glass rear guide rail from the door

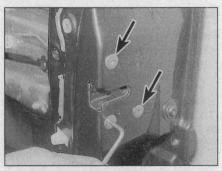

13.19 Unscrew the three lock securing screws

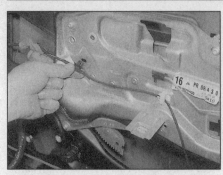

13.21 Release the wiring clips from the door mechanism mounting plate

13.22a Door mechanism mounting plate securing screws (arrowed)

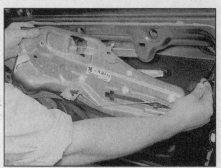

13.22b Removing the door mechanism mounting plate

Refitting

24 Refitting is a reversal of removal, bearing in mind the following points **(see illustration)**.

a) *Where applicable, use new rivets to secure the lock to the mounting plate.*

b) *Ensure that the lock button operating rod passes through the hole in door when refitting the assembly.*

c) *Ensure that the lug on the top of the door mechanism mounting plate engages with the corresponding hole in the door.*

d) *When refitting the mounting plate/lock assembly to the door, tighten the three lock-to-door screws before tightening the mounting plate-to-door screws.*

e) *Ensure that all lock operating rods are correctly reconnected and routed as noted before removal.*

f) *Ensure that the window glass rear guide rail is correctly located inside the door.*

g) *Refit the door window glass as described in Section 14.*

h) *Refit the door interior and exterior handles as described previously in this Section.*

l) *Refit the plastic sealing sheet and the door inner trim panel (see Section 12).*

---

14 Door window glass and regulator - removal and refitting

Front door window glass

Removal

1 Fully close the window.

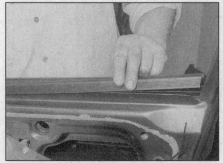

14.3 Unclip the weatherstrip from the window aperture

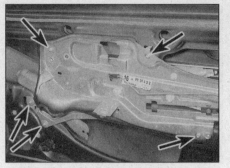

13.23 Door lock securing rivets (arrowed)

2 Remove the door inner trim panel and the plastic sealing sheet as described in Section 12.

3 Unclip the inner weatherstrip from the lower edge of the window aperture **(see illustration)**.

4 Support the window glass (the glass can be secured to the top of the door frame using strong adhesive tape) then, working at the top of the door aperture, remove the two screws securing the glass to the regulator mechanism **(see illustration)**.

5 Temporarily refit the window regulator handle, or reconnect the battery negative lead and the electronic control unit and switch, as applicable, and move the window regulator mechanism so that the window glass support rail is fully lowered.

6 Lift the glass out through the outside of the window aperture by tilting it forwards.

Refitting

7 Refitting is a reversal of removal, but ensure

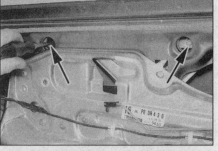

14.4 Remove the two screws (arrowed) securing the glass to the regulator mechanism

13.24 Ensure that the lug (arrowed) engages with the hole in the door

that the weatherstrip is securely refitted, and refit the plastic sheet and the door inner trim panel with reference to Section 12.

Rear door window glass

Removal

8 Proceed as described in paragraphs 1 to 3.

9 Working at the rear outside corner of the door, remove the exterior trim plate, by pushing it firmly upwards to release the lower edge from the door **(see illustration)**.

10 Proceed as described in paragraphs 4 to 6.

Refitting

11 Refitting is a reversal of removal, but ensure that the weatherstrip is securely refitted, and refit the plastic sheet and the door inner trim panel with reference to Section 12.

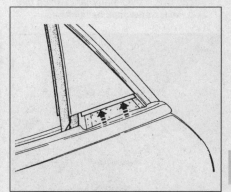

14.9 Remove the exterior trim plate from the rear corner of the door

11

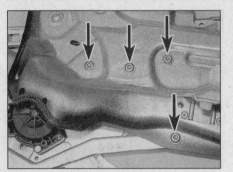

14.15a Unscrew the four securing screws (arrowed) . . .

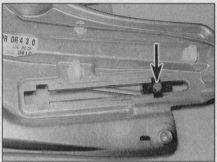

14.15b . . . then slide the regulator runner (arrowed) from the slot

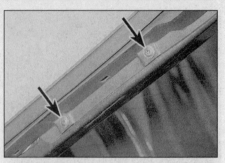

15.3 Unscrew the screws (arrowed) and remove the plastic wiring housing - Hatchback models

Door window regulator

Removal

Note: *On some models, the regulator mechanism is integral with the door mechanism mounting plate, and cannot be removed independently. Check with a Renault dealer on the availability of spares before attempting to remove a regulator assembly.*

12 Remove the door window glass as described previously in this Section.

13 Remove the door lock assembly, as described in Section 13.

14 On some models, the regulator mechanism is integral with the door mechanism mounting plate (removed complete with the lock), and cannot be renewed independently. If the regulator mechanism is faulty, the complete door mechanism mounting plate assembly must be renewed.

15 On models with a renewable regulator mechanism, unscrew the four screws securing the assembly to the mounting plate, then slide the regulator runner from the slots in the mounting plate, and withdraw the assembly **(see illustrations)**.

16 On some models with electric windows, the regulator motors can be renewed with reference to Section 19.

Refitting

17 Refitting is a reversal of removal, bearing in mind the following points.

a) *Refit the door mechanism mounting plate/lock assembly as described in Section 13, noting the order in which the securing screws must be tightened.*

b) *Refit the door window glass as described previously in this Section.*

c) *Refit the plastic sealing sheet and the door trim panel with reference to Section 12.*

15 Tailgate and support struts - removal, refitting and adjustment

Tailgate - Hatchback models

Removal

1 Disconnect the battery negative terminal (refer to *Disconnecting the battery* in the Reference Section of this manual).

2 Remove the securing screws, and withdraw the tailgate rear (inner) trim panel.

3 Working at the left-hand side of the tailgate, unscrew the securing screws, and release the plastic wiring housing **(see illustration)**.

4 Disconnect the wiring from all electrical components mounted in the tailgate.

5 Release the wiring from any clips inside the tailgate.

6 Pull the wiring grommet from the apertures in the tailgate.

7 If the original tailgate is to be refitted, tie a length of string to the ends of all relevant wiring, then feed the wiring through the top of the tailgate. Untie the string, leaving it in position in the tailgate to assist refitting.

8 Support the tailgate, then prise out the support strut spring clips, and pull the struts from the balljoints on the tailgate **(see illustration)**.

9 Unscrew the nut on each side of the tailgate, securing the splined hinge-pin in position.

10 Using a pin-punch, drive out the hinge-pins **(see illustration)**.

11 Unscrew the bolt on each side securing the tailgate to the hinge, then carefully lift the tailgate from the vehicle.

Refitting and adjustment

12 If a new tailgate is to be fitted, transfer all serviceable components (lock components, wiper motor, etc) to it.

13 Refitting is a reversal of removal, bearing in mind the following points **(see illustration)**.

a) *If the original tailgate is refitted, draw the wiring through the tailgate using the string.*

b) *If necessary, adjust the plastic buffers to obtain a good fit when the tailgate is shut. The position of the buffers can be altered by loosening the securing screws.*

c) *If necessary, adjust the position of the tailgate lock striker within its elongated holes to achieve satisfactory lock operation (remove the luggage compartment rear trim panel for access to the lock striker).*

Tailgate - Estate models

Removal

14 Disconnect the battery negative terminal (refer to *Disconnecting the battery* in the Reference Section of this manual).

15 Remove the securing screws, and withdraw the tailgate inner trim panel.

16 Disconnect the wiring from all electrical components mounted in the tailgate.

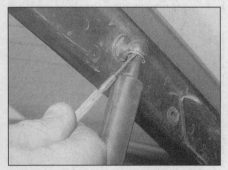

15.8 Prise out the support strut spring clips - Hatchback models

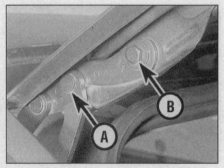

15.10 Tailgate hinge pin (A) and bolt (B) - Hatchback models

15.13 Tailgate plastic buffer adjustment screw (arrowed) - Hatchback models

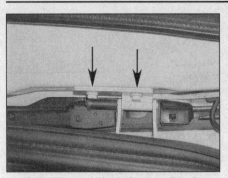

15.21 Unscrew the bolts securing the tailgate to the hinges - Estate models

17 Release the wiring from any clips inside the tailgate.
18 Pull the wiring grommet from the apertures in the tailgate.
19 If the original tailgate is to be refitted, tie a length of string to the ends of all relevant wiring, then feed the wiring through the top of the tailgate. Untie the string, leaving it in position in the tailgate to assist refitting.
20 Support the tailgate, then prise out the support strut spring clips, and pull the struts from the balljoints on the tailgate.
21 Unscrew the bolts on each side securing the tailgate to the hinge, then carefully lift the tailgate from the vehicle (see illustration).

Refitting and adjustment

22 If a new tailgate is to be fitted, transfer all serviceable components (lock components, wiper motor, etc) to it.

16.2 Removing a tailgate rear trim panel side securing screw - Hatchback models

15.26 Releasing a tailgate support strut lower spring clip

23 Refitting is a reversal of removal, bearing in mind the following points.

a) If the original tailgate is refitted, draw the wiring through the tailgate using the string.

b) If necessary, adjust the plastic buffers to obtain a good fit when the tailgate is shut. The position of the buffers can be altered by loosening the securing screws.

c) If necessary, adjust the position of the tailgate lock striker within its elongated holes to achieve satisfactory lock operation (remove the luggage compartment rear trim panel for access to the lock striker).

Support strut

Removal

24 Support the tailgate in the open position, with the help of an assistant, or using a stout piece of wood.
25 Using a suitable flat-bladed screwdriver, release the spring clip, and pull the support strut from its balljoint on the tailgate.
26 Similarly, release the strut from the balljoint on the body, and withdraw the strut from the vehicle (see illustration).

Refitting

27 Refitting is a reversal of removal, but ensure that the spring clips are correctly engaged.

16 Tailgate lock components - removal and refitting

Lock

Removal

1 Disconnect the battery negative terminal (refer to *Disconnecting the battery* in the Reference Section of this manual).
2 Remove the securing screws, and withdraw the tailgate rear (inner) trim panel. Note that it will be necessary to remove the rear light access panels for access to the side securing screws. Note also that one of the trim panel securing screws is located in the recess in the panel above the tailgate lock (see illustration).
3 Working through the aperture in the tailgate, disconnect the operating rod from the lock cylinder assembly (see illustration).
4 Remove the three securing screws, and withdraw the lock from the tailgate. Where applicable, disconnect the wiring plug from the lock as it is withdrawn (see illustration).

Refitting

5 Refitting is a reversal of removal, but check the operation of the lock on completion, and if necessary adjust the position of the lock striker within its elongated holes to achieve satisfactory lock operation.

Lock cylinder

Removal

6 Remove the securing screws, and withdraw the tailgate rear (inner) trim panel.
7 Working through the aperture in the tailgate, unscrew the two lock cylinder securing nuts.
8 Disconnect the lock operating rod and the central locking motor wiring plug, then withdraw the lock cylinder assembly (see illustration). Note that on Estate models, considerable manipulation is necessary to allow the lock cylinder to pass through the aperture in the tailgate. Try it one way, then the other, go for a cup of coffee and come back and try again. Eventually it will come free!

16.3 Disconnecting the operating rod from the lock cylinder assembly - Hatchback models

16.4 Disconnecting the wiring plug from the tailgate lock - Hatchback models

16.8 Withdrawing the tailgate lock cylinder assembly - Hatchback models

11

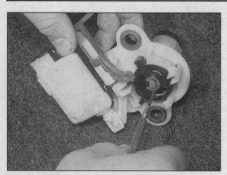

16.9a Prise off the circlip . . .

16.9b . . . then lift off the lock lever . . .

16.9c . . . and slide out the lock cylinder

9 To separate the lock cylinder from the housing, prise the circlip from the rear of the lock, then lift off the lock lever and slide out the lock cylinder **(see illustrations)**.

Refitting

10 Refitting is a reversal of removal, but check the operation of the lock before refitting the tailgate trim panel. If the lock cylinder has been separated from the housing, ensure that the lock lever is located behind the metal lock operating lever on refitting.

Lock striker

Removal

11 Working in the luggage compartment, remove the securing screws and clips, and withdraw the luggage compartment rear trim panel.
12 Unscrew the securing bolts, and remove the striker.

Refitting

13 Refitting is a reversal of removal, but check the operation of the lock on completion, and if necessary adjust the position of the lock striker within its elongated holes to achieve satisfactory lock operation.

HAYNES HINT

If the fuel filler flap release cable is broken, the flap can be opened by unclipping the right-hand rear light bulb access panel, and pulling out the sound insulation panel, then pulling on the now-exposed red release handle

17 Fuel filler flap lock and release cable - removal and refitting

Note: *If the fuel filler flap release cable is broken, refer to the* **Haynes Hint**.

Removal

1 Working in the passenger compartment, next to the driver's seat, unclip the trim plate from the fuel flap release handle to expose the handle securing screw **(see illustration)**.
2 Remove the securing screw, then slide the handle forwards to remove it from the lever assembly.
3 Pull back the carpet panel to expose the lever assembly securing nuts, then unscrew the nuts.
4 Working inside the car, remove the sill trim panels to expose the cable (see Section 26).
5 Similarly, working in the luggage compartment, remove the side trim panels (see Section 26). On left-hand-drive models, it will be necessary to remove the trim panels on both sides of the luggage compartment, and also the luggage compartment rear trim panel.
6 Open the fuel filler flap then unscrew the nut securing the filler flap lock **(see illustration)**.
7 Release the cable from the clips on the body. Note the routing of the cable to aid refitting.
8 Reach in through the aperture in the rear wing panel, then withdraw the lock assembly, and feed the cable through until the assembly

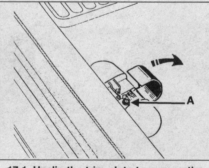

17.1 Unclip the trim plate to expose the fuel flap release handle securing screw (A)

can be withdrawn. The lock and cable are integral, and cannot be separated.

Refitting

9 Refitting is a reversal of removal, bearing in mind the following points.
a) *Ensure that the cable is routed as noted before removal.*
b) *Check the operation of the release mechanism before refitting the trim panels.*

18 Central locking system components - removal and refitting

Door lock motor

Removal

1 Remove the door lock as described in Section 13.
2 The lock motor can be removed from the lock by driving out the securing roll-pin, and disconnecting the lock operating lever. Check with a Renault dealer regarding the availability of spares before removing the motor.

Refitting

3 Refitting is a reversal of removal, but refit the door lock as described in Section 13.

Tailgate lock motor

Removal

4 Remove the tailgate lock cylinder as described in Section 16.

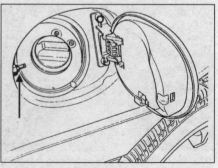

17.6 Fuel filler flap lock securing nut (arrowed)

18.5 Unscrewing a tailgate lock motor securing screw

18.9 Removing the central locking electronic control unit

18.15 Removing the central locking remote control receiver unit

5 Remove the securing screws, then withdraw the motor from the lock cylinder (see illustration).

Refitting

6 Refitting is a reversal of removal, but ensure that the lock motor operating lever engages correctly with the lock cylinder, and refit the lock cylinder as described in Section 16.

Electronic control unit

Removal

7 The control unit is mounted behind the driver's side sill trim panel.
8 Where applicable remove the securing screw, then pull back the front edge of the driver's side sill trim panel to expose the control unit.
9 Push the unit upwards to release it from its mounting (see illustration).
10 Depress the securing clips and disconnect the control unit wiring connectors.
11 Withdraw the unit from the sill.

Refitting

12 Refitting is a reversal of removal, but ensure that the control unit is securely clipped into position.

Remote control receiver unit

Removal

13 The receiver unit is integral with the receiver cover, and the ultrasonic intruder sensors, where applicable.
14 Disconnect the battery negative lead.
15 Slide the receiver unit/cover forwards from the roof console panel and remove the unit (see illustration).
16 Disconnect the wiring plug from the receiver unit, then unclip the unit from the roof console.

Refitting

17 Refitting is a reversal of removal.

Remote control transmitter batteries - renewal

18 Remove the securing screw, and separate the two halves of the transmitter unit.
19 Remove the two batteries, noting which way round they are fitted.
20 Fit the two new batteries, ensuring that they are fitted the correct way round; the

battery and transmitter terminals are marked '+' and '-' to avoid confusion.
21 Clip the transmitter back together and refit the securing screw.

---

19 Electric window components - removal and refitting

Window switches

1 Refer to Chapter 12, Section 4.

Window regulator motors

Removal

Note: *On some models, the motors are integral with the regulator mechanism, and cannot be renewed independently. Check with a Renault dealer on the availability of spares before attempting to remove a motor.*

2 On models where the regulator mechanism and motor is integral with the door mechanism mounting plate, the complete door mechanism mounting plate/lock assembly must be renewed as described in Section 13.
3 On models where the motor can be renewed, remove the door mechanism mounting plate/lock assembly as described in Section 13, then remove the securing screws and withdraw the motor assembly.

Refitting

4 Refitting is a reversal of removal, but refit the door mechanism mounting plate/lock assembly with reference to Section 13.

19.6 Electric windows electronic control unit (arrowed)

Electronic control unit

General

5 Certain models are fitted with an additional control unit, which is integral with the central locking electronic control unit (see Section 18), and automatically closes the windows and the sunroof if they are left open. The windows and sunroof are automatically closed when the central locking remote control transmitter is operated by holding the button down for at least two seconds.

Removal

6 The control unit is located on the driver's door, behind the door inner trim panel (see illustration).
7 Disconnect the battery negative terminal (refer to *Disconnecting the battery* in the Reference Section of this manual).
8 Remove the door inner trim panel as described in Section 12.
9 Disconnect the control unit wiring plug.
10 Remove the two securing screws, and withdraw the control unit from the door.

Refitting

11 Refitting is a reversal of removal, but refit the door inner trim panel with reference to Section 12.

---

20 Exterior mirrors and associated components - removal and refitting

Manually-adjustable mirror

Removal

1 Working at the inside edge of the door, unclip the front edge of the mirror trim plate from the door, then pull the trim plate rearwards to release it from the door. Note that the mirror adjustment lever cover is integral with the trim plate.
2 Unscrew the nut securing the mirror control cable to the mirror cover plate (see illustration overleaf).
3 Unscrew the three securing screws, and remove the mirror cover plate.
4 Remove the cover plug from the front edge of the door trim panel.

11

20.2 Mirror control cable securing nut (A) and mirror cover plate securing screws (B)

5 Support the mirror, then unscrew the two nuts and the bolt (accessible through the aperture in the door trim panel) securing the mirror to the door.
6 Take great care not to drop the nuts and screws into the door behind the trim panel.
7 Lift the mirror from the door, and where applicable disconnect the wiring from the outside temperature sensor mounted in the mirror housing.

Refitting

8 Refitting is a reversal of removal, but ensure that the mirror locating pin engages with the corresponding hole in the edge of the door.

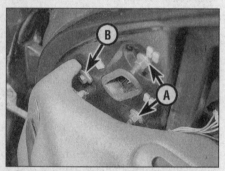

20.13a Unscrew the two nuts (A) and the bolt (B) . . .

20.13b . . . then remove the mirror

20.11 Removing the mirror cover plate

Electric mirror

Removal

9 Disconnect the battery negative terminal (refer to *Disconnecting the battery* in the Reference Section of this manual).
10 Working at the inside edge of the door, unclip the edge of the mirror trim plate from the door, then pull the trim plate rearwards to release it from the door.
11 Unscrew the three securing screws, and remove the mirror cover plate **(see illustration)**.
12 Disconnect the mirror wiring connector **(see illustration)**.
13 Proceed as described in paragraphs 4 to 7 **(see illustrations)**.

Refitting

14 Refitting is a reversal of removal, but ensure that the mirror locating pins engage with the corresponding holes in the edge of the door.

Mirror glass

Removal

15 Tilt the mirror assembly outwards (towards the front of the vehicle).
16 Press carefully on the outside edge of the mirror glass, until it is possible to insert your fingers under the inside edge of the glass **(see illustration)**.
17 Carefully pull the inside edge of the glass until the clips release. Take care not to break the glass.
18 Withdraw the glass and, where applic-

20.16 Press on the outside edge of the glass until it is possible to insert your fingers under the inside edge of the glass

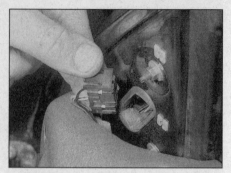

20.12 Disconnecting the mirror wiring connector

able, disconnect the heating element wires from the rear of the glass.

Refitting

19 Where applicable, reconnect the wires to the rear of the glass.
20 Align the glass locating lugs with the corresponding holes in the mirror assembly, then carefully push the glass into position until the securing clips engage.

Mirror rear cover

Removal

21 Remove the mirror glass, as described previously in this Section.
22 Working at the outer edge of the mirror housing, release the two securing clips, then pull the outer edge of the mirror rear cover back until the securing lug at the inner edge of the cover is released from the housing **(see illustration)**.

Refitting

23 Refitting is a reversal of removal, but ensure that the inner securing lug is engaged with the housing before pushing the outer edge of the cover into position.

21 Windscreen, tailgate and fixed side window glass - general information

These areas of glass are secured by the tight fit of the weatherstrip in the body aperture, and are bonded in position with a special adhesive.

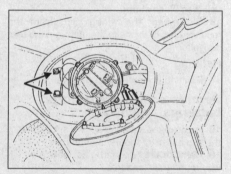

20.22 Mirror rear cover outer securing clips (arrowed)

23.11 Unscrew the two scuttle panel securing screws on each side

23.13 Unclip the weatherstrip from the scuttle panel

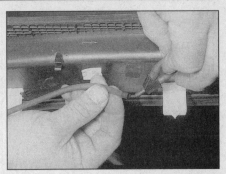

23.15 Disconnect the washer fluid hose from the adapter

Renewal of such fixed glass is a difficult, messy and time-consuming task, which is considered beyond the scope of the home mechanic. It is difficult, unless one has plenty of practice, to obtain a secure, waterproof fit. Furthermore, the task carries a high risk of breakage; this applies especially to the laminated glass windscreen. In view of this, owners are strongly advised to have this sort of work carried out by one of the many specialist windscreen fitters.

22 Sunroof - general information

> **HAYNES HINT**
>
> *If the sunroof mechanism is faulty, and the roof panel is stuck open, the panel can be closed manually as follows.*
> a) *Remove the roof console panel as described in Section 26.*
> b) *Insert a 4 mm Allen key in the hole provided in the sunroof motor spindle, then use the Allen key to turn the motor and close the roof panel.*

The factory-fitted sunroof is of the electric tilt/slide type.

Due to the complexity of the sunroof mechanism, considerable expertise is required to repair, replace or adjust the sunroof components successfully. Removal of the roof first requires the headlining to be removed, which is not a task to be undertaken lightly. Therefore, any problems with this type of sunroof should be referred to a Renault dealer.

23 Body exterior fittings - removal and refitting

Radiator grille panel

1 Refer to Section 7.

Rear spoiler

Removal

2 Open the tailgate, then remove the securing

screws and withdraw the tailgate (interior) rear trim panel.
3 Unscrew the two spoiler centre nuts.
4 Working at each corner of the tailgate, unscrew the two side spoiler securing screws on each side.
5 Lift the spoiler from the tailgate.

Refitting

6 Refitting is a reversal of removal.

Centre body pillar trim panel

Removal

7 Open both the front and rear doors.
8 Unscrew the two upper securing screws, and the lower securing screw and remove the trim panel.

Refitting

9 Refitting is a reversal of removal.

Scuttle cover panel(s)

Removal

10 Remove the wiper arms as described in Chapter 12. A lever may be required for wiper arm removal.
11 Unscrew the two screws at each side, securing the scuttle cover panel to the scuttle **(see illustration)**.
12 On later models with two-piece scuttle cover panels, unscrew the centre panel securing screw.
13 Unclip the weatherstrip from the edge of the scuttle panel **(see illustration)**.
14 Pull the scuttle panel forwards to release the rear clips securing the panel under the windscreen. Take care not to break the clips.
15 Disconnect the windscreen washer jet hose from the adapter, then withdraw the scuttle cover panel **(see illustration)**.

Refitting

16 Refitting is a reversal of removal, ensuring that the panel securing clips are securely engaged under the windscreen.

Wheel arch liners, mud shields and engine undershield

17 The wheel arch liners and engine undershield (where applicable) are secured by a combination of self-tapping screws, and push-fit clips. Removal is self-evident, and normally the clips can be released by pulling

the liner away from the wheel arch.
18 The mud shields are secured in a similar manner, although certain panels may be secured using pop-rivets. Where applicable, drill out the pop-rivets, and use new rivets on refitting.

Body trim strips and badges

19 The various body trim strips and badges are held in position with a special adhesive tape. Removal requires the trim/badge to be heated, to soften the adhesive, and then cut away from the surface. Due to the high risk of damage to the vehicle paintwork during this operation, it is recommended that this task should be entrusted to a Renault dealer.

24 Seats - removal and refitting

Front seat

> ⚠️ **Warning: On models fitted with seat belt tensioners, observe the following precautions before attempting to remove the seat.**
> a) *Remove the ignition key.*
> b) *Disconnect the battery negative terminal (refer to Disconnecting the battery in the Reference Section of this manual), and wait for five minutes before carrying out any further work.*
> c) *Disconnect the wiring plugs from the seat belt tensioner/air bag electronic control unit (see Chapter 12).*

Removal

1 On models fitted with seat belt tensioners, disconnect the battery negative terminal (refer to *Disconnecting the battery* in the Reference Section of this manual), and observe the precautions given at the start of this Section.
2 Apply the handbrake, then jack up the front of the vehicle and support securely on axle stands (see *Jacking and vehicle support*).
3 Working under the vehicle, remove the securing bolts and withdraw the intermediate exhaust heat shield to expose the rear inner seat securing bolt.
4 Again working under the vehicle, unscrew the four seat securing bolts **(see illustration)**.

11

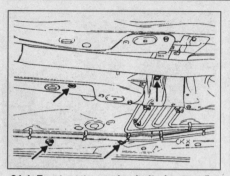

24.4 Front seat securing bolts (arrowed) - viewed with intermediate exhaust heat shield removed

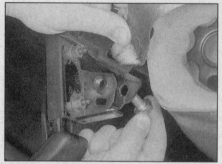

24.8 Removing the seat belt lower anchor bolt from the front seat

24.12 Seat back securing nut (arrowed)

5 On models fitted with seat belt tensioners, separate the two halves of the connector under the seat.

6 Working inside the vehicle, lift out the seat, and tilt it for access to the lower seat belt anchor bolt.

7 Unscrew the two securing screws (located at the side and rear of the panel), then lift up the rear of the seat side trim panel, and slide the panel forwards to remove it from the seat.

8 Prise off the plastic cap, then unscrew the now-exposed lower seat belt anchor bolt **(see illustration)**.

9 Disconnect the lower seat belt anchor from the seat, then lift the seat from the vehicle.

⚠️ **Warning: Do not tamper with the pre-tensioner unit in any way, and do not attempt to test the unit. Note that the unit is triggered if the mechanism is supplied with an electrical**

current (including via an ohmmeter), or if the assembly is subjected to a temperature of greater than 100°C.

Refitting

10 Refitting is a reversal of removal, but ensure that the lug on the lower seat belt anchor plate engages with the corresponding hole in the seat frame, and tighten the anchor bolt to the specified torque.

Rear seat back

Removal

11 Fold the rear seat cushion forwards.

12 Working at the bottom of the seat back, remove the securing nuts **(see illustration)**.

13 Unclip the seat belts from the seat back, then release the upper securing catches, and withdraw the seat back, feeding the seat belts over it as it is withdrawn.

Refitting

14 Refitting is a reversal of removal.

Rear seat cushion

Removal

15 Fold the seat cushion forwards, then slide the plastic clips from the hinges, and pull the cushion upwards to release it from the hinges.

Refitting

16 Refitting is a reversal of removal.

---

25 Seat belt components - removal and refitting

Front seat belt

Removal

1 To improve access, remove the front seat as described in Section 24.

2 Pull the button from the seat belt height adjuster lever on the body pillar **(see illustration)**.

3 Prise off the trim, and unscrew the seat belt upper anchor bolt. Note that the bolt is captive in the upper anchor plate **(see illustration)**.

4 Open the front and rear doors, and unclip the weatherstrips from the edges of the centre pillar trim panels.

5 Pull the top of the upper centre pillar trim panel away from the pillar to release the securing clips, then withdraw the panel upwards to release it from the bottom panel **(see illustration)**.

6 If not already done, unscrew the two securing screws, then lift up the rear of the seat side trim panel, and slide the panel forwards to remove it from the nut. Prise off the plastic cap, then unscrew the now-exposed lower seat belt anchor bolt.

7 Unclip the sill trim panels (where necessary, remove the securing screws) from the lower centre pillar trim panel **(see illustration)**.

8 Where applicable, unscrew the securing screws from the lower centre pillar trim panel, then withdraw the panel **(see illustrations)**.

9 Unscrew the inertia reel securing bolt, then

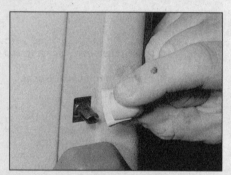

25.2 Pull the button from the seat belt height adjuster

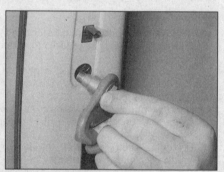

25.3 Unscrew the seat belt upper anchor bolt

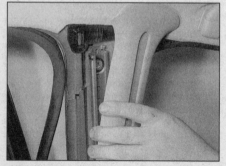

25.5 Withdraw the upper centre pillar trim panel

25.7 Unclip the sill trim panels

25.8a Unscrew the upper . . .

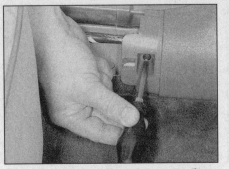

25.8b . . . and lower securing screws from the lower centre pillar trim panel

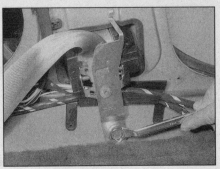

25.9 Unscrewing the front seat belt inertia reel securing bolt

tilt the assembly upwards to release the upper securing lug, and withdraw the seat belt assembly **(see illustration)**.

Refitting

10 Refitting is a reversal of removal, but tighten all seat belt mountings to the specified torque.

Front seat belt stalk/seat belt tensioner

⚠ *Warning: On models fitted with seat belt tensioners, observe the following precautions before attempting to remove the seat belt stalk.*
a) Remove the ignition key.
b) Disconnect the battery negative terminal (refer to Disconnecting the battery in the Reference Section of this manual), and wait for five minutes before carrying out any further work.

c) Disconnect the wiring plugs from the seat belt tensioner/air bag electronic control unit (see Chapter 12).

Removal

11 To improve access, remove seat as described in Section 24.
12 On models fitted with front seat belt tensioners, disconnect the battery negative terminal (refer to *Disconnecting the battery* in the Reference Section of this manual), and observe the precautions given at the start of this Section.
13 Unscrew the trim panel securing screw, then unscrew the seat belt stalk securing bolt, and remove the plastic trim panel and the seat belt stalk from the seat **(see illustration)**.
14 On models with seat belt tensioners, the tensioner assembly is attached to the trim panel. Pull the tensioner from the trim panel, and unclip the tensioner wiring from the trim

plate. Pull the tape from the tensioner wiring connector, then disconnect the connector, and remove the tensioner.

⚠ *Warning: Do not tamper with the pre-tensioner unit in any way, and do not attempt to test the unit. Note that the unit is triggered if the mechanism is supplied with an electrical current (including via an ohmmeter), or if the assembly is subjected to a temperature of greater than 100°C.*

Refitting

15 Refitting is a reversal of removal, but tighten the stalk securing bolt to the specified torque, and refit the seat with reference to Section 24.

Rear side seat belt

Removal

16 Fold the rear seat cushion forwards to expose the seat belt lower anchor bolt, then unscrew the bolt **(see illustration)**.
17 On Estate models, remove the luggage compartment trim panel as described in Section 26 for access to the inertia reel. On Hatchback models, fold down the rear seat back, then unscrew the rear parcel shelf support panel securing screws. Two screws are located at the rear of the panel, and one screw at the front of the panel **(see illustration)**.
18 Carefully prise the securing clip from the side of the front of the panel, then unclip the panel from the body **(see illustration)**.
19 Remove securing screws, and withdraw the luggage compartment rear corner trim panel **(see illustration)**.

25.13 Removing the trim panel and the seat belt stalk from the front seat

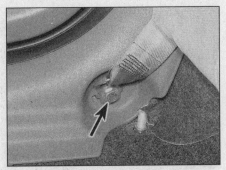

25.16 Unscrew the seat belt lower anchor bolt

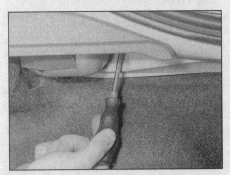

25.17 Unscrewing the parcel shelf support panel rear securing screws

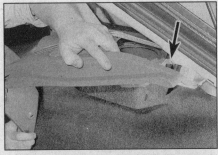

25.18 Unclipping the parcel shelf support panel from the body. Note rear locating lug (arrowed)

25.19 Withdraw the luggage compartment rear corner trim panel

11

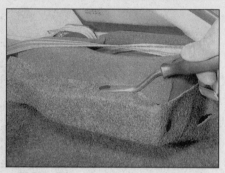

25.20a Prise out the securing clips . . .

20 Prise out the securing clips, and pull the luggage compartment side trim from the body **(see illustrations)**.
21 Twist the loudspeaker anti-clockwise to release it from the body panel, then lift out the insulating foam, noting its orientation **(see illustrations)**.
22 Unscrew the now-exposed inertia reel securing bolt **(see illustrations)**.
23 Working at the front of the parcel shelf side support panel, unclip the seat belt surround from the panel.
24 Feed the seat belt webbing, buckle and lower anchor plate through the parcel shelf side support panel, then withdraw the seat belt from the vehicle.

Refitting

25 Refitting is a reversal of removal, but ensure that all seat belt mountings are tightened to the specified torque given at the start of this Chapter.

25.21a Remove the loudspeaker . . .

25.22 . . . then unscrew the inertia reel securing bolt (arrowed)

25.20b . . . and pull the side trim panel from the body

Rear centre seat belt

26 The procedure is as described previously for the rear side seat belts, noting that there is no need to feed the belt through the trim panel, and that the inertia reel securing bolt is accessed from underneath the assembly **(see illustration)**.

Rear seat belt stalks

Removal

27 The assemblies can simply be unbolted from the floor panel, after folding the rear seat cushion forwards. Note the locations of any washers and/or spacers to ensure correct refitting.

Refitting

28 Refitting is a reversal of removal. Ensure that all washers and/or spacers are positioned as noted before removal, and tighten all mounting bolts to the specified torque.

25.21b . . . and the insulating foam . . .

25.26 Unscrewing the rear centre seat belt inertia reel securing bolt

26 Interior trim - removal and refitting

General

1 The interior trim panels are secured by a combination of clips and screws. Removal and refitting is generally self-explanatory, noting that it may be necessary to remove or loosen surrounding panels to allow a particular panel to be removed. The following paragraphs describe the removal and refitting of the major panels in more detail.

Door trim panels

2 Refer to Section 12.

Sill trim panels

Front panel

3 If desired, to improve access, remove the front seat, as described in Section 24.
4 Open the front door and carefully unclip the weatherstrip from the edge of the panel.
5 Pull the panel from the sill to release the securing clips.
6 Refitting is a reversal of removal, but make sure that the weatherstrip is correctly refitted.

Rear panel

7 Open the front door and carefully unclip the weatherstrip from the edge of the panel.
8 Fold the rear seat cushion forwards, then unscrew the lower seat belt anchor bolt from the panel.
9 Fold the rear seat back down, and unscrew the sill trim panel securing screws.
10 Unscrew the lower securing screw from the rear parcel shelf side support panel.
11 Pull the panel from the body to release the securing clips, then manipulate the panel out.
12 Refitting is a reversal of removal, but ensure that the weatherstrips are securely clipped into position, and tighten the seat belt anchor bolt to the specified torque.

Centre pillar trim panels

Removal

13 Carefully pull the button from the seat belt height adjuster lever.
14 Prise off the trim, and unscrew the seat belt upper anchor bolt.
15 Open the front and rear doors, and unclip the weatherstrips from the edges of the centre pillar trim panels.
16 Pull the top of the upper centre pillar trim panel away from the pillar to release the securing clips, then withdraw the panel upwards to release it from the bottom panel.
17 Unclip the sill trim panels (where necessary, remove the securing screws) from the lower centre pillar trim panel.
18 Where applicable, unscrew the securing screws from the lower centre pillar trim panel, then withdraw the panel.

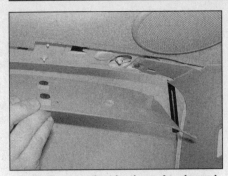

26.27 Remove the plastic roof end panel from the upper centre of the tailgate aperture - Estate models

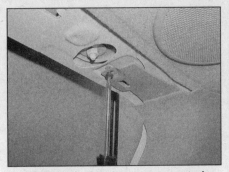

26.28 Undo the screw now exposed securing the upper rear corner of the side trim panel to the roof - Estate models

26.29 Release the access cover and undo the screw (arrowed) in the aperture securing the side trim panel to the rear body pillar - Estate models

Refitting

19 Refitting is a reversal of removal, but tighten the seat belt anchor bolt to the specified torque.

Rear parcel shelf support panel - Hatchback models

Removal

20 Open the tailgate, and fold down the rear seat back.

21 Unscrew the two securing screws from the rear of the panel, and the single screw from the front edge of the panel.

22 Carefully prise the securing clip from the side of the front of the panel.

23 If the panel is to be completely removed from the vehicle, unbolt the rear side seat belt lower anchor bolt, then carefully prise the seat

belt surround from the panel, and feed the seat belt webbing, buckle and anchor plate through the aperture in the panel.

24 Unclip the panel from the body.

Refitting

25 Refitting is a reversal of removal but, where applicable tighten the seat belt anchor bolt to the specified torque, and ensure that the sound-proofing is correctly located.

Luggage compartment trim panels - Estate models

Removal

26 Open the tailgate, and peel back the rubber weatherstrip from the top and sides of the tailgate aperture.

27 Carefully unclip and remove the plastic

roof end panel from the upper centre of the tailgate aperture (see illustration).

28 Undo the screw now exposed securing the upper rear corner of the side trim panel to the roof (see illustration).

29 Release the access cover and undo the screw in the aperture securing the side trim panel to the rear body pillar (see illustration).

30 Release the panel at the rear, and from the side retaining clips under the window, and remove the panel (see illustrations).

31 Undo the screws and remove the seat belt cover panel from the rear door pillar (see illustrations).

32 Peel back the rubber weatherstrip from the rear of the rear door aperture (see illustration).

33 Undo the screw and remove the small plastic trim panel around the rear seat back catch (see illustration).

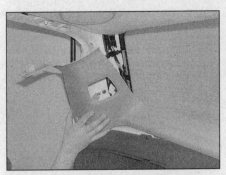

26.30a Release the panel at the rear . . .

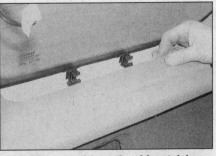

26.30b . . . and from the side retaining clips under the window, and remove the side trim panel - Estate models

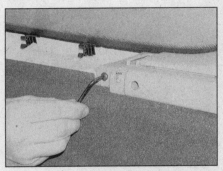

26.31a Undo the screws . . .

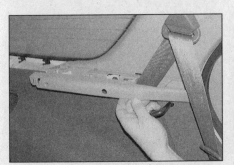

26.31b . . . and remove the seat belt cover panel from the rear door pillar - Estate models

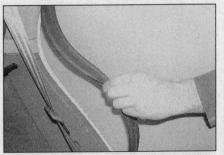

26.32 Peel back the rubber weatherstrip from the rear of the rear door aperture - Estate models

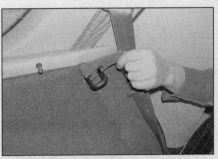

26.33 Undo the screw and remove the small plastic trim panel around the rear seat back catch - Estate models

11

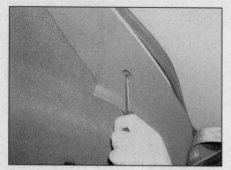

26.34a Undo the screws securing the door rear aperture plastic panel . . .

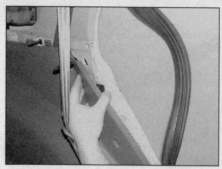

26.34b . . . release the clips and remove the panel - Estate models

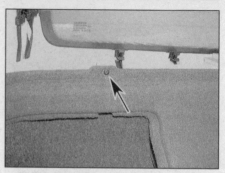

26.36a Undo the screws along the top edge (arrowed) . . .

34 Undo the screws, release the clips and remove the door rear aperture plastic panel **(see illustrations)**.

35 Remove the storage compartment lid on the side trim panel.

36 Undo the screws along the top edge, bottom and rear of the side trim panel **(see illustrations)**.

37 Release the clips and withdraw the panel from the luggage compartment **(see illustration)**.

Refitting

38 Refitting is a reversal of removal ensuring that the retaining clips correctly located.

Tailgate trim panel - Hatchback models

Removal

39 Open the tailgate and prise out the rear light access panels.

40 Undo the trim panel securing screws located on the panel, in the rear light apertures and in the recess in the panel above the tailgate lock.

41 Release the panel retaining clips and remove the panel from the tailgate.

Refitting

42 Refitting is a reversal of removal ensuring that the retaining clips correctly located.

Tailgate trim panel - Estate models

Removal

43 Open the tailgate and carefully prise out the screw caps using a small screwdriver **(see illustration)**.

44 Undo the trim panel securing screws, release the panel retaining clips and remove the panel from the tailgate **(see illustrations)**.

Refitting

45 Refitting is a reversal of removal ensuring that the retaining clips correctly located.

Roof console panel

Removal

46 Disconnect the battery negative terminal (refer to *Disconnecting the battery* in the Reference Section of this manual).

47 Slide the central locking remote control receiver unit cover, or trim panel, as applicable, forwards from the roof console panel.

48 Remove the two now-exposed securing screws, then tilt the console panel down to release the rear clips **(see illustration)**.

49 Disconnect the wiring from the components mounted in the console panel, then withdraw the panel.

Refitting

50 Refitting is a reversal of removal.

26.36b . . . bottom edge (arrowed) . . .

26.36c . . . and rear of the side trim panel . . .

26.37 . . . then release the clips and remove the panel - Estate models

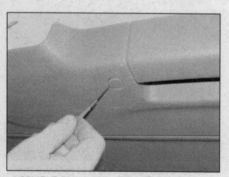

26.43 Prise out the tailgate trim panel screw caps using a small screwdriver

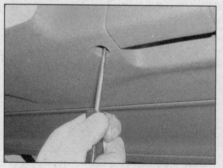

26.44a Undo the trim panel securing screws . . .

26.44b . . . release the panel retaining clips and remove the panel from the tailgate - Estate models

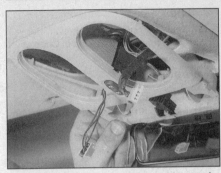

26.48 Removing the roof console panel

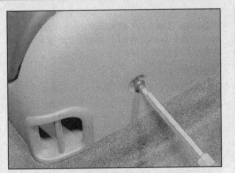

27.2 Unscrewing a centre console rear securing screw

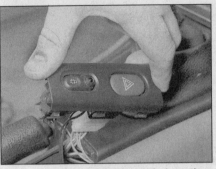

27.3 Prise the switch assembly from the console

Carpets

51 The passenger compartment floor carpet is in several pieces, and is secured along the edges by screws or various types of clips.

52 Carpet removal and refitting is reasonably straightforward, but time-consuming, due to the fact that all adjoining trim panels must be released, and the seats and centre console must be removed.

Headlining

53 The headlining is clipped to the roof, and can be withdrawn only once all fittings such as the grab handles, sun visors, sunroof, windscreen, centre and rear pillar trim panels, and associated components have been removed. The door, tailgate and sunroof aperture weatherstrips will also have to be prised clear.

54 Note that headlining removal requires considerable skill and experience if it is to be carried out without damage, and is therefore best entrusted to an expert.

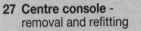

27 Centre console - removal and refitting

Removal

1 Disconnect the battery negative terminal (refer to *Disconnecting the battery* in the Reference Section of this manual).

2 Push the front seats as far forward as possible, then unscrew the two centre console rear securing screws, one screw on each side of the console **(see illustration)**.

3 Carefully prise the switch assembly from

the front of the console, and disconnect the wiring plugs **(see illustration)**.

4 Unclip the trim plate from below the handbrake lever to expose the centre console securing nut. Unscrew the nut **(see illustration)**.

5 Unclip the gear lever gaiter surround/lever trim plate from the top of the centre console **(see illustration)**.

6 Unclip the ashtray from its housing **(see illustration)**.

7 Unscrew the two securing screws, then unclip the ashtray housing from the front of the console (reach in and pull on the bottom edge of the housing), and disconnect the wiring from the cigarette lighter, and the ashtray light, as applicable **(see illustrations)**.

8 Working through the ashtray housing aperture, unscrew the two console front securing screws **(see illustration)**.

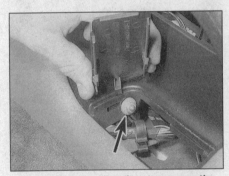

27.4 Unclip the trim plate to expose the console securing nut (arrowed)

27.5 Unclip the gear lever gaiter

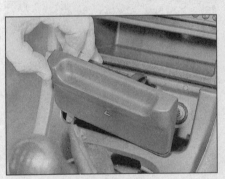

27.6 Unclip the ashtray . . .

27.7a . . . then unscrew the two screws . . .

27.7b . . . and unclip the ashtray housing

27.8 Unscrew the two console front securing screws

11

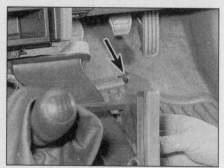

27.9 Removing the centre console - front securing lug arrowed

9 Working at the front of the console, pull the edges of the console outwards to release the securing lugs, then pull the console rearwards to free it from its mountings **(see illustration)**.

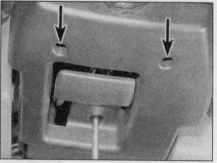

28.2a Remove the three lower steering column shroud securing screws

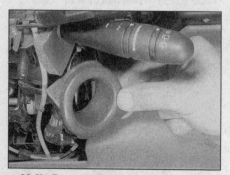

28.2b Recover the ignition switch trim plate

10 Pull the handbrake lever fully up, then withdraw the console. Recover the centre securing bolt and spacer, and the rear securing plates if they are loose.

Refitting

11 Refitting is a reversal of removal, but ensure that the centre securing bolt (complete with spacer) and the locating blocks are in place before offering the console into position.

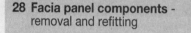

28 Facia panel components - removal and refitting

Steering column shrouds

Removal

1 Remove the steering wheel as described in Chapter 10.
2 Working under the steering column, remove the three securing screws, and withdraw the lower steering column shroud. Recover the trim plate from the ignition switch **(see illustrations)**.
3 Where applicable, unclip the cover from the radio/cassette player remote control switch, then slacken the securing screw **(see illustration)**.
4 Remove the two securing screws, and withdraw the upper steering column shroud **(see illustration)**.

28.3 Unclip the cover from the remote control switch to expose the switch securing screw (arrowed)

Refitting

5 Refitting is a reversal of removal, but refit the steering wheel as described in Chapter 10.

Glovebox

Removal

6 On models fitted with a glovebox light, disconnect the battery negative terminal (refer to *Disconnecting the battery* in the Reference Section of this manual).
7 Open the glovebox then, where applicable, prise out the glovebox light and disconnect the wiring.
8 Remove the upper glovebox securing screws **(see illustration)**.
9 Carefully peel back the lower carpet trim panel to expose the lower glovebox screws.
10 Remove the lower securing screws, and withdraw the glovebox from the facia **(see illustrations)**. Where applicable, disconnect the wiring from the glovebox light switch as the glovebox is withdrawn.

Refitting

11 Refitting is a reversal of removal.

Glovebox lock barrel

Removal

12 Remove the glovebox as described previously in this Section.

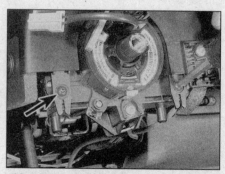

28.4 Remove the upper shroud securing screws

28.8 Remove the glovebox upper securing screws . . .

28.10a . . . and the lower securing screws . . .

28.10b . . . then withdraw the glovebox

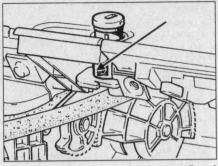

28.13 Push the securing tab (arrowed) and withdraw the glovebox lock barrel

28.16 Glovebox lock mounting plate securing clips (arrowed) - viewed from behind with facia removed

28.18 Unclip the documentation tray . . .

13 Push the securing tab, and withdraw the lock barrel from the top of the facia (see illustration).

Refitting

14 Refitting is a reversal of removal, ensuring that the securing tab engaged securely.

Glovebox lock assembly

Removal

15 Remove the glovebox as described previously in this Section.
16 Working at the rear edge of the lock mounting plate, carefully lever off the two metal clips securing the assembly to the facia, then withdraw the assembly (see illustration).

Refitting

17 Refitting is a reversal of removal, ensuring that the securing clips are correctly refitted.

Passenger's side lower facia panel

Removal

18 Remove the securing screws, and unclip the documentation tray from under the facia (see illustration).
19 Remove the securing screws, and withdraw the carpet trim from under the facia (see illustration).

Refitting

20 Refitting is a reversal of removal.

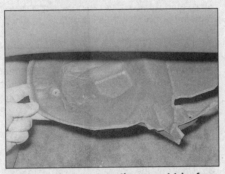

28.19 . . . then remove the carpet trim from under the facia

Complete facia assembly

Removal

21 Disconnect the battery negative terminal (refer to *Disconnecting the battery* in the Reference Section of this manual).
22 Remove the steering wheel as described in Chapter 10, and the steering column shrouds as described previously in this Section.
23 On models fitted with a passenger's side air bag, remove the passenger's side air bag unit as described in Chapter 12.
24 Remove the centre console (Section 27).
25 Where applicable, remove the radio/cassette player as described in Chapter 12.

28.26a Unscrew the two lower . . .

26 Unscrew the two lower and two upper securing screws from the radio/cassette player housing (see illustrations).
27 Reach into the storage tray to release the securing clips, and remove the storage tray from the radio/cassette player housing, then withdraw the radio/cassette player housing from the facia (see illustrations).
28 Working under the heater/ventilation control unit, unscrew the two securing screws. On models fitted with automatic air conditioning, withdraw the control unit from the facia, and disconnect the wiring plugs (see illustrations).
29 Carefully lever up the lower edge of the clock/temperature/radio/cassette player display

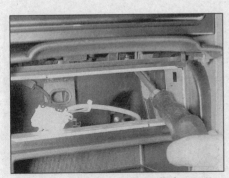

28.26b . . . and two upper radio/cassette player housing securing screws

28.27a Remove the storage tray . . .

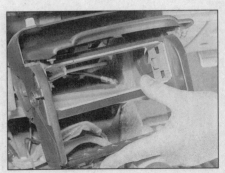

28.27b . . . then withdraw the radio/cassette player housing

11

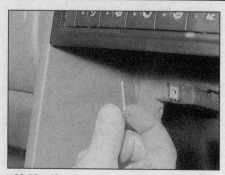

28.28a Unscrew the securing screws . . .

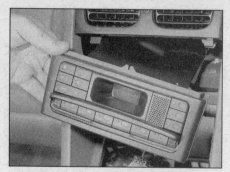

28.28b . . . and withdraw the heater/ ventilation control unit from the facia

28.29 Remove the clock/temperature/ radio/cassette player surround panel . . .

surround panel, to release the securing clips, then pull the panel forwards to release the rear lugs **(see illustration)**. Take care as the clips are easily broken.

30 Remove the three securing screws, then withdraw the clock/temperature/radio/cass-ette player display and disconnect the wiring plug(s) **(see illustration)**.

31 Working at the driver's side of the facia, remove the screw from the bottom of the facia switch/corner trim panel **(see illustration)**. Pull the panel downwards to release the upper securing lugs then, where applicable, disconnect the wiring from the switch(es) and withdraw the panel.

32 Unscrew the screws, then withdraw the steering column stalk switches, and disconnect the wiring plugs. Where applic-

able, also remove the radio/cassette player remote control switch, as described in Chap-ter 12.

33 Loosen the securing screw, and withdraw the rotary switch/stalk switch mounting plate assembly from the steering column. Disconnect the rotary connector wiring plug and, where applicable, unclip the wiring plug from the switch mounting plate, then withdraw the assembly **(see illustrations)**.

34 Unscrew the upper and lower screws securing the instrument panel surround, then withdraw the panel surround.

35 Unscrew the upper and lower instrument panel securing screws, then pull the instrument panel forwards from the facia, and disconnect the wiring plugs, and the speedometer cable, where applicable.

 On models with a speed-ometer cable, it will prove significantly easier to pull the instrument panel forwards from the facia if the speedometer cable is first disconnected at the transmission as described in Chapter 12.

36 Withdraw the instrument panel, and recover the locating rubbers from the sides of the panel if they are loose.

37 Carefully pull the trim panels from the windscreen pillars **(see illustration)**.

38 Working on each side of the facia in turn, carefully prise up the front edge of the facia-mounted loudspeaker, then pivot the speaker up to release the rear securing lugs **(see**

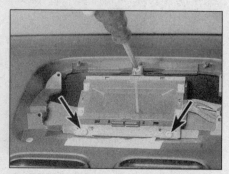

28.30 . . . for access to the display securing screws

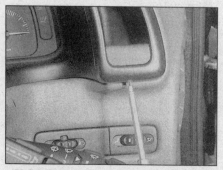

28.31 Remove the screw from the facia corner trim panel

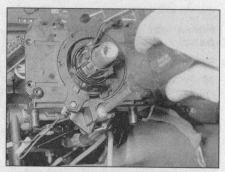

28.33a Loosen the securing screw . . .

28.33b . . . and withdraw the rotary switch/stalk switch mounting plate

28.37 Prise the trim panels from the windscreen pillars

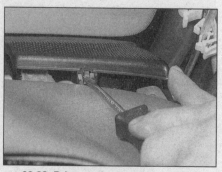

28.38 Prise up the front edge of the loudspeaker

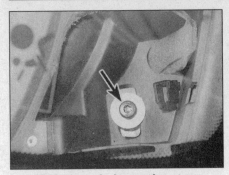

28.39 Upper facia securing screw (arrowed) as viewed through the windscreen

28.40 Unscrew the facia securing bolt (arrowed) from the fusebox

28.41 Prise out the blanking plates to expose the facia side securing bolts (arrowed)

illustration). Withdraw the speakers from the facia and disconnect the wiring.

39 Working through the loudspeaker apertures, unscrew the two upper facia securing screws **(see illustration)**.

40 Release the securing clips, and lower the fusebox cover, then unscrew the facia securing bolt from the upper edge of the fusebox **(see illustration)**.

41 Fully open the front doors, and prise out the blanking plates from each corner of the facia. Unscrew the now-exposed facia side securing bolts, one on each side of the facia **(see illustration)**.

42 Unscrew the two facia securing screws from the bottom of the instrument panel housing **(see illustration)**.

43 Working through the aperture in the centre of the facia, unscrew the centre facia securing screw **(see illustration)**.

44 Working in the passenger's footwell, reach up under the facia and unscrew the lower facia securing screw **(see illustration)**.

45 With the aid of an assistant, carefully pull the facia assembly forwards to enable the wiring connectors to be disconnected. Where

applicable, disconnect the glovebox light wiring from the passenger's side of the facia. Disconnect the wiring plugs from the rear of the fusebox assembly on the driver's side of the facia.

46 Pull the top edge of the facia upwards, then pull the facia forwards, and disconnect any remaining wiring. Release the wiring harnesses from any clips and brackets on the facia, and take careful note of the wiring harness routing to aid refitting.

47 Withdraw the facia through one of the front door apertures **(see illustration)**.

Refitting

48 Refitting is a reversal of removal, bearing in mind the following points.

a) Ensure that the facia is correctly centred in the passenger compartment.

b) Ensure that all wiring harnesses are correctly routed as noted before removal, and ensure that all wiring connectors are securely reconnected.

c) Where applicable, reconnect the speedometer cable before refitting the instrument panel.

28.42 Unscrew the screws (arrowed) from the bottom of the instrument panel housing

d) Ensure that the locating rubbers are in place at the sides of the instrument panel.

e) Refit the centre console with reference to Section 27.

f) Where applicable, have the air bag system checked by a Renault dealer, before refitting the air bag units - refer to Chapter 12 for details.

g) Refit the steering wheel (see Chapter 10).

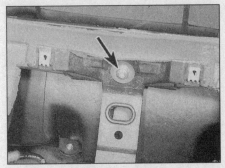

28.43 Unscrew the centre facia securing screw (arrowed)

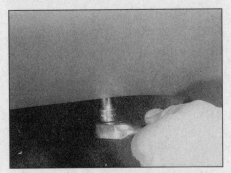

28.44 Unscrew the lower facia securing screw from the passenger's footwell

28.47 Withdraw the facia through one of the door apertures

11

Chapter 12
Body electrical system

Contents

Degrees of difficulty

Easy, suitable for novice with little experience	Fairly easy, suitable for beginner with some experience	Fairly difficult, suitable for competent DIY mechanic	Difficult, suitable for experienced DIY mechanic	Very difficult, suitable for expert DIY or professional

Specifications

General

System type .... 12-volt negative earth

Fuses

Refer to label on fusebox cover

Bulbs	Type	Wattage
Headlight:		
Up to May 1998:		
Main beam	H1	55
Dipped beam	H1	55
May 1998 onwards:		
Main beam	H7	55
Dipped beam	H7	55
Front sidelight	Push-fit	5
Front direction indicator light	Bayonet-fit	21
Front direction indicator side repeater light	Push-fit	5
Front foglight	H1	55
Tail/stop light	Bayonet-fit	21/5
Rear direction indicator light	Bayonet-fit	21
Reversing light	Bayonet-fit	21
Rear foglight	Bayonet-fit	21
Number plate light	Push-fit	5
Front courtesy and map reading lights	Push-fit	5
Rear courtesy lights	Bayonet-fit	5
Glovebox and luggage compartment lights	Double-ended	7

Torque wrench settings	Nm	lbf ft
Air bag securing screws	5	4
Air bag electronic control unit nuts	4	3

1 General information and precautions

The electrical system is of 12-volt negative earth type. Power for the lights and all electrical accessories is supplied by a lead/acid type battery, which is charged by the alternator.

This Chapter covers repair and service procedures for the various electrical components not associated with engine. Information on the battery, alternator and starter motor can be found in Chapter 5A.

It should be noted that, prior to working on any component in the electrical system, the battery negative terminal should first be disconnected, to prevent the possibility of electrical short-circuits and/or fires.

Precautions

⚠️ Warning: Before carrying out any work on the electrical system, read through the precautions given in Safety first! at the beginning of this manual, and in Chapter 5A.

⚠️ Warning: Later models are equipped with an air bag system. When working on the electrical system, refer to the precautions given in Section 25, to avoid the possibility of personal injury.

Caution: Before proceeding, refer to Disconnecting the battery in the Reference Section of this manual for further information.

2 Electrical fault finding - general information

Note: Refer to the precautions given in Safety first! and in Section 1 of this Chapter before starting work. The following tests relate to testing of the main electrical circuits, and should not be used to test delicate electronic circuits (such as anti-lock braking systems), particularly where an electronic control module is used.

General

1 A typical electrical circuit consists of an electrical component, any switches, relays, motors, fuses, fusible links or circuit breakers related to that component, and the wiring and connectors which link the component to both the battery and the chassis. To help to pinpoint a problem in an electrical circuit, wiring diagrams are included at the end of this Chapter.

2 Before attempting to diagnose an electrical fault, first study the appropriate wiring diagram, to obtain a more complete understanding of the components included in the particular circuit concerned. The possible sources of a fault can be narrowed down by noting whether other components related to the circuit are operating properly. If several components or circuits fail at one time, the problem is likely to be related to a shared fuse or earth connection.

3 Electrical problems usually stem from simple causes, such as loose or corroded connections, a faulty earth connection, a blown fuse, a melted fusible link, or a faulty relay (refer to Section 3 for details of testing relays). Visually inspect the condition of all fuses, wires and connections in a problem circuit before testing the components. Use the wiring diagrams to determine which terminal connections will need to be checked, in order to pinpoint the trouble-spot.

4 The basic tools required for electrical fault-finding include a circuit tester or voltmeter (a 12-volt bulb with a set of test leads can also be used for certain tests); a self-powered test light (sometimes known as a continuity tester); an ohmmeter (to measure resistance); a battery and set of test leads; and a jumper wire, preferably with a circuit breaker or fuse incorporated, which can be used to bypass suspect wires or electrical components. Before attempting to locate a problem with test instruments, use the wiring diagram to determine where to make the connections.

5 To find the source of an intermittent wiring fault (usually due to a poor or dirty connection, or damaged wiring insulation), a 'wiggle' test can be performed on the wiring. This involves wiggling the wiring by hand, to see if the fault occurs as the wiring is moved. It should be possible to narrow down the source of the fault to a particular section of wiring. This method of testing can be used in conjunction with any of the tests described in the following sub-Sections.

6 Apart from problems due to poor connections, two basic types of fault can occur in an electrical circuit - open-circuit, or short-circuit.

7 Open-circuit faults are caused by a break somewhere in the circuit, which prevents current from flowing. An open-circuit fault will prevent a component from working, but will not cause the relevant circuit fuse to blow.

8 Short-circuit faults are caused by a 'short' somewhere in the circuit, which allows the current flowing in the circuit to 'escape' along an alternative route, usually to earth. Short-circuit faults are normally caused by a breakdown in wiring insulation, which allows a feed wire to touch either another wire, or an earthed component such as the bodyshell. A short-circuit fault will normally cause the relevant circuit fuse to blow.

Finding an open-circuit

9 To check for an open-circuit, connect one lead of a circuit tester or voltmeter to either the negative battery terminal or a known good earth.

10 Connect the other lead to a connector in the circuit being tested, preferably nearest to the battery or fuse.

11 Switch on the circuit, bearing in mind that some circuits are live only when the ignition switch is moved to a particular position.

12 If voltage is present (indicated either by the tester bulb lighting or a voltmeter reading, as applicable), this means that the section of the circuit between the relevant connector and the battery is problem-free.

13 Continue to check the remainder of the circuit in the same fashion.

14 When a point is reached at which no voltage is present, the problem must lie between that point and the previous test point with voltage. Most problems can be traced to a broken, corroded or loose connection.

Finding a short-circuit

15 To check for a short-circuit, first disconnect the load(s) from the circuit (loads are the components which draw current from a circuit, such as bulbs, motors, heating elements, etc).

16 Remove the relevant fuse from the circuit, and connect a circuit tester or voltmeter to the fuse connections.

17 Switch on the circuit, bearing in mind that some circuits are live only when the ignition switch is moved to a particular position.

18 If voltage is present (indicated either by the tester bulb lighting or a voltmeter reading, as applicable), this means that there is a short-circuit.

19 If no voltage is present, but the fuse still blows with the load(s) connected, this indicates an internal fault in the load(s).

Finding an earth fault

20 The battery negative terminal is connected to 'earth' - the metal of the engine/transmission and the car body - and most systems are wired so that they only receive a positive feed, the current returning via the metal of the car body. This means that the component mounting and the body form part of that circuit. Loose or corroded mountings can therefore cause a range of electrical faults, ranging from total failure of a circuit, to a puzzling partial fault. In particular, lights may shine dimly (especially when another circuit sharing the same earth point is in operation), motors (eg wiper motors or the radiator cooling fan motor) may run slowly, and the operation of one circuit may have an apparently-unrelated effect on another. Note that on many vehicles, earth straps are used between certain components, such as the engine/transmission and the body, usually where there is no metal-to-metal contact between components, due to flexible rubber mountings, etc.

21 To check whether a component is properly earthed, disconnect the battery, and connect one lead of an ohmmeter to a known good earth point. Connect the other lead to the wire or earth connection being tested. The resistance reading should be zero; if not, check the connection as follows.

22 If an earth connection is thought to be

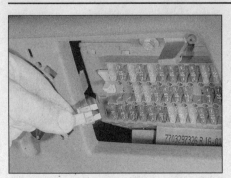

3.6 Using the plastic tool to remove a fuse

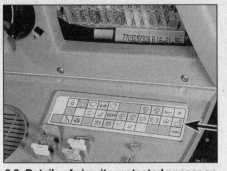

3.9 Details of circuits protected appear on the label (arrowed)

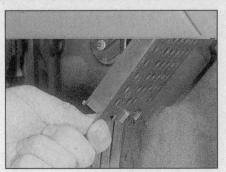

3.13 Unclipping the relay cover plate from under the fusebox

faulty, dismantle the connection, and clean back to bare metal both the bodyshell and the wire terminal or the component earth connection mating surface. Be careful to remove all traces of dirt and corrosion, then use a knife to trim away any paint, so that a clean metal-to-metal joint is made. On reassembly, tighten the joint fasteners securely; if a wire terminal is being refitted, use serrated washers between the terminal and the bodyshell, to ensure a clean and secure connection. When the connection is remade, prevent the onset of corrosion in the future by applying a coat of petroleum jelly or silicone-based grease, or by spraying on (at regular intervals) a proprietary ignition sealer.

3 Fuses and relays -
general information

Fuses

1 Fuses are designed to break a circuit when a predetermined current is reached, in order to protect the components and wiring which could be damaged by excessive current flow. Any excessive current flow will be due to a fault in the circuit, usually a short-circuit (see Section 2).

2 The main fuses are located in the fusebox, below the driver's side of the facia.

3 For access to the fuses, squeeze the securing clips and lower the fusebox cover.

4 A blown fuse can be recognised from its melted or broken wire.

5 To remove a fuse, first ensure that the relevant circuit is switched off.

6 Using the plastic tool provided on the fusebox cover, pull the fuse from its location **(see illustration)**.

7 Spare fuses are provided in the blank terminal positions in the fusebox cover.

8 Before renewing a blown fuse, trace and rectify the cause, and always use a fuse of the correct rating. Never substitute a fuse of a higher rating, or make temporary repairs using wire or metal foil; more serious damage, or even fire, could result.

9 Note that the fuses are colour-coded as

follows. Refer to the label on the fusebox cover for details of the circuits protected **(see illustration)**.

Colour	Rating
Orange	5A
Red	10A
Blue	15A
Yellow	20A
Clear or white	25A
Green	30A

10 On some models, additional fuses may be located in the electrical connector box next to the battery in the engine compartment.

Relays

11 A relay is an electrically-operated switch, which is used for the following reasons:
  a) A relay can switch a heavy current remotely from the circuit in which the current is flowing, allowing the use of lighter-gauge wiring and switch contacts.
  b) A relay can receive more than one control input, unlike a mechanical switch.
  c) A relay can have a timer function - for example, the intermittent wiper relay.

12 Most of the relays are located under the facia, above and below the main fusebox.

13 Access to the relays under the fusebox can be obtained by reaching up under the facia and unclipping the relay cover plate. Lower the cover plate, and pull the relevant relay from the relay board **(see illustration)**. Note that high-rating fuses and circuit-breakers may also be fitted to the relay board.

14 Access to the relays above the fusebox is very difficult with the facia in position. It may be possible to reach certain relays through the voice synthesiser loudspeaker aperture in the fusebox housing, or through the steering column aperture or instrument panel aperture once the steering column shrouds and instrument panel have been removed.

15 If a circuit or system controlled by a relay develops a fault, and the relay is suspect, operate the system. If the relay is functioning, it should be possible to hear it 'click' as it is energised. If this is the case, the fault lies with the components or wiring of the system. If the relay is not being energised, then either the relay is not receiving a main supply or a switching voltage, or the relay itself is faulty.

Testing is by the substitution of a known good unit, but be careful - while some relays are identical in appearance but and in operation, others look similar but perform different functions.

16 To remove a relay, first ensure that the relevant circuit is switched off. The relay can then simply be pulled out from the socket, and pushed back into position.

4 Switches -
removal and refitting

Note: *Disconnect the battery negative terminal (refer to Disconnecting the battery in the Reference Section of this manual), before removing any switch, and reconnect the terminal after refitting the switch.*

Ignition switch/ steering column lock

1 Refer to Chapter 10.

Steering column combination switches

Removal

2 Remove the steering wheel as described in Chapter 10.

3 Remove the steering column shrouds, with reference to Chapter 11, Section 28.

4 Unscrew the two securing screws, and slide the switch assembly out from the housing **(see illustration)**.

4.4 Unscrew the stalk switch securing screws

4.5 Disconnect the stalk switch wiring plugs

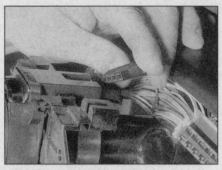

4.10 Disconnect the wiring plug from the rear of the rotary switch

4.11a Depress the upper retaining tabs . . .

4.11b . . . and withdraw the switch assembly

5 Disconnect the switch wiring connector(s) **(see illustration)**.
6 If the lighting stalk switch is being removed, where applicable, disconnect the horn wiring spade connectors.

Refitting

7 Refitting is a reversal of removal, but, where applicable, ensure that the warning buzzer contacts are correctly refitted, and refit the steering wheel as described in Chapter 10.

Steering column (air bag/ cruise control) rotary switch

Removal

8 The rotary switch is used to provide an electrical connection between the steering column and the steering wheel on models with an air bag and/or cruise control.
9 Ensure that the front wheels are in the straight-ahead position, then remove the

steering wheel as described in Chapter 10, and the steering column shrouds as described in Chapter 11, Section 28.
10 Disconnect the wiring plug from the rear of the switch assembly **(see illustration)**.
11 Depress the two upper retaining tabs, and withdraw the switch assembly from the column **(see illustrations)**.

Refitting

12 Refitting is a reversal of removal, bearing in mind the following points.
a) Ensure that the front wheels are in the straight-ahead position.
b) If a new switch assembly is being fitted, it will be supplied ready-centred, and held in position by an adhesive label which will tear the first time the steering wheel is turned - do not remove the label before the steering wheel is refitted.
c) If the switch assembly has been removed

without the front wheels in the straight-ahead position, the switch ribbon cable can be centred manually by moving it whilst pressing the centre section of the switch. Note that with the front wheels in the straight-ahead position, the switch hub on the steering column locks in position - make sure that the switch hub is locked, and that the arrows at the top of the rotary switch are aligned, then refit the rotary switch.
d) Where applicable, feed the horn wiring through the centre of the switch as it is refitted.
e) Refit the steering wheel as described in Chapter 10.

Radio/cassette player remote control switch

Removal

13 Working under the steering column, unscrew the securing screws, and withdraw the lower steering column shroud.
14 Turn the steering wheel as necessary, then carefully prise the cover from the radio/cassette player remote control switch to reveal the securing screw.
15 Unscrew the switch securing screw, and withdraw the switch from the upper shroud **(see illustration)**.
16 Remove the radio/cassette player as described in Section 21, and disconnect the switch wiring plug from the rear of the unit.
17 Feed the switch wiring behind the facia, noting its routing, then withdraw the switch.

Refitting

18 Refitting is a reversal of removal, but ensure that the wiring is routed as noted before removal.

Facia-mounted pushbutton switches

19 Remove the screw from the bottom of the facia switch/corner trim panel. Pull the panel downwards to release the upper securing lugs, then disconnect the wiring from the switch(es) and withdraw the panel.
20 Working at the rear of the panel, unscrew the two securing screws, then withdraw the switch from the panel.
21 Refitting is a reversal of removal.

Centre console-mounted switches

22 Carefully prise the switch panel assembly from the front of the console, and disconnect the wiring plugs **(see illustration)**.
23 Working at the rear of the panel, remove the switch securing screws, then withdraw the switch from the panel **(see illustration)**.
24 Refitting is a reversal of removal.

Instrument panel illumination rheostat

25 Reach up from under the facia, and use a small screwdriver to release the rheostat securing clips.

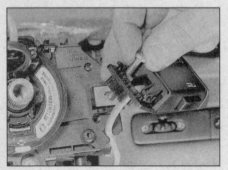

4.15 Removing the radio/cassette player remote control switch

4.22 Disconnecting the wiring from the centre console-mounted switches

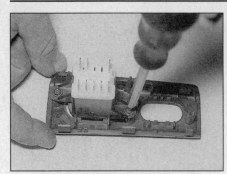

4.23 Unscrewing a centre console-mounted switch securing screw

4.26 Lowering the instrument panel illumination rheostat from the facia

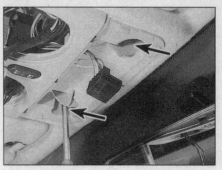

4.33 Unscrew the roof console securing screws (arrowed)

26 Lower the rheostat and disconnect the wiring plug **(see illustration)**.
27 Refitting is a reversal of removal.

Heater blower motor switch

28 The switch is integral with the heater control unit, and cannot be renewed separately.

Headlight adjuster switch

29 Refer to Section 9.

Roof console-mounted switches

30 The light control switches are integral with the light units, and cannot be renewed separately.
31 The sunroof control switch can be removed as follows.
32 Slide the roof console front panel/central locking remote control receiver forwards, then unclip it from the roof console. Where applicable, disconnect the wiring, and remove the panel.
33 Unscrew the two now-exposed screws. Pivot the roof console down, and disconnect the wiring from the lights, and the switch. Withdraw the roof console **(see illustration)**.
34 Working at the rear of the console, remove the two securing screws, and withdraw the sunroof switch from the console.
35 Refitting is a reversal of removal.

Door-mounted switches

36 Remove the securing screw, then unclip the hand-grip plate/switch panel from the top of the armrest **(see illustration)**. If necessary, carefully lever the plate away using a flat-bladed screwdriver.

4.36 Remove the securing screw from the hand-grip plate/switch panel . . .

37 Disconnect the wiring from the switches in the panel, and withdraw the panel **(see illustration)**.
38 Working at the rear of the panel, remove the two securing screws, then withdraw the switch.
39 Refitting is a reversal of removal.

Courtesy light switches
Door pillar-mounted switch

40 Pull the rubber cover from the switch.
41 Twist the switch to align the cut-outs in the edge of the switch with the corresponding holes in the door pillar.
42 Insert a small rod, such as a rivet or twist drill, into each of the holes in the door pillar to release the switch retaining clips **(see illustration)**.
43 Carefully prise out the switch using a screwdriver, then disconnect the wiring plug **(see illustration)**.

4.37 . . . then disconnect the wiring from the switches

44 Refitting is a reversal of removal, but refit the rubber cover to the switch before pushing the switch into position.

Light-mounted switches

45 The switches are integral with the light units, and cannot be renewed separately.

Glovebox light switch

46 Remove the glovebox (see Chapter 11, Section 28).
47 Working at the rear of the glovebox, depress the retaining clips, then push the switch out **(see illustration)**.
48 Refitting is a reversal of removal.

Luggage compartment light switch

49 Remove the tailgate lock as described in Chapter 11.
50 Working at the rear of the lock, depress the retaining clips, and remove the switch.

4.42 Insert rivets into the holes in the door pillar . . .

4.43 . . . then prise out the switch

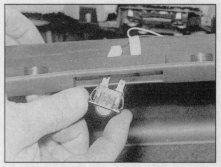

4.47 Removing the glovebox light switch

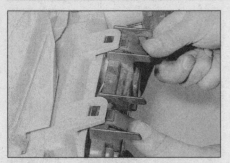

5.2 Withdrawing the plastic cover from the rear of the headlight - viewed with headlight removed for clarity

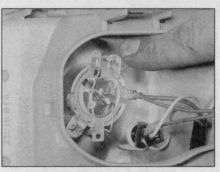

5.5a Compress the spring clip . . .

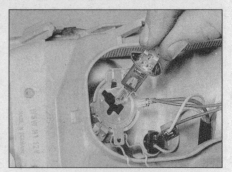

5.5b . . . and withdraw the bulb - viewed with headlight removed for clarity

51 Refitting is a reversal of removal.

Cruise control (steering wheel mounted) switches

52 Carefully prise the switch from the housing in the steering wheel and disconnect the wiring plug.

53 Refitting is a reversal of removal.

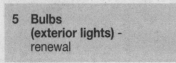

5 Bulbs (exterior lights) - renewal

1 Whenever a bulb is renewed, note the following points.

 a) *Disconnect the battery negative terminal (refer to Disconnecting the battery in the Reference Section of this manual), before starting work.*

 b) *Remember that, if the light has just been in use, the bulb may be extremely hot.*

 c) *Always check the bulb contacts and holder, ensuring that there is clean metal-to metal contact between the bulb and its live(s) and earth. Clean off any corrosion or dirt before fitting a new bulb.*

 d) *Wherever bayonet-type bulbs are fitted (see Specifications), ensure that the live contact(s) bear firmly against the bulb contact.*

 e) *Always ensure that the new bulb is of the correct rating, and that it is completely clean before fitting it; this applies particularly to headlight/foglight bulbs (see below).*

Headlight

Note 1: *On models with automatic transmission, it will be necessary to release the transmission electronic control unit for access to the left-hand side headlight unit. To do this, detach the rubber retaining strap, or lift the retaining hook, as applicable, and move the unit to one side.*

Note 2: *On 1.9 litre diesel engine models, it will be necessary to disconnect the intake air hose in front of the battery for access to the left-hand side headlight unit.*

2 Working in the engine compartment, depress the securing clips (where fitted), and withdraw the plastic cover from the rear of the headlight **(see illustration)**.

3 Separate main and dipped beam bulbs are fitted. Both bulbs are removed in exactly the same way.

4 Disconnect the bulb wiring.

5 Release the spring clip by compressing its ends, then withdraw the relevant bulb **(see illustrations)**.

6 When handling the new bulb, use a tissue or clean cloth, to avoid touching the glass with the fingers; moisture and grease from the skin can cause blackening and rapid failure of this type of bulb. If the glass is accidentally touched, wipe it clean using methylated spirit.

7 Install the new bulb, ensuring that its locating tabs are correctly seated in the light cut-outs. Secure the bulb in position with the spring clip, and reconnect the wiring.

8 Make sure that the rubber seal is correctly seated in the headlight cover (check the condition of the seal, and renew if necessary), then refit the cover.

Front sidelight

9 The sidelight bulbs are located in the headlight units.

10 Working in the engine compartment, depress the securing clips (where fitted), and withdraw the plastic cover from the rear of the headlight.

11 Twist the bulbholder anti-clockwise, and withdraw it from the headlight.

12 The bulb is a push-fit in the bulbholder **(see illustration)**.

13 Refitting is a reversal of removal.

Front direction indicator light

14 On models with separate direction indicator light units, unclip the direction indicator light retaining spring from the lug on the body, then withdraw the light unit from the front wing panel **(see illustration)**. Twist the bulbholder anti-clockwise, and withdraw it from the light unit.

15 On models with combined direction indicator/headlight units, twist the bulbholder anti-clockwise and withdraw it from the rear of the headlight unit.

16 The bulb is a bayonet-fit in the bulbholder **(see illustration)**.

17 Refitting is a reversal of removal but, where applicable, ensure that the light unit retaining spring is securely engaged.

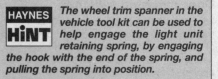

HAYNES HiNT *The wheel trim spanner in the vehicle tool kit can be used to help engage the light unit retaining spring, by engaging the hook with the end of the spring, and pulling the spring into position.*

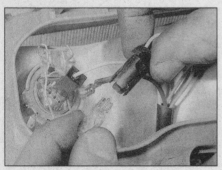

5.12 Removing a sidelight bulb

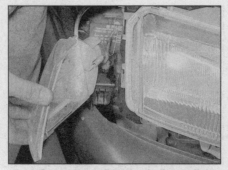

5.14 Removing a direction indicator light unit

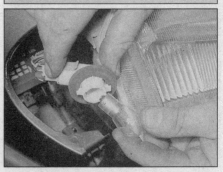

5.16 Removing a direction indicator light bulb

5.18a Remove the securing screw and withdraw the foglight cover plate . . .

5.18b . . . then unscrew the securing bolt . . .

5.18c . . . and withdraw the foglight unit - pre-1998 models

Front foglight

18 On pre-May 1998 models, remove the securing screw, and withdraw the cover plate from the front spoiler to reveal the light unit securing bolt . Unscrew the securing bolt, and manipulate the light unit out from the front of the bumper **(see illustrations)**.

19 On May 1998 models onward, undo the mounting bolt under the bumper, then release the upper mounting lugs and pull the light unit forward out of the bumper.

20 Disconnect the wiring plug.

21 Working at the rear of the light unit, twist the cover anticlockwise and remove it.

22 Release the spring clip by compressing its ends, then withdraw the bulb **(see illustration)**.

23 When handling the new bulb, use a tissue or clean cloth, to avoid touching the glass

with the fingers; moisture and grease from the skin can cause blackening and rapid failure of this type of bulb. If the glass is accidentally touched, wipe it clean using methylated spirit.

24 Install the new bulb, ensuring that it locates correctly in the light unit. Secure the bulb in position with the spring clip, and refit the cover to the rear of the light unit.

25 Refit the light unit using a reversal of the removal procedure.

26 If necessary, the foglight beam alignment can be adjusted using the screw provided at the top inside corner of the light unit **(see illustration)**.

Front direction indicator side repeater light

27 Carefully prise the light unit from the door panel, using a small flat-bladed screwdriver

(see illustration).

28 Twist the bulbholder anti-clockwise, and withdraw it from the light unit **(see illustration)**.

29 The bulb is a push-fit in the bulbholder.

30 Fit the new bulb and refit the light unit using a reversal of the removal procedure.

Rear lights

Rear wing-mounted lights

31 Open the tailgate, then depress the retaining clips, and remove the cover panel from the rear of the luggage compartment for access to the light assembly.

32 Carefully pull out the sound insulation to expose the bulbholder **(see illustrations)**.

33 Depress the retaining clips, and withdraw the bulbholder from the rear of the light unit **(see illustration)**.

5.22 Removing the foglight bulb

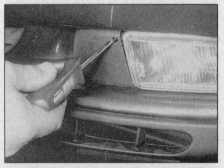

5.26 The foglight beam alignment can be adjusted using the screw provided

5.27 Prise the indicator side repeater light unit from the door panel

5.28 Removing the bulbholder from the side repeater light unit

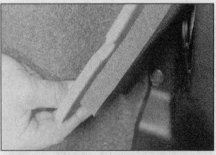

5.32a Pull out the sound insulation to expose the rear light bulbholder on Hatchback models . . .

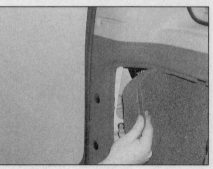

5.32b . . . and on Estate models

12

5.33 Depress the retaining clips, and withdraw the bulbholder from the rear of the light unit - Estate model shown

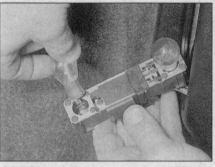

5.34 Removing a rear wing-mounted light bulb

5.36a Removing a rear light cover panel from the tailgate

5.36b Removing a rear light bulbholder from the tailgate

34 The bulbs are a bayonet-fit in the bulbholder **(see illustration)**.
35 Refitting is a reversal of removal, but

5.43 Press the tab on the side of the bulbholder and withdraw the bulbholder from the number plate surround - Estate models

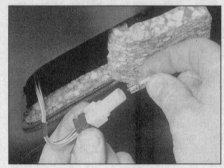

5.41 Removing a number plate light bulb - Hatchback models

ensure that the sound insulation is correctly seated on the rear of the light unit.

Tailgate-mounted lights

36 Proceed as described previously for the rear wing-mounted lights, noting that the lights are accessed by removing the outer cover panels from the tailgate **(see illustrations)**.

High-level stop light

37 Where fitted, the high-level stop light is a sealed unit. Any work should be referred to a Renault dealer.

Number plate light

Hatchback models

38 Open the tailgate, then depress the retaining clips, and remove the relevant inner

cover panel from the rear of the tailgate for access to the light assembly.
39 Where applicable, carefully pull out the sound insulation to expose the bulbholder.
40 Reach up into the tailgate, and pull the bulbholder from the rear of the light unit.
41 The bulb is a push-fit in the bulbholder **(see illustration)**.
42 Refitting is a reversal of removal, but ensure that the sound insulation is correctly seated on the rear of the light unit.

Estate models

43 Press the tab on the side of the bulbholder and withdraw the bulbholder from the number plate surround **(see illustration)**.
44 Remove the lens from the bulbholder and withdraw the bulb from the contacts **(see illustrations)**.
45 Refitting is a reversal of removal.

6 Bulbs (interior lights) - renewal

General

1 Refer to Section 5, paragraph 1.

Courtesy lights and map reading light

2 Carefully prise the light unit from the roof console **(see illustration)**.

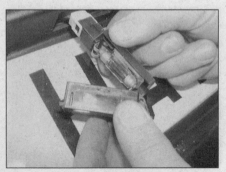

5.44a Remove the lens from the bulbholder . . .

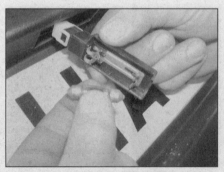

5.44b . . . and withdraw the bulb from the contacts - Estate models

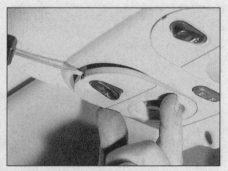

6.2 Prising the map reading light from the roof console

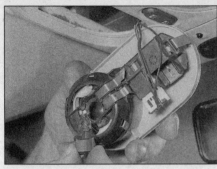

6.3 Removing the map reading light bulbholder

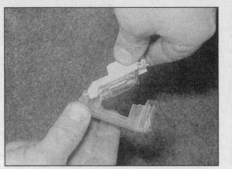

6.7 Unclipping the lens from the luggage compartment light

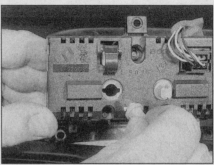

6.14 Removing a clock/temperature/radio/cassette player display bulb

3 Twist the bulbholder anti-clockwise and remove it from the rear of the light unit **(see illustration)**.
4 The bulb is a push-fit in the bulbholder.
5 Refitting is a reversal of removal.

Glovebox light and luggage compartment light

6 Open the tailgate or glovebox, as applicable, then depress the retaining clips, and prise out the light unit.
7 Unclip the lens from the light unit, then pull the bulb from the spring contacts **(see illustration)**.
8 Refitting is a reversal of removal.

Instrument panel illumination and warning light bulbs

9 Remove the instrument panel as described in Section 10.
10 Twist the relevant bulbholder anti-clockwise to remove it from the rear of the panel.
11 The bulbs are integral with the bulbholders.
12 Refitting is a reversal of removal.

Digital clock/temperature/audio player display illumination bulb

13 Remove the clock/temperature/audio player display as described in Section 12.
14 Proceed as described in paragraphs 10 to 12 **(see illustration)**.

Pushbutton switch illumination bulbs

15 The bulbs are integral with the switches, and cannot be renewed independently.

Cigarette lighter illumination bulb

16 Remove the complete cigarette lighter assembly as described in Section 13.
17 Unclip the cover from the bulb, the pull the bulb from the bulbholder.
18 Refitting is a reversal of removal.

Heater/ventilation control unit illumination bulbs

19 Remove the control unit from the facia as described in Chapter 3. Note that, where applicable, there is no need to disconnect the control cables.
20 Working at the top of the control unit, twist the bulbholder anti-clockwise, and withdraw it from the panel **(see illustration)**.
21 The bulb is integral with the bulbholder.

---

7 Exterior light units - removed and refitting

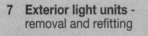

Note: *Disconnect the battery negative terminal (refer to Disconnecting the battery in the Reference Section of this manual), before removing any light unit, and reconnect the lead after refitting the unit.*

Headlight

Removal

1 On pre-May 1998 models, remove the front direction indicator light unit as described later in this Section.

6.20 Removing a heater/ventilation control unit bulb

2 Working at the rear of the light unit, disconnect the headlight wiring connector and the beam adjustment motor wiring connector **(see illustration)**.
3 Remove the radiator grille panel with reference to Chapter 11. On May 1998 models onward, also remove the front bumper as described in Chapter 11.
4 Unscrew the lower and upper securing bolts, then withdraw the headlight from the front of the vehicle **(see illustrations)**.

Refitting

5 Refitting is a reversal of removal, bearing in mind the following points.
   a) *Ensure that the two positioning lugs at the top of the light unit engage with the body front panel.*
   b) *Refit the radiator grille and front bumper (where applicable) as described in Chapter 11.*

7.2 Disconnecting the headlight wiring connector

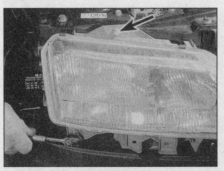

7.4a Unscrew the securing bolts . . .

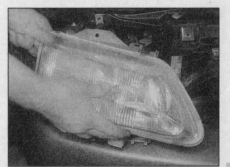

7.4b . . . and withdraw the headlight

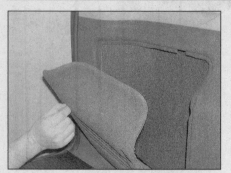

7.11a Remove the storage compartment lid on the side trim panel . . .

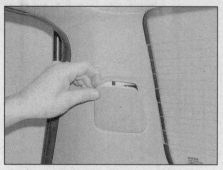

7.11b . . . and unclip the access hatch on the rear body pillar - Estate models

7.14 Withdrawing a rear wing-mounted light unit - Hatchback model shown

c) On completion, have the headlight beam alignment checked at the earliest opportunity with reference to Section 8.

Front direction indicator light

Removal

Note: *On later models, the direction indicator light is incorporated in the headlight unit and cannot be removed separately.*

6 Working in the engine compartment, at the rear of the light unit, unclip the direction indicator light retaining spring from the lug on the body, then withdraw the light unit from the front wing panel.

7 Disconnect the wiring plug, and remove the light unit.

Refitting

8 Refitting is a reversal of removal, but ensure that the light unit retaining spring is securely engaged.

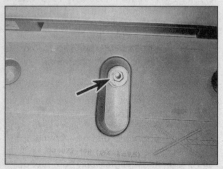

7.18 Remove the reflector panel securing nut (arrowed)

Front foglight

9 Removal and refitting is described as part of the bulb renewal procedure in Section 5.

Front direction indicator side repeater light

10 Removal and refitting is described as part of the bulb renewal procedure in Section 5.

Rear lights

Rear wing-mounted lights

11 On Hatchback models, open the tailgate, and unclip the access hatch from the rear corner of the luggage compartment. On Estate models, open the tailgate and remove the storage compartment lid on the side trim panel. Also unclip the access hatch on the rear body pillar **(see illustrations)**.

12 Pull the soundproofing from the rear of the light unit.

13 Disconnect the wiring from the bulbholder.

14 Unscrew the securing bolts, and withdraw the light unit from the rear of the wing panel **(see illustration)**.

15 Refitting is a reversal of removal.

Tailgate-mounted lights

16 The tailgate-mounted rear lights are integral with the tailgate reflector panel.

17 Remove the number plate.

18 Remove the reflector panel nut, exposed by removal of the number plate **(see illustration)**.

19 Working inside the tailgate, remove the securing screws, and withdraw the tailgate rear trim panel.

20 Disconnect the wiring from the rear lights.

21 Depress the retaining clips, and remove the number plate light bulbholders from the reflector/light assembly.

22 Unscrew the eight reflector/light assembly securing nuts from inside the tailgate. Note the locations of any brackets and clips secured by the nuts **(see illustration)**.

23 Withdraw the assembly from the rear of the tailgate **(see illustration)**.

24 Refitting is a reversal of removal, but ensure that any brackets and clips are located as noted before removal.

High-level stop light

Hatchback models

25 Open the tailgate and undo the two stop light unit mounting screws.

26 Withdraw the unit from the tailgate glass and disconnect the wiring connector.

27 Refitting is a reversal of removal.

Estate models

28 Open the tailgate and undo the screws at each end, and in the centre, securing the stop light mounting/deflector panel to the tailgate **(see illustrations)**.

29 Pull the panel off the tailgate to release the retaining clips. Disconnect the stop light wiring and the tailgate washer hose and remove the panel **(see illustrations)**.

7.22 Note the locations of any brackets secured by the inner panel securing nuts

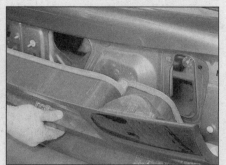

7.23 Removing the tailgate light/reflector assembly

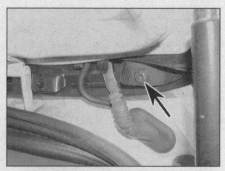

7.28a Undo the screws at each end (arrowed) . . .

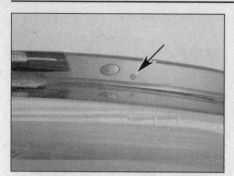

7.28b . . . and in the centre (arrowed) securing the stop light mounting/deflector panel to the tailgate - Estate models

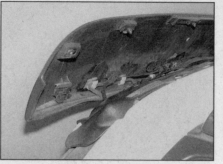

7.29a Pull the stop light mounting/deflector panel off the tailgate to release the retaining clips . . .

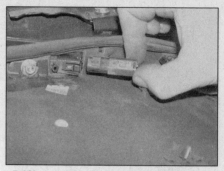

7.29b . . . then disconnect the wiring . . .

30 The stop light unit is secured to the mounting/deflector panel by two screws and a very strong adhesive. Undo the screws then release the adhesive using a sharp knife, while at the same time carefully prising the two components apart with a screwdriver.

31 Refitting is a reversal of removal but use a suitable adhesive (available from Renault dealers) to bond the light unit to the mounting/deflector panel.

Number plate light

32 The number plate lights are integral with the tailgate-mounted rear lights/reflector assembly. Refer to paragraphs 16 to 25 for details.

---

8 Headlight beam alignment - general information

1 Accurate adjustment of the headlight beam is only possible using optical beam-setting equipment, and this work should therefore be carried out by a Renault dealer or suitably-equipped workshop.

2 All vehicles are equipped with a four-position electrical vertical beam adjuster unit - this can be used to adjust the headlight beam, to compensate for the relevant load which the vehicle is carrying. An adjuster switch is provided on the facia. The adjuster switch should be positioned as follows, according to the load being carried in the vehicle.

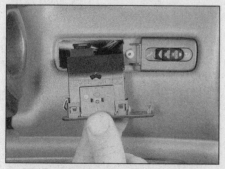

9.3 Removing the headlight adjuster switch

Hatchback models

Position 0	Front seat(s) occupied, luggage compartment empty
Position 1	Front and rear seats occupied, luggage compartment empty
Position 2	Front and rear seats occupied and luggage compartment fully loaded
Position 3	Driver's seat only occupied and luggage compartment fully loaded
Position 4	Not used

Estate models

Position 0	Front seat(s) occupied, luggage compartment empty
Position 1	Front seat(s) occupied, rear occasional seats occupied by children, luggage compartment empty
Position 2	Front and rear seats occupied, rear occasional seats occupied by children, luggage compartment empty
Position 3	Not used
Position 4	Front and rear seats occupied and luggage compartment fully loaded

---

9 Headlight beam adjustment components - removal and refitting

General

1 Refer to Section 8.

Adjuster switch

Removal

2 Disconnect the battery negative terminal (refer to *Disconnecting the battery* in the Reference Section of this manual).

3 Carefully prise the switch from the facia, and disconnect the wiring plug **(see illustration)**.

Refitting

4 Refitting is a reversal of removal.

7.29c . . . and the washer hose - Estate models

Adjuster motor

Removal

5 Remove the relevant headlight unit as described in Section 7.

6 Twist the adjuster motor through an eighth-of-a-turn clockwise, then slide the unit upwards to release the motor balljoint from the adjuster lever **(see illustration)**. Take care, as the adjuster lever is easily broken.

7 Withdraw the motor.

Refitting

8 If a new adjuster motor is being fitted, proceed as follows, otherwise proceed to paragraph 10.

9 It is now necessary to check on which type of headlights are fitted. If Valeo headlight units are fitted, then the adjusters can be refitted as described in paragraph 10 onwards. If Hella headlight units are fitted, proceed as follows.

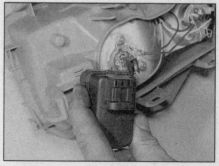

9.6 Twist the headlight adjuster motor through an eighth of a turn

10.2 Remove the facia switch/corner trim panel

10.3a Remove the upper . . .

10.3b . . . and lower securing screws . . .

a) *Connect the wiring plug to the adjuster motor, and reconnect the battery negative lead (do not refit the adjuster motor at this stage).*
b) *Switch on the ignition, and move the adjuster switch on the facia to position 4.*
c) *Switch off the ignition and disconnect the wiring plug and the battery negative lead.*
d) *Turn the adjuster screw on the motor unit until the dimension between the end of the motor balljoint, and the end of the balljoint housing is as shown.*

10 Slide the motor balljoint into engagement with the headlight adjuster lever, then engage the motor casing with the headlight, and twist clockwise to lock the motor in position.
11 Refit the headlight as described in Section 7.

10 Instrument panel - removal and refitting

Removal

Caution: The gauges in the instrument panel are damped using silicone fluid. Once the instrument panel has been removed, it must be stored upright, to prevent the silicone from escaping. If the silicone escapes from the instruments, the relevant instruments must be renewed.

1 Disconnect the battery negative terminal (refer to *Disconnecting the battery* in the Reference Section of this manual).
2 Working at the driver's side of the facia,

remove the screw from the bottom of the facia switch/corner trim panel. Pull the panel downwards to release the upper securing lugs then, where applicable, disconnect the wiring from the switch(es) and withdraw the panel **(see illustration)**.
3 Unscrew the upper and lower screws securing the instrument panel surround, then withdraw the panel surround **(see illustrations)**.
4 Unscrew the upper and lower instrument panel securing screws, then pull the instrument panel forwards from the facia, and disconnect the wiring plugs, and the speedometer cable, where applicable **(see illustrations)**.
5 Withdraw the instrument panel, and recover the locating rubbers from the sides of the panel if they are loose.

Refitting

6 Refitting is a reversal of removal, but ensure that the locating rubbers are in place at the sides of the panel, and make sure that the wiring plugs, and where applicable, the speedometer cable are securely reconnected.

11 Instrument panel components - removal and refitting

Caution: The gauges in the instrument panel are damped using silicone fluid. Once the instrument panel has been removed, it must be stored upright, to prevent the silicone from escaping. If the

10.3c . . . and withdraw the instrument panel surround

instruments are tilted for more than ten minutes, the silicone is likely to escape. If the silicone escapes from the instruments, the relevant instruments must be renewed. Caution: On models fitted with a trip computer, and all later (May 1998 onward) models, the instrument panel cannot be dismantled. If any of the components are faulty, refer to a Renault dealer for advice - it is likely that the complete instrument panel will have to be renewed.

Instruments - Jaeger instrument panel

Removal

1 With the instrument panel removed as described in Section 10, proceed as follows.
2 Working at the front of the panel, carefully pull off the trip counter button rubber and, where applicable, the clock reset button rubber.

10.4a Unscrew the securing screws . . .

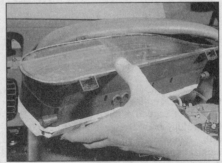

10.4b . . . and withdraw the instrument panel

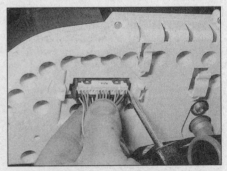

10.4c Using a screwdriver to release an instrument panel wiring plug clip

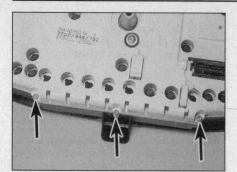

11.3 Three of the instrument panel rear cover securing screws (arrowed) - Jaeger instrument panel

3 Working at the rear of the panel, remove the nine securing screws, securing the rear cover to the main casing, and the two screws securing the speedometer **(see illustration)**.
4 Separate the rear cover from the main casing assembly, and remove the binnacle/lens assembly from the front of the main casing **(see illustration)**.
5 Working at the rear of the main assembly, unscrew the three nuts securing the printed circuit board to the clock.
6 Release the fuel and temperature gauge contacts (and the rev. counter contacts, where applicable) from the clips on the printed circuit board, then carefully separate the circuit board from the rear of the instruments. Do not lever the circuit board from the instruments - take great care not to damage the circuit board.
7 Separate the front panel, in which the gauges are mounted, from the plastic casing.
8 To remove an instrument, first carefully pull off the needle/hands from the front of the panel.
9 Remove the securing screws, and withdraw the instrument from the rear of the panel. If the clock is being removed, recover the resetting components as the assembly is removed, noting the locations of the components.

Refitting

10 Reassembly is a reversal of dismantling, bearing in mind the following points.
 a) If the clock is being refitted, before refitting the assembly, position the resetting pinions on their shafts, and reposition the reset button and its spring. Note that the pinion shafts are tapered, so the pinions must be fitted the correct way round. If a new clock is being fitted, a special tool is provided with the new clock to aid refitting of the hands.
 b) Do not overtighten the instrument fixings, as the casing is easily broken.
 c) Take care not to damage the printed circuit board during refitting.
 d) Refit the instrument panel with reference to Section 10.

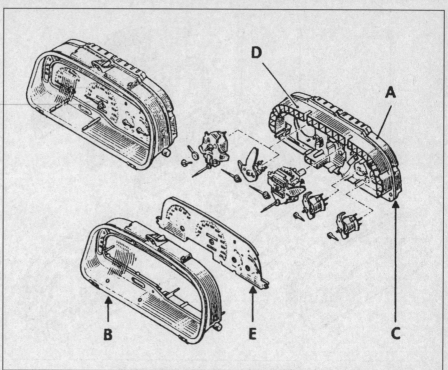

11.4 Jaeger instrument panel components

A Rear cover	C Printed circuit
B Binnacle/lens	D Main casing

E Front panel

Instruments - Sagem instrument panel

Removal

11 With the instrument panel removed as described in Section 10, proceed as follows.
12 Working at the front of the panel, carefully pull off the trip counter button rubber and, where applicable, the clock reset button rubber.
13 Working at the rear of the panel, remove the two screws securing the rear cover to the main casing, then separate the rear cover, by levering the four securing clips to release them **(see illustration)**.

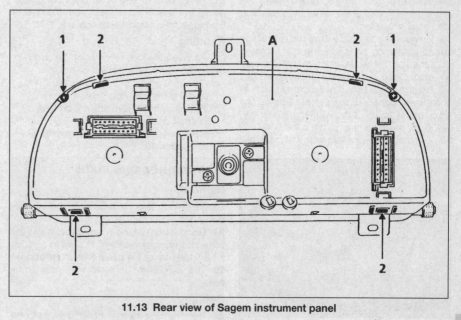

11.13 Rear view of Sagem instrument panel

1 Rear cover securing screws	2 Rear cover securing clips

A Rear cover

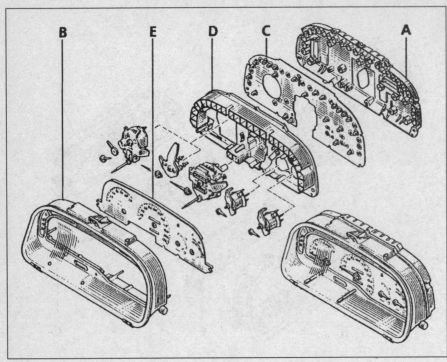

11.14 Sagem instrument panel components

A Rear cover   C Printed circuit   E Front panel
B Binnacle/lens   D Main casing

14 Again working at the rear of the panel, remove the six screws securing the panel components together **(see illustration)**.
15 Release the fuel and temperature gauge contacts (and the rev. counter contacts, where applicable) from the clips on the printed circuit board, then carefully separate the circuit board from the rear of the instruments. Do not lever the circuit board from the instruments - take great care not to damage the circuit board.
16 Remove the two screws at the rear of the speedometer to separate the main casing from the front panel (in which the instruments are mounted) and the binnacle/lens assembly.
17 Remove the two small screws (one at each lower corner of the panel) securing the front panel to the binnacle/lens assembly. Withdraw the lower part of the panel first.
18 To remove an instrument, first carefully

pull off the needle/hands from the front of the panel.
19 To remove the speedometer or rev. counter, unscrew the two securing screws from the rear of the panel, then withdraw the instrument.
20 To remove the clock, carefully release the five securing clips at the rear of the panel. Take care, as the clips are easily broken.
21 To remove the fuel or temperature gauge, unclip the U-shaped bracket from the rear of the panel, then withdraw the gauge.

Refitting

22 Reassembly is a reversal of dismantling, bearing in mind the following points.
    a) Do not overtighten the instrument fixings, as the casing is easily broken.
    b) Take care not to damage the printed circuit board during refitting.
    c) Refit the instrument panel with reference to Section 10.

Instrument panel bulbs

Removal

23 Remove the instrument panel as described in Section 10.
24 Using a pair of long-nosed pliers, twist the relevant bulbholder anti-clockwise to remove it from the rear of the panel **(see illustration)**.
25 The bulbs are integral with the bulbholders.

Refitting

26 Refitting is a reversal of removal, but refit the instrument panel with reference to Section 10.

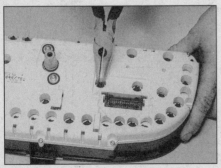

11.24 Using a pair of pliers to remove an instrument panel bulb

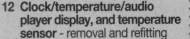

12 Clock/temperature/audio player display, and temperature sensor - removal and refitting

Clock/temperature/audio player display

Removal

1 Disconnect the battery negative terminal (refer to *Disconnecting the battery* in the Reference Section of this manual).
2 Carefully lever up the lower edge of the clock surround panel, to release the securing clips, the pull the panel forwards to release the rear lugs. Take care as the clips are easily broken.
3 Remove the three securing screws, then withdraw the clock/temperature/radio/cassette player display and disconnect the wiring plug(s).

Refitting

4 Refitting is a reversal of removal.

Outside temperature sensor

Removal

5 The sensor is located in the bottom of the passenger's side exterior mirror housing.
6 Remove the mirror glass as described in Chapter 11.
7 Remove the screw securing the sensor in the mirror housing **(see illustration)**.
8 Working inside the door, prise the mirror trim panel from the front edge of the door.
9 Unscrew the three securing screws and remove the wiring connector cover.
10 Separate the two halves of the wiring connector, then feed the wiring through into the mirror housing, and withdraw the sensor, complete with the wiring.
11 Refitting is a reversal of removal, noting the following points.
    a) It is advisable to solder the new wire connections.
    b) Ensure that the wiring connections are adequately insulated.
    c) Refit the mirror glass with reference to Chapter 11.

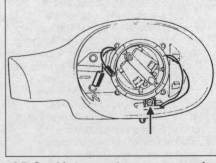

12.7 Outside temperature sensor securing screw

13 Cigarette lighter - removal and refitting

Removal

1 Disconnect the battery negative terminal (refer to *Disconnecting the battery* in the Reference Section of this manual).
2 Unclip the ashtray from its housing.
3 Remove the two securing screws, and withdraw the ashtray housing from the facia. Disconnect the wiring from the cigarette lighter as the housing is removed **(see illustration)**.
4 Pull the cigarette lighter element from the metal sleeve.
5 To remove the metal sleeve, push the rear of the sleeve, and simultaneously depress the two securing lugs on the inner face of the sleeve.
6 To remove the plastic housing, push the housing, from the rear, out of the ashtray housing.

Refitting

7 Refitting is a reversal of removal.

14 'Lights-on' warning buzzer - general information

The purpose of this system is to inform the driver that the lights have been left on once the ignition has been switched off; the buzzer will sound when a door is opened. The system consists of a buzzer unit which is linked to the driver's door courtesy light switch.

The buzzer unit is located with the fuses behind the facia (see Section 3).

Refer to Section 4 for details of courtesy light switch removal.

15 Horn - removal and refitting

Removal

1 The horns are located behind the left-hand side of the bumper.
2 Disconnect the battery negative terminal (refer to *Disconnecting the battery* in the Reference Section of this manual).
3 Working under the vehicle, where applicable, remove the engine undershield.
4 Disconnect the horn wiring plug.
5 Unscrew the securing nut and remove the horn **(see illustration)**.

Refitting

6 Refitting is a reversal of removal.

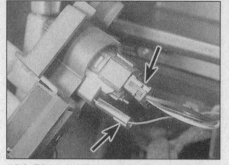

13.3 Disconnect the wiring (arrowed) from the cigarette lighter

16 Speedometer cable - removal and refitting

Removal

1 Remove the instrument panel as described in Section 10.
2 Working in the engine compartment, locate the end of the speedometer cable at the transmission, then squeeze the securing lugs and disconnect the cable from the transmission.
3 Working at the engine compartment bulkhead, release the speedometer cable grommet from the bulkhead. Release the cable from any clips and brackets in the engine compartment.
4 Working in the passenger compartment, pull the cable through the bulkhead, and withdraw it from the vehicle.

Refitting

5 Refitting is a reversal of removal. Ensure that the cable is routed as noted before removal.

17 Wiper arm - removal and refitting

Removal

1 Operate the wiper motor, then switch it off so that the wiper arm returns to the at-rest position.

17.2a Unscrewing a wiper arm nut

15.5 Horn securing nut (arrowed)

HAYNES HiNT	*Stick a piece of masking tape along the edge of the wiper blade, to use as an alignment aid on refitting.*

2 Lift up the wiper arm spindle nut cover, then slacken and remove the spindle nut. Lift the blade off the glass, and pull the wiper arm off its spindle. Note that on some models, the wiper arms may be very tight on the spindle splines - it should be possible to lever the arm off the spindle, using a flat-bladed screwdriver (take care not to damage the scuttle cover panel). If the arm cannot be levered off, a puller must be used **(see illustrations)**.

Refitting

3 Ensure that the wiper arm and spindle splines are clean and dry, then refit the arm to the spindle. Where applicable, align the wiper blade with the tape fitted on removal.
4 Refit the spindle nut, tightening it securely, and clip the nut cover back into position.

18 Windscreen wiper motor and linkage - removal and refitting

Removal

1 Disconnect the battery negative terminal (refer to *Disconnecting the battery* in the Reference Section of this manual).
2 Remove the wiper arms as described in Section 17.

17.2b Using a puller to remove a wiper arm

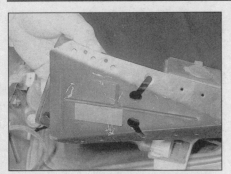

18.5 Lifting the alarm siren and lock bracket assembly from the scuttle

18.7a Unscrew the left-hand . . .

7 Unscrew the five bolts securing the motor and linkage assembly to the scuttle, then lift the assembly from the scuttle (see illustrations).
8 If desired, the motor can be separated from the linkage as follows.
  a) *Make alignment marks on the linkage drive link and the motor spindle, then unscrew the spindle nut.*
  b) *Unscrew the three nuts securing the motor to the mounting plate, then withdraw the motor from the linkage assembly.*

Refitting

9 Refitting is a reversal of removal, noting the following points.
  a) *Ensure that the motor is in the 'parked' position before refitting.*
  b) *If the motor has been removed from the linkage, ensure that the marks made on the linkage drive link and motor spindle are aligned on refitting.*
  c) *Refit the wiper arms with reference to Section 17.*

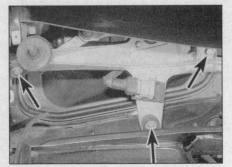

18.7b . . . and right-hand wiper motor/ linkage securing bolts (arrowed) . . .

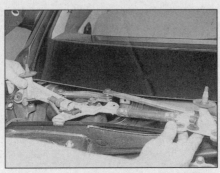

18.7c . . . and withdraw the assembly

3 Fully open the bonnet.
4 Remove the scuttle cover panels as described in Chapter 11, Section 23.
5 Where applicable, unscrew the two securing nuts, and lift the alarm siren and lock

bracket assembly from the scuttle. Move the assembly to one side, taking care not to strain the wiring (see illustration).
6 Disconnect the windscreen wiper motor wiring connector.

19 Tailgate wiper motor - removal and refitting

Removal

1 Disconnect the battery negative terminal (refer to *Disconnecting the battery* in the Reference Section of this manual).
2 Remove the wiper arm (see Section 17).
3 Remove the tailgate interior trim panel as described in Chapter 11, Section 26.
4 Disconnect the tailgate wiper motor wiring plug (see illustration).
5 Unscrew the three bolts (Hatchback models), or four bolts (Estate models) securing the motor mounting plate to the tailgate, then manipulate the assembly out through the aperture in the tailgate (see illustrations).
6 On Hatchback models, the motor can be separated from the linkage as follows (see illustration).
  a) *Make alignment marks on the linkage drive link and the motor spindle, then unscrew the spindle nut. If the spindle nut is not accessible because it is obscured by the linkage, check on the steering*

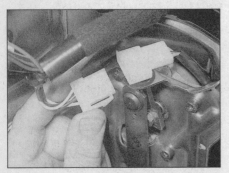

19.4 Disconnecting the tailgate wiper motor wiring plug

19.5a Unscrew the three securing bolts (arrowed) . . .

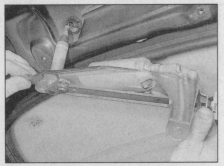

19.5b . . . then withdraw the tailgate wiper motor assembly - Hatchback models

19.5c Tailgate wiper motor mounting plate securing bolts - Estate models

19.6 Tailgate wiper linkage positioned for access to spindle nut (arrowed) - Hatchback models

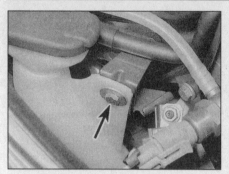

20.5a Unscrew the upper . . .

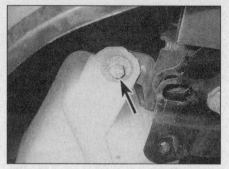

20.5b . . . and lower washer fluid reservoir securing bolts (arrowed)

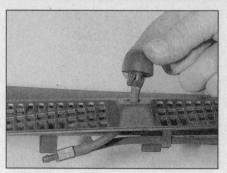

20.13 Removing a windscreen washer fluid nozzle

column stalk switch that the motor is in the tailgate wiper is switched off (motor in 'parked' position), then temporarily reconnect the battery and the motor wiring connector, and alter the position of the linkage by using the stalk switch. - ignition must be used to stop motor, otherwise motor always parks in same position Disconnect the battery and the motor wiring plug once the spindle nut can be reached.

b) Unscrew the three bolts securing the motor to the mounting plate, then withdraw the motor from the linkage assembly.

7 On Estate models, the motor drives the wiper arm directly and a linkage is not used. To remove the motor, undo the mounting bolts and remove it from the mounting plate.

Refitting

8 Refitting is a reversal of removal, noting the following points.

a) Ensure that the motor is in the 'parked' position before refitting.

b) On Hatchback models, if the motor has been removed from the linkage, ensure that the marks made on the linkage drive link and motor spindle are aligned on refitting.

c) Refit the wiper arm with reference to Section 17.

20 Windscreen/tailgate washer system components - removal and refitting

Washer fluid reservoir

Note: Prior to removing the reservoir, empty the contents of the reservoir, or be prepared for fluid spillage.

Removal

1 Disconnect the battery negative terminal (refer to *Disconnecting the battery* in the Reference Section of this manual).

2 Apply the handbrake, then jack up the front of the vehicle and support securely on axle stands (see *Jacking and vehicle support*).

3 Remove the securing screws, and withdraw the splash guard from the bottom of the wing panel to expose the reservoir.

4 Disconnect the wiring plug from the fluid pump

5 Unscrew upper and lower securing bolts, then disconnect the fluid hoses from the pump, and lower the reservoir from the wing panel **(see illustrations)**.

Refitting

6 Refitting is a reversal of removal.

Washer fluid pump

Note: Prior to removing the pump, empty the contents of the reservoir, or be prepared for fluid spillage.

Removal

7 Proceed as described in paragraphs 1 to 3.

8 Disconnect the wiring plug from the pump.

9 Carefully pull the pump from the sealing grommet in the reservoir.

10 Mark the fluid hoses to ensure that they are reconnected in their original locations, the disconnect the hoses from the pump.

Refitting

11 Refitting is a reversal of removal, but check the condition of the sealing grommet, and renew if necessary.

Windscreen washer nozzle
Removal

12 Remove the scuttle cover panel as described in Chapter 11, Section 23.

13 Working at the rear of the panel, release the securing clips, and push the nozzle out of the panel **(see illustration)**.

14 Disconnect fluid hose from the nozzle.

Refitting

15 Refitting is a reversal of removal.

Tailgate washer nozzle
Removal

16 On Hatchback models, release the securing clips, and lower the rear of the headlining from the roof. Reach in and unscrew the securing nut, then tilt the nozzle towards the driver's side of the vehicle, and manipulate it out through the top of the roof panel **(see illustration)**.

17 On Estate models, carefully prise the nozzle assembly from the tailgate deflector panel **(see illustration)**.

18 Disconnect the fluid hose from the nozzle. Make sure that the hose does not fall into the roof or tailgate whilst the nozzle is removed.

Refitting

19 Refitting is a reversal of removal.

21 Radio/cassette player - removal and refitting

Note: *On models with a security-coded radio/cassette player, once the battery has been disconnected, the unit cannot be re-activated until the appropriate security code has been entered. Do not remove the unit unless the appropriate code is known. The following information applies to radio/cassette players having standard DIN fixings.*

20.16 Tilt the tailgate washer nozzle towards the driver's side of the vehicle and withdraw it from the roof panel - Hatchback models

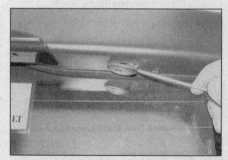

20.17 Carefully prise the tailgate washer nozzle assembly from the tailgate deflector panel - Estate models

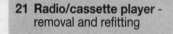

21.5 Using DIN tools to remove the radio/cassette player

Removal

1 Disconnect the battery negative terminal (refer to *Disconnecting the battery* in the Reference Section of this manual).
2 Open the radio/cassette player cover.
3 In order to release the retaining clips, two DIN removal tools will be required. These tools comprise two U-shaped rods, with cut-outs in the ends, which engage with the radio/cassette player securing clips (these tools are often supplied with the vehicle when new if a DIN standard audio unit is fitted). Suitable tools can easily be obtained from car accessory shops or audio specialists.
4 Slide the removal tools into the holes in the front of the radio/cassette player, until they are felt to engage with the securing clips.
5 Pull the unit from the facia using the tools, until the wiring connector(s) and aerial lead can be disconnected from the rear of the unit **(see illustration)**.

Refitting

6 Reconnect the wiring plug(s) and the aerial lead, then push the unit into its housing until the securing clips engage.
7 On completion, reconnect the battery negative lead and, where applicable enter the security code.

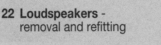

22 Loudspeakers -
   removal and refitting

Facia-mounted loudspeakers

Removal

1 Disconnect the battery negative terminal (refer to *Disconnecting the battery* in the Reference Section of this manual).
2 Carefully pull the trim panel from the windscreen pillar.
3 Carefully prise up the front edge of the loudspeaker, then pivot the speaker up to release the rear securing lugs. Withdraw the speaker from the facia and disconnect the wiring **(see illustration)**.

Refitting

4 Refitting is a reversal of removal.

Front door-mounted loudspeakers

Removal

5 Disconnect the battery negative lead.
6 Starting at the bottom, carefully unclip the loudspeaker cover panel. Take care, as the clips are easily broken.
7 Unscrew the securing screws, then withdraw the loudspeaker from the housing in the door, and disconnect the wiring **(see illustrations)**.

Refitting

8 Refitting is a reversal of removal.

Rear side-mounted loudspeakers

Removal

9 Fold down the rear seat back, then unscrew the rear parcel shelf support panel securing screws. Two screws are located at the rear of the panel, and one screw at the front of the panel.
10 Carefully prise the securing clip from the side of the front of the panel, then unclip the panel from the body **(see illustration)**.
11 Disconnect the loudspeaker wiring plug.
12 Twist the loudspeaker anti-clockwise to release it from body panel, then withdraw the loudspeaker **(see illustration)**.

Refitting

13 Refitting is a reversal of removal, but make sure that the loudspeaker insulating foam is correctly positioned.

Rear roof-mounted loudspeakers

Removal

14 Turn the speaker cover anti-clockwise to release the internal mounting lugs and withdraw the cover **(see illustration)**.

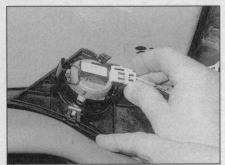

22.3 Disconnecting the wiring plug from a facia-mounted loudspeaker

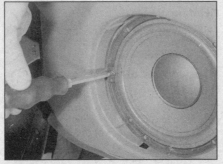

22.7a Unscrew the securing screws . . .

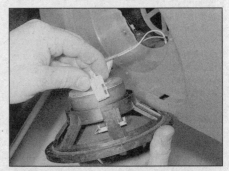

22.7b . . . then withdraw the loudspeaker and disconnect the wiring plug

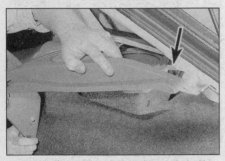

22.10 Removing the rear parcel shelf support panel - rear side mounted loudspeakers

22.12 Removing a rear loudspeaker - rear side mounted loudspeakers

22.14 Turn the speaker cover anti-clockwise to release the internal mounting lugs and withdraw the cover - rear roof mounted loudspeakers

15 Twist the loudspeaker anti-clockwise to release it from roof panel, then withdraw the loudspeaker **(see illustration)**.
16 Disconnect the loudspeaker wiring plug.

Refitting

17 Refitting is a reversal of removal.

23 Radio aerial - removal and refitting

Removal

1 The aerial mast can be unscrewed from the base for renewal. To remove the complete aerial assembly, proceed as follows.
2 Disconnect the battery negative terminal (refer to *Disconnecting the battery* in the Reference Section of this manual).
3 Slide the central locking remote control receiver unit cover, or trim panel, as applicable, forwards from the roof console panel.
4 Remove the two now-exposed securing screws, then tilt the console panel down to release the rear clips.
5 Disconnect the wiring from the components mounted in the console panel, then withdraw the panel.
6 Unscrew the now-exposed aerial securing nut, and disconnect the lead from the aerial stud.
7 Lift the aerial assembly from the roof panel.

Refitting

8 Refitting is a reversal of removal.

24 Anti-theft alarm system and engine immobiliser - general information

General information

Certain vehicles are equipped with an anti-theft alarm system and/or and engine immobiliser system. Various types of system may be fitted depending on vehicle specification, and market.

The anti-theft alarm system, and the engine immobiliser are automatically activated by the central locking remote control transmitter. If for some reason the remote control central locking transmitter fails whilst the alarm is armed, the alarm can be disarmed using the dedicated key in the switch provided beneath the fusebox cover. On some models, the engine immobiliser can be temporarily disarmed by entering the dedicated four-digit code supplied with the vehicle when new (on models without a code, a Renault dealer must be consulted to disarm the system). The method of entering this code varies, depending on model - refer to the vehicle handbook, or a Renault dealer for further information.

The alarm system has switches on the bonnet, tailgate and each of the doors. It also

22.15 Twist the loudspeaker anti-clockwise to release it from roof panel - rear roof mounted loudspeakers

has ultrasonic sensing, which detects movement inside the vehicle via sensors mounted in the roof console.

When working on the vehicle electrical system, the alarm siren can be isolated using the dedicated key in the switch provided under the bonnet. Pull off the plastic cover for access to the switch. When the switch has been used, take care to securely refit the cover to prevent moisture from entering the switch.

Any faults with the system should be referred to a Renault dealer.

Disconnecting the vehicle battery

The following precautions should be observed when disconnecting the and reconnecting the battery leads on a vehicle equipped with an alarm system.
a) Before disconnecting the battery, de-activate the alarm siren, using the dedicated key.
b) When reconnecting the battery, as soon as the battery is reconnected, the alarm is automatically activated. Use the remote control transmitter to turn off the alarm, then activate the alarm siren using the dedicated key.

25 Air bag system - general information, precautions and system de-activation

General information

A driver's side air bag is fitted as standard equipment on some models, and is available as an option on others. The air bag is fitted to the steering wheel centre pad.

Similarly, a passenger's side air bag is also fitted as standard equipment, or as an option, depending on model.

The system is armed only when the ignition is switched on, however, a reserve power source maintains a power supply to the system in the event of a break in the main electrical supply. The system is activated by a 'g' sensor (deceleration sensor), incorporated in the electronic control unit. Note that the electronic control unit also controls the front seat belt tensioners.

The air bags are inflated by gas generators, which force the bags out from their locations in the steering wheel, and the passenger's side facia, where applicable.

Precautions

⚠️ **Warning: The following precautions must be observed when working on vehicles equipped with an air bag system, to prevent the possibility of personal injury.**

General precautions

The following precautions must be observed when carrying out work on a vehicle equipped with an air bag.
a) *Do not disconnect the battery with the engine running.*
b) *Before carrying out any work in the vicinity of the air bag, removal of any of the air bag components, or any welding work on the vehicle, de-activate the system as described in the following sub-Section.*
c) *Do not attempt to test any of the air bag system circuits using test meters or any other test equipment.*
d) *If the air bag warning light comes on, or any fault in the system is suspected, consult a Renault dealer without delay. Do not attempt to carry out fault diagnosis, or any dismantling of the components.*

Precautions to be taken when handling an air bag

a) *Transport the air bag by itself, bag upward.*
b) *Do not put your arms around the air bag.*
c) *Carry the air bag close to the body, bag outward.*
d) *Do not drop the air bag or expose it to impacts.*
e) *Do not attempt to dismantle the air bag unit.*
f) *Do not connect any form of electrical equipment to any part of the air bag circuit.*

Precautions to be taken when storing an air bag unit

a) *Store the unit in a cupboard with the air bag upward.*
b) *Do not expose the air bag to temperatures above 80°C.*
c) *Do not expose the air bag to flames.*
d) *Do not attempt to dispose of the air bag - consult a Renault dealer.*
e) *Never refit an air bag which is known to be faulty or damaged.*

De-activation of air bag system

The system must be de-activated as follows, before carrying out any work on the air bag components or surrounding area.
a) *Switch off the ignition.*
b) *Remove the ignition key.*
c) *Switch off all electrical equipment.*
d) *Disconnect the battery negative terminal.*
e) *Insulate the battery negative terminal and the end of the battery negative lead to prevent any possibility of contact.*

12

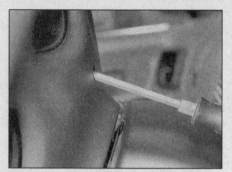

26.6 Unscrewing a driver's side air bag unit securing screw

f) *Remove the air bag/seat belt tensioner system fuse from the fusebox.*
g) *Wait for at least five minutes before carrying out any further work.*

Activation of air bag system

Before reconnecting the air bag wiring connector, the operation of the system must be checked using a dummy air bag unit. This operation **must** be entrusted to a Renault dealer who will have access to the appropriate equipment. Once the system has been checked, a Renault dealer will be able to re-activate the system.

⚠ *Warning: Failure to have the air bag system checked before reconnecting the air bag wiring connector may result in incorrect operation or accidental triggering of the air bag or seat belt tensioner systems.*

26 Air bag system components - removal and refitting

⚠ *Warning: Refer to the precautions given in Section 25 before attempting to carry out work on the air bag components. Note that the system operation must be checked by a Renault dealer before reconnecting the air bag wiring plug.*

General

1 The air bag sensor is integral with the electronic control unit.
2 Any suspected faults with the air bag system should be referred to a Renault dealer - under no circumstances attempt to carry out any work other than removal and refitting of the air bag units and the control unit, as described in the following paragraphs, or the rotary switch (see Section 4).

Driver's side air bag unit
Removal

3 The air bag unit is an integral part of the steering wheel centre pad.
4 De-activate the air bag system as described in Section 25.
5 Move the steering wheel as necessary for access to the two air bag unit securing

26.7 Withdraw the air bag unit and disconnect the orange wiring connector

screws. The screws are located at the rear of the steering wheel centre pad.
6 Remove the two air bag unit securing screws (**see illustration**).
7 Withdraw the air bag unit from the steering wheel, and disconnect the **orange** wiring connector from the rear of the unit (**see illustration**).

⚠ *Warning: The orange air bag connector must always be disconnected before disconnecting the rotary switch wiring connector.*

Refitting

Note: *Before reconnecting the air bag wiring connector, the operation of the system must be checked using a dummy air bag unit. This operation* **must** *be entrusted to a Renault dealer who will have access to the appropriate equipment. Once the system has been checked, a Renault dealer will be able to re-activate the system.*

⚠ *Warning: Failure to have the air bag system checked before reconnecting the air bag wiring connector may result in incorrect operation or accidental triggering of the air bag or seat belt tensioner systems.*

8 Before reconnecting the air bag wiring connector, the system must be checked by a Renault dealer.
9 Refitting is a reversal of removal, but tighten the air bag securing screws to the specified torque.

Passenger's side air bag unit
Removal

Note: *If the passenger's air bag unit has been triggered, the complete facia assembly must be renewed, as the air bag mountings will be damaged.*

10 On early models, the passenger's air bag unit is mounted in the location normally occupied by the glovebox in the facia. On later models the air bag is mounted above the glovebox.
11 De-activate the air bag system as described in Section 25.
12 To remove the air bag on later models, remove the glovebox as described in Chapter 11, Section 28. Disconnect the wiring connector, undo the four bolts and remove the unit from the facia. Depress the two tabs on the side of the air bag module to release the module from the facia trim.
13 To remove the air bag on early models, proceed as follows.
14 Remove the rubber mat from the storage tray on the passenger's side of the facia.
15 Peel off the 'tamper-proof' label to reveal the screws.
16 Remove the two screws, and withdraw the upper cover plate to reveal the three cover screws (**see illustration**).
17 Unscrew the three screws securing the cover, and lift off the cover to expose the lower trim securing screws.
18 Remove the securing screws and withdraw the lower trim to expose the three lower air bag module securing screws (**see illustration**).

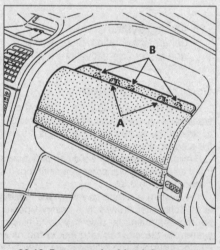

26.16 Passenger's side air bag cover details - early models

A *Upper cover plate screws*
B *Cover screws*

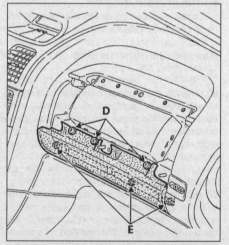

26.18 Passenger's side air bag lower trim details - early models

D *Lower trim securing screws*
E *Lower air bag module securing screws*

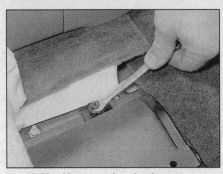

26.28a Unscrew the plastic nuts . . .

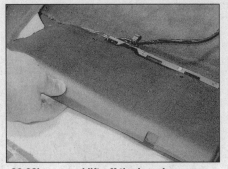

26.28b . . . and lift off the housing cover - early models

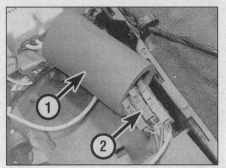

26.29 Slide the foam insulation (1) from the wiring connectors (2) - early models

19 Unscrew the three securing screws, then lift out the air bag unit, and disconnect the two wiring connectors.

Refitting

Note: *Before reconnecting the air bag wiring connector, the operation of the system must be checked using a dummy air bag unit. This operation **must** be entrusted to a Renault dealer who will have access to the appropriate equipment. Once the system has been checked, a Renault dealer will be able to re-activate the system.*

⚠️ **Warning: Failure to have the air bag system checked before reconnecting the air bag wiring connector may result in incorrect operation or accidental triggering of the air bag or seat belt tensioner systems.**

20 Before reconnecting the air bag wiring connector, the system must be checked by a Renault dealer.
21 Refitting is a reversal of removal, bearing in mind the following points.
a) *Tighten the air bag securing screws to the specified torque.*
b) *Fit a new 'tamper-proof' label (obtainable from a Renault dealer) to the upper cover plate on early models.*
c) *Ensure that no foreign bodies (nuts, screws, clips, etc) are left between the air bag unit and the covers.*

Electronic control unit

Removal

22 The electronic control unit controls the air bag(s) and the seat belt tensioners, where applicable. The unit is mounted in a housing under the front passenger's seat on early models, or under the centre console on later models.
23 De-activate the air bag system as described in Section 25.
24 To remove the control unit on later models, remove the centre console as described in Chapter 11. Disconnect the wiring connector, undo the mounting bolts and remove the control unit from the car.
25 To remove the control unit on early models, proceed as follows.
26 Move the front passenger's seat as far forwards as possible (access is much easier if

the seat is removed as described in Chapter 11).
27 Release the securing clips and lift up the carpet panel from the top of the control unit housing.
28 Unscrew the plastic nuts and lift off the housing cover **(see illustrations)**.
29 Slide the foam insulation from the wiring connectors, then separate the two halves of each connector **(see illustration)**.
30 Unscrew the four securing nuts, and lift the control unit from the housing.

Refitting

⚠️ **Warning: It advisable to consult a Renault dealer for advice regarding any precautions to be observed when refitting the electronic control unit and re-activating the system.**

31 Refitting is a reversal of removal, bearing in mind the following points.
a) *The unit must be refitted with the arrow on the label facing the front of the vehicle.*
b) *Refit the unit and tighten the securing nuts to the specified torque before reconnecting the wiring plugs.*

Air bag rotary switch

32 Refer to Section 4.

27 Cruise control system - general information

The cruise control system is vacuum-operated, and comprises the following components.
a) *Vacuum pump.*
b) *Vacuum-operated throttle actuator.*
c) *Electronic control unit (ECU).*
d) *Road speed sensor.*
e) *Control switches mounted on the facia, steering wheel, and brake and clutch pedals.*

The system allows a constant road speed to be maintained without the need to operate the accelerator pedal. The desired 'cruising' speed can be set manually at speeds above 30 mph (50 km/h).

The speed is controlled by moving the throttle lever, by means of the throttle actuator. The throttle actuator is supplied with vacuum from the vacuum pump. The vacuum

pump is controlled by the electronic control unit according to information provided by the road speed sensor and control switches.

The system does not affect the operation of the throttle pedal (although the pedal will move in accordance with the movement of the throttle actuator), and the system can be overridden at any time by depressing the accelerator, brake or clutch pedals, or using the main control switch.

28 Cruise control system components - removal and refitting

Vacuum pump

Removal

1 The pump is located behind the bumper on the right-hand side of the vehicle.
2 Disconnect the battery negative terminal (refer to *Disconnecting the battery* in the Reference Section of this manual).
3 Remove the front bumper as described in Chapter 11.
4 Unscrew the two vacuum pump securing bolts, and lift the assembly from the body panel **(see illustration)**.
5 Where applicable, remove the cover from the assembly to expose the vacuum and wiring connections.

28.4 Cruise control vacuum pump location (arrowed) under right-hand wheel arch

12

6 Disconnect the wiring plugs and the vacuum hoses, noting their locations to aid refitting, then withdraw the pump.

Refitting

7 Refitting is a reversal of removal, but ensure that the pump wiring plugs and vacuum hoses are correctly reconnected as noted before removal.

Throttle actuator

Removal

8 Disconnect the battery negative terminal (refer to *Disconnecting the battery* in the Reference Section of this manual).
9 Disconnect the vacuum hose from the actuator **(see illustration)**.
10 Disconnect the throttle operating rod/cable from the actuator.
11 Unscrew the securing bolts, and remove the actuator complete with its mounting bracket.

Refitting

12 Refitting is a reversal of removal, but on completion, check the adjustment of the throttle operating rod/cable as follows.
13 With the actuator in its rest (disengaged) position, and the throttle in the idle position, there should be 1.5 mm of free-play at the actuator end of the rod/cable.
14 The free-play can be adjusted by adjusting the length of the throttle operating rod.

Electronic control unit

Removal

15 The electronic control unit is located in a housing under the passenger's seat.
16 Disconnect the battery negative terminal (refer to *Disconnecting the battery* in the Reference Section of this manual).
17 Move the front passenger's seat as far forwards as possible (access is much easier if the seat is removed as described in Chapter 11).
18 Release the securing clips and lift up the carpet panel from the top of the control unit housing.
19 Unscrew the plastic nuts and lift off the housing cover.
20 Unclip the control unit from the housing, and disconnect the wiring plug(s) **(see illustration)**.

Refitting

21 Refitting is a reversal of removal.

Road speed sensor

22 The vehicle speed sensor is located in the speedometer cable, either in the engine compartment, or in the driver's footwell, depending on model. Removal and refitting of the sensor is self-explanatory.

Control switches

23 Refer to Section 4.

Pedal switches

24 Refer to the procedure for stop-light removal and refitting in Chapter 9.

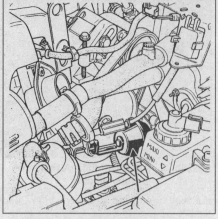

28.9 Cruise control throttle actuator location (arrowed)

29 Trip computer - general information

General information

1 Certain models are fitted with a trip computer, which provides data on fuel consumption and range, and also a readout of the mileage to be covered before the next service is due. The unit analyses information supplied by a the fuel level sensor, coolant temperature sensor, oil level sensor, oil temperature sensor, fuel flowmeter, and a vehicle speed sensor.
2 The trip computer is integral with the instrument panel (refer to Section 10 for details of instrument panel removal and refitting).
3 Note that the instrument panel cannot be dismantled. A self-diagnostic system is built into the trip computer control unit, which senses any faults in the system components, and stores fault codes which can be used by a Renault dealer to analyse any problems.

Service indicator resetting

Note: *If the mileage before the next due service is less than 1250 miles (2000 km), the*

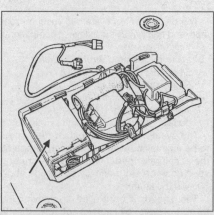

28.20 Cruise control electronic control unit location (arrowed)

spanner symbol on the display will flash each time the ignition is switched on.
4 Within 10 seconds of switching on the ignition, press the re-set button below the speedometer, and hold the button depressed until the number of miles displayed begins to flash.
5 Hold the button depressed - the number of miles on the display will move left, along the display, and the figures for the re-set value will appear on the right of the display. Continue to hold the button depressed until the desired re-set number is displayed in its entirety, then release the button.

30 Voice synthesiser/ warning system - general information

General information

1 Certain models are fitted with a voice synthesiser/warning system which provides spoken warnings of various faults. The unit analyses information provided by various sensors, and provides warnings on low fluid levels, low oil pressure, engine overheating, defective light bulbs, etc.
2 The warning system control unit is integral with the instrument panel (refer to Section 10 for details of instrument panel removal and refitting).
3 Any problems with the system should be referred to a Renault dealer.

Component removal and refitting

Loudspeaker

4 The loudspeaker is located under the fusebox cover, next to the fusebox.
5 To remove the loudspeaker, open the fusebox cover, and remove the loudspeaker securing screws.
6 Withdraw the loudspeaker and disconnect the wiring.
7 Refitting is a reversal of removal.

Bulb failure monitor unit

8 The unit is under the passenger's seat.
9 Disconnect the battery negative terminal (refer to *Disconnecting the battery* in the Reference Section of this manual).
10 Push the seat as far back as possible, then remove the two screws securing the plastic cover to the control unit housing.
11 Unclip the control unit from the housing, and disconnect the wiring plug(s).
12 Refitting is a reversal of removal.

Electronic control unit

13 The control unit is integral with the instrument panel. Note that the instrument panel cannot be dismantled, and if the unit is faulty, the complete instrument panel must be renewed.
14 Refer to Section 10 for details of instrument panel removal and refitting.

RENAULT LAGUNA wiring diagrams

Diagram 1

Key to symbols

Bulb	⊗
Switch	
Multiple contact switch (ganged)	
Fuse/fusible link and rating	F24 30A
Resistor	
Variable resistor	
Item no.	15
Pump/motor	(M)
Earth and location (via lead)	E1
Gauge/meter	
Diode	
Light emitting diode (LED)	
Internal connection (connecting wires)	
Wire splice or connector	
Solenoid actuator	
Connections to other circuits. Direction of arrow denotes current flow.	*Diagram 3, Arrow A* **High beam warning light**
Wire colour (Red wire/white tracer)	R/W
Screened cable	
Denotes alternative wiring variation (brackets)	
Box shape denotes part of a larger component	
30 Terminal identification (i.e. battery +ve)	30 A10
A10 Connector pin number	

Earth locations

E1	Below RH rear light cluster
E2	Below LH rear light cluster
E3	Below LH rear light cluster
E4	RH driver's inner sill
E5	LH passenger's front inner sill
E6	LH passenger's rear inner sill
E7	RH side engine (petrol) LH side engine (Diesel)
E8	Front of engine compartment' below LH headlight

Terminal identification

15	Ignition switch 'ignition' position
15	Ignition switch 'ignition' position
30	Battery +ve
31	Earth
50	Ignition switch 'start' position
85	Relay winding input
86	Relay winding earth
87	Relay output
87a	Relay output
D+	Charge warning light

Key to circuits

Diagram 1	Information for wiring diagrams
Diagram 2	Starting, charging, Diesel fuel shut-off, engine cooling fan,
Diagram 3	Diesel fuel heater, pre and post heating
Diagram 4	Turbo Diesel pre and post heating, ABS
Diagram 5	Automatic transmission, air bag/pretensioners, variable power steering
Diagram 6	Fuel injection Bosch monopoint
Diagram 7	Fuel injection (Bendix Siemens MPi)
Diagram 8	Instrument cluster
Diagram 9	Instrument cluster
Diagram 10	Speed sensor, clock/external temperature gauge, heater blower
Diagram 11	Heated front/rear screen, heated washer jets, windscreen wash/wipe
Diagram 12	Rear wash/wipe, headlight washer, sidelights and headlights
Diagram 13	Stop, reversing,fog and direction indicator lights
Diagram 14	Headlight levelling, interior lighting
Diagram 15	Rheostat interior lighting, audio system, central locking
Diagram 16	Electric mirrors and windows

Typical passenger compartment fuse box

Fuse	Rating	Circuit protected
F1	20A	Cooling fan
F2	25A	Horn
F3	15A	RH main beam
F4	15A	LH main beam
F5	10A	Reversing light (automatic transmission)
F6	10A	Clock/radio and memory units, electric mirrors, alarm
F7	25A	Front wiper park position
F8	15A	Direction indicators and hazard warning light
F9	25A	Windscreen wiper
F10	15A	Instrument panel, air bag, pretensioners, alarm, memory seats
F11	25A	Central locking
F12	30A	+ve supply after ignition switch
F13	5A	Variable power steering
F14	5A	ABS
F15	5A	Automatic transmission
F16	15A	RH dipped beam headlight
F17	15A	LH dipped beam headlight, headlight levelling
F18	15A	Stop lights, cruise control, flasher unit, bulb failure unit
F19	15A	Heated seats
F20	20A	Rear screen wiper, heated front/rear screen, reversing lights, lights on buzzer, heater controls
F23	15A	Variable shock absorbers
F24	10A	Clock, display illunination, alarm, memory seats
F25	10A	Rear fog light
F26	20A	Radio, heater controls, cigar lighter
F27	25A	Memory seats
F28	25A	Front fog lights
F29	15A	Boot and interior lights
F30	5A	Injection
F31	10A	Heated mirrors
F32	30A	Sunroof
F33	5A	Radio telephone
F34	10A	LH side light, lights, bulb failure unit
F35	40A	Heated rear screen
F37	40A	Air conditioning
F38	40A	Driver's electric window
F39	40A	Passenger's electric window
F40	40A	Power passenger seat

Typical engine compartment fuse box

Fuse	Rating	Circuit protected
F51	60A	Accessory cut-off shunt
F52	60A	+ battery passenger compartment
F53	60A	+ ignition switch
F54	60A	After ignition relay
F55	40A	RH cooling fan
F56	40A	LH cooling fan
F57	30A	ABS
F58	40A	Headlight washers
F60	30/70A	Fuel injection (30A), Diesel pre-heating (70A)
F65	70A	Heated windscreen relay

12

H31764

Wire colours

BA	White	JA	Yellow
BE	Blue	MA	Brown
BJ	Beige	NO	Black
CY	Clear	OR	Orange
GR	Grey	RG	Red
SA	Pink	VI	Mauve
VE	Green		

Key to items

1 Battery
2 Ignition switch
3 Engine compartment fuse box
4 Passenger compartment fuse box
5 Starter motor
6 Alternator
7 Starter relay
8 Diesel fuel shut-off valve
9 Cooling fan switch (single temperature)
10 Cooling fan switch (dual temperature)
11 Cooling fan motor
12 Cooling fan relay
13 Cooling fan 1st speed relay
14 Cooling fan 2nd speed relay
15 Cooling fan resistor

Diagram 2

H31765

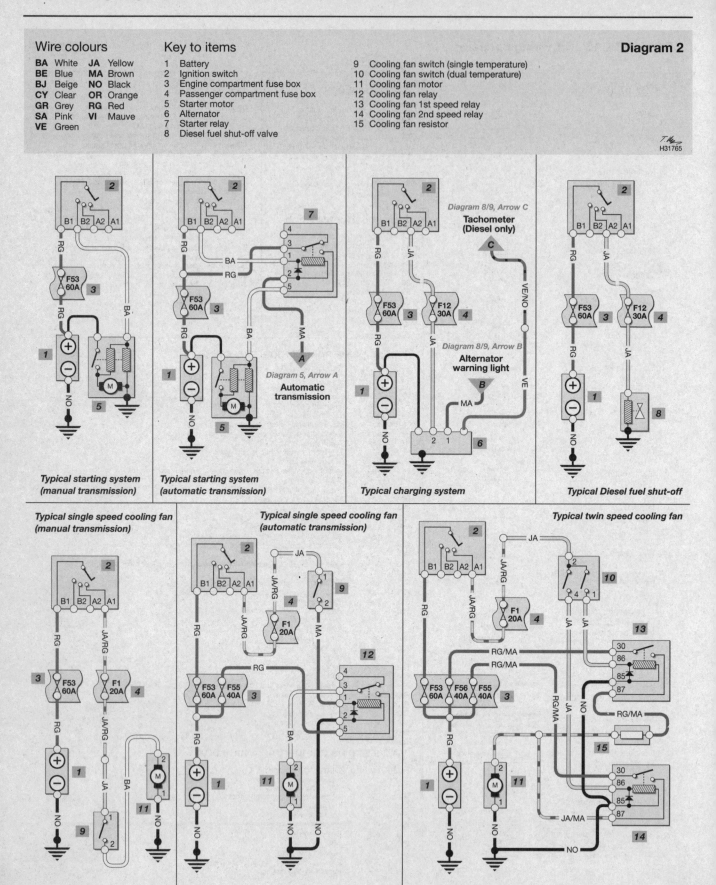

Typical starting system (manual transmission)

Typical starting system (automatic transmission)

Typical charging system

Typical Diesel fuel shut-off

Typical single speed cooling fan (manual transmission)

Typical single speed cooling fan (automatic transmission)

Typical twin speed cooling fan

Wire colours

BA	White	JA	Yellow
BE	Blue	MA	Brown
BJ	Beige	NO	Black
CY	Clear	OR	Orange
GR	Grey	RG	Red
SA	Pink	VI	Mauve
VE	Green		

Key to items

1 Battery
2 Ignition switch
3 Engine compartment fuse box
4 Passenger compartment fuse box
17 Fuel filter heater
18 Fuel heater temperature switch
19 Preheater unit
20 Glow plugs
21 Pump unit
  a = advance/retard valve
  b = EGR switch
  c = throttle position switch
  d = pump advance solenoid
22 Altitude relay
23 Altitude capsule
24 Coolant temperature sensor
25 Fast idle solenoid valve
26 Clutch pedal switch
27 EGR timer relay
28 EGR temperature switch
29 EGR valve

Diagram 3

H31766

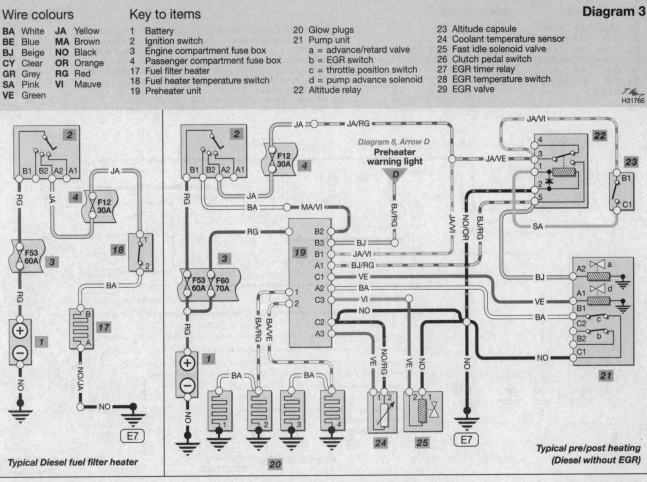

Typical Diesel fuel filter heater

Typical pre/post heating (Diesel without EGR)

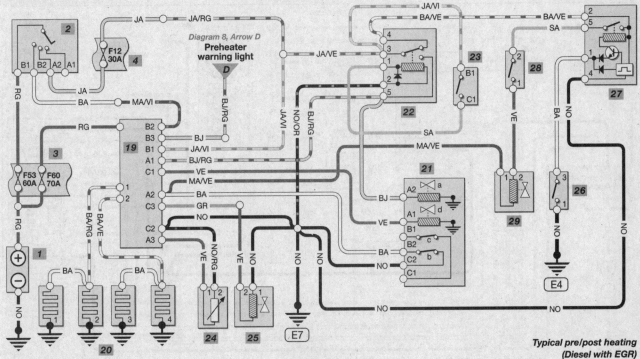

Typical pre/post heating (Diesel with EGR)

12

Diagram 4
H31767

Wire colours

BA	White	JA	Yellow
BE	Blue	MA	Brown
BJ	Beige	NO	Black
CY	Clear	OR	Orange
GR	Grey	RG	Red
SA	Pink	VI	Mauve
VE	Green		

Key to items

1 Battery
2 Ignition switch
3 Engine compartment fuse box
4 Passenger compartment fuse box
19 Preheater unit
20 Glow plugs
21 Pump unit
 a = advance/retard valve
 d = pump advance solenoid
24 Coolant temperature switch
25 Fast idle solenoid valve
27 EGR relay
29 EGR valve
32 Throttle potentiometer
33 Speed threshold sensor
34 Diagnostic socket
35 Air temperature sensor
36 ABS auxiliary relay
37 ABS connection plate
 a = ABS main relay
 b = ABS pump relay
38 ABS hydraulic unit
39 ABS soleniod valve unit
40 Pedal travel sensor
41 Wheel sensor
42 ABS ECU
43 Stop light switch

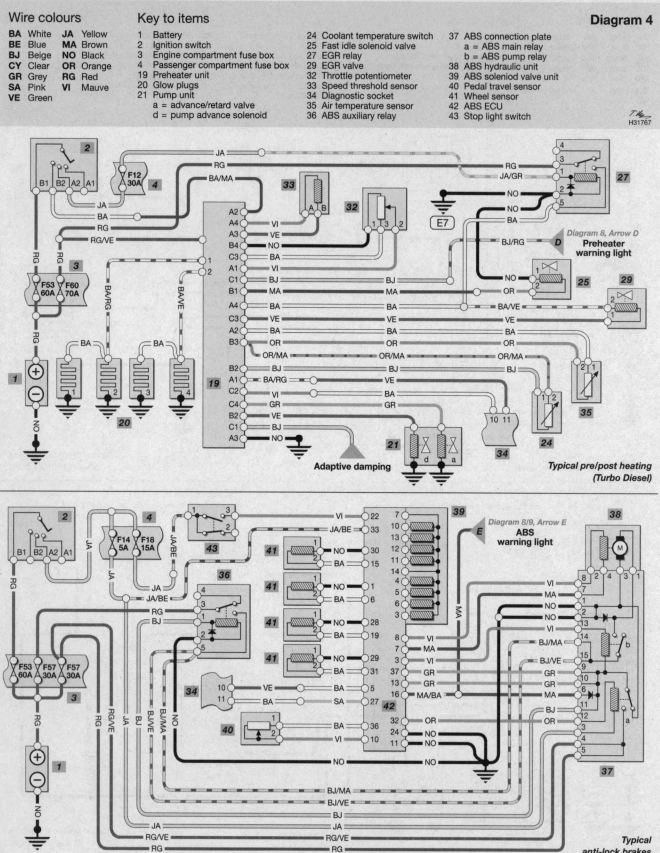

Typical pre/post heating
(Turbo Diesel)

Adaptive damping

Diagram 8, Arrow D
Preheater warning light

Diagram 8/9, Arrow E
ABS warning light

Typical anti-lock brakes

Wire colours

BA	White	**JA**	Yellow
BE	Blue	**MA**	Brown
BJ	Beige	**NO**	Black
CY	Clear	**OR**	Orange
GR	Grey	**RG**	Red
SA	Pink	**VI**	Mauve
VE	Green		

Key to items

1 Battery
2 Ignition switch
3 Engine compartment fuse box
4 Passenger compartment fuse box
34 Diagnostic socket
43 Stop light switch
46 Auto. trans. control unit
47 Auto. trans. ECU
48 Line pressure sensor
49 Throttle potentiometer
50 Speed sensor
51 Multifunction switch
52 Kick down switch
53 Shift speed control switch
54 Selector light
55 Airbag control unit
56 Driver's airbag/cruise control switch
57 Passenger's airbag
58 Driver's seatbelt pretensioner
59 Passenger's seatbelt pretensioner
60 Power steering ECU
61 Power steering speed sensor
62 Power steering motor

Diagram 5

H31768

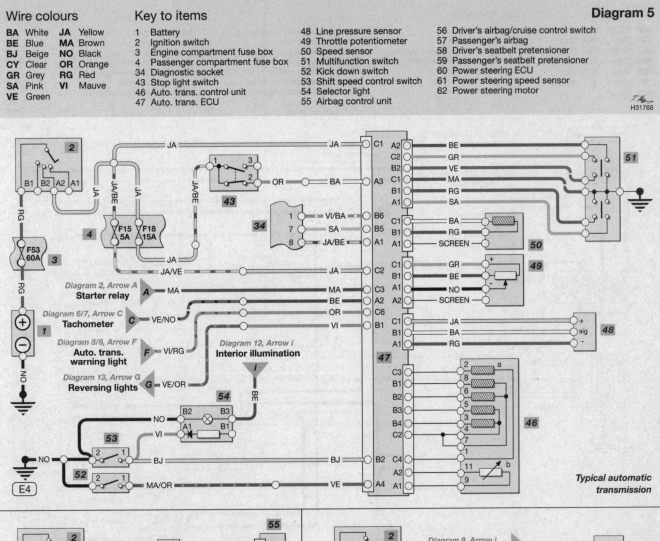

Typical automatic transmission

Diagram 2, Arrow A — **Starter relay** — A
Diagram 6/7, Arrow C — **Tachometer** — C
Diagram 8/9, Arrow F — **Auto. trans. warning light** — F
Diagram 12, Arrow i — **Interior illumination** — i
Diagram 13, Arrow G — **Reversing lights** — G

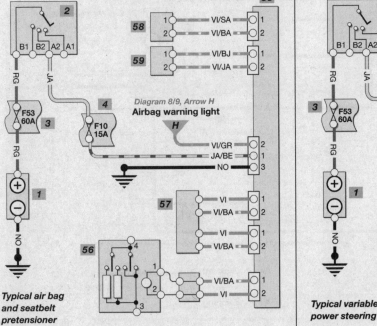

Typical air bag and seatbelt pretensioner

Diagram 8/9, Arrow H — **Airbag warning light** — H

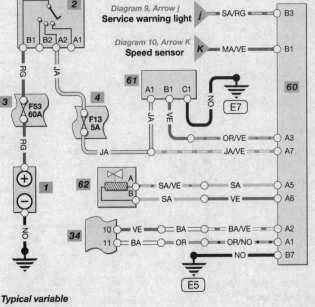

Typical variable power steering

Diagram 9, Arrow j — **Service warning light** — j
Diagram 10, Arrow K — **Speed sensor** — K

12

Wire colours

BA	White	JA	Yellow
BE	Blue	MA	Brown
BJ	Beige	NO	Black
CY	Clear	OR	Orange
GR	Grey	RG	Red
SA	Pink	VI	Mauve
VE	Green		

Key to items

1 Battery
2 Ignition switch
3 Engine compartment fuse box
4 Passenger compartment fuse box
34 Diagnostic socket
65 Fuel injection ECU
66 Oxygen sensor

67 Ignition power module
68 Fuel pump relay
69 Injection locking relay
70 Fuel pump
71 Crankshaft sensor
72 Canister purge solenoid valve
73 Coolant temperature sensor

74 Knock sensor
75 MAP sensor
76 Throttle body
  a = throttle potentiometer
  b = idle speed regulator
  c = fuel injection
  d = air temperature sensor

Diagram 6

H31769

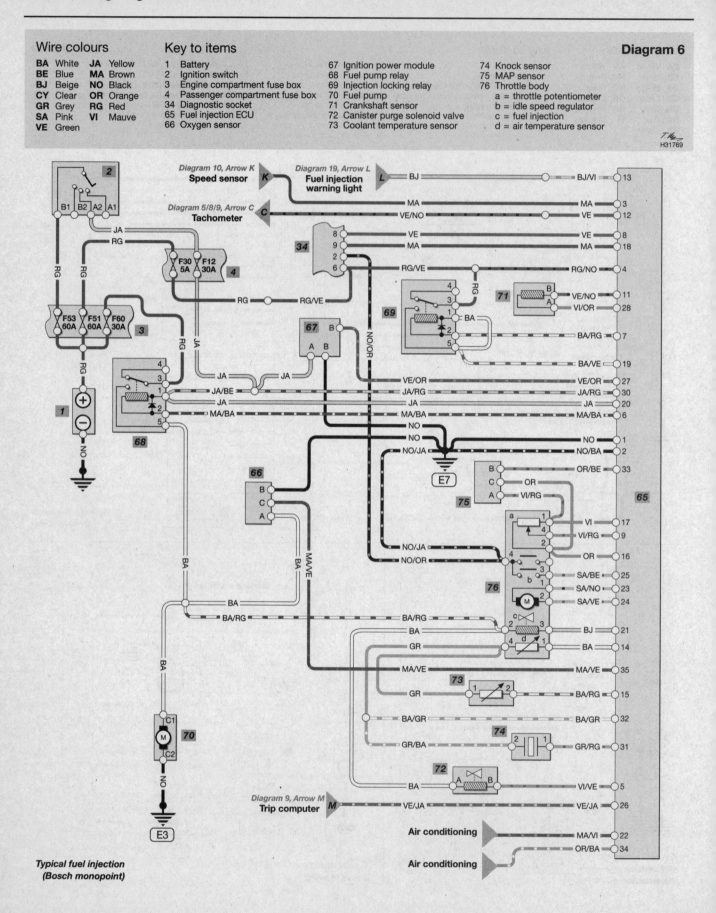

*Typical fuel injection
(Bosch monopoint)*

Wire colours

BA	White	**JA**	Yellow
BE	Blue	**MA**	Brown
BJ	Beige	**NO**	Black
CY	Clear	**OR**	Orange
GR	Grey	**RG**	Red
SA	Pink	**VI**	Mauve
VE	Green		

Key to items

1 Battery
2 Ignition switch
3 Engine compartment fuse box
4 Passenger compartment fuse box
34 Diagnostic socket
65 Fuel injection ECU
66 Oxygen sensor
67 Ignition power module
68 Fuel pump relay
69 Injection locking relay
70 Fuel pump
71 Crankshaft sensor
72 Canister purge solenoid valve
73 Coolant temperature sensor
74 Knock sensor
75 MAP sensor
77 Throttle potentiometer
78 Idle speed regulator
79 Air temperature sensor
80 Power steering pressure switch
81 Fuel injectors

Diagram 7

H31770

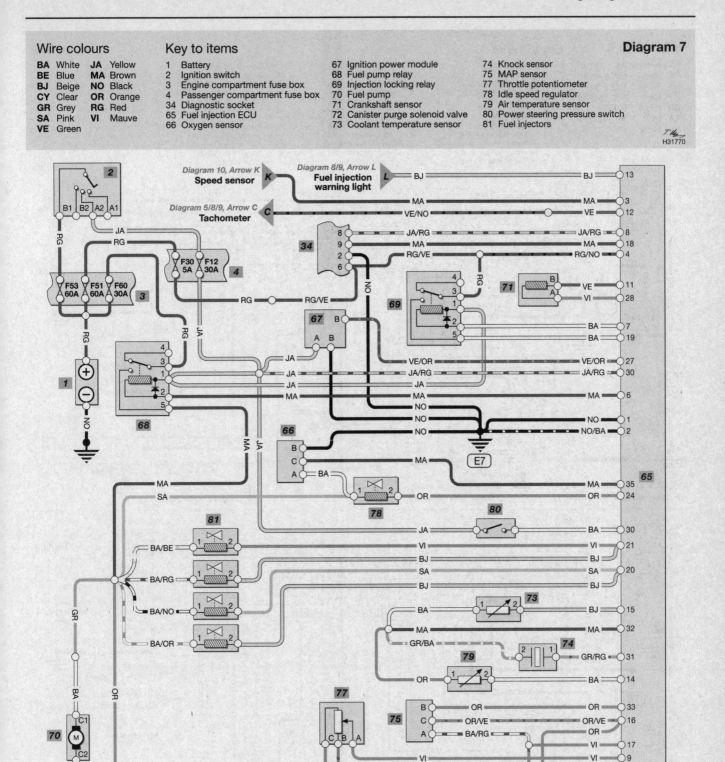

*Typical fuel injection
(Bendix Siemens MPi)*

12

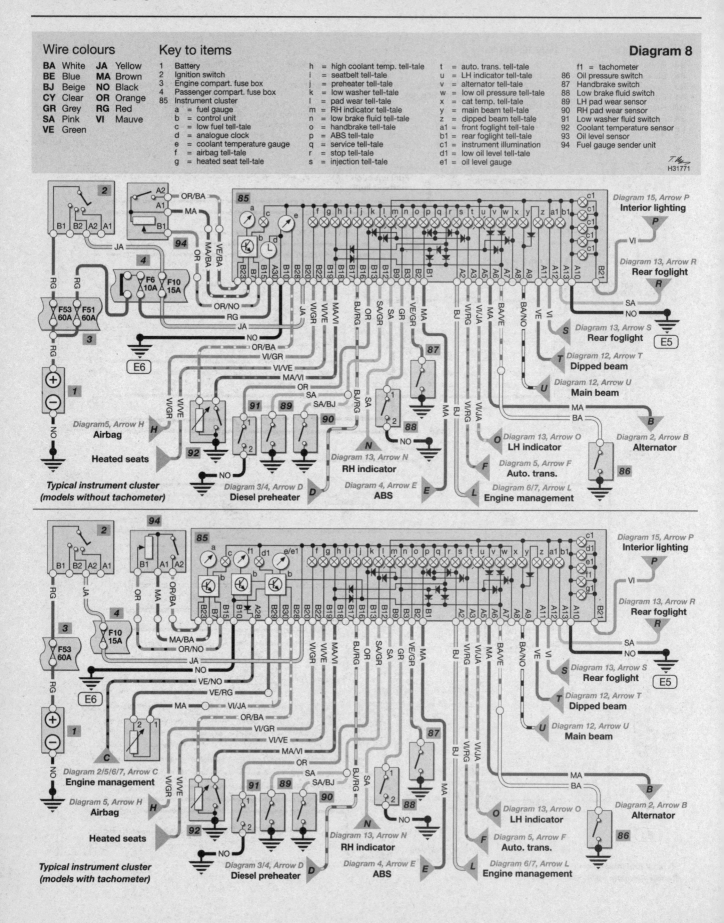

H31771

Wire colours

BA	White	**JA**	Yellow
BE	Blue	**MA**	Brown
BJ	Beige	**NO**	Black
CY	Clear	**OR**	Orange
GR	Grey	**RG**	Red
SA	Pink	**VI**	Mauve
VE	Green		

Key to items

1 Battery
2 Ignition switch
3 Engine compart. fuse box
4 Passenger compart. fuse box
34 Diagnostic socket
85 Instrument cluster
86 Oil pressure switch

88 Low brake fluid switch
89 LH pad wear sensor
90 RH pad wear sensor
91 Low washer fluid switch
92 Coolant temperature sensor
93 Oil level sensor (Diesel)
94 Fuel gauge sender unit

95 Oil temperature sensor (Diesel)
96 Combined oil level/temperature
    sensor (petrol)

Diagram 9

H31772

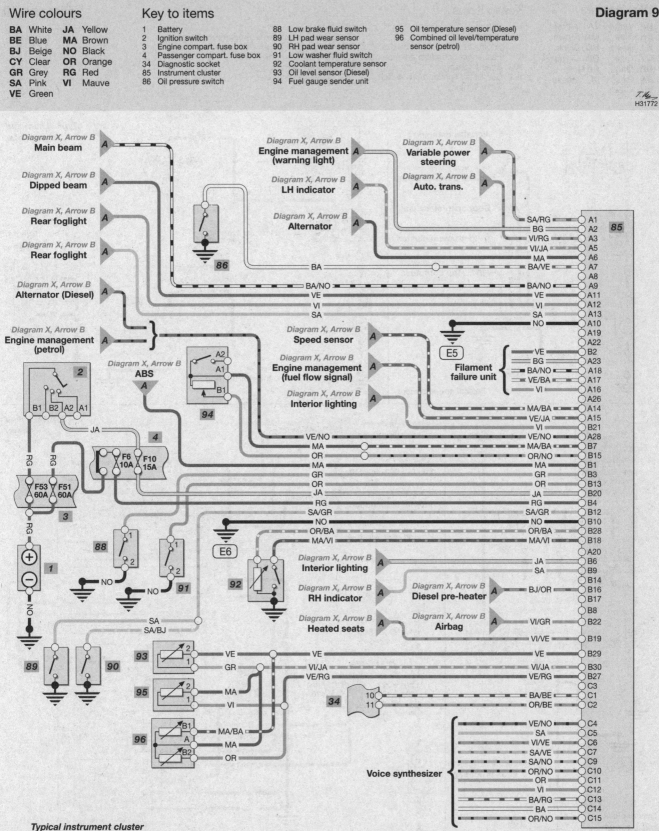

Typical instrument cluster
(models with on-board computer)

Wire colours

BA	White	JA	Yellow
BE	Blue	MA	Brown
BJ	Beige	NO	Black
CY	Clear	OR	Orange
GR	Grey	RG	Red
SA	Pink	VI	Mauve
VE	Green		

Key to items

1   Battery
2   Ignition switch
3   Engine compartment fuse box
4   Passenger compartment fuse box
100   Speed sensor
101   Combined lighting/horn switch
102   Cigar lighter
103   Horn
104   Clock and external temperature gauge
105   Passenger side electric mirror
106   Heater blower motor
107   Heater switch
108   Heater resistor unit

Diagram 10

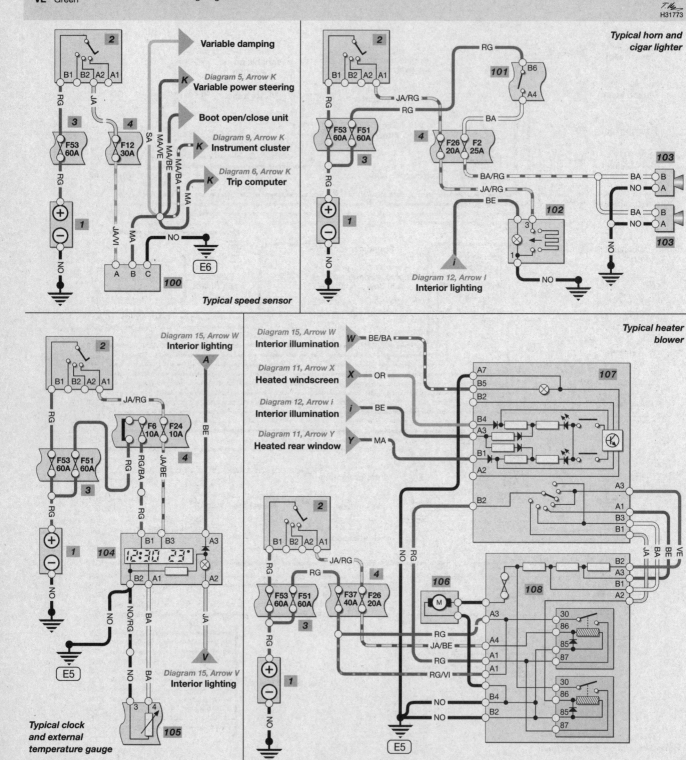

Variable damping

Diagram 5, Arrow K
Variable power steering

Boot open/close unit

Diagram 9, Arrow K
Instrument cluster

Diagram 6, Arrow K
Trip computer

Typical speed sensor

Typical horn and cigar lighter

Diagram 12, Arrow I
Interior lighting

Typical heater blower

Diagram 15, Arrow W
Interior lighting

Diagram 15, Arrow W
Interior illumination

Diagram 11, Arrow X
Heated windscreen

Diagram 12, Arrow i
Interior illumination

Diagram 11, Arrow Y
Heated rear window

Diagram 15, Arrow V
Interior lighting

Typical clock and external temperature gauge

Wire colours

BA	White	**JA**	Yellow
BE	Blue	**MA**	Brown
BJ	Beige	**NO**	Black
CY	Clear	**OR**	Orange
GR	Grey	**RG**	Red
SA	Pink	**VI**	Mauve
VE	Green		

Key to items

1 Battery
2 Ignition switch
3 Engine compartment fuse box
4 Passenger compartment fuse box
110 Heated rear window relay
111 Ignition relay 1
112 Heated rear window
113 Heated windscreen relay
114 Heated windscreen
115 Heated washer jet
116 Windscreen wiper timer
117 Wash/wipe combination switch
118 Front wiper motor
119 Front/rear washer pump

Diagram 11

H31774

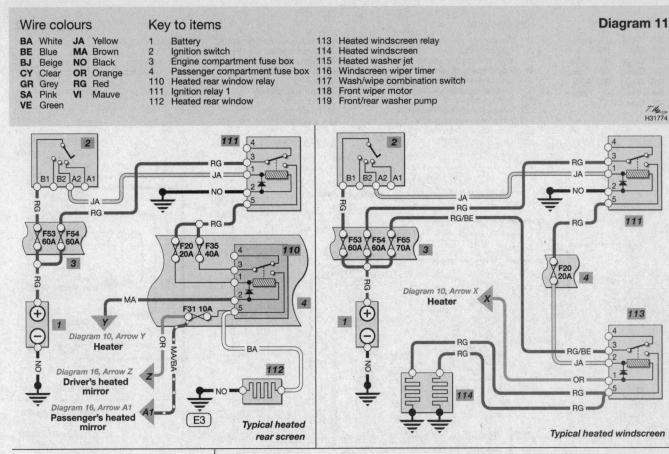

Diagram 10, Arrow Y
Heater

Diagram 16, Arrow Z
Driver's heated mirror

Diagram 16, Arrow A1
Passenger's heated mirror

Typical heated rear screen

Diagram 10, Arrow X
Heater

Typical heated windscreen

Typical windscreen wash/wipe

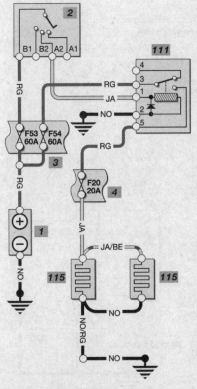

Typical heated washer jets

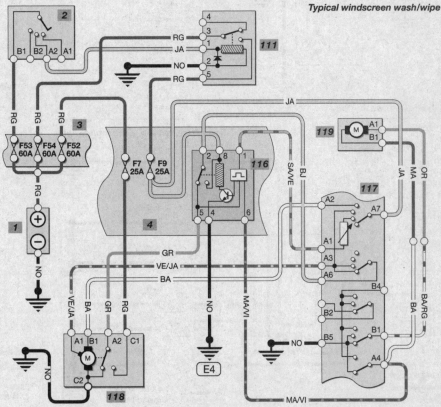

12

Wire colours

BA	White	**JA**	Yellow
BE	Blue	**MA**	Brown
BJ	Beige	**NO**	Black
CY	Clear	**OR**	Orange
GR	Grey	**RG**	Red
SA	Pink	**VI**	Mauve
VE	Green		

Key to items

1   Battery
2   Ignition switch
3   Engine compartment fuse box
4   Passenger compartment fuse box
101   Combined lighting/horn switch
110   Heated rear window relay
111   Ignition relay 1
117   Wash/wipe combination switch
119   Front/rear washer pump
120   Rear wiper timer relay
121   Rear wiper motor

122   Headlight washer timer relay
123   Headlight washer pump
124   Number plate light
125   LH rear light cluster
    a = tail light
126   RH rear light cluster
    a = tail light
127   LH headlight unit
    a = sidelight
    b = dip beam
    c = main beam

128   RH headlight unit
    a = sidelight
    b = dip beam
    c = main beam

Diagram 12

H31775

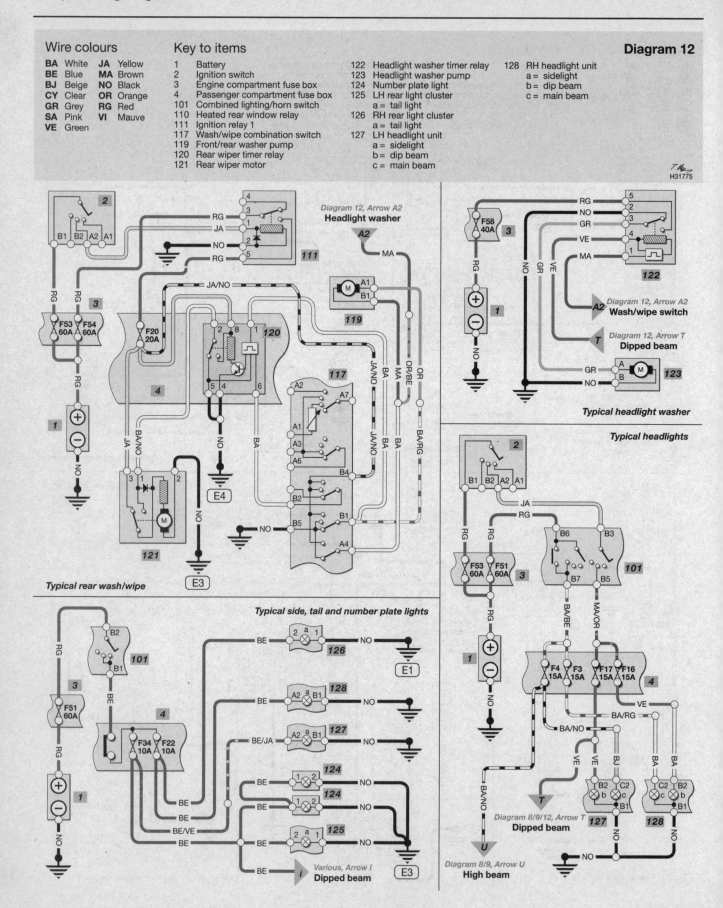

Typical rear wash/wipe

Typical side, tail and number plate lights

Typical headlight washer

Typical headlights

Diagram 12, Arrow A2
Headlight washer

Diagram 12, Arrow A2
Wash/wipe switch

Diagram 12, Arrow T
Dipped beam

Diagram 8/9/12, Arrow T
Dipped beam

Various, Arrow i
Dipped beam

Diagram 8/9, Arrow U
High beam

Wire colours

BA	White	JA	Yellow
BE	Blue	MA	Brown
BJ	Beige	NO	Black
CY	Clear	OR	Orange
GR	Grey	RG	Red
SA	Pink	VI	Mauve
VE	Green		

Key to items

1   Battery
2   Ignition switch
3   Engine compartment fuse box
4   Passenger compartment fuse box
43 Stop light switch
101 Combined lighting/horn switch
111 Ignition relay 1
125 LH rear light cluster
    b = stop light
    c = direction indicator

126 RH rear light cluster
    b = stop light
    c = direction indicator
130 LH reversing light
131 RH reversing light
132 Front foglight relay
133 Reversing light switch
134 Rear foglight
135 LH front foglight

136 RH front foglight
137 LH front direction indicator
138 LH direction indicator side repeater
139 RH front direction indicator
140 RH direction indicator side repeater
141 Hazard warning light
142 Direction indicator flasher unit

Diagram 13

H31776

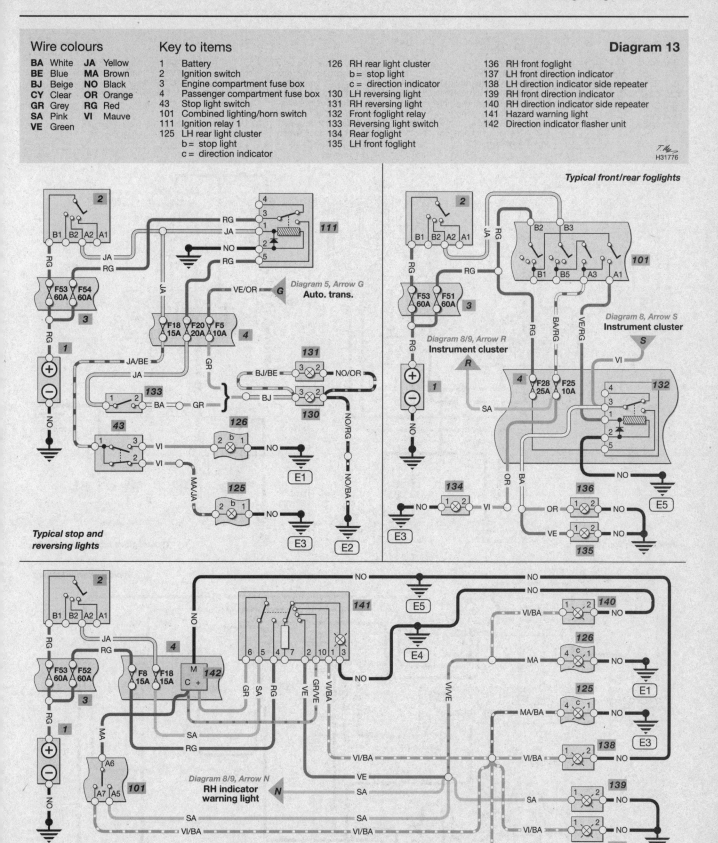

Typical front/rear foglights

Diagram 5, Arrow G
Auto. trans.

Diagram 8/9, Arrow R
Instrument cluster

Diagram 8, Arrow S
Instrument cluster

Typical stop and
reversing lights

Diagram 8/9, Arrow N
RH indicator
warning light

Diagram 8/9, Arrow O
LH indicator
warning light

Typical direction indicator
and hazard warning lights

12

Diagram 14

Wire colours

BA	White	**JA**	Yellow
BE	Blue	**MA**	Brown
BJ	Beige	**NO**	Black
CY	Clear	**OR**	Orange
GR	Grey	**RG**	Red
SA	Pink	**VI**	Mauve
VE	Green		

Key to items

1 Battery
2 Ignition switch
3 Engine compartment fuse box
4 Passenger compartment fuse box
101 Combined lighting/horn switch
145 Headlight levelling switch
146 LH headlight adjustment motor
147 RH headlight adjustment motor
148 Glove box light

149 Glove box light switch
150 Luggage compartment light
151 Luggage compartment light switch
152 Interior lighting/central locking control unit
153 Driver's door switch
154 Passenger's door switch
155 LH rear door switch
156 RH rear door switch
157 Map reading light

158 Front interior light
159 LH rear interior light
160 RH rear interior light
161 Infrared sensor

H31777

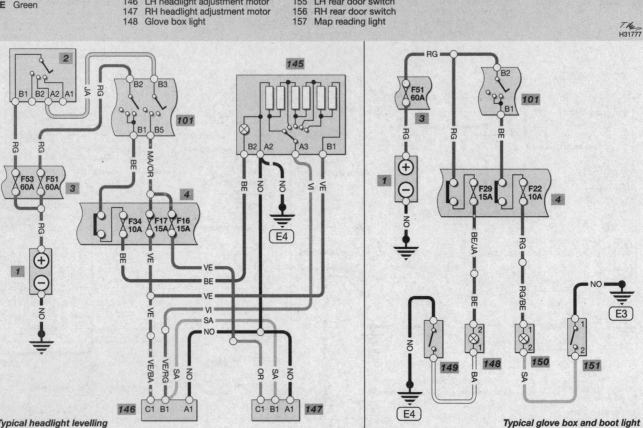

Typical headlight levelling

Typical glove box and boot light

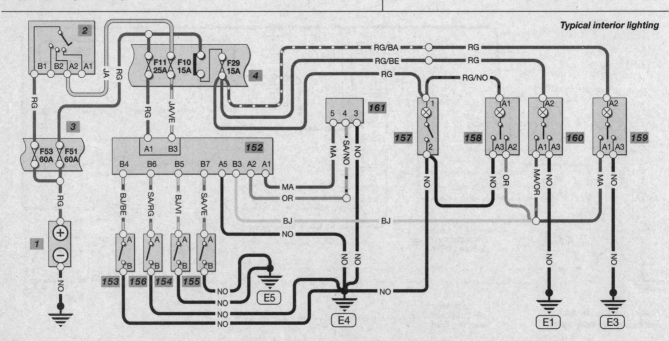

Typical interior lighting

Wire colours

BA	White	**JA**	Yellow
BE	Blue	**MA**	Brown
BJ	Beige	**NO**	Black
CY	Clear	**OR**	Orange
GR	Grey	**RG**	Red
SA	Pink	**VI**	Mauve
VE	Green		

Key to items

1 Battery
2 Ignition switch
3 Engine compartment fuse box
4 Passenger compartment fuse box
101 Combined lighting/horn switch
152 Interior lighting/central locking control unit
161 Infrared sensor
165 Lighting rheostat relay
166 Interior lighting rheostat
167 Audio unit
168 Satellite cointrol unit
169 LH front speaker
170 RH front speaker
171 LH rear speaker
172 RH rear speaker
173 LH tweeter
174 RH tweeter
175 Central locking control switch
176 Driver's central locking motor
177 Passenger's central locking motor
178 LH rear central locking motor
179 RH rear central locking motor
180 Tailgate lock motor

Diagram 15

H31778

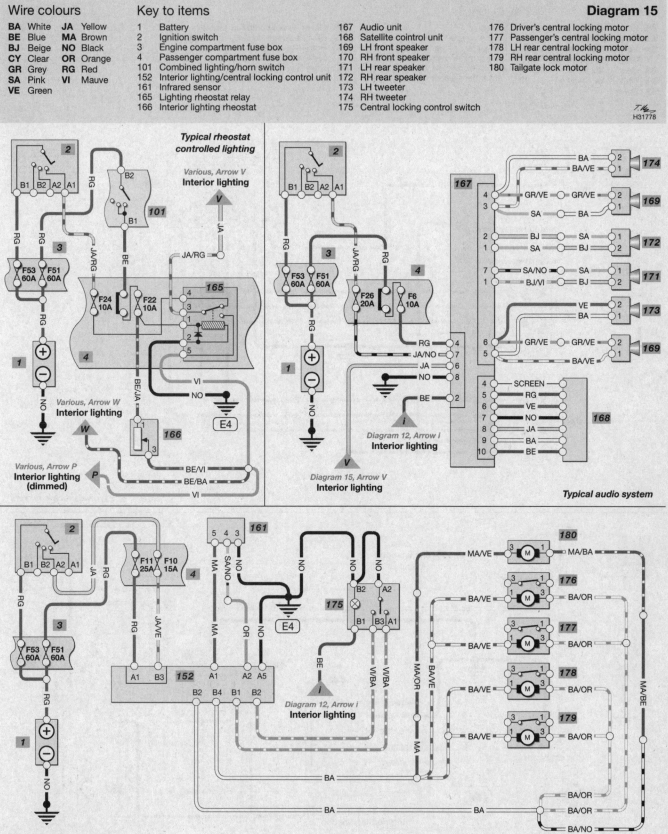

Typical rheostat controlled lighting

Various, Arrow V **Interior lighting**

Various, Arrow W **Interior lighting**

Various, Arrow P **Interior lighting (dimmed)**

Diagram 12, Arrow i **Interior lighting**

Diagram 15, Arrow V **Interior lighting**

Typical audio system

Diagram 12, Arrow i **Interior lighting**

Typical central locking

Wire colours

BA	White	JA	Yellow
BE	Blue	MA	Brown
BJ	Beige	NO	Black
CY	Clear	OR	Orange
GR	Grey	RG	Red
SA	Pink	VI	Mauve
VE	Green		

Key to items

1 Battery
3 Engine compartment fuse box
4 Passenger compartment fuse box
185 Electric mirror switch
186 Driver's electric mirror
187 Passenger's electric mirror
188 Driver's electric window switch
189 Driver's switch for passenger window
190 Passenger's electric window switch
191 'One touch' control unit
192 Driver's window motor
193 Passenger's window motor

Diagram 16

H31779

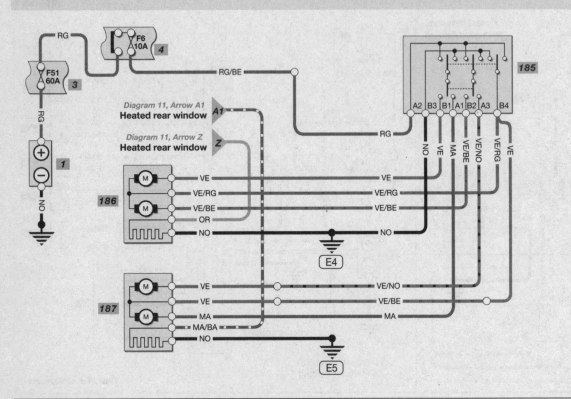

Typical electric mirrors

Typical electric windows

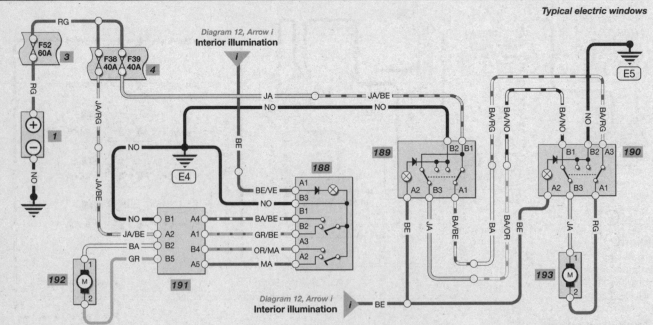

Dimensions and weights

Note: *All figures are approximate, and may vary according to model. Refer to manufacturer's data for exact figures.*

Dimensions

Overall length:
   Hatchback models .... 4508 mm
   Estate models .... 4628 mm
Overall width (excluding wing mirrors) .... 1752 mm
Overall height (unladen):
   Hatchback models .... 1433 mm
   Estate models .... 1470 mm
Wheelbase .... 2654 mm

Weights

Kerb weight* .... 1225 to 1475 kg
Maximum towing weight:**
   Unbraked trailer .... 610 to 750 kg
   Braked trailer .... 1000 to 1700 kg
Maximum roof rack load .... 70 kg
*Depending on model and specification.
**Refer to a Renault dealer for exact recommendations

Conversion factors

Length (distance)

Inches (in)	x 25.4	= Millimetres (mm)	x 0.0394	= Inches (in)
Feet (ft)	x 0.305	= Metres (m)	x 3.281	= Feet (ft)
Miles	x 1.609	= Kilometres (km)	x 0.621	= Miles

Volume (capacity)

Cubic inches (cu in; in³)	x 16.387	= Cubic centimetres (cc; cm³)	x 0.061	= Cubic inches (cu in; in³)
Imperial pints (Imp pt)	x 0.568	= Litres (l)	x 1.76	= Imperial pints (Imp pt)
Imperial quarts (Imp qt)	x 1.137	= Litres (l)	x 0.88	= Imperial quarts (Imp qt)
Imperial quarts (Imp qt)	x 1.201	= US quarts (US qt)	x 0.833	= Imperial quarts (Imp qt)
US quarts (US qt)	x 0.946	= Litres (l)	x 1.057	= US quarts (US qt)
Imperial gallons (Imp gal)	x 4.546	= Litres (l)	x 0.22	= Imperial gallons (Imp gal)
Imperial gallons (Imp gal)	x 1.201	= US gallons (US gal)	x 0.833	= Imperial gallons (Imp gal)
US gallons (US gal)	x 3.785	= Litres (l)	x 0.264	= US gallons (US gal)

Mass (weight)

Ounces (oz)	x 28.35	= Grams (g)	x 0.035	= Ounces (oz)
Pounds (lb)	x 0.454	= Kilograms (kg)	x 2.205	= Pounds (lb)

Force

Ounces-force (ozf; oz)	x 0.278	= Newtons (N)	x 3.6	= Ounces-force (ozf; oz)
Pounds-force (lbf; lb)	x 4.448	= Newtons (N)	x 0.225	= Pounds-force (lbf; lb)
Newtons (N)	x 0.1	= Kilograms-force (kgf; kg)	x 9.81	= Newtons (N)

Pressure

Pounds-force per square inch (psi; lbf/in²; lb/in²)	x 0.070	= Kilograms-force per square centimetre (kgf/cm²; kg/cm²)	x 14.223	= Pounds-force per square inch (psi; lbf/in²; lb/in²)
Pounds-force per square inch (psi; lbf/in²; lb/in²)	x 0.068	= Atmospheres (atm)	x 14.696	= Pounds-force per square inch (psi; lbf/in²; lb/in²)
Pounds-force per square inch (psi; lbf/in²; lb/in²)	x 0.069	= Bars	x 14.5	= Pounds-force per square inch (psi; lbf/in²; lb/in²)
Pounds-force per square inch (psi; lbf/in²; lb/in²)	x 6.895	= Kilopascals (kPa)	x 0.145	= Pounds-force per square inch (psi; lbf/in²; lb/in²)
Kilopascals (kPa)	x 0.01	= Kilograms-force per square centimetre (kgf/cm²; kg/cm²)	x 98.1	= Kilopascals (kPa)
Millibar (mbar)	x 100	= Pascals (Pa)	x 0.01	= Millibar (mbar)
Millibar (mbar)	x 0.0145	= Pounds-force per square inch (psi; lbf/in²; lb/in²)	x 68.947	= Millibar (mbar)
Millibar (mbar)	x 0.75	= Millimetres of mercury (mmHg)	x 1.333	= Millibar (mbar)
Millibar (mbar)	x 0.401	= Inches of water (inH₂O)	x 2.491	= Millibar (mbar)
Millimetres of mercury (mmHg)	x 0.535	= Inches of water (inH₂O)	x 1.868	= Millimetres of mercury (mmHg)
Inches of water (inH₂O)	x 0.036	= Pounds-force per square inch (psi; lbf/in²; lb/in²)	x 27.68	= Inches of water (inH₂O)

Torque (moment of force)

Pounds-force inches (lbf in; lb in)	x 1.152	= Kilograms-force centimetre (kgf cm; kg cm)	x 0.868	= Pounds-force inches (lbf in; lb in)
Pounds-force inches (lbf in; lb in)	x 0.113	= Newton metres (Nm)	x 8.85	= Pounds-force inches (lbf in; lb in)
Pounds-force inches (lbf in; lb in)	x 0.083	= Pounds-force feet (lbf ft; lb ft)	x 12	= Pounds-force inches (lbf in; lb in)
Pounds-force feet (lbf ft; lb ft)	x 0.138	= Kilograms-force metres (kgf m; kg m)	x 7.233	= Pounds-force feet (lbf ft; lb ft)
Pounds-force feet (lbf ft; lb ft)	x 1.356	= Newton metres (Nm)	x 0.738	= Pounds-force feet (lbf ft; lb ft)
Newton metres (Nm)	x 0.102	= Kilograms-force metres (kgf m; kg m)	x 9.804	= Newton metres (Nm)

Power

Horsepower (hp)	x 745.7	= Watts (W)	x 0.0013	= Horsepower (hp)

Velocity (speed)

Miles per hour (miles/hr; mph)	x 1.609	= Kilometres per hour (km/hr; kph)	x 0.621	= Miles per hour (miles/hr; mph)

Fuel consumption*

Miles per gallon, Imperial (mpg)	x 0.354	= Kilometres per litre (km/l)	x 2.825	= Miles per gallon, Imperial (mpg)
Miles per gallon, US (mpg)	x 0.425	= Kilometres per litre (km/l)	x 2.352	= Miles per gallon, US (mpg)

Temperature

Degrees Fahrenheit = (°C x 1.8) + 32   Degrees Celsius (Degrees Centigrade; °C) = (°F - 32) x 0.56

It is common practice to convert from miles per gallon (mpg) to litres/100 kilometres (l/100km), where mpg x l/100 km = 282

Spare parts are available from many sources, including manufacturer's appointed garages, accessory shops, and motor factors. To be sure of obtaining the correct parts, it will sometimes be necessary to quote the vehicle identification number. If possible, it can also be useful to take the old parts along for positive identification. Items such as starter motors and alternators may be available under a service exchange scheme - any parts returned should always be clean.

Our advice regarding spare part sources is as follows.

Officially-appointed garages

This is the best source of parts which are peculiar to your vehicle, and which are not otherwise generally available (eg badges, interior trim, certain body panels, etc). It is also the only place at which you should buy parts if the vehicle is still under warranty.

Accessory shops

These are very good places to buy materials and components needed for the maintenance of your vehicle (oil, air and fuel filters, spark plugs, light bulbs, drivebelts, oils and greases, brake pads, touch-up paint, etc). Components of this nature sold by a reputable shop are of the same standard as those used by the vehicle manufacturer.

Besides components, these shops also sell tools and general accessories, usually have convenient opening hours, charge lower prices, and can often be found not far from home. Some accessory shops have parts counters where the components needed for almost any repair job can be purchased or ordered.

Motor factors

Good factors will stock all the more important components which wear out comparatively quickly, and can sometimes supply individual components needed for the overhaul of a larger assembly (eg brake seals and hydraulic parts, bearing shells, pistons, valves, alternator brushes). They may also handle work such as cylinder block reboring, crankshaft regrinding and balancing, etc.

Tyre and exhaust specialists

These outlets may be independent, or members of a local or national chain. They frequently offer competitive prices when compared with a main dealer or local garage, but it will pay to obtain several quotes before making a decision. When researching prices, also ask what "extras" may be added - for instance, fitting a new valve and balancing the wheel are both commonly charged on top of the price of a new tyre.

Other sources

Beware of parts or materials obtained from market stalls, car boot sales or similar outlets. Such items are not invariably sub-standard, but there is little chance of compensation if they do prove unsatisfactory. In the case of safety-critical components such as brake pads, there is the risk not only of financial loss but also of an accident causing injury or death.

Second-hand components or assemblies obtained from a car breaker can be a good buy in some circumstances, but this sort of purchase is best made by the experienced DIY mechanic.

Vehicle identification

Modifications are a continuing and unpublicised process in vehicle manufacture, quite apart from major model changes. Spare parts manuals and lists are compiled upon a numerical basis, the individual vehicle identification numbers being essential to correct identification of the component concerned.

When ordering spare parts, always give as much information as possible. Quote the car model, year of manufacture, body and engine numbers as appropriate.

The *Vehicle Identification Number (VIN)* plate is riveted to the bulkhead at the rear of the engine compartment on models up to early 1995. From early 1995, the VIN plate is replaced by an adhesive label located in the luggage compartment, in the spare wheel housing - an additional plate is also located on the right-hand centre door pillar. The VIN number may also be stamped into the top of the right-hand suspension turret in the engine compartment **(see illustrations)**.

The *engine number* location varies depending on engine type. On all petrol engines except 2.0 litre (16-valve) engines, the engine number plate is riveted to the front left-hand corner of the cylinder block. On 2.0 litre (16-valve) engines, the engine number is stamped on a label attached to the timing cover, or engraved on the rear of the cylinder block, behind the coolant pump. On diesel engines, the engine number stamped on a label attached to the timing belt cover at the right-hand end of the engine, or riveted to a plate attached to the front left-hand corner of the cylinder block **(see illustrations)**.

Note: *The first part of the engine number gives the engine code - eg, G8T.*

The *chassis number* is stamped into the top of the right-hand suspension turret, directly after the VIN number.

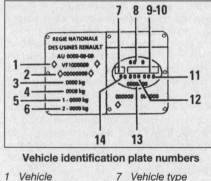

Vehicle identification plate numbers

1 Vehicle Identification Number (VIN)	7 Vehicle type
	8 Vehicle symbol
	9 Equipment number
2 Chassis number	10 Options
3 Max. all-up weight	11 Equipment level
4 Max. total train weight	12 Original paint code
5 Max. front axle load	13 Fabrication no
6 Max. rear axle load	14 Trim code

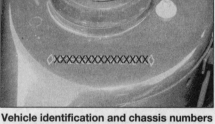

Vehicle identification and chassis numbers stamped on suspension turret

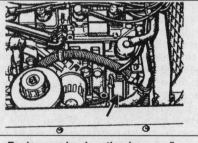

Engine number location (arrowed) - petrol engine models

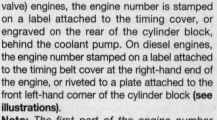

Vehicle identification plate location (arrowed) on bulkhead

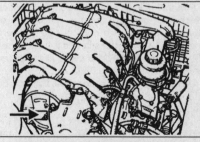

Engine number location (arrowed) - diesel engine models

Whenever servicing, repair or overhaul work is carried out on the car or its components, observe the following procedures and instructions. This will assist in carrying out the operation efficiently and to a professional standard of workmanship.

Joint mating faces and gaskets

When separating components at their mating faces, never insert screwdrivers or similar implements into the joint between the faces in order to prise them apart. This can cause severe damage which results in oil leaks, coolant leaks, etc upon reassembly. Separation is usually achieved by tapping along the joint with a soft-faced hammer in order to break the seal. However, note that this method may not be suitable where dowels are used for component location.

Where a gasket is used between the mating faces of two components, a new one must be fitted on reassembly; fit it dry unless otherwise stated in the repair procedure. Make sure that the mating faces are clean and dry, with all traces of old gasket removed. When cleaning a joint face, use a tool which is unlikely to score or damage the face, and remove any burrs or nicks with an oilstone or fine file.

Make sure that tapped holes are cleaned with a pipe cleaner, and keep them free of jointing compound, if this is being used, unless specifically instructed otherwise.

Ensure that all orifices, channels or pipes are clear, and blow through them, preferably using compressed air.

Oil seals

Oil seals can be removed by levering them out with a wide flat-bladed screwdriver or similar implement. Alternatively, a number of self-tapping screws may be screwed into the seal, and these used as a purchase for pliers or some similar device in order to pull the seal free.

Whenever an oil seal is removed from its working location, either individually or as part of an assembly, it should be renewed.

The very fine sealing lip of the seal is easily damaged, and will not seal if the surface it contacts is not completely clean and free from scratches, nicks or grooves. If the original sealing surface of the component cannot be restored, and the manufacturer has not made provision for slight relocation of the seal relative to the sealing surface, the component should be renewed.

Protect the lips of the seal from any surface which may damage them in the course of fitting. Use tape or a conical sleeve where possible. Lubricate the seal lips with oil before fitting and, on dual-lipped seals, fill the space between the lips with grease.

Unless otherwise stated, oil seals must be fitted with their sealing lips toward the lubricant to be sealed.

Use a tubular drift or block of wood of the appropriate size to install the seal and, if the seal housing is shouldered, drive the seal down to the shoulder. If the seal housing is unshouldered, the seal should be fitted with its face flush with the housing top face (unless otherwise instructed).

Screw threads and fastenings

Seized nuts, bolts and screws are quite a common occurrence where corrosion has set in, and the use of penetrating oil or releasing fluid will often overcome this problem if the offending item is soaked for a while before attempting to release it. The use of an impact driver may also provide a means of releasing such stubborn fastening devices, when used in conjunction with the appropriate screwdriver bit or socket. If none of these methods works, it may be necessary to resort to the careful application of heat, or the use of a hacksaw or nut splitter device.

Studs are usually removed by locking two nuts together on the threaded part, and then using a spanner on the lower nut to unscrew the stud. Studs or bolts which have broken off below the surface of the component in which they are mounted can sometimes be removed using a stud extractor. Always ensure that a blind tapped hole is completely free from oil, grease, water or other fluid before installing the bolt or stud. Failure to do this could cause the housing to crack due to the hydraulic action of the bolt or stud as it is screwed in.

When tightening a castellated nut to accept a split pin, tighten the nut to the specified torque, where applicable, and then tighten further to the next split pin hole. Never slacken the nut to align the split pin hole, unless stated in the repair procedure.

When checking or retightening a nut or bolt to a specified torque setting, slacken the nut or bolt by a quarter of a turn, and then retighten to the specified setting. However, this should not be attempted where angular tightening has been used.

For some screw fastenings, notably cylinder head bolts or nuts, torque wrench settings are no longer specified for the latter stages of tightening, "angle-tightening" being called up instead. Typically, a fairly low torque wrench setting will be applied to the bolts/nuts in the correct sequence, followed by one or more stages of tightening through specified angles.

Locknuts, locktabs and washers

Any fastening which will rotate against a component or housing during tightening should always have a washer between it and the relevant component or housing.

Spring or split washers should always be renewed when they are used to lock a critical component such as a big-end bearing retaining bolt or nut. Locktabs which are folded over to retain a nut or bolt should always be renewed.

Self-locking nuts can be re-used in non-critical areas, providing resistance can be felt when the locking portion passes over the bolt or stud thread. However, it should be noted that self-locking stiffnuts tend to lose their effectiveness after long periods of use, and should then be renewed as a matter of course.

Split pins must always be replaced with new ones of the correct size for the hole.

When thread-locking compound is found on the threads of a fastener which is to be re-used, it should be cleaned off with a wire brush and solvent, and fresh compound applied on reassembly.

Special tools

Some repair procedures in this manual entail the use of special tools such as a press, two or three-legged pullers, spring compressors, etc. Wherever possible, suitable readily-available alternatives to the manufacturer's special tools are described, and are shown in use. In some instances, where no alternative is possible, it has been necessary to resort to the use of a manufacturer's tool, and this has been done for reasons of safety as well as the efficient completion of the repair operation. Unless you are highly-skilled and have a thorough understanding of the procedures described, never attempt to bypass the use of any special tool when the procedure described specifies its use. Not only is there a very great risk of personal injury, but expensive damage could be caused to the components involved.

Environmental considerations

When disposing of used engine oil, brake fluid, antifreeze, etc, give due consideration to any detrimental environmental effects. Do not, for instance, pour any of the above liquids down drains into the general sewage system, or onto the ground to soak away. Many local council refuse tips provide a facility for waste oil disposal, as do some garages. If none of these facilities are available, consult your local Environmental Health Department, or the National Rivers Authority, for further advice.

With the universal tightening-up of legislation regarding the emission of environmentally-harmful substances from motor vehicles, most vehicles have tamperproof devices fitted to the main adjustment points of the fuel system. These devices are primarily designed to prevent unqualified persons from adjusting the fuel/air mixture, with the chance of a consequent increase in toxic emissions. If such devices are found during servicing or overhaul, they should, wherever possible, be renewed or refitted in accordance with the manufacturer's requirements or current legislation.

OIL CARE
FOLLOW THE CODE
OIL BANK LINE
0800 66 33 66
www.oilbankline.org.uk

Note: It is antisocial and illegal to dump oil down the drain. To find the location of your local oil recycling bank, call this number free.

The jack supplied with the vehicle tool kit should only be used for changing the roadwheels - see Wheel changing at the front of this manual. When carrying out any other kind of work, raise the vehicle using a hydraulic (or trolley) jack, and always supplement the jack with axle stands positioned under the vehicle jacking points.

When using a hydraulic jack or axle stands, always position the jack head or axle stand head under, or adjacent to one of the relevant wheel changing jacking points under the sills. Use a block of wood between the jack or axle stand and the sill - the block of wood should have a groove cut into it, in which the weld flange of the sill will locate (see illustrations).

The front of the vehicle can be raised using a substantial wooden block located across both body side-members, just behind the front crossmember. Place the jack under the wooden block.

Do not attempt to jack the vehicle under the front crossmember, the sump, or any of the suspension components.

The jack supplied with the vehicle locates in the jacking points on the underside of the sills - see Wheel changing at the front of this manual. Ensure that the jack head is correctly engaged before attempting to raise the vehicle.

⚠️ **Warning: Never work under, around, or near a raised vehicle, unless it is adequately supported in at least two places.**

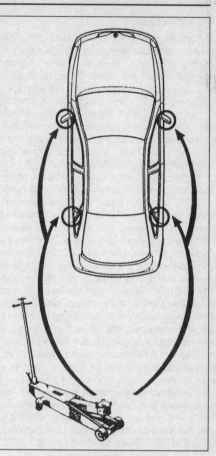

Vehicle jacking points

Use a wooden block between the jack or axle stands and sill

Disconnecting the battery

Several systems fitted to the vehicle require battery power to be available at all times, either to ensure their continued operation (such as the clock) or to maintain control unit memories which could be erased if the battery were to be disconnected. Whenever the battery is to be disconnected therefore, first note the following, to ensure that there are no unforeseen consequences of this action:

a) First, on any vehicle with central locking, it is a wise precaution to remove the key from the ignition, and to keep it with you, so that it does not get locked in if the central locking should engage accidentally when the battery is reconnected.

b) If a security-coded audio unit is fitted, and the unit and/or the battery is disconnected, the unit will not function again on reconnection until the correct security code is entered. Details of this procedure, which varies according to the unit fitted and vehicle model, are given in the vehicle owner's handbook. Where necessary, ensure you have the correct code before you disconnect the battery. If you do not have the code or details of the correct procedure, but can supply proof of ownership and a legitimate reason for wanting this information, a Renault dealer may be able to help.

c) On vehicles equipped with an original equipment anti-theft alarm system, before disconnecting the battery, de-activate the alarm siren, using the dedicated key. When reconnecting the battery, as soon as the battery is reconnected, the alarm is automatically activated. Use the remote control transmitter to turn off the alarm, then activate the alarm siren using the dedicated key.

Devices known as 'memory-savers' (or 'code-savers') can be used to maintain an electrical supply to various circuits. Precise details vary according to the device used. Typically, it is plugged into the cigarette lighter, and is connected by its own wires to a spare battery; the vehicle's own battery is then disconnected from the electrical system, leaving the 'memory-saver' to pass sufficient current to maintain audio unit security codes and any other memory values, and also to run permanently-live circuits such as the clock.

⚠️ **Warning: Some of these devices allow a considerable amount of current to pass, which can mean that many of the vehicle's systems are still operational when the main battery is disconnected. If a 'memory saver' is used, ensure that the circuit concerned is actually 'dead' before carrying out any work on it!**

Introduction

A selection of good tools is a fundamental requirement for anyone contemplating the maintenance and repair of a motor vehicle. For the owner who does not possess any, their purchase will prove a considerable expense, offsetting some of the savings made by doing-it-yourself. However, provided that the tools purchased meet the relevant national safety standards and are of good quality, they will last for many years and prove an extremely worthwhile investment.

To help the average owner to decide which tools are needed to carry out the various tasks detailed in this manual, we have compiled three lists of tools under the following headings: *Maintenance and minor repair, Repair and overhaul,* and *Special.* Newcomers to practical mechanics should start off with the *Maintenance and minor repair* tool kit, and confine themselves to the simpler jobs around the vehicle. Then, as confidence and experience grow, more difficult tasks can be undertaken, with extra tools being purchased as, and when, they are needed. In this way, a *Maintenance and minor repair* tool kit can be built up into a *Repair and overhaul* tool kit over a considerable period of time, without any major cash outlays. The experienced do-it-yourselfer will have a tool kit good enough for most repair and overhaul procedures, and will add tools from the *Special* category when it is felt that the expense is justified by the amount of use to which these tools will be put.

Maintenance and minor repair tool kit

The tools given in this list should be considered as a minimum requirement if routine maintenance, servicing and minor repair operations are to be undertaken. We recommend the purchase of combination spanners (ring one end, open-ended the other); although more expensive than open-ended ones, they do give the advantages of both types of spanner.

☐ *Combination spanners:*
Metric - 8 to 19 mm inclusive
☐ *Adjustable spanner - 35 mm jaw (approx.)*
☐ *Spark plug spanner (with rubber insert) - petrol models*
☐ *Spark plug gap adjustment tool - petrol models*
☐ *Set of feeler gauges*
☐ *Brake bleed nipple spanner*
☐ *Screwdrivers:*
Flat blade - 100 mm long x 6 mm dia
Cross blade - 100 mm long x 6 mm dia
Torx - various sizes (not all vehicles)
☐ *Combination pliers*
☐ *Hacksaw (junior)*
☐ *Tyre pump*
☐ *Tyre pressure gauge*
☐ *Oil can*
☐ *Oil filter removal tool*
☐ *Fine emery cloth*
☐ *Wire brush (small)*
☐ *Funnel (medium size)*
☐ *Sump drain plug key (not all vehicles)*

Repair and overhaul tool kit

These tools are virtually essential for anyone undertaking any major repairs to a motor vehicle, and are additional to those given in the *Maintenance and minor repair* list. Included in this list is a comprehensive set of sockets. Although these are expensive, they will be found invaluable as they are so versatile - particularly if various drives are included in the set. We recommend the half-inch square-drive type, as this can be used with most proprietary torque wrenches.

The tools in this list will sometimes need to be supplemented by tools from the *Special* list:

☐ *Sockets (or box spanners) to cover range in previous list (including Torx sockets)*
☐ *Reversible ratchet drive (for use with sockets)*
☐ *Extension piece, 250 mm (for use with sockets)*
☐ *Universal joint (for use with sockets)*
☐ *Flexible handle or sliding T "breaker bar" (for use with sockets)*
☐ *Torque wrench (for use with sockets)*
☐ *Self-locking grips*
☐ *Ball pein hammer*
☐ *Soft-faced mallet (plastic or rubber)*
☐ *Screwdrivers:*
Flat blade - long & sturdy, short (chubby), and narrow (electrician's) types
Cross blade – long & sturdy, and short (chubby) types
☐ *Pliers:*
Long-nosed
Side cutters (electrician's)
Circlip (internal and external)
☐ *Cold chisel - 25 mm*
☐ *Scriber*
☐ *Scraper*
☐ *Centre-punch*
☐ *Pin punch*
☐ *Hacksaw*
☐ *Brake hose clamp*
☐ *Brake/clutch bleeding kit*
☐ *Selection of twist drills*
☐ *Steel rule/straight-edge*
☐ *Allen keys (inc. splined/Torx type)*
☐ *Selection of files*
☐ *Wire brush*
☐ *Axle stands*
☐ *Jack (strong trolley or hydraulic type)*
☐ *Light with extension lead*
☐ *Universal electrical multi-meter*

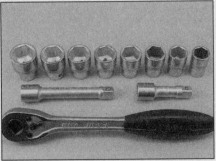
Sockets and reversible ratchet drive

Brake bleeding kit

Torx key, socket and bit

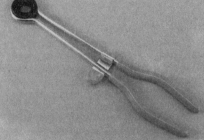
Hose clamp

Angular-tightening gauge

Special tools

The tools in this list are those which are not used regularly, are expensive to buy, or which need to be used in accordance with their manufacturers' instructions. Unless relatively difficult mechanical jobs are undertaken frequently, it will not be economic to buy many of these tools. Where this is the case, you could consider clubbing together with friends (or joining a motorists' club) to make a joint purchase, or borrowing the tools against a deposit from a local garage or tool hire specialist. It is worth noting that many of the larger DIY superstores now carry a large range of special tools for hire at modest rates.

The following list contains only those tools and instruments freely available to the public, and not those special tools produced by the vehicle manufacturer specifically for its dealer network. You will find occasional references to these manufacturers' special tools in the text of this manual. Generally, an alternative method of doing the job without the vehicle manufacturers' special tool is given. However, sometimes there is no alternative to using them. Where this is the case and the relevant tool cannot be bought or borrowed, you will have to entrust the work to a dealer.

☐ Angular-tightening gauge
☐ Valve spring compressor
☐ Valve grinding tool
☐ Piston ring compressor
☐ Piston ring removal/installation tool
☐ Cylinder bore hone
☐ Balljoint separator
☐ Coil spring compressors (where applicable)
☐ Two/three-legged hub and bearing puller
☐ Impact screwdriver
☐ Micrometer and/or vernier calipers
☐ Dial gauge
☐ Stroboscopic timing light
☐ Dwell angle meter/tachometer
☐ Fault code reader
☐ Cylinder compression gauge
☐ Hand-operated vacuum pump and gauge
☐ Clutch plate alignment set
☐ Brake shoe steady spring cup removal tool
☐ Bush and bearing removal/installation set
☐ Stud extractors
☐ Tap and die set
☐ Lifting tackle
☐ Trolley jack

Buying tools

Reputable motor accessory shops and superstores often offer excellent quality tools at discount prices, so it pays to shop around.

Remember, you don't have to buy the most expensive items on the shelf, but it is always advisable to steer clear of the very cheap tools. Beware of 'bargains' offered on market stalls or at car boot sales. There are plenty of good tools around at reasonable prices, but always aim to purchase items which meet the relevant national safety standards. If in doubt, ask the proprietor or manager of the shop for advice before making a purchase.

Care and maintenance of tools

Having purchased a reasonable tool kit, it is necessary to keep the tools in a clean and serviceable condition. After use, always wipe off any dirt, grease and metal particles using a clean, dry cloth, before putting the tools away. Never leave them lying around after they have been used. A simple tool rack on the garage or workshop wall for items such as screwdrivers and pliers is a good idea. Store all normal spanners and sockets in a metal box. Any measuring instruments, gauges, meters, etc, must be carefully stored where they cannot be damaged or become rusty.

Take a little care when tools are used. Hammer heads inevitably become marked, and screwdrivers lose the keen edge on their blades from time to time. A little timely attention with emery cloth or a file will soon restore items like this to a good finish.

Working facilities

Not to be forgotten when discussing tools is the workshop itself. If anything more than routine maintenance is to be carried out, a suitable working area becomes essential.

It is appreciated that many an owner-mechanic is forced by circumstances to remove an engine or similar item without the benefit of a garage or workshop. Having done this, any repairs should always be done under the cover of a roof.

Wherever possible, any dismantling should be done on a clean, flat workbench or table at a suitable working height.

Any workbench needs a vice; one with a jaw opening of 100 mm is suitable for most jobs. As mentioned previously, some clean dry storage space is also required for tools, as well as for any lubricants, cleaning fluids, touch-up paints etc, which become necessary.

Another item which may be required, and which has a much more general usage, is an electric drill with a chuck capacity of at least 8 mm. This, together with a good range of twist drills, is virtually essential for fitting accessories.

Last, but not least, always keep a supply of old newspapers and clean, lint-free rags available, and try to keep any working area as clean as possible.

Micrometers

Dial test indicator ("dial gauge")

Strap wrench

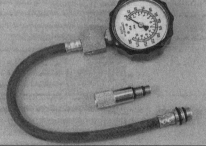

Compression tester

Fault code reader

This is a guide to getting your vehicle through the MOT test. Obviously it will not be possible to examine the vehicle to the same standard as the professional MOT tester. However, working through the following checks will enable you to identify any problem areas before submitting the vehicle for the test.

Where a testable component is in borderline condition, the tester has discretion in deciding whether to pass or fail it. The basis of such discretion is whether the tester would be happy for a close relative or friend to use the vehicle with the component in that condition. If the vehicle presented is clean and evidently well cared for, the tester may be more inclined to pass a borderline component than if the vehicle is scruffy and apparently neglected.

It has only been possible to summarise the test requirements here, based on the regulations in force at the time of printing. Test standards are becoming increasingly stringent, although there are some exemptions for older vehicles.

An assistant will be needed to help carry out some of these checks.

The checks have been sub-divided into four categories, as follows:

1 Checks carried out **FROM THE DRIVER'S SEAT**

2 Checks carried out **WITH THE VEHICLE ON THE GROUND**

3 Checks carried out **WITH THE VEHICLE RAISED AND THE WHEELS FREE TO TURN**

4 Checks carried out on **YOUR VEHICLE'S EXHAUST EMISSION SYSTEM**

1 Checks carried out **FROM THE DRIVER'S SEAT**

Handbrake

☐ Test the operation of the handbrake. Excessive travel (too many clicks) indicates incorrect brake or cable adjustment.
☐ Check that the handbrake cannot be released by tapping the lever sideways. Check the security of the lever mountings.

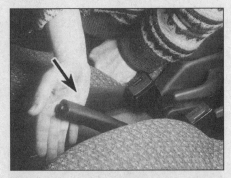

Footbrake

☐ Depress the brake pedal and check that it does not creep down to the floor, indicating a master cylinder fault. Release the pedal, wait a few seconds, then depress it again. If the pedal travels nearly to the floor before firm resistance is felt, brake adjustment or repair is necessary. If the pedal feels spongy, there is air in the hydraulic system which must be removed by bleeding.

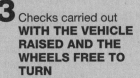
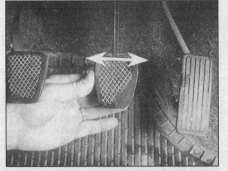

☐ Check that the brake pedal is secure and in good condition. Check also for signs of fluid leaks on the pedal, floor or carpets, which would indicate failed seals in the brake master cylinder.
☐ Check the servo unit (when applicable) by operating the brake pedal several times, then keeping the pedal depressed and starting the engine. As the engine starts, the pedal will move down slightly. If not, the vacuum hose or the servo itself may be faulty.

Steering wheel and column

☐ Examine the steering wheel for fractures or looseness of the hub, spokes or rim.
☐ Move the steering wheel from side to side and then up and down. Check that the steering wheel is not loose on the column, indicating wear or a loose retaining nut. Continue moving the steering wheel as before, but also turn it slightly from left to right.
☐ Check that the steering wheel is not loose on the column, and that there is no abnormal

movement of the steering wheel, indicating wear in the column support bearings or couplings.

Windscreen, mirrors and sunvisor

☐ The windscreen must be free of cracks or other significant damage within the driver's field of view. (Small stone chips are acceptable.) Rear view mirrors must be secure, intact, and capable of being adjusted.

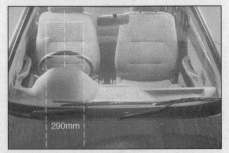

290mm

☐ The driver's sunvisor must be capable of being stored in the "up" position.

Seat belts and seats

Note: *The following checks are applicable to all seat belts, front and rear.*

☐ Examine the webbing of all the belts (including rear belts if fitted) for cuts, serious fraying or deterioration. Fasten and unfasten each belt to check the buckles. If applicable, check the retracting mechanism. Check the security of all seat belt mountings accessible from inside the vehicle.

☐ Seat belts with pre-tensioners, once activated, have a "flag" or similar showing on the seat belt stalk. This, in itself, is not a reason for test failure.

☐ The front seats themselves must be securely attached and the backrests must lock in the upright position.

Doors

☐ Both front doors must be able to be opened and closed from outside and inside, and must latch securely when closed.

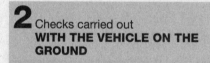

2 Checks carried out **WITH THE VEHICLE ON THE GROUND**

Vehicle identification

☐ Number plates must be in good condition, secure and legible, with letters and numbers correctly spaced – spacing at (A) should be at least twice that at (B).

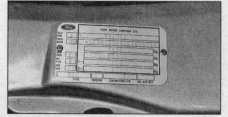

☐ The VIN plate and/or homologation plate must be legible.

Electrical equipment

☐ Switch on the ignition and check the operation of the horn.

☐ Check the windscreen washers and wipers, examining the wiper blades; renew damaged or perished blades. Also check the operation of the stop-lights.

☐ Check the operation of the sidelights and number plate lights. The lenses and reflectors must be secure, clean and undamaged.

☐ Check the operation and alignment of the headlights. The headlight reflectors must not be tarnished and the lenses must be undamaged.

☐ Switch on the ignition and check the operation of the direction indicators (including the instrument panel tell-tale) and the hazard warning lights. Operation of the sidelights and stop-lights must not affect the indicators - if it does, the cause is usually a bad earth at the rear light cluster.

☐ Check the operation of the rear foglight(s), including the warning light on the instrument panel or in the switch.

☐ The ABS warning light must illuminate in accordance with the manufacturers' design. For most vehicles, the ABS warning light should illuminate when the ignition is switched on, and (if the system is operating properly) extinguish after a few seconds. Refer to the owner's handbook.

Footbrake

☐ Examine the master cylinder, brake pipes and servo unit for leaks, loose mountings, corrosion or other damage.

☐ The fluid reservoir must be secure and the fluid level must be between the upper (**A**) and lower (**B**) markings.

☐ Inspect both front brake flexible hoses for cracks or deterioration of the rubber. Turn the steering from lock to lock, and ensure that the hoses do not contact the wheel, tyre, or any part of the steering or suspension mechanism. With the brake pedal firmly depressed, check the hoses for bulges or leaks under pressure.

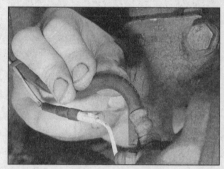

Steering and suspension

☐ Have your assistant turn the steering wheel from side to side slightly, up to the point where the steering gear just begins to transmit this movement to the roadwheels. Check for excessive free play between the steering wheel and the steering gear, indicating wear or insecurity of the steering column joints, the column-to-steering gear coupling, or the steering gear itself.

☐ Have your assistant turn the steering wheel more vigorously in each direction, so that the roadwheels just begin to turn. As this is done, examine all the steering joints, linkages, fittings and attachments. Renew any component that shows signs of wear or damage. On vehicles with power steering, check the security and condition of the steering pump, drivebelt and hoses.

☐ Check that the vehicle is standing level, and at approximately the correct ride height.

Shock absorbers

☐ Depress each corner of the vehicle in turn, then release it. The vehicle should rise and then settle in its normal position. If the vehicle continues to rise and fall, the shock absorber is defective. A shock absorber which has seized will also cause the vehicle to fail.

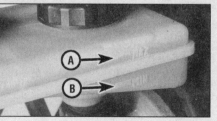

Exhaust system

☐ Start the engine. With your assistant holding a rag over the tailpipe, check the entire system for leaks. Repair or renew leaking sections.

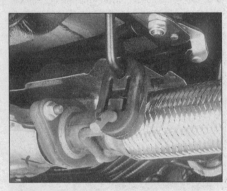

3 Checks carried out WITH THE VEHICLE RAISED AND THE WHEELS FREE TO TURN

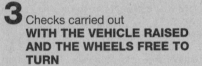

Jack up the front and rear of the vehicle, and securely support it on axle stands. Position the stands clear of the suspension assemblies. Ensure that the wheels are clear of the ground and that the steering can be turned from lock to lock.

Steering mechanism

☐ Have your assistant turn the steering from lock to lock. Check that the steering turns smoothly, and that no part of the steering mechanism, including a wheel or tyre, fouls any brake hose or pipe or any part of the body structure.
☐ Examine the steering rack rubber gaiters for damage or insecurity of the retaining clips. If power steering is fitted, check for signs of damage or leakage of the fluid hoses, pipes or connections. Also check for excessive stiffness or binding of the steering, a missing split pin or locking device, or severe corrosion of the body structure within 30 cm of any steering component attachment point.

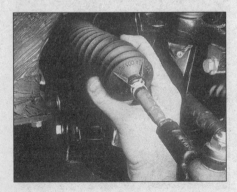

Front and rear suspension and wheel bearings

☐ Starting at the front right-hand side, grasp the roadwheel at the 3 o'clock and 9 o'clock positions and rock gently but firmly. Check for free play or insecurity at the wheel bearings, suspension balljoints, or suspension mountings, pivots and attachments.
☐ Now grasp the wheel at the 12 o'clock and 6 o'clock positions and repeat the previous inspection. Spin the wheel, and check for roughness or tightness of the front wheel bearing.

☐ If excess free play is suspected at a component pivot point, this can be confirmed by using a large screwdriver or similar tool and levering between the mounting and the component attachment. This will confirm whether the wear is in the pivot bush, its retaining bolt, or in the mounting itself (the bolt holes can often become elongated).

☐ Carry out all the above checks at the other front wheel, and then at both rear wheels.

Springs and shock absorbers

☐ Examine the suspension struts (when applicable) for serious fluid leakage, corrosion, or damage to the casing. Also check the security of the mounting points.
☐ If coil springs are fitted, check that the spring ends locate in their seats, and that the spring is not corroded, cracked or broken.
☐ If leaf springs are fitted, check that all leaves are intact, that the axle is securely attached to each spring, and that there is no deterioration of the spring eye mountings, bushes, and shackles.

☐ The same general checks apply to vehicles fitted with other suspension types, such as torsion bars, hydraulic displacer units, etc. Ensure that all mountings and attachments are secure, that there are no signs of excessive wear, corrosion or damage, and (on hydraulic types) that there are no fluid leaks or damaged pipes.
☐ Inspect the shock absorbers for signs of serious fluid leakage. Check for wear of the mounting bushes or attachments, or damage to the body of the unit.

Driveshafts (fwd vehicles only)

☐ Rotate each front wheel in turn and inspect the constant velocity joint gaiters for splits or damage. Also check that each driveshaft is straight and undamaged.

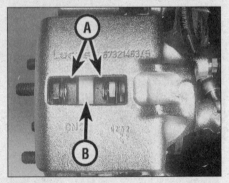

Braking system

☐ If possible without dismantling, check brake pad wear and disc condition. Ensure that the friction lining material has not worn excessively, (A) and that the discs are not fractured, pitted, scored or badly worn (B).

☐ Examine all the rigid brake pipes underneath the vehicle, and the flexible hose(s) at the rear. Look for corrosion, chafing or insecurity of the pipes, and for signs of bulging under pressure, chafing, splits or deterioration of the flexible hoses.
☐ Look for signs of fluid leaks at the brake calipers or on the brake backplates. Repair or renew leaking components.
☐ Slowly spin each wheel, while your assistant depresses and releases the footbrake. Ensure that each brake is operating and does not bind when the pedal is released.

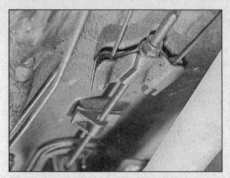

☐ Examine the handbrake mechanism, checking for frayed or broken cables, excessive corrosion, or wear or insecurity of the linkage. Check that the mechanism works on each relevant wheel, and releases fully, without binding.

☐ It is not possible to test brake efficiency without special equipment, but a road test can be carried out later to check that the vehicle pulls up in a straight line.

Fuel and exhaust systems

☐ Inspect the fuel tank (including the filler cap), fuel pipes, hoses and unions. All components must be secure and free from leaks.

☐ Examine the exhaust system over its entire length, checking for any damaged, broken or missing mountings, security of the retaining clamps and rust or corrosion.

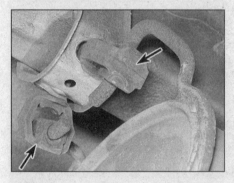

Wheels and tyres

☐ Examine the sidewalls and tread area of each tyre in turn. Check for cuts, tears, lumps, bulges, separation of the tread, and exposure of the ply or cord due to wear or damage. Check that the tyre bead is correctly seated on the wheel rim, that the valve is sound and properly seated, and that the wheel is not distorted or damaged.

☐ Check that the tyres are of the correct size for the vehicle, that they are of the same size and type on each axle, and that the pressures are correct.

☐ Check the tyre tread depth. The legal minimum at the time of writing is 1.6 mm over at least three-quarters of the tread width. Abnormal tread wear may indicate incorrect front wheel alignment.

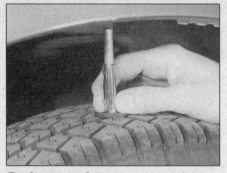

Body corrosion

☐ Check the condition of the entire vehicle structure for signs of corrosion in load-bearing areas. (These include chassis box sections, side sills, cross-members, pillars, and all suspension, steering, braking system and seat belt mountings and anchorages.) Any corrosion which has seriously reduced the thickness of a load-bearing area is likely to cause the vehicle to fail. In this case professional repairs are likely to be needed.

☐ Damage or corrosion which causes sharp or otherwise dangerous edges to be exposed will also cause the vehicle to fail.

4 Checks carried out on **YOUR VEHICLE'S EXHAUST EMISSION SYSTEM**

Petrol models

☐ Have the engine at normal operating temperature, and make sure that it is in good tune (ignition system in good order, air filter element clean, etc).

☐ Before any measurements are carried out, raise the engine speed to around 2500 rpm, and hold it at this speed for 20 seconds. Allow the engine speed to return to idle, and watch for smoke emissions from the exhaust tailpipe. If the idle speed is obviously much too high, or if dense blue or clearly-visible black smoke comes from the tailpipe for more than 5 seconds, the vehicle will fail. As a rule of thumb, blue smoke signifies oil being burnt (engine wear) while black smoke signifies unburnt fuel (dirty air cleaner element, or other carburettor or fuel system fault).

☐ An exhaust gas analyser capable of measuring carbon monoxide (CO) and hydrocarbons (HC) is now needed. If such an instrument cannot be hired or borrowed, a local garage may agree to perform the check for a small fee.

CO emissions (mixture)

☐ At the time of writing, for vehicles first used between 1st August 1975 and 31st July 1986 (P to C registration), the CO level must not exceed 4.5% by volume. For vehicles first used between 1st August 1986 and 31st July 1992 (D to J registration), the CO level must not exceed 3.5% by volume. Vehicles first

used after 1st August 1992 (K registration) must conform to the manufacturer's specification. The MOT tester has access to a DOT database or emissions handbook, which lists the CO and HC limits for each make and model of vehicle. The CO level is measured with the engine at idle speed, and at "fast idle". The following limits are given as a general guide:

At idle speed -
CO level no more than 0.5%
At "fast idle" (2500 to 3000 rpm) -
CO level no more than 0.3%
(Minimum oil temperature 60°C)

☐ If the CO level cannot be reduced far enough to pass the test (and the fuel and ignition systems are otherwise in good condition) then the carburettor is badly worn, or there is some problem in the fuel injection system or catalytic converter (as applicable).

HC emissions

☐ With the CO within limits, HC emissions for vehicles first used between 1st August 1975 and 31st July 1992 (P to J registration) must not exceed 1200 ppm. Vehicles first used after 1st August 1992 (K registration) must conform to the manufacturer's specification. The MOT tester has access to a DOT database or emissions handbook, which lists the CO and HC limits for each make and model of vehicle. The HC level is measured with the engine at "fast idle". The following is given as a general guide:

At "fast idle" (2500 to 3000 rpm) -
HC level no more than 200 ppm
(Minimum oil temperature 60°C)

☐ Excessive HC emissions are caused by incomplete combustion, the causes of which can include oil being burnt, mechanical wear and ignition/fuel system malfunction.

Diesel models

☐ The only emission test applicable to Diesel engines is the measuring of exhaust smoke density. The test involves accelerating the engine several times to its maximum unloaded speed.

Note: *It is of the utmost importance that the engine timing belt is in good condition before the test is carried out.*

☐ The limits for Diesel engine exhaust smoke, introduced in September 1995 are:
Vehicles first used before 1st August 1979:
Exempt from metered smoke testing, but must not emit "dense blue or clearly visible black smoke for a period of more than 5 seconds at idle" or "dense blue or clearly visible black smoke during acceleration which would obscure the view of other road users".
Non-turbocharged vehicles first used after 1st August 1979: 2.5m⁻¹
Turbocharged vehicles first used after 1st August 1979: 3.0m⁻¹

☐ Excessive smoke can be caused by a dirty air cleaner element. Otherwise, professional advice may be needed to find the cause.

Engine

- Engine fails to rotate when attempting to start
- Engine rotates, but will not start
- Engine difficult to start when cold
- Engine difficult to start when hot
- Starter motor noisy or excessively-rough in engagement
- Engine starts, but stops immediately
- Engine idles erratically
- Engine misfires at idle speed
- Engine misfires throughout the driving speed range
- Engine hesitates on acceleration
- Engine stalls
- Engine lacks power
- Engine backfires
- Oil pressure warning light illuminated with engine running
- Engine runs-on after switching off
- Engine noises

Cooling system

- Overheating
- Overcooling
- External coolant leakage
- Internal coolant leakage
- Corrosion

Fuel and exhaust systems

- Excessive fuel consumption
- Fuel leakage and/or fuel odour
- Excessive noise or fumes from exhaust system

Clutch

- Pedal travels to floor - no pressure or very little resistance
- Clutch fails to disengage (unable to select gears)
- Clutch slips (engine speed increases, with no increase in vehicle speed)
- Judder as clutch is engaged
- Noise when depressing or releasing clutch pedal

Manual transmission

- Noisy in neutral with engine running
- Noisy in one particular gear
- Difficulty engaging gears
- Jumps out of gear
- Vibration
- Lubricant leaks

Automatic transmission

- Fluid leakage
- Transmission fluid brown, or has burned smell
- General gear selection problems
- Transmission will not downshift (kickdown) with accelerator fully depressed
- Engine will not start in any gear, or starts in gears other than Park or Neutral
- Transmission slips, shifts roughly, is noisy, or has no drive in forward or reverse gears

Driveshafts

- Clicking or knocking noise on turns (at slow speed on full-lock)
- Vibration when accelerating or decelerating

Braking system

- Vehicle pulls to one side under braking
- Noise (grinding or high-pitched squeal) when brakes applied
- Excessive brake pedal travel
- Brake pedal feels spongy when depressed
- Excessive brake pedal effort required to stop vehicle
- Judder felt through brake pedal or steering wheel when braking
- Brakes binding
- Rear wheels locking under normal braking

Suspension and steering systems

- Vehicle pulls to one side
- Wheel wobble and vibration
- Excessive pitching and/or rolling around corners, or during braking
- Wandering or general instability
- Excessively-stiff steering
- Excessive play in steering
- Lack of power assistance
- Tyre wear excessive

Electrical system

- Battery will not hold a charge for more than a few days
- Ignition/no-charge warning light remains illuminated with engine running
- Ignition/no-charge warning light fails to come on
- Lights inoperative
- Instrument readings inaccurate or erratic
- Horn inoperative, or unsatisfactory in operation
- Windscreen/tailgate wipers inoperative, or unsatisfactory in operation
- Windscreen/tailgate washers inoperative, or unsatisfactory in operation
- Electric windows inoperative, or unsatisfactory in operation
- Central locking system inoperative, or unsatisfactory in operation

Introduction

The vehicle owner who does his or her own maintenance according to the recommended service schedules should not have to use this section of the manual very often. Modern component reliability is such that, provided those items subject to wear or deterioration are inspected or renewed at the specified intervals, sudden failure is comparatively rare. Faults do not usually just happen as a result of sudden failure, but develop over a period of time. Major mechanical failures in particular are usually preceded by characteristic symptoms over hundreds or even thousands of miles. Those components which do occasionally fail without warning are often small and easily carried in the vehicle.

With any fault-finding, the first step is to decide where to begin investigations. Sometimes this is obvious, but on other occasions, a little detective work will be necessary. The owner who makes half a dozen haphazard adjustments or replacements may be successful in curing a fault (or its symptoms), but will be none the wiser if the fault recurs, and ultimately may have spent more time and money than was necessary. A calm and logical approach will be found to be more satisfactory in the long run. Always take into account any warning signs or abnormalities that may have been noticed in the period preceding the fault - power loss, high or low gauge readings, unusual smells, etc - and remember that failure of components such as fuses or spark plugs may only be pointers to some underlying fault.

The pages which follow provide an easy-reference guide to the more common problems which may occur during the operation of the vehicle. These problems and their possible causes are grouped under headings denoting various components or systems, such as Engine, Cooling system, etc. The general Chapter which deals with the problem is also shown in brackets; refer to the relevant part of that Chapter for system-specific information. Whatever the fault, certain basic principles apply. These are as follows:

Verify the fault. This is simply a matter of being sure that you know what the symptoms are before starting work. This is particularly important if you are investigating a fault for someone else, who may not have described it very accurately.

Don't overlook the obvious. For example, if the vehicle won't start, is there petrol in the tank? (Don't take anyone else's word on this particular point, and don't trust the fuel gauge either!) If an electrical fault is indicated, look for loose or broken wires before digging out the test gear.

Cure the disease, not the symptom. Substituting a flat battery with a fully-charged one will get you off the hard shoulder, but if the underlying cause is not attended to, the new battery will go the same way. Similarly, changing oil-fouled spark plugs for a new set will get you moving again, but remember that the reason for the fouling (if it wasn't simply an incorrect grade of plug) will have to be established and corrected.

Don't take anything for granted. Particularly, don't forget that a 'new' component may itself be defective (especially if it's been rattling around in the boot for months), and don't leave components out of a fault diagnosis sequence just because they are new or recently-fitted. When you do finally diagnose a difficult fault, you'll probably realise that all the evidence was there from the start.

Engine

Engine fails to rotate when attempting to start

- [ ] Battery terminal connections loose or corroded (Weekly Checks).
- [ ] Battery discharged or faulty (Chapter 5).
- [ ] Broken, loose or disconnected wiring in the starting circuit (Chapter 5).
- [ ] Defective starter solenoid or switch (Chapter 5).
- [ ] Defective starter motor (Chapter 5).
- [ ] Starter pinion or flywheel ring gear teeth loose or broken (Chapters 2 and 5).
- [ ] Engine earth strap broken or disconnected (Chapter 5).
- [ ] Automatic transmission not in Park/Neutral position, or multi-function switch faulty or incorrectly adjusted (Chapter 7).

Engine rotates, but will not start

- [ ] Fuel tank empty.
- [ ] Battery discharged (engine rotates slowly) (Chapter 5).
- [ ] Battery terminal connections loose or corroded (Weekly checks).
- [ ] Ignition components damp or damaged (Chapters 1 and 5).
- [ ] Broken, loose or disconnected wiring in the ignition circuit (Chapters 1 and 5).
- [ ] Worn, faulty or incorrectly-gapped spark plugs (Chapter 1).
- [ ] Fuel injection system fault (Chapter 4).
- [ ] Major mechanical failure (eg camshaft drive) (Chapter 2).

Engine difficult to start when cold

- [ ] Battery discharged (Chapter 5).
- [ ] Battery terminal connections loose or corroded (Weekly checks).
- [ ] Worn, faulty or incorrectly-gapped spark plugs (Chapter 1).
- [ ] Fuel injection system fault (Chapter 4).
- [ ] Other ignition system fault (Chapters 1 and 5).
- [ ] Low cylinder compressions (Chapter 2).

Engine difficult to start when hot

- [ ] Air filter element dirty or clogged (Chapter 1).
- [ ] Fuel injection system fault (Chapter 4).
- [ ] Other ignition system fault (Chapters 1 and 5).
- [ ] Low cylinder compressions (Chapter 2).

Starter motor noisy or excessively-rough in engagement

- [ ] Starter pinion or flywheel ring gear teeth loose or broken (Chapter 2).
- [ ] Starter motor mounting bolts loose or missing (Chapter 5).
- [ ] Starter motor internal components worn or damaged (Chapter 5).

Engine starts, but stops immediately

- [ ] Loose or faulty electrical connections in the ignition circuit (Chapters 1 and 5).
- [ ] Vacuum leak at the throttle body/housing or inlet manifold (Chapter 4).
- [ ] Blocked injector/fuel injection system fault (Chapter 4).

Engine idles erratically

- [ ] Air filter element clogged (Chapter 1).
- [ ] Vacuum leak at the throttle body/housing, inlet manifold or associated hoses (Chapter 4).
- [ ] Worn, faulty or incorrectly-gapped spark plugs (Chapter 1).
- [ ] Uneven or low cylinder compressions (Chapter 2).
- [ ] Camshaft lobes worn (Chapter 2).
- [ ] Timing belt incorrectly fitted (Chapter 2).
- [ ] Blocked injector/fuel injection system fault (Chapter 4).

Engine misfires at idle speed

- [ ] Worn, faulty or incorrectly-gapped spark plugs (Chapter 1).
- [ ] Faulty spark plug HT leads (Chapter 1).
- [ ] Faulty ignition coil (Chapter 5).
- [ ] Vacuum leak at the throttle body/housing, inlet manifold or associated hoses (Chapter 4).
- [ ] Blocked injector/fuel injection system fault (Chapter 4).
- [ ] Distributor cap (where fitted) cracked or tracking internally (Chapter 1).
- [ ] Uneven or low cylinder compressions (Chapter 2).
- [ ] Disconnected, leaking, or perished crankcase ventilation hoses (Chapter 4).

Engine misfires throughout the driving speed range

- [ ] Fuel filter choked (Chapter 1).
- [ ] Fuel pump faulty, or delivery pressure low (Chapter 4).
- [ ] Fuel tank vent blocked, or fuel pipes restricted (Chapter 4).
- [ ] Vacuum leak at the throttle body/housing, inlet manifold or associated hoses (Chapter 4).
- [ ] Worn, faulty or incorrectly-gapped spark plugs (Chapter 1).
- [ ] Faulty spark plug HT leads (Chapter 1).
- [ ] Distributor cap (where fitted) cracked or tracking internally (Chapter 1).
- [ ] Faulty ignition coil (Chapter 5).
- [ ] Uneven or low cylinder compressions (Chapter 2).
- [ ] Blocked injector/fuel injection system fault (Chapter 4).

Engine hesitates on acceleration

- [ ] Worn, faulty or incorrectly-gapped spark plugs (Chapter 1).
- [ ] Vacuum leak at the throttle body/housing, inlet manifold or associated hoses (Chapter 4).
- [ ] Blocked injector/fuel injection system fault (Chapter 4).

Engine stalls

- [ ] Vacuum leak at the throttle body/housing, inlet manifold or associated hoses (Chapter 4).
- [ ] Fuel filter choked (Chapter 1).
- [ ] Fuel pump faulty, or delivery pressure low (Chapter 4.
- [ ] Fuel tank vent blocked, or fuel pipes restricted (Chapter 4).
- [ ] Blocked injector/fuel injection system fault (Chapter 4).

Engine (continued)

Engine lacks power

- [ ] Timing belt incorrectly fitted (Chapter 2).
- [ ] Fuel filter choked (Chapter 1).
- [ ] Fuel pump faulty, or delivery pressure low (Chapter 4).
- [ ] Uneven or low cylinder compressions (Chapter 2).
- [ ] Worn, faulty or incorrectly-gapped spark plugs (Chapter 1).
- [ ] Vacuum leak at the throttle body/housing, inlet manifold or associated hoses (Chapter 4).
- [ ] Blocked injector/fuel injection system fault (Chapter 4).
- [ ] Brakes binding (Chapters 1 and 9).
- [ ] Clutch slipping - manual transmission models (Chapter 6).

Engine backfires

- [ ] Timing belt incorrectly fitted (Chapter 2).
- [ ] Vacuum leak at the throttle body/housing, inlet manifold or associated hoses (Chapter 4).
- [ ] Blocked injector/fuel injection system fault (Chapter 4).

Oil pressure warning light illuminated with engine running

- [ ] Low oil level, or incorrect oil grade (Weekly checks).
- [ ] Faulty oil pressure sensor (Chapter 5).
- [ ] Worn engine bearings and/or oil pump (Chapter 2).
- [ ] High engine operating temperature (Chapter 3).
- [ ] Oil pressure relief valve defective (Chapter 2).
- [ ] Oil pick-up strainer clogged (Chapter 2).

Engine runs-on after switching off

- [ ] Excessive carbon build-up in engine (Chapter 2).
- [ ] High engine operating temperature (Chapter 3).
- [ ] Fuel injection system fault (Chapter 4).

Engine noises

Pre-ignition (pinking) or knocking during acceleration or under load

- [ ] Ignition system fault (Chapters 1 and 5).
- [ ] Incorrect grade of spark plug (Chapter 1).
- [ ] Incorrect grade of fuel (Chapter 1).
- [ ] Vacuum leak at the throttle body/housing, inlet manifold or associated hoses (Chapter 4).
- [ ] Excessive carbon build-up in engine (Chapter 2).
- [ ] Blocked injector/fuel injection system fault (Chapter 4).

Whistling or wheezing noises

- [ ] Leaking inlet manifold or throttle body/housing gasket (Chapter 4).
- [ ] Leaking exhaust manifold gasket or pipe-to-manifold joint (Chapter 4).
- [ ] Leaking vacuum hose (Chapter 4).
- [ ] Blowing cylinder head gasket (Chapter 2).

Tapping or rattling noises

- [ ] Worn valve gear or camshaft (Chapter 2).
- [ ] Ancillary component fault (coolant pump, alternator, etc) (Chapters 3, 5, etc).

Knocking or thumping noises

- [ ] Worn big-end bearings (regular heavy knocking, perhaps less under load) (Chapter 2).
- [ ] Worn main bearings (rumbling and knocking, perhaps worsening under load) (Chapter 2).
- [ ] Piston slap (most noticeable when cold) (Chapter 2).
- [ ] Ancillary component fault (coolant pump, alternator, etc) (Chapters 3, 5, etc).

Cooling system

Overheating

- [ ] Insufficient coolant in system (Weekly checks).
- [ ] Thermostat faulty (Chapter 3).
- [ ] Radiator core blocked, or grille restricted (Chapter 3).
- [ ] Electric cooling fan or thermoswitch faulty (Chapter 3).
- [ ] Pressure cap faulty (Chapter 3).
- [ ] Ignition system fault (Chapters 1 and 5).
- [ ] Inaccurate temperature gauge sender unit (Chapter 3).
- [ ] Airlock in cooling system (Chapter 1).

Overcooling

- [ ] Thermostat faulty (Chapter 3).
- [ ] Inaccurate temperature gauge sender unit (Chapter 3).

External coolant leakage

- [ ] Deteriorated or damaged hoses or hose clips (Chapter 1).
- [ ] Radiator core or heater matrix leaking (Chapter 3).
- [ ] Pressure cap faulty (Chapter 3).
- [ ] Coolant pump seal leaking (Chapter 3).
- [ ] Boiling due to overheating (Chapter 3).
- [ ] Cylinder block core plug leaking (Chapter 2).

Internal coolant leakage

- [ ] Leaking cylinder head gasket (Chapter 2).
- [ ] Cracked cylinder head or cylinder bore (Chapter 2).

Corrosion

- [ ] Infrequent draining and flushing (Chapter 1).
- [ ] Incorrect coolant mixture or inappropriate coolant type (Chapter 1).

Fuel and exhaust systems

Excessive fuel consumption

- [ ] Air filter element dirty or clogged (Chapter 1).
- [ ] Fuel injection system fault (Chapter 4).
- [ ] Ignition system fault (Chapters 1 and 5).
- [ ] Tyres under-inflated (Weekly checks).

Fuel leakage and/or fuel odour

- [ ] Damaged or corroded fuel tank, pipes or connections (Chapter 4).

Excessive noise or fumes from exhaust system

- [ ] Leaking exhaust system or manifold joints (Chapters 1 and 4).
- [ ] Leaking, corroded or damaged silencers or pipe (Chapters 1 and 4).
- [ ] Broken mountings causing body or suspension contact (Chapter 1).

Clutch

Pedal travels to floor - no pressure or very little resistance

- ☐ Broken clutch cable (Chapter 6).
- ☐ Incorrect clutch cable adjustment (Chapter 6).
- ☐ Broken clutch release bearing or fork (Chapter 6).
- ☐ Broken diaphragm spring in clutch pressure plate (Chapter 6).

Clutch fails to disengage (unable to select gears).

- ☐ Incorrect clutch cable adjustment (Chapter 6).
- ☐ Clutch plate sticking on gearbox input shaft splines (Chapter 6).
- ☐ Clutch plate sticking to flywheel or pressure plate (Chapter 6).
- ☐ Faulty pressure plate assembly (Chapter 6).
- ☐ Clutch release mechanism worn or incorrectly assembled (Chapter 6).

Clutch slips (engine speed increases, with no increase in vehicle speed).

- ☐ Incorrect clutch cable adjustment (Chapter 6).
- ☐ Clutch plate linings excessively worn (Chapter 6).
- ☐ Clutch plate linings contaminated with oil or grease (Chapter 6).
- ☐ Faulty pressure plate or weak diaphragm spring (Chapter 6).

Judder as clutch is engaged

- ☐ Clutch plate linings contaminated with oil or grease (Chapter 6).
- ☐ Clutch plate linings excessively worn (Chapter 6).
- ☐ Clutch cable sticking or frayed (Chapter 6).
- ☐ Faulty or distorted pressure plate or diaphragm spring (Chapter 6).
- ☐ Worn or loose engine or gearbox mountings (Chapter 2).
- ☐ Clutch plate hub or gearbox input shaft splines worn (Chapter 6).

Noise when depressing or releasing clutch pedal

- ☐ Worn clutch release bearing (Chapter 6).
- ☐ Worn or dry clutch pedal bushes (Chapter 6).
- ☐ Faulty pressure plate assembly (Chapter 6).
- ☐ Pressure plate diaphragm spring broken (Chapter 6).
- ☐ Broken clutch plate cushioning springs (Chapter 6).

Manual transmission

Noisy in neutral with engine running

- ☐ Input shaft bearings worn (noise apparent with clutch pedal released, but not when depressed) (Chapter 7).*
- ☐ Clutch release bearing worn (noise apparent with clutch pedal depressed, possibly less when released) (Chapter 6).

Noisy in one particular gear

- ☐ Worn, damaged or chipped gear teeth (Chapter 7).*

Difficulty engaging gears

- ☐ Clutch fault (Chapter 6).
- ☐ Oil level low (Chapter 1).
- ☐ Worn or damaged gearchange linkage (Chapter 7).
- ☐ Incorrectly-adjusted gearchange linkage (Chapter 7).
- ☐ Worn synchroniser units (Chapter 7).*

Jumps out of gear

- ☐ Worn or damaged gearchange linkage (Chapter 7).
- ☐ Incorrectly-adjusted gearchange linkage (Chapter 7).
- ☐ Worn synchroniser units (Chapter 7).*
- ☐ Worn selector forks (Chapter 7).*

Vibration

- ☐ Lack of oil (Chapter 1).
- ☐ Worn bearings (Chapter 7).*

Lubricant leaks

- ☐ Leaking differential output oil seal (Chapter 7).
- ☐ Leaking housing joint (Chapter 7).*
- ☐ Leaking input shaft oil seal (Chapter 7).*

*Although the corrective action necessary to remedy the symptoms described is beyond the scope of the home mechanic, the above information should be helpful in isolating the cause of the condition, so that the owner can communicate clearly with a professional mechanic.

Automatic transmission

Note: Due to the complexity of the automatic transmission, it is difficult for the home mechanic to properly diagnose and service this unit. For problems other than the following, the vehicle should be taken to a dealer service department or automatic transmission specialist. Do not be too hasty in removing the transmission if a fault is suspected, as most of the testing is carried out with the unit still fitted.

Fluid leakage

- ☐ Automatic transmission fluid is usually dark in colour. Fluid leaks should not be confused with engine oil, which can easily be blown onto the transmission by airflow.
- ☐ To determine the source of a leak, first remove all built-up dirt and grime from the transmission housing and surrounding areas using a degreasing agent, or by steam-cleaning. Drive the vehicle at low speed, so airflow will not blow the leak far from its source. Raise and support the vehicle, and determine where the leak is coming from. The following are common areas of leakage:

a) Oil pan - where applicable (Chapter 1).
b) Dipstick tube - where applicable (Chapter 1).
c) Transmission-to-fluid cooler pipes/unions (Chapter 7).

Transmission fluid brown, or has burned smell

- ☐ Transmission fluid level low, or fluid in need of renewal (Chapter 1).

General gear selection problems

- ☐ Chapter 7 deals with checking and adjusting the selector cable on automatic transmissions. The following are common problems which may be caused by a poorly-adjusted cable:

a) Engine starting in gears other than Park or Neutral.
b) Indicator panel indicating a gear other than the one actually being used.
c) Vehicle moves when in Park or Neutral.
d) Poor gearshift quality or erratic gearchanges
- ☐ Refer to Chapter 7 for the selector cable adjustment procedure.

Automatic transmission (continued)

Transmission will not downshift (kickdown) with accelerator pedal fully depressed

☐ Low transmission fluid level (Chapter 1).
☐ Incorrect selector cable adjustment (Chapter 7).
☐ Incorrect kickdown cable adjustment (Chapter 7).
☐ Electronic control system fault (Chapter 7).

Engine will not start in any gear, or starts in gears other than Park or Neutral

☐ Incorrect selector cable adjustment (Chapter 7).
☐ Incorrect multi-function switch adjustment (Chapter 7).

Transmission slips, is noisy, or has no drive in forward or reverse gears

☐ There are many probable causes for the above problems, but the home mechanic should be concerned with only one possibility - fluid level. Before taking the vehicle to a dealer or transmission specialist, check the fluid level and condition of the fluid as described in Chapter 1. Correct the fluid level as necessary, or change the fluid and filter if needed. If the problem persists, professional help will be necessary.

Driveshafts

Clicking or knocking noise on turns (at slow speed on full-lock).

☐ Lack of constant velocity joint lubricant, possibly due to damaged gaiter (Chapter 8).
☐ Worn outer constant velocity joint (Chapter 8).

Vibration when accelerating or decelerating

☐ Worn inner constant velocity joint (Chapter 8).
☐ Bent or distorted driveshaft (Chapter 8).

Braking system

Note: *Before assuming that a brake problem exists, make sure that the tyres are in good condition and correctly inflated, that the front wheel alignment is correct, and that the vehicle is not loaded with weight in an unequal manner. Apart from checking the condition of all pipe and hose connections, any faults occurring on the anti-lock braking system should be referred to a Nissan dealer for diagnosis.*

Vehicle pulls to one side under braking

☐ Worn, defective, damaged or contaminated brake pads/shoes on one side (Chapters 1 and 9).
☐ Seized or partially-seized front brake caliper or rear wheel cylinder/caliper piston (Chapters 1 and 9).
☐ A mixture of brake pad/shoe lining materials fitted between sides (Chapters 1 and 9).
☐ Brake caliper or backplate mounting bolts loose (Chapter 9).
☐ Worn or damaged steering or suspension components (Chapters 1 and 10).

Noise (grinding or high-pitched squeal) when brakes applied

☐ Brake pad or shoe friction lining material worn down to metal backing (Chapters 1 and 9).
☐ Excessive corrosion of brake disc or drum. (May be apparent after the vehicle has been standing for some time (Chapters 1 and 9).
☐ Foreign object (stone chipping, etc) trapped between brake disc and shield (Chapters 1 and 9).

Excessive brake pedal travel

☐ Inoperative rear brake self-adjust mechanism - drum brake models (Chapters 1 and 9).
☐ Faulty master cylinder (Chapter 9).
☐ Air in hydraulic system (Chapter 9).
☐ Faulty vacuum servo unit (Chapters 1 and 9).

Brake pedal feels spongy when depressed

☐ Air in hydraulic system (Chapter 9).
☐ Deteriorated flexible rubber brake hoses (Chapters 1 and 9).
☐ Master cylinder mounting nuts loose (Chapter 9).
☐ Faulty master cylinder (Chapter 9).

Excessive brake pedal effort required to stop vehicle

☐ Faulty vacuum servo unit (Chapters 1 and 9).
☐ Disconnected, damaged or insecure brake servo vacuum hose (Chapter 9).
☐ Primary or secondary hydraulic circuit failure (Chapter 9).
☐ Seized brake caliper or wheel cylinder piston(s) (Chapter 9).
☐ Brake pads or brake shoes incorrectly fitted (Chapter 9).
☐ Incorrect grade of brake pads or brake shoes fitted (Chapter 9).
☐ Brake pads or brake shoe linings contaminated (Chapter 9).

Judder felt through brake pedal or steering wheel when braking

☐ Excessive run-out or distortion of discs/drums (Chapter 9).
☐ Brake pad or brake shoe linings worn (Chapters 1 and 9).
☐ Brake caliper or brake backplate mounting bolts loose (Chapter 9).
☐ Wear in suspension or steering components or mountings (Chapters 1 and 10).

Brakes binding

☐ Seized brake caliper or wheel cylinder piston(s) (Chapter 9).
☐ Incorrectly-adjusted handbrake mechanism (Chapter 1).
☐ Faulty master cylinder (Chapter 9).

Rear wheels locking under normal braking

☐ Rear brake pad/shoe linings contaminated (Chapters 1 and 9).
☐ Faulty brake pressure regulator (Chapter 9).

Suspension and steering

Note: *Before diagnosing suspension or steering faults, be sure that the trouble is not due to incorrect tyre pressures, mixtures of tyre types, or binding brakes.*

Vehicle pulls to one side

- [ ] Defective tyre (Weekly checks).
- [ ] Excessive wear in suspension or steering components (Chapters 1 and 10).
- [ ] Incorrect front/rear wheel alignment (Chapter 1).
- [ ] Accident damage to steering or suspension components (Chapter 1).

Wheel wobble and vibration

- [ ] Front roadwheels out of balance (vibration felt mainly through the steering wheel) (Chapters 1 and 10).
- [ ] Rear roadwheels out of balance (vibration felt throughout the vehicle) (Chapters 1 and 10).
- [ ] Roadwheels damaged or distorted (Chapters 1 and 10).
- [ ] Faulty or damaged tyre (Weekly checks).
- [ ] Worn steering or suspension joints, bushes or components (Chapters 1 and 10).
- [ ] Wheel bolts loose (Chapters 1 and 10).

Excessive pitching and/or rolling around corners, or during braking

- [ ] Defective shock absorbers (Chapters 1 and 10).
- [ ] Broken or weak spring and/or suspension component (Chapters 1 and 10).
- [ ] Worn or damaged anti-roll bar or mountings (Chapter 10).

Wandering or general instability

- [ ] Incorrect front/rear wheel alignment (Chapter 1).
- [ ] Worn steering or suspension joints, bushes or components (Chapters 1 and 10).
- [ ] Roadwheels out of balance (Chapters 1 and 10).
- [ ] Faulty or damaged tyre (Weekly checks).
- [ ] Wheel bolts loose (Chapters 1 and 10).
- [ ] Defective shock absorbers (Chapters 1 and 10).

Excessively-stiff steering

- [ ] Lack of steering gear lubricant (Chapter 10).
- [ ] Seized track rod end balljoint or suspension balljoint (Chapters 1 and 10).
- [ ] Broken or incorrectly-adjusted auxiliary drivebelt - power steering (Chapter 1).
- [ ] Incorrect front wheel alignment (Chapter 1).
- [ ] Steering rack or column bent or damaged (Chapter 10).

Excessive play in steering

- [ ] Worn steering track rod end balljoints (Chapters 1 and 10).
- [ ] Worn rack-and-pinion steering gear (Chapter 10).
- [ ] Worn steering or suspension joints, bushes or components (Chapters 1 and 10).

Lack of power assistance

- [ ] Broken or incorrectly-adjusted auxiliary drivebelt (Chapter 1).
- [ ] Incorrect power steering fluid level (Weekly checks).
- [ ] Restriction in power steering fluid hoses (Chapter 1).
- [ ] Faulty power steering pump (Chapter 10).
- [ ] Faulty rack-and-pinion steering gear (Chapter 10).

Tyre wear excessive

Tyres worn on inside or outside edges

- [ ] Tyres under-inflated (wear on both edges) (Weekly checks).
- [ ] Incorrect camber or castor angles (wear on one edge only) (Chapter 1).
- [ ] Worn steering or suspension joints, bushes or components (Chapters 1 and 10).
- [ ] Excessively-hard cornering.
- [ ] Accident damage.

Tyre treads exhibit feathered edges

- [ ] Incorrect toe setting (Chapter 1).

Tyres worn in centre of tread

- [ ] Tyres over-inflated (Weekly checks).

Tyres worn on inside and outside edges

- [ ] Tyres under-inflated (Weekly checks).

Tyres worn unevenly

- [ ] Tyres/wheels out of balance (Chapter 1).
- [ ] Excessive wheel or tyre run-out (Chapter 1).
- [ ] Worn shock absorbers (Chapters 1 and 10).
- [ ] Faulty tyre (Weekly checks).

Electrical system

Note: *For problems associated with the starting system, refer to the faults listed under Engine earlier in this Section.*

Battery will not hold a charge for more than a few days

- [ ] Battery defective internally (Chapter 5).
- [ ] Battery terminal connections loose or corroded (Weekly checks).
- [ ] Auxiliary drivebelt worn or incorrectly adjusted (Chapter 1).
- [ ] Alternator not charging at correct output (Chapter 5).
- [ ] Alternator or voltage regulator faulty (Chapter 5).
- [ ] Short-circuit causing continual battery drain (Chapters 5 and 12).

Ignition/no-charge warning light remains illuminated with engine running

- [ ] Auxiliary drivebelt broken, worn, or incorrectly adjusted (Chapter 1).
- [ ] Alternator brushes worn, sticking, or dirty (Chapter 5).
- [ ] Alternator brush springs weak or broken (Chapter 5).
- [ ] Internal fault in alternator or voltage regulator (Chapter 5).
- [ ] Broken, disconnected, or loose wiring in charging circuit (Chapter 5).

Ignition/no-charge warning light fails to come on

- [ ] Warning light bulb blown (Chapter 12).
- [ ] Broken, disconnected, or loose wiring in warning light circuit (Chapter 12).
- [ ] Alternator faulty (Chapter 5).

Electrical system (continued)

Lights inoperative

- ☐ Bulb blown (Chapter 12).
- ☐ Corrosion of bulb or bulbholder contacts (Chapter 12).
- ☐ Blown fuse (Chapter 12).
- ☐ Faulty relay (Chapter 12).
- ☐ Broken, loose, or disconnected wiring (Chapter 12).
- ☐ Faulty switch (Chapter 12).

Instrument readings inaccurate or erratic

Instrument readings increase with engine speed

- ☐ Faulty voltage regulator (Chapter 12).

Fuel or temperature gauges give no reading

- ☐ Faulty gauge sender unit (Chapters 3 and 4).
- ☐ Wiring open-circuit (Chapter 12).
- ☐ Faulty gauge (Chapter 12).

Fuel or temperature gauges give continuous maximum reading

- ☐ Faulty gauge sender unit (Chapters 3 and 4).
- ☐ Wiring short-circuit (Chapter 12).
- ☐ Faulty gauge (Chapter 12).

Horn inoperative, or unsatisfactory in operation

Horn operates all the time

- ☐ Horn push either earthed or stuck down (Chapter 12).
- ☐ Horn cable-to-horn push earthed (Chapter 12).

Horn fails to operate

- ☐ Blown fuse (Chapter 12).
- ☐ Cable or cable connections loose, broken or disconnected (Chapter 12).
- ☐ Faulty horn (Chapter 12).

Horn emits intermittent or unsatisfactory sound

- ☐ Cable connections loose (Chapter 12).
- ☐ Horn mountings loose (Chapter 12).
- ☐ Faulty horn (Chapter 12).

Windscreen/tailgate wipers inoperative, or unsatisfactory in operation

Wipers fail to operate, or operate very slowly

- ☐ Wiper blades stuck to screen, or linkage seized or binding (Chapters 1 and 12).
- ☐ Blown fuse (Chapter 12).
- ☐ Cable or cable connections loose, broken or disconnected (Chapter 12).
- ☐ Faulty relay (Chapter 12).
- ☐ Faulty wiper motor (Chapter 12).

Wiper blades sweep over too large or too small an area of the glass

- ☐ Wiper arms incorrectly positioned on spindles (Chapter 1).
- ☐ Excessive wear of wiper linkage (Chapter 12).
- ☐ Wiper motor or linkage mountings loose or insecure (Chapter 12).

Wiper blades fail to clean the glass effectively

- ☐ Wiper blade rubbers worn or perished (Weekly checks).
- ☐ Wiper arm tension springs broken, or arm pivots seized (Chapter 12).
- ☐ Insufficient windscreen washer additive to adequately remove road film (Weekly checks).

Windscreen/tailgate washers inoperative, or unsatisfactory in operation

One or more washer jets inoperative

- ☐ Blocked washer jet (Chapter 1 or 12).
- ☐ Disconnected, kinked or restricted fluid hose (Chapter 12).
- ☐ Insufficient fluid in washer reservoir (Weekly checks).

Washer pump fails to operate

- ☐ Broken or disconnected wiring or connections (Chapter 12).
- ☐ Blown fuse (Chapter 12).
- ☐ Faulty washer switch (Chapter 12).
- ☐ Faulty washer pump (Chapter 12).

Washer pump runs for some time before fluid is emitted from jets

- ☐ Faulty one-way valve in fluid supply hose (Chapter 12).

Electric windows inoperative, or unsatisfactory in operation

Window glass will only move in one direction

- ☐ Faulty switch (Chapter 12).

Window glass slow to move

- ☐ Incorrectly-adjusted door glass guide channels (Chapter 11).
- ☐ Regulator seized or damaged, or in need of lubrication (Chapter 11).
- ☐ Door internal components or trim fouling regulator (Chapter 11).
- ☐ Faulty motor (Chapter 11).

Window glass fails to move

- ☐ Incorrectly-adjusted door glass guide channels (Chapter 11).
- ☐ Blown fuse (Chapter 12).
- ☐ Faulty relay (Chapter 12).
- ☐ Broken or disconnected wiring or connections (Chapter 12).
- ☐ Faulty motor (Chapter 11).

Central locking system inoperative, or unsatisfactory in operation

Complete system failure

- ☐ Blown fuse (Chapter 12).
- ☐ Faulty relay (Chapter 12).
- ☐ Broken or disconnected wiring or connections (Chapter 12).
- ☐ Faulty control unit (Chapter 11).

Latch locks but will not unlock, or unlocks but will not lock

- ☐ Faulty master switch (Chapter 12).
- ☐ Broken or disconnected latch operating rods or levers (Chapter 11).
- ☐ Faulty relay (Chapter 12).
- ☐ Faulty control unit (Chapter 11).

One solenoid/motor fails to operate

- ☐ Broken or disconnected wiring or connections (Chapter 12).
- ☐ Faulty solenoid/motor (Chapter 11).
- ☐ Broken, binding or disconnected latch operating rods or levers (Chapter 11).
- ☐ Fault in door latch (Chapter 11).

A

ABS (Anti-lock brake system) A system, usually electronically controlled, that senses incipient wheel lockup during braking and relieves hydraulic pressure at wheels that are about to skid.

Air bag An inflatable bag hidden in the steering wheel (driver's side) or the dash or glovebox (passenger side). In a head-on collision, the bags inflate, preventing the driver and front passenger from being thrown forward into the steering wheel or windscreen.

Air cleaner A metal or plastic housing, containing a filter element, which removes dust and dirt from the air being drawn into the engine.

Air filter element The actual filter in an air cleaner system, usually manufactured from pleated paper and requiring renewal at regular intervals.

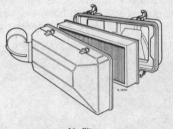

Air filter

Allen key A hexagonal wrench which fits into a recessed hexagonal hole.

Alligator clip A long-nosed spring-loaded metal clip with meshing teeth. Used to make temporary electrical connections.

Alternator A component in the electrical system which converts mechanical energy from a drivebelt into electrical energy to charge the battery and to operate the starting system, ignition system and electrical accessories.

Ampere (amp) A unit of measurement for the flow of electric current. One amp is the amount of current produced by one volt acting through a resistance of one ohm.

Anaerobic sealer A substance used to prevent bolts and screws from loosening. Anaerobic means that it does not require oxygen for activation. The Loctite brand is widely used.

Antifreeze A substance (usually ethylene glycol) mixed with water, and added to a vehicle's cooling system, to prevent freezing of the coolant in winter. Antifreeze also contains chemicals to inhibit corrosion and the formation of rust and other deposits that would tend to clog the radiator and coolant passages and reduce cooling efficiency.

Anti-seize compound A coating that reduces the risk of seizing on fasteners that are subjected to high temperatures, such as exhaust manifold bolts and nuts.

Asbestos A natural fibrous mineral with great heat resistance, commonly used in the composition of brake friction materials.

Asbestos is a health hazard and the dust created by brake systems should never be inhaled or ingested.

Axle A shaft on which a wheel revolves, or which revolves with a wheel. Also, a solid beam that connects the two wheels at one end of the vehicle. An axle which also transmits power to the wheels is known as a live axle.

Axleshaft A single rotating shaft, on either side of the differential, which delivers power from the final drive assembly to the drive wheels. Also called a driveshaft or a halfshaft.

B

Ball bearing An anti-friction bearing consisting of a hardened inner and outer race with hardened steel balls between two races.

Bearing The curved surface on a shaft or in a bore, or the part assembled into either, that permits relative motion between them with minimum wear and friction.

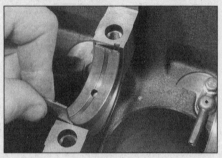

Bearing

Big-end bearing The bearing in the end of the connecting rod that's attached to the crankshaft.

Bleed nipple A valve on a brake wheel cylinder, caliper or other hydraulic component that is opened to purge the hydraulic system of air. Also called a bleed screw.

Brake bleeding Procedure for removing air from lines of a hydraulic brake system.

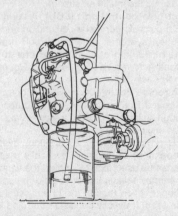

Brake bleeding

Brake disc The component of a disc brake that rotates with the wheels.

Brake drum The component of a drum brake that rotates with the wheels.

Brake linings The friction material which contacts the brake disc or drum to retard the vehicle's speed. The linings are bonded or riveted to the brake pads or shoes.

Brake pads The replaceable friction pads that pinch the brake disc when the brakes are applied. Brake pads consist of a friction material bonded or riveted to a rigid backing plate.

Brake shoe The crescent-shaped carrier to which the brake linings are mounted and which forces the lining against the rotating drum during braking.

Braking systems For more information on braking systems, consult the *Haynes Automotive Brake Manual*.

Breaker bar A long socket wrench handle providing greater leverage.

Bulkhead The insulated partition between the engine and the passenger compartment.

C

Caliper The non-rotating part of a disc-brake assembly that straddles the disc and carries the brake pads. The caliper also contains the hydraulic components that cause the pads to pinch the disc when the brakes are applied. A caliper is also a measuring tool that can be set to measure inside or outside dimensions of an object.

Camshaft A rotating shaft on which a series of cam lobes operate the valve mechanisms. The camshaft may be driven by gears, by sprockets and chain or by sprockets and a belt.

Canister A container in an evaporative emission control system; contains activated charcoal granules to trap vapours from the fuel system.

Canister

Carburettor A device which mixes fuel with air in the proper proportions to provide a desired power output from a spark ignition internal combustion engine.

Castellated Resembling the parapets along the top of a castle wall. For example, a castellated balljoint stud nut.

Castor In wheel alignment, the backward or forward tilt of the steering axis. Castor is positive when the steering axis is inclined rearward at the top.

Catalytic converter A silencer-like device in the exhaust system which converts certain pollutants in the exhaust gases into less harmful substances.

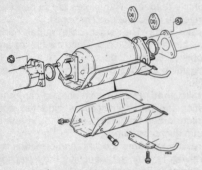

Catalytic converter

Circlip A ring-shaped clip used to prevent endwise movement of cylindrical parts and shafts. An internal circlip is installed in a groove in a housing; an external circlip fits into a groove on the outside of a cylindrical piece such as a shaft.

Clearance The amount of space between two parts. For example, between a piston and a cylinder, between a bearing and a journal, etc.

Coil spring A spiral of elastic steel found in various sizes throughout a vehicle, for example as a springing medium in the suspension and in the valve train.

Compression Reduction in volume, and increase in pressure and temperature, of a gas, caused by squeezing it into a smaller space.

Compression ratio The relationship between cylinder volume when the piston is at top dead centre and cylinder volume when the piston is at bottom dead centre.

Constant velocity (CV) joint A type of universal joint that cancels out vibrations caused by driving power being transmitted through an angle.

Core plug A disc or cup-shaped metal device inserted in a hole in a casting through which core was removed when the casting was formed. Also known as a freeze plug or expansion plug.

Crankcase The lower part of the engine block in which the crankshaft rotates.

Crankshaft The main rotating member, or shaft, running the length of the crankcase, with offset "throws" to which the connecting rods are attached.

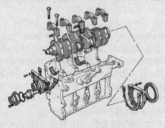

Crankshaft assembly

Crocodile clip See Alligator clip

D

Diagnostic code Code numbers obtained by accessing the diagnostic mode of an engine management computer. This code can be used to determine the area in the system where a malfunction may be located.

Disc brake A brake design incorporating a rotating disc onto which brake pads are squeezed. The resulting friction converts the energy of a moving vehicle into heat.

Double-overhead cam (DOHC) An engine that uses two overhead camshafts, usually one for the intake valves and one for the exhaust valves.

Drivebelt(s) The belt(s) used to drive accessories such as the alternator, water pump, power steering pump, air conditioning compressor, etc. off the crankshaft pulley.

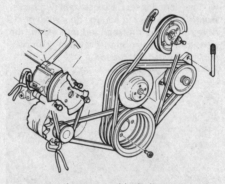

Accessory drivebelts

Driveshaft Any shaft used to transmit motion. Commonly used when referring to the axleshafts on a front wheel drive vehicle.

Drum brake A type of brake using a drum-shaped metal cylinder attached to the inner surface of the wheel. When the brake pedal is pressed, curved brake shoes with friction linings press against the inside of the drum to slow or stop the vehicle.

E

EGR valve A valve used to introduce exhaust gases into the intake air stream.

Electronic control unit (ECU) A computer which controls (for instance) ignition and fuel injection systems, or an anti-lock braking system. For more information refer to the *Haynes Automotive Electrical and Electronic Systems Manual.*

Electronic Fuel Injection (EFI) A computer controlled fuel system that distributes fuel through an injector located in each intake port of the engine.

Emergency brake A braking system, independent of the main hydraulic system, that can be used to slow or stop the vehicle if the primary brakes fail, or to hold the vehicle stationary even though the brake pedal isn't depressed. It usually consists of a hand lever that actuates either front or rear brakes mechanically through a series of cables and linkages. Also known as a handbrake or parking brake.

Endfloat The amount of lengthwise movement between two parts. As applied to a crankshaft, the distance that the crankshaft can move forward and back in the cylinder block.

Engine management system (EMS) A computer controlled system which manages the fuel injection and the ignition systems in an integrated fashion.

Exhaust manifold A part with several passages through which exhaust gases leave the engine combustion chambers and enter the exhaust pipe.

F

Fan clutch A viscous (fluid) drive coupling device which permits variable engine fan speeds in relation to engine speeds.

Feeler blade A thin strip or blade of hardened steel, ground to an exact thickness, used to check or measure clearances between parts.

Feeler blade

Firing order The order in which the engine cylinders fire, or deliver their power strokes, beginning with the number one cylinder.

Flywheel A heavy spinning wheel in which energy is absorbed and stored by means of momentum. On cars, the flywheel is attached to the crankshaft to smooth out firing impulses.

Free play The amount of travel before any action takes place. The "looseness" in a linkage, or an assembly of parts, between the initial application of force and actual movement. For example, the distance the brake pedal moves before the pistons in the master cylinder are actuated.

Fuse An electrical device which protects a circuit against accidental overload. The typical fuse contains a soft piece of metal which is calibrated to melt at a predetermined current flow (expressed as amps) and break the circuit.

Fusible link A circuit protection device consisting of a conductor surrounded by heat-resistant insulation. The conductor is smaller than the wire it protects, so it acts as the weakest link in the circuit. Unlike a blown fuse, a failed fusible link must frequently be cut from the wire for replacement.

G

Gap The distance the spark must travel in jumping from the centre electrode to the side electrode in a spark plug. Also refers to the spacing between the points in a contact breaker assembly in a conventional points-type ignition, or to the distance between the reluctor or rotor and the pickup coil in an electronic ignition.

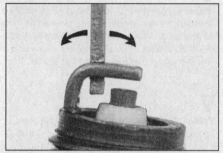

Adjusting spark plug gap

Gasket Any thin, soft material - usually cork, cardboard, asbestos or soft metal - installed between two metal surfaces to ensure a good seal. For instance, the cylinder head gasket seals the joint between the block and the cylinder head.

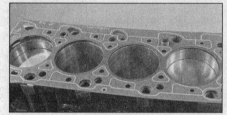

Gasket

Gauge An instrument panel display used to monitor engine conditions. A gauge with a movable pointer on a dial or a fixed scale is an analogue gauge. A gauge with a numerical readout is called a digital gauge.

H

Halfshaft A rotating shaft that transmits power from the final drive unit to a drive wheel, usually when referring to a live rear axle.

Harmonic balancer A device designed to reduce torsion or twisting vibration in the crankshaft. May be incorporated in the crankshaft pulley. Also known as a vibration damper.

Hone An abrasive tool for correcting small irregularities or differences in diameter in an engine cylinder, brake cylinder, etc.

Hydraulic tappet A tappet that utilises hydraulic pressure from the engine's lubrication system to maintain zero clearance (constant contact with both camshaft and valve stem). Automatically adjusts to variation in valve stem length. Hydraulic tappets also reduce valve noise.

I

Ignition timing The moment at which the spark plug fires, usually expressed in the number of crankshaft degrees before the piston reaches the top of its stroke.

Inlet manifold A tube or housing with passages through which flows the air-fuel mixture (carburettor vehicles and vehicles with throttle body injection) or air only (port fuel-injected vehicles) to the port openings in the cylinder head.

J

Jump start Starting the engine of a vehicle with a discharged or weak battery by attaching jump leads from the weak battery to a charged or helper battery.

L

Load Sensing Proportioning Valve (LSPV) A brake hydraulic system control valve that works like a proportioning valve, but also takes into consideration the amount of weight carried by the rear axle.

Locknut A nut used to lock an adjustment nut, or other threaded component, in place. For example, a locknut is employed to keep the adjusting nut on the rocker arm in position.

Lockwasher A form of washer designed to prevent an attaching nut from working loose.

M

MacPherson strut A type of front suspension system devised by Earle MacPherson at Ford of England. In its original form, a simple lateral link with the anti-roll bar creates the lower control arm. A long strut - an integral coil spring and shock absorber - is mounted between the body and the steering knuckle. Many modern so-called MacPherson strut systems use a conventional lower A-arm and don't rely on the anti-roll bar for location.

Multimeter An electrical test instrument with the capability to measure voltage, current and resistance.

N

NOx Oxides of Nitrogen. A common toxic pollutant emitted by petrol and diesel engines at higher temperatures.

O

Ohm The unit of electrical resistance. One volt applied to a resistance of one ohm will produce a current of one amp.

Ohmmeter An instrument for measuring electrical resistance.

O-ring A type of sealing ring made of a special rubber-like material; in use, the O-ring is compressed into a groove to provide the sealing action.

Overhead cam (ohc) engine An engine with the camshaft(s) located on top of the cylinder head(s).

Overhead valve (ohv) engine An engine with the valves located in the cylinder head, but with the camshaft located in the engine block.

Oxygen sensor A device installed in the engine exhaust manifold, which senses the oxygen content in the exhaust and converts this information into an electric current. Also called a Lambda sensor.

P

Phillips screw A type of screw head having a cross instead of a slot for a corresponding type of screwdriver.

Plastigage A thin strip of plastic thread, available in different sizes, used for measuring clearances. For example, a strip of Plastigage is laid across a bearing journal. The parts are assembled and dismantled; the width of the crushed strip indicates the clearance between journal and bearing.

Plastigage

Propeller shaft The long hollow tube with universal joints at both ends that carries power from the transmission to the differential on front-engined rear wheel drive vehicles.

Proportioning valve A hydraulic control valve which limits the amount of pressure to the rear brakes during panic stops to prevent wheel lock-up.

R

Rack-and-pinion steering A steering system with a pinion gear on the end of the steering shaft that mates with a rack (think of a geared wheel opened up and laid flat). When the steering wheel is turned, the pinion turns, moving the rack to the left or right. This movement is transmitted through the track rods to the steering arms at the wheels.

Radiator A liquid-to-air heat transfer device designed to reduce the temperature of the coolant in an internal combustion engine cooling system.

Refrigerant Any substance used as a heat transfer agent in an air-conditioning system. R-12 has been the principle refrigerant for many years; recently, however, manufacturers have begun using R-134a, a non-CFC substance that is considered less harmful to the ozone in the upper atmosphere.

Rocker arm A lever arm that rocks on a shaft or pivots on a stud. In an overhead valve engine, the rocker arm converts the upward movement of the pushrod into a downward movement to open a valve.

Rotor In a distributor, the rotating device inside the cap that connects the centre electrode and the outer terminals as it turns, distributing the high voltage from the coil secondary winding to the proper spark plug. Also, that part of an alternator which rotates inside the stator. Also, the rotating assembly of a turbocharger, including the compressor wheel, shaft and turbine wheel.

Runout The amount of wobble (in-and-out movement) of a gear or wheel as it's rotated. The amount a shaft rotates "out-of-true." The out-of-round condition of a rotating part.

S

Sealant A liquid or paste used to prevent leakage at a joint. Sometimes used in conjunction with a gasket.

Sealed beam lamp An older headlight design which integrates the reflector, lens and filaments into a hermetically-sealed one-piece unit. When a filament burns out or the lens cracks, the entire unit is simply replaced.

Serpentine drivebelt A single, long, wide accessory drivebelt that's used on some newer vehicles to drive all the accessories, instead of a series of smaller, shorter belts. Serpentine drivebelts are usually tensioned by an automatic tensioner.

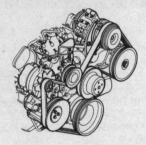

Serpentine drivebelt

Shim Thin spacer, commonly used to adjust the clearance or relative positions between two parts. For example, shims inserted into or under bucket tappets control valve clearances. Clearance is adjusted by changing the thickness of the shim.

Slide hammer A special puller that screws into or hooks onto a component such as a shaft or bearing; a heavy sliding handle on the shaft bottoms against the end of the shaft to knock the component free.

Sprocket A tooth or projection on the periphery of a wheel, shaped to engage with a chain or drivebelt. Commonly used to refer to the sprocket wheel itself.

Starter inhibitor switch On vehicles with an automatic transmission, a switch that prevents starting if the vehicle is not in Neutral or Park.

Strut See MacPherson strut.

T

Tappet A cylindrical component which transmits motion from the cam to the valve stem, either directly or via a pushrod and rocker arm. Also called a cam follower.

Thermostat A heat-controlled valve that regulates the flow of coolant between the cylinder block and the radiator, so maintaining optimum engine operating temperature. A thermostat is also used in some air cleaners in which the temperature is regulated.

Thrust bearing The bearing in the clutch assembly that is moved in to the release levers by clutch pedal action to disengage the clutch. Also referred to as a release bearing.

Timing belt A toothed belt which drives the camshaft. Serious engine damage may result if it breaks in service.

Timing chain A chain which drives the camshaft.

Toe-in The amount the front wheels are closer together at the front than at the rear. On rear wheel drive vehicles, a slight amount of toe-in is usually specified to keep the front wheels running parallel on the road by offsetting other forces that tend to spread the wheels apart.

Toe-out The amount the front wheels are closer together at the rear than at the front. On front wheel drive vehicles, a slight amount of toe-out is usually specified.

Tools For full information on choosing and using tools, refer to the *Haynes Automotive Tools Manual*.

Tracer A stripe of a second colour applied to a wire insulator to distinguish that wire from another one with the same colour insulator.

Tune-up A process of accurate and careful adjustments and parts replacement to obtain the best possible engine performance.

Turbocharger A centrifugal device, driven by exhaust gases, that pressurises the intake air. Normally used to increase the power output from a given engine displacement, but can also be used primarily to reduce exhaust emissions (as on VW's "Umwelt" Diesel engine).

U

Universal joint or U-joint A double-pivoted connection for transmitting power from a driving to a driven shaft through an angle. A U-joint consists of two Y-shaped yokes and a cross-shaped member called the spider.

V

Valve A device through which the flow of liquid, gas, vacuum, or loose material in bulk may be started, stopped, or regulated by a movable part that opens, shuts, or partially obstructs one or more ports or passageways. A valve is also the movable part of such a device.

Valve clearance The clearance between the valve tip (the end of the valve stem) and the rocker arm or tappet. The valve clearance is measured when the valve is closed.

Vernier caliper A precision measuring instrument that measures inside and outside dimensions. Not quite as accurate as a micrometer, but more convenient.

Viscosity The thickness of a liquid or its resistance to flow.

Volt A unit for expressing electrical "pressure" in a circuit. One volt that will produce a current of one ampere through a resistance of one ohm.

W

Welding Various processes used to join metal items by heating the areas to be joined to a molten state and fusing them together. For more information refer to the *Haynes Automotive Welding Manual*.

Wiring diagram A drawing portraying the components and wires in a vehicle's electrical system, using standardised symbols. For more information refer to the *Haynes Automotive Electrical and Electronic Systems Manual*.

Note: *References throughout this index are in the form* **"Chapter number"** • **"Page number"**

Haynes Manuals – The Complete List

Title	Book No.
ALFA ROMEO Alfasud/Sprint (74 - 88) up to F *	0292
Alfa Romeo Alfetta (73 - 87) up to E *	0531
AUDI 80, 90 & Coupe Petrol (79 - Nov 88) up to F	0605
Audi 80, 90 & Coupe Petrol (Oct 86 - 90) D to H	1491
Audi 100 & 200 Petrol (Oct 82 - 90) up to H	0907
Audi 100 & A6 Petrol & Diesel (May 91 - May 97) H to P	3504
Audi A4 Petrol & Diesel (95 - Feb 00) M to V	3575
AUSTIN A35 & A40 (56 - 67) up to F *	0118
Austin/MG/Rover Maestro 1.3 & 1.6 Petrol (83 - 95) up to M	0922
Austin/MG Metro (80 - May 90) up to G	0718
Austin/Rover Montego 1.3 & 1.6 Petrol (84 - 94) A to L	1066
Austin/MG/Rover Montego 2.0 Petrol (84 - 95) A to M	1067
Mini (59 - 69) up to H	0527
Mini (69 - 01) up to X	0646
Austin/Rover 2.0 litre Diesel Engine (86 - 93) C to L	1857
AUSTIN HEALEY 100/6 & 3000 (56 - 68) up to G *	0049
BEDFORD CF Petrol (69 - 87) up to E	0163
Bedford/Vauxhall Rascal & Suzuki Supercarry (86 - Oct 94) C to M	3015
BMW 316, 320 & 320i (4-cyl) (75 - Feb 83) up to Y *	0276
BMW 320, 320i, 323i & 325i (6-cyl) (Oct 77 - Sept 87) up to E	0815
BMW 3- & 5-Series Petrol (81 - 91) up to J	1948
BMW 3-Series Petrol (Apr 91 - 96) H to N	3210
BMW 3-Series Petrol (Sept 98 - 03) S-reg. on	4067
BMW 520i & 525e (Oct 81 - June 88) up to E	1560
BMW 525, 528 & 528i (73 - Sept 81) up to X *	0632
BMW 1500, 1502, 1600, 1602, 2000 & 2002 (59 - 77) up to S *	0240
CHRYSLER PT Cruiser Petrol (00 - 03) W-reg. on	4058
CITROËN 2CV, Ami & Dyane (67 - 90) up to H	0196
Citroën AX Petrol & Diesel (87 - 97) D to P	3014
Citroën BX Petrol (83 - 94) A to L	0908
Citroën C15 Van Petrol & Diesel (89 - Oct 98) F to S	3509
Citroën CX Petrol (75 - 88) up to F	0528
Citroën Saxo Petrol & Diesel (96 - 01) N to X	3506
Citroën Visa Petrol (79 - 88) up to F	0620
Citroën Xantia Petrol & Diesel (93 - 98) K to S	3082
Citroën XM Petrol & Diesel (89 - 00) G to X	3451
Citroën Xsara Petrol & Diesel (97 - Sept 00) R to W	3751
Citroën Xsara Picasso Petrol & Diesel (00 - 02) W-reg. onwards	3944
Citroën ZX Diesel (91 - 98) J to S	1922
Citroën ZX Petrol (91 - 98) H to S	1881
Citroën 1.7 & 1.9 litre Diesel Engine (84 - 96) A to N	1379
FIAT 126 (73 - 87) up to E *	0305
Fiat 500 (57 - 73) up to M *	0090
Fiat Bravo & Brava Petrol (95 - 00) N to W	3572
Fiat Cinquecento (93 - 98) K to R	3501
Fiat Panda (81 - 95) up to M	0793
Fiat Punto Petrol & Diesel (94 - Oct 99) L to V	3251
Fiat Punto Petrol (Oct 99 - July 03) V-reg on	4066
Fiat Regata Petrol (84 - 88) A to F	1167
Fiat Tipo Petrol (88 - 91) E to J	1625
Fiat Uno Petrol (83 - 95) up to M	0923
Fiat X1/9 (74 - 89) up to G *	0273
FORD Anglia (59 - 68) up to G *	0001

Title	Book No.
Ford Capri II (& III) 1.6 & 2.0 (74 - 87) up to E	0283
Ford Capri II (& III) 2.8 & 3.0 V6 (74 - 87) up to E	1309
Ford Cortina Mk III 1300 & 1600 (70 - 76) up to P*	0070
Ford Escort Mk I 1100 & 1300 (68 - 74) up to N*	0171
Ford Escort Mk I Mexico, RS 1600 & RS 2000 (70 - 74) up to N *	0139
Ford Escort Mk II Mexico, RS 1800 & RS 2000 (75 - 80) up to W *	0735
Ford Escort (75 - Aug 80) up to V *	0280
Ford Escort Petrol (Sept 80 - Sept 90) up to H	0686
Ford Escort & Orion Petrol (Sept 90 - 00) H to X	1737
Ford Escort & Orion Diesel (Sept 90 - 00) H to X	4081
Ford Fiesta (76 - Aug 83) up to Y	0334
Ford Fiesta Petrol (Aug 83 - Feb 89) A to F	1030
Ford Fiesta Petrol (Feb 89 - Oct 95) F to N	1595
Ford Fiesta Petrol & Diesel (Oct 95 - 01) N-reg. on	3397
Ford Fiesta (02 - 04) 02-reg. onwards	4170
Ford Focus Petrol & Diesel (98 - 01) S to Y	3759
Ford Focus Petrol & Diesel (01 - 04) Y-reg. on	4167
Ford Galaxy Petrol & Diesel (95 - Aug 00) M to W	3984
Ford Granada Petrol (Sept 77 - Feb 85) up to B	0481
Ford Granada & Scorpio Petrol (Mar 85 - 94) B to M	1245
Ford Ka (96 - 02) P-reg. onwards	3570
Ford Mondeo Petrol (93 - Sept 00) K to X	1923
Ford Mondeo Petrol & Diesel (Oct 00 - Jul 03) X to 03	3990
Ford Mondeo Diesel (93 - 96) L to N	3465
Ford Orion Petrol (83 - Sept 90) up to H	1009
Ford Sierra 4-cyl Petrol (82 - 93) up to K	0903
Ford Sierra V6 Petrol (82 - 91) up to J	0904
Ford Transit Petrol (Mk 2) (78 - Jan 86) up to C	0719
Ford Transit Petrol (Mk 3) (Feb 86 - 89) C to G	1468
Ford Transit Diesel (Feb 86 - 99) C to T	3019
Ford 1.6 & 1.8 litre Diesel Engine (84 - 96) A to N	1172
Ford 2.1, 2.3 & 2.5 litre Diesel Engine (77 - 90) up to H	1606
FREIGHT ROVER Sherpa Petrol (74 - 87) up to E	0463
HILLMAN Avenger (70 - 82) up to Y	0037
Hillman Imp (63 - 76) up to R *	0022
HONDA Accord (76 - Feb 84) up to A	0351
Honda Civic (Feb 84 - Oct 87) A to E	1226
Honda Civic (Nov 91 - 96) J to N	3199
Honda Civic Petrol (Mar 95 - 00) M to X	4050
HYUNDAI Pony (85 - 94) C to M	3398
JAGUAR E Type (61 - 72) up to L	0140
Jaguar MkI & II, 240 & 340 (55 - 69) up to H *	0098
Jaguar XJ6, XJ & Sovereign; Daimler Sovereign (68 - Oct 86) up to D	0242
Jaguar XJ6 & Sovereign (Oct 86 - Sept 94) D to M	3261
Jaguar XJ12, XJS & Sovereign; Daimler Double Six (72 - 88) up to F	0478
JEEP Cherokee Petrol (93 - 96) K to N	1943
LADA 1200, 1300, 1500 & 1600 (74 - 91) up to J	0413
Lada Samara (87 - 91) D to J	1610
LAND ROVER 90, 110 & Defender Diesel (83 - 95) up to N	3017
Land Rover Discovery Petrol & Diesel (89 - 98) G to S	3016
Land Rover Freelander Petrol & Diesel (97 - 02) R-reg. onwards	3929
Land Rover Series IIA & III Diesel (58 - 85) up to C	0529
Land Rover Series II, IIA & III 4-cyl Petrol (58 - 85) up to C	0314
MAZDA 323 (Mar 81 - Oct 89) up to G	1608

Title	Book No.
Mazda 323 (Oct 89 - 98) G to R	3455
Mazda 626 (May 83 - Sept 87) up to E	0929
Mazda B-1600, B-1800 & B-2000 Pick-up Petrol (72 - 88) up to F	0267
Mazda RX-7 (79 - 85) up to C *	0460
MERCEDES-BENZ 190, 190E & 190D Petrol & Diesel (83 - 93) A to L	3450
Mercedes-Benz 200 D, 240 D, 240 TD, 300 D & 300 TD 123 Series Diesel (Oct 76 - 85) up to C	1114
Mercedes-Benz 250 & 280 (68 - 72) up to L	0346
Mercedes-Benz 250 & 280 123 Series Petrol (Oct 76 - 84) up to B *	0677
Mercedes-Benz 124 Series Petrol & Diesel (85 - Aug 93) C to K	3253
Mercedes-Benz C-Class Petrol & Diesel (93 - Aug 00) L to W	3511
MG A (55 - 62) *	0475
MGB (62 - 80) up to W	0111
MG Midget & Austin-Healey Sprite (58 - 80) up to W	0265
MITSUBISHI Shogun & L200 Pick-Ups Petrol (83 - 94) up to M	1944
MORRIS Ital 1.3 (80 - 84) up to B	0705
Morris Minor 1000 (56 - 71) up to K	0024
NISSAN Almera Petrol (95 - Feb 00) N to V	4053
Nissan Bluebird (May 84 - Mar 86) A to C	1223
Nissan Bluebird Petrol (Mar 86 - 90) C to H	1473
Nissan Cherry (Sept 82 - 86) up to D	1031
Nissan Micra (83 - Jan 93) up to K	0931
Nissan Micra (93 - 99) K to T	3254
Nissan Primera Petrol (90 - Aug 99) H to T	1851
Nissan Stanza (82 - 86) up to D	0824
Nissan Sunny Petrol (May 82 - Oct 86) up to D	0895
Nissan Sunny Petrol (Oct 86 - Mar 91) D to H	1378
Nissan Sunny Petrol (Apr 91 - 95) H to N	3219
OPEL Ascona & Manta (B Series) (Sept 75 - 88) up to F	0316
Opel Ascona Petrol (81 - 88) (Not available in UK see Vauxhall Cavalier 0812)	3215
Opel Astra Petrol (Oct 91 - Feb 98) (Not available in UK see Vauxhall Astra 1832)	3156
Opel Astra & Zafira Diesel (Feb 98 - Sept 00) (See Vauxhall/Opel Astra & Zafira Diesel Book No. 3797)	
Opel Astra & Zafira Petrol (Feb 98 - Sept 00) (See Vauxhall/Opel Astra & Zafira Petrol Book No. 3758)	
Opel Calibra (90 - 98) (See Vauxhall/Opel Calibra Book No. 3502)	
Opel Corsa Petrol (83 - Mar 93) (Not available in UK see Vauxhall Nova 0909)	3160
Opel Corsa Petrol (Mar 93 - 97) (Not available in UK see Vauxhall Corsa 1985)	3159
Opel Corsa Diesel (Mar 93 - Oct 00) (See Vauxhall/Opel Corsa Diesel Book No. 4087)	
Opel Corsa Petrol (Apr 97 - Oct 00) (See Vauxhall/Opel Corsa Petrol Book No. 3921)	
Opel Corsa Petrol & Diesel (Oct 00 - Sept 03) (See Vauxhall/Opel Corsa Petrol & Diesel Book No. 4079)	
Opel Frontera Petrol & Diesel (91 - 98) (See Vauxhall/Opel Frontera Book No. 3454)	
Opel Kadett Petrol (Nov 79 - Oct 84) up to B	0634
Opel Kadett Petrol (Oct 84 - Oct 91) (Not available in UK see Vauxhall Astra & Belmont 1136)	3196
Opel Omega & Senator Petrol (Nov 86 - 94) (NA in UK see Vauxhall Carlton & Senator 1469)	3157
Opel Omega (94 - 99) (See Vauxhall/Opel Omega Book No. 3510)	
Opel Rekord Petrol (Feb 78 - Oct 86) up to D	0543

* Classic reprint

Title	Book No.
Opel Vectra Petrol (Oct 88 - Oct 95)	
(Not available in UK see Vauxhall Cavalier 1570)	**3158**
Opel Vectra (95 - Feb 99)	
(See Vauxhall/Opel Vectra Book No. 3396)	
Opel Vectra (Mar 99 - May 02)	
(See Vauxhall/Opel Vectra Book No. 3930)	
Opel Diesel Engine *(See Vauxhall/Opel 1.5, 1.6 & 1.7 litre*	
Diesel Engine Book No. 1222)	
PEUGEOT 106 Petrol & Diesel (91 - 02) J-reg. on	**1882**
Peugeot 205 Petrol (83 - 97) A to P	**0932**
Peugeot 206 Petrol & Diesel (98 - 01) S to X	**3757**
Peugeot 306 Petrol & Diesel (93 - 99) K to T	**3073**
Peugeot 307 Petrol & Diesel (01 - 04) Y-reg. on	**4147**
Peugeot 309 Petrol (86 - 93) C to K	**1266**
Peugeot 405 Petrol (88 - 97) E to P	**1559**
Peugeot 405 Diesel (88 - 97) E to P	**3198**
Peugeot 406 Petrol & Diesel (96 - Mar 99) N to T	**3394**
Peugeot 406 Petrol & Diesel	
(Mar 99 - 02) T-reg. onwards	**3982**
Peugeot 505 Petrol (79 - 89) up to G	**0762**
Peugeot 1.7/1.8 & 1.9 litre Diesel Engine	
(82 - 96) up to N	**0950**
Peugeot 2.0, 2.1, 2.3 & 2.5 litre Diesel Engines	
(74 - 90) up to H	**1607**
PORSCHE 911 (65 - 85) up to C	**0264**
Porsche 924 & 924 Turbo (76 - 85) up to C	**0397**
PROTON (89 - 97) F to P	**3255**
RANGE ROVER V8 Petrol (70 - Oct 92) up to K	**0606**
RELIANT Robin & Kitten (73 - 83) up to A *	**0436**
RENAULT 4 (61 - 86) up to D *	**0072**
Renault 5 Petrol (Feb 85 - 96) B to N	**1219**
Renault 9 & 11 Petrol (82 - 89) up to F	**0822**
Renault 18 Petrol (79 - 86) up to D	**0598**
Renault 19 Petrol (89 - 96) F to N	**1646**
Renault 19 Diesel (89 - 96) F to N	**1946**
Renault 21 Petrol (86 - 94) C to M	**1397**
Renault 25 Petrol & Diesel (84 - 92) B to K	**1228**
Renault Clio Petrol (91 - May 98) H to R	**1853**
Renault Clio Diesel (91 - June 96) H to N	**3031**
Renault Clio Petrol & Diesel	
(May 98 - May 01) R to Y	**3906**
Renault Clio Petrol & Diesel	
(June 01 - 04) Y-reg. onwards	**4168**
Renault Espace Petrol & Diesel (85 - 96) C to N	**3197**
Renault Laguna Petrol & Diesel (94 - 00) L to W	**3252**
Renault Mégane & Scénic Petrol & Diesel	
(96 - 98) N to R	**3395**
Renault Mégane & Scénic Petrol & Diesel	
(Apr 99 - 02) T-reg. onwards	**3916**
ROVER 213 & 216 (84 - 89) A to G	**1116**
Rover 214 & 414 Petrol (89 - 96) G to N	**1689**
Rover 216 & 416 Petrol (89 - 96) G to N	**1830**
Rover 211, 214, 216, 218 & 220 Petrol &	
Diesel (Dec 95 - 98) N to R	**3399**
Rover 25 & MG ZR Petrol & Diesel	
(Oct 99 - 03) V-reg. onwards	**4145**
Rover 414, 416 & 420 Petrol & Diesel	
(May 95 - 98) M to R	**3453**
Rover 618, 620 & 623 Petrol (93 - 97) K to P	**3257**
Rover 820, 825 & 827 Petrol (86 - 95) D to N	**1380**
Rover 3500 (76 - 87) up to E *	**0365**
Rover Metro, 111 & 114 Petrol	
(May 90 - 98) G to S	**1711**
SAAB 95 & 96 (66 - 76) up to R *	**0198**
Saab 90, 99 & 900 (79 - Oct 93) up to L	**0765**
Saab 900 (Oct 93 - 98) L to R	**3512**
Saab 9000 (4-cyl) (85 - 98) C to S	**1686**

Title	Book No.
Saab 9-5 Petrol (Sept 97 - 03) R-reg. onwards	**4156**
SEAT Ibiza & Cordoba Petrol & Diesel	
(Oct 93 - Oct 99) L to V	**3571**
Seat Ibiza & Malaga Petrol (85 - 92) B to K	**1609**
SKODA Estelle (77 - 89) up to G	**0604**
Skoda Favorit (89 - 96) F to N	**1801**
Skoda Felicia Petrol & Diesel (95 - 01) M to X	**3505**
SUBARU 1600 & 1800 (Nov 79 - 90) up to H	**0995**
SUNBEAM Alpine, Rapier & H120	
(67 - 74) up to N *	**0051**
SUZUKI SJ Series, Samurai & Vitara (4-cyl)	
Petrol (82 - 97) up to P	**1942**
TALBOT Alpine, Solara, Minx & Rapier	
(75 - 86) up to D	**0337**
Talbot Horizon Petrol (78 - 86) up to D	**0473**
Talbot Samba (82 - 86) up to D	**0823**
TOYOTA Carina E Petrol (May 92 - 97) J to P	**3256**
Toyota Corolla (80 - 85) up to C	**0683**
Toyota Corolla (Sept 83 - Sept 87) A to E	**1024**
Toyota Corolla (Sept 87 - Aug 92) E to K	**1683**
Toyota Corolla Petrol (Aug 92 - 97) K to P	**3259**
Toyota Hi-Ace & Hi-Lux Petrol	
(69 - Oct 83) up to A	**0304**
TRIUMPH GT6 & Vitesse (62 - 74) up to N *	**0112**
Triumph Herald (59 - 71) up to K *	**0010**
Triumph Spitfire (62 - 81) up to X	**0113**
Triumph Stag (70 - 78) up to T *	**0441**
Triumph TR2, TR3, TR3A, TR4 & TR4A	
(52 - 67) up to F *	**0028**
Triumph TR5 & 6 (67 - 75) up to P *	**0031**
Triumph TR7 (75 - 82) up to Y *	**0322**
VAUXHALL Astra Petrol (80 - Oct 84) up to B	**0635**
Vauxhall Astra & Belmont Petrol	
(Oct 84 - Oct 91) B to J	**1136**
Vauxhall Astra Petrol (Oct 91 - Feb 98) J to R	**1832**
Vauxhall/Opel Astra & Zafira Petrol	
(Feb 98 - Sept 00) R to W	**3758**
Vauxhall/Opel Astra & Zafira Diesel	
(Feb 98 - Sept 00) R to W	**3797**
Vauxhall/Opel Calibra (90 - 98) G to S	**3502**
Vauxhall Carlton Petrol (Oct 78 - Oct 86) up to D	**0480**
Vauxhall Carlton & Senator Petrol	
(Nov 86 - 94) D to L	**1469**
Vauxhall Cavalier Petrol (81 - Oct 88) up to F	**0812**
Vauxhall Cavalier Petrol (Oct 88 - 95) F to N	**1570**
Vauxhall Chevette (75 - 84) up to B	**0285**
Vauxhall/Opel Corsa Diesel (Mar 93 - Oct 00) K to X	**4087**
Vauxhall Corsa Petrol (Mar 93 - 97) K to R	**1985**
Vauxhall/Opel Corsa Petrol	
(Apr 97 - Oct 00) P to X	**3921**
Vauxhall/Opel Corsa Petrol & Diesel	
(Oct 00 - Sept 03) X-reg onwards	**4079**
Vauxhall/Opel Frontera Petrol & Diesel	
(91 - Sept 98) J to S	**3454**
Vauxhall Nova Petrol (83 - 93) up to K	**0909**
Vauxhall/Opel Omega Petrol (94 - 99) L to T	**3510**
Vauxhall/Opel Vectra Petrol & Diesel	
(95 - Feb 99) N to S	**3396**
Vauxhall/Opel Vectra Petrol & Diesel	
(Mar 99 - May 02) T-reg. onwards	**3930**
Vauxhall/Opel 1.5, 1.6 & 1.7 litre Diesel Engine	
(82 - 96) up to N	**1222**
VOLKSWAGEN 411 & 412 (68 - 75) up to P *	**0091**
Volkswagen Beetle 1200 (54 - 77) up to S	**0036**
Volkswagen Beetle 1300 & 1500	
(65 - 75) up to P	**0039**
Volkswagen Beetle 1302 & 1302S	
(70 - 72) up to L *	**0110**

Title	Book No.
Volkswagen Beetle 1303, 1303S & GT	
(72 - 75) up to P	**0159**
Volkswagen Beetle Petrol & Diesel	
(Apr 99 - 01) T-reg. onwards	**3798**
Volkswagen Golf & Bora Petrol & Diesel	
(April 98 - 00) R to X	**3727**
Volkswagen Golf & Jetta Mk 1 Petrol 1.1 & 1.3	
(74 - 84) up to A	**0716**
Volkswagen Golf, Jetta & Scirocco Mk 1 Petrol	
1.5, 1.6 & 1.8 (74 - 84) up to A	**0726**
Volkswagen Golf & Jetta Mk 1 Diesel	
(78 - 84) up to A	**0451**
Volkswagen Golf & Jetta Mk 2 Petrol	
(Mar 84 - Feb 92) A to J	**1081**
Volkswagen Golf & Vento Petrol & Diesel	
(Feb 92 - Mar 98) J to R	**3097**
Volkswagen Golf (01 - 04) X-reg. onwards	**4169**
Volkswagen LT Petrol Vans & Light Trucks	
(76 - 87) up to E	**0637**
Volkswagen Passat & Santana Petrol	
(Sept 81 - May 88) up to E	**0814**
Volkswagen Passat 4-cyl Petrol & Diesel	
(May 88 - 96) E to P	**3498**
Volkswagen Passat 4-cyl Petrol & Diesel	
(Dec 96 - Nov 00) P to X	**3917**
Volkswagen Polo & Derby (76 - Jan 82) up to X	**0335**
Volkswagen Polo (82 - Oct 90) up to H	**0813**
Volkswagen Polo Petrol (Nov 90 - Aug 94) H to L	**3245**
Volkswagen Polo Hatchback Petrol & Diesel	
(94 - 99) M to S	**3500**
Volkswagen Scirocco (82 - 90) up to H	**1224**
Volkswagen Transporter 1600 (68 - 79) up to V	**0082**
Volkswagen Transporter 1700, 1800 & 2000	
(72 - 79) up to V *	**0226**
Volkswagen Transporter (air-cooled) Petrol	
(79 - 82) up to Y	**0638**
Volkswagen Transporter (water-cooled) Petrol	
(82 - 90) up to H	**3452**
Volkswagen Type 3 (63 - 73) up to M *	**0084**
VOLVO 120 & 130 Series (& P1800)	
(61 - 73) up to M *	**0203**
Volvo 142, 144 & 145 (66 - 74) up to N *	**0129**
Volvo 240 Series Petrol (74 - 93) up to K	**0270**
Volvo 262, 264 & 260/265 (75 - 85) up to C *	**0400**
Volvo 340, 343, 345 & 360 (76 - 91) up to J	**0715**
Volvo 440, 460 & 480 Petrol (87 - 97) D to P	**1691**
Volvo 740 & 760 Petrol (82 - 91) up to J	**1258**
Volvo 850 Petrol (92 - 96) J to P	**3260**
Volvo 940 Petrol (90 - 96) H to N	**3249**
Volvo S40 & V40 Petrol (96 - 99) N to V	**3569**
Volvo S70, V70 & C70 Petrol (96 - 99) P to V	**3573**

AUTOMOTIVE TECHBOOKS

Title	Book No.
Automotive Air Conditioning Systems	**3740**
Automotive Carburettor Manual	**3288**
Automotive Diagnostic Fault Codes Manual	**3472**
Automotive Diesel Engine Service Guide	**3286**
Automotive Electrical and Electronic Systems	
Manual	**3049**
Automotive Engine Management and Fuel	
Injection Systems Manual	**3344**
Automotive Gearbox Overhaul Manual	**3473**
Automotive Service Summaries Manual	**3475**
Automotive Timing Belts Manual - Austin/Rover	**3549**
Automotive Timing Belts Manual - Ford	**3474**
Automotive Timing Belts Manual - Peugeot/Citroën	**3568**
Automotive Timing Belts Manual - Vauxhall/Opel	**3577**
Automotive Welding Manual	**3053**

CL16.03/04

Preserving Our Motoring Heritage

< The Model J Duesenberg Derham Tourster. Only eight of these magnificent cars were ever built – this is the only example to be found outside the United States of America

Almost every car you've ever loved, loathed or desired is gathered under one roof at the Haynes Motor Museum. Over 300 immaculately presented cars and motorbikes represent every aspect of our motoring heritage, from elegant reminders of bygone days, such as the superb Model J Duesenberg to curiosities like the bug-eyed BMW Isetta. There are also many old friends and flames. Perhaps you remember the 1959 Ford Popular that you did your courting in? The magnificent 'Red Collection' is a spectacle of classic sports cars including AC, Alfa Romeo, Austin Healey, Ferrari, Lamborghini, Maserati, MG, Riley, Porsche and Triumph.

A Perfect Day Out

Each and every vehicle at the Haynes Motor Museum has played its part in the history and culture of Motoring. Today, they make a wonderful spectacle and a great day out for all the family. Bring the kids, bring Mum and Dad, but above all bring your camera to capture those golden memories for ever. You will also find an impressive array of motoring memorabilia, a comfortable 70 seat video cinema and one of the most extensive transport book shops in Britain. The Pit Stop Cafe serves everything from a cup of tea to wholesome, home-made meals or, if you prefer, you can enjoy the large picnic area nestled in the beautiful rural surroundings of Somerset.

> John Haynes O.B.E., Founder and Chairman of the museum at the wheel of a Haynes Light 12.

< Graham Hill's Lola Cosworth Formula 1 car next to a 1934 Riley Sports.

The Museum is situated on the A359 Yeovil to Frome road at Sparkford, just off the A303 in Somerset. It is about 40 miles south of Bristol, and 25 minutes drive from the M5 intersection at Taunton.
Open 9.30am - 5.30pm (10.00am - 4.00pm Winter) 7 days a week, *except Christmas Day, Boxing Day and New Years Day*
Special rates available for schools, coach parties and outings Charitable Trust No. 292048